W9-AUO-584

PEARSON

ALWAYS LEARNING

Managing People in Organizations

An Integration of Human Resource Management and Organizational Behaviour

Second Edition for University of Guelph

Taken from:
Human Resources Management in Canada, Canadian Twelfth Edition
by Gary Dessler, Nita Chhinzer, and Nina D. Cole

Organizational Behaviour: Concepts, Controversies, Applications, Sixth
Canadian Edition
by Nancy Langton, Stephen P. Robbins, and Timothy A. Judge

Management: A Skills Approach, Second Edition
by Phillip L. Hunsaker

Cover Art: Courtesy of EyeWire/Getty Images, Digital Vision/Getty Images, Rubberball Productions/Getty Images, Blend Images/Getty Images, and Photodisc/Getty Images.

Taken from:

Human Resources Management in Canada, Canadian Twelfth Edition
by Gary Dessler, Nita Chhinzer, and Nina D. Cole
Copyright © 2014, 2011, 2008, 2005, 2002, 1992 by Pearson Canada, Inc.
Published by Prentice Hall

Organizational Behaviour: Concepts, Controversies, Applications, Sixth Canadian Edition
by Nancy Langton, Stephen P. Robbins, and Timothy A. Judge
Copyright © 2013, 2010, 2007, 2003, 2001, 1999 by Pearson Canada, Inc.
Published by Prentice Hall
Toronto, Ontario

Management: A Skills Approach, Second Edition
by Phillip L. Hunsaker
Copyright © 2005, 2001 by Pearson Education, Inc.
Published by Prentice Hall
Upper Saddle River, New Jersey 07458

This special edition published in cooperation with Pearson Learning Solutions.

All trademarks, service marks, registered trademarks, and registered service marks are the property of their respective owners and are used herein for identification purposes only.

Pearson Learning Solutions, 501 Boylston Street, Suite 900, Boston, MA 02116
A Pearson Education Company
www.pearsoned.com

Printed in Canada

1 2 3 4 5 6 7 8 9 10 XXXX 18 17 16 15 14 13

000200010271763682

LF

ISBN 10: 1-269-33363-1
ISBN 13: 978-1-269-33363-4

BRIEF CONTENTS

Chapters 2-6, 13-14, 18-20, 25-26, and their respective Endnotes and Photo Credits are taken from *Organizational Behaviour: Concepts, Controversies, Applications,* Sixth Canadian Edition, by Nancy Langton, Stephen P. Robbins, and Timothy A. Judge.

Chapters 1, 7-12, 15-17, 21-24, and their respective Endnotes and Photo Credits are taken from *Human Resources Management in Canada,* Canadian Twelfth Edition, by Gary Dessler, Nita Chhinzer, and Nina D. Cole.

Appendix A is taken from *Management: A Skills Approach,* Second Edition, by Phillip L. Hunsaker.

CONTENTS

1

The Changing Legal Emphasis

Compliance and Impact on
Canadian Workplaces

The Legal Framework for Employment Law in Canada

A 2011 survey conducted by Queen's University in partnership with the Human Resources Institute of Alberta (HRIA) and the International Personnel Management Association (IPMA) asked 451 HR professionals to identify the top five critical pieces of knowledge required in their roles. While business acumen was identified as the most critical piece of knowledge, employment law/legislative awareness and talent management were tied for second position.[1] While HR professionals are expected to provide guidance, training, programs, and policy developments that are legally defensible, the actions of supervisors and managers as agents of the organization must also abide by legislated rules and regulations. The risk of expensive lawsuits and their impact on employer branding or reputation requires an awareness of employment law within the organization that extends well beyond just the HR professionals.

There are a number of distinct sets of responsibilities that exist between the employee and employer, including formal and informal expectations. There is a mutual expectation of each party to maintain the employment relationship by fulfilling their own responsibilities within the relationship. For example, there may be an implied, informal expectation from an employee's point of view that as long as they attend work for the scheduled number of hours, they can expect job security and continued employment from the employer. Such informal and personalized expectations are difficult to manage and correct if one party feels that the other has violated the expectations within the mutual relationship. As a result, the influence and impact of formal expectations (largely established through legislation and the interpretation of it) plays a significant role in the Canadian workplace.

The primary objective of most employment legislation in Canada is to prevent employers from exploiting paid workers, assuming that an implicit power imbalance exists in the employment relationship (in favour of the employer).[2] While employers have a right to modify employee work terms and arrangements according to legitimate business needs, employees have a right to be protected from harmful business practices. In this regard, the government's role is to balance employee and employer needs through the development and maintenance of employment legislation. The judicial system provides a forum for interpreting legislation according to the precedents past judicial rulings have established.

Canadian employment legislation is largely modelled on the US National Labor Relations Act with three significant differences. First, the Canadian population is more inclined to accept and expect government-mandated regulations about organizational activities, since Canadians are generally more receptive to governmental regulatory intervention than the US public.[3]

Second, in the United States the historical notion of "employment at will" allowed either the employee or employer to break the relationship (with no liability) provided that no autonomous employment contract exists and employees are not represented by a collective bargaining unit. In Canada, employers are permitted to terminate employment without a reason provided they ensure reasonable notice is given to workers. In return, the employee is permitted to quit, strike, or otherwise cease employment without penalty, provided that they align with the legislation pertaining to such events.

Finally, the US employment legislation model is largely centralized. In contrast, the primary responsibility for employment-related laws resides with the provinces and territories in Canada. Today, provincial/territorial employment laws govern approximately 90 percent of Canadian workers. The remaining 10 percent of the workforce are employed in the federal civil service, Crown corporations and agencies, or businesses engaged in transportation, banking, and communications, which are all governed by federal employment legislation. Thus there are 14 jurisdictions—10 provinces, 3 territories, and Canada as a whole—for employment law.

As highlighted in Exhibit 1-1, at the broadest level all persons residing in Canada are guaranteed protection under constitutional law, particularly the Charter of Rights and Freedoms. The regulations set forth in the Charter are not employment specific, but all employers must abide by them because they are fundamental, guaranteed rights to all persons residing in Canada. There are also provincial human rights codes that ensure the rights of every Canadian are protected and that all persons are treated with equality and respect. Discrimination based on protected grounds highlighted in the legislation is prohibited not only in the employment relationship but also in the delivery of goods and services. Therefore, while the Charter of Rights and Freedom and human rights codes extend beyond just the employment relationship, they both have a significant impact on workplace practices.

There is also a series of employment-specific legislation in Canada that employers must abide by, such as the Employment Standards Act, which vary slightly by jurisdiction. There is a great deal of commonality to the legislation, but there are also some differences. For example, vacations, statutory holidays, and minimum wage standards are provided by all jurisdictions, but specific entitlements may vary from one jurisdiction to the next. Therefore, a company with employees in different provinces/territories must monitor the legislation in each of those jurisdictions and remain current as legislation changes. Ensuring legality across multiple jurisdictions can be complex, since it is possible for a policy, practice, or procedure to be legal in one jurisdiction yet illegal in others.

There are laws that specifically regulate some areas of HRM—occupational health and safety (occupational health and safety acts are reviewed in Chapter 22), union relations (labour relations acts are reviewed in Chapter 24), and pensions and compensation (pay equity acts, the Income Tax Act, and others are discussed briefly in Chapter 17).

Yet even more specific is the issue of contract law, which governs collective agreements and individual employment contracts. Such laws impose specific requirements

Government of Canada
http://canada.gc.ca

EXHIBIT 1-1 Multiple Layers of Canadian Legislation Affecting Workplace Practices

Affects general population

Canadian Charter of Rights and Freedom—Basic rights guaranteed to all persons residing in Canada

Human Rights Legislation—Protection from discrimination in employment relationships and the delivery of goods and services

Employment Standards Legislation—Establishes minimum terms and conditions of the employment relationship within each jurisdiction (e.g., minimum wages, hours of work, maternity leave)

Ordinary Laws—Protection under context- or content-specific laws affecting workplaces (like Occupational Health and Safety)

Collective Bargaining Agreement—A legally binding agreement establishing minimum terms and conditions of employment affecting unionized positions

Employment Contract—A contract between an individual employee and their employer regarding specified employment conditions in specified roles

Affects specific employees and conditions

Source: Chhinzer, 2011.

and constraints on management and employee policies, procedures, and practices. For example, a collective bargaining agreement is a contract regarding the terms and conditions of employment that both employees and employers must abide by legally. In non-unionized roles, individual employment contracts are often signed prior to the commencement of the employment relationship and create an individualized legal contract that employees and employers must abide by.

In addition to the legislation above, Canada has also inherited the English system of tort law. Tort law is primarily judge-based law, where the precedent and jurisprudences set by one judge through his or her assessment of a case establishes how similar cases will be interpreted. Tort laws are often separated into two categories: intentional torts (for example, assault, battery, trespass, intentional affliction of mental distress) and unintentional torts (for example, negligence based on events where harm is caused by carelessness).

To avoid flooding the courts with complaints and the prosecutions of relatively minor infractions, the government in each jurisdiction creates special regulatory bodies to enforce compliance with the law and aid in its interpretation. Such bodies, which include human rights commissions and ministries of labour, develop legally binding rules called **regulations** and evaluate complaints.

Within these various levels of legislation there is a sense of hierarchy. The more general the impact of the legislation, the more it supersedes lower levels of legislation. For example, a collective bargaining agreement cannot agree to wages less than the minimum wage established in the provincial Employment Standards Act. Likewise, the Employment Standards Act cannot violate the minimums set forth in the Charter of Rights and Freedom.

There are two opposing interpretations of Canadian legislation. Employees often choose to view the regulations as a statutory floor and expect to receive higher than the minimum requirements (more than the minimum wage, minimum entitlement for vacation days, minimum entitlement for severance pay, and so on). In contrast, employers often prefer to view legislated guidelines as a contractual ceiling and align maximum commitment levels to the minimums established in the guidelines. HR professionals play a critical role in balancing these divergent sets of expectations, with obligations toward both the employees and employers.

Legislation Protecting the General Population

Human rights legislation makes it illegal to discriminate, even unintentionally, against various groups. Reactive (complaint driven) in nature, the focus of such legislation is on the types of acts in which employers should *not* engage. Included in this category are

1. *The Charter of Rights and Freedoms*, federal legislation that is the cornerstone of human rights in Canada, and

2. *Human rights legislation*, which is present in every jurisdiction.

The Charter of Rights and Freedoms

The cornerstone of Canada's legislation pertaining to issues of human rights is the Constitution Act, which contains the **Charter of Rights and Freedoms**. The Charter applies to the actions of all levels of government (federal, provincial/territorial, and municipal) and agencies under their jurisdiction as they go about their work of creating laws. The Charter takes precedence over all other laws, which means that all legislation must meet Charter standards; thus, it is quite far-reaching in scope.

There are two notable exceptions to this generalization. The Charter allows laws to infringe on Charter rights if they can be demonstrably justified as reasonable limits in a "free and democratic society." Since "demonstrably justified" and "reasonable" are

Hints | **TO ENSURE LEGAL COMPLIANCE**

regulations Legally binding rules established by special regulatory bodies created to enforce compliance with the law and aid in its interpretation.

Charter of Rights and Freedoms Federal law enacted in 1982 that guarantees fundamental freedoms to all Canadians.

open to interpretation, many issues challenged under the Charter eventually end up before the Supreme Court of Canada, its ultimate interpreter. The second exception occurs when a legislative body invokes the "notwithstanding" provision, which allows the legislation to be exempted from challenge under the Charter.

The Charter provides the following fundamental rights and freedoms to every Canadian, including but not limited to:

1. Freedom of conscience and religion

2. Freedom of thought, belief, opinion, and expression, including freedom of the press and other media of communication

3. Freedom of peaceful assembly

4. Freedom of association

In addition, the Charter provides Canadian multicultural heritage rights, First Nations' rights, minority language education rights, equality rights, the right to live and work anywhere in Canada, the right to due process in criminal proceedings, and the right to democracy.[4]

Section 15—**equality rights**—provides the basis for human rights legislation, as it guarantees the right to equal protection and benefit of the law without discrimination, in particular without discrimination based on race, national or ethnic origin, colour, religion, sex, age, or mental or physical disability.[5]

Human Rights Legislation

Every person residing in Canada is protected by **human rights legislation**, which prohibits intentional and unintentional discrimination in employment situations and the delivery of goods and services. Human rights legislation is extremely broad in scope, affecting almost all aspects of HRM when applied to the employment relationship. An important feature of human rights legislation is that it supersedes the terms of any employment contract or collective agreement.[6] For these reasons, supervisors and managers must be thoroughly familiar with the human rights legislation of their jurisdiction and their legal obligations and responsibilities specified therein.

Human rights legislation prohibits discrimination against all Canadians in a number of areas, including employment. To review individual provincial and territorial human rights laws would be confusing because of the many but generally minor differences among them, often only in terminology (for example, some provinces use the term "creed," others "religion"). As indicated in Exhibit 1-2, most provincial/territorial laws are similar to the federal statute in terms of scope, interpretation, and application. All jurisdictions prohibit discrimination on the grounds of race, colour, religion/creed, sex, marital status, age, disability, and sexual orientation. Some, but not all, jurisdictions further prohibit discrimination on the basis of family status, nationality or ethnic origin, and various other grounds.

Discrimination Defined

Central to human rights laws is the concept of **discrimination**. When someone is accused of discrimination, it generally means that he or she is perceived to be acting in an unfair or prejudiced manner within the context of prohibited grounds for discrimination. For example, if an employee was discriminated against based on his or her initials or if they wore a black top to work that day, this would fall outside the scope of human rights legislation. The law prohibits unfair discrimination—making choices on the basis of perceived but inaccurate differences to the detriment of specific individuals or groups. Standards pertaining to unfair discrimination have changed over time. Both intentional and unintentional discrimination is prohibited.

Supreme Court of Canada
www.scc-csc.gc.ca

Government of Canada
http://canada.gc.ca

Canadian Human Rights Tribunal
www.chrt-tcdp.gc.ca

equality rights Section 15 of the Charter of Rights and Freedoms, which guarantees the right to equal protection and benefit of the law without discrimination.

human rights legislation Jurisdictions specific legislation that prohibits intentional and unintentional discrimination in employment situations and in the delivery of goods and services.

discrimination As used in the context of human rights in employment, a distinction, exclusion, or preference based on one of the prohibited grounds that has the effect of nullifying or impairing the right of a person to full and equal recognition and exercise of his or her human rights and freedoms.

EXHIBIT 1-2 Prohibited Grounds of Discrimination in Employment by Jurisdiction

Prohibited Grounds of Discrimination	Federal	Alta.	B.C.	Man.	N.B.	N.L.	N.S.	Ont.	P.E.I.	Que.	Sask.	N.W.T.	Y.T.	Nunavut
Race	◆	◆	◆	◆	◆	◆	◆	◆	◆	◆	◆	◆	◆	◆
Colour	◆	◆	◆	◆	◆	◆	◆	◆	◆	◆	◆	◆	◆	◆
Creed or religion	◆	◆	◆	◆	◆	◆	◆	◆	◆	◆	◆	◆	◆	◆
Sex	◆	◆	◆	◆	◆	◆	◆	◆	◆	◆	◆	◆	◆	◆
Marital status	◆	◆	◆	◆	◆	◆	◆	◆	◆	◆	◆	◆	◆	◆
Age	◆	18+	19–65	◆	◆	19–65	◆	18+	◆	◆	18–64	◆	◆	◆
Mental & physical disability	◆	◆	◆	◆	◆	◆	◆	◆	◆	◆	◆	◆	◆	◆
Sexual orientation	◆	◆	◆	◆	◆	◆	◆	◆	◆	◆	◆	◆	◆	◆
National or ethnic origin	◆			◆	◆	◆	◆	◆	◆	◆	◆	◆	◆	◆
Family status	◆	◆	◆	◆			◆	◆	◆	◆	◆	◆	◆	◆
Ancestry or place of origin		◆	◆	◆	◆			◆			◆	◆	◆	◆
Political belief			◆		◆	◆	◆		◆	◆			◆	
Association				◆	◆		◆	◆	◆			◆	◆	◆
Source of income		◆		◆			◆			◆	◆			
Social condition or origin				◆		◆				◆			◆	
Language								◆		◆			◆	
Pardoned conviction	◆											◆	◆	◆
Record of criminal conviction										◆			◆	
Assignment, attachment, or seizure of pay						◆								

Source: Prohibited Grounds of Discrimination in Canada. http://www.chrc-ccdp.ca/pdf/prohibit_en.pdf, Canadian Human Rights Commission, 2006. Reproduced with the permission of the Ministry of Public Works and Government Services Canada, 2012.

Intentional Discrimination

Except in specific circumstances that will be described later, intentional discrimination is prohibited. An employer cannot discriminate *directly* by deliberately refusing to hire, train, or promote an individual, for example, on any of the prohibited grounds. It is important to realize that deliberate discrimination is not necessarily overt. In fact, overt (blatant) discrimination is relatively rare today. But subtle, indirect discrimination can be difficult to prove. For example, if a 60-year-old applicant is not selected for a job and is told that there was a better-qualified candidate, it is often difficult for the rejected job seeker to determine if someone else truly did more closely match the firm's specifications or if the employer discriminated on the basis of age.

An employer is also prohibited from intentional discrimination in the form of **differential or unequal treatment**. No individuals or groups may be treated differently in any aspects or terms and conditions of employment based on any of the prohibited grounds. For example, it is illegal for an employer to request that only female applicants for a factory job demonstrate their lifting skills or to insist that any candidates with a physical disability undergo a pre-employment medical, unless all applicants are being asked to do so.

differential or unequal treatment
Treating an individual differently in any aspect of terms and conditions of employment based on any of the prohibited grounds.

It is also illegal for an employer to engage in intentional discrimination *indirectly* through another party. This means that an employer may not ask someone else to discriminate on his or her behalf. For example, an employer cannot request that an employment agency refer only male candidates for consideration as management trainees or instruct supervisors that racial minorities are to be excluded from consideration for promotions.

Discrimination because of association is another possible type of intentional discrimination listed specifically as a prohibited ground in several Canadian jurisdictions. It involves the denial of rights because of friendship or other relationship with a protected group member. An example would be the refusal of a firm to promote a highly qualified male into senior management on the basis of the assumption that his wife, who was recently diagnosed with multiple sclerosis, will require too much of his time and attention and that her needs may restrict his willingness to travel on company business.

Unintentional Discrimination

Unintentional discrimination (also known as **constructive** or **systemic discrimination**) is the most difficult to detect and combat. Typically, it is embedded in policies and practices that appear neutral on the surface and that are implemented impartially, but have an adverse impact on specific groups of people for reasons that are not job related or required for the safe and efficient operation of the business. Examples are shown in Exhibit 1-3.

Permissible Discrimination via Bona Fide Occupational Requirements

Employers are permitted to discriminate if employment preferences are based on a **bona fide occupational requirement (BFOR)**, defined as a justifiable reason for discrimination based on business necessity, such as the requirement for the safe and efficient operation of the organization (for example, a person who is blind cannot be employed as a truck driver or bus driver). In some cases, a BFOR exception to human rights protection is fairly obvious. For example, when casting in the theatre, there may be specific roles that justify using age, sex, or national origin as a recruitment and selection criterion.

EXHIBIT 1-3 Examples of Systemic Discrimination

- Minimum height and weight requirements, which screen out disproportionate numbers of women and people from Asia, who tend to be shorter in stature.
- Internal hiring policies or word-of-mouth hiring in workplaces that have not embraced diversity.
- Limited accessibility to company premises, which poses a barrier to persons with mobility limitations.
- Culturally biased or non-job-related employment tests, which discriminate against specific groups.
- Job evaluation systems that are not gender-neutral; that is, they undervalue traditional female-dominated jobs.
- Promotions based exclusively on seniority or experience in firms that have a history of being white-male-dominated.
- Lack of a harassment policy or guidelines, or an organizational climate in which certain groups feel unwelcome and uncomfortable.

Source: Based on material provided by the Ontario Women's Directorate and the Canadian Human Rights Commission.

---

discrimination because of association Denial of rights because of friendship or other relationship with a protected group member.

unintentional/constructive/ systemic discrimination Discrimination that is embedded in policies and practices that appear neutral on the surface and are implemented impartially, but have an adverse impact on specific groups of people for reasons that are not job related or required for the safe and efficient operation of the business.

bona fide occupational requirement (BFOR) A justifiable reason for discrimination based on business necessity (that is, required for the safe and efficient operation of the organization) or a requirement that can be clearly defended as intrinsically required by the tasks an employee is expected to perform.

The Meiorin case (Supreme Court of Canada, 1999) established three criteria that are now used to assess if the discrimination qualifies as a bona fide occupational requirement. First, is the question of rationale: Was the policy or procedure that resulted in the discrimination based on a legitimate, work-related purpose? Second, is the question of good faith: Did the decision makers or other agents of the organization honestly believe that the requirement was necessary to fulfill the requirements of the role? Third, (and this one is often the most difficult to prove) is the question of reasonable necessity: Was it impossible to accommodate those who have been discriminated against without imposing undue hardship on the employer?

The issue of BFORs gets more complicated in situations in which the occupational requirement is less obvious; the onus of proof is then placed on the employer. There are a number of instances in which BFORs have been established. For example, adherence to the tenets of the Roman Catholic Church has been deemed a BFOR when selecting faculty to teach in a Roman Catholic school.[7] The Royal Canadian Mounted Police has a requirement that guards be of the same sex as prisoners being guarded, which was also ruled to be a BFOR.[8]

Reasonable Accommodation

The Job Accommodation Network
http://askjan.org/

An important feature of human rights legislation is the requirement for **reasonable accommodation.** Employers are required to adjust employment policies and practices so that no individual is prevented from doing his or her job on the basis of prohibited grounds for discrimination. Accommodation may involve scheduling adjustments to accommodate religious beliefs or workstation redesign to enable an individual with a physical disability to perform a particular task. Employers are expected to accommodate to the point of **undue hardship**, meaning that the financial cost of the accommodation (even with outside sources of funding) or health and safety risks to the individual concerned or other employees would make accommodation impossible.[9] Failure to make every reasonable effort to accommodate employees is a violation of human rights legislation in all Canadian jurisdictions. The term "reasonable" is relatively vague and open to interpretation, which can be found in the precedent that has been established in the legal system. The Supreme Court of Canada recently clarified the scope of the duty to accommodate by stating that it does not require an employer to completely alter the essence of the employment contract, whereby the employee has a duty to perform work in exchange for remuneration. For example, if the characteristics of an illness are such that the employee remains unable to work for the foreseeable future, even though the employer has tried to accommodate the employee, the employer will have satisfied the test of undue hardship.[10]

Human Rights Case Examples

Alberta Human Rights Commission
www.albertahumanrights.ab.ca

In claims of discrimination, it does not matter if the protected grounds were the primary or heaviest weighted factor in the decision being challenged or if it was one of many considerations made in the decision. If there were 20 criteria used to make a decision, and even one of those criteria violated protection against discrimination as per the applicable human rights legislation, then the entire decision made by the employer can be deemed illegal. Provincial/Territorial human rights commissions most often encounter cases related to disability (roughly 50%), gender (including pregnancy) and harassment (roughly 20% combined), and race or ethnicity (roughly 15%), with the remaining protected clauses accounting for an estimated 10% of discrimination claims.[11] In order to clarify how the human rights legislation is applied and the types of discrimination prohibited, a few examples follow.

Disability

Claims of discrimination based on disability make up almost half of all human rights claims. A disability in human rights legislation includes a wide range of conditions,

reasonable accommodation The adjustment of employment policies and practices that an employer may be expected to make so that no individual is denied benefits, disadvantaged in employment, or prevented from carrying out the essential components of a job because of grounds prohibited in human rights legislation.

undue hardship The point to which employers are expected to accommodate employees under human rights legislative requirements.

some which are visible and some which are not. In general, a distinction can be drawn between a physical disability and a mental one. A disability may be present from birth, caused by an accident, or develop over time and may include (depending on the jurisdiction) physical, mental, and learning disabilities; mental disorders; hearing or vision disabilities; epilepsy; drug and alcohol dependencies; environmental sensitivities; as well as other conditions. Temporary illnesses are generally not considered to be disabilities under human rights legislation (unless related to a workplace safety claim), but mental disorders, even temporary ones, are included in the definition of a disability. The intent of providing protection from discrimination based on past, present, or perceived disabilities is largely based on the principle of having an inclusive society with a barrier-free design and equal participation of persons with varying levels of ability.[12] Because employers set standards or requirements, they therefore "owe an obligation to be aware of both the differences between individuals, and differences that characterize groups of individuals. They must build conceptions of equality into workplace [or other] standards."[13]

According to the Supreme Court of Canada, the focus of a disability is not simply the presence of it, but the effect of the disability. In a case heard by the Supreme Court of Canada in 2000 against the City of Boisbriand and Communauté urbaine de Montréal, the city had dismissed an employee, Palmerino Troilo, from his position as a police officer because he suffered from Crohn's disease. Crohn's disease is linked to problems with a person's immune system response and people with it have (ongoing) inflammation of their gastrointestinal tract. There is no known cure for Crohn's at the moment.[14] Medical evidence presented in the case indicated that Troilo could perform normal functions of his job, but the city argued that the illness was permanent and could be interpreted subjectively as an indication of future job-related challenges. The judge found that the illness did not actually result in any functional limitations and held that Troilo had been a victim of discriminatory exclusion. In this case, it was not the presence of a disability that was of concern to employment-related legislation, but the impact of that disability on creating job-related functional limitations.

The Supreme Court of Canada has suggested three broad inquiries to determine if discrimination has taken place:

1. **Differential treatment:** Was there substantively differential treatment due to a distinction, exclusion, or preference or because of a failure to take into account the complainant's already disadvantaged position within Canadian society?

2. **An enumerated ground** (a condition or clause that is explicitly protected by legislation): Was the differential treatment based on an enumerated ground?

3. **Discrimination in a substantive sense:** Does the differential treatment discriminate by imposing a burden upon or withholding a benefit from a person? Does the differential treatment amount to discrimination because it makes distinctions that are offensive to human dignity?

Accommodation   Although each situation is unique, there are general principles for accommodating persons with disabilities.

First, the accommodation should be provided in a manner that most respects the dignity of the person, including an awareness of privacy, confidentiality, autonomy, individuality, and self-esteem. For example, the requirement for a person in a wheelchair to enter the workplace through the loading dock or garbage room is undignified. Each person's needs are unique and must be considered independently when an accommodation request is made. Persons with disabilities have the fundamental right to integration and full participation; therefore, barriers should be removed to the point of undue hardship. Workplace programs and policies should be designed

British Columbia Human Rights Tribunal
www.bchrt.bc.ca

Manitoba Human Rights Commission
www.gov.mb.ca/hrc

New Brunswick Human Rights Commission
www.gnb.ca/hrc-cdp/index-e.asp

Newfoundland and Labrador Human Rights Commission
www.justice.gov.nl.ca/hrc

Northwest Territories Human Rights Commission
www.nwthumanrights.ca

Nova Scotia Human Rights Commission
www.gov.ns.ca/humanrights

Nunavut Human Rights Tribunal
www.nhrt.ca

Ontario Human Rights Commission
www.ohrc.on.ca

Prince Edward Island Human Rights Commission
www.gov.pe.ca/humanrights/

Québec Commission des droits de la personne et des droits de la jeunesse
www.cdpdj.qc.ca

Saskatchewan Human Rights Commission
www.shrc.gov.sk.ca

Yukon Human Rights Commission
www.yhrc.yk.ca

by inclusion to combat "social handicapping," in which societal attitudes and actions create non-inclusive thinking against people who have no or few limitations. Providing equal access to employment is largely based on the removal of physical, attitudinal, and systemic barriers. Even when all of these factors are considered, there might still be a need for accommodation.

Second, if discrimination does exist it must be legally defensible, in the sense that the company must demonstrate individualized attempts to accommodate the disability to the point of undue hardship. The Meiorin test discussed earlier is used to establish if the company reached the point of undue hardship. Employers have the legal duty to accommodate persons with disability, and the employees have a responsibility to seek accommodation, cooperate in the process, exchange relevant information, and explore accommodation solutions together.[15] Examples of employer and employee responsibilities associated with the duty to accommodate disabilities are highlighted in Exhibit 1-4. Often, accommodations can be made easily and at minimal cost, such as increased flexibility in work hours or break times; providing reading material in digitized, Braille, or large print formats; installing automatic doors and making washrooms accessible; job restructuring, retraining, or assignment to an alternative position within the company.

Third, the duty to accommodate requires the most appropriate accommodation to be undertaken to the point of undue hardship. The principle underlying this condition is that accommodations are unique, numerous, part of a process, and a matter of degree. Rather than an all-or-nothing approach, there may be many options available to accommodate an employee's disability with varying degrees of complexity, resource demands, and effects on work processes. An accommodation can be considered appropriate if it results in equal opportunity to attain the same level of performance, benefits,

---

EXHIBIT 1-4 Duty to Accommodate Disabilities: Shared Responsibilities

As a person with a disability

- Tell your employer or union what your disability-related needs are as they relate to your job duties.
- Provide supporting information about your disability-related needs, including medical or other expert opinions where necessary.
- Participate in exploring possible accommodation solutions.

As an employer or union

- Accept requests for accommodation from employees in good faith.
- Request only information that is required to provide the accommodation. For example, you need to know that an employee's loss of vision prevents them from using printed material, but you do not need to know they have diabetes.
- Take an active role in examining accommodation solutions that meet individual needs.
- Deal with accommodation requests as quickly as possible, even if it means creating a temporary solution while a long-term one is developed.
- Maximize confidentiality for the person seeking accommodation and be respectful of his or her dignity.
- Cover the costs of accommodations, including any necessary medical or other expert opinion or documentation.

Source: Policy and Guidelines on Disability and the Duty to Accommodate, published by the Ontario Human Rights Commission in 2000 and found on the Commission's website at http://www.ohrc.on.ca/en/policy-and-guidelines-disability-and-duty-accommodate. © Queen's Printer for Ontario, 2000. Reproduced with permission.

and privileges others experience, or if it is adopted for the purpose of achieving equal opportunity and meets the individual's disability-related needs. In cases where alternative options preserve the same level of dignity and respect, employers are entitled to select the less expensive or less disruptive option.

Accommodation of employees with "invisible" disabilities, such as chronic fatigue syndrome, fibromyalgia, and mental illnesses, is becoming more common. An employee with bipolar disorder was terminated when he began to exhibit pre-manic symptoms after waiting for a response from management regarding his request for accommodation. A human rights tribunal in 2008 found that the company had not investigated the nature of his condition or possible accommodations and awarded the employee over $80 000 in damages.[16]

Harassment

The most historic battle for protection against harassment was initiated in 1982, at a time when it was largely interpreted that sexual harassment was not a form of sex discrimination (therefore, not illegal) and it was perceived that employers were not responsible for the actions of their employees. As indicated in the Workforce Diversity box, perspectives on sexual harassment and employers' responsibilities toward protecting employees from sexual harassment have shifted significantly over the last three decades, largely due to a Supreme Court ruling on a case initiated by two young waitresses.

Some jurisdictions prohibit harassment on all prescribed grounds, while others only expressly ban sexual harassment. **Harassment** includes unwelcome behaviour that demeans, humiliates, or embarrasses a person and that a reasonable person should have known would be unwelcome.[17] Examples of harassment are included in Exhibit 1-5. Minority women often experience harassment based on both sex and race.[18]

EXHIBIT 1-5 Examples of Harassment

Some examples of harassment include:

- unwelcome remarks, slurs, jokes, taunts, or suggestions about a person's body, clothing, race, national or ethnic origin, colour, religion, age, sex, marital status, family status, physical or mental disability, sexual orientation, pardoned conviction, or other personal characteristics;
- unwelcome sexual remarks, invitations, or requests (including persistent, unwanted contact after the end of a relationship);
- display of sexually explicit, sexist, racist, or other offensive or derogatory material;
- written or verbal abuse or threats;
- practical jokes that embarrass or insult someone;
- leering (suggestive staring) or other offensive gestures;
- unwelcome physical contact, such as patting, touching, pinching, hitting;
- patronizing or condescending behaviour;
- humiliating an employee in front of co-workers;
- abuse of authority that undermines someone's performance or threatens his or her career;
- vandalism of personal property; and
- physical or sexual assault.

Source: Anti-Harassment Policies for the Workforce: An Employer's Guide, www.chrc-ccdp.ca/pdf/ AHPoliciesWorkplace_en.pdf, Canadian Human Rights Commission, 2006. Reproduced by permission of the Ministry of Public Works and Government Services Canada, 2012.

harassment Unwelcome behaviour that demeans, humiliates, or embarrasses a person and that a reasonable person should have known would be unwelcome.

Psychological harassment is often called bullying.

One type of intentional harassment that is receiving increasing attention is bullying, which involves repeated and deliberate incidents of negative behaviour that cumulatively undermine a person's self-image. This psychological form of harassment is much more prevalent and pervasive in workplaces than physical violence.[19] In 2004, a Quebec law prohibiting workplace psychological harassment came into effect with the intent of ending bullying in the workplace. In the first year more than 2500 complaints were received, surpassing expectations to such a degree that the number of investigators was increased from 10 to 34.[20] Saskatchewan prohibits psychological harassment in its occupational health and safety legislation.[21]

This issue is a concern in other countries as well.

Employer Responsibility   The Supreme Court has made it clear that protecting employees from harassment is part of an employer's responsibility to provide a safe and healthy working environment. If harassment is occurring and employers are aware or ought to have been aware, they can be charged as well as the alleged harasser.[22] Employer responsibility also includes employee harassment by clients or customers once it has been reported. In a recent Ontario case, Bell Mobility was ordered to pay an employee more than $500 000 after a supervisor assaulted her in the office and she developed post-traumatic stress disorder. The company was found vicariously liable for the supervisor's aggressive behaviours and was found to have breached its duty of care to provide a safe and harassment-free working environment.[23]

Sexual Harassment   The type of harassment that has attracted the most attention in the workplace is **sexual harassment**. Sexual harassment is offensive or humiliating behaviour that is related to a person's sex, as well as behaviour of a sexual nature that creates an intimidating, unwelcome, hostile, or offensive work environment or that could reasonably be thought to put sexual conditions on a person's job or employment opportunities.

Sexual harassment can be divided into two categories: sexual coercion and sexual annoyance.[24] **Sexual coercion** involves harassment of a sexual nature that results in some direct consequence to the worker's employment status or some gain in or loss of tangible job benefits. Typically, this involves a supervisor using control over employment, pay, performance appraisal results, or promotion to attempt to coerce an employee to grant sexual favours. If the worker agrees to the request, tangible job benefits follow; if the worker refuses, job benefits are denied or taken away.

Sexual annoyance is sexually related conduct that is hostile, intimidating, or offensive to the employee but has no direct link to tangible job benefits or loss thereof. Rather, a "poisoned work environment" is created for the employee, the tolerance of which effectively becomes a term or condition of employment. An Alberta court upheld the dismissal of a male employee who had used profane language, sexually infused talk and jokes, and displayed pornographic and graphically violent images. The employee claimed that he was a misunderstood jokester who had never worked with a female engineer before and blamed the company for not training him on appropriate conduct. However, the court found that the company had embarked on a campaign to recruit women into trade positions many years earlier and that all employees had been provided with diversity training. In addition, the company had also implemented and widely publicized an anti-harassment policy.[25]

Harassment Policies   To reduce liability, employers should establish sound harassment policies, communicate such policies to all employees, enforce the policies in a fair and

Sexual Harassment: Your Rights and Responsibilities
www.ohrc.on.ca/en/ sexual-and-gender-based- harassment-know-your-rights

sexual harassment Offensive or humiliating behaviour that is related to a person's sex, as well as behaviour of a sexual nature that creates an intimidating, unwelcome, hostile, or offensive work environment or that could reasonably be thought to put sexual conditions on a person's job or employment opportunities.

sexual coercion Harassment of a sexual nature that results in some direct consequence to the worker's employment status or some gain in or loss of tangible job benefits.

sexual annoyance Sexually related conduct that is hostile, intimidating, or offensive to the employee but has no direct link to tangible job benefits or loss thereof.

Hints | TO ENSURE LEGAL COMPLIANCE

consistent manner, and take an active role in maintaining a working environment that is free of harassment. Effective harassment policies should include[26]

1. An anti-harassment policy statement, stating the organization's commitment to a safe and respectful work environment and specifying that harassment is against the law;

2. Information for victims (for example, identifying and defining harassment);

3. Employees' rights and responsibilities (for example, respecting others, speaking up, reporting harassment);

4. Employers' and managers' responsibilities (for example, putting a stop to harassment, being aware, listening to employees);

5. Anti-harassment policy procedures (what to do if you are being harassed, what to do if you are accused of harassment, what to do if you are a third-party employee, investigation guidelines, remedies for the victim and corrective action for harassers, guidelines for handling unsubstantiated complaints and complaints made in bad faith, confidentiality);

6. Penalties for retaliation against a complainant;

7. Guidelines for appeals;

8. Other options such as union grievance procedures and human rights complaints;

9. How the policy will be monitored and adjusted.

Race and Colour

Discrimination on the basis of race and colour is illegal in every Canadian jurisdiction. For example, the British Columbia Human Rights Tribunal found that two construction companies had discriminated against 38 Latin American workers brought in to work on a public transit project; the Latin Americans were treated differently than workers brought in from European countries in that they were paid lower wages and provided with inferior accommodation. As a result, the Tribunal awarded each worker $100 000.[27]

Urban Alliance on Race Relations
www.tgmag.ca/magic/uarr.html

Racism and Racial Harassment: Your Rights and Responsibilities
www.ohrc.on.ca/en/racial-harassment-know-your-rights

Religion

Discrimination on the basis of religion can take many forms in Canada's multicultural society. For example, it is a violation of human rights laws across Canada to deny time to pray or to prohibit clothing recognized as religiously required (for example, a hijab for Muslim women or a turban for Sikh men). According to a recent survey in Toronto, discriminatory hiring practices and workplace racism toward Muslim women are quite common. Of the 32 women surveyed, 29 said that their employer had commented on their hijab, and 13 said they were told that they would have to stop wearing their hijab if they wanted the job.[28]

A well-recognized case on religion involved Canadian National Railway (CN). An employee, Mr. Bhinder, worked as a maintenance electrician in the Toronto coach yard. As a practising Sikh, he wore a turban both on and off work premises. Four years after Bhinder first started working for CN, the company introduced a rule requiring all employees working in the coach yard to wear a hard hat, citing safety reasons. Bhinder informed management that he was unable to wear the hard hat since his faith prohibited him from wearing anything other than the turban and there was no way he could wear anything under or over it. He was fired and subsequently launched a discrimination case against CN. In 1981, the Canadian Human Rights Tribunal found that the company did discriminate against Bhinder on religious grounds. The company appealed, and two years later the Federal Court of Appeal overturned the Tribunal's ruling, identifying the hard hat as a BFOR. The case was appealed again, and in 1995 the Supreme Court of Canada did find that the rule discriminated against Bhinder on religious grounds, but that the requirement was bona fide. Therefore, it was not considered to be a discriminatory process and CN did not have a duty to accommodate Bhinder.

This case highlights a significant area of concern in dealing with human rights complaints—the length of time and multiple opportunities for appeal that exist within the legislative systems in Canada. This puts considerable pressure on HR and management to be aware of and proactively manage programs and policies in a legally defensible way to at least try to mitigate the likelihood of lengthy and often expensive court proceedings.

Sexual Orientation

Discrimination on the basis of sexual orientation is prohibited in all jurisdictions in Canada. As a result of lawsuits by same-sex couples, the Supreme Court ruled that all laws must define "common-law partners" to include both same-sex and opposite-sex couples.[29] In a recent federal case, a lesbian employee alleged that she was harassed by a co-worker. She made a complaint to her supervisors but felt the complaint was not investigated properly. She alleged that she was given a poor performance review because of her complaint and that her request for a transfer to another work site was denied. The Canadian Human Rights Commission ordered her employer to provide a letter of apology, financial compensation for pain and suffering, and a transfer to another work site. The Commission also ordered a meeting with the employer's harassment coordinator to talk about the complainant's experiences with the internal complaint process.[30]

An Ethical | Dilemma

Your company president tells you not to hire any gay or lesbian employees to work as part of his office staff because it would make him uncomfortable. What would you do?

Sexual Orientation: Your Rights and Responsibilities
www.ohrc.on.ca/en/sexual-orientation-and-human-rights

Age

Many employers believe that it is justifiable to specify minimum or maximum ages for certain jobs. In actual fact, evidence is rarely available to support the position that age is an accurate indicator of a person's ability to perform a particular type of work.[31] For example, because of an economic downturn, an Ontario company was forced to lay off staff. The complainant, a foreman, had worked for the company for more than 32 years and was 57 at the time he was selected for termination along with another foreman who was aged 56. Both were offered a generous retirement package. The two foremen who remained were younger than the two released. The vice-president had prepared a note indicating that the two older workers who were terminated were told of the need to reduce people and that they "hoped to keep people with career potential." The Ontario Human Rights Tribunal found that the company engaged in age discrimination on the basis of the good employment record of the complainant, the ages of those selected for layoff compared with those retained, and the vice-president's statement, which was found to be a "euphemism; its meaning concerns age."[32]

Family Status

The Canadian Council on Rehabilitation and Work
www.workink.com

Decisions regarding the specific meaning of discrimination based on family status (the status of being in a parent–child relationship) are evolving.[33] In a recent BC case, an employee whose shift was changed by the employer requested a return to her previous shift because the new shift time made it difficult for her to find a caregiver that could provide for her son's special needs. The employer refused, and an arbitrator upheld the decision, saying that family status did not encompass the many circumstances that arise in regard to childcare needs. However, a court of appeal overturned the arbitrator's decision and adopted a middle ground between a narrow definition of family status as being a parent and a broad definition encompassing all possible parental obligations.[34]

Enforcement

Enforcement of human rights acts is the responsibility of the human rights commission in each jurisdiction. It should be noted that all costs are borne by the commission, not by the complainant, which makes the process accessible to all employees, regardless of financial means. The commission itself can initiate a complaint if it has reasonable grounds to assume that a party is engaging in a discriminatory practice.

Challenges of human rights legislation are heard by the human rights tribunal. The tribunal's primary role is to provide a speedy and accessible process to help parties affected by discrimination claims resolve the conflict through mediation. Once a claim is filed with the human rights commission or tribunal, the organization is notified and given a relatively short period of time (for example, 30 calendar days) to prepare their case. Regardless of whether a formal complaint or an informal accusation has been filed against a company, the employer has a duty to investigate claims of discrimination. Fulfilling the duty to investigate starts with the selection of an appropriate investigator. A checklist to be reviewed when selecting an investigator is provided in Exhibit 1-6.

An employer's obligations include the following:

1. Demonstrating an awareness of the issues of discrimination or harassment, including having an antidiscrimination/antiharassment policy in place, a complaint mechanism, and training available for employees

2. Fulfilling post-complaint actions, including assessing the seriousness of the complaint, launching an investigation promptly, focusing on employee welfare, and taking actions based on the complaint

3. Resolving the complaint by demonstrating reasonable resolution and communication

---

EXHIBIT 1-6 A Checklist for Employers when Selecting a Workplace Investigator

1. Internal or external investigators: Many employers select trained internal HR experts to conduct workplace investigations, while others rely on external investigators. Selection is dependent on the resources (time and money) of the firm, the complexities of the case (potential conflicts of interest), the expertise of the in-house staff, and the severity of the case.

2. One investigator or two: The nature of the case may warrant the need for more than one investigator (e.g., one male and one female in the case of a sexual harassment claim).

3. Respecting the mandate: Investigators should be able to maintain the role within the mandate of the task they have been assigned (e.g., fact finder or adviser) and not stray too far off track. Assigned investigators are perceived as agents of the organization, therefore the organization can be held partially accountable for investigator actions.

4. Impartiality or neutrality: Investigators should have no conflict of interest vested in the conditions, persons, or context of the case they are handling.

5. Reliable, thorough, and professional: Although these qualities should go without saying, an investigator is expected to be a competent, effective, and professional communicator throughout the investigation, and must be capable of making credible assessments.

6. Quality of the written report: The details and word selection in the written report can become evidence in a case. Therefore, a high-quality report details "what happened" and assists counsel in their defence.

7. Respects confidentiality: The investigator should only discuss the investigation when required and respect the confidentiality of all parties affected by the investigation.

Source: Chhinzer, N., summary from Module 4 at the HR Law Certificate Program at Osgoode Hall Law School, 2011.

EXHIBIT 1-7 Common Remedies Issued by the Human Rights Tribunals	
Systemic Remedies (forward looking)	**Restitution Remedies (penalties for past events)**
• cease and desist the discriminatory practice • change a program to eliminate discriminatory elements, such as offering same-sex benefits under an employee benefit plan • make physical modifications to work places as mandated • develop non-discriminatory action plans • develop employment equity plans • post notices regarding provisions and protection offered to employees under the human rights code • develop information-sharing practices for future programs to allow monitoring of progress toward antidiscrimination goals	• payment of retroactive benefits • reinstatement of employment • payment for lost wages • compensation for insult to dignity, mental anguish, or infringement of rights under the human rights code • make a public apology

Source: Raj Anand, "Human Rights and the Professional Regulator in the 21st Century," pp. 17–18, November 4, 2011. Used with permission from Raj Anand, Partner, WeirFoulds LLP.

If discrimination is found, two forms of remedies can be imposed. **Systemic remedies** (forward looking) require the respondent to take positive steps to ensure compliance with legislation, both in respect to the current complaint and with respect to any future practices. If a pattern of discrimination is detected, the employer will be ordered to cease such practices and may be required to attend a training session or hold regular human rights workshops. **Restitutional remedies** include monetary compensation for the complainant to put him or her back to the position he or she would be in if the discrimination had not occurred (this includes compensation for injury to dignity and self-respect). A written letter of apology may also be required.

The most common reason for restitutional remedies is compensation for lost wages; others include compensation for general damages, complainant expenses, and pain and humiliation. The violator is generally asked to restore the rights, opportunities, and privileges denied the victim, such as employment or promotion. The total compensation received by the complainant is generally between $0 and $20 000, with a general range of $10 000 to $20 000 for cases where evidence confirmed discrimination occurred and a restitution was ordered. Exhibit 1-7 highlights examples of common remedies issued by a human rights tribunal.

systemic remedies Forward looking solutions to discrimination that require respondents to take positive steps to ensure compliance with legislation, both in respect to the current complaint and any future practices.

restitutional remedies Monetary compensation for the complainant to put him or her back to the position he or she would be in if the discrimination had not occurred (this includes compensation for injury to dignity and self-respect), and may include an apology letter.

occupational segregation The existence of certain occupations that have traditionally been male dominated and others that have been female dominated.

glass ceiling An invisible barrier, caused by attitudinal or organizational bias, that limits the advancement opportunities of qualified designated group members.

Employment Equity Legislation

The Charter of Rights and Freedoms legalizes employment equity initiatives, which go beyond human rights laws in that they are proactive programs developed by employers to remedy past discrimination or prevent future discrimination. Human rights laws focus on prohibiting various kinds of discrimination; however, over time it became obvious that there were certain groups for whom this complaint-based, reactive approach was insufficient. Investigation revealed that four identifiable groups—women, Aboriginal people, persons with disabilities, and visible minorities—had been subjected to pervasive patterns of differential treatment by employers, as evidenced by lower pay on average, occupational segregation, higher rates of unemployment, underemployment, and concentration in low-status jobs with little potential for career growth. An example of **occupational segregation** is that the majority of women worked in a very small number of jobs, such as nursing, teaching, sales, and secretarial/clerical work. Advancement of women and other designated group members into senior management positions has been hindered by the existence of a **glass ceiling**, an "invisible" barrier caused by attitudinal or organizational bias that limits the advancement opportunities

EXHIBIT 1-8 The Catalyst Pyramid—Canadian Women in Business

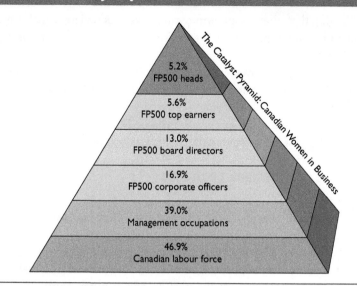

The Catalyst Pyramid: Canadian Women in Business

5.2%
FP500 heads

5.6%
FP500 top earners

13.0%
FP500 board directors

16.9%
FP500 corporate officers

39.0%
Management occupations

46.9%
Canadian labour force

Source: Catalyst, 2008 Catalyst Census of Women Corporate Officers and Top Earners of the FP500 (2009); Catalyst, 2007 Census of Women Board Directors of the FP500: Voices of the Boardroom (2008); Statistics Canada, Labour Force Survey (2008). Reproduced by permission of Catalyst, www. catalystwomen.org.

of qualified individuals. As you can see in Exhibit 1-8, a survey from 2008 confirmed that the glass ceiling is still intact.

After realizing that simple prohibition of discrimination would not correct these patterns, a number of jurisdictions passed employment equity legislation aimed at identifying and eliminating systemic barriers to employment opportunities that adversely affect these four groups. Employment equity legislation is focused on bringing the four traditionally disadvantaged groups identified above into the mainstream of Canada's labour force. The use of the term "employment equity" distinguishes Canada's approach from the "affirmative action" approach used in the United States. Affirmative action has come to be associated with quotas, which is a divisive political issue.[35]

Employment equity legislation is intended to remove employment barriers and promote equality for the members of the four designated groups. Employers under federal jurisdiction must prepare an annual plan with specific goals to achieve better representation of the designated group members at all levels of the organization and timetables for goal implementation. Employers must also submit an annual report on the company's progress in meeting its goals, indicating the representation of designated group members by occupational groups and salary ranges and providing information on those hired, promoted, and terminated. In addition, the Federal Contractors Program requires firms bidding on federal contracts of $200 000 or more to implement an employment equity plan.

In contrast, mandatory employment equity programs are virtually non-existent in provincial and territorial jurisdictions. Some provinces have employment equity policies that encourage employment equity plans in provincial departments and ministries. Quebec has a contract compliance program where employers in receipt of more than $100 000 in provincial funding must implement an employment equity plan.[36]

An **employment equity program** is designed to achieve a balanced representation of designated group members in the organization. It is a major management exercise because existing employees must become comfortable working with others from diverse backgrounds, cultures, religions, and so on, and this represents a major change in the work environment. A deliberately structured process is involved, which can be tailored to suit the unique needs of the firm. The employment equity process usually takes six

employment equity program
A detailed plan designed to identify and correct existing discrimination, redress past discrimination, and achieve a balanced representation of designated group members in the organization.

months. The first step is the demonstration of senior management commitment and support, which leads to data collection and analysis of the current workforce demographics. Following that, there is an employment systems review, which leads to plan development and eventual plan implementation. The last step is monitoring, evaluating, and revising the plan.

Although embracing employee equity or diversity offers opportunities to enhance organizational effectiveness, transforming an organizational culture presents a set of challenges that must be handled properly. Diversity initiatives should be undertaken slowly, since they involve a complex change process. Resistance to change may have to be overcome, along with stereotyped beliefs or prejudices and employee resentment.

The Plight of the Four Designated Groups

Women

Canadian Association of Administrators of Labour Legislation
www.caall-acalo.org

Workplace Standards
www.workplace.ca/laws/employ_standard_comp.html

Women accounted for 47 percent of the employed workforce in 2006. Two-thirds of all employed women were working in teaching, nursing and related health occupations, clerical or other administrative positions, and sales and service occupations. There has been virtually no change in the proportion of women employed in these traditionally female-dominated occupations over the past decade. Women continue to be under-represented in engineering, natural sciences, and mathematics, a trend unlikely to change in the near future since women are still under-represented in university programs in these fields.[37]

Every jurisdiction in Canada has legislation incorporating the principle of *equal pay for equal work*. In most jurisdictions, this entitlement is found in the employment (labour) standards legislation; otherwise, it is in the human rights legislation. **Equal pay for equal work** specifies that an employer cannot pay male and female employees differently if they are performing the same or substantially similar work. Pay differences based on a valid merit or seniority system or employee productivity are permitted; it is only sex-based discrimination that is prohibited. This principle makes it illegal, for example, for the Canadian government to employ nurses (mostly women) as "program administrators" and doctors (mainly men) as "health professionals" to do the same job adjudicating Canada Pension Plan disability claims and pay the men twice as much.[38]

It is illegal in every jurisdiction in Canada to discriminate on the basis of disability.

Aboriginals

Most Aboriginal employees in the workforce are concentrated in low-skill, low-paid jobs such as trades helpers. The unemployment rate for Aboriginal people is significantly higher than the rate among non-Aboriginals, and their income is significantly lower.[39]

People with Disabilities

Equal pay for equal work specifies that an employer cannot pay male and female employees differently if they are performing the same or substantially similar work.

About 45 percent of people with disabilities are in the labour force, compared with almost 80 percent of the non-disabled population. Although 63 percent of people with a mild disability are in the workforce, only 28 percent of those with a severe to very severe disability are working. The median employment income of workers with disabilities is 83 percent of that of other Canadian workers.[40]

Visible Minorities

According to the federal Employment Equity Act, a visible minority is defined as "persons, other than Aboriginal peoples, who are non-Caucasian in race or non-white in colour." Often the terms "visible minority" and "immigrant" are used interchangeably, but these two terms are actually distinct. An immigrant represents a person who was not born in Canada, but resides in Canada for the purpose of settlement. In the 2006 Canadian census, there were almost 6.2 million immigrants in the Canadian population. There were almost 5.1 million persons who self-identified as visible minorities, with the largest representation among South Asians and Chinese, followed by persons who self-identified as black, Filipino, and Latin American. In 1981, 55.5 percent of new immigrants to Canada were visible minorities, but by 2001 that proportion reached 72.9 percent.[41] This suggests that almost three out of every ten immigrants in the last decade were not visible minorities, while there are millions of people born in Canada who are visible minorities, but not immigrants.

Traditionally, visible minorities were typically unable to obtain employment that took full advantage of their knowledge, skills, and abilities (**KSAs**), and thus faced **underemployment.** As a result, visible minorities were included as a designated group. A recent study on diversity in the Greater Toronto Area (GTA) highlighted the continuing disadvantaged status of visible minorities. The study looked at 3257 leaders in the GTA in all sectors and found that just 13 percent were visible minorities (even though visible minorities make up half of the GTA population).[42]

Employment/Labour Standards Legislation

All employers and employees in Canada, including unionized employees, are covered by **employment (labour) standards legislation.** The intent of an employment standards act (ESA) is to establish minimum terms and conditions for workplaces pertaining to such issues as wages; paid holidays and vacations; maternity, parental, or adoption leave (or some mix thereof); bereavement leave; compassionate care leave; termination notice; and overtime pay. They also set the maximum number of hours of work permitted per day or week; overtime pay is required for any work in excess of the maximum.

While employer and employee agreements or practices can exceed minimums established in the ESA, neither party can choose to opt out of or waive their rights as established in the ESA. For example, if the ESA minimum requirement establishes a minimum vacation rate of 4 percent of pay, an employment agreement cannot have a provision for only 3 percent of pay as vacation pay, even if both parties consent.

In contrast, the minimums established in the ESA can be exceeded in employment contracts, through collective bargaining agreements (in unionized positions), or based on common law (precedent established by the judicial system). An employer or employee can agree to 5 percent of pay as vacation pay without violating the ESA, for example.

If there is a conflict between the ESA and another contract, the principle of greater benefit is applied. For example, an employment policy or contract that is communicated to employees stating that in the case of a layoff, employees will be provided with one month notice for every year that they worked if they are laid off. The ESA minimum requires the provision of only one week notice per year that an employee worked, up to an eight-week maximum. In this example, an employee who worked for 10 years would be given the greater benefit (10 months of notice before a layoff), not the minimum under the ESA, to preserve the greater benefit to the employee.

While the ESA provides minimum terms and conditions of employment, it is not totally inclusive. Often, students on work exchange programs, inmates on work projects,

KSAs Knowledge, skills, and abilities.

underemployment Being employed in a job that does not fully utilize one's knowledge, skills, and abilities (KSAs).

employment (labour) standards legislation Laws present in every Canadian jurisdiction that establish minimum employee entitlements and set a limit on the maximum number of hours of work permitted per day or week.

police officers, independent officers, and others are explicitly excluded from protection under the ESA. In addition, regulations for specific occupations such as doctors, lawyers, managers, architects, and specific types of salespersons modify the applicability of certain sections of the ESA.

Enforcement of the ESA

Governed by federal, provincial, or territorial employment standards acts (ESAs), enforcement is complaint based, and violators can be fined. This occurs through the filing of a formal written or electronic complaint against the violator to the appropriate authorities (often the provincial or territorial ministry of labour). A person, union, or corporation can file a complaint with the ministry for violations, given that the ESA has an interest in mitigating the employment relationships between employee and employers.

Employees are required to give up their rights to sue an employer in civil court once a claim is filed with the ministry of labour. This protects employers from dual proceedings on the same issue, and protects courts from being overwhelmed with duplicate cases. There are also strict limitation periods, establishing the maximum amount of time that can elapse between the violation and the filing of a complaint, with these limits differing based on the violation (unpaid wages, vacation pay, and so on). There is also a general maximum claim limit (for example, $10 000 under the Ontario ESA) for unpaid wages. Under the ESA, employees have been awarded compensation for actual unpaid wages and direct earnings losses, time required to find a new job and expenses to seek a new job, benefit plan entitlements, severance pay, and loss of "reasonable expectation" of continued employment.

Respecting Employee Privacy

Privacy Commissioner of Canada
www.priv.gc.ca

Information and Privacy
Commissioner of Ontario
www.ipc.on.ca

Today's employers are grappling with the problem of how to balance employee privacy rights with their need to monitor the use of technology-related tools in the workplace. Employers must maintain the ability to effectively manage their employees and prevent liability to the company, which can be held legally liable for the actions of its employees.[43] They want to eliminate time wasted (on web surfing, playing computer games, and so on) and abuse of company resources (such as use of the Internet and email at work for personal and possibly illegal uses, such as gambling or visiting pornographic sites).[44] For example, one employee used workplace computers to access hundreds of pornographic websites, to surf Internet dating sites for hours at a time, and to maintain personal files with sexually explicit images. The employee was dismissed and an arbitrator upheld the decision, stating that the employee had engaged in serious culpable misconduct.[45] Another concern is employee blogging, as a posting intended to be seen by a few friends that includes confidential company information or comments about management can easily make its way to a national media outlet without the author even knowing it.[46]

Hints | **TO ENSURE LEGAL COMPLIANCE**

Employees are concerned with privacy—their control over information about themselves and their freedom from unjustifiable interference in their personal life. The Personal Information Protection and Electronic Documents Act (PIPEDA) governs the collection, use, and disclosure of personal information across Canada, including employers' collection and dissemination of personal information about employees. Any information beyond name, title, business address, and telephone number is regarded as personal and private, including health-related information provided to insurers. Employers must obtain consent from employees whenever personal information is collected, used, or disclosed.[47]

Some employers have resorted to electronic monitoring, which is becoming easier and less expensive as new software is developed, that can track websites visited by workers and the time spent on each.[48] In general, courts in Canada have permitted electronic surveillance as long as there is proper balancing of opposing interests. Employers are given substantial leeway in monitoring their employees' use of the Internet and email, and they are in an even stronger position if there is a written policy in place. The policy should be updated regularly to reflect changes in technology and should address the use of all company technological equipment away from the employer's premises, including laptops, cellphones, BlackBerrys, and so on.[49] Exhibit 1-9 provides a sample company email and Internet usage policy.

Video Surveillance

Some employers install video surveillance equipment to prevent employee theft and vandalism and to monitor productivity. Employees must be made aware of the surveillance. Unions often file grievances against video surveillance, and arbitrators

---

EXHIBIT 1-9 Sample Company Email and Internet Usage Policy

1. Employees shall not use the Internet or email in any manner that may harm the business interests of the employer, subject the employer to liability, or be offensive to other employees.

2. Employees may use the Internet and email for reasonable limited personal use providing such use does not interfere with job performance or employee productivity.

3. Employee personal email shall include a disclaimer that the views expressed therein are not the views, representations, or position of the company.

4. Employees shall not send, retrieve, or archive any material that may be considered discriminatory, harassment, or creates a hostile work environment.

5. Employees shall post no junk mail or spam.

6. Employees shall not access, attach, or store any information that may compromise the bandwidth of the employer's system.

7. Employees acknowledge the employer has the right to and does monitor both Internet and email use.

8. Employees acknowledge that the employer has the right to keep and store any information resulting from this monitoring.

9. Employees acknowledge the employer has the right to block access and filter any material that the employer determines to be inappropriate, offensive, or a threat to the security of the employer Internet and email system.

10. Employer shall consent to give employees the right to store personal information in "personal" files provided said files do not violate any provisions of this Internet and email policy.

11. Employee agrees that the employer may access any email or computer storage file, including personal files, to protect the interests of the employer.

12. Employer shall disclose to all employees the extent of monitoring, the type of reports, the level of detail, and who will receive these reports.

13. Employer shall disclose to all employees who is responsible for enforcement of email and Internet policy, clarifying interpretation of policy, granting employee use exceptions, and resolving disputes.

14. Employer shall disclose to all employees the penalties for violation of the Internet and email acceptable use policy.

15. Employer and employees shall establish a procedure for both parties' involvement in design and implementation of the company's Internet and email policy, including a system for continual evaluation of that policy and procedures for making changes to it as necessary.

An Ethical | Dilemma

Is it ethical to use video surveillance of employees? Do you think employees need to be told of surveillance tools if they are used?

have been reluctant to support it because of privacy concerns. Courts typically assess whether the surveillance was reasonable and whether there were reasonable alternatives available. Generally, they have decided that video surveillance is not reasonable and that other means could be used.[50] The federal, British Columbia, and Alberta privacy commissioners have jointly issued video surveillance guidelines, which are shown in Exhibit 1-10.

EXHIBIT 1-10 Video Surveillance Guidelines

1. Determine whether a less privacy-invasive alternative to video surveillance would meet your needs.
2. Establish the business reason for conducting video surveillance and use video surveillance only for that reason.
3. Develop a policy on the use of video surveillance.
4. Limit the use and viewing range of cameras as much as possible.
5. Inform the public that video surveillance is taking place.
6. Store any recorded images in a secure location with limited access, and destroy them when they are no longer required for business purposes.
7. Be ready to answer questions from the public. Individuals have the right to know who is watching them and why, as well as what information is being captured and what is being done with recorded images.
8. Give individuals access to information about themselves. This includes video images.
9. Educate camera operators about the obligation to protect the privacy of individuals.
10. Periodically evaluate the need for video surveillance.

Source: Office of the Privacy Commissioner of Canada, "Ten Things to Do," *Guidelines for Overt Video Surveillance in the Private Sector* (March 2008). Reprinted with permission. www.priv.gc.ca/information/ guide/2008/gl_vs0803063.pdf.

2

Perception, Personality, and Emotions

Walmart Canada.[1] Just the thought of the retailer being in Canada upsets some people. There was strong resistance when Walmart first announced it was coming to Canada in 1994, and a belief that the retailer would somehow destroy the fabric of Canadian society. Eighteen years after its arrival, Mississauga, Ontario-based Walmart Canada serves more than 1 million Canadians each day, employs more than 85 000 Canadians in 325 stores across Canada, and is Canada's third-largest employer. The company was ranked as one of Canada's best employers on the Hewitt Associates survey of Canada's Best Employers five times between 2001 and 2007. It has also appeared on KPMG's list of Canada's 25 Most Admired Corporate Cultures, most recently in 2009. It was one of Workplace Institute's winners in 2011 for Best Employers Award for 50-Plus Canadians, which it's won several times previously. In presenting the award, Workplace Institute noted, "Wal-Mart has exceptional hiring and recognition programs and a workplace culture that supports diversity." With all of these positive statements about Walmart Canada, customers are not necessarily convinced of Walmart's greatness. When asked in a 2011 survey how likely they would be to change their shopping habits once Target opens stores in Canada, 57 percent of Walmart shoppers indicated a willingness to shop at Target. Less than 20 percent of Canadian Tire, Shoppers Drug Mart, and Costco customers indicated a willingness to shop at Target. How can the perception of the company be so negative for some individuals?

All of our behaviour is somewhat shaped by our perceptions, personalities, emotions, and experiences. In this chapter, we consider the role that perception plays in affecting the way we see the world and the people around us. We also consider how personality characteristics affect our attitudes toward people and situations. We then consider how emotions shape many of our work-related behaviours.

Perception

1 What is perception?

Perception is the process by which individuals organize and interpret their impressions to give meaning to their environment. However, what we perceive can be substantially different from objective reality. We often disagree about what is real. As we have seen, Walmart Canada has won many awards, but not every Canadian respects the retailer.

Why is perception important in the study of organizational behaviour (OB)? Simply because people's behaviour is based on their perception of what reality is, not on reality itself. *The world as it is perceived is the world that is behaviourally important.* A 2010 study of political behaviour suggests that once individuals hold particular perceptions, it can be quite difficult to change their minds, even if they are shown contrary evidence.[2]

Factors Influencing Perception

How do we explain that individuals may look at the same thing, yet perceive it differently, and both be right? A number of factors operate to shape and sometimes distort perception. These factors can reside in the *perceiver*; in the object, or *target*, being perceived; or in the context of the *situation* in which the perception is made. Exhibit 2-1 summarizes the factors that influence perception.

What causes people to have different perceptions of the same situation?

The Perceiver

When you ("the perceiver") look at a target and attempt to interpret what you see, that interpretation is heavily influenced by your personal characteristics. Characteristics that affect perception include your attitudes, personality, motives, interests, past experiences, and expectations. For instance, if you expect police officers to be authoritative, young people to be lazy, or individuals holding public office to be corrupt, you may perceive them as such, regardless of their actual traits. A 2010 study found that one's perceptions of others reveals a lot about the person themselves.[3] People with positive perceptions of others tended to describe themselves (and be described by others) as "enthusiastic, happy, kind-hearted, courteous, emotionally stable and capable."

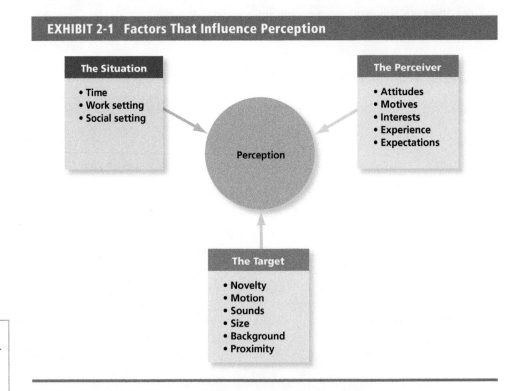

EXHIBIT 2-1 Factors That Influence Perception

The Situation
- Time
- Work setting
- Social setting

The Perceiver
- Attitudes
- Motives
- Interests
- Experience
- Expectations

Perception

The Target
- Novelty
- Motion
- Sounds
- Size
- Background
- Proximity

perception The process by which individuals organize and interpret their impressions in order to give meaning to their environment.

Negative perceptions of others were related to increased narcissism and antisocial behaviour.

The Target

A target's characteristics also affect what we perceive. Loud people are more likely to be noticed in a group than are quiet ones. So too are extremely attractive or unattractive individuals. Novelty, motion, sounds, size, and other characteristics of a target shape the way we see it.

Because we don't look at targets in isolation, the relationship of a target to its background influences perception. For instance, we often perceive women, First Nations, Asians, or members of any other group that has clearly distinguishable characteristics as alike in other, unrelated ways as well.

The Situation

The situation or context is also important. The time at which we see an object or event can influence attention, as can location, light, heat, or any number of situational factors. For example, at a nightclub on Saturday night, you may not notice a young guest "dressed to the nines." Yet that same person so attired for your Monday morning management class would certainly catch your attention (and that of the rest of the class). Neither the perceiver nor the target changed between Saturday night and Monday morning, but the situation is different.

Perceptual Errors

Perceiving and interpreting why others do what they do takes time. As a result, we develop techniques to make this task more manageable. These techniques are frequently valuable—they allow us to make accurate perceptions rapidly and provide valid data for making predictions. However, they are not foolproof. They can and do get us into trouble. Some of the errors that distort the perception process are attribution theory, selective perception, halo effect, contrast effects, projection, and stereotyping.

Can people be mistaken in their perceptions?

Attribution Theory

Attribution theory tries to explain the ways we judge people differently, depending on the meaning we attribute to a given behaviour.[4] Basically, the theory suggests that when we observe what seems like atypical behaviour by an individual, we try to make sense of it. We consider whether the individual is responsible for the behaviour (the cause is internal), or whether something outside the individual caused the behaviour (the cause is external). *Internally* caused behaviour is believed to be under the personal control of the individual. *Externally* caused behaviour is believed to result from outside causes; we see the person as having been forced into the behaviour by the situation. For example, if a student is late for class, the instructor might attribute his lateness to partying into the wee hours of the morning and then oversleeping. This would be an internal attribution. But if the instructor assumes a major automobile accident tied up traffic on the student's regular route to school, that is making an external attribution. In trying to determine whether behaviour is internally or externally caused, we rely on three rules about the behaviour: (1) distinctiveness, (2) consensus, and (3) consistency. Let's discuss each of these in turn.

Whom do you tend to blame when someone makes a mistake? Ever wonder why?

attribution theory The theory that when we observe what seems like atypical behaviour by an individual, we attempt to determine whether it is internally or externally caused.

Distinctiveness **Distinctiveness** refers to whether an individual acts similarly across a variety of situations. Is the student who arrives late for class today also the one who is always goofing off in team meetings, and not answering urgent emails? What we want to know is whether this behaviour is unusual. If it is, we are likely to give it an external attribution. If it's not, we will probably judge the behaviour to be internal.

Consensus If everyone who is faced with a similar situation responds in the same way, we can say the behaviour shows **consensus**. The tardy student's behaviour would meet this criterion if all students who took the same route to school were also late. From an attribution perspective, if consensus is high, you would probably give an external attribution to the student's tardiness. But if other students who took the same route made it to class on time, you would attribute the cause of lateness for the student in question to an internal cause.

Consistency Finally, an observer looks for **consistency** in a person's actions. Does the person respond the same way over time? If a student is usually on time for class, being 10 minutes late will be perceived differently from the student who is late almost every class. The more consistent the behaviour, the more we are inclined to attribute it to internal causes.

Exhibit 2-2 summarizes the key elements in attribution theory. It illustrates, for instance, how to evaluate an employee's behaviour on a new task. To do this, you might note that employee Kim Randolph generally performs at about the same level on other related tasks as she does on her current task (low distinctiveness). You see that other employees frequently perform differently—better or worse—than Kim does on that current task (low consensus). Finally, if Kim's performance on this current task is consistent over time (high consistency), you or anyone else who is judging Kim's work is likely to hold her primarily responsible for her task performance (internal attribution).

Have you ever misjudged a person? Do you know why?

How Attributions Get Distorted One of the more interesting findings from attribution theory is that there are errors or biases that distort attributions. When we judge the behaviour of other people, we tend to underestimate the influence of external factors

distinctiveness A behavioural rule that considers whether an individual acts similarly across a variety of situations.

consensus A behavioural rule that considers if everyone faced with a similar situation responds in the same way.

consistency A behavioural rule that considers whether the individual has been acting in the same way over time.

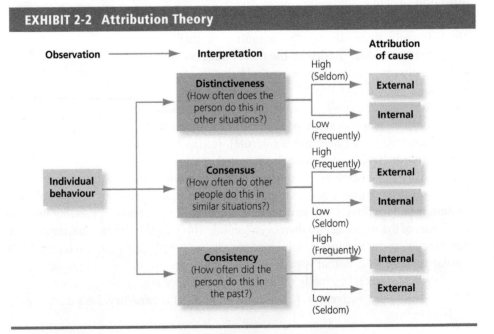

EXHIBIT 2-2 Attribution Theory

EXHIBIT 2-3 Percentage of Individuals Rating Themselves Above Average on Each Attribute

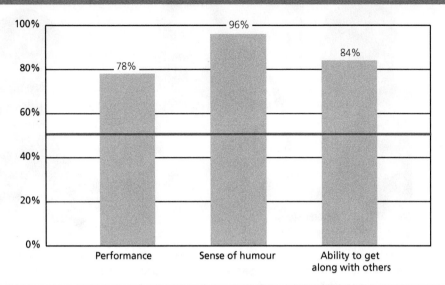

Source: Based on C. Merkle and M. Weber, *True Overconfidence—The Inability of Rational Information Processing to Account for Overconfidence* (March 2009). Available at SSRN: http://ssrn.com/abstract=1373675

and overestimate the influence of internal, or personal, factors.[5] This **fundamental attribution error** can explain why a sales manager attributes the poor performance of his or her sales agents to laziness rather than acknowledging the impact of the innovative product line introduced by a competitor. A 2011 study suggests this same error occurs when we judge leaders to be charismatic, based on limited information.[6] For instance, Steve Jobs, CEO of Apple, gave spellbinding presentations that led him to be considered a charismatic visionary. What the audience does not see is "the ten hours of practice Jobs [committed] to every ten minute pitch," which might make him look less charismatic.[7]

We use **self-serving bias** when we judge ourselves, however. This means that when we are successful, we are more likely to believe it was because of internal factors, such as ability or effort. When we fail, however, we blame external factors, such as luck. In general, people tend to believe that their own behaviour is more positive than the behaviour of those around them. Research suggests, however, that individuals tend to overestimate their own good behaviour, and underestimate the good behaviour of others.[8] Exhibit 2-3 illustrates this point.

Selective Perception

Because it's impossible for us to see everything, any characteristic that makes a person, object, or event stand out will increase the probability that it will be perceived. This tendency explains why you are more likely to notice cars that look like your own. It also explains why some people may be reprimanded by their manager for doing something that goes unnoticed when other employees do it. Since we cannot observe everything going on about us, we engage in **selective perception**.

But how does selectivity work as a shortcut in judging other people? Since we cannot take in all that we observe, we take in bits and pieces. But we do not choose randomly; rather, we select according to our interests, background, experience, and attitudes. Selective perception allows us to speed-read others, but not without the risk of coming to an inaccurate conclusion. Because we see what we want to see, we can draw unwarranted conclusions from an ambiguous situation. Selective perception led the Law Society of BC to discriminate against lawyers who suffer from a mental illness.

fundamental attribution error The tendency to underestimate the influence of external factors and overestimate the influence of internal factors when making judgments about the behaviour of others.

self-serving bias The tendency for individuals to attribute their own successes to internal factors while putting the blame for failures on external factors.

selective perception People's selective interpretation of what they see based on their interests, background, experience, and attitudes.

The behaviours that both women and men engage in can affect the perceptions that others have about their ability to become senior managers. A 2010 study found that assertiveness and independence were top qualities to exhibit, and individuals who did not do so were deemed less suited to be CEOs.[9] Those judging the suitability were engaging in selective perception.

Halo Effect

When we draw a general impression of an individual on the basis of a single characteristic, such as intelligence, likeability, or appearance, a **halo effect** operates.[10] If you are a critic of Prime Minister Stephen Harper, try listing 10 things you admire about him. If you are an admirer, try listing 10 things you dislike about him. No matter which group describes you, odds are that you will not find this an easy exercise! That is the halo effect: Our general views contaminate our specific ones.

The reality of the halo effect was confirmed in a classic study. Subjects were given a list of traits and asked to evaluate the person to whom those traits applied.[11] When traits such as intelligent, skillful, practical, industrious, determined, and warm were used, the person was judged to be wise, humorous, popular, and imaginative. When cold was substituted for warm, a completely different set of perceptions was obtained, though otherwise the list was identical. Clearly, the subjects were allowing a single trait to influence their overall impression of the person being judged.

Contrast Effects

There is an old saying among entertainers: "Never follow an act that has children or animals in it." Why? Audiences love children and animals so much that you will look bad in comparison.

This example demonstrates how **contrast effects** can distort perceptions. We don't evaluate a person in isolation. Our reaction to one person is often influenced by other people we have recently encountered.

In a series of job interviews, for instance, interviewers can make distortions in any given candidate's evaluation as a result of his or her place in the interview schedule. The candidate is likely to receive a more favourable evaluation if preceded by mediocre applicants, and a less favourable evaluation if preceded by strong applicants.

Projection

It's easy to judge others if we assume that they are similar to us. For instance, if you want challenge and responsibility in your job, you assume that others want the same. Or you are honest and trustworthy, so you take it for granted that other people are equally reliable. This tendency to attribute our own characteristics to other people is called **projection**.

halo effect Drawing a general impression of an individual on the basis of a single characteristic.

contrast effects The concept that our reaction to one person is often influenced by other people we have recently encountered.

projection Attributing one's own characteristics to other people.

Aboriginal hip-hop artists, led by Winnipeg's Most (pictured here), have created a coalition against the negative stereotyping of Indigenous rappers by the mainstream media. This initiative is an opportunity for Indigenous hip hop to define itself in a sustainable and healthy manner for the future. Aboriginal musician Jarrett Martineau says that hip hop is popular with Aboriginal youth because it deals with oppression and dispossession and because First Nations culture has a strong tradition of storytelling.[12]

People who engage in projection tend to perceive others according to what they themselves are like, rather than perceiving others as they really are. Because they always judge people as being similar to themselves, when they observe someone who is actually like them, their perceptions are naturally correct. But when they observe others who are not like them, their perceptions are not as accurate. Managers who engage in projection compromise their ability to respond to individual differences. They tend to see people as more homogeneous than they really are.

Stereotyping

When we judge someone on the basis of our perception of the group to which he or she belongs, we are using the shortcut called **stereotyping**.

We rely on generalizations every day because they help us make decisions quickly. They are a means of simplifying a complex world. It's less difficult to deal with an unmanageable number of stimuli if we use **heuristics** (judgment shortcuts in decision making) or stereotypes. For example, it does make sense to assume that Tre, the new employee from accounting, is going to know something about budgeting, or that Allie from finance will be able to help you figure out a forecasting problem. The problem occurs, of course, when we generalize inaccurately or too much. In organizations, we frequently hear comments that represent stereotypes based on gender, age, race, religion, ethnicity, and even weight:[13] "Women will not relocate for a promotion," "men are not interested in child care," "older workers cannot learn new skills," "Asian immigrants are hard-working and conscientious," "overweight people lack discipline." Stereotypes can be so deeply ingrained and powerful that they influence life-and-death decisions. One study showed that, controlling for a wide array of factors (such as aggravating or mitigating circumstances), the degree to which black defendants in murder trials looked "stereotypically black" essentially doubled their odds of receiving a death sentence if convicted.[14]

One of the problems of stereotypes is that they *are* widespread and often useful generalizations, despite the fact that they may not contain a shred of truth when applied to a particular person or situation. So we constantly have to check ourselves to make sure we are not unfairly or inaccurately applying a stereotype in our evaluations and decisions. Stereotypes are an example of the warning, "The more useful, the more danger

stereotyping Judging someone on the basis of one's perception of the group to which that person belongs.

heuristics Judgment shortcuts in decision making.

Muslim women in Canada often experience discrimination in being hired, or how their co-workers treat them, when they wear a hijab. Some co-workers of nurse practitioner Sharon Hoosein, shown here, were surprised that she returned to work following her maternity leave. They assumed that because of her religion she would be expected to stay at home to raise children rather than work.

from misuse." Stereotypes can lead to strong negative reactions, such as prejudice, which we describe below.

Prejudice **Prejudice** is an unfounded dislike of a person or group based on their belonging to a particular stereotyped group. For instance, an individual may dislike people of a particular religion, or state that they do not want to work with someone of a particular ethnicity. Prejudice can lead to negative consequences in the workplace and, in particular, to discrimination. For instance, an individual of a particular ethnic group might be passed over for a management position because of the belief that employees might not see that person as a good manager. In another instance, an individual in his 50s who is looking for work but cannot find a job may be discriminated against because of the belief that younger workers are more appealing than older workers. Prejudice generally starts with stereotypes and then has negative emotional content added. Prejudice is harmful to the person who is the target of the behaviour. A 2011 study by researchers from the University of Toronto found that Asian women are more likely to take racism than sexism personally and were more negatively affected by racism.[15]

Why Do Perception and Judgment Matter?

People in organizations are always judging one another. Managers must appraise their employees' performances. We evaluate how much effort our co-workers are putting into their jobs. When a new person joins a work team, the other members immediately "size her up." Individuals even make judgments about people's virtues based on whether they exercise, as a recent study by McMaster University professor Kathleen Martin Ginis showed.[16] In many cases, judgments have important consequences for the organization. A 2010 study found that in organizations that did not seem to value innovation, employees who wanted to see change were often afraid to speak out, due to fear of negative perceptions from co-workers who valued the status quo.[17] Another 2010 study found that positive employee perceptions of an organization

Can perception really affect outcomes?

prejudice An unfounded dislike of a person or group based on their belonging to a particular stereotyped group.

have a positive impact on retention, customer loyalty, and financial outcomes.[18] A 2011 study noted that individuals who misperceive how well they have done on a task (positively or negatively) tended to prepare less and to perform poorly in subsequent tasks.[19]

Let's briefly look at a few of the most obvious applications of judgment shortcuts in the workplace: employment interviews, performance expectations, and performance evaluations.

Employment Interviews

It's fair to say that few people are hired without undergoing an interview. But interviewers make perceptual judgments that are often inaccurate[20] and draw early impressions that quickly become entrenched. Research shows we form impressions of others within a tenth of a second, based on our first glance.[21] If these first impressions are negative, they tend to be more heavily weighted in the interview than if that same information came out later.[22] Most interviewers' decisions change very little after the first four or five minutes of an interview. As a result, information that comes out early in the interview carries greater weight than information that comes out later, and a "good applicant" is probably characterized more by the absence of unfavourable characteristics than by the presence of favourable ones.

Performance Expectations

People attempt to validate their perceptions of reality even when they are faulty.[23] The terms **self-fulfilling prophecy** and *Pygmalion effect* describe how an individual's behaviour is determined by others' expectations. If a manager expects big things from her people, they are not likely to let her down. Similarly, if she expects only minimal performance, they will likely meet those low expectations. Expectations become reality. The self-fulfilling prophecy has been found to affect the performance of students, soldiers, and even accountants.[24]

Performance Evaluations

Performance evaluations very much depend on the perceptual process.[25] An employee's future is closely tied to the appraisal—promotion, pay raises, and continuation of employment are among the most obvious outcomes. Although the appraisal can be objective (for example, a salesperson is appraised on how many dollars of sales he generates in his territory), many jobs are evaluated in subjective terms. Subjective evaluations, though often necessary, are problematic because all the errors we have discussed thus far—selective perception, contrast effects, halo effect, and so on—affect them. Ironically, sometimes performance ratings say as much about the evaluator as they do about the employee!

As you can see, perception plays a large role in how people are evaluated. Personality, which we review next, is another major factor affecting how people relate to and evaluate one another in the workplace.

Personality

Walmart faced great outrage from Canadians when it first entered Canada in 1994.[26] Target will arrive in Canada in 2013, taking over more than 130 Zellers locations. Walmart and Target have different personalities. "Target stocks its shelves with low-cost bedspreads, shower curtains, and clothes with bright colors and funky designs. Walmart is for the necessities: cheap Cheerios, laundry detergent, bulk meat, paper plates."

The image of Target is fun, while Walmart's image is frugal. In other words, they have different personalities.

2 What is personality and how does it affect behaviour?

self-fulfilling prophecy A concept that proposes a person will behave in ways consistent with how he or she is perceived by others.

Organizational personalities can be interesting, but even more interesting is the impact of individual personalities on organizational behaviour. Why are some people quiet and passive, while others are loud and aggressive? Are certain personality types better adapted for certain job types? Before we can answer these questions, we need to address a more basic one: What is personality?

What Is Personality?

When we talk of personality, we don't mean that a person has charm, a positive attitude toward life, a smiling face, or is a finalist for "Happiest and Friendliest." When psychologists talk of personality, they mean a dynamic concept describing the growth and development of a person's whole psychological system.

Gordon Allport produced the most frequently used definition of *personality* more than 70 years ago. He said personality is "the dynamic organization within the individual of those psychophysical systems that determine his unique adjustments to his environment."[27] For our purposes, you should think of **personality** as the stable patterns of behaviour and consistent internal states that determine how an individual reacts to and interacts with others. It's most often described in terms of measurable traits that a person exhibits.

Measuring Personality

The most important reason managers need to know how to measure personality is that research has shown that personality tests are useful in hiring decisions. Scores on personality tests help managers forecast who is the best fit for a job.[28] Some managers use personality tests to better understand and more effectively manage the people who work for them. The most common means of measuring personality is through self-report surveys, with which individuals evaluate themselves on a series of factors, such as "I worry a lot about the future." Though self-report measures work well when well constructed, one weakness of these measures is that the respondent might lie or practise impression management—that is, the person could "fake it" on the test to create a good impression. Evidence shows that when people know that their personality scores are going to be used for hiring decisions, they rate themselves as about half a standard deviation more conscientious and emotionally stable than if they are taking the test just to learn more about themselves.[29] Another problem is accuracy. A perfectly good candidate could have just been in a bad mood when the survey was taken.

Observer ratings provide an independent assessment of personality. Here, a co-worker or another observer does the rating (sometimes with the subject's knowledge and sometimes without). Though the results of self-reports and observer ratings are strongly correlated, research suggests that observer ratings are a better predictor of success on the job.[30] However, each can tell us something unique about an individual's behaviour in the workplace.

Personality Determinants

An early argument in personality research centred on whether an individual's personality was predetermined at birth or the result of the individual's interaction with his or her environment. Clearly, there is no simple answer. Personality appears to be a result of both influences. In addition, today we recognize a third factor—the situation. Thus, an adult's personality is now generally considered to be made up of both hereditary and environmental factors, moderated by situational conditions.

Heredity

Heredity refers to those factors that were determined at conception. Physical stature, facial attractiveness, gender, temperament, muscle composition and reflexes, energy

personality The stable patterns of behaviour and consistent internal states that determine how an individual reacts to and interacts with others.

level, and biological rhythms are characteristics that are generally considered to be either completely or substantially influenced by your parents' biological, physiological, and inherent psychological makeup. The heredity approach argues that the ultimate explanation of an individual's personality is a person's genes.

Are people born with their personalities?

If heredity played little or no part in determining personality, you would expect to find few similarities between identical twins who were separated at birth and raised separately. But researchers who looked at more than 100 sets of separated twins found a lot in common.[31] For almost every behavioural trait, a significant part of the variation between the twins turned out to be associated with genetic factors. For instance, one set of twins, who had been separated for 39 years and raised 70 kilometres apart, were found to drive the same model and colour car, chain-smoke the same brand of cigarette, own dogs with the same name, and regularly vacation within three blocks of each other in a beach community 2000 kilometres away.

Researchers have found that genetics can explain about 50 percent of the personality differences and more than 30 percent of the variation in occupational and leisure interests found in individuals. In other words, blood-related siblings are likely to have more similar personalities, occupations, and leisure interests than unrelated people.

Does personality change over one's lifetime? Most research in this area suggests that while some aspects of our personalities do change over time, the rank orderings do not change very much. For example, people's scores on measures of conscientiousness tend to increase as they get older. However, there are still strong individual differences in conscientiousness, and despite the fact that most of us become more responsible over time, people tend to change by about the same amount, so that the rank order stays roughly the same.[32] For instance, if you are more conscientious than your sibling now, that is likely to be true in 20 years, even though you both should become more conscientious over time. Consistent with the notion that the teenage years are periods of great exploration and change, research has shown that personality is more changeable in adolescence and more stable among adults.[33]

Personality Traits

The early work in the structure of personality revolved around attempts to identify and label enduring characteristics that describe an individual's behaviour. Popular characteristics include shy, aggressive, submissive, lazy, ambitious, loyal, and timid. Those characteristics, when they are exhibited in a large number of situations, are called **personality traits**.[34] The more consistent the characteristic and the more frequently it occurs in diverse situations, the more important that trait is in describing the individual.

A number of early research efforts tried to identify the *primary* traits that govern behaviour.[35] However, for the most part, they resulted in long lists of traits that were difficult to generalize from and provided little practical guidance to organizational decision makers. Two exceptions are the Myers-Briggs Type Indicator and the Big Five Personality Model, the dominant frameworks for identifying and classifying traits.

Keep in mind that each of us reacts differently to personality traits. This is partially a function of how we perceive those traits. In Exhibit 2-4, you will note that Lucy tells Linus a few things about his personality.

The Myers-Briggs Type Indicator

The **Myers-Briggs Type Indicator (MBTI)** is the most widely used personality-assessment instrument in the world.[36] It's a 100-question personality test that asks people how they usually feel or act in particular situations. On the basis of their

personality traits Enduring characteristics that describe an individual's behaviour.

Myers-Briggs Type Indicator (MBTI) A personality test that taps four characteristics and classifies people into 1 of 16 personality types.

EXHIBIT 2-4

Source: Peanuts, reprinted by permission of Universal Uclick.

answers, individuals are classified as extraverted or introverted (E or I), sensing or intuitive (S or N), thinking or feeling (T or F), and judging or perceiving (J or P). These terms are defined as follows:

- *Extraverted/introverted.* Extraverted individuals are outgoing, sociable, and assertive. Introverts are quiet and shy. E/I measures where we direct our energy when dealing with people and things.

- *Sensing/intuitive.* Sensing types are practical and prefer routine and order. They focus on details. Intuitives rely on unconscious processes and look at the "big picture." This dimension looks at how we process information.

- *Thinking/feeling.* Thinking types use reason and logic to handle problems. Feeling types rely on their personal values and emotions.

- *Judging/perceiving.* Judging types want control and prefer their world to be ordered and structured. Perceiving types are flexible and spontaneous.

These classifications together describe 16 personality types. To illustrate, let's look at three examples:

- *INTJs are visionaries.* They usually have original minds and great drive for their own ideas and purposes. They are skeptical, critical, independent, determined, and often stubborn.

- *ESTJs are organizers.* They are realistic, logical, analytical, decisive, and have a natural head for business or mechanics. They like to organize and run activities.

- *ENTPs are conceptualizers.* They are innovative, individualistic, versatile, and attracted to entrepreneurial ideas. They tend to be resourceful in solving challenging problems, but may neglect routine assignments.

A book profiling 13 contemporary business people who created super-successful firms including Apple Computer, FedEx, Honda Motor, Microsoft, and Sony found that all are intuitive thinkers (NTs).[37] This result is particularly interesting because intuitive thinkers represent only about 5 percent of the population.

The MBTI is widely used by organizations including Apple Computer, AT&T, Citigroup, GE, 3M, many hospitals and educational institutions, and even the US Armed Forces. In spite of its popularity, the evidence is mixed as to whether the MBTI is a valid measure of personality—with most of the evidence suggesting that it is not.[38] One problem is that it forces a person into either one type or another (that is, you are either introverted or extraverted). There is no in-between, though people can be both extraverted and introverted to some degree. The best we can say is that the MBTI can be a valuable tool for increasing self-awareness and providing career guidance. But because results tend to be unrelated to job performance, managers probably should not use it as a selection test for job candidates.

The Big Five Personality Model

The MBTI may lack valid supporting evidence, but that cannot be said for the **Big Five Personality Model**. An impressive body of research supports the notion that five basic personality dimensions underlie all others and encompass most of the significant variation in human personality.[39] The Big Five personality factors are as follows:

- **Extraversion**. This dimension captures a person's comfort level with relationships. Extraverts tend to be gregarious, assertive, and sociable. Introverts tend to be reserved, timid, and quiet.

- **Agreeableness**. This dimension refers to a person's propensity to defer to others. Highly agreeable people are cooperative, warm, and trusting. People who score low on agreeableness are cold, disagreeable, and antagonistic.

- **Conscientiousness**. This dimension is a measure of reliability. A highly conscientious person is responsible, organized, dependable, and persistent. Those who score low on this dimension are easily distracted, disorganized, and unreliable.

- **Emotional stability**. This dimension—often labelled by its converse, *neuroticism*—taps into a person's ability to withstand stress. People with positive emotional stability tend to be calm, self-confident, and secure. Those with high negative scores tend to be nervous, anxious, depressed, and insecure.

- **Openness to experience**. The final dimension addresses a person's range of interests and fascination with novelty. Extremely open people are creative, curious, and artistically sensitive. Those at the other end of the openness category are conventional and find comfort in the familiar.

Researchers at the University of Toronto have recently created a "fake proof" personality test to measure the Big Five factors.[40] Professor Jordan Peterson, one of the researchers, noted that it is common for people to try to "make themselves look better than they actually are on these questionnaires. . . . This sort of faking can distort the predictive validity of these tests, with significant negative economic consequences. We wanted to develop a measure that could predict real-world performance even in the absence of completely honest responding."[41]

Exhibit 2-5 shows the characteristics for the high and low dimensions of each Big Five personality factor.

RESEARCH FINDINGS: The Big Five

Research on the Big Five has found a relationship between the personality dimensions and job performance.[42] As the authors of the most-cited review put it, "The preponderance of evidence shows that individuals who are dependable, reliable, careful, thorough, able to plan, organized, hardworking, persistent, and achievement-oriented tend to have higher job performance in most if not all occupations."[43] In addition, employees who score higher in conscientiousness develop higher levels of job knowledge, probably because highly conscientious people learn more (a review of 138 studies revealed conscientiousness was rather strongly related to grade point average).[44] Higher levels of job knowledge then contribute to higher levels of job performance.[45]

Although conscientiousness is the Big Five trait most consistently related to job performance, the other traits are related to aspects of performance in some situations. All five traits also have other implications for work and for life. Let's look at the implications of these traits, one at a time. (Exhibit 2-6 summarizes the discussion.)

Big Five Personality Model A personality assessment model that taps five basic dimensions.

extraversion A personality factor that describes the degree to which a person is sociable, talkative, and assertive.

agreeableness A personality factor that describes the degree to which a person is good-natured, cooperative, and trusting.

conscientiousness A personality factor that describes the degree to which a person is responsible, dependable, persistent, and achievement-oriented.

emotional stability A personality dimension that characterizes someone as calm, self-confident, secure (positive) vs. nervous, depressed, and insecure (negative).

openness to experience A personality factor that describes the degree to which a person is imaginative, artistically sensitive, and curious.

EXHIBIT 2-5 Big Five Personality Factors

Low   **Extraversion**   **High**

Reserved	Gregarious
Timid	Assertive
Quiet	Sociable

Agreeableness

Cold	Cooperative
Disagreeable	Warm
Antagonistic	Empathetic
	Trusting

Conscientiousness

Easily distracted	Responsible
Disorganized	Organized
Unreliable	Dependable
	Persistent

Emotional Stability

Hostile	Calm
Anxious	Self-confident
Depressed	Secure
Insecure	

Openness to Experience

Unimaginative	Creative
Inflexible	Flexible
Literal-minded	Curious
Dull	Artistic

EXHIBIT 2-6 How the Big Five Traits Influence OB

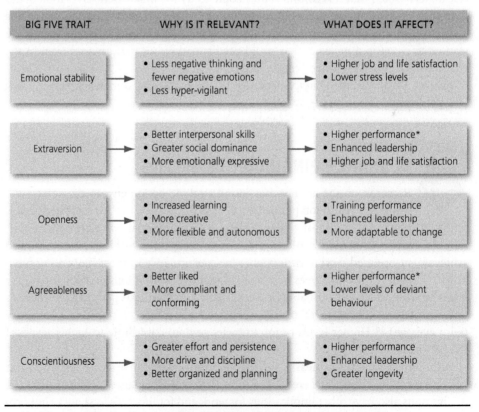

BIG FIVE TRAIT	WHY IS IT RELEVANT?	WHAT DOES IT AFFECT?
Emotional stability	• Less negative thinking and fewer negative emotions • Less hyper-vigilant	• Higher job and life satisfaction • Lower stress levels
Extraversion	• Better interpersonal skills • Greater social dominance • More emotionally expressive	• Higher performance* • Enhanced leadership • Higher job and life satisfaction
Openness	• Increased learning • More creative • More flexible and autonomous	• Training performance • Enhanced leadership • More adaptable to change
Agreeableness	• Better liked • More compliant and conforming	• Higher performance* • Lower levels of deviant behaviour
Conscientiousness	• Greater effort and persistence • More drive and discipline • Better organized and planning	• Higher performance • Enhanced leadership • Greater longevity

*In jobs requiring significant teamwork or frequent interpersonal interactions.

Emotional stability. People who score high on emotional stability are happier than those who score low. Of the Big Five traits, emotional stability is most strongly related to life satisfaction, job satisfaction, and low stress levels. This is probably true because high scorers are more likely to be positive and optimistic in their thinking and experience fewer negative emotions. People low on emotional stability are hyper-vigilant (looking for problems or impending signs of danger), and are especially vulnerable to the physical and psychological effects of stress.

Extraversion. Extraverts tend to be happier in their jobs and in their lives as a whole. They experience more positive emotions than do introverts, and they more freely express these feelings. They also tend to perform better in jobs that require significant interpersonal interaction, perhaps because they have more social skills—they usually have more friends and spend more time in social situations than introverts. Finally, extraversion is a relatively strong predictor of leadership emergence in groups; extraverts are more socially dominant, "take charge" sorts of people, and they are generally more assertive than introverts.[46] One downside of extraversion is that extraverts are more impulsive than introverts; they are more likely to be absent from work and engage in risky behaviour such as unprotected sex, drinking, and other impulsive or sensation-seeking acts.[47] One study also found that extraverts were more likely to lie during job interviews than introverts.[48]

Openness to experience. Individuals who score high on openness to experience are more creative in science and in art than those who score low. Because creativity is important to leadership, open people are more likely to be effective leaders. They also are more comfortable with ambiguity and change than are those who score lower on this trait. As a result, open people cope better with organizational change and are more adaptable in changing contexts.[49] Recent evidence also suggests, however, that they are especially susceptible to workplace accidents.[50]

Agreeableness. You might expect agreeable people to be happier than disagreeable people, and they are, but only slightly. When people choose romantic partners, friends, or organizational team members, agreeable individuals are usually their first choice. Thus, agreeable individuals are better liked than disagreeable people, which explains why they tend to do better in interpersonally oriented jobs such as customer service. They also are more compliant and rule abiding and less likely to get into accidents as a result. Agreeable children do better in school and as adults are less likely to get involved

Indra Nooyi, CEO and chair of PepsiCo, scores high on all personality dimensions of the Big Five Model. She is described as sociable, agreeable, conscientious, emotionally stable, and open to experiences. These personality traits have contributed to Nooyi's high job performance and career success at PepsiCo and are the reason she landed the CEO position.

It is unusual for two people to share the CEO role, but Ronnen Harary (left) and Anton Rabie (right), co-CEOs of Toronto-based toy company Spin Master (pictured with executive vice-president Ben Varadi), like the arrangement. Rabie is an extrovert, while Harary is an introvert. The childhood friends feel their personalities complement each other, making an ideal management team.

in drugs or excessive drinking.[51] They also are less likely to engage in organizational deviance. One downside of agreeableness is that it is associated with lower levels of career success (especially earnings). Agreeable individuals may be poorer negotiators; they are so concerned with pleasing others that they often don't negotiate as much for themselves as they might.[52]

Conscientiousness. Conscientious people live longer than less conscientious people because they tend to take better care of themselves (eat better, exercise more) and engage in fewer risky behaviours (smoking, drinking/drugs, risky sexual or driving behaviour).[53] Still, probably because they are so organized and structured, conscientious people don't adapt as well to changing contexts. They are generally performance-oriented and have more trouble learning complex skills early in the training process because their focus is on performing well rather than on learning. Finally, they are often less creative than less conscientious people, especially artistically.[54]

Other Personality Attributes Influencing OB

Although the Big Five traits have proven highly relevant to OB, they don't exhaust the range of traits that can describe someone's personality. Now we will look at other, more specific attributes that are powerful predictors of behaviour in organizations. The first relates to one's core self-evaluation. The others are Machiavellianism, narcissism, self-monitoring, propensity for risk-taking, and Type A and B and proactive personalities. We shall briefly introduce these attributes and summarize what we know about their ability to explain and predict employee behaviour.

Core Self-Evaluation

core self-evaluation The degree to which an individual likes or dislikes himself or herself, whether the person sees himself or herself as capable and effective, and whether the person feels in control of his or her environment or powerless over the environment.

People who have positive **core self-evaluations** like themselves and see themselves as effective, capable, and in control of their environment. Those with negative core self-evaluations tend to dislike themselves, question their capabilities, and view themselves as powerless over their environment.[55]

People with positive core self-evaluations perform better than others because they set more ambitious goals, are more committed to their goals, and persist longer at attempting to reach these goals. For example, one study of life-insurance agents found that core self-evaluations were critical predictors of performance. In life-insurance sales, 90 percent of sales calls end in rejection, so an agent has to believe in him- or herself to persist. In fact, this study showed that the majority of successful salespersons had positive core self-evaluations.[56] Such people also provide better customer service, are more popular co-workers, and have careers that both begin on better footing and ascend more rapidly over time.[57]

You might wonder whether someone can be too positive. What happens when someone thinks he is capable, but he is actually incompetent? One study of *Fortune* 500 CEOs, for example, showed that many are overconfident, and their perceived infallibility often causes them to make bad decisions.[58] While many people are overconfident, just as many people sell themselves short and are less happy and effective than they could be because of lack of confidence. If we decide we cannot do something, for example, we won't try, and not doing it only reinforces our self-doubts.

Machiavellianism

The personality characteristic of **Machiavellianism** (Mach) is named after Niccolò Machiavelli, who wrote in the sixteenth century on how to gain and use power. An individual high in Machiavellianism is pragmatic, maintains emotional distance, and believes that ends can justify means. "If it works, use it" is consistent with a high-Mach perspective.

A considerable amount of research has related high- and low-Mach personalities to certain behavioural outcomes.[59] High Machs manipulate more, win more, are persuaded less, and persuade others more than do low Machs.[60] They like their jobs less, are more stressed by their work, and engage in more deviant work behaviours.[61] Yet high-Mach outcomes are moderated by situational factors. It has been found that high Machs do better (1) when they interact face to face with others rather than indirectly; (2) when the situation has a minimum number of rules and regulations, thus allowing room for improvising; and (3) when emotional involvement with details irrelevant to winning distracts low Machs.[62]

Should we conclude that high Machs make good employees? That answer depends on the type of job and whether you consider ethical implications in evaluating performance. In jobs that require bargaining skills (such as labour negotiation) or that offer substantial rewards for winning (as in commissioned sales), high Machs will be productive. But if the ends cannot justify the means, if there are absolute standards of behaviour, or if the three situational factors noted in the preceding paragraph are not in evidence, our ability to predict a high Mach's performance will be severely limited.

Narcissism

Hans likes to be the centre of attention. He likes to look at himself in the mirror a lot. He has extravagant dreams and seems to consider himself a person of many talents. Hans is a narcissist. The term is from the Greek myth of Narcissus, the story of a man so vain and proud that he fell in love with his own image. In psychology, **narcissism** describes a person who has a grandiose sense of self-importance, requires excessive admiration, has a sense of entitlement, and is arrogant.[63] Are today's youth narcissistic? Despite claims to that effect, the evidence is unclear. High school seniors in 2006 were more likely than in 1975 to agree they would be "very good" spouses (56 percent of 2006 seniors, compared with 37 percent in 1975), parents (54 percent of 2006 seniors, 36 percent in 1975), and workers (65 percent of 2006 seniors, 49 percent in 1975). On the other hand, scores on the Narcissistic Personality Inventory—the most common measure of narcissism—have not increased since 1982.[64]

Whether it is increasing or not, narcissism can have pretty toxic consequences. A 2011 study found that narcissists were more likely to cheat on exams than others, in

Machiavellianism The degree to which an individual is pragmatic, maintains emotional distance, and believes that ends can justify means.

narcissism The tendency to be arrogant, have a grandiose sense of self-importance, require excessive admiration, and have a sense of entitlement.

part because they did not feel guilty doing so.[65] A study found that while narcissists thought they were *better* leaders than their colleagues, their supervisors actually rated them as *worse*. For example, an Oracle executive described that company's CEO, Larry Ellison, as follows: "The difference between God and Larry is that God does not believe he is Larry."[66] Because narcissists often want to gain the admiration of others and receive affirmation of their superiority, they tend to "talk down" to those who threaten them, treating others as if they were inferior. Narcissists also tend to be selfish and exploitive, and they often carry the attitude that others exist for their benefit.[67] Studies indicate that narcissists are rated by their bosses as less effective at their jobs than others, particularly when it comes to helping other people.[68] Despite these negative outcomes, one 2011 study found that having two or more narcissists on a team can lead to more creativity.[69] Because narcissists want admiration from their peers, they will attempt to outdo one another, raising the competitiveness within the team.

Self-Monitoring

Self-monitoring refers to an individual's ability to adjust his or her behaviour to external, situational factors.[70] Individuals high in self-monitoring show considerable adaptability in adjusting their behaviour to external situational factors. They are highly sensitive to external cues and can behave differently in different situations. High self-monitors are capable of presenting striking contradictions between their public personae and their private selves. Low self-monitors cannot disguise themselves in the same way. They tend to display their true dispositions and attitudes in every situation. There is high behavioural consistency between who they are and what they do.

Research suggests that high self-monitors tend to pay closer attention to the behaviour of others and are more capable of conforming than are low self-monitors.[71] High self-monitoring managers tend to be more mobile in their careers and receive more promotions (both internal and cross-organizational) and are more likely to occupy central positions in an organization.[72] High self-monitors also receive better performance ratings, are more likely to emerge as leaders, and show less commitment to their organizations.[73]

Risk-Taking

People differ in their willingness to take chances, a quality that affects how much time and information managers require before they make a decision. In one study, 79 managers worked on simulated exercises that required them to make hiring decisions.[74] High **risk-taking** managers made more rapid decisions and used less information in making their choices than did the low risk-taking managers. Interestingly, the decision accuracy was the same for both groups.

Although previous studies have shown managers in large organizations to be more risk averse than are growth-oriented entrepreneurs who actively manage small businesses, recent findings suggest that managers in large organizations may actually be more willing to take risks than entrepreneurs.[75] The work population as a whole also differs in risk propensity.[76] It makes sense to recognize these differences and even to consider aligning risk-taking propensity with specific job demands. A high risk-taking propensity may lead to more effective performance for a stock trader in a brokerage firm because that type of job demands rapid decision making. On the other hand, a willingness to take risks might prove a major obstacle to an accountant who performs auditing activities. The latter job might be better filled by someone with a low risk-taking propensity.

Type A and Type B Personalities

Do you know people who are excessively competitive and always seem to be chronically pushed for time? If you do, it's a good bet that those people have a Type A personality.

self-monitoring A personality trait that measures an individual's ability to adjust behaviour to external, situational factors.

risk-taking A personality willingness to take chances or risks.

A person with a **Type A personality** is "aggressively involved in a chronic, incessant struggle to achieve more and more in less and less time, and, if required to do so, against the opposing efforts of other things or other persons."[77] In North American culture, such characteristics tend to be highly prized and positively associated with ambition and the successful acquisition of material goods.

Type As tend to have the following characteristics:

- Are always moving, walking, and eating rapidly

- Feel impatient with the rate at which most events take place

- Strive to think or do two or more things at once

- Cannot cope with leisure time

- Are obsessed with numbers, measuring their success in terms of how many or how much of everything they acquire

Do you think it is better to be a Type A or a Type B personality?

A person with a **Type B personality** is exactly the opposite of a Type A, "rarely harried by the desire to obtain a wildly increasing number of things or participate in an endless growing series of events in an ever-decreasing amount of time."[78]

Type Bs tend to have the following characteristics:

- Never suffer from a sense of time urgency, with its accompanying impatience

- Feel no need to display or discuss either their achievements or accomplishments unless such exposure is demanded by the situation

- Play for fun and relaxation, rather than to exhibit their superiority at any cost

- Can relax without guilt

Type As operate under moderate to high levels of stress. They subject themselves to more or less continuous time pressure, creating a life of deadlines. These characteristics result in some rather specific behavioural outcomes. Type As are fast workers because they emphasize quantity over quality. In managerial positions, Type As demonstrate their competitiveness by working long hours and, not infrequently, making poor decisions because they make them too fast.

Stressed Type As are also rarely creative. Because of their concern with quantity and speed, they rely on past experiences when faced with problems. They will not take the time that is necessary to develop unique solutions to new problems. They rarely vary in their responses to specific challenges in their environment. As a result, their behaviour is easier to predict than that of Type Bs.

Are Type As or Type Bs more successful in organizations? Type As do better than Type Bs in job interviews because they are more likely to be judged as having desirable traits such as high drive, competence, aggressiveness, and success motivation.[79] Despite the hard work of Type As, Type Bs are the ones who appear to make it to the top. Great salespeople are usually Type As; senior executives are usually Type Bs. Why? The answer lies in the tendency of Type As to trade off quality of effort for quantity. Promotions in corporate and professional organizations "usually go to those who are wise rather than to those who are merely hasty, to those who are tactful rather than to those who are hostile, and to those who are creative rather than to those who are merely agile in competitive strife."[80]

Proactive Personality

Did you ever notice that some people actively take the initiative to improve their current circumstances or create new ones? These are people with a proactive personality.[81] People with a **proactive personality** identify opportunities, show initiative,

Type A personality A personality with aggressive involvement in a chronic, incessant struggle to achieve more and more in less and less time and, if necessary, against the opposing efforts of other things or other people.

Type B personality A personality that is described as easy-going, relaxed, and patient.

proactive personality A person who identifies opportunities, shows initiative, takes action, and perseveres until meaningful change occurs.

take action, and persevere until meaningful change occurs. They create positive change in their environment, regardless or even in spite of constraints or obstacles.[82] Not surprisingly, proactives have many behaviours that organizations desire. They are more likely to be seen as leaders and more likely to act as change agents within the organization.[83]

Other actions of proactives can be positive or negative, depending on the organization and the situation. Proactives are more likely to challenge the status quo or voice their displeasure when situations are not to their liking.[84] If an organization requires people with entrepreneurial initiative, proactives make good candidates; however, they are also more likely to leave an organization to start their own business.[85] As individuals, proactives are more likely to achieve career success.[86] They select, create, and influence work situations in their favour. Proactives are more likely to seek out job and organizational information, develop contacts in high places, engage in career planning, and demonstrate persistence in the face of career obstacles.

Emotions

3 Can emotions help or get in the way when we are dealing with others?

Despite the fact that Walmart Canada has won numerous "Best Employer" and "Best Culture" awards, which are based partly on responses of employees, not all Walmart employees agree with those findings.[87] Comments from Walmart employees at RateMyEmployer.ca show a range of emotions from "love it" to "hate it." Over the past 10 years, at least 20 different groups of Walmart employees across the country have tried to unionize. A recent drive in Trail, BC, told fellow employees that unionizing would be "making Walmart an even BETTER place to work." Obviously there are strong feelings about the employer. Could emotions affect how individual employees perceive Walmart?

Each of us has a range of personality characteristics, but we also bring with us a range of emotions. Given the obvious role that emotions play in our everyday life, it might surprise you to learn that, until very recently, the topic of emotions was given little or no attention within the field of OB.[88] Why? We offer two possible explanations.

First is the *myth of rationality*.[89] Until very recently, the protocol of the work world kept a damper on emotions. A well-run organization did not allow employees to express frustration, fear, anger, love, hate, joy, grief, or similar feelings thought to be the antithesis of rationality. Though researchers and managers knew emotions were an inseparable part of everyday life, they tried to create organizations that were emotion-free. Of course, that was not possible.

The second explanation is that many believed emotions of any kind were disruptive.[90] Researchers looked at strong negative emotions—especially anger—that interfered with an employee's ability to work effectively. They rarely viewed emotions as constructive or contributing to enhanced performance.

Certainly some emotions, particularly when exhibited at the wrong time, can reduce employee performance. But employees do bring their emotions to work every day, and no study of OB would be complete without considering their role in workplace behaviour.

affect A broad range of feelings that people experience.

emotions Intense feelings that are directed at someone or something.

moods Feelings that tend to be less intense than emotions and that lack a contextual stimulus.

What Are Emotions and Moods?

Let's look at three terms that are closely intertwined: *affect*, *emotions*, and *moods*. **Affect** is a generic term that covers a broad range of feelings people experience, including both emotions and moods.[91] **Emotions** are intense feelings that are directed at someone or something.[92] **Moods** are feelings that are less intense than emotions and that lack a contextual stimulus.[93]

Most experts believe emotions are more fleeting than moods.[94] For example, if someone is rude to you, you would likely feel angry. That intense feeling probably comes and goes fairly quickly, maybe even in a matter of seconds. When you are in a bad mood, though, you can feel bad for several hours.

Emotions are reactions to a person (seeing a friend at work may make you feel glad) or an event (dealing with a rude client may make you feel angry). You show your emotions when you are "happy about something, angry at someone, afraid of something."[95] Moods, in contrast, are not usually directed at a person or an event. But emotions can turn into moods when you lose focus on the event or object that started the feeling. And, by the same token, good or bad moods can make you more emotional in response to an event. So when a colleague criticizes how you spoke to a client, you might show emotion (anger) toward a specific object (your colleague). But as the specific emotion starts to go away, you might just feel generally dispirited. You cannot attribute this feeling to any single event; you are just not your normal self. You might then overreact to other events. This affect state describes a mood. Exhibit 2-7 shows the relationships among affect, emotions, and mood.

First, as the exhibit shows, *affect* is a broad term that encompasses emotions and moods. Second, there are differences between emotions and moods. Some of these differences—that emotions are more likely to be caused by a specific event, and emotions are more fleeting than moods—we just discussed. Other differences are subtler. For example, unlike moods, emotions like anger and disgust tend to be more clearly revealed by facial expressions. Also, some researchers speculate that emotions may be more action oriented—they may lead us to some immediate action—while moods may be more cognitive, meaning they may cause us to think or brood for a while.[96]

Finally, the exhibit shows that emotions and moods are closely connected and can influence each other. Getting your dream job may generate the emotion of joy, which can put you in a good mood for several days. Similarly, if you are in a good or bad mood, it might make you experience a more intense positive or negative emotion than otherwise. In a bad mood, you might blow up in response to a co-worker's comment that would normally have generated only a mild reaction.

Affect, emotions, and moods are separable in theory; in practice the distinction isn't always crystal clear. In some areas, researchers have studied mostly moods, in other areas mainly emotions. So, when we review the OB topics on emotions and moods, you

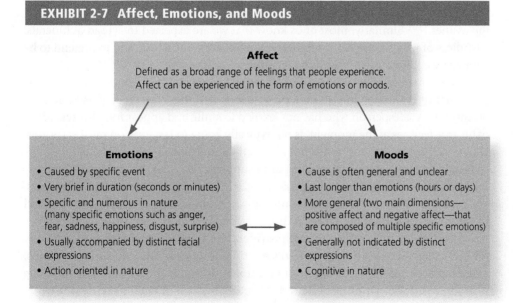

EXHIBIT 2-7 Affect, Emotions, and Moods

Affect
Defined as a broad range of feelings that people experience.
Affect can be experienced in the form of emotions or moods.

Emotions
- Caused by specific event
- Very brief in duration (seconds or minutes)
- Specific and numerous in nature (many specific emotions such as anger, fear, sadness, happiness, disgust, surprise)
- Usually accompanied by distinct facial expressions
- Action oriented in nature

Moods
- Cause is often general and unclear
- Last longer than emotions (hours or days)
- More general (two main dimensions— positive affect and negative affect—that are composed of multiple specific emotions)
- Generally not indicated by distinct expressions
- Cognitive in nature

may see more information on emotions in one area and on moods in another. This is simply the state of the research.

Choosing Emotions: Emotional Labour

If you have ever had a job working in retail sales or waiting on tables in a restaurant, you know the importance of projecting a friendly demeanour and smiling. Even though there were days when you did not feel cheerful, you knew management expected you to be upbeat when dealing with customers. So you faked it. Every employee expends physical and mental labour by putting body and mind into the job. But jobs also require **emotional labour**, an employee's expression of organizationally desired emotions during interpersonal transactions at work.[97]

Ever wonder why the grocery clerk is always smiling?

The concept of emotional labour emerged from studies of service jobs. Airlines expect their flight attendants, for instance, to be cheerful; we expect funeral directors to be sad; and we expect doctors to be emotionally neutral. But really, emotional labour is relevant to almost every job. Your managers expect you, for example, to be courteous, not hostile, in interactions with co-workers. The true challenge arises when employees have to project one emotion while simultaneously feeling another.[98] This difference is **emotional dissonance**, and it can take a heavy toll on employees. Bottled-up feelings of frustration, anger, and resentment can eventually lead to emotional exhaustion and burnout.[99] It is because of emotional labour's increasing importance in effective job performance that an understanding of emotion has gained heightened relevance within the field of OB.

Emotional labour creates dilemmas for employees. There are people with whom you have to work that you just don't like. Maybe you consider their personality abrasive. Maybe you know they have said negative things about you behind your back. Regardless, your job requires you to interact with these people on a regular basis. So you are forced to pretend to be friendly.

It can help you, on the job especially, if you separate emotions into *felt* or *displayed* emotions.[100] **Felt emotions** are an individual's actual emotions. In contrast, **displayed emotions** are those that the organization requires employees to show and considers appropriate in a given job. They are not natural; they are learned. "The ritual look of delight on the face of the first runner-up as the [winner] is announced is a product of the display rule that losers should mask their sadness with an expression of joy for the winner."[101] Similarly, most of us know that we are expected to act sad at funerals, regardless of whether we consider the person's death to be a loss, and to pretend to be happy at weddings, even if we don't feel like celebrating.[102]

Effective managers have learned to be serious when giving an employee a negative performance evaluation and to hide their anger when they have been passed over for promotion. A salesperson who has not learned to smile and appear friendly, regardless of his true feelings at the moment, is not typically going to last long on most sales jobs. How we *experience* an emotion is not always the same as how we *show* it.[103]

Displaying fake emotions requires us to suppress real ones. **Surface acting** is hiding one's inner feelings and hiding emotional expressions in response to display rules. For example, when an employee smiles at a customer even when he does not feel like it, he is surface acting. **Deep acting** is trying to modify one's true inner feelings based on display rules. A health care provider trying to genuinely feel more empathy for her patients is deep acting.[104] Surface acting deals with one's *displayed* emotions, and deep acting deals with one's *felt* emotions. Research shows that surface acting is more stressful to employees than deep acting because it entails faking one's true emotions.[105] Displaying emotions we don't really feel is exhausting, so it is important

emotional labour When an employee expresses organizationally desired emotions during interpersonal interactions.

emotional dissonance Inconsistencies between the emotions people feel and the emotions they show.

felt emotions An individual's actual emotions.

displayed emotions Emotions that are organizationally required and considered appropriate in a given job.

surface acting Hiding one's inner feelings to display what is expected.

deep acting Trying to modify one's true inner feelings to match what is expected.

to give employees who engage in surface displays a chance to relax and recharge. A study that looked at how cheerleading instructors spent their breaks from teaching found those who used their breaks to rest and relax were more effective instructors after their breaks.[106] Instructors who did chores during their breaks were only about as effective after their break as they were before. Though much of the research on emotional labour shows negative consequences for those displaying false positive emotions, a 2011 study suggests that as people age, engaging in positive emotions and attitudes, even when the circumstances warrant otherwise, actually enhances emotional well-being.[107]

Why Should We Care About Emotions in the Workplace?

Research is increasingly showing that emotions are actually critical to rational thinking.[108] We must have the ability to experience emotions to be rational. Why? Because our emotions provide important information about how we understand the world around us. Would we really want a manager to make a decision about firing an employee without regarding either his or the employee's emotions? The key to good decision making is to employ both thinking *and* feeling in our decisions.

There are other reasons to be concerned about understanding emotions in the workplace.[109] People who know their own emotions and are good at reading others' emotions may be more effective in their jobs. That, in essence, is the theme underlying contemporary research on emotional intelligence. The entire workplace can be affected by positive or negative workplace emotions, another issue we consider below. Finally, we consider affective events theory, which has increased our understanding of emotions at work.

Emotional Intelligence

Diane Marshall is an office manager. Her awareness of her own and others' emotions is almost zero. She is moody and unable to generate much enthusiasm or interest in her employees. She does not understand why employees get upset with her. She often overreacts to problems and chooses the most ineffectual responses to emotional situations.[110] Diane Marshall has low emotional intelligence. **Emotional intelligence (EI)** is a person's ability to (1) be self-aware (to recognize one's own emotions when one experiences them), (2) detect emotions in others, and (3) manage emotional cues and information. People who know their own emotions and are good at reading emotional cues—for instance, knowing why they are angry and how to express themselves without violating norms—are most likely to be effective.[111] One simulation study showed that students who were good at identifying and distinguishing among their feelings were able to make more profitable investment decisions.[112]

The most recent study on EI (2011) reviewed and analyzed most of the previous studies on EI and concluded that EI is strongly and positively correlated with job performance—emotionally intelligent people are better workers.[113] Another illuminating study looked at the successes and failures of 11 American presidents—from Franklin Roosevelt to Bill Clinton. They were evaluated on six qualities—communication, organization, political skill, vision, cognitive style, and emotional intelligence. It was found that the key quality that differentiated the successful (such as Roosevelt, Kennedy, and Reagan) from the unsuccessful (such as Johnson, Carter, and Nixon) was EI.[114] Some researchers argue that EI is particularly important for leaders.[115]

EI has been a controversial concept in OB. It has supporters and detractors. In the following sections, we review the arguments for and against the effectiveness of EI in OB.

The Case for EI

The arguments in favour of EI include its intuitive appeal, the fact that EI predicts criteria that matter, and the idea that EI is biologically based.

emotional intelligence (EI) An assortment of noncognitive skills, capabilities, and competencies that influence a person's ability to succeed in coping with environmental demands and pressures.

Intuitive Appeal   There is a lot of intuitive appeal to the EI concept. Almost everyone would agree that it is good to possess street smarts and social intelligence. People who can detect emotions in others, control their own emotions, and handle social interactions well will have a powerful leg up in the business world, so the thinking goes.[116] As just one example, partners in a multinational consulting firm who scored above the median on an EI measure delivered $1.2 million more in business than did the other partners.[117]

EI Predicts Criteria That Matter   More and more evidence suggests that a high level of EI means a person will perform well on the job. One study found that EI predicted the performance of employees in a cigarette factory in China.[118] Another study found that being able to recognize emotions in others' facial expressions and to emotionally "eavesdrop" (that is, pick up subtle signals about people's emotions) predicted peer ratings of how valuable those people were to their organization.[119] Finally, a review of 59 studies indicated that, overall, EI correlated moderately with job performance.[120]

EI Is Biologically Based   One study has shown that people with damage to the part of the brain that governs emotional processing (lesions in an area of the prefrontal cortex) score significantly lower than others on EI tests. Even though these brain-damaged people scored no lower on standard measures of intelligence than people without similar brain damage, they were still impaired in normal decision making. But they scored significantly lower on EI tests and were impaired in normal decision making, as demonstrated by their poor performance in a card game with monetary rewards. This study suggests that EI is neurologically based in a way that is unrelated to standard measures of intelligence.[121] There is also evidence EI is genetically influenced, further supporting the idea that it measures a real underlying biological factor.[122]

The Case Against EI

For all its supporters, EI has just as many critics. Its critics say that EI is vague and impossible to measure, and they question its validity.

EI Is Too Vague a Concept   To many researchers, it's not clear what EI is. Is it a form of intelligence? Most of us would not think that being self-aware or self-motivated or having empathy is a matter of intellect. Moreover, different researchers often focus on different skills, making it difficult to get a definition of EI. One researcher may study self-discipline, another empathy, another self-awareness. As one reviewer noted, "The concept of EI has now become so broad and the components so variegated that . . . it is no longer even an intelligible concept."[123]

EI Cannot Be Measured   Many critics have raised questions about measuring EI. Because EI is a form of intelligence, they argue, there must be right and wrong answers about it on tests. Some tests do have right and wrong answers, although the validity of some questions is doubtful. One measure asks you to associate particular feelings with specific colours, as if purple always makes us feel cool and not warm. Other measures are self-reported, meaning that there is no right or wrong answer. For example, an EI test question might ask you to respond to the statement "I'm good at 'reading' other people," and have no right or wrong answers. The measures of EI are diverse, and researchers have not subjected them to as much rigorous study as they have measures of personality and general intelligence.[124]

The Validity of EI Is Suspect   Some critics argue that because EI is so closely related to intelligence and personality, once you control for these factors, EI has nothing unique to offer. There is some foundation to this argument. EI appears to be highly correlated with measures of personality, especially emotional stability.[125] If this is true, then the evidence for a biological component to EI is not valid, and biological markers such as brain activity and heritability are attributable to other well known and much more researched psychological variables. But there has not been enough research on whether EI adds insight beyond measures of personality and general intelligence in predicting job performance. Still, EI is wildly popular among consulting firms and in the popular press. One company's promotional materials for an EI measure claimed, "EI accounts for more than 85 percent of star performance in top leaders."[126] To say the least, it's difficult to validate this statement with the research literature.

Weighing the arguments for and against EI, it's still too early to tell whether the concept is useful. It *is* clear, though, that the concept is here to stay.

Negative Workplace Emotions

Negative emotions can lead to a number of deviant workplace behaviours. Anyone who has spent much time in an organization realizes that people often engage in voluntary actions that violate established norms and threaten the organization, its members, or both. These actions are called **employee deviance**.[127] Deviant actions fall into categories such as production (leaving early, intentionally working slowly); property (stealing, sabotage); political (gossiping, blaming co-workers); and personal aggression (sexual harassment, verbal abuse).[128]

Many of these deviant behaviours can be traced to negative emotions. For instance, envy is an emotion that occurs when you resent someone for having something you don't, and strongly desire—such as a better work assignment, larger office, or higher salary.[129] It can lead to malicious deviant behaviours, such as hostility, "backstabbing," and other forms of political behaviour that negatively distort others' successes and positively distort your own accomplishments.[130] Angry people look for other people to blame for their bad mood, interpret other people's behaviour as hostile, and have trouble considering others' points of view.[131] It's not hard to see how these thought processes, too, can lead directly to verbal or physical aggression. Evidence suggests that people who feel negative emotions, particularly those who feel angry or hostile, are more likely than others to engage in deviant behaviour at work.[132]

Managing emotions in the workplace becomes important both to ward off negative behaviour and to encourage positive behaviour in those around us. You may be surprised to learn the extent to which your mood can affect the mood of others. Once aggression starts, it's likely that other people will become angry and aggressive, so the stage is set for a serious escalation of negative behaviour.

Affective Events Theory

Understanding emotions at work has been significantly helped by a model called **affective events theory (AET)**.[133] AET demonstrates that employees react emotionally to things that happen to them at work, and that this emotional reaction influences their job performance and satisfaction.

Exhibit 2-8 summarizes AET. The theory begins by recognizing that emotions are a response to an event in the work environment. The work environment includes everything surrounding the job—characteristics of the job, such as the variety of tasks and degree of autonomy, job demands, and requirements for expressing emotional labour. This environment creates work events that can be hassles, uplifting events, or both. Examples of hassles are colleagues who refuse to carry their share of work, conflicting directions by different managers, and excessive time pressures. Uplifting events include meeting a goal, getting support from a colleague, and receiving recognition for an accomplishment.[134]

These work events trigger positive or negative emotional reactions, to which employees' personalities and moods predispose them to respond with greater or lesser inten-

employee deviance Voluntary actions that violate established norms and threaten the organization, its members, or both.

affective events theory (AET) The theory that employees react emotionally to things that happen to them at work and that this emotional reaction influences their job performance and satisfaction.

EXHIBIT 2-8 Affective Events Theory

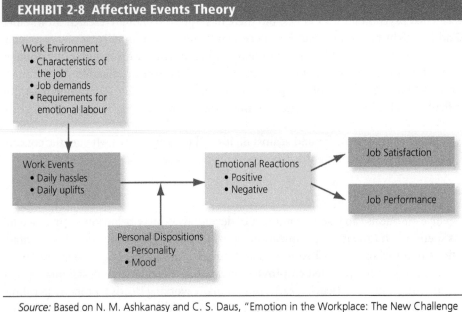

Source: Based on N. M. Ashkanasy and C. S. Daus, "Emotion in the Workplace: The New Challenge for Managers," *Academy of Management Executive,* February 2002, p. 77.

sity. People who score low on emotional stability are more likely to react strongly to negative events. In addition, a person's emotional response to a given event can change depending on his or her mood. Finally, emotions influence a number of job performance and satisfaction variables, such as organizational citizenship behaviour (OCB), organizational commitment, intentions to quit, level of effort, and workplace deviance.

Tests of affective events theory suggest the following:[135]

- An emotional episode is actually a series of emotional experiences, precipitated by a single event and containing elements of both emotions and mood cycles.

- Current emotions influence job satisfaction at any given time, along with the history of emotions surrounding the event.

- Because moods and emotions fluctuate over time, their effect on performance also fluctuates.

- Emotion-driven behaviours are typically short in duration and of high variability.

- Because emotions, even positive ones, tend to be incompatible with behaviours required to do a job, they typically have a negative influence on job performance.

An example might help better explain AET.[136] You work as an aeronautical engineer for Bombardier. Because of the downturn in the demand for commercial jets, you have just learned that the company is considering laying off several thousand employees. This could include you. This event is likely to elicit a negative emotional reaction: You are fearful that you might lose your job and primary source of income. Also, because you are prone to worry a lot and obsess about problems, your feelings of insecurity are increased. This event also puts into place a series of subevents that create an episode: You talk with your boss and he assures you that your job is safe; you hear rumours that your department is high on the list to be eliminated; you run into a former colleague who was laid off six months ago and still has not found work. These, in turn, create emotional ups and downs. One day, you are feeling more upbeat and sure that you will survive the cuts. The next day, you might be depressed and anxious, convinced that your department will be eliminated. These swings in your emotions take your attention away from your work and result in reduced job performance and satisfaction. Finally, your response is magnified because this is the fourth large layoff that Bombardier has initiated in the past three years.

In summary, AET offers two important messages.[137] First, emotions provide valuable insights into how workplace hassles and uplifting events influence employee performance and satisfaction. Second, employees and managers should not ignore emotions or the events that cause them, even when they appear minor, because they accumulate.

GLOBAL **IMPLICATIONS**

In considering potential global differences in this chapter's concepts, let's consider the four areas that have attracted the most research: (1) perception, (2) attributions, (3) personality, and (4) emotions.

Perception

Several studies have examined how people observe the world around them.[138] In one study, researchers showed East Asians and US subjects a photo with a focal object (like a train) with a busy background and tracked their eye movements. They found that the US subjects were more likely to look at the focal object, whereas the East Asian subjects were more likely to look at the background. Thus, the East Asians appeared to focus more on the context or environment than on the most important object in it. As one of the researchers concluded, "If people are seeing different things, it may be because they are looking differently at the world."[139]

Perceptual differences across cultures have been found to be rooted in the brain's architecture. Using a functional Magnetic Resonance Imaging (fMRI) device to scan subjects' brains, one researcher found that when Singaporeans were shown pictures where either the foreground or background was varied, their brains were less attuned to new foreground images and more attuned to new background images than those of US subjects.[140] This finding suggests that perception is not universal, and that the cultural tendency to focus on either an object/person or a context is part of the "hard wiring" of our brains.

Finally, culture affects what we remember as well. When asked to remember events, US subjects recall more about personal details and their own personal characteristics, whereas Asians recall more about personal relationships and group activities.[141]

As a set, these studies provide striking evidence that Eastern and Western cultures differ in one of the deepest aspects of organizational behaviour: how we see the world around us.

Attributions

The evidence on cultural differences in perception is mixed, but most studies suggest that there *are* differences across cultures in the attributions people make.[142]

Asians overall are less likely to make the fundamental attribution error. The Japanese in particular are less likely to attribute a person's behaviour to internal factors than external or situational forces. A study also found Korean managers less likely to use the self-serving bias—they tended to accept responsibility for group failure "because I was not a capable leader" instead of attributing failure to group members.[143] On the other hand, Asian managers are more likely to lay blame on institutions or whole organizations, whereas Western observers are more likely to believe individual managers should be the focus of blame or praise.[144] That probably explains why US newspapers prominently report the names of individual executives when firms do poorly, whereas

Asian media provide more coverage of how the firm as a whole has failed. This tendency to make group-based attributions also explains why individuals from Asian cultures are more likely to make group-based stereotypes.[145] Attribution theory was developed largely based on experiments with US and Western European workers. But these studies suggest caution in making attribution theory predictions in non-Western societies, especially in countries with strong collectivistic traditions.

These differences in attribution tendencies don't mean that the basic concepts of attribution and blame completely differ across cultures, though. Recent studies suggest that Chinese managers assess blame for mistakes using the same distinctiveness, consensus, and consistency cues Western managers use.[146] Chinese managers also become angry and punish those who are deemed responsible for failure, a reaction shown in many studies of Western managers. This finding means that the basic process of attribution applies across cultures but that it takes more evidence for Asian managers to conclude someone else should be blamed.

Personality

The five personality factors identified in the Big Five model appear in almost all cross-cultural studies.[147] These studies have included a wide variety of diverse cultures—such as China, Israel, Germany, Japan, Spain, Nigeria, Norway, Pakistan, and the United States. Differences tend to be in the emphasis on particular dimensions and whether countries are predominantly individualist or collectivist. For example, Chinese managers use the dimension of conscientiousness more often and agreeableness less often than do US managers. The Big Five appear to predict behaviour more accurately in individualistic cultures than collectivistic cultures.[148] However, there is a surprisingly high amount of agreement that the Big Five variables are useful predictors, especially among individuals from developed countries. A comprehensive review of studies covering people from what was then the 15-nation European Community found conscientiousness to be a valid predictor of performance across jobs and occupational groups.[149] US studies have reached the same conclusion.

Emotions

People vary in the degree to which they experience emotions. In China, for example, people report experiencing fewer positive and negative emotions than people in other cultures, and the emotions they experience are less intense than what other cultures report. Compared with mainland Chinese, Taiwanese are more like Canadian employees in their experience of emotions: On average, Taiwanese report more positive and fewer negative emotions than their Chinese counterparts.[150] In general, people in most cultures appear to experience certain positive and negative emotions, but the frequency of their experience and their intensity varies to some degree.[151]

In general, people from all over the world interpret negative and positive emotions the same way. We all view negative emotions, such as hate, terror, and rage, as dangerous and destructive. And we all desire positive emotions, such as joy, love, and happiness. However, some cultures value certain emotions more than others. For example, Americans value enthusiasm, while the Chinese consider negative emotions to be more useful and constructive. In general, pride is seen as a positive emotion in Western, individualistic cultures such as the United States, but Eastern cultures such as China and Japan tend to view pride as undesirable.[152]

The norms for the expression of emotions vary by culture as well. For example, some fundamentalist Muslims see smiling as a sign of sexual attraction, so women have learned not to smile at men so as not to be misinterpreted.[153] And research has shown that in collectivistic countries, people are more likely to believe that the emotional displays of another have something to do with their own relationship with the person expressing the emotion, while people in individualistic cultures don't think that another's emotional expressions are directed at them. Evidence indicates that in Canada a bias exists against expressing emotions, especially intense negative emotions. French retail clerks, in contrast, are infamous for being surly toward customers (a report from the French government itself confirmed this). Reports also indicate that serious German shoppers have been turned off by Walmart's friendly greeters and helpful personnel.[154]

3

Values, Attitudes, and Diversity in the Workplace

Regina-based SaskGaming, which operates two casinos (Casino Regina and Casino Moose Jaw), faces an interesting perception problem.[1] Not everyone thinks that gambling is okay, and a number of studies show the negative impact of gambling. Still, gambling is legal, and SaskGaming is committed to being a good employer. In fact, it was named one of Canada's Top 100 Employers in both 2008 and 2009, one of Saskatchewan's Top 10 Employers for the third year in a row in 2009, and one of Canada's Best Diversity Employers in 2010.

SaskGaming lists its four organizational values on its website: respect, integrity, passion, and innovation. These values operate under the company's mandate: to "offer casino entertainment in a socially responsible manner, generating quality employment, economic benefit to the community and profit for Saskatchewan people in partnership with First Nations."

Generally, we expect that an organization's values, like those of an individual, will be reflected in corresponding behaviour and attitudes. If a company stated that it valued gambling in a socially responsible manner, and yet no behaviour followed from that statement, we would question whether that value was really so important to the company. However, in SaskGaming's case, the company backs up its value statements with concrete policies and actions to show support for its values. Does having strong values make for a better workplace?

In this chapter, we look more carefully at how values influence behaviour, and consider the relationship between values and attitudes. We then consider two specific issues that arise from our discussion of values and attitudes: job satisfaction and workforce diversity.

Values

① What are values?

Is capital punishment right or wrong? How about racial or gender quotas in hiring—are they right or wrong? If a person likes power, is that good or bad? The answers to these questions are value-laden. Some might argue, for example, that capital punishment is right because it is an appropriate response to crimes such as murder. However, others might argue just as strongly that no government has the right to take anyone's life.

Values represent basic convictions that "a specific mode of conduct or end-state of existence is personally or socially preferable to an opposite or converse mode of conduct or end-state of existence."[2] They contain a judgmental element in that they carry an individual's ideas as to what is right, good, or desirable. Values have both content and intensity attributes. The content attribute says a mode of conduct or end-state of existence is *important*. The intensity attribute specifies *how important* it is. When we rank an individual's values in terms of their intensity, we obtain that person's **value system**. All of us have a hierarchy of values that forms our value system, and these influence our attitudes and behaviour.[3]

Values tend to be relatively stable and enduring.[4] Most of our values are formed in our early years—with input from parents, teachers, friends, and others. As children, we were told that certain behaviours or outcomes are always desirable or always undesirable. There were few grey areas. It is this absolute or "black-or-white" learning of values that more or less ensures their stability and endurance.

Below we examine two frameworks for understanding values: Milton Rokeach's terminal and instrumental values, and Kent Hodgson's general moral principles.

Rokeach Value Survey

Milton Rokeach created the Rokeach Value Survey (RVS), which consists of two sets of values, each containing 18 individual value items.[5] One set, called **terminal values**, refers to desirable end-states of existence. These are the goals that individuals would like to achieve during their lifetime. They include

- A comfortable life (a prosperous life)
- An exciting life (a stimulating, active life)
- A sense of accomplishment (lasting contribution)
- Equality (brotherhood, equal opportunity for all)
- Inner harmony (freedom from inner conflict)
- Happiness (contentedness)[6]

The other set, called **instrumental values**, refers to preferable ways of behaving, or means for achieving the terminal values. They include

- Ambitious (hard-working, aspiring)
- Broad-minded (open-minded)
- Capable (competent, effective)
- Courageous (standing up for your beliefs)
- Imaginative (daring, creative)
- Honest (sincere, truthful)[7]

Several studies confirm that RVS values vary among groups.[8] People in the same occupations or categories (corporate managers, union members, parents, students)

values Basic convictions that a specific mode of conduct or end-state of existence is personally or socially preferable to an opposite or converse mode of conduct or end-state of existence.

value system A hierarchy based on a ranking of an individual's values in terms of their intensity.

terminal values Goals that individuals would like to achieve during their lifetime.

instrumental values Preferable ways of behaving.

EXHIBIT 3-1	Value Ranking of Executives, Union Members, and Activists (Top Five Only)				
EXECUTIVES		**UNION MEMBERS**		**ACTIVISTS**	
Terminal	**Instrumental**	**Terminal**	**Instrumental**	**Terminal**	**Instrumental**
1. Self-respect	1. Honest	1. Family security	1. Responsible	1. Equality	1. Honest
2. Family security	2. Responsible	2. Freedom	2. Honest	2. A world of peace	2. Helpful
3. Freedom	3. Capable	3. Happiness	3. Courageous	3. Family security	3. Courageous
4. A sense of accomplishment	4. Ambitious	4. Self-respect	4. Independent	4. Self-respect	4. Responsible
5. Happiness	5. Independent	5. Mature love	5. Capable	5. Freedom	5. Capable

Source: Based on W. C. Frederick and J. Weber, "The Values of Corporate Managers and Their Critics: An Empirical Description and Normative Implications," in *Business Ethics: Research Issues and Empirical Studies,* ed. W. C. Frederick and L. E. Preston (Greenwich, CT: JAI Press, 1990), pp. 123–144.

tend to hold similar values. One study compared corporate executives, members of the steelworkers' union, and members of a community activist group. Although there was a good deal of overlap among the three groups,[9] there were also some very significant differences (see Exhibit 3-1). The activists ranked "equality" as their most important terminal value; executives and union members ranked this value 12 and 13, respectively. Activists ranked "helpful" as their second-highest instrumental value. The other two groups both ranked it 14. Because executives, union members, and activists all have a vested interest in what corporations do, these differences can create serious conflicts when these groups have to reach agreement on the organization's economic and social policies.[10]

Hodgson's General Moral Principles

Ethics is the study of moral values or principles that guide our behaviour and inform us whether actions are right or wrong. Thus, ethical values are related to moral judgments about right and wrong.

In recent years, there has been concern that individuals are not grounded in moral values. It is believed that this lack of moral roots has resulted in a number of business scandals, such as those at WorldCom, Enron, Hollinger International, and even in the sponsorship scandal of the Canadian government. We discuss the issue of ethics further in Chapter 5.

Management consultant Kent Hodgson has identified seven general moral principles that individuals should follow when making decisions about behaviour. He calls these "the Magnificent Seven" and suggests that they are universal values that managers should use to make *principled*, *appropriate*, and *defensible* decisions.[11]

ethics The study of moral values or principles that guide our behaviour and inform us whether actions are right or wrong.

Assessing Cultural Values

SaskGaming's decision to value diversity in its workplace reflects a dominant value of Canada as a multicultural country.[12] The approach to diversity is very different in the United States, which considers itself a melting pot with respect to different cultures. SaskGaming has other values that guide employees. These include respect, integrity, passion, and innovation. What do we know about the values of other countries? What values make Canada unique?

 2 How can we understand values across cultures?

We noted that managers have to become capable of working with people from different cultures. Thus, it is important to understand how values differ across cultures.

Hofstede's Framework for Assessing Cultures

One of the most widely referenced approaches for analyzing variations among cultures was done in the late 1970s by Geert Hofstede.[13] He surveyed more than 116 000 IBM employees in 40 countries about their work-related values, and found that managers and employees vary on 5 value dimensions of national culture:

- *Power distance.* **Power distance** describes the degree to which people in a country accept that power in institutions and organizations is distributed unequally. A high rating on power distance means that large inequalities of power and wealth exist and are tolerated in the culture, as in a class or caste system that discourages upward mobility. A low power distance rating characterizes societies that stress equality and opportunity.

- *Individualism vs. collectivism.* **Individualism** is the degree to which people prefer to act as individuals rather than as members of groups and believe in individual rights above all else. **Collectivism** emphasizes a tight social framework in which people expect others in groups of which they are a part to look after them and protect them.

- *Masculinity vs. femininity.* Hofstede's construct of **masculinity** is the degree to which the culture favours traditional masculine roles, such as achievement, power, and control, as opposed to viewing men and women as equals. A high masculinity rating indicates the culture has separate roles for men and women, with men dominating the society. A high **femininity** rating means the culture sees little differentiation between male and female roles and treats women as the equals of men in all respects.

- *Uncertainty avoidance.* The degree to which people in a country prefer structured over unstructured situations defines their uncertainty avoidance. In cultures that score high on uncertainty avoidance, people have an increased level of anxiety about uncertainty and ambiguity, and use laws and controls to reduce uncertainty. Cultures low on **uncertainty avoidance** are more accepting of ambiguity and are less rule-oriented, take more risks, and more readily accept change.

- *Long-term vs. short-term orientation.* This newest addition to Hofstede's typology measures a society's long-term devotion to traditional values. People in a culture with **long-term orientation** look to the future and value thrift, persistence, and tradition. In a culture with **short-term orientation**, people value the here and now; they accept change more readily and don't see commitments as impediments to change.

How do different countries score on Hofstede's dimensions? Exhibit 3-2 shows the ratings for the countries for which data are available. For example, power distance is higher in Malaysia and Slovak Republic than in any other countries. Canada is tied with the Netherlands as one of the top five individualistic countries in the world, falling just behind the United States, Australia, and Great Britain. Canada also tends to be short term in orientation and is low in power distance (people in Canada tend not to accept built-in class differences among people). Canada is also relatively low on uncertainty avoidance, meaning that most adults are relatively tolerant of uncertainty and ambiguity. Canada scores relatively high on masculinity (meaning that most people emphasize traditional gender roles) in comparison with countries such as Denmark, Finland, Norway, and Sweden, although its score is lower than that of the United States.

power distance A national culture attribute that describes the extent to which a society accepts that power in institutions and organizations is distributed unequally.

individualism A national culture attribute that describes the degree to which people prefer to act as individuals rather than as members of groups.

collectivism A national culture attribute that describes a tight social framework in which people expect others in groups of which they are a part to look after them and protect them.

masculinity A national culture attribute that describes the extent to which the culture favours traditional masculine work roles of achievement, power, and control. Societal values are characterized by assertiveness and materialism.

femininity A national culture attribute that sees little differentiation between male and female roles; women are treated as the equals of men in all respects.

uncertainty avoidance A national culture attribute that describes the extent to which a society feels threatened by uncertain and ambiguous situations and tries to avoid them.

long-term orientation A national culture attribute that emphasizes the future, thrift, and persistence.

short-term orientation A national culture attribute that emphasizes the past and present, respect for tradition, and fulfillment of social obligations.

Exhibit 3-2 Hofstede's Cultural Values by Nation

Country Index	Power Distance Index	Individualism Index	Masculinity Index	Uncertainty Avoidance Index	Long-Term Orientation
Argentina	49	46	56	86	20
Australia	36	90	61	51	21
Austria	11	55	79	70	60
Belgium	65	75	54	94	82
Brazil	69	38	49	76	44
Canada	39	80	52	48	36
Canada French	54	73	45	60	na
Chile	63	23	28	86	31
China	80	20	66	30	87
Colombia	67	13	64	80	13
Costa Rica	35	15	21	86	na
Czech Republic	57	58	57	74	70
Denmark	18	74	16	23	35
Ecuador	78	8	63	67	na
El Salvador	66	19	40	94	20
Finland	33	63	26	59	38
France	68	71	43	86	63
Germany	35	67	66	65	83
Great Britain	35	89	66	35	51
Greece	60	35	57	112	45
Guatemala	95	6	37	101	na
Hong Kong	68	25	57	29	61
India	77	48	56	40	51
Indonesia	78	14	46	48	62
Iran	58	41	43	59	14
Ireland	28	70	68	35	24
Israel	13	54	47	81	38
Italy	50	76	70	75	61
Jamaica	45	39	68	13	na
Japan	54	46	95	92	88
Korea (South)	60	18	39	85	100
Malaysia	104	26	50	36	41
Mexico	81	30	69	82	24
Netherlands	38	80	14	53	67
New Zealand	22	79	58	49	33
Norway	31	69	8	50	35
Pakistan	55	14	50	70	50
Panama	95	11	44	86	na
Peru	64	16	42	87	25
Philippines	94	32	64	44	27
Poland	68	60	64	93	38
Portugal	63	27	31	104	28
Singapore	74	20	48	8	72
Slovak Republic	104	52	110	51	77
South Africa (white)	49	65	83	49	na
Spain	57	51	42	86	48
Sweden	31	71	5	29	53
Switzerland	34	68	70	58	74
Taiwan	58	17	45	69	93
Thailand	64	20	34	64	32
Turkey	66	37	45	85	46
United States	40	91	62	46	26
Uruguay	61	36	38	100	26
Venezuela	81	12	73	76	16
Vietnam	70	20	40	30	57

Scores range from 0 = extremely low on dimension to 100 = extremely high.

Source: Geert Hofstede, Gert Jan Hofstede, Michael Minkov, *Cultures and Organizations, Software of the Mind*, Third Revised Edition, McGrawHill 2010, ISBN 0-07-166418-1. By permission of the author.

You will notice regional differences. Western and Northern nations such as Canada and the Netherlands tend to be more individualistic. Poorer countries such as Mexico and the Philippines tend to be higher on power distance. South American nations tend to be higher than other countries on uncertainty avoidance, and Asian countries tend to have a long-term orientation.

How do countries differ in their values?

Hofstede's cultural dimensions have been enormously influential on OB researchers and managers. Nevertheless, his research has been criticized. First, although Hofstede's work was updated and reaffirmed by a Canadian researcher at the Chinese University of Hong Kong (Michael Bond), who conducted research on values in 22 countries on 5 continents,[14] the original work is more than 30 years old and was based on a single company (IBM). A lot has happened in the world scene since then. Some of the most obvious changes include the fall of the Soviet Union, the transformation of Central and Eastern Europe, the end of apartheid in South Africa, the spread of Islam throughout the world today, and the rise of China as a global power. Second, few researchers have read the details of Hofstede's methodology closely and are therefore unaware of the many decisions and judgment calls he had to make (for example, reducing the number of cultural values to just five). Some results are unexpected. For example, Japan, which is often considered a highly collectivistic nation, is considered only average on collectivism under Hofstede's dimensions.[15] Despite these concerns, many of which Hofstede refutes,[16] he has been one of the most widely cited social scientists ever, and his framework has left a lasting mark on OB.

The GLOBE Framework for Assessing Cultures

Begun in 1993, the Global Leadership and Organizational Behavior Effectiveness (GLOBE) research program is an ongoing cross-cultural investigation of leadership and national culture. Using data from 825 organizations in 62 countries, the GLOBE team identified nine dimensions on which national cultures differ.[17] Some—such as power distance, individualism/collectivism, uncertainty avoidance, gender differentiation (similar to masculinity vs. femininity), and future orientation (similar to long-term vs. short-term orientation)—resemble the Hofstede dimensions. The main difference is that the GLOBE framework added dimensions, such as humane orientation (the degree to which a society rewards individuals for being altruistic, generous, and kind to others) and performance orientation (the degree to which a society encourages and rewards group members for performance improvement and excellence).

Which framework is better? That is hard to say, and each has its adherents. We give more emphasis to Hofstede's dimensions here because they have stood the test of time and the GLOBE study confirmed them. However, researchers continue to debate the differences between these frameworks, and future studies may, in time, favour the more nuanced perspective of the GLOBE study.[18]

Values in the Canadian Workplace

 Are there unique Canadian values?

Studies have shown that when individual values align with organizational values, the results are positive. Individuals who have an accurate understanding of the job requirements and the organization's values adjust better to their jobs, and have greater levels of satisfaction and organizational commitment.[19] In addition, shared values between the employee and the organization lead to more positive work attitudes,[20] lower turnover,[21] and greater productivity.[22]

Individual and organizational values do not always align. Moreover, within organizations, individuals can have very different values. Two major factors lead to a potential clash of values in the Canadian workplace: generational differences and cultural differences.

Let's look at the findings and implications of generational and cultural differences in Canada.

Generational Differences

Research suggests that generational differences exist in the workplace among the Baby Boomers (born between the mid-1940s and the mid-1960s), the Generation Xers (born between the mid-1960s and the late 1970s), and the Generation Ys (born between 1979 through 1994).[23] Gen-Xers are squeezed in the workplace between the much larger Baby Boomer and Gen-Y groups. With Generation Y starting to climb the ladder in organizations, while Boomers are continuing to hold on to their jobs rather than retire, the impact of having these two large generations—one younger and one older—in the workplace is gaining attention. Bear in mind that our discussion of these generations presents broad generalizations, and you should certainly avoid stereotyping individuals on the basis of these generalizations. There are individual differences in values. For instance, there is no law that says a Baby Boomer cannot think like someone from Generation Y. Despite these limitations, values do change over generations.[24] We can gain some useful insights from analyzing values this way to understand how others might view things differently from ourselves, even when they are exposed to the same situation.

Baby Boomers

Baby Boomers (called *Boomers* for short) are a large cohort born after World War II, when veterans returned to their families and times were good. Boomers entered the workforce from the mid-1960s through the mid-1980s. They brought with them a large measure of the "hippie ethic" and distrust of authority. But they placed a great deal of emphasis on achievement and material success. They work hard and want to enjoy

Robert Dutton, president and CEO of Boucherville, Quebec-based Rona, started working at the company under a grandfather, and then later found himself working with fellow Baby Boomers. Recently he has realized that Generation Y is starting to make up a larger portion of Rona's dealers, and finds that it has changed his life to "have the chance to work with young people—to share ideas with them, their thoughts, their vision for the future."[25] Dutton started the group Young Rona Business Leaders to help develop the talent that will be the future of Rona.

the fruits of their labours. They are pragmatists who believe ends can justify means. Boomers see the organizations that employ them merely as vehicles for their careers. Terminal values such as a sense of accomplishment and social recognition rank high with them.

Generation X

The lives of Gen-Xers (Generation Xers) have been shaped by globalization, two-career parents, MTV, AIDS, and computers. They value flexibility, life options, and the achievement of job satisfaction. Family and relationships are very important to this cohort. Gen-Xers are skeptical, particularly of authority. They also enjoy team-oriented work. In search of balance in their lives, Gen-Xers are less willing to make personal sacrifices for the sake of their employer than previous generations were. On the Rokeach Value Survey, they rate high on true friendship, happiness, and pleasure.

Generation Y

The most recent entrants to the workforce, *Generation Y* (also called *Millennials*, *Netters*, *Nexters*, and *Generation Nexters*), grew up during prosperous times. They have high expectations and seek meaning in their work. Gen-Ys have life goals more oriented toward becoming rich (81 percent) and famous (51 percent) than do Generation Xers (62 percent and 29 percent, respectively), but they also see themselves as socially responsible. Gen-Ys are at ease with diversity and are the first generation to take technology for granted. More than other generations, they tend to be questioning, electronically networked, and entrepreneurial. At the same time, some

Are Gen-Ys really different from their elders?

When Sean Durfy, CEO of Calgary-based WestJet, announced in March 2011 that he was stepping down from the position, he said it was for "family reasons." While that has often been code for "being let go," in Durfy's case it was more likely the truth. His wife had been ill for four years, and the couple has young children. Instead, there was talk that Durfy's announcement was the start of what might be expected from other Generation X-ers, who "work to live rather than live to work." Baby Boomers were expected to sacrifice one's family to climb the corporate ladder. But this may no longer be true of younger generations.

have described Gen-Ys as entitled and needy. They grew up with parents who watched (and praised) their every move. One employer said, "This is the most high-maintenance workforce in the history of the world. The good news is they're also going to be the most high-performing."[26] Bruce Tulgan, author of *Not Everyone Gets a Trophy: How to Manage Generation Y*, suggests that managers need to give Gen-Ys extra direction, encouragement, and feedback to keep them focused and loyal.[27]

The Generations Meet in the Workplace

An understanding that individuals' values differ but tend to reflect the societal values of the period in which they grew up can be a valuable aid in explaining and predicting behaviour. Baby Boomers currently dominate the workplace, but their years of being in charge are limited. In 2013, half of them will be at least 55 and 18 percent will be over 60.[28] Recent research suggests that Baby Boomers and Generation Y have a significant amount in common in their views toward the workplace, and that this might have profound effects on the organization of the workplace in the future.[29] Members of these two generations, much more than those from Generation X, want more flexible workplaces, more opportunity for time off to explore themselves, and more work-life balance. Generation Y will certainly change the face of the workplace in significant ways. Its members have mastered a communication and information system that many of their parents have yet to understand. In Chapter 14, we discuss further motivational differences between the Baby Boomers and Gen-Ys.

Cultural Differences

Canada is a multicultural country. One in five Canadians is an immigrant, according to the 2006 Census (the 2011 Census was still being conducted at the time of writing).[30] In 2006, 46 percent of Metropolitan Toronto's population, 40 percent of Vancouver's population, and 21 percent of Montreal's population were made up of immigrants.[31] The 2006 Census found that 20.1 percent of Canada's population spoke neither of the country's two official languages as their first language. In Vancouver and Toronto, this rate was 41 percent and 44 percent, respectively, so considerably more than one-third of the population of those two cities does not speak either English or French as a first language.[32] Of those who speak other languages, 16 percent speak Chinese (mainly Mandarin or Cantonese). The other dominant languages in Canada are Italian (in fourth place), followed by German, Punjabi, and Spanish.[33] These figures indicate the very different cultures that are part of the Canadian fabric of life.

Though we live in a multicultural society, there are some tensions among people from different races and ethnic groups. For instance, a Statistics Canada survey on ethnic diversity found that while most Canadians (93 percent) say they have never or rarely experienced unfair treatment because of ethnic or cultural characteristics, 20 percent of visible minorities reported having been unfairly treated sometimes or often.[34] Canadians often define themselves as "not Americans" and point out differences in the values of the two countries. Ipsos Reid recently conducted a national survey of Americans and Canadians, ages 18 to 34, and found a number of differences between the two countries' young adults. Both groups rated health care, education, and employment as their top concerns. "When we compare the lifestyles of young adults in the United States and Canada, one could describe the Americans as more 'traditional' and more 'domestic' in their values and focus, whereas Canadians are more of the 'free-spirit' type," said Samantha McAra, senior research manager with Ipsos Reid.[35] Exhibit 3-3 shows some of the other differences between Canadian and American young adults.

In his book *Fire and Ice*, Michael Adams finds that there is a growing dissimilarity between Canadian and American values. The two groups differ in 41 of the 56 values

EXHIBIT 3-3 Differences between Canadian and American Young Adults, 18 to 34	Canada	United States
Text messages per week (sent and received)	78.7	129.6
Online social media	Facebook: 81% had a profile MySpace: 23% had registered a profile	Facebook: 57% had registered a profile MySpace: 54% had registered a profile
Married	25%	39%
Domestic partnerships	18%	7%
Own a home	35%	45%
Employed on a full- or part-time basis or self-employed	62%	64%
Some post-secondary education	76%	68%
Actively participate in a recycling program	88%	72%
Use public transportation once a week or more often	33%	20%
Favourite sport	NHL hockey (58%)	NFL football (57%)

Source: Based on Ipsos Reid, *A Check-up on the Habits and Values of North America's Young Adults (Part 1)* (Calgary: Ipsos Reid, 2009), http://www.ipsos-na.com/news-polls/pressrelease.aspx?id=4532

that Adams examined. For 24 values the gap has actually widened between 1992 and 2000, indicating that Canadians' social values are growing more distinct from those of Americans.[36] Adams suggests that the September 11 attacks have had an impact on the American personality. He finds Americans are more accepting of patriarchy and hierarchy these days, and he concludes that it is "the supposedly bold, individualistic Americans who are the nodding conformists, and the supposedly shy, deferential and law-abiding Canadians who are most likely to assert their personal autonomy and political agency."[37]

In what follows, we identify a number of cultural values that influence workplace behaviour in Canada. Be aware that these are generalizations, and it would be a mistake to assume that everyone coming from the same cultural background acts similarly. Rather, these overviews are meant to encourage you to think about cultural differences and similarities so that you can better understand people's behaviour.

Francophone and Anglophone Values

Quebec is generally seen as culturally, linguistically, politically, and legally distinct from the rest of Canada.[38] French, not English, is the dominant language in Quebec, and Roman Catholicism, not Protestantism, is the dominant religion. Unlike the rest of Canada, where the law is based on English common law principles, Quebec's legal system is based on the French civil code. From time to time, Quebec separatists threaten that the province will leave Canada. Thus, it will be of interest to managers and employees in Canadian firms to be aware of some of the potential cultural differences when managing in francophone environments compared with anglophone environments.

A number of studies have shown that English-speaking Canadians and French-speaking Canadians have distinctive value priorities. In general, Canadian anglophone managers are seen to be more individualistic than Canadian francophone managers,[39] although more recent research finds greater similarity between anglophone and francophone middle managers in terms of their individualistic-collectivistic orientation.[40] Francophones have also been shown to be more concerned about the interpersonal aspects of the workplace than task competence.[41] They have also been found to be more committed to their work organizations.[42] Earlier studies suggested that anglophones took more risks,[43] but more recent studies have found that this point has become less true and that French-speaking Canadians had the highest values for "reducing or avoiding ambiguity and uncertainty at work."[44]

Canadian anglophone business people have been found to use a more cooperative negotiating style when dealing with one another, compared with Canadian francophone business people.[45] However, Canadian francophones are more likely than Canadian anglophones to use a more cooperative approach during cross-cultural negotiations.[46] Other studies indicate that anglophone managers tend to value autonomy and intrinsic job values, such as achievement, and thus are more achievement-oriented, while francophone managers tend to value affiliation and extrinsic job values, such as technical supervision.[47] A recent study conducted at the University of Ottawa and Laval University suggests that some of the differences reported in previous research may be decreasing.[48] Another study suggests that anglophones and francophones are not very different personality-wise.[49] Yet another study indicates that French Canadians have become more like English Canadians in valuing autonomy and self-fulfillment.[50] These studies are consistent with a recent study that suggests there are few differences between francophones and anglophones.[51]

Professor Carolyn Egri of the business school at Simon Fraser University led a cross-cultural study that found that Canadian anglophone and francophone managers tend to use somewhat different influence styles.[52] Specifically, Canadian anglophone managers are significantly more likely to use behaviours that are beneficial to the organization than Canadian francophone managers. Canadian francophone managers are more likely to focus on their own needs more than the organization's and use destructive/legal (what the authors term "get out of my way or get trampled") and destructive/illegal (what the authors term "burn, pillage and plunder") behaviour dimensions than Canadian anglophone managers. The study also examined the influence styles of American and Mexican managers and found that Mexican managers scored significantly higher than Canadian francophone managers on the use of destructive behaviours, with American managers' use of these behaviours more similar to Canadian anglophones. The results of this study suggest that Canadian francophone managers might serve as a bridge between Mexican managers at one end and American and Canadian anglophone managers on the other, as the francophone style is sometimes a blend of the other groups. The study's authors concluded that Canadian francophones would do well in "joint ventures, business negotiations, and other organizational interactions that involve members of more divergent cultural groups. For example, a national Canadian firm may find it strategically advantageous to utilize Canadian-Francophones in negotiating business contracts with Mexican firms."[53]

Despite some cultural and lifestyle value differences, both francophone and anglophone managers today would have been exposed to more of the same types of organizational theories during their training in post-secondary school, which might also influence their outlooks as managers. Thus we would not expect to find large differences in the way that firms in francophone Canada are managed, compared with those in the rest of Canada. Throughout the textbook, you will find examples of Quebec-based businesses that support this conclusion.

Aboriginal Values

Entrepreneurial activity among Canada's Aboriginal peoples has been increasing at the same time that there are more partnerships and alliances between Aboriginal and non-Aboriginal businesses. Because of these business interactions, it is important to examine the types of differences we might observe in how each culture manages its businesses. For instance, sustainability is an important value in Aboriginal logging companies. Chilanko Forks, BC-based Tsi Del Del, a logging company, received the 2011 Aboriginal Forest Products Business Leadership Award because of the substantial amount of revenues the company put into education.[54] For every cubic metre harvested, the Alexis Creek First Nations–owned company puts 50 cents into a post-secondary educational fund. The fund is used to train the next generation of loggers. Andrew Gage, vice-president of the Forest Products Association of Canada, says that it's a wise investment for the company. "You are not going to find a group of people that are more committed to sustainable harvesting. They share those values that our industry has been trying to get to for the last decade or so."[55]

What can you learn about OB from Aboriginal culture?

"Aboriginal values are usually perceived (by non-Aboriginals) as an impediment to economic development and organizational effectiveness."[56] These values include reluctance to compete, a time orientation different from the Western one, and an emphasis on consensus decision making.[57] Aboriginal people do not necessarily agree that these values are business impediments, however.

Specifically, although Canadian businesses and government have historically assumed that "non-Native people must teach Native people how to run their own organizations," the First Nations of Canada are not convinced.[58] They believe that traditional culture, values, and languages do not have to be compromised in the building of a self-sustaining economy. Moreover, they believe that their cultural values may actually be a positive force in conducting business.[59]

In recent years, Canadian businesses facing Native land claims have met some difficulties in trying to accommodate demands for appropriate land usage. In some cases, accommodation can mean less logging or mining by businesses until land claims are worked out. Cliff Hickey and David Natcher, two anthropologists from the University of Alberta, collaborated with the Little Red River Cree Nation in northern Alberta to develop a new model for forestry operations on First Nations land and achieve better communication between businesses and Native leaders.[60] The anthropologists sought to balance the Native community's traditional lifestyle with the economic concerns of forestry operations. Johnson Sewepegaham, chief of the Little Red River Cree, said his community would use these recommendations to resolve difficulties on treaty lands for which Vernon, BC-based Tolko Industries and Vancouver-based Ainsworth jointly hold forest tenure. The two companies presented their general development plan to the Cree in fall 2008.[61] In 2009, the Cree were effective in persuading Tolko to revise its tree harvesting activities in a way that recognizes and respects the First Nations' ecological and cultural needs.[62]

Lindsay Redpath of Athabasca University has noted that Aboriginal cultures are more collectivist in orientation than are non-Aboriginal cultures in Canada and the United States.[63] Aboriginal organizations are much more likely to reflect and advance the goals of the community. There is also a greater sense of family within the workplace, with greater affiliation and loyalty. Power distance in Aboriginal cultures is smaller than in non-Aboriginal cultures of Canada and the United States, and there is an emphasis on consensual decision making. Aboriginal cultures are lower on uncertainty avoidance than non-Aboriginal cultures in Canada and the United States. Aboriginal organizations and cultures tend to have fewer rules and regulations. Each of these differences suggests that businesses created by Aboriginal people will differ from non-Aboriginal businesses, and both research and anecdotal evidence support this conjecture.[64] For instance, Richard Prokopanko, director of government relations for Vancouver-based

Alcan, says that shifting from handling issues in a generally legalistic, contract-oriented manner to valuing more dialogue and collaboration has helped ease some of the tension that had built up over 48 years between Alcan and First Nations people.[65]

Asian Values

The largest visible minority group in Canada are the Chinese. Over 1 million Chinese live in Canada, representing 26 percent of the country's visible minority population.[66] The Chinese in this country are a diverse group; they come from different countries, speak different languages, and practise different religions. The Chinese are only one part of the entire East and Southeast Asian population that influences Canadian society. It's predicted that by 2017 almost one-half of all visible minorities in Canada will come from two groups, South Asian and Chinese, and that these groups will be represented in almost equal numbers.[67] As well, many Canadian organizations, particularly those in British Columbia, conduct significant business with Asian firms. Asian cultures differ from Canadian culture on many of the GLOBE dimensions discussed earlier. For instance, Asian cultures tend to exhibit greater power distance and greater collectivism. These differences in values can affect individual interactions.

What would you need to know to set up a business in Asia?

Professor Rosalie Tung of Simon Fraser University and her student Irene Yeung examined the importance of *guanxi* (personal connections with the appropriate authorities or individuals) for a sample of North American, European, and Hong Kong firms doing business with companies in mainland China.[68] They suggest that their findings are also relevant in understanding how to develop relationships with firms from Japan, South Korea, and Hong Kong.

"*Guanxi* refers to the establishment of a connection between two independent individuals to enable a bilateral flow of personal or social transactions. Both parties must derive benefits from the transaction to ensure the continuation of such a relationship."[69]*Guanxi* relations are based on reciprocation, unlike Western networked relationships, which may be characterized more by self-interest. *Guanxi* relationships are meant to be long-term and enduring, in contrast with the immediate gains sometimes expected in Western relationships. *Guanxi* also relies less on institutional law, and more on personal power and authority, than do Western relationships. Finally, *guanxi* relations are governed more by the notion of shame (that is, external pressures on performance), while Western relations often rely on guilt (that is, internal pressures on performance) to maintain agreements. *Guanxi* is seen as extremely important for business success in China—more than such factors as the right location, price, or strategy, or product differentiation and quality. For Western firms wanting to do business with Asian firms, an understanding of *guanxi* and an effort to build relationships are important strategic advantages.

Our discussion about differences in cross-cultural values should suggest to you that understanding other cultures matters. When Canadian firms develop operations across Canada, south of the border, or overseas, employees need to understand other cultures to work more effectively and get along with others.

Attitudes

Despite recognition over the years as a good employer, the employees at SaskGaming's Casino Regina went on strike for almost two months in June and July 2010.[70] The employees had been without a collective agreement since May 2009.

Fran Mohr, spokesperson for the Public Service Alliance of Canada (PSAC), which represents the striking employees, was relieved to see the strike end. "We are happy it's finally over.

4 What are attitudes and why are they important?

I feel like a lot of weight has been lifted off my shoulders," said Mohr. "It's a big thing having 400 people walking a picket line day after day. It's a really good feeling to be going back. It feels like we've been gone a long time."

Though the casino had to run much shorter hours, public attitude seemed to favour the employees during the course of the strike. Those on the picket line received frequent donations of food and money. Mohr, a cashier at the casino, said the public understood why the employees went on strike. "We love what we do and no one wants to go on strike, but at some point you have to stand up for yourself. We have our families to consider and I think our clientele really respects that." The attitudes of the striking employees toward their employer were considerably negative before the strike began and became stronger as the strike progressed. So how do employees' attitudes get formed, and can they really be changed?

Attitudes are evaluative statements—either positive or negative—about objects, people, or events. They reflect how we feel about something. When I say, "I like my job," I am expressing my attitude about work.

Specific attitudes tend to predict specific behaviours, whereas general attitudes tend to predict general behaviours. For instance, asking an employee about her intention to stay with an organization for the next six months is likely to better predict turnover for that person than asking her how satisfied she is with her job. On the other hand, overall job satisfaction would better predict a general behaviour, such as whether the employee is engaged in her work or motivated to contribute to her organization.[71]

In organizations, attitudes are important because they affect job behaviour.[72] Employees may believe, for example, that supervisors, auditors, managers, and time-and-motion engineers are all conspiring to make them work harder for the same or less money. This may then lead to a negative attitude toward management when an employee is asked to stay late for help on a special project.

Employees may also be negatively affected by the attitudes of their co-workers or clients.

A person can have thousands of attitudes, but OB focuses our attention on a limited number of work-related attitudes.[73] Below we consider four important attitudes that affect organizational performance: job satisfaction, organizational commitment, job involvement, and employee engagement.

Job Satisfaction

Our definition of **job satisfaction**—a positive feeling about a job resulting from an evaluation of its characteristics—is clearly broad.[74] A survey conducted by Mercer in 2011 found that Canadians are not all that satisfied: 36 percent said they were thinking about leaving their employers and another 20 percent were ambivalent about staying or going.[75]

What Causes Job Satisfaction?

Think about the best job you have ever had. What made it so? Chances are you liked the work you did and the people with whom you worked. Interesting jobs that provide training, variety, independence, and control satisfy most employees.[76] There is also a strong correspondence between how well people enjoy the social context of their workplace and how satisfied they are overall. Interdependence, feedback, social support, and interaction with co-workers outside the workplace are strongly related to job satisfaction even after accounting for characteristics of the work itself.[77]

You have probably noticed that pay comes up often when people discuss job satisfaction. For people who are poor (for example, living below the poverty line) or who live in poor countries, pay does correlate with job satisfaction and overall happiness. But once an individual reaches a level of comfortable living (in Canada, that occurs at about

attitudes Positive or negative feelings about objects, people, or events.

job satisfaction A positive feeling about a job resulting from an evaluation of its characteristics.

$40 000 a year, depending on the region and family size), the relationship between pay and job satisfaction virtually disappears. People who earn $80 000 are, on average, no happier with their jobs than those who earn close to $40,000.[78] High-paying jobs have average satisfaction levels no higher than those that pay much less. One researcher even found no significant difference when he compared the overall well-being of the richest people on the *Forbes* 400 list with that of Maasai herders in East Africa.[79]

Money does motivate people, as we will discover in Chapter 13. But what motivates us is not necessarily the same as what makes us happy. A recent poll found that entering first-year university students rated becoming "very well off financially" first on a list of 19 goals, ahead of choices such as helping others, raising a family, or becoming proficient in an academic pursuit. Maybe your goal isn't to be happy. But if it is, money is probably not going to do much to get you there.[80]

Job satisfaction is not just about job conditions. Personality also plays a role. Research has shown that people who have positive **core self-evaluations**—who believe in their inner worth and basic competence—are more satisfied with their jobs than those with negative core self-evaluations. Not only do they see their work as fulfilling and challenging, they are more likely to gravitate toward challenging jobs in the first place. Those with negative core self-evaluations set less ambitious goals and are more likely to give up when confronting difficulties. Thus, they are more likely to be stuck in boring, repetitive jobs than those with positive core self-evaluations.[81]

So what are the consequences of job satisfaction? We examine this question on the next page.

Job Satisfaction and Productivity

The idea that "happy workers are productive workers" developed in the 1930s and 1940s, largely as a result of the Hawthorne studies at Western Electric. Based on those conclusions, managers focused on working conditions and the work environment to make employees happier. Then, in the 1980s, an influential review of the research suggested that the relationship between job satisfaction and job performance was not particularly high. The authors of that review even labelled it "illusory."[83]

More recently, a review of more than 300 studies corrected some errors in that earlier review and found the correlation between job satisfaction and job performance is moderately strong, even across international contexts. This conclusion also appears to

When asked "On a scale of 1 (not at all) to 7 (completely) how satisfied are you with your life?" *Forbes* magazine's "richest Americans" averaged 5.8 and an East African Maasai tribe, who engage in traditional herding and lead nomadic lives, averaged 5.7. The results of this study suggest that money does not buy life satisfaction.[82]

core self-evaluation Bottom-line conclusions individuals have about their capabilities, competence, and worth as a person.

be generalizable across international contexts. The correlation is higher for complex jobs that provide employees with more discretion to act on their attitudes.[84] A review of 16 studies that assessed job performance and satisfaction over time also linked job satisfaction to job performance[85] and suggested the relationship mostly works one way: Satisfaction was a likely cause of better performance, but higher performance was not a cause of higher job satisfaction.

We cannot be entirely sure, however, whether satisfaction causes productivity or productivity causes satisfaction.[86] In other words, if you do a good job, you intrinsically feel good about it. In addition, your higher productivity should increase your recognition, your pay level, and your likelihood of promotion. Cumulatively, these rewards, in turn, increase your level of satisfaction with the job. Most likely, satisfaction can lead to high levels of performance for some people, while for others, high performance is satisfying.

As we move from the individual to the organization level, we also find support for the satisfaction-performance relationship.[87] When we gather satisfaction and productivity data for the organization as a whole, we find organizations with more satisfied employees tend to be more effective than organizations with less satisfied employees.

Job Satisfaction and Organizational Citizenship Behaviour

In Chapter 1, we defined **organizational citizenship behaviour (OCB)** as discretionary behaviour that is not part of an employee's formal job requirements and is not usually rewarded, but that nevertheless promotes the effective functioning of the organization.[88] Individuals who are high in OCB will go beyond their usual job duties, providing performance that is beyond expectations. Examples of such behaviour include helping colleagues with their workloads, taking only limited breaks, and alerting others to work-related problems.[89] More recently OCB has been associated with the following workplace behaviours: "altruism, conscientiousness, loyalty, civic virtue, voice, functional participation, sportsmanship, courtesy, and advocacy participation." [90] Organizational citizenship is important, as it can help the organization function more efficiently and more effectively.[91]

It seems logical to assume that job satisfaction should be a major determinant of an employee's OCB.[92] Satisfied employees would seem more likely to talk positively about an organization, help others, and go beyond the normal expectations in their jobs.[93] They might go beyond the call of duty because they want to reciprocate their positive experiences. Consistent with this thinking, evidence suggests job satisfaction is moderately correlated with OCBs; people who are more satisfied with their jobs are more likely to engage in OCBs.[94] Why? Fairness perceptions help explain the relationship.[95] Those who feel their co-workers support them are more likely to engage in helpful behaviours, whereas those who have antagonistic relationships with co-workers are less likely to do so.[96]

Job Satisfaction and Customer Satisfaction

As we noted in Chapter 1, employees in service jobs often interact with customers. Since service organization managers should be concerned with pleasing customers, it is reasonable to ask: Is employee satisfaction related to positive customer outcomes? For front-line employees who have regular contact with customers, the answer is yes. Satisfied employees increase customer satisfaction and loyalty.[97]

Why? In service organizations, customer retention and defection are highly dependent on how front-line employees deal with customers. Satisfied employees are more likely to be friendly, upbeat, and responsive—which customers appreciate. Because satisfied employees are less prone to turnover, customers are more likely to encounter familiar faces and receive experienced service. These qualities build customer satisfaction and loyalty. In addition, the relationship seems to apply in reverse: Dissatisfied customers can increase an employee's job dissatisfaction. Employees who interact

organizational citizenship behaviour (OCB) Discretionary behaviour that is not part of an employee's formal job requirements, but that nevertheless promotes the effective functioning of the organization.

Service organizations know that whether customers are satisfied and loyal depends on how front-line employees deal with customers. Singapore Airlines has earned a reputation among world travellers for outstanding customer service. The airline's "putting people first" philosophy applies to both its employees and customers. In recruiting flight attendants, the airline selects people who are warm, hospitable, and happy to serve others. Through extensive training, Singapore Airlines moulds recruits into attendants focused on complete customer satisfaction.

with rude, thoughtless, or unreasonably demanding customers report lower job satisfaction.[98]

Job Satisfaction and Absenteeism and Turnover   We find a consistent negative relationship between satisfaction and absenteeism, but it is moderate to weak.[99] While it certainly makes sense that dissatisfied employees are more likely to miss work, other factors affect the relationship. Organizations that provide liberal sick leave benefits are encouraging all their employees—including those who are highly satisfied—to take days off. You can find work satisfying yet still want to enjoy a three-day weekend if those days come free with no penalties. When numerous alternative jobs are available, dissatisfied employees have high absence rates, but when there are few they have the same (low) rate of absence as satisfied employees.[100]

The relationship between job satisfaction and turnover is stronger than between satisfaction and absenteeism.[101] The satisfaction-turnover relationship also is affected by alternative job prospects. If an employee is presented with an unsolicited job offer, job dissatisfaction is less predictive of turnover because the employee is more likely leaving because of "pull" (the lure of the other job) than "push" (the unattractiveness of the current job). Similarly, job dissatisfaction is more likely to translate into turnover when employment opportunities are plentiful because employees perceive it is easy to move. Finally, when employees have high "human capital" (high education, high ability), job dissatisfaction is more likely to translate into turnover because they have, or perceive, many available alternatives.[102]

How Employees Can Express Dissatisfaction

Job dissatisfaction and antagonistic relationships with co-workers predict a variety of behaviours organizations find undesirable, including unionization attempts, substance abuse, stealing at work, undue socializing, and tardiness. Researchers argue that these behaviours are indicators of a broader syndrome called *deviant behaviour in the workplace* (or *employee withdrawal*).[103] If employees don't like their work environment, they will respond somehow, though it is not always easy to forecast exactly *how*. One worker might quit. Another might use work time to surf the Internet or take work supplies home for personal use. In short, workers who don't like their jobs "get even" in various ways—and because those ways can be quite creative, controlling only one behaviour, such as with an absence control policy, leaves the root cause untouched. To effectively control the undesirable consequences of job dissatisfaction, employers should attack the source of the problem—the dissatisfaction—rather than try to control the different responses.

Exhibit 3-4 presents a model—the exit-voice-loyalty-neglect framework—that can be used to examine individual responses to job dissatisfaction along two dimensions: whether they are constructive or destructive and whether they are active or passive. Four types of behaviour result:[104]

- **Exit**. Actively attempting to leave the organization, including looking for a new position as well as resigning. This is a destructive action from the point of view of the organization.

- **Voice**. Actively and constructively attempting to improve conditions, including suggesting improvements, discussing problems with superiors, and some forms of union activity.

- **Loyalty**. Passively but optimistically waiting for conditions to improve, including speaking up for the organization in the face of external criticism and trusting the organization and its management to "do the right thing."

- **Neglect**. Passively allowing conditions to worsen, including chronic absenteeism or lateness, reduced effort, and increased error rate. This is a destructive action from the point of view of the organization.

Exit and neglect behaviours reflect employee choices of lowered productivity, absenteeism, and turnover in the face of dissatisfaction. But this model also presents constructive behaviours such as voice and loyalty that allow individuals to tolerate unpleasant situations or to work toward satisfactory working conditions. It helps us understand situations, such as those we sometimes find among unionized workers, where low job satisfaction is coupled with low turnover.[105] Union members often

exit Dissatisfaction expressed by actively attempting to leave the organization.

voice Dissatisfaction expressed by actively and constructively attempting to improve conditions.

loyalty Dissatisfaction expressed by passively waiting for conditions to improve.

neglect Dissatisfaction expressed by passively allowing conditions to worsen.

EXHIBIT 3-4 Responses to Job Dissatisfaction

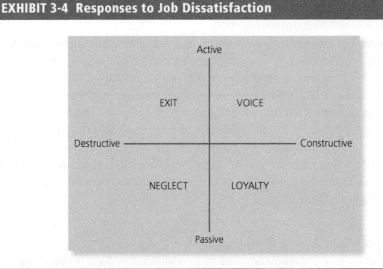

Source: "When Bureaucrats Get the Blues: Responses to Dissatisfaction Among Federal Employees" by Caryl Rusbult, David Lowery. *Journal of Applied Social Psychology 15*, no. 1, p. 83. Copyright © 1985, John Wiley and Sons.

express dissatisfaction through the grievance procedure or through formal contract negotiations. These voice mechanisms allow them to continue in their jobs while convincing themselves that they are acting to improve the situation.

Managers Often "Don't Get It"

Given the evidence we have just reviewed, it should come as no surprise that job satisfaction can affect the bottom line. One study by a management consulting firm separated large organizations into high morale (where more than 70 percent of employees expressed overall job satisfaction) and medium or low morale (fewer than 70 percent). The stock prices of companies in the high morale group grew 19.4 percent, compared with 10 percent for the medium or low morale group. Despite these results, many managers are unconcerned about employee job satisfaction. Still others overestimate how satisfied employees are with their jobs, so they don't think there's a problem when there is. In one study of 262 large employers, 86 percent of senior managers believed their organization treated its employees well, but only 55 percent of the employees agreed. Another study found 55 percent of managers thought morale was good in their organization, compared with only 38 percent of employees.[106] Managers first need to care about job satisfaction, and then they need to measure it rather than just assume that everything is going well.

Organizational Commitment

In **organizational commitment** an employee identifies with a particular organization and its goals, and wishes to remain a member.[107]

Professor John Meyer at the University of Western Ontario and his colleagues have identified and developed measures for three types of commitment:[108]

- **Affective commitment**. An individual's emotional attachment to an organization and a belief in its values. For example, a PetSmart employee may be affectively committed to the company because of its involvement with animals.

- **Normative commitment**. The obligation an individual feels to stay with an organization for moral or ethical reasons. An employee spearheading a new initiative may remain with an employer because she feels she would "leave the employer in the lurch" if she left.

- **Continuance commitment**. An individual's perceived economic value of remaining with an organization. An employee may be committed to an employer because she is paid well and feels it would hurt her family to quit.

A positive relationship appears to exist between organizational commitment and job productivity, but it is a modest one.[109] A review of 27 studies suggested that the relationship between commitment and performance is strongest for new employees, and considerably weaker for more experienced employees.[110] The research evidence demonstrates negative relationships between organizational commitment and both absenteeism and turnover.[111]

Different forms of commitment have different effects on behaviour. One study found managerial affective commitment more strongly related to organizational performance than was continuance commitment.[112] Another study showed that continuance commitment was related to a lower intention to quit but an increased tendency to be absent and lower job performance. These results make sense in that continuance commitment really isn't a commitment at all. Rather than an allegiance (affective commitment) or an obligation (normative commitment) to an employer, a continuance commitment describes an employee "tethered" to an employer simply because there isn't anything better available.[113]

organizational commitment The degree to which an employee identifies with a particular organization and its goals, and wishes to maintain membership in the organization.

affective commitment An individual's emotional attachment to and identification with an organization, and a belief in its values.

normative commitment The obligation an individual feels to stay with an organization.

continuance commitment An individual's calculation to stay with an organization based on the perceived costs of leaving the organization.

A major focus of Nissan Motor Company's Diversity Development Office in Japan is helping female employees develop their careers. Nissan provides women such as the assembly-line workers shown here with one-on-one counselling services of career advisers and training programs to develop applicable skills. Women can also visit Nissan's corporate intranet to read interviews with "role models," women who have made substantial contributions to the company. Nissan believes that hiring more women and supporting their careers will contribute to the company's competitive edge.

How can companies increase organizational commitment? Research on a number of companies known for employees with high organizational commitment identified five reasons why employees commit themselves:[114]

- They are proud of [the company's] aspirations, accomplishments, and legacy; they share its values.

- They know what each person is expected to do, how performance is measured, and why it matters.

- They are in control of their own destinies; they savour the high-risk, high-reward work environment.

- They are recognized mostly for the quality of their individual performance.

- They have fun and enjoy the supportive and highly interactive environment.

These findings suggest a variety of ways for organizations to increase the commitment of employees. Earlier in the chapter, we discussed the role of satisfaction on organizational citizenship behaviour (OCB). We should also note that when individuals have high organizational commitment, they are likely to engage in more OCB.

Job Involvement

job involvement The degree to which a person identifies with a job, actively participates in it, and considers performance important to self-worth.

psychological empowerment Employees' belief in the degree to which they affect their work environment, their competence, the meaningfulness of their job, and their perceived autonomy in their work.

Related to job satisfaction is **job involvement**,[115] which measures the degree to which people identify psychologically with their job and consider their perceived performance level important to self-worth.[116] Employees with a high level of job involvement strongly identify with and really care about the kind of work they do. Another closely related concept is **psychological empowerment**, employees' beliefs in the degree to which they influence their work environment, their competence, the meaningfulness of their job, and their perceived autonomy.[117] High levels of both job involvement and psychological empowerment are positively related to organizational citizenship and job performance.[118] High job involvement is also related to reduced absences and lower resignation rates.[119]

Employee Engagement

A new concept that comes out of the work on job involvement is **employee engagement**, an individual's involvement with, satisfaction with, and enthusiasm for the work he or she does. For example, we might ask employees about the availability of resources and the opportunities to learn new skills, whether they feel their work is important and meaningful, and whether their interactions with co-workers and supervisors are rewarding.[120] Highly engaged employees have a passion for their work and feel a deep connection to their company; disengaged employees have essentially "checked out"—putting time but not energy or attention into their work.[121] Calgary-based Vista Projects, an engineering procurement and construction management firm, consults with its employees for engagement ideas. Doing so has resulted in educational initiatives, opportunities for company ownership, and time off for religious holidays.[122] To encourage engagement, the president of Charlottetown, PEI-based Holland College visits the college's 13 sites routinely to give employees an opportunity to raise concerns.

A study of nearly 8000 business units in 36 companies found that those whose employees had high average levels of engagement had higher levels of customer satisfaction, were more productive, had higher profits, and had lower levels of turnover and accidents than at other companies.[123] Toronto-based Molson Coors Canada found that engaged employees were five times less likely to have safety incidents, and when one did occur, it was much less serious, and less costly for the engaged employee than for a disengaged one ($63 per incident vs. $392).

Such promising findings have earned employee engagement a following in many business organizations and management consulting firms. However, the concept is relatively new and still generates active debate about its usefulness. One review of the literature concluded that the meaning of the term is ambiguous for both practitioners and academics,[124] while another reviewer called engagement "an umbrella term for whatever one wants it to be."[125] Still, a 2011 study that draws from the best current research to create a model of work engagement suggests that there is a lot of promise to this concept.[126]

Organizations will likely continue using employee engagement, and it will remain a subject of research. The ambiguity surrounding it arises from its newness and may also, ironically, reflect its popularity. Engagement is a very general concept, perhaps broad enough to capture the intersection of the other variables we have discussed. In other words, it may be what these attitudes have in common.

Managing Diversity in the Workplace

Managers at SaskGaming consider managing diversity part of their contribution to supporting the future of Saskatchewan.[127] The 1000 employees working in two casinos—Casino Regina and Casino Moose Jaw—represent considerable diversity: 42.5 percent are of Aboriginal descent, 5.8 percent are persons with disabilities, and 11.5 percent are visible minorities. The company provides quality employment, helping young people develop skills and leadership abilities. SaskGaming's training program is also intended to "provide a foundation for our employees to assume leadership roles within their communities." The company invests in the communities where employees live and work as well. In 2010, it contributed $750 000 and considerable volunteer hours to community organizations and events. Why does managing diversity well make a difference?

5 How do we respond to diversity in the workplace?

---

employee engagement An individual's involvement with, satisfaction with, and enthusiasm for the work he or she does.

biographical characteristics Personal characteristics—such as age, gender, race, and length of tenure—that are objective and easily obtained from personnel records. These characteristics are representative of surface-level diversity.

ability An individual's capacity to perform the various tasks in a job.

Organizations increasingly face diversity concerns as workplaces become more heterogeneous. **Biographical characteristics** such as age, gender, race, disability, and length of service are some of the most obvious ways employees differ. Others include length of service (tenure), religion, sexual orientation, and gender identity. There is also diversity in **ability**, an individual's current capacity to perform the various tasks in a job. Earlier in the chapter, we discussed cultural and generational differences and their implications in the Canadian workplace.

Many organizations have attempted to incorporate workforce diversity initiatives into their workplaces to improve relations among co-workers. For example, Dell Canada is one of a number of companies in Canada that have developed diversity policies for their workplace. Dell Canada's policy states the following:

> *Diversity, inclusiveness and respect for all Dell employees form the basis of Dell's Winning Culture and are essential to Dell's success. Dell values each individual's distinct contribution and leverages our collective strengths to ensure that Dell remains the technology solutions company of choice for customers around the world.*[128]

Dell's statement on diversity is typical of statements found in company annual reports and employee information packets to signal corporate values to those who interact with the company. Some corporations choose to signal the value of diversity because they think it is an important strategic goal. Other organizations recognize that the purchasing power of diverse groups is substantial.

When companies design and then publicize statements about the importance of diversity, they are essentially producing value statements. The hope, of course, is that the statements will influence the behaviour of members of the organization, particularly since preference for people who are ethnically like ourselves may be ingrained in us at an early age. In a study published in 2011, researchers from Concordia University and the University of Montreal found that Asian Canadian and French Canadian preschoolers preferred to interact with kids of their own ethnic group.[129]

There is little research showing that values can be changed successfully.[130] Because values tend to be relatively stable, workplaces try to address diversity issues through education aimed at changing attitudes.

Effective Diversity Programs

Joan Vogelesang, CEO of Montreal-based animation software company Toon Boom, says that Canadian companies do not make use of the diversity in employees they have. She thinks Canadian companies need to look beyond imperfect English and cultural customs when hiring. She practises what she preaches: Most of her executive team are first-generation immigrants. Her employees speak 20 languages among them. "Two of our staff members speak Japanese. You can hardly do business in Japan if you don't speak it," she says.[131]

Vogelesang's description of diversity as a competitive advantage speaks to the need for effective diversity programs that have three distinct components. First, they should teach people about the legal framework for equal employment opportunity and encourage fair treatment of all people, regardless of their demographic characteristics. Second, they should teach people how a diverse workforce will be better able to serve a diverse market of customers and clients. Third, they should foster personal development practices that bring out the skills and abilities of all workers, acknowledging how differences in perspective can be a valuable way to improve performance for everyone.[132] A 2011 study by researchers at the University of Toronto Scarborough found that focusing on the positive benefits of diversity, rather than telling people what they should and should not do, was more likely to reduce people's prejudices toward other groups.[133]

Much concern about diversity has to do with fair treatment.[134] Most negative reactions to employment discrimination are based on the idea that discriminatory treatment is unfair. Regardless of race or gender, people are generally in favour of diversity-oriented programs if they believe the policies ensure everyone has a fair opportunity to show their skills and abilities.

A major study of the consequences of diversity programs came to what might seem a surprising conclusion.[135] Organizations that provided diversity training were not

Joan Vogelesang, CEO of Montreal-based animation software company Toon Boom, says that Canadian companies do not make use of the diversity in employees they have. She thinks Canadian companies need to look beyond imperfect English and cultural customs when hiring. She practises what she preaches: Most of her executive team are first-generation immigrants. Her employees speak 20 languages among them. She is pictured with Francisco Del Cueto, CTO (left), and Steven Chu, COO (right).

consistently more likely to have women and minorities in upper management positions than organizations that did not. On closer examination, though, these results are not surprising. Experts have long known that one-shot training sessions without strategies to encourage effective diversity management back on the job are not likely to be very effective. Some diversity programs, such as those of Toronto-based Corus Entertainment, Ottawa-based Health Canada, Regina-based Information Services Corporation, and Brampton, Ontario-based Loblaw Companies, are truly effective in improving representation in management. They include strategies to measure the representation of women and minorities in managerial positions, and they hold managers accountable for achieving more demographically diverse management teams.

Organizational leaders should examine their workforce to determine whether the **protected groups** covered by Canada's Employment Equity Act (women, people with disabilities, Aboriginal people, and visible minorities) have been underutilized. If groups of employees are not proportionally represented in top management, managers should look for any hidden barriers to advancement. They can often improve recruiting practices, make selection systems more transparent, and provide training for those employees who have not had adequate exposure to necessary work-related experiences in the past. Exhibit 3-5 presents examples of what some of the leading companies are doing as part of their diversity initiatives.[136]

Management should also clearly communicate the company's diversity policies and their rationale to employees so they can understand how and why certain practices are followed. Communications should focus as much as possible on qualifications and job performance; emphasizing that certain groups need more assistance could well backfire.

To ensure the top-level management team represents the diversity of its workforce and client base, Safeway implemented the Retail Leadership Development (RLD) program, a formal career development program. This program is open to all employees, so it is inclusive, but women and underrepresented racial or ethnic groups are particularly encouraged to participate. Interested individuals take tests to determine whether they

protected groups The four groups designated by the Employment Equity Act as the beneficiaries of employment equity (women, people with disabilities, Aboriginal people, and visible minorities).

EXHIBIT 3-5 Practices Used by 45 of Canada's Most Welcoming Places to Work

Company (Location)	Industry	Number of Employees	Diversity Activities
Bell Aliant Regional Communications (Halifax)	Wired telecommunications carriers	7460	Created a diversity team that represents women, Aboriginal people, visible minorities, people with disabilities, new Canadians, LGBT, and francophone employees
Cameco Corp. (Saskatoon)	Mining	2800	Partners with the Mining Industry Human Resources Council and Women in Mining to study employment barriers women face in the mining industry
Bombardier Aerospace (Dorval)	Aircraft manufacturing	16 659	Launched a network for female employees in 2008 and is developing a recruitment strategy to attract and retain women
Ontario Public Service (Toronto)	Government support	64 725	Provides a "quiet room" to meet employees' diverse religious and spiritual needs
City of Vancouver	Government	6901	Provides diversity training workshops to new employees. Translated training materials into various languages
Newalta Corp. (Calgary)	Recycling and industrial waste management	1669	Created an online diversity area with e-learning modules and newsletters to keep employees up-to-date on best practices

Source: Based on MediaCorp Canada, "Canada's Best Diversity Employers, 2011," *Canada's Top 100 Employers*, February 2011, http://www.canadastop100.com/diversity/

have management potential. Safeway managers are charged with providing promising RLD participants with additional training and development opportunities to ensure they have the skills needed for advancement, and are given performance bonuses if they meet concrete diversity goals. The RLD program has increased the number of white women store managers by 31 percent since its inception, and the number of women-of-colour store managers by 92 percent.[137]

Just because the company's managers may value diversity, this does not mean that all employees will share that value. Consequently, even if they are required to attend diversity training, employees may exhibit negative attitudes toward individuals because of their gender or ethnicity. Additionally, what attitudes are appropriately displayed outside of the workplace may be questioned by some employers. Finally, the workplace is not the only place where people's attitudes toward racial diversity gets displayed, underscoring that the responsibility for education about reacting to diversity goes beyond employers. In September 2011, at an exhibition game between the Philadelphia Flyers and the Detroit Red Wings played in London, Ontario, someone from the audience threw a banana at Flyers' player Wayne Simmonds, one of the few black players in the NHL. Retired Montreal Canadiens forward Georges Laraque, when asked to comment on the incident, noted that "throughout [my] career, [I] had to endure the 'N' word a number of times."[138]

Cultural Intelligence

Are some individuals better than others at dealing with people from different cultures? Management professors Christopher Earley of the London School of Business and Elaine Mosakowski of the University of Colorado at Boulder have recently introduced the idea of **cultural intelligence**, or CQ, to suggest that people vary in how they deal with other cultures. This term is defined as "the seemingly natural ability to interpret someone's unfamiliar and ambiguous gestures in just the way that person's compatriots and colleagues would, even to mirror them."[139]

Earley and Mosakowski suggest that CQ "picks up where emotional intelligence leaves off." Those with CQ try to figure out whether a person's behaviour is representative of all members of a group or just that person. Thus, for example, a person with high CQ who encounters two German engineers would be able to determine which of the engineers' conduct is explained by the fact of being an engineer, by being German, and by behaviour that is simply particular to the individual. A 2010 study found that CQ is particularly helpful to expatriates on international assignment because the ability to be confident about and interested in being in new cultural environments makes it easier to adjust to the demands of foreign assignments.[140]

RESEARCH FINDINGS

RESEARCH FINDINGS: Cultural Intelligence

According to the researchers, "cultural intelligence resides in the body [the physical] and the heart [the emotional/motivational], as well as the head [the cognitive]." Individuals who have high *cognitive* CQ look for clues to help them identify a culture's shared understandings. Specifically, an individual does this by looking for consistencies in behaviours across a variety of people from the same cultural background. Individuals with high *physical* CQ learn the customs and gestures of those from other cultures and therefore act more like them. This increases understanding, trust, and openness between people of different cultures. One study found that job candidates who used some of the mannerisms of recruiters who had different cultural backgrounds from themselves were more likely to receive job offers than those who did not do so.[141] Those with high *emotional/motivational* CQ believe that they are capable of understanding people from other cultures, and will keep trying to do so, even if they are faced with difficulties in doing so.

Based on their research, Earley and Mosakowski have discovered that most managers fall into the following cultural intelligence profiles:

- *Provincial*. They work best with people of similar background, but have difficulties working with those from different backgrounds.

- *Analyst*. They analyze a foreign culture's rules and expectations to figure out how to interact with others.

- *Natural*. They use intuition rather than systematic study to understand those from other cultural backgrounds.

- *Ambassador*. They communicate convincingly that they fit in, even if they do not know much about the foreign culture.

- *Mimic*. They control actions and behaviours to match others, even if they do not understand the significance of the cultural cues observed.

- *Chameleon*. They have high levels of all three CQ components. They could be mistaken as being from the foreign culture. According to research, only about 5 percent of managers fit this profile.

Exhibit 3-6 can help you assess your own CQ.

cultural intelligence The ability to understand someone's unfamiliar and ambiguous gestures in the same way as would people from that person's culture.

EXHIBIT 3-6 Measuring Your Cultural Intelligence

Rate the extent to which you agree with each statement, using the following scale:

1 = strongly disagree
2 = disagree
3 = neutral
4 = agree
5 = strongly agree

_____ Before I interact with people from a new culture, I ask myself what I hope to achieve.
_____ If I encounter something unexpected while working in a new culture, I use this experience to figure out new ways to approach other cultures in the future.
_____ I plan how I'm going to relate to people from a different culture before I meet them.
_____ When I come into a new cultural situation, I can immediately sense whether something is going well or something is wrong.

Total _____ ÷ 4 = **Cognitive CQ**

_____ It's easy for me to change my body language (for example, eye contact or posture) to suit people from a different culture.
_____ I can alter my expression when a cultural encounter requires it.
_____ I modify my speech style (for example, accent or tone) to suit people from a different culture.
_____ I easily change the way I act when a cross-cultural encounter seems to require it.

Total _____ ÷ 4 = **Physical CQ**

_____ I have confidence that I can deal well with people from a different culture.
_____ I am certain that I can befriend people whose cultural backgrounds are different from mine.
_____ I can adapt to the lifestyle of a different culture with relative ease.
_____ I am confident that I can deal with a cultural situation that is unfamiliar.

Total _____ ÷ 4 = **Emotional/motivational CQ**

Interpretation: Generally, an average of less than 3 would indicate an area calling for improvement, while an average of greater than 4.5 reflects a true CQ strength.

Source: P. C. Earley and E. Mosakowski, "Cultural Intelligence," _Harvard Business Review_ 82, no. 10 (October 2004), pp. 139–146. Reprinted by permission of _Harvard Business Review_.

GLOBAL IMPLICATIONS

Although a number of topics were covered in this chapter, we review only three in terms of their application beyond Canada and the United States. First, we consider whether job satisfaction is simply a US concept. Second, we examine whether employees in Western cultures are more satisfied with their jobs than people from other cultures. Finally, we look at international differences in how diversity is managed.

Is Job Satisfaction a US Concept?

Most of the research on job satisfaction has been conducted in the United States. So, is job satisfaction a US concept? The evidence strongly suggests it is _not_; people in other cultures can and do form judgments of job satisfaction. Moreover, similar factors seem to cause, and result from, job satisfaction across cultures: We noted earlier that pay is positively, but relatively weakly, related to job satisfaction. This relationship appears to hold in other industrialized nations as well.

Are Employees in Western Cultures More Satisfied with Their Jobs?

Although job satisfaction appears relevant across cultures, that does not mean there are no cultural differences in job satisfaction. Evidence suggests that employees in Western cultures have higher levels of job satisfaction than those in Eastern cultures.[142] Do employees in Western cultures have better jobs? Or are they simply more positive (and less self-critical)? Although both factors are probably at play, evidence suggests that people in Eastern cultures find negative emotions less disagreeable than do people in Western cultures, who tend to emphasize positive emotions and individual happiness.[143] That may be why employees in Western cultures such as the United States and Scandinavia are more likely to have higher levels of satisfaction.

Does organizational commitment vary cross-nationally? A recent study explored this question and compared the organizational commitment of Chinese employees with that of Canadian and South Korean employees.[144] Although results revealed that the three types of commitment—normative, affective, and continuance—are present in all three cultures, they differ in importance. In addition, the study found that Canadians and South Koreans are closer to each other in values than either is with the Chinese. Normative commitment (an obligation to remain with an organization for moral or ethical reasons) and affective commitment (an emotional attachment to the organization and belief in its values) were highest among Chinese employees. Continuance commitment (the perceived economic value of remaining with an organization) was *lower* among Chinese employees than among Canadian, British, and South Korean employees.

Is Diversity Managed Differently across Cultures?

Besides the mere presence of diversity in international work settings, there are international differences in how diversity is managed. Each country has its own legal framework for dealing with diversity, and these frameworks are a powerful reflection of the diversity-related concerns of each country. Many countries require specific targets and quotas for achieving employment equity goals, whereas the legal framework in Canada specifically forbids their use. The types of demographic differences considered important for diversity management also vary across countries. For example, in India the nondiscrimination framework includes quotas and set-aside programs for individuals from lower castes.[145] A case study of the multinational Finnish company TRANSCO found that it was possible to develop a consistent global philosophy for diversity management. However, differences in legal and cultural factors across nations forced TRANSCO to develop unique policies to match the cultural and legal frameworks of each country in which it operated.[146]

LESSONS LEARNED

- Values represent basic convictions about what is important, right, and good.
- Attitudes tend to predict behaviours.
- Job satisfaction leads to better performance.

4

Organizational Culture

SECTION TWO

ORGANIZATIONAL CULTURE,

STRUCTURE, DECISION MAKING

AND CREATIVITY

When you walk into a Boston Pizza restaurant in BC, Ontario, or Quebec, you will find many similarities, but a few differences too.[1] The Quebec restaurants carry poutine, while the Ontario restaurants have a meatball sub on the menu and use a different type of pepperoni on the pizzas than those made in BC and Quebec.

Despite these menu differences, the similarity that binds the Richmond, BC-based Boston Pizza restaurants throughout Canada and the United States is the strong organizational culture created by the company's co-owners, Jim Treliving and George Melville. The two men believe that a strong culture makes for a strong organization, and they emphasize the importance of finding the right people, having good systems in place, training employees, and communicating effectively.

The emphasis on a strong culture seems to be paying off for Boston Pizza. It has been named one of Canada's 10 Most Admired Corporate Cultures, and its three-year average revenue growth far exceeded industry standards and the TSX 60 Composite index.

In this chapter, we show that every organization has a culture. We examine how that culture reveals itself and the impact it has on the attitudes and behaviours of members of that organization. An understanding of what makes up an organization's culture and how it is created, sustained, and learned enhances our ability to explain and predict the behaviour of people at work.

What Is Organizational Culture?

1 What is the purpose of organizational culture?

When Henry Mintzberg, professor at McGill University and one of the world's leading management experts, was asked to compare organizational structure and corporate culture, he said, "Culture is the soul of the organization—the beliefs and values, and how they are manifested. I think of the structure as the skeleton, and as the flesh and blood. And culture is the soul that holds the thing together and gives it life force."[2]

Mintzberg's culture metaphor provides a clear image of how to think about culture. Culture provides stability to an organization and gives employees a clear understanding of "the way things are done around here." Culture sets the tone for how an organization operates and how individuals within the organization interact. Think of the different impressions you have when a receptionist tells you that "Ms. Dettweiler" will be available in a moment, while at another organization you are told that "Emma" will be with you as soon as she gets off the phone. It's clear that in one organization the rules are more formal than in the other.

As we discuss organizational culture, you may want to remember that organizations differ considerably in the cultures they adopt. Consider the different cultures of Calgary-based WestJet Airlines and Montreal-based Air Canada. WestJet is viewed as having a "young, spunky, can-do environment, where customers will have more fun."[3] Air Canada, by contrast, is considered less helpful and friendly. One analyst even suggested that Air Canada staff "tend to make their customers feel stressed" by their confrontational behaviour.[4] Our discussion of culture should help you understand how these differences across organizations occur.

As you start to think about different organizations where you might work, you will want to research their cultures. For instance, some organizations' cultures are admired more than others: Toronto-based Shoppers Drug Mart, Calgary-based WestJet Airlines, Vancouver-based Ledcor Group, and Toronto-based ING Direct are 4 of the 10 companies named "Most Admired Corporate Cultures" of 2011. An organization that expects employees to work 15 hours a day may not be where you would like to work.

Definition of *Organizational Culture*

Organizational culture refers to a system of shared meaning held by members that distinguishes the organization from other organizations.[5]

Seven primary characteristics capture the essence of an organization's culture:[6]

- *Innovation and risk-taking.* The degree to which employees are encouraged to be innovative and take risks.

- *Attention to detail.* The degree to which employees are expected to work with precision, analysis, and attention to detail.

- *Outcome orientation.* The degree to which management focuses on results, or outcomes, rather than on the techniques and processes used to achieve these outcomes.

- *People orientation.* The degree to which management decisions take into consideration the effect of outcomes on people within the organization.

- *Team orientation.* The degree to which work activities are organized around teams rather than individuals.

- *Aggressiveness.* The degree to which people are aggressive and competitive rather than easygoing and supportive.

- *Stability.* The degree to which organizational activities emphasize maintaining the status quo in contrast to growth.

organizational culture A system of shared meaning held by members that distinguishes the organization from other organizations.

Each of these characteristics exists on a continuum from low to high.

When individuals consider their organization in terms of these seven characteristics, they get a composite picture of the organization's culture. This picture becomes the basis for feelings of shared understanding that members have about the organization, how things are done in it, and the way members are supposed to behave. Exhibit 4-1 demonstrates how these characteristics can be mixed to create highly diverse organizations.

Levels of Culture

Because organizational culture has multiple levels,[7] the metaphor of an iceberg has often been used to describe it.[8] However, a simmering volcano may better represent the layers of culture: beliefs, values, assumptions bubble below the surface, producing observable aspects of culture at the surface. Exhibit 4-2 reminds us that culture is very visible at the level of **artifacts**. These are what you see, hear, and feel when you encounter an organization's culture. You may notice, for instance, that employees in two offices have very different dress policies, or one office displays great works of art while another posts company mottos on the wall. These visible artifacts emerge from the organization's culture.

Vancouver-based Playland amusement park hires hundreds of young people each summer to run the rides, sell tickets, and manage the games booths. Managers want to make sure that new employees will fit into the "fun culture" of the environment. Instead of one-on-one interviews, applicants are put into teams where they solve puzzles together, while managers watch the group dynamics. Amy Nguyen (left) and Chloe Wong are two of the teens hired after they did well in the group interview.

Exhibit 4-2 also shows us that beliefs, values, and assumptions, unlike artifacts, are not always readily observable. Instead, we rely on the visible artifacts (material symbols, special language used, rituals carried out, and stories told to others) to help us uncover the organization's beliefs, values, and assumptions. **Beliefs** are the understandings of how objects and ideas relate to each other. **Values** are the stable, long-lasting beliefs about what is important. For instance, Winnipeg-based Palliser Furniture, a manufacturer of leather- and fabric-upholstered furniture, promotes the following corporate values: "demonstrate integrity in all relationships; promote the dignity and value of each other; respect the environment; support our community; and strive for excellence in all we do."[9] **Assumptions** are the taken-for-granted notions of how something should be. When basic assumptions are held by the entire group, members will have difficulty conceiving

---

EXHIBIT 4-1 Contrasting Organizational Cultures

Organization A	Organization B
• Managers must fully document all decisions.	• Management encourages and rewards risk-taking and change.
• Creative decisions, change, and risks are not encouraged.	• Employees are encouraged to "run with" ideas, and failures are treated as "learning experiences."
• Extensive rules and regulations exist for all employees.	• Employees have few rules and regulations to follow.
• Productivity is valued over employee morale.	• Productivity is balanced with treating its people right.
• Employees are encouraged to stay within their own department.	• Team members are encouraged to interact with people at all levels and functions.
• Individual effort is encouraged.	• Many rewards are team-based.

artifacts Aspects of an organization's culture that you see, hear, and feel.

beliefs The understandings of how objects and ideas relate to each other.

values The stable, long-lasting beliefs about what is important.

assumptions The taken-for-granted notions of how something should be.

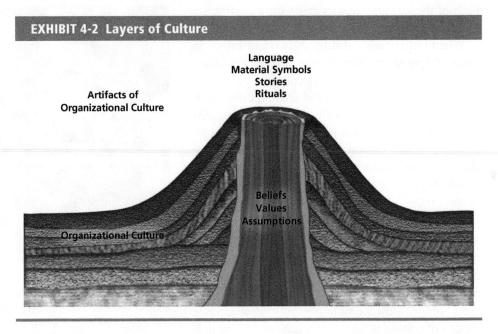

EXHIBIT 4-2 Layers of Culture

Language
Material Symbols
Stories
Rituals

Artifacts of
Organizational Culture

Beliefs
Values
Assumptions

Organizational Culture

of another way of doing things. For instance, in Canada, some students hold a basic assumption that universities should not consider costs when setting tuition, and should keep tuition low for greater access by students. Beliefs, values, and assumptions, if we can uncover them, help us understand why organizations do the things that we observe.

Culture's Functions

Culture performs a number of functions within an organization:

- It has a boundary-defining role because it creates distinction between one organization and others.

- It conveys a sense of identity to organization members.

- It helps create commitment to something larger than an individual's self-interest.

- It enhances stability; it is the social glue that helps hold the organization together by providing appropriate standards for what employees should say and do.

- It serves as a control mechanism that guides and shapes the attitudes and behaviour of employees, and helps them make sense of the organization.

This last function is of particular interest to us.[10] As the following quotation makes clear, culture defines the rules of the game:

Culture by definition is elusive, intangible, implicit, and taken for granted. But every organization develops a core set of assumptions, understandings, and implicit rules that govern day-to-day behaviour in the workplace. Until newcomers learn the rules, they are not accepted as full-fledged members of the organization. Transgressions of the rules on the part of high-level executives or front-line employees result in universal disapproval and powerful penalties. Conformity to the rules becomes the primary basis for reward and upward mobility.[11]

Today's trend toward decentralized organizations makes culture more important than ever, but ironically it also makes establishing a strong culture more difficult. When formal authority and control systems are reduced, culture's *shared meaning* points everyone in the same direction. However, employees organized in teams may show greater allegiance to their team and its values than to the values of the organization as a whole. In virtual organizations, the lack of frequent face-to-face contact makes establishing a common set of norms very difficult. Strong leadership that communicates frequently about common goals and priorities is especially important in innovative organizations.[12]

What does organizational culture do?

Culture Creates Climate

If you have worked with someone whose positive attitude inspired you to do your best, or with a lacklustre team that drained your motivation, you have experienced the effects of climate. **Organizational climate** refers to the shared perceptions organizational members have about their organization and work environment.[13] This aspect of culture is like team spirit at the organizational level. When everyone has the same general feelings about what is important or how well things are working, the effect of these attitudes will be more than the sum of the individual parts. The same appears true for organizations. One meta-analysis found that across dozens of different samples, psychological climate was strongly related to individuals' level of job satisfaction, involvement, commitment, and motivation.[14] A positive overall workplace climate has been linked to higher customer satisfaction and financial performance as well.[15]

Dozens of dimensions of climate have been studied, including safety, justice, diversity, and customer service, to name a few.[16] A person who encounters a positive climate for performance will think about doing a good job more often and will believe others support his or her success. Someone who encounters a positive climate for diversity will feel more comfortable collaborating with co-workers regardless of their demographic background. Climate also influences the habits people adopt. If the climate for safety is positive, everyone wears safety gear and follows safety procedures even if individually they would not normally think very often about being safe.

Do Organizations Have Uniform Cultures?

Organizational culture represents a common perception the organization's members hold. We should expect, therefore, that individuals with different backgrounds or at different levels in the organization will tend to describe its culture in similar terms.[17]

The fact that organizational culture has common properties does not mean that there cannot be subcultures within it. Most large organizations have a dominant culture and numerous sets of subcultures.[18] A **dominant culture** expresses the core values that are shared by a majority of the organization's members. When we talk about an organization's culture, we are referring to its dominant culture, which gives an organization its distinct personality.[19] **Subcultures** tend to develop in large organizations to reflect common problems, situations, or experiences faced by groups of members in the same department or location. The purchasing department can have a subculture that includes the **core values** of the dominant culture plus additional values unique to members of the purchasing department.

If organizations were composed only of numerous subcultures, organizational culture as an independent variable would be significantly less powerful. It is the "shared meaning" aspect of culture that makes it such a potent device for guiding and shaping behaviour. This is what allows us to say that Microsoft's culture values aggressiveness and risk-taking,[20] and then to use that information to better understand the behaviour of Microsoft executives and employees. But many organizations also have subcultures that can influence the behaviour of members.

organizational climate The shared perceptions organizational members have about their organization and work environment.

dominant culture A system of shared meaning that expresses the core values shared by a majority of the organization's members.

subcultures Mini-cultures within an organization, typically defined by department designations and geographical separation.

core values The primary or dominant values that are accepted throughout the organization.

Organizational culture guides and shapes the attitudes of employees at New Zealand Air. One of the airline's guiding principles is to champion and promote New Zealand and its national heritage both within the country and overseas. In this photo, a cabin crew member dressed in traditional Maori clothing and a pilot touch noses to represent the sharing of a single breath following a ceremony for the airline's purchase of a Boeing airplane in Everett, Washington. This expression of representing their country with pride creates a strong bond among employees.

Strong vs. Weak Cultures

It is possible to differentiate between strong and weak cultures.[21] If most employees (responding to management surveys) have the same opinions about the organization's mission and values, the culture is strong; if opinions vary widely, the culture is weak.

In a **strong culture**, the organization's core values are both intensely held and widely shared.[22] The more members who accept the core values and the greater their commitment to those values, the stronger the culture is. A strong culture will have a great influence on the behaviour of its members because the high degree of shared experiences and intensity create an internal climate of high behavioural control. American retailer Nordstrom has developed one of the strongest service cultures in the retailing industry. Nordstrom employees know what is expected of them, and these expectations go a long way in shaping their behaviour.

A strong culture builds cohesiveness, loyalty, and organizational commitment. These qualities, in turn, lessen employees' tendency to leave the organization.[23]

Reading an Organization's Culture

 How do you read an organization's culture?

Boston Pizza claims to be Canada's number one casual dining restaurant. It has reached that status by developing a strong organizational culture.[24] The company's reward structure is designed to encourage all employees to meet corporate targets. "We feel strongly that everyone should participate and everyone should be rewarded in company growth and success," says the company's president and CEO, Mark Pacinda.

As part of its emphasis on building a strong culture, the company pays careful attention to its hiring strategy. The company also provides long-term incentives for employees to stay at Boston Pizza, so that there is a stable set of individuals in place to help socialize new employees into the culture.

strong culture A culture in which the core values are intensely held and widely shared.

Co-owner George Melville recognizes that when hiring franchisees, business skills and money are not enough. Employees have to fit into the culture as well. He reports that they once hired a person who had money and superb business skills, but who "was basically a jerk." The senior management realized that they had to let him go after six months. "The idea that you can build a team around somebody who isn't a team builder is a mistake," says Melville. Why does culture have such a strong influence on people's behaviour?

As we noted in Exhibit 4-2, the artifacts of culture inform outsiders and employees about the underlying values and beliefs of the organization's culture. These artifacts, or physical manifestations of culture, include stories, rituals, material symbols, and language. The extent to which organizations have artifacts of their culture indicates whether they have strong or weak cultures. *From Concepts to Skills* on pages 392–393 offers additional ideas on how to "read" an organization's culture.

> What kind of organizational culture would work best for you?

Stories

When Toronto-based Bank of Montreal (BMO) decided several years ago to become a leader in customer service in the banking industry, it needed a way of communicating this message to the bank's employees. The decision: "Every meeting starts with a customer story." No matter what kind of meeting is being held, one staff member has to tell a recent story about an interaction with a customer—ranging from feel-good stories to horror stories of something that went wrong for the customer. By focusing on customer stories, employees know they need to pay attention to interactions so that they can share the stories. Susan Brown, a senior VP with BMO, explains the importance of the story focus for the bank: "If you want to change culture, a great way to do it is the customer story. It's part of the evolution of developing a customer-centric culture."[25] Stories circulate through many organizations. They typically tell about the organization's founders, rule breaking, rags-to-riches successes, reductions in the workforce, relocation

Legend has it that a woman who was a frequent flyer on Southwest Airlines complained constantly about the service, dispiriting the customer service department. Finally, the head of customer relations asked Herb Kelleher, the founder, what they should do. Kelleher's response to the customer was brief: "Dear Mrs. X, We will miss you. Love, Herb." Employees were thrilled to get this kind of support from their CEO.

of employees, reactions to past mistakes, and organizational coping.[26] These stories anchor the present in the past and explain and legitimize current practices.[27]

Rituals

Rituals are repetitive sequences of activities that express and reinforce the key values of the organization; what goals are most important; and which people are important and which are expendable.[28]

One well-known corporate ritual is Walmart's company chant. Begun by the company's founder, Sam Walton, as a way to motivate and unite his workforce, "Gimme a W, gimme an A, gimme an L, give me an M, A, R, T!" has become a company ritual that bonds Walmart employees and reinforces Walton's belief in the importance of his employees to the company's success. Similar corporate chants are used by IBM, Ericsson, Novell, Deutsche Bank, and PricewaterhouseCoopers.[29]

Material Symbols

The layout of corporate headquarters, the types of cars given to top executives, and the presence or absence of corporate aircraft are a few examples of **material symbols**. Others include the size of offices, the elegance of furnishings, executive perks, and dress code.[30] In addition, corporate logos, signs, brochures, and advertisements reveal aspects of the organization's culture.[31] These material symbols convey to employees, customers, and clients who is important, the degree of egalitarianism top management desires, and the kinds of behaviour (for example, risk-taking, conservative, authoritarian, participative, individualistic, social) that are appropriate. For instance, pictures of all Creo employees hang in the Burnaby, BC-based company's entrance lobby, which visibly conveys Creo's anti-hierarchical culture.

Companies differ in how much separation they make between their executives and employees. This plays out in how material benefits are distributed to executives. Some companies provide their top executives with chauffeur-driven limousines and,

rituals Repetitive sequences of activities that express and reinforce the key values of the organization; what goals are most important; and which people are important and which are expendable.

material symbols What conveys to employees who is important, the degree of egalitarianism top management desires, and the kinds of behaviour that are appropriate.

At Walmart, culture is transmitted to employees through the daily ritual of the "Walmart cheer." The cheer is performed at both US and international stores. Employees are asked to do the cheer in every morning meeting. Shown here are employees of a Walmart store in Evergreen Park, Illinois, chanting the motivational cheer that helps preserve a small-family spirit and work environment within the world's largest retailer.

when they travel by air, unlimited use of the corporate jet. Other companies might pay for car and air transportation for top executives, only the car is a Chevrolet with no driver, and the jet seat is in the economy section of a commercial airliner. At Bolton, Ontario-based Husky Injection Molding Systems, a more egalitarian culture is favoured. Employees and management share the parking lot, dining room, and even washrooms.

Language

Many organizations and units within organizations use language to help identify with the culture, show their acceptance of it, and help preserve it. Baristas at Starbucks call drinks *short, tall,* or *grande,* not *small, medium,* or *large,* and they know the difference between a half-decaf double tall almond skinny mocha and an iced short schizo skinny hazelnut cappuccino with wings.[32] Students and employees at Grant MacEwan College are informed by the philosophy of the college's namesake. Dr. Grant MacEwan, historian, writer, politician, and environmentalist, was never a formal part of the management of the organization. However, many phrases from his writing and creed have found their way into formal college publications and calendars, as well as informal communications, including his most well known, "I have tried to leave things in the vineyard better than I found them."[33]

Over time, organizations often develop unique terms to describe equipment, offices, key staff, suppliers, customers, or products that relate to their business. New employees are frequently overwhelmed with acronyms and jargon that, after six months on the job, have become fully part of their language. Once assimilated, this terminology acts as a common denominator that unites members of a given culture or subculture.

Creating and Sustaining an Organization's Culture

One of the challenges Boston Pizza co-owners Jim Treliving and George Melville face in managing the 325 restaurants and more than 16 000 employees across Canada is making sure that everyone is on the same page.[34] The individual restaurants in the chain are not owned by the company. Instead, franchisees invest a considerable amount of money in order to gain the right to own a Boston Pizza restaurant. Thus, there could be a conflict between what the co-founders want done, and what a franchisee feels is best for his or her investment.

Treliving and Melville try to prevent this conflict by carefully vetting franchise candidates. Potential franchisees are informed of the initial $60 000 fee and start-up costs that could run between $1.5 and $2.4 million. Despite the size of their investment, franchisees must demonstrate a "willingness to adhere to the Boston Pizza system." Franchisees are given a lot of help in starting out, however.

When Hank Van Poelgeest opened up the first Boston Pizza restaurant in St. John's, Newfoundland, in January 2006, he naturally worried. A lot of preparation had gone into the opening, which involved months of planning, and a careful choice of location, and a team of nine people had been sent from head office to help hire and train staff. The new staff did a dress rehearsal of the grand opening four times to make sure nothing went wrong.

The preparation was so thorough that the opening exceeded all expectations. "We wanted to use the first couple of weeks as a slow beginning," says Van Poelgeest, "but we've never had a slow beginning." What role does culture play in creating high-performing employees?

3 How do you create and maintain organizational culture?

An organization's culture does not pop out of thin air, and once established, it rarely fades away. What forces influence the creation of a culture? What reinforces and sustains these forces once they are in place? Exhibit 4-3 summarizes how an organization's culture is established and sustained. We describe each part of this process next.

EXHIBIT 4-3 How Organizational Cultures Form

How a Culture Begins

An organization's current customs, traditions, and general way of doing things are largely due to what it has done before and how successful it was in doing it. This leads us to the ultimate source of an organization's culture: its founders.[35]

Is culture the same as rules?

Founders traditionally have a major impact on an organization's early culture. Free of previous customs or ideologies, they have a vision of what the organization should be. Because new organizations are typically small, it's possible for the founders to impose their vision on all organizational members. Jim Treliving, the co-owner of Boston Pizza, keeps his vision alive by stopping in at every Boston Pizza wherever he is travelling, shaking hands with the staff, and thanking them for their hard work. According to Treliving, "you take people in as franchisees and they become part of your family."[36]

Culture creation occurs in three ways.[37] First, founders only hire and keep employees who think and feel the way they do. Second, they indoctrinate and socialize these employees to their way of thinking and feeling. Finally, the founders' own behaviour encourages employees to identify with the founders and thereby internalize those beliefs, values, and assumptions. When the organization succeeds, the founders' vision is viewed as a primary determinant of that success. At that point, the founders' personality becomes embedded in the culture of the organization.

The culture at Toronto-based PCL, the largest general contracting organization in Canada, is still strongly influenced by the vision of Ernest Poole, who founded the company in 1906. "Poole's rules," which include "Employ highest grade people obtainable" and "Encourage integrity, loyalty and efficiencies," still influence the way the company hires and trains its employees long after the founder's death.[38] Other contemporary examples of founders who have had an immeasurable impact on their organizations' cultures are Ted Rogers of Toronto-based Rogers Communications, Frank Stronach of Aurora, Ontario-based Magna International, and Richard Branson of UK-based Virgin Group.

Keeping a Culture Alive

Once a culture is in place, practices within the organization maintain it by giving employees a set of similar experiences.[39] The selection process, performance evaluation criteria, training and career development activities, and promotion procedures ensure that those hired fit in with the culture, reward those who support it, and penalize (and even expel) those who challenge it. Three forces play a particularly important part in sustaining a culture: *selection* practices, the actions of *top management*, and *socialization* methods. Let's take a closer look at each.

Selection

The explicit goal of the selection process is to identify and hire individuals who have the knowledge, skills, and abilities to perform successfully.

The final decision, because it is significantly influenced by the decision maker's judgment of how well the candidates will fit into the organization, identifies people whose values are essentially consistent with at least a good portion of the organization's values.[40]

Selection also provides information about the organization to applicants. Windsor, Ontario-based Windsor Family Credit Union makes job candidates go through a process that has as many as eight steps so that the organization and the employee can determine if they are a good fit for each other.[41] To signal to job candidates that dignity and respect are important parts of Kitchener, Ontario-based Mennonite Savings and Credit Union's culture, job candidates are provided with interview questions in advance. The credit union encourages two-way communication throughout the hiring process.[42]

Careful hiring practices mean that those who perceive a conflict between their values and those of the organization can remove themselves from the applicant pool. Selection, therefore, becomes a two-way street: It allows the employer or applicant to avoid a mismatch and sustains organizational culture by selecting out those individuals who might attack or undermine the organization's core values.

Top Management

The actions of top management also have a major impact on the organization's culture.[43] Through words and behaviour, senior executives establish norms that filter through the organization about, for instance, whether risk-taking is desirable; how much freedom managers should give their employees; what is appropriate dress; and what actions will pay off in terms of pay raises, promotions, and other rewards.

Socialization

No matter how effectively the organization recruits and selects new employees, they are not fully indoctrinated in the organization's culture and can disrupt beliefs and customs already in place. The process that helps new employees adapt to the prevailing culture is called **socialization**.[44] As a 2011 study suggests, socialization done well will develop a new employee's self-efficacy, hope, optimism, and resilience.[45]

Monique Leroux, chair of the board, president, and CEO of Desjardins Group, recently led an organizational restructuring at Desjardins. To help accomplish this goal, she established 10 multidisciplinary teams with equal numbers of women and men on each, sending a clear message about gender equality to the cooperative. Leroux is a mentor to many women, and among her many activities geared to supporting women in a traditionally male-dominated financial industry, Leroux has also helped Desjardins launch scholarships and internships for young women interested in finance. Desjardins was named one of Canada's 10 Most Admired Corporate Cultures in 2010.

socialization The process that adapts new employees to an organization's culture.

EXHIBIT 4-4

"I don't know how it started, either. All I know is that it's part of our corporate culture."

Source: © Mick Stevens/ The New Yorker Collection/ www.cartoonbank.com

New employees at the Japanese electronics company Sanyo are socialized through a particularly long training program. At their intensive five-month course, trainees eat and sleep together in company-subsidized dorms and are required to vacation together at company-owned resorts. They learn the Sanyo way of doing everything—from how to speak to managers to proper grooming and dress.[46] The company considers this program essential for transforming young employees, fresh out of school, into dedicated *kaisha senshi*, or corporate warriors.

Starbucks does not go to the extreme that Sanyo does, but it seeks the same outcome.[47] All new employees go through 24 hours of training. Classes cover everything necessary to transform new employees into brewing consultants. They learn the Starbucks philosophy, the company jargon, and even how to help customers make decisions about beans and grind, as well as about espresso machines. The result is employees who understand Starbucks' culture and who project an enthusiastic and knowledgeable image to customers.

An organization continues to socialize its employees throughout their career in the organization, which further contributes to sustaining the culture. (Sometimes, however, employees are not fully socialized. For instance, you will note in Exhibit 4-4 that employees had learned they were supposed to wear checkerboard caps to work, but clearly did not know why.) As part of its continual socialization process, the CEO of Windsor, Ontario-based Windsor Family Credit Union takes employees to breakfast quarterly to find out about their questions, concerns, and their work.[48] This provides an opportunity to make sure employees understand the overall goals of the organization.

We can think of socialization as a process composed of three stages: prearrival, encounter, and metamorphosis.[49] This process (illustrated in Exhibit 4-5) has an impact on the new employee's work productivity, commitment to the organization's objectives, and eventual decision to stay with the organization.

The Prearrival Stage   The **prearrival stage** explicitly recognizes that each individual arrives with a set of values, attitudes, and expectations about both the work to be done and the organization. One major purpose of a business school, for example, is to socialize business students to the attitudes and behaviours business firms want. Newcomers to high-profile organizations with a strong market position will make their own assumptions about what it must be like to work there.[50] What people know before they join the organization and how proactive their personality is are critical predictors of how well they adjust to a new culture.[51]

EXHIBIT 4-5 A Socialization Model

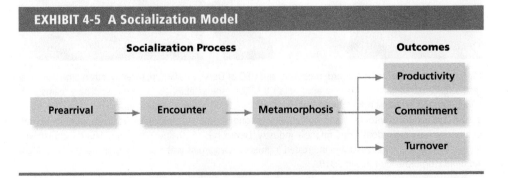

Socialization Process   **Outcomes**

Prearrival → Encounter → Metamorphosis → Productivity / Commitment / Turnover

prearrival stage The period of learning in the socialization process that occurs before a new employee joins the organization.

One way to capitalize on the importance of prehire characteristics is to use the selection process to inform prospective employees about the organization as a whole. We have also seen how the selection process ensures the inclusion of the "right type"—those who will fit in. "Indeed, the ability of the individual to present the appropriate face during the selection process determines his or her ability to move into the organization in the first place. Thus, success depends on the degree to which the aspiring member has correctly anticipated the expectations and desires of those in the organization in charge of selection."[52]

The Encounter Stage Upon entering the organization, the new employee begins the **encounter stage**,and confronts the possibility that expectations—of the job, co-workers, boss, and the organization in general—may differ from reality. If the employee's expectations are fairly accurate, the encounter stage merely reaffirms earlier perceptions.

However, this is often not the case. At the extreme, new members may become totally disillusioned with the realities of their job and resign. Proper selection should significantly reduce the probability of that outcome, and so too should encouraging friendship ties in the organization—newcomers are more committed when friends and co-workers help them "learn the ropes."[54] A 2011 study by professor Alan Saks of the Rotman School of Business at the University of Toronto and professor Jamie Gruman of the School of Hospitality and Tourism Management at the University of Guelph demonstrates the benefits of orientation, training, and mentorship programs for new employees. These activities help employees adjust better because they make them feel happier, more confident that they will more likely fit with the organization, and therefore more engaged.[55]

The Metamorphosis Stage Finally, to work out any problems discovered during the encounter stage, the new employee changes or goes through the **metamorphosis stage**. The options presented in Exhibit 4-6 are designed to bring about the desired metamorphosis. The more management relies on formal, collective, fixed, and serial socialization programs and emphasizes divestiture, the more likely that newcomers' differences and perspectives will be stripped away and replaced by standardized and predictable behaviours. These *institutional* practices are common in police departments, fire departments, and other organizations that value rule following and order. Programs that are informal, individual, random, variable, and disjunctive and emphasize investiture are more likely to give newcomers an innovative sense of their role and methods of working. Creative fields, such as research and development, advertising, and filmmaking, rely on these *individual* practices. Most research suggests high levels of institutional practices encourage person-organization fit and high levels of commitment, whereas individual practices produce more role innovation.[56]

encounter stage The stage in the socialization process in which a new employee sees what the organization is really like and confronts the possibility that expectations and reality may diverge.

metamorphosis stage The stage in the socialization process in which a new employee adjusts to the values and norms of the job, work group, and organization.

New employees at Broad Air Conditioning in Changsha, China, are indoctrinated in the company's military-style culture by going through a 10-day training session of boot camp, where they are divided into platoons and live in barracks. Boot camp prepares new hires for the military formality that prevails at Broad, where employees begin their work week standing in formation during a flag-raising ceremony of two company flags and the flag of China. All employees live in dorms on the company campus and receive free food and lodging. To motivate its workers, Broad has scattered throughout the campus 43 life-size bronze statues of inspirational leaders from Confucius to Jack Welch, the former CEO of General Electric.

We can say that metamorphosis and the entry socialization process is complete when

- The new employee has become comfortable with the organization and his or her job
- The new employee has internalized the norms of the organization and the work group, and understands and accepts these norms

---

EXHIBIT 4-6 Entry Socialization Options

Formal vs. Informal The more a new employee is segregated from the ongoing work setting and differentiated in some way to make explicit his or her newcomer's role, the more formal socialization is. Specific orientation and training programs are examples. Informal socialization puts the new employee directly into his or her job, with little or no special attention.

Individual vs. Collective New members can be socialized individually. This describes how it's done in many professional offices. They can also be grouped together and processed through an identical set of experiences, as in military boot camp.

Fixed vs. Variable This refers to the time schedule in which newcomers make the transition from outsider to insider. A fixed schedule establishes standardized stages of transition. This characterizes rotational training programs. It also includes probationary periods, such as the 8- to 10-year "associate" status accounting and law firms use before deciding whether to name a candidate as a partner. Variable schedules give no advance notice of their transition timetable. Variable schedules describe the typical promotion system, where individuals are not advanced to the next stage until they are "ready."

Serial vs. Random Serial socialization is characterized by the use of role models who train and encourage the newcomer. Apprenticeship and mentoring programs are examples. In random socialization, role models are deliberately withheld. The new employee is left on his or her own to figure things out.

Investiture vs. Divestiture Investiture socialization assumes that the newcomer's qualities and qualifications are the necessary ingredients for job success, so these qualities and qualifications are confirmed and supported. Divestiture socialization tries to strip away certain characteristics of the recruit. Fraternity and sorority "pledges" go through divestiture socialization to shape them into the proper role.

Sources: Based on J. Van Maanen, "People Processing: Strategies of Organizational Socialization," *Organizational Dynamics,* Summer 1978, pp. 19–36; and E. H. Schein, "Organizational Culture," *American Psychologist,* February 1990, p. 116.

- The new employee feels accepted by his or her peers as a trusted and valued individual, is self-confident that he or she has the competence to complete the job successfully, and understands the system—not only his or her own tasks but also the rules, procedures, and informally accepted practices

- The new employee understands how he or she will be evaluated and knows what criteria will be used to measure and appraise his or her work; he or she knows what is expected and what constitutes a job "well done"

As Exhibit 4-5 on page 96 shows, successful metamorphosis should have a positive impact on the new employee's productivity and commitment to the organization. It should reduce the tendency to leave the organization.

The Liabilities of Organizational Culture

Culture enhances organizational commitment and increases the consistency of employee behaviour.[57] These are clearly benefits to an organization. From an employee's standpoint, culture is valuable because it spells out how things are done and what is important. However, we should not ignore the potentially dysfunctional aspects of culture, especially of a strong culture, on an organization's effectiveness. Below, we consider culture's impact on change, diversity, and mergers and acquisitions.

4 Can organizational culture have a downside?

Barrier to Change

Culture is a liability when the shared values are not in agreement with those that will further the organization's effectiveness. For example, when an organization's environment is undergoing rapid change, its entrenched culture may no longer be appropriate.[58] Consistency of behaviour, an asset in a stable environment, may then burden the organization and make it difficult to respond to changes. For many organizations with strong cultures, practices that led to previous successes can lead to failure when those practices no longer match up well with environmental needs.[59]

Barrier to Diversity

Hiring new employees who differ from the majority in race, gender, disability, or other characteristics creates a paradox:[60] Management demonstrates support for the differences that these employees bring to the workplace, but newcomers who wish to fit in must accept the organization's core cultural values. Because diverse behaviours and unique strengths are likely to diminish as people attempt to assimilate, strong cultures can become liabilities when they effectively eliminate these advantages.

By limiting the range of values and styles that are acceptable, strong cultures put considerable pressure on employees to conform. It's not a coincidence that employees at Disney theme parks appear to be almost universally attractive, clean, and wholesome-looking, with bright smiles. That is the image Walt Disney Company wants to project. It selects employees who will maintain that image. Once the theme-park employees are on the job, a strong culture—supported by formal rules and regulations—ensures that they will act in a relatively uniform and predictable way.

Organizations seek out and hire diverse individuals because of the new strengths these people bring to the workplace. Yet these diverse behaviours and strengths are likely to diminish in strong cultures as people try to fit in. Strong cultures, therefore, can be liabilities when they effectively eliminate the unique strengths that people of different backgrounds bring to the organization. Moreover, strong cultures can also be liabilities when they support institutional bias or become insensitive to people who are different.

Barrier to Mergers and Acquisitions

Historically, when management looked at merger or acquisition decisions, the key factors were related to financial advantages or product synergy. In recent years, cultural compatibility has become the primary concern.[61] All things being equal, whether the merger or acquisition actually works seems to have more to do with how well the two organizations' cultures match up.

Strategies for Merging Cultures

Organizations can use several strategies when considering how to merge the cultures of two organizations:[62]

- *Assimilation.* The entire new organization is determined to take on the culture of one of the merging organizations. This strategy works best when one of the organizations has a relatively weak culture. However, if a culture is simply imposed on an organization, it rarely works.

- *Separation.* The organizations remain separate and keep their individual cultures. This strategy works best when the organizations have little overlap in the industries in which they operate.

- *Integration.* A new culture is formed by merging parts of each of the organizations. This strategy works best when aspects of each organization's culture need to be improved.

Potential merger partners might do well to conduct a **bicultural audit** before concluding that a merger should occur. Through questionnaires, interviews, and/or focus groups, potential merger partners should examine differences in the "vision, values, structure, management practices and behaviours" of the merging parties.[63] This examination should indicate whether there are commonalities from which to build a successful merger, or differences that could cause extreme difficulties in merging the two organizations. If the decision after a bicultural audit is to merge, the management team should bridge any existing culture gaps by[64]

- Defining a structure that is appropriate for both organizations, along with a reorganization plan

- Identifying and implementing a management style that is appropriate for both organizations

- Reinforcing internal communication to make sure that employees are kept aware of changes that will occur

- Getting agreement on what will be considered in performance evaluations, including expected behaviours and performance criteria

Changing Organizational Culture

5 How do you change organizational culture?

Boston Pizza co-owners Jim Treliving and George Melville did not actually found the company.[65] It was started in Edmonton in 1964 by Greek immigrant Gus Agioritis. Treliving was an RCMP officer who became excited about the Boston Pizza concept, and opened his first franchise restaurant in Penticton, BC. In 1973, Melville became Treliving's business partner, after being his accountant for four years. By 1983, the two men owned 16 of the Boston Pizza restaurants, and decided to buy the entire Western-Canada–based chain of 46 restaurants. They hoped to expand the chain across the country.

To achieve a successful expansion, Treliving and Melville recognized the importance of introducing a number of systems and operating standards that would apply to all of the restaurants.

bicultural audit An examination of the differences between two potential merger partners prior to a merger to determine whether the cultures will be able to work together.

They developed the Three Pillar Success Strategy, "which emphasizes continually improving guest experience, franchise profitability and building the brand, to promote expansion." The strategy is continuously communicated to all members of the organization. As president Mark Pacinda says: "We make sure we're constantly communicating and being very consistent with our message, our goals and our objectives." Why have Treliving and Melville been so successful in creating an organizational culture that enabled a small franchise to expand across the country?

Trying to change the culture of an organization is quite difficult and requires that many aspects of the organization change at the same time, especially the reward structure. Culture is such a challenge to change because it often represents the established mindset of employees and managers.

John Kotter, professor of leadership at Harvard Business School, has created a detailed approach for implementing change.[66] Efforts directed at changing organizational culture do not usually yield immediate or dramatic results. Cultural change is actually a lengthy process—measured in years, not months. But we can ask the question, "Can culture be changed?" And the answer is, "Yes!"

Below we consider two particular kinds of changes organizations might want to make to their culture: creating an ethical culture and creating a positive organizational culture.

Creating an Ethical Culture

The organizational culture most likely to shape high ethical standards among its members is one that is high in risk tolerance, low to moderate in aggressiveness, and focuses on means, as well as outcomes.[67] This type of culture also takes a long-term perspective and balances the rights of multiple stakeholders, including the communities in which the business operates, its employees, and its stockholders. Managers are supported for taking risks and innovating, are discouraged from engaging in unbridled competition, and guided to pay attention not just to *what* goals are achieved but also to *how*.

If the culture is strong and supports high ethical standards, it should have a very powerful and positive influence on employee behaviour. Johnson & Johnson, for example, has a strong culture that has long stressed corporate obligations to customers, employees, the community, and shareholders, in that order. When poisoned Tylenol (a Johnson & Johnson product) was found on store shelves some years ago, company employees across the United States independently pulled the product from these stores before management had even issued a statement about the tampering. No one had to tell these individuals what was morally right; they knew what Johnson & Johnson would expect them to do.

What can management do to create a more ethical culture? Research suggests managers can have an effect on the ethical behaviour of employees by adhering to the following principles:[68]

- *Be a visible role model.* Employees will look to the actions of top management as a benchmark for appropriate behaviour. Senior managers who take the ethical high road provide a positive message for all employees.

- *Communicate ethical expectations.* Minimize ethical ambiguities by creating and disseminating an organizational code of ethics. It should state the organization's primary values and the ethical rules that employees are expected to follow.

- *Provide ethics training.* Set up seminars, workshops, and similar ethics training programs. Use these to reinforce the organization's standards of conduct, to clarify what practices are and are not permissible, and to address possible ethical dilemmas.

- *Visibly reward ethical acts and punish unethical ones.* Include in managers' performance appraisals a point-by-point evaluation of how their decisions measured against the organization's code of ethics. Review the means taken to achieve goals, as well as the ends themselves. Visibly reward those who act ethically. Just as importantly, conspicuously punish unethical acts.

- *Provide protective mechanisms.* Provide formal mechanisms so employees can discuss ethical dilemmas and report unethical behaviour without fear of reprimand. These might include ethics counsellors, ombudspersons, or ethics officers.

Setting a positive ethical climate has to start at the top of the organization.[69] A study of 195 managers demonstrated that when top management emphasizes strong ethical values, supervisors are more likely to practise ethical leadership. This positive ethical attitude transfers down to line employees, who show lower levels of deviant behaviour and higher levels of cooperation and assistance. The general ethical behaviour and attitudes of other members of the department matter too for shaping individual ethical behaviour. Finally, employees whose ethical values are similar to those of their department are more likely to be promoted, so we can think of ethical culture as flowing from the bottom up as well.[70]

Creating a Positive Organizational Culture

At first blush, creating a positive culture may sound hopelessly naive, or like a Dilbert-style conspiracy. The one thing that makes us believe this trend is here to stay is that there are signs that management practice and OB research are converging.

A **positive organizational culture** emphasizes building on employee strengths, rewards more often than it punishes, and emphasizes individual vitality and growth.[71] Let's consider each of these areas.

Building on Employee Strengths

A lot of OB, and management practice, considers how to fix employee problems. Although a positive organizational culture does not ignore problems, it emphasizes showing employees how they can capitalize on their strengths. As management guru Peter Drucker said, "Most [employees] do not know what their strengths are. When you ask them, they look at you with a blank stare, or they respond in terms of subject knowledge, which is the wrong answer." Do you know what your strengths are? Wouldn't it be better to be in an organizational culture that helped you discover those, and learn ways to make the most of them?

Larry Hammond used this approach—finding and exploiting employee strengths—when you would least expect it: during the darkest days of his business. Hammond is CEO of Auglaize Provico, an agribusiness company. The company was in the midst of its worst financial struggles and had to lay off one-quarter of its workforce. At that low point, Hammond decided to try a different approach. Rather than dwell on what was wrong, he took advantage of what was right. "If you really want to [excel], you have to know yourself—you have to know what you're good at, and you have to know what you're not so good at," says Hammond. With the help of Gallup consultant Barry Conchie, Auglaize Provico focused on discovering and using employee strengths and helped turn the company around. "You ask Larry [Hammond] what the difference is, and he'll say that it's individuals using their natural talents," says Conchie.[72]

positive organizational culture
A culture that emphasizes building on employee strengths, rewards more than punishes, and emphasizes individual vitality and growth.

Rewarding More Often Than Punishing

Although most organizations are sufficiently focused on extrinsic rewards like pay and promotions, they often forget about the power of smaller (and cheaper) rewards like praise. Part of creating a positive organizational culture is "catching employees doing something right." Another part is articulating praise. Many managers withhold praise either because they are afraid employees will coast, or because they think praise is not valued. Because employees generally don't ask for praise, managers usually don't realize the costs of failing to do it. Failing to praise can become a "silent killer" like escalating blood pressure.

Take the example of Elzbieta Górska-Kolodziejczyk, a plant manager for International Paper's facility in Kwidzyn, Poland. The job environment at the plant is bleak and difficult. Employees work in a windowless basement. Staffing is only roughly one-third of its prior level, while production has tripled. These challenges had done in the previous three managers. So when Górska-Kolodziejczyk took over, she knew she had her work cut out for her. Although she had many items on her list of ways to transform the organization, at the top of her list was recognition and praise. She initially found it difficult to give praise to those who were not used to it, especially men. "They were like cement at the beginning," she said. "Like cement." Over time, however, she found they valued and even reciprocated praise. One day a department supervisor pulled her over to tell her she was doing a good job. "This I do remember, yes," she said.[73]

Emphasizing Vitality and Growth

A positive organizational culture emphasizes not only organizational effectiveness, but individuals' growth as well. No organization will get the best out of employees who see themselves as mere tools or parts of the organization. A positive culture realizes the difference between a job and a career and supports not only what the employee does to contribute to organizational effectiveness, but also what the organization can do to make the employee more effective (personally and professionally).

Limits of Positive Culture

Is a positive culture the answer to all organizational problems? Though companies such as WestJet, GE, Xerox, Boeing, and 3M have embraced aspects of a positive organizational culture, it is a new enough area that there is some uncertainty about how and when it works best.

Not all cultures value being positive as much as Canadian and US cultures do, and, even within these countries, there surely are limits to how far we should go to preserve a positive culture. For example, Admiral, a British insurance company, has established a Ministry of Fun in its call centres to organize such events as poem writings, foosball, conker (a British game involving chestnuts) competitions, and fancy dress days. When does the pursuit of a positive culture start to seem coercive or even Orwellian? As one critic notes, "Promoting a social orthodoxy of positiveness focuses on a particular constellation of desirable states and traits but, in so doing, can stigmatize those who fail to fit the template."[74]

Our point is that there may be benefits to establishing a positive culture, but an organization also needs to be careful to be objective and not pursue it past the point of effectiveness.

GLOBAL IMPLICATIONS

We considered global cultural values (collectivism and individualism, power distance, and so on) in Chapter 3. Here, our focus is a bit narrower: How is organizational culture affected by a global context?

Organizational cultures often reflect national culture. The culture at AirAsia, a Malaysian-based airline, emphasizes informal dress so as not to create status differences. The carrier has lots of parties, participative management, and no private offices, reflecting Malaysia's relatively collectivistic culture. However, the culture of Air Canada does not reflect the same degree of informality. If Air Canada were to set up operations in Malaysia or merge with AirAsia, it would need to take these cultural differences into account. So when an organization opens up operations in another country, it ignores the local culture at its own risk.

Three times a week, employees at the Canadian unit of Japanese video game maker Tecmo Koei begin the day by standing next to their desks, facing their boss, and saying "Good morning" in unison. Employees then deliver short speeches on topics that range from corporate principles to 3D game engines. Tecmo Koei also has employees punch a time clock and asks women to serve tea to top executive guests. Although these practices are consistent with Tecmo Koei's culture, they do not fit Canadian culture very well. "It's kind of like school," says one Canadian employee.[75]

The management of ethical behaviour is one area where national culture can rub up against corporate culture.[76] Many strategies for improving ethical behaviour are based on the values and beliefs of the host country. Canadian managers tend to endorse the supremacy of anonymous market forces and implicitly or explicitly view profit maximization as a moral obligation for business organizations. This worldview sees bribery, nepotism, and favouring personal contacts as highly unethical. Any action that deviates from profit maximization may indicate that inappropriate or corrupt behaviour may be occurring. In contrast, managers in developing economies are more likely to see ethical decisions as embedded in a social environment. That means doing special favours for family and friends is not only appropriate but may even be an ethical responsibility. Managers in many nations also view capitalism skeptically and believe the interests of employees should be put on a par with the interests of shareholders.

5

Decision Making, Creativity, and Ethics

EElana Rosenfeld and Leo Johnson are the founders and owners of Invermere, BC-based Kicking Horse Coffee Company, the top organic fair trade coffee company in Canada.[1] The decision to create a fair trade coffee company reflects the values the two have toward their employees and the farmer co-ops in Mexico, Nicaragua, Peru, and other countries from which they buy their coffee. When the two travel to the coffee plantations for weeks at a time, they rely on their employees to keep everything running smoothly back in BC.

"Knowing we can leave the shop in good hands allows us to develop a personal relationship with local suppliers," Rosenfeld says. "In turn, we can report back to our employees and customers on how fair trade coffee makes a real difference to the lives of those who were often exploited. That message encourages further support for the company's mission and products."

Rosenfeld and Johnson started roasting coffee in their garage in 1996, with their small children in tow. Two years later they were one of the first companies to join TransFair Canada (now known as Fairtrade Canada), an organization that encourages Canadian organizations to make choices that would improve the working conditions of farmers and workers in the developing world. By 2003 Kicking Horse Coffee made the decision to purchase and roast only 100 percent certified organic coffee beans.

In this chapter, we describe how decisions in organizations are made, as well as how creativity is linked to decision making. We also look at the ethical and socially responsible aspects of decision making as part of our discussion. Decision making affects people at all levels of the organization, and it is engaged in by both individuals and groups. Therefore, we also consider the special characteristics of group decision making.

How Should Decisions Be Made?

1 Is there a right way to make decisions?

A **decision** is the choice made from two or more alternatives. Decision making happens at all levels of an organization. Top managers determine their organization's goals, what products or services to offer, how best to finance operations, or where to locate a new high-tech research and development facility. Middle- and lower-level managers determine production schedules, select new employees, and decide how pay raises are to be allocated. Nonmanagerial employees decide how much effort to put forward once at work and whether to comply with a request from their manager. In recent years organizations have been empowering their nonmanagerial employees with decision-making authority that was historically reserved for managers alone. Thus, nonmanagerial employees may have the authority to make decisions about initiating some new project or solving certain customer-related problems without consulting their managers.

Knowing how to make decisions is an important part of everyday life. Below we consider various decision-making models that apply to both individual and group choices. (Later in the chapter, we discuss special aspects of group decision making.) We start with the rational model, which describes decision making in the ideal world, a situation that rarely exists. We then look at alternatives to the rational model, and how decisions actually get made.

The Rational Decision-Making Process

The **rational** decision maker makes consistent, value-maximizing choices within specified constraints.[2] These choices are made following a six-step **rational decision-making model**.[3] Moreover, specific assumptions underlie this model.

The Rational Model

The six steps in the rational decision-making model are presented in Exhibit 5-1.

First, the decision maker must *define the problem*. If you calculate your monthly expenses and find you are spending $50 more than your monthly earnings, you have defined a problem. Many poor decisions can be traced to the decision maker overlooking a problem or defining the wrong problem.

EXHIBIT 5-1 Steps in the Rational Decision-Making Model

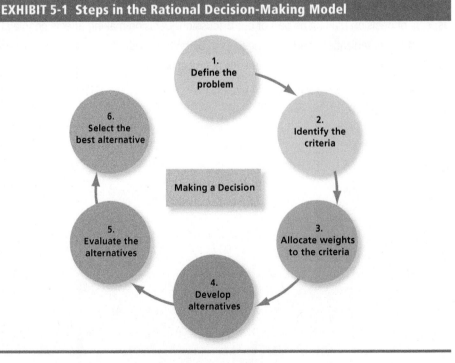

decision The choice made from two or more alternatives.

rational Refers to choices that are consistent and value-maximizing within specified constraints.

rational decision-making model A six-step decision-making model that describes how individuals should behave in order to maximize some outcome.

The decision maker then needs to *identify the criteria* that are relevant to making the decision. This step brings the decision maker's interests, values, and similar personal preferences into the process, because not all individuals will consider the same factors relevant for any particular decision.

To understand the types of criteria that might be used to make a decision, consider how Toronto-based Canadian Imperial Bank of Commerce (CIBC) handles the many sponsorship requests it receives each year. When it makes a decision about whether to support a request, the bank takes into account a number of criteria. Specifically, to be eligible for funding, a request must

- Be aligned to youth, education or health

- Be for a Canadian organization, using funds in Canada

- Be for a registered charity with a Canada Revenue Agency Charitable Registration Number or a non-profit organization

- Have a record of achievement or potential for success in line with our overall goals

- Address a community need and provide direct impact to the community served

- Include planned outcomes, supported by a measurement and evaluation process

- Have audited financial statements for the organization, sound financial practices and a sustainable funding model[4]

If the sponsorship request does not meet these criteria, it is not funded.

Because the criteria identified are rarely all equal in importance, the third step requires the decision maker to *allocate weights to the criteria*.

The fourth step requires the decision maker to *develop alternatives* that could succeed in resolving the problem.

The decision maker then critically *evaluates the alternatives*, using the previously established criteria and weights.

Finally, the decision maker *selects the best alternative* by evaluating each alternative against the weighted criteria and selecting the alternative with the highest total score.

Assumptions of the Model

The rational decision-making model we just described contains a number of assumptions.[5] Let's briefly outline those assumptions:

- *Problem clarity.* The problem is clear and unambiguous and complete information is available.

- *Known options.* It's assumed that the decision maker can identify all relevant criteria, all workable alternatives, and their consequences.

- *Clear preferences.* The criteria and alternatives can be ranked and weighted to reflect their importance.

- *Constant preferences.* The specific decision criteria are constant and the weights assigned to them are stable over time.

- *No time or cost constraints.* The decision maker can obtain full information about criteria and alternatives because there are no time or cost constraints.

- *Maximum payoff.* The decision maker will choose the alternative that yields the highest perceived value.

During his 10-year tenure as CEO of Symantec, John Thompson made a decision in reaction to the problem of an explosion of Internet viruses. Thompson, now chairman of the board of directors, said, "About every 15 to 18 months, there's a new form of attack that makes old technologies less effective." So he decided to acquire 13 companies that specialize in products such as personal firewalls, intrusion detection, and early warning systems that protect everything from corporate intranets to consumer email inboxes.

How Do Individuals Actually Make Decisions?

2 How do people actually make decisions?

In 1996, when Elana Rosenfeld and Leo Johnson were just getting their Kicking Horse Coffee Company started, they had one goal: "get everyone to drink good coffee."[6] Obviously, people differ as to what they perceive good coffee to be. Some like Tim Hortons the best. Others enjoy Starbucks. Fans of one company complain about the coffee of the other. Rosenfeld felt she knew what really good coffee was, and it started with fair trade beans. When she first began educating her customers about her product, they thought she meant "free trade." To change customer perceptions, Rosenfeld said they "did a good job of marketing and explaining it on our packaging." They also knew that some people thought good coffee meant Italian coffee, which Kicking Horse does not sell. So they created fun names for the coffee, such as *454 Horse Power* and *Hoodoo Jo* to appeal to a broader number of consumers. What sorts of perceptual biases might affect the decisions people make?

When decision makers are faced with a simple problem with few alternative courses of action, and when the cost of searching out and evaluating alternatives is low, the rational model provides a fairly accurate description of the decision process.[7] However, such situations are the exception. Most decisions in the real world don't follow the rational model. People are usually content to find an acceptable or reasonable solution to their problem rather than an optimal one. Choices tend to be confined to the problem symptom and to the current alternative. As one expert in decision making has concluded, "Most significant decisions are made by judgment, rather than by a defined prescriptive model."[8] What is more, people are remarkably unaware of making suboptimal decisions.[9]

In the following sections, we indicate areas where the reality of decision making conflicts with the rational model.[10] None of these ways of making decisions should be considered *irrational*; they simply depart from the rational model when information is unavailable or too costly to collect.

Bounded Rationality in Considering Alternatives

When you considered which university or college to attend, did you look at *every* workable alternative? Did you carefully identify all the criteria that were important in your decision? Did you evaluate each alternative against the criteria in order to find the optimum school? The answer to these questions is probably "no." But don't feel bad, because few people selected their educational institution this way.

Do people really consider every alternative when making a decision?

It's difficult for individuals to identify and consider every possible alternative available to them. Realistically speaking, people are limited by their ability to interpret, process, and act on information. This is called **bounded rationality**.[11]

How does bounded rationality work for the typical individual? Once we have identified a problem, we begin to search for criteria and alternatives. But the list of criteria is likely to be far from exhaustive. We identify a limited list of the most obvious choices, which usually represent familiar criteria and tried-and-true solutions. Next, we begin reviewing them, but our review will not be comprehensive. Instead, we focus on alternatives that differ only in a relatively small degree from the choice currently in effect. Following familiar and well-worn paths, we review alternatives only until we identify one that is "good enough"—that meets an acceptable level of performance. That ends our search. So the solution represents a **satisficing** choice—the first *acceptable* one we encounter—rather than an optimal one. In practice, this might mean that rather than interview 10 job candidates for a position and then make a hiring decision, a manager interviews one at a time until someone that is "good enough" is found. This process of satisficing is not always a bad idea—using a simple process may frequently be more sensible than the traditional rational decision-making model.[12]

bounded rationality Limitations on a person's ability to interpret, process, and act on information.

satisficing To provide a solution that is both satisfactory and sufficient.

Intuition

Perhaps the least rational way of making decisions is to rely on intuition. **Intuitive decision making** is a nonconscious process created from distilled experience.[13] Its defining qualities are that it occurs outside conscious thought; it relies on holistic associations, or links between disparate pieces of information; it's fast; and it's affectively charged, meaning that it usually engages the emotions.[14]

Intuition is not rational, but that does not necessarily make it wrong. Nor does it always operate in opposition to rational analysis; rather, the two can complement each other. Intuition can be a powerful force in decision making. But intuition is not superstition, or the product of some magical or paranormal sixth sense. As one recent review noted, "Intuition is a highly complex and highly developed form of reasoning that is based on years of experience and learning."[15]

As the example of the chess players shows, those who use intuition effectively often rely on their experiences to help guide and assess their intuitions. That is why many managers turn to intuition.

For most of the twentieth century, experts believed that decision makers' use of intuition was irrational or ineffective. That is no longer the case.[16] We now recognize that rational analysis has been overemphasized and that, in certain instances, relying on intuition can improve decision making.[17] But, we cannot rely on it too much. Because it is so unquantifiable, it's hard to know when our hunches are right or wrong. A 2010 study that examined people's ability to "use their gut" to make decisions found that not everyone's gut is reliable. For some people, the physiological feelings that one associates with intuition works, but for others it does not.[18] The key is not to either abandon or rely solely on intuition, but to supplement it with evidence and good judgment.

Is it okay to use intuition when making decisions?

Judgment Shortcuts

Decision makers engage in bounded rationality, but they also allow systematic biases and errors to creep into their judgments.[19] To minimize effort and avoid difficult trade-offs, people tend to rely too heavily on experience, impulses, gut feelings, and convenient rules of thumb. In many instances, these shortcuts are helpful. However, they can lead to distortions of rationality.

In what follows, we discuss some of the most common judgment shortcuts to alert you to mistakes that are often made when making decisions.

Why is it that we sometimes make bad decisions?

Overconfidence Bias

It's been said that "no problem in judgment and decision making is more prevalent and more potentially catastrophic than overconfidence."[20]

When we are given factual questions and asked to judge the probability that our answers are correct, we tend to be far too optimistic. This is known as **overconfidence bias**. When people say they are 65 to 70 percent confident that they are right, they are actually correct only about 50 percent of the time.[21] When they say they are 100 percent sure, they tend to be right about 70 to 85 percent of the time.[22]

Individuals whose intellectual and interpersonal abilities are *weakest* are most likely to overestimate their performance and ability.[23] So as managers and employees become more knowledgeable about an issue, they become less likely to display overconfidence.[24] Overconfidence is most likely to surface when organizational members are considering issues or problems that are outside their area of expertise.[25]

intuitive decision making A nonconscious process created out of a person's many experiences.

overconfidence bias Error in judgment that arises from being far too optimistic about one's own performance.

Anchoring Bias

The **anchoring bias** is a tendency to fixate on initial information and fail to adequately adjust for subsequent information.[26] It occurs because the mind appears to give a disproportionate amount of emphasis to the first information it receives.[27] Anchors are widely used by people in professions where persuasion skills are important—such as advertising, management, politics, real estate, and law. For instance, in a mock jury trial, the plaintiff's attorney asked one set of jurors to make an award in the range of $15 million to $50 million. The plaintiff's attorney asked another set of jurors for an award in the range of $50 million to $150 million. Consistent with the anchoring bias, the median awards were $15 million and $50 million, respectively.[28]

Consider the role of anchoring in negotiations. Any time a negotiation takes place, so does anchoring. As soon as someone states a number, your ability to ignore that number has been compromised. For instance, when a prospective employer asks how much you were making in your prior job, your answer typically anchors the employer's offer. You may want to keep this in mind when you negotiate your salary, but remember to set the anchor only as high as you realistically can. Finally, the more precise your anchor, the smaller the adjustment. Some research suggests people think of adjustment after an anchor is set as rounding off a number. If you suggest an initial target salary of $55 000, your boss will consider $50 000 to $60 000 a reasonable range for negotiation, but if you mention $55 650, your boss is more likely to consider $55 000 to $56 000 the range of likely values for negotiation.[29]

Confirmation Bias

The rational decision-making process assumes that we objectively gather information. But we don't. We *selectively* gather it. The **confirmation bias** represents a specific case of selective perception. We seek out information that reaffirms our past choices, and we discount information that contradicts them.[30] We also tend to accept at face value information that confirms our preconceived views, while we are critical and skeptical of information that challenges these views. Therefore, the information we gather is typically biased toward supporting views we already hold. This confirmation bias influences where we go to collect evidence because we tend to seek out sources most likely to tell us what we want to hear. It also leads us to give too much weight to supporting information and too little to contradictory information.[31]

Availability Bias

The **availability bias** is the tendency for people to base their judgments on information that is readily available.[32] Events that evoke emotions, that are particularly vivid, or that have occurred more recently tend to be more available in our memory. As a result, we tend to overestimate unlikely events, such as airplane crashes, compared with more likely events, such as car crashes. The availability bias can also explain why managers, when doing annual performance appraisals, tend to give more weight to recent behaviours of an employee than to those of six or nine months ago.

Escalation of Commitment

Some decision makers escalate commitment to a failing course of action.[33] **Escalation of commitment** refers to staying with a decision even when there is clear evidence that it's wrong. For example, a friend has been dating a man for about four years. Although she admits that things are not going well, she is determined to marry him anyway. Her justification: "I have a lot invested in the relationship!"

Individuals escalate commitment to a failing course of action when they view themselves as responsible for the failure.[34] That is, they "throw good money after bad" to demonstrate that their initial decision was not wrong and to avoid having to admit they

anchoring bias A tendency to fixate on initial information, from which one then fails to adequately adjust for subsequent information.

confirmation bias The tendency to seek out information that reaffirms past choices and to discount information that contradicts past judgments.

availability bias The tendency for people to base their judgments on information that is readily available to them rather than complete data.

escalation of commitment An increased commitment to a previous decision despite negative information.

made a mistake.[35] In fact, people who carefully gather and consider information consistent with the rational decision-making model are *more* likely to engage in escalation of commitment than those who spend less time thinking about their choices.[36] Perhaps they have invested so much time and energy into making their decisions that they have convinced themselves they are taking the right course of action and don't update their knowledge in the face of new information. Many organizations have suffered large losses because a manager was determined to prove his or her original decision was right by continuing to commit resources to a lost cause.

Randomness Error

Human beings have a lot of difficulty dealing with chance. Most of us like to believe we have some control over our world and our destiny. Our tendency to believe we can predict the outcome of random events is the **randomness error**.

Decision making becomes impaired when we try to create meaning out of random events, particularly when we turn imaginary patterns into superstitions.[37] These can be completely contrived, such as "I never make important decisions on Friday the 13th." They can also evolve from a certain pattern of behaviour that has been reinforced previously. For example, before every game, former NHL star goalie Patrick Roy would skate "backwards towards the net before turning around at the last second, an act he believed made the goal shrink."[38] Superstitious behaviour can be debilitating when it affects daily judgments or biases major decisions.

Risk Aversion

Mathematically, we should find a 50–50 flip of the coin for $100 to be worth as much as a sure promise of $50. After all, the expected value of the gamble over a number of trials is $50. However, most people don't consider these options equally valuable. Rather, nearly everyone but committed gamblers would rather have the sure thing than a risky prospect.[39] For many people, a 50–50 flip of a coin even for $200 might not be worth as much as a sure promise of $50, even though the gamble is mathematically worth twice as much as the sure thing! This tendency to prefer a sure thing over a risky outcome is **risk aversion**.

Risk aversion has important implications. Ambitious people with power that can be taken away (most managers) appear to be especially risk averse, perhaps because they don't want to lose on a gamble everything they have worked so hard to achieve.[40] CEOs at risk of being terminated are also exceptionally risk averse, even when a riskier investment strategy is in their firms' best interests.[41]

Because people are less likely to escalate commitment where there is a great deal of uncertainty, the implications of risk aversion are not all bad.[42] When a risky investment is not paying off, most people would rather play it safe and cut their losses, but if they think the outcome is a sure thing, they will keep escalating.

Risk preference is sometimes reversed: People prefer to take their chances when trying to prevent a negative outcome.[43] They would rather take a 50–50 gamble on losing $100 than accept the certain loss of $50. Thus they will risk losing a lot of money at trial rather than settle out of court. Trying to cover up wrongdoing instead of admitting a mistake, despite the risk of truly catastrophic press coverage or even jail time, is another example. Stressful situations can make these risk preferences stronger. People will more likely engage in risk-seeking behaviour for negative outcomes, and risk-averse behaviour for positive outcomes, when under stress.[44]

Hindsight Bias

The **hindsight bias** is the tendency to believe falsely, after the outcome of an event is actually known, that we could have accurately predicted that outcome.[45] When we have accurate feedback on the outcome, we seem to be pretty good at concluding it was

randomness error The tendency of individuals to believe that they can predict the outcome of random events.

risk aversion The tendency to prefer a sure gain of a moderate amount over a riskier outcome, even if the riskier outcome might have a higher expected payoff.

hindsight bias The tendency to believe falsely, after an outcome of an event is actually known, that one could have accurately predicted that outcome.

obvious. As Malcolm Gladwell, author of *Blink, Outliers*, and *The Tipping Point*, writes, "What is clear in hindsight is rarely clear before the fact. It's an obvious point, but one that nonetheless bears repeating."[46]

The hindsight bias reduces our ability to learn from the past. It lets us think that we are better predictors than we really are, and can make us falsely confident. If your actual predictive accuracy is only 40 percent, but you think it's 90 percent, you are likely to be less skeptical about your predictive skills.

Improving Decision Making through Knowledge Management

3 How can knowledge management improve decision making?

The process of organizing and distributing an organization's collective wisdom so the right information gets to the right people at the right time is called **knowledge management (KM)**.[47] When done properly, KM provides an organization with both a competitive edge and improved organizational performance because it makes its employees smarter.

A growing number of companies—including the Royal Bank of Canada, Cisco Systems, British Telecom, and Johnson & Johnson—have realized the value of KM. In fact, one survey found that 81 percent of the leading organizations in Europe and the United States say they have, or are at least considering adopting, some kind of KM system.[48]

KM is increasingly important today for at least three reasons:[49]

- Organizations that can quickly and efficiently tap into their employees' collective experience and wisdom are more likely to "outsmart" their competition.

- As Baby Boomers begin to leave the workforce, there is an increasing awareness that they represent a wealth of knowledge that will be lost if there are no attempts to capture it.

- A well-designed KM system reduces redundancy and makes the organization more efficient. For instance, when employees in a large organization undertake a new project, they need not start from scratch. They can access what former employees have learned and avoid repeating previous mistakes.

How do organizations record the knowledge and expertise of their employees and make that information easily accessible? First, organizations need to develop *computer databases* of pertinent information that employees can readily access. This process includes identifying what knowledge matters to the organization.[50]

Second, organizations need to create a *culture* that promotes, values, and rewards sharing knowledge. As we discussed in Chapter 8, information that is important and scarce can be a potent source of power. Moreover, people who hold that power are often reluctant to share it with others. KM will not work unless the culture supports information sharing.[51]

Finally, organizations need to develop *mechanisms* that allow employees who have built up valuable expertise and insights to share them with others.[52] *More* knowledge is not necessarily *better* knowledge. Information overload needs to be avoided by designing the system to capture only pertinent information and then organizing it so it can be quickly accessed by the people whom it can help. Royal Bank of Canada, for instance, created a KM system with customized email distribution lists carefully broken down by employees' specialty, title, and area of interest; set aside a dedicated site on the company's intranet that serves as a central information repository; and created separate in-house websites featuring "lessons learned" summaries, where employees with various expertise can share new information with others.[53]

knowledge management (KM)
The process of organizing and distributing an organization's collective wisdom so that the right information gets to the right people at the right time.

Group Decision Making

While a variety of decisions in both life and organizations are made at the individual level, the belief—characterized by juries—that two heads are better than one has long been accepted as a basic component of North American and many other countries' legal systems. Today, many decisions in organizations are made by groups, teams, or committees. In this section, we review group decision making and compare it with individual decision making.

 4 What factors affect group decision making?

Groups vs. the Individual

Decision-making groups may be widely used in organizations, but are group decisions preferable to those made by an individual alone? The answer to this depends on a number of factors we consider below.[54] See Exhibit 5-2 for a summary of our major points.

Strengths of Group Decision Making

Groups generate *more complete information and knowledge.* By combining the resources of several individuals, groups bring more input into the decision process. They offer *increased diversity of views.* This opens up the opportunity to consider more approaches and alternatives. Finally, groups lead to *increased acceptance of a solution.*[55] Many decisions fail after they are made because people don't accept them. Group members who participated in making a decision are likely to support the decision enthusiastically and encourage others to accept it.

Weaknesses of Group Decision Making

Group decisions have their drawbacks. They are *time-consuming* because groups typically take more time to reach a solution. There are *conformity pressures.* The desire by group members to be accepted and considered an asset to the group can result in squashing any overt disagreement. Group discussion can be *dominated by one or a few members.* If they are low- and medium-ability members, the group's overall effectiveness will suffer. Finally, group decisions suffer from *ambiguous responsibility.* In an individual decision, it's clear who is accountable for the final outcome. In a group decision, the responsibility of any single member is watered down.

Effectiveness and Efficiency

Whether groups are more effective than individuals depends on how you define effectiveness. Group decisions are generally more *accurate* than the decisions of the average

EXHIBIT 5-2 Group vs. Individual Decision Making		
Criteria of Effectiveness	**Groups**	**Individuals**
More complete information	√	
Diversity of views	√	
Decision quality	√	
Accuracy	√	
Creativity	√	
Degree of acceptance	√	
Speed		√
Efficiency		√

individual in a group, but they are less accurate than the judgments of the most accurate group member.[56] If decision effectiveness is defined in terms of *speed*, individuals are superior. If *creativity* is important, groups tend to be more effective than individuals. And if effectiveness means the degree of *acceptance* the final solution achieves, the nod again goes to the group.[57]

But we cannot consider effectiveness without also assessing efficiency. Groups almost always stack up as a poor second to the individual decision maker. With few exceptions, group decision making consumes more work hours than if an individual were to tackle the same problem alone. The exceptions tend to be the instances in which, to achieve comparable quantities of diverse input, the single decision maker must spend a great deal of time reviewing files and talking to people. Because groups can include members from diverse areas, the time spent searching for information can be reduced. However, as we noted, these advantages in efficiency tend to be the exception. Groups are generally less efficient than individuals. In deciding whether to use groups, then, consideration should be given to assessing whether increases in effectiveness are more than enough to offset the reductions in efficiency.

Groupthink and Groupshift

Two by-products of group decision making have the potential to affect the group's ability to appraise alternatives objectively and arrive at quality solutions: groupthink and groupshift.

Groupthink

Have you ever felt like speaking up in a meeting, classroom, or informal group, but decided against it? One reason may have been shyness. On the other hand, you may have been a victim of **groupthink**, a phenomenon in which group pressures for conformity prevent the group from critically appraising unusual, minority, or unpopular views. The individual's mental efficiency, reality testing, and moral judgment deteriorate as a result of group pressures.[58]

We have all seen the symptoms of the groupthink phenomenon:[59]

- *Illusion of invulnerability.* Group members become overconfident among themselves, allowing them to take extraordinary risks.

- *Assumption of morality.* Group members believe highly in the moral rightness of the group's objectives and do not feel the need to debate the ethics of their actions.

- *Rationalized resistance.* Group members rationalize any resistance to the assumptions they have made. No matter how strongly the evidence may contradict their basic assumptions, members behave so as to reinforce those assumptions continually.

- *Peer pressure.* Group members apply direct pressure on those who momentarily express doubts about any of the group's shared views or who question the validity of arguments supporting the alternative favoured by the majority.

- *Minimized doubts.* Those group members who have doubts or hold differing points of view seek to avoid deviating from what appears to be group consensus by keeping silent about misgivings and even minimizing to themselves the importance of their doubts.

- *Illusion of unanimity.* If someone does not speak, it's assumed that he or she is in full accord. In other words, abstention becomes viewed as a yes vote.

groupthink A phenomenon in which group pressures for conformity prevent the group from critically appraising unusual, minority, or unpopular views.

One place where groupthink has been shown to happen is among stock analysts. Groupthink appears to be closely aligned with the conclusions Solomon Asch drew in his experiments with a lone dissenter, which we describe in Chapter 18. Individuals

Young adults rioting in the streets of Vancouver after the Canucks' loss to the Boston Bruins in Game 7 of the 2011 NHL playoffs may have been affected by groupthink as they got carried away, smashing windows, looting, and setting fires. It is unlikely that everyone who participated in the riots had carefully planned out their activities in advance of the riots starting.

who hold a position that is different from that of the dominant majority are under pressure to suppress, withhold, or modify their true feelings and beliefs. As members of a group, we find it more pleasant to be in agreement—to be a positive part of the group—than to be a disruptive force, even if disruption is necessary to improve the effectiveness of the group's decisions.

Do all groups suffer from groupthink? No. It seems to occur most often where there is a clear group identity, where members hold a positive image of their group, which they want to protect, and where the group perceives a collective threat to this positive image.[60] So groupthink is less a dissenter-suppression mechanism than a means for a group to protect its positive image.

What can managers do to minimize groupthink?[61]

- *Monitor group size.* People grow more intimidated and hesitant as group size increases, and, although there is no magic number that will eliminate groupthink, individuals are likely to feel less personal responsibility when groups get larger than about 10.

- *Encourage group leaders to play an impartial role.* Leaders should actively seek input from all members and avoid expressing their own opinions, especially in the early stages of deliberation.

- *Appoint one group member to play the role of devil's advocate.* This member's role is to overtly challenge the majority position and offer divergent perspectives.

- *Stimulate active discussion of diverse alternatives to encourage dissenting views and more objective evaluations.* Group members might delay discussion of possible gains so they can first talk about the dangers or risks inherent in a decision. Requiring members to first focus on the negatives of an alternative makes the group less likely to stifle dissenting views and more likely to gain an objective evaluation.

While considerable anecdotal evidence indicates the negative implications of groupthink in organizational settings, not much actual empirical work has been conducted in organizations in this area.[62] In fact, researchers on groupthink have been criticized for suggesting that its effect is uniformly negative[63] and for overestimating the link between the decision-making process and its outcome.[64] A study of groupthink using 30 teams from 5 large corporations suggests that elements of groupthink may affect decision making differently. For instance, the illusion of invulnerability, assumption of morality, and illusion of unanimity were positively associated with team performance.[65] The most recent research suggests that we should be aware of groupthink conditions that lead to poor decisions, while realizing that not all groupthink symptoms harm decision making.

Groupshift

There are differences between group decisions and the individual decisions of group members.[66] Sometimes group decisions are more conservative. More often, they lean toward greater risk.[67] In either case, participants have engaged in **groupshift**, a phenomenon in which the initial positions of individual group members become exaggerated because of the interactions of the group.

What appears to happen in groups is that the discussion leads members toward a more extreme view of the position they already held. Conservative types become more cautious and more aggressive types assume more risk. The group discussion tends to exaggerate the initial position of the group.

The greater shift toward risk has generated several explanations.[68] It has been argued, for instance, that the discussion makes members more comfortable with one another, and, thus, more bold and daring. Another argument is that the group diffuses responsibility. Group decisions free any single member from accountability for the group's final choice, so greater risks can be taken. It's also likely that people take on extreme positions because they want to demonstrate how different they are from the outgroup.[69] People on the fringes of political or social movements take on more and more extreme positions just to prove they are really committed to the cause.

How should you use the findings on groupshift? Recognize that group decisions exaggerate the initial position of the individual members, that the shift has been shown more often to be toward greater risk, and that which way a group will shift is a function of the members' pre-discussion inclinations.

Group Decision-Making Techniques

Groups can use a variety of techniques to stimulate decision making. We outline four of them below.

Interacting Groups

The most common form of group decision making takes place in **interacting groups**. Members meet face to face and rely on both verbal and nonverbal interaction to communicate with one another. But as our discussion of groupthink demonstrated, interacting groups often censor themselves and pressure individual members toward conformity of opinion. *Brainstorming*, the *nominal group technique*, and *electronic meetings* have been proposed as ways to reduce many of the problems inherent in the traditional interacting group.

Brainstorming

Brainstorming uses an idea-generation process that specifically encourages any and all alternatives, in a criticism-free environment.

In a typical brainstorming session, 6 to 12 people sit around a table. The group leader states the problem in a clear manner so that all participants understand it. Members then "free-wheel" as many alternatives as they can in a given period of time. No criticism is allowed, and all the alternatives are recorded for later discussion and analysis. One idea stimulates others, and judgments of even the most bizarre suggestions are withheld until later to encourage group members to "think the unusual."

groupshift A phenomenon in which the initial positions of individual group members become exaggerated because of the interactions of the group.

interacting groups Typical groups, where members interact with each other face to face.

brainstorming An idea-generation process that specifically encourages any and all alternatives, while withholding any criticism of those alternatives.

Brainstorming may indeed generate ideas—but not in a very efficient manner. Research consistently shows that individuals working alone generate more ideas than a group in a brainstorming session.[70] One reason for this is "production blocking." When people generate ideas in a group, many people are talking at once, which blocks the thought process and eventually impedes the sharing of ideas.[71] Another reason suggested by a 2011 study is fixation—group members start to fixate early on a limited number of solutions rather than continue to look for others.[72] One recent study suggests that goal-setting approaches might make brainstorming more effective.[73] The following two techniques go further than brainstorming by offering methods that help groups arrive at a preferred solution.[74]

Nominal Group Technique

The **nominal group technique** restricts discussion or interpersonal communication during the decision-making process, hence the term *nominal* (which means "in name only"). Group members are all physically present, as in a traditional committee meeting, but they operate independently. Specifically, a problem is presented and then the group takes the following steps:

- Members meet as a group, but before any discussion takes place, each member independently writes down his or her ideas on the problem.

- After this silent period, each member presents one idea to the group. Group members take turns presenting a single idea until all ideas have been presented and recorded. No discussion takes place until all ideas have been recorded.

- The group discusses the ideas for clarity and evaluates them.

- Each group member silently and independently ranks the ideas. The idea with the highest aggregate ranking determines the final decision.

The steps of the nominal group technique are illustrated in Exhibit 5-3. The chief advantage of the technique is that it permits the group to meet formally but does not restrict independent thinking, as does the interacting group. Research generally shows that nominal groups outperform brainstorming groups.[75]

Electronic Meetings

The most recent approach to group decision making blends the nominal group technique with sophisticated computer technology.[76] It's called the computer-assisted group, or **electronic meeting**. Up to 50 people sit around a horseshoe-shaped table, which is empty except for a series of networked laptops. Issues are presented to participants and they type their responses into their computers. Individual comments (which are anonymous), as well as aggregate votes, are displayed on a projection screen.

The major advantages of electronic meetings are anonymity, honesty, and speed. This group decision-making approach also allows people to be brutally honest without

nominal group technique A group decision-making method in which individual members meet face to face to pool their judgments in a systematic but independent fashion.

electronic meeting A meeting where members interact on computers, allowing for anonymity of comments and aggregation of votes.

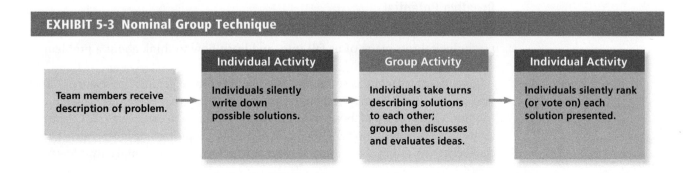

EXHIBIT 5-3 Nominal Group Technique

Team members receive description of problem. → **Individual Activity** Individuals silently write down possible solutions. → **Group Activity** Individuals take turns describing solutions to each other; group then discusses and evaluates ideas. → **Individual Activity** Individuals silently rank (or vote on) each solution presented.

EXHIBIT 5-4 Evaluating Group Effectiveness				
		Type of Group		
Effectiveness Criteria	Interacting	Brainstorming	Nominal	Electronic
Number and quality of ideas	Low	Moderate	High	High
Social pressure	High	Low	Moderate	Low
Money costs	Low	Low	Low	High
Speed	Moderate	Moderate	Moderate	Moderate
Task orientation	Low	High	High	High
Potential for interpersonal conflict	High	Low	Moderate	Low
Commitment to solution	High	Not applicable	Moderate	Moderate
Development of group cohesiveness	High	High	Moderate	Low

Source: Based on J. K. Murnighan, "Group Decision Making: What Strategies Should You Use?" *Academy of Management Review*, February 1981, p. 61.

penalty. It's fast because chit-chat is eliminated, discussions don't digress, and many participants can "talk" at once without stepping on one another's toes. Early evidence, however, indicates that electronic meetings don't achieve most of their proposed benefits. They actually lead to *decreased* group effectiveness, require *more* time to complete tasks, and result in *reduced* member satisfaction compared with face-to-face groups.[77] Nevertheless, current enthusiasm for computer-mediated communications suggests that this technology is here to stay and is likely to increase in popularity in the future.

Each of these four group decision techniques has its own strengths and weaknesses. The choice depends on what criteria you want to emphasize and the cost-benefit trade-off. As Exhibit 5-4 indicates, an interacting group is good for achieving commitment to a solution, brainstorming develops group cohesiveness, the nominal group technique is an inexpensive means for generating a large number of ideas, and electronic meetings minimize social pressures and conflicts.

Creativity in Organizational Decision Making

5 How can we get more creative decisions?

Although following the steps of the rational decision-making model will often improve decisions, a rational decision maker also needs **creativity**; that is, the ability to produce novel and useful ideas.[78] These are ideas that are different from what has been done before but that are appropriate to the problem or opportunity presented.

Why is creativity important to decision making? It allows the decision maker to more fully appraise and understand the problem, including seeing problems others cannot see. Such thinking is becoming more important.

Creative Potential

Most people have useful creative potential. But to unleash it, they have to escape the psychological ruts many of us fall into, and learn how to think about a problem in divergent ways.

Exceptional creativity is scarce. We all know of creative geniuses in science (Albert Einstein), art (Pablo Picasso), and business (Steve Jobs). But what about the typical individual? Intelligent people and those who score high on openness to experience (see Chapter 2) are more likely to be creative.[79] Other traits of creative people include independence, self-confidence, risk-taking, a positive core self-evaluation, tolerance for ambiguity, a low need

creativity The ability to produce novel and useful ideas.

Sometimes desperation can lead to creative decisions. General Motors Canada saw the challenge of producing the much-in-demand Chevrolet Equinox and GMC Terrain crossover utility vehicles as an opportunity to think creatively.[80] Rather than adding a new paint shop to GM's Ingersoll, Ontario-based Cami Automotive, which would have been expensive and time-consuming, management decided to ship the unpainted cars to an underutilized GM plant in Oshawa for painting and finishing. It was an unprecedented move, but one that allows the car to be produced much more quickly.

for structure, and perseverance.[81] A study of the lifetime creativity of 461 men and women found that fewer than 1 percent were exceptionally creative.[82] However, 10 percent were highly creative and about 60 percent were somewhat creative. These findings suggest that most of us have creative potential; we just need to learn to unleash it.

Three-Component Model of Creativity

What can individuals and organizations do to stimulate employee creativity? The best answer lies in the **three-component model of creativity**,[83] which proposes that individual creativity essentially requires expertise, creative-thinking skills, and intrinsic task motivation (see Exhibit 5-5). Studies confirm that the higher the level of each of these three components, the higher the creativity.

> Why are some people more creative than others?

Expertise is the foundation for all creative work. Film writer, producer, and director Quentin Tarantino spent his youth working in a video rental store, where he built up an encyclopedic knowledge of movies. The potential for creativity is enhanced when individuals have abilities, knowledge, proficiencies, and similar expertise in their field of endeavour. You would not expect someone with a minimal knowledge of programming to be very creative as a software engineer.

The second component is *creativity skills*. This encompasses personality characteristics associated with creativity, the ability to use analogies, and the talent to see the familiar in a different light.

A meta-analysis of 102 studies found that positive moods increase creativity, but it depended on what sort of positive mood was considered.[84] Moods such as happiness that encourage interaction with the world are more conducive to creativity than passive moods such as calm. This finding means that the common advice to relax and clear your mind to develop creative ideas may be misplaced. It would be better to get in an upbeat mood and then frame your work as an opportunity to have fun and experiment. Further, negative moods don't always affect creativity in the same way. Passive

three-component model of creativity The proposition that individual creativity requires expertise, creative-thinking skills, and intrinsic task motivation.

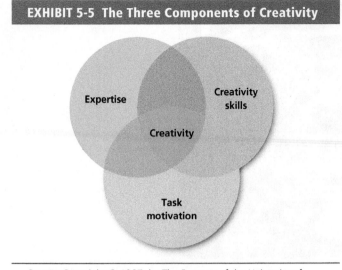

EXHIBIT 5-5 The Three Components of Creativity

Source: Copyright © 1997, by The Regents of the University of California. Reprinted from *The California Management Review* 40, no. 1. By permission of The Regents.

negative moods such as sadness don't seem to have much effect, but avoidance-oriented negative moods such as fear and anxiety decrease creativity. Feeling threatened reduces your desire to try new activities; risk aversion increases when you are scared. Active negative moods, such as anger, however, appear to enhance creativity, especially if you are taking your task seriously.

Being around others who are creative can make us more inspired, especially if we are creatively "stuck."[85] One study found that "weak ties" to creative people—knowing them but not well—facilitates creativity because the people are there as a resource if we need them, but they are not so close as to stunt our own independent thinking.[86]

Analogies allow decision makers to apply an idea from one context to another. One of the most famous examples was Alexander Graham Bell's observation that it might be possible to apply the way the ear operates to his "talking box." He noticed that the bones in the ear are operated by a delicate, thin membrane. He wondered why, then, a thicker and stronger piece of membrane should not be able to move a piece of steel. From that analogy, the telephone was conceived. Thinking in terms of analogies is a complex intellectual skill, which helps explain why cognitive ability is related to creativity. Demonstrating this effect, one study found that children who got high scores on cognitive ability tests at age 13 were significantly more likely to have made creative achievements in their professional lives 25 years later.[87]

Some people have developed their creativity skills because they are able to see problems in a new way. They are able to make the strange familiar and the familiar strange.[88] For instance, most of us think of hens laying eggs. But how many of us have considered that a hen is only an egg's way of making another egg?

The final component in the three-component model of creativity is intrinsic *task motivation*. This is the desire to work on something because it's interesting, involving, exciting, satisfying, or personally challenging. It is what turns creativity *potential* into *actual* creative ideas. Environmental stimulants that foster creativity include a culture that encourages the flow of ideas; fair and constructive judgment of ideas; rewards and recognition for creative work; sufficient financial, material, and information resources; freedom to decide what work is to be done and how to do it; a supervisor who communicates effectively, shows confidence in others, and supports the work group; and work group members who support and trust one another.[89]

Organizational Factors That Affect Creativity

Five organizational factors have been found to block your creativity at work:[90]

- *Expected evaluation.* Focusing on how your work is going to be evaluated.

- *Surveillance.* Being watched while you are working.

- *External motivators.* Focusing on external, tangible rewards.

- *Competition.* Facing win-lose situations with peers.

- *Constrained choice.* Being given limits on how you can do your work.

Canadian Tire built a better tent by giving people an environment that encouraged them to think creatively.

Shahrzad Rafati, founder and CEO of Vancouver-based BroadbandTV, made Fast Company's 2011 list of the top 100 most creative people in business, the only Canadian to do so. When she was still an undergraduate computer science major at UBC, she came up with the idea of taking video uploaded to sites like YouTube and merging it with online advertising opportunities—bringing together both "pirates" and corporate content providers. "We're helping companies identify and take control of their content and generate revenue from it," she explained.

What About Ethics in Decision Making?

The owners of Invermere, BC-based Kicking Horse Coffee Company are committed to providing their customers with the best coffee possible.[91] "Quality is our number-one difference from others," says Elana Rosenfeld. "We take that seriously; we don't want to disappoint people if they are paying for this coffee." In 2007, the company faced a dilemma: how to respond to the increasing demand for more "green" coffee beans. The company had marketed itself as selling only organic beans, and those beans are harder to find, and more expensive. Nevertheless, Kicking Horse decided that despite supply challenges, they no longer purchase any coffee beans that are not fair trade in origin. How can ethics influence business strategy?

6 What is ethics, and how can it be used for better decision making?

No contemporary examination of decision making would be complete without the discussion of ethics, because ethical considerations should be an important criterion in organizational decision making. **Ethics** is the study of moral values or principles that guide our behaviour and inform us whether actions are right or wrong. Ethical principles help us "do the right thing." In this section, we present four ways to ethically frame decisions and examine the factors that shape an individual's ethical decision-making behaviour. We also examine organizational responses to the demand for ethical behaviour, as well as consideration of ethical decisions when doing business in other cultures.

Four Ethical Decision Criteria

An individual can use four criteria in making ethical choices.[92] The first is **utilitarianism**, in which decisions are made solely on the basis of their outcomes, ideally to provide the greatest good for the greatest number. This view dominates business decision making. It is consistent with goals such as efficiency, productivity, and high profits. By maximizing profits, for instance, business executives can argue that they are securing the greatest good for the greatest number—as they hand out dismissal notices to 15 percent of employees.

A second ethical criterion is to make decisions consistent with fundamental liberties and privileges as set forth in documents such as the Canadian Charter of Rights and Freedoms. An emphasis on *rights* in decision making means respecting and protecting the

ethics The study of moral values or principles that guide our behaviour and inform us whether actions are right or wrong.

utilitarianism A decision focused on outcomes or consequences that emphasizes the greatest good for the greatest number.

Stewart Leibl, president of Perth's, a Winnipeg dry-cleaning chain, is a founding sponsor of the "Koats for Kids" program. The company's outlets are a drop-off point for no-longer-needed children's coats, which Perth's cleans free of charge before distributing them to children who don't have winter coats. Each year, over 5000 freshly cleaned coats and parkas are distributed to children in need. Leibl is going beyond utilitarian criteria when he says, "We all have a responsibility to contribute to the society that we live in." He is also looking at social justice.

basic rights of individuals, such as the rights to privacy, free speech, and due process. This criterion protects **whistle-blowers** when they report unethical or illegal practices by their organizations to the media or to government agencies, using their right to free speech.

A third criterion is to impose and enforce rules fairly and impartially to ensure *justice* or an equitable distribution of benefits and costs. Union members typically favour this view. It justifies paying people the same wage for a given job, regardless of performance differences, and using seniority as the primary determination in making layoff decisions. A focus on justice protects the interests of the underrepresented and less powerful, but it can encourage a sense of entitlement that reduces risk-taking, innovation, and productivity.

A fourth ethical criterion is *care*. The ethics of care can be stated as follows: "The morally correct action is the one that expresses care in protecting the special relationships that individuals have with each other."[93] The care criterion suggests that we should be aware of the needs, desires, and well-being of those to whom we are closely connected. This perspective does remind us of the difficulty of being impartial in all decisions.

Decision makers, particularly in for-profit organizations, tend to feel safe and comfortable when they use utilitarianism, framing decisions as being in the best interests of "the organization" and stockholders. Critics of this perspective note that it can result in ignoring the rights of some individuals, particularly those with minority representation in the organization.[94] Using nonutilitarian criteria presents a solid challenge to today's managers because doing so involves far more ambiguities.

Factors That Influence Ethical Decision-Making Behaviour

What accounts for unethical behaviour in organizations? Is it immoral individuals or work environments that promote unethical activity? The answer is, *both!* The evidence indicates that ethical or unethical actions are largely a function of both the individual's characteristics and the environment in which he or she works.[95] The model in Exhibit 5-6 illustrates factors affecting ethical decision-making behaviour and emphasizes three factors: stage of moral development, locus of control, and the organizational environment.

whistle-blowers Individuals who report unethical practices by their employer to outsiders.

EXHIBIT 5-6 Factors Affecting Ethical Decision-Making Behaviour

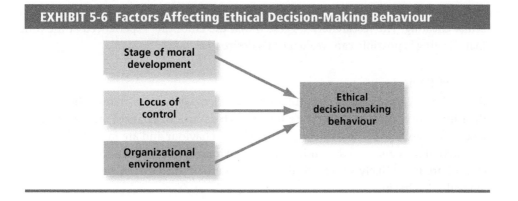

Stages of Moral Development

Stages of moral development assess a person's capacity to judge what is morally right.[96] Research suggests that there are three levels of moral development.[97] The higher a person's moral development, the less dependent he or she is on outside influences and the more he or she will be predisposed to behave ethically. The first level is the preconventional level, the second is the conventional level, and the third, or highest, level is the principled level. These levels and their stages are described in Exhibit 5-7.

Research indicates that people proceed through the stages one step at a time, though they do not necessarily reach the highest stage.[98] Most adults are at a mid-level of moral development—they are strongly influenced by peers and will follow an organization's rules and procedures. Those individuals who have progressed to the higher stages place increased value on the rights of others, regardless of the majority's opinion, and are likely to challenge organizational practices they personally believe are wrong. Those at the higher stages are most likely to make ethical decisions. A 2011 study by three psychologists from the University of Toronto found

Why do some people make more ethical decisions than others?

stages of moral development The developmental stages that explain a person's capacity to judge what is morally right.

EXHIBIT 5-7 Stages of Moral Development

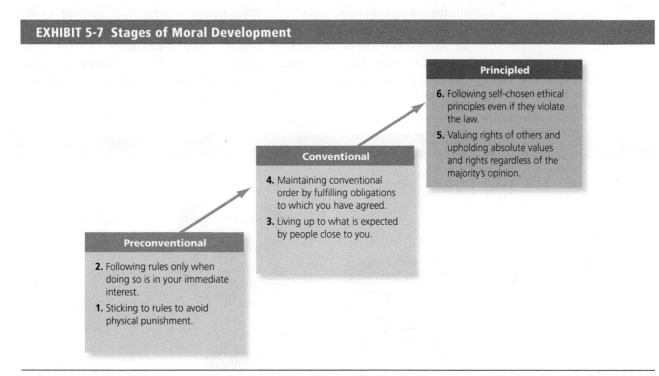

Source: Based on L. Kohlberg, "Moral Stages and Moralization: The Cognitive-Developmental Approach," in *Moral Development and Behaviour: Theory, Research, and Social Issues,* ed. T. Lickona (New York: Holt, Rinehart and Winston, 1976), pp. 34–35.

that people were likely to predict they would cheat more often than they engaged in actual cheating. The researchers suggested that the emotions experienced at the time that cheating is possible can weaken one's desire to cheat.[99]

Locus of Control

Research indicates that people with an external *locus of control* (that is, they believe their lives are controlled by outside forces, such as luck or chance) are less likely to take responsibility for the consequences of their behaviour and are more likely to rely on external influences to determine their behaviour. Those with an internal locus of control are more likely to rely on their own internal standards of right or wrong to guide their behaviour.

Organizational Environment

The *organizational environment* refers to an employee's perception of organizational expectations. Does the organizational culture encourage and support ethical behaviour by rewarding it or discourage unethical behaviour by punishing it? Characteristics of an organizational environment that are likely to foster high ethical decision making include written codes of ethics; high moral behaviour by senior management; realistic performance expectations; performance appraisals that evaluate means as well as ends; visible recognition and promotions for individuals who display high moral behaviour; and visible punishment for those who act unethically. The Canadian Forces recently distributed a guide to its forces to underscore the need for ethical behaviour in warfare.

In summary, people who lack a strong moral sense are much less likely to make unethical decisions if they are constrained by an organizational environment that frowns on such behaviours. Conversely, righteous individuals can be corrupted by an organizational environment that permits or encourages unethical practices. In the next section, we consider how to formulate an ethical decision.

Making Ethical Decisions

While there are no clear-cut ways to differentiate ethical from unethical decision making, there are some questions you should consider.

Exhibit 5-8 illustrates a decision tree to guide ethical decisions.[100] This tree is built on three of the ethical decision criteria—utilitarianism, rights, and justice—presented above. The first question you need to answer addresses self-interest vs. organizational goals.

EXHIBIT 5-8 Is a Decision Ethical?

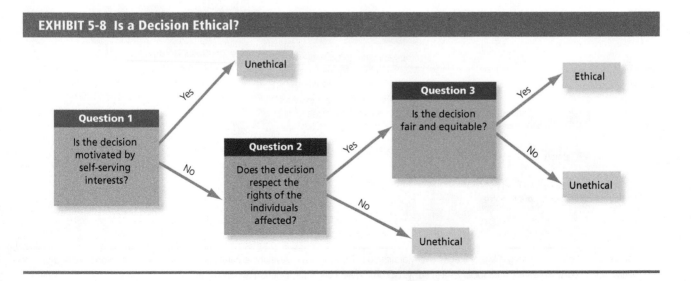

Paul Nielsen (shown with his wife, Dayle) owns Calgary-based DumpRunner Waste Systems, a specialty garbage and debris removal company. He encourages an ethical approach to dealing with both clients and employees. He notes that in Calgary, business is built on handshakes and being true to your word, and people are expected to act ethically. Ethical behaviour may be easier for Nielsen than for some others. He says he is guided by his passion for being in business, rather than a "quest for money."

The second question concerns the rights of other parties. If the decision violates the rights of someone else (the person's right to privacy, for instance), then the decision is unethical.

The final question that needs to be addressed relates to whether the decision conforms to standards of equity and justice. The department head who inflates the performance evaluation of a favoured employee and deflates the evaluation of a disfavoured employee—and then uses these evaluations to justify giving the former a big raise and nothing to the latter—has treated the disfavoured employee unfairly.

Unfortunately, the answers to the questions in Exhibit 5-8 are often argued in ways to make unethical decisions seem ethical. Powerful people, for example, can become very adept at explaining self-serving behaviours in terms of the organization's best interests. Similarly, they can persuasively argue that unfair actions are really fair and just. Our point is that immoral people can justify almost any behaviour. Those who are powerful, articulate, and persuasive are the most likely to be able to get away with unethical actions successfully. When faced with an ethical dilemma, try to answer the questions in Exhibit 5-8 truthfully.

Corporate Social Responsibility

Elana Rosenfeld and Leo Johnson, founders of Kicking Horse Coffee Company, are committed to making the best coffee possible, but they also want to do so in ways that highlight corporate social responsibility.[101] They start with their employees, with whom they have built a relationship based on "trust, employee autonomy and a shared sense of mission." They restrict their purchases to fair trade growers, who provide healthy working environments for employees. Rosenfeld and Johnson travel to visit their coffee bean suppliers in South America and other places, which enables them to report first-hand to their customers and employees "how fair trade coffee makes a real difference to the lives of those who were often exploited." Rosenfeld and Johnson also take the environment seriously. The cans their coffee is sold in are made of recycled steel, which can be recycled many times over. To what extent should companies be socially responsible?

7 What is corporate social responsibility?

Corporate social responsibility is an organization's responsibility to consider the impact of its decisions on society. Thus, organizations may try to better society through such things as charitable contributions or providing better wages to employees working in offshore factories. Organizations may engage in these practices because they feel pressured by society to do so, or they may seek ways to improve society because they feel it is the right thing to do.

Canadians want businesses to give back to society, according to a 2010 poll which found that Canadians' views of corporations are largely affected by whether businesses support charitable causes and protect the environment.[102] Oakville, Ontario-based Tim Hortons, which makes customers aware of its Children's Foundation, is well regarded by Canadians.[103]

Not everyone agrees that organizations should assume social responsibility. For example, economist Milton Friedman remarked in *Capitalism and Freedom* that "few trends could so thoroughly undermine the very foundations of our free society as the acceptance by corporate officials of a social responsibility other than to make as much money for their stockholders as possible."[104]

Joel Bakan, professor of law at the University of British Columbia, author of *The Corporation*,[105] and co-director of the documentary of the same name, is more critical of organizations than Friedman. Bakan suggests that today's corporations have many of the same characteristics as a psychopathic personality (for example, self-interested, lacking empathy, manipulative, and reckless in their disregard of others). Bakan notes that even though companies have a tendency to act psychopathically, this is not why they are fixated on profits. Rather, their only legal responsibility is to maximize organizational profits for stockholders. He suggests changes in laws to encourage corporations to behave more socially responsibly.

Canadian senior executives have mixed feelings about the extent to which businesses should get involved in charitable giving, or forcing industry standards on foreign corporations. A 2011 poll found that 45 percent believe individual shareholders, not the company, should make personal decisions about giving to charity. Another 35 percent, however, felt corporations should donate to charities. One CEO explained, "Being a good corporate citizen means assisting those less fortunate—as long as it is done in the context of the entities' aims, objectives and employees' desires."[106] A 2011 poll conducted by COMPAS found that Canadian business leaders were not about imposing Canadian management values on Chinese employers, however. "We don't have the right to tell China how to run its economy," said one CEO. "We have the choice to buy, or not to buy."[107]

A recent survey found that Canadian and American MBA students are very interested in the subject of corporate social responsibility. Over 80 percent of respondents "believed business professionals should take into account social and environmental impacts when making decisions." Almost two-thirds of these respondents felt that corporate social responsibility should be part of core MBA classes, and 60 percent said "they would seek socially responsible employment."[108]

GLOBAL IMPLICATIONS

When considering potential global differences in this chapter's concepts, let's consider two areas among this chapter's concepts that have attracted the most research: decision making and ethics.

Decision Making

The rational model makes no acknowledgment of cultural differences, nor does the bulk of OB research literature on decision making. A recent review of cross-cultural OB research covered 25 areas, but cultural influence on decision making was not among them. Another recent review identified 15 topics, but the result was the same: No research on culture and decision making.[109]

corporate social responsibility
An organization's responsibility to consider the impact of its decisions on society.

However, Indonesians, for instance, don't necessarily make decisions the same way Australians do. Therefore, we need to recognize that the cultural background of a decision maker can have a significant influence on the selection of problems, the depth of analysis, the importance placed on logic and rationality, and whether organizational decisions should be made autocratically by an individual manager or collectively in groups.[110]

Cultures differ in their time orientation, the importance of rationality, their belief in the ability of people to solve problems, and their preference for collective decision making. Differences in time orientation help us understand why managers in Egypt make decisions at a much slower and more deliberate pace than their US counterparts. While rationality is valued in North America, that is not true elsewhere in the world. A North American manager might make an important decision intuitively but know it's important to appear to proceed in a rational fashion because rationality is highly valued in the West. In countries such as Iran, where rationality is not as paramount as other factors, efforts to appear rational are not necessary.

Some cultures emphasize solving problems, while others focus on accepting situations as they are. Canada falls in the first category; Thailand and Indonesia are examples of the second. Because problem-solving managers believe they can and should change situations to their benefit, Canadian managers might identify a problem long before their Thai or Indonesian counterparts would choose to recognize it as such. Decision making by Japanese managers is much more group-oriented than in Canada. The Japanese value conformity and cooperation. So before Japanese CEOs make an important decision, they collect a large amount of information, which they use in consensus-forming group decisions.

In short, there are probably important cultural differences in decision making, but unfortunately not yet much research to identify them.

Ethics

There are no global ethical standards,[111] as contrasts between Asia and the West illustrate.[112] Because bribery is commonplace in countries such as China, a Canadian working in China might face a dilemma: Should I pay a bribe to secure business if it is an accepted part of that country's culture? A manager of a large US company operating in China caught an employee stealing. Following company policy, she fired him and turned him over to the local authorities. Later, she was horrified to learn the employee had been summarily executed.[113]

Although ethical standards may seem ambiguous in the West, criteria defining right and wrong are actually much clearer there than in Asia, where few issues are black and white and most are grey. In Japan, people doing business together often exchange gifts, even expensive ones. This is part of Japanese tradition. When North American and European companies started doing business in Japan, most North American executives were not aware of the Japanese tradition of exchanging gifts and wondered whether this was a form of bribery. Most have come to accept this tradition now, and have even set different limits on gift giving in Japan than in other countries.[114]

Global organizations must establish ethical principles for decision makers in countries such as India and China and modify them to reflect cultural norms if they want to uphold high standards and consistent practices. Having agreements among countries to police bribery may not be enough, however. The 34 countries of the Organisation for Economic Co-operation and Development (OECD) entered into an agreement to tackle corporate bribery in 1997. However, a 2011 study by Berlin-based Transparency International found that 21 of the OECD countries are "doing little or nothing" to enforce the agreement. Canada came under strong criticism for being "the only G7 country in the little or no enforcement category." The United States and Germany rated highest on number of cases filed. Transparency International noted that Canada needed to enforce more of its laws in this area.[115]

LESSONS LEARNED

- Individuals often short-cut the decision making process and do not consider all options.
- Intuition leads to better results when supplemented with evidence and good judgment.
- Exceptional creativity is rare, but expertise, creative-thinking skills, and intrinsic task motivation encourage creativity.

6

Organizational Structure

Geoff Flood, president of Toronto-based T4G, a technical services company, has some strong feelings about bureaucracy. "Bureaucracy," he proclaims, "is nonsense that gets in the way. It is cost, pure cost."[1] He believes he has a better idea: He structured his company into a loose portfolio of business units led by different people in turn, depending on the project they are working on and their expertise. "It is a roles-based design," explains Flood. "There has never been an organizational chart in the company. And there won't be an organizational chart until I'm gone."

Flood feels that the flat structure improves communication and decision making. "In a typical business there is a hierarchy, and if there was one in this business it would be an inverted pyramid and I'd be on the bottom," he says. "I report to the people on the front lines."

Other T4G initiatives include enabling virtual teams, so that the highly qualified professionals they hire can work from wherever they like.

Flood is part of a new breed of executives who tailor organizational structure to employee needs. The company locates its offices where "smart people want to live and raise their families." The result is competitive advantage through high staff retention rates and the fostering of innovation and creativity.

The theme of this chapter is that organizations have different structures, determined by specific forces, and that these structures have a bearing on employee attitudes and behaviour. Organizations need to think carefully about the best way to organize how people inside and outside the organization are connected to each other. These connections form the basis for organizational structure.

What Is Organizational Structure?

 What are the key elements of organizational structure?

An **organizational structure** defines how job tasks are formally divided, grouped, and coordinated. Managers need to address six key elements when they design their organization's structure: work specialization, departmentalization, chain of command, span of control, centralization and decentralization, and formalization.[2] Exhibit 6-1 presents all of these elements as answers to an important structural question.

Work Specialization

We use the term **work specialization**, or *division of labour*, to describe the degree to which tasks in the organization are subdivided into separate jobs. The essence of work specialization is that, rather than an entire job being completed by one individual, it's broken down into a number of steps, with each step being completed by a separate individual. In essence, individuals specialize in doing part of an activity rather than the entire activity.

What happens when a person performs the same task over and over again?

Specialization can be efficient. Employee skills at performing a task improve through repetition. Less time is spent in changing tasks, in putting away tools and equipment from a prior step in the work process, and in preparing for another. It's easier and less costly to find and train employees to do specific and repetitive tasks. This is especially true of highly sophisticated and complex operations. For example, could Montreal-based Bombardier produce even one Canadian regional jet a year if one person had to build the entire plane alone? Not likely! Finally, work specialization increases efficiency and productivity by encouraging the creation of special inventions and machinery.

However, specialization can lead to boredom, fatigue, stress, low productivity, poor quality, increased absenteeism, and high turnover, so it is not always the best way to organize employees. Giving employees a variety of activities to do, allowing them to do a whole and complete job, and putting them into teams with interchangeable skills can result in significantly higher output and increased employee satisfaction.

Most managers today recognize that specialization provides economies in certain types of jobs but problems when it's carried too far. High work specialization helps McDonald's make and sell hamburgers and fries efficiently, and aids medical specialists working in hospitals. Other companies, on the other hand, have achieved success by reducing specialization.

organizational structure How job tasks are formally divided, grouped, and coordinated.

work specialization The degree to which tasks in the organization are subdivided into separate jobs.

EXHIBIT 6-1 Six Key Questions That Managers Need to Answer in Designing the Proper Organizational Structure

The Key Question	The Answer Is Provided By
1. To what degree are tasks subdivided into separate jobs?	*Work specialization*
2. On what basis will jobs be grouped together?	*Departmentalization*
3. To whom do individuals and groups report?	*Chain of command*
4. How many individuals can a manager efficiently and effectively direct?	*Span of control*
5. Where does decision-making authority lie?	*Centralization and decentralization*
6. To what degree will there be rules and regulations to direct employees and managers?	*Formalization*

Work is specialized at the Russian factories that manufacture the wooden nesting dolls called *matryoshkas*. At this factory outside Moscow, individuals specialize in doing part of the doll production, from the craftsmen who carve the dolls to the painters who decorate them. Work specialization brings efficiency to doll production, as some 50 employees can make 100 *matryoshkas* every two days.

Departmentalization

Once jobs are divided up through work specialization, they must be grouped so that common tasks can be coordinated. The basis on which jobs are grouped together is called **departmentalization**. One of the concerns related to departmental groups is that they can become *silos* within an organization. Often, departments start protecting their own turf and not interacting well with other departments, which can lead to a narrow vision with respect to organizational goals.

Functional Departmentalization

One of the most popular ways to group activities is by *functions* performed. For example, a manufacturing company might separate engineering, accounting, manufacturing, human resource, and purchasing specialists into common departments. Similarly, a hospital might have departments devoted to research, patient care, accounting, and so forth. The major advantage to functional groupings is obtaining efficiencies from putting people with common skills and orientations together into common units.

Product Departmentalization

Tasks can also be departmentalized by the type of *product* the organization produces. Procter & Gamble groups each major product—such as Tide, Pampers, Charmin, and Pringles—under an executive who has complete global responsibility for it. The major advantage to this type of grouping is increased accountability for product performance, since all activities related to a specific product line are under the direction of a single manager.

Geographic Departmentalization

Another way to departmentalize is on the basis of geography, or territory. The sales function, for instance, may be divided regionally with departments for British Columbia, the Prairies, Central Canada, and Atlantic Canada. Each of these regions is, in effect, a department organized around geography. If an organization's customers are scattered over a large geographic area and have similar needs based on their location, then this form of departmentalization can be valuable.

departmentalization The basis on which jobs are grouped together.

The Carillon Generating Station on the Ottawa River (shown here) is one of Montreal-based Hydro-Québec's hydroelectric power stations. Hydro-Québec organizes its operations by functions so that the company can be more responsive to growth outside Quebec. It has four divisions: Hydro-Québec Production, Hydro-Québec TransÉnergie, Hydro-Québec Distribution, and Hydro-Québec Équipement/Société d'énergie de la Baie James.

Process Departmentalization

Some companies organize departments by the processing that occurs. For example, an aluminum tubing manufacturer might have the following departments: casting; press; tubing; finishing; and inspecting, packing, and shipping. This is an example of process departmentalization, because each department specializes in one specific phase in the production of aluminum tubing. Since each process requires different skills, this method offers a basis for the homogeneous categorizing of activities.

Process departmentalization can be used for processing customers, as well as products. For example, in some provinces, you may go through a series of steps handled by several departments before receiving your driver's licence: (1) validation by a motor vehicles division; (2) processing by the licensing department; and (3) payment collection by the treasury department.

Customer Departmentalization

Yet another way to departmentalize is on the basis of the particular type of customer the organization seeks to reach. Microsoft, for example, is organized around four customer markets: consumers, large corporations, software developers, and small businesses. Customers in each department have a common set of problems and needs best met by having specialists for each.

Large organizations may use all the forms of departmentalization we have described. A major Japanese electronics firm organizes each of its divisions along functional lines, its manufacturing units around processes, sales around seven geographic regions, and each sales region into four customer groupings. In a strong recent trend among organizations of all sizes, rigid functional departmentalization is increasingly complemented by teams that cross traditional departmental lines. As we described in Chapter 18, as tasks have become more complex, and more diverse skills are needed to accomplish those tasks, management has turned to cross-functional teams.

Chain of Command

While the chain of command was once a basic cornerstone in the design of organizations, it has far less importance today.[3] But contemporary managers should still consider its implications. The **chain of command** is the continuous line of authority that extends from upper organizational levels to the lowest level and clarifies who reports to whom. It helps employees answer questions such as, "Who do I go to if I have a problem?" and "To whom do I report?"

We cannot discuss the chain of command without also discussing authority and unity of command. **Authority** refers to the rights inherent in a managerial position to give orders and expect them to be obeyed. To facilitate coordination, each managerial position is given a place in the chain of command, and each manager is given a degree of authority in order to meet his or her responsibilities. The principle of **unity of command** helps preserve the concept of an unbroken line of authority. It says a person should have one and only one superior to whom he or she is directly responsible. If the unity of command is broken, an employee might have to cope with conflicting demands or priorities from several superiors.

Because managers have limited time and knowledge, they may choose to delegate some of their responsibilities to other employees. **Delegation** is the assignment of authority to another person to carry out specific duties, allowing the employee to make some of the decisions. Delegation is an important part of a manager's job, as it can ensure that the right people are part of the decision-making process. Through delegation, employees are being empowered to make decisions that previously were reserved for management.

Times change, and so do the basic tenets of organizational design. A low-level employee today can access information in seconds that was available only to top managers a generation ago. Networked computers allow employees anywhere in an organization to communicate with anyone else without going through formal channels. Operating employees are empowered to make decisions previously reserved for management. Add the popularity of self-managed and cross-functional teams and the creation of new structural designs that include multiple bosses, and you can see why authority and unity of command hold less relevance. Many organizations still find they can be most productive by enforcing the chain of command. There just seem to be fewer of them today.

Span of Control

Span of control refers to the number of employees who report to a manager. This number will vary by organization, and by unit within an organization, and is determined by the number of employees a manager can efficiently and effectively direct. In an assembly-line factory, a manager may be able to direct numerous employees, because the work is well defined and controlled by machinery. A sales manager, by contrast, might have to give one-on-one supervision to individual sales reps, and, therefore, fewer would report to the sales manager. All things being equal, the wider or larger the span, the more efficient the organization. An example can illustrate the validity of this statement.

Assume that we have two organizations, both of which have approximately 4100 operative-level employees. As Exhibit 6-2 illustrates, if one has a uniform span of 4 and the other a span of 8, the wider span would have 2 fewer levels and approximately 800 fewer managers. If the average manager earned $56 000 a year, the wider span would save about $45 million a year in management salaries. Obviously, wider spans are more efficient in terms of cost. However, at some point when supervisors no longer have time to provide the necessary leadership and support, they reduce effectiveness and employee performance suffers.

Narrow or small spans have their advocates. By keeping the span of control to 5 or 6 employees, a manager can maintain close control.[4] But narrow spans have three major drawbacks. First, as already described, they are expensive because they add levels of management. Second, they make vertical communication in the organization more

chain of command The continuous line of authority that extends from upper organizational levels to the lowest level and clarifies who reports to whom.

authority The rights inherent in a managerial position to give orders and to expect the orders to be obeyed.

unity of command The idea that a subordinate should have only one superior to whom he or she is directly responsible.

delegation Assignment of authority to another person to carry out specific duties, allowing the employee to make some of the decisions.

span of control The number of employees that report to a manager.

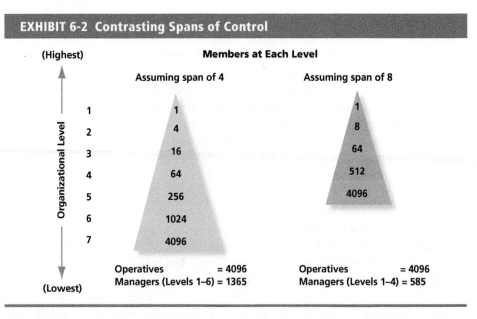

EXHIBIT 6-2 Contrasting Spans of Control

	(Highest)		**Members at Each Level**	
			Assuming span of 4	Assuming span of 8
Organizational Level	1		1	1
	2		4	8
	3		16	64
	4		64	512
	5		256	4096
	6		1024	
	7		4096	
	(Lowest)		Operatives = 4096 Managers (Levels 1–6) = 1365	Operatives = 4096 Managers (Levels 1–4) = 585

complex. The added levels of hierarchy slow down decision making and tend to isolate upper management. Third, narrow spans of control encourage overly tight supervision and discourage employee autonomy.

The trend in recent years has been toward wider spans of control.[5] Wider spans of control are consistent with recent efforts by companies to reduce costs, cut overhead, speed up decision making, increase flexibility, get closer to customers, and empower employees. However, to ensure that performance does not suffer because of these wider spans, organizations have been investing heavily in employee training. Managers recognize that they can handle a wider span when employees know their jobs inside and out or can turn to their co-workers when they have questions.

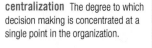
centralization The degree to which decision making is concentrated at a single point in the organization.

decentralization The degree to which decision making is distributed to lower-level employees.

When Surrey, BC, RCMP decentralized its offices, the results were positive. Merchants, local politicians, and police in Surrey say they are happy with the results. Some crime statistics have dropped, and the police feel that they are closer to the people they serve. The RCMP split its force into five units operating at regional stations, rather than out of one headquarters opposite Surrey's city hall. The advantage is that "regional offices can concentrate on the unique problems of the various areas."

Centralization and Decentralization

Centralization refers to the degree to which decision making is concentrated at a single point in the organization. In centralized organizations, top managers make all the decisions, and lower-level managers merely carry out their directives. In organizations at the other extreme, decentralized decision making is pushed down to the managers closest to the action.

The concept of centralization includes only formal authority; that is, the rights inherent in one's position. An organization characterized by centralization is inherently different structurally from one that is decentralized. An organization characterized by **decentralization** can act more quickly to solve problems, more people provide input into decisions, and employees are less likely to feel alienated from those who make decisions that affect their work lives. Decentralized departments make it easier to address customer concerns as well. As Dilbert points out in Exhibit 6-3, however,

EXHIBIT 6-3

Source: Dilbert, reprinted by permission of Universal Uclick.

some organizations do not seem able to decide upon an appropriate level of decentralization.

Management efforts to make organizations more flexible and responsive have produced a recent trend toward decentralized decision making by lower-level managers, who are closer to the action and typically have more detailed knowledge about problems than top managers. Big retailers such as The Bay and Sears Canada have given their store managers considerably more discretion in choosing what merchandise to stock. This allows those stores to compete more effectively against local merchants.

Formalization

Formalization refers to the degree to which jobs within the organization are standardized. In organizations that are highly formalized, there are explicit job descriptions, lots of organizational rules, and clearly defined procedures covering work processes. Employees can be expected always to handle the same input in exactly the same way, resulting in a consistent and uniform output where there is high formalization. Where formalization is low, job behaviours are relatively nonprogrammed, and employees have a great deal of freedom to exercise discretion in their work. Standardization not only eliminates the possibility of employees engaging in alternative behaviours but also removes the need for employees to consider alternatives.

McDonald's is an example of a company where employee routines are highly formalized. Employees are instructed in such things as how to greet the customer (smile, be sincere, make eye contact), ask for and receive payment (state amount of order clearly

formalization The degree to which jobs within the organization are standardized.

The job of these women sorting cookies at a factory in Perugia, Italy, is highly standardized. There is really only one way for them to complete their task, and they are not required to make major decisions to do so. Individual differences influence how these employees respond to their high work formalization. For these women, formalization may be a source of job satisfaction because it provides the security of a routine and gives them the chance to socialize on the job because they don't have to pay close attention to what they are doing.

and loudly, announce the amount of money the customer gives to the employee, count change out loud and efficiently), and thank the customer (give a sincere thank you, make eye contact, ask customer to come again). McDonald's includes this information in training and employee handbooks, and managers are given a checklist of these behaviours so that they can observe their employees to ensure that the proper procedures are followed.[6]

The degree of formalization can vary widely among organizations and within organizations. Certain jobs, for instance, are well known to have little formalization. Publishing representatives who call on college and university professors to inform them of their company's new publications have a great deal of freedom in their jobs. They have only a general sales pitch, which they tailor as needed, and rules and procedures governing their behaviour may be little more than the requirement to submit a weekly sales report and suggestions on what to emphasize in forthcoming titles. At the other extreme, clerical and editorial employees in the same publishing houses may need to be at their desks by 8 a.m. and follow a set of precise procedures dictated by management.

Common Organizational Designs

 What are some examples of traditional organizational designs?

We now turn to describing some of the more common organizational designs: the *simple structure*, the *bureaucracy*, and the *matrix structure*.

The Simple Structure

What do a small retail store, a start-up electronics firm run by a hard-driving entrepreneur, a new Planned Parenthood office, and an airline "war room" in the midst of a company-wide pilots' strike have in common? They probably all use the **simple structure**.

The simple structure is said to be characterized most by what it is *not* rather than by what it is. The simple structure is not elaborate.[7] It has a low degree of departmentalization, wide spans of control, authority centralized in a single person, and little formalization. It is a "flat" organization; it usually has only two or three vertical levels, a loose body of employees, and one individual in whom the decision-making authority is centralized.

simple structure An organizational design characterized by a low degree of departmentalization, wide spans of control, authority centralized in a single person, and little formalization.

The simple structure is most widely practised in small businesses in which the manager and the owner are one and the same, such as the local corner grocery store.

The strength of the simple structure lies in its simplicity. It's fast, flexible, and inexpensive to maintain, and accountability is clear. One major weakness is that it's difficult to maintain in anything other than small organizations. It becomes increasingly inadequate as an organization grows because its low formalization and high centralization tend to create information overload at the top. As size increases, decision making typically becomes slower and can eventually come to a standstill as the single executive tries to continue making all the decisions. This often proves to be the undoing of many small businesses. When an organization begins to employ 50 or 100 people, it's very difficult for the owner-manager to make all the choices. If the structure is not changed and made more elaborate, the firm often loses momentum and can eventually fail. The simple structure's other weakness is that it's risky—everything depends on one person. One serious illness can literally destroy the organization's information and decision-making centre.

The Family Business

Family businesses represent 70 percent of Canadian employment and more than 30 percent of the gross domestic product. Some of the most prominent family businesses in Canada over the past 50 years include Montreal, Quebec-based Seagram Company (the Bronfman family), Calgary, Alberta-based Shaw Communications (the Shaw family), Montreal, Quebec-based Birks jewellers (the Birk family), Saint John, New Brunswick-based Irving Paper conglomerate (the Irving family), Montreal, Quebec-based Molson Coors Brewing Company (the Molson family), and Florenceville, New Brunswick-based McCain Foods (the McCain family). Not all family businesses are as large as these, however, and many have relatively simple structures.

Family businesses have more complex dynamics than nonfamily businesses, because they face both family/personal relations and business/management relations. These companies generally have shareholders (family members and perhaps others), although the businesses may be public companies listed on the stock exchange. For instance, of the companies mentioned above, Seagram Company, Shaw Communications, and Molson Coors Brewing Company are public companies. Shaw Communications has an interesting structure—only family members have voting shares.

Mississauga, Ontario-based Furlani's Food Corporation uses a "family business" mentality to govern its approach to employees. The business is run in a non-hierarchical manner and no formal or impersonal HR processes dictate employee behaviour. Employees are encouraged to share ideas openly, which keeps morale high. For a recent improvement project, employees from different levels and areas collaborated to make the process go smoothly.

Unlike nonfamily businesses, family businesses must manage the conflicts found within families, as well as the normal business issues that arise for any business. As John Davis of Harvard Business School notes, "In a family business, the business, the family, and the ownership group all need governance." Good governance structures can help family businesses manage the conflicts that may arise. Good governance includes "a sense of direction, values to live by or work by, and well-understood and accepted policies that tell organization members how they should behave."[8]

One area in which governance can play a key role is in CEO succession. Family businesses need to figure out rules of succession for when the CEO retires, and also rules for who in the family gets to work in the business. Succession in family-owned businesses often does not work "because personal and emotional factors determine who the next leader will be," rather than suitability.[9] For instance, a father may want his first-born son to take over the business, even if one of the daughters might make a better CEO.

The issues become more complex when second- and third-generation family members become involved in the family business.

So what makes family businesses unique? Founders of family businesses seek to "build businesses that are also family institutions."[10] As a result, there is added pressure on the business, which needs to balance business needs and family needs. Family businesses may have different goals than nonfamily businesses as well, emphasizing the importance of family values in maintaining and growing the business rather than wealth maximization.

The Bureaucracy

Standardization! That is the key concept underlying all bureaucracies. Take a look at the bank where you keep your chequing account, the department store where you buy your clothes, or the government offices that collect your taxes, enforce health regulations, or provide local fire protection. They all rely on standardized work processes for coordination and control. Bureaucracy is a dirty word in many people's minds. However, it does have advantages. Its primary strength is its ability to perform standardized activities in a highly efficient manner. Putting like specialties together in functional departments results in economies of scale, minimum duplication of personnel and equipment, and employees who have the opportunity to talk "the same language" among their peers.

A **bureaucracy** is characterized by highly routine operating tasks achieved through specialization, formalized rules and regulations, tasks that are grouped into functional departments, centralized authority, narrow spans of control, and decision making that follows the chain of command.

Strengths of Bureaucracy

German sociologist Max Weber, writing in the early 1900s, described bureaucracy as an alternative to the traditional administrative form. In the traditional model, leaders could be quite arbitrary, with authority based on personal relations. There were no general rules, and no separation between the leader's "private" and "public" business. Bureaucracy solved some of the problems of leaders who took advantage of their situation.

The primary strength of the bureaucracy lies in its ability to perform standardized activities in a highly efficient manner. Bureaucracies can get by nicely with less talented—and, hence, less costly—middle- and lower-level managers. Rules and regulations substitute for managerial discretion. Standardized operations, coupled with high formalization, allow decision making to be centralized. There is little need for innovative and experienced decision makers below the level of senior executives. In short, bureaucracy is an effective structure for ensuring consistent application of policies and practices and for ensuring accountability.

bureaucracy An organizational design with highly routine operating tasks achieved through specialization, formalized rules and regulations, tasks that are grouped into functional departments, centralized authority, narrow spans of control, and decision making that follows the chain of command.

Weaknesses of Bureaucracy

Bureaucracy is not without its problems. Listen in on a dialogue among four executives in one company: "You know, nothing happens in this place until we produce something," said the production executive. "Wrong," commented the research and development manager. "Nothing happens until we design something!" "What are you talking about?" asked the marketing executive. "Nothing happens here until we sell something!" The exasperated accounting manager responded, "It doesn't matter what you produce, design, or sell. No one knows what happens until we tally up the results!" This conversation highlights that specialization creates subunit conflicts in which functional-unit goals can override the overall goals of the organization. Each department acts like a silo, focusing more on what it perceives as its own value and contribution to the organization. Each silo fails to understand that departments are really interdependent, with each having to perform well for the company as a whole to survive. The conflict that can happen among functional units means that sometimes functional unit goals can override the overall goals of the organization.

Bureaucracy can sometimes lead to power being concentrated in the hands of just a few people, with others expected to follow their orders unquestioningly. This chapter's *Ethical Dilemma Exercise* on page 506 illustrates what can happen when someone higher in the authority chain pressures someone below him or her to perform unethical tasks.

The other major weakness of a bureaucracy is something we have all experienced: obsessive concern with following the rules. When cases arise that don't precisely fit the rules, there is no room for modification. The bureaucracy is efficient only as long as employees confront problems that they have previously encountered and for which programmed decision rules have already been established.

The Matrix Structure

Another popular organizational design option is the **matrix structure**. You will find it being used in advertising agencies, aerospace firms, research and development laboratories, construction companies, hospitals, government agencies, universities, management consulting firms, and entertainment companies.[11] It combines two forms of departmentalization: functional and product.

The strength of functional departmentalization is putting like specialists together, which minimizes the number necessary while allowing the pooling and sharing of specialized resources across products. Its major disadvantage is the difficulty of coordinating the tasks of diverse functional specialists on time and within budget. Product departmentalization has exactly the opposite benefits and disadvantages. It facilitates coordination among specialties to achieve on-time completion and meet budget targets. It provides clear responsibility for all activities related to a product but with duplication of activities and costs. The matrix attempts to gain the strengths of each, while avoiding their weaknesses.

The most obvious structural characteristic of the matrix is that it breaks the unity-of-command concept. Employees in the matrix have two bosses—their functional department managers and their product managers.

Exhibit 6-4 shows the matrix structure used in a faculty of business administration. The academic departments of accounting, administrative studies, finance, and so forth are functional units. Specific programs (that is, products) are overlaid on the functions. Thus, members in a matrix structure have a dual chain of command: to their functional department and to their product groups. A professor of accounting who is teaching an undergraduate course reports to the director of undergraduate programs, as well as to the chair of the accounting department.

Advantages of a Matrix Structure

The strength of the matrix is its ability to foster coordination when the organization has a number of complex and interdependent activities. Information permeates the

matrix structure An organizational design that combines functional and product departmentalization; it has a dual chain of command.

EXHIBIT 6-4 Matrix Structure for a Faculty of Business Administration

Programs / Academic departments	Undergraduate	Master's	PhD	Research	Executive development	Community service
Accounting						
Administrative studies						
Finance						
Information and decision sciences						
Marketing						
Organizational behaviour						
Quantitative methods						

organization and more quickly reaches those people who need it. Furthermore, the matrix reduces "bureaupathologies." The dual lines of authority reduce tendencies of departmental members to become so busy protecting their little worlds that the organization's overall goals become secondary. A matrix also achieves economies of scale and facilitates the allocation of specialists by providing both the best resources and an effective way of ensuring their efficient deployment.

Disadvantages of a Matrix Structure

The major disadvantages of the matrix lie in the confusion it creates, its tendency to foster power struggles, and the stress it places on individuals.[12] Without the unity-of-command concept, ambiguity about who reports to whom is significantly increased and often leads to conflict. It's not unusual for product managers to fight over getting the best specialists assigned to their products. Bureaucracy reduces the potential for power grabs by defining the rules of the game. When those rules are "up for grabs," power struggles between functional and product managers result. For individuals who desire security and absence of ambiguity, this work climate can be stressful. Reporting to more than one manager introduces role conflict, and unclear expectations introduce role ambiguity. The comfort of bureaucracy's predictability is replaced by insecurity and stress.

What happens when you report to two bosses?

New Design Options

3 What do newer organizational structures look like?

Geoff Flood says that one of the best things about T4G's flat, project team-based structure is that it helps foster employee creativity, passion, and dedication by eliminating bureaucratic barriers.[13] Flood is passionate about managing the structure of his organization around the needs of his employees. This has led Flood to open offices in Halifax, Moncton, Fredericton, Saint John, Toronto, Vancouver, and Saco, Maine.

Flood's employees seem to agree with his approach to organizational structure. T4G was named one of the Best Workplaces in Canada in the under 1000 employee category in 2008, and continued to make that list each year since. Flood explains this success as follows:

"Everyone at T4G has a 'Go Do' attitude to put their hearts into the work and do the right thing for our customers at all times. We embrace change and refuse wasting time and money." Can new forms of organization always lead to better ways to get things done? What downsides might there be?

Organizational theorists Jay Galbraith and Edward Lawler have argued that there is a "new logic of organizing" for organizations.[14] They suggest that new-style organizations are considerably more flexible than older-style organizations. Exhibit 6-5 compares characteristics of new-style and old-style organizations.

The new structural options for organizations involve breaking down boundaries in some fashion, either internally, externally, or a combination of the two. In this section, we describe three such designs: the *team structure*, which modifies internal boundaries; the *virtual organization*, which modifies external organizational boundaries; and the *boundaryless organization*, which attempts to break down both internal and external boundaries.[15] We also discuss how downsizing can lead to leaner organizations.

The Team Structure

As described in Chapter 18, teams have become an extremely popular means around which to organize work activities. When management uses teams as its central coordination device, you have a **team structure**. The primary characteristics of the team structure are that it breaks down departmental barriers and decentralizes decision making to the level of the work team. Team structures also require employees to be generalists as well as specialists.[16]

In smaller companies, the team structure can define the entire organization. For instance, Toyota Canada's parts distribution centre in Toronto reorganized its workforce into work teams in 1995. Employees have a team-focused mission statement, and the staff are split into six work teams, each with its own leader. Among larger organizations, such as Xerox Canada and GM Canada, the team structure often complements what is typically a bureaucratic structure. This allows the organization to achieve the efficiency of bureaucracy's standardization while gaining the flexibility that teams provide.

EXHIBIT 6-5 New-Style vs. Old-Style Organizations

New	Old
Dynamic, learning	Stable
Information rich	Information is scarce
Global	Local
Small and large	Large
Product/customer oriented	Functional oriented
Skills oriented	Job oriented
Team oriented	Individual oriented
Involvement oriented	Command/control oriented
Lateral/networked	Hierarchical
Customer oriented	Job requirements oriented

Source: J. R. Galbraith and E. E. Lawler III, "Effective Organizations: Using the New Logic of Organizing," in *Organizing for the Future: The New Logic for Managing Complex Organizations*, ed. J. R. Galbraith, E. E. Lawler III, and associates (San Francisco: Jossey-Bass, 1993). Copyright © 1993 Jossey-Bass Inc. Publishers. Reprinted with permission of John Wiley & Sons, Inc.

team structure The use of teams as the central device to coordinate work activities.

The Virtual Organization

Why own when you can rent? That question captures the essence of the **virtual organization** (also sometimes called the *network organization* or *modular organization*).[17] The virtual organization can take several different forms, depending on its degree of centralization. In some instances, a small, core organization outsources major business functions. In this case, the core organization would have more of the control. In more extreme forms, the virtual organization "is a continually evolving network of independent companies—suppliers, customers, even competitors—linked together to share skills, costs, and access to one another's markets."[18] In this case, participants give up some of their control and act more interdependently. Thus, virtual organizations may not have a central office, an organizational chart, or a hierarchy. Typically, the organizations come together to exploit specific opportunities or attain specific strategic objectives.

The prototype of the virtual structure is today's movie-making organization. In Hollywood's golden era, movies were made by huge, vertically integrated corporations. Studios such as MGM, Warner Brothers, and 20th Century Fox owned large movie lots and employed thousands of full-time specialists—set designers, camera people, film editors, directors, and even actors. Today, most movies are made by a collection of individuals and small companies who come together and make films project by project.[19] This structural form allows each project to be staffed with the talent best suited to its demands rather than just the people employed by the studio. It minimizes bureaucratic overhead because there is no lasting organization to maintain. As well, it lessens long-term risks and their costs because there is no long term—a team is assembled for a finite period and then disbanded.

About one in nine Canadian companies engages in some sort of alliance. These alliances take many forms, ranging from precompetitive consortia to coproduction, cross-equity arrangements, and equity joint ventures with separate legal entities.[20] Amazon.ca partners with Canada Post in such an arrangement. Orders placed on Amazon.ca's website are fulfilled and shipped by Assured Logistics, which is part of Canada Post. Assured Logistics operates a Toronto-area warehouse that stores books, music, and movies so that they can be shipped when ordered, thus eliminating the need for Amazon to set up its own warehouse facility in Canada. Newman's Own, the food products company founded by Paul Newman, sells over $120 million in food every year yet employs only 19 people. This is possible because it outsources almost everything: manufacturing, procurement, shipping, and quality control.

What is going on here? A quest for maximum flexibility. These virtual organizations have created networks of relationships that allow them to contract out manufacturing, distribution, marketing, or any other business function management feels others can do better or more cheaply. The virtual organization stands in sharp contrast to the typical bureaucracy and concentrates on what it does best, which is typically design or marketing.

Exhibit 6-6 shows a virtual organization in which management outsources all the primary functions of the business. The core of the organization is a small group of executives whose job is to oversee directly any activities done in house and to coordinate relationships with the other organizations that manufacture, distribute, and perform other crucial functions for the virtual organization. The dotted lines represent the relationships typically maintained under contracts. In essence, managers in virtual structures spend most of their time coordinating and controlling external relations, typically by way of computer-network links.

The major advantage of the virtual organization is its flexibility, which allows individuals with an innovative idea and little money to successfully compete against the likes of Sony, Hitachi, and Sharp Electronics. This structural form allows organizations to share costs and skills, provide access to global markets, and increase market responsiveness.

virtual organization A continually evolving network of independent companies—suppliers, customers, even competitors—linked together to share skills, costs, and access to one another's markets.

Virtual organizations' drawbacks have become increasingly clear as their popularity has grown.[21] They are in a state of perpetual flux and reorganization, which means roles, goals, and responsibilities are unclear: This sets the stage for political behaviour. Those who work frequently with virtual organizations also note cultural alignment and shared goals can be lost because of the low degree of interaction among members. Team members who are geographically dispersed and communicate only intermittently find it difficult to share information and knowledge, which can limit innovation and slow response time. Ironically, some virtual organizations are less adaptable and innovative than those with well-established communication and collaboration networks. A leadership presence that reinforces the organization's purpose and facilitates communication is thus especially valuable.

EXHIBIT 6-6 A Virtual Organization

The Boundaryless Organization

Virtual organizations break down external boundaries of the organization without generally affecting the internal workings of each of the cooperating organizations. Some organizations, however, strive to break down both the internal and external boundaries. Former General Electric chairman Jack Welch coined the term **boundaryless organization** to describe his idea of what he wanted GE to become: a "family grocery store."[22] That is, in spite of GE's monstrous size (2010 revenues were over $150 billion), Welch wanted to eliminate vertical and horizontal boundaries within it and break down external barriers between the company and its customers and suppliers. Although GE has not yet achieved this boundaryless state—and probably never will—it has made significant progress toward that end. So

Can an organization really have no boundaries?

BMW Group operates as a boundaryless organization in designing, developing, and producing its BMW, Rolls-Royce, and Mini cars. The automaker uses virtual tools such as computer-aided design and simulation models and a flexible production network of 17 plants in 6 countries to respond quickly to fluctuations in the market and individual customer preferences. BMW's boundaryless structure drives innovative ideas by eliminating vertical and horizontal barriers among employees and creating an environment of learning and experimentation. From their first day on the job, employees are encouraged to build a network of relationships from all functional areas and across all divisions to speed innovation and problem solving.

boundaryless organization An organization that seeks to eliminate the chain of command, have limitless spans of control, and replace departments with empowered teams.

have other companies, such as Hewlett-Packard, AT&T, Motorola, and 3M. Let's see what a boundaryless organization looks like and what some firms are doing to make it a reality.[23]

The boundaryless organization breaks down barriers internally by flattening the hierarchy, creating cross-hierarchical teams (which include top executives, middle managers, supervisors, and operative employees), and using participative decision-making practices and 360-degree performance appraisals (where peers and others above and below the employee evaluate his or her performance). Another way management can cut through barriers is to use lateral transfers, rotating people into and out of different functional areas. This approach turns specialists into generalists. The boundaryless organization also breaks down barriers to external constituencies (suppliers, customers, regulators, etcetera) and barriers created by geography. Globalization, strategic alliances, supplier-organization and customer-organization linkages, and teleworking are all examples of practices that reduce external boundaries.

One of the drawbacks of boundaryless organizations is that they are difficult to manage. It's difficult to overcome the political and authority boundaries inherent in many organizations. It can also be time-consuming and difficult to manage the coordination necessary with so many different stakeholders. That said, the well-managed boundaryless organization offers the best talents of employees across several different organizations; enhances cooperation across functions, divisions, and external groups; and potentially offers much quicker response time to the environment.

The Leaner Organization: Organization Downsizing

The goal of the new organizational forms we have described is to improve agility by creating a lean, focused, and flexible organization. Companies may need to cut divisions that are not adding value. Downsizing is a systematic effort to make an organization leaner by selling off business units, closing locations, or reducing staff. It has been very controversial because of its potential negative impacts on employees.

The radical shrinking of Chrysler and General Motors in recent years was a case of downsizing due to loss of market share and changes in consumer demand. Similarly, delays in getting their PlayBook to market along with anemic sales of BlackBerrys forced Waterloo-based Research In Motion (RIM) to announce in June 2011 that jobs would be lost over the coming months. These companies probably needed to downsize just to survive. Others downsize to direct all their efforts toward their core competencies. When Cisco announced in early 2011 that it was shutting down production of the Flip video camera, just a year after it had bought the rights to it, fans of the camera were shocked. But Cisco does not have a retail presence—that is not its core competency (however, selling routers and switches to the technology and telecommunications industries is). So gaining shelf space or developing consumer advertising came difficult to the company.[24] Some companies focus on lean management techniques to reduce bureaucracy and speed decision making. For example, Starbucks has done so to improve coffee quality, produce more consistent taste outcomes, and decrease the serving time for customers.[25]

Despite the advantages of being a lean organization, the impact of downsizing on organizational performance has been very controversial.[26] Reducing the size of the workforce has an immediately positive outcome in the huge reduction in wage costs. Companies downsizing to improve strategic focus often see positive effects on stock prices after the announcement. On the other hand, among companies that only cut employees but don't restructure, profits and stock prices usually decline. Part of the problem is the effect of downsizing on employee attitudes. Those who remain often feel worried about future layoffs and may be less committed to the organization.[27] Stress reactions can lead to increased sickness absences, lower concentration on the job, and lower creativity. In companies that don't invest much in their employees, downsizing can also lead to more voluntary turnover, so vital human capital is lost. The result is a company that is more anemic than lean.

Companies can reduce negative impacts by preparing for the post-downsizing environment in advance, thus alleviating some employee stress and strengthening support for the new strategic direction.[28] The following are some effective strategies for downsizing and suggestions for implementing them. Most are closely linked to the principles for organizational justice we discussed in Chapter 13:

- *Investment.* Companies that downsize to focus on core competencies are more effective when they invest in high-involvement work practices afterward.

- *Communication.* When employers make efforts to discuss downsizing with employees early, employees are less worried about the outcomes and feel the company is taking their perspective into account.

- *Participation.* Employees worry less if they can participate in the process in some way. In some companies, voluntary early retirement programs or severance packages can help achieve leanness without layoffs.

- *Assistance.* Providing severance, extended health care benefits, and job search assistance demonstrates a company does really care about its employees and honours their contributions.

Companies that make themselves lean can be more agile, efficient, and productive—but only if they make cuts carefully and help employees through the process.

Why Do Structures Differ?

We have described organizational designs ranging from the highly structured bureaucracy to the amorphous boundaryless organization. The other designs we discussed exist somewhere between these extremes.

Exhibit 6-7 recaps our discussions by presenting two extreme models of organizational design. One we will call the **mechanistic model**. It's generally synonymous with the bureaucracy in that it has highly standardized processes for work, high formalization, and more managerial hierarchy. The other extreme, the **organic model**, looks a lot like the boundaryless organization. It's flat, has fewer formal procedures for making decisions, has multiple decision makers, and favours flexible practices.[29]

4 Why do organizational structures differ?

EXHIBIT 6-7 Mechanistic vs. Organic Models

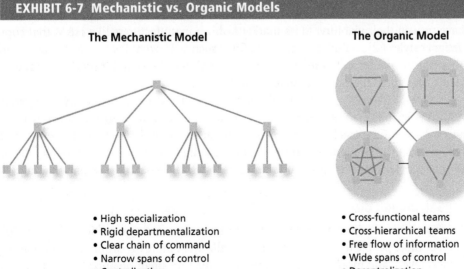

The Mechanistic Model

- High specialization
- Rigid departmentalization
- Clear chain of command
- Narrow spans of control
- Centralization
- High formalization

The Organic Model

- Cross-functional teams
- Cross-hierarchical teams
- Free flow of information
- Wide spans of control
- Decentralization
- Low formalization

mechanistic model A structure characterized by high specialization, rigid departmentalization, a clear chain of command, narrow spans of control, a limited information network, and centralization.

organic model A structure that is flat, uses cross-functional and cross-hierarchical teams, possesses a comprehensive information network, has wide spans of control, and has low formalization.

With these two models in mind, let's ask a few questions: Why are some organizations structured along more mechanistic lines, whereas others follow organic characteristics? What forces influence the choice of design? In the following pages, we present the major causes, or determinants, of an organization's structure: strategy, organizational size, technology, and environment.[30] The *Working with Others Exercise* on page 504 gives you the opportunity to create different organizational structures and see how they can affect productivity.

Strategy

An organization's structure is a means to help management achieve its objectives. Since objectives are derived from the organization's overall strategy, it's only logical that the structure should support the strategy.[31]

Most current strategy frameworks focus on three strategy dimensions—innovation, cost minimization, and imitation—and the structural design that works best with each.[32]

Innovation Strategy

To what degree does an organization introduce major new products or services? An **innovation strategy** strives to achieve meaningful and unique innovations. Obviously, not all firms pursue innovation. Apple and 3M do, but it certainly is not a strategy pursued by McDonald's. Innovative firms will use competitive pay and benefits to attract top candidates and motivate employees to take risks. Some degree of mechanistic structure can actually benefit innovation. Well-developed communication channels, policies for enhancing long-term commitment, and clear channels of authority all may make it easier to make rapid changes smoothly.

Cost-Minimization Strategy

An organization pursuing a **cost-minimization strategy** tightly controls costs, refrains from incurring unnecessary innovation or marketing expenses, and cuts prices in selling a basic product. This would describe the strategy pursued by Walmart, as well as the sellers of generic grocery products. Cost-minimizing organizations pursue fewer policies meant to develop commitment among their workforce.

Imitation Strategy

Organizations following an **imitation strategy** try to both minimize risk and maximize opportunity for profit, moving into new products or new markets only after innovators have proven their viability. Mass-market fashion manufacturers like H&M that copy designer styles follow this strategy, as do firms such as Hewlett-Packard and Caterpillar. They follow smaller and more innovative competitors with superior products, but only after competitors have demonstrated that the market is there.

Exhibit 6-8 describes the structural option that best matches each strategy. Innovators need the flexibility of the organic structure, while cost minimizers seek the efficiency and stability of the mechanistic structure. Imitators combine the two structures. They use a mechanistic structure in order to maintain tight controls and low costs in their current activities, but create organic subunits in which to pursue new undertakings.

Organizational Size

An organization's size significantly affects its structure.[33] Organizations that employ 2000 or more people tend to have more specialization, more departmentalization, more vertical levels, and more rules and regulations than do small organizations. However, size becomes less important as an organization expands. Why is this? At around 2000

innovation strategy A strategy that emphasizes the introduction of major new products and services.

cost-minimization strategy A strategy that emphasizes tight cost controls, avoidance of unnecessary innovation or marketing expenses, and price cutting.

imitation strategy A strategy of moving into new products or new markets only after their viability has already been proven.

EXHIBIT 6-8 The Strategy-Structure Relationship	
Strategy	**Structural Option**
Innovation	*Organic:* A loose structure; low specialization, low formalization, decentralized
Cost minimization	*Mechanistic:* Tight control; extensive work specialization, high formalization, high centralization
Imitation	*Mechanistic and organic:* Mix of loose with tight properties; tight controls over current activities and looser controls for new undertakings

employees an organization is already fairly mechanistic. An additional 500 employees will not have much impact. But adding 500 employees to an organization that has only 300 members is likely to significantly shift it toward a more mechanistic structure.

Technology

Technology describes the way an organization transfers its inputs into outputs. Every organization has at least one technology for converting financial, human, and physical resources into products or services. Ford Motor Company uses an assembly-line process to make its vehicles. Universities may use a number of instruction technologies to teach students—the ever-popular formal lecture method, the case-analysis method, the experiential exercise method, or the programmed learning method. Regardless, organizational structures adapt to their technology.

So what does *technology* mean?

Variations in Technology

Numerous studies have examined the technology-structure relationship.[34] The common theme that differentiates technologies is their *degree of routineness*. Routine activities are characterized by automated and standardized operations, such as an assembly line, where one might affix a car door to a car at set intervals, automated transaction processing of sales transactions, and printing and binding of this book. Nonroutine activities are customized, such as furniture restoring, custom shoemaking, and genetic research.

Environment

An organization's **environment** includes outside institutions or forces that can affect the organization's performance, such as suppliers, customers, competitors, government regulatory agencies, and public pressure groups. Moreover, an organization's structure can be affected by environmental uncertainty. Static environments create significantly less uncertainty for managers than do dynamic ones. Because uncertainty is a threat to an organization's effectiveness, management will try to minimize it through adjustments in the organization's structure. They may, for example, broaden their structure to sense and respond to threats. Most companies, including Pepsi and WestJet, have added social networking departments to their structure so as to respond to negative information posted on blogs. Or companies may form strategic alliances with other companies; for example, Microsoft and Yahoo! joined forces to better compete with Google.[35]

Why should an organization's structure be affected by its environment? The answer is environmental uncertainty. Some organizations face relatively static environments—few forces in their environment are changing. There is, for example, no new competition, no new technological breakthroughs by current competitors, or little activity by public pressure groups to influence the organization. Other organizations face dynamic environments—rapidly changing government regulations affecting their business, new

technology The way in which an organization transfers its inputs into outputs.

environment Those institutions or forces outside the organization that potentially affect the organization's performance.

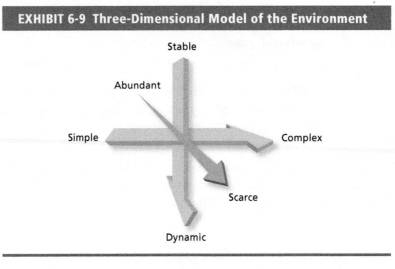

EXHIBIT 6-9 Three-Dimensional Model of the Environment

competitors, difficulties in acquiring raw materials, continually changing product preferences by customers, and so on. Static environments create significantly less uncertainty for managers than do dynamic ones. Since uncertainty is a threat to an organization's effectiveness, management will try to minimize it. One way to reduce environmental uncertainty is through adjustments in the organization's structure.[36]

Recent research has helped clarify what is meant by environmental uncertainty. It has been found that there are three key dimensions to any organization's environment: capacity, volatility, and complexity.[37]

The *capacity* of an environment refers to the degree to which it can support growth. Rich and growing environments generate excess resources, which can buffer the organization in times of relative scarcity.

Volatility describes the degree of instability in an environment. A dynamic environment with a high degree of unpredictable change makes it difficult for management to make accurate predictions. Because information technology changes at such a rapid pace, for instance, more organizations' environments are becoming volatile. Turmoil in the US financial markets in 2008 caught many by surprise and created a lot of instability. Canada's credit market faced significant tightening as a result, making it more difficult for corporations and individuals to borrow money. The US financial crisis was a valuable reminder to all organizations that they are operating in a global environment.

Finally, *complexity* is the degree of heterogeneity and concentration among environmental elements. Simple environments—like the tobacco industry, which has relatively few players—are homogeneous and concentrated. Environments characterized by heterogeneity and dispersion—like the broadband industry—are complex and diverse, with numerous competitors.

Exhibit 6-9 summarizes our definition of the environment along its three dimensions. The arrows in this figure are meant to indicate movement toward higher uncertainty. Organizations that operate in environments characterized as scarce, dynamic, and complex face the greatest degree of uncertainty because they have high unpredictability, little room for error, and a diverse set of elements in the environment to monitor constantly.

Given this three-dimensional definition of *environment*, we can offer some general conclusions about environmental uncertainty and structural arrangements. The more scarce, dynamic, and complex the environment, the more organic a structure should be. The more abundant, stable, and simple the environment, the more mechanistic a structure should be.

Organizational Designs and Employee Behaviour

5 What are the behavioural implications of different organizational designs?

We opened this chapter by implying that an organization's structure can have significant effects on its members. What might those effects be?

A review of the evidence leads to a pretty clear conclusion: You cannot generalize! Not everyone prefers the freedom and flexibility of organic structures. Different factors stand out in different structures as well. In highly formalized, heavily structured, mechanistic organizations, the level of fairness in formal policies and procedures is a very important predictor of satisfaction. In more personal, individually adaptive organic organizations, employees value interpersonal justice more.[38] Some people are most productive and satisfied when work tasks are standardized and ambiguity minimized—that is, in mechanistic structures. So any discussion of the effect of organizational design on employee behaviour has to address individual differences. To do so, let's consider employee preferences for work specialization, span of control, and centralization.[39]

The evidence generally indicates that work specialization contributes to higher employee productivity—but at the price of reduced job satisfaction. However, work specialization is not an unending source of higher productivity. Problems start to surface, and productivity begins to suffer, when the human diseconomies of doing repetitive and narrow tasks overtake the economies of specialization. As the workforce has become more highly educated and desirous of jobs that are intrinsically rewarding, we seem to reach the point at which productivity begins to decline more quickly than in the past.

There is still a segment of the workforce that prefers the routine and repetitiveness of highly specialized jobs. Some individuals want work that makes minimal intellectual demands and provides the security of routine; for them, high work specialization is a source of job satisfaction. The question, of course, is whether they represent 2 percent of the workforce or 52 percent. Given that some self-selection operates in the choice of careers, we might conclude that negative behavioural outcomes from high specialization are most likely to surface in professional jobs occupied by individuals with high needs for personal growth and diversity.

It is probably safe to say no evidence supports a relationship between span of control and employee performance. Although it is intuitively attractive to argue that large spans might lead to higher employee performance because they provide more distant supervision and more opportunity for personal initiative, the research fails to support this notion. At this point it's impossible to state that any particular span of control is best for producing high performance or high satisfaction among employees. Some people like to be left alone; others prefer the security of a boss who is quickly available at all times. Consistent with several of the contingency theories of leadership discussed in Chapter 20, we would expect factors such as employees' experiences and abilities and the degree of structure in their tasks to explain when wide or narrow spans of control are likely to contribute to their performance and job satisfaction. However, some evidence indicates that a manager's job satisfaction increases as the number of employees supervised increases.

We find fairly strong evidence linking centralization and job satisfaction. In general, organizations that are less centralized have a greater amount of autonomy. And autonomy appears positively related to job satisfaction. But, again, individual differences surface. While one employee may value freedom, another may find autonomous environments frustratingly ambiguous.

Our conclusion: To maximize employee performance and satisfaction, managers must take into account individual differences, such as experience, personality, and the work task. Culture should factor in, too.

We can draw one obvious insight: People don't select employers randomly. They are attracted to, are selected by, and stay with organizations that suit their personal characteristics.[40] Job candidates who prefer predictability are likely to seek out and take employment in mechanistic structures, and those who want autonomy are more likely to end up in an organic structure. So the effect of structure on employee behaviour is undoubtedly reduced when the selection process facilitates proper matching of individual characteristics with organizational characteristics.

GLOBAL IMPLICATIONS

When we think about how culture influences how organizations are to be structured, several questions come to mind. First, does culture really matter to organizational structure? Second, do employees in different countries vary in their perceptions of different types of organizational structures? Finally, how do cultural considerations fit with our discussion of the boundaryless organization? Let's tackle each question in turn.

Culture and Organizational Structure

Does culture really affect organizational structure? The answer might seem obvious—yes!—but there are reasons it may not matter as much as you think. The US model of business has been very influential on organizational structures in other countries. Moreover, US and Canadian structures themselves have been influenced by structures in other countries (especially Japan, Great Britain, and Germany). However, cultural concerns still might be important. Bureaucratic structures still dominate in many parts of Europe and Asia. One management expert argues that US management often places too much emphasis on individual leadership, which may be jarring in countries where decision making is more decentralized.[41]

Culture and Employee Structure Preferences

Although research is slim, it does suggest national culture influences the preference for structure.[42] Organizations that operate with people from high power-distance cultures, such as Greece, France, and most of Latin America, find that their employees are much more accepting of mechanistic structures than are employees from low power-distance countries. So consider cultural differences along with individual differences when predicting how structure will affect employee performance and satisfaction.

Culture and the Boundaryless Organization

When fully operational, the boundaryless organization also breaks down barriers created by geography. Today most large US companies and some Canadian companies see themselves as global corporations and may well do as much business overseas as at home (as does Coca-Cola, for example). As a result, many companies struggle with the problem of how to incorporate geographic regions into their structure. The boundaryless organization provides one solution because it considers geography more of a tactical, logistical issue than a structural one. In short, the goal of the boundaryless organization is to break down cultural barriers.

One way to do so is through strategic alliances. Firms such as NEC Corporation, Boeing, and Apple each have strategic alliances or joint partnerships with dozens of companies. These alliances blur the distinction between one organization and another as employees work on joint projects. Moreover, some companies allow customers to perform functions previously done by management. Some AT&T units receive bonuses

LESSONS LEARNED

- Organizational structure determines the level of autonomy an individual has.
- Strategy, organizational size, technology, and environment determine an organization's structure.
- There is no one best structure, and individuals differ in their preference of organizational structure.

based on customer evaluations of the teams that serve them. Finally, teleworking is blurring organizational boundaries. The security analyst with Merrill Lynch who does his job from his ranch in Alberta or the software designer in Winnipeg who works for a Waterloo firm are just two of the millions of employees who work outside the physical boundaries of their employers' premises.

OB on the EDGE

Stress @Work

Long-haul truck driving is not an easy job. Drivers face heavy traffic, demanding schedules, challenges accessing healthy food, and fatigue. Surrey, BC-based Coastal Pacific Xpress (CPx) looks after its drivers and, for this, won an Award of Excellence from the British Columbia Medical Association in June 2011.[1] The award specifically noted CPx's "Focus on Fitness Friday," where drivers and staff get healthy meals and snacks, and are encouraged to exercise by walking. All employees have free access to pedometers, and CPx donates $2 to charity for every 1000 steps recorded on its pedometers on Focus on Fitness Fridays.

Employees are also encouraged to track their heart rate, Body Mass Index, weight, oxygen saturation levels, and other vital signs using on-site LifeClinic kiosks. Laurie Forbes, vice-president of administration, notes that "healthy drivers cope better with stress, have less downtime due to illness, are better-rested and safer drivers."

Being sensitive to workplace stress is putting increased responsibilities on managers. When Janie Toivanen was diagnosed with severe depression, she approached her employer, Vancouver-based Electronic Arts (EA) Canada, to request indefinite stress leave.[2] Instead, just days later, she was fired. After working there for six years, she "felt like she had been thrown away." Toivanen thought EA cared about its employees, and could not believe it would not do anything to help her as she struggled to overcome her illness. She subsequently filed a complaint with the BC Human Rights Tribunal and was awarded, among other things, $20 000 for injury to her dignity, feelings, and self-respect and $19 744 in severance pay.

Are We Overstressed?

Stress appears to be a major factor in the lives of many Canadians. A 2010 survey conducted by Statistics Canada found that Canadians experience a great deal of stress, with those from Quebec topping the list.[3] The survey also found that women were more stressed than men. The inset *Stressed Quite a Lot, 2010* reports the findings.

The impact of stress on the Canadian economy is huge, costing an estimated $33 billion a year in lost productivity, and considerably more than that in medical costs. To address these costs, Prime Minister Stephen Harper announced the creation of the Mental Health Commission of Canada in 2007. At the launch of the commission, Harper noted that mental health disorders are "now the fastest-growing category of disability insurance claims in Canada."[4]

Shannon Wagner, a clinical psychologist and a specialist in workplace stress research at the University of Northern British Columbia, notes that changes in the nature of jobs may be increasing the levels of stress in the workplace. While many jobs are not as physically demanding, they are often more mentally demanding. "A lot of people now are identifying techno-stress and the 24/7 workday, which we didn't have even 10 or 15 years ago, this feeling of being constantly plugged in, of checking email 500 times a day."[5]

An additional problem is that employees are increasingly asked to donate labour to their employers, according to Professor Linda Duxbury of Carleton University's Sprott School of Business and Professor Chris Higgins of the Richard Ivey School of Business at the University of Western Ontario. Their survey of 31 571 Canadians found that in the previous month half of them had worked an extra 2.5 days of unpaid overtime, and more than half had donated 3.5 days of working at home to catch up.[6] Canadians are frequently reporting that they want more balance in their work and family lives.[7]

Jobs and Stress Levels

How do jobs rate in terms of stress? The inset *The Most and Least Stressful Jobs* on page 124 shows how selected occupations ranked in an evaluation of 250 jobs. Among the criteria used in the rankings were overtime, quotas, deadlines, competitiveness, physical demands, environmental conditions, hazards encountered, initiative required, stamina required, win-lose situations, and working in the public eye.

Stress is not something that can be ignored in the workplace. A recent poll by Ipsos Reid found that 66 percent of the CEOs surveyed said that "stress, burnout or other physical and mental health issues" have a negative effect on productivity.[8] A study conducted in 15 developed countries found that individuals who report that they are stressed in their jobs are 25 percent more likely to quit and 25 percent more likely to miss days of work.[9] Canadian, French, and Swedish employees reported the highest stress levels. In Canada, 41 percent of employees noted that they "often" or "always" experience stress at work, while only 31 percent of employees in Denmark and Switzerland reported stress levels this high. "In the wake of years of fiscal downsizing, workers across all sectors are working harder and longer than ever while trying to balance family responsibilities," said Scott Morris, former head of the Vancouver-based consulting firm Priority Management Systems.[10] Daniel Ondrack, a professor at the Rotman School of Management at the

Stressed Quite a Lot, 2010 (Percent)

	Males	Females
Canada	22.0	24.9
Newfoundland and Labrador	16.6	14.6
Prince Edward Island	12.4*	14.3
Nova Scotia	17.0	21.1
New Brunswick	18.6	21.9
Quebec	24.0	29.5
Ontario	22.2	25.1
Manitoba	17.7	23.3
Saskatchewan	19.1	19.5
Alberta	21.2	23.1
British Columbia	23.0	22.6
Yukon	15.7	20.4
Northwest Territories	14.9	19.0*
Nunavut	18.7*	17.7*

*Use with caution.

Note: Population aged 15 and older who reported experiencing quite a lot or extreme stress most days of their lives.

Source: From "Perceived life stress, quite a lot, by sex, by province and territory," Statistics Canada's Summary Tables, http://www40.statcan.ca/l01/cst01/health107b-eng.htm, July 14, 2011

University of Toronto, notes that "one of the major reasons for absenteeism is the logistical problems workers face in just getting to work, including transporting children to school and finding daycare. Single parents, especially female, have to juggle all the daycare and family responsibilities, and that makes it extremely difficult for people to keep up with work demands."[11]

What Is Stress?

Stress is a dynamic condition in which an individual is confronted with an opportunity, demand, or resource related to what the individual desires and for which the outcome is perceived to be both uncertain and important.[12] This is a complicated definition. Let's look at its components more closely.

Stress is not necessarily bad in and of itself. Although stress is typically discussed in a negative context, it also has a positive value.[13] Consider, for example, the superior performance that an athlete or stage performer gives in "clutch" situations. Such individuals often use stress positively to rise to the occasion and perform at or near their maximum. Similarly, many professionals see the pressures of heavy workloads and deadlines as positive challenges that enhance the quality of their work and the satisfaction they get from their job. In short, some stress can be good, and some can be bad.

Recently, researchers have argued that *challenge stressors*—or stressors associated with workload, pressure to complete tasks, and time urgency—operate quite differently from *hindrance stressors*—or stressors that keep you from reaching your goals (red tape, office politics, confusion over job responsibilities). Although research has just started to accumulate, early evidence suggests that challenge stressors produce less strain than hindrance stressors.[14] Role ambiguity, role con-

flict, role overload, job insecurity, environmental uncertainty, and situational constraints were all consistently negatively related to job performance.[16] Evidence also suggests that challenge stress improves job performance in a supportive work environment, whereas hindrance stress reduces job performance in all work environments.[17] It appears that employees who have a stronger affective commitment to their organization can transfer psychological stress into greater focus and higher sales performance, whereas employees with low levels of commitment perform worse under stress.[18]

More typically, stress is associated with *demands* and *resources*. Demands are responsibilities, pressures, obligations, and even uncertainties that individuals face in the workplace. Resources are things within an individual's control that can be used to resolve the demands. For example, when you take a test, you feel stress because you confront opportunities and performance pressures. To the extent that you can apply resources to the demands on you—such as being prepared for the exam—you will feel less stress.

Under the demands-resources perspective, having resources to cope with stress is just as important in offsetting it as demands are in increasing it.[19]

Causes of Stress

The workplace provides a variety of stressors:[20]

- *Environmental factors.* Uncertainty is the biggest reason people have trouble coping with organizational changes.[21] Two types of environmental uncertainty are economic and technological. Changes in the business cycle create *economic uncertainties*. When the economy is contracting, for example, people become increasingly anxious about their job security. Because new innovations can make an employee's skills and experience obsolete in a very short time, computers, robotics, automation, and similar forms of *technological change* are a threat to many people and cause them stress.

- *Organizational factors.* There is no shortage of factors within an organization that can cause

---

The Most and Least Stressful Jobs

How do jobs rate in terms of stress? According to *Health* magazine, the top 10 most and least stressful jobs are as follows.[15]

Ten Most Stressful Jobs
1. Inner-city high school teacher
2. Police officer
3. Miner
4. Air traffic controller
5. Medical intern
6. Stockbroker
7. Journalist
8. Customer-service/ complaint worker
9. Secretary
10. Waiter

Ten Least Stressful Jobs
1. Forester
2. Bookbinder
3. Telephone line worker
4. Toolmaker
5. Millwright
6. Repairperson
7. Civil engineer
8. Therapist
9. Natural scientist
10. Sales representative

stress. Pressures to avoid errors or complete tasks in a limited time, work overload, a demanding and insensitive boss, and unpleasant co-workers are a few examples. We have categorized these factors around task, role, and interpersonal demands.[22]

- *Task demands* relate to a person's job. They include the design of the individual's job (autonomy, task variety, degree of automation), working conditions, and the physical work layout. Assembly lines can put pressure on people when they perceive the line's speed to be excessive. Working in an overcrowded room or in a visible location where noise and interruptions are constant can increase anxiety and stress.[23] As customer service grows ever more important, emotional labour becomes a source of stress.[24] Do you think you could put on a happy face when you are having a bad day?

- *Role demands* relate to pressures placed on a person as a function of the particular role he or she plays in the organization.

- *Interpersonal demands* are pressures created by other employees. Lack of social support from colleagues and poor interpersonal relationships can cause stress, especially among employees with a high social need. A rapidly growing body of research has also shown that negative coworker and supervisor behaviours, including fights, bullying, incivility, racial harassment, and sexual harassment, are especially strongly related to stress at work.[25]

- *Personal factors.* The typical individual works about 40 to 50 hours a week. But the experiences and problems that people encounter in the other 120-plus nonwork hours can spill over to the job. Our final category, then, encompasses factors in the employee's personal life: family issues, personal economic problems, and personality characteristics.

- National surveys consistently show that people hold *family* and personal relationships dear. Marital difficulties, the breaking off of a relationship, caring for elderly parents, and discipline troubles with children create stress employees often cannot leave at the front door when they arrive at work.[26]

- Regardless of income level—people who make $100 000 per year seem to have as much trouble handling their finances as those who earn $20 000—some people are poor money managers or have wants that exceed their earning capacity. The *economic* problems of overextended financial resources create stress and take attention away from work.

- Studies in three diverse organizations found that participants who reported stress symptoms before beginning a job accounted for most of the variance in stress symptoms reported nine months later.[27] The researchers concluded that some people may have an inherent tendency to accentuate negative aspects of the world in general. If this is true, then stress symptoms expressed on the job may actually originate in the person's *personality*.

When we review stressors individually, it's easy to overlook that stress is an additive phenomenon—it builds up.[28] Each new and persistent stressor adds to an individual's stress level. A single stressor may seem relatively unimportant in and of itself, but if it is added to an already high level of stress, it can be "the straw that breaks the camel's back."

Consequences of Stress

Stress manifests itself in a number of ways, such as high blood pressure, ulcers, irritability, difficulty in making routine decisions, loss of appetite, accident proneness, and the like. These symptoms can be placed under three general categories: physiological, psychological, and behavioural symptoms.[30]

- *Physiological symptoms.* Most early research concerned with stress was

---

FACTBOX

- About 8% of full-time employees in Canada missed work in any given week for personal reasons in 2010.

- The average employee missed 8 days of work in 2000, compared with 9.1 days in 2010, which means that about 100 million work-days were lost in 2010 due to absenteeism.

- In 2008, 21.2% of males and 23.4% of females aged 15 or older reported that most days were "quite a bit or extremely stressful."

- 24% of employed Canadians did not take all of their vacation days in 2009, giving back an average of 2.03 days of unused vacation time.[29]

directed at physiological symptoms because most researchers in this area were specialists in the health and medical sciences. Their work led to the conclusion that stress could create changes in metabolism, increase heart and breathing rates, increase blood pressure, cause headaches, and induce heart attacks. Because symptoms are complex and difficult to measure objectively, researchers concluded there were few, if any, consistent relationships.[31] More recently, some evidence suggests stress may have harmful physiological effects. One study linked stressful job demands to increased susceptibility to upper respiratory illnesses and poor immune system functioning, especially for individuals with low self-efficacy.[32] Furthermore, stress hits workers at all ages, and it is not unusual for employees in their 20s, 30s, and 40s to suffer long-term disabilities, claiming illnesses that are either psychiatric (such as depression) or more difficult to diagnose (such as chronic fatigue syndrome or fibromyalgia, a musculoskeletal discomfort). The increase in disability claims may be the result of downsizing taking its toll on the psyches of those in the workforce.[33]

- *Psychological symptoms.* Job dissatisfaction is "the simplest and most obvious psychological effect" of stress.[34] But stress also shows itself in other psychological states—for instance, tension, anxiety, irritability, boredom, and procrastination.

    The evidence indicates that when people are placed in jobs that make multiple and conflicting demands or in which there is a lack of clarity as to the person's duties, authority, and responsibilities, both stress and dissatisfaction increase.[35] Similarly, the less control people

have over the pace of their work, the greater the stress and dissatisfaction. Although more research is needed to clarify the relationship, jobs providing a low level of variety, significance, autonomy, feedback, and identity create stress and reduce satisfaction and involvement in the job.[36]

- *Behavioural symptoms.* Behaviourally related stress symptoms include changes in productivity, absence, and turnover, as well as changes in eating habits, increased smoking or consumption of alcohol, rapid speech, fidgeting, and sleep disorders. More recently, stress has been linked to aggression and violence in the workplace.

Why Do Individuals Differ in Their Experience of Stress?

Some people thrive on stressful situations, while others are overwhelmed by them. What differentiates people in terms of their ability to handle stress? What individual difference variables moderate the relationship between *potential* stressors and *experienced* stress? At least four variables—perception, job experience, social support, and personality—are relevant.

- *Perception.* Individuals react in response to their *perception* of reality rather than to reality itself. Perception, therefore, moderates the relationship between a potential stress condition and an employee's reaction to it. Layoffs may cause one person to fear losing his job, while another sees an opportunity to get a large severance allowance and start her own business.[37] So stress potential does not lie in objective conditions; instead it lies

in an employee's interpretation of those conditions.

- *Job experience.* Experience on the job tends to be negatively related to work stress. Two explanations have been offered.[38] First is selective withdrawal. Voluntary turnover is more probable among people who experience more stress. Therefore, people who remain with the organization longer are those with more stress-resistant traits or those who are more resistant to the stress characteristics of their organization. Second, people eventually develop coping mechanisms to deal with stress. Because this takes time, senior members of the organization are more likely to be fully adapted and should experience less stress.

- *Social support.* Collegial relationships with co-workers or supervisors can buffer the impact of stress.[39] Social support helps ease the negative effects of even high-strain jobs. Outside the job, involvement with family, friends, and community can provide the support if it is missing at work.

- *Personality.* Personality affects not only the degree to which people experience stress but also how they cope with it. Perhaps the most widely studied personality trait in stress is *Type A personality*, discussed in Chapter 2. Type A—particularly that aspect that manifests itself in hostility and anger—is associated with increased levels of stress and risk for heart disease.[40] People who are quick to anger, maintain a persistently hostile outlook, and project a cynical mistrust of others are at increased risk of experiencing stress in situations. Stressed Type As recover from stressful situations slower than Type B personalities, which suggests Type A individuals

tend to have higher rates of death associated with hypertension, coronary heart disease, and coronary artery disease.[41]

How Do We Manage Stress?

Below we discuss ways that individuals can manage stress, and what programs organizations use to help employees manage stress.

Individual Approaches

An employee can take personal responsibility for reducing his or her stress level. Individual strategies that have proven effective include time management techniques, physical exercise, relaxation techniques, and a close social support network.

- *Time management.* Many people manage their time poorly. The well-organized employee, like the well-organized student, can often accomplish twice as much as the person who is poorly organized. So understanding and using basic time management principles can help individuals cope better with tensions created by job demands.[42] A few of the more well-known time management principles are (1) making daily lists of activities to be accomplished; (2) prioritizing activities by importance and urgency; (3) scheduling activities according to the priorities set; and (4) knowing your daily productivity cycle and handling the most demanding parts of your job during the high part of your cycle, when you are most alert and productive.[43]

- *Physical activity.* Physicians have recommended noncompetitive physical exercise, such as aerobics, walking, jogging, swimming, and riding a bicycle as a way to deal with excessive stress levels. These forms of physical exercise increase heart capacity, lower at-rest heart rate, provide a mental diversion from work pressures, and slow the physical and mental effects of aging.[44]

- *Relaxation techniques.* Individuals can teach themselves to reduce tension through relaxation techniques such as meditation, hypnosis, and biofeedback. The objective is to reach a state of deep relaxation, in which you feel somewhat detached from the immediate environment and from body sensations.[45] Deep relaxation for 15 or 20 minutes a day releases tension and provides a pronounced sense of peacefulness, as well as significant changes in heart rate, blood pressure, and other physiological factors.

- *Building social supports.* Having friends, family, or colleagues to talk to provides an outlet when stress levels become excessive. Expanding your social support network provides you with someone to listen to your problems and to offer a more objective perspective on the situation.

The inset *Tips for Reducing Stress* offers additional ideas for managing stress.

Organizational Approaches

Employees who work at Montreal-based Ericsson Canada, a global telecommunications supplier, have access to a comprehensive wellness program. They can engage in activities that address their intellectual, emotional, social, physical, and spiritual well-being. "The program has really evolved over the years," says Louise Leonhardt, manager of human resources. "We've found it helps people balance their life, just like the on-site daycare does."

Employees who work at Toronto-based BCS Group, a publishing, advertising, and public relations agency, receive biweekly shiatsu massages, paid for by the company. The company spends about $700 a month for the massages, equivalent to the amount it used to spend providing coffee to the employees. "It's in my company's best interest to have my employees be healthy," says Caroline Tapp-McDougall, BCS Group publisher.[47]

Most firms that have introduced wellness programs have found significant benefits. Health Canada reports that businesses get back $3.39 for each corporate dollar they invest in wellness initiatives. For individuals with three to five risk factors (such as

Tips for Reducing Stress

- At least two or three times a week, spend time with supportive friends or family.
- Ask for support when you are under pressure. This is a sign of health, not weakness.
- If you have spiritual or religious beliefs, increase or maintain your involvement.
- Use a variety of methods to reduce stress. Consider exercise, nutrition, hobbies, positive thinking, and relaxation techniques such as meditation or yoga.[46]

high cholesterol, being overweight, or smoking) the return was $2.04 for each dollar spent.[48] The savings come about because there is less turnover, greater productivity, and reduced medical claims.[49] While many Canadian businesses report having wellness initiatives, only 24 percent have "fully implemented wellness strategies" (which includes multi-year goals and an evaluation of results), according to a 2010 survey.[50]

So what can organizations do to reduce employee stress? In general, strategies to reduce stress include improved processes for choosing employees, placement of employees in appropriate jobs, realistic goal setting, designing jobs with employee needs and skills in mind, increased employee involvement, improved organizational communication, offering employee sabbaticals, and, as mentioned, establishment of corporate wellness programs.

Certain jobs are more stressful than others, but individuals also differ in their response to stress situations. We know, for example, that individuals with little experience or an external locus of control tend to be more prone to stress. Selection and placement decisions should take these facts into consideration. Although management should not restrict hiring to only experienced individuals with an internal locus of control, such individuals may adapt better to high-stress jobs and perform those jobs more effectively.

Individuals perform better when they have specific and challenging goals and receive feedback on how well they are progressing toward them.[51] Goals can reduce stress as well as provide motivation.[52] Specific goals that are perceived as attainable clarify performance expectations. Additionally, goal feedback reduces uncertainties as to actual job performance. The result is

Toward Less Stressful Work

- Avoid high-stress jobs—such as stockbroker, customer service/complaint worker, police officer, waiter, medical intern, secretary, and air traffic controller—unless you are confident in your ability to handle stress.

- If you do experience stress at work, try to find a job that has plenty of control (so you can decide how to perform your work) and supportive co-workers.

- Lack of money is the top stressor reported by people under age 30, so pursue a career that pays you well but does not have a high degree of stress.[53]

less employee frustration, role ambiguity, and stress.

Redesigning jobs to give employees more responsibility, more meaningful work, more autonomy, and increased feedback can reduce stress because these factors give the employee greater control over work activities and lessen dependence on others. Of course, not all employees want jobs with increased responsibility. The right design for employees with a low need for growth might be less responsibility and increased specialization. If individuals prefer structure and routine, more structured jobs should also reduce uncertainties and stress levels.

Role stress is detrimental to a large extent because employees feel uncertain about goals, expectations, how they will be evaluated, and the like. By giving these employees a voice in the decisions that directly affect their job performance, management can increase employee control and reduce role stress. So managers should consider *increasing employee involvement* in decision making.[54]

Increasing formal organizational communication with employees reduces uncertainty by lessening role ambiguity and role conflict. Given the

importance that perceptions play in moderating the stress-response relationship, management can also use effective communication as a means to shape employee perceptions. Remember that what employees categorize as demands, threats, or opportunities are merely interpretations, and those interpretations can be affected by the symbols and actions communicated by management.

Some employees need an occasional escape from the frenetic pace of their work. In recent years, companies such as Charles Schwab, DuPont, L.L.Bean, Nike, and 3Com have begun to provide extended voluntary leaves.[55] These *sabbaticals*—ranging in length from a few weeks to several months—allow employees to travel, relax, or pursue personal projects that consume time beyond normal vacation weeks. Proponents say that these sabbaticals can revive and rejuvenate workers who might be headed for burnout.

Our final suggestion is to offer organizationally supported wellness programs. These typically provide workshops to help people quit smoking, control alcohol use, lose weight, eat better, and develop a regular

exercise program; they focus on the employee's total physical and mental condition.[56] A study of 36 programs designed to reduce stress (including wellness programs) showed that interventions to help employees reframe stressful situations and use active coping strategies led to an appreciable reduction in stress levels.[57] Most wellness programs assume that employees need to take personal responsibility for their physical and mental health and that the organization is merely a means to that end. The inset *Toward Less Stressful Work* offers additional ideas.

RESEARCH EXERCISES

1. Look for data on stress levels in other countries. How do these data compare with the Canadian data presented above? Are the sources of stress the same in different countries? What might you conclude about how stress affects people in different cultures?

2. Find out what three Canadian organizations in three different industries have done to help employees manage stress. Are there common themes in these programs? Did you find any unusual programs? To what extent are these programs tailored to the needs of the employees in those industries?

YOUR PERSPECTIVE

1. Think of all the technical avenues enabling employees to be connected 24/7 to the workplace: email, texting, company web pages. A generation ago, most employees could go home after a day at work and not be "on call." What are the positive benefits of this change? What are the down-

F A C E O F F

When organizations provide on-site daycare facilities, they are filling a needed role in parents' lives, and making it easier for parents to attend to their job demands rather than worry about child-care arrangements.

When employees expect organizations to provide child care, they are shifting their responsibilities to their employers, rather than keeping their family needs and concerns private. Moreover, it is unfair to offer child-care benefits when not all employees have children.

sides? As an employee facing the demand to "stay connected" to your workplace, how would you try to maintain a balance in your life?

2. How much responsibility should individuals take for managing their own stress? To what extent should organizations become involved in the personal lives of their employees when trying to help them manage stress? What are the pros and cons for whether employees or organizations take responsibility for managing stress?

WANT TO KNOW MORE?

If you are wondering how stressed you are, go to **www.heartandstroke.ca** and click on "Health Information," "Heart Disease," and then "Other Resources for Heart Disease" to take a stress test. The site also offers tips on reducing stress.

7

Designing and Analyzing Jobs

SECTION THREE

JOB ANALYSIS, RECRUITMENT

AND SELECTION

Fundamentals of Job Analysis

Job analysis is a process by which information about jobs is systematically gathered and organized. Job analysis is sometimes called the cornerstone of HRM.

A **job** consists of a group of related activities and duties. Ideally, the duties of a job should be clear and distinct from those of other jobs, and they should involve natural units of work that are similar and related. This approach helps to minimize conflict and enhance employee performance. A job may be held by a single employee or may have a number of incumbents. The collection of tasks and responsibilities performed by one person is known as a **position**. To clarify, in a department with 1 supervisor, 1 clerk, 40 assemblers, and 3 tow-motor operators, there are 45 positions and 4 jobs.

Uses of Job Analysis Information

Job analysis is the procedure firms use to determine the tasks, duties, and responsibilities of each job, and the human attributes (in terms of knowledge, skills, and abilities) required to perform it. Once this information has been gathered it is used for developing job descriptions (what the job entails) and job specifications (what the human requirements are). As illustrated in Exhibit 7-1, the information gathered, evaluated, and summarized through job analysis is the basis for a number of interrelated HRM activities.

Human Resources Planning

Knowing the actual requirements of an organization's various jobs is essential for planning future staffing needs. When this information is combined with knowledge about the skills and qualifications of current employees, it is possible to determine which jobs can be filled internally and which will require external recruitment.

Recruitment and Selection

The job description and job specification information should be used to decide what sort of person to recruit and hire. Identifying bona fide occupational requirements and ensuring that all activities related to recruitment and selection (such as advertising, screening, and testing) are based on these requirements is necessary for legal compliance in all Canadian jurisdictions.

job A group of related activities and duties, held by a single employee or a number of incumbents.

position The collection of tasks and responsibilities performed by one person.

job analysis The procedure for determining the tasks, duties, and responsibilities of each job, and the human attributes (in terms of knowledge, skills, and abilities) required to perform it.

EXHIBIT 7-1 Uses of Job Analysis Information

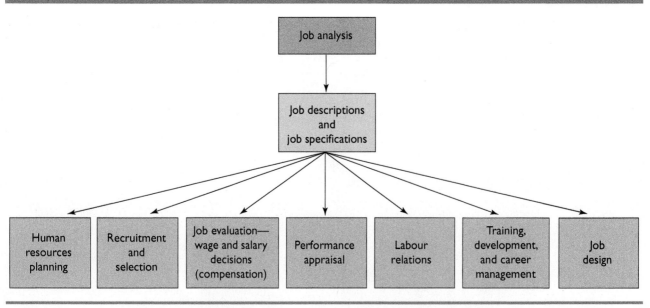

Compensation

Job analysis information is also essential for determining the relative value of and appropriate compensation for each job. Job evaluation should be based on the required skills, physical and mental demands, responsibilities, and working conditions—all assessed through job analysis. The relative value of jobs is one of the key factors used to determine appropriate compensation and justify pay differences if challenged under human rights or pay equity legislation. Information about the actual job duties is also necessary to determine whether a job qualifies for overtime pay and for maximum-hours purposes, as specified in employment standards legislation.

Performance Management

To be legally defensible, the criteria used to assess employee performance must be directly related to the duties and responsibilities identified through job analysis. For many jobs involving routine tasks, especially those of a quantifiable nature, performance standards are determined through job analysis. For more complex jobs, performance standards are often jointly established by employees and their supervisors. To be realistic and achievable, such standards should be based on actual job requirements as identified through job analysis.

Labour Relations

In unionized environments, the job descriptions developed from the job analysis information are generally subject to union approval before being finalized. Such union-approved job descriptions then become the basis for classifying jobs and bargaining over wages, performance criteria, and working conditions. Once approved, significant changes to job descriptions may have to be negotiated.

Training, Development, and Career Management

By comparing the knowledge, skills, and abilities (KSAs) that employees bring to the job with those that are identified by job analysis, managers can determine gaps that require training programs. Having accurate information about jobs also means that employees can prepare for future advancement by identifying gaps between their current KSAs and those specified for the jobs to which they aspire.

Restructuring

Job analysis is useful for ensuring that all of the duties that need to be done have actually been assigned and for identifying areas of overlap within duties. Also, having an accurate description of each job may lead to the identification of unnecessary requirements, areas of conflict or dissatisfaction, or health and safety concerns that can be eliminated through job redesign or restructuring.

Steps in Job Analysis

There are six critical steps involved in analyzing jobs. Organizations collect details about jobs on a relatively continuous basis for many uses, such as the ones outlined above (planning, recruitment and selection, performance management, compensation, and so on). Traditionally, organizations would first determine the intended use of job analysis information, since this determined the types of data that should be collected and the techniques used. However, this preliminary step has been largely abolished in practice given the diverse uses of job analysis information and the continual need for such information.

The six steps involved in job analysis are as follows:

1. Relevant organizational information is reviewed.

2. Jobs are selected to be analyzed.

3. Using one or more job analysis techniques, data are collected on job activities.

4. The information collected in Step 3 is then verified and modified, if required.

5. Job descriptions and specifications are developed based on the verified information.

6. The information is then communicated and updated on an as-needed basis.

The structure of this chapter aligns with the six steps of job analysis.

Step 1: Review Relevant Background Information

An organization consists of one or more employees who perform various tasks. The relationships between people and tasks must be structured so that the organization achieves its strategic goals in an efficient and effective manner through a motivated and engaged workforce. There are many ways to distribute work among employees, and careful consideration of how this is done can provide a strategic advantage over competitors.

Organizational structure refers to the formal relationships among jobs in an organization. An **organization chart** is often used to depict the structure. As illustrated in Exhibit 7-2, the chart indicates the types of departments established and the title of each manager's job. By means of connecting lines, it clarifies the chain of command and shows who is accountable to whom. An organization chart presents a "snapshot" of the firm at a particular point in time, but it does not provide details about actual communication patterns, degree of supervision, amount of power and authority, or specific duties and responsibilities. In the example provided in Figure 7.2, there may be the expectation that Auditor Plant A will have to report some information to Manager Plant A. Often an organizational chart will exclude this information or identify secondary reporting responsibilities using a dotted line.

organizational structure The formal relationships among jobs in an organization.

organization chart A "snapshot" of the firm, depicting the organization's structure in chart form at a particular point in time.

Online Organization Charts
www.nakisa.com

EXHIBIT 7-2 A Sample Organization Chart

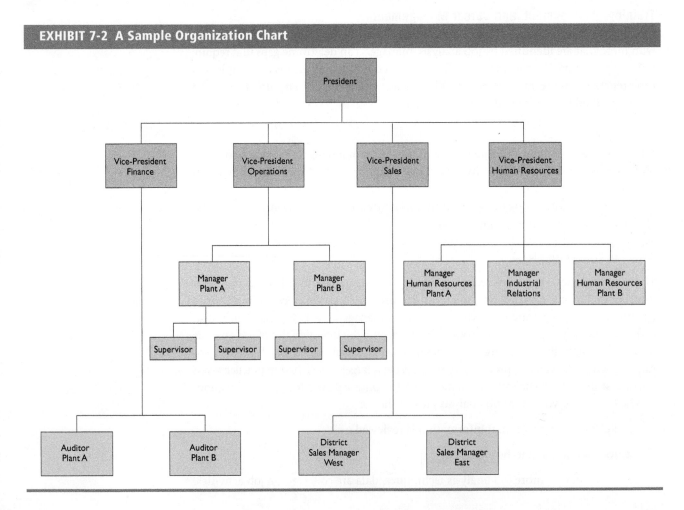

Designing an organization involves choosing a structure that is appropriate given the company's strategic goals. Exhibit 7-3 depicts three common types of organizational structure: bureaucratic, flat, and matrix. In flatter organizations, managers have

EXHIBIT 7-3 Bureaucratic, Flat, and Matrix Organizational Structures

Structure	Characteristics

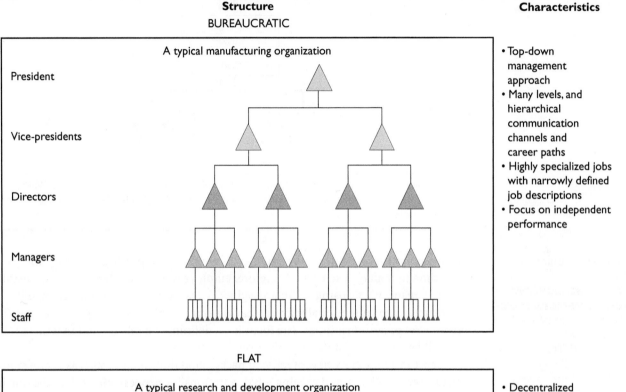

BUREAUCRATIC

A typical manufacturing organization

President
Vice-presidents
Directors
Managers
Staff

- Top-down management approach
- Many levels, and hierarchical communication channels and career paths
- Highly specialized jobs with narrowly defined job descriptions
- Focus on independent performance

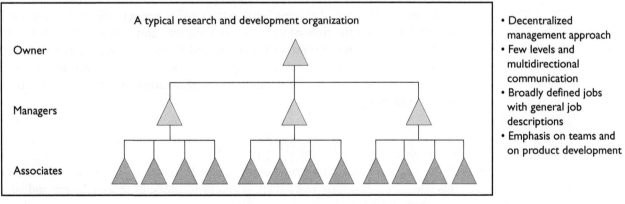

FLAT

A typical research and development organization

Owner
Managers
Associates

- Decentralized management approach
- Few levels and multidirectional communication
- Broadly defined jobs with general job descriptions
- Emphasis on teams and on product development

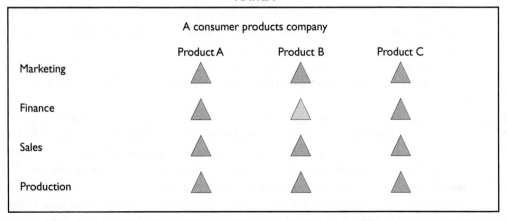

MATRIX

A consumer products company

Product A   Product B   Product C

Marketing
Finance
Sales
Production

- Each job has two components: functional and product
- Finance personnel for product B are responsible to both the finance executive and the product B executive

EXHIBIT 7-4 Process Chart for Analyzing a Job's Workflow

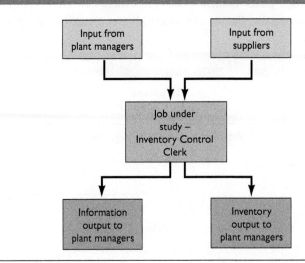

Source: Henderson, Richard I. (ed.), *Compensation Management in a Knowledge-based World*, 10th ed. (Upper Saddle River, NJ: Pearson Education, Inc., 2006), p. 114. Reprinted by permission of the publisher.

Example of Online Organization Charts
www.forces.gc.ca/site/about-notresujet/org-eng.asp or http://office.microsoft.com/en-us/templates/business-organizational-chart-TC006088976.aspx

increased spans of control (the number of employees reporting to them) and thus less time to manage each one. Therefore, employees' jobs involve more responsibility. In organizations using self-managed work teams, employees' jobs change daily, so management intentionally avoids having employees view their jobs as a specific, narrow set of responsibilities. The focus is on defining the job at hand in terms of the overall best interests of the organization, as is the case at IKEA.

Step 1 includes the review of relevant background information, such as organization charts, process charts, and existing job descriptions.[1] A **process chart** (like the one in Exhibit 7-4) shows the flow of inputs to and outputs from the job under study. (In Exhibit 7-4, the inventory control clerk is expected to receive inventory from suppliers, take requests for inventory from the two plant managers, provide requested inventory to these managers, and give information to the plant accountant on the status of in-stock inventories.)

Step 2: Select Jobs to be Analyzed

The next step involves the selection of representative positions and jobs to be analyzed. This selection is necessary when there are many incumbents in a single job and when a number of similar jobs are to be analyzed because it would be too time-consuming to analyze every position and job.

Job design is the process of systematically organizing work into the tasks that are required to perform a specific job. An organization's strategy and structure influence the ways in which jobs are designed. In bureaucratic organizations, for example, because a hierarchical division of labour exists, jobs are generally highly specialized. In addition, effective job design also takes into consideration human and technological factors.

In the twenty-first century, the traditional meaning of a "job" as a set of well-defined and clearly delineated responsibilities has changed. Companies are grappling with challenges such as rapid product and technological change, global competition, deregulation, political instability, demographic changes, and a shift to a service economy. This has increased the need for firms to be responsive, flexible, and much more competitive. In turn, the organizational methods managers use to accomplish this have helped weaken this traditional definition of a "job." Requiring employees to limit themselves

process chart A diagram showing the flow of inputs to and outputs from the job under study.

job design The process of systematically organizing work into tasks that are required to perform a specific job.

to narrow jobs runs counter to the need to have them willingly switch from task to task as jobs and team assignments change.

All these changes have led to work becoming more cognitively complex, more team-based and collaborative, more dependent on social skills, more dependent on technological competence, more time pressured, more mobile, and less dependent on geography.[2] This situation has led some organizations to focus on personal competencies and skills in job analysis, hiring, and compensation management, rather than on specific duties and tasks.

The Evolution of Jobs and Job Design

In most organizations, work is divided into manageable units and, ultimately, into jobs that can be performed by employees. The term "job" as it is known today is largely an outgrowth of the efficiency demands of the Industrial Revolution. As the substitution of machine power for people power became more widespread, experts wrote glowingly about the positive correlation between (1) job specialization and (2) productivity and efficiency.[3] The popularity of specialized, short-cycle jobs soared—at least among management experts and managers.

Work simplification evolved from scientific management theory. It is based on the premise that work can be broken down into clearly defined, highly specialized, repetitive tasks to maximize efficiency. This approach to job design involves assigning most of the administrative aspects of work (such as planning and organizing) to supervisors and managers, while giving lower-level employees narrowly defined tasks to perform according to methods established and specified by management.

Work simplification can increase operating efficiency in a stable environment and may be very appropriate in settings employing individuals with intellectual disabilities or those lacking education and training (as in some operations in the developing world); it is not effective, however, in a changing environment in which customers/clients demand custom-designed products and/or high-quality services, or one in which employees want challenging work. Moreover, among educated employees, simplified jobs often lead to lower satisfaction, higher rates of absenteeism and turnover, and sometimes to a demand for premium pay to compensate for the repetitive nature of the work.

Another important contribution of scientific management was the study of work. **Industrial engineering**, which evolved with this movement, is concerned with analyzing work methods and establishing time standards to improve efficiency. Industrial engineers systematically identify, analyze, and time the elements of each job's work cycle and determine which, if any, elements can be modified, combined, rearranged, or eliminated to reduce the time needed to complete the cycle.

Too much emphasis on the concerns of industrial engineering—improving efficiency and simplifying work methods—may result in human considerations being neglected or downplayed. For example, an assembly line, with its simplified and repetitive tasks, embodies the principles of industrial engineering but may lead to repetitive strain injuries, high turnover, and low satisfaction because of the lack of psychological fulfillment. Thus, to be effective, job design must also satisfy human psychological and physiological needs.

By the mid-1900s, reacting to what they viewed as the "dehumanizing" aspects of highly repetitive and specialized jobs, various management theorists proposed ways of broadening the activities employees engaged in. **Job enlargement**, also known as **horizontal loading**, involves assigning workers additional tasks at the same level of responsibility to increase the number of tasks they have to perform. Thus, if the work was assembling chairs, the worker who previously only bolted the seat to the legs might take on the additional tasks of assembling the legs and attaching the back as well. Job enlargement reduces monotony and fatigue by expanding the job cycle and drawing on a wider range of employee skills.

work simplification An approach to job design that involves assigning most of the administrative aspects of work (such as planning and organizing) to supervisors and managers, while giving lower-level employees narrowly defined tasks to perform according to methods established and specified by management.

industrial engineering A field of study concerned with analyzing work methods; making work cycles more efficient by modifying, combining, rearranging, or eliminating tasks; and establishing time standards.

job enlargement (horizontal loading) A technique to relieve monotony and boredom that involves assigning workers additional tasks at the same level of responsibility to increase the number of tasks they have to perform.

Another technique to relieve monotony and employee boredom is **job rotation**. This involves systematically moving employees from one job to another. Although the jobs themselves don't change, workers experience more task variety, motivation, and productivity. The company gains by having more versatile, multiskilled employees who can cover for one another efficiently.

It has also been suggested that the best way to motivate workers is to build opportunities for challenge and achievement into jobs through **job enrichment**, also known as **vertical loading**.[4] This is defined as any effort that makes an employee's job more rewarding or satisfying by adding more meaningful tasks and duties. Job enrichment involves increasing autonomy and responsibility by allowing employees to assume a greater role in the decision-making process.

Enriching jobs can be accomplished through activities such as

- Increasing the level of difficulty and responsibility of the job;
- Assigning workers more authority and control over outcomes;
- Providing feedback about individual or unit job performance directly to employees;
- Adding new tasks requiring training, thereby providing an opportunity for growth; and
- Assigning individuals entire tasks or responsibility for performing a whole job rather than only parts of it, such as conducting an entire background check rather than just checking educational credentials.

Job enrichment is not always the best approach. It is more successful in some jobs and settings than in others; for example, not all employees want additional responsibilities and challenges. Some people prefer routine jobs and may resist job redesign efforts. In addition, job redesign efforts almost always fail when employees lack the physical or mental skills, abilities, or education needed to perform the job.

By the late twentieth century, it became apparent that in addition to considering psychological needs, effective job design also required taking physiological needs and health and safety issues into account. **Ergonomics** seeks to integrate and accommodate the physical needs of workers into the design of jobs. It aims to adapt the entire job system—the work, environment, machines, equipment, and processes—to match human characteristics. Doing so results in eliminating or minimizing product defects, damage to equipment, and worker injuries or illnesses caused by poor work design.

Competency-Based Job Analysis

Not coincidentally, many employers and job analysis experts say traditional job analysis procedures can't go on playing a central role in HR management.[5] Their basic concern is this: In high-performance work environments in which employers need workers to seamlessly move from job to job and exercise self-control, job descriptions based on lists of job-specific duties may actually inhibit (or fail to encourage) the flexible behaviour companies need. Employers are therefore shifting toward newer approaches for describing jobs, such as competency-based analysis.

Competency-based job analysis basically means writing job descriptions based on competencies rather than job duties. It emphasizes what the employee must be capable of doing, rather than a list of the duties he or she must perform. **Competencies** are demonstrable characteristics of a person that enable performance. Job competencies are always observable and measurable behaviours that comprise part of a job. The job's required competencies can be identified by simply completing this sentence: "In order to perform this job competently, the employee should be able to . . ."

Competency-based job analysis means describing the job in terms of the measurable, observable behavioural competencies (knowledge, skills, or behaviours)

---

job rotation A technique to relieve monotony and employee boredom that involves systematically moving employees from one job to another.

job enrichment (vertical loading) Any effort that makes an employee's job more rewarding or satisfying by adding more meaningful tasks and duties.

ergonomics An interdisciplinary approach that seeks to integrate and accommodate the physical needs of workers into the design of jobs. It aims to adapt the entire job system—the work, environment, machines, equipment, and processes—to match human characteristics.

competencies Demonstrable characteristics of a person that enable performance of a job.

competency-based job analysis Describing a job in terms of the measurable, observable behavioural competencies an employee must exhibit to do a job well.

that an employee doing that job must exhibit to do the job well. This contrasts with the traditional way of describing a job in terms of job duties and responsibilities. Traditional job analysis focuses on "what" is accomplished—on duties and responsibilities. Competency-based analysis focuses more on "how" the worker meets the job's objectives or actually accomplishes the work. Traditional job analysis is thus job focused; competency-based analysis is worker focused—specifically, what must he or she be competent to do?

Three Reasons to Use Competency Analysis

There are three reasons to describe jobs in terms of competencies rather than duties. First, as mentioned earlier, traditional job descriptions (with their lists of specific duties) may actually backfire if a *high-performance work system* is the goal. The whole thrust of these systems is to encourage employees to work in a self-motivated way: by organizing the work around teams, by encouraging team members to rotate freely among jobs (each with its own skill set), by pushing more responsibility for things like day-to-day supervision down to the workers, and by organizing work around projects or processes in which jobs may blend or overlap. Employees here must be enthusiastic about learning and moving among jobs. Giving someone a job description with a list of specific duties may simply breed a "that's-not-my-job" attitude by pigeonholing workers too narrowly.

Second, describing the job in terms of the skills, knowledge, and competencies the worker needs is *more strategic*. For example, a company with a strategic emphasis on miniaturization and precision manufacturing should encourage some employees to develop their expertise in these two strategically crucial areas.

Third, measurable skills, knowledge, and competencies support the employer's *performance management process*. Training, appraisals, and rewards should be based on fostering and rewarding the skills and competencies required to achieve work goals. Describing the job in terms of skills and competencies facilitates understanding of those required competencies.

Examples of Competencies

In practice, managers often write paragraph-length competencies for jobs and organize these into two or three clusters. For example, the job's required competencies might include *general or core competencies* (such as reading, writing, and mathematical reasoning), *leadership competencies* (such as leadership, strategic thinking, and teaching others), and *technical/task/functional competencies* (which focus on the specific technical competencies required for specific types of jobs or occupations).

So, some technical competencies for the job of systems engineer might include the following:

- Design complex software applications, establish protocols, and create prototypes.
- Establish the necessary platform requirements to efficiently and completely coordinate data transfer.
- Prepare comprehensive and complete documentation including specifications, flow diagrams, process patrols, and budgets.[6]

Similarly, for a corporate treasurer, technical competencies might include the following:

- Formulate trade recommendations by studying several computer models for currency trends and using various quantitative techniques to determine the financial impact of certain financial trades.
- Recommend specific trades and when to make them.

At a Nissan factory in Tokyo, Japan, workers meet at a productivity session, surrounded by unfinished car frames hanging along the assembly line. Work teams like this are part of the trend toward a multiskilled, cross-functional, self-directed team organization that allows workers greater autonomy in meeting goals. In plants like these, broadly described jobs that emphasize employees' required competencies are replacing narrowly defined jobs.

- Present recommendations and persuade others to follow the recommended course of action.[7] (Note: Exhibiting this competency presumes the treasurer has certain knowledge and skills that one could measure.)

Comparing Traditional versus Competency-Based Job Analysis

In practice, in almost any job description today some of the job's listed duties and responsibilities are competency-based, while most are not. For example, consider the typical duties you might find in a marketing manager's job description. Which of the duties would complete this phrase: "In order to perform this job competently, the employee should be able to . . ."?

Some familiar duties and responsibilities would not easily fit these requirements. For example, "works with writers and artists and oversees copywriting, design, layout, and production of promotional materials" is not particularly measurable. How can the extent to which the employee "works with writers and artists" or "oversees copywriting, design, and layout" be measured? Put another way, in analyzing this job, how would one determine whether the person had been adequately trained to work with writers and artists? In fact, what sort of training would that duty and responsibility even imply? It's not clear at all.

On the other hand, some of the job's typical duties and responsibilities are more easily expressed as competencies. For example, the phrase "to perform this job competently, the employee should be able to . . ." could easily be completed with "conduct marketing surveys on current and new-product concepts; prepare marketing activity reports; and develop and execute marketing plans and programs."

Team-Based Job Designs

A logical outgrowth of job enrichment and the job characteristics model has been the increasing use of **team-based job designs**, which focus on giving a **team**, rather than an individual, a whole and meaningful piece of work to do. Team members are empowered to decide among themselves how to accomplish the work.[8] Often they are cross-trained and then rotated through different tasks. Team-based designs are best suited to flat and matrix organization structures. Increasingly, organizations are using "virtual teams"—people working together effectively and efficiently across boundaries of time and space and using software to make team meetings more productive.[9]

Step 3: Collecting Job Analysis Information

Various qualitative and quantitative techniques are used to collect information about the duties, responsibilities, and requirements of the job; the most important ones will be discussed in this section. In practice, when the information is being used for multiple purposes, ranging from developing recruitment criteria to compensation decisions, several techniques may be used in combination.

Collecting job analysis data usually involves a joint effort by an HR specialist, the incumbent, and the jobholder's supervisor. The HR specialist (an HR manager, job analyst, or consultant) might observe and analyze the work being done and then develop a job description and specification. The supervisor and incumbent generally also get involved, perhaps by filling out questionnaires. The supervisor and incumbent typically review and verify the job analyst's conclusions regarding the job's duties, responsibilities, and requirements.

team-based job designs Job designs that focus on giving a team, rather than an individual, a whole and meaningful piece of work to do and empowering team members to decide among themselves how to accomplish the work.

team A small group of people with complementary skills who work toward common goals for which they hold joint responsibility and accountability.

The Interview

The interview is probably the most widely used method for determining the duties and responsibilities of a job. Three types of interviews are used to collect job analysis data: *individual interviews* with each employee; *group interviews* with employees who have the same job; and *supervisory interviews* with one or more supervisors who are thoroughly knowledgeable about the job being analyzed. The group interview is used when a large number of employees are performing similar or identical work, and it can be a quick and inexpensive way of learning about the job. As a rule, the immediate supervisor attends the group session; if not, the supervisor should be interviewed separately to get that person's perspective on the duties and responsibilities of the job.

The most fruitful interviews follow a structured or checklist format. A job analysis questionnaire, like the one presented in Exhibit 7-5, may be used to interview job incumbents or may be filled out by them. It includes a series of detailed questions regarding such matters as the general purpose of the job; responsibilities and duties; the education, experience, and skills required; physical and mental demands; and working conditions.

Interview Guidelines

When conducting a job analysis interview, supervisors and job analysts should keep several things in mind:

1. The job analyst and supervisor should work together to identify the employees who know the job best as well as those who might be expected to be the most objective in describing their duties and responsibilities.

2. Rapport should be established quickly with the interviewee by using the individual's name, speaking in easily understood language, briefly reviewing the purpose of the interview (job analysis, not performance appraisal), and explaining how the person came to be chosen.

Tips | **FOR THE FRONT LINE**

3. A structured guide or checklist that lists questions and provides spaces for answers should be used. Using a form ensures that crucial questions are identified ahead of time, that complete and accurate information is gathered, and that all interviewers (if there is more than one) glean the same types of data, thereby helping to ensure comparability of results. However, leeway should also be permitted by including some open-ended questions, such as "Is there anything that we didn't cover with our questions?"

4. When duties are not performed in a regular manner—for instance, when the incumbent doesn't perform the same tasks or jobs over and over again many times a day—the incumbent should be asked to list his or her duties *in order of importance and frequency of occurrence*. This will ensure that crucial activities that occur infrequently—like a nurse's occasional emergency room duties—aren't overlooked.

5. The data should be reviewed and verified by both the interviewee and his or her immediate supervisor.

Questionnaire

Having employees or supervisors fill out questionnaires to describe job-related duties and responsibilities is another good method of obtaining job analysis information. There are two major decisions around questionnaires.

The first is determining how structured the questionnaire should be and what questions to include. Some questionnaires involve structured checklists: Each employee is presented with a long list of specific duties or tasks (such as "change and splice wire") and is asked to indicate whether or not he or she performs each and, if so, how much time is

EXHIBIt 7-5 Job Analysis Questionnaire

Job title: _____ Job grade: _____
Department: _____ Location: _____
Prepared by: _____ Date: _____

1. Purpose of job
- What is the purpose of the job? Why does the job exist?

_____
_____
_____

2. Major responsibilities and essential functions (list in order of importance)
- What are the responsibilities?
- How are they done?
- Percentage of time?
- Why is the activity performed?
- What is the measure of success?
- What direction of others is involved?

_____
_____
_____
_____

3. Knowledge
- What techniques and/or practices are necessary? Why?

_____
_____

- List specific education requirement(s).

_____
_____

- List experience requirement(s) and number of years required in each.

_____
_____

- List required licences or certificates.

_____
_____

4. Problem solving and decision making
- List how the jobholder solves problems (i.e., planning, scheduling, creativity techniques, complexity of procedures, degree of independent thinking, and resourcefulness or ingenuity required). List examples of required development of new methods. What are the consequences if problems are not solved?

_____
_____
_____
_____
_____

5. Resource responsibility
- List annual pay of personnel who report to jobholder: _____
- List annual operating budget (include pay): _____

continued

- List any other financial resources (i.e., annual project value/cost, shop order value, total sales, total unit payroll, gross sales booked, purchasing/contracts volume, transportation costs, facilities budget, assets, investment income, program development costs, gross sales billed):

_____

_____

- What is the jobholder's role in planning, organizing, acquiring, or monitoring these resources?

_____

_____

- What is the jobholder's impact in planning, organizing, acquiring, or monitoring these resources?

_____

_____

6. Skills of persuasion
- Describe the communication skills required in the job (e.g., explaining, convincing, selling).
- Are contacts inside or outside?
- What are the levels of contacts?
- What type of oral or written communications are involved?
- Who is communicated with and why?

_____

_____

_____

_____

_____

_____

7. Working conditions
Read the list of working conditions below and put a check mark if they impact on your job.

Condition	Amount of Exposure		
	Occasional	*Regular*	*Frequent*
Dust, dirt, fumes	_____	_____	_____
Heat, cold	_____	_____	_____
Noise	_____	_____	_____
Vibration	_____	_____	_____
Inclement weather	_____	_____	_____
Lighting	_____	_____	_____

Describe any health or safety hazards related to the job.

_____

_____

_____

Source: Carswell's Compensation Guide, ed. D.E. Tyson, CHRP, Tab 3 Job Analysis and Evaluation, Chapter 9, "Job Analysis and Job Descriptions," by T.J. Hackett and E.G. Vogeley, adapted by S. Weeks, P. Drouillard and D.E. Tyson, pages 9–21 and 9–23. Reprinted by permission of Carswell, a division of Thomson Reuters Canada Limited.

normally spent on the task. At the other extreme, the questionnaire can be open-ended and simply ask the employee to describe the major duties of his or her job. In practice, a typical job analysis questionnaire often falls between the two extremes.

The second major decision is determining who will complete the questionnaire. Employees may inflate requirements and supervisors may be unaware of all components of the job. Technology often assists with overcoming this challenge in that questionnaires can be relatively easily and affordably posted online to allow for multiple respondents.

One of the most popular pre-developed, structured job analysis questionnaires is the **Position Analysis Questionnaire (PAQ)**, a portion of which is shown in Exhibit 7-6.[10] The PAQ itself is filled in by a job analyst, who should already be acquainted with the particular job to be analyzed. The PAQ contains 194 items, each of which represents a basic element that may or may not play an important role in the job. The job analyst decides whether each item plays a role in the job and, if so, to what extent (using a five-point scale). If, for example, "written materials" received a rating of four, this would indicate that materials such as books, reports, and office notes play a considerable role in this job.

The advantage of the PAQ is that it provides a quantitative score or profile of the job in terms of how that job rates on six basic dimensions: (1) information input, (2) mental processes, (3) work output (physical activities and tools), (4) relationships with others, (5) job context (the physical and social environment), and (6) other job characteristics (such as pace and structure). Because it allows for the assignment of a quantitative score to each job based on these six dimensions, the PAQ's real strength is in classifying jobs. Results can be used to compare jobs with one another; this information can then be used to determine appropriate pay levels.[11]

Functional Job Analysis (FJA) is also a regularly used pre-established questionnaire that rates a job on responsibilities for data, people, and things from simple to complex. For example, working with "things" literally means the physical interaction with tangibles such as desktop equipment (pencils, paper clips, telephone), groceries, luggage, or a bus. Physical involvement with tangibles such as a telephone may not seem very important in tasks primarily concerned with data (such as data analysis) or people (such as nursing), but its importance is quickly apparent for a worker with a disability. This technique also identifies performance standards and training requirements. Thus, FJA allows the analyst to answer the question: "To do this task and meet these standards, what training does the worker require?"[12]

Observations

Observation involves watching employees perform their work and recording the frequency of behaviours or the nature of performance. This can be done using information that is prepared in advance (structured), or in real time with no advance information provided to the observer (unstructured), or a combination of the two.

Direct observation is especially useful when jobs consist mainly of observable physical activities. Jobs like those of a janitor, assembly-line worker, and accounting clerk are examples. Third-party observation focuses more on reality than perception. As a result, third-party observation is often viewed as having more credibility, since there is minimal incentive to distort the results.

A challenge is that observations can influence job behaviour. Additionally, observation is usually not appropriate when the job entails a lot of immeasurable mental activity (e.g., lawyers or design engineers). Nor is it useful if the employee engages in important activities that might occur only occasionally, such as compiling year-end reports. Often, direct observation and interviewing are used together.

Participant Diary/Log

Another technique involves asking employees to keep a **diary/log** or list of what they do during the day. Each employee records every activity in which he or she is involved

Position Analysis Questionnaire (PAQ) A questionnaire used to collect quantifiable data concerning the duties and responsibilities of various jobs.

Functional Job Analysis (FJA) A quantitative method for classifying jobs based on types and amounts of responsibility for data, people, and things. Performance standards and training requirements are also identified.

diary/log Daily listings made by employees of every activity in which they engage, along with the time each activity takes.

EXHIBIt 7-6 Position Analysis Questionnaire (Excerpt)

A1. Visual Sources of Job Information

Using the response scale at the left, rate each of the following items on the basis of the extent to which it is used by the worker as a source of information in performing the job.

1. **Written materials**
   E.g., books, reports, office notes, articles, job instructions, or signs

2. **Quantitative materials**
   Materials that deal with quantities or amounts, e.g., graphs, accounts, specifications, or tables of numbers

3. **Pictorial materials**
   Pictures or picturelike materials used as sources of information, e.g., drawings, blueprints, diagrams, maps, tracings, photographic films, x-ray films, or TV pictures

4. **Patterns or related devices**
   E.g., templates, stencils, or patterns used as sources of information when observed during use (Do not include materials described in item 3.)

5. **Visual displays**
   E.g., dials, gauges, signal lights, radarscopes, speedometers, or clocks

6. **Measuring devices**
   E.g., rules, calipers, tire pressure gauges, scales, thickness gauges, pipettes, thermometers, or protractors used to obtain visual information about physical measurements (Do not include devices described in item 5.)

7. **Mechanical devices**
   E.g., tools, equipment, or machinery that are sources of information when observed during use or operation

8. **Materials in process**
   E.g., parts, materials, or objects which are sources of information when being modified, worked on, or otherwise processed, such as bread dough being mixed, a workpiece being turned in a lathe, fabric being cut, or a shoe being resoled

9. **Materials not in process**
   E.g., parts, materials, or objects not in the process of being changed or modified, which are sources of information when being inspected, handled, packaged, distributed, or selected, such as items or materials in inventory, storage, or distribution channels, or items being inspected

10. **Features of nature**
    E.g., landscapes, fields, geological samples, vegetation, cloud formations, and other natural features that are observed or inspected to provide information

11. **Constructed features of environment**
    E.g., structures, buildings, dams, highways, bridges, docks, railroads, and other "constructed" or altered aspects of the indoor or outdoor environment which are observed or inspected to provide job information (Do not consider equipment, machines, etc., that individuals use in their work, as covered by item 7.)

12. **Behaviour**
    Observing the actions of people or animals, e.g., in teaching, supervising, or sports officiating, where the behaviour is a source of job information

13. **Events or circumstances**
    Events the worker observed and may participate in, such as flow of traffic, movement of materials, or airport control tower operations

14. **Art or décor**
    Artistic or decorative objects or arrangements used as *sources* of job information, e.g., paintings, sculpture, jewellery, window displays, or interior design

Note: The 194 PAQ elements are grouped into six dimensions. This figure exhibits 14 of the "information input" questions or elements. Other PAQ pages contain questions regarding mental processes, work output, relationships with others, job context, and other job characteristics.

Source: E.J. McCormick, P.R. Jeanneret, and R.D. Mecham, *Position Analysis Questionnaire.* West Lafayette, IN: Purdue Research Foundation, 1989. Copyright © 1989 by Purdue Research Foundation. Reprinted with permission.

(along with the time spent) in a log. This can produce a very complete picture of the job, especially when supplemented with subsequent interviews with the employee and his or her supervisor. The employee might, of course, try to exaggerate some activities and underplay others. However, the detailed, chronological nature of the log tends to minimize this problem.

The National Occupational Classification

The **National Occupational Classification (NOC)**, the product of systematic, field-based research by Human Resources and Skills Development Canada (HRSDC), is an excellent source of standardized job information. It was updated and revised in 2011 and contains comprehensive descriptions of approximately 40 000 occupations and the requirements for each. To illustrate the types of information included, the NOC listing for specialists in human resources is shown in Exhibit 7-7.

Organizations can readily access information regarding the activities, requirements, competencies, and so on required by job title. However, it is highly recommended that companies who use external sources such as the NOC:

1. Adjust information based on their organizational strategy and structure;

2. Update information as required (for example, in Exhibit 7-7 the term "personnel" is used in reference to educational attainment. While this was an appropriate term in the late 1990s when the data was collected, the evolution of HR has made this term obsolete); and

3. Engage in the verification techniques in detail as per Step 4 (which we will discuss shortly).

The NOC and its counselling component, the *Career Handbook* (2nd ed.), both focus on occupations rather than jobs. An **occupation** is defined as a collection of jobs that share some or all of a set of main duties. The list of examples of job titles within each of the 520 Unit Groups in the NOC provides a frame of reference for the boundaries of that occupational group. The jobs within each group are characterized by similar skills.

To provide a complete representation of work in the Canadian economy, the NOC classifies occupations into Major Groups based on two key dimensions—skill level and skill type. The Major Groups, which are identified by two-digit numbers, are then broken down further into Minor Groups, with a third digit added, and Unit Groups, at which level a fourth digit is added. Within these three levels of classification, a Unit Group provides the actual profile of an occupation.[13] For example:

Major Group 31—Professional Occupations in Health
Minor Group 311—Physicians, Dentists, and Veterinarians
Unit Group 3113—Dentists

> Occupational Information Network
> **www.job-analysis.net**
>
> **National Occupational Classification (NOC)** A reference tool for writing job descriptions and job specifications. Compiled by the federal government, it contains comprehensive, standardized descriptions of about 40 000 occupations and the requirements for each.
>
> **occupation** A collection of jobs that share some or all of a set of main duties.

Using Multiple Sources of Job Analysis Information

An Ethical | Dilemma

If a job analyst is on the other side of the world from an employee who completed a web-based job analysis questionnaire, should another method of job analysis also be used to confirm the accuracy of the information?

Job analysis information can be obtained from individual workers, groups, supervisors, or observers. Interviews, observations, or questionnaires can be used. Some firms use a single approach, but one study suggests that using just one source is not wise because each approach has drawbacks. For example, in a group interview, some group members may feel pressure to go along with the group's consensus, or an individual employee may be careless about how he or she completes a questionnaire. Thus, collecting job analysis data from only one source may lead to inaccurate conclusions, so when possible, job analysis data should be collected from several sources.

EXHIBIt 7-7 NOC Job Description for Specialists in Human Resources

Specialists in Human Resources develop, implement, and evaluate human resources and labour relations policies, programs, and procedures and advise managers and employees on personnel matters. Specialists in Human Resources are employed throughout the private and public sectors, or may be self-employed.

Examples of titles classified in this unit group

Business Agent, Labour Organization
Classification Officer—human resources
Classification Specialist
Compensation Research Analyst
Conciliator
Consultant, Human Resources
Employee Relations Officer
Employment Equity Officer
Human Resources Research Officer
Job Analyst
Labour Relations Officer
Mediator
Union Representative
Wage Analyst

Main duties

Specialists in Human Resources perform some or all of the following duties:

- Plan, develop, implement, and evaluate personnel and labour relations policies, programs, and procedures to address an organization's human resource requirements
- Advise managers and employees on the interpretation of personnel policies, compensation and benefit programs, and collective agreements
- Negotiate collective agreements on behalf of employers or workers, mediate labour disputes and grievances, and provide advice on employee and labour relations
- Research and prepare occupational classifications, job descriptions, salary scales, and competency appraisal measures and systems
- Plan and administer staffing, total compensation, training and career development, employee assistance, employment equity, and affirmative action programs
- Manage programs and maintain human resources information and related records systems
- Hire and oversee training of staff
- Coordinate employee performance and appraisal programs
- Research employee benefit and health and safety practices and recommend changes or modifications to existing policies

Employment requirements

- A university degree or college diploma in a field related to personnel management, such as business administration, industrial relations, commerce, or psychology
  or
  Completion of a professional development program in personnel administration is required.
- Some experience in a clerical or administrative position related to personnel administration is required.

Additional information

- Progression to management positions is possible with experience.

Classified elsewhere

- *Human Resources Managers* (0112)
- *Personnel and Recruitment Officers* (1223)
- *Personnel Clerks* (1442)
- *Professional Occupations in Business Services to Management* (1122)
- Training officers and instructors (in 4131 *College and Other Vocational Instructors*)

Source: Adapted from Human Resources and Skills Development Canada, *National Occupational Classification*, 2001. Reproduced with the permission of Her Majesty The Queen in Right of Canada 2009. http://www5.hrsdc.gc.ca/noc/English/NOC/2006/QuickSearch.aspx?val65=1121 (Accessed March 29, 2009).

Step 4: Verifying Information

The job analysis information should be verified with any workers performing the job and with the immediate supervisor. This corroboration will help to confirm that the information is factually correct and complete, and it can also help gain the employees' acceptance of the job analysis data.

The knowledge that information will be verified increases the reliability and validity of the results in two ways. First, areas of inconsistency or concern can be further probed to develop awareness as to why the inconsistency exists and what should be done about it. Second, participants in the data collection techniques will be more honest and consistent knowing that they may later be held accountable for their contributions.

Step 5: Writing Job Descriptions and Job Specifications

Job Descriptions

A **job description** is a written statement of *what* the jobholder actually does, *how* he or she does it, and *under what conditions* the job is performed. The description in Exhibit 7-8—in this case for a vice-president of human resources, Asia-Pacific region—provides an example. As can be seen, the description is quite comprehensive and includes such essential elements as job identification, summary, and duties and responsibilities, as well as the human qualifications for the job.

No standard format is used in writing job descriptions, but most include the following types of information: job identification, job summary, relationships, duties and responsibilities, authority of incumbent, performance standards, and working conditions. As mentioned previously, job specifications (human qualifications) may also be included, as is the case in Exhibit 7-8.

Job Identification

As in Exhibit 7-8, the job identification section generally contains several categories of information. The *position title* specifies the title of the job, such as vice-president, marketing manager, recruiter, or inventory control clerk. The *department* and *location* are also indicated, along with the title of the immediate supervisor—in this case under the heading *reports to*.

Job Summary

The *job summary* should describe the general nature of the job, listing only its major functions or activities. Thus (as in Exhibit 7-8), the vice-president of human resources, Asia-Pacific region, will "develop, recommend, and implement approved HRM strategies, policies, and practices that will facilitate the achievement of the company's stated business and HRM objectives." For the job of materials manager, the summary might state that he or she will "purchase economically, regulate deliveries of, store, and distribute all materials necessary on the production line," while the summary for a mailroom supervisor might indicate that he or she will "receive, sort, and deliver all incoming mail properly, and he or she will handle all outgoing mail, including the accurate and timely posting of such mail."[14]

Relationships

The *relationships* section indicates the jobholder's relationships with others inside and outside the organization, as shown in Exhibit 7-8. Others directly and indirectly supervised are included, along with peers, superiors, and outsiders relevant to the job.

job description A list of the duties, responsibilities, reporting relationships, and working conditions of a job—one product of a job analysis.

EXHIBIt 7-8 Sample Job Description

Sample Job Description

Position:	Vice-President, Human Resources, Asia-Pacific
Location:	Hong Kong
Division:	Asia-Pacific
Department:	Human Resources
Reports to:	President Asia-Pacific (administrative), Vice-President, Human Resources—Corporate (functional)
Date:	April 2, 2013

Job Summary

Under the administrative direction of the President, Asia-Pacific, and the functional guidance of the Vice-President, Human Resources—Corporate, develop, recommend, and implement approved HRM strategies, policies, and practices that will facilitate the achievement of the company's stated business and HRM objectives.

Duties and Responsibilities

- Develop and recommend HRM strategies, policies and practices that promote employee commitment, competence, motivation, and performance, and that facilitate the achievement of the Asia-Pacific region's business objectives.
- Provide policy guidance to senior management regarding the acquisition, development, reward, maintenance, and existence of the division's human resources so as to promote the status of the company as an ethical and preferred employer of choice.
- Identify, analyze, and interpret for Asia-Pacific regional senior management and corporate HR management influences and changes in the division's internal and external environment and their impact on HRM and divisional business objectives, strategies, policies, and practices.

Relationships

Internally, relate with senior line and functional managers within the Asia-Pacific region and corporate headquarters in Vancouver. Externally, successfully relate with senior academic, business, government, and trade union personnel. Directly supervise the following positions: Manager, Compensation and Benefits, Asia-Pacific and Manager, Training and Development, Asia-Pacific. Functionally supervise the HR managers in 13 geographic locations within the Asia-Pacific region.

Problem Solving

Diverse cultures and varying stages of economic development within the Asia-Pacific region create a unique and tough business environment. The incumbent will often face complex HR and business problems demanding solutions that need to be creative and, at the same time, sensitive to local and company requirements.

Authority

This position has the authority to:

- approve expenditures on budgeted capital items up to a total value of $100 000 in any one financial year
- hire and fire subordinate personnel in accordance with company policies and procedures
- approve expense accounts for subordinate personnel in accordance with company policies and procedures
- authorize all non-capital item expenditures within approved budgetary limit
- exercise line authority over all direct reporting positions

continued

Accountability

Employees: 3000. Sales: $4 billion. Direct budget responsibility: $2.7 million. Assets controlled: $780 000. Locations: Australia, China, Hong Kong, India, Indonesia, Japan, South Korea, Malaysia, New Zealand, the Philippines, Singapore, Taiwan, Thailand.

Special Circumstances

Successful performance requires the incumbent to work long hours, to travel extensively (50–60 percent of the time), to quickly adapt to different cultures and business conditions, to successfully handle high-stress situations, and to constantly work under pressure in a complex and very competitive business environment.

Performance Indicators

Performance indicators will include both quantitative and qualitative measures as agreed by the President, Asia-Pacific Division, and Vice-President, Human Resources—Corporate and the incumbent. Indicators may be market based (e.g., share price improvement), business based (e.g., division profitability, budget control, days lost through industrial unrest, positive changes in employee commitment, job satisfaction, and motivation), and individual based (e.g., performance as a leader and manager as assessed by superiors, peers, and subordinates). Performance expectations and performance indicators generally will be defined on an annual basis. A formal performance appraisal will be conducted at least once a year.

Source: Adapted from R.J. Stone, *Human Resource Management*, 4th ed. Milton, Queensland: John Wiley & Sons, 2002, pp. 131–132. Reprinted with permission of the author.

Duties and Responsibilities

This section presents a detailed list of the job's major duties and responsibilities. As in Exhibit 7-8, each of the job's major duties should be listed separately and described in a few sentences. In the figure, for instance, the duties of the vice-president of human resources, Asia-Pacific region, include developing and recommending HRM strategies, policies, and practices; providing policy guidance; and identifying, analyzing, and interpreting internal and external environmental changes. Typical duties of other jobs might include maintaining balanced and controlled inventories, making accurate postings to accounts payable, maintaining favourable purchase price variances, or repairing production line tools and equipment.

An Ethical | Dilemma

In view of the fact that job descriptions are not required by law and that some organizations have found them no longer relevant, would abolishing job descriptions raise any moral or legal concerns?

Most experts state unequivocally that "one item frequently found that should *never* be included in a job description is a 'cop-out clause' like 'other duties, as assigned.'" This phrase leaves open the nature of the job and the people needed to staff it, and it can be subject to abuse.[15]

Authority

This section of a job description should define the limits of the jobholder's authority, including his or her decision-making authority, direct supervision of other employees, and budgetary limitations. For example, the vice-president of human resources, Asia-Pacific region (in Exhibit 7-8) has the authority to approve all budgeted non-capital expenditures and budgeted capital expenditures up to $100 000; approve expense accounts for subordinates; hire and fire subordinates; and exercise line authority over direct reporting positions.

Performance Standards/Indicators

Some job descriptions also contain a performance standards/indicators section, which indicates the standards the employee is expected to achieve in each of the job description's main duties and responsibilities.

Setting standards is never easy. Most managers soon learn, however, that just telling employees to "do their best" doesn't provide enough guidance to ensure top performance. One straightforward way of setting standards is to finish the statement: "I will be completely satisfied with your work when . . ." This sentence, if completed for each duty listed in the job description, should result in a usable set of performance standards.[16] Some examples would include the following:

Duty: Accurately Posting Accounts Payable

- All invoices received are posted within the same working day.
- All invoices are routed to the proper department managers for approval no later than the day following receipt.
- No more than three posting errors per month occur, on average.
- The posting ledger is balanced by the end of the third working day of each month.

Duty: Meeting Daily Production Schedule

- Work group produces no fewer than 426 units per working day.
- No more than 2 percent of units are rejected at the next workstation, on average.
- Work is completed with no more than 5 percent overtime per week, on average.

Working Conditions and Physical Environment

The job description should also list the general working conditions involved in the job. This section generally includes information about noise level, temperature, lighting, degree of privacy, frequency of interruptions, hours of work, amount of travel, and hazards to which the incumbent may be exposed.

Job Descriptions and Human Rights Legislation

Human rights legislation requires employers to ensure that there is no discrimination on any of the prohibited grounds in any aspect of the terms and conditions of employment. To ensure that job descriptions comply with this legislation, a few key points should be kept in mind:

- Job descriptions are not legally required but are highly advisable.
- Essential job duties should be clearly identified in the job description. Indicating the percentage of time spent on each duty or listing duties in order of importance are strategies used to differentiate between essential and non-essential tasks and responsibilities.
- When assessing suitability for employment, training program enrollment, and transfers or promotions, and when appraising performance, the only criteria examined should be the knowledge, skills, and abilities (KSAs) required for the essential duties of the job.
- When an employee cannot perform one or more of the essential duties because of reasons related to a prohibited ground, such as a physical disability or religion, reasonable accommodation to the point of undue hardship is required.

Hints | **TO ENSURE LEGAL COMPLIANCE**

Job Specifications

Writing the **job specification** involves examining the duties and responsibilities of the job and answering the question, "What human traits and experience are required to do this job?" Much of this information can be obtained from the job analysis questionnaire. The job specification clarifies what kind of person to recruit and which qualities that person should be tested for. It is sometimes included with the job description.

job specification A list of the "human requirements," that is, the requisite knowledge, skills, and abilities needed to perform the job—another product of a job analysis.

Complying with human rights legislation means keeping a few pointers in mind:

- All listed qualifications are bona fide occupational requirements (BFORs) based on the current job duties and responsibilities.

- Unjustifiably high educational or lengthy experience requirements can lead to systemic discrimination.

- The qualifications of the current incumbent should not be confused with the minimum requirements, since he or she might be underqualified or overqualified.

- For entry-level jobs, identifying the actual physical and mental demands is critical. For example, if the job requires detailed manipulation on a circuit-board assembly line, finger dexterity is extremely important and is something for which candidates should be tested. A **physical demands analysis**—which identifies the senses used and the type, frequency, and amount of physical effort involved in the job—is often used to supplement the job specification. A sample form is included in Exhibit 7-9. Having such detailed information is particularly beneficial when determining accommodation requirements. The mental and emotional demands of a job are typically missing from job analysis information. They should be specified so that the mental and emotional competencies of job applicants can be assessed and any need for accommodation can be identified.

Identifying the human requirements for a job can be accomplished through a judgmental approach (based on educated guesses of job incumbents, supervisors, and HR managers) or statistical analysis (based on the relationship between some human trait or skill and some criterion of job effectiveness). Basing job specifications on statistical analysis is more legally defensible. For example, the Personality-Related Position Requirements Form (PPRF) is a survey instrument designed to assist managers in identifying potential personality-related traits that may be important in a job. Identifying personality dimensions is difficult when using most job analysis techniques, because they tend to be much better suited to unearthing human aptitudes and skills—like manual dexterity. The PPRF uses questionnaire items to assess the relevance of such basic personality dimensions as agreeableness, conscientiousness, and emotional stability to the job under study. The relevance of these personality traits can then be assessed through statistical analysis.[17]

An Ethical | Dilemma

Are personality traits really part of the KSAs and bona fide occupational requirements/essential duties of a job?

Completing the Job Specification Form

Once the required human characteristics have been determined, whether using statistical analysis or a judgmental approach, a job specification form should be completed. To illustrate the types of information and amount of detail that should be provided in a well-written job specification, a sample has been included in Exhibit 7-10.

Writing Competency-Based Job Descriptions

Defining the job's competencies and writing them up involves a process that is similar in most respects to traditional job analysis. In other words, the manager will interview job incumbents and their supervisors, ask open-ended questions regarding job responsibilities and activities, and perhaps identify critical incidents that pinpoint success on the job. These job descriptions can be particularly useful in organizations that use competency-based pay, as discussed in Chapter 15.

physical demands analysis
Identification of the senses used and the type, frequency, and amount of physical effort involved in a job.

EXHIBIT 7-9 Physical Demands Analysis

Division:	Job Title:
Job Code:	Level:
Date:	Date of Last Revision:

Physical Requirements
Review the chart below. Indicate which of the following are essential to perform the functions of this job, with or without accommodation. Check one box in each section.

Section 1				Section 2		Section 3			Section 4	
Incumbent Uses:	NA	Right	Left	Both	Repetitive motion	The job requires the use of the first category up to 2 hours per day	The job requires the use of the first category up to 4 hours per day	The job requires the use of the first category up to 8 hours per day	Frequent breaks: Normal breaks plus those caused by performing jobs outside of the area.	Limited breaks: Two short breaks and one lunch break.
					Y	N					
Hands: (requires manual manipulation)											
Feet: (functions requiring foot pedals and the like)											

Lifting capacity: Indicate, by checking the appropriate box, the amount of lifting necessary for this job, with or without accommodation.

	NA	Occasionally (As Needed)	Often (Up to 4 Hours Per Day)	Frequently (Up to 8 Hours Per Day)
5 kg				
5–10 kg				
10–25 kg				
25–50 kg				
50+ kg				

Mobility: Indicate which category the job functions fall under by placing a check next to those that apply.
☐ Sits constantly (6 hours or more with two breaks and one lunch break)
☐ Sits intermittently (6 hours or more with frequent change, due to breaks and getting up to perform jobs outside of the area)
☐ Stands intermittently (6 hours or more with frequent changes, due to breaks and getting up to perform jobs outside of the area)
☐ Bending constantly (4 hours or more with two breaks and one lunch break)
☐ Bending intermittently (4 hours or more with frequent changes, due to breaks and getting up to perform jobs outside of the area)
☐ Walks constantly (6 hours or more with two breaks and one lunch break)
☐ Walks intermittently (6 hours or more with frequent changes, due to breaks and getting up to perform jobs outside of the area)

Visual acuity: Indicate the minimum acceptable level, with or without accommodation, necessary for the job
☐ Excellent visual acuity
☐ Good visual acuity
☐ Not relevant to the job

continued

Auditory acuity: Indicate the minimum acceptable level, with or without accommodation, necessary for the job.
☐ Excellent auditory acuity
☐ Good auditory acuity
☐ Not relevant to the job

Source: M. Rock and D.R. Berger, eds., *The Compensation Handbook: A State-of-the-Art Guide to Compensation Strategy and Design*, 4th ed. Columbus, OH: McGraw-Hill, 2000, pp. 69–70. © 2000 The McGraw-Hill Companies, Inc.

EXHIBIT 7-10 Job Specification

Job Title: Lifeguard   **Location:** Lethbridge Community Pool
Job Code: LG1   **Supervisor:** Head Lifeguard
Department: Recreation   **Division:** Parks and Recreation
Date: May 1, 2013

Job Summary
The incumbent is required to safeguard the health of pool users by patrolling the pool, rescuing swimmers in difficulty, treating injuries, advising pool users of safety rules, and enforcing safety rules.

Skill
Formal Qualifications: Royal Life Saving Society Bronze Medallion or equivalent
Experience: No prior experience required but would be an asset.
Communication Skills: Good oral communication skills are required. Proficiency in one or more foreign languages would be an asset. The incumbent must be able to communicate courteously and effectively. Strong interpersonal skills are required. All interaction with the public must be handled with tact and diplomacy.

Effort
Physical Effort: The incumbent is required to stand during the majority of working hours. In the event of an emergency where a swimmer is in distress, the incumbent must initiate rescue procedures immediately, which may involve strenuous physical exertion.
Mental Effort: Continuous mental attention to pool users. Must remain vigilant despite many simultaneous demands on his or her attention.
Emotional Effort: Enforcement of safety rules and water rescue can be stressful. Must maintain a professional demeanour when dealing with serious injuries or death.

Working Conditions
Job is performed in humid indoor environment, temperature-controlled. No privacy. Shift work to cover pool hours from 7 A.M. to 11 P.M., seven days a week. Some overtime and split shifts may be required.

Approval Signatures
Incumbent: _____
Supervisor: _____ Date: _____

Step 6: Communication and Preparations for Revisions

Organizations are often affected by internal and external factors, that influence organizational strategy, structure, or processes. Most organizations adopt strategies with a three- to five-year target, and many are forced to adjust according to environmental factors much sooner. Significant organizational changes like restructuring, new product development, technological changes, and competition modify the nature of how work is done, resulting in a need for revisions to the existing job descriptions and specifications.

Job analysis must be structured enough to allow for modifications as required while still providing current and future employees with an understanding of what they are expected to do. Once a system is developed to collect data, an organization may choose to (1) regularly update the data collected in a proactive manner, (2) develop systems to collect data on an ongoing basis, or (3) adjust job analysis activities in a reactive manner after a significant organizational change is initiated.

Information provided from the job analysis must be communicated to all relevant stakeholders. For example, employees must be aware of the core job requirements to help drive desired performance. Line managers must be aware of information provided in the job analysis to help align expectations of various jobs, manage performance, and manage HR planning activities. Recruiters use this information to determine and assess the desired knowledge, skills, abilities, and other characteristics (KSAO's) of potential candidates and to develop job ads. Compensation specialists can use this information to develop or modify pay scales according to job-related act ivities. Overall, the job analysis process is a fundamental component of HRM and a cornerstone that is critical to other organizational activities related to labour and work processes.

Recruitment

The Strategic Importance of Recruitment

Human talent is beginning to be referred to as the world's most sought-after commodity.[1] The quality of an organization's human resources begins with a strategic perspective in the management of recruitment. **Recruitment** is the process of searching out and attracting qualified job applicants. It begins with the identification of a position that requires staffing and is completed when résumés or completed application forms are received from an adequate number of applicants. A Watson Wyatt study found that organizations with superior recruiting practices financially outperform those with less effective programs and that successful recruiting is a strong indicator of higher shareholder value.[2]

Authority for recruitment is generally delegated to HR staff members, except in small businesses where line managers usually recruit their own staff. In large organizations where recruiting is done on a continual basis, the HR team typically includes specialists, known as **recruiters**, whose job is to find and attract qualified applicants. Recruiters are becoming increasingly critical to achieving an organization's strategic objectives as competition for the employees necessary for strategy implementation increases due to the growing talent shortage.

Organizations are increasingly seeking the high profile given to an "employer of choice," such as those included in lists such as Mediacorp's "Top 100 Employers," the Hewitt Associates "50 Best Employers," and the *Financial Post*'s "Ten Best Companies to Work for." Employers such as Scotiabank, Purolator, Tim Hortons, and many others are also applying the marketing concept of branding to strengthen their recruitment activities.[3]

Employer Branding

Gabriel Bouchard, founder of the Monster Canada online job board, says, "In an increasingly tight job market, employers must remain permanently visible to potential employees, establishing and maintaining relationships with potential candidates before they even begin pursuing a new job. This is particularly crucial when it comes to hard-to-fill or mission-critical positions."[4] Proactive employers are trying to obtain a competitive advantage in recruitment by establishing themselves as employers of choice through employer branding. The purpose of an employer brand is to attract people to apply to work at the organization and to earn the loyalty of current employees.

Employer branding is the image or impression of an organization as an employer based on the perceived benefits of being employed by the organization. It is the experience of an employee when working for a company, based on feelings, emotions, senses, realities, and benefits (functional benefits such as personal development, economic benefits such as monetary rewards, and psychological benefits such as feelings of purpose, belonging, and recognition). It is essentially a promise made to employees and their perception of how well that promise is delivered.[5]

Employer branding is particularly important during the recruitment process, not just for applicants who are eventually hired but also for those not hired who are out in the marketplace communicating their experience as an applicant to other job seekers.[6] Inconsiderate recruiting practices can be brand suicide for companies. Branding includes the experiences a candidate goes through while interacting with a company throughout the recruitment process, including[7]

- what candidates experience when they go to the company's website,

- whether HR sends an acknowledgement letter or email thanking each candidate who sends in a résumé,

- how candidates are greeted by the receptionist when they make initial contact by phone or in person, and

- whether the HR person who interviews candidates is a good spokesperson who can articulate the organization's values and culture.

Recruiters Café
www.recruiterscafe.com

Great Place to Work Institute Canada
www.greatplacetowork.ca

recruitment The process of searching out and attracting qualified job applicants, which begins with the identification of a position that requires staffing and is completed when résumés or completed application forms are received from an adequate number of applicants.

recruiter A specialist in recruitment whose job is to find and attract capable candidates.

employer branding The image or impression of an organization as an employer based on the benefits of being employed by the organization.

Employer branding involves three steps.[8] Step 1 is to define the target audience, where to find them, and what they want from an employer. The target group may be one of the four generations in today's workforce, the underemployed, or the four employment equity groups. McDonald's may target potential Generation Y employees who are seeking career development. At Southland Transportation, a school bus service provider in Alberta, the target audience is retired police officers, recent retirees, and parents with young children.[9]

Step 2 is to develop the employee value proposition—the specific reasons why the organization is a unique place to work and a more attractive employer for the target audience compared to other organizations. The use of concrete facts, programs, policies, survey results, and information will clearly portray the organization as an employer of choice. It is also important to ensure that current managers are prepared to deliver the value proposition by guiding and mentoring employees.[10] Loblaw and Fairmont Hotels offer potential employees the opportunity to participate in "green" environmental initiatives.[11] At PCL Construction of Alberta, 80 percent of employees own stock in the company.[12]

Step 3 is to communicate the brand by incorporating the value proposition into all recruitment efforts. The communication should reinforce and remind current and potential employees of promises in the employee value proposition and of the organization's ability to deliver it through their managers. An integrated marketing approach to internal and external communication should use various channels, such as television, radio, print, websites, social media, and so on.[13]

McDonald's used focus groups to identify the interests of one of their target markets for recruitment (young people). The results of the focus groups suggest that this target market is interested in balancing their own freedom and goals with making money. As a result, McDonald's offered flexible hours, uniform choices, scholarships, and discount cards to support its value proposition slogan "We take care of our employees." This value proposition was also communicated through television ads and a recruiting website. Following the introduction of this branding initiative, McDonald's saw a surge in the number of young people who recognized McDonald's as a great place to work.[14] With the right branding strategy, job seekers line up to apply for jobs. A successful brand results in job seekers saying "I'd like to work there."[15]

McDonald's Recruiting
www.worksforme.ca/mcd

The Recruitment Process

As illustrated in Exhibit 8-1, the recruitment process has a number of steps:

1. Job openings are identified through HR planning (based on the organization's strategic plan) or manager request. HR plans play a vital role in the identification process, because they indicate present and future openings and specify which should be filled internally and which externally. Openings do arise unexpectedly, though, when managers request that a new employee be hired.

2. The job requirements are determined. This step involves reviewing the job description and the job specifications and updating them, if necessary. Chapter 7 included a discussion of job analysis, which outlined how to collect and interpret job descriptions and specifications.

3. Appropriate recruiting source(s) and method(s) are chosen. The major decision here is whether to start with internal or external recruiting. There is no single, best recruiting technique, and the most appropriate for any given position depends on a number of factors, which will be discussed in the next section.

4. A pool of qualified recruits is generated. The requirements of employment equity legislation (if any) and the organization's diversity goals should be reflected in the applicant pool.

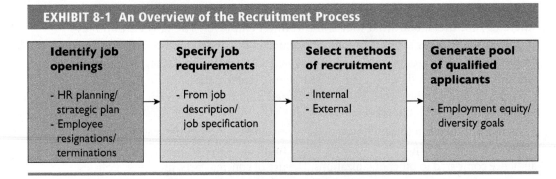

EXHIBIT 8-1 An Overview of the Recruitment Process

Identify job openings	Specify job requirements	Select methods of recruitment	Generate pool of qualified applicants
- HR planning/ strategic plan - Employee resignations/ terminations	- From job description/ job specification	- Internal - External	- Employment equity/ diversity goals

A recruiter must be aware of constraints affecting the recruitment process to be successful in his or her job. Constraints arise from organizational policies, such as promote-from-within policies, which mean that a recruiter cannot start recruiting externally for a specified period, even if he or she is aware that there are no suitable internal candidates. Constraints also arise from compensation policies, since they influence the attractiveness of the job to potential applicants. If there is an employment equity plan, it will specify goals for increasing recruitment from the designated groups. Monetary and non-monetary inducements offered by competitors impose a constraint, since recruiters must try to meet the prevailing standards of the company or use alternative inducements.

Perhaps the biggest constraint on recruiting activity at this time is the current labour shortage, which makes recruiting more difficult. One survey by Hewitt Associates found that recruitment practices will have to undergo "enormous change" over the next several years.[16] Some initiatives are already underway to attract foreign recruits.

Developing and Using Application Forms

For most employers, completion of an application form is the last step in the recruitment process. An application form provides an efficient means of collecting verifiable historical data from each candidate in a standardized format; it usually includes information about education, prior work history, and other job-related skills.

A completed application form can provide the recruiter with information on the applicant's education and experience, a brief overview of the applicant's career progress and growth, and information that can be used to predict whether or not the candidate will succeed on the job. Even when detailed résumés have been submitted, most firms also request that a standardized company application form be completed. There are many reasons for this practice:

- Candidate comparison is facilitated because information is collected in a uniform manner.

- The information that the company requires is specifically requested, rather than just what the candidate wants to reveal.

- Candidates are typically asked to complete an application form while on the company premises, and thus it is a sample of the candidate's own work (obtaining assistance with résumés is common, given that many job boards offer online résumé building options).

- Application forms typically ask the candidate to provide written authorization for reference checking.

- Candidates are asked to acknowledge that the information provided is true and accurate, which protects the company from applicants who falsify their credentials.

Tips | **FOR THE FRONT LINE**

- Many application forms today have an optional section regarding designated group member status. An example is provided in Exhibit 8-2. The data collected are used for employment equity tracking purposes.

One type of application form that can be used to predict performance is a **biographical information blank (BIB)**, also known as a biodata form. Essentially, it is a more detailed version of an application form, focusing on biographical data found to be predictive of job success. Questions relating to age, gender, race, or other grounds prohibited under human rights legislation cannot be used. Candidates respond to a series of questions about their background, experiences, and preferences, including willingness to travel and leisure activities. Because biographical questions rarely have right or wrong answers, BIBs are difficult to fake. The development of a BIB requires that the items that are valid predictors of job success be identified and that scores be established for different responses to these items. By totalling the scores for each item, it is possible to obtain a composite score for each applicant.

There has been a shift in the format of the forms from the traditional pen and paper methods to online applications given the exposure to the World Wide Web and the advances in human resource information systems. Exhibit 8-3 provides an example of an online application used by Canadian Tire to collect the same information that was traditionally collected in pen and paper format. Online applications significantly reduce the risk of lost applications, increase the exposure level of the job ad (global reach), and can reduce the likelihood of biases associated with other forms of face-to-face recruitment.

However, online application forms can result in a large number of applicants (for example, Google receives over 3000 applications per day[18]), therefore putting pressure on staff to manage the high volume of applicants. HRIS can be extremely useful here in automatically coding and storing applications, allowing HR professionals to search through the applications using specified search functions. The HRIS can also pre-screen applicants against predetermined criteria, providing an automated shortlist of qualified candidates. This significantly reduces the need for HR staff to screen résumés, but increases the importance of the content of the résumés and the validity of the pre-screening criteria. Due to the convenience and ubiquity of web browsers, application forms are increasingly being used online to allow applicants to build a profile and submit information directly or indirectly to potential employers. This offers around-

---

EXHIBIT 8-2 Self-Identification for Employment Equity Purposes

Employee Self-Identification Form

(Confidential when completed)

- This form is designed to collect information on the composition of the Public Service workforce to comply with legislation on employment equity and to facilitate the planning and implementation of employment equity activities. Your response is **voluntary** and you may identify in more than one designated group.

- The information you provide will be used in compiling statistics on employment equity in the federal Public Service. With your consent (see Box E), it may also be used by the employment equity coordinator of your department for human resource management purposes. This includes referral for training and developmental assignments and, in the case of persons with disabilities, facilitating appropriate accommodation in the workplace.

- Employment equity information will be retained in the Employment Equity Data Bank (EEDB) of the Treasury Board Secretariat and its confidentiality is protected under the *Privacy Act*. You have the right to review and correct information about yourself and can be assured that it will not be used for unauthorized purposes.

Step 1: Complete boxes A to E. In boxes B, C and D, refer to the definitions provided.

Step 2: Sign and date the form and return it to your department's EE coordinator.

biographical information blank (BIB) A detailed job application form requesting biographical data found to be predictive of success on the job, pertaining to background, experiences, and preferences. Responses are scored.

continued

Thank you for your cooperation.

TBS/PPB 300-02432
TBS/SCT 330-78 (Rev. 1999–02)

A.

[_____]   [_____]

Family Name   Given Name and Initial

[_____]

Department or Agency/Branch

( )   [_____]

Telephone # (office)   Personal Record Identifier (PRI)

○ Female   ○ Male

B. A person with a disability . . . (i) . . . has a long-term or recurring physical, mental, sensory, psychiatric, or learning impairment and

1. considers himself/herself to be disadvantaged in employment by reason of that impairement, or,

2. believes that an employer or potential employer is likely to consider him/her to be disadvantaged in employment by reason of that impairment,
    and includes persons whose functional limitations owing to their impairment have been accommodated in their current job or workplace.

ARE YOU A PERSON WITH A DISABILITY?

○ No

○ Yes, check all that apply

11 ○ **Co-ordination or dexterity** *(difficulty using hands or arms, for example, grasping or handling a stapler or using a keyboard)*

12 ○ **Mobility** *(difficulty moving around, for example, from one office to another or up and down stairs)*

16 ○ **Blind or visual impairment** *(unable to see or difficulty seeing)*

19 ○ **Deaf or hard of hearing** *(unable to hear or difficulty hearing)*

13 ○ **Speech impairment** *(unable to speak or difficulty speaking and being understood)*

23 ○ **Other disability** *(including learning disabilities, developmental disabilities and all other types of disabilities)*

(Please specify) _____

C. An Aboriginal person . . .
    . . . is a North American Indian or a member of a First Nation or who is Métis or Inuit. North American Indians or members of a First Nation include status, treaty or registered Indians, as well as non-status and non-registered Indians.

ARE YOU AN ABORIGINAL PERSON

○ No

○ Yes, check the appropriate circle

03 ○ North American Indian/First Nation

02 ○ Métis

01 ○ Inuit

D. A person in a visible minority . . .
    . . . in Canada is someone (other than an Aboriginal person as defined in C above) who is non-white in colour/race, regardless of place of birth.

ARE YOU IN A VISIBLE MINORITY GROUP

○ No

○ Yes, check the circle which best describes your visible minority group or origin

41 ○ Black

45 ○ Chinese

continued

51 ○ Filipino

47 ○ Japanese

48 ○ Korean

56 ○ South Asian/East Indian *(including Indian from India; Bangladeshi; Pakistani; East Indian from Guyana; Trinidad; East Africa; etc.)*

58 ○ Southeast Asian *(including Burmese; Cambodian; Laotian; Thai; Vietnamese; etc.)*

57 ○ Non-White West Asian, North African and Arab *(including Egyptian; Libyan; Lebanese; Iranian; etc.)*

42 ○ Non-White Latin American *(including indigenous persons from Central and South America, etc.)*

44 ○ Persons of Mixed Origin *(with one parent in one of the visible minority groups listed above)*

59 ○ Other Visible Minority Group

(Please specify) _____

E. 99○ The information in this form may be used for human resources management

_____   _____
Signature   Date (DD/MM/YY)

Source: Employee Self-Identification Form, www.tbs-sct.gc.ca/gui/iden2-eng.asp, Treasury Board of Canada Secretariat, 2002. Reproduced with the permission of the Minister of Public Works and Government Services Canada, 2012.

EXHIBIT 8-3 Sample Online Application Form—Canadian Tire

Source: Reproduced with permission of Canadian Tire.

---

the-clock convenience since applicants can create and submit applications or résumés on an ongoing and continuous real-time basis.

Recruiting from within the Organization

Although recruiting often brings job boards and employment agencies to mind, current employees are generally the largest source of recruits. Filling open positions with inside candidates has several advantages. According to human capital theory, the accumulation of firm-specific knowledge and experience involves a joint investment by both the employee and employer, therefore, both parties benefit from maintaining a long-term relationship. Employees see that competence is rewarded, thus enhancing their commitment, morale, and performance. Having already been with the firm for some time, insiders may be more committed to the company's goals and less likely to leave. Managers (as agents of the organization) are provided with a longer-term perspective when making business decisions. It is generally safer to promote from within, because the firm is likely to have a more accurate assessment of the person's skills and performance level than would otherwise be the case. In addition, inside candidates require less orientation than outsiders do.

Recruiting from within also has a number of drawbacks. Employees who apply for jobs and don't get them may become discontented (informing unsuccessful applicants as to why they were rejected and what remedial action they might take to be more successful in the future is thus essential).[19] Managers may be required to post all job openings and interview all inside candidates, even when they already know whom they want to hire, thus wasting considerable time and creating false hope on the part of those employees not genuinely being considered. Employees may be less satisfied with and accepting of a boss appointed from within their own ranks than they would be with a newcomer; it is sometimes difficult for a newly chosen leader to adjust to no longer being "one of the gang."[20] There is also a possibility of "inbreeding." When an entire management team has been brought up through the ranks, they may have a tendency to make decisions "by the book" and to maintain the status quo when a new and innovative direction is needed.

Internal Recruitment Methods

Recruiting from within can be accomplished by using job posting, human resources records, and skills inventories.

Job Posting

Job posting is a process of notifying current employees about vacant positions. Most companies now use computerized job-posting systems, where information about job vacancies can be found on the company's intranet. This involves a notice outlining the job title, duties (as listed in the job description), qualifications (taken from the job specification), hours of work, pay range, posting date, and closing date, as shown in Figure 8.4. Not all firms use intranets. Some post jobs on bulletin boards or in employee publications. As illustrated in Exhibit 8-5, there are advantages and disadvantages to using job postings to facilitate the transfer and promotion of qualified internal candidates.

An Ethical | Dilemma

Suppose a manager has already made up his or her mind about who will be selected for an internal position. But an internal job posting and subsequent interviews have shown another equally qualified candidate. Who should be offered the position?

Human Resources Records

Human resources records are often consulted to ensure that qualified individuals are notified, in person, of vacant positions. An examination of employee files, including résumés and application forms, may uncover employees who are working in jobs below their education or skill levels, people who already have the requisite KSAs, or individuals with the potential to move into the vacant position if given some additional training.

Skills Inventories

Skills inventories are an even better recruitment tool. Although such inventories may be used instead of job postings, they are more often used as a supplement. Whether computerized or manual, referring to such inventories ensures that qualified internal candidates are identified and considered for transfer or promotion when opportunities arise.

job posting The process of notifying current employees about vacant positions.

EXHIBIT 8-4 Sample Job Posting: University of Alberta

Faculty of Physical Education and Recreation—Academic Programs

Competition No.: A103814421   Closing Date: June 3, 2011

The Academic Programs area of the Faculty of Physical Education and Recreation oversees and manages the academic programs of approximately 920 undergraduates in four undergraduate degree programs and 135 graduate students at the master's and doctoral level. The goal of this unit is to provide an optimal learning experience for our students. It is also responsible for the appointment and management of Sessional Instructors for the Fall and Winter courses and a combination of Graduate Teaching Assistants (GTAs) and Sessional staff for the Spring and Summer courses.

In order to aid in the overall strategic direction and planning of this unit, as well as undertaking necessary day-to-day service functions, this unit is seeking an Academic Programs Administrative Professional Officer (APO) who will lead important administrative aspects in a collegial working environment. Out of the 11 continuing staff members who work in the Academic Programs Unit, this position is one of two that reports directly to the Vice Dean. The APO is accountable for establishing/coordinating an efficient and effective administrative support system for the teaching and service functions of the Academic Programs Unit.

Responsibilities:

- Identifies, recruits, conducts preliminary interviews and makes final decision on appointments regarding the hiring of Sessional Academic Staff (Contract Academic Staff: Teaching (CAST)); prepares all data for the production of the CAST contracts for Fall and Winter terms and advises the Vice Dean on these appointments
- Manages and supervises the Faculty's Sessional teaching instructors including preparing and monitoring the Faculty's CAST budget
- Responsible for all human resource functions for seven full-time support staff including supervision and performance evaluations
- Responsible for the administrative support of the Faculty Evaluation Committee (FEC) process within the Faculty; for this activity the position is responsible to the Dean, as Chair of FEC within the Faculty
- Responsible for the preparation of the annual Academic Programs operating budget
- Advises the Academic Planning Committee on the relevant Faculty and University policies in all areas of operation
- Contributes to the development of policies and procedures for the Academic Unit and represents the best interests of the unit through membership on Faculty ad hoc task forces, committees, etc.
- Responsible for the Faculty of Physical Education and Recreation's section of the UofA calendar
- Schedules academic courses, final exams, course restrictions, and Management & Balancing Lab/Seminar sections
- Maintains and upgrades the functionality of the Faculty's Teaching Assignment database

Qualifications

- Bachelor's degree in Physical Education, Recreation, Kinesiology, or a related allied health field preferred; undergraduate degrees in other disciplines may be considered
- Excellent interpersonal, communication and written skills
- Ability to work effectively both in a team environment and independently
- Ability to work under tight timelines and make decisions involving the recruitment and appointment of CAST instructional staff
- Excellent PeopleSoft skills with both Campus Solutions and Human Capital Management
- Superior information systems skills including: MS Office Suite, WWW, etc.
- Superior analytical, problem-solving and critical-thinking skills
- Demonstrated ability to provide precise and concise information/advice to all areas in the unit
- Demonstrated strong leadership capabilities and organizational skills
- Strong financial analysis/reporting skills and attention to detail; ability to develop and monitor operating budgets in the Academic Programs Unit
- Well-developed planning and organization skills
- Extensive knowledge of University and Faculty Policies & Procedures

In accordance with the Administrative Professional Officer agreement, this full-time continuing position offers a comprehensive benefits package and annual salary range of $55,388–$92,316 (subject to current negotiations).

How to Apply

Apply Online

Note: Online applications are accepted until midnight Mountain Standard Time of the closing date.

Mail

Dr. Dan Syrotuik, Vice Dean   **Email**
Academic Programs Office   Dan.Syrotuik@ualberta.ca
Faculty of Physical Education and Recreation
University of Alberta   **Fax**
E407 Van Vliet Centre   (780) 492-6583
EDMONTON, Alberta, T6G 2H9

The University of Alberta hires on the basis of merit. We are committed to the principle of equity in employment. We welcome diversity and encourage applications from all qualified women and men, including persons with disabilities, members of visible minorities and Aboriginal persons.)

Source: Raj Anand, "Human Rights and the Professional Regulator in the 21st Century," pp. 17–18, November 4, 2011. Used with permission from Raj Anand, Partner, WeirFoulds LLP.

> **EXHIBIT 8-5 Advantages and Disadvantages of Job Posting**
>
> ## Advantages
>
> - Provides every qualified employee with a chance for a transfer or promotion.
> - Reduces the likelihood of special deals and favouritism.
> - Demonstrates the organization's commitment to career growth and development.
> - Communicates to employees the organization's policies and guidelines regarding promotions and transfers.
> - Provides equal opportunity to all qualified employees.
>
> ## Disadvantages
>
> - Unsuccessful job candidates may become demotivated, demoralized, discontented, and unhappy if feedback is not communicated in a timely and sensitive manner.
> - Tensions may rise if it appears that a qualified internal candidate was passed over for an equally qualified or less qualified external candidate.
> - The decision about which candidate to select may be more difficult if there are two or more equally qualified candidates.

Source: Raj Anand, "Human Rights and the Professional Regulator in the 21st Century," pp. 17–18, November 4, 2011. Used with permission from Raj Anand, Partner, WeirFoulds LLP.

Limitations of Recruiting from Within

It is rarely possible to fill all non-entry-level jobs with current employees. Middle- and upper-level jobs may be vacated unexpectedly, with no internal replacements yet qualified or ready for transfer or promotion; or the jobs may require such specialized training and experience that there are no potential internal replacements. Even in firms with a policy of promoting from within, potential external candidates are increasingly being considered to meet strategic objectives. Hiring someone from outside may be preferable in order to acquire the latest knowledge and expertise or to gain new ideas and revitalize the department or organization.[21]

Recruiting from Outside the Organization

Unless there is a workforce reduction, even in firms with a promote from within policy, a replacement from outside must eventually be found to fill the job left vacant once all eligible employees have been given the opportunity for transfer or promotion. In addition, most entry-level positions must be filled by external candidates. The advantages of external recruitment include the following:

- The generation of a larger pool of qualified candidates, which may have a positive impact on the quality of the selection decision

- The availability of a more diverse applicant pool, which can assist in meeting employment equity goals and timetables

- The acquisition of skills or knowledge not currently available within the organization or the introduction of new ideas and creative problem-solving techniques

- The elimination of rivalry and competition caused by employees jockeying for transfers and promotions, which can hinder interpersonal and interdepartmental cooperation

- The potential cost savings resulting from hiring individuals who already have the required skills, rather than providing extensive training

Planning External Recruitment

When choosing the external recruitment method(s), several factors should be considered in addition to the constraints mentioned earlier. The type of job to be filled has a major impact on the recruitment method selected. For example, most firms normally rely on professional search firms for recruiting executive-level employees. In contrast, Internet advertising is commonly used for recruiting other salaried employees.

Yield ratios help to indicate which recruitment methods are the most effective at producing qualified job candidates. A **yield ratio** is the percentage of applicants that proceed to the next stage of the selection process. A recruiting yield pyramid, such as that shown in Exhibit 8-6, can be devised for each method by calculating the yield ratio for each step in the selection process.

The hypothetical firm in Exhibit 8-6 typically hires 50 entry-level accountants each year. As the figure illustrates, this company knows that if they recruit 1 200 potential new hires only 200 will be invited for interviews (a 6:1 ratio of leads generation to candidates interviewed). In other words, of six leads generated through college/university recruiting efforts, one applicant is invited to attend an interview. Of those, only 150 will actually make it to the interview process with a mere 100 being offered a position, and of those only 50 will accept and eventually be hired. The firm calculates that this method leads to a ratio of offers made to actual new hires of two to one (about half of the candidates to whom offers are made accept). The firm also knows that the ratio of candidates interviewed to offers made is three to two, while the ratio of candidates invited for interviews to candidates actually interviewed is generally four to three. Finally, the firm knows that the ratio between leads generated and candidates selected for interviews is six to one. Given these ratios, the firm knows that using this particular recruitment method, 1 200 leads must be generated to hire 50 new accountants. While this example identifies how yields are calculated and used, each organization typically determines their own desired yields based on industry, position, size, and resources of the organization to determine their own internal yield targets.

The average number of days from when the company initiates a recruitment method to when the successful candidate begins to work is called *time-lapse data*. Assume that the accounting company in the above example found the following scenario: Six days elapsed between submission of application forms and résumés to invitation for an interview; five days then passed from invitation to actual interview; five days from interview to job offer; six days from job offer to acceptance; and 23 days from acceptance of job offer to commencement of work. These data indicate that, using on-campus recruiting, the firm must initiate recruitment efforts at least 45 days before the anticipated job opening date. Calculating time-lapse data for each recruitment method means that the amount of lead time available can be taken into account when deciding which strategy or strategies would be most appropriate.

External Recruitment Methods

EXHIBIT 8-6 Recruiting Yield Pyramid

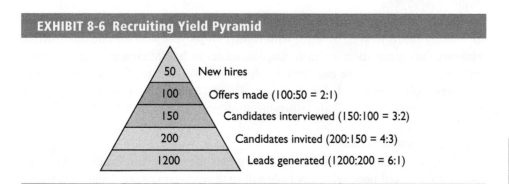

- 50 — New hires
- 100 — Offers made (100:50 = 2:1)
- 150 — Candidates interviewed (150:100 = 3:2)
- 200 — Candidates invited (200:150 = 4:3)
- 1200 — Leads generated (1200:200 = 6:1)

yield ratio The percentage of applicants that proceed to the next stage of the selection process.

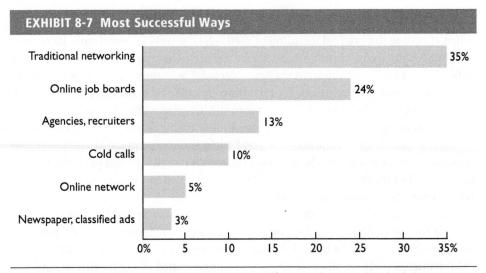

EXHIBIT 8-7 Most Successful Ways

Note: Often candidates rely on more than one method (for example, networking leads to an awareness about a job posted online in a colleague's company). The above survey forced respondents to identify only one tool that they used to find their most recent job.

Source: Survey by Right Management, published in "Networking Gets the Job Done," *Canadian HR Reporter* (August 15, 2011), p. 4.

Many methods of recruiting from the external labour market are in use. A 2010 study by Right Management of 5 858 job seekers found that the most successful way to find a job was through traditional networking, followed by online job boards. The results of the study are highlighted in Exhibit 8-7. Traditional networking includes employee referrals, former employees who have remained in contact with the organization, concentrated job fairs based on relationships formed with educational institutes, professional and trade associations, labour organizations, and military personnel. Online job boards include traditional online job boards, corporate websites, and government-initiated job boards.

Employee Referrals

Some organizations encourage applications from friends and relatives of current employees by mounting an employee referral campaign. Openings are announced in the company's intranet or newsletter along with a request for referrals. Cash awards or prizes may be offered for referrals that culminate in a new hire. Because no advertising or agency fees are involved, paying bonuses still represents a low recruiting cost.

The disadvantages associated with employee referrals include the potential for inbreeding and **nepotism** to cause morale problems and dissatisfaction among employees whose referrals are not hired. Perhaps the biggest drawback, however, is that this method may result in systemic discrimination.

Former Employees

In these times of talent shortage and diminishing employee loyalty, some organizations are making efforts to keep in touch with former employees who may be interested in rejoining the organization in future. Organizations such as Microsoft, Ernst & Young, and Procter & Gamble are establishing alumni networks that offer benefits such as healthcare, job boards, and alumni parties. About 25 percent of hires at the manager level and above at Microsoft are returning employees, known as "boomerangs."[22]

Educational Institutions

Recruiting at educational institutions is extremely effective when candidates require formal training but need relatively little full-time work experience. High schools can

nepotism A preference for hiring relatives of current employees.

provide recruits for clerical and some blue-collar jobs. For example, Encana, an oil and gas company headquartered in Calgary, is facing an ongoing shortage of skilled workers. It has started a program called "Oil and Gas Production Field Operator Career Pathway," which offers high school students an opportunity to earn credits while learning about field production work. Beginning in Grade 10, students in participating high schools can sign up for a distance-learning course supplied by Calgary-based Southern Alberta Institute of Technology (SAIT). Students who progress through the course in all three years will graduate with a production field operation certificate from SAIT. Students will have a chance of getting one of at least six paid 8-week summer internship positions with Encana following each year.[23]

Many companies take recruitment campaigns into high schools to sell careers to a younger generation. This type of recruitment helps a variety of industries meet future recruitment demands. Here, students learn how to work on a car.

Most high schools, colleges, and universities have counselling centres that provide job-search assistance to students through such activities as skills assessment testing and workshops on résumé preparation and interview strategies. Sometimes they arrange for onsite job fairs, at which employers set up displays outlining the types of job opportunities available. The Halifax Career Fair, a partnership among Nova Scotia's universities and colleges, is the foremost recruiting event in Atlantic Canada. Every year the event attracts about 100 companies from across the country and 1200 students.[24]

Cooperative (co-op) education and field placement programs have become increasingly popular in Canada. These programs require students to spend a specified amount of time working in organizations as an integral part of the academic program, thereby gaining some hands-on skills in an actual work setting. Co-op programs are offered in some high schools, as well as in colleges and universities.

Career Edge
www.careeredge.ca

Job Postings (Student Job Magazine)
www.jobpostings.ca

Halifax Career Fair
www.halifaxcareerfair.com

Summer internship programs hire college or university students to complete summer projects between their second-last and final year of study. Their performance is assessed, and those who are judged to be superior are offered permanent positions following graduation. Other firms offer internship opportunities to graduates, thereby enabling them to acquire hands-on skills to supplement their education. As with student internships, outstanding performers are often offered full-time employment at the end of the program. It is now possible for firms to recruit graduate interns online through Career Edge, an organization committed to helping university, college, and high school graduates gain essential career-related experience through internships. Career Edge uses the Internet as its sole means of bringing companies and youth together. More than 8 000 young Canadians have started their careers through the program in more than 1 000 organizations. Within a few months of completing their internship, nearly 80 percent of interns have found permanent employment with competitive salaries, and nearly 60 percent of the interns are hired by host organizations on a full-time basis.[25]

Internship, co-op, and field placement programs can produce a win–win result. The employer is provided with an inexpensive opportunity to assess potential employees while benefiting from the current knowledge and enthusiasm of bright, talented individuals. Because co-op students and interns have been exposed to the organization, they are less likely to leave shortly after permanent hire than recruits with no previous exposure to the firm.[26] Recognizing these benefits has made such programs a major recruitment method in many organizations.

Open Houses and Job Fairs

Another popular recruitment method involves holding an open house. Common in retail firms looking to staff a new store from the ground up, open houses have also been the choice of corporations trying to draw out scarce talent in an ultra-tight job market. A similar recruitment method involves holding a job fair onsite. At such events, recruiters share information about the organization and job opportunities with those attending in an informal, relaxed setting. Some organizations are now holding job fairs online (known as virtual job fairs) to connect with a wider geographical audience. Top prospects are invited to visit the firm or to return at a later date for a more in-depth assessment.

Professional and Trade Associations

Professional and trade associations can be extremely helpful when recruiters are seeking individuals with specialized skills in such fields as IT, engineering, HR, and accounting, particularly if experience is a job requirement. Many such associations conduct ongoing placement activities on behalf of their members, and most regularly send their members newsletters or magazines in which organizations can place job advertisements. Such advertising may attract individuals who hadn't previously thought about changing jobs, as well as those actively seeking employment. For example, the Human Resources Professionals Association (HRPA) in Ontario has an employment service called the Hire Authority. For a nominal fee, employers can post HR-related employment opportunities on the HRPA website, where they can be viewed by HRPA members. Additionally, employers can pay for access to an online database of member résumés and can search, sort, and pre-screen qualified candidates for vacant positions.[27]

Labour Organizations

Some firms, particularly in the construction industry, obtain recruits through union hiring halls. The union maintains a roster of members (typically skilled trades people, such as carpenters, pipe fitters, welders, plumbers, and electricians), whom it sends out on assignment as requests from employers are received. Once the union members have completed their contracted work at one firm, they notify the union of their availability for another assignment.

Military Personnel

Military reservists are also potential recruits. The Canadian Forces Liaison Council (CFLC) is responsible for promoting the hiring of reservists by civilian employers. The CFLC also encourages civilian employers to give reservists time off for military training. Reserve force training develops skills and attributes sought after in the civilian workforce, such as leadership, planning, coordination, and teamwork.[28] Many organizations—such as Home Depot Canada and Énergie New Brunswick Power—have recognized the value of such leave and have joined the 4 700 organizations in Canada that have signed a statement of support for the reserve forces with the CFLC.[29] The CFLC's Reserve Employment Assistance Program (REAP) allows employers to place job postings for skilled personnel at more than 300 military units across the country at no charge.[30]

Online Recruiting

The majority of companies now use *online recruitment*, and a majority of Canadian workers use the Internet to research prospective employers, review job postings, complete online applications, and post their résumés. The Internet provides recruiters with a large audience for job postings and a vast talent pool. Online recruiting can involve accessing one or more Internet job boards, using a corporate website, or using social networking sites.

Internet Job Boards   Online job boards are fast, easy, and convenient and allow recruiters to search for candidates for positions in two ways. First, companies can post a job opening online (often for a fee) and customize it by using corporate logos and adding details about the company benefits and culture. Job seekers can search through the job postings, often by job type, region, or other criterion, and apply for the position online through the job board. The popularity of Internet job boards among job seekers is high because of the number of job postings available on one site.

Second, job seekers can post their résumés on job boards, and firms can search the database. Canada has hundreds of job boards, ranging from the two largest, Workopolis and Monster, to many smaller job boards serving specific fields from tourism to medicine.[31] Job board meta-crawlers such as simplyhired. ca enable job seekers to search multiple job boards with one query.

The advantages of job boards include candidate assistance with self-assessment and résumé writing, and pre-screening assistance for recruiters. One problem with Internet job boards is their vulnerability to privacy breaches. Fake job postings can lead to identity theft from submitted résumés, and résumés are sometimes copied onto competing job boards or other sites.[32] As a result, job boards are now providing tips for job seekers on maintaining privacy and confidentiality.[33]

Corporate Websites   With the overabundance of applicants found on most online job boards, employers are now using their own corporate websites to recruit. Career pages provide a single platform for recruitment that promotes the employer brand, educates the applicant about the company, captures data about the applicant, and provides an important link to job boards where a company's positions may be advertised.[34] Virtual workplace tours using video can be provided to attract top talent aligned with the employer brand.[35] Corporate websites also help the company create a pool of candidates who have already expressed interest in the organization.[36]

Using pre-screening strategies is essential, however. The volume of résumés definitely does not diminish when the firm accepts them online. At Hewlett-Packard, for example, more than 1 million online applications are received each year.[37] One way of coping with this volume is to generate automatic replies acknowledging receipt of applications.[38] Applicant tracking software is available to help recruiters track individual candidates through the recruitment and selection processes and to enable candidates to keep their profiles up to date.

Active job seekers are not the only potential future employees who visit corporate websites. Customers, investors, and competitors also visit them.[39] Many of those visiting career websites are "happily employed" individuals (known as "passive" job seekers) who are likely to arrive at the career site after browsing the company's main pages for other reasons, such as research into products or services. Therefore, it is important that a firm have a prominently positioned link on the homepage leading directly to the careers section to make it easy for passive job seekers to pursue job opportunities within the company.[40]

Best practices for career websites include the following:

- Include candid information about company culture, career paths, and business prospects.

- Include third-party sources of information on your company, such as articles, rankings, and awards.

- Design separate sections for different types of job seekers, such as students and part-timers.

- Have a direct link from the homepage to the career page.

- Have a job search tool that allows applicants to search open job positions by location and job category.

- Have a standardized application or résumé builder to allow for easy applicant screening.

- Use "email to a friend" options for visitor referrals.[41]

Tips | FOR THE FRONT LINE

Job Bank
www.jobbank.gc.ca

Training and Careers
www.jobsetc.gc.ca

Human Resources and Skills Development Canada (HRSDC)

Through various programs, including those for youth, Aboriginals, and persons with disabilities, HRSDC helps unemployed individuals find suitable jobs and helps employers locate qualified candidates to meet their needs—at no cost to either party. The Job Bank is the largest web-based network of job postings available to Canadian employers free of charge, and it provides access to 700 000 new jobs each year, with more than 40 000 jobs at any given time and up to 2 000 new jobs posted every day. HRSDC also operates Job Match, a web-based recruitment tool that can match employers' skill requirements with individuals' skill sets. Job seekers receive a list of employers with a matching job vacancy and employers receive a list of qualified candidates.[42]

Executive Search Firms

Employers use executive search firms to fill critical positions in a firm, usually middle- to senior-level professional and managerial positions. Such firms often specialize in a particular type of talent, such as executives, sales, scientific, or middle-management employees. They typically know and understand the marketplace, have many contacts, and are especially adept at contacting qualified candidates who are employed and not actively looking to change jobs (which is why they have been given the nickname "headhunters"). Generally, one-third of the fee is payable as a retainer at the outset. Compared with the value of the time savings realized by the client firm's executive team, however, such a fee often turns out to be insignificant.

Using this recruitment method has some potential pitfalls.[43] Executive search firms cannot do an effective job if they are given inaccurate or incomplete information about the job or the firm. It is therefore essential for employers to explain in detail the type of candidate required—and why. A few headhunters are more salespeople than professionals, and they are more interested in persuading the employer to hire a candidate rather than in finding one who really meets the job specifications. Some firms have also been known to present an unpromising candidate to a client simply to make their one or two other prospects look that much better. The Association of Canadian Search, Employment, and Staffing Services (ACSESS) sponsors the Certified Personnel Consultant (CPC) designation, which signifies that recruiters have met specific educational and testing requirements and confirms an individual's commitment to best industry practices.[44]

Association of Canadian Search, Employment, and Staffing Services (ACSESS)
www.acsess.org

Private Employment Agencies

Private employment agencies are often called on to provide assistance to employers seeking clerical staff, functional specialists, and technical employees. The "staffing" business has grown into a $6 billion industry that places hundreds of thousands of job seekers each year.[45] Generally, it is the employer who pays the agency fee. It is not uncommon for employers to be charged a fee equal to 15 to 30 percent of the first year's salary of the individual hired through agency referral. This percentage may vary depending on the volume of business provided by the client and the type of employee sought.

These agencies take an employer's request for recruits and then solicit job seekers, relying primarily on Internet job boards, advertising, and walk-ins/write-ins. Employment agencies serve two basic functions: (1) expanding the applicant pool and (2) performing preliminary interviewing and screening. Specific situations in which an employment agency might be used for recruiting include the following:

- The organization does not have an HR department or does not have anyone with the requisite time and/or expertise.

- The firm has experienced difficulty in generating a pool of qualified candidates for the position or a similar type of position in the past.

- A particular opening must be filled quickly.

- There is a desire to recruit a greater number of designated group members than the firm has been able to attract on its own.

- The recruitment effort is aimed at reaching individuals who are currently employed and might therefore feel more comfortable answering ads placed by and dealing with an employment agency.

It should be noted, however, that the amount of service provided varies widely, as does the level of professionalism and the calibre of staff. Although most agencies carefully screen applicants, some simply provide a stream of applicants and let the client's HR department staff do the screening. Agency staff is usually paid on a commission basis, and their desire to earn a commission may occasionally compromise their professionalism (for example, encouraging job seekers to accept jobs for which they are neither qualified nor suited).

Cold Calls: Walk-Ins and Write-Ins

Individuals who go to organizations in person to apply for jobs without referral or invitation are called walk-ins. People who submit unsolicited résumés to organizations are known as write-ins. Walk-ins and write-ins are an inexpensive recruitment method. Their résumés are generally screened by the HR department and if an applicant is considered suitable, his or her résumé is retained on file for three to six months or passed on to the relevant department manager if there is an immediate or upcoming opening for which the applicant is qualified. Some organizations, such as RBC Financial Group, are using computer databases to store the information found on the résumés and application forms of walk-in and write-in candidates. Whether the original document is paper based or submitted online, it can be scanned and stored in databases for fast, easy access using a few key words.[46]

Online Networking Sites

Many organizations are turning to social networking sites like Facebook to find young, tech-savvy recruits. Some create virtual recruitment booths and others create a company profile where they can post jobs and publicize their employer brand. Other users seeking jobs can become "friends" of potential employers and upload their profiles, which contain more information than résumés. Ernst & Young is one firm that has used this approach—it has even established its own company social networking site for employees and alumni.[47]

The advantage of using social networking for recruitment purposes is the opportunity to connect with millions of other users at little or no cost. One disadvantage is the possibility of unhappy employees or customers posting negative comments on the site.[48]

An Ethical | Dilemma

Is it ethical to use personal information on social networking sites to assess job candidates?

Print Advertising

Despite the advent of online recruiting, traditional advertising in newspapers and other print media is still a very common method of recruiting.[49] For advertising to bring the desired results, two issues must be addressed: the media to be used and the construction of the ad.[50] The selection of the best medium—whether it is the local newspaper, a national newspaper, a technical journal, or even a billboard—depends on the types of positions for which the organization is recruiting. Reaching individuals who are already employed and not actively seeking alternative employment requires a different medium than is appropriate to attract those who are unemployed.

To achieve optimum results from an advertisement, the following four-point guide, called AIDA, should be kept in mind as the ad is being constructed:

Tips | **FOR THE FRONT LINE**

1. The ad should *attract attention*. The ads that stand out have borders, a company logo or picture, and effective use of empty white space. To attract attention, key positions should be advertised in display ads, rather than classified ads.

2. The ad should develop *interest* in the job. Interest can be created by the nature of the job itself, by pointing out the range of duties or the amount of challenge or responsibility involved. Sometimes other aspects of the job, such as its location or working conditions, are useful in attracting interest. To ensure that the individuals attracted are qualified, the job specifications should always be included.

3. The ad should create a *desire* for the job. This may be done by capitalizing on the interesting aspects of the job itself or by pointing out any unique benefits or opportunities associated with it, such as the opportunity for career development or travel. Desire may also be created by stressing the employer's commitment to employment equity. The target audience should be kept in mind as the ad is being created.

4. The ad should instigate *action*. To prompt action, ads often include a closing date and a statement such as "Call today," "Send your résumé today," "Check out our website for more information," or "Go to the site of our next job fair."

When properly constructed, advertisements can be an effective instrument for recruiting, as well as for communicating the organization's corporate image to the general public.

There are two general types of newspaper advertisements: want ads and blind ads. **Want ads** describe the job and its specifications, the compensation package, and the hiring employer. Although the content pertaining to the job, specifications, and compensation is identical in **blind ads**, such ads omit the identity and address of the hiring employer. Although many job seekers do not like responding to blind ads because there is always the danger of unknowingly sending a résumé to the firm at which they are currently employed, such ads do result in the opening remaining confidential (which may be necessary if the position is still staffed).

Many factors make advertising a useful recruiting method. Employers can use advertisements to reach and attract potential job applicants from a diverse labour market in as wide or narrow a geographical area as desired. To meet employment equity goals and timetables, ads can be placed in publications read by designated group members, such as a minority-language newspaper or the newsletter of a not-for-profit agency assisting individuals who have a particular mental or physical disability.

Recruiting Non-Permanent Staff

In recent years, many companies have increased their use of contingent workers to attain labour flexibility and acquire employees with special skills on an as needed basis. In these firms, recruiters are spending more time seeking temporary (term, seasonal, casual) and contract workers and less time recruiting permanent staff.[51] Two common sources of non-permanent staff are temporary help agencies and contract workers.

Temporary Help Agencies

Temporary help agencies, such as Kelly Services and Office Overload, exist in major cities in Canada. They specialize in providing temporary workers to cover for employees who are ill, on vacation, or on a leave of absence. Firms also use temporary employees to handle seasonal work, peak workloads, and special projects for which no current employees have the time or expertise. Temporary workers (temps) are agency employees and are reassigned to another employer when their services are no longer required.

Temps provide employers with three major benefits:

want ad A recruitment ad describing the job and its specifications, the compensation package, and the hiring employer. The address to which applications or résumés should be submitted is also provided.

blind ad A recruitment ad in which the identity and address of the employer are omitted.

1. They cost much less than permanent employees, as they generally receive less compensation than permanent staff. There are also savings related to the hiring and training costs associated with permanent employees. In fact, training has become the central investment in the business strategy of many temporary employment agencies. For example, Accountemps invests in the skills and training of employees after they have worked for a specified amount of time. This training includes online tutoring in software they may use on the job and tuition reimbursement for skills training.[52]

2. If a temp performs unsatisfactorily, a substitute can be requested immediately. Generally, a suitable replacement is sent to the firm within one business day.

3. Individuals working as temps who are seeking full-time employment are often highly motivated, knowing that many firms choose full-time employees from the ranks of their top-performing temps.

The number of temporary and freelance workers is increasing all over the world. Freelancing allows employers to match their job needs to independent workers who complete tasks on an as needed basis.

Contract Workers

Contract workers are employees who develop work relationships directly with the employer for a specific type of work or period of time.[53] For example, Parc Aviation is a major supplier of contract workers to the airline industry. Airline organizations benefit from the services of contract engineers by having them cover seasonal or unplanned peaks in business, carry out special tasks or projects, and reduce the necessity for airlines to downsize permanent staff during cyclical downturns.[54]

Many professionals with specialized skills become contract workers, including project managers, accountants, and lawyers. Some have consciously made a decision to work for themselves; others have been unable to obtain full-time employment in their field of expertise or have found themselves out of a full-time job because of cutbacks. Thus, some want to remain self-employed; others work a contract while hoping to obtain a full-time position eventually. Some firms hire former employees (such as retirees) on a contract basis.

An Ethical | Dilemma

Is it ethical to keep extending the contracts of contract workers rather than hiring them as permanent employees to avoid the cost of employee benefits?

Recruiting a More Diverse Workforce

Recruiting a diverse workforce is not just socially responsible—it's a necessity. As noted previously, the composition of Canada's workforce is changing dramatically. Trends of particular significance include the increasing necessity of hiring older employees, a decrease in the availability of young workers, and an increase in the number of women, visible minorities, Aboriginal people, and persons with disabilities in the workforce.

Prime50
www.prime50.com

Attracting Older Workers

Many employers, recognizing the fact that the workforce is aging, are encouraging retirement-age employees to stay with the company or are actively recruiting employees who are at or beyond retirement age. For example, 20 percent of Home Depot Canada's workforce is over the age of 50.[55] Hiring and retaining older employees has significant benefits. These workers typically have high job satisfaction, a strong sense of loyalty and

contract workers Employees who develop work relationships directly with the employer for a specific type of work or period of time.

organizational commitment, a strong work ethic, good people skills, and a willingness to work in a variety of roles, including part time.[56]

To make a company attractive to older workers, it is important to deal with stereotypical attitudes toward older workers through education, ensure that HR policies do not discourage recruitment of older workers, develop flexible work arrangements, and redesign jobs to accommodate decreased dexterity and strength. Canadian employers have been encouraged to take action to retain and recruit older workers as they represent a large, underutilized, skilled labour pool, but so far little effort has been made to attract these people.[57] A 2008 Conference Board of Canada study found that the most common recruitment strategy for older workers was rehiring former employees and retirees. Less than 20 percent were using recruitment campaigns directed specifically at mature workers.[58]

Attracting Younger Employees

Many firms are recognizing the benefits of a multigenerational workforce and are not only trying to attract older workers, but are also taking steps to address the pending shortage of younger employees. Although older employees have comparatively wider experience and wisdom, the young bring energy, enthusiasm, and physical strength to their positions.

Successful organizations balance these different kinds of experience. McDonald's Restaurants of Canada (one of the largest employers of youth in the country and an active recruiter of seniors) feels that it is critical for organizations in the service industry to have employees who mirror their customer base. Its experience is that each member of the multi-age teams brings a particular strength, which leads to synergy, respect, and team building.[59]

Younger members of the workforce are part of the Generation X and Generation Y cohorts. To appeal to Generation Xers, it is important to stress that they will be able to work independently and that work–life balance is supported. Potential employees from Generation Y will want to know that they will be working with experts from across the organization and that the will have a variety of experiences. They will be attracted by organizations that value social responsibility, diversity, and creativity.[60] Accounting firm Meyers Norris Penny built an award-winning student recruiting campaign around the question "What do you want?" which resulted in continuously improving the quality of the students hired.[61]

After struggling to restart his career in Canada, Sibaway Issah found the assistance he needed with Career Edge, a not-for-profit agency that links qualified immigrants with possible employers.

Recruiting Designated Group Members

Most of the recruitment methods already discussed can be used to attract members of designated groups (Aboriginal people, women, visible minorities, and persons with disabilities), provided that the employer's commitment to equality and diversity is made clear to all involved in the recruitment process—whether it is employees who are asked for referrals or private employment agencies. This can also be stressed in all recruitment advertising. Alternative publications targeted at designated group members should be considered for advertising, and linkages can be formed with organizations and agencies specializing in assisting designated group members. Specific examples follow.

The Aboriginal Human Resource Council, headquartered in Saskatoon, Saskatchewan, sponsors the Aboriginal Inclusion Network, which offers a job board, résumé database, and other tools to hire, retain, and promote

Aboriginal talent. The Inclusion Network is linked to 350 Aboriginal employment centres across Canada, and the number of job seekers on the network increased 70 percent from 2009 to 2011.[62]

The Society for Canadian Women in Science and Technology (SCWIST) is a not-for-profit, volunteer organization aimed at improving attitudes and stereotypes about and assisting women in scientific, technological, and engineering careers. Employers can access valuable resources such as websites, employment agencies, and publications to attract professional women for employment opportunities in industries where they generally have a low representation.[63]

WORKink is Canada's most powerful online career development and employment portal for Canadians with disabilities. The WORKink site offers a full complement of employment and recruitment resources and services for job seekers with disabilities and for employers looking to create an inclusive workplace. WORKink is sponsored by the Canadian Council on Rehabilitation and Work. Employers can post job openings free of charge, browse résumés of people with disabilities, or access information on how to adapt the work environment to accommodate people with disabilities in their region.[64]

The Ontario Ministry of Community and Social Services sponsors a program called Paths to Equal Opportunity intended to provide links to information on removing and preventing barriers so that people with disabilities can work, learn, and play to their fullest potential. In conjunction with the Canadian Abilities Foundation, the program publishes a resource booklet called *Abilities @ Work*, which provides specific information to employers who want to find out about recruiting, interviewing, hiring, and working with people with disabilities. It also provides information to employees and job seekers with disabilities who want information on looking for work, accommodation in the workplace, and maintaining employment.

Another useful tool is the guidebook *Tapping the Talents of People with Disabilities: A Guidebook for Employers*, which is available through the Conference Board of Canada.

Aboriginal Human Resource Council
http://aboriginalhr.ca

Canadian Council on Rehabilitation and Work
www.ccrw.org

WORKink
www.workink.com

HireImmigrants.ca
www.hireimmigrants.ca

9

Selection

The Strategic Importance of Employee Selection

Selection is the process of choosing among individuals who have been recruited to fill existing or projected job openings. Whether considering current employees for a transfer or promotion or outside candidates for a first-time position with the firm, information about the applicants must be collected and evaluated. Selection begins when a pool of applicants has submitted their résumés or completed application forms as a result of the recruiting process.

The selection process has important strategic significance. More and more managers have realized that the quality of the company's human resources is often the single most important factor in determining whether the firm is going to survive and be successful in reaching the objectives specified in its strategic plan. Those individuals selected will be implementing strategic decisions and, in some cases, creating strategic plans. Thus, successful candidates must fit with the strategic direction of the organization. For example, if the organization is planning to expand internationally, language skills and international experience will become important selection criteria.

When a poor selection decision is made and the individual selected for the job is not capable of acceptable performance in the job, strategic objectives will not be met. In addition, when an unsuccessful employee must be terminated, the recruitment and selection process must begin all over again, and the successor must be properly oriented and trained. The "hidden" costs are frequently even higher, including internal disorganization and disruption and customer alienation. For example, the City of Waterloo was forced to fire its new chief administrative officer after three weeks on the job when it was found that he had provided inaccurate and misleading information to city council in a previous job.[1]

There are also legal implications associated with ineffective selection. Human rights legislation in every Canadian jurisdiction prohibits discrimination in all aspects, terms, and conditions of employment on such grounds as race, religion or creed, colour, marital status, gender, age, and disability. Firms must ensure that all their selection procedures are free of both intentional and systemic discrimination. Organizations required by law to implement an employment equity plan must ensure that all their employment systems, including selection, are bias-free and do not have an adverse impact on members of the four designated groups—women, visible minorities, Aboriginal people, and persons with disabilities.

An Ethical | Dilemma

As the company recruiter, how would you handle a request from the CEO that you hire her son for a summer job, knowing that, given current hiring constraints, the sons and daughters of other employees will not be able to obtain such positions?

Another legal implication is employer liability for negligent or wrongful hiring. Courts are increasingly finding employers liable when employees with unsuitable backgrounds are hired and subsequently engage in criminal activities falling within the scope of their employment. British Columbia has a law that requires schools, hospitals, and employers of childcare workers to conduct criminal record checks for all new employees.[2]

Suggested guidelines for avoiding negative legal consequences, such as human rights complaints, liability for negligent hiring, and wrongful dismissal suits, include the following:

1. Ensure that all selection criteria and strategies are based on the job description and the job specifications.

2. Adequately assess the applicant's ability to meet performance standards or expectations.

3. Carefully scrutinize all information supplied on application forms and résumés.

Hints | **TO ENSURE LEGAL COMPLIANCE**

selection The process of choosing among individuals who have been recruited to fill existing or projected job openings.

4. Obtain written authorization for reference checking from prospective employees, and check references carefully.

5. Save all records and information obtained about the applicant during each stage of the selection process.

6. Reject applicants who make false statements on their application forms or résumés.

Supply Challenges

Although it is desirable to have a large, qualified pool of recruits from which to select applicants, this is not always possible. Certain vacant positions may be subject to a labour shortage (based on job requirements, location, work environment, and so on), while other simultaneous vacant positions may be subject to a labour surplus (due to external environment factors, training and education levels, immigration patterns, and so on). A **selection ratio** is the ratio of the number of applicants hired to the total number of applicants available, as follows:

Number of Applicants Hired ÷ Total Number of Applicants = Selection Ratio

A small selection ratio, such as 1:2, may be indicative of a limited number of applicants from which to select, and it may also mean low-quality recruits. If this is the case, it is generally better to start the recruitment process over again, even if it means a hiring delay, rather than taking the risk of hiring an employee who will be a marginal performer at best.

A large selection ratio, such as 1:400, may be indicative that the job ad is too vague, that the organization's HR team may need to automate the screening process, or that there is a need for more resources to find the right job candidate amongst the high number of applicants.

The Selection Process

Most firms use a sequential selection system involving a series of successive steps—a **multiple-hurdle strategy**. Only candidates clearing a "hurdle" (selection techniques including pre-screening, testing, interviewing, and background/reference checking) are permitted to move on to the next step. Clearing the hurdle requires meeting or exceeding the minimum requirements established for that hurdle. Thus, only candidates who have cleared all of the previous hurdles remain in contention for the position at the time that the hiring decision is being made.

To assess each applicant's potential for success on the job, organizations typically rely on a number of sources of information. The number of steps in the selection process and their sequence vary with the organization. The types of selection instruments and screening devices used are also not standardized across organizations. Even within a firm, the number and sequence of steps often vary with the type and level of the job, as well as the source and method of recruitment. Exhibit 9-1 illustrates the steps commonly involved.

At each step in the selection process, carefully chosen selection criteria must be used to determine which applicants will move on to the next step. It is through job analysis that the duties, responsibilities, and human requirements for each job are identified. By basing selection criteria on these requirements, firms can create a legally defensible hiring system.[3] Individuals hired after thorough screening against these carefully developed selection criteria (based directly on the job description and job specifications) learn their jobs readily, are productive, and generally adjust to their jobs with a minimum of difficulty.

selection ratio The ratio of the number of applicants hired to the total number of applicants.

multiple-hurdle strategy An approach to selection involving a series of successive steps or hurdles. Only candidates clearing the hurdle are permitted to move on to the next step.

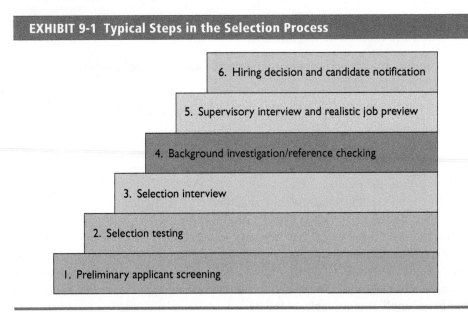

EXHIBIT 9-1 Typical Steps in the Selection Process

6. Hiring decision and candidate notification

5. Supervisory interview and realistic job preview

4. Background investigation/reference checking

3. Selection interview

2. Selection testing

1. Preliminary applicant screening

Designing an effective selection process involves composing a series of job-related questions to be asked of all applicants for a particular job. There are also a few job-related, candidate-specific questions. Doing so involves the following five steps, the first two of which should occur before recruitment:[4]

1. Decide who will be involved in the selection process and *develop selection criteria.* Specifying selection criteria involves clarifying and weighting the information in the job description and job specifications and holding discussions among the interview-team members, especially those most familiar with the job and co-workers.

2. *Specify musts and wants and weight the wants.* Once agreed on, the selection criteria should be divided into the two categories: musts and wants.[5] **Must criteria** are those that are absolutely essential for the job, include a measurable standard of acceptability, or are absolute. There are often only two musts: a specific level of education (or equivalent combination of education and work experience) and a minimum amount of prior work experience. These criteria can be initially screened, based on the applicants' résumés or applications. The **want criteria** include skills and abilities that cannot be screened on paper (such as verbal skills) or are not readily measurable (such as leadership ability, teamwork skills, and enthusiasm), as well as qualifications that are desirable but not critical.

3. Determine assessment strategies and *develop an evaluation form.* Once the must and want criteria have been identified, appropriate strategies for learning about each should be specified. For some qualifications, especially those that are critically important, the team may decide to use several assessment strategies. For example, leadership skills might be assessed through behavioural questions, situational questions, a written test, and an assessment centre. Once all want criteria have been agreed on and weighted, it becomes the basis for candidate comparison and evaluation, as illustrated in Exhibit 9-2.

4. *Develop interview questions* to be asked of all candidates. Questions should be developed for each KSA to be assessed during the interview. *Job-knowledge questions* and *worker-requirements questions* to gauge the applicants' motivation and willingness to perform under prevailing working conditions, such as shift work or travel, should also be included.

must criteria Requirements that are absolutely essential for the job, include a measurable standard of acceptability, or are absolute and can be screened initially on paper.

want criteria Those criteria that represent qualifications that cannot be screened on paper or are not readily measurable, as well as those that are highly desirable but not critical.

EXHIBIT 9-2 Worksheet—Comparison of Candidates for an Administrative Assistant Position

Criteria		A Smith		B Brown		C Yuill	
				Alternatives			
Must		Info	Go/No	Info	Go/No	Info	Go/No
Education — Office Admin. diploma or equivalent experience (3 years' clerical/secretarial experience)		Office admin. diploma	Go	Office admin. diploma	Go	No diploma, 1 year related experience	No Go
Experience — At least 2 years' secretarial/clerical experience		3 years' experience	Go	2 years' experience	Go		

Wants	Wt.	Info	Sc.	Wt. Sc.	Info	Sc.	Wt. Sc.	Info	Sc.	Wt. Sc.
Keyboarding/word processing	10	Word processing test			Word processing test	9	90	Word processing test	10	100
Good oral communication	9	Interview assessment			Interview assessment	9	81	Interview assessment	9	81
Good spelling/grammar	9	Test results			Test results	8	72	Test results	9	81
Organizational ability	9	Interview questions/simulation/ reference checking			Interview questions/simulation/ reference checking	8	72	Interview questions/simulation/ reference checking	9	81
Initiative	8	Interview questions/simulation/ reference checking			Interview questions/simulation/ reference checking	7	56	Interview questions/simulation/ reference checking	8	64
High ethical standards	7	Interview questions/simulation/ reference checking			Interview questions/simulation/ reference checking	7	49	Interview questions/simulation/ reference checking	7	49
Shorthand skills (or speed writing)	4	Interview question and test results			Interview question and test results	4	16		0	0
Designated group member, other than white female	2	Application form			Application form	2	4		0	0
							440			456

<u>TOP CANDIDATE</u>

5. *Develop candidate-specific questions.* A few open-ended, job-related questions that are candidate specific should be planned, based on each candidate's résumé and application form.

Acquiring Employees and the Law

Hints | **TO ENSURE LEGAL COMPLIANCE**

The entire recruitment and selection procedure must comply with human rights legislation. All information collected from the time an ad is posted to the time that the selection decision is made must be free from questions that would directly or indirectly classify candidates on the basis of any of the prohibited grounds under human rights legislation; potential employers cannot ask for a photograph, information about illnesses, disabilities or workers' compensation claims, or information that could lead to direct, intentional discrimination, such as age, gender, sexual orientation, marital status, maiden name, date of birth, place of origin, number of dependents, and so on.

If the process collects any information that is considered a prohibited ground for discrimination, an unsuccessful candidate may challenge the legality of the entire recruitment and selection processes. In such cases, the burden of proof is on the employer. Thus, taking human rights legislation requirements into consideration when designing effective recruitment and selection procedures is imperative. Specific guidelines regarding questions that can and cannot be asked on application forms are available through the human rights commissions in each jurisdiction.

Managing the process in a legally defensible way involves keeping the following guidelines in mind:

1. Selection personnel cannot ask questions that would violate human rights legislation, either directly or indirectly. Questions cannot be asked about candidates' marital status, childcare arrangements, ethnic background, or workers' compensation history, for example.

2. All candidates must be treated in the same manner. Any agent of the organization cannot ask only female factory position applicants to demonstrate their lifting abilities, for example, or question female sales applicants about their willingness to travel but not ask male candidates. However, accommodation must be provided to applicants with disabilities.

3. Cutting short an interview based on preconceived notions about the gender or race of the "ideal" candidate must also be avoided, because this is another example of illegal differential treatment.

4. A helpful phrase to keep in mind when designing selection criteria is "This job requires . . ." Organization representatives who focus on the job description and job specifications can gather all the information required to assess applicants without infringing on the candidates' legal rights.

Step 1: Preliminary Applicant Screening

Initial applicant screening is generally performed by members of the HR department. Application forms and résumés are reviewed, and those candidates not meeting the essential selection criteria are eliminated first. Then, the remaining applications are examined and those candidates who most closely match the remaining job specifications are identified and given further consideration.

The use of technology is becoming increasingly popular to help HR professionals improve the initial screening process. Almost all large firms or firms with high turnover use technological applications to help screen large numbers of candidates and generate short lists of individuals who will move on to the next step in the selection process.

Step 2: Selection Testing

Selection testing is a common screening device used by approximately two-thirds of Canadian organizations to assess specific job-related skills as well as general intelligence, personality characteristics, mental abilities, interests, and preferences.[6] Testing techniques provide efficient, standardized procedures for screening large numbers of applicants. Several thousand psychological and personality tests are on the market.[7]

The Importance of Reliability and Validity

Tests and other selection techniques are only useful if they provide reliable and valid measures.[8] All reputable tests will provide information to users about the reliability and validity of the test.

Reliability

The degree to which interviews, tests, and other selection procedures yield comparable data over time is known as **reliability**. Reliability is the degree of dependability, consistency, or stability of the measures used. For example, a test that results in widely variable scores (for example, if the same candidate completes the test three times and secures scores of 60 percent, 82 percent, and 71 percent) when it is administered on different occasions to the same individual is unreliable. Reliability also refers to the extent to which two or more methods yield the same results or are consistent. For example, applicants with high scores on personality tests for impulsivity or lack of self-control are correlated with the likelihood of failing background checks due to criminal behaviour.[9] Reliability also means the extent to which there is agreement between two or more raters (inter-rater reliability).

When dealing with tests, another measure of reliability that is taken into account is internal consistency. For example, suppose a vocational interest test has 10 items, all of which were supposed to measure, in one way or another, the person's interest in working outdoors. To assess internal reliability, the degree to which responses to those 10 items vary together would be statistically analyzed (which is one reason that tests often include questions that appear rather repetitive). Reliability can be diminished when questions are answered randomly, when the test setting is noisy or uncomfortable, and when the applicant is tired or unwell.

Validity

Validity, in the context of selection, is an indicator of the extent to which data from a selection technique, such as a test or interview, are related to or predictive of subsequent performance on the job. For example, high impulsivity is correlated with low productivity.[10] Separate validation studies of selection techniques should be conducted for different subgroups, such as visible minorities and women, to assess **differential validity**. In some cases, the technique may be a valid predictor of job success for one group (such as white males) but not for other applicants, thereby leading to systemic discrimination.

Three types of validity are particularly relevant to selection: criterion-related, content, and construct validity.

Criterion-Related Validity The extent to which a selection tool predicts or significantly correlates with important elements of work behaviour is known as **criterion-related validity**. Demonstrating criterion-related validity requires proving that those who exhibit strong sales ability on a test or in an interview, for example, also have high sales on the job, and that those individuals who do poorly on the test or in the interview have poor sales results.

reliability The degree to which interviews, tests, and other selection procedures yield comparable data over time; in other words, the degree of dependability, consistency, or stability of the measures used.

validity The accuracy with which a predictor measures what it is intended to measure.

differential validity Confirmation that the selection tool accurately predicts the performance of all possible employee subgroups, including white males, women, visible minorities, persons with disabilities, and Aboriginal people.

criterion-related validity The extent to which a selection tool predicts or significantly correlates with important elements of work behaviour.

Content Validity When a selection instrument, such as a test, adequately samples the knowledge and skills needed to perform the job, **content validity** is assumed to exist. The closer the content of the selection instrument is to actual samples of work or work behaviour, the greater the content validity. For example, asking a candidate for a secretarial position to demonstrate word processing skills, as required on the job, has high content validity.

Construct Validity The extent to which a selection tool measures a theoretical construct or trait deemed necessary to perform the job successfully is known as **construct validity**. Intelligence, verbal skills, analytical ability, and leadership skills are all examples of constructs. Measuring construct validity requires demonstrating that the psychological trait or attribute is related to satisfactory job performance, as well as showing that the test or other selection tool used accurately measures the psychological trait or attribute. As an example of poor construct validity, an accounting firm was selecting applicants for auditor positions based on a test for high extroversion, when the job in fact required working alone with data. A test to select applicants with high introversion would have had higher construct validity and would have helped to avoid the high turnover rate the firm was experiencing.[11]

Professional standards for psychologists require that tests be used as supplements to other techniques, such as interviews and background checks; that tests be validated in the organization where they will be used; that a certified psychologist be used to choose, validate, administer, and interpret tests; and that private, quiet, well-lit, and well-ventilated settings be provided to all applicants taking the tests.[12]

Tests of Cognitive Abilities

Ensuring validity of selection tools when assessing candidates with disabilities may require accommodation of the disability. Included in the category of tests of cognitive abilities are tests of general reasoning ability (intelligence), tests of emotional intelligence, and tests of specific cognitive abilities, like memory and inductive reasoning.

Intelligence Tests

Intelligence (IQ) tests are tests of general intellectual abilities (also referred to as general mental abilities) and have been used since the end of World War I.[13] They measure not a single "intelligence" trait, but rather a number of abilities, including memory, vocabulary, verbal fluency, and numerical ability. An IQ score is actually a *derived* score, reflecting the extent to which the person is above or below the "average" adult's intelligence score. Empirical research suggests that general mental ability is the strongest general predictor of job performance at one's chosen occupation.[14] Intelligence is often measured with individually administered tests, such as the Stanford-Binet test or the Wechsler test. Other IQ tests, such as the Wonderlic Personnel Test, can be administered to groups of people. These are relatively quick pen and paper or online tests that can be accessed for a nominal fee.

Emotional Intelligence Tests

Emotional intelligence (EI) tests measure a person's ability to monitor his or her own emotions and the emotions of others and to use that knowledge to guide thoughts and actions. Someone with a high emotional quotient (EQ) is self-aware, can control his or her impulses, is self-motivated, and demonstrates empathy and social awareness. Many people believe that EQ, which can be modified through conscious effort and practice, is actually a more important determinant of success than a high IQ. However, there is extremely limited and somewhat highly controversial empirical evidence to support the importance of EI in the workplace.[15] Self-assessment EI tests include the Emotional Quotient Inventory (EQ-i), the EQ Map, the Mayer-Salovey-Caruso Emotional Intelligence Test (MSCEIT), and the Emotional Intelligence Questionnaire (EIQ). The

content validity The extent to which a selection instrument, such as a test, adequately samples the knowledge and skills needed to perform the job.

construct validity The extent to which a selection tool measures a theoretical construct or trait deemed necessary to perform the job successfully.

intelligence (IQ) tests Tests that measure general intellectual abilities, such as verbal comprehension, inductive reasoning, memory, numerical ability, speed of perception, spatial visualization, and word fluency.

emotional intelligence (EI) tests Tests that measure a person's ability to monitor his or her own emotions and the emotions of others and to use that knowledge to guide thoughts and actions.

EXHIBIT 9-3 Two Problems from the Test of Mechanical Comprehension

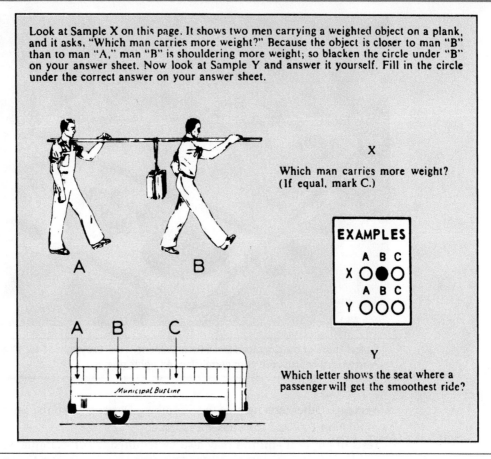

Look at Sample X on this page. It shows two men carrying a weighted object on a plank, and it asks, "Which man carries more weight?" Because the object is closer to man "B" than to man "A," man "B" is shouldering more weight; so blacken the circle under "B" on your answer sheet. Now look at Sample Y and answer it yourself. Fill in the circle under the correct answer on your answer sheet.

X

Which man carries more weight?
(If equal, mark C.)

EXAMPLES

Y

Which letter shows the seat where a passenger will get the smoothest ride?

Source: Sample Items from the Bennet Mechanical Comprehension Test. Copyright 1942, 1967–1970, and 1980 by NCS Pearson, Inc. Reproduced with permission. All rights reserved. "Bennet Mechanical Comprehension Test" and "BMCT" are trademarks in the US and/or other countries, of Pearson Education, Inc. or its affiliates(s).

Emotional Competence Inventory (ECI) is a 360-degree assessment in which several individuals evaluate one person to get a more complete picture of the individual's emotional competencies.[16]

Emotional Intelligence Consortium
www.eiconsortium.org

Specific Cognitive Abilities

There are also measures of specific thinking skills, such as inductive and deductive reasoning, verbal comprehension, memory, and numerical ability. Tests in this category are often called **aptitude tests**, since they purport to measure the applicant's aptitude for the job in question, that is, the applicant's potential to perform the job once given proper training. An example is the test of mechanical comprehension illustrated in Exhibit 9-3. It tests the applicant's understanding of basic mechanical principles. It may therefore reflect a person's aptitude for jobs—like that of machinist or engineer—that require mechanical comprehension. Multidimensional aptitude tests commonly used in applicant selection include the General Aptitude Test Battery (GATB).

Tests of Motor and Physical Abilities

There are many *motor abilities* that a firm might want to measure. These include finger dexterity, manual dexterity, speed of arm movement, and reaction time. The Crawford Small Parts Dexterity Test, as illustrated in Exhibit 9-4, is an example. It measures the speed and accuracy of simple judgment, as well as the speed of finger, hand, and arm

Hints | TO ENSURE LEGAL COMPLIANCE

aptitude tests Tests that measure an individual's aptitude or potential to perform a job, provided he or she is given proper training.

EXHIBIT 9-4 Crawford Small Parts Dexterity Test

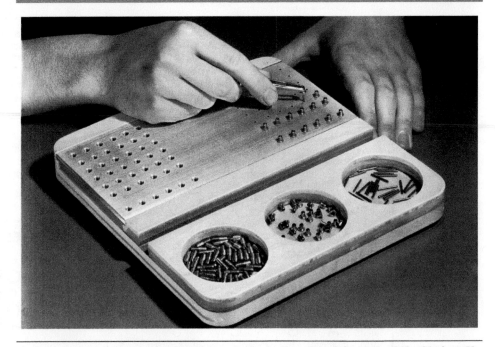

Source: Photo of the Crawford Small Parts Dexterity Test. Copyright 1946, 1956, 1981 by NCS Pearson, Inc. Reproduced with permission. All rights reserved.

movements. Other tests include the Stromberg Dexterity Test, the Minnesota Rate of Manipulation Test, and the Purdue Pegboard.

Tests of physical abilities may also be required.[17] For example, some firms are now using functional abilities evaluations (FAE) to assist with placement decisions. An FAE, which measures a whole series of physical abilities—ranging from lifting, to pulling and pushing, sitting, squatting, climbing, and carrying—is particularly useful for positions with a multitude of physical demands, such as a firefighter or police officer.[18] Ensuring that physical abilities tests do not violate human rights legislation requires basing such tests on job duties identified through job analysis and a physical demands analysis, ensuring that the tests duplicate the actual physical requirements of the job, developing and imposing such tests honestly and in good faith, ensuring that those administering the tests are properly trained and administer the tests in a consistent manner, and ensuring that testing standards are objectively related to job performance.[19]

Measuring Personality and Interests

A person's mental and physical abilities are seldom sufficient to explain his or her job performance. Other factors, such as the person's motivation and interpersonal skills, are important too. Personality and interest inventories are sometimes used as predictors of such intangibles.

Personality tests can measure basic aspects of an applicant's personality, such as introversion, stability, and motivation. The use of such tests for selection assumes that it is possible to find a relationship between a measurable personality trait (such as conscientiousness) and success on the job.[20] Many of these tests are *projective*. In the Thematic Apperception Test, an ambiguous stimulus (like an inkblot or clouded picture) is presented to the test taker, and he or she is asked to interpret or react to it. Because the pictures are ambiguous, the person's interpretation must come from within—the viewer supposedly *projects* into the picture his or her own emotional attitudes about life. Thus,

personality tests Instruments used to measure basic aspects of personality, such as introversion, stability, motivation, neurotic tendency, self-confidence, self-sufficiency, and sociability.

EXHIBIT 9-5 Sample Picture from Thematic Apperception Test: How Do You Interpret It?

a security-oriented person might have a very different description of what he or she sees compared to someone who is not.

The Myers-Briggs Type Indicator instrument, which has been in use for more than 50 years, is believed to be the most widely used personality inventory in the world. More than 2 million assessments are administered annually in the United States alone.[21] Another example of a common personality test is the Minnesota Multiphasic Personality Inventory (MMPI), which measures traits like hypochondria and paranoia.

Research studies confirm that personality tests can help companies hire more effective workers. For example, industrial psychologists often talk in terms of the "Big Five" personality dimensions as they apply to employment testing: *extroversion, emotional stability, agreeableness, conscientiousness,* and *openness to experience.*[22] These dimensions can be measured using the NEO Five-Factor Inventory (NEO-FFI) and similar tests. One study focused on the extent to which these dimensions predicted performance (in terms of job and training proficiency, for example) for professionals, police officers, managers, sales workers, and skilled/semi-skilled workers. Conscientiousness showed a consistent relationship with all performance criteria for every occupation. Extroversion was a valid predictor of performance for managers and sales employees—the two occupations involving the most social interaction. Both openness to experience and extroversion predicted training proficiency for all occupations.[23]

There has been an ongoing debate in the research world on whether personality can be faked. In a test of 77 experienced assessors, over 70 percent agreed that "faking is a serious threat to the validity of personality inventory in the assessment process."[24] Evidence supports two specific trends in personality tests and faking: (1) people can fake personality inventories when they are motivated to do so, and (2) individual differences exist in the ability to fake.[25]

Interest inventories compare a candidate's interests with those of people in various occupations. Thus, a person taking the Strong-Campbell Interest Inventory would receive a report comparing his or her interests with those of people already in occupations such as accountant, engineer, manager, or medical technologist. Interest inventories have many uses. One is career planning, since people generally do better in jobs involving activities in which they have an interest. Another is selection. If the firm can select people whose interests are roughly the same as those of high-performing incumbents in the jobs for which it is hiring, the new employees are more likely to be successful.[26]

Psychometric Assessments
www.psychometrics.com

Research INSIGHT

Research Psychologists Press
www.rpp.on.ca

interest inventories Tests that compare a candidate's interests with those of people in various occupations.

Achievement Tests

An **achievement test** is basically a measure of what a person has learned. Most of the tests taken in school are achievement tests. They measure knowledge or proficiency in such areas as economics, marketing, or HRM. Achievement tests are also widely used in selection. For example, the Purdue Test for Machinists and Machine Operators tests the job knowledge of experienced machinists with such questions as "What is meant by 'tolerance'?" Other tests are available for electricians, welders, carpenters, and so forth. In addition to job knowledge, achievement tests measure the applicant's abilities; a keyboarding test is one example.

Work Sampling

achievement tests Tests used to measure knowledge or proficiency acquired through education, training, or experience.

management assessment centre A comprehensive, systematic procedure used to assess candidates' management potential that uses a combination of realistic exercises, management games, objective testing, presentations, and interviews.

Work samples focus on measuring job performance directly and thus are among the best predictors of job performance. In developing a work-sampling test, experts first list all the possible tasks that jobholders would be required to perform. Then, by listing the frequency of performance and relative importance of each task, key tasks are identified. Each applicant then performs the key tasks, and his or her work is monitored by the test administrator, who records the approach taken. Finally, the work-sampling test is validated by determining the relationship between the applicants' scores on the work samples and their actual performance on the job. Once it is shown that the work sample is a valid predictor of job success, the employer can begin using it for selection.[27]

A management game or simulation is a typical component in a management assessment centre.

Management Assessment Centres

In a two- to three-day **management assessment centre**, the management potential of 10 or 12 candidates is assessed by expert appraisers who observe them performing realistic management tasks. The centre may be a plain conference room, but it is often a special room with a one-way mirror to facilitate unobtrusive observations. Examples of the types of activities and exercises involved include the following:

1. *An in-basket exercise.* Each candidate is faced with an accumulation of reports, memos, messages from incoming phone calls, letters, and other materials collected in the in-basket of the simulated job that he or she is to take over and is required to take appropriate action. For example, he or she must write letters, return phone calls, and prepare meeting agendas. The trained evaluators then review the results.

2. *A leaderless group discussion.* A leaderless group is given a discussion question and told to arrive at a group decision. The raters evaluate each candidate's interpersonal skills, acceptance by the group, leadership ability, and individual influence.

3. *Management games.* Participants engage in realistic problem solving, usually as members of two or more simulated companies that are competing in the marketplace. Decisions might have to be made about issues such as how to advertise and manufacture and how much inventory to keep in stock.

4. *Individual presentations.* During oral presentations on an assigned topic, each participant's communication skills and persuasiveness are evaluated.

5. *Objective tests.* Candidates may be asked to complete paper and pencil or computer-based personality, aptitude, interest, or achievement tests.

6. *An interview.* Most centres also require an interview between at least one of the expert assessors and each participant to evaluate interests, background, past performance, and motivation.

Situational Testing

In **situational tests**, candidates are presented with hypothetical situations representative of the job for which they are applying (often on video) and are evaluated on their responses.[28] Several of the assessment centre exercises described above are examples of situational tests. In a typical test, a number of realistic scenarios are presented and each is followed by a multiple-choice question with several possible courses of action, from which candidates are asked to select the "best" response, in their opinion.[29] The level of each candidate's skills is then evaluated, and an assessment report can be easily generated, making the simulation easier and less expensive to administer than other screening tools. Simulations also provide a realistic job preview by exposing candidates to the types of activities they will encounter on the job.

A research study of situational testing on 160 civil service employees demonstrated the validity of the situational test in predicting overall job performance as well as three performance dimensions: core technical proficiency, job dedication, and interpersonal facilitation. The situational test provided valid predictive information over and above cognitive ability tests, personality tests, and job experience.[30]

Micro-Assessments

An entirely performance-based testing strategy that focuses on individual performance is a **micro-assessment**. In a micro-assessment, each applicant completes a series of verbal, paper-based, or computer-based questions and exercises that cover the range of activities required on the job for which he or she is applying. In addition to technical exercises, participants are required to solve a set of work-related problems that demonstrate their ability to perform well within the confines of a certain department or corporate culture. Exercises are simple to develop because they are taken directly from the job.

Physical Examination, Substance Abuse Testing, and Polygraph Tests

The use of medical examinations in selection has decreased, in part because of the loss of physically demanding manufacturing and natural resource jobs. Before 1980, 25 percent of new hires underwent a medical exam, but by 2001, only 11 percent were required to do so.[31] Three main reasons that firms may include a medical examination as a step in the selection process are (1) to determine that the applicant *qualifies for the physical requirements* of the position and, if not, to document any *accommodation requirements*; (2) to establish a *record and baseline* of the applicant's health for the purpose of future insurance or compensation claims; and (3) to *reduce absenteeism and accidents* by identifying any health issues or concerns that need to be addressed, including communicable diseases of which the applicant may have been unaware. Medical exams are only permitted after a written offer of employment has been extended (except in the case of bona fide occupational requirements, as for food handlers).

The purpose of pre-employment substance abuse testing is to avoid hiring employees who would pose unnecessary risks to themselves and others or perform

Interactive employment tests administered on the computer are becoming popular as screening devices at many firms.

below expectations. However, in Canada, employers are not permitted to screen candidates for substance abuse. Alcohol and drug addiction is considered to be a disability under human rights codes, and an employee cannot be discriminated against during the selection process based on a disability.[32]

A polygraph test (also referred to as a lie detector test) involves using a series of controlled questions while simultaneously assessing physiological conditions of individuals such as blood pressure, pulse, respiration, and skin conductivity, with the assumption that deceptive responses produce different physiological responses than truthful responses. Such tests have been widely rejected by the scientific community since they have failed to produce valid or reliable results. In Ontario, the Employment Standards Act specifically prohibits use of polygraphs in pre-employment selection. Validated tests of honesty or integrity are more useful and reliable in the selection process.

Step 3: The Selection Interview

The interview is used by virtually all organizations for selecting job applicants. The **selection interview**, which involves a process of two-way communication between the interviewee and the interviewer, can be defined as "a procedure designed to predict future job performance on the basis of applicants' oral responses to oral inquiries."[33]

Interviews are considered to be one of the most important aspects of the selection process and generally have a major impact on both applicants and interviewers. Interviews significantly influence applicants' views about the job and organization, enable employers to fill in any gaps in the information provided on application forms and résumés, and supplement the results of any tests administered. They may also reveal entirely new types of information.

A major reason for the popularity of selection interviews is that they meet a number of the objectives of both the interviewer and interviewee. Interviewer objectives include assessing applicants' qualifications and observing relevant aspects of applicants' behaviour, such as verbal communication skills, degree of self-confidence, and interpersonal skills; providing candidates with information about the job and expected duties and responsibilities; promoting the organization and highlighting its attractiveness; and determining how well the applicants would fit into the organization. Typical objectives of job applicants include presenting a positive image of themselves, selling their skills and marketing their positive attributes to the interviewer(s), and gathering information about the job and the organization so that they can make an informed decision about the job, career opportunities in the firm, and the work environment.[34]

Types of Interviews

Selection interviews can be classified according to the degree of structure, their content, and the way in which the interview is administered.

The Structure of the Interview

First, interviews can be classified according to the degree to which they are structured. In an **unstructured interview**, questions are asked as they come to mind. Thus, interviewees for the same job may or may not be asked the same or similar questions, and the interview's unstructured nature allows the interviewer to ask questions based on the candidate's last statements and to pursue points of interest as they develop. Unstructured interviews generally have low reliability and validity.[35]

The interview can also be structured. In the classical **structured interview**, the questions and acceptable responses are specified in advance and the responses are rated for appropriateness of content.[36] In practice, however, most structured interviews do not involve specifying and rating responses in advance. Instead, each candidate is asked a series of predetermined, job-related questions based on the job description and specifications.

selection interview A procedure designed to predict future job performance on the basis of applicants' oral responses to oral inquiries.

unstructured interview An unstructured, conversational-style interview. The interviewer pursues points of interest as they come up in response to questions.

structured interview An interview following a set sequence of questions.

Such interviews are generally high in validity and reliability. However, a totally structured interview does not provide the flexibility to pursue points of interest as they develop, which may result in an interview that seems quite mechanical to all concerned.

Between these two extremes is the **mixed (semi-structured) interview**, which involves a combination of pre-set, structured questions based on the job description and specification, and a series of candidate-specific, job-related questions based on information provided on the application form or résumé. The questions asked of all candidates facilitate candidate comparison, while the job-related, candidate-specific questions make the interview more conversational. A realistic approach that yields comparable answers and indepth insights, the mixed interview format is extremely popular.

A study of 92 real employment interviews found that the interviewers using high levels of structure in the interview process evaluated applicants less favourably than those who used semi-structured or unstructured interviews, and those applicants who were evaluated using a semi-structured interview were rated slightly higher than those evaluated by unstructured interviews. Additionally, the study found that significant differences occur in the way that female and male interviewers evaluate their applicants. Although male interviewers' ratings were unaffected by the interview structure, female interviewers' ratings were substantially higher in unstructured and semi-structured interviews than in highly structured interviews.[37]

The Content of the Interview

Interviews can also be classified according to the content of their questions. A **situational interview** is one in which the questions focus on the individual's ability to project what his or her *future* behaviour would be in a given situation.[38] The underlying premise is that intentions predict behaviour. For example, a candidate for a supervisory position might be asked how he or she would respond to an employee coming to work late three days in a row. The interview can be both *structured* and *situational*, with predetermined questions requiring the candidate to project what his or her behaviour would be. In a structured situational interview, the applicant could be evaluated, say, on whether he or she would try to determine if the employee was experiencing some difficulty in getting to work on time or would simply issue a verbal or written warning to the employee.

The **behavioural interview**, also known as a **behaviour description interview (BDI)**, involves describing various situations and asking interviewees how they behaved *in the past* in such situations.[39] The underlying assumption is that the best predictor of future performance is past performance in similar circumstances.

Administering the Interview

Interviews can also be classified based on how they are administered:

- One-on-one or by a panel of interviewers
- Sequentially or all at once
- Face-to-face or technology aided (such as videoconferencing or by phone)

The majority of interviews are sequential, face-to-face, and one-on-one. In a *sequential* interview the applicant is interviewed by several persons in sequence before a selection decision is made. In an *unstructured sequential* interview each interviewer may look at the applicant from his or her own point of view, ask different questions, and form an independent opinion of the candidate. Conversely, in a *structured sequential* (or serialized) interview, each interviewer rates the candidate on a standard evaluation form, and the ratings are compared before the hiring decision is made.[40]

A **panel interview** involves the candidate being interviewed simultaneously by a group (or panel) of interviewers, including an HR representative, the hiring manager,

mixed (semi-structured) interview An interview format that combines the structured and unstructured techniques.

situational interview A series of job-related questions that focus on how the candidate would behave in a given situation.

behavioural interview or behaviour description interview (BDI) A series of job-related questions that focus on relevant past job-related behaviours.

panel interview An interview in which a group of interviewers questions the applicant.

A panel interview is an efficient and cost-effective way of permitting a number of qualified persons to assess a candidate's KSAs.

and potential co-workers, superiors, or reporting employees. The key advantages associated with this technique are the increased likelihood that the information provided will be heard and recorded accurately; varied questions pertaining to each interviewer's area of expertise; minimized time and travel/accommodation expenses as each interviewee only attends one interview; reduced likelihood of human rights/employment equity violations since an HR representative is present; and less likelihood of interviewer error, because of advanced planning and preparation.

A more stressful variant of the panel interview is the *mass interview*, which involves a panel simultaneously interviewing several candidates. The panel poses a problem to be solved and then sits back and watches which candidate takes the lead in formulating an answer.

Common Interviewing Mistakes

Several common interviewing errors that can undermine the usefulness of interviews are discussed in the following pages. These interviewer errors can be reduced by properly planning and training interviewers on the process, as well as educating interviewers about these risks.

Poor Planning

Many selection interviews are simply not carefully planned and may be conducted without having prepared written questions in advance. Lack of planning often leads to a relatively unstructured interview, in which whatever comes up is discussed. The end result may be little or no cross-candidate job-related information. The less structured the interview is, the less reliable and valid the evaluation of each candidate will be.[41]

Snap Judgments

One of the most consistent literature findings is that interviewers tend to jump to conclusions—make snap judgments—during the first few minutes of the interview or even before the interview begins based on the candidates' test scores or résumé data. Thus, candidates feel pressure to start off on the right foot with the interviewer. However, snap judgments are not accurate or reliable in the selection process and should be avoided.

Negative Emphasis

Many interviewers seem to have a consistent negative bias. They are generally more influenced by unfavourable than favourable information about the candidate. Also, their impressions are much more likely to change from favourable to unfavourable than vice versa. Providing information about the value or weight of criteria in the selection process can ensure that the interviewer assesses the criteria accordingly.

Halo Effect

It is also possible for a positive initial impression to distort an interviewer's rating of a candidate, because subsequent information is judged with a positive bias. This is known as the **halo effect**. Having gained a positive impression of the candidate on one or more factors, the interviewer may not seek contradictory information when listening to the candidate's answers to the questions posed or may interpret/frame all responses positively.

Poor Knowledge of the Job

Interviewers who do not know precisely what the job entails and what sort of candidate is best suited for it usually make their decisions based on incorrect stereotypes about

halo effect A positive initial impression that distorts an interviewer's rating of a candidate because subsequent information is judged with a positive bias.

what a good applicant is. Interviewers who have a clear understanding of what the job entails conduct more effective interviews.

Contrast (Candidate-Order) Error

Contrast or candidate-order error means that the order in which applicants are seen can affect how they are rated. In one study, managers were asked to evaluate a candidate who was "just average" after first evaluating several "unfavourable" candidates. The average candidate was evaluated more favourably than he or she might otherwise have been because, in contrast to the unfavourable candidates, the average one looked better than he or she actually was.

Influence of Nonverbal Behaviour

Interviewers are also influenced by the applicant's nonverbal behaviour, and the more eye contact, head moving, smiling, and other similar nonverbal behaviours, the higher the ratings. These nonverbal behaviours often account for more than 80 percent of the applicant's rating. This finding is of particular concern since nonverbal behaviour is tied to ethnicity and cultural background. An applicant's attractiveness and gender also play a role. Research has shown that those rated as being more physically attractive are also rated as more suitable for employment, well ahead of those rated average looking and those regarded as physically unattractive. Although this bias is considered to be unconscious, it may have serious implications for aging employees.[42]

Leading

Some interviewers are so anxious to fill a job that they help the applicants to respond correctly to their questions by asking leading questions or guiding the candidate to the expected answer. An obvious example might be a question like: "This job calls for handling a lot of stress. You can do that, right?" The leading is not always so obvious. Subtle cues regarding the preferred response, such as a smile or nod, are also forms of leading.[43]

Too Much/Too Little Talking

If the applicant is permitted to dominate the interview, the interviewer may not have a chance to ask his or her prepared questions and often learns very little about the candidate's job-related skills. At the other extreme, some interviewers talk so much that the interviewee is not given enough time to answer questions. One expert suggests using the 30/70 rule: During a selection interview, encourage the candidate to speak 70 percent of the time, and restrict the interviewer speaking to just 30 percent of the time.[44]

Similar-to-Me Bias

Interviewers tend to provide more favourable ratings to candidates who possess demographic, personality, and attitudinal characteristics similar to their own, regardless of the value of those characteristics to the job.[45] The result can be a lack of diversity in the organization and a poor fit with the job if secured.

Designing an Effective Interview

Problems like those just described can be avoided by designing and conducting an effective interview. Combining several of the interview formats previously discussed enables interviewers to capitalize on the advantages of each.[46] To allow for probing and to prevent the interview from becoming too mechanical in nature, a semi-structured format is recommended. Given their higher validity in predicting job performance, the focus should be on situational and behavioural questions.

Conducting an Effective Interview

Although the following discussion focuses on a semi-structured panel interview, the steps described apply to all selection interviews.[47]

contrast or candidate-order error An error of judgment on the part of the interviewer because of interviewing one or more very good or very bad candidates just before the interview in question.

Planning the Interview

Before the first interview, agreement should be reached on the procedure that will be followed. Sometimes all members of the team ask a question in turn; in other situations, only one member of the team asks questions and the others serve as observers. Sitting around a large table in a conference room is much more appropriate and far less stressful than having all panel members seated across from the candidate behind a table or desk, which forms both a physical and a psychological barrier. As noted earlier, special planning is required when assessing candidates with disabilities.

The rapport established with a job applicant not only puts the person at ease but also reflects the company's attitude toward its public.

Establishing Rapport

The main purpose of an interview is to find out as much as possible about the candidate's fit with the job specifications, something that is difficult to do if the individual is tense and nervous. The candidate should be greeted in a friendly manner and put at ease.

Asking Questions

The questions written in advance should then be asked in order. Interviewers should listen carefully, encourage the candidate to express his or her thoughts and ideas fully, and record the candidate's answers briefly but thoroughly. Taking notes increases the validity of the interview process, since doing so (1) reduces the likelihood of forgetting job-relevant information and subsequently reconstructing forgotten information in accordance with biases and stereotypes; (2) reduces the likelihood of making a snap judgment and helps to prevent the halo effect, negative emphasis, and candidate-order errors; and (3) helps to ensure that all candidates are assessed on the same criteria.[48] Some examples of appropriate interview questions are shown in Exhibit 9-6.

EXHIBIT 9-6 Suggested Supplementary Questions for Interviewing Applicants

1. How did you choose this profession?
2. What did you enjoy most about your previous job?
3. What did you like least about your previous job?
4. Why did you leave your last job? What were the circumstances?
5. What has been your greatest frustration on your current job? Why?
6. Why should we be hiring you?
7. What do you expect from us?
8. What are three things you will not do in your next job?
9. What would your last employer say your three weaknesses are?
10. What would your last employer say your three major strengths are?
11. How can your manager best help you obtain your goals?
12. How did your manager rate your job performance?
13. Would you change your last supervisor? How?
14. What are your career goals during the next 1–3 years? 5–10 years?
15. How will working for this company help you reach those goals?
16. What did you do the last time you received instructions with which you disagreed?
17. What are some of the disagreements between you and your manager? What did you do?
18. Which do you prefer, working alone or working with teams?
19. What motivated you to do better at your last job?
20. Do you consider your progress on that job representative of your ability? Why?
21. Do you have any questions about the duties of the job for which you have applied?
22. How do you think you can perform the essential functions of the job for which you have applied?

Source: Based on www.HR.BLR.com

Closing the Interview

Toward the end of the interview, time should be allocated to answer any questions that the candidate may have and, if appropriate, to advocate for the firm and position. It is useful to also inform the candidate about the next steps and timelines that the organization will follow at this point.

Evaluating the Candidate

Immediately following each interview, the applicant's interview performance should be rated by each panel member independently, based on a review of his or her notes or an observation form like the one shown in Exhibit 9-7. Since interviews are only one step in the process, and since a final decision cannot be reached until all assessments (including reference checking) have been completed, these evaluations should not be shared at this time.

EXHIBIT 9-7 Interview Evaluation Form

Name of candidate:
Date interviewed:
Position:

Completed by:
Date:

Instructions: Circle one number for each criterion, then add them together for a total.

KNOWLEDGE OF SPECIFIC JOB AND JOB-RELATED TOPICS

0. No knowledge evident.
1. Less than we would prefer.
2. Meets requirements for hiring.
3. Exceeds our expectations of average candidates.
4. Thoroughly versed in job and very strong in associated areas.

EXPERIENCE

0. None for this job; no related experience either.
1. Would prefer more for this job. Adequate for job applied for.
2. More than sufficient for job.
3. Totally experienced in job.
4. Strong experience in all related areas.

COMMUNICATION

0. Could not communicate. Will be severely impaired in most jobs.
1. Some difficulties. Will detract from job performance.
2. Sufficient for adequate job performance.
3. More than sufficient for job.
4. Outstanding ability to communicate.

INTEREST IN POSITION AND ORGANIZATION

0. Showed no interest.
1. Some lack of interest.
2. Appeared genuinely interested.
3. Very interested. Seems to prefer type of work applied for.
4. Totally absorbed with job content. Conveys feeling only this job will do.

OVERALL MOTIVATION TO SUCCEED

0. None exhibited.
1. Showed little interest in advancement.
2. Average interest in advancement.
3. Highly motivated. Strong desire to advance.
4. Extremely motivated. Very strong desire to succeed and advance.

POISE AND CONFIDENCE

0. Extremely distracted and confused. Displayed uneven temper.
1. Sufficient display of confusion or loss of temper to interfere with job performance.
2. Sufficient poise and confidence to perform job.
3. No loss of poise during interview. Confidence in ability to handle pressure.
4. Displayed impressive poise under stress. Appears unusually confident and secure.

continued

COMPREHENSION

0. Did not understand many points and concepts.
1. Missed some ideas or concepts.
2. Understood most new ideas and skills discussed.
3. Grasped all new points and concepts quickly.
4. Extremely sharp. Understood subtle points and underlying motives.

_____ **TOTAL POINTS**

ADDITIONAL REMARKS:

Step 4: Background Investigation/Reference Checking

Background investigation and reference checking are used to verify the accuracy of the information provided by candidates on their application forms and résumés. In an ideal world, every applicant's story would be completely accurate, but in real life this is often not the case, as illustrated in Exhibit 9-8. At least one-third of applicants lie—overstating qualifications or achievements, attempting to hide negative information, or being deliberately evasive or untruthful.[49]

Unfortunately, some employers do not check references, which can have grave consequences. Background checks are thus necessary to avoid negligent hiring lawsuits when others are placed in situations of unnecessary and avoidable risk.[50] Cases in Canada have included a nurse who practised in a Toronto hospital for almost two years without a registered nurse qualification, a manufacturing plant payroll officer who embezzled almost $2 million, and a teacher arrested for possessing child pornography.[51] Other problems can also be addressed through background checks. Loblaw recently took action to reduce its $1 billion disappearing goods problem by making criminal record checks mandatory for all prospective employees. As a result, 7.5 percent of prospective hires have been eliminated because of criminal records.[52]

Surveys indicate that at least 90 percent of Canadian organizations conduct background checks.[53] Many firms use reference-checking services or hire a consultant to perform this task. Obtaining such assistance may be a small price to pay to avoid the time and legal costs associated with the consequences of failing to do a thorough background check.

Whether requesting reference information in writing or asking for such information over the telephone, questions should be written down in advance. If enough time is taken and the proper questions are asked, such checking is an inexpensive

CKR Global
www.ckrglobal.com

BackCheck
www.backcheck.ca

Investigative Research Group
www.irgcanada.com

EXHIBIT 9-8 Top Seven Résumé Lies

1 Dates of employment

2 Job title (inflated rank)

3 Salary level

4 Criminal records

5 Education (bogus degrees, diploma mills)

6 Professional licence (MD, RN, etc.)

7 "Ghost" company (self-owned business)

and straightforward way of verifying factual information about the applicant. This may include current and previous job titles, salary, dates of employment, and reasons for leaving, as well as information about the applicant's fit with the prospective job and organizational culture.

Information to Be Verified

A basic background check includes a criminal record check, independent verification of educational qualifications, and verification of at least five years' employment, together with checks of three performance-related references from past supervisors. For financially sensitive positions, a credit check may also be included.

Obtaining Written Permission

As a legal protection for all concerned, applicants should be asked to indicate, in writing, their willingness for the firm to check with current or former employers and other references. There is generally a section on the application form for this purpose. Many employers will not give out any reference information until they have received a copy of such written authorization. Because background checks may provide information on age or other prohibited grounds for discrimination, some employers do not conduct background checks until a conditional offer of employment has been extended.[54]

However, other employers do not hesitate to seek out information in the public domain at any time, without permission. A recent survey found that almost one-quarter of employers are using social networking sites like Facebook to gather information on job applicants. A third of those employers find enough negative information (such as the items listed in Exhibit 9-9) to eliminate a candidate from further consideration, and one-quarter of them find favourable content that supports the candidate's application.[55]

Providing References

In providing reference information, the concept of *qualified privilege* is important. Generally speaking, if comments are made in confidence for a public purpose, without malice, and are honestly believed, the defence of qualified privilege exists. Thus, if honest, fair, and candid references are given by an individual who is asked to provide confidential information about the performance of a job applicant, then the doctrine

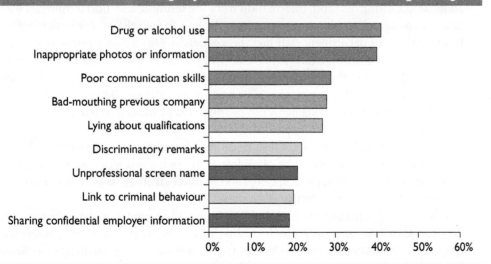

EXHIBIT 9-9 Online Postings by Job Candidates that Concern Hiring Managers

Source: Data from R. Zupek, "Is Your Future Boss Researching You Online?" CareerBuilder.ca, www.careerbuilder.ca/blog/2008/10/09/cb-is-your-future-boss-researching-you-online (accessed May 24, 2009).

of qualified privilege generally protects the reference giver, even if negative information is imparted about the candidate.[56] An overly positive reference, however, describing an employee dismissed for theft as "trustworthy," for example, can be considered *negligent misrepresentation* if the former employee steals from a new employer.[57] Due to concerns about the possibility of civil litigation, some Canadian companies have adopted a "no reference" policy regarding previous employees or are only willing to confirm the position held and dates of employment—especially in the case of discharged employees.[58]

Step 5: Supervisory Interview and Realistic Job Preview

The two or three top candidates typically return for an interview with the immediate supervisor, who usually makes the final selection decision. The supervisory interview is important because the supervisor knows the technical aspects of the job, is most qualified to assess the applicants' job knowledge and skills, and is best equipped to answer any job-specific questions from the candidate. Also, the immediate supervisor generally has to work closely with the selected individual and must feel comfortable with that person. The selected individual must fit with the current members of the hiring department, something that the supervisor is often best able to assess. When a supervisor makes a hiring recommendation, he or she is usually committed to the new employee's success and will try to provide assistance and guidance. If the new hire is not successful, the supervisor is more likely to accept some of the responsibility.

A **realistic job preview (RJP)** should be provided at the time of the supervisory interview. The purpose of an RJP is to create appropriate expectations about the job by presenting realistic information about the job demands, the organization's expectations, and the work environment.[59] Studies have reported that RJPs lead to improved employee job satisfaction, reduced voluntary turnover, and enhanced communication.[60] Although some candidates may choose not to accept employment with the firm after an RJP, those individuals probably would not have remained with the firm long had they accepted the job offer.[61]

Step 6: Hiring Decision and Candidate Notification

To make the hiring decision, information from the multiple selection techniques used must be combined, and the applicant who is the best fit with the selection criteria must be identified. HR department staff members generally play a major role in compiling all the data. It is the immediate supervisor who is usually responsible for making the final hiring decision, though. Firms generally make a subjective evaluation of all the information gleaned about each candidate and arrive at an overall judgment. The validity and reliability of these judgments can be improved by using tests that are objectively scored and by devising a candidate-rating sheet based on the weighted want criteria.

Another approach involves combining all the pieces of information according to a formula and giving the job to the candidate with the highest score. Research studies have indicated that this approach, called a **statistical strategy**, is generally more reliable and valid than is a subjective evaluation.[62]

Regardless of collection methodology, all information used in making the selection decision should be kept in a file, including interview notes, test results, reference-checking information, and so on. In the event of a human rights challenge, negligent hiring charge, or union grievance about the selection decision, such data are critical.

Once the selection decision has been made, a job offer is extended to the successful candidate. Often, the initial offer is made by telephone, but it should be followed up

realistic job preview (RJP) A strategy used to provide applicants with realistic information—both positive and negative—about the job demands, the organization's expectations, and the work environment.

statistical strategy A more objective technique used to determine whom the job should be offered to; involves identifying the most valid predictors and weighting them through statistical methods, such as multiple regression.

with a written employment offer that clearly specifies important terms and conditions of employment, such as starting date, starting salary, probation period, and so on.

Candidates should be given a reasonable length of time in which to think about the offer and not be pressured into making an immediate decision. If there are two candidates who are both excellent and the first-choice candidate declines the offer, the runner-up can then be offered the job.

An Ethical | Dilemma

As the HR manager, how much feedback should you provide to those individuals not selected for a position?

10 Orientation and Training

The terms "orientation" and "training" are associated, but actually represent slightly different variations of employee assimilation efforts. Orientation refers to a long-term, continuous socialization process in which employee and employer expectations or obligations are considered. With a focus on organization-specific topics, orientation attempts to transfer learning into behaviour using disciplined, consistent efforts.[1] In comparison, training refers to short-term, discrete efforts in which organizations impart information and instructions in an effort to help the recipient gain the required skills or knowledge to perform the job at adequate levels. Given that training often occurs after the orientation process, this chapter first reviews the process of orienting employees, followed by a review of the training process.

Orienting Employees

Once employees have been recruited and selected, the next step is orienting them to their new company and their new job. A strategic approach to recruitment and retention of employees includes a well-integrated orientation program, both before and after hiring.[2] New employees need a clear understanding of company policies, expectations regarding their performance, and operating procedures. In the long term, a comprehensive orientation (also called onboarding) program can lead to reductions in turnover, increased morale, fewer instances of corrective discipline, and fewer employee grievances. It can also reduce the number of workplace injuries, particularly for young workers.[3] The bottom-line implications of successful orientation can be dramatic.

Purpose of Orientation Programs

Employee orientation (onboarding) provides new employees with basic background information about the employer and specific information that they need to perform their jobs satisfactorily. At the Law Society of Upper Canada, any time a new employee walks through the door the organization acts quickly to help the person get started on the right foot. The Law Society views orientation as an investment in the retention of talent. The essence of the orientation program is to introduce people to the culture, give them a common bond, teach the importance of teamwork in the workplace, and provide the tools and information to be successful at the Law Society.[4]

Orientation is actually one component of the employer's new-employee socialization process. **Socialization** is the ongoing process of instilling in all employees the prevailing attitudes, standards, values, and patterns of behaviour that are expected by the organization.[5] During the time required for socialization to occur, a new employee is less than fully productive. A strong onboarding program can speed up the socialization process and result in the new employee achieving full productivity as quickly as possible.

Orientation helps the employee to perform better by providing necessary information about company rules and practices. It helps to clarify the organization's expectations of an employee regarding his or her job, thus helping to reduce the new employee's first-day jitters and **reality shock** (also referred to as **cognitive dissonance**)—the discrepancy between what the new employee expected from his or her new job and its realities.

An important part of any effective orientation program is sitting down and deciding on work-related goals with the new employee. These goals provide the basis for early feedback and establish a foundation for ongoing performance management.[6] Orientation is the first step in helping the new employee manage the learning curve; it helps new employees become productive more quickly than they might otherwise.

Some organizations commence orientation activity before the first day of employment. At Ernst & Young, the firm keeps in touch with people who have been hired but have not yet started work by sending them internal newsletters, inviting them

employee orientation (onboarding) A procedure for providing new employees with basic background information about the firm and the job.

socialization The ongoing process of instilling in all employees the prevailing attitudes, standards, values, and patterns of behaviour that are expected by the organization.

reality shock (cognitive dissonance) The state that results from the discrepancy between what the new employee expected from his or her new job and the realities of it.

to drop by for chats, and hosting dinners for them.[7] Others use orientation as an ongoing "new-hire development process" and extend it in stages throughout the first year of employment to improve retention levels and reduce the overall costs of recruitment.[8]

Online onboarding systems that can be provided to new employees as soon as they accept the job offer are increasingly being used to engage employees more quickly and accelerate employee performance.[9] Online onboarding provides strategic benefits starting with building the brand as an employer of choice. This approach engages new hires in a personalized way and accelerates their time-to-productivity by completing benefits decisions, payroll forms, new-hire data, introduction of policies and procedures, and preliminary socialization using videos and graphics before the first day on the job, leading to a productive day one.[10]

Content of Orientation Programs

Orientation programs range from brief, informal introductions to lengthy, formal programs. In the latter, the new employee is usually given (over an extended period of time) the following:

- Internal publications, including employee handbooks that cover matters such as company history, current mission, activities, products, and people

- Facility tour and staff introductions

- Job-related documents, including an explanation of job procedures, duties and responsibilities, working hours, and attendance expectations; vacations and holidays; payroll, employee benefits, and pensions; and work regulations and policies such as personal use of company technology

- Expected training to be received (when and why)

- Performance appraisal criteria, including the estimated time to achieve full productivity.

Note that some courts have found employee handbook contents to represent a contract with the employee. Therefore, disclaimers should be included that make it clear that statements of company policies, benefits, and regulations do not constitute the terms and conditions of an employment contract, either express or implied. Firms should think twice before including such statements in the handbook as "No employee will be terminated without just cause," or statements that imply or state that employees have tenure; these could be viewed as legal and binding commitments.

Hints | TO ENSURE LEGAL COMPLIANCE

Responsibility for Orientation

The first day of the orientation usually starts with the HR specialist, who explains such matters as working hours and vacation. The employee is then introduced to his or her new supervisor, who continues the orientation by explaining the exact nature of the job, introducing the person to his or her new colleagues, and familiarizing the new employee with the workplace. Sometimes, another employee at a peer level will be assigned as a "buddy" or mentor for the newly hired employee for the first few weeks or months of employment.[11] It is a good idea for the HR department to follow up with each new employee about three months after the initial orientation to address any remaining questions.

In an orientation, the supervisor explains the exact nature of the job, introduces new colleagues, and familiarizes new employees with the workplace.

Special Orientation Situations

Diverse Workforce

In an organization that has not had a diverse workforce in the past, orienting new employees from different backgrounds poses a special challenge. The values of the organization may be new to the new employees if these values were not part of their past experience. New employees should be advised to expect a variety of reactions from current employees to someone from a different background and be given some tips on how to deal with these reactions. In particular, they need to know which reactions are prohibited under human rights legislation and how to report these, should they occur. In addition, as diversity of the internal workforce increases, existing employees can be oriented toward a broader range of employee perceptions and effective communication techniques.

Mergers and Acquisitions

Employees of a newly merged company need to receive information about the details of the merger or acquisition as part of the information on company history. They also need to be made aware of any ongoing, as-yet-unresolved difficulties regarding day-to-day operational issues related to their work. A further orientation issue arises with respect to the existing employees at the time of the merger or acquisition: A new company culture will evolve in the merged organization, and everyone will experience a resocialization process. This presents an opportunity for the merged organization to emphasize the new organizational values and beliefs, thereby reinforcing corporate culture and furthering the new organization's business objectives.[12]

Union versus Non-Union Employees

New employees in unionized positions need to be provided with a copy of the collective bargaining agreement and be told which information relates specifically to their particular job. They also need to be introduced to their union steward, have payroll deduction of union dues explained, and be informed of the names of union executive members. New employees, both unionized and non-unionized, need to be made aware of which jobs are unionized and which ones are not.

Multi-Location Organizations

New employees in a multi-location company need to be made aware of where the other locations are and what business functions are performed in each location. The Ontario Ministry of Education is one such organization, and it uses a web-based, online orientation to deliver corporate-level information.[13] All employees have equal access regardless of their location, and the same message is delivered to each one. Updates can be made instantaneously, and employees can view the information at their own pace.

IBM has been piloting two virtual onboarding programs for interns in China and India. In the Chinese pilot, US-based HR staff and Chinese interns create individual avatars to build relationships, learn about their functions, and hold meetings within Second Life (an online artificial 3-D world). In India, IBM is using another virtual tool called Plane Shift to allow virtual teams to simulate project work.[14]

Problems with Orientation Programs

A number of potential problems can arise with orientation programs. Often, *too much information* is provided in a short time (usually one day) and the new employee is overwhelmed. New employees commonly find themselves inundated with forms to fill out for payroll, benefits, pensions, and so on. Another problem is that *little or no orientation* is provided, which means that new employees must personally seek answers to each question that arises and work without a good understanding of what is expected of them. This is a common problem for part-time and contract workers. Finally, the orientation information provided by the HR department can be *too broad* to be meaningful to a new employee, especially on the first day; whereas the orientation information provided by the immediate supervisor may be *too detailed* to realistically be remembered by the new employee.

Evaluation of Orientation Programs

Orientation programs should be evaluated to assess whether they are providing timely, useful information to new employees in a timely and cost-effective manner. Three approaches to evaluating orientation programs are as follows:

1. *Employee reaction.* Interview or survey new employees for their opinion on the usefulness of the orientation program. Also, evaluate job performance within specified time periods to assess transference of learning and behaviours where possible.

2. *Socialization effects.* Review new employees at regular intervals to assess progress toward understanding and acceptance of the beliefs, values, and norms of the organization.

3. *Cost/benefit analysis.* Compare (1) orientation costs, such as printing handbooks and time spent orienting new employees by HR staff and immediate supervisors, with (2) benefits of orientation, including reduction in errors, rate of productivity, efficiency levels, and so on.

Executive Integration

The orientation process is a continuous, long-term process aimed at moulding desired behaviours and aligning values of the employee and the organization. As such, there is a formal component of orientation that often occurs when a new employee first joins the organization. There is also an ongoing informal orientation process, with the aim to build a strong employee bond with organizational values, history, and tradition. This can include staff involvement such as mentoring, management guidance (by using high level staff, firms communicate the importance of messages and experiences in a more meaningful way), and through employee empowerment (indoctrination of values and information to guide workplace behaviour).

Additionally, newly hired or promoted executives typically do not participate in formal orientation activities, and there is little planning regarding how they will be integrated into their new position and company. The common assumption is that the new executive is a professional and will know what to do, but full executive integration can take up to 18 months. [15] To make things even more difficult, executives are often brought in as change agents, in which case they can expect to face considerable resistance. Thus, a lack of attention to executive integration can result in serious problems with assimilation and work effectiveness. It is common to perceive executive integration as an orientation issue, but integration at senior levels in the organization requires an ongoing process that can continue for months as the new executive learns about the unspoken dynamics of the organization that are not covered in orientation programs, such as how decisions are really made and who holds what type of power.[16]

Executive integration is of critical importance to a productive relationship between a new executive and his or her organization, and it is important to review previous successes

An Ethical | Dilemma

Is it ethical to withhold information from an incoming executive about critical problems that he or she will face?

and failures at executive integration on an ongoing basis. Key aspects of the integration process include the following:

- Identifying position specifications (particularly the ability to deal with and overcome jealousy)

- Providing realistic information to job candidates and providing support regarding reality shock

- Assessing each candidate's previous record at making organizational transitions

- Announcing the hiring with enthusiasm

- Stressing the importance of listening as well as demonstrating competency, and promoting more time spent talking with the boss

- Assisting new executives who are balancing their work to change cultural norms while they themselves are part of the culture itself.[17]

The Training Process

Training employees involves a learning process in which workers are provided with the information and skills that they need to successfully perform their jobs. Training might mean showing a production worker how to operate a new machine, a new salesperson how to sell the firm's product, or a new supervisor how to interview and appraise employees. Whereas *training* focuses on skills and competencies needed to perform employees' current jobs, *development* is training of a long-term nature. Its aim is to prepare current employees for future jobs within the organization.

It is important to ensure that business and training goals are aligned and that training is part of an organization's strategic plan.[18] A training professional in today's business world has to understand the organization's business, speak its language, and demonstrate the business value of training investment.[19] Purolator, one of Canada's largest courier services, has 12 500 employees in Canada, and Stephen Gould, senior vice-president of HR, says it's critical to the success of the business that the company's trainers understand the business strategy.[20]

In today's service-based economy, highly knowledgeable workers can be the company's most important assets. Thus, it is important to treat training as a strategic investment in human capital.[21] For example, Vancouver's Sierra Systems, an information technology consulting company, offers ongoing in-house training and more than 2 000 online courses for its employees. Their senior HR manager explains: "Training and development is critical to our business. We're a professional services firm and our people are how we deliver our business."[22] Unfortunately, formal training levels have been reducing over the last few years.

A federal government report concluded that:

> To remain competitive and keep up with the accelerating pace of technological change, Canada must continuously renew and upgrade the skills of its workforce. We can no longer assume that the skills acquired in youth will carry workers through their active lives. Rather, the working life of most adults must be a period of continuous learning.[23]

Already, a skills crisis has arisen in the manufacturing sector, where lack of qualified personnel is a major problem. Skills in greatest need of improvement are problem solving, communications, and teamwork.[24] Training is therefore moving to centre stage as a necessity for improving employers' competitiveness. The federal government has called for businesses to increase spending on training, and business has asked the government to expand programs for professional immigrants to get Canadian qualifications in their

Canadian Society for Training and Development (CSTD)
www.cstd.ca

training The process of teaching employees the basic skills/competencies that they need to perform their jobs.

fields. In response, the Canadian Council on Learning was created by the federal government to promote best practices in workplace learning. The Quebec government has legislated that all firms with a payroll of more than $250 000 must spend 1 percent of payroll on employee training (or else pay a tax in the same amount).[25]

Another benefit of increased training is the fact that training can strengthen employee commitment. It implies faith in the future of the company and of the individual employee. Few things can better illustrate a firm's commitment to its employees than continuing developmental opportunities to improve themselves, and such commitment is usually reciprocated.[26] This loyalty is one reason that a high-commitment firm like the Bank of Montreal provides seven days of training per year for all employees at a cost of $1 800 per employee—more than double the national average.[27] Today's young employees view learning and growth as the pathway to a successful and secure future and are attracted to organizations that have a commitment to keeping and growing their talent.[28]

Training and Learning

Training is essentially a learning process. To train employees, therefore, it is useful to know something about how people learn. For example, people have three main learning styles: *auditory*, learning through talking and listening; *visual*, learning through pictures and print; and *kinesthetic*, tactile learning through a whole-body experience. Training effectiveness can be enhanced by identifying learning styles and personalizing the training accordingly.[29]

First, it is easier for trainees to understand and remember material that is meaningful. At the start of training, provide the trainees with an overall picture of the material to be presented. When presenting material, use as many visual aids as possible and a variety of familiar examples. Organize the material so that it is presented in a logical manner and in meaningful units. Try to use terms and concepts that are already familiar to trainees.

Research | INSIGHT

Second, make sure that it is easy to transfer new skills and behaviours from the training site to the job site. Maximize the similarity between the training situation and the work situation and provide adequate training practice. Give trainees the chance to use their new skills immediately on their return to work. Train managers first and employees second to send a message about the importance of the training, and control contingencies by planning rewards for trainees who successfully complete and integrate the new training.[30]

Third, motivate the trainee. Motivation affects training outcomes independently of any increase in cognitive ability. Training motivation is affected by individual characteristics like conscientiousness and by the training climate.[31] Therefore, it is important to try to provide as much realistic practice as possible. Trainees learn best at their own pace and when correct responses are immediately reinforced, perhaps with a quick "Well done." For many younger employees, the use of technology can motivate learning. Simulations, games, virtual worlds, and online networking are revolutionizing how people learn and how learning experiences are designed and delivered. Learners who are immersed in deep experiential learning in highly visual and interactive environments become intellectually engaged in the experience.[32]

Fourth, effectively prepare the trainee. Research evidence shows that the trainee's pre-training preparation is a crucial step in the training process. It is important to create a perceived need for training in the minds of participants.[33] Also, provide preparatory information that will help to set the trainees' expectations about the events and consequences of actions that are likely to occur in the training environment (and, eventually, on the job). For example, trainees learning to become first-line supervisors might face stressful conditions, high workload, and difficult employees. Studies suggest that the negative impact of such events can be reduced by letting trainees know ahead of time what might occur.[34]

International Personnel Assessment
Council
www.ipacweb.org

Legal Aspects of Training

Under human rights and employment equity legislation, several aspects of employee training programs must be assessed with an eye toward the program's impact on designated group members.[35] For example, if relatively few women or visible minorities are selected for the training program, there may be a requirement to show that the admissions procedures are valid—that they predict performance on the job for which the person is being trained. It could turn out that the reading level of the training manuals is too advanced for many trainees for whom English is not their first language, which results in their doing poorly in the program, quite aside from their aptitude for the jobs for which they are being trained. The training program might then be found to be unfairly discriminatory. On the other hand, employees who refuse a lawful and reasonable order to attend a training program may be considered to have abandoned their position.[36]

Negligent training is another potential problem. **Negligent training** occurs when an employer fails to train adequately, and an employee subsequently harms a third party. Also, employees who are dismissed for poor performance or disciplined for safety infractions may claim that the employer was negligent in that the employee's training was inadequate.

The Five-Step Training Process

A typical training program consists of five steps, as summarized in Exhibit 10-1. The purpose of the *needs analysis* step is to identify the specific job performance skills needed, to analyze the skills and needs of the prospective trainees, and to develop specific, measurable knowledge and performance objectives. Managers must make sure that the performance deficiency is amenable to training rather than caused by, say, poor morale because of low salaries. In the second step, *instructional design*, the actual content of the training program is compiled and produced, including workbooks, exercises, and activities. The third step is *validation*, in which the bugs are worked out of the training program by presenting it to a small, representative audience. Fourth, the training program is *implemented*, using techniques like those discussed in this chapter and the next (such as on-the-job training and programmed learning). Fifth, there should be an *evaluation* and follow-up step in which the program's successes or failures are assessed.

Step 1: Training Needs Analysis

The first step in training is to determine what training is required, if any. The main task in assessing the training needs of new employees is to determine what the job entails and to break it down into subtasks, each of which is then taught to the new employee. Assessing the training needs of current employees can be more complex, because it involves the added task of deciding whether or not training is the solution. For example, performance may be down not because of lack of training but because the standards are not clear or because the person is not motivated.

Task analysis and performance analysis are the two main techniques for identifying training needs. **Task analysis**—an analysis of the job's requirements—is especially appropriate for determining the training needs of employees who are *new* to their jobs. **Performance analysis** appraises the performance of *current* employees to determine whether training could reduce performance problems (such as excess scrap or low output). Other techniques used to identify training needs include supervisors' reports, HR records, management requests, observations, tests of job knowledge, and questionnaire surveys.[37]

Whichever technique is used—task analysis, performance analysis, or some other—employee input is essential. It is often true that no one knows as much about the job as the people actually doing it, so soliciting employee input is usually wise.[38]

---

negligent training Occurs when an employer fails to adequately train an employee who subsequently harms a third party.

task analysis A detailed study of a job to identify the skills and competencies it requires so that an appropriate training program can be instituted.

performance analysis Verifying that there is a performance deficiency and determining whether that deficiency should be rectified through training or through some other means (such as transferring the employee).

EXHIBIT 10-1 The Five Steps in the Training and Development Process

1. NEEDS ANALYSIS

- Identify specific job performance skills needed to improve performance and productivity.
- Analyze the audience to ensure that the program will be suited to their specific levels of education, experience, and skills, as well as their attitudes and personal motivations.
- Use research to develop specific measurable knowledge and performance objectives.

2. INSTRUCTIONAL DESIGN

- Gather instructional objectives, methods, media, description of and sequence of content, examples, exercises, and activities. Organize them into a curriculum that supports adult learning theory and provides a blueprint for program development.
- Make sure all materials (such as video scripts, leaders' guides, and participants' workbooks) complement each other, are written clearly, and blend into unified training geared directly to the stated learning objectives.
- Carefully and professionally handle all program elements—whether reproduced on paper, film, or tape—to guarantee quality and effectiveness.

3. VALIDATION

- Introduce and validate the training before a representative audience. Base final revisions on pilot results to ensure program effectiveness.

4. IMPLEMENTATION

- When applicable, boost success with a train-the-trainer workshop that focuses on presentation knowledge and skills in addition to training content.

5. EVALUATION AND FOLLOW-UP

- Assess program success according to

  REACTION—Document the learners' immediate reactions to the training.

  LEARNING—Use feedback devices or pre- and post-tests to measure what learners have actually learned.

  BEHAVIOUR—Note supervisors' reactions to learners' performance following completion of the training. This is one way to measure the degree to which learners apply new skills and knowledge to their jobs.

  RESULTS—Determine the level of improvement in job performance and assess needed maintenance.

Source: This article was originally published in IOMA's monthly newsletter *HRFocus*® and is republished here with the express written permission of IOMA. © 2009. Further use of, electronic distribution, or reproduction of this material requires the permission of IOMA. www.ioma.com

Task Analysis: Assessing the Training Needs of New Employees

Task analysis—identifying the broad competencies and specific skills required to perform job-related tasks—is used for determining the training needs of employees who are new to their jobs. Particularly with entry-level workers, it is common to hire inexperienced people and train them.[39] Thus, the aim is to develop the skills and knowledge required for effective performance—like soldering (in the case of an assembly worker) or interviewing (in the case of a supervisor).

The job description and job specifications are helpful here. These list the specific duties and skills required on the job and become the basic reference point in determining the training required to perform the job.

Task Analysis Record Form

Some employers supplement the current job description and specification with a task analysis record form. This consolidates information regarding the job's required tasks and skills in a form that is especially helpful for determining training requirements. As illustrated in Table 10.1, a task analysis record form contains six types of information:

1. *Column 1, Task List.* Here, the job's main tasks and subtasks are listed.

2. *Column 2, When and How Often Performed.* Here, the frequency with which the tasks and subtasks are performed is indicated.

3. *Column 3, Quantity and Quality of Performance.* Here, the standards of performance for each task and subtask are described in measurable terms, like "tolerance of 0.007 inches," or "within two days of receiving the order," for instance.

4. *Column 4, Conditions Under Which Performed.* This column indicates the conditions under which the tasks and subtasks are to be performed.

5. *Column 5, Competencies and Specific Knowledge Required.* This is the heart of the task analysis form. Here, the competencies and specific skills or knowledge required for each task and subtask are listed, specifying exactly what knowledge or skills must be taught. Thus, for the subtask "Set cutting distance," the trainee must be taught how to read the gauge.

6. *Column 6, Where Best Learned.* The decision as to whether the task is learned best on or off the job is based on several considerations. Safety is one: For example, prospective jet pilots must learn something about the plane off the job in a simulator before actually getting behind the controls.

Once the essential skills involved in doing the job are determined, new employees' proficiency in these skills can be assessed and training needs identified for each individual.

Performance Analysis: Determining the Training Needs of Current Employees

Performance analysis means verifying whether there is a significant performance deficiency and, if so, determining whether that deficiency should be rectified through training or some other means (such as transferring the employee). The first step is to appraise the employee's performance because, to improve it, the firm must first compare the person's current performance with what it should be. Examples of specific performance deficiencies follow:

"Salespeople are expected to make ten new contacts per week, but John averages only six."

"Other plants our size average no more than two serious accidents per month; we are averaging five."

Distinguishing between *can't do* and *won't do* problems is at the heart of performance analysis. First, the firm must determine whether it is a *can't do* problem and, if so, its specific causes. For example, the employees do not know what to do or what the standards are; there are obstacles in the system (such as a lack of tools or supplies); job aids

TABLE 10.1 Task Analysis Record Form

Task List	When and How Often Performed	Quantity and Quality of Performance	Conditions Under Which Performed	Competencies and Specific Knowledge Required	Where Best Learned
1. Operate paper cutter	4 times per day		Noisy press room:		
1.1 Start motor			distractions		
1.2 Set cutting distance		tolerance of 0.007 in.		Read gauge	On the job
1.3 Place paper on cutting table		Must be completely even to prevent uneven cut		Lift paper correctly	On the job
1.4 Push paper up to cutter				Must be even	On the job
1.5 Grasp safety release with left hand	100% of time, for safety			Essential for safety	On the job but practise first with no distractions
1.6 Grasp cutter release with right hand				Must keep both hands on releases	On the job but practise first with no distractions
1.7 Simultaneously pull safety release with left hand and cutter release with right hand					
1.8 Wait for cutter to retract	100% of time, for safety			Must keep both hands on releases	On the job but practise first with no distractions
1.9 Retract paper				Wait till cutter retracts	On the job but practise first with no distractions
1.10 Shut off	100% of time, for safety				On the job but practise first with no distractions
2. Operate printing press					
2.1 Start motor					
.					
.					
.					

Note: Task analysis record form showing some of the tasks and subtasks performed by a right-handed printing press operator.

are needed; poor selection has resulted in hiring people who do not have the skills to do the job; or training is inadequate. Conversely, it might be a *won't do* problem. In this case, employees *could* do a good job if they wanted to. If so, the reward system might have to be changed, perhaps by implementing an incentive program.

Training Objectives

Once training needs have been identified, training objectives can be established, which should be concrete and measurable. Objectives specify what the trainee should be able to accomplish after successfully completing the training program. They thus provide a focus for the efforts of both the trainee and the trainer and provide a benchmark for evaluating the success of the training program. A training program can then be developed and implemented with the intent to achieve these objectives. These objectives must be accomplished within the organization's training budget.

Step 2: Instructional Design

After the employees' training needs have been determined and training objectives have been set, the training program can be designed. Descriptions of the most popular traditional training techniques and more recent e-learning techniques follow.

Traditional Training Techniques

On-the-Job Training

On-the-job training (OJT) involves having a person learn a job by actually performing it. Virtually every employee—from mailroom clerk to company president—gets some on-the-job training when he or she joins a firm. In many companies, OJT is the only type of training available. It usually involves assigning new employees to experienced workers or supervisors who then do the actual training.[40]

OJT has several advantages: it is relatively inexpensive, trainees learn while producing, and there is no need for expensive off-job facilities, like classrooms or manuals. The method also facilitates learning, since trainees learn by actually doing the job and get quick feedback about the quality of their performance.

Apprenticeship Training

More employers are going "back to the future" by implementing apprenticeship training programs, an approach that began in the Middle Ages. Apprenticeship training basically involves having the learner/apprentice study under the tutelage of a master craftsperson.

Apprentices become skilled workers through a combination of classroom instruction and on-the-job training. Apprenticeships are widely used to train individuals for many occupations, including those of electrician and plumber. In Canada, close to 170 established trades have recognized apprenticeship programs.[41]

Apprenticeship training is critical today as more than half of skilled trades workers are expecting to retire by 2020. Federal, provincial, and territorial governments are increasing their funding of apprenticeship training programs to meet this growing need for more trades people.[42]

Informal Learning

About two-thirds of industrial training is not "formal" at all but rather results from day-to-day unplanned interactions between the new worker and his or her colleagues. Informal learning may be defined as "any learning that occurs in which the learning process is not determined or designed by the organization."[43]

On-the-job training is structured and concrete. Here, a supervisor teaches an employee to use a drum-forming machine.

Job Instruction Training

Many jobs consist of a logical sequence of steps and are best taught step by step. This step-by-step process is called **job instruction training (JIT)**. To begin, all necessary steps in the job are listed, each in its proper sequence. Alongside each step, a corresponding "key point" (if any) should be noted. The steps show *what* is to be done, while the key points show *how* it is to be done and *why*. Here is an example of a job instruction training sheet for teaching a right-handed trainee how to operate a large, motorized paper cutter:

Steps	Key Points
1. Start motor	None
2. Set cutting distance	Carefully read scale to prevent wrong-sized cut
3. Place paper on cutting table	Make sure paper is even to prevent uneven cut
4. Push paper up to cutter	Make sure paper is tight to prevent uneven cut
5. Grasp safety release with left hand	Do not release left hand to prevent hand from being caught in cutter
6. Grasp cutter release with right hand	Do not release right hand to prevent hand from being caught in cutter
7. Simultaneously pull cutter and safety releases	Keep both hands on corresponding releases to avoid hands being on cutting table
8. Wait for cutter to retract	Keep both hands on releases to avoid having hands on cutting table
9. Retract paper	Make sure cutter is retracted; keep both hands away from releases
10. Shut off motor	None

In today's service economy, job instruction training for step-by-step manual work is being superseded by behaviour modelling for service workers. Behaviour modelling is discussed in the next chapter.

Classroom Training

Classroom training continues to be the primary method of providing corporate training in Canada, and lectures are a widely used method of classroom training delivery. Lecturing has several advantages. It is a quick and simple way of providing knowledge to large groups of trainees, as when the sales force must be taught the special features of a new product.

Classroom learning has evolved to maintain its relevance in the technological age. For Generation Y employees familiar with Web 2.0 features such as wikis, blogs, and podcasts, learning opportunities must reflect their new abilities and needs. Blended learning, using a combination of instructor-led training and online e-learning, has been found to provide better learning results and higher learner engagement and enthusiasm than expected. In blended learning, the in-class training becomes tightly integrated with the online experience, and the relevance to the learner is vastly improved. Thus the classroom has evolved to include interactions with remote colleagues and instructors, e-learning in many forms, coaching, assessment, and feedback.[44]

Audiovisual Techniques

Audiovisual techniques (CDs or DVDs) can be very effective and are widely used. Audiovisuals can be more expensive than conventional lectures to develop, but

job instruction training (JIT) The listing of each job's basic tasks along with key points to provide step-by-step training for employees.

offer some advantages. Trainers should consider using them in the following situations:

1. *When there is a need to illustrate how a certain sequence should be followed over time,* such as when teaching wire soldering or telephone repair. The stop-action, instant-replay, or fast- or slow-motion capabilities of audiovisuals can be useful.

2. *When there is a need to expose trainees to events not easily demonstrable in live lectures,* such as a visual tour of a factory or open-heart surgery.

3. *When the training is going to be used organization-wide* and it is too costly to move the trainers from place to place.

There are three options when it comes to audiovisual material: buying an existing product, making one, or using a production company. Dozens of businesses issue catalogues that list audiovisual programs on topics ranging from applicant interviewing to zoo management.

Videoconferencing, in which an instructor is televised live to multiple locations, is now a common method for training employees. It has been defined as "a means of joining two or more distant groups using a combination of audio and visual equipment."[45] Videoconferencing allows people in one location to communicate live with people in another city or country or with groups in several places at once. It is particularly important to prepare a training guide ahead of time, as most or all of the learners will not be in the same location as the trainer. It is also important for the trainer to arrive early and test all equipment that will be used.

Programmed Learning

Whether the programmed instruction device is a textbook or a computer, **programmed learning** consists of three functions:

1. Presenting questions, facts, or problems to the learner

2. Allowing the person to respond

3. Providing feedback on the accuracy of his or her answers

The main advantage of programmed learning is that it reduces training time by about one-third.[46] Programmed instruction can also facilitate learning because it lets trainees learn at their own pace, provides immediate feedback, and (from the learner's point of view) reduces the risk of error. However, trainees do not learn much more from programmed learning than they would from a traditional textbook. Therefore, the cost of developing the manuals or software for programmed instruction has to be weighed against the accelerated but not improved learning that should occur.

Vestibule or Simulated Training

Vestibule or simulated training is a technique by which trainees learn on the actual or simulated equipment that they will use on the job, but they are trained off the job. Therefore, it aims to obtain the advantages of on-the-job training without actually putting the trainee on the job. Vestibule training is virtually a necessity when it is too costly or dangerous to train employees on the job. Putting new assembly-line workers right to work could slow production, for instance, and when safety is a concern—as with pilots— vestibule training may be the only practical alternative.

Vestibule training may just place a trainee in a separate room with the equipment that he or she will actually be using on the job; however, it often involves the use of equipment simulators. In pilot training, for instance, the main advantages of flight simulators are safety, learning efficiency, and cost savings (on maintenance costs, pilot cost, fuel cost, and the cost of not having the aircraft in regular service).[47]

videoconferencing Connecting two or more distant groups by using audiovisual equipment. Charter of Rights and Freedoms Federal law enacted in 1982 that guarantees fundamental freedoms to all Canadians.

programmed learning A systematic method for teaching job skills that involves presenting questions or facts, allowing the person to respond, and giving the learner immediate feedback on the accuracy of his or her answers.

vestibule or simulated training Training employees on special off-the-job equipment, as in airplane pilot training, whereby training costs and hazards can be reduced.

E-Learning

Electronic training techniques have been developed that allow trainers to provide learning in a more flexible, personalized, and cost-effective manner. **E-learning** is the delivery and administration of learning opportunities and support via computer, networked, and web-based technology to enhance employee performance and development. Canadian employers are using e-learning to become more productive and innovative and to make self-directed, lifelong learners of their employees.[48]

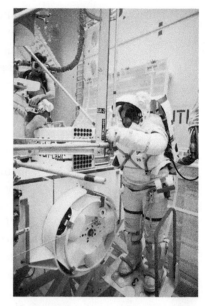

Vestibule training simulates flight conditions at NASA headquarters.

Effective e-learning requires good instructional design. It is critical to motivate learners by describing the benefits they will gain from the training, providing content designed to the learner's specific needs, and offering interactivity, such as application of the material to common problems in the context of the learner's workplace and intrinsic feedback.[49]

The Canadian Society for Training and Development has found that e-learning is generally as effective as other forms of learning, but at a reduced cost. The primary users of e-learning in Canada are professional and technical employees; clerical, service, and support employees; and managers. Interestingly, learners are more satisfied when web-based learning involves high levels of human interaction.[50] Mobile technologies are growing in influence in training and development. Short videos, instant messages, podcasts, and email are examples of smartphone features that can be used for training.[51]

There are three major types of e-learning: computer-based training, online training, and electronic performance support systems (EPSS).

Computer-Based Training

In computer-based training (CBT), the trainee uses a computer-based system to interactively increase his or her knowledge or skills. Computer-based training almost always involves presenting trainees with integrated computerized simulations and using multimedia (including video, audio, text, and graphics) to help the trainee learn how to do the job.[52] Cisco Systems developed a binary math game intended to improve the effectiveness of network engineers and made it available for free on its website and for use on mobile devices. This simple game solved a key training problem and also turned out to be an effective corporate marketing tool.[53]

A new generation of simulations has been developed to simulate role-play situations designed to teach behavioural skills and emotional intelligence. Body language, facial expressions, and subtle nuances are programmed in. These new simulations offer authentic and relevant scenarios involving pressure situations that tap users' emotions and force them to act.[54] At L'Oréal Canada, new product managers participate in a training program that combines e-learning and a virtual simulation where they apply their new skills. Teams of trainees compete as virtual companies in the marketplace and continue to learn when they see their results compared to the others.[55]

A higher percentage of Canadian firms use CBT compared with American firms, primarily because of Canada's geography. CBT is often more cost-effective than traditional training methods, which require instructors or trainees to travel long distances to training sites.[56] Alberta Pacific Forest Industries (Al-Pac) had such good results from using CBT as a staple of its training program that it launched a new component to enable employees to learn the skills of another trade. Employees benefit from having training that is accessible 24 hours a day, which addresses shift work and different learning styles. This training program also helps to keep non-union staff members satisfied, as the multi-skilling resulting from CBT enables many employees to rotate jobs.[57]

CBT programs can be very beneficial. Advantages include instructional consistency (computers, unlike human trainers, do not have good days and bad days), mastery of learning (if the trainee does not learn it, he or she generally cannot move on to the next step in the CBT), flexibility for the trainee, and increased trainee motivation (resulting from the responsive feedback of the CBT program).

e-learning Delivery and administration of learning opportunities and support via computer, networked, and web-based technology to enhance employee performance and development.

Online Training

Web-based training is now commonly used by Canadian organizations. It is generally estimated that online training costs about 50 percent less than traditional classroom-based training. Also, online learning is ideal for adults, who learn what they want, when they want, and where they want. Online training is often the best solution for highly specialized business professionals who have little time available for ongoing education. Students (the workers of tomorrow) thrive in online learning environments. They do not find it to be an isolated or lonely experience, and they find that they have more time to reflect on the learning material, which leads to livelier interaction.[58] Further, online training is ideal for global organizations that want consistent training for all employees worldwide. Alcan Inc. is using this approach to standardize its training programs for 72 000 employees in 55 countries.[59]

However, critics point out that content management, sound educational strategy, learner support, and system administration should receive more attention, as they are often the critical determining factors in successful training outcomes. In the last few years, "learner content management systems" have been developed to deliver personalized content in small "chunks" or "nuggets" of learning. These systems complement "learning management systems" that are focused on the logistics of managing learning. Together, they form a powerful combination for an e-learning platform. This development is considered part of the "second wave" of e-learning, involving greater standardization and the emergence of norms. Another problem is that the freedom of online learning means that unless learners are highly motivated, they may not complete the training. It is estimated that learners don't complete 50 to 90 percent of online courses. In general, it is important to seek "blended learning," including both personal interaction and online training tools.[60]

Electronic Performance Support Systems (EPSS)

Electronic performance support systems (EPSS) are computer-based job aids, or sets of computerized tools and displays, that automate training, documentation, and phone support. EPSS provides support that is faster, cheaper, and more effective than traditional paper-based job aids, such as manuals. When a customer calls a Dell Computer service representative about a problem with a new computer, for example, the representative is probably asking questions prompted by an EPSS, which takes the service representative and the customer through an analytical sequence, step by step. Without the EPSS, Dell would have to train its service representatives to memorize an unrealistically large number of solutions. Learners say that an EPSS provides significant value in maximizing the impact of training. If a skill is taught but the trainees don't need to use it until several weeks or months later, the learning material is always available through the EPSS.[61]

Steps 3 and 4: Validation and Implementation

Validation of the training program that has been designed is an often-overlooked step in the training process. In order to ensure that the program will accomplish its objectives, it is necessary to conduct a pilot study, or "run through," with a representative group of trainees. The results of the pilot study are used to assess the effectiveness of the training.

Revisions to the program can be made to address any problems encountered by the pilot group of trainees in using the training material and experiences provided to them. Testing at the end of the pilot study can measure whether or not the program is producing the desired improvement in skill level. If the results fall below the level of the training objectives, then more work must be undertaken to strengthen the instructional design.

Once the program has been validated, it is ready to be implemented by professional trainers. In some cases, a train-the-trainer workshop may be required to familiarize

electronic performance support systems (EPSS) Computer-based job aids, or sets of computerized tools and displays, that automate training, documentation, and phone support.

trainers with unfamiliar content or with unique and innovative new methods for presenting the training content.

Step 5: Evaluation of Training

It is important to assess the return on investment in human capital made through training by determining whether the training actually achieved the objectives. **Transfer of training** is the application of the skills acquired during the training program into the work environment and the maintenance of these skills over time. A number of actions can be taken before, during, and after a training program to enhance transfer of training.[62]

Before training, potential trainees can be assessed on their level of ability, aptitude, and motivation regarding the skill to be taught, and those with higher levels can be selected for the training program. Trainees can be involved in designing the training, and management should provide active support at this stage.

During the training, it is important to provide frequent feedback, opportunities for practice, and positive reinforcement. After the training program, trainees can use goal-setting and relapse-prevention techniques to increase the likelihood of applying what they have learned. Management can enhance transfer of training by providing opportunities to apply new skills and by continuing to provide positive reinforcement of the new skills while being tolerant of errors.

After trainees complete their training (or at planned intervals during the training), the program should be evaluated to see how well its objectives have been met and the extent to which transfer of training has occurred. Thus, if assemblers should be able to solder a junction in 30 seconds, or a photocopier technician repair a machine in 30 minutes, then the program's effectiveness should be measured based on whether these objectives are attained. For example, are trainees learning as *much* as they can? Are they learning as *fast* as they can? Is there a *better method* for training them? These are some of the questions that are answered by properly evaluating training efforts.

Overall, there is little doubt that training and development can be effective. Formal studies of training programs substantiate the potential positive impact of such programs. Profitable companies spend the most on training, and those rated as being among the 100 best companies to work for in Canada spend the most per employee on training.[63]

There are two basic issues to address when evaluating a training program. The first is the design of the evaluation study and, in particular, whether controlled experimentation will be used. The second is the training effect to be measured.

Controlled experimentation is the best method to use in evaluating a training program. A controlled experiment uses both a training group and a control group (that receives no training). Data (for example, on quantity of production or quality of soldered junctions) should be obtained both before and after the training effort in the training group, and before and after a corresponding work period in the control group. In this way, it is possible to determine the extent to which any change in performance in the training group resulted from the training itself, rather than from some organization-wide change like a raise in pay, which would likely have affected employees in both groups equally.

Training Effects to Measure

Four basic categories of training outcomes can be measured:[64]

1. *Reaction.* First, evaluate trainees' reactions to the program. Did they like the program? Did they think it worthwhile? One expert suggests using an evaluation form like the one shown in Exhibit 10-2 to evaluate employee reaction to the training program.[65]

transfer of training Application of the skills acquired during the training program into the work environment and the maintenance of these skills over time.

controlled experimentation Formal methods for testing the effectiveness of a training program, preferably with a control group and with tests before and after training.

EXHIBIT 10-2 Sample Training Evaluation Form

PROGRAM NAME: _____   DATE: _____

YOUR NAME (Optional): _____   FACILITATOR(S): _____

OVERALL PROGRAM RATING	Poor		Fair		Good		Excellent
	1	2	3	4	5	6	7

What did you like **best** about the program?	What did you like **least** about the program?	What would you like to have spent **more** time on?

Please complete this form to help us assess how well this program met your needs and our objectives. Your feedback is important to us and will be used in our continuous efforts to improve the quality and usefulness of this program. Circle the number that best expresses your reaction to each item.

	Strongly Disagree		Disagree		Agree		Strongly Agree
1. The program was well-organized	1	2	3	4	5	6	7
2. The sequence of material presented was logical	1	2	3	4	5	6	7
3. The content of the program was understandable	1	2	3	4	5	6	7
4. The program activities were effective in helping me learn the concepts and skills presented	1	2	3	4	5	6	7
5. The objectives of the program were clear	1	2	3	4	5	6	7
6. The program met its stated objectives	1	2	3	4	5	6	7
7. The facilitator(s) grasped the material and activities they presented	1	2	3	4	5	6	7
8. The knowledge and skills learned in this program will help me do my job better	1	2	3	4	5	6	7

9. The length of the program   was appropriate   should be shorter   should be longer

Thank you for your participation and feedback!

Source: Reproduced, with permission, from the *Ultimate HR Manual*, published by and copyright CCH Canadian Limited, Toronto, Ontario.

2. *Learning.* Second, test the trainees to determine whether they learned the principles, skills, and facts that they were supposed to learn.

3. *Behaviour.* Next, ask whether the trainees' behaviour on the job changed because of the training program. For example, are employees in the store's complaint department more courteous toward disgruntled customers than they were previously? These measures determine the degree of transfer of training.

4. *Results.* Last, but probably most important, ask questions such as these: "Did the number of customer complaints about employees drop?" "Did the rejection rate improve?" "Was turnover reduced?" "Are production quotas now being met?" and so on. Improvements in these "metrics"—specific measures of workplace results—are especially important. The training program may succeed in terms of the reactions from trainees, increased learning, and even changes in behaviour, but if the results are not achieved, then in the final analysis the training has not achieved its goals. If so, the problem may be related to inappropriate use of a training program. For example, training is ineffective when environmental factors are the cause of poor performance.

Although the four basic categories are understandable and widely used, there are several things to keep in mind when using them to measure training effects. First, there are usually only modest correlations among the four types of training criteria (that is, scoring "high" on learning does not necessarily mean that behaviour or results will also score "high," and the converse is true as well). Similarly, studies show that "reaction" measures (for example, asking trainees "How well did you like the program?") may provide some insight into how trainees felt about the program, but probably will not provide much insight into what they learned or how they will behave once they are back on the job.

Training for Special Purposes

Training increasingly does more than just prepare employees to perform their jobs effectively. Training for special purposes—increasing literacy and adjusting to diversity, for instance—is required too. The following is a sampling of such special-purpose training programs.

Literacy and Essential Skills Training

Functional illiteracy is a serious problem for many employers. As the Canadian economy shifts from goods to services, there is a corresponding need for workers who are more skilled, more literate, and better able to perform at least basic arithmetic. Not only does enhanced literacy give employees a better chance for success in their careers, but it also improves bottom-line performance of the employer—through time savings, lower costs, and improved quality of work.[66]

National Adult Literacy Database
www.nald.ca

In 2008, the Canadian Council on Learning reported that almost half of Canadian adults are below the internationally accepted literacy standard for coping in a modern society.[67] A 2010 update of this research suggests that Canada's largest cities (like Toronto, Vancouver, and Ottawa) will see a substantial increase in the illiteracy rate of the workforce, largely due to the spike in the number of seniors and the growing number of immigrants.[68] Research by University of Ottawa economists for Statistics Canada has shown that investments in essential skills training to improve literacy and numeracy pay off. For every increase of 1 percent in national literacy scores relative to the international average, a country will realize a 2.5 percent gain in productivity and a 1.5 percent increase in per capita GDP over the long term.[69]

Employers are responding to this issue in two main ways. Organizations such as diamond mining company BHP Billiton, steel giant Dofasco, the Construction Sector Council, and the Canadian Trucking Human Resources Council have implemented a training strategy with the objective of raising the essential skills of their workforce. Essential skills of workers can be measured with the Test of Workplace Essential Skills (TOWES), developed by Bow Valley College in Calgary. In 2005, the federal government made funding available for training professionals to develop enhanced language training (ELT) to provide job-specific English instruction to help immigrants gain employment in their area of expertise.70

Training for Global Business and Diverse Workforces

With increasingly diverse workforces and customers, there is a strong business case for implementing global business and diversity training programs. Research by Healthy Companies International has found that success in the global marketplace is predicted by developing leaders at all levels of business and by placing a high value on multicultural experience and competencies. The research identified four global literacies, or critical competencies, required to succeed in the global economy:

- Personal literacy—understanding and valuing oneself

- Social literacy—engaging and challenging other people

- Business literacy—focusing and mobilizing the business

- Cultural literacy—understanding and leveraging cultural differences[71]

Diversity training enhances cross-cultural sensitivity among supervisors and non-supervisors, with the aim of creating more harmonious working relationships among a firm's employees. It also enhances the abilities of salespeople to provide effective customer service.[72]

Two broad approaches to diversity training are cross-cultural communication training and cultural sensitivity training. *Cross-cultural communication training* focuses on workplace cultural etiquette and interpersonal skills. *Cultural sensitivity training* focuses on sensitizing employees to the views of different cultural groups toward work so that employees from diverse backgrounds can work together more effectively. All employees should be involved in managing diversity, and diversity initiatives should be planned and supported as any other business opportunity would be.[73]

Diversity Training
www.diversityatwork.org
www.diversitytraining.com

Customer Service Training

More and more retailers are finding it necessary to compete based on the quality of their service, and many are therefore implementing customer service training programs. The basic aim is to train all employees to (1) have excellent product knowledge and (2) treat the company's customers in a courteous and hospitable manner. The saying "The customer is always right" is emphasized by countless service companies today. However, putting the customer first requires employee customer service training.

The Canadian retail industry has struggled in the past with poorly trained workers who were not equipped to provide quality customer service. Retailers now understand that they need to make a serious investment in their employees.[74] The Retail Council of Canada offers a national customer service certification program for retail sales associates and retail first-level managers, based on national occupational standards and essential skills profiles for each group. Certification requires the completion of a workbook, a multiple-choice exam, an in-store evaluation-of-performance interview, and experience (600 hours for sales associates, one year for first-level managers). The certification program for sales associates includes the topics of professionalism, customer service and sales, inventory, store appearance, security and safety, and communication. Topics for first-level managers include professionalism, communication, leadership, human resources, operations, marketing, sales, customer service, administration, and planning.[75]

Training for Teamwork

An increasing number of firms today use work teams to improve their effectiveness. However, many firms find that teamwork does not just happen and that employees must be trained to be good team members.

Some firms use outdoor training—such as Outward Bound programs—to build teamwork. Outdoor training usually involves taking a group of employees out into rugged terrain, where, by overcoming physical obstacles, they learn team spirit, cooperation, and the need to trust and rely on each other.[76] An example of one activity is the "trust fall." Here, an employee has to slowly lean back and fall backward from a height of, say, three metres into the waiting arms of five or ten team members. The idea is to build trust in one's colleagues.

Not all employees are eager to participate in such activities. Firms like Outward Bound have prospective participants fill out extensive medical evaluations to make sure that participants can safely engage in risky outdoor activities. Others feel that the outdoor activities are too contrived to be applicable back at work. However, they do illustrate the lengths to which employers will go to build teamwork.

Training for First-Time Supervisors/Managers

As Baby Boomers head into retirement, young employees are rising to positions of authority quickly and in large numbers. They are assuming supervisory and managerial roles at much younger ages than their counterparts were only 10 to 15 years ago, with some university graduates being hired into management training programs right after graduation. Along with the steep learning curve that all first-time supervisors/managers face, the latest group faces the challenges of managing employees from previous generations who are still present in the workforce.

New supervisors/managers are often chosen for their technical ability, and their interpersonal and communication skills get overlooked. But it is precisely these skills that will determine success as a manager, which requires networking and the ability to get work done through other people. New managers also need to learn to define their personal management style, how to give and receive feedback, how to motivate others, and how to manage conflict.[77]

The transition demands crucial training because first-time supervisors/managers need to learn a new set of skills. Formal training is required, and higher-level managers need to coach, mentor, and provide performance feedback to new young supervisors.[78] This type of training can be provided by external organizations like the Canadian Management Centre.

An Ethical | Dilemma

Is it ethical to require employees to participate in weekend and evening training programs if they do not want to because it is going to take time that they would otherwise be spending on personal and family responsibilities?

Canadian Management Centre
www.cmctraining.org

11 Career Development

Career Planning and Development

Career planning has become a critical strategic issue for CEOs and boards of directors, as well as HR executives.[1] The aging workforce and shifts in occupations and employment patterns have created a sense of urgency regarding the development of careers for the next generation of managers and executives. Increasing competition for talent is expected to create a serious challenge for retaining high-potential employees. Proactive organizations have already started to take action to manage the need for more managerial talent.

At the same time, there is an increasing need for employees who are interested in global careers, in virtual work as a key aspect of their careers, in careers that involve continuously changing technology, and many other variations on traditional career paths. HRM activities play an important role in **career planning and development**. Career-related programs help HR professionals maintain employee commitment—an employee's identification with and agreement to pursue the company's or the unit's strategic goals. Most employees appreciate and respond well to having their skills and potential enhanced, and to knowing that they will be more marketable. Developmental activities, such as providing the educational and training resources required to help employees identify and develop their promotion and career potential, are extremely important to younger employees today. Career-oriented firms also stress career-oriented appraisals that link the employee's past performance, career preferences, and developmental needs in a formal career plan.

Career planning can play a significant role in retaining employees in the organization and reducing turnover of valued workers. The key factors in employee retention today are an organizational culture that values and nurtures talented employees, fair processes in "people" decisions, and managers who understand what motivates employees.[2] Employers and employees also recognize the need for lifelong learning. Retention can be strengthened by providing extensive continuing training—from basic remedial skills to advanced decision-making techniques—throughout employees' careers.

Before proceeding, it would be useful to clarify some of the terms that will be used throughout this chapter.[3] A **career** is a series of work-related positions, paid or unpaid, that help a person to grow in job skills, success, and fulfillment. *Career development* is the lifelong series of activities (such as workshops) that contribute to a person's career exploration, establishment, success, and fulfillment. Career development for older workers is just as important as it is for younger employees. *Career planning* is the deliberate process through which someone becomes aware of personal skills, interests, knowledge, motivations, and other characteristics; acquires information about opportunities and choices; identifies career-related goals; and establishes action plans to attain specific goals.

The Evolution of Career Development

In the early stages of career development research, career patterns were assumed to be stable, predictable, linear, and based on hierarchies. Career stages were seen as influential on the employee's knowledge of and preference for various occupations, and were often associated to the concept that based on an employee's age, their career stage could be established. Later studies, like the Vocational Preference Test (VPT) by John Holland suggested that a person's personality (including values, motives, and needs) determines his or her **occupational orientation**, which is another important factor in career choices.

Based on research with the Vocational Preference Test (VPT), six basic personality types or orientations were identified:

Career Planning Exercises
www.careerstorm.com

Career Networking
www.careerkey.com

Research | INSIGHT

career planning and development The deliberate process through which a person becomes aware of personal career-related attributes and the lifelong series of activities that contribute to his or her career fulfillment.

career A series of work-related positions, paid or unpaid, that help a person to grow in job skills, success, and fulfillment.

occupational orientation The theory, that there are six basic personal orientations that determine the sorts of careers to which people are drawn.

1. *Realistic orientation.* These people are attracted to occupations that involve physical activities requiring skill, strength, and coordination. Examples include forestry, farming, and agriculture.

2. *Investigative orientation.* Investigative people are attracted to careers that involve cognitive activities (thinking, organizing, and understanding) rather than affective activities (feeling, acting, or interpersonal and emotional tasks). Examples include biologists, chemists, and university professors.

3. *Social orientation.* These people are attracted to careers that involve interpersonal rather than intellectual or physical activities. Examples include clinical psychology, foreign service, and social work.

4. *Conventional orientation.* A conventional orientation favours careers that involve structured, rule-regulated activities, as well as careers in which it is expected that the employee subordinate his or her personal needs to those of the organization. Examples include accountants and bankers.

5. *Enterprising orientation.* Verbal activities aimed at influencing others are attractive to enterprising personalities. Examples include managers, lawyers, and public relations executives.

6. *Artistic orientation.* People here are attracted to careers that involve self-expression, artistic creation, expression of emotions, and individualistic activities. Examples include artists, advertising executives, and musicians.

Most people have more than one orientation (they might be social, realistic, and investigative, for example). Holland believes that the more similar or compatible these orientations are, the less internal conflict or indecision a person will face in making a career choice.

New Approaches to Career Development

The beginning of the twenty-first century was marked by a new social arrangement and diversification of approaches to work, which have begun to challenge traditional theories of career development. Job transitions are more frequent, therefore occupational prospects and linear career patterns lose definability and predictability.

As a result, a new concept of career development emerged, in which the primary stakeholder of a career is the person, not the organization.[4] Therefore, a more dynamic and holistic approach to career development is emerging, with a focus on lifelong learning, flexibility, and adaptability. As such, a number of individual and organizational considerations need to be made.

Identify Skills and Aptitudes

Successful performance depends not just on motivation, but also on ability. Someone may have a conventional orientation, but whether he or she has the skills to be an accountant, banker, or credit manager will largely determine the specific occupation ultimately chosen. Therefore, each individual's skills must be identified based on his or her education and experience. In organizations using competency- or skill-based pay, a formal system for evaluating skills will already be in place.

For career-planning purposes, a person's aptitudes are usually measured with a test battery, such as the general aptitude test battery (GATB). This instrument measures various aptitudes, including intelligence and mathematical ability. Considerable work has been done to relate aptitudes, such as those measured by the GATB, to specific occupations.

Identify Career Anchors

Edgar Schein says that career planning is a continuing process of self-discovery. As a person learns more about him- or herself, a dominant **career anchor** may become

career anchor A concern or value that a person will not give up if a choice has to be made.

apparent. Career anchors, as their name implies, are concerns or values that a person will not give up if a choice has to be made. Schein identified eight career anchors:

1. *Technical/functional:* People who have a strong technical/functional career anchor tend to avoid decisions that would drive them toward general management. Instead, they make decisions that will enable them to remain and grow in their chosen technical or functional fields.

2. *Managerial competence:* Other people show a strong motivation to become managers, and their career experience convinces them that they have the skills and values required to rise to general management positions. A management position of high responsibility is their ultimate goal.

3. *Creativity:* People who become successful entrepreneurs have a need to build or create something that is entirely their own product—a product or process that bears their name, a company of their own, or a personal fortune that reflects their accomplishments.

4. *Autonomy and independence:* Some people seem driven to be on their own, free of the dependence that can arise when a person works in a large organization where promotions, transfers, and salary decisions make them subordinate to others.

5. *Security:* Some people are mostly concerned with long-run career stability and job security. A stable future with one organization that offers a good retirement program and benefits or maintaining similar geographic surroundings may be important.

6. *Service/dedication:* More and more people feel a need to do something meaningful in a larger context. Information technology has made global problems, such as the environment, overpopulation, and poverty, highly visible.

7. *Pure challenge:* A small group of people define their career in terms of overcoming impossible odds, solving unsolved problems, and winning out over competitors.

8. *Lifestyle:* A growing number of people, particularly dual-career couples, define their careers as part of a larger lifestyle, integrating two careers and two sets of personal and family concerns.

Focus on Life Trajectories

Issues of work–life balance are becoming more significant in a person's reflections about their career aspirations. In addition, the growth in the number of people employed in the contingent workforce (temporary, part time, contractual, freelance, casual, and so on) makes managing interactions between work and life domains more critical in career planning.

As a result, career development can be envisioned as a *life trajectory*, in which a person designs and builds his or her career and life simultaneously. This increases the importance of ensuring that employees are empowered decision makers when an organization engages in career planning. As well, the value of career development initiatives must extend beyond adding value to the employer to also include an explicit discussion of the transferability and value of the initiatives to the employee.[5]

The focus on life trajectories requires a shift in thinking about career development, as outlined below:

1. *From traits and states to context:* Research on personality traits and ability factors to guide occupation-driven careers relied on stability and predictability. In the new economy, career patterns should be viewed as professional identities that

are dynamic. Understanding the range of factors that are outside of the organization's control is critical to the new approach of career development.

2. *From prescriptive to process:* On average, people up to the age of 36 change their jobs every 2 years. Traditional career paths involving a single, committed occupational choice are no longer a reality. Instead, career planners must stay informed about all of the job-specific requirements and offer a best fit of career patterns, focusing on adding information and content to enable employees to achieve a range of career ambitions.

3. *From linear to non-linear:* Traditional career development was very deductive in that it assumed past employment patterns were valid predictors of future career ambitions. Thus, there is a necessary shift to a more holistic life design for career development, with an awareness of non-linear, often mutually dependant, causalities. Career plans must be frequently reevaluated and updated involving an iterative strategy between organizational agents and employees.

4. *From scientific facts to narrative evaluations:* The old path of completing all desired education, securing a job, then establishing a family is no longer a reality for many Canadians; there is growing diversity of individual realities. Career development must empower employees to self-assess and interpret their own life experiences (often in the form of a narrative) and assist employees in making sense of their distinct perspective and implementing co-evolution.

5. *From describing to modelling:* Career development must adapt to individual experiences, ambitions, abilities, opportunities, and perspectives. Thus, the use of simple descriptive or scientific statistics alone undermines the complexity of career development. Career forecasting in this sense should develop a number of possible configurations and continuously monitor interacting variables to increase the success of career development.

Become a Learning Organization

Learning is a survival technique for both individuals and organizations. Today, employees at all levels know that they must engage in lifelong learning to remain employable and have a satisfying career. A **learning organization** is an organization skilled at creating, acquiring, and transferring knowledge and at modifying its behaviour to reflect new knowledge and insights. The HR department is often the driving force behind ensuring that the training and development opportunities necessary to create a learning organization are in place, particularly in transferring knowledge, learning from experience, experimentation through searching for and testing new knowledge, learning from others, and systematic problem solving.

Roles in Career Development

The individual, the manager, and the employer all have roles in the individual's career development. Ultimately, however, it is the *individual* who must accept responsibility for his or her own career, since workers are often seen as collaborators in the organizations that employ them.[6] This requires an entrepreneurial, goal-oriented approach that uses four key skills: self-motivation, independent learning, effective time and money management, and self-promotion.[7] Younger workers today are increasingly expecting to develop these skills by pursuing a career path that involves moving through multiple organizations.[8] **Networking** is the foundation of active career management and is essential for accessing the most valuable career resource—people. Networking is an organized process whereby the individual arranges and conducts a series of face-to-face meetings with his or her colleagues and contacts, plus individuals that they recommend.

learning organization An organization skilled at creating, acquiring, and transferring knowledge and at modifying its behaviour to reflect new knowledge and insights.

networking An organized process whereby the individual arranges and conducts a series of face-to-face meetings with his or her colleagues and contacts, plus individuals that they recommend.

EXHIBIT 11-1 **Personal Networking Chart**

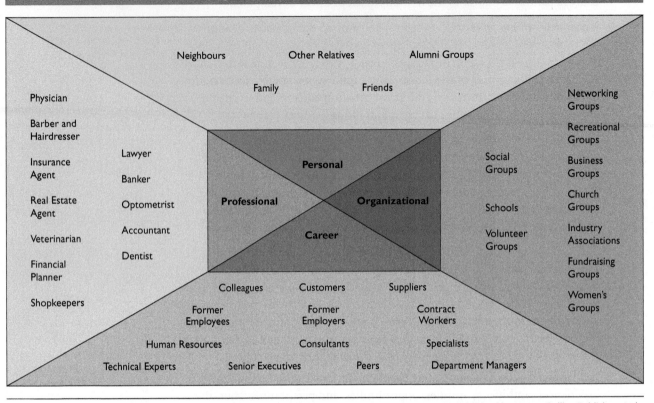

Networking does not involve asking for a job and it is not a one-sided encounter where only one individual benefits, but rather is a mutual sharing process. Its objectives are to let people know about background and career goals, and to exchange information, advice, and referrals.[9] A personal networking chart is shown in Exhibit 11-1.

Within the organization, the individual's *manager* plays a role in career development, too. The manager should provide timely and objective performance feedback, offer developmental assignments and support, and participate in career development discussions. The manager acts as a coach, an appraiser, an adviser, and a referral agent by listening to and clarifying the individual's career plans, giving feedback, generating career options, and linking the employee to organizational resources and career options.

Finally, the *employer* also plays a career development role. For example, an organization wanting to retain good employees should provide career-oriented training and development opportunities, offer career information and career programs, and give employees a variety of career options. Most employees will ultimately assess their employers on the extent to which the organization allowed them to excel and to become the people they believed they had the potential to become. How well an employer fulfills this career development role will help determine an employee's overall job satisfaction and commitment to his or her employer.[10]

Managing Transfers and Promotions

Transfers and promotions are significant career-related decisions that managers make on an ongoing basis. These decisions have important career development implications for the transferred or promoted employee and substantial benefits for the organization in terms of creating a pool of potential future managers with broad experience throughout the firm.

Managing Transfers

Employees may seek transfers into jobs that offer greater possibility for career advancement or opportunities for personal enrichment, or into those that are more interesting or more convenient—better hours, location of work, and so on.[11]

Employers may transfer a worker to fill a vacant position or, more generally, to find a better fit for the employee within the firm. Transfers are thus increasingly used as a way to give employees opportunities for diversity of job assignment and, therefore, personal and career growth. Many organizations are recognizing that future leaders will need international experience to effectively manage their organizations in the increasingly globalized world of business, and they are providing international assignments as a career development experience.

Policies of routinely transferring employees from locale to locale, either to give their employees more exposure to a wider range of jobs or to fill open positions with trained employees, have fallen into disfavour, partly because of the cost of relocating employees and partly because of the assumption that frequent transfers have a bad effect on an employee's family life. Companies are facing a record number of rejections of their relocation offers. About two-thirds of all transfer refusals are due to family or spousal concerns. Providing reassurances that relocation costs will be covered is often no longer enough to persuade employees to upset their lifestyles, their spouses' careers, and their children's activities. To overcome this problem, companies are offering spousal support in the form of career transition programs to encourage employees to accept transfers.[12]

Making Promotion Decisions

Employers must decide on the criteria on which to promote employees, and the way that these decisions are made will affect the employees' motivation, performance, and commitment.

Decision 1: Is Seniority or Competence the Rule?

From the point of view of motivation, promotion based on competence is best. However, union agreements often contain a clause that emphasizes seniority in promotions, meaning that only *substantial differences in abilities* can be taken into account in such situations.[13]

Hints | TO ENSURE LEGAL COMPLIANCE

Decision 2: How is Competence Measured?

If promotion is to be based on competence, how will competence be defined and measured? Defining and measuring *past* performance are relatively straightforward matters, but promotion also requires predicting the person's *potential*; thus, there must be a valid procedure for predicting a candidate's future performance. Tests and assessment centres can be used to evaluate employees and identify those with executive potential.[14]

Decision 3: Is the Process Formal or Informal?

Many employers still depend on an informal system where the availability and requirements of open positions are kept secret. Key managers make promotion decisions among employees whom they know personally and who have impressed them.[15] The problem is that when employees are not made aware of the jobs that are available, the criteria for promotion, and how promotion decisions are made, the link between performance and promotion is severed, thereby diminishing the effectiveness of promotion as a reward. For this reason, many employers establish formal, published promotion policies and procedures that describe the criteria by which promotions are awarded. Skills inventories, replacement charts, and replacement summaries (like those discussed in Chapter 21) can be used to compile detailed information about the qualifications of hundreds or even thousands of employees. The net effect of such actions is twofold: (1) an employer ensures that all qualified employees are considered for openings, and (2) promotion becomes more closely linked with performance in the minds of employees, which also increases the legal defensibility of the decision.

Management Development

Management development is any attempt to improve managerial performance by imparting knowledge, changing attitudes, or increasing skills. Management development is particularly important as Baby Boomers enter retirement and the next generation of managers assumes senior management responsibilities. It can also help attract top talent or achieve employer-of-choice status. The ultimate aim of management development programs is to achieve business strategy. For this reason, the management development process consists of (1) assessing the company's human resources needs to achieve its strategic objectives, (2) creating a talent pool, and (3) developing the managers themselves.[16]

Another critical issue in management development is training local managers in other parts of the world to take over from the original expatriate managers first sent out to initiate operations. Many organizations are focusing on management development in the Asia-Pacific region.

Succession Planning

Most organizations take special measures to plan ahead to develop replacements for senior executives because of their key strategic role. This process is called **succession planning**. Succession planning provides "a significant competitive advantage to companies that take it seriously—and serious risks to those that do not."[17] Although succession planning has traditionally been focused only on management jobs, many organizations today include other strategic positions as well. When an organization loses a top salesperson or a talented engineer, the loss will not make headlines but the impact on the bottom line could still be significant. A vacant position can mean that important decisions are delayed or made by other employees with less knowledge and expertise.[18]

Successful succession planning begins with the following steps:[19]

1. Establishing a strategic direction for the organization and jobs that are critical to achieving that strategic direction

2. Identifying core skills and competencies needed in jobs that are critical to achieve the strategy

3. Identifying people inside the organization who have, or can acquire, those skills and providing them with developmental opportunities (being prepared to recruit externally as well)

Succession planning for senior managers needs to be overseen by the CEO, as it can easily become an emotional issue for ambitious managers and can evoke political behaviour that can only be dealt with at the highest level.[20] HR staff ensure that all the required information for effective succession planning (such as skills inventories) is available, help to ensure objectivity in the process, and provide the development activities required for employees identified in the succession plan.[21]

Once potential successors have been identified, a *replacement chart* is often prepared. As shown in Exhibit 11-2, this chart summarizes potential candidates and their development needs for each job in the succession management plan.[22] It is important to ensure that these plans are implemented and carefully managed. A recent survey showed that half of North American companies with succession plans did not actively manage them.[23]

management development Any attempt to improve current or future management performance by imparting knowledge, changing attitudes, or increasing skills.

succession planning A process through which senior-level and critical strategic job openings are planned for and eventually filled.

EXHIBIT 11-2 Replacement Chart Showing Development Needs of Future Divisional Vice-President

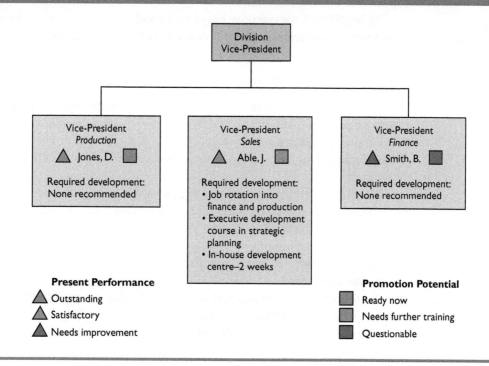

Employees should be encouraged to be proactive and accept responsibility for their own careers, including seeking out opportunities for leadership training. Employees who feel empowered and motivated to be the initiators of their own management development process may already be demonstrating leadership potential. Empowering employees in the organization to be part of a mutual succession-planning process increases the potential for its success.[24]

Management Development Techniques

Management development can include both on-the-job and off-the-job techniques. On-the-job development techniques are very popular, including developmental job rotation, the coaching/understudy approach, and action learning approach.

Developmental Job Rotation

Developmental job rotation involves moving management trainees from department to department to broaden their understanding of all parts of the business.[25] The trainee—often a recent college or university graduate—may work for several months in each department; this not only helps to broaden his or her experience, but it also helps the trainee discover which jobs he or she prefers. For example, Labatt Breweries' global management trainee program is helping to ensure a supply of future leaders.

In addition to providing a well-rounded training experience for each person, job rotation helps to prevent stagnation through the constant introduction of new points of view in each department. It also tests the trainee and helps to identify the person's strong and weak points.[26] Job rotation is more appropriate for developing general line managers than functional staff experts.

Coaching/Understudy Approach

In the *coaching/understudy approach*, the trainee works directly with the person that he or she is to replace; the latter is, in turn, responsible for the trainee's coaching. Normally, the trainee relieves the executive of certain responsibilities and learns the job by doing

developmental job rotation
A management training technique that involves moving a trainee from department to department to broaden his or her experience and identify strong and weak points.

it.[27] This helps to ensure that the employer will have trained managers to assume key positions.

To be effective, the executive has to be a good coach and mentor. His or her motivation to train the replacement will depend on the quality of the relationship between them.

Action Learning

Action learning releases managers from their regular duties so that they can work full time on projects, analyzing and solving problems in departments other than their own. The trainees meet periodically with a project group of four or five people with whom their findings and progress are discussed and debated. TD Bank Group and TELUS use this method.[28]

The idea of developing managers in this way has pros and cons. It gives trainees real experience with actual problems, and to that extent it can develop skills like problem analysis and planning. Furthermore, working with the others in the group, the trainees can and do find solutions to major problems. The main drawback is that, in releasing trainees to work on outside projects, the employer loses the full-time services of a competent manager.

There are many techniques that are used to develop managers off the job, perhaps in a conference room at headquarters or off the premises entirely at a university or special seminar. These options are addressed next.

Outside Seminars

Adventure learning participants enhance their leadership skills, team skills, and risk-taking behaviour.

Niagara Institute
www.niagarainstitute.com

Many organizations offer special seminars and conferences aimed at providing skill-building training for managers. For example, the Niagara Institute in Niagara-on-the-Lake, Ontario, offers programs that develop skills essential for strong leadership; and the Canadian Management Professionals Association offers a professional accreditation program leading to the Canadian Management Professional (CMP) designation.[29] Outdoor experiential expeditions, or adventure learning experiences, are sometimes used to enhance leadership skills, team skills, and risk-taking behaviour.[30]

College/University-Related Programs

Colleges and universities provide three types of management development activities. First, many schools provide *executive development programs* in leadership, marketing, HRM, operations management, and so on. The programs use cases and lectures to provide senior-level managers with the latest management skills, as well as practice in analyzing complex organizational problems. Most of these programs take the executives away from their jobs, putting them in university-run learning environments for their entire stay.

Second, many colleges and universities also offer *individualized courses* in areas like business, management, and healthcare administration. Managers can take these courses to fill gaps in their backgrounds. Thus, a prospective division manager with a gap in experience with accounting controls might sign up for a two-course sequence in managerial accounting.

Finally, many schools also offer *degree programs*, such as the MBA or Executive MBA. The latter is a Master of Business Administration degree program geared especially to middle managers and above, who generally take the courses on weekends and proceed through the program with the same group of colleagues.

The employer usually plays a role in university-related programs.[31] First, many employers offer *tuition refunds* as an incentive for employees to develop job-related skills. Thus, engineers may be encouraged to enroll in technical courses aimed at

action learning A training technique by which management trainees are allowed to work full time, analyzing and solving problems in other departments.

keeping them abreast of changes in their field. Supervisors may be encouraged to enroll in programs to develop them for higher-level management jobs. Employers are also increasingly granting technical and professional employees extended *sabbaticals*—periods of time off—to attend a college or university to pursue a higher degree or to upgrade skills.

In-House Development Centres

Some employers have **in-house development centres**, also called "corporate universities." These centres usually combine classroom learning (lectures and seminars, for instance) with other techniques, like assessment centres, in-basket exercises, and role-playing, to help develop employees and other managers. The number of corporate universities in North America has grown exponentially over the last several years because of their effectiveness in recruiting and retaining the brightest minds and in developing employee loyalty.[32] In Canada, BMO Financial Group, Canada Post, the City of Richmond, and many others all find that corporate universities can create a competitive advantage.[33]

BMO Financial Group
www.bmo.com/home

Behaviour Modelling

From the career development perspective, learning techniques can assist in the short-term or long-term career development of employees using behaviour modelling.

Behaviour modelling involves (1) showing employees the right (or "model") way of doing something, (2) letting each person practice the right way to do it, and (3) providing feedback regarding each employee's performance.[34] It has been used to train first-line supervisors to better handle common supervisor–employee interactions; this includes giving recognition, disciplining, introducing changes, and improving poor performance. It has also been used to train middle managers to better handle interpersonal situations, such as performance problems and undesirable work habits. Finally, it has been used to train employees and their supervisors to take and give criticism, give and ask for help, and establish mutual trust and respect.

The basic behaviour-modelling procedure can be outlined as follows:

1. *Modelling:* First, trainees watch films that show model persons behaving effectively in a problem situation. In other words, trainees are shown the right way to behave in a simulated but realistic situation. The film or video might thus show a supervisor effectively disciplining an employee, if teaching how to discipline is the aim of the training program.

2. *Role-playing:* Next, the trainees are given roles to play in a simulated situation; here they practice and rehearse the effective behaviours demonstrated by the models.

3. *Social reinforcement:* The trainer provides reinforcement in the form of praise and constructive feedback based on how the trainee performs in the role-playing situation.

4. *Transfer of training:* Finally, trainees are encouraged to apply their new skills when they are back on their jobs.

Critical elements of behaviour modelling include case studies, role-playing, management games, and simulations. The **case study method** presents a trainee with a written description of an organizational problem. The person then analyzes the case in private, diagnoses the problem, and presents his or her findings and solutions in a discussion with other trainees.[35] The case study method is aimed at giving trainees realistic experience in identifying and analyzing complex problems in an

Tips | FOR THE FRONT LINE

in-house development centre A company-based method for exposing prospective managers to realistic exercises to develop improved management skills.

behaviour modelling A training technique in which trainees are first shown good management techniques, then asked to play roles in a simulated situation, and finally given feedback regarding their performance.

case study method A development method in which a trainee is presented with a written description of an organizational problem to diagnose and solve.

environment in which their progress can be subtly guided by a trained discussion leader. Through the class discussion of the case, trainees learn that there are usually many ways to approach and solve complex organizational problems. Trainees also learn that their own needs and values often influence their solutions.

The aim of **role-playing** is to create a realistic situation and then have the trainees assume the parts (or roles) of specific people in that situation.[36] When combined with the general instructions for the role-playing exercise, roles like these for all of the participants can trigger a spirited discussion among the role-players, particularly when they all throw themselves into the roles. The idea of the exercise is to solve the problem at hand and thereby develop trainees' skills in areas like leadership and delegation.

In a computerized **management game**, trainees are divided into five- or six-person companies, each of which has to compete with the others in a simulated marketplace. Each company sets a goal (for example, "maximize sales") and is told that it can make several decisions, such as (1) how much to spend on advertising, (2) how much to produce, (3) how much inventory to maintain, and (4) how many of which product to produce. As in the real world, each company usually cannot see what decisions the other firms have made, although these decisions do affect their own sales. Management games can be good development tools. People learn best by getting involved in the activity itself, and the games can be useful for gaining such involvement. They help trainees develop their problem-solving and leadership skills, as well as foster cooperation and teamwork.

Several things can be done to increase the effectiveness of behaviour modelling approaches. If possible, the cases should be actual scenarios from the trainees' own firms; this will help ensure that trainees understand the background of the situation, as well as make it easier for trainees to transfer what they learn to their own jobs and situations. Instructors have to guard against dominating the behaviour modelling sessions and make sure that they remain no more than a catalyst or coach. Finally, they must carefully debrief employees about the intended versus actual behaviour as part of the learning process.[37]

Trainees participating in a case study discussion

Mentoring

Another approach to behaviour modelling includes mentoring. **Mentoring** has traditionally been defined as the use of an experienced individual (the mentor) to teach and train someone (the protégé) with less knowledge in a given area. Through individualized attention, "the mentor transfers needed information, feedback, and encouragement to the protégé," and in that way, the opportunities for the protégé to optimize his or her career success are improved. Effective mentoring builds trust both ways in the mentor–protégé relationship. Mentoring provides benefits to mentors, who demonstrate enhanced attitudes and job performance, and protégés, who become more self-confident and productive and experience greater career satisfaction and faster career growth.[38]

Organizational mentoring may be formal or informal. Informally, of course, middle- and senior-level managers will often voluntarily take up-and-coming employees under their wings, not only to train them but also to give career advice and to help them steer around political pitfalls. However, many employers also establish formal mentoring programs. Here, employers actively encourage mentoring relationships to take place and may pair protégés with potential mentors.[39] Training may be provided to facilitate the

Queen's School of Business: Executive Education
http://business.queensu.ca/executiveeducation/index.php

Development Dimensions International
www.ddiworld.com

Peer Resources
www.mentors.ca

role-playing A training technique in which trainees act the parts of people in a realistic management situation.

management game A computerized development technique in which teams of managers compete with one another by making decisions regarding realistic but simulated companies.

mentoring The use of an experienced individual (the mentor) to teach and train someone (the protégé) with less knowledge in a given area.

mentoring process and, in particular, to aid both mentor and protégé in understanding their respective responsibilities in the mentoring relationship.

A new development in mentoring is *reverse mentoring* programs, where younger employees provide guidance to senior executives on how to use technology for messaging, buying products and services, finding new business opportunities, and so forth. Procter & Gamble, General Electric, and the Wharton Business School are all using reverse mentoring. The relationship that develops often provides benefits to the young mentor as well when the technology-challenged older manager reciprocates in the form of career advice and guidance. Younger employees can also contribute toward understanding the ever-changing consumer marketplace.[40]

Through reverse mentoring, a younger employee can provide an older one with guidance in using modern technology.

Leadership Development

Canada is facing a shortage of leadership talent. At the same time, leadership values are evolving. The traditional command-and-control leadership style is losing its effectiveness, and there is a growing need for leaders who can listen to others and tolerate mistakes made in good faith as part of a learning process. Organizations can gain competitive advantage by addressing this leadership gap.[41]

Bob Hedley, vice-president of people and leadership at Maple Leaf Foods, says, "Where I lose sleep right now is we still don't have enough bench strength. One of the challenges is to acquire enough talent within the company and grow them fast enough so that we are ready to grow ourselves."[42] Maple Leaf Foods believes that employees' success guarantees the success of the company. They call it the "Leadership Edge"—thousands of high-performing people thriving in a high-performance culture. Employees are provided with ongoing feedback about their performance through a state-of-the-art performance assessment and development process. Employees receive recognition for both their accomplishments and their potential. This feedback is followed up with well-targeted developmental activities to ensure continued growth and development.[43]

At the executive level, 70 percent of learning comes from job experience, 20 percent comes from other individuals such as mentors and coaches, and 10 percent comes from formal training.[44] Many companies are trying to enhance learning from others by providing one-on-one executive coaching by independent coaches as part of the executive development process. In some cases, company managers are being provided with training in coaching skills, indicating the growing interest in developing coaching competencies throughout the management ranks.[45] For example, SaskEnergy created a long-term coaching program for 200 managers from all levels to help them develop successful leadership behaviours and provide skills they could apply to their teams. Coaching goals were tied to organizational strategy and succession planning, and senior management actively supported the program. The success of the program is helping to build leaders and position SaskEnergy for future success.[46]

The leadership development programs at the Banff Centre in Alberta focus on building leadership capability in five crucial areas that make up the leadership system: self, team, business unit, organization, and community/society. Leading in increasingly complex situations requires a systematic approach to successfully understand and navigate the interdependencies and linkages among all parts of the system, from the self through to the greater community. For this reason, the Banff Centre

EXHIBIT 11-3 Banff Centre Competency Matrix Model

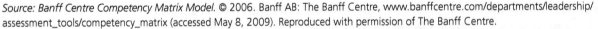

Source: Banff Centre Competency Matrix Model. © 2006. Banff AB: The Banff Centre, www.banffcentre.com/departments/leadership/
assessment_tools/competency_matrix (accessed May 8, 2009). Reproduced with permission of The Banff Centre.

uses an integrated approach to develop leaders.[47] The Banff Centre believes that the three basic requirements of successful leadership are knowledge, competency, and character. Exhibit 11-3 illustrates the Banff Centre Competency Matrix Model, which is based on six categories of competencies—self-mastery, futuring (vision), sense making (thinking), design of intelligent action, aligning people to action (leading), and adaptive learning.

Today it is critical that leadership development be a strategic priority for organizations to successfully cope with the coming exodus of Boomer executives. Without new executive talent that is trained and ready to assume senior-level responsibilities, Canadian companies will find it difficult to continue to compete successfully in the global economy.

12 Performance Management

The Strategic Importance of Performance Management

In any organization, achieving strategic objectives requires employee productivity above all else as organizations strive to create a high-performance culture by using a minimum number of employees. Thus, it has been suggested that better performance management represents a largely untapped opportunity to improve company profitability.[1] Many companies are still dealing with the reality that their performance management systems are ineffective—for example, they need to downsize poor performers, but performance appraisal records indicate that all employees are performing adequately.

Performance management is a process encompassing all activities related to improving employee performance, productivity, and effectiveness. It includes *goal setting, pay for performance, training and development, career management,* and *disciplinary action.* The performance management system must provide an integrated network of procedures across the organization that will influence all work behaviour.[2] There are three major purposes of performance management: it aligns employee actions with strategic goals, it is a vehicle for culture change, and it provides input into other HR systems such as development and remuneration.[3]

The Performance Management Process

Performance management is of considerable strategic importance to today's organizations because the most effective way for firms to differentiate themselves in a highly competitive, service-oriented, global marketplace is through the quality of its employees.[4] The performance management process contains five steps:[5]

1. Defining performance expectations and goals

2. Providing ongoing feedback and coaching

3. Conducting performance appraisal and evaluation discussions

4. Determining performance rewards/consequences

5. Conducting development and career opportunities discussions

Robert Thorndike researched performance management processes and suggests that employment decisions (such as a performance appraisal system) must be valid, practical, reliable, and free from bias.[6] Failure to measure and use appraisal results effectively in human resource decision making and career development negates the primary purpose of performance evaluations. Effective performance management thus begins with defining the job and its performance standards, which will now be discussed.

Step 1: Defining Performance Expectations

Defining performance expectations and goals is a critical step in employees' understanding of how their work makes a contribution to achieving business results. Over the last 30 years there has been more recognition that job performance is a multidimensional construct which can be split into what has become widely acknowledged as *task* versus *contextual* performance.[7]

Task performance reflects an individual's direct contribution to their job-related processes. Focusing on tasks means that performance expectations are grounded in realistic job demands and align with the organization's strategic objectives and implementation plans. They may also be partially based on previous performance evaluations.

However, as part of the movement toward more corporate social responsibility, expectations are beginning to extend beyond job skills and skills required for promotion to addressing the concept of whole person development (aligned with the direction,

performance management The process encompassing all activities related to improving employee performance, productivity, and effectiveness.

task performance An individual's direct contribution to their job related processes.

attitudes, motivation, and advancement opportunities of the employee). In addition to task performance, contextual performance is often evaluated as a second factor contributing to an employee's overall work-related performance. **Contextual performance** reflects an individual's indirect contribution to the organization by improving the organizational, social, and psychological behaviours that contribute to organizational effectiveness beyond those specified for the job. This includes extra-role behaviours and contextual factors like "demonstrates a positive attitude" and "pitches in to help others when needed," which have surfaced as contextual performance expectations.[8] These goals may be informally known, but not formally defined, which can become problematic in performance management. Employees also need to be aware of which behaviours are expected and which are discretionary to maintain the legitimacy of the performance management system.

Research finds that most employees require much more clarification of their performance expectations and how these contribute to the organization's overall results.[9] For example, the sales associate job description may list such duties as "supervise support staff" and "be responsible for all customer liaisons." However, one particular sales associate may be expected to personally sell at least $600 000 worth of products per year by handling the division's two largest accounts, to keep the sales assistants happy, and to keep customers away from company executives.[10]

Ultimately, the performance management process cannot be separated from performance measurement. Performance expectations need to be developed in a legally defensible (correlated with job activities), clear, and measurable way. In addition, they must be communicated and supported as such by the organization. Aligned with the sales associate example, a "personal selling" activity can be measured in terms of how many dollars of sales the associate is to generate personally. "Keeping customers away from executives" can be measured with a standard of no more than 10 customer complaints per year being the sales associate's target. In general, employees should always know ahead of time how and on what basis they will be appraised. It is important to note that expectations cannot discriminate directly or indirectly against anyone on protected grounds (gender, age, disability, and so on).

In global companies, performance appraisal criteria may need to be modified to be consistent with cultural norms and values. An interesting study found that some criteria are acceptable in many cultures.

Hints | TO ENSURE LEGAL COMPLIANCE

Step 2: Providing Ongoing Coaching and Feedback

Throughout the performance management process, managers and their reports should continue to discuss progress. Exhibit 12-1 provides an example of a performance improvement plan (often referred to as a PIP) that can be used to focus such discussions and facilitate ongoing performance improvement. It is important to have open two-way communication, and both the employee and the manager need to check in frequently throughout the performance management process to talk about progression toward goals.

In some organizations, strategies and objectives change quickly. In such cases, managers and employees may need to change their goals to be consistent. Employees are responsible for monitoring their own performance and asking for help. This promotes employee ownership and control over the process.

Step 3: Performance Appraisal and Evaluation Discussion

The appraisal itself is generally conducted with the aid of a predetermined and formal method, like one or more of those described in this section.

contextual performance An individual's indirect contribution to the organization by improving the organizational, social, and psychological behaviours that contribute to organizational effectiveness beyond those specified for the job.

EXHIBIT 12-1 Example of a Performance Improvement Plan

Sample Performance Improvement Plan

TO: [Employee's Name]

FROM: [ ]

SUBJECT: [30/60/90] Day Performance Improvement Plan

DATE: [ ]

This memorandum is written as a [30/60/90] Day Performance Improvement Plan designed to focus your attention on substantially improving your performance in several key areas.

[As was discussed in your most recent performance review dated __________ , you received several "1's" in key areas and an overall rating of "1" meaning you did not meet expectations.]

[Since your performance review on ________, your performance has been unsatisfactory in several respects. For example, ______________________________________ .]

This being the case, I have outlined the following Performance Improvement Plan which sets forth objectives that you must accomplish in order to bring your performance up to minimal acceptable standards. The plan is as follows:

1.

2.

3. [list fair objectives – they can be both objective and subjective – in clear terms that could reasonably be accomplished within the required time frame]

4.

5.

You have [30/60/90] days from today to meet these objectives. I will meet with you twice over the next [30/60/90] days to discuss your progress. Our first meeting will be on __________________ at ________________ and the second meeting will be on ________ at __________________ . Both meetings will be in my office.

It is your responsibility to contact me at anytime during this time period regarding your performance and to seek assistance in removing roadblock(s) you may come up against which may impede your progress.

MILW_513764.1

Source: Docstoc, Documents & Resources for Small Businesses & Professionals, www.docstoc.com/docs/4960973/Sample-Performance-Improvement-Plan-TO-FROM-SUBJECT-DATE-Employee.

Formal Appraisal Methods

Graphic Rating Scale

The **graphic rating scale** is the simplest and most popular technique for appraising performance. Exhibit 12-2 shows a typical rating scale. It lists traits (such as reliability) and a range of performance values (from unsatisfactory to outstanding) for each one. The supervisor rates each employee by circling or checking the score that best describes his or her performance for each trait. The assigned values are then totalled.

Instead of appraising generic traits or factors, many firms specify the duties to be appraised. For a payroll coordinator, these might include being the liaison with accounting and benefits staff, continually updating knowledge regarding relevant legislation, maintenance of payroll records, data entry and payroll calculations, and ongoing responses to employee inquiries regarding payroll issues.

Alternation Ranking Method

Ranking employees from best to worst on a trait or traits is another method for evaluating employees. Because it is usually easier to distinguish between the worst and best employees than to rank them, an **alternation ranking method** is popular. First, list all employees to be rated, and then cross out the names of any not known well enough to rank. Then, on a form such as that shown in Exhibit 12-3, indicate the employee who is the highest on the characteristic being measured and also the one who is the lowest. Then choose the next highest and the next lowest, alternating between highest and lowest until all the employees to be rated have been ranked.

Paired Comparison Method

The **paired comparison method** helps to make the ranking method more precise. For every trait (quantity of work, quality of work, and so on), every employee is paired with and compared with every other employee.

Suppose that five employees are to be rated. In the paired comparison method, a chart is prepared, as in Exhibit 12-4, of all possible pairs of employees for each trait. Then, for each trait, indicate (with a + or −) who is the better employee of the pair. Next, the number of times that an employee is rated as better is added up. In Exhibit 12-4, employee Maria was ranked highest (she has the most + marks) for quality of work, while Art was ranked highest for creativity.

Forced Distribution Method

Jack Welch, retired chief executive officer of General Electric (GE), is most often associated with the **forced distribution method**, which places predetermined percentages of ratees in performance categories. At GE, the bell curve was used to identify the top 10–20% of the workforce (which are then identified as those exceeding expectations, with a focus on receiving the highest compensation increases and advancement opportunities), the bottom 10% (which are identified as those not meeting expectations, with a focus on coaching for improvement or possible termination). The remaining employees, by default, are considered the backbone of the workforce and receive moderate compensation increases and development opportunities. While the method allows for a concentration of effort and resources on those deemed to be top performers, this method has been criticized as being demotivating since the majority of the workforce are classified as at or below average.[11]

Critical Incident Method

With the **critical incident method**, the supervisor keeps a log of desirable or undesirable examples or incidents of each employee's work-related behaviour. Then, every six months or so, the supervisor and employee meet to discuss the latter's performance by using the specific incidents as examples.

graphic rating scale A scale that lists a number of traits and a range of performance for each. The employee is then rated by identifying the score that best describes his or her level of performance for each trait.

alternation ranking method Ranking employees from best to worst on a particular trait.

paired comparison method Ranking employees by making a chart of all possible pairs of employees for each trait and indicating the better employee of the pair.

forced distribution method Predetermined percentages of ratees are placed in various performance categories.

critical incident method Keeping a record of uncommonly good or undesirable examples of an employee's work-related behaviour and reviewing the list with the employee at predetermined times.

EXHIBIT 12-2 Sample Graphic Rating Scale Form

Sample Performance Rating Form

Employee's Name _____   Level: Entry-level employee

Manager's Name _____

Key Work Responsibilities   Results/Goals to be Achieved
1. _____   1. _____
2. _____   2. _____
3. _____   3. _____
4. _____   4. _____

Communication

	1	2	3	4	5

Below Expectations	Meets Expectations	Role Model
Even with guidance, fails to prepare straight-forward communications, including forms, paperwork, and records, in a timely and accurate manner; products require extensive corrections. Even with guidance, fails to adapt style and materials to communicate straightforward information.	With guidance, prepares straightforward communications, including forms, paperwork, and records, in a timely and accurate manner; products require minimal corrections. With guidance, adapts style and materials to communicate straightforward information.	Independently prepares communications, such as forms, paperwork, and records, in a timely, clear, and accurate manner; products require few, if any, corrections. Independently adapts style and materials to communicate information.

Organizational Know-How

	1	2	3	4	5

Below Expectations	Meets Expectations	Role Model
<performance standards appear here>	<performance standards appear here>	<performance standards appear here>

Personal Effectiveness

	1	2	3	4	5

Below Expectations	Meets Expectations	Role Model
<performance standards appear here>	<performance standards appear here>	<performance standards appear here>

Teamwork

	1	2	3	4	5

Below Expectations	Meets Expectations	Role Model
<performance standards appear here>	<performance standards appear here>	<performance standards appear here>

Achieving Business Results

	1	2	3	4	5

Below Expectations	Meets Expectations	Role Model
<performance standards appear here>	<performance standards appear here>	<performance standards appear here>

continued

Results Assessment

Accomplishment 1: _____

1	2	3	4	5
Low Impact		**Moderate Impact**		**High Impact**
The efficiency or effectiveness of operations remained the same or improved only minimally. The quality of products remained the same or improved only minimally.		The efficiency or effectiveness of operations improved quite a lot. The quality of products improved quite a lot.		The efficiency or effectiveness of operations improved tremendously. The quality of products improved tremendously.

Accomplishment 2: _____

1	2	3	4	5
Low Impact		**Moderate Impact**		**High Impact**
The efficiency or effectiveness of operations remained the same or improved only minimally. The quality of products remained the same or improved only minimally.		The efficiency or effectiveness of operations improved quite a lot. The quality of products improved quite a lot.		The efficiency or effectiveness of operations improved tremendously. The quality of products improved tremendously.

Narrative

_____

_____

_____

_____

_____

Areas to Be Developed	Actions	Completion Date

Manager's Signature _____ Date _____

Employee's Signature _____ Date _____

The above employee signature indicates receipt of, but not necessarily concurrence with, the evaluation herein.

Source: Adapted from Elaine Pulakos, *Performance Management* (SHRM Foundation, 2004) pp. 16–17. Reprinted by permission of Society for Human Resource Management Foundation.

EXHIBIT 12-3 Alternation Ranking Scale

ALTERNATION RANKING SCALE

For the Trait: _____

For the trait you are measuring, list all the employees you want to rank. Put the highest-ranking employee's name on line 1. Put the lowest-ranking employee's name on line 20. Then list the next highest ranking on line 2, the next lowest ranking on line 19, and so on. Continue until all names are on the scale.

Highest-ranking employee

1. _____ 11. _____
2. _____ 12. _____
3. _____ 13. _____
4. _____ 14. _____
5. _____ 15. _____
6. _____ 16. _____
7. _____ 17. _____
8. _____ 18. _____
9. _____ 19. _____
10. _____ 20. _____

Lowest-ranking employee

EXHIBIT 12-4 Ranking Employees by the Paired Comparison Method

FOR THE TRAIT "QUALITY OF WORK"

As Compared with:	A Art	B Maria	C Chuck	D Diane	E José
A Art		+	+	−	−
B Maria	−		−	−	−
C Chuck	−	+		+	−
D Diane	+	+	−		+
E José	+	+	+	−	

Maria Ranks Highest Here

FOR THE TRAIT "CREATIVITY"

As Compared with:	A Art	B Maria	C Chuck	D Diane	E José
A Art		−	−	−	−
B Maria	+		−	+	+
C Chuck	+	+		−	+
D Diane	+	−	+		−
E José	+	−	−	+	

Art Ranks Highest Here

Note: "+" means "better than" and "−" means "worse than." For each chart, add up the number of + signs in each column to get the highest-ranked employee.

This method has several advantages. It provides specific hard facts for explaining the appraisal. It also ensures that a manager thinks about the employee's appraisal throughout the year, because the incidents must be accumulated; therefore, the rating does not just reflect the employee's most recent performance. Keeping a running list of critical incidents should also provide concrete examples of what an employee can do to eliminate any performance deficiencies.

The critical incident method can be adapted to the specific job expectations laid out for the employee at the beginning of the year. Thus, in the example presented in Table 12.1, one of the assistant plant manager's continuing duties is to supervise procurement and to minimize inventory costs. The critical incident shows that the assistant plant manager let inventory storage costs rise 15 percent; this provides a specific example of what performance must be improved in the future.

The critical incident method is often used to supplement another appraisal technique, like a ranking system. It is useful for identifying specific examples of good and poor performance and for planning how deficiencies can be corrected. It is not as useful by itself for comparing employees nor, therefore, for making salary decisions.

Narrative Forms

Some employers use narrative forms to evaluate employees. For example, the form in Exhibit 12-1 presented a suggested format for identifying a performance issue and presenting a *performance improvement plan* (PIP). The performance problem is described in specific detail, and its organizational impact is specified. The improvement plan identifies measurable improvement goals, provides directions regarding training and any other suggested activities to address the performance issue, and encourages the employee to add ideas about steps to be taken to improve performance. Therefore, a PIP essentially facilitates a constructive discussion between an employee and his or her manager, and provides clarity as to how to improve work performance. Finally, the outcomes and consequences, both positive and negative, are explicitly stated. A summary performance appraisal discussion then focuses on problem solving.[12]

Behaviourally Anchored Rating Scales

A **behaviourally anchored rating scale (BARS)** combines the benefits of narratives, critical incidents, and quantified ratings by anchoring a series of quantified scales, one for each performance dimension, with specific behavioural examples of good or poor performance. The guiding principle to BARS is that by elaboration of the dimension and rating scale, it gives raters a uniform interpretation as to the types of behaviour being measured.[13] BARS usually involves a scale of nine anchors, although seven and five anchors have also been used.[14]

The midpoint scales are more difficult to develop in a standardized format than the scale extremes. Recent efforts have focused on addressing midpoint scale development to influence inter-rater reliability and inter-rater agreement.[15] The research suggests that all levels of the scale be anchored with statements reflecting how users are to interpret

behaviourally anchored rating scale (BARS) An appraisal method that aims to combine the benefits of narratives, critical incidents, and quantified ratings by anchoring a quantified scale with specific narrative examples of good and poor performance.

TABLE 12.1 Task Analysis Record Form		
Continuing Duties	**Targets**	**Critical Incidents**
Schedule production for plant	Full utilization of employees and machinery in plant; orders delivered on time	Instituted new production scheduling system; decreased late orders by 10 percent last month; increased machine utilization in plant by 20 percent last month
Supervise procurement of raw materials and inventory control	Minimize inventory costs while keeping adequate supplies on hand	Let inventory storage costs rise 15 percent last month; overordered parts "A" and "B" by 20 percent; underordered part "C" by 30 percent
Supervise machinery maintenance	No shutdowns because of faulty machinery	Instituted new preventative maintenance system for plant; prevented a machine breakdown by discovering faulty part

them to increase uniform use of the scale. As well, developers of the scales should be involved in the training of users to increase the consistency in how the scale is used, which increases the effectiveness and legal defensibility of the performance appraisal. Exhibit 12-5 provides an example of a BARS for one performance dimension: "sales skills."

Developing a BARS can be more time-consuming than developing other appraisal tools, like graphic rating scales. But BARS may also have important advantages:[16]

1. *A more accurate measure.* People who know the job and its requirements better than anyone else does develop BARS. The result should therefore be a good measure of performance on that job.

2. *Clearer standards.* The critical incidents along the scale help to clarify what is meant by extremely good performance, average performance, and so forth.

3. *Feedback.* The critical incidents may be more useful in providing feedback to appraisees than simply informing them of their performance rating without providing specific behavioural examples.

4. *Independent dimensions.* Systematically clustering the critical incidents into five or six performance dimensions (such as "knowledge and judgment") should help to make the dimensions more independent of one another. For example, a rater should be less likely to rate an employee high on all dimensions simply because he or she was rated high in "conscientiousness."

5. *Consistency.* BARS evaluations also seem to be relatively consistent and reliable in that different raters' appraisals of the same person tend to be similar.[17]

EXHIBIT 12-5 Behaviourally Anchored Rating Scale

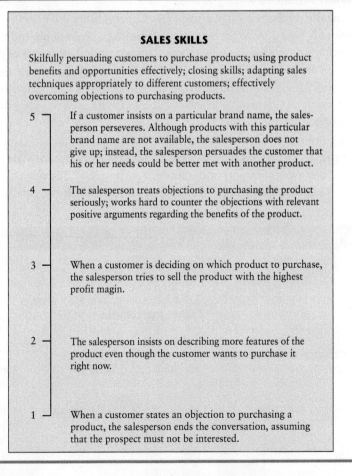

SALES SKILLS

Skilfully persuading customers to purchase products; using product benefits and opportunities effectively; closing skills; adapting sales techniques appropriately to different customers; effectively overcoming objections to purchasing products.

5 — If a customer insists on a particular brand name, the salesperson perseveres. Although products with this particular brand name are not available, the salesperson does not give up; instead, the salesperson persuades the customer that his or her needs could be better met with another product.

4 — The salesperson treats objections to purchasing the product seriously; works hard to counter the objections with relevant positive arguments regarding the benefits of the product.

3 — When a customer is deciding on which product to purchase, the salesperson tries to sell the product with the highest profit magin.

2 — The salesperson insists on describing more features of the product even though the customer wants to purchase it right now.

1 — When a customer states an objection to purchasing a product, the salesperson ends the conversation, assuming that the prospect must not be interested.

Management by Objectives (MBO)

Stripped to its essentials, **management by objectives (MBO)** requires the manager and employee to jointly set specific measurable goals and periodically discuss progress toward these goals, aligned with a comprehensive, *organization-wide goal-setting and appraisal program*. When managers and employees set goals collaboratively, employees become more engaged and committed to the goal, leading to a higher rate of success.[18] While there is a notion that difficult goals (also referred to as "stretch goals") can increase personal growth and professional development, and improve organizational effectiveness,[19] it is important to set objectives that match the job description and the person's abilities. Goals that push an employee too far beyond his or her abilities may lead to burnout.[20] To motivate performance, the objectives must be fair and attainable.

1. *Set the organization's goals.* Establish an organization-wide plan for the next year and set goals.

2. *Set departmental goals.* Department heads and their superiors jointly set goals for their departments.

3. *Discuss departmental goals.* Department heads discuss the department's goals with all employees in the department (often at a department-wide meeting) and ask them to develop their own individual goals; in other words, how can each employee contribute to the department's attainment of its goals?

4. *Define expected results* (set individual goals). Here, department heads and employees set short-term performance targets.

5. *Performance reviews: Measure the results.* Department heads compare the actual performance of each employee with the expected results.

6. *Provide feedback.* Department heads hold periodic performance review meetings with employees to discuss and evaluate progress in achieving expected results.

Problems to Avoid   Using MBO has three potential problems. *Setting unclear, unmeasurable objectives* is the main one. Such an objective as "will do a better job of training" is useless. Conversely, "will have four employees promoted during the year" is a measurable objective. Second, MBO is *time-consuming*. Taking the time to set objectives, measure progress, and provide feedback can take several hours per employee per year, over and above the time already spent doing each person's appraisal. Third, setting objectives with an employee sometimes turns into a *tug of war*; managers push for higher goals and employees push for lower ones. It is thus important to know the job and the person's ability. To motivate performance, the objectives must be fair and attainable.

Mixing the Methods

Most firms combine several appraisal techniques. The form shown in Exhibit 12-2 is a graphic rating scale with behavioural incidents included to define values for the traits being measured. The quantifiable ranking method permits comparisons of employees and is therefore useful for making salary, transfer, and promotion decisions. The critical incidents provide specific examples of performance relative to expectations and can be used to develop the high and low anchors for the BARS technique.[21] Ultimately, no one single solution is best for all performance management systems. Instead, resource constraints (time, money, people) and organizational factors (budget, turnover, strategy) will help determine which of the options is best for each organization.

management by objectives (MBO) Involves setting specific measurable goals with each employee and then periodically reviewing the progress made.

The Use of Technology in Performance Appraisals

Over the past few years, web-based performance management has moved from being a leading-edge approach adopted by only large companies to a mainstream practice that is quickly becoming an industry standard among medium and small organizations.[22] It enables managers to keep computerized notes on employees, combine these with ratings on several performance traits, and then generate written text to support each part of the appraisal.

But the true value in web-based performance management goes beyond simply automating time-consuming, tedious tasks like tracking down paper-based appraisal forms. They ultimately improve the overall performance management process, starting with higher completion rates, which can dramatically increase the value of performance management within organizations of all sizes. Performance management systems provide employees with a clear development path and a better understanding of how their goals are aligned with those of the organization, which in turn increases their support of the process. Managers have the information they need to ensure development plans are relevant and executed. Executives have a clear picture of the organization's talent strategy and how it ties into the bottom line.

Most web-based performance management systems provide advanced reporting capabilities, which allow managers to track the status of performance management initiatives easily. Goal management functions enable organizations to link individual goals to strategic corporate goals, meaning that executives have insight into the progress being made on corporate objectives. Succession planning tools provide executives with a clear plan to build a talent pool to meet the organization's business needs and address potential attrition.

In a relatively short time, employee performance management has undergone a rapid evolution with the development of powerful, web-based tools. HR professionals are no longer mired in paperwork and other mundane administrative tasks. They have more time to focus on meeting strategic objectives, better tools to implement best practices programs, and access to critical workforce metrics they can share with their executive team.

Electronic performance monitoring (EPM) is in some respects the ultimate in computerized appraising. Electronic performance monitoring means having supervisors electronically observe the employee's output or whereabouts. This typically involves using computer networks and wireless audio or video links to monitor and record employees' work activities. It includes, for instance, monitoring a data clerk's hourly keystrokes, tracking via GPS the whereabouts of delivery drivers, and monitoring the calls of customer service clerks.

electronic performance monitoring (EPM) Having supervisors electronically monitor the amount of computerized data an employee is processing per day and thereby his or her performance.

This food service supervisor is conducting a feedback session about an employee's performance during a major banquet to keep communications open and build employee commitment.

Performance Appraisal Problems and Solutions

Few of the things a manager does are fraught with more peril than appraising employees' performance. Employees in general tend to be overly optimistic about what their ratings will be, and they also know that their raises, career progress, and peace of mind may well hinge on how they are rated. Thus, an honest appraisal inevitably involves an emotional component, which is particularly difficult when managers are not trained on formal appraisal discussion skills. The result is often dishonest appraisals or avoidance of appraisals.[23]

Even more problematic, however, are the numerous structural problems that can cast serious doubt on just how fair the whole process is. Fortunately, research shows that action by management to implement a more acceptable performance appraisal system can increase employee trust in management.[24] According to several studies, the majority of organizations view their performance management systems as ineffective. More focus on the execution of performance appraisal is required instead of searching for new techniques and methods.[25] Some of the main appraisal problems and how to solve them, as well as several other pertinent appraisal issues, will now be reviewed.

Validity and Reliability

Appraisal systems must be based on performance criteria that are valid for the position being rated and must be reliable, in that their application must produce consistent ratings for the same performance. Employee concerns about appraisal fairness are influenced by these characteristics of the performance appraisal system.

Criteria used in performance appraisal must be accurate, or valid, to produce useful results. Criteria must be (1) relevant to the job being appraised, (2) broad enough to cover all aspects of the job requirements, and (3) specific. For example, including a broad criterion, such as "leadership," may not be relevant to non-management jobs and may be so vague that it can be interpreted in many different ways.

Effective appraisal criteria are precise enough to result in consistent measures of performance when applied across many employees by many different raters. This is difficult to achieve without quantifiable and measurable criteria.

Rating Scale Problems

Seven main problems can undermine appraisal tools like graphic rating scales: unclear standards, the halo effect, central tendency, leniency or strictness, appraisal bias, the recency effect, and the similar-to-me bias.

The problem of **unclear performance standards** is illustrated in Table 12.2. Although the graphic rating scale seems objective, it would probably result in unfair appraisals because the traits and degrees of merit are open to interpretation. For example, different supervisors would probably differently define "good" performance, "fair" performance, and so on. The same is true of traits, such as "quality of work" or "creativity." There are several ways in which to rectify this problem. The best way is to develop and include descriptive phrases that define each trait, as in Exhibit 12-2. There, the form specified what was meant by "outstanding," "very good," and "good" quality of work. This specificity results in appraisals that are more consistent and more easily explained.

The **halo effect** means that the rating of an employee on one trait (such as "gets along with others") biases the way that person is rated on other traits (such as "reliability"). This problem often occurs with employees who are especially friendly (or unfriendly) toward the supervisor. For example, an unfriendly employee will often be rated unsatisfactory for all traits rather than just for the trait "gets along well with others." Being aware of this problem is a major step toward avoiding it. Supervisory training can also alleviate the problem.[26]

Many supervisors have a **central tendency** when filling in rating scales. For example, if the rating scale ranges from one to seven, they tend to avoid the highs (six and seven) and lows (one and two) and rate most of their employees between three and five. If a graphic rating scale is used, this central tendency could mean that all employees are simply rated "average." Such a restriction can distort the evaluations, making them less useful for promotion, salary, or counselling purposes. Ranking employees instead of using a graphic rating scale can avoid this central tendency problem, because all employees must be ranked and thus cannot all be rated average.

Some supervisors tend to rate all of their employees consistently high (or low), just as some instructors are notoriously high graders and others are not. Fear of interpersonal conflict is often the reason for leniency.[27] Conversely, evaluators tend to give more weight to negative attributes than to positive ones.[28] This **strictness/leniency** problem is especially serious with graphic rating scales, since supervisors are not necessarily required to avoid giving all of their employees low (or high) ratings. However,

unclear performance standards An appraisal scale that is too open to interpretation of traits and standards.

halo effect In performance appraisal, the problem that occurs when a supervisor's rating of an employee on one trait biases the rating of that person on other traits.

central tendency A tendency to rate all employees in the middle of the scale.

strictness/leniency The problem that occurs when a supervisor has a tendency to rate all employees either low or high.

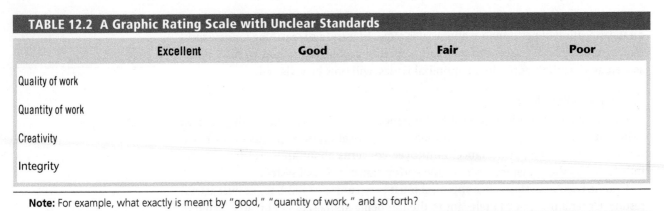

	Excellent	Good	Fair	Poor
Quality of work				
Quantity of work				
Creativity				
Integrity				

TABLE 12.2 A Graphic Rating Scale with Unclear Standards

Note: For example, what exactly is meant by "good," "quantity of work," and so forth?

when ranking employees, a manager is forced to distinguish between high and low performers. Thus, strictness/leniency is not a problem with the ranking or forced distribution approaches.

Individual differences among ratees in terms of a wide variety of characteristics, such as age, race, and sex, can affect their ratings, often quite apart from their actual performance.[29] In fact, research shows that less than half of performance evaluation ratings are actually related to employee performance and that most of the rating is based on idiosyncratic factors.[30] This is known as **appraisal bias**. Not only does this bias result in inaccurate feedback, but it is also illegal under human rights legislation. Although age-related bias is typically thought of as affecting older workers, one study found a negative relationship between age and performance evaluation for entry-level jobs in public accounting firms.[31]

Interestingly, the friendliness and likeability of an employee have been found to have little effect on that person's performance ratings.[32] However, an employee's previous performance can affect the evaluation of his or her current performance.[33] The actual error can take several forms. Sometimes the rater may systematically overestimate improvement by a poor worker or decline by a good worker, for instance. In some situations—especially when the change in behaviour is more gradual—the rater may simply be insensitive to improvement or decline. In any case, it is important to rate performance objectively. Such factors as previous performance, age, or race should not be allowed to influence results.

The **recency effect** occurs when ratings are based on the employee's most recent performance, whether good or bad. To the extent that this recent performance does not exemplify the employee's average performance over the appraisal period, the appraisal is biased.

If a supervisor tends to give higher ratings to employees with whom he or she has something in common, the **similar-to-me bias** is occurring. This bias can be discriminatory if it is based on similarity in race, gender, or other prohibited grounds.

How to Avoid Appraisal Problems

There are at least four ways in which managers can minimize the impact of appraisal problems, such as bias and central tendency. First, raters must be familiar with the problems just discussed. Understanding the problem can help to prevent it.

Second, training supervisors on how to eliminate rating errors, such as the halo effect, leniency, and central tendency, can help them avoid these problems.[34] In a typical training program, raters are shown videos of jobs being performed and are asked to rate the worker. Ratings made by each participant are then placed on a flip chart and the various errors (such as leniency and halo) are explained. For example, if a trainee rated all criteria (such as quality, quantity, and so on) about the same, the trainer

Canadian Human Rights
Commission
www.chrc-ccdp.ca

appraisal bias The tendency to allow individual differences, such as age, race, and sex, to affect the appraisal ratings that these employees receive.

recency effect The rating error that occurs when ratings are based on the employee's most recent performance rather than on performance throughout the appraisal period.

similar-to-me bias The tendency to give higher performance ratings to employees who are perceived to be similar to the rater in some way.

might explain that a halo error had occurred. Typically, the trainer gives the correct rating and then illustrates the rating errors made by the participants.[35] According to one study, computer-assisted appraisal training improved managers' ability to conduct performance appraisal discussions with their employees.[36]

Rater training will not eliminate all rating errors or ensure absolute accuracy. In practice, several factors—including the extent to which pay is tied to performance ratings, union pressure, employee turnover, time constraints, and the need to justify ratings—may be more important than training. This means that improving appraisal accuracy calls not only for training but also for reducing outside factors, such as union pressure and time constraints.[37] It has also been found that employee reaction to current performance reviews is affected by past appraisal feedback, which is beyond the control of the current manager.[38]

Third, raters must choose the right appraisal tool. Each tool, such as the graphic rating scale or critical incident method, has its own advantages and disadvantages. For example, the ranking method avoids central tendency but can cause ill feelings when employees' performances are, in fact, all "high" (see Table 12.3).

Fourth, errors in performance appraisals can be reduced by using multiple raters in the evaluation. Multiple raters increase the validity and accuracy of the rating by controlling for individual biases or idiosyncrasies. Also, responsibility for poor appraisals is diffused; therefore, raters are more comfortable giving a poor rating. When raters are accountable for their rating, reliability also increases.[39] As an additional benefit, multiple ratings may be more legally defensible.

Who Should Do the Appraising?

Who should actually rate an employee's performance? Several options exist as to who can be involved in the performance management appraisal process.

TABLE 12.3 Important Advantages and Disadvantages of Appraisal Tools

	Excellent	Good
Graphic rating scale	Simple to use; provides a quantitative rating for each employee.	Standards may be unclear; halo effect, central tendency, leniency, and bias can also be problems.
Alternation ranking	Simple to use (but not as simple as graphic rating scale); avoids central tendency and other problems of rating scales.	Can cause disagreements among employees and may be unfair if all employees are, in fact, excellent.
Paired comparison method	A more precise ranking method that involves multiple traits.	Difficult to use as employee numbers increase; differences may not be noticeable enough to rank.
Forced distribution method	End up with a predetermined number of people in each group.	Appraisal results depend on the adequacy of the original choice of cutoff points.
Critical incident method	Helps specify what is "right" and "wrong" about the employee's performance; forces the supervisor to evaluate employees on an ongoing basis.	Difficult to rate or rank employees relative to one another; cannot be used to defend salary decisions.
Narrative form	Explicitly states improvement goals and associated outcomes or consequences.	Employees may take these too personally.
Behaviourally anchored rating scale (BARS)	Provides behavioural "anchors"; very accurate; high inter-rater reliability.	Difficult to develop.
Management by objectives	Tied to jointly agreed-upon performance objectives.	Risk of unclear performance measures, time-consuming, and inflated/deflated goals due to tug of war.

The best performance appraisal systems are those in which the supervisor or manager makes an ongoing effort to coach and monitor employees instead of leaving evaluation to the last minute.

Supervisors

Supervisors' ratings are still the heart of most appraisal systems. Getting a supervisor's appraisal is relatively easy and also makes a great deal of sense. The supervisor should be—and usually is—in the best position to observe and evaluate the performance of employees reporting to him or her and is responsible for their performance.

Self

Employees' self-ratings of performance are sometimes used, generally in conjunction with supervisors' ratings. Employees value the opportunity to participate in performance appraisal more for the opportunity to be heard than for the opportunity to influence the end result.[40] Nevertheless, the basic problem with self-ratings is that employees usually rate themselves higher than they are rated by supervisors or peers.[41] In one study, for example, it was found that when asked to rate their own job performance, 40 percent of the employees in jobs of all types placed themselves in the top 10 percent ("one of the best"), while virtually all remaining employees rated themselves either in the top 25 percent ("well above average") or at least in the top 50 percent ("above average"). Usually no more than 1 percent or 2 percent will place themselves in a below-average category, and then almost invariably in the top below-average category. However, self-ratings have been found to correlate more highly with performance measures if employees know that this comparison will be made and if they are instructed to compare themselves with others.[42]

Supervisors requesting self-appraisals should know that their appraisals and their employees' self-appraisals may accentuate appraiser–appraisee differences, and rigidify positions.[43] Furthermore, even if self-appraisals are not formally requested, each employee will enter the performance review meeting with his or her own self-appraisal in mind, and this will usually be higher than the supervisor's rating.

Peers

The appraisal of an employee by his or her peers can be effective in predicting future management success. Peers may have more opportunity to observe ratees and to observe them at more revealing times than supervisors do. One potential problem is *logrolling;* here, all the peers simply get together to rate each other highly.

With more firms using self-managing teams, peer or team appraisals are becoming more popular. One study found that peer ratings had an immediate positive impact on perceptions of open communication, motivation, group cohesion, and satisfaction, and these were not dependent on the ratio of positive to negative feedback.[44] Thus, peer appraisals would appear to have great potential for work teams.

Committees

Many employers use rating committees to evaluate employees. These committees usually comprise the employee's immediate supervisor and three or four other supervisors. Using multiple raters can be advantageous. Although there may be a discrepancy in the ratings made by individual supervisors, the composite ratings tend to be more reliable, fair, and valid.[45] Using several raters can help cancel out problems like bias and the halo effect on the part of individual raters. Furthermore, when there are variations in raters' ratings, they usually stem from the fact that raters often observe different facets of an employee's performance and the appraisal ought to reflect these differences.[46] Even when a committee is not used, it is common to have the appraisal reviewed by the manager immediately above the one who makes the appraisal.

Subordinates

Traditionally, supervisors feared that being appraised by their employees would undermine their management authority. However, with today's flatter organizations and empowered workers, much managerial authority is a thing of the past, and employees are in a good position to observe managerial performance.[47] Thus, more firms today are letting employees anonymously evaluate their supervisors' performance, a process many call *upward feedback*.[48] When conducted throughout the firm, the process helps top managers diagnose management styles, identify potential "people" problems, and take corrective action with individual managers as required. Such employee ratings are especially valuable when used for developmental rather than evaluative purposes.[49] Managers who receive feedback from employees who identify themselves view the upward appraisal process more positively than do managers who receive anonymous feedback; however, employees (not surprisingly) are more comfortable giving anonymous responses, and those who have to identify themselves tend to provide inflated ratings.[50] Research comparing employee and peer ratings of managers found them to be comparable. [51]

Upward feedback from reporting employees is quite effective in terms of improving the supervisor's behaviour, according to the research evidence. One study examined data for 92 managers who were rated by one or more reporting employees in each of four administrations of an upward feedback survey over two and a half years. The reporting employees were asked to rate themselves and their managers in surveys that consisted of 33 behavioural statements. The feedback to the managers also contained results from previous administrations of the survey so that they could track their performance over time.

According to the researchers, managers whose initial performance level was lower than the average employee performance level improved performance by the next performance assessment and sustained this improvement two years later. Interestingly, the results also suggest that it is not necessarily the specific feedback that caused the performance improvement, because low-performing managers seemed to improve over time even if they did not receive any feedback. Instead, learning what the critical supervisory behaviours were (as a result of themselves filling out the appraisal surveys) and knowing that they might be appraised may have been enough to result in the improved supervisory behaviours. In a sense, therefore, it is the existence of the formal upward feedback program rather than the actual feedback itself that may signal and motivate supervisors to get their behaviours in line with what they should be.[52]

Research | INSIGHT

360-Degree Appraisal

Many Canadian firms are now using what is called **360-degree appraisal**, or "multisource feedback." Here, as shown in Exhibit 12-6, performance information is collected "all around" an employee—from his or her supervisors, subordinates, peers, and internal or external customers.[53] This feedback was originally used only for training and development purposes, but it has rapidly spread to the management of performance and pay.[54] The 360-degree approach supports the activities of performance feedback, coaching, leadership development, succession planning, and rewards and recognition.[55]

There are a number of reasons for the rapid growth of 360-degree appraisal, despite the significant investment of time required for it to function successfully. Today's flatter organizations employ a more open communicative climate conducive to such an approach, and 360-degree appraisal fits closely with the goals of organizations committed to continuous learning. A multiple-rater system is also more meaningful in today's reality of complex jobs, with matrix and team reporting relationships. A 360-degree appraisal can be perceived as a jury of peers, rather than the supervisor as a single judge, which enhances perceptions of fairness.[56]

360-degree appraisal A performance appraisal technique that uses multiple raters including peers, employees reporting to the appraisee, supervisors, and customers.

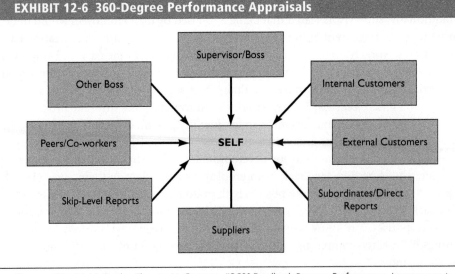

EXHIBIT 12-6 360-Degree Performance Appraisals

Most 360-degree appraisal systems contain several common features (including Internet-based 360-degree feedback systems, as described in Chapter 3). They are usually applied in a confidential and anonymous manner. Appropriate parties—peers, superiors, employees, and customers, for instance—complete survey questionnaires about an individual. The questionnaires must be custom-designed and linked to the organization's strategic direction, vision, and values.[57] All this information is then compiled into individualized reports. When the information is being used for self-development purposes only, the report is presented to the person being rated, who then meets with his or her own supervisor and information pertinent for the purpose of developing a self-improvement plan is shared. When the information is being used for management of performance or pay, the information is also provided to the ratee's supervisor, and a supportive and facilitative process to follow up is required to ensure that the behavioural change required for performance improvement is made.[58]

Research | INSIGHT

An Ethical | Dilemma

Is it fair to factor in employee self-ratings in 360-degree performance appraisal, when we know that these appraisals tend to be inflated?

There is a limited amount of research data on the effectiveness of 360-degree feedback. Some organizations have abandoned it for appraisal purposes because of negative attitudes from employees and inflated ratings.[59] Some studies have found that the different raters often disagree on performance ratings.[60] A recent study by researchers at Concordia University in Montreal found that 360-degree feedback is popular among Canadian employers, despite such problems as the amount of time and effort involved, lack of trust in the system by employees, and lack of fit with strategic goals and other HR practices. The results showed that organizations that successfully implemented 360-degree feedback were those that had the most clarity on what their initial objectives were. Organizations that rely exclusively on external consultants to establish 360-degree appraisal have less success than organizations that are more sensitive to contextual factors, such as the readiness of employees and the culture of the organization.[61]

Some experts suggest that 360-degree feedback be used for developmental purposes only.[62] In general, it is advisable to use 360-degree feedback for developmental/career-planning purposes initially, and then to determine whether the organization is ready to use it for evaluative appraisal purposes. A pilot test in one department is often recommended. Once a decision to use 360-degree appraisal has been made, organizations should consider the following advice:[63]

- Have the performance criteria developed by a representative group that is familiar with each job.

- Be clear about who will have access to reports.

- Provide training for all supervisors, raters, and ratees.

- Assure all raters that their comments will be kept anonymous.

- Plan to evaluate the 360-degree feedback system for fine-tuning.

Tips | **FOR THE FRONT LINE**

Formal Appraisal Discussions

The essence of a performance appraisal is the feedback provided in a one-on-one conversation called the **formal appraisal discussion**. This is an interview in which the supervisor and employee review the appraisal and make plans to remedy deficiencies and reinforce strengths. Unfortunately, surveys show that less than half of companies describe their performance appraisal systems as effective or very effective because of weak execution due to managers abdicating their responsibility for screening out poor performers.[64] This discussion is often avoided by supervisors and managers who have not been trained to provide constructive feedback and to deal with defensive employees. Ultimately, feedback should be ongoing, making the formal appraisal discussion one of many performance discussions.

Types of Interviews

There are three basic types of formal appraisal discussions, each with its own objectives:[65]

Formal Appraisal Discussion Type	Formal Appraisal Discussion Objective
(1) Satisfactory performance— Promotable employee	(1) Make development plans
(2) Satisfactory performance— Nonpromotable employee	(2) Maintain performance
(3) Unsatisfactory performance—Correctable	(3) Plan correction

If the employee's performance is unsatisfactory and the situation uncorrectable, there is usually no need for any formal appraisal discussion because the person's performance is not correctable anyway. Either the person's poor performance is tolerated for now, or he or she is dismissed.

Satisfactory—Promotable

Here, the person's performance is satisfactory and there is a promotion ahead. This is the easiest of the three formal appraisal discussions. The objective is to discuss the person's career plans and to develop a specific action plan for the educational and professional development that the person needs to move to the next job.

Satisfactory—Not Promotable

This interview is for employees whose performance is satisfactory but for whom promotion is not possible. Perhaps there is no more room in the company; some employees are happy where they are and do not want a promotion.[66] The objective here is not to improve or develop the person but to maintain satisfactory performance.

This situation is not easy. The best option is usually to find incentives that are important to the person and are enough to maintain satisfactory performance. These might include extra time off, a small bonus, additional authority to handle a slightly enlarged job, and verbal reinforcement in the form of "Well done!"

formal appraisal discussion An interview in which the supervisor and employee review the appraisal and make plans to remedy deficiencies and reinforce strengths.

Unsatisfactory—Correctable

When the person's performance is unsatisfactory but correctable, the interview objective is to lay out an *action plan* (as explained later) for correcting the unsatisfactory performance.

Preparing for the Formal Appraisal Discussion

An important component of the performance management process is the effective use of feedback. This often happens in a formal appraisal discussion after the performance has been evaluated. There are three things to do in preparation for the interview.[67] First, assemble the data. Study the person's job description, compare the employee's performance to the standards, and review the files of the employee's previous appraisals. Next, prepare the employee. Give the employee at least a week's notice to review his or her own work, read over his or her job description, analyze problems he or she may be dealing with, and gather questions and comments for the interview. Finally, find a mutually agreeable time and place and allow plenty of time for the interview. Interviews with non-supervisory staff should take no more than an hour. Appraising management employees often takes two or three hours. Be sure that the interview is conducted in a private place where there will be no interruptions. It is important to keep in mind what is said and how it is said.

How to Conduct the Interview

Tips | **FOR THE FRONT LINE**

Constructive feedback is considered a positive and motivating experience.[68] There are four things to keep in mind when conducting a formal appraisal discussion to ensure the feedback is constructive.[69]

1. *Be direct and specific.* Talk in terms of objective work data. Use examples, such as absences, tardiness, quality records, inspection reports, scrap or waste, orders processed, productivity records, material used or consumed, timeliness of tasks or projects, control or reduction of costs, numbers of errors, costs compared with budgets, customers' comments, product returns, order processing time, inventory level and accuracy, accident reports, and so on.

2. *Do not get personal.* Do not say, "You are too slow in producing those reports." Instead, try to compare the person's performance with a standard ("These reports should normally be done within 10 days"). Similarly, do not compare the person's performance with that of other people ("He is quicker than you are").

3. *Encourage the person to talk.* Stop and listen to what the person is saying; ask open-ended questions, such as, "What do you think we can do to improve the situation?" Use phrases such as, "Go on," or "Tell me more." Restate the person's last point as a question, such as, "You do not think that you can get the job done?"

4. *Develop an action plan.* Do not get personal, but do make sure that by the end of the interview you have (a) provided specific examples of performance that does and does not need attention or improvement, (b) made sure the person understands how he or she should improve his or her performance, (c) obtained an agreement from the person that he or she understands the reasons for the appraisal, and (d) developed an action plan that shows steps to achieving specified goals and the results expected. Be sure that a timeline is included in the plan.

How to Handle Criticism and Defensive Employees

When criticism is required, it should be done in a manner that lets the person maintain his or her dignity and sense of worth. Specifically, criticism should be provided constructively, in private, and immediately following poor performance. Provide examples of critical incidents and specific suggestions of what could be done and why. Finally, ensure that criticism is objective and free of any personal biases.

When poor performance by an employee is described, the first reaction will often be denial. By denying the fault, the person avoids having to question his or her own competence. Others react to criticism with anger and aggression. This helps them let off steam and postpones confronting the immediate problem until they are able to cope with it. Still others react to criticism by retreating into a shell.

Understanding and dealing with defensiveness is an important appraisal skill that requires the following:[70]

1. Recognize that defensive behaviour is normal.

2. Never attack a person's defences. Do not try to "explain someone" to himself or herself by saying things like, "You know the real reason you are using that excuse is that you cannot bear to be blamed for anything." Instead, try to concentrate on the act itself ("sales are down") rather than on the person ("you are not selling enough").

3. Postpone action. Sometimes it is best to do nothing at all. People frequently react to sudden threats by instinctively hiding behind their "masks." Given sufficient time, however, a more rational reaction usually takes over.

4. Recognize human limitations. Do not expect to be able to solve every problem that comes up, especially the human ones. More importantly, remember that a supervisor should not try to be a psychologist. Offering employees understanding is one thing; trying to deal with deep psychological problems is another matter entirely.

Ensuring That the Formal Appraisal Discussion Leads to Improved Performance

It is important to clear up performance problems by setting goals and a schedule for achieving them. However, even if you have obtained agreement from your employees about the areas for performance improvement, they may or may not be satisfied with their appraisal. In one study, researchers found that whether or not employees expressed satisfaction with their formal appraisal discussion depended mostly on three factors: (1) not feeling threatened during the interview, (2) having an opportunity to present their ideas and feelings and to influence the course of the interview, and (3) having a helpful and constructive supervisor conduct the interview.[71]

Ultimately, the main objective of performance apprasials is to improve employee performance, keeping performance expectations clear and targeted on activities that build value for the organization. In dealing with employee performance issues, legal experts suggest that management follow seven steps to ensure that performance appraisals have the desired effect and are legally defensible:

1. Let the employee know that his or her performance is unacceptable and explain your minimum expectations.

2. Ensure that your expectations are reasonable.

3. Let employees know that warnings play a significant role in the process of establishing just cause; employees must be warned and told that discharge will result if they continue to fail to meet minimum standards.

4. Ensure that you take prompt corrective measures when required; failure to do so could lead to a finding that you condoned your employee's conduct.

5. Avoid sending mixed messages, such as a warning letter together with a "satisfactory" performance review.

6. Provide the employee with a reasonable amount of time to improve performance.

7. Be prepared to provide your employees with the necessary support to facilitate improvement.[72]

How to Handle a Formal Written Warning

There will be times when an employee's performance is so poor that a formal written warning is required. Such written warnings serve two purposes: (1) They may serve to shake the employee out of his or her bad habits, and (2) they can help the manager defend his or her rating of the employee, both to his or her boss and (if needed) to a court or human rights commission.

Written warnings should identify the standards under which the employee is judged, make it clear that the employee was aware of the standard, specify any violation of the standard, indicate that the employee has had an opportunity to correct his or her behaviour, and specify what the employee must now do to correct his or her behaviour.

Step 4: Determine Performance Rewards/Consequences

Some time after the performance review has taken place, the manager should use the salary planning guidelines to determine the appropriate rewards or consequences, comparing actual performance against the defined levels. Performance rewards are given through merit pay or extra payment such as a cash bonus. The two most important aspects used to determine the appropriate reward/consequence are achievement of goals and how the employee meets the defined standards. Further detail on compensation and rewards is provided in Chapters 15 and 16.

Step 5: Career Development Discussion

During this discussion, the manager and employee discuss opportunities for development to strengthen or improve the employee's knowledge, skills, and abilities. Business needs must be balanced with the employee's preferences. These opportunities may focus on actions to boost performance in the area of current goals or to develop new knowledge aimed at a future career plan. Further detail on career planning and development is provided in Chapter 11.

Legal and Ethical Issues in Performance Management

Ethics should be the bedrock of performance management. Accurate, well-documented performance records and performance appraisal feedback are necessary to avoid legal penalties and to defend against charges of bias based on grounds prohibited under human rights legislation, such as age, sex, and so on. As one commentator puts it,

> The overall objective of high-ethics performance reviews should be to provide an honest assessment of performance and to mutually develop a plan to improve the individual's effectiveness. That requires that we tell people where they stand and that we be straight with them.[73]

Ashland Canada Ltd., an automotive products marketing company in British Columbia, was fined $20 000 for dismissing a sales employee based on an "unacceptable" performance rating even though the employee had exceeded his sales goals. The British Columbia Supreme Court found that the performance rating was unwarranted and undeserved, and criticized Ashland's human resources department for a "reprehensible and substantial departure" from good faith dealings with the employee.[74] In another case, a worker in a government mental health facility was terminated for unsatisfactory performance after 10 years of work with no performance evaluations and no disciplinary record. An adjudicator determined that the employer had failed to establish that the worker's job performance was unsatisfactory, that she had not been given a chance to improve, and that the employer did not have just cause for termination. The employer was required to pay compensation in lieu of reinstatement.[75]

Guidelines for developing an effective appraisal process include the following:[76]

1. Conduct a job analysis to ascertain characteristics (such as "timely project completion") required for successful job performance. Use this information to create job performance standards.

2. Incorporate these characteristics into a rating instrument. (The professional literature recommends rating instruments that are tied to specific job behaviours, that is, BARS.)

3. Make sure that definitive performance standards are provided to all raters and ratees.

4. Use clearly defined individual dimensions of job performance (like "quantity" or "quality") rather than undefined, global measures of job performance (like "overall performance").

5. When using a graphic rating scale, avoid abstract trait names (such as "loyalty," "honesty") unless they can be defined in terms of observable behaviours.

6. Employ subjective supervisory ratings (essays, for instance) as only one component of the overall appraisal process.

7. Train supervisors to use the rating instrument properly. Give instructions on how to apply performance appraisal standards ("outstanding," "satisfactory," and so on) when making judgments. Ensure that subjective standards are not subject to bias.

8. Allow appraisers regular contact with the employee being evaluated.

9. Whenever possible, have more than one appraiser conduct the appraisal, and conduct all such appraisals independently. This process can help to cancel out individual errors and biases.

10. Use formal appeal mechanisms and a review of ratings by upper-level managers.

11. Document evaluations and reasons for any termination decision.

12. Where appropriate, provide corrective guidance to assist poor performers in improving their performance.

The Future of Performance Management

Effective appraisals are the basis for successful performance management. Although performance appraisal is a difficult interpersonal task for managers, it cannot be eliminated.

Managers need some way to review employees' work-related behaviour, and no one has offered any concrete alternative. Despite the difficulties involved, performance management is still the basis for fostering and managing employee skills and talents, and it can be a key component of improved organizational effectiveness. Performance management techniques in high- and low-performing organizations are essentially the same, but managers in high-performing organizations tend to conduct and implement appraisals and manage performance on a daily basis more effectively.[77]

Recent research indicates that effective performance management involves

- Linking individual goals and business strategy,

- Showing leadership and accountability at all levels of the organization,

- Ensuring close ties among appraisal results, rewards, and recognition outcomes,

- Investing in employee development planning, and

- Having an administratively efficient system with sufficient communication support. [78]

The key success factor for effective performance appraisal that will lead to optimum employee performance is the quality of the performance appraisal dialogue between a manager and an employee.[79] Managers need to engage in training on an ongoing basis to ensure that they are in a position to engage in high-quality formal appraisal discussions.

Overall, the solution is to create more effective appraisals, as described in this chapter. Effective appraisals are essential to managing the performance required of an organization's employees to achieve that organization's strategic objectives.

13

Theories of Motivation

Patrick Chan, currently Canada's number one male figure skater, is motivated.[1] After placing a disappointing fifth in the Vancouver 2010 Winter Olympics, despite skating a personal best in the free skate program, he had to make a decision. Chan had to either introduce the very challenging quadruple jump (the hallmark of elite skaters such as Kurt Browning) into his routines or continue to hope that a quadruple was not necessary for champion skaters.

Chan took the loss in the Olympics with grace. "I think after overcoming the Olympics and not doing your best, that's the biggest challenge and that's the Mount Everest of athletes. I think now I can go to Worlds in March [2010] and say, you know, this is a walk in the park."

In preparing for the World Figure Skating Championships, Chan had to consider the impact of figure skating's judging system. At one time, the perfect score was 6.0, although it was not quite clear how that score was achieved. Under the new system introduced in 2004, every element—"from jumps to spins to the step sequences in between—[has] an assigned value." Judges then add or subtract points based on how well the skater executes each element.

Chan won a gold medal at the 2010 Grand Prix Finals in Beijing. Then at the 2011 Moscow Worlds, he not only won gold but also set three world records in doing so. At the end of 2011, Chan had won his second consecutive gold in the Grand Prix Finals held in Quebec City. By January 2012, he had won his fifth national title. So what made Chan's loss at the Olympics motivational rather than make him want to quit skating completely?

In this chapter, we examine the subjects of motivation and rewards. We look at what motivation is, and how needs can be used to motivate individuals. We also present theories of motivation, and then consider the roles that fairness, reinforcement, and ethics play in motivation.

What is Motivation?

1 What is motivation?

We define **motivation** as the process that accounts for an individual's intensity, direction, and persistence of effort toward reaching a goal.[2]

The three key elements in our definition are intensity, direction, and persistence. *Intensity* describes how hard a person tries. This is the element most of us focus on when we talk about motivation. However, high intensity is unlikely to lead to favourable job-performance outcomes unless the effort is channelled in a *direction* that is beneficial. Therefore, we consider the quality of effort as well as its intensity. Finally, the effort requires *persistence*. This measures how long a person can maintain effort. Motivated individuals stay with a task long enough to achieve their goal.

Many people incorrectly view motivation as a personal trait—something some people have and others don't. Along these lines, Douglas McGregor proposed two distinct views of human beings. **Theory X**, which is basically negative, suggests that employees dislike work, will attempt to avoid it, and must be coerced, controlled, or threatened with punishment to achieve goals. **Theory Y**, which is basically positive, suggests that employees like work, are creative, seek responsibility, and will exercise self-direction and self-control if they are committed to the objectives.[3]

Our knowledge of motivation tells us that neither theory alone fully accounts for employee behaviour. What we know is that motivation is the result of the interaction of the individual and the situation. Certainly, individuals differ in their basic motivational drive. But the same employee who is quickly bored when pulling the lever on a drill press may enthusiastically pull a slot machine lever in Casino Windsor for hours on end. You may read the latest bestseller at one sitting, yet find it difficult to concentrate on a textbook for more than 20 minutes. It's not necessarily you—it's the situation. So as we analyze the concept of motivation, keep in mind that the level of motivation varies both *among* individuals and *within* individuals at different times.

You should also realize that what motivates people will also vary among individuals and situations. Motivation theorists talk about **intrinsic motivators** and **extrinsic motivators**. Extrinsic motivators come from outside the person and include such things as pay, bonuses, and other tangible rewards. Intrinsic motivators come from a person's internal desire to do something, due to such things as interest, challenge, and personal satisfaction. Individuals are intrinsically motivated when they genuinely care about their work, look for better ways to do it, and are energized and fulfilled by doing it well.[4] The rewards the individual gets from intrinsic motivation come from the work itself rather than from external factors such as increases in pay or compliments from the boss.

Are individuals primarily intrinsically or extrinsically motivated? Theory X suggests that people are almost exclusively driven by extrinsic motivators. However, Theory Y suggests that people are more intrinsically motivated. This view is consistent with that of Alfie Kohn, author of *Punished by Rewards*, who suggests that it's only necessary to provide the right environment, and people will be motivated.[5] We discuss his ideas further in Chapter 14.

Intrinsic and extrinsic motivation may reflect the situation, however, rather than individual personalities. For example, suppose your mother has asked you or your brother to take her to a meeting an hour away. You may be willing to drive her, without any thought of compensation, because it will make you feel good to do something for her. That is intrinsic motivation. But if you have a love-hate relationship with your brother, you may insist that he buy you lunch for helping out. Lunch would then be an extrinsic motivator—something that came from outside yourself and motivated you to do the task. Later in the chapter, we review the evidence regarding the significance of extrinsic vs. intrinsic rewards, and also examine how to increase intrinsic motivation. Meanwhile, you might consider whether you can motivate yourself through self-talk.

motivation The intensity, direction, and persistence of effort a person shows in reaching a goal.

Theory X The assumption that employees dislike work, will attempt to avoid it, and must be coerced, controlled, or threatened with punishment to achieve goals.

Theory Y The assumption that employees like work, are creative, seek responsibility, and will exercise self-direction and self-control if they are committed to the objectives.

intrinsic motivators A person's internal desire to do something, due to such things as interest, challenge, and personal satisfaction.

extrinsic motivators Motivation that comes from outside the person and includes such things as pay, bonuses, and other tangible rewards.

Needs Theories of Motivation

Theories of motivation generally fall into two categories: needs theories and process theories. *Needs theories* describe the types of needs that must be met to motivate individuals. *Process theories* help us understand the actual ways in which we and others can be motivated. There are a variety of needs theories, including Maslow's hierarchy of needs, Alderfer's ERG theory, Herzberg's motivation-hygiene theory (sometimes called the *two-factor theory*), and McClelland's theory of needs. We briefly review these to illustrate the basic properties of needs theories.

Needs theories are widely criticized for not standing up to scientific review. However, you should know them because (1) they represent a foundation from which contemporary theories have grown, and (2) practising managers still regularly use these theories and their terminology in explaining employee motivation.

2 How do needs motivate people?

Maslow's Hierarchy of Needs Theory

It's probably safe to say that the most well-known theory of motivation is Abraham Maslow's **hierarchy of needs theory**.[6] Maslow hypothesized that within every human being there exists a hierarchy of five needs:

- *Physiological.* Includes hunger, thirst, shelter, sex, and other bodily needs.

- *Safety.* Includes security and protection from physical and emotional harm.

- *Social.* Includes affection, belongingness, acceptance, and friendship.

- *Esteem.* Includes internal esteem factors such as self-respect, autonomy, and achievement; and external esteem factors such as status, recognition, and attention.

- *Self-actualization.* Includes growth, achieving one's potential, and self-fulfillment. This is the drive to become what one is capable of becoming.

Although no need is ever fully met, a substantially satisfied need no longer motivates. Thus, as each of these needs becomes substantially satisfied, the next need becomes dominant. This is what Maslow means by moving up the steps of the hierarchy. So if you want to motivate someone, according to Maslow, you need to understand what level of the hierarchy that person is currently on and focus on satisfying the needs at or above that level. Exhibit 13-1 identifies Maslow's hierarchy of needs on the left, and then illustrates how these needs are applied in the workplace.[7]

Maslow separated the five needs into higher and lower orders. Physiological and safety needs were **lower-order needs**, and social, esteem, and **self-actualization** were **higher-order needs**. The differentiation between the two orders was made on the

hierarchy of needs theory A hierarchy of five needs—physiological, safety, social, esteem, and self-actualization—in which, as each need is substantially satisfied, the next need becomes dominant.

lower-order needs Needs that are satisfied externally, such as physiological and safety needs.

self-actualization The drive to become what a person is capable of becoming.

higher-order needs Needs that are satisfied internally, such as social, esteem, and self-actualization needs.

EXHIBIT 13-1 Maslow's Hierarchy of Needs Applied to the Workplace

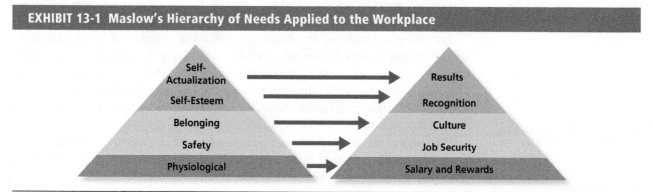

Source: How Great Companies Get Their Mojo From Maslow by Chip Conley and Tony Hsieh. Copyright © 2007, Jossey-Bass. Reprinted with permission of John Wiley & Sons, Inc.

premise that higher-order needs are satisfied internally (within the person), whereas lower-order needs are mainly satisfied externally (by such things as pay, union contracts, and tenure).

Maslow's needs theory continues to receive wide recognition, particularly among practising managers. It is intuitively logical and easy to understand, even though there is little research supporting the theory. Maslow himself provided no empirical evidence, and there is little evidence that need structures are organized along the dimensions proposed by Maslow, that unsatisfied needs motivate, or that a satisfied need activates movement to a new need level.[8] One 2011 study differs in its findings, however. Using data from 123 countries, the study found that Maslow's needs are universally related to individual happiness, but that the order of need fulfillment had little bearing on life satisfaction and enjoyment. Lower-order needs were related to positive life evaluation, while higher-order needs were linked to enjoying life. The researchers concluded that the findings overall supported Maslow's theory.[9]

ERG Theory

Clayton Alderfer reworked Maslow's hierarchy of needs to align it more closely with the empirical research. His revised need hierarchy is called **ERG theory**.[10]

Alderfer argued that there are three groups of core needs—*existence* (similar to Maslow's physiological and safety needs), *relatedness* (similar to Maslow's social needs), and *growth* (similar to Maslow's esteem needs and self-actualization). Unlike Maslow, Alderfer did not assume that these needs existed in a rigid hierarchy. An individual could focus on all three need categories simultaneously. Despite these differences, empirical research has not been any more supportive of ERG theory than it has of Maslow's theory.[11]

Motivation-Hygiene Theory

Psychologist Frederick Herzberg proposed the **motivation-hygiene theory** (also called the *two-factor theory*).[12] Believing that an individual's relationship to work is basic and that attitude toward this work can very well determine success or failure, Herzberg investigated the question, "What do people want from their jobs?" He asked people to describe, in detail, situations in which they felt exceptionally good or bad about their jobs. He then tabulated and categorized the response. Exhibit 13-2 illustrates factors affecting job attitudes, as reported in 12 investigations conducted by Herzberg.

Herzberg concluded that the replies people gave when they felt good about their jobs significantly differed from when they felt bad. As shown in Exhibit 13-2, intrinsic factors, such as achievement, recognition, the work itself, responsibility, advancement, and growth, seem to be related to job satisfaction. Respondents who felt good about their work tended to attribute these characteristics to themselves. On the other hand, dissatisfied respondents tended to cite extrinsic factors, such as company policy and administration, supervision, interpersonal relations, and work conditions.

According to Herzberg, the data suggest that the opposite of satisfaction is not dissatisfaction, as was traditionally believed. Removing dissatisfying characteristics from a job does not necessarily make the job satisfying. As illustrated in Exhibit 13-3, Herzberg proposes that his findings indicate the existence of a dual continuum: the opposite of "Satisfaction" is "No Satisfaction," and the opposite of "Dissatisfaction" is "No Dissatisfaction."

Herzberg explained that the factors leading to job satisfaction (motivators) are separate and distinct from those that lead to job dissatisfaction (hygiene factors). Therefore, managers who seek to eliminate factors that create job dissatisfaction may bring about peace but not necessarily motivation. They will be placating rather than motivating their employees. As a result, Herzberg characterized conditions such as quality of supervision, pay, company policies, physical working conditions, relationships

ERG theory A theory that posits three groups of core needs: existence, relatedness, and growth.

motivation-hygiene theory A theory that relates intrinsic factors to job satisfaction and associates extrinsic factors with dissatisfaction. Also called the *two-factor theory*.

EXHIBIT 13-2 Comparison of Satisfiers and Dissatisfiers

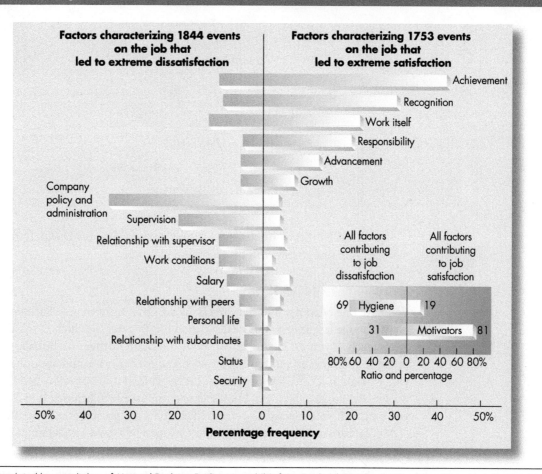

with others, and job security as **hygiene factors**. When they are adequate, people will not be dissatisfied; but neither will they be satisfied. If we want to motivate people in their jobs, Herzberg suggested emphasizing factors associated with the work itself or with outcomes directly derived from it, such as promotional opportunities, personal growth opportunities, recognition, responsibility, and achievement. These are the characteristics people find intrinsically rewarding. The motivation-hygiene theory is not without its critics, who suggest the following:[13]

- *The procedure that Herzberg used is limited by its methodology.* When things are going well, people tend to take credit themselves. Contrarily, they blame failure on the external environment.

- *The reliability of Herzberg's methodology is questionable.* Raters have to make interpretations, so they may contaminate the findings by interpreting one response in one manner while treating a similar response differently.

- *No overall measure of satisfaction was used.* A person may dislike part of their job, yet still think the job is acceptable overall.

- *Herzberg assumed that a relationship exists between satisfaction and productivity.* But the research methodology he used looked only at satisfaction, not at productivity. To make such research relevant, one must assume a strong relationship between satisfaction and productivity.[14]

hygiene factors Factors—such as company policy and administration, supervision, and salary—that, when adequate in a job, placate employees. When these factors are adequate, people will not be dissatisfied.

EXHIBIT 13-3 Contrasting Views of Satisfaction and Dissatisfaction

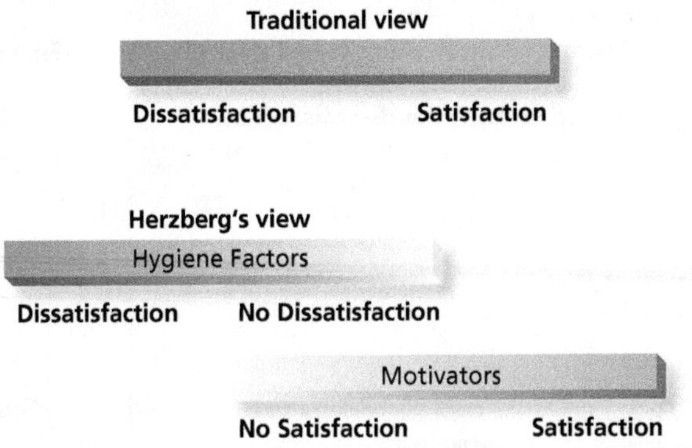

Traditional view

Dissatisfaction   Satisfaction

Herzberg's view

Hygiene Factors

Dissatisfaction   No Dissatisfaction

Motivators

No Satisfaction   Satisfaction

Regardless of these criticisms, Herzberg's theory has been widely read, and few managers are unfamiliar with his recommendations.

McClelland's Theory of Needs

You have one beanbag, and five targets are set up in front of you. Each target is farther away than the last and thus more difficult to hit. Target A is a cinch. It sits almost within arm's reach. If you hit it, you get $2. Target B is a bit farther out, but about 80 percent of the people who try can hit it. It pays $4. Target C pays $8, and about half the people who try can hit it. Very few people can hit Target D, but the payoff is $16 for those who do. Finally, Target E pays $32, but it's almost impossible to achieve. Which target would you try for? If you selected C, you are likely to be a high achiever. Why? Read on.

McClelland's theory of needs was developed by David McClelland and his associates.[15] The theory focuses on three needs, defined as follows:

- **Need for achievement (nAch).** The drive to excel, to achieve in relation to a set of standards, to strive to succeed.

- **Need for power (nPow).** The need to make others behave in a way that they would not have behaved otherwise.

- **Need for affiliation (nAff).** The desire for friendly and close interpersonal relationships.

Of the three needs, McClelland and subsequent researchers focused most of their attention on nAch. High achievers perform best when they perceive their probability of success as 0.5—that is, a 50–50 chance of success.[16] They dislike gambling with high odds because they get no achievement satisfaction from success that comes by pure chance. Similarly, they dislike low odds (high probability of success) because then there is no challenge to their skills. They like to set goals that require stretching themselves a little.

Relying on an extensive amount of research, we can make some reasonably well-supported predictions of the relationship between achievement need and job performance. Although less research has been done on power and affiliation needs, findings are consistent there, too. First, when jobs have a high degree of personal responsibility, feedback, and an intermediate degree of risk, high achievers are strongly motivated. They are successful in entrepreneurial activities such as running their own businesses, for example, and managing self-contained units within large organizations.[17] Second, a high need to achieve does not necessarily make someone a good manager, especially in large organizations. People with a high achievement need are interested in how well they do personally and not in influencing others to do well. High-nAch salespeople do not necessarily

McClelland's theory of needs Achievement, power, and affiliation are three important needs that help explain motivation.

need for achievement (nAch) The drive to excel, to achieve in relation to a set of standards, to strive to succeed.

need for power (nPow) The need to make others behave in a way that they would not have behaved otherwise.

need for affiliation (nAff) The desire for friendly and close interpersonal relationships.

make good sales managers, and the good general manager in a large organization does not typically have a high need to achieve.[18] Third, needs for affiliation and power tend to be closely related to managerial success. The best managers are high in their need for power and low in their need for affiliation.[19] In fact, a high power motive may be a requirement for managerial effectiveness.[20]

McClelland's theory has had the best research support of the different needs theories. Unfortunately, it has less practical effect than the others. Because McClelland argued that the three needs are subconscious—meaning we may be high on them but not know it—measuring them is not easy. In the most common approach, a trained expert presents pictures to individuals, asks them to tell a story about each, and then scores their responses in terms of the three needs. However, the process is time consuming and expensive, and few organizations have been willing to invest time and resources in measuring McClelland's concept.

Anne Sweeney, co-chair of Disney Media Networks and president of Disney/ABC Television Group, is a high achiever. Sweeney's Disney/ABC Television Group was the first media company to feature television content on new platforms, such as the iPod and iPad. More recently, she was instrumental in Disney's becoming an equity partner in Hulu.com. Sweeney's unofficial motto is "create what's next."

Summarizing Needs Theories

The needs theories we have just reviewed all propose a similar idea: Individuals have needs that, when unsatisfied, will result in motivation. For instance, if you have a need to be praised, you may work harder at your task in order to receive recognition from your manager or other co-workers. Similarly, if you need money and you are asked to do something (within reason) that offers money as a reward, you will be motivated to complete that task.

Where needs theories differ is in the types of needs they consider and whether they propose a hierarchy of needs (where some needs have to be satisfied before others) or simply a list of needs. Exhibit 13-4 illustrates the relationship among the four needs theories that we discussed, and Exhibit 13-5 indicates whether the theory proposes a hierarchy of needs, and the contribution of and empirical support for each theory.

What can we conclude from needs theories? We can safely say that individuals do have needs, and that they can be highly motivated to achieve those needs. The types of needs, and their importance, vary by individual, and probably vary over time for the same individual as well. When rewarding individuals, you should consider their specific needs. Obviously, in a workplace, it would be difficult to design a reward structure that could completely take into account the specific needs of every employee. To better understand what might motivate you in the workplace.

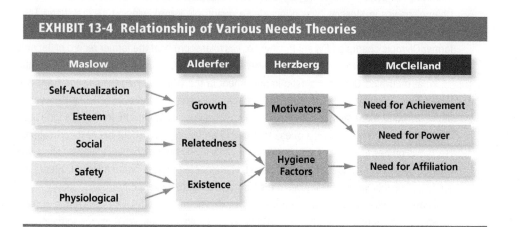

EXHIBIT 13-4 Relationship of Various Needs Theories

EXHIBIT 13-5 Summarizing the Various Needs Theories

Theory	Maslow	Alderfer	Herzberg	McClelland
Is there a hierarchy of needs?	The theory argues that lower-order needs must be satisfied before one progresses to higher-order needs.	More than one need can be important at the same time. If a higher-order need is not being met, the desire to satisfy a lower-level need increases.	Hygiene factors must be met if a person is not to be dissatisfied. They will not lead to satisfaction, however. Motivators lead to satisfaction.	People vary in the types of needs they have. Their motivation and how well they perform in a work situation are related to whether they have a need for achievement, power, or affiliation.
What is the theory's impact/contribution?	The theory enjoys wide recognition among practising managers. Most managers are familiar with it.	The theory is seen as a more valid version of the need hierarchy. It tells us that achievers will be motivated by jobs that offer personal responsibility, feedback, and moderate risks.	The popularity of giving employees greater responsibility for planning and controlling their work can be attributed to this theory (see, for instance, the job characteristics model in Chapter 5). It shows that more than one need may operate at the same time.	The theory tells us that high-need achievers do not necessarily make good managers, since high achievers are more interested in how they do personally.
What empirical support/criticisms exist?	Research has not validated the hierarchical nature of needs. However, a 2011 study found that the needs are universally related to individual happiness.	It ignores situational variables.	It is not really a theory of motivation: It assumes a link between satisfaction and productivity that was not measured or demonstrated.	It has mixed empirical support, but the theory is consistent with our knowledge of individual differences among people. Good empirical support exists on needs achievement in particular.

Process Theories of Motivation

3 Are there other ways to motivate people?

After finishing fifth at the Vancouver 2010 Winter Olympics, Patrick Chan had to work on improving his performance.[21] A year later, Chan placed first at the 2011 World Figure Skating Championships in Moscow (which included a quadruple jump), winning his first World Title, and breaking records in doing so. His short program score broke the record previously held by former Olympic champion Evgeni Plushenko. His total score beat the former record of Japan's Daisuke Takahashi (who won the bronze medal in the 2010 Olympics) by more than 16 points.

What motivated Chan's dramatic improvement in the year between the Olympics and the World Figure Skating Championships? Chan acknowledges that the disappointing experience at the Olympics made him "push himself and improve in order to capture the world's top spot." But winning his first World Title does not make Chan feel at ease about his next competition. He knows he has to keep practising to improve. "It's funny but I didn't feel totally satisfied with my free [skate] in Moscow. I felt that I wasn't as connected to the Phantom [of the Opera] as I am to this new program which gives me goose bumps when I skate it."

Chan is motivated by a mix of intrinsic and extrinsic motivation. Like any talented athlete, he wants to be number one. But he also gets joy out of skating well. What makes someone like Patrick Chan show up at the skating rink, day after day, practising his routines?

Process theories go beyond individual needs and focus on the broader picture of how one motivates one's self and others. Process theories include expectancy theory, goal-setting theory (and its application, management by objectives), and self-efficacy theory.

Expectancy Theory

Currently, one of the most widely accepted explanations of motivation is Victor Vroom's **expectancy theory**.[22]

From a practical perspective, expectancy theory says that employees will be motivated to exert a high level of effort when they believe the following:

- That the effort will lead to good performance

- That good performance will lead to organizational rewards, such as a bonus, a salary increase, or a promotion

- That the rewards will satisfy employees' personal goals

The theory focuses on the three relationships (expectancy, instrumentality, and valence) illustrated in Exhibit 13-6 and described in the following pages. This exhibit also provides an example of how you might apply the theory.

Effort-Performance Relationship

The effort-performance relationship is commonly called **expectancy**. It answers the question: *If I give a maximum effort, will it be recognized in my performance appraisal?* For many employees, the answer is "no." Why? Their skill level may be deficient, which means that no matter how hard they try, they are not likely to be high performers. The organization's performance appraisal system may be designed to assess nonperformance factors such as loyalty, initiative, or courage, which means more effort will not necessarily result in a higher evaluation. Another possibility is that employees, rightly or wrongly, think the boss does not like them. As a result, they expect to get a poor appraisal, regardless of level of effort. These examples suggest one possible source of low motivation is employees' belief that, no matter how hard they work, the likelihood of getting a good performance appraisal is low. Expectancy can be expressed as a probability, and ranges from 0 to 1.

expectancy theory The theory that individuals act based on their evaluation of whether their effort will lead to good performance, whether good performance will be followed by a given outcome, and whether that outcome is attractive.

expectancy The belief that effort is related to performance.

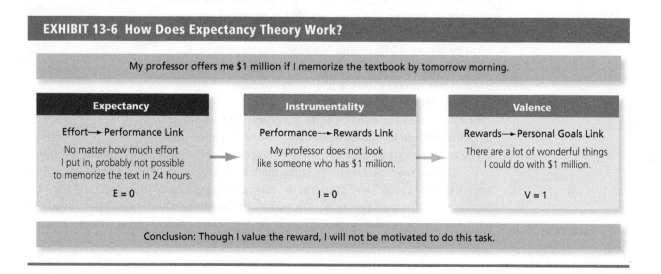

EXHIBIT 13-6 How Does Expectancy Theory Work?

My professor offers me $1 million if I memorize the textbook by tomorrow morning.

Expectancy	Instrumentality	Valence
Effort → Performance Link	Performance → Rewards Link	Rewards → Personal Goals Link
No matter how much effort I put in, probably not possible to memorize the text in 24 hours.	My professor does not look like someone who has $1 million.	There are a lot of wonderful things I could do with $1 million.
E = 0	I = 0	V = 1

Conclusion: Though I value the reward, I will not be motivated to do this task.

Using employee performance software, convenience-store retailer 7-Eleven measures the efforts of store managers and employees at its 8800 North American stores. The company ties employee compensation to performance outcomes based on 7-Eleven's five fundamental strategic initiatives—product assortment, value, quality, service, and cleanliness—as well as meeting goals set for new products. Many other companies reward simply on sales, which does not capture the full range of value-added services that employees provide.

Performance-Rewards Relationship

The performance-rewards relationship is commonly called **instrumentality**. It answers the question: *If I get a good performance appraisal, will it lead to organizational rewards?* Many organizations reward a lot of things besides performance. When pay is based on factors such as having seniority, being cooperative, or "kissing up" to the boss, employees are likely to see the performance–rewards relationship as weak and demotivating. Instrumentality ranges from –1 to +1. A negative instrumentality indicates that high performance reduces the chances of getting the desired outcome. An instrumentality of 0 indicates that there is no relationship between performance and receiving the desired outcome.

> Are managers manipulating employees when they link rewards to productivity? Is this ethical?

Rewards-Personal Goals Relationship

The rewards-personal goals relationship is commonly called **valence**. It answers the question: *If I'm rewarded, are the rewards attractive to me?* The employee works hard in the hope of getting a promotion but gets a pay raise instead. Or the employee wants a more interesting and challenging job but receives only a few words of praise. Or the employee puts in extra effort to be relocated to the Paris office but instead is transferred to Singapore. It's important to tailor rewards to individual employee needs. Unfortunately, many managers are limited in the rewards they can distribute, which makes it difficult to personalize rewards. Moreover, some managers incorrectly assume that all employees want the same thing. They overlook the motivational effects of differentiating rewards. In either case, employee motivation may be lower because the specific need the employee has is not being met through the reward structure. Valence ranges from –1 (very undesirable reward) to +1 (very desirable reward).

> Why do some managers do a better job of motivating people than others?

instrumentality The belief that performance is related to rewards.

valence The value or importance an individual places on a reward.

Golfers such as Hamilton, Ontario's Alena Sharp, who won the 25th Canadian Women's PGA Championship in September 2011, illustrate the effectiveness of the expectancy theory of motivation, where rewards are tied to effort and outcome. Players on the LPGA tour are paid strictly according to their performance, unlike members of professional sports teams. Sharp's first LPGA Tour victory came in 2004. As Sharp has put more effort into her play, she has been increasing her earnings. In 2010, she earned $163 000 compared to $97 000 in 2006.[23]

Vancouver-based Radical Entertainment, creator of such digital entertainment as *Prototype* and *Crash of the Titans*, makes sure the company meets the needs of its employees, because it does not want to lose them to the United States.[24] The company employs a "Radical fun guru" whose job is to make the workplace so much fun no one wants to leave. The company provides free food all day, including catered lunches a few times a week, and there is a log cabin on-site, fitted out with big screens, DVDs, and gaming equipment, where employees can take time out to recharge during their long workdays. Radical Entertainment offers these benefits to meet the needs of its young employees, who find greater motivation from being part of a cool workplace than having a bigger pension plan.

Expectancy Theory in the Workplace

Does expectancy theory work? Although it has its critics,[25] most of the research evidence supports the theory.[26] Research in cross-cultural settings has also indicated support for expectancy theory.[27]

Exhibit 13-7 gives some suggestions for what a manager can do to increase the motivation of employees, using insights from expectancy theory.

EXHIBIT 13-7 Steps to Increasing Motivation, Using Expectancy Theory

Improving Expectancy	Improving Instrumentality	Improving Valence
Improve the ability of the individual to perform.	Increase the individual's belief that performance will lead to reward.	Make sure that the reward is meaningful to the individual.
• Make sure employees have skills for the task. • Provide training. • Assign reasonable tasks and goals.	• Observe and recognize performance. • Deliver rewards as promised. • Indicate to employees how previous good performance led to greater rewards.	• Ask employees what rewards they value. • Give rewards that are valued.

Hasso Plattner, co-founder of the German software firm SAP, motivates employees by setting stretch goals. Plattner set a shockingly optimistic goal of 15 percent annual growth for SAP's software licence revenues. Employees responded by achieving an even higher growth rate of 18 percent. Plattner set another stretch goal by announcing a bonus plan that would pay $381 million to hundreds of managers and key employees if they could double the company's market capitalization, from a starting point of $57 billion, by the end of 2010. For Plattner, setting stretch goals is a way to inject entrepreneurial energy into the 40-year-old company.

The Importance of Providing Performance Feedback

For employees to understand the relationship between rewards and performance, as well as considering whether rewards are equitable, they need to be given performance feedback. Many managers, however, find providing performance feedback to employees so unpleasant[28] they have to be pressured by organizational policies and controls to do so.[29] Why the reluctance to give performance feedback? There seem to be at least three reasons.

First, managers are often uncomfortable discussing performance weaknesses directly with employees. Even though almost every employee could stand to improve in some areas, managers fear a confrontation when presenting negative feedback.

Second, employees become defensive when their weaknesses are pointed out. Some employees challenge the evaluation by criticizing the manager or redirecting blame to someone else. A survey of 151 area managers, for instance, found that 98 percent encountered some type of aggression after giving employees negative appraisals.[30]

Finally, employees tend to have an inflated assessment of their own performance. By definition, half of all employees must be below-average performers, but the average employee estimates his or her own performance level at around the 75th percentile.[31] So even when managers are providing good news, employees are likely to perceive it as not good enough.

An effective review—one in which the employee perceives the appraisal as fair, the manager as sincere, and the climate as constructive—can result in the employee's leaving the interview in an upbeat mood, informed about the performance areas needing improvement, and determined to correct the deficiencies.[32] In addition, the performance review should be more like a counselling activity than a judgment process, allowing the review to evolve out of the employee's own self-evaluation.

Goal-Setting Theory

You have heard the phrase a number of times: "Just do your best. That's all anyone can ask for." But what does "do your best" mean? Do we ever know if we have achieved that vague goal? Might you have done better in your high school English class if your parents had said, "You should strive for 75 percent or higher on all your work in English" instead of "do your best"?

The research on **goal setting theory** by Edwin Locke and his colleague, professor Gary Latham at the University of Toronto, shows that intentions to work toward a **goal** are a major source of work motivation.[33] Goals tell an employee what needs to be done and how much effort will need to be expended.[34]

Goal-setting theory has an impressive base of research support.[35] But as a manager, how do you make it operational? That is often left up to the individual manager or leader. Some managers explicitly set aggressive performance targets—what General Electric called "stretch goals." For example, some CEOs, such as Procter & Gamble's A. G. Laffey and SAP's Hasso Plattner, are known for the demanding performance goals they set. The problem with leaving it up to the individual manager is that, in many cases, managers don't set goals. A recent survey revealed that when asked whether their job had clearly defined goals, only a minority of employees agreed.[36]

goal-setting theory A theory that says that specific and difficult goals, with feedback, lead to higher performance.

goal What an individual is trying to accomplish.

A more systematic way to utilize goal setting is with a **management by objectives (MBO)** program.[37] In MBO, managers and employees jointly set performance goals that are tangible, verifiable, and measurable; progress on goals is periodically reviewed, and rewards are allocated on the basis of this progress.

A relatively new way of using goal setting in the workplace is by creating a Results-Only Work Environment (ROWE). In this type of environment, employees focus only on achieving results and manage their time accordingly.

ROWE is effective because it encourages intrinsic motivation. Employees working under ROWE have more autonomy, they work on things that really matter, and they feel that the work they do actually makes a difference.[38]

How Does Goal Setting Motivate?

According to Locke, goal setting motivates in four ways (see Exhibit 13-8):[39]

- *Goals direct attention.* Goals indicate where individuals should direct their efforts when they are choosing among things to do. For instance, recognizing that an important assignment is due in a few days, goal setting may encourage you to say no when friends invite you to a movie this evening.

- *Goals regulate effort.* Goals suggest how much effort an individual should put into a given task. For instance, if earning a high mark in accounting is more important to you than earning a high mark in organizational behaviour, you will likely put more effort into studying accounting.

- *Goals increase persistence.* Persistence represents the effort spent on a task over time. When people keep goals in mind, they will work hard on them, even in the face of obstacles.

- *Goals encourage the development of strategies and action plans.* Once goals are set, individuals can develop plans for achieving those goals. For instance, a goal to become more fit may include plans to join a gym, work out with friends, and change eating habits.

In order for goals to be effective, they should be "SMART." SMART stands for

- **Specific:** Individuals know exactly what is to be achieved.

- **Measurable:** The goals proposed can be tracked and reviewed.

- **Attainable:** The goals, even if difficult, are reasonable and achievable.

- **Results-oriented:** The goals should support the vision of the organization.

- **Time-bound:** The goals are to be achieved within a stated time.

EXHIBIT 13-8 Locke's Model of Goal Setting

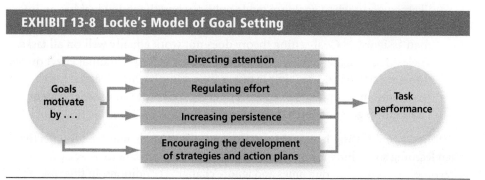

Source: Adapted from E. A. Locke and G. P. Latham, *A Theory of Goal Setting and Task Performance* (Englewood Cliffs, NJ: Prentice Hall, 1980). Reprinted by permission of Edwin A. Locke.

management by objectives (MBO) An approach to goal setting in which specific measurable goals are jointly set by managers and employees; progress on goals is periodically reviewed, and rewards are allocated on the basis of this progress.

GLOBAL IMPLICATIONS

RESEARCH FINDINGS: The Effects of Goal Setting

Locke and his colleagues have spent considerable time studying the effects of goal setting in various situations. The evidence strongly supports the value of goals. More to the point, we can say the following:

- *Specific goals increase performance, under certain conditions.* In early research, specific goals were linked to better performance.[40] However, other research indicates that specific goals can lead to poorer performance in complex tasks. Employees may be too goal-focused on complex tasks, and therefore not consider alternative and better solutions to such tasks.[41]

- *Difficult goals, when accepted, result in higher performance than do easy goals.* Research clearly shows that goal difficulty leads to positive performance for the following reasons.[42] First, challenging goals get our attention and thus tend to help us focus. Second, difficult goals energize us because we have to work harder to attain them. Third, when goals are difficult, people persist in trying to attain them. Finally, difficult goals lead us to discover strategies that help us perform the job or task more effectively. If we have to struggle to solve a difficult problem, we often think of a better way to go about it. However, this relationship does not hold when employees view the goals as impossible, rather than just difficult.[43]

- *Feedback leads to higher performance.* Feedback allows individuals to know how they are doing, relative to their goals.[44] Feedback encourages individuals to adjust their direction, effort, and action plans if they are falling short of their goals. Self-generated feedback—with which employees are able to monitor their own progress—has been shown to be a more powerful motivator than externally generated feedback.[45]

- *Goals are equally effective whether participatively set, assigned, or self-set.* Research indicates that how goals are set is not clearly related to performance.[46] In some cases, participatively set goals yielded superior performance; in others, individuals performed best when assigned goals by their boss. But a major advantage of participation may be that it increases acceptance of the goal as a desirable one toward which to work.[47] Commitment is important. If participation isn't used, then the individual assigning the goal needs to clearly explain its purpose and importance.[48]

- *Goal commitment affects whether goals are achieved.* Goal-setting theory assumes that an individual is committed to the goal and is determined not to lower or abandon it. In terms of behaviour, the individual (1) believes he or she can achieve the goal and (2) wants to achieve it.[49] Goal commitment is most likely to occur when goals are made public, when the individual has an internal locus of control (see Chapter 12), and when the goals are self-set rather than assigned.[50] Goal-setting theory does not work equally well on all tasks. The evidence suggests that goals seem to have a more substantial effect on performance when tasks are simple rather than complex, well learned rather than novel, and independent rather than interdependent.[51] On interdependent tasks, group goals are preferable.

Although goal setting has positive outcomes, some goals may be too effective.[52] When learning something is important, goals related to performance may cause people to become too focused on outcomes and ignore changing conditions. In this case, a goal to learn and generate alternative solutions will be more effective than a goal to perform. Some authors have also argued that goals can lead employees to be too focused on a single standard to the exclusion of all others. Consider the narrow focus on short-term stock prices in many businesses—so much attention to this one standard for performance may have led organizations to ignore long-term success, and even to engage in such unethical behaviour as accounting fraud or excessively risky investments. Of course it is possible for organizations to establish goals for ethical performance. Despite differences of opinion, most researchers do agree that goals are powerful in shaping behaviour. Managers should make sure they are actually aligned with the company's objectives.

Goal-setting theory is consistent with expectancy theory. The goals can be considered the effort-performance link—in other words, the goals determine what must be done. Feedback can be considered the performance-reward relationship, where the individual's efforts are recognized. Finally, the implication of goal setting is that the achievement of the goals will result in intrinsic satisfaction (and may of course be linked to external rewards).

Self-Efficacy Theory

Self-efficacy refers to an individual's belief that he or she is capable of performing a task.[53] The higher your self-efficacy, the more confidence you have in your ability to succeed in a task. So, in difficult situations, people with low self-efficacy are more likely to lessen their effort or give up altogether, while those with high self-efficacy will try harder to master the challenge.[54] In addition, individuals high in self-efficacy seem to respond to negative feedback with increased effort and motivation, while those low in self-efficacy are likely to lessen their effort when given negative feedback.[55] How can managers help their employees achieve high levels of self-efficacy? By bringing together goal-setting theory and self-efficacy theory (also known as *social cognitive theory* or *social learning theory*).

Goal-setting theory and self-efficacy theory don't compete with one another; rather, they complement each other. As Exhibit 13-9 shows, when a manager sets difficult goals for employees, this leads employees to have a higher level of self-efficacy, and also leads them to set higher goals for their own performance. Why? Research has shown that setting difficult goals for people communicates your confidence in them. For example, imagine that your boss sets a higher goal for you than for your co-workers. How would you interpret this? As long as you did not feel you were being picked on, you would probably think, "Well, I guess my boss thinks I'm capable of performing better than others." This sets in motion a psychological process in which you are more confident in yourself (higher self-efficacy) and you set higher personal goals, causing you to perform better both in the workplace and outside it.

The researcher who developed self-efficacy theory, Albert Bandura, argues that there are four ways self-efficacy can be increased:[56]

- *Enactive mastery.* Gaining relevant experience with the task or job. If you have been able to do the job successfully in the past, then you are more confident that you will be able to do it in the future.

- *Vicarious modelling.* Becoming more confident because you see someone else doing the task. For example, if your friend loses weight, then it increases your confidence that you can lose weight, too. Vicarious modelling is most effective when you see yourself as similar to the person you are observing.

- *Verbal persuasion.* Becoming more confident because someone convinces you that you have the skills necessary to be successful. Motivational speakers use this tactic a lot.

- *Arousal.* An energized state, which drives a person to complete a task. The person gets "psyched up" and performs better. But if the task is something that requires a steady, lower-key perspective (say, carefully editing a manuscript), arousal may in fact hurt performance.

What are the OB implications of self-efficacy theory? Well, it's a matter of applying Bandura's sources of self-efficacy to the work setting. Training programs often make

self-efficacy An individual's belief that he or she is capable of performing a task.

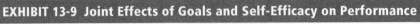

EXHIBIT 13-9 Joint Effects of Goals and Self-Efficacy on Performance

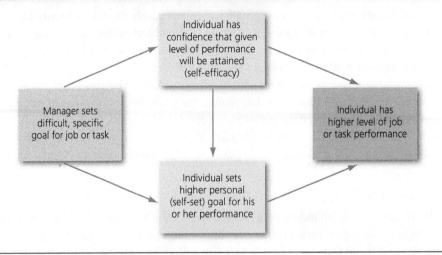

Source: Based on E. A. Locke and G. P. Latham, "Building a Practically Useful Theory of Goal Setting and Task Motivation: A 35-Year Odyssey," *American Psychologist*, September 2002, pp. 705–717.

use of enactive mastery by having people practise and build their skills. In fact, one of the reasons training works is because it increases self-efficacy.[57]

The best way for a manager to use verbal persuasion is through the *Pygmalion effect* or the *Galatea effect*. The Pygmalion effect is a form of a self-fulfilling prophecy in which believing something can make it true (also see Chapter 2). The Pygmalion effect increases self-efficacy by communicating to an individual's teacher or supervisor that the person is of high ability. In some studies, teachers were told their students had very high IQ scores, when in fact they had a range of IQs—some high, some low, and some in between. Consistent with the Pygmalion effect, the teachers spent more time with the students they *thought* were smart, gave them more challenging assignments, and expected more of them—all of which led to higher student self-efficacy and better student grades.[58] This has also been used in the workplace.[59] The Galatea effect occurs when high performance expectations are communicated directly to an employee. Sailors who were told, in a convincing manner, that they would not get seasick in fact were much less likely to get seasick.[60]

Note that intelligence and personality are absent from Bandura's list. Much research shows that intelligence and personality (especially conscientiousness and emotional stability) can increase self-efficacy.[61] Those individual traits are so strongly related to self-efficacy (people who are intelligent, conscientious, and emotionally stable are much more likely to have high self-efficacy than those who score low on these characteristics) that some researchers would argue that self-efficacy does not exist.[62] They believe it is simply a by-product in a smart person with a confident personality. Although Bandura strongly disagrees with this conclusion, more research is needed.

Responses to the Reward System

 Do equity and fairness matter?

After the new judging system for figure skating and ice dancing was put into place in 2004, Skate Canada immediately had analysts review how points would be allocated for figure skating, and Canadian skaters were instructed on how to make best use of the system.[63]

"We were fortunate with how well-educated our federation made us about the system," said Jeff Buttle, who won a silver medal for Canada at the 2005 World Figure Skating Championships in Moscow after finishing 15th under the old system in 2003. "We sat down right from the beginning of that first season and talked about what we needed to be focusing on to maximize our scores."

Still, the new system was not without controversy. While it allows gifted "total" skaters—like Jeff Buttle, Patrick Chan, and Joannie Rochette—to earn high scores on overall skating skills rather than focusing on jumps, the scoring is still somewhat subjective. This subjectivity causes frustration for the skaters. At the 2009 World Championships in Los Angeles, the Canadian team was surprised when Brian Joubert of France beat Patrick Chan, who is well regarded for "footwork, transitions and overall skating skills." As Buttle pointed out, "Joubert may be a better jumper in the sense that he can do the quad, but people who don't even watch skating could easily see the difference in quality between Patrick and Brian." Outcomes like this can make the system seem unfair, with individuals giving the best performances not getting the highest marks. When individuals encounter unfairness in rewards systems, how do they respond?

To a large extent, motivation theories are about rewards. The theories suggest that individuals have needs and will exert effort in order to have those needs met. The needs theories specifically identify those needs. Goal-setting and expectancy theories portray processes by which individuals act and then receive desirable rewards (intrinsic or extrinsic) for their behaviour.

Three additional process theories ask us to consider how individuals respond to rewards. Equity theory suggests that individuals evaluate and interpret rewards. Fair process goes one step further, suggesting that employees are sensitive to a variety of fairness issues in the workplace that extend beyond the reward system but also affect employee motivation. Cognitive evaluation theory examines how individuals respond to the introduction of extrinsic rewards for intrinsically satisfying activities.

Equity Theory

Jane Pearson graduated from university last year with a degree in accounting. After interviews with a number of organizations on campus, she accepted an articling position with one of the nation's largest public accounting firms and was assigned to the company's Edmonton office. Jane was very pleased with the offer she received: challenging work with a prestigious firm, an excellent opportunity to gain valuable experience, and the highest salary any accounting major at her university was offered last year—$5500 a month. But Jane was the top student in her class; she was ambitious and articulate, and fully expected to receive a commensurate salary.

Twelve months have passed since Jane joined her employer. The work has proved to be as challenging and satisfying as she had hoped. Her employer is extremely pleased with her performance; in fact, she recently received a $300-a-month raise. However, Jane's motivational level has dropped dramatically in the past few weeks. Why? Her employer has just hired a new graduate from Jane's university, who lacks the one-year experience Jane has gained, for $5850 a month—$50 more than Jane now makes! It would be an understatement to describe Jane as irate. Jane is even talking about looking for another job.

How important is fairness to you?

Jane's situation illustrates the role that equity plays in motivation. We perceive what we get from a job situation (outcomes such as salary levels, raises, recognition, challenging assignments, working conditions) in relation to what we put into it (inputs such as effort, experience, education, competence, creativity), and then we compare our outcome-input ratio with that of relevant others. (This idea is illustrated in Exhibit 13-10.) If we perceive our ratio to be equal to that of the relevant others with whom we compare ourselves, a state of equity is said to exist. We perceive our situation as fair and justice prevails. When we see the ratio as unequal, we experience equity tension. When we see ourselves as underrewarded, the tension creates anger; when we see ourselves as overrewarded, it creates guilt. J. Stacy Adams has proposed that this negative state of tension provides the motivation to do something to correct it.[64]

EXHIBIT 13-10 Equity Theory

Ratio of Output to Input	Person 1's Perception
Person 1 / Person 2	Inequity, underrewarded
Person 1 / Person 2	Equity
Person 1 / Person 2	Inequity, overrewarded

To Whom Do We Compare Ourselves?

The referent that an employee selects when making comparisons adds to the complexity of **equity theory**.[65] There are four referent comparisons that an employee can use:

- *Self-inside.* An employee's experiences in a different position inside his or her current organization.

- *Self-outside.* An employee's experiences in a situation or position outside his or her current organization.

- *Other-inside.* Another individual or group of individuals inside the employee's organization.

- *Other-outside.* Another individual or group of individuals outside the employee's organization.

Employees might compare themselves with friends, neighbours, co-workers, colleagues in other organizations, or compare their present job with previous jobs they have had. Which referent an employee chooses will be influenced by the information the employee holds about referents, as well as by the attractiveness of the referent. Four moderating variables are gender, length of tenure, level in the organization, and amount of education or professionalism.[66]

Gender Research shows that both men and women prefer same-sex comparisons. Women are typically paid less than men in comparable jobs and have lower pay expectations than men for the same work.[67] For instance, in 2005 full-time female employees earned, on average, 70.5 cents for every dollar earned by full-time male employees.[68] So a woman who uses another woman as a referent tends to have a lower comparative standard for pay than a woman who uses a man as the referent. If women are to be paid equally to men in comparable jobs, the standard of comparison—as used by both employees and employers—needs to be expanded to include both sexes.

Length of Tenure Employees with short tenure in their current organizations tend to have little information about others inside the organization, so they rely on their own personal experiences. Employees with long tenure rely more heavily on co-workers for comparison.

equity theory A theory that says that individuals compare their job inputs and outcomes with those of others and then respond to eliminate any inequities.

Level in the Organization and Amount of Education   Upper-level employees, those in the professional ranks, and those with more education tend to have better information about people in other organizations and will make more other-outside comparisons.

What Happens When We Feel Treated Inequitably?

Based on equity theory, employees who perceive an inequity will make one of six choices.[69]

- *Change their inputs* (exert less effort if underpaid, or more if overpaid; for example, Patrick Chan decided to practise even harder to place first in subsequent competitions).

> What can you do if you think your salary is unfair?

- *Change their outcomes* (individuals paid on a piece-rate basis can increase their pay by producing a higher quantity of units of lower quality).

- *Adjust perceptions of self* ("I used to think I worked at a moderate pace, but now I realize I work a lot harder than everyone else.")

- *Adjust perceptions of others* ("Mike's job isn't as desirable as I thought.")

- *Choose a different referent* ("I may not make as much as my brother-in-law, but I'm doing a lot better than my Dad did when he was my age.")

- *Leave the field* (quit the job).

RESEARCH FINDINGS: Inequitable Pay

Some of these propositions have been supported, but others have not.[70]
First, inequities created by overpayment do not seem to have a very significant impact on behaviour in most work situations. Apparently, people have a great deal more tolerance of overpayment inequities than of underpayment inequities or are better able to rationalize them. It's pretty damaging to a theory when half the equation (how people respond to overreward) falls apart. Second, not all people are equity sensitive.[71] A small part of the working population actually prefers outcome-input ratios less than the referent comparisons. Predictions from equity theory are not likely to be very accurate with these "benevolent types."

Note too that while most research on equity theory has focused on pay, employees seem to look for equity in the distribution of other organizational rewards. High-status job titles and large and lavishly furnished offices may function as outcomes for some employees in their equity equation.[72]

Fair Process and Treatment

Recent research has expanded the meaning of equity, or fairness.[73] Historically, equity theory focused on **distributive justice**, or the perceived fairness of the *amount* and *allocation* of rewards among individuals. But, increasingly, equity is thought of from the standpoint of **organizational justice**, or the overall larger perception of what is fair in the workplace. Employees perceive their organizations as just when they believe the outcomes they have received and the way they received them are fair.[74] One key element of organizational justice is an individual's *perception* of justice. In other words, fairness or equity can be subjective, residing in our perception. What one person sees as unfair, another may see as perfectly appropriate. In general, people have an egocentric, or self-serving, bias. They see allocations or procedure favouring themselves as fair.[75] In a recent poll, 61 percent of respondents said they are paying their fair share of taxes, but an almost equal number (54 percent) felt the system as a whole is unfair, saying some people skirt it.[76]

> **distributive justice** The perceived fairness of the amount and allocation of rewards among individuals.
>
> **organizational justice** An overall perception of what is fair in the workplace, composed of distributive, procedural, and interactional justice.

Beyond its focus on perceptions of fairness, the other key element of organizational justice is the view that justice is multidimensional. How much we get paid relative to what we think we should be paid (distributive justice) is obviously important. But, according to researchers, *how* we get paid is just as important. Thus, people also care about **procedural justice**—the perceived fairness of the *process* used to determine the distribution of rewards.[77] Two key elements of procedural justice are process control and explanations. *Process control* is the opportunity to present your point of view about desired outcomes to decision makers. *Explanations* are clear reasons management gives for the outcome. Thus, for employees to see a process as fair, they need to feel they have some control over the outcome and that they were given an adequate explanation about why the outcome occurred. It's also important that a manager is *consistent* (across people and over time), is *unbiased,* makes decisions based on *accurate information,* and is *open to appeals.*[78] Exhibit 13-11 shows a model of organizational justice.

A recent addition to research on organizational justice is **interactional justice**, an individual's perception of the degree to which she is treated with dignity, concern, and respect. When people are treated in an unjust manner (at least in their own eyes), they respond by retaliating (for example, badmouthing a supervisor).[79] Because people intimately connect interactional justice or injustice to the person who communicates the information (usually one's supervisor), we would expect perceptions of injustice to be more closely related to one's supervisor. Generally, that is what the evidence suggests.[80]

Of these three forms of organizational justice, distributive justice is most strongly related to organizational commitment satisfaction with outcomes such as pay. Procedural justice relates most strongly to job satisfaction, employee trust, withdrawal from the organization, job performance, and organizational citizenship behaviour. There is less evidence on how interactional justice affects employee behaviour.[81]

Managers can help foster employees' perceptions of fairness. First, they should realize that employees are especially sensitive to unfairness in procedures when bad news has to be communicated (that is, when distributive justice is low). Thus, it's especially

EXHIBIT 13-11 Model of Organizational Justice

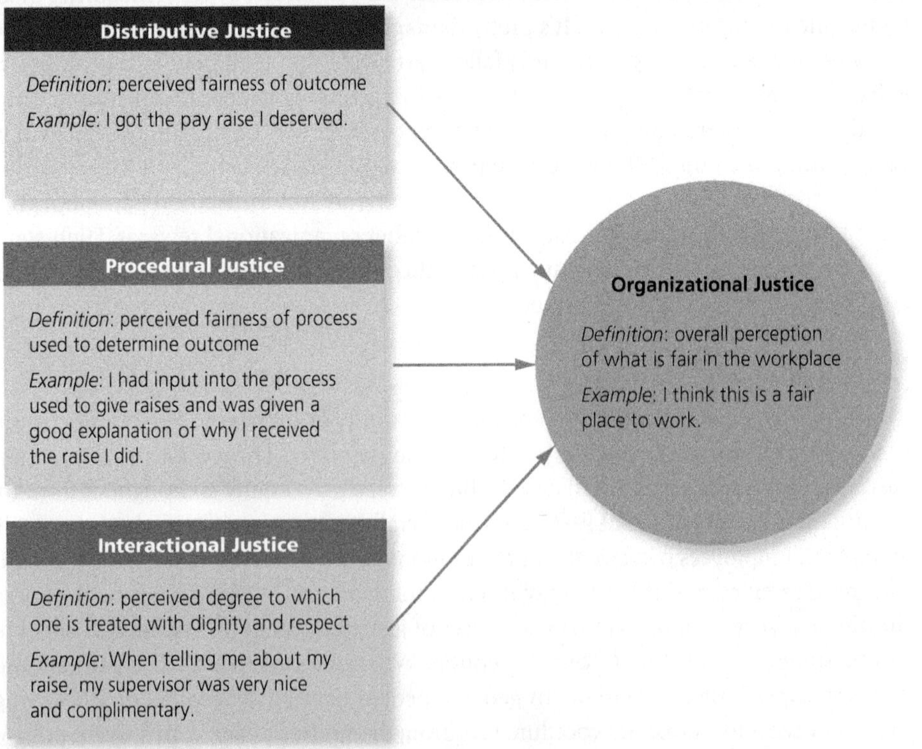

Distributive Justice

Definition: perceived fairness of outcome

Example: I got the pay raise I deserved.

Procedural Justice

Definition: perceived fairness of process used to determine outcome

Example: I had input into the process used to give raises and was given a good explanation of why I received the raise I did.

Interactional Justice

Definition: perceived degree to which one is treated with dignity and respect

Example: When telling me about my raise, my supervisor was very nice and complimentary.

Organizational Justice

Definition: overall perception of what is fair in the workplace

Example: I think this is a fair place to work.

procedural justice The perceived fairness of the process used to determine the distribution of rewards.

interactional justice The perceived quality of the interpersonal treatment received from a manager.

important to openly share information about how allocation decisions are made, follow consistent and unbiased procedures, and engage in similar practices to increase the perception of procedural justice. Second, when addressing perceived injustices, managers need to focus their actions on the source of the problem. Professor Daniel Skarlicki of the Sauder School of Business at the University of British Columbia has found that it is when unfavourable outcomes are combined with unfair procedures or poor interpersonal treatment that resentment and retaliation (for example, theft, badmouthing, and sabotage) are most likely.[82]

Self-Determination Theory

"It's strange," said Marcia. "I started work at the Humane Society as a volunteer. I put in fifteen hours a week helping people adopt pets. And I loved coming to work. Then, three months ago, they hired me full-time at eleven dollars an hour. I'm doing the same work I did before. But I'm not finding it near as much fun."

Does Marcia's reaction seem counterintuitive? There is an explanation for it. It's called **self-determination theory**, which proposes that people prefer to feel they have control over their actions, so anything that makes a previously enjoyed task feel more like an obligation than a freely chosen activity will undermine motivation.[83] Much research on self-determination theory in OB has focused on **cognitive evaluation theory**, which hypothesizes that extrinsic rewards will reduce intrinsic interest in a task. When people are paid for work, it feels less like something they *want* to do and more like something they *have* to do. Self-determination theory also proposes that in addition to being driven by a need for autonomy, people seek ways to achieve competence and positive connections to others. A large number of studies support self-determination theory.[84] As we will show, its major implications relate to work rewards.

Extrinsic vs. Intrinsic Rewards

Historically, motivation theorists have generally assumed that intrinsic motivators are independent of extrinsic motivators. That is, the stimulation of one would not affect the other. But cognitive evaluation theory suggests otherwise. It argues that when extrinsic rewards are used by organizations as payoffs for superior performance, the intrinsic rewards, which are derived from individuals doing what they like, are reduced.

When organizations use extrinsic rewards as payoffs for superior performance, employees feel less like they are doing a good job because of their own intrinsic desire to excel and more like they are doing a good job because that is what the organization wants. Eliminating extrinsic rewards can also shift from an external to an internal explanation of an individual's perception of why she works on a task. If you are reading a novel a week because your contemporary literature instructor requires you to, you can attribute your reading behaviour to an external source. If you stop reading novels the moment the course ends, this is more evidence that your behaviour was due to an external source. However, if you find yourself continuing to read a novel a week when the course ends, your natural inclination is to say, "I must enjoy reading novels, because I'm still reading one a week!"

Recent studies examining how extrinsic rewards increased motivation for some creative tasks suggests we might need to place cognitive evaluation theory's predictions in a broader context.[85] Goal setting is more effective in improving motivation, for instance, when we provide rewards for achieving the goals. The original authors of self-determination theory acknowledge that extrinsic rewards such as verbal praise and feedback about competence can improve even intrinsic motivation under specific circumstances. Deadlines and specific work standards do, too, if people believe they are in control of their behaviour.[86] This is consistent with the central theme of self-determination theory: rewards and deadlines diminish motivation if people see them as coercive.

What does self-determination theory suggest for providing rewards? Consider two situations. If a senior sales representative really enjoys selling and making the deal, a

self-determination theory A theory of motivation that is concerned with the beneficial effects of intrinsic motivation and the harmful effects of extrinsic motivation.

cognitive evaluation theory Offering extrinsic rewards (for example, pay) for work effort that was previously rewarding intrinsically will tend to decrease the overall level of a person's motivation.

commission indicates she has been doing a good job at this valued task. The reward will increase her sense of competence by providing feedback that could improve intrinsic motivation. On the other hand, if a computer programmer values writing code because she likes to solve problems, a reward for working to an externally imposed standard she does not accept could feel coercive, and her intrinsic motivation would suffer. She would be less interested in the task and might reduce her effort.

A recent outgrowth of cognitive evaluation research is **self-concordance**, which considers how strongly people's reasons for pursuing goals are consistent with their interests and core values.[87] If individuals pursue goals because of an intrinsic interest, they are more likely to attain their goals, and are happy even if they do not attain them. Why? Because the process of striving toward them is fun. In contrast, people who pursue goals for extrinsic reasons (money, status, or other benefits) are less likely to attain their goals and are less happy even when they do achieve them. Why? Because the goals are less meaningful to them.[88] OB research suggests that people who pursue work goals for intrinsic reasons are more satisfied with their jobs, feel like they fit into their organizations better, and may perform better.[89]

Of course, organizations cannot simply ignore financial rewards. When people feel they are being treated unfairly in the workplace, pay often becomes a focal point of their concerns. If tasks are dull or unpleasant, extrinsic rewards will probably increase intrinsic motivation.[90] Even when a job is inherently interesting, there still exists a powerful norm for extrinsic payment.[91] But creating fun, challenging, and empowered workplaces may do more for motivation and performance than focusing simply on the compensation system.

Increasing Intrinsic Motivation

Our discussion of motivation theories and our discussion of how to apply motivation theories in the workplace has focused heavily on improving extrinsic motivation. Professor Kenneth Thomas of the Naval Postgraduate School in Monterey, California, developed a model of intrinsic motivation that draws from the job characteristics model (see Chapter 14) and cognitive evaluation theory.[92] He identified four key rewards that increase an individual's intrinsic motivation:

- *Sense of choice.* The opportunity to select what one will do and perform the way one thinks best. Individuals can use their own judgment to carry out the task.

- *Sense of competence.* The feeling of accomplishment for doing a good job. Individuals are more likely to feel a sense of accomplishment when they carry out challenging tasks.

- *Sense of meaningfulness.* The opportunity to pursue worthwhile tasks. Individuals feel good about what they are doing and believe that what they are doing matters.

- *Sense of progress.* The feeling of accomplishment that one is making progress on a task, and that it is moving forward. Individuals feel that they are spending their time wisely in doing their jobs.

Thomas also identified four sets of behaviours managers can use to build intrinsic rewards for their employees:

- *Leading for choice.* Empowering employees and delegating tasks.

- *Leading for competence.* Supporting and coaching employees.

- *Leading for meaningfulness.* Inspiring employees and modelling desired behaviours.

- *Leading for progress.* Monitoring and rewarding employees.

Exhibit 13-12 describes what managers can do to increase the likelihood that intrinsic rewards are motivational.

self-concordance The degree to which a person's reasons for pursuing a goal is consistent with the person's interests and core values.

EXHIBIT 13-12 Building Blocks for Intrinsic Rewards

Leading for Choice	Leading for Competence
• Delegated authority • Trust in workers • Security (no punishment) for honest mistakes • A clear purpose • Information	• Knowledge • Positive feedback • Skill recognition • Challenge • High, noncomparative standards
Leading for Meaningfulness	**Leading for Progress**
• A noncynical climate • Clearly identified passions • An exciting vision • Relevant task purposes • Whole tasks	• A collaborative climate • Milestones • Celebrations • Access to customers • Measurement of improvement

Source: Reprinted with permission of the publisher. From *Intrinsic Motivation at Work: Building Energy and Commitment.* Copyright © K. Thomas. 1997. Berrett-Koehler Publishers Inc., San Francisco, CA. All rights reserved. www.bkconnection.com.

Motivating through Reinforcement

Patrick Chan did not win a medal in the Vancouver 2010 Winter Olympics.[93] Though he performed a personal best in the free skate program, it was not enough. Some wondered whether he should have mastered a quadruple and put the jump into his program. Although he practised quadruple jumps in the run-up to the Olympics, several weeks before the start of the games, he decided not to risk it. "My decision is pretty certain now that I don't want to make any changes and risk putting the quad in the most important competition of probably my life," he said. "We kind of went the way of sticking with two triple Axels and a good solid program."

Though he might have been playing it too safe, American Evan Lysacek (who won the gold medal) did not have any quads in his program. Russian Evgeni Plushenko (who won the silver medal) successfully performed the quad in his free skate, but was bitter about his scores. He said his jumps were the hardest that any of the male finalists attempted and added: "You need to skate, you need to spin, you need to skate, yes, but figure skating is not only skating, you need to jump, hard jumps like quad." He also said that without a quad, men's figure skating was merely "dancing." He vowed to perfect a double quad for his next competition to regain his position at number one.

This threat may have been enough to motivate Chan to add quadruple jumps to his repertoire. When he won the 2011 Moscow World Figure Skating Championships, he landed two quadruple jumps at the start of his program. When asked whether quad jumps were really necessary to compete at the highest level, Chan responded, "No doubt it does make a difference and there is also the respect you get for having one." Chan intends to ride the momentum coming out of the World Championships by defending his title in 2012, and then going back to the Olympics in 2014. Meanwhile, he will add a new quad salchow to his program. So how does reinforcement work, and does it motivate?

5 What role does reinforcement play in motivation?

The motivation theories we have covered to this point emphasize how people's needs and thought processes can be used to motivate them. As a behaviourist, B. F. Skinner found it "pointless to explain behaviour in terms of unobservable inner states such as needs, drives, attitudes, or thought processes."[94]

Skinner's view of motivation is much simpler. He suggested that people learn how to behave to get something they want or to avoid something they don't want.[95] This idea

EXHIBIT 13-13 Types of Reinforcement	
Reinforcement Type	**Example**
Positive reinforcement	A manager praises an employee for a job well done.
Negative reinforcement	An instructor asks a question and a student looks through her lecture notes to avoid being called on. She has learned that looking busily through her notes prevents the instructor from calling on her.
Punishment	A manager gives an employee a two-day suspension from work without pay for showing up drunk.
Extinction	An instructor ignores students who raise their hands to ask questions. Hand-raising becomes extinct.

is known as **operant conditioning**, which means behaviour is influenced by the reinforcement or lack of reinforcement brought about by the consequences of the behaviour.

Skinner argued that creating pleasing consequences to follow specific forms of behaviour would increase the frequency of that behaviour. People will most likely engage in desired behaviours if they are positively reinforced for doing so. Rewards are most effective if they immediately follow the desired behaviour. In addition, behaviour that is not rewarded, or is punished, is less likely to be repeated.

You see illustrations of operant conditioning everywhere. For example, any situation where reinforcements are contingent on some action on your part involves the use of operant conditioning. Your instructor says that if you want a high grade in the course, you must supply correct answers on the test. A commissioned salesperson who wants to earn a high income must generate high sales in her territory. Of course, the linkage can also work to teach the individual to engage in behaviours that work against the best interests of the organization. Assume that your boss tells you that if you will work overtime during the next three-week busy season, you will be compensated for it at the next performance appraisal. However, when performance appraisal time comes, you find that you are given no positive reinforcement for your overtime work. The next time your manager asks you to work overtime, you will probably decline! Your behaviour can be explained by operant conditioning: If a behaviour fails to be positively reinforced, the probability that the behaviour will be repeated declines.

Methods of Shaping Behaviour

There are four ways in which to shape behaviour: through positive reinforcement, negative reinforcement, punishment, and extinction.

Following a response with something pleasant is called *positive reinforcement*. Following a response with the termination or withdrawal of something unpleasant is called *negative reinforcement*. *Punishment* is causing an unpleasant condition in an attempt to eliminate an undesirable behaviour. Eliminating any reinforcement that is maintaining a behaviour is called *extinction*. Exhibit 13-13 presents examples of each type of reinforcement. Negative reinforcement should not be confused with punishment: Negative reinforcement strengthens a behaviour because it takes away an unpleasant situation.

Schedules of Reinforcement

While consequences have an effect on behaviour, the timing of those consequences or reinforcements is also important. The two major types of reinforcement schedules are *continuous* and *intermittent*. A **continuous reinforcement** schedule reinforces the desired behaviour each and every time it is demonstrated. Take, for example, the case of someone who has historically had trouble arriving at work on time. Every time he

operant conditioning A type of conditioning in which desired voluntary behaviour leads to a reward or prevents a punishment.

continuous reinforcement A desired behaviour is reinforced each and every time it is demonstrated.

EXHIBIT 13-14 Schedules of Reinforcement

Reinforcement Schedule	Nature of Reinforcement	Effect on Behaviour	Example
Continuous	Reward given after each desired behaviour	Fast learning of new behaviour but rapid extinction	Compliments
Fixed-interval	Reward given at fixed time intervals	Average and irregular performance with rapid extinction	Weekly paycheques
Variable-interval	Reward given at variable time intervals	Moderately high and stable performance with slow extinction	Pop quizzes
Fixed-ratio	Reward given at fixed amounts of output	High and stable performance attained quickly but also with rapid extinction	Piece-rate pay
Variable-ratio	Reward given at variable amounts of output	Very high performance with slow extinction	Commissioned sales

is not tardy, his manager might compliment him on his desirable behaviour. In an intermittent schedule, on the other hand, not every instance of the desirable behaviour is reinforced, but reinforcement is given often enough to make the behaviour worth repeating. Evidence indicates that the intermittent, or varied, form of reinforcement tends to promote more resistance to extinction than does the continuous form.[96]

An **intermittent reinforcement** schedule can be of a ratio or interval type. Ratio schedules depend on how many responses the subject makes. The individual is reinforced after giving a certain number of specific types of behaviour. Interval schedules depend on how much time has passed since the previous reinforcement. With interval schedules, the individual is reinforced on the first appropriate behaviour after a particular time has elapsed. A reinforcement can also be classified as fixed or variable. When these factors are combined, four types of intermittent schedules of reinforcement result: **fixed-interval schedule**, **variable-interval schedule**, **fixed-ratio schedule**, and **variable-ratio schedule**.

Exhibit 13-14 summarizes the five schedules of reinforcement and their effects on behaviour.

Reinforcement in the Workplace

Managers want employees to behave in ways that most benefit the organization. Therefore, they look for ways to reinforce positive behaviour and extinguish negative behaviour. Consider the situation in which an employee's behaviour is significantly different from that sought by management. If management rewarded the individual only when he or she showed desirable responses, there might be very little reinforcement taking place. Instead, managers can reinforce each successive step that moves the individual closer to the desired response. If an employee who usually turns in his work two days late succeeds in turning in his work only one day late, managers can reinforce that improvement. Reinforcement would increase as responses more closely approximated the desired behaviour.

While variable-ratio and variable-interval reinforcement schedules produce the best results for improving behaviour, most work organizations rely on fixed-interval (weekly or monthly) pay or fixed-ratio (piece-rate) pay. In the next chapter, we will discuss the idea of variable pay, as well as reactions to it. We will also look at how rewards in general are used in the workplace.

intermittent reinforcement A desired behaviour is reinforced often enough to make the behaviour worth repeating, but not every time it is demonstrated.

fixed-interval schedule The reward is given at fixed time intervals.

variable-interval schedule The reward is given at variable time intervals.

fixed-ratio schedule The reward is given at fixed amounts of output.

variable-ratio schedule The reward is given at variable amounts of output.

Motivation for Whom?

6 What are the ethics behind motivation theories?

A current debate among organizational behaviour scholars is, Who benefits from the theories of motivation?[97] Some argue that motivation theories are only intended to help managers get more productivity out of employees, and are little concerned with employees beyond improvements in productivity. Thus, needs theories, process theories, and theories concerned with fairness could be interpreted not as ways to help employees get what they want or need, but rather as means to help managers get what they want from employees. In his review of "meaningful work" literature, professor Christopher Michaelson of the Wharton School at the University of Pennsylvania finds that researchers propose that organizations have a moral obligation to provide employees with "free choice to enter, honest communication, fair and respectful treatment, intellectual challenge, considerable independence to determine work methods, democratic participation in decision making, moral development, due process and justice, nonpaternalism, and fair compensation."[98]

Michaelson suggests that scholars concerned with meaningful work should focus on the conditions of the workplace and improving those conditions. He also suggests that researchers have a moral obligation to make workplaces better for employees. While productivity may be a by-product of better work conditions, the important thing is for employers to treat employees well, and to consider the needs of employees as an end in itself. By contrast, he argues, mainstream motivation theory does not consider the moral obligation of employers to their employees, but it does consider ways to ensure employees are more productive.

While this debate is not easily resolved, and may well guide the elaboration of motivation theories in years to come, it does inspire a provocative analysis of why employers provide the workplace conditions they do.

Putting it all Together

While it's always dangerous to synthesize a large number of complex ideas into a few simple guidelines, the following suggestions summarize the essence of what we know about motivating employees in organizations:

- *Recognize individual differences.* Employees have different needs and should not be treated alike. Managers should spend the time necessary to understand what is important to each employee and then align goals, level of involvement, and rewards with individual needs.

- *Use goals and feedback.* Employees should have challenging, specific goals, as well as feedback on how well they are doing in pursuit of those goals.

- *Allow employees to participate in decisions that affect them.* Employees can contribute to a number of decisions that affect them: setting work goals, choosing their own benefits packages, solving productivity and quality problems, and the like. This can increase employee productivity, commitment to work goals, motivation, and job satisfaction.

- *When giving rewards, be sure that they reward desired performance.* Rewards should be linked to the type of performance expected. It is important that employees perceive a clear linkage. How closely rewards are actually correlated to performance criteria is less important than the perception of this relationship. If individuals perceive this relationship to be low, the results will be low performance, a decrease in job satisfaction, and an increase in turnover and absenteeism.

- *Check the system for equity.* Employees should be able to perceive rewards as equating with the inputs they bring to the job. At a simplistic level, this means that experience, skills, abilities, effort, and other obvious inputs should explain differences in performance and, hence, pay, job assignments, and other obvious rewards.

GLOBAL IMPLICATIONS

Most current motivation theories were developed in the United States and Canada.[99] Goal-setting and expectancy theories emphasize goal accomplishment as well as rational and individual thought—characteristics consistent with Canadian and American culture. Let's look at several motivation theories and consider their cross-cultural transferability.

Needs Theories

Maslow's needs theory says people start at the physiological level and progress up the hierarchy to safety, social, esteem, and self-actualization needs. This hierarchy, if it applies at all, aligns with Canadian and US culture. In Japan, Greece, and Mexico, where uncertainty-avoidance characteristics are strong, security needs would be on top of the hierarchy. Countries that score high on nurturing characteristics—Denmark, Sweden, Norway, the Netherlands, and Finland—would have social needs on top.[100] Group work will motivate employees more when the country's culture scores high on the nurturing criterion.

The view that a high achievement need acts as an internal motivator presupposes two cultural characteristics—willingness to accept a moderate degree of risk (which excludes countries with strong uncertainty avoidance characteristics) and concern with performance (which applies to countries with strong achievement characteristics). This combination is found in Anglo-American countries such as the United States, Canada, and Great Britain[101] and much less so in Chile and Portugal.

Goal Setting

Setting specific, difficult, individual goals may have different effects in different cultures. Most goal-setting research has been done in the United States and Canada, where individual achievement and performance are most highly valued. To date, research has not shown that group-based goals are more effective in collectivistic than in individualistic cultures. There is evidence that in collectivistic and high-power-distance cultures, achievable moderate goals can be more highly motivating than difficult ones.[102] Finally, assigned goals appear to generate greater goal commitment in high rather than low power-distance cultures.[103] Much more research is needed to assess how goal constructs might differ across cultures.

Equity Theory

Equity theory has gained a strong following in Canada and the United States because the reward systems assume that employees are highly sensitive to equity in reward allocations. In Canada and the United States, equity is meant to closely tie pay to performance. However, in collectivistic cultures, especially the former socialist countries of Central and Eastern Europe, employees expect rewards to reflect their individual needs as well as their performance.[104] Consistent with a legacy of communism and centrally planned economies, employees exhibited an entitlement attitude—that is, they expected outcomes to be *greater* than their inputs.[105] These findings suggest that Canadian-style pay practices may need modification, especially in Russia and former communist countries, to be perceived as fair by employees.

Intrinsic and Extrinsic Motivation

A recent study found interesting differences in managers' perceptions of employee motivation.[106] The study examined managers from three distinct cultural regions: North America, Asia, and Latin America. The results of the study revealed that North American managers perceive their employees as being motivated more by extrinsic factors (for example, pay) than intrinsic factors (for example, doing meaningful work). Asian managers perceive their employees as being motivated by both extrinsic and intrinsic factors, while Latin American managers perceive their employees as being motivated by intrinsic factors.

Even more interesting, these differences affected evaluations of employee performance. As expected, Asian managers focused on both types of motivation when evaluating their employees' performance, and Latin American managers focused on intrinsic motivation. Oddly, North American managers, though believing that employees are motivated primarily by extrinsic factors, actually focused more on intrinsic factors when evaluating employee performance. Why the paradox? One explanation is that North Americans value uniqueness, so any deviation from the norm—such as being perceived as being unusually high in intrinsic motivation—is rewarded.

Latin American managers' focus on intrinsic motivation when evaluating employees may be related to a cultural norm termed *simpatía*, a tradition that compels employees to display their internal feelings. Consequently, Latin American managers are more sensitized to these displays and can more easily notice their employees' intrinsic motivation.

Cross-Cultural Consistencies

Don't assume that there are *no* cross-cultural consistencies. The desire for interesting work seems important to almost all employees, regardless of their national culture. In a study of 7 countries, employees in Belgium, Britain, Israel, and the United States ranked work number 1 among 11 work goals, and employees in Japan, the Netherlands, and Germany ranked it either second or third.[107] In a study comparing job-preference outcomes among graduate students in the United States, Canada, Australia, and Singapore, growth, achievement, and responsibility had identical rankings as the top three.[108] Meta-analytic evidence shows that individuals in both individualistic and collectivistic cultures prefer an equitable distribution of rewards (the most effective employees get paid the most) over an equal division (everyone gets paid the same regardless of performance).[109] Across nations, the same basic principles of procedural justice are respected, and employees around the world prefer rewards based on performance and skills over rewards based on seniority.[110]

14 Motivation in Action

John Mackey, the CEO of Austin, Texas-based Whole Foods, a fast-growing upscale grocery retailer with stores in Vancouver, West Vancouver, Toronto, Oakville, London (England), and cities across the United States recently implemented an incentive program to help his employees engage in healthier living. By meeting certain health requirements, employees can earn up to an extra 10 percent discount on the store's products (in addition to the 20 percent discount they already receive).[1]

To be eligible to participate in the program, employees must be non-smokers with a body mass index (BMI) below 30. Eligible participants are screened for their cholesterol count, blood pressure, and BMI, and awarded a discount from 2 percent to 10 percent, based on the measurements. The bonuses are awarded as follows: Bronze (2 percent), Silver (5 percent), Gold (7 percent), and Platinum (10 percent). To earn Bronze level, an employee must have a blood pressure of 140/90, total cholesterol count of 195 or less, and a BMI of 30 or less. Platinum level demands blood pressure of 110/70, total cholesterol count below 150, and a BMI of less than 24.

The thinking behind Mackey's program is that incentives might help his employees achieve new fitness levels. The program was widely criticized when it was announced. Rosemary Bennett, senior communications officer for the Ontario Human Rights Commission, says that even though the program is voluntary, weight issues are sometimes treated as a disability. "If it's an incentive program, it should be for an incentive people can do things about. Human rights are about accommodation and equality and providing as level a playing field as you possibly can, and the way you do that is to look at the individual circumstances." Does it make sense for Mackey to motivate his employees this way?

In this chapter, we focus on how to apply motivation concepts. We review a number of reward programs and consider whether rewards are overrated. We also discuss how to create more motivating jobs and workplaces, both of which have been shown to be alternatives to rewards in motivating individuals.

From Theory to Practice: The Role of Money

1 Is money an important motivator?

The most commonly used reward in organizations is money. As one author notes, "Money is probably the most emotionally meaningful object in contemporary life: only food and sex are its close competitors as common carriers of such strong and diverse feelings, significance, and strivings."[2] A 2010 survey of Canadian employees found that overall, 46 percent believe they are underpaid. More employees in Quebec think they are underpaid (54 percent) than those in Ontario (38 percent). The survey's results are similar to a 2011 poll conducted in the United States, in which 45 percent felt they were underpaid.[3]

The motivation theories we have presented only give us vague ideas of how money relates to individual motivation. For instance, Theory X suggests that individuals need to be extrinsically motivated. Money is certainly one such extrinsic motivator. According to Maslow's hierarchy of needs, individuals' basic needs must be met, including food, shelter, and safety. Generally, money can be used to satisfy those needs. Herzberg's motivation-hygiene theory, on the other hand, suggests that money (and other extrinsic motivators) are necessary but not sufficient conditions for individuals to be motivated. Process theories are relatively silent about the role of money specifically, indicating more how rewards motivate, without specifying particular types of rewards. Expectancy theory does note that individuals need to value the reward, or it won't be very motivational.

Despite the importance of money in attracting and retaining employees, and rewarding and recognizing them, not enough research has been done on this topic.[4] With respect to job satisfaction, one 2010 study found that pay level was only moderately correlated, and concluded that a person could be satisfied with his or her pay level, and still not have job satisfaction.[5] A 2011 study concluded that "money leads to autonomy but it does not add to well-being or happiness."[6] Supporting this idea, recent research suggests that money is not the sole motivator for Generation Y and Baby Boomer employees. Both generations find having "a great team, challenging assignments, a range of new experiences, and explicit performance evaluation and recognition" as important as money.[7] Exhibit 14-1 illustrates the key differences and similarities of what the two generations value in addition to money.

A number of studies suggest that there are personality traits and demographic factors that correlate with an individual's attitude toward money.[8] People who highly value money score higher on "attributes like sensation seeking, competitiveness, materialism, and control." People who desire money score higher on self-esteem, need for achievement, and Type A personality measures. Men seem to value money more than women, who value recognition for doing a good job more.[9]

EXHIBIT 14-1 What Baby Boomers and Generation Y Value as Much as Compensation

Baby Boomers	Generation Y
High-quality colleagues	High-quality colleagues
An intellectually stimulating workplace	Flexible work arrangements
Autonomy regarding work tasks	Prospects for advancement
Flexible work arrangements	Recognition from one's company or boss
Access to new experiences and challenges	A steady rate of advancement and promotion
Giving back to the world through work	Access to new experiences and challenges
Recognition from one's company or boss	

Source: S. A. Hewlett, L. Sherbin, and K. Sumberg, "How Gen Y & Boomers Will Reshape Your Agenda," *Harvard Business Review,* July/August 2009, p. 76.

What these findings suggest is that when organizations develop reward programs, they need to consider very carefully the importance to the individual of the specific rewards offered.

Creating Effective Reward Systems

At Whole Foods, departments are organized around teams because the retailer is determined not to have an "us vs. them" mindset in the workplace.[10] The team is responsible for managing the department and is given a set of guidelines for doing so. Teams have decision-making responsibility in a number of areas, including recruiting. In order to make sure that individuals function together as a team, bonus payments are based on team performance. Sales and margin figures for all departments are available for employees to inspect at any time.

Whole Foods fosters team spirit through various incentives, including the following:[11]

- self-directed teams that meet regularly to discuss issues, solve problems, and appreciate each other's contributions
- gainsharing and other team member incentive programs
- stock options and stock purchase plan
- commitment to make jobs more fun by combining work and play and through friendly competition to improve the stores.

To encourage a shared collective vision, Whole Foods also has a salary cap "that limits the maximum cash compensation (wages plus profit incentive bonuses) paid to any Team Member in the calendar year to 19 times the company-wide annual average salary of all full-time Team Members."[12]

All of these actions signal to employees that they are valued as important contributors to the company's success. What else can a company do to make sure its employees feel valued?

2 What does an effective reward system look like?

As we saw in Chapter 3, pay is not a primary factor driving job satisfaction. However, it does motivate people, and companies often underestimate the importance of pay in keeping top talent. A recent study found that although only 45 percent of employers thought that pay was a key factor in losing top talent, 71 percent of top performers indicated that it was a main reason.[13]

Given that pay is so important, we need to understand what to pay employees and how to pay them. To do that, management must make some strategic decisions. Will the organization lead, match, or lag the market in pay? How will individual contributions be recognized? In this section, we consider four major strategic rewards decisions that need to be made: (1) what to pay employees (which is decided by establishing a pay structure); (2) how to pay individual employees (which is decided through variable-pay plans and skill-based pay plans); (3) what benefits to offer, especially whether to offer employees choice in benefits (flexible benefits); and (4) how to construct employee recognition programs.

What to Pay: Establishing a Pay Structure

When organizations set pay rates, they balance *internal equity*—the worth of the job to the organization (usually established through a technical process called *job evaluation*)—and *external equity*—the external competitiveness of an organization's pay relative to pay elsewhere in its industry (usually established through pay surveys). Obviously, the best pay system pays the job what it is worth (internal equity) while also paying competitively relative to the labour market.

Pay is often the highest single operating cost for an organization, and it's a strategic decision with clear trade-offs. Paying above the market results in better-qualified, more highly motivated employees who will stay with the organization longer. Paying below the market results in higher turnover as people are lured to better-paying jobs. Companies often underestimate the importance of pay in keeping top talent. A recent study found that competitive pay led to more satisfied customers as well as employees with higher morale and increased productivity.[14]

How to Pay: Rewarding Individuals through Variable-Pay Programs

"Why should I put any extra effort into this job?" asks a frustrated grade 4 teacher. "I can excel or I can do the bare minimum. It makes no difference. I get paid the same. Why do anything above the minimum to get by?" Similar comments have been voiced by schoolteachers (and some other unionized employees) for decades because pay increases are tied to seniority.

A number of organizations—business firms as well as school districts and other government agencies—are moving away from paying people based solely on credentials or length of service and toward using variable-pay programs. Piece-rate wages, merit-based pay, bonuses, gainsharing, profit-sharing plans, stock options, and employee stock ownership plans are all forms of **variable-pay programs**, which base a portion of an employee's pay on some individual, group, and/or organizational measure of performance. Earnings therefore fluctuate up and down with the measure of performance,[15] as Jason Easton, corporate communications manager at Toronto-based GM Canada, explains: "In any given year the variable pay can actually be zero, below the target or above the target, depending on how the company has performed."[16]

Burnaby, BC-based TELUS and Hamilton, Ontario-based ArcelorMittal Dofasco are just a couple of examples of companies that use variable pay with rank-and-file employees. About 10 to 15 percent of the base pay of ArcelorMittal Dofasco's blue-collar workers is subject to variable compensation, while more than half of the CEO's compensation is based on variable pay.[17] GM Canada gave performance-based bonuses to its salaried employees in 2011, generating discontent among union employees who had no such provision in their collective agreement.[18]

Variable-pay plans have long been used to compensate salespeople and executives. Recently they have begun to be applied to other employees. A recent international survey by Hewitt Associates of large organizations in 46 countries found that more than 80 percent offered variable pay in 2010. In Canada, 9.6 percent of the payroll, on average, goes to variable pay.[19]

The fluctuation in variable pay is what makes these programs attractive to management. It turns part of an organization's fixed labour costs into a variable cost, thus reducing expenses when performance declines. When the economy falters, companies with variable pay are able to reduce their labour costs much faster than others.[20] When pay is tied to performance, the employee's earnings recognize contribution rather than become a form of entitlement. Low performers find, over time, that their pay stagnates, while high performers enjoy pay increases commensurate with their contributions.

Despite some reservations by employees, management professor Maria Rotundo of the Rotman School of Management at the University of Toronto noted that merit pay can work. "It all hinges on fair measures" during the performance appraisal. Managers need to explain why people get different amounts of money, or people "get angry, jealous and disenchanted."[21]

Individual-Based Incentives

There are four major forms of individual-based variable-pay programs: piece-rate wages, merit-based pay, bonuses, and skill-based pay.

Piece-Rate Wages The **piece-rate pay plan** has long been popular as a means for compensating production employees by paying a fixed sum for each unit of production completed. A pure piece-rate plan provides no base salary and pays the employee only for what he or she produces. People who work at baseball parks selling peanuts and soft drinks frequently are paid this way. At a rate of 25 cents for every bag of peanuts sold, they make $50 if they sell 200 bags during a game, and $10 if they sell only

variable-pay programs A reward program in which a portion of an employee's pay is based on some individual and/or organizational measure of performance.

piece-rate pay plan An individual-based incentive plan in which employees are paid a fixed sum for each unit of production completed.

40 bags. The Vancouver Canucks' four best players were well paid for the 2011–2012 season: The Sedin twins were paid $6.1 million, Roberto Luongo was paid $5.3 million, and Ryan Kesler earned $5 million, regardless of how many games they helped their team win.[22] Would it be better to pay each of them a fixed amount for each win? It seems unlikely they would accept such a deal, and it may cause unanticipated consequences as well (such as cheating). So, although incentives are motivating and relevant for some jobs, it is unrealistic to think they can constitute the only piece of some employees' pay.

Merit-Based Pay **Merit-based pay plans** pay for individual performance based on performance appraisal ratings. Most large organizations have merit-based pay plans, especially for salaried employees. IBM Canada's merit pay plan, for example, provides increases to employees' base salary based on their annual performance evaluation. Since the 1990s, when the economy stumbled badly, an increasing number of Japanese companies have abandoned seniority-based pay in favour of merit-based pay. Koichi Yanashita of Takeda Chemical Industries commented, "The merit-based salary system is an important means to achieve goals set by the company's top management, not just a way to change wages."[23]

The thinking behind merit pay is that people who are high performers should be given bigger raises. For merit pay to be effective, however, individuals need to perceive a strong relationship between their performance and the rewards they receive.[24] Unfortunately, the evidence suggests that this is not the case.[25]

Despite the intuitive appeal of paying for performance, merit-based pay plans have several limitations. One is that they are typically based on an annual performance appraisal and thus are only as valid as the performance ratings. Another limitation is that the pay raise pool fluctuates based on economic or other conditions that have little to do with an individual employee's performance. One year, a colleague at a top university who performed very well in teaching and research was given a pay raise of $300. Why? Because the budget for pay raises was very small. Yet that is hardly pay for performance. Unions typically resist merit-based pay plans and prefer seniority-based pay, where all employees get the same raises.

Finally, merit pay systems may result in gender and racial discrimination in pay. A 2010 study found that when organizations have merit-based cultures, managers tend to favour male employees over female employees, with men getting larger monetary rewards. The researchers conclude that there may be "unrecognized risks behind certain organizational efforts used to reward merit."[26]

Bonuses An annual **bonus** is a significant component of total compensation for many jobs.[27] Bonuses reward employees for recent performance rather than historical performance and are one-time rewards rather than ongoing entitlements. They are used by such companies as Ontario Hydro Energy, the Bank of Montreal, and Molson Coors Brewing Company. The incentive effects of performance bonuses should be higher because, rather than paying for performance that may have occurred years ago (and was rolled into their base pay), bonuses reward only recent performance. Moreover, when times are bad, firms can cut bonuses to reduce compensation costs. Steel company Nucor, for example, guarantees its employees only about $10 per hour, but bonuses can be substantial. In 2006, the average Nucor employee made roughly $91 000. When the recession hit, bonuses were cut dramatically: In 2009, total pay had dropped 40 percent.[28]

Bonuses are not free from organizational politics (which we discuss in Chapter 25), and they can sometimes result in negative behaviour, when employees engage in negative behaviours to ensure they will receive bonuses.

The collapse of so many financial institutions at once suggests that rewarding individuals based on financial measures can cause problems.

merit-based pay plan An individual-based incentive plan based on performance appraisal ratings.

bonus An individual-based incentive plan that rewards employees for recent performance rather than historical performance.

Skill-Based Pay   **Skill-based pay** (also called competency-based or knowledge-based pay) is an alternative to job-based pay and bases pay levels on the basis of how many skills employees have or how many jobs they can do.[29] Frito-Lay Corporation ties its compensation for front-line operations managers to developing their skills in leadership, workforce development, and functional excellence. For employers, the lure of skill-based pay plans is that they increase the flexibility of the workforce: Filling staffing needs is easier when employee skills are interchangeable. Skill-based pay also facilitates communication across the organization because people gain a better understanding of each other's jobs.

What about the downside? People can "top out"—that is, they can learn all the skills the program calls for them to learn. This can frustrate employees after they have been challenged by an environment of learning, growth, and continual pay raises. Finally, skill-based plans don't address level of performance. They deal only with whether someone can perform the skill.

Group-Based Incentives

There is one major form of group-based pay-for-performance program: gainsharing.

Gainsharing   **Gainsharing** is a formula-based group incentive plan that uses improvements in group productivity from one period to another to determine the total amount of money to be shared.[30] For instance, if last month a company produced 1000 items using 10 000 person hours, and this month production of the same number of items was produced with only 9000 person hours, the company experiences a savings of 1000 person hours, at the average cost per hour to hire a person. Productivity savings can be divided between the company and employees in any number of ways, but 50-50 is fairly typical. Approximately 45 percent of *Fortune* 1000 firms have implemented gainsharing plans.[31]

Gainsharing differs from profit sharing, discussed below, in that it ties rewards to productivity gains rather than profits. Employees in a gainsharing plan can receive incentive awards even when the organization is not profitable. Because the benefits accrue to groups of employees, high-performing employees pressure weaker performers to work harder, improving performance for the group as a whole.[32] Delta, BC-based Avcorp Industries, and governments, such as Ontario's Town of Ajax and Kingston Township, have introduced gainsharing. It has been found to improve productivity in a majority of cases, and often has a positive impact on employee attitudes.[33]

Organizational-Based Incentives

There are two major forms of organizational-based pay-for-performance programs: profit-sharing and stock option plans, which include employee stock ownership plans.

Profit-Sharing Plans   A **profit-sharing plan** is an organization-wide plan in which the employer shares profits with employees based on a predetermined formula. The plan can distribute direct cash outlays or stock options. Though senior executives are most likely to be rewarded through profit-sharing plans, employees at any level can be recipients. Burlington, Ontario-based O.C. Tanner Canada pays all of its employees' bonuses based on profits, twice a year.

Profit-sharing plans do not necessarily focus employees on the future, because employees and managers look for ways to cut costs today, without considering longer-term organizational needs. They also tend to ignore factors such as customer service and employee development, which may not be seen as having a direct link to profits. Employees can see inconsistent rewards with such a plan. Gregg Saretsky, WestJet's

skill-based pay An individual-based incentive plan that sets pay levels on the basis of how many skills employees have or how many jobs they can do.

gainsharing A group-based incentive plan in which improvements in group productivity determine the total amount of money to be shared.

profit-sharing plan An organization-wide incentive plan in which the employer shares profits with employees based on a predetermined formula.

president and CEO, worries about the flatness of the company's stock price compared with how it soared after the company's initial public offering in 1999. With 84 percent owning shares, most of WestJet employees' compensation is affected by stock prices. However, pay is not the only motivator at WestJet. "You have to have fun and feel you can make a contribution and drive a difference. WestJetters have that in spades," says Saretsky.[34] Vancouver-based 1-800-GOT-JUNK? made no payment in 2007 when the company used its profits to invest in international expansion. Tania Hall, senior PR manager, acknowledged that the lack of a reward cheque could "test employee staying power. This is an opportunity to grow and be part of shaping the future, and you're either in or not."[35]

Three Canadian studies by Professor Richard J. Long of the University of Saskatchewan's College of Commerce show that a profit-sharing plan is most effective in workplaces where there is more involvement by employees, more teamwork, and a managerial philosophy that encourages participation.[36] Employees working under profit-sharing plans have a greater feeling of psychological ownership.[37]

Employee Stock Ownership Plans and Stock Options An **employee stock ownership plan (ESOP)**[38] is a company-established benefit plan in which employees acquire stock as part of their benefits. Stock options give employees the right to buy stocks in the company at a later date for a guaranteed price. In either case, the idea is that employees will be more likely to think about the consequences of their behaviour on the bottom line if they own part of the company.

Canadian companies lag far behind the United States in the use of ESOPs because Canada's tax environment is less conducive to such plans. Nevertheless, Edmonton-based PCL Constructors has been owned by its employees since 1977, with 80 percent of employees owning shares. Ross Grieve, the company's president and CEO, says that ownership "elevates [the employees'] commitment to the organization."[39] Toronto-based I Love Rewards and Edmonton-based Cybertech are other examples of companies that have employee stock ownership plans.

RESEARCH FINDINGS: ESOPs

The research on ESOPs indicates that while they increase employee satisfaction,[40] their impact on performance is less clear. A study by the Toronto Stock Exchange found positive results for public companies with ESOPs:[41]

- Five-year profit growth was 123 percent higher.
- Net profit margin was 95 percent higher.
- Productivity, measured by revenue per employee, was 24 percent higher.
- Return on average total equity was 92.3 percent higher.
- Return on capital was 65.5 percent higher.

ESOPs have the potential to increase employee job satisfaction and work motivation. For this potential to be realized, employees need to psychologically experience ownership.[42] In addition to their financial stake in the company, they need to be kept regularly informed on the status of the business, and have the opportunity to exercise influence over it to achieve significant improvements in the organization's performance.[43] ESOPs for top management can reduce unethical behaviour. CEOs are more likely to manipulate firm earnings reports to make themselves look good in the short run when they don't have an ownership share, even though this manipulation will eventually lead to lower stock prices. However, when CEOs own a large value of stock, they report earnings accurately because they don't want the negative consequences of declining stock prices.[44]

employee stock ownership plan (ESOP) A company-established benefit plan in which employees acquire stock as part of their benefits.

RESEARCH FINDINGS: Variable-Pay Programs

Do variable-pay programs increase motivation and productivity? The answer is a qualified "yes." Studies generally support the idea that organizations with profit-sharing plans have higher levels of profitability than those without them.[45] Similarly, gainsharing has been found to improve productivity in a majority of cases, and often has a positive impact on employee attitudes.[46] Another study found that although piece-rate pay-for-performance plans stimulated higher levels of productivity, this positive effect was not observed for risk-averse employees. Thus, American economist Ed Lazear generally seems right when he says, "Workers respond to prices just as economic theory predicts. Claims by sociologists and others that monetizing incentives may actually reduce output are unambiguously refuted by the data."[47] However, that does not mean everyone responds positively to variable-pay programs.[48]

Teamwork, unions, public sector employees, and ethical considerations present distinct challenges to pay-for-performance programs.

Teamwork   Incentive pay, especially when it is awarded to individuals, can have a negative effect on group cohesiveness and productivity, and in some cases it may not offer significant benefits to a company.[49] For example, Montreal-based National Bank of Canada offered a $5 employee bonus for every time employees referred clients for loans, mutual funds, or other bank products. But the bonus so upset employees that the plan was abandoned after just three months.[50] Tellers complained that the bonus caused colleagues to compete against one another. Meanwhile, the bank could not determine whether the referrals actually generated new business.

If an organization wants a group of individuals to function as a "team" (which we define in Chapter 18), emphasis needs to be on team-based rewards, rather than individual rewards. We will discuss the nature of team-based rewards in Chapter 18.

Unions   In Canada, there are considerably more unionized workplaces than there are in the United States. Consequently, the unionized context must be considered when motivation theories and practices are examined. Unionized employees are typically paid on the basis of seniority and job categories, with very little range within a category, and few opportunities to receive performance-based pay.

Moreover, organized labour is, in general, cool to the idea of pay for performance. Prem Benimadhu, an analyst at The Conference Board of Canada, notes, "Canadian unions have been very allergic to variable compensation."[51] Andrew Jackson, senior economist for the Canadian Labour Congress in Ottawa, adds that "it hurts co-operation in the workplace. It can lead to competition between workers, speeding up the pace of work. It's a bad thing if it creates a stressful work environment where older workers can't keep up."[52] Union members are also concerned that factors out of their control might affect whether bonuses are awarded.

> What is the impact of unions on pay for performance?

Public Sector Employees   There are special challenges in pay-for-performance programs for public sector employees (those who work for local, provincial, or federal governments). Because public sector work is often of a service nature, it can be hard to measure productivity in the same way manufacturing or retail firms do. One might be able to count how many children an employee places in foster homes, but this might not really address the quality of those placements. Therefore, it becomes more difficult to make a meaningful link between rewards and productivity.

Because pay-for-performance programs can be difficult to administer in the public sector, several researchers have suggested that goal-setting theory be used to improve performance in public sector organizations instead.[53] More recently, another researcher found that goal difficulty and goal specificity, as well as the belief that the goal could be achieved, significantly improved motivation of public sector employees.[54] Because many public sector employees are also unionized, the challenges faced in motivating unionized employees also apply to government employees.

Ethical Considerations   Organizations need to consider the ethical implications of their performance-based plans. The recent collapse of financial institutions in the United States provides one example of employees manipulating performance results to increase their bonuses. Walmart has been accused by a number of employees of demanding that they work many unpaid hours.[55] According to company policy, Walmart's store managers are told to keep payroll costs below fixed targets and not to allow employees to work overtime. Yet they are reprimanded and face possible demotion or dismissal if they miss their targets. When store managers pressure employees to do work without recording the hours on time sheets, they are simply following practices to ensure that they will be rewarded for performance by their superiors.

Flexible Benefits: Developing a Benefits Package

Alain Bourdeau and Yasmin Murphy have very different needs in terms of employee benefits. Alain is married and has three young children and a wife who is at home full time. Yasmin, too, is married, but her husband has a high-paying job with the federal government, and they have no children. Alain is concerned about having a good dental plan and enough life insurance to support his family in case it's needed. In contrast, Yasmin's husband already has her dental needs covered on his plan, and life insurance is a low priority for both Yasmin and her husband. Yasmin is more interested in extra vacation time and long-term financial benefits such as a tax-deferred savings plan.

A standardized benefits package for all employees at an organization would be unlikely to satisfactorily meet the needs of both Alain and Yasmin. Some organizations, therefore, cover both sets of needs by offering flexible benefits.

Consistent with expectancy theory's thesis that organizational rewards should be linked to each individual employee's personal goals, **flexible benefits** individualize rewards by allowing each employee to choose the compensation package that best satisfies his or her current needs. It replaces the traditional "one-benefit-plan-fits-all" programs designed for a male with a wife and two children at home that dominated organizations for more than 50 years.[56] The average organization provides fringe benefits worth approximately 40 percent of an employee's salary. Flexible benefits can be uniquely tailored to accommodate differences in employee needs based on age, marital status, spouse's benefit status, number and age of dependants, and the like.

The three most popular types of benefits plans are modular plans, core-plus plans, and flexible spending accounts.[57] *Modular plans* are predesigned packages of benefits, with each module put together to meet the needs of a specific group of employees. A module designed for single employees with no dependants might include only essential benefits. Another, designed for single parents, might have additional life insurance, disability insurance, and expanded health coverage. *Core-plus plans* consist of a core of essential benefits and a menu-like selection of other benefit options from which employees can select. Typically, each employee is given "benefit credits," which allow the "purchase" of additional benefits that uniquely meet his or her needs. *Flexible spending accounts* allow employees to set aside pretax dollars up to the dollar amount offered in the plan to pay for particular benefits, such as eye care and dental premiums. Flexible spending accounts can increase employee take-home pay because employees don't pay taxes on the dollars they spend out of these accounts.

flexible benefits   A benefits plan that allows each employee to put together a benefits package individually tailored to his or her own needs and situation.

Intrinsic Rewards: Employee Recognition Programs

A few years ago, 1500 employees were surveyed in a variety of work settings to find out what they considered to be the most powerful workplace motivator. Their response? Recognition, recognition, and more recognition![58]

Expectancy theory tells us that a key component of motivation is the link between performance and rewards (that is, having your behaviour recognized). Employee recognition programs cover a wide spectrum of activities. They range from a spontaneous and private "thank you" on up to widely publicized formal programs in which specific types of behaviour are encouraged and the procedures for attaining recognition are clearly identified.[59] Some research suggests financial incentives may be more motivating in the short term, but in the long run it's nonfinancial incentives that are motivating.[60]

Toronto-based software developer RL Solutions developed a formal program for employees to recognize co-workers who go above and beyond in working with clients or in other aspects of their work. Those recognized by their co-workers receive cash and/ or other rewards. Employees are also recognized with bonuses when they refer good job candidates to the company.[61] Brian Scudamore, CEO of Vancouver-based 1-800-GOT-JUNK? understands the importance of showing employees that they are appreciated. "I believe that the best way to engage someone is with heartfelt thanks. We have created a culture of peer recognition, and 'thank yous' have become contagious. Whether it's a card, kudos at the huddle or basic one-on-one thanks, gratitude goes a long way toward building team engagement, loyalty and, of course, happiness."[62] Scudamore says that actions like these keep the company growing, and employees having fun.

A recent survey of Canadian firms found that 34 percent of companies recognize individual or group achievements with cash or merchandise.[63] Other ways of recognizing performance include sending employees personal thank-you notes or emails for good performance, putting employees on prestigious committees, sending employees for training, and giving an employee an assistant for a day to help clear backlogs. Recognition and praise, however, need to be meaningful.

Beware the Signals That Are Sent by Rewards

Perhaps more often than we would like, organizations engage in what has been called "the folly of rewarding A, while hoping for B"[64]; in other words, hoping employees will engage in one type of behaviour, while managers reward for another type. Expectancy theory suggests that individuals will generally perform in ways that raise the probability of receiving the rewards offered. Exhibit 14-2 provides examples of common management reward follies. By focusing on test scores (easy to measure) rather than learning (harder to measure), administrators in the Atlanta, Georgia, school district encouraged teachers to change students' answers on tests.

Ever wonder why employees do some strange things?

Research suggests that there are three major obstacles to ending these follies:[65]

1. *Individuals are unable to break out of old ways of thinking about reward and recognition practices.* Management often emphasizes quantifiable behaviours to the exclusion of nonquantifiable behaviours; management is sometimes reluctant to change the existing performance system; and employees sometimes have an entitlement mentality (they don't want change because they are comfortable with the current system for rewards).

2. *Organizations often don't look at the big picture of their performance system.* Consequently, rewards are allocated at subunit levels, with the result that units often compete against each other.

3. *Both management and shareholders often focus on short-term results.* They don't reward employees for longer-range planning.

EXHIBIT 14-2 Management Reward Follies

We hope for . . .	But we reward . . .
Teamwork and collaboration	The best team members
Innovative thinking and risk-taking	Proven methods and not making mistakes
Development of people skills	Technical achievements and accomplishments
Employee involvement and empowerment	Tight control over operations and resources
High achievement	Another year's effort
Long-term growth; environmental responsibility	Quarterly earnings
Commitment to total quality	Shipping on schedule, even with defects
Candour; surfacing bad news early	Reporting good news, whether it's true or not; agreeing with the manager, whether or not (s)he's right

Sources: Constructed from S. Kerr, "On the Folly of Rewarding A, While Hoping for B," *Academy of Management Executive* 9, no. 1 (1995), pp. 7–14; and "More on the Folly," *Academy of Management Executive* 9, no. 1 (1995), pp. 15–16. Copyright © Academy of Management, 1990.

Organizations would do well to ensure that they do not send the wrong message when offering rewards. When organizations outline an organizational objective of "team performance," for example, but reward each employee according to individual productivity, this does not send a message that teams are valued. When a retailer tells commissioned employees that they are responsible for monitoring and replacing stock, those employees will nevertheless concentrate on making sales. Employees motivated by the promise of rewards will do those things that earn them the rewards they value.

Gordon Nixon, president and CEO of the Royal Bank of Canada, highlights changes RBC made to be sure it was rewarding the right things: "We constantly reinforce the values of the organization and ensure it is living up to those values by the way we respect people, the way we compensate and promote people, the way we recognize [them]. We changed our review process to ensure there is alignment with respect to values and culture—that there is alignment between our values and how people are recognized and rewarded."[66]

Can We Eliminate Rewards?

Alfie Kohn, in his book *Punished by Rewards,* argues that "the desire to do something, much less to do it well, simply cannot be imposed; in this sense, it is a mistake to talk about motivating other people. All we can do is set up certain conditions that will maximize the probability of their developing an interest in what they are doing and remove the conditions that function as constraints."[67]

Are rewards overrated?

Based on his research and consulting experience, Kohn proposes a number of actions that organizations can take to create a more supportive, motivating work environment.

Abolish Incentive Pay   Pay employees generously and fairly so they don't feel exploited. They will be more able to focus on the goals of the organization, rather than have their paycheque as their main goal.

Re-evaluate Evaluation   Instead of making performance appraisals look and feel like a punitive effort—who gets raises, who gets promoted, who is told they are performing poorly—structure the performance evaluation system more like a two-way conversation to trade ideas and questions. The discussion of performance should not be tied to compensation. "Providing feedback that employees can use to do a better job ought never to be confused or combined with controlling them by offering (or withholding) rewards."[68]

Create the Conditions for Authentic Motivation   A noted economist summarized the evidence about pay for productivity as follows: "Changing the way workers are *treated* may boost productivity more than changing the way they are *paid*."[69] There is some consensus about what the conditions for authentic motivation might be: helping employees rather than putting them under surveillance; listening to employee concerns and thinking about problems from their viewpoint; and providing plenty of feedback so they know what they have done right and what they need to improve.[70]

Encourage Collaboration   People are more likely to perform better in well-functioning groups where they can get feedback and learn from one another.[71] Therefore, it's important to provide the necessary supports to create well-functioning teams.

Enhance Content   People are generally the most motivated when their jobs give them an opportunity to learn new skills, provide variety in the tasks that are performed, and enable them to demonstrate competence. Some of this can be fostered by carefully matching people to their jobs, and by giving them the opportunity to try new jobs. It's also possible to increase the meaningfulness of many jobs, as we discuss later in this chapter.

But what about jobs that don't seem inherently interesting? One psychologist suggests that in cases where the jobs are fundamentally unappealing, the manager might acknowledge frankly that the task is not fun, give a meaningful rationale for why it must be done, and then give people as much choice as possible in how the task is completed.[72] One sociologist studying a group of garbage collectors in San Francisco discovered that they were quite satisfied with their work because of the way it was organized: Relationships among the crew were important, tasks and routes were varied to provide interest, and each worker owned a share of the company, and thus felt "pride of ownership."[73]

Provide Choice   "We are most likely to become enthusiastic about what we are doing—and do it well—when we are free to make decisions about the way we carry out a task."[74] Extrinsic rewards (and punishments) remove choice, because they focus us on rewards, rather than on tasks or goals. Research suggests that burnout, dissatisfaction, absenteeism, stress, and coronary heart disease are related to situations where individuals did not have enough control over their work situations.[75] By *choice* we do not mean lack of management, but rather, involving people in the decisions that are to be made. A number of studies indicate that participative management, when it includes full participation by everyone, is successful.[76]

It would be difficult for many organizations to implement these ideas immediately and expect that they would work. Managers would need to relinquish control and take on the job of coach. Employees would need to believe that their participation and input mattered. Nevertheless, these actions, when implemented, can lead to quite a different workplace than what we often see. Moreover, Kohn suggests that sometimes it's not the type or amount of rewards that makes a difference as much as whether the work itself is intrinsically interesting.

Below we examine how to create more motivating jobs and workplaces in order to make work itself more intrinsically rewarding for employees.

Motivating by Job Redesign

3 How can jobs be designed to increase motivation?

Research in **job design** suggests that the way the elements in a job are organized can act to increase or decrease effort. This research also offers detailed insights into just what those elements are. We will first review the job characteristics model and then discuss some ways jobs can be redesigned. Finally, we will explore some alternative work arrangements.

job design The way the elements in a job are organized.

EXHIBIT 14-3 Examples of High and Low Job Characteristics

Skill Variety

High variety	The owner-operator of a garage who does electrical repair, rebuilds engines, does body work, and interacts with customers
Low variety	A body shop worker who sprays paint eight hours a day

Task Identity

High identity	A cabinet maker who designs a piece of furniture, selects the wood, builds the object, and finishes it to perfection
Low identity	A worker in a furniture factory who operates a lathe solely to make table legs

Task Significance

High significance	Nursing the sick in a hospital intensive care unit
Low significance	Sweeping hospital floors

Autonomy

High autonomy	A telephone installer who schedules his or her own work for the day, makes visits without supervision, and decides on the most effective techniques for a particular installation
Low autonomy	A telephone operator who must handle calls as they come according to a routine, highly specified procedure

Feedback

High feedback	An electronics factory worker who assembles a radio and then tests it to determine if it operates properly
Low feedback	An electronics factory worker who assembles a radio and then routes it to a quality control inspector who tests it for proper operation and makes needed adjustments

Source: G. Johns, *Organizational Behavior: Understanding and Managing Life at Work*, 4th ed. Copyright © 1997. Adapted by permission of Pearson Education, Inc., Upper Saddle River, NJ.

The Job Characteristics Model

Developed by OB researchers J. Richard Hackman from Harvard University and Greg Oldham from the University of Illinois, the **job characteristics model (JCM)** says we can describe any job in terms of five core job dimensions:[77]

- **Skill variety.** The degree to which the job requires a variety of different activities so the employee can use a number of different skills and talents.

- **Task identity.** The degree to which the job requires completion of a whole and identifiable piece of work.

- **Task significance**. The degree to which the job has an impact on the lives or work of other people.

- **Autonomy**. The degree to which the job provides substantial freedom, independence, and discretion to the individual in scheduling the work and determining the procedures to be used in carrying it out.

- **Feedback**. The degree to which carrying out the work activities required by the job results in the individual obtaining direct and clear information about the effectiveness of his or her performance.

Jobs can be rated as high or low on these dimensions. Examples of jobs with high and low ratings appear in Exhibit 14-3.

job characteristics model (JCM) A model that proposes that any job can be described in terms of five core job dimensions: skill variety, task identity, task significance, autonomy, and feedback.

skill variety The degree to which the job requires a variety of different activities.

task identity The degree to which the job requires completion of a whole and identifiable piece of work.

task significance The degree to which the job has a substantial impact on the lives or work of other people.

autonomy The degree to which the job provides substantial freedom, independence, and discretion to the individual in scheduling the work and determining the procedures to be used in carrying it out.

feedback The degree to which carrying out the work activities required by the job results in the individual obtaining direct and clear information about the effectiveness of his or her performance.

EXHIBIT 14-4 The Job Characteristics Model

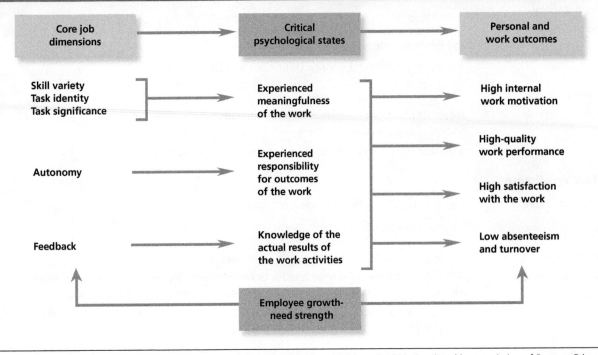

Source: J. RICHARD HACKMAN & GREG R. OLDHAM, WORK REDESIGN, 1st Edition, © 1980. Reprinted by permission of Pearson Education, Inc., Upper Saddle River, NJ.

Exhibit 14-4 presents the job characteristics model. Note how the first three dimensions—skill variety, task identity, and task significance—combine to create meaningful work the incumbent will view as important, valuable, and worthwhile. Note, too, that jobs with high autonomy give incumbents a feeling of personal responsibility for the results and that, if a job provides feedback, employees will know how effectively they are performing. From a motivational standpoint, the JCM proposes that individuals obtain internal rewards when they learn (knowledge of results) that they personally (experienced responsibility) have performed well on a task they care about (experienced meaningfulness).[78] The more these three psychological states are present, the greater will be employees' motivation, performance, and satisfaction, and the lower their absenteeism and likelihood of leaving. As Exhibit 14-4 shows, individuals with a high growth need are more likely to experience the critical psychological states when their jobs are enriched—and respond to them more positively—than are their counterparts with low growth need. Autonomy does not mean the same for every person.

A survey of college and university students highlights the underlying theme of the JCM. When the students were asked about what was most important to them as they thought about their careers, their top four answers were as follows:

- Having idealistic and committed co-workers (very important to 68 percent of the respondents)

- Doing work that helps others (very important to 65 percent)

- Doing work that requires creativity (very important to 47 percent)

- Having a lot of responsibility (very important to 39 percent)[79]

Salary and prestige ranked lower in importance than these four job characteristics.

Motivating Potential Score

motivating potential score (MPS)
A predictive index suggesting the motivation potential in a job.

We can combine the core dimensions into a single predictive index, called the **motivating potential score (MPS)**, which is calculated as follows:

Working on a fish-processing line requires being comfortable with job specialization. One person cuts off heads, another guts the fish, a third removes the scales. Each person performs the same task repetitively as fish move down the line. Such jobs are low on skill variety, task identity, task significance, autonomy, and feedback.

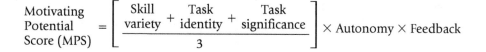

$$\text{Motivating Potential Score (MPS)} = \left[\frac{\text{Skill variety} + \text{Task identity} + \text{Task significance}}{3} \right] \times \text{Autonomy} \times \text{Feedback}$$

To be high on motivating potential, jobs must be high on at least one of the three factors that lead to experienced meaningfulness and high on both autonomy and feedback. If jobs score high on motivating potential, the model predicts motivation, performance, and satisfaction will improve and absence and turnover will be reduced.

RESEARCH FINDINGS: JCM

Most evidence supports the JCM concept that the presence of a set of job characteristics—variety, identity, significance, autonomy, and feedback—generates higher and more satisfying job performance and reduces absenteeism and turnover costs.[80] However, we can better calculate motivating potential by simply adding the characteristics rather than using the formula.[81] On the critical issue of productivity, the evidence is inconclusive.[82] In some situations, job enrichment increases productivity; in others, it decreases productivity. However, even when productivity goes down, there does seem to be consistently more conscientious use of resources and a higher quality of product or service.

When might job redesign be most appropriate?

While many employees want challenging, interesting, and complex work, some people prosper in simple, routinized work.[83] The variable that seems to best explain who prefers a challenging job is the strength of an individual's higher-order needs.[84] Individuals with high growth needs are more responsive to challenging work.

Many employees meet their higher-order needs *off* the job. There are 168 hours in a week, and work rarely consumes more than 30 percent of them. That leaves considerable opportunity, even for individuals with strong growth needs, to find higher-order need satisfaction outside the workplace.

Job Redesign in the Canadian Context: The Role of Unions

Labour unions have been largely resistant to participating in discussions with management over job redesign issues. Redesigns often result in loss of jobs, and labour unions try to prevent job loss. Union head offices, however, can sometimes be at odds with their membership over the acceptance of job redesign. Some members value the opportunity for skill development and more interesting work.

Some of the larger unions have been more open to discussions about job redesign. For instance, the Communications, Energy and Paperworkers Union of Canada (CEP) asserted that unions should be involved in the decisions and share in the benefits of work redesign.[85] The CEP believes that basic wages, negotiated through a collective agreement, must remain the primary form of compensation, although the union is open to other forms of compensation as long as they do not detract from basic wages determined through collective bargaining.

While managers may regard job redesign as more difficult under a collective agreement, the reality is that for change to be effective in the workplace, management must gain employees' acceptance of the plan whether or not they are unionized.

How Can Jobs Be Redesigned?

Let's look at some of the ways to put JCM into practice to make jobs more motivating.

Job Rotation

If employees suffer from overroutinization, one alternative is **job rotation**, or the periodic shifting of an employee from one task to another with similar skill requirements at the same organizational level (what many call *cross-training*). When an activity is no longer challenging, the employee is rotated to another job at the same level that has similar skill requirements.[86]

At McDonald's, this approach is used as a way to make sure that the new employees learn all of the tasks associated with making, packaging, and serving hamburgers and other items. At Singapore Airlines, a ticket agent may take on the duties of a baggage handler. Extensive job rotation is one of the reasons Singapore Airlines is rated one of the best airlines in the world and a highly desirable place to work.

A Statistics Canada survey found that about 19 percent of firms with 10 or more employees engaged in job rotation.[87] Employees in technical trades and clerical and administrative positions were more likely to rotate jobs than managerial and professional employees.

The strengths of job rotation are that it reduces boredom, increases motivation, and helps employees better understand how their work contributes to the organization. An indirect benefit is that employees with a wider range of skills give management more flexibility in scheduling work, adapting to changes, and filling vacancies.[88]

However, job rotation has drawbacks. Training costs are increased, and productivity is reduced by moving an employee into a new position just when efficiency at the prior job is creating organizational economies. Job rotation also creates disruptions when members of the work group have to adjust to the new employee. The manager may also have to spend more time answering questions and monitoring the work of the recently rotated employee.

job rotation The periodic shifting of an employee from one task to another.

Job Enrichment

Job enrichment expands jobs by increasing the degree to which the employee controls the planning, execution, and evaluation of the work. An enriched job organizes tasks to allow the employee to do a complete activity, increases the employee's freedom and independence, increases responsibility, and provides feedback so individuals can assess and correct their own performance.[89]

Some newer versions of job enrichment concentrate more specifically on improving the meaningfulness of work. One significant method is to relate employee experiences to customer outcomes, simply by providing employees with stories from customers who benefited from the company's products or services. Researchers recently found that when university fundraisers briefly interacted with the undergraduates who would receive the scholarships they raised, they persisted 42 percent longer, and raised nearly twice as much money, as those who did not interact with potential recipients.[90] Another method for improving the meaningfulness of work is providing employees with mutual assistance programs.[91] Employees who can help one another directly through their work come to see themselves, and the organizations for which they work, in more positive, pro-social terms. This, in turn, can increase employee affective commitment.

The evidence on job enrichment shows it reduces absenteeism and turnover costs and increases satisfaction, but not all job enrichment programs are equally effective.[92] A review of 83 organizational interventions designed to improve performance management showed that frequent, specific feedback related to solving problems was linked to consistently higher performance, but infrequent feedback that focused more on past problems than future solutions was much less effective.[93] Some recent evidence suggests job enrichment works best when it compensates for poor feedback and reward systems.[94] One recent study showed employees with a higher preference for challenging work experienced larger reductions in stress following job redesign than individuals who did not prefer challenging work.[95]

Alternative Work Arrangements

Beyond redesigning work itself and including employees in decisions, another approach to motivation is to alter work arrangements. Below we consider how flextime, job sharing, and telework might address one of Kohn's ideas for increasing motivation that we discussed above: creating better work environments for people. These arrangements are likely to be especially important for a diverse workforce of dual-earner couples, single parents, and employees caring for a sick or aging relative.

How can flexible workplaces increase motivation?

Do employers really like flexible arrangements?

Flextime

Flextime is short for "flexible work time." Employees must work a specific number of hours a week, but they are free to vary the hours of work within certain limits. As shown in Exhibit 14-5, each day consists of a common core, usually six hours, with a flexibility band surrounding it. The core may be 9 a.m. to 3 p.m., with the office actually opening at 6 a.m. and closing at 6 p.m. All employees are required to be at their jobs during the common core period, but they may accumulate their other two hours before and/or after the core time. Some flextime programs allow extra hours to be accumulated and turned into a free day off each month.

Flextime has become an extremely popular scheduling option, although in Canada women are less likely than men to have flexible work schedules.[96] More managers

job enrichment The vertical expansion of jobs, which increases the degree to which the employee controls the planning, execution, and evaluation of the work.

flextime An arrangement where employees work during a common core period each day but can form their total workday from a flexible set of hours outside the core.

EXHIBIT 14-5 Examples of Flextime Schedules

Schedule 1

Percent Time:	100% = 40 hours per week
Core Hours:	9:00 a.m.–5:00 p.m., Monday through Friday (1 hour lunch)
Work Start Time:	Between 8:00 a.m. and 9:00 a.m.
Work End Time:	Between 5:00 p.m. and 6:00 p.m.

Schedule 2

Percent Time:	100% = 40 hours per week
Work Hours:	8:00 a.m.–6:30 p.m., Monday through Thursday (1/2 hour lunch)
	Friday off
Work Start Time:	8:00 a.m.
Work End Time:	6:30 p.m.

Schedule 3

Percent Time:	90% = 36 hours per week
Work Hours:	8:30 a.m.–5:00 p.m., Monday through Thursday (1/2 hour lunch)
	8:00 a.m.–Noon Friday (no lunch)
Work Start Time:	8:30 a.m. (Monday–Thursday); 8:00 a.m. (Friday)
Work End Time:	5:00 p.m. (Monday–Thursday); Noon (Friday)

Schedule 4

Percent Time:	80% = 32 hours per week
Work Hours:	8:00 a.m.–6:00 p.m., Monday through Wednesday (1/2 hour lunch)
	8:00 a.m.–11:30 a.m. Thursday (no lunch)
	Friday off
Work Start Time:	Between 8:00 a.m. and 9:00 a.m.
Work End Time:	Between 5:00 p.m. and 6:00 p.m.

(42.4 percent) enjoy the freedom of flextime than do manufacturing employees (23.3 percent).[97]

Most of the performance evidence stacks up favourably. Flextime tends to reduce absenteeism and frequently improves employee productivity and satisfaction,[98] probably for several reasons. Employees can schedule their work hours to align with personal demands, reducing tardiness and absences, and they can work when they are most productive. Other research on the impact of flextime on the Canadian workplace has found that employees have positive attitudes and view it as their most preferred option.[99] Managers are in favour,[100] and women with flextime suffer less stress.[101]

Flextime can help employees balance work and family lives, as happens at Goodfish Lake, Alberta-based Goodfish Lake Development Corporation (GFLDC). GFLDC is an Aboriginal business that provides dry-cleaning, clothing manufacturing and repair, protective clothing rentals, and bakery services to Fort McMurray. Many of the company's employees are women who have husbands that work full time in Fort McMurray. This can make it difficult for GFLDC's female employees to care for their children, so the company created flexible schedules to help employees balance work and home life.[102] A 2010 study by University of Toronto researchers found that flextime can lead to longer hours of work overall and more multi-tasking. These in turn lead to greater work-life conflict and stress.[103] So the management of flextime is an important issue for employees.

Flextime's other major drawback is that it is not applicable to every job. It works well with clerical tasks where an employee's interaction with people outside his or her department is limited. It is not a viable option for receptionists, salespeople in retail stores, or similar jobs where people must be at their workstations at fixed times that suit the needs of customers and clients.

Job Sharing

Job sharing allows two or more people to split a 40-hour-a-week job. While popular in Europe, it is not a common arrangement in Canada. In 2007, about 14 percent of Canadian employers offered this arrangement.[104] Reasons it is not more widely adopted are likely the difficulty of finding compatible partners to share a job and the historically negative perceptions of individuals not completely committed to their job and employer.[105]

Job sharing allows the organization to draw upon the talents of more than one individual in a given job. A bank manager who oversees two job sharers describes it as an opportunity to get two heads, but "pay for one."[106] It also opens up the opportunity to acquire skilled employees—for instance, women with young children, retirees, and others desiring flexibility—who might not be available on a full-time basis.[107] Many Japanese firms are increasingly considering job sharing—but for a very different reason.[27] Because Japanese executives are extremely reluctant to fire people, job sharing is seen as a potentially humanitarian means of avoiding layoffs due to overstaffing.[108]

From the employee's perspective, job sharing increases flexibility and can increase motivation and satisfaction for those for whom a 40-hour-a-week job is just not practical. But the major drawback from management's perspective is finding compatible pairs of employees who can successfully coordinate the demands of one job. "Job sharing must be well planned, and needs clear job descriptions," says Julianna Cantwell, HR consultant with Edmonton-based Juna Consulting.[110]

Job sharing can be a creative solution to some organizational problems. For example, Nunavut has had great difficulty finding doctors willing to commit to serving the territory for more than short periods of time.[111] Dr. Sandy MacDonald, director of Medical Affairs and Telehealth for Nunavut, allows doctors to work for three months at a time. "In the past, the government was trying to get some of them to sign up for two or three years, and most people don't want to do that initially, or they would leave positions unfilled because someone would only come for two or three weeks or a month," he says. Meanwhile, doctors working in Nunavut were overworked because there were not enough doctors on call. MacDonald's approach has changed that—now more doctors are available because of the job-sharing solution.

> **job sharing** The practice of having two or more people split a 40-hour-a-week job.

In response to the recession of 2008, the Canadian government included a job-sharing incentive as an alternative to layoffs. Over 165 000 Canadian employees benefited from the program, which allowed employees to draw employment insurance benefits to compensate them for their reduced wages. Calgary-based Standen's, run by president and CEO Mel Svendsen (in forefront), makes heat-treated alloy steel parts and was able to get through the recession without laying off a single member of the team, in part by using this program. While most of the stimulus funding support ended on March 31, 2011, the job-sharing support was extended into 2011.[109]

Bob Fortier, president of the Canadian Telework Association, says, "Mobile work is here to stay." He says that telework has many benefits: It helps attract employees who are looking for flexible work, reduces turnover, and reduces carbon emissions. However, some managers worry about supervising employees who work off-site. "In an ideal situation, teleworkers work from home or on the road a set number of hours a week, but come into the office to work and interact with managers for the rest of the time. This gives them a healthy balance," says Fortier.[113]

Telework

Telework refers to employees working anywhere away from the office that they have access to smartphones, tablets, and other mobile computing devices.[112] (A closely related term—*the virtual office*—is increasingly being used to describe employees who work out of their home on a relatively permanent basis.)

More than 1 billion people worldwide worked remotely at the end of 2010, and it is forecast that more than one-third of all workers will be mobile by 2013.[114] About 40 percent of Canadian companies offered telework in 2008, up from 25 percent in 2007.[115] Bob Fortier, president of the Canadian Telework Association, estimates that between 1.5 million and 2 million individuals worked remotely in Canada in 2011, compared with 100 000 in the late 1980s.[116] At Cisco's downtown Toronto office, there are 200 desks for 500 employees. "Everyone else works remotely and just comes in occasionally for meetings," said Jeff Seifert, chief technology officer for Cisco's Canadian division. An internal survey in 2009 of Cisco employees found increased productivity and satisfaction due to the teleworking. It also saved the company $277 million in a year.[117] Longueuil, Quebec-based SICO Paints, Manitoba Hydro, and the Saskatchewan Government are other examples of workplaces that encourage telework.

> Would you find telework motivating?

What kinds of jobs lend themselves to telework? There are three categories: routine information-handling tasks, mobile activities, and professional and other knowledge-related tasks.[118] Writers, attorneys, analysts, and employees who spend the majority of their time on computers or the phone—telemarketers, customer-service representatives, reservation agents, and product-support specialists—are natural candidates for telework. As teleworkers, they can access information on their computer screens at home as easily as on the company screen in any office.

RESEARCH FINDINGS: Telework

A recent Ipsos Reid study found that 42 percent of employees reported that they would be more likely to stay with their current employer, or enticed to take a new job, if the employer offered the opportunity to telework.[119] Other researchers looking at teleworking in Canada have found that it results in increased productivity,[120] decreased stress,[121] and better service to customers and clients.[122] Teleworking has been found to reduce turnover[123] and decrease absenteeism.[124] Further potential pluses for management include a larger labour pool from which to select and reduced office-space costs. A positive relationship exists between teleworking and supervisor performance ratings.[125]

The major downside for management is less direct supervision of employees. In addition, in today's team-focused workplace, teleworking may make it more difficult

telework An arrangement where employees do their work outside the office anywhere they have access to smartphones, tablets, and other mobile computing devices.

for management to coordinate teamwork.[126] From the employee's standpoint, teleworking offers a considerable increase in flexibility—but not without costs. For employees with a high social need, teleworking can increase feelings of isolation and reduce job satisfaction. And all teleworkers are vulnerable to the "out of sight, out of mind" effect.[127] Employees who are not at their desks, who miss meetings, and who don't share in day-to-day informal workplace interactions may be at a disadvantage when it comes to raises and promotions. Finally, a 2011 study by University of Toronto researchers found greater psychological stress for women than men when employees were contacted frequently at home by supervisors, co-workers, or clients. The researchers concluded that women may face greater difficulties balancing work and home life while working at home.[128]

The Social and Physical Context of Work

The job characteristics model shows most employees are more motivated and satisfied when their intrinsic work tasks are engaging. However, having the most interesting workplace characteristics in the world may not always lead to satisfaction if you feel isolated from your co-workers, and having good social relationships can make even the most boring and onerous tasks more fulfilling. Research demonstrates that social aspects and work context are as important as other job design features.[129] Policies such as job rotation, employee empowerment, and employee participation have positive effects on productivity, at least partially because they encourage more communication and a positive social environment.

Some social characteristics that improve job performance include interdependence, social support, and interactions with other people outside work. Social interactions are strongly related to positive moods and give employees more opportunities to clarify their work role and how well they are performing. Social support gives employees greater opportunities to obtain assistance with their work. Constructive social relationships can bring about a positive feedback loop as employees assist one another in a "virtuous circle."

The work context is also likely to affect employee satisfaction. Work that is hot, loud, and dangerous is less satisfying than work conducted in climate-controlled, relatively quiet, and safe environments. This is probably why most people would rather work in a coffee shop than a metalworking foundry. Physical demands make people physically uncomfortable, which is likely to show up in lower levels of job satisfaction.

To assess why an employee is not performing to her best level, look at the work environment to see whether it's supportive. Does the employee have adequate tools, equipment, materials, and supplies? Does the employee have favourable working conditions, helpful co-workers, supportive work rules and procedures, sufficient information to make job-related decisions, adequate time to do a good job, and the like? If not, performance will suffer.

Employee Involvement

Those who work at Whole Foods demonstrate high employee involvement.[130] Employees have the freedom to make decisions, including helping each other, figuring out how to manage breaks, and solving customer problems. To make this level of involvement work well, employees are given training and development opportunities, feedback, and targets.

One particularly effective practice that encourages employee involvement is the annual visits employees make to other store branches. Comparable teams from different stores are encouraged to learn from one another and give feedback, which encourages healthy rivalry and cross-fertilization of ideas. What other ways can companies encourage employee involvement?

4 How do employees become more involved in the workplace?

What is **employee involvement**? It's a participative process that uses employees' input to increase their commitment to the organization's success. The logic is that if we engage employees in decisions that affect them and increase their autonomy and control over their work lives, they will become more motivated, more committed to the organization, more productive, and more satisfied with their jobs.[131]

Examples of Employee Involvement Programs

Let's look at two major forms of employee involvement—participative management and representative participation—in more detail.

Participative Management

The distinct characteristic common to all **participative management** programs is joint decision making, in which subordinates share a significant degree of decision-making power with their immediate superiors. Participative management has, at times, been promoted as the solution for poor morale and low productivity. But for it to work, the issues in which employees are engaged must be relevant to their interests so they will be motivated, employees must have the competence and knowledge to make a useful contribution, and trust and confidence must exist among all parties.[132]

Dozens of studies have been conducted on the participation-performance relationship. The findings, however, are mixed.[133] Organizations that institute participative management do have higher stock returns, lower turnover rates, and higher estimated labour productivity, although these effects are typically not large.[134] A careful review of the research at the individual level shows participation typically has only a modest influence on variables such as employee productivity, motivation, and job satisfaction. Of course, this does not mean participative management cannot be beneficial under the right conditions. What it says, however, is that it is not a sure means for improving employee performance.

Representative Participation

Almost every country in western Europe requires companies to practise **representative participation**, called "the most widely legislated form of employee involvement around the world."[135] Its goal is to redistribute power within an organization, putting labour on a more equal footing with the interests of management and stockholders by letting employees be represented by a small group of employees who actually participate.

The two most common forms are works councils and board representatives.[136] Works councils are groups of nominated or elected employees who must be consulted when management makes decisions about employees. Board representatives are employees who sit on a company's board of directors and represent the interests of the firm's employees.

The influence of representative participation on working employees seems to be minimal.[137] Works councils are dominated by management and have little impact on employees or the organization. While participation might increase the motivation and satisfaction of employee representatives, there is little evidence this effect trickles down to the operating employees they represent. Overall, "the greatest value of representative participation is symbolic. If one is interested in changing employee attitudes or in improving organizational performance, representative participation would be a poor choice."[138]

Linking Employee Involvement Programs and Motivation Theories

Employee involvement draws on a number of the motivation theories we discussed in Chapter 13. Theory Y is consistent with participative management and Theory X with the more traditional autocratic style of managing people. In terms of Herzberg's two-factor theory, employee involvement programs could provide intrinsic motivation by increasing opportunities for growth, responsibility, and involvement in the work itself. The opportunity to make and implement decisions—and then see them work out—can help satisfy an employee's needs for responsibility, achievement, recognition, growth, and enhanced self-esteem. And extensive employee involvement programs clearly have the potential to increase employee intrinsic motivation in work tasks.

employee involvement A participative process that uses the input of employees and is intended to increase employee commitment to an organization's success.

participative management A process in which subordinates share a significant degree of decision-making power with their immediate superiors.

representative participation A system in which employees participate in organizational decision making through a small group of representative employees.

Motivation: Putting It All Together

In Chapter 13, we reviewed basic theories of motivation, considering such factors as how needs affect motivation, the importance of linking performance to rewards, and the need for fair process. In this chapter, we considered various ways to pay and recognize people, and looked at job design and creating more flexible workplaces. Three Harvard University professors recently completed two studies that suggest a way to put all of these ideas together to understand (1) what motivates people and (2) how to use this knowledge to make sure that organizational processes motivate.[139]

5 Can we simplify how we think about motivation?

According to the study authors, research suggests that four basic emotional drives (needs) guide individuals.[140] These are the drive to acquire; the drive to bond; the drive to comprehend; and the drive to defend. People want to acquire any number of scarce goods, both tangible and intangible (such as social status). They want to bond with other individuals and groups. They want to understand the world around them. As well, they want to protect against external threats to themselves and others, and want to ensure justice occurs.

Understanding these different drives makes it possible to motivate individuals more effectively. As the study authors point out, "each drive is best met by a distinct organizational lever." The drive to acquire is met through organizational rewards. The drive to bond can be met by "creat[ing] a culture that promotes teamwork, collaboration, openness, and friendship." The drive to comprehend is best met through job design and creating jobs that are "meaningful, interesting, and challenging." The drive to defend can be accomplished through an organization's performance management and resource allocation processes; this includes fair and transparent processes for managing performance and adequate resources to do one's job. Exhibit 14-6 indicates concrete ways that organizational characteristics can address individual drives.

EXHIBIT 14-6 How to Fulfill the Drives That Motivate Employees

DRIVE	PRIMARY LEVER	ACTIONS
1 Acquire	**Reward System**	• Sharply differentiate good performers from average and poor performers • Tie rewards clearly to performance • Pay as well as your competitors
2 Bond	**Culture**	• Foster mutual reliance and friendship among co-workers • Value collaboration and teamwork • Encourage sharing of best practices
3 Comprehend	**Job Design**	• Design jobs that have distinct and important roles in the organization • Design jobs that are meaningful and foster a sense of contribution to the organization
4 Defend	**Performance Management and Resource Allocation Processes**	• Increase the transparency of all processes • Emphasize their fairness • Build trust by being just and transparent in granting rewards, assignments, and other forms of recognition

Source: N. Nohria, B. Groysberg, and L.-E. Lee, "Employee Motivation: A Powerful New Model," *Harvard Business Review* 86, no. 7–8 (July–August 2008), p. 82. Reprinted by permission of *Harvard Business Review*.

GLOBAL **IMPLICATIONS**

Do the motivational approaches we have discussed vary by culture? Because we have covered some very different approaches in this chapter, let's break down our analysis by approach. Not every approach has been studied by cross-cultural researchers, so we consider cross-cultural differences in (1) variable pay, (2) flexible benefits, (3) job characteristics and job enrichment, (4) telework, and (5) employee involvement.

Variable Pay

You would probably think individual pay systems (such as merit pay or pay-for-performance) work better in individualistic cultures such as the United States than in collectivistic cultures such as China or Venezuela. Similarly, you would probably hypothesize that group-based rewards such as gainsharing or profit sharing work better in collectivistic cultures than in individualistic cultures. Unfortunately, there isn't much research on the issue. One recent study did suggest, though, that beliefs about the fairness of a group incentive plan were more predictive of pay satisfaction for employees in the United States than for employees in Hong Kong. One interpretation of these findings is that US employees are more critical in appraising a group pay plan, and therefore it's more critical that the plan be communicated clearly and administered fairly.[141]

Flexible Benefits

Today, almost all major corporations in the United States offer flexible benefits. They are becoming the norm in other countries, too. A recent survey of 136 Canadian organizations found that 93 percent have adopted or will adopt flexible benefits in the near term.[142] And a similar survey of 307 firms in the United Kingdom found that while only 16 percent have flexible benefits programs in place, another 60 percent are either in the process of implementing them or are seriously considering it.[143]

In Exhibit 14-7, we show the link between a country's rating on GLOBE/Hofstede cultural dimensions, which we discussed in Chapter 3, and its preferences for particular

---

EXHIBIT 14-7 Reward Preferences in Different Countries

GLOBE/Hofstede Cultural Dimension	Reward Preference	Examples
High uncertainty avoidance	Certainty in compensation systems: • Seniority-based pay • Skill-based pay	Greece, Portugal, Japan
Individualism	Compensation based on individual performance: • Pay for performance • Individual incentives • Stock options	Australia, United Kingdom, United States
Humane orientation (Hofstede's masculinity vs. femininity dimension)	Social benefits and programs: • Flexible benefits • Workplace child-care programs • Career-break schemes • Maternity leave programs	Sweden, Norway, the Netherlands

Source: Based on R. S. Schuler and N. Rogovsky, "Understanding Compensation Practice Variations across Firms: The Impact of National Culture," *Journal of International Business Studies* 29, no. 1 (First Quarter 1998), pp. 159–177. Reprinted by permission of Palgrave/Macmillan.

types of rewards. Countries that put a high value on uncertainty avoidance prefer pay based on objective measures, such as skill or seniority, because the outcomes are more certain. Countries that put a high value on individualism place more emphasis on an individual's responsibility for performance that leads to rewards. Countries that put a high value on humane orientation offer social benefits and programs that provide work-family balance, such as child care, maternity leave, and sabbaticals.[144] Managers who receive overseas assignments should consider a country's cultural orientation when designing and implementing reward practices.

Job Characteristics and Job Enrichment

A few studies have tested the job characteristics model in different cultures, but the results are not very consistent.[145] One study suggested that when employees are "other oriented" (concerned with the welfare of others at work), the relationship between intrinsic job characteristics and job satisfaction is weaker. The fact that the job characteristics model is relatively individualistic (considering the relationship between the employee and his or her work) suggests job enrichment strategies may not have the same effects in collectivistic cultures as in individualistic cultures (such as the United States).[146] However, another study suggested the degree to which jobs had intrinsic job characteristics predicted job satisfaction and job involvement equally well for US, Japanese, and Hungarian employees.[147]

Telework

Does the degree to which employees telework vary by nation? Does its effectiveness depend on culture? First, one study suggests that telework is more common in the United States than in all the European Union (EU) nations except the Netherlands. In the study, 24.6 percent of US employees engaged in teleworking, compared with only 13.0 percent of EU employees. Of the EU countries, the Netherlands had the highest rate of teleworking (26.4 percent); the lowest rates were in Spain (4.9 percent) and Portugal (3.4 percent). What about the rest of the world? Unfortunately, there are few data comparing teleworking rates in other parts of the world. Similarly, we don't really know whether teleworking works better in the United States than in other countries. However, the same study that compared telework rates between the United States and the EU determined that employees in Europe appeared to have the same level of interest in telework: regardless of country, interest is higher among employees than among employers.[148]

Employee Involvement

Employee involvement programs differ among countries.[149] A study comparing the acceptance of employee involvement programs in four countries, including the United States and India, confirmed the importance of modifying practices to reflect national culture.[150] Specifically, while US employees readily accepted these programs, managers in India who tried to empower their employees through employee involvement programs were rated low by those employees. These reactions are consistent with India's high power-distance culture, which accepts and expects differences in authority. Similarly, Chinese employees who were very accepting of traditional Chinese values showed few benefits from participative decision making, but employees who were less traditional were more satisfied and had higher performance ratings under participative management.[151] This study illustrates the substantial differences in how management practices are perceived by individuals within as well as between countries.

LESSONS LEARNED

- Money is not a motivator for all individuals.
- Effective reward systems link pay to performance.
- Jobs characterized by variety, autonomy, and feedback are more motivating.

15

Strategic Pay Plans

The Strategic Importance of Total Employment Rewards

Compensation and rewards management is extremely important to every employee. **Total employment rewards** refer to an integrated package of all rewards gained by employees arising from their employment. These rewards encompass everything that employees value in the employment relationship.

There are a variety of models that attempt to define the elements of total employee rewards. Some models segment rewards based on the monetary (extrinsic), non monetary (intrinsic) divide, with further differentiation between bash payments and benefits that have are a cash expense for the organization, but are not paid as cash to the employees, as illustrated in Exhibit 15-1.[1]

Alternatively, WorldatWork conceptualized the total rewards model within three broad categories:

Compensation (extrinsic), *benefits (extrinsic)*, and *non-monetary rewards (intrinsic)*. Recently, the work experience category was further refined by splitting it into three parts—work–life programs, performance and recognition, and development and career opportunities—resulting in five categories of total rewards, as shown in Exhibit 15-2.

The total rewards approach, as opposed to the previous approach of managing different elements of compensation in isolation, has arisen from the changing business environment of the last several decades. The economies of developed nations like Canada have evolved from a largely industrialized base to become far more virtual, knowledge-based, and service-based, where employees are increasingly regarded as drivers of productivity. A total rewards approach considers individual reward components as part of an integrated whole to determine the best mix of rewards that are aligned with business strategy and that provide employee value, all within the cost constraints of the organization. Alignment is the extent to which rewards support outcomes that are important to achieving the organization's strategic objectives. For example, when competitive advantage relies on relentless customer service, this behaviour should be reinforced. Employee value is created when rewards are meaningful to employees and influence their affiliation with the organization.[2]

EXHIBIT 15-1 Employment Rewards: An Integrated Package of Rewards

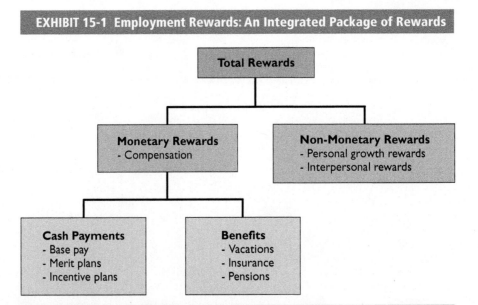

total employment rewards An integrated package of all rewards (monetary and non-monetary, extrinsic and intrinsic) gained by employees arising from their employment.

EXHIBIT 15-2 The Total Rewards Model

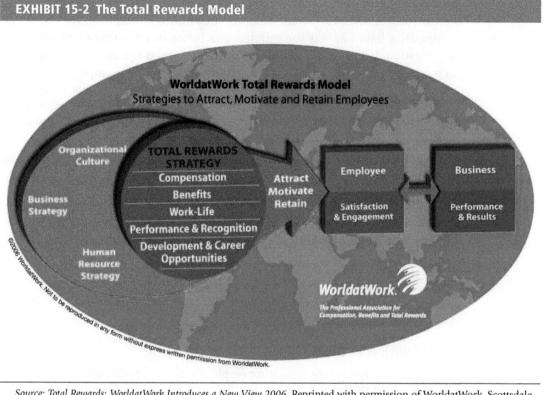

Source: Total Rewards: WorldatWork Introduces a New View 2006. Reprinted with permission of WorldatWork, Scottsdale, AZ. www.worldatwork.org.

The Five Components of Total Rewards

1. *Compensation.* This category includes direct financial payments in the form of wages, salaries, incentives, commissions, and bonuses. Wages and salaries are discussed in this chapter, and other direct financial payments are discussed in Chapter 16.

2. *Benefits.* This category includes indirect payments in the form of financial benefits, like employer-paid insurance and vacations. It also includes employee services, as discussed in Chapter 17.

3. *Work–life programs.* This category of rewards relates to programs that help employees do their jobs effectively, such as flexible scheduling, telecommuting, childcare, and so on. Work–life programs are discussed in Chapter 17.

4. *Performance and recognition.* This category includes pay-for-performance and recognition programs. These programs are discussed in Chapter 16.

5. *Development and career opportunities.* This category of rewards focuses on planning for the advancement or change in responsibilities to best suit individual skills, talents, and desires. Tuition assistance, professional development, sabbaticals, coaching and mentoring opportunities, succession planning, and apprenticeships are all examples of career-enhancing programs.

The world's most admired companies excel at taking a total rewards approach.

Impact of Rewards

The purposes of rewards are to attract, retain, motivate, and engage employees. *Engagement* refers to a positive emotional connection to the employer and a clear understanding of the strategic significance of the job, which results in discretionary

Towers Perrin (now known as Towers Watson)
www.towerswatson.com

effort on the part of the employee. The *2007–2008 Global Workforce Study* by Towers Perrin (now known as Towers Watson) consultants found that, for Canadians, competitive base pay was the number one factor in attracting employees to an organization, having excellent career opportunities was the most important factor in retaining employees, and senior management's interest in employee well-being was the top factor influencing employee engagement.[3] Similarly, a study of 446 organizations across Canada by Western Compensation and Benefits Consultants found that the most effective attraction strategy was offering competitive base salaries, and the top reason for turnover among employees was dissatisfaction with cash compensation. Opportunities for advancement, work–life balance programs, and competitive benefits programs are also used by over 70 percent of Canadian companies to attract talent.[4]

Basic Considerations in Determining Pay Rates

Four basic considerations influence the formulation of any pay plan: legal requirements, union issues, compensation policy, and equity.

Legal Considerations in Compensation

All of the 14 jurisdictions regulating employment in Canada (ten provinces, three territories, and the federal jurisdiction) have laws regulating compensation. Thus, HR managers must pay careful attention to which legislation affects their employees. Further, these laws are constantly changing and require continual monitoring to ensure compliance. Legislation affecting compensation administration is discussed below.

Hints | TO ENSURE LEGAL COMPLIANCE

Employment/Labour Standards Acts (Canada Labour Code)

Employment/labour laws set minimum standards regarding pay, including minimum wage, maximum hours of work, overtime pay, paid vacation, paid statutory holidays, termination pay, record keeping of pay information, and more. There are variations in some of the minimum standards for students, trainees, domestics, nannies, seasonal agricultural workers, and others. Executive, administrative, and professional employees are generally exempt from the overtime pay requirements.

Pay Equity Acts

Pay equity laws were enacted to address the historical undervaluation of "women's work" by providing equal pay for work of equal (or comparable) value performed by men and women. Employers are required to identify male- and female-dominated jobs, and then use a gender-neutral job evaluation system based on specific compensable factors (such as skill, effort, responsibility, and working conditions) to evaluate the jobs. Pay for female-dominated jobs that are equivalent in value to male-dominated jobs must be increased to the pay level of the comparable male-dominated job. Not all Canadian jurisdictions have pay equity laws, as will be discussed later in this chapter.

Human Rights Acts

All jurisdictions have enacted human rights laws to protect Canadians from discrimination on a number of grounds in employment and other areas. These grounds differ somewhat among jurisdictions, but most prohibit discrimination in employment (such as in compensation and promotion) on the basis of age, sex, colour, race/ancestry/place of origin, religion/creed, marital/family status, and physical or mental disability.

Canada/Quebec Pension Plan

All employees and their employers must contribute to the Canada/Quebec Pension Plan throughout the employee's working life. Pension benefits based on the employee's average earnings are paid during retirement. Details of these and other benefits are provided in Chapter 17.

Other Legislation Affecting Compensation

Each province and territory, as well as the federal government, has its own *workers' compensation laws*. The objective of these laws is to provide a prompt, sure, and reasonable income to victims of work-related accidents and illnesses. The Employment Insurance Act is aimed at protecting Canadian workers from total economic destitution in the event of employment termination that is beyond their control. Employers and employees both contribute to the benefits provided by this act. This act also provides up to 45 weeks of compensation for workers unemployed through no fault of their own (depending on the unemployment rate in the claimant's region and other factors). Maternity leave, parental leave, and compassionate care leave benefits are also provided under the Employment Insurance Act.[5]

Association of Workers' Compensation Boards of Canada **www.awcbc.org**

Union Influences on Compensation Decisions

Unions and labour relations laws also influence how pay plans are designed. Historically, wage rates have been the main issue in collective bargaining. However, other issues—including time off with pay, income security (for those in industries with periodic layoffs), cost-of-living adjustments, and pensions—are also important.[6]

The Canada Industrial Relations Board and similar bodies in each province and territory oversee employer practices and ensure that employees are treated in accordance with their legal rights. Their decisions underscore the need to involve union officials in developing the compensation package.

Work stoppages may reflect employee dissatisfaction with pay plans and other forms of compensation, such as pensions.

Union Attitudes toward Compensation Decisions

Several classic studies shed light on union attitudes toward compensation plans and on commonly held union fears.[7] Many union leaders fear that any system used to evaluate the worth of a job can become a tool for management malpractice. They tend to believe that no one can judge the relative value of jobs better than the workers themselves. In addition, they believe that management's usual method of using several compensable factors (like "degree of responsibility") to evaluate and rank the worth of jobs can be a manipulative device for restricting or lowering the pay of workers. One implication is that the best way in which to gain the cooperation of union members in evaluating the worth of jobs is to get their active involvement in this process and in assigning fair rates of pay to these jobs. However, management has to ensure that its prerogatives—such as the right to use the appropriate job evaluation technique to assess the relative worth of jobs—are not surrendered.

Research INSIGHT

Compensation Policies

An employer's compensation policies provide important guidelines regarding the wages and benefits that it pays. A number of factors are taken into account when developing a compensation policy, including whether the organization wants to be a leader or a follower regarding pay, business strategy, and the cost of different types of compensation. Important policies include the basis for salary increases, promotion and demotion policies, overtime pay policy, and policies regarding probationary pay and leaves for military service, jury duty, and holidays. Compensation policies are usually written by the HR or compensation manager in conjunction with senior management.[8]

Equity and Its Impact on Pay Rates

A crucial factor in determining pay rates is the need for equity, specifically **external equity** and **internal equity**. Research has indicated that employee perceptions of fairness are one of the two key conditions for effective reward programs.[9] Externally, pay must compare favourably with rates in other organizations or an employer will find it hard to attract and retain qualified employees. Pay rates must also be equitable internally: Each employee should view his or her pay as equitable given other pay rates in the organization.

Establishing Pay Rates

In practice, the process of establishing pay rates that are both externally and internally equitable requires three stages:

1. Determine the worth of jobs within the organization through job evaluation (to ensure internal equity), and group jobs with similar worth into pay grades.

2. Conduct a wage/salary survey of what other employers are paying for comparable jobs (to ensure external equity).

3. Combine the job evaluation (internal) and salary survey (external) information to determine pay rates for the jobs in the organization.

Each of these stages will be explained in turn.

Stage 1: Job Evaluation

Job evaluation is aimed at determining a job's relative worth. It is a formal and systematic comparison of jobs within a firm to determine the worth of one job relative to another, and it eventually results in a job hierarchy. The basic procedure is to compare the content of jobs in relation to one another, for example, in terms of their effort, responsibility, skills, and working conditions. Job evaluation usually focuses on **benchmark jobs** that are critical to the firm's operations or that are commonly found in other organizations. Rohm and Haas, a multinational chemical company, ensures that its benchmark jobs represent all the various business units and departments in the organization, are drawn from all levels of the organization, have large numbers of incumbents, are clear and well known in the industry, are stable and easily understood in terms of purpose and work content, and are visible and well understood by all employees.[10] The resulting evaluations of benchmark jobs are used as reference points around which other jobs are arranged in order of relative worth.

external equity Employees perceives his or her pay as fair given the pay rates in other organizations.

internal equity Employees perceives his or her pay as fair given the pay rates of others in the organization.

job evaluation A systematic comparison to determine the relative worth of jobs within a firm.

benchmark job A job that is critical to the firm's operations or that is commonly found in other organizations.

compensable factor A fundamental, compensable element of a job, such as skill, effort, responsibility, and working conditions.

Compensable Factors

Jobs can be compared intuitively by deciding that one job is "more important" or "of greater value or worth" than another without digging any deeper into why in terms of specific job-related factors. This approach, called the *ranking method*, is hard to defend to employees or others who may not agree with the resulting job hierarchy. As an alternative, jobs can be compared by focusing on certain basic factors that they have in common. In compensation management, these basic factors are called **compensable factors**. They are the factors that determine the definition of job content, establish how the jobs compare with one another, and set the compensation paid for each job.

Some employers develop their own compensable factors. However, most use factors that have been popularized by packaged job evaluation systems or by legislation. For example, most of the pay equity acts in Canada focus on four compensable factors: *skill, effort, responsibility,* and *working conditions*. As another example, the job evaluation method popularized by the Hay Group consulting firm focuses on four compensable factors: *know-how, problem solving, accountability,* and *working conditions*. Often, different job evaluation systems are used for different departments, employee groups, or business units.

Identifying compensable factors plays a pivotal role in job evaluation. All jobs in each employee group, department, or business unit are evaluated *using the same compensable factors*. An employer thus evaluates the same elemental components for each job within the work group and is then better able to compare jobs—for example, in terms of the degree of skill, effort, responsibility, and working conditions present in each.[11]

Job Evaluation Committee

Job evaluation is largely a judgmental process and one that demands close cooperation among supervisors, compensation specialists, and the employees and their union representatives. The main steps involved include identifying the need for the program, getting cooperation, and choosing an evaluation committee; the committee then carries out the actual job evaluation.[12]

A **job evaluation committee** is established to ensure the representation of the points of view of various people who are familiar with the jobs in question, each of whom may have a different perspective regarding the nature of the jobs. The committee may include employees, HR staff, managers, and union representatives.

The evaluation committee first identifies 10 or 15 key benchmark jobs. These will be the first jobs to be evaluated and will serve as the anchors or benchmarks against which the relative importance or value of all other jobs can be compared. Then the committee turns to its most important function—actually evaluating the worth of each job. For this, the committee will probably use either the job classification method or the point method.

The job evaluation committee typically includes several employees and has the important task of evaluating the worth of each job using compensable factors.

Classification Method

The **classification/grading method** involves categorizing jobs into groups. The groups are called **classes** if they contain similar jobs or **grades** if they contain jobs that are similar in difficulty but otherwise different.

This method is widely used in the public sector. The federal government's UT (University Teaching) job group is an example of a job class because it contains similar jobs involving teaching, research, and consulting. Conversely, the AV (Audit, Commerce, and Purchasing) job group is an example of a job grade because it contains dissimilar jobs, involving auditing, economic development consulting, and purchasing.

There are several ways in which to categorize jobs. One is to draw up class descriptions (similar to job descriptions) and place jobs into classes based on their correspondence to these descriptions. Another is to draw up a set of classifying rules for each class (for instance, the amount of independent judgment, skill, physical effort, and so on that the class of jobs requires). Then the jobs are categorized according to these rules.

The usual procedure is to choose compensable factors and then develop class or grade descriptions that describe each class in terms of the amount or level of compensable factor(s) in jobs. The federal government's classification system, for example, employs different compensable factors for various job groups. Based on these compensable factors, a **grade/group description** (like that in Exhibit 15-3) is written. Then, the evaluation committee reviews all job descriptions and slots each job into its appropriate class or grade.

The job classification method has several advantages. The main one is that most employers usually end up classifying jobs anyway, regardless of the job evaluation method that they use. They do this to avoid having to work with and develop pay rates for an unmanageable number of jobs; with the job classification method, all jobs are already grouped into several classes. The disadvantages are that it is difficult to write the class or grade descriptions and that considerable judgment is required in applying them. Yet many employers use this method with success.

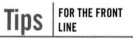
FOR THE FRONT LINE

job evaluation committee
A diverse group (including employees, HR staff, managers, and union representatives) established to ensure the fair and comprehensive representation of the nature and requirements of the jobs in question.

classification/grading method
A method for categorizing jobs into groups.

classes Groups of jobs based on a set of rules for each class, such as amount of independent judgment, skill, physical effort, and so forth. Classes usually contain similar jobs—such as all secretaries.

grades Groups of jobs based on a set of rules for each grade, where jobs are similar in difficulty but otherwise different. Grades often contain dissimilar jobs, such as secretaries, mechanics, and firefighters.

grade/group description A written description of the level of compensable factors required by jobs in each grade; sed to combine similar jobs into grades or classes.

EXHIBIT 15-3 Example of a Group Definition in the Federal Government

Correctional Services (CX) Group Definition

The Correctional Services Group comprises positions that are primarily involved in the custody, control and correctional influence of inmates in the institutions of Correctional Service Canada and the training of staff engaged in custodial and correctional work at a Staff College of Correctional Service Canada.

Inclusions

Notwithstanding the generality of the foregoing, for greater certainty, it includes positions that have as their primary purpose, responsibility for one or more of the following activities:

1. the custody and control of inmates and the security of the institution;
2. the custody and control of detainees being held under Immigration and Refugee Protection Act (IRPA) Security Certificates;
3. the correctional influence of inmates with the continuing responsibility to relate actively and effectively to inmates;
4. the admission and discharge of inmates, and the control of inmate visits and correspondence;
5. the organization and implementation of recreational activities, the surveillance and control of inmates engaged in these activities and the custody and issue of recreational equipment;
6. the training of staff in custodial and correctional procedures and techniques; and
7. the leadership of any of the above activities.

Exclusions

Positions excluded from the Correctional Services Group are those whose primary purpose is included in the definition of any other group or those in which one or more of the following activities is of primary importance:

1. the operation of heating plant, sewage facilities and water supplies and the provision of maintenance services;
2. the provision of patient care that requires the application of a comprehensive knowledge of or specialized expertise in physical and mental health care;
3. the provision of services and supplies to inmates; and
4. the instruction of inmates in workshops, crafts and training programs.

Source: Correctional Services (CX) Classification Standard. www.tbs-sct.gc.ca/cla/def/cx-eng.asp, Treasury Board of Canada Secretariat, 2004. Reproduced with the permission of the Minister of Public Works and Government Services Canada, 2012.

Point Method

The **point method** is widely used in the private sector and requires identifying several compensable factors. The extent or degree to which each factor is present in the job is evaluated, a corresponding number of points is assigned for each factor, and the number of points for each factor is summed to arrive at an overall point value for the job.

1. *Preliminary steps.* To use the point method, it is necessary to have current job descriptions and job specifications based on a thorough job analysis. The foundation of the job evaluation plan is a number of compensable factors that must be agreed upon. In Canada, four compensable factors are commonly used: skill, effort, responsibility, and working conditions. These factors are general and can mean different things in different workplaces. Therefore sub-factors of each one may also be determined to clarify the specific meaning of each factor, as shown below.

Factor	Sub-Factors
Skill	Education and Experience Interpersonal Skill
Effort	Physical Effort Mental Effort
Responsibility	Supervision of Others Planning
Working Conditions	Physical Environment Travel

point method A job evaluation method in which a number of compensable factors are identified, the degree to which each of these factors is present in the job is determined, and an overall point value is calculated.

Each sub-factor must be carefully defined to ensure that the evaluation committee members will apply them consistently. An example of a sub-factor definition is presented in Exhibit 15-4.

EXHIBIT 15-4 Sub-Factor Definition

Responsibility for Others

This sub-factor is used to measure the responsibility that the incumbent of the position assumes for the direction and/or supervision of volunteers, external suppliers/contractors and staff. The following characteristics of the work are to be considered in selecting a level: the nature of supervision given, based either on accountability for results or functional guidance (how-to), and the number of employees or others directed/supervised. Occasional supervision, such as that performed during the absence of the supervisor on vacation or sick leaves, is not to be considered. **This sub-factor does NOT include the academic supervision of students or the activities of others outside of an employee-type relationship.**

Source: Based on McMaster University CAW Local 555 Job Evaluation Plan, www.workingatmcmaster. ca/jjesc (accessed March 23, 2009).

2. *Determine factor weights and degrees.* The next step is to decide on the maximum number of points (called "weight") to assign to each factor. Assigning factor weights is generally done by the evaluation committee. The committee members carefully study each factor and determine the relative value of the factors. For example:

Skill	30 percent
Effort	30 percent
Responsibility	30 percent
Working conditions	10 percent
	100 percent

Then definitions of varying amounts (called "degrees" or "levels") of each sub-factor (or overall factor if no sub-factors are used) are prepared so that raters can judge the degree of a sub-factor/factor existing in a job. Thus, sub-factor "physical environment" for the factor "working conditions" might have three degrees—occasional, frequent, continuous—defined as follows:

Degree 1: Occasional—less than 30 percent of the time on an annual basis. Typically occurs once in a while, but not every day, or every day for less than 30 percent of the day.

Degree 2: Frequent—30 percent to 60 percent of the time on an annual basis. A regular feature of the job that occurs during any given day, week, or season.

Degree 3: Continuous—More than 60 percent of the time on an annual basis. Typically occurs for most of the regular work day, all year round (on average).

The number of degrees usually does not exceed five or six, and the actual number depends mostly on judgment. It is not necessary to have the same number of degrees for each factor, and degrees should be limited to the number necessary to distinguish among jobs.

3. *Assign points for each degree of each sub-factor.* Points are then assigned to each factor, as in Table 15.1. For example, suppose that it is decided to use a total number of 1 000 points in the point plan. Then, since the factor "skill" had a weight of 30 percent, it would be assigned a total of 30 percent of 1 000 = 300 points. This automatically means that the highest degree for each sub-factor of the skill factor would be 300 points. Points are then assigned to the other degrees for this factor, in equal amounts from the lowest to the highest degree. This step is repeated for each factor and its sub-factors, resulting in the final job evaluation plan, as shown in Table 15.1. All these decisions are recorded in a job evaluation manual to be used by the job evaluation committee.

TABLE 15.1 Point Method Job Evaluation Plan

Factor	Sub-Factors	Degrees					Maximum Weight	Points
		1	**2**	**3**	**4**			
Skill	Education and Experience	50	100	150	200	200		
	Interpersonal Skill	25	50	75	100	100		
							300	30%
Effort	Physical Effort	25	50	75	100	100		
	Mental Effort	50	100	150	200	200		
							300	30%
Responsibility	Supervision of Others	50	100	150		150		
	Planning	50	100	150		150		
							300	30%
Working Conditions	Physical Environment	20	40	60		60		
	Travel	10	20	30	40	40		
							100	10%
							1000	100%

4. *Evaluate the jobs.* Once the manual is complete, the actual evaluations can begin. Each job is evaluated factor by factor to determine the number of points that should be assigned to it. First, committee members determine the degree (first degree, second degree, and so on) to which each factor is present in the job. Then they note the corresponding points (see Table 15.1) that were assigned to each of these degrees. Finally, they add up the points for all factors, arriving at a total point value for the job. Raters generally start by rating benchmark jobs and obtaining consensus on these, and then they rate the rest of the jobs.

Point systems involve a quantitative technique that is easily explained to and used by employees. However, it can be difficult and time-consuming to develop a point plan and to effectively train the job evaluation user group. This is one reason why many organizations adopt a point plan developed and marketed by a consulting firm. In fact, the availability of a number of ready-made plans probably accounts in part for the wide use of point plans in job evaluation.

If the committee assigned pay rates to each individual job, it would be difficult to administer since there might be different pay rates for hundreds or even thousands of jobs. Even in smaller organizations there is a tendency to try to simplify wage and salary structures as much as possible. Therefore, the committee will probably want to group similar jobs (in terms of their number of points, for instance) into grades for pay purposes. Then, instead of having to deal with pay rates for hundreds of jobs, it might only have to focus on pay rates for 10 or 12 groupings of jobs.

A **pay grade** comprises jobs of approximately equal value or importance, as determined by job evaluation. If the point method was used, the pay grade consists of jobs falling within a range of points. If the classification system was used, then the jobs are already categorized into classes or grades. The next stage is to obtain information on market pay rates by conducting a wage/salary survey.

Stage 2: Conduct a Wage/Salary Survey

Compensation or **wage/salary surveys** play a central role in determining pay rates for jobs.[13] An employer may use wage/salary surveys in three ways. First, survey data

pay grade Comprises jobs of approximately equal value.

wage/salary survey A survey aimed at determining prevailing wage rates. A good salary survey provides specific wage rates for comparable jobs. Formal written questionnaire surveys are the most comprehensive.

are used to determine pay rates for benchmark jobs that serve as reference points or anchors for the employer's pay scale, meaning that other jobs are then paid based on their relative worth compared to the benchmark jobs. Second, an increasing number of positions are paid solely based on the marketplace (rather than relative to the firm's benchmark jobs).[14]

As a result of the current shift away from long-term employment, compensation is increasingly shaped by market wages and less by how it fits into the hierarchy of jobs in one organization. Finally, surveys also collect data on employee benefits, work–life programs, pay-for-performance plans, recognition plans, and so on to provide a basis on which to make decisions regarding other types of rewards.

Formal and Informal Surveys by the Employer

Most employers rely heavily on formal or informal surveys of what other employers are paying.[15] Informal telephone surveys are good for collecting data on a relatively small number of easily identified and quickly recognized jobs, such as when a bank's HR director wants to determine the salary at which a newly opened customer service representative's job should be advertised. Informal discussions among human resources specialists at regular professional association meetings are other occasions for informal salary surveys. Some employers use formal questionnaire surveys to collect compensation information from other employers, including things like number of employees, overtime policies, starting salaries, and paid vacations.

Commercial, Professional, and Government Salary Surveys

Many employers also rely on surveys published by various commercial firms, professional associations, or government agencies. For example, Statistics Canada provides monthly data on earnings by geographic area, by industry, and by occupation. Table 15.2 provides an example of earnings data by industry and occupation.

The Toronto Board of Trade conducts five compensation surveys annually, covering executive; management; professional, supervisory, and sales; information technology; and administrative and support positions. The surveys include information from small, medium, and large employers in the Greater Toronto Area. A separate survey of employee benefits and employment practices is also conducted.

Private consulting or executive recruiting companies, such as Towers Watson, Mercer, and Hewitt Associates, annually publish data covering the compensation of senior and middle managers and members of boards of directors. Professional organizations, such as the Certified General Accountants and Professional Engineers Ontario, conduct surveys of compensation practices among members of their associations.

For some jobs, salaries are determined directly based on formal or informal salary surveys like those available from Monster.ca. In most cases, though, surveys are used to price benchmark jobs around which other jobs are then slotted based on their relative worth as determined through job evaluation.

Monster.ca Salary & Benefits Centre
http://career-advice.monster.ca/ Salary-Benefits/careers.aspx

Salary Survey Interpretation and Use

Data from the Hay Group consulting firm indicate that large organizations participate in an average of 11 compensation surveys and use information from seven of them to administer their own compensation practices.[16]

Upward bias can be a problem regardless of the type of compensation survey used. At least one compensation expert argues that the way in which most surveys are constructed, interpreted, and used leads almost invariably to a situation in which firms set higher wages than they otherwise might. For example, "companies like to compare themselves against well-regarded, high-paying, and high-performing companies," so baseline salaries tend to be biased upward. Similarly, "companies that sponsor surveys often do so with an implicit (albeit unstated) objective: to show the company [is]

TABLE 15.2 Average Weekly Earnings by Industry 2004–2009

Geography = Canada
Type of employees = All employees
Overtime = Including overtime

North American Industry Classification System (NAICS)	2004	2005	2006	2007	2008	2009
Industrial aggregate excluding unclassified businesses	709.41	737.29	755.48	788.06	810.52	823.53
Mining, quarrying, and oil and gas extraction	1,278.11	1,296.35	1,325.73	1,437.44	1,527.90	1,594.04
Utilities	1,261.08	1,298.32	1,350.66	1,421.49	1,424.73	1,500.79
Construction	846.38	877.34	900.32	961.16	1,014.51	1,048.42
Manufacturing	862.60	896.35	904.69	940.67	949.54	917.73
Wholesale trade	826.89	865.92	905.24	937.14	956.59	988.89
Retail trade	425.65	441.18	449.86	458.80	475.17	486.70
Transportation and warehousing	807.78	828.07	834.40	864.51	883.28	874.69
Information and cultural industries	916.99	952.30	955.52	1,003.44	1,003.54	1,077.16
Finance and insurance	887.00	921.01	951.17	998.93	1,002.03	1,036.81
Real estate and rental and leasing	654.56	698.06	710.73	756.11	772.87	771.83
Professional, scientific and technical services	937.42	989.94	1,016.41	1,060.36	1,093.67	1,129.10
Management of companies and enterprises	1,012.41	1,005.19	1,050.28	1,086.16	1,087.91	1,144.86
Admistrative and support, waste management and remediation services	546.15	583.67	600.98	648.97	673.97	671.44

Source: Statistics Canada, CANSIM database, Table 281-0027, 2011. Available for free at www.statcan.gc.ca/pub/72-002-x/72-002-x2011002-eng.pdf.

paying either competitively or somewhat below the market, so as to justify positive corrective action." For these and similar reasons, it is probably wise to review survey results with a skeptical eye and to acknowledge that upward bias may exist and should perhaps be considered when making decisions.[17]

Tips | **FOR THE FRONT LINE**

Whatever the source of the survey, the data must be carefully assessed for accuracy before they are used to make compensation decisions. Problems can arise when the organization's job descriptions only partially match the descriptions contained in the survey, the survey data were collected several months before the time of use, the participants in the survey do not represent the appropriate labour market for the jobs being matched, and so on.[18]

Now all the information necessary to move to the next stage—determining pay for jobs—has been obtained.

Stage 3: Combine the Job Evaluation and Salary Survey Information to Determine Pay for Jobs

The final stage is to assign pay rates to each pay grade. (Of course, if jobs were not grouped into pay grades, individual pay rates would have to be assigned to each job.) Assigning pay rates to each pay grade (or to each job) is usually accomplished with a **wage curve**.

The wage curve graphically depicts the market pay rates currently being paid for jobs in each pay grade, relative to the job evaluation points for each job or grade. An

wage curve A graphic description of the relationship between the value of the job and the average wage paid for this job.

example of a wage curve is presented in Exhibit 15-5. Note that pay rates are shown on the vertical axis, while the points for pay grades are shown along the horizontal axis. The purpose of the wage curve is to show the relationship between the value of the job as determined by one of the job evaluation methods and the current average pay rates for each job or grade.

There are several steps in determining pay for pay grades using a wage curve. First, find the average pay for each pay grade, since each of the pay grades consists of several jobs. Next, plot the pay rates for each pay grade, as was done in Exhibit 15-5. Then fit a line (called a "wage line") through the points just plotted. This can be done either freehand or by using a statistical method known as regression analysis. Finally, determine pay for jobs. Wages along the wage line are the target wages or salary rates for the jobs in each pay grade.

An Ethical | Dilemma

What should employers do when there is a shortage of a certain type of skill and they cannot attract any workers unless they pay a market rate above the maximum of their salary range for that job? How should other jobs (without a skills shortage) in the same company in the same salary range be paid?

Developing Rate Ranges

Most employers do not just pay one rate for all jobs in a particular pay grade. Instead, they develop **pay ranges** for each grade so that there might, for instance, be 10 levels or "steps" and 10 corresponding pay rates within each pay grade. This approach is illustrated in Table 15.3, which shows the pay rates and levels for some of the federal government pay grades. As of the time of this pay schedule, for instance, employees in positions that were classified in grade CX-1 could be paid annual salaries between $52 604 and $66 413, depending on the level at which they were hired into the grade, the amount of time they were in the grade, and their merit increases (if any). Another way to depict the rate ranges for each grade is with a wage structure, as in Exhibit 15-6. The wage structure graphically depicts the range of pay rates (in this case, per hour) to be paid for each grade.

The use of pay ranges for each pay grade has several benefits. First, the employer can take a more flexible stance with respect to the labour market; for example, some flexibility makes it easier to attract experienced, higher-paid employees into a pay grade where the starting salary for the lowest step may be too low to attract such experienced people. Pay ranges also allow employers to provide for performance differences

---

EXHIBIT 15-5 Plotting a Wage Curve

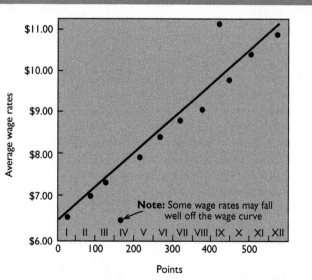

Note: The average market pay rate for jobs in each grade (Grade I, Grade II, Grade III, etc.) is plotted, and the wage curve is fitted to the resulting points.

pay ranges A series of steps or levels within a pay grade, usually based on years of service.

TABLE 15.3 Federal Government Pay Schedules CX-1 and CX-2

Rate Levels within Grade					
Grade	1	2	3	4	5
CX-1	$52 604	55 761	59 107	62 652	66 413
CX-2	$55 826	59 176	62 726	66 489	70 477

Source: CX - Correctional Services Group Annual Rates of Pay, www.tbs-sct.gc.ca/pubs_pol/hrpubs/coll_agre/cx/cx08-eng.asp, Treasury Board of Canada Secretariat, 2006. Reproduced with the permission of the Minister of Public Works and Government Services Canada, 2012.

between employees within the same grade or between those with differing seniority. As in Exhibit 15-6, most employers structure their pay ranges to overlap a bit so that an employee with greater experience or seniority may earn more than an entry-level person in the next higher pay grade.

Broadbanding

The trend today is for employers to reduce their salary grades and ranges from 10 or more down to three to five, a process that is called **broadbanding**. Broadbanding means combining salary grades and ranges into just a few wide levels or "bands," each of which then contains a relatively wide range of jobs and salary levels (see Exhibit 15-7).

Broadbanding a pay system involves several steps. First, the number of bands is decided on and each is assigned a salary range. The bands usually have wide salary

EXHIBIT 15-6 Wage Structure

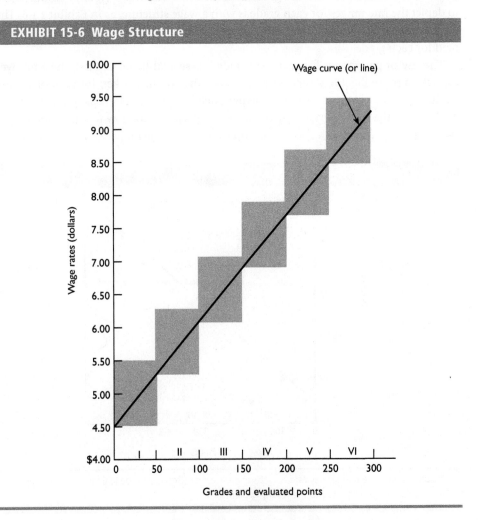

broadbanding Reducing the number of salary grades and anges into just a few wide levels or "bands," each of which then contains a relatively wide range of jobs and salary levels.

EXHIBIT 15-7 Broadbanding

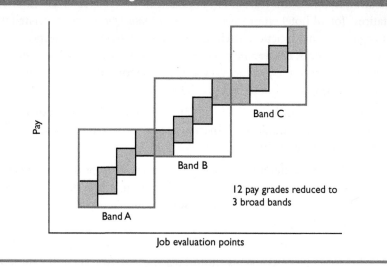

Band C

Band B

Band A

12 pay grades reduced to
3 broad bands

Pay

Job evaluation points

ranges and also overlap substantially. As a result, there is much more flexibility to move employees from job to job within bands and less need to "promote" them to new grades just to give them higher salaries.

Broadbanding's basic advantage is that it injects greater flexibility into employee compensation.[19] The new, broad salary bands can include both supervisors and those reporting to them. Broadbanding also facilitates less specialized, boundaryless jobs and organizations. Less specialization and more participation in cross-departmental processes generally mean enlarged duties or capabilities and more possibilities for alternative career tracks.

Correcting Out-of-Line Rates

The actual wage rate for a job may fall well off the wage line or well outside the rate range for its grade. This means that the average pay for that job is currently too high or too low relative to other jobs in the firm. If a point falls well below the line, a pay raise for the job may be required. If the plot falls well above the wage line, pay cuts or a pay freeze may be required.

Underpaid employees should have their wages raised to the minimum of the rate range for their pay grade, assuming that the organization wants to retain the employees and has the funds. This can be done either immediately or in one or two steps.

Pay rates of overpaid employees are often called **red circle pay rates**, and there are several ways to cope with this problem. One is to freeze the rate paid to employees in this grade until general salary increases bring the other jobs into line with it. A second alternative is to transfer or promote some or all of the employees involved to jobs for which they can legitimately be paid their current pay rates. The third alternative is to freeze the rate for six months, during which time attempts are made to transfer or promote the overpaid employees. If this is not possible, then the rate at which these employees are paid is cut to the maximum in the pay range for their grade.

Pay for Knowledge

Pay-for-knowledge systems are known as *competency-based pay* (for management and professional employees) and *skill-based pay* (for manufacturing employees). These plans pay employees for the range, depth, and types of knowledge that they are capable of using, rather than for the job that they currently hold. Competencies are individual knowledge, skills, and behaviours that are critical to successful individual or corporate performance based on their relation to the organization's visions, values, and business strategy.[20]

red circle pay rate A rate of pay that is above the pay range maximum.

Core competencies describe knowledge and behaviours that employees throughout the organization must exhibit for the organization to succeed, such as "customer service orientation" for all hotel employees. *Functional competencies* are associated with a particular organizational function, such as "negotiation skills" for salespeople, or "safety orientation" for pilots. *Behavioural competencies* are expected behaviours, such as "always walking a customer to the product they are looking for rather than pointing."[21] A pay-for-knowledge program should include the following:

- Competencies and skills—directly important to job performance—that can be defined in measurable and objective terms. Skills tend to be easier to define and measure than competencies.

Construction workers today are often compensated for their work through the method of skill-based pay.

- New and different competencies that replace obsolete competencies or competencies that are no longer important to job performance. If additional competencies are needed, the obsolete competency should be removed from the program.

- On-the-job training, not "in the classroom" training. Those who possess the competencies or skills should teach them. Also include on-the-job assessment, which can be supplemented by paper-and-pencil exams administered on the job.[22]

As an example, in a manufacturing plant setting, workers would be paid based on their attained skill levels. In a three-level plan:

1. Level 1 would indicate limited ability, such as knowledge of basic facts and ability to perform simple tasks without direction.

2. Level 2 would mean that the employee has attained partial proficiency and could, for instance, apply technical principles on the job.

3. Level 3 would mean that the employee is fully competent in the area and could, for example, analyze and solve production problems.

Increased workforce flexibility is one of the most significant advantages of pay for knowledge. Employees rotate between different jobs or production areas to encourage the learning of new competencies and skills. This process fosters flexibility by encouraging workers to learn multiple competencies and skills and to willingly switch tasks.[23]

Experience has shown that competency-based pay is more efficient in the first years of its existence. The greatest challenge is measurement of competencies. As time goes on, employees often become dissatisfied if these measurements are not valid or if the people responsible for assessing competencies are considered incompetent or biased.[24]

Another major employee concern is that pay be linked sufficiently to performance as well as competencies. Some compensation consultants suggest that firms should not pay for competencies at the exclusion of rewards for high performance results. For example, competencies could be linked to the determination of base salary combined with bonuses that are based on performance.[25] One final issue for many Canadian companies is that pay-for-knowledge systems do not meet pay equity requirements.[26]

Although only about 15 to 20 percent of workplaces use pay for knowledge at present, experts predict that the viewpoint that people, rather than jobs, provide advantages to organizations will continue to grow in popularity. They foresee the emergence of new pay systems combining competencies and market values.[27]

Pay for Executive, Managerial, and Professional Jobs

Developing a compensation plan to pay executive, managerial, and professional employees is similar in many respects to developing a plan for other employees.[28] The basic aims of the plan are the same in that the goal is to attract good employees and maintain their commitment. Yet for executive, managerial, and professional jobs, job evaluation provides only a partial answer to the question of how to pay these employees. Executives, managers, and professionals are almost always paid based on their performance as well as on the basis of static job demands, like working conditions.

Compensating Executives and Managers

There are five elements in an executive/managerial compensation package: salary, benefits, short-term incentives, long-term incentives, and perquisites.[29] The amount of salary paid usually depends on the value of the person's work to the organization and how well the person is honouring his or her responsibilities. Salary is the cornerstone of executive compensation, because it is the element on which the others are layered, with benefits, incentives, and perquisites often awarded in some proportion to base pay.

Executive compensation tends to emphasize performance incentives more than other employee pay plans do, since organizational results are likely to reflect the contributions of executives more directly than those of other employees. The heavy incentive component of executive compensation can be illustrated by using some of Canada's best-paid executives as an example.[30] The highest paid executive in Canada in 2010 was Hank Swartout, CEO of Precision Drilling Corporation, who earned a total compensation of $74 824 331, of which $840 000 was base salary. Hunter Harrison, CEO of Canadian National Railway, received total compensation of $56 219 494, which included his base salary of $1 665 950. A study on CEO pay determined that firm size accounts for 40 percent of the variance of total CEO pay, while firm performance accounts for less than 5 percent of the variance.[31]

An Ethical | Dilemma

Is it right that CEOs earn enormous amounts of money when most employees are getting small increases each year (sometimes even less than inflation)?

Research | INSIGHT

There has been considerable debate regarding whether top executives are worth what they are paid. Some argue that the job of an executive is increasingly difficult. The stakes are high, and job tenure is often short. Expectations are getting higher, the questions from shareholders are more direct, and the challenge of navigating an organization through difficult economic times has never been so great. However, shareholder activism regarding executive pay has attempted to tighten the restrictions on what firms pay their top executives.

Some believe that pay for performance is taking hold, with companies now making stronger links between company performance and CEO total compensation. Others believe that linking pay to performance is still inadequate in the majority of companies. Most agree that better disclosure of executive pay is required, and groups such as the Canadian Securities Administrators and the Canadian Coalition for Good Governance are pressing for dramatic changes in executive compensation disclosure.[32]

Compensating Professional Employees

Compensating non-supervisory professional employees, like engineers and scientists, presents unique problems. Analytical jobs require creativity and problem solving, compensable factors not easily compared or measured. Furthermore, the professional's economic impact on the firm is often related only indirectly to the person's actual efforts; for example, the success of an engineer's invention depends on many factors, like how well it is produced and marketed.

In theory, the job evaluation methods explained previously can be used for evaluating professional jobs.[33] The compensable factors here tend to focus on problem solving, creativity, job scope, and technical knowledge and expertise. The job classification method is commonly used—a series of grade descriptions are written, and each position is slotted into the grade having the most appropriate definition.

In practice, traditional methods of job evaluation are rarely used for professional jobs since it is so difficult to identify compensable factors and degrees of factors that meaningfully capture the value of professional work. "Knowledge and the skill of applying it," as one expert notes, "are extremely difficult to quantify and measure."[34]

As a result, most employers use a *market-pricing approach* in evaluating professional jobs. They price professional jobs in the marketplace to the best of their ability to establish the values for benchmark jobs. These benchmark jobs and the employer's other professional jobs are then slotted into a salary structure. Specifically, each professional discipline (like mechanical engineering or electrical engineering) usually ends up having four to six grade levels, each of which requires a fairly broad salary range. This approach helps ensure that the employer remains competitive when bidding for professionals whose attainments vary widely and whose potential employers are found literally worldwide.[35]

Pay Equity

Historically, the average pay for Canadian women has been considerably lower than that for men. In 1967, women's average wages were 46.1 percent of men's average wages. Table 15.4 shows the most recent wage gap statistics. Some of this gap is due to the fact that women do more part-time work than men, but even when full-year, full-time workers are compared, the gap has stalled at approximately 30 percent since 1998. The wage gap is narrower for single women over those who are married, and for younger women when compared to those who are older.[36]

Moreover, the gap persists even when women have the same qualifications and do the same type of work as men. A 2004 study showed that, two years after graduation, female university graduates in the Maritime provinces working full time earned 78 percent of the weekly wage of males, even after accounting for differences in field of study, occupation, location, and hours worked.[37]

TABLE 15.4 Male–Female Average Earnings Ratio* for Full-Year, Full-Time Workers, 1998–2008

Geography = Canada
Work activity = Full-year full-time workers

Earnings	Average earnings, females (dollars)	Average earnings, males (dollars)	Female-to-male average earnings ratio (percent)
1998	40,500	56,300	71.9
1999	38,900	56,900	68.4
2000	40,200	56,900	70.6
2001	40,600	58,100	69.9
2002	40,800	58,200	70.2
2003	40,700	57,900	70.2
2004	42,000	59,900	70.1
2005	41,800	59,400	70.5
2006	43,200	60,000	71.9
2007	44,100	61,700	71.4
2008	44,700	62,600	71.3

*Earnings stated in constant year 2006 dollars.
Source: Statistics Canada, CANSIM Table 202-0102, http://estat.statcan.gc.ca/cgi-win/CNSMCGI.EXE (accessed August 20, 2011).

Although such factors as differences in hours worked, experience levels, education levels, and level of unionization contribute to the wage gap, systemic discrimination is also present.[38] The purpose of pay equity legislation is to redress systemic gender discrimination in compensation for work performed by employees in female-dominated job classes. **Pay equity** requires that equal wages be paid for jobs of equal value or "worth" to the employer, as determined by gender-neutral (i.e., free of any bias based on gender) job evaluation techniques.

The legal process involved can be lengthy. A final decision is still pending in a pay equity complaint filed against Canada Post in 1983 claiming that 6 000 clerical workers had been subjected to systemic discrimination.[39] In 2006, the Supreme Court of Canada ruled against a Canadian Human Rights Tribunal decision that female Air Canada flight attendants' jobs could not be compared with those of mainly male mechanics and pilots and sent the case back to the tribunal. The court condemned Air Canada's use of legal technicalities to delay the case, which began in 1991.[40]

Saskatchewan workers demonstrate for pay equity.

Six provinces (Ontario, Quebec, Manitoba, Nova Scotia, New Brunswick, and Prince Edward Island) have created separate proactive legislation that specifically requires that pay equity be achieved. Ontario and Quebec require pay equity in both the public and the private sectors, whereas the legislation in the other four provinces applies only to the public sector. In the federal jurisdiction and the Yukon (public sector only), human rights legislation requires equal pay for work of equal value.

The wage gap has narrowed since the introduction of pay equity legislation, but there is still no explanation other than systemic discrimination for much of the 30 percent gap that still persists.[41] In the long term, the best way to remove the portion of the wage gap resulting from systemic discrimination is to eliminate male- and female-dominated jobs by ensuring that women have equal access to and are equally represented in all jobs.

pay equity Providing equal pay to male-dominated job classes and female-dominated job classes of equal value to the employer.

16

Pay-for-Performance and Financial Incentives

Money and Motivation

The use of financial incentives—financial rewards paid to workers whose production exceeds some predetermined standard—is not new; it was popularized by Frederick Taylor in the late 1800s. As a supervisory employee of the Midvale Steel Company, Taylor had become concerned with the tendency of employees to work at the slowest pace possible and produce at the minimum acceptable level. What especially intrigued him was the fact that some of these same workers still had the energy to run home and work on their cabins, even after a 12-hour day. Taylor knew that if he could find some way to harness this energy during the workday, huge productivity gains would be achieved.

Today's efforts to achieve the organization's strategy through motivated employees include fixed and variable compensation plans. **Fixed pay** represents compensation that is independent of the performance level of the individual, group, or organization. Fixed compensation includes base pay and other forms of relatively consistent compensation (for example, allowances) that satisfy the need for income stability. In contrast, **variable pay** represents any plan that links pay with productivity, profitability, or some other measure of organizational performance. Employers continue to increase their use of variable pay plans while holding salary increases or fixed compensation at modest levels. On average, organizations spend roughly 11 percent of total pay-related spending on variable pay-related expenses. More than 84 percent of Canadian employers have one or more types of variable pay plans in place.[1] As shown in Exhibit 16-1, cash bonuses or incentives are the most common form of short-term incentives, used in 87 percent of organizations that have short-term incentive plans in place.

Variable pay facilitates management of total compensation by keeping base pay inflation controlled. The fundamental premise of variable pay plans is that top performers must get top pay to secure their commitment to the organization. Thus, accurate performance appraisal or measurable outcomes is a precondition of effective pay-for-performance plans. Another important prerequisite for effective variable pay plans is "line of sight", or the extent to which an employee can relate his or her daily work to the achievement of overall corporate goals. Employees need to understand corporate strategy and how their work as individual employees is important to the achievement of strategic objectives.[2]

The entire thrust of such programs is to treat workers like partners and get them to think of the business and its goals as their own. It is thus reasonable to pay them more

fixed pay Compensation that is independent of the performance level of the individual, group, or organization.

variable pay Any plan that ties pay to productivity or profitability.

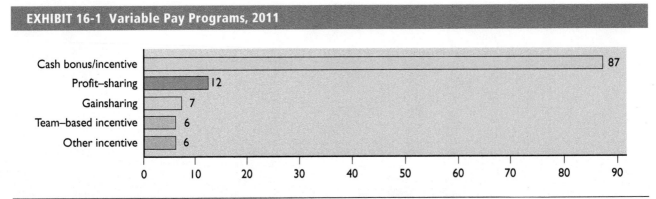

EXHIBIT 16-1 Variable Pay Programs, 2011

Cash bonus/incentive	87
Profit–sharing	12
Gainsharing	7
Team–based incentive	6
Other incentive	6

Note: n = 323; percent based on organizations with at least one annual variable pay plan in place.
Figures do not add to 100 because some respondents have more than one plan.

Source: A. Cowan, *Compensation Planning Outlook 2011* (Ottawa, ON: Conference Board of Canada, 2010), p. 7. Reprinted by permission of The Conference Board of Canada, Ottawa.

like partners, too, by linking their pay more directly to performance. For example, the owners of a Surrey, British Columbia–based trucking company handed out bonus cheques totalling more than $400 000 to more than 400 employees in August 2005. Over the preceding five years, the owners had grown Coastal Pacific Xpress (CPX) by 500 percent and decided to reward their employees for their hard work.[3]

Types of Incentive Plans

There are several types of incentive plans. Individual incentive programs give income over and above base salary to individual employees who meet a specific individual performance standard. Informal incentives may be awarded, generally to individual employees, for accomplishments that are not readily measured by a standard, such as "to recognize the long hours that this employee put in last month," or "to recognize exemplary customer service this week." Group incentive programs are like individual incentive plans, but they provide payments over and above base salary to all team members when the group or team collectively meets a specified standard for performance, productivity, or other work-related behaviour. Organization-wide incentive plans provide monetary incentives to all employees of the organization. Examples are profit-sharing plans that provide employees with a share of the organization's profits in a specified period, and gainsharing programs designed to reward employees for improvements in organizational productivity. Finally, non-monetary recognition programs motivate employees through praise and expressions of appreciation for their work.

It is important to ensure that whatever incentive is being provided is appealing to the individual receiving it. Demographic factors can have an impact on what is appealing,.

For simplicity, these plans will be discussed as follows: incentives for operations employees; incentives for senior managers and executives; incentives for salespeople; incentives primarily for other managers and professional employees (merit pay); and organization-wide incentives.

Incentives for Operations Employees

Piecework Plans

Several incentive plans are particularly well suited for use with operations employees, such as those doing production work.[4] **Piecework** is the oldest incentive plan and still the most commonly used. Earnings are tied directly to what the worker produces—the person is paid a piece rate for each unit that he or she produces. Thus, if Tom Smith gets $0.40 per piece for stamping out door jambs, then he would make $40 for stamping out 100 a day and $80 for stamping out 200.

Developing a workable piece-rate plan requires both job evaluation and (usually) industrial engineering. Job evaluation enables firms to assign an hourly wage rate to the job in question. The crucial issue in piece-rate planning is the production standard, however, and this standard is usually developed by industrial engineers. Production standards are stated in terms of a standard number of minutes per unit or a standard number of units per hour. In Tom Smith's case, the job evaluation indicated that his door-jamb stamping job was worth $10 per hour. The industrial engineer determined that 20 jambs per hour was the standard production rate. Therefore, the piece rate (for each door jamb) was $10 , 20 = $0.50 per door jamb.

With a **straight piecework plan**, Tom Smith would be paid on the basis of the number of door jambs that he produced; there would be no guaranteed minimum wage. However, after passage of employment/labour standards legislation, it became necessary for most employers to guarantee their workers a minimum wage. With a

piecework A system of pay based on the number of items processed by each individual worker in a unit of time, such as items per hour or items per day.

straight piecework plan A set payment for each piece produced or processed in a factory or shop.

guaranteed piecework plan, Tom Smith would be paid the minimum wage whether or not he stamped out the number of door jambs required to make minimum wage—for example, 18 pieces if minimum wage is $9 per hour. As an incentive he would, however, also be paid at the piece rate of $0.50 for each unit that he produced over the number required to make minimum wage.

"Piecework" generally implies straight piecework, a strict proportionality between results and rewards regardless of the level of output. Thus, in Smith's case, he continues to get $0.50 apiece for stamping out door jambs, even if he stamps out many more than planned (say, 500 per day). Other types of piece-work incentive plans call for a sharing of productivity gains between worker and employer such that the worker does not receive full credit for all production above normal.[5]

The **differential piece-rate plan** is like the standard piece-rate plan with one major difference: With a piece-rate plan, the worker is paid a particular rate for each piece that he or she produces; with the differential piece rate plan, the worker is rewarded by a *premium that equals the percentage by which his or her performance exceeds the standard*. The plan assumes the worker has a guaranteed base rate.

As an example, suppose that the base rate for Smith's job is $10 per hour. (The base rate may, but need not, equal the hourly rate determined by the job evaluation; however, it must meet or exceed the minimums established in the applicable Employment Standards Act.) Assume also that the production standard for Smith's job is 20 units per hour, or three minutes per unit. Suppose that in one day (eight hours) Smith produces 200 door jambs. According to the production standard, this should have taken Smith 10 hours (200 ÷ 20 per hour); instead it took him eight hours. He produced at a rate that was 25 percent higher than the standard rate. The standard rate would be eight hours × 20 (units per hour) = 160: Smith actually produced 40 more, for a total of 200. He will, therefore, be paid at a differential piece rate of 25 percent (40/160) above his base rate for the day. His base rate was $10 per hour times eight hours, which equals $80, so he will be paid 1.25 times $80, or $100 for the day.

Advantages and Disadvantages

Piecework incentive plans have several advantages. They are simple to calculate and easily understood by employees. Piece-rate plans appear equitable in principle, and their incentive value can be powerful since rewards are directly tied to performance.

Piecework also has some disadvantages. A main one is its somewhat unsavoury reputation among many employees, based on some employers' habits of arbitrarily raising production standards whenever they found their workers earning "excessive" wages. In addition, piece rates are stated in monetary terms (like $0.50 per piece). Thus, when a new job evaluation results in a new hourly wage rate, the piece rate must also be revised; this can be a big clerical chore. Another disadvantage is more subtle: Since the piece rate is quoted on a per-piece basis, in workers' minds production standards become tied inseparably to the amount of money earned. When an attempt is made to revise production standards it meets considerable worker resistance, even if the revision is fully justified.[6]

In fact, the industrial-engineered specificity of piecework plans represents the seeds of piecework's biggest disadvantage these days. Piecework plans tend to be tailor-made for relatively specialized jobs in which employees do basically the same narrow set of tasks over and over again many times a day. This, in turn, fosters a certain rigidity—employees become preoccupied with producing the number of units needed and are less willing to concern themselves with meeting quality standards or switching from job to job (since doing so could reduce the person's productivity).[7] Employees tend to be trained to perform only a limited number of tasks. Similarly, attempts to introduce new technology or innovative processes may be more likely to fail, insofar as they require major adjustments to engineered standards and negotiations with employees. Equipment tends not to be as well maintained, since employees are focusing on maximizing each machine's output.

guaranteed piecework plan The minimum hourly wage plus an incentive for each piece produced above a set number of pieces per hour.

differential piece-rate plan A plan by which a worker is paid a basic hourly rate plus an extra percentage of his or her base rate for production exceeding the standard per hour or per day. It is similar to piecework payment but is based on a percentage premium.

The differential piece-rate plan has most of the advantages of the piecework plan and is fairly simple to compute and easy to understand. The incentive is expressed in units of time instead of in monetary terms (as it is with the standard piece-rate system). Therefore, there is less of a tendency on the part of workers to link their production standard with their pay. Furthermore, the clerical job of recomputing piece rates whenever hourly wage rates are re-evaluated is avoided.

Such problems as these have led some firms to drop their piecework plans and to substitute team-based incentive plans or programs, like gainsharing, which will be discussed later in this chapter.

Team or Group Incentive Plans

There are several ways in which to implement **team or group incentive plans**.[8] One is to set work standards for each member of the group and maintain a count of the output of each member. Members are then paid based on one of three formulas: (1) All members receive the pay earned by the highest producer; (2) all members receive the pay earned by the lowest producer; or (3) all members receive payment equal to the average pay earned by the group.

The second approach is to set a production standard based on the final output of the group as a whole; all members then receive the same pay, based on the piece rate that exists for the group's job. The group incentive can be based on either the piece rate or standard hour plan, but the latter is somewhat more prevalent.

A third option is to choose a measurable definition of group performance or productivity that the group can control. For instance, broad criteria, such as total labour hours per final product, could be used; piecework's engineered standards are thus not necessarily required here.[9]

There are several reasons to use team incentive plans. Sometimes, several jobs are interrelated, as they are on project teams. Here, one worker's performance reflects not only his or her own effort but that of co-workers as well; thus, team incentives make sense. Team plans also reinforce group planning and problem solving and help to ensure that collaboration takes place. In Japan, employees are rewarded as a group to reduce jealousy, make group members indebted to one another (as they would be to the group), and encourage a sense of cooperation. There tends to be less bickering among group members over who has "tight" production standards and who has "loose" ones. Group incentive plans also facilitate on-the-job training, since each member of the group has an interest in getting new members trained as quickly as possible.[10]

A group incentive plan's chief disadvantage is that each worker's rewards are no longer based solely on his or her own effort. To the extent that the person does not see his or her effort leading to the desired reward, a group plan may be less effective at motivating employees than an individual plan is.

Group incentive plans have been found to be more effective when there are high levels of communication with employees about the specifics of the plan, when there is strong worker involvement in the plan's design and implementation, and when group members perceive the plan as fair.[11]

Research | INSIGHT

Incentives for Senior Managers and Executives

Most employers award their senior managers and executives a bonus or an incentive because of the role they play in determining divisional and corporate profitability.[12]

Short-Term Incentives: The Annual Bonus

More than 90 percent of firms in Canada with variable pay plans provide an *annual bonus*.[13] Unlike salaries, which rarely decline with reduced performance, short-term incentive bonuses can easily result in an increase or decrease of up to 70 percent or

team or group incentive plan A plan in which a production standard is set for a specific work group and its members are paid incentives if the group exceeds the production standard.

more in total pay relative to the previous year. Three basic issues should be considered when awarding short-term incentives: eligibility, fund-size determination, and individual awards.

Jim Balsillie, former co-CEO of Research In Motion, received very high bonuses in addition to his regular compensation.

Eligibility

Eligibility is usually decided in one of three ways. The first criterion is *key position*. Here, a job-by-job review is conducted to identify the key jobs (typically only line jobs) that have a measurable impact on profitability. The second approach to determining eligibility is to set a *salary-level* cut-off point; all employees earning over that threshold amount are automatically eligible for consideration for short-term incentives. Finally, eligibility can be determined by *salary grade*. This is a refinement of the salary cut-off approach and assumes that all employees at a certain grade or above should be eligible for the short-term incentive program. The simplest approach is just to use salary level as a cut-off.[14]

The size of the bonus is usually greater for top-level executives. Thus, an executive earning $150 000 in salary may be able to earn another 80 percent of his or her salary as a bonus, while a manager in the same firm earning $80 000 can earn only another 30 percent. Similarly, a supervisor might be able to earn up to 15 percent of his or her base salary in bonuses. Average bonuses range from a low of 10 percent to a high of 80 percent or more: A typical company might establish a plan whereby executives could earn 45 percent of base salary, managers 25 percent, and supervisors 12 percent.

How Much to Pay Out (Fund Size)

Next, a decision must be made regarding the fund size—the total amount of bonus money that will be available—and there are several formulas to do this. Some companies use a *non-deductible formula*. Here a straight percentage (usually of the company's net income) is used to create the short-term incentive fund. Others use a *deductible formula* on the assumption that the short-term incentive fund should begin to accumulate only after the firm has met a specified level of earnings.

In practice, what proportion of profits is usually paid out as bonuses? In fact, there are no hard-and-fast rules about what an ideal payout size would be, and some firms do not even have a formula for developing the bonus fund. One alternative is to reserve a minimum amount of the profits, say 10 percent, for safeguarding shareholders' investments, and then to establish a fund for bonuses equal to 20 percent of the corporate operating profit before taxes in excess of this base amount. Thus, if the operating profits were $100 000, then the management bonus fund might be 20 percent of $90 000, or $18 000.

Determining Individual Awards

The third issue is determining the *individual awards* to be paid. In some cases, the amount is determined on a discretionary basis (usually by the employee's boss), but typically a target bonus is set for each eligible position and adjustments are then made for greater or less than targeted performance. A maximum amount, perhaps double the target bonus, may be set. Performance ratings are obtained for each manager, and preliminary bonus estimates are computed. Estimates for the total amount of money to be spent on short-term incentives are thereby made and compared with the bonus fund available. If necessary, the individual estimates are then adjusted.

A related question is whether managers will receive bonuses based on individual performance, team performance, corporate performance, or some combination of these. Keep in mind that there is a difference between a profit-sharing plan and a true individual incentive bonus. In a profit-sharing plan, each person gets a bonus based on the company's results, regardless of the person's actual effort. With a true individual incentive, it is the manager's individual effort and performance that are rewarded with a bonus.

Here, again, there are no hard-and-fast rules. Top-level executive bonuses are generally tied to overall corporate results (or divisional results if the executive is, say, the vice-president of a major division). The assumption is that corporate results reflect the person's individual performance. However, as one moves further down the chain of command, corporate profits become a less accurate gauge of a manager's contribution. For supervisory staff or the heads of functional departments, the person's individual performance, rather than corporate results, is a more logical determinant of his or her bonus.

Many experts argue that, in most organizations, managerial and executive-level bonuses should be tied to both organizational and individual performance, and there are several ways to do this.[15] Perhaps the simplest is the *split-award method*, which breaks the bonus into two parts. Here, the manager actually gets two separate bonuses, one based on his or her individual effort and one based on the organization's overall performance. Thus, a manager might be eligible for an individual performance bonus of up to $10 000 but receive an individual performance bonus of only $8 000 at the end of the year, based on his or her individual performance evaluation. In addition, though, the person might also receive a second bonus of $8 000 based on the company's profits for the year. Thus, even if there were no company profits, the high-performing manager would still get an individual performance bonus.

One drawback to this approach is that it pays too much to the marginal performer, who, even if his or her own performance is mediocre, at least gets that second, company-based bonus. One way to get around this problem is to use the *multiplier method*. For example, a manager whose individual performance was "poor" might not even receive a company-performance-based bonus, on the assumption that the bonus should be a *product* of individual *and* corporate performance. When either is very poor, the product is zero.

Whichever approach is used, outstanding performers should get substantially larger awards than do other managers. They are people that the company cannot afford to lose, and their performance should always be adequately rewarded by the organization's incentive system. Conversely, marginal or below-average performers should never receive awards that are normal or average, and poor performers should be awarded nothing. The money saved on those people should be given to above-average performers.[16]

Long-Term Incentives

Long-term incentives are intended to motivate and reward top management for the firm's long-term growth and prosperity and to inject a long-term perspective into executive decisions. If only short-term criteria are used, a manager could, for instance, increase profitability in one year by reducing plant maintenance; this tactic might, however, reduce profits over the next two or three years. This issue of long- versus short-term perspective has received considerable attention in the past several years as shareholders have become increasingly critical of management focus on short-term returns at the expense of long-term increase in share price. The deep economic recession that began in late 2008 fol-

The Conference Board of Canada
www.conferenceboard.ca

lowing the sub-prime mortgage lending crisis resulted in increasing regulatory focus on this type of compensation.

Long-term incentives are also intended to encourage executives to stay with the company by giving them the opportunity to accumulate capital (in the form of company shares) based on the firm's long-term success. Long-term incentives, or **capital accumulation programs**, are most often reserved for senior executives but have more recently begun to be extended to employees at lower organizational levels.[17] Approximately 60 percent of Canadian private sector organizations provide long-term incentives. They are rarely provided to public sector employees.[18]

Some of the most common long-term incentive plans (for capital accumulation) in Canada are stock options, performance share unit plans, restricted share unit plans, and deferred share unit plans.[19] The popularity of these plans changes over time because of economic conditions and trends, internal company financial pressures, changing attitudes toward long-term incentives, and changes in tax law, as well as other factors. Exhibit 16-2 illustrates the popularity of various long-term incentive plans.

Stock Options

The **stock option** is the most popular long-term incentive in Canada, but its use is decreasing. Forty-six percent of organizations using long-term incentives provided stock options in 2011, compared with 57 percent in 2005 and 72 percent in 2002.[20] A stock option is the right to purchase a specific number of shares of company stock at a specific price at some point in the future.

Often a vesting (waiting) period is required to ensure that the employee has contributed to any increase in stock price, which also aligns the stock option with the goal of long-term retention of talent. The executive thus hopes to profit by exercising his or her option to buy the shares in the future but at today's price. The assumption is that the price of the stock will go up rather than going down or staying the same. For example, if shares provided at an option price of $20 per share are exercised (bought) later for $20 when the market price is $60 per share and sold on the stock market when

capital accumulation programs Long-term incentives most often reserved for senior executives.

stock option The right to purchase a stated number of shares of a company stock at today's price at some time in the future.

EXHIBIT 16-2 Long-Term Incentive Plans, 2011

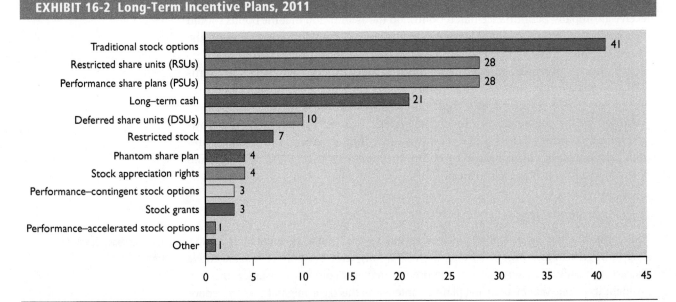

Notes: n = 170; percent based on organizations with at least one LTIP in place.
Figures do not add to 100 because some respondents have more than one plan.

Source: A. Cowan, *Compensation Planning Outlook 2011* (Ottawa, ON: Conference Board of Canada, 2010), p. 11. Reprinted by permission of The Conference Board of Canada, Ottawa.

the market price is $80 per share, a cash gain of $60 per share results. The difference between fair market value of the stock at the time the option is sold and the amount paid by the employee to acquire it is treated as a taxable benefit. Often, the employee benefits since they are only required to pay capital gains tax on 50 percent of the gain. In comparison, from the employer's perspective, capital gains from cash incentive plans and stock purchase plans are taxed at full income inclusion levels. Thus, stock option plans are often seen as a cash windfall with no downside risk but unlimited upside potential.[21]

Unfortunately, stock price depends to a significant extent on considerations outside the executive's control, such as general economic conditions and investor sentiment. An executive performing valiantly in a declining market or troubled industry may receive nothing, since stock options are worthless if share prices don't rise. This is a particularly important concern in today's volatile stock market.[22] However, stock price is affected relative to the overall stock market by the firm's profitability and growth, and to the extent that the executive can affect these factors, the stock option can be an incentive.

As shown in Exhibit 16-3, stock options have traditionally been treated as a tool to attract and retain highly skilled workers. In 2007, the average stock option deduction was $53 000, with only 2 percent of claimants earning less than $100 000 per year and more than three-quarters of claimants earning more than $500 000 per year. One of the interesting trends in stock options as long-term incentives is that, increasingly, they are being used for non-managers and non-executives. PepsiCo, Starbucks, TELUS, and many other companies have broad-based stock option plans that include employees below the executive level. The trend toward broad-based plans is aimed at providing support for the competitive strategies being pursued by many firms today. Such companies have been asking more from employees than ever before, but employees often feel that they are corporate "partners" in name only, working harder but receiving little in return. In response,

> [c]ompanies are increasingly interested in drawing employees into the new deal by implementing broad-based stock option plans. By giving stock options to non-executives, companies make good the promise of letting employees share in the company's success.[23]

EXHIBIT 16-3 Distribution of Stock Option Deduction by Income, 2007

Individual's total income[1] ($)	Number of individuals claiming a stock option deduction	Stock option deduction claimed		
		Average amount ($)	Aggregate amount ($ millions)	% of total
Under 100,000	32,483	3,000	100	2%
100,000 to 500,000	38,034	23,000	890	22%
Over 500,000	7,985	393,000	3,140	75%
Total	78,502	53,000	4,130	100%

[1] Including stock option benefits
Source: Tax filer data for the 2007 taxation year.
Numbers may not add due to rounding.

Source: Archived - Annex 5: Tax Measures: Supplementary Information and Notices of Ways and Means Motions, http://www.budget.gc.ca/2010/plan/anx5-eng.html#a20, Department of Finance Canada, 2010. Reproduced with the permission of the Minister of Public Works and Government Services Canada, 2012.

Proposals have been made to require that stock options be shown as an expense on company financial statements because the excessive issuing of options dilutes share values for shareholders and creates a distorted impression of the true value of a company. Guidelines used by the Canada Pension Plan Investment Board state the following:

> Stock options are a less effective and less efficient form of compensation than direct share ownership in aligning the interests of directors with those of shareholders, [and] it does not motivate the executive to enhance long-term corporate performance. Stock-based compensation is superior to option-based compensation plans for three broad reasons:
>
> - It provides better alignment of interest of employees with shareholders (across a wide range of future share prices);
> - It is a more efficient form of compensation (in terms of the perceived value received by the executive); and
> - It alters the capital structure in a more predictable way (with less potential dilution and more straightforward accounting treatment).[24]

Plans Providing Share "Units"

Although the use of stock options persists, a new approach based on providing "units" instead of stock has become increasingly common.[25] Executives are granted a specified number of units whose value is equal to (and fluctuates with) a company's share price, subject to certain conditions. A *performance share unit plan* provides units subject to the achievement of predetermined financial targets, such as profit or growth in earnings per share (often over a multiyear period). If the performance goals are met, then the value of the units is paid to the executive in cash or stock. The units have no value if the pre-established performance criteria are not met. In a *restricted share unit plan*, units are promised to the executive but will be forfeited if an executive leaves the company before a vesting period (typically three years). If the executive is still employed at the company after the vesting period, the full value of the units based on the current stock price is payable in cash or stock. In a *deferred share unit plan*, units are promised to the executive but are only payable when the executive leaves the company.

Relating Strategy to Executive Compensation

Executive compensation is more likely to be effective if it is appropriately linked to corporate strategy.[26] Few HR practices have as much connection to strategy as does how the company crafts its long-term incentives. Whether expanding sales through joint ventures abroad, consolidating operations and downsizing the workforce, or some other tactic, few strategies can be accomplished in just one or two years. As a result, the long-term signals that are sent to executives regarding the results and activities that will (or will not) be rewarded can have an impact on whether or not the firm's strategy is implemented effectively. For example, a strategy to boost sales by expanding abroad might suggest linking incentives to increased sales abroad. A cost-reduction strategy might instead emphasize linking incentives to improved profit margins.

Therefore, compensation experts suggest defining the strategic context for the executive compensation plan before creating the compensation package itself, as follows:[27]

1. Define the internal and external issues that face the company and its business objectives—boosting sales abroad, downsizing, and so on.

2. Based on the strategic aims, shape each component of the executive compensation package and then group the components into a balanced whole. Include a stock option plan to give the executive compensation package the special character it needs to meet the unique needs of the executives and the company.

3. Check the executive compensation plan for compliance with all legal and regulatory requirements and for tax effectiveness.

4. Install a process for reviewing and evaluating the executive compensation plan whenever a major business change occurs.

Incentives for Salespeople

Sales compensation plans have typically relied heavily on incentives (sales commissions), although this varies by industry. In the real estate industry, for instance, salespeople are paid entirely via commissions, while in the pharmaceutical industry, salespeople tend to be paid a salary. However, the most prevalent approach is to use a combination of salary and commissions to compensate salespeople.[28]

The widespread use of incentives for salespeople is due to three factors: tradition, the unsupervised nature of most sales work, and the assumption that incentives are needed to motivate salespeople. The pros and cons of salary, commission, and combination plans follow.

Sales Compensation **www.davekahle.com/article/ getem.html**

Salary Plan

In a salary plan, salespeople are paid a fixed salary, although there may be occasional incentives in the form of bonuses, sales contest prizes, and the like. There are several reasons to use straight salary. It works well when the main sales objective is prospecting (finding new clients) or when the salesperson is mostly involved in account servicing, such as developing and executing product training programs for a distributor's sales force or participating in national and local trade shows.[29] Jobs like these are often found in industries that sell technical products. This is one reason why the aerospace and transportation equipment industries have a relatively heavy emphasis on salary plans for their salespeople.

There are advantages to paying salespeople on a straight salary basis. Sales-people know in advance what their income will be, and the employer also has fixed, predictable sales force expenses. Straight salary makes it simple to switch territories or quotas or to reassign salespeople, and it can develop a high degree of loyalty among the sales staff. Commissions tend to shift the salesperson's emphasis to making the sale rather than to prospecting and cultivating long-term customers. A long-term perspective is encouraged by straight salary compensation.

The main disadvantage is that salary plans do not depend on results.[30] In fact, salaries are often tied to seniority rather than to performance, which can be demotivating to potentially high-performing salespeople who see seniority—not performance—being rewarded.

Commission Plan

Commission plans pay salespeople in direct proportion to their sales—they pay for results and only for results. The commission plan has several advantages. Salespeople have the greatest possible incentive, and there is a tendency to attract high-performing salespeople who see that effort will clearly lead to rewards. Sales costs are proportional to sales rather than fixed, and the company's selling investment is reduced. The commission basis is also easy to understand and compute.

The commission plan also has drawbacks, however. Salespeople focus on making a sale and on high-volume items; cultivating dedicated customers and working to push hard-to-sell items may be neglected. Wide variances in income between salespeople may occur and this can lead to a feeling that the plan is inequitable. More serious is the fact that salespeople are encouraged to neglect other duties, like servicing small accounts. In addition, pay is often excessive in boom times and very low in recessions.

An Ethical | Dilemma

Is it fair to compensate sales employees on a 100 percent commission basis with no financial security?

Research | INSIGHT

Recent research evidence presents further insights into the impact of sales commissions. One study addressed whether paying salespeople on commission "without a financial net" might induce more salespeople to leave. The participants in this study were 225 field sales representatives from a telecommunications company. Results showed that paying salespeople a commission accounting for 100 percent of pay was the situation that resulted in the highest turnover of salespersons by far. Turnover was much lower in the situation in which salespeople are paid a combination of a base salary plus commissions.[31] These findings suggest that although 100 percent commissions can drive higher sales by focusing the attention of strong-willed salespeople on maximizing sales, without a financial safety net it can also undermine the desire of salespeople to stay.

The effects on the salesperson of a commission pay plan could also depend on that person's personality. A second study investigated 154 sales representatives who were responsible for contacting and renewing existing members and for identifying and adding new members. A number of the sales reps in this study were more extroverted than were the others—they were more sociable, outgoing, talkative, aggressive, energetic, and enthusiastic.[32] It might be expected that extroverted salespeople would usually generate higher sales than less extroverted ones, but in this study extroversion was positively associated with higher performance (in terms of percentage of existing members renewing their memberships and the count of new members paying membership fees) *only when the salespeople were explicitly rewarded for accomplishing these tasks.* Thus, being extroverted did not always lead to higher sales; extroverts only sold more than those less extroverted when their rewards were contingent on their performance.

Combination Plan

There has been a definite movement away from the extremes of straight commission or fixed salary to combination plans for salespeople. Combination plans provide some of the advantages of both straight salary and straight commission plans and also some of their disadvantages. Salespeople have a floor to their earnings. Furthermore, the company can direct its salespeople's activities by detailing what services the salary component is being paid for, while the commission component provides a built-in incentive for superior performance.

However, the salary component is not tied to performance, and the employer is therefore trading away some incentive value. Combination plans also tend to become complicated, and misunderstandings can result. This might not be a problem with a simple "salary plus commission" plan, but most plans are not so simple. For example, there is a "commission plus drawing account" plan, whereby a salesperson is paid basically on commissions but can draw on future earnings to get through low sales periods. Similarly, in the "commission plus bonus" plan, salespeople are again paid primarily on the basis of commissions, but they are also given a small bonus for directed activities, like selling slow-moving items.

An example can help to illustrate the complexities of the typical combination plan. In one company, the following three-step formula is applied:

- Step 1: Sales volume up to $18 000 a month—Base salary plus 7 percent of gross profits plus 0.5 percent of gross sales.

- Step 2: Sales volume from $18 000 to $25 000 a month—Base salary plus 9 percent of gross profits plus 0.5 percent of gross sales.

- Step 3: Sales volume more than $25 000 a month—Base salary plus 10 percent of gross profits plus 0.5 percent of gross sales.

In all cases, base salary is paid every two weeks, while the earned percentage of gross profits and gross sales is paid monthly. It should be remembered that setting sales goals or targets is complex and requires careful planning and analysis. Answers to such questions as why $18 000 and $25 000 were chosen as break points must be available.[33]

The sales force also may get various special awards.[34] Trips and high-tech items such as BlackBerrys and iPhones are commonly used as sales prizes.

Tips | FOR THE FRONT LINE

Sales Compensation in the E-commerce Era

Traditional product-based sales compensation focuses on the amount of product sold. In the Internet age, an integrated team of individuals works together to position the company with prospects, make sales, and service accounts. All sales team members work to deepen customer relationships. This new approach is due to the fact that, for customers who know what they want, rapid low-cost purchases can be made over the Internet. Face-to-face sales are now reserved for high-volume customers and higher-margin services.

Sales incentive plans now need to encourage the sales force to focus on the customer, integrate with e-commerce, and support rapid change. Cross-selling incentives (making multiple sales of different product lines to the same customer) are more important, along with incentives for relationship management and customer satisfaction. Experts recommend setting sales salaries at 50 to 75 percent of total expected compensation, plus incentives. A portion of the incentive should be tied to team-based sales results to encourage sharing, hand-offs, and peer pressure.[35]

Incentives for other Managers and Professionals

Merit pay or a **merit raise** is any salary increase that is awarded to an employee based on his or her individual performance. It is different from a bonus in that it usually represents a continuing increment, whereas the bonus represents a one-time payment. Although the term "merit pay" can apply to the incentive raises given to any employees—office or factory, management or non-management—the term is more often used with respect to white-collar employees, and particularly professional, office, and clerical employees.

Merit pay has both advocates and detractors and is the subject of much debate.[36] Advocates argue that only pay or other rewards tied directly to performance can motivate improved performance. They contend that the effect of awarding identical pay raises to all employees (without regard to individual performance) may actually detract from performance by showing employees that they will be rewarded the same regardless of how they perform.

Conversely, merit pay detractors present good reasons why merit pay can backfire. One is that the usefulness of the merit pay plan depends on the validity of the performance appraisal system, because if performance appraisals are viewed as unfair, so too will the merit pay that is based on them. Second, supervisors often tend to minimize differences in employee performance when computing merit raises. They give most employees about the same raise, either because of a reluctance to alienate some employees or a desire to give everyone a raise that will at least help them to stay even with the cost of living. A third problem is that almost every employee thinks that he or she is an above-average performer; being paid a below-average merit increase can thus be demoralizing. Finally, some believe that merit pay pits employees against each other and harms team spirit.[37]

merit pay (merit raise) Any salary increase awarded to an employee based on his or her individual performance.

However, although problems like these can undermine a merit pay plan, the consensus of opinion is that merit pay can and does improve performance. It is critical, however, that performance appraisals be carried out effectively.[38]

Traditional merit pay plans have two basic characteristics: (1) Merit increases are usually granted to employees at a designated time of the year in the form of a higher base salary (or *raise*); and (2) the merit raise is usually based exclusively on individual performance, although the overall level of company profits may affect the total sum available for merit raises.[39] In some cases, merit raises are awarded in a single lump sum once a year, without changing base salary. Occasionally, awards are tied to both individual and organizational performance.

Incentives for Professional Employees

Professional employees are those whose work involves the application of learned knowledge to the solution of the employer's problems. They include lawyers, doctors, economists, and engineers. Professionals almost always reach their positions through prolonged periods of formal study.[40]

Pay decisions regarding professional employees involve unique problems. One is that, for most professionals, money has historically been somewhat less important as an incentive than it has been for other employees. This is true partly because professionals tend to be paid well anyway and partly because they are already driven by the desire to produce high-calibre work and receive recognition from colleagues.

However, that is not to say that professionals do not want financial incentives. For example, studies in industries like pharmaceuticals and aerospace consistently show that firms with the most productive research and development groups have incentive pay plans for their professionals, usually in the form of bonuses. However, professionals' bonuses tend to represent a relatively small portion of their total pay. The time cycle of the professionals' incentive plans also tends to be longer than a year, reflecting the long time spent in designing, developing, and marketing a new product.

There are also many non-salary items that professionals must have to do their best work. Not strictly incentives, these items range from better equipment and facilities and a supportive management style to support for professional journal publications.

Organization-Wide Incentive Plans

Many employers have incentive plans in which virtually all employees can participate. These include profit-sharing, employee stock ownership, and gainsharing plans.

Profit-Sharing Plans

In a **profit-sharing plan**, most or all employees receive a share of the company's profits. Fewer than 15 percent of Canadian organizations offer profit-sharing plans.[41] These plans are easy to administer and have a broad appeal to employees and other company stakeholders. In addition to helping attract, retain, and motivate workers, profit-sharing plans have tax advantages for employees, including tax deferrals and income splitting. The main weakness of profit-sharing plans is "line of sight." It is unlikely that most employees perceive that they personally have the ability to influence overall company profit. It has been found that these plans produce a one-time productivity improvement but no change thereafter. Another weakness of these plans is that they typically provide an annual payout, which is not as effective as more frequent payouts.[42]

There are several types of profit-sharing plans. In *cash plans*, the most popular, a percentage of profits (usually 15 to 20 percent) is distributed as profit shares at regular intervals. One example is Atlas-Graham Industries in Winnipeg. There, a profit-sharing pool is calculated by deducting 2 percent of sales from pre-tax profit and then taking

profit-sharing plan A plan whereby most or all employees share in the company's profits.

30 percent of the result. The pool is distributed equally among all employees. Other plans provide cash and deferred benefits. Fisheries Products International in St. John's, Newfoundland, contributes 10 percent of pre-tax income to a profit-sharing pool that is divided up, just before Christmas, based on each employee's earnings. The first 75 percent of each employee's share is paid in cash, and the remaining 25 percent is allocated to pension plan improvements.[43]

Employee Share Purchase/Stock Ownership Plan

Employee share purchase/stock ownership plans (ESOPs) are in place at approximately 60 percent of Canadian organizations with publicly traded stock.[44] A trust is established to purchase shares of the firm's stock for employees by using cash from employee (and sometimes employer) contributions. Employers may also issue treasury shares to the trust instead of paying cash for a purchase on the open market. The trust holds the stock in individual employee accounts and distributes it to employees, often on retirement or other separation from service. Some plans distribute the stock to employees once a year.

The corporation receives a tax deduction equal to the fair market value of the shares that are purchased by the trustee by using employer contributions, but not for any treasury shares issued. The value of the shares purchased with employer contributions, and of any treasury shares issued, is a taxable benefit to the employees in the year of purchase of the shares. This tax treatment can create two problems. First, if the plan requires employees to complete a certain period of service before taking ownership of the shares and the employee leaves before being eligible for ownership, the employee has paid tax on the value of shares that he or she never owns. Therefore, most plans have immediate vesting.[45] Second, if the value of the shares drops, employees may have paid tax on a greater amount than they will receive when they eventually sell the shares.

ESOPs can encourage employees to develop a sense of ownership in and commitment to the firm, particularly when combined with good communication, employee involvement in decision making, and employee understanding of the business and the economic environment.[46] For example, one employee at Creo, a digital products company in Burnaby, British Columbia, that offers an ESOP said, "It's not just the shares. It's the way of thinking. I'm extremely happy here."[47]

Gainsharing Plans

A **gainsharing plan** is an incentive plan that engages many or all employees in a common effort to achieve a company's productivity objectives; any resulting incremental cost-saving gains are shared among employees and the company.[48] Popular types of gainsharing plans include the Rucker and improshare plans.

The basic difference between these plans is in the formula used to determine employee bonuses.[49] The Rucker formula uses sales value minus materials and supplies, all divided into payroll expenses. It includes participative management systems that use committees. The improshare plan creates production standards for each department. It does not include a participative management component but instead considers participation an outcome of the bonus plan.

The financial aspects of a gainsharing program can be quite straightforward. Assume that a supplier wants to boost quality. Doing so would translate into fewer customer returns, less scrap and rework, and therefore higher profits. Historically, $1 million in output results in $20 000 (2 percent) scrap, returns, and rework. The company tells its employees that if next month's production results in only 1 percent scrap, returns, and rework, the 1 percent saved would be a gain to be split 50/50 with the workforce, less a small amount reserved for months in which scrap exceeds 2 percent. Awards are often posted monthly but allocated quarterly.[50]

Hints | TO ENSURE LEGAL COMPLIANCE

National Center for Employee Ownership
www.nceo.org

employee share purchase/stock ownership plan (ESOP) A plan whereby a trust is established to hold shares of company stock purchased for or issued to employees. The trust distributes the stock to employees on retirement, separation from service, or as otherwise prescribed by the plan.

gainsharing plan An incentive plan that engages employees in a common effort to achieve productivity objectives and share the gains.

Gainsharing works well in stable organizations with predictable goals and measures of performance, but is less flexible and useful in dynamic industries that require rapid business adjustment. In general, most of their cost savings are generated in the early years.[51] For example, in 2011, US Airways announced that its employees would receive profit-sharing payouts totalling more than $47 million associated with the previous year's financial performance success. US Airways' chair and chief executive officer, Doug Parker, said, "Thank you and congratulations to our professional team members on an outstanding 2010. Our team ran a safe, reliable airline in 2010, completing more scheduled flights and delivering baggage more reliably than our network peers. Our customers have noticed the turnaround and our financial results reflect these positive results." Individual employee payouts vary by the employee's base salary and collective bargaining agreement. In addition, US Airways' employees also received more than $25 million in operational incentive bonuses and individual employee recognition rewards in 2010.[52]

Developing Effective Incentive Plans

There are two major practical considerations in developing an effective incentive plan: when to use it and how to implement it.

When to Use Incentives

Before deciding to implement an incentive plan, it is important to remember several points:

1. *Performance pay cannot replace good management.* Performance pay is supposed to motivate workers, but lack of motivation is not always the culprit. Ambiguous instructions, lack of clear goals, inadequate employee selection and training, unavailability of tools, and a hostile workforce (or management) are just a few of the factors that impede performance.

2. *Firms get what they pay for.* Psychologists know that people often put their effort where they know they will be rewarded. However, this can backfire. An incentive plan that rewards a group based on how many pieces are produced could lead to rushed production and lower quality. Awarding a plant-wide incentive for reducing accidents may simply reduce the number of reported accidents.

3. *"Pay is not a motivator."*[53] Psychologist Frederick Herzberg makes the point that money only buys temporary compliance; as soon as the incentive is removed, the "motivation" disappears too. Instead, Herzberg says, employers should provide adequate financial rewards and then build other motivators, like opportunities for achievement and psychological success, into their jobs.

4. *Rewards rupture relationships.* Incentive plans have the potential for reducing teamwork by encouraging individuals (or individual groups) to blindly pursue financial rewards for themselves.

5. *Rewards may undermine responsiveness.* Since the employees' primary focus is on achieving some specific goal, like cutting costs, any changes or extraneous distractions mean that achieving that goal will be harder. Incentive plans can, therefore, mediate against change and responsiveness.

Research by two professors at the University of Alberta focused on resolving a longstanding debate about whether extrinsic rewards can backfire by reducing intrinsic motivation, or whether extrinsic rewards boost performance and enhance intrinsic motivation. The authors concluded that *careful* management of rewards does enhance performance. Common problem areas to be avoided include not tying rewards to performance, not delivering on all rewards initially promised, and delivering rewards in an authoritarian style or manner.[54]

Potential pitfalls like these do not mean that financial incentive plans cannot be useful or should not be used. They do suggest, however, that goals need to be reasonable and achievable, but not so easily attained that employees view incentives as entitlements.[55] In general, any incentive plan is more apt to succeed if implemented with management support, employee acceptance, and a supportive culture characterized by teamwork, trust, and involvement at all levels.[56] This probably helps to explain why some of the longest-lasting incentive plans, like the improshare and Rucker plans, depend heavily on two-way communication and employee involvement in addition to incentive pay.

Nelson Motivation Inc.
www.drbobnelson.com

Therefore, in general, it makes more sense to use an incentive plan when units of output can be measured, the job is standardized, the workflow is regular, and delays are few or consistent. It is also important that there be a clear relationship between employee effort and quantity of output and that quality is less important than quantity, or, if quality is important, that it is easily measured and controlled.

How to Implement Incentive Plans

There are several specific common-sense considerations in establishing any incentive plan. Of primary importance is "line of sight." The employee or group must be able to see their own impact on the goals or objectives for which incentives are being provided.[57]

Research indicates that there are seven principles that support effective implementation of incentive plans that lead to superior business results:

1. Pay for performance—and make sure that performance is tied to the successful achievement of critical business goals.

2. Link incentives to other activities that engage employees in the business, such as career development and challenging opportunities.

3. Link incentives to measurable competencies that are valued by the organization.

4. Match incentives to the culture of the organization—its vision, mission, and operation principles.

5. Keep group incentives clear and simple—employee understanding is the most important factor differentiating effective from ineffective group incentive plans.

6. Overcommunicate—employees become engaged when they hear the message that they are neither faceless nor expendable.

7. Remember that the greatest incentive is the work itself. For example, highly skilled engineers at MacDonald Dettwiler and Associates Ltd. in Richmond, British Columbia, feel valued and appreciated when they are chosen by their peers to work on project teams, to work on the Canada space arm, or to work on a project to save the rainforest, and they don't require large financial incentives to work hard.

Tips | FOR THE FRONT LINE

Employee Recognition Programs

In today's fast-changing environment, recognition is emerging as a critical component of the total rewards mix.[58] Why? Because lack of recognition and praise is the number one reason that employees leave an organization. The traditional role of recognition plans has been to reward employees for long service, but today's employees value being appreciated by an employer throughout their career. In fact, recent Japanese research has shown that people get as excited about receiving a compliment as they do about receiving a cash reward because both activate the same reward centre in the brain (the striatum).[59]

An employee's introduction to a corporate recognition culture needs to start on the day he or she is hired. For example, the employee could receive a welcome note, a nameplate, and a personalized gift pack that includes a company T-shirt and coffee mug. These things are all very easy to do, and they send a clear message to a new employee.[60] Recognition and other simple incentives are particularly effective in smaller entrepreneurial companies.

Employees consistently say that they receive little recognition. One study found that only 50 percent of managers give recognition for high performance, and that up to 40 percent of workers feel that they never get recognized for outstanding performance. Nurses are one group of employees that has long suffered from lack of respect. They feel ignored and undervalued as subservient assistants to doctors. The shortage of nurses in Canada has forced employers to consider treating nurses with the respect and recognition they deserve as invaluable contributors of knowledge and skills to the healthcare system.[61]

Some believe that this lack of recognition occurs because expressing generous appreciation means talking about feelings in public, which may make managers feel vulnerable. However, when lack of recognition and praise is resulting in the loss of valued employees, managers need to confront such apprehension and start recognizing their employees for their achievements. Why? Because employees favour recognition from supervisors and managers by a margin of two-to-one over recognition from other sources.[62] Thus, line managers are critical to the success of recognition programs.

Recognition is also cost-effective. It takes 5 to 15 percent of pay to have an impact on behaviour when a cash reward is provided, but only 3 to 5 percent when a non-cash form of reward is used (such as recognition and modest gifts).[63] Company DNA, an incentives provider, offers an online points system where recognition points can be spent on merchandise with merchant partners, such as Eddie Bauer, La Senza, Canadian Tire, and Future Shop.[64] There appears to be a growing interest by employees in having recognition awards linked to "green" or charitable causes, such as time off for volunteering.[65] The most common recognition awards are shown in Exhibit 16-4.

Effective recognition is specific, immediate, personal, and spontaneous. Making time to recognize the individual in front of his or her colleagues is critical to the success of the program. Personal attention and public celebration create recognition that is personal in nature and that addresses the deep needs that we all have for belonging and contributing to something worthwhile. By making it memorable, the recognition experience will continue to evoke emotion and make the employee feel that his or her individual effort made a difference.

Recognition programs are more effective than cash in achieving improved employee attitudes, increased workloads and hours of work, and improved productivity (speed of work/intensity of work). They can build confidence, create a positive and supportive environment, build a sense of pride in accomplishments, inspire people to increase their efforts, and help people feel valued. Recognition can act as a strategic change effort if recognition criteria are aligned with business strategy, employee input is solicited regarding program design and implementation, and a recognition culture is created.[66]

Recognition is also important for high performers, who focus on what needs to be done to exceed expectations. These employees are driven by internal motivation and look to reward programs to add fuel to their achievements. Recognition satisfies "wants" rather than "needs" (where cash bonuses often go); such programs eliminate guilt about owning luxury items, provide bragging rights, and create a lasting impression in the employee's memory.[67]

Recognition Plus, Inc.
www.recognitionplusinc.com

Recognition Professionals International
www.recognition.org

O.C. Tanner Recognition Co.
www.octanner.ca

EXHIBIT 16-4 Common Recognition Awards

Certificates and plaques continue to be the most common form of recognition to employees, according to a survey of 614 North American organizations by WorldatWork and the National Association for Employee Recognition in 2005. Nearly nine out of every ten organizations (89 percent) offer some form of recognition to staff. Below is a list of various items and the percentage of respondents that offer them.

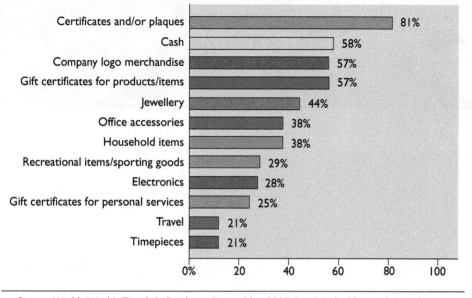

Source: *WorldatWork's Trends in Employee Recognition 2005.* Reprinted with permission of WorldatWork, Scottsdale, AZ. www.worldatwork.org.

Finally, recognition programs are key corporate communication tools that can achieve several goals—saying thank you, encouraging good workers, and encouraging behaviour that supports strategic objectives.[68] RBC Financial Group, Fairmont Hotels and Resorts, Research In Motion, Procor Limited, Montana's Cookhouse, Minto Developments Inc., Alberta Milk, Southland Transportation, and Snow Valley Edmonton are just some of the Canadian companies that are reaping the benefits of employee recognition programs.[69]

17

Employee Benefits and Services

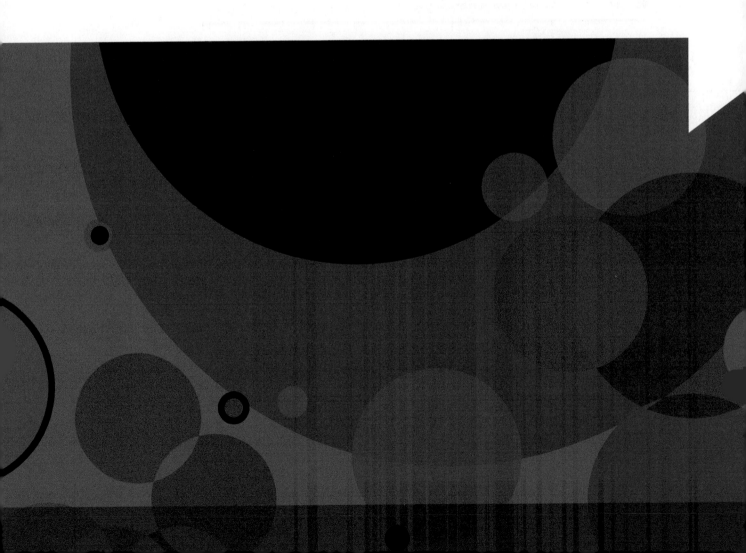

The Strategic Role of Employee Benefits

Employee benefits and services can be defined as all the indirect financial payments that an employee receives during his or her employment with an employer.[1] Benefits are generally provided to all of a firm's employees and include such things as time off with pay, supplementary health and life insurance, and employee assistance plans. Employee services, traditionally a minor aspect of compensation, are becoming more sought after by today's employees in the post-job-security era. Research indicates that benefits do matter to employees and that, if they are aligned with business strategy, they can help to attract and retain the right people to achieve business objectives.[2] Alberta's AltaGas Ltd. uses benefits to help them compete for talented workers in the ultra-competitive Alberta labour market.

Employee benefits are an important part of most employees' compensation, particularly given today's reality of modest salary increases.[3] For the aging workforce, healthcare benefits are becoming increasingly important. Employee benefits are in the midst of an evolution based on the aging population, the looming labour shortage in Canada, and advances in healthcare. Each of these factors is expected to increase the cost of benefits, which is already at an all-time high.[4]

Administering benefits today represents an increasingly specialized task, because workers are more financially sophisticated and demanding and because benefit plans must comply with a wide variety of laws. Providing and administering benefits is also an increasingly expensive task. Benefits as a percentage of payroll (for public and private sectors combined) are approximately 37 percent today (compared with about 15 percent in 1953). Most employees do not realize the market value and high cost to the employer of their benefits.

Certain benefits are mandated by law, and most Canadian companies voluntarily provide additional employee benefits such as group life insurance, health and dental care insurance, and retirement benefits. In the remainder of this chapter, government-sponsored benefits, voluntary employer-sponsored benefits, employee services, flexible benefits, and benefits administration will be discussed.

Government-Mandated Benefits

Canada has one of the world's finest collections of social programs to protect its citizens when they cannot earn income. Employers and employees provide funding for these plans, along with general tax revenues.

Employment Insurance (EI)

Employment insurance (EI) is a federal program intended to provide temporary financial assistance to eligible persons who experience interruption to their work through no fault of their own. EI benefits are not payable when an employee is terminated for just cause—for example, for theft of company property—or when an employee quits for no good reason. EI is perceived to be a benefit, since it provides employees who are laid off, terminated without just cause, or who quit their job for a justifiable reason (such as harassment) with an alternative form of government income until they secure employment.

In addition to loss of employment through no fault of the employee, eligibility is also restricted to persons who have paid into the account (for example, a contractor who does not contribute to the EI account is ineligible for the benefit), have worked a minimum number of hours in a specified time, and are willing and able to work.

The EI benefit is generally 55 percent of average earnings during the last 14 to 45 weeks of the qualifying period or a maximum weekly rate (for example, as of January 1, 2012, in Ontario the maximum weekly rate was $485), depending on the regional

---

Benefits Interface
www.benefits.org

Employee Benefit Research Institute
www.ebri.org

BenefitsLink.com
www.benefitslink.com

Benefits Canada
www.benefitscanada.ca

employee benefits Indirect financial payments given to employees. They may include supplementary health and life insurance, vacation, pension plans, education plans, and discounts on company products.

employment insurance (EI) A federal program intended to provide temporary financial assistance to eligible persons who experience interruption to their work through no fault of their own.

unemployment rate. The benefit is payable for up to 45 weeks, depending on factors like the regional unemployment rate. To continue receiving EI benefits, individuals must demonstrate that they are actively seeking work. Claimants are encouraged to work part time, as they can earn up to 25 percent of their EI benefit amount before these earnings will be deducted from the benefit.

To receive benefits, an employee must first have worked a minimum number of hours during a minimum number of weeks called a *qualifying period* (the number of hours and weeks varies among regions of the country). Then there is a waiting period from the last day of work until benefits begin. The waiting period varies but is often two weeks. If the employee was provided with severance pay or holiday pay at the time of losing the job, these payments must run out before the waiting period begins.

The EI program is funded by contributions from eligible employees and their employers. Employee contributions are collected by payroll deduction, and employers pay 1.4 times the employee contribution. Employer contributions can be reduced if the employer provides a wage loss replacement plan for employee sick leave.

A supplemental unemployment benefit (SUB) plan is an agreement between an employer and the employees (often the result of collective bargaining) for a plan that enables employees who are eligible for EI benefits to receive additional benefits from a SUB fund created by the employer. SUB plans help employees maintain their standard of living during periods of unemployment (most often maternity leave) by receiving a combined benefit closer to their actual working wage. Most SUBs provide benefits of 90 percent of the working wage or greater.[5] Work-sharing programs are a related arrangement in which employees work a reduced workweek and receive EI benefits for the remainder of the week. The Canada Employment Insurance Commission must approve SUB plans and work-sharing programs.

Hints | TO ENSURE LEGAL COMPLIANCE

Income Security Programs
www.hrsdc.gc.ca/eng/corporate/ about_us/hrsdc_branches. shtml#issd

Pay on Termination of Employment

Employment/labour standards legislation requires that employees whose employment is being terminated by the employer be provided with termination pay when they leave. The amount to be paid varies among jurisdictions and with the circumstances, as follows. Specifically, it should be noted that often employees confuse severance pay with reasonable advanced notice pay.

Reasonable Advance Notice Periods

An employee must be provided with advance written notice if the employer is going to terminate his or her employment, unless the employee is working on a short-term contract or is being fired for just cause (such as continued poor performance, theft, or if the employee initiated the termination of employment). The amount of advance notice that is required applies only to employees whose employment relationship is terminated through no cause of their own, increases with the length of employment of the employee (e.g. one week per year of employment to a specified maximum), and varies among jurisdictions. In practice, many employers do not provide advance written notice. Instead, they ask the employee to cease working immediately and provide the employee with a lump-sum equal to their pay for the notice period. This amount is called **pay in lieu of reasonable notice**.

Severance Pay

Employees only in Ontario and the federal jurisdiction may be eligible for severance pay in addition to pay in lieu of notice in certain termination situations (no other jurisdictions mandate severance pay). For example, in Ontario, employees with five or more years of service may be eligible for severance pay if (1) the employer's annual Ontario payroll is $2.5 million or more, or (2) the employer is closing down the business and

pay in lieu of reasonable notice
A lump-sum equal to an employee's pay for the notice period provided to employees who cease working immediately.

50 or more employees will be losing their jobs within a six-month period. The amount of the severance pay is one week's pay for each year of employment (maximum 26 weeks). In the federal jurisdiction system, employees who have been employed for 12 months or more receive the greater of either two days' worth of wages for every year employed with the company or a total of five days' wages (for example, an employee who has been with the company for one year would be entitled to five days' worth of severance, which is the greater of the two options above). Severance pay is an additional payout on top of the minimum notice period requirements and only applies if the specific conditions in the applicable jurisdiction are met.

Pay for Mass Layoffs

The provinces of British Columbia, Manitoba, Ontario, New Brunswick, and Newfoundland and Labrador require that additional pay be provided when a lay-off of 50 or more employees occurs. The rationale behind this regulation is that larger layoffs result in longer time to re-employment, so in cases of larger layoffs the employees are given longer reasonable notice periods. In Nova Scotia and Saskatchewan, additional pay is required if 10 or more employees are being laid off. The amount of additional pay ranges from 6 weeks to 18 weeks, depending on the province and the number of employees being laid off.

Leaves of Absence

All provinces and territories and the federal jurisdiction require unpaid leaves of absence to be provided to employees in certain circumstances. Maternity/parental leave is provided in every jurisdiction (usually after one year of service). The amount of maternity leave is 17 or 18 weeks in each jurisdiction (15 weeks in Alberta), but parental and adoption leaves range from 34 to 52 weeks. Employees who take these leaves of absence are guaranteed their old job or a similar job when they return to work. Parental leave benefits can be taken by one parent or split between both parents.

Bereavement leave on the death of a family member is provided for employees in some but not all jurisdictions. The amount of time off varies by jurisdiction and depends on the closeness of the relationship between the employee and the deceased. Bereavement leave is usually unpaid, but in some cases it can be partially or fully paid. All jurisdictions except Alberta provide compassionate care leave for employees who are caring for a critically or terminally ill relative (six weeks of EI is payable during these leaves).[6] Quebec has extended compassionate leave to cover situations where close family members are victims of criminal acts, commit suicide, or where a child disappears.[7]

Some employers provide full or partial pay for all or part of legally required unpaid leaves by "topping up" what employees receive from EI, such that the total amount they receive more closely matches their regular salary. For example, in some cases bereavement leave may be partially or fully paid by the employer.

Having a clear procedure for any leave of absence is essential. An application form, such as the one in Exhibit 17-1, should be the centrepiece of any such procedure. In general, no employee should be given a leave until it is clear what the leave is for. If the leave is for medical or family reasons, medical certification should be obtained from the attending physician or medical practitioner. A form like this creates a record of the employee's expected return date and the fact that, without an authorized extension, his or her employment may be terminated.

Although these leaves are unpaid, it is incorrect to assume that the leave is costless to the employer. For example, one study concluded that the costs associated with recruiting new temporary workers, training replacement workers, and compensating for the lower level of productivity of these workers could represent a substantial expense over and above what employers would normally pay their full-time employees.[8]

EXHIBIT 17-1 Sample Application for Leave of Absence

APPLICATION FOR LEAVE
(SUPPORT STAFF)

This form is used by all Support Staff employees to record applications for leave of one-half day duration or longer.

UNB
UNIVERSITY OF
NEW BRUNSWICK

HR USE ONLY

| LAST NAME | | FIRST NAME | | DATATEL / EMPLOYEE ID# | |

DEPARTMENT ○ **UNBF** ○ **UNBSJ**

TYPE OF LEAVE	DATES (use separate forms for each year) Specify first and last day of leave for those longer than 1 day. Show A.M. or P.M. for half days.	# OF WORK DAYS
VACATION		
SICK		

	START DATE	END DATE		HR USE ONLY
MATERNITY				
PARENTAL				

	START DATE	END DATE	# of DAYS	
BEREAVEMENT				Relative:
EMERGENCY				Reason:
LEAVE WITHOUT PAY if over 30 days needs VP approval				Reason:
OTHER				Reason:

ADDITIONAL DETAILS:

EMPLOYEE SIGNS HERE _____

09-07-14

DATE

APPROVAL

_____   _____   _____
RECOMMENDED   POSITION   DATE

_____   _____   _____
APPROVED   POSITION   DATE

FORWARD COMPLETED FORMS TO:

UNBF
 HUMAN RESOURCES
 ROOM 102
 I.U.C. COMPLEX

UNBSJ
 FINANCIAL & ADMINISTRATIVE SERVICES
 ROOMS 114,115
 OLAND HALL

HR USE ONLY   POSTED ON:

Source: Prepared by University of New Brunswick Human Resources. Used by permission.

Canada/Quebec Pension Plan (C/QPP)

The **Canada/Quebec Pension Plans (C/QPP)** were introduced in 1966 to provide working Canadians with a basic level of financial security on retirement or disability. Four decades later, these benefits do indeed provide a significant part of most Canadians' retirement income. Almost all employed Canadians between the ages of 18 and 65 are covered, including self-employed individuals. Casual and migrant workers are excluded, as are people who are not earning any employment income, such as homemakers or volunteers. The benefits are portable, meaning that pension rights are not affected by changes in job or residence within Canada. Both contributions and benefits are based only on earnings up to the "year's maximum pensionable earnings" (intended to approximate the average industrial wage), as defined in the legislation. Benefits are adjusted based on inflation each year in line with the consumer price index. Contributions made by employees (4.95 percent of pensionable earnings as of January 2012) are matched by employers.

Three types of benefits are provided: retirement pensions, disability pensions, and survivor benefits. The *retirement pension* is calculated as 25 percent of the average earnings (adjusted for inflation up to the average inflation level during the last five years before retirement) over the years during which contributions were made. Plan members can choose to begin receiving benefits at any time between the ages of 60 and 70. Benefits are reduced on early retirement before age 65 and are increased in the case of late retirement after age 65. *Disability benefits* are only paid for severe disabilities that are expected to be permanent or to last for an extended period. The disability benefit is 75 percent of the pension benefit earned at the date of disability, plus a flat-rate amount per child. *Survivor benefits* are paid on the death of a plan member. A lump-sum payment is made to the plan member's estate, and a monthly pension is also payable to the surviving spouse and each dependent child.

Workers' Compensation

Workers' compensation laws are aimed at providing sure, prompt income and medical benefits to victims of work-related accidents or illnesses or their dependants, regardless of fault. Every province and territory and the federal jurisdiction has its own workers' compensation law. These laws impose compulsory collective liability for workplace accidents and work-related illnesses. This means that employees and employers cannot sue each other regarding the costs of workplace accidents or illnesses. Workers' compensation is, in effect, a "no fault" insurance plan designed to help injured or ill workers get well and return to work. For an injury or illness to be covered by workers' compensation, one must only prove that it arose while the employee was on the job. It does not matter that the employee may have been at fault; if he or she was on the job when the injury or illness occurred, he or she is entitled to workers' compensation. For example, suppose all employees are instructed to wear safety goggles when working at their machines, and one does not and is injured. Workers' compensation benefits will still be provided. The fact that the worker was at fault in no way waives his or her claim to benefits.

Employers collectively pay the full cost of the workers' compensation system, which can be an onerous financial burden for small businesses. The cost varies by industry and with actual employer costs; employer premiums are tax deductible. Workers' compensation boards (or equivalent bodies) exist in each jurisdiction to determine and collect payments from employers, determine rights to compensation, and pay workers the amount of benefit to which they are entitled under the legislation in their jurisdiction. Employers and employees have some representation on these boards, but usually both parties believe they should have more control.

Workers' compensation benefits include payment of expenses for medical treatment and rehabilitation, and income benefits during the time in which the worker is

---

Canada Pension Plan
www.hrsdc.gc.ca/eng/isp/cpp/cpptoc.shtml

Association of Workers' Compensation Boards of Canada
www.awcbc.org

Canada/Quebec Pension Plans (C/QPP) Programs that provide three types of benefits: retirement income; survivor or death benefits payable to the employee's dependants regardless of age at time of death; and disability benefits payable to employees with disabilities and their dependants. Benefits are payable only to those individuals who make contributions to the plans or to their family members.

workers' compensation Workers' compensation provides income and medical benefits to victims of work-related accidents or illnesses or their dependants, regardless of fault.

unable to work (temporarily or permanently) because of his or her disability (partial or total). Survivor benefits are payable if a work-related death occurs. All benefits are non-taxable.

Controlling Workers' Compensation Costs

All parties agree that a renewed focus on accident prevention is the best way to manage workers' compensation costs over the long term. Minimizing the number of workers' compensation claims is an important goal for all employers. Although workers' compensation boards pay the claims, the premiums for most employers depend on the number and amount of claims that are paid. Minimizing such claims is thus important.

In practice, there are two basic approaches to reducing workers' compensation claims. First, firms try to reduce accident- or illness-causing conditions in facilities by instituting effective *safety and health programs* and complying with government safety standards. Second, since workers' compensation costs increase the longer an employee is unable to return to work, employers have become involved in instituting *rehabilitation programs* for injured or ill employees. These include physical therapy programs and career counselling to guide such employees into new, less strenuous or stressful positions. Workers are required to cooperate with return-to-work initiatives, such as modified work.[9] When Purolator's workers' compensation costs came to $13 million, it decided to use both of these approaches to reduce costs. The company hired occupational nurses, conducted physical demands analyses of many of its jobs, strengthened its return-to-work program, tied injury reduction to managers' bonuses, and increased its interaction with doctors.[10]

Vacations and Holidays

Labour/employment standards legislation sets out a minimum amount of paid vacation that must be provided to employees, usually two weeks per year, but the requirements vary by jurisdiction. The actual number of paid employee vacation days also varies considerably from employer to employer. Many employers provide additional paid holidays and paid vacation over and above the amount required by law. Thus, a typical vacation policy might call for

- two weeks for the first 5 years of service

- three weeks for 6 to 10 years of service

- four weeks for 11 to 15 years of service

- five weeks for 16 to 25 years of service

- six weeks after 25 years of service

The number of paid holidays similarly varies considerably from one jurisdiction to another, from a minimum of five to a maximum of nine. The most common paid holidays include New Year's Day, Good Friday, Canada Day, Labour Day, and Christmas and Boxing Day. Other common holidays include Victoria Day, Thanksgiving Day, and Remembrance Day. Additional holidays may be observed in each province, such as Saint-Jean-Baptiste Day in Quebec.

Paid Breaks

While vacation requirements mandate paid time off, in terms of full days of work off, there are also mandated paid and unpaid time off requirements within a work day at the provincial, territorial, or federal level. For example, in Nova Scotia, an employee shift of over five hours requires a minimum 30-minute uninterrupted break. If the employee

Tips | FOR THE FRONT LINE

is under direct control of the employer and expected to be available for work during this time, then the break must be paid. If not, then it can be unpaid. Similar conditions apply in Ontario. Contrary to popular belief, coffee or other rest breaks in addition to the eating period are often not government mandated. If the employee is free to leave the workplace, then the employer does not have to pay for the time.

Voluntary Employer-Sponsored Benefits

Although they are not required to do so, employers often provide many other employee benefits. Several of the most common types of employee benefits will now be described.

Life Insurance

Virtually all employers provide **group life insurance** plans for their employees. As a group, employees can obtain lower rates than if they bought such insurance as individuals. In addition, group plans usually contain a provision for coverage of all employees—including new ones—regardless of health or physical condition.

In most cases, the employer pays 100 percent of the base premium, which usually provides life insurance equal to about two years' salary. Additional life insurance coverage is sometimes made available to employees on an optional, employee-paid basis. *Accidental death and dismemberment* coverage provides a fixed lump-sum benefit in addition to life insurance benefits when death is accidental. It also provides a range of benefits in case of accidental loss of limbs or sight and is often paid for by the employer.

Critical illness insurance provides a lump-sum benefit to an employee who is diagnosed with and survives a life-threatening illness. This benefit bridges the gap between life insurance and disability insurance by providing immediate funds to relieve some the financial burden associated with the illness (such as paying for out-of-country treatment or experimental treatment) or enabling employees to enjoy their remaining time by pursuing activities that would normally be beyond their financial means.[11]

Supplementary Healthcare/Medical Insurance

Most employers provide their employees with supplementary healthcare/medical insurance (over and above that provided by provincial healthcare plans). Along with life insurance and long-term disability, these benefits form the cornerstone of almost all benefits programs.[12] Supplementary healthcare insurance is aimed at providing protection against medical costs arising from off-the-job accidents or illness.

Most supplementary health insurance plans provide insurance at group rates, which are usually lower than individual rates and are generally available to all employees—including new ones—regardless of health or physical condition. Supplementary healthcare plans provide major medical coverage to meet medical expenses not covered by government healthcare plans, including prescription drugs, private or semi-private hospital rooms, private duty nursing, physiotherapy, medical supplies, ambulance services, and so on. In most employer-sponsored drug plans, employees must pay a specified amount of **deductible** expense (typically $25 or $50) per year before plan benefits begin. Many employers also sponsor health-related insurance plans that cover expenses like vision care, hearing aids, and dental services, often with deductibles. In a majority of cases, the participants in such plans have their premiums paid for entirely by their employers.[13]

Reducing Health Benefit Costs

Dramatic increases in healthcare costs are the biggest issue facing benefits managers in Canada today. Exhibit 17-2 shows how increases in medical and dental plan costs have continued to escalate since 2006. The main reasons for these increases are increased

group life insurance Life insurance provided at lower rates for all employees, including new employees, regardless of health or physical condition.

deductible The annual amount of health/dental expenses that an employee must pay before insurance benefits will be paid.

EXHIBIT 17-2 Increases in Health Plan Costs, 2006–2010

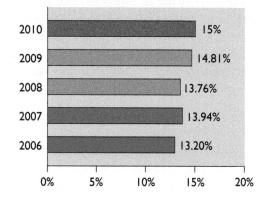

Overall Blended Health Care Trend

2010	15%
2009	14.81%
2008	13.76%
2007	13.94%
2006	13.20%

Source: Canadian Health Care Trend Survey Results 2010 (Toronto ON: Buck Consultants, 2010), p. 2. Reprinted with permission of Buck Consultants, an ACS Company.

use of expensive new drugs and rising drug use by an aging population.[14] Despite government healthcare plans, Canadian employers pay about 30 percent of all healthcare expenses in Canada, most of this for prescription drugs.[15]

Many Canadian managers now find controlling and reducing healthcare costs topping their to-do lists. The simplest approach to reducing health-benefit costs is to *increase the amount of healthcare costs paid by employees*. This can be accomplished by increasing employee premiums, increasing deductibles, reducing company **coinsurance** levels, instituting or lowering annual maximums on some services, or even eliminating coverage for spouses, private hospital rooms, and other benefits. An Angus Reid poll of 1 500 Canadians found that three-quarters of the respondents were willing to pay higher premiums to cover the high cost of prescription drugs.[16]

Another cost-reduction strategy is to publish a *restricted list of drugs* that will be paid for under the plan to encourage the use of generic rather than more expensive brand-name drugs. New drugs may not be covered if equally effective, cheaper alternatives are available. This approach should be combined with employee education to effectively manage the demand for drugs.[17]

A third approach is *health promotion*. In-house newsletters can caution workers to take medication properly and advertise programs on weight management, smoking cessation, exercise classes, onsite massage therapy, nutrition counselling, and other wellness programs. After 10 years of providing an onsite exercise program for employees, Canada Life Assurance Company found that absenteeism dropped 24 percent for employees who exercised two to three times per week.[18] Employee assistance programs can help to combat alcohol and drug addiction and provide stress-management counselling.

A fourth approach is to implement *risk-assessment* programs. Such programs are being used by CIBC and other companies. A third party conducts a confidential survey of the health history and lifestyle choices of employees to identify common health risk factors, such as those associated with heart disease or mental health, so that problem-specific programs can be implemented.[19]

Tips FOR THE FRONT LINE

Public Health Agency of Canada
www.publichealth.gc.ca

coinsurance The percentage of expenses (in excess of the deductible) that are paid for by the insurance plan.

An onsite employee fitness centre

Finally, *healthcare spending accounts* (HCSA) are offered by more than 90 percent of Canadian employers, either alone or in combination with a standard healthcare plan.[20] The employer establishes an annual account for each employee containing a certain amount of money (determined by the employer to control costs). The employee can spend the money on healthcare costs as he or she wants. This provides flexibility for the employee. These accounts are governed by the Income Tax Act, which allows expenses not normally covered under employer-sponsored healthcare plans (such as laser eye surgery) and defines dependants more broadly than most employer plans.[21] HCSAs are very popular with employees, particularly those in Generation Y.

Retiree Health Benefits

Another concern is the cost of health benefits provided to retirees. These benefits typically include life insurance, drugs, and private/semi-private hospital coverage. Some continue coverage to a surviving spouse. Retiree benefit costs are already exceeding the costs for active employees in some organizations, in part because many early retirees between the ages of 50 and 65 are not yet eligible for government health benefits that start at age 65. Employers are required to disclose liabilities for retiree benefits in their financial statements. These liabilities are not required to be pre-funded and thus are at risk in the case of business failure.[22]

An Ethical Dilemma

Should it be the employer's responsibility to cover healthcare costs for early retirees until they become eligible for government healthcare benefits at age 65?

Employers can cut costs by increasing retiree contributions, increasing deductibles, tightening eligibility requirements, and reducing maximum payouts.[23] The last few years have seen a trend away from employer-provided retiree health benefits. This trend is expected to continue as a result of rising healthcare costs, growing retiree populations, uncertain business profitability, and federal regulations that provide only limited opportunities for funding retiree medical benefits.[24]

Short-Term Disability Plans and Sick Leave Plans

Short-term disability plans (also known as salary continuation plans) provide a continuation of all or part of an employee's earnings when the employee is absent from work because of non-work-related illness or injury. Usually a medical certificate is required if the absence extends beyond two or three days. These plans typically provide full pay for some period (often two or three weeks) and then gradually reduce the percentage of earnings paid as the period of absence lengthens. The benefits cease when the employee returns to work or when the employee qualifies for long-term disability. These plans are some-times provided through an insurance company.

Sick leave plans operate quite differently from short-term disability plans. Most sick leave policies grant full pay for a specified number of permissible sick days—usually up to about 12 per year (often accumulated at the rate of one day per month of service). Most jurisdictions require a few days of sick leave (unpaid) as a minimum standard. Sick leave pay creates difficulty for many employers. The problem is that, although many employees use their sick days only when they are legitimately sick, others simply use their sick leave as extensions to their vacations, whether they are sick or not. Also, seriously ill or injured employees get no pay once their sick days are used up.

Some employers now buy back unused sick leave at the end of the year by paying their employees a daily equivalent pay for each sick leave day not used. The drawback is that the policy can encourage legitimately sick employees to come to work despite their illness. Others have experimented with holding monthly lotteries in which only employees with perfect monthly attendance are able to participate; those who participate are eligible to win a cash prize. Still others aggressively investigate

short-term disability and sick leave Plans that provide pay to an employee when he or she is unable to work because of a non-work-related illness or injury.

all absences, for instance by calling the absent employee at their home when they are off sick.

Long-Term Disability

Long-term disability insurance is aimed at providing income protection or compensation for loss of income because of long-term illness or injury that is not work related. The disability payments usually begin when normal short-term disability or sick leave is used up and may continue to provide income to age 65 or beyond. The disability benefits usually range from 50 to 75 percent of the employee's base pay.

The number of long-term disability claims in Canada is rising sharply. This trend is expected to accelerate as the average age of the workforce continues to increase because the likelihood of chronic illness, such as arthritis, heart disease, and diabetes, increases with age. Therefore, disability management programs with a goal of returning workers safely back to work are becoming a priority in many organizations.[25] For example, employers are beginning to put more effort into managing employees with episodic disabilities, which are chronic illnesses such as HIV, lupus, multiple sclerosis, arthritis, and some cancers and mental illnesses that are unpredictable. These employees may have long periods of good health followed by unpredicted episodes of poor health.[26]

Disability management is a proactive, employer-centred process that coordinates the activities of the employer, the insurance company, and healthcare providers in an effort to minimize the impact of injury, disability, or disease on a worker's capacity to successfully perform his or her job. Maintaining contact with a worker who is ill or injured is imperative in disability management so that the worker can be involved in the return-to-work process from the beginning. Ongoing contact also allows the employer to monitor the employee's emotional well-being, which is always affected by illness or injury.[27]

Effective disability management programs include prevention, early assessment and intervention regarding employee health problems, monitoring and management of employee absences, and early and safe return-to-work policies.[28] The three most common approaches to returning a worker with a disability to work are reduced work hours, reduced work duties, and workstation modification.[29] Evaluating the physical capabilities of the worker is an important step in designing work modifications to safely reintegrate injured workers. In many cases, the cost of accommodating an employee's disability can be quite modest.

Mental Health Benefits

Mental health issues continue to be the leading cause of short- and long-term disability claims in Canada. Psychiatric disabilities are the fastest growing of all occupational disabilities, with depression being the most common (even though only 32 percent of those afflicted seek treatment, as they do not want to admit it to their employer).[30]

For Canadian employers, the cost of mental health benefits is about $51 billion annually.[31] Despite the staggering costs, depression is not being addressed in a systematic way, and employers are unprepared to deal with stress, depression, and anxiety in the workplace. Some of the challenges involved in improving this situation are shown in Exhibit 17-3. Only one-third of employers have implemented return-to-work programs specific to mental health. Companies such as Bell Canada, Alcan, and Superior Propane are trying to help reduce costs with prevention and early intervention programs, including psychiatric counselling and peer-support groups.[32]

National Institute of Disability Management and Research **www.nidmar.ca**

Canadian Council on Rehabilitation and Work **www.ccrw.org**

World Federation for Mental Health **www.wfmh.org**

disability management A proactive, employer-centred process that coordinates the activities of the employer, the insurance company, and healthcare providers in an effort to minimize the impact of injury, disability, or disease on a worker's capacity to successfully perform his or her job.

EXHIBIT 17-3 The Top Challenges in Improving How Mental Health Issues Are Addressed in the Workplace

1. Employee perceptions and stigma related to mental health issues	60%
2. Lack of front-line manager awareness	54%
3. Inability to identify suitable modified work	40%
4. Inability to introduce significant flexibility options	39%
5. Lack of tools and supports	29%
6. Lack of funds/budget for program enhancements	23%
7. Lack of senior management buy-in	20%
8. Don't know where to start	14%
9. Other	8%

Source: "What Are the Top Challenges You Face in Improving How Mental Health Issues Are Addressed in Your Workplace?" 2008 Mental Health in the Workplace National Survey (Toronto, ON: Mercer and Canadian Alliance on Mental Illness and Mental Health, 2008), p. 22. Reprinted with permission of Mercer.

Sabbaticals

A few employers provide sabbatical leaves for employees who want time off to rejuvenate or to pursue a personal goal. Sabbatical leaves are usually unpaid, but some employers provide partial or full pay. Sabbaticals can help to retain employees and to avoid employee burnout, without the employee losing job security or seniority.

Retirement Benefits

Employer-sponsored **pension plans** are intended to supplement an employee's government-sponsored retirement benefits, which, on average, makeup 50 percent of the average Canadian's retirement income.[33] Unlike government-provided retirement benefits, employer-sponsored pension plans are pre-funded. Money is set aside in a pension fund to accumulate with investment income until it is needed to pay benefits at retirement. Pension fund assets have grown rapidly over the past 40 years. Much of this money is invested in Canadian stocks and bonds because of laws restricting the investment of these assets in foreign securities.

Two Categories of Pension Plans

Pension plans fall into two categories—defined benefit pension plans and defined contribution pension plans. A **defined benefit pension plan** contains a formula for determining retirement benefits so that the actual benefits to be received are defined ahead of time. For example, the plan might include a formula, such as 2 percent of final year's earnings for each year of service, which would provide a pension of 70 percent of final year's earnings to an employee with 35 years of service.

A **defined contribution pension plan** specifies what contribution the employer will make to a retirement fund set up for the employee. The defined contribution plan does not define the eventual benefit amount, only the periodic contribution to the plan. In a defined benefit plan, the employee knows ahead of time what his or her retirement benefits will be on retirement. With a defined contribution plan, the employee cannot be sure of his or her retirement benefits until retirement, when his or her share of the money in the pension fund is used to buy an annuity. Thus, benefits depend on both the amounts contributed to the fund and the retirement fund's investment earnings.

pension plans Plans that provide income when employees reach a predetermined retirement age.

defined benefit pension plan A plan that contains a formula for determining retirement benefits.

defined contribution pension plan A plan in which the employer's contribution to the employees' retirement fund is specified.

There are two other types of defined contribution arrangements. Under a *group reg-istered retirement savings plan* (*group RRSP*), employees can have a portion of their compensation (which would otherwise be paid in cash) put into an RRSP by the employer. The employee is not taxed on those set-aside dollars until after he or she retires (or removes the money from the plan). Most employers do not match all or a portion of what the employee contributes to the group RRSP because employer contributions are considered taxable income to employees. Instead, the employer often establishes a **deferred profit-sharing plan (DPSP)** and contributes a portion of company profits into the DPSP fund, where an account is set up for each employee. No employee contributions to a DPSP are allowed under Canadian tax law. Group RRSP/DPSP combinations are popular in Canada because no tax is paid until money is received from the plans at the time of the employee's death or termination of employment (at retirement or otherwise).

As shown in Table 17-1, both plans are quite popular, and a few companies use combination or other forms of pension plans.

The entire area of pension planning is complicated, a result of the laws governing pensions. For example, companies want to ensure that their pension contributions are tax deductible and must therefore adhere to the Income Tax Act. The provincial and federal jurisdictions also have laws governing employer-sponsored pension plans. In some cases, the complicated and overlapping federal and provincial legislation can make employers question whether or not to sponsor a pension plan.[34] Legislation regarding pension plans varies around the world, and Canada's regulators can learn important lessons from other countries' successes and failures.

Employers must pay careful attention to their obligation to educate and inform (but not advise) plan members about pension investments. There have been cases where plan members who were unhappy with the information provided by the employer and surprised by small benefits have sued their employers and won. Conversely, the University of Western Ontario plan converted to defined contribution in 1970, and faculty members are retiring with incomes greater than their working salaries.[35]

Canadian Association for Retired Persons
www.carp.ca

Benefits and Pensions Monitor
www.bpmmagazine.com

Association of Canadian Pension Management
www.acpm.com

deferred profit-sharing plan (DPSP) A plan in which a certain amount of company profits is credited to each employee's account, payable at retirement, termination, or death.

TABLE 17-1 Registered Pension Plans by Type, 2006–2010

A	B	C	D	E	F
	2006	2007	2008	2009	2010
Defined benefit plans	50.30%	59.46%	60.15%	61.05%	61.40%
Defined contribution plans	47.56%	38.51%	37.35%	35.88%	35.47%
Composite or combination plans[1]	0.99%	0.77%	0.73%	0.71%	0.66%
Defined benefit and contribution plans	0.59%	0.78%	1.30%	2.03%	2.21%
Other types of plans[2]	1.14%	1.26%	1.78%	2.36%	2.47%

[1]In composite or combination plans, the pension has both defined benefit and defined contribution characteristics.

[2]These plans may be for different classes of employees or one benefit type may be for current employees and the other for new employees or these plans may be hybrid plans where the pension benefit is the better of that provided by defined benefit or defined contribution provisions.

Source: Adapted from Statistics Canada, CANSIM, table 280-0016, "Registered pension plans (RPPs) and members, by type of plan and sector," http://www.statcan.gc.ca/tables-tableaux/sum-som/l01/cst01/famil120a-eng.htm.

Workers rally in Windsor, Ontario, after the provincial government refuses to expand pension guarantees.

The severe economic recession that began in late 2008 resulted in major shrinkage in the value of pension funds and highlighted issues with both types of plans. For defined benefit plans, the recession necessitated major increases in contributions to pension funds in order to maintain their required funding levels.[36] Although some jurisdictions eased the funding rules temporarily to allow more time to repay funding shortfalls, defined benefit plans began to be called an "endangered species."[37] For defined contribution plans, many plan members nearing retirement saw no other option but to defer retirement and continue working until the markets recovered and their pension fund account balance recovered to an amount that would provide them with the retirement income they needed. These issues created considerable debate about the adequacy of retirement savings for future generations.

When designing a pension plan, there are several legal and policy issues to consider:[38]

Hints | TO ENSURE LEGAL COMPLIANCE

- *Membership requirements.* For example, at what minimum number of years of service do employees become eligible to join the plan?

- *Benefit formula* (defined benefit plans only). This usually ties the pension to the employee's final earnings, or an average of his or her last three to five years' earnings.

- *Retirement age.* Traditionally, the normal retirement age in Canada has been 65. However, since mandatory retirement is now prohibited by human rights laws across the country, employees cannot be required to retire at age 65. Some plans call for "30 and out." This permits an employee to retire after 30 years of continuous service, regardless of the person's age.

- *Funding.* The question of how the plan is to be funded is another key issue. One aspect is whether the plan will be contributory or non-contributory. In the former, contributions to the pension fund are made by both employees and the employer. In a non-contributory fund, only the employer contributes.

- *Vesting.* Employee **vesting** rights is another critical issue in pension planning. Vesting refers to the money that the employer has placed in the pension fund that cannot be forfeited for any reason; the employees' contributions can never be forfeited. An employee is vested when he or she has met the requirements set out in the plan, whereby, on termination of employment, he or she will receive future benefits based on the contributions made to the plan by the *employer* on behalf of the employee. In most provinces, pension legislation requires that employer contributions be vested once the employee has completed two years of service. Plans may vest more quickly than required by law. If the employee terminates employment before being vested, he or she is only entitled to a refund of his or her own contributions plus interest (unless the employer has decided to be more generous). Once an employee is vested, all contributions are "locked in" and cannot be withdrawn by the employee on termination of employment; that is, employees must wait until retirement to receive a pension from the plan. Most plans permit the employee to transfer the amount into a locked-in RRSP (see the discussion on portability below), but the money cannot be accessed until retirement.

An Ethical | Dilemma

Should an employer with a pension plan that covers employees in several provinces give each group the minimum vesting and portability benefits for their province, or take the most generous of these and provide it to all employees?

vesting A provision that employer money placed in a pension fund cannot be forfeited for any reason.

- *Portability.* Canadian employers today are required by pension legislation to make their pensions more "portable" for employees on termination of employment. **Portability** means that employees in defined contribution plans can take the money in their company pension account to a new employer's plan or roll it over into a locked-in RRSP. For defined benefit plans, the lump-sum value of the benefit earned can be transferred.

Phased Retirement

The labour shortage is resulting in employers seeking to retain older employees. At the same time, many Canadians wishing to retire early are finding that they are not in a financial position to do so and that they need to continue working to age 60, 65, or even later.[39] The idea of **phased retirement**, whereby employees gradually ease into retirement using reduced workdays or shortened workweeks, has been increasing in Canada, as shown in Exhibit 17-4. Constraints under the Income Tax Act and pension legislation in some jurisdictions are slowly being loosened, and it is now possible for older workers to receive some benefits from their pension plan while they are being paid to continue to work.[40]

Supplemental Employee Retirement Plans (SERPs)

The Income Tax Act has not changed the maximum pension benefit permissible under the act (for tax deductibility of plan contributions) since 1976. Thus, many Canadians have their pension benefits capped at less than what their defined benefit plan formula would otherwise provide. Originally this situation only created problems for highly paid executives, but in recent years more and more employees have been affected. **Supplemental employee retirement plans (SERPs)** are intended to provide the difference in pension benefit and thus restore pension adequacy for high earners.

A Towers Perrin survey found that nearly three-quarters of employers provide SERPs (including about two-thirds of small employers with fewer than 500 employees). The survey also found that 53 percent of SERP sponsors cover employees below the executive

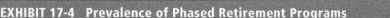

EXHIBIT 17-4 Prevalence of Phased Retirement Programs

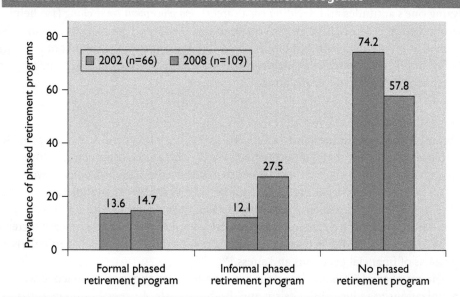

Source: K. Thorpe, Harnessing the Power: Recruiting, Engaging, and Retaining Mature Workers (Ottawa, ON: The Conference Board of Canada, October 2008), p. 23. Reprinted by permission of The Conference Board of Canada, Ottawa.

portability A provision that employees who change jobs can transfer the lump-sum value of the pension they have earned to a locked-in RRSP or their new employer's pension plan.

phased retirement An arrangement whereby employees gradually ease into retirement by using reduced workdays or shortened workweeks.

supplemental employee retirement plans (SERPs) Plans that provide the additional pension benefit required for employees to receive their full pension benefit in cases where their full pension benefit exceeds the maximum allowable benefit under the Income Tax Act.

level in "broad-based" plans. Most SERPs are "pay-as-you-go" plans; that is, they do not have a fund established to accumulate money to pay the benefits (because contributions are not tax deductible). However, the security of SERP benefits has been improving, as 41 percent of plans are now secured in some manner.[41]

Employee Services

Although an employee's time off and insurance and retirement benefits account for the largest portion of an organization's benefits costs, many employers also provide a range of services, including personal services (such as counselling), job-related services (such as childcare facilities), and executive perquisites (such as company cars and planes for executives).

Personal Services

First, many companies provide personal services that most employees need at one time or another. These include credit unions, counselling, employee assistance plans, and social and recreational opportunities. The intent of these services is to help employees balance work–life issues, aid them in dealing with non-work issues that may affect work-related issues, and provide employees with a sense of overall well-being.

Credit Unions

Credit unions are usually separate businesses established with the assistance of the employer. Employees usually become members of a credit union by purchasing a share of the credit union's stock for $5 or $10. Members can then deposit savings that accrue interest at a rate determined by the credit union's board of directors. Perhaps more important to most employees, loan eligibility and the rate of interest paid on the loan are usually more favourable than those found in banks and finance companies.

Counselling Services

Employers are also providing a wider range of counselling services to employees. These include *financial counselling* (for example, how to overcome existing debt problems), *family counselling* (for marital problems and so on), *career counselling* (for example, analyzing one's aptitudes and deciding on a career), *job placement counselling* (for helping terminated or disenchanted employees find new jobs), and *pre-retirement counselling* (aimed at preparing retiring employees for what many find is the trauma of retiring). Many employers also make available to employees a full range of *legal counselling* services through legal insurance plans.[42]

Employee Assistance Plans (EAPs)

An **employee assistance plan (EAP)** is a formal employer program that provides employees (and often their family members) with confidential counselling or treatment programs for problems such as mental health issues, marital/family problems, work–life balance issues, stress, legal problems, substance abuse, and other addictions such as gambling. They are particularly important for helping employees who suffer workplace trauma—ranging from harassment to physical assault. There was a significant increase in EAP usage during the economic recession that began in late 2008, particularly in the areas of financial problems and stress.[43]

The number of EAPs in Canada is growing because they are a proactive way for organizations to reduce absenteeism and disability costs. A general estimate is that 10 percent of employees use EAP services. With supervisory training in how to identify employees who may need an EAP referral, usage can be expanded to more employees who need help.[44]

Family Services Employee
Assistance Programs
www.familyserviceseap.com

hepell.fgi
www.shepellfgi.com

employee assistance plan (EAP)
A company-sponsored program to help employees cope with personal problems that are interfering with or have the potential to interfere with their job performance, as well as issues affecting their well-being or the well-being of their families.

EAP counsellors can be employed in-house, or the company can contract with an external EAP firm.[45] It is important to assess the services provided by external EAP providers before using them, as quality levels vary. Whatever the model, an EAP provider should be confidential, accessible to employees in all company locations, and timely in providing service, and should offer highly educated counsellors and provide communication material to publicize the plan to employees. They should also provide utilization reports on the number of employees using the service and the types of services being provided, without compromising confidentiality.[46]

Other Personal Services

Finally, some employers also provide various social and recreational opportunities for their employees, including company-sponsored athletic events, dances, annual summer picnics, craft activities, and parties. In practice, the benefits offered are limited only by creativity in thinking up new benefits. For example, pharmaceutical giant Pfizer Inc. provides employees with free drugs made by the company, including Viagra.[47]

Job-Related Services

Job-related services aimed directly at helping employees perform their jobs, such as educational subsidies and childcare centres, constitute a second group of services.

Subsidized Childcare

Eighty percent of Canadian families with young children have both parents working.[48] Subsidized childcare is offered to assist in balancing these work and life responsibilities.

Many employers simply investigate the childcare facilities in their communities and recommend certain ones to interested employees, but more employers are setting up company-sponsored childcare facilities themselves, both to attract young parents to the payroll and to reduce absenteeism. In this case, the centre is a separate, privately run venture, paid for by the firm. IKEA, Husky Injection Molding Systems, IBM, and the Kanata Research Park have all chosen this option. Where successful, the hours of operation are structured around parents' schedules, the childcare facility is close to the workplace (often in the same building), and the employer provides 50 to 75 percent of the operating costs. Two emerging benefits are childcare for mildly ill children and emergency backup childcare.[49]

Subsidizing childcare facilities for children of employees has many benefits for the employer, including lower employee absenteeism.

To date, the evidence regarding the actual effects of employer-sponsored childcare on employee absenteeism, turnover, productivity, recruitment, and job satisfaction is positive, particularly with respect to reducing obstacles to coming to work and improving workers' attitudes.[50]

Eldercare

With the average age of the Canadian population rising, eldercare is increasingly a concern for many employers and individuals. It is a complex, unpredictable, and exhausting process that creates stress for the caregiver, the family, and co-workers. Eldercare is expected to become a more common workplace issue than childcare as the twenty-first century progresses.[51]

Company eldercare programs are designed to assist employees who must help elderly parents or relatives who are not fully able to care for themselves, up to and including palliative care of the dying. Eldercare benefits include flexible hours, support groups, counselling, free pagers, and adult daycare programs. Referral services to help employees connect with the wide variety of services for the elderly are particularly helpful for employees with eldercare responsibilities.[52] For example, BMO Financial Group's EAP can be used to find nursing homes by entering a postal code and using the list of questions provided to assist in selecting the best one. BMO employee Yasmin Meralli says, "It helped me with my work because it reduced the amount of time I had to spend outside of work doing other stuff... It really felt to me that I worked for a company that cared."[53]

Subsidized Employee Transportation

Some employers also provide subsidized employee transportation. An employer can negotiate with a transit system to provide free year-round transportation to its employees. Other employers facilitate employee carpooling, perhaps by acting as the central clearinghouse to identify employees from the same geographic areas who work the same hours.

Food Services

Food services are provided in some form by many employers; they allow employees to purchase meals, snacks, or coffee onsite, usually at relatively low prices. Even employers that do not provide full dining facilities generally make available food services, such as coffee wagons or vending machines, for the convenience of employees.

Educational Subsidies

Educational subsidies, such as tuition refunds, have long been a popular benefit for employees seeking to continue or complete their education. Payments range from all tuition and expenses to some percentage of expenses to a flat fee per year of, say, $500 to $600. Most companies pay for courses directly related to an employee's present job. Many also reimburse tuition for courses that are not job related (such as a secretary taking an accounting class) that pertain to the company business, and those that are part of a degree or diploma program. In-house educational programs include remedial work in basic literacy and training for improved supervisory skills.

Family-Friendly Benefits

Research INSIGHT

Boomers are the "Sandwich Generation," caring for both children and elderly parents.

One of the top drivers of workforce commitment in Canada is management's recognition of personal and family life. Ninety percent of responding employees in one survey said work–life benefits were "important" or "very important" to them.[54] Recognition of the pressures of balancing work and family life has led many employers to bolster what they call their "family-friendly" benefits. Examples include flexible work hours, onsite childcare, and eldercare benefits.

Family-friendly benefits are intended to reduce the extent to which work–family conflicts spill over into the employee's job and undermine the person's job satisfaction and performance. Research has found that "the relationship between job satisfaction and various [work–family] conflict measures is strong and negative across all samples; people with high levels of [work–family] conflict tend to be less satisfied with their jobs."[55] Similarly, there was a strong negative correlation between work–family conflict and the extent to which the employees were satisfied with their lives in general. Managers should therefore understand that providing their employees with family-friendly benefits can have very positive effects on the employees, one of which is making them more satisfied with their work and their jobs.

Executive Perquisites

Perquisites (perks, for short) are usually given to only a few top executives. Perks can range from the substantial to the almost insignificant. A bank chairperson may have a chauffeur-driven limousine and use of a bank-owned property in the Caribbean. Executives of large companies often use a corporate jet for business travel. At the other extreme, perks may entail little more than the right to use a company car.56

A multitude of popular perks fall between these extremes. These include management loans (which typically enable senior officers to use their stock options); salary guarantees (also known as *golden parachutes*) to protect executives if their firms are the targets of acquisitions or mergers; financial counselling (to handle top executives' investment programs); and relocation benefits, often including subsidized mortgages, purchase of the executive's current house, and payment for the actual move. A potpourri of other executive perks include outplacement assistance, company cars, chauffeured limousines, security systems, company planes and yachts, executive dining rooms, legal services, tax assistance, liberal expense accounts, club memberships, season tickets, credit cards, and subsidized education for their children. Perks related to wellness and quality of life (such as physical fitness programs) are highly valued in today's stressful environment. An increasingly popular new perk offered at KPMG, TELUS, and Ernst & Young is concierge service, intended to carry out errands, such as grocery shopping or organizing a vacation, for busy executives.[57]

An Ethical | Dilemma

Is it ethical for e xecutive perquisites to continue if the company is facing financial problems?

Flexible Benefits Programs

Research conducted more than 30 years ago found that an employee's age, marital status, and sex influenced his or her choice of benefits.58 For example, preference for pensions increased significantly with employee age, and preference for the family dental plan increased sharply as the number of dependants increased. Thus, benefits that one worker finds attractive, may be unattractive to another. In the last 25 years in Canada, there has been a significant increase in **flexible benefits programs** that permit employees to develop individualized benefits packages for themselves by choosing the benefits options they prefer. In 1980, there were no flex plans in Canada, but by 2005, 41 percent of employers offered flex benefits plans. Benefit consultants Hewitt Associates report that 85 percent of Canadian employers either have a flex plan in place or expect to implement one at some point. Fifty-three percent either have a full flex plan now or are in the process of creating one.[59]

Employers derive several advantages from offering flexible benefit plans: the two most important being cost containment and the ability to meet the needs of an increasingly diverse workforce. Hewitt Associates' surveys have found that, over the years, the most important advantage of implementing flexible benefits has been meeting diverse employee needs. However, in 2005, for the first time in survey history, the concern about containing benefit cost increases surpassed meeting diverse employee needs as the most significant reason to implement flexible plans. In the 2006 survey, 100 percent of respondents reported that their flex plans were meeting or exceeding their expectations regarding meeting employee needs, and the level of satisfaction with flex plans as a cost containment measure was 78 percent.[60]

Flexible benefits plans empower the employee to put together his or her own benefit package, subject to two constraints. First, the employer must carefully limit total cost for each total benefits package. Second, each benefit plan must include certain items that are not optional. These include, for example, Canada/Quebec Pension Plan, workers' compensation, and employment insurance. Subject to these two constraints, employees can pick and choose from the available options. Thus, a young parent might opt for

flexible benefits programs
Individualized benefit plans to accommodate employee needs and preferences.

EXHIBIT 17-5   Advantages and Disadvantages of Flexible Benefit Programs

ADVANTAGES

1. Employees choose packages that best satisfy their unique needs.
2. Flexible benefits help firms meet the *changing* needs of a *changing* workforce.
3. Increased involvement of employees and families improves understanding of benefits.
4. Flexible plans make introduction of new benefits less costly. The new option is added merely as one among a wide variety of elements from which to choose.
5. Cost containment—the organization sets the dollar maximum. Employee chooses within that constraint.

DISADVANTAGES

1. Employees make bad choices and find themselves not covered for predictable emergencies.
2. Administrative burdens and expenses increase.
3. Adverse selection—employees pick only benefits they will use. The subsequent high benefit utilization increases its cost.

Source: G.T. Milkovich, J.M. Newman, N.D. Cole, Compensation, 3rd Canadian ed. (Toronto: McGraw Hill Ryerson). © 2010. Reprinted with permission of McGraw-Hill Ryerson Ltd.

the company's life and dental insurance plans, while an older employee opts for an improved pension plan. The list of possible options that the employer might offer can include many of the benefits discussed in this chapter—vacations, insurance benefits, pension plans, educational services, and so on.

Benefits Design, Inc
www.benefitsdesign.com

International Foundation of Employee Benefit Plans
www.ifebp.org

Advantages and disadvantages of flexible benefit programs are summarized in Exhibit 17-5. The flexibility is, of course, the main advantage. Although most employees favour flexible benefits, some do not like to spend time choosing among available options, and some choose inappropriate benefits. Communication regarding the choices available in a flexible plan is considered the biggest challenge for employers. A majority of flex plan sponsors provide a plan website. However, even with new technology employers still find face-to-face communication is the preferred method for providing initial information about a new flex plan.[61] The recent rapid increase in the number of flexible plans in Canada indicates that the pros outweigh the cons.

Benefits Administration

Canadian Pension and Benefits Institute
www.cpbi-icra.ca

Whether it is a flexible benefits plan or a more traditional one, benefits administration is a challenge. Even in a relatively small company with 40 to 50 employees, the administrative problems of keeping track of the benefits status of each employee can be a time-consuming task as employees are hired and separated and as they use or want to change their benefits. However, software is available to assist with this challenge. Many companies make use of some sort of benefits spreadsheet software to facilitate tracking benefits and updating information. Another approach is outsourcing benefits administration to a third-party expert. The major advantages are greater efficiency and consistency, and enhanced service. [62]

Keeping Employees Informed

Benefits communication, particularly regarding pension plans and flexible ben-efits, is increasingly important as a large number of people are approaching retirement. Correct information must be provided in a timely, clear manner. Pension legislation across Canada specifies what information must be disclosed to plan members and their spouses. Court challenges concerning information on benefits plans are on the rise as people's awareness of their right to informa-tion grows. [63]

Increasingly, organizations are using new technology, such as intranets, to ensure that up-to-date information is provided in a consistent manner. Some companies are now using real-time e-statements. At Hewlett Packard (Canada), an electronic pension booklet is available on the company's intranet, and a pension-modelling tool can be accessed through the web. The modelling soft-ware allows employees to fill in their personal information to calculate various "what if" scenarios. [64]

18

Groups and Teamwork

Quebec-based Cirque du Soleil is recognized worldwide for the many creative shows it has produced since its start in 1984.[1] The company has 5000 employees, with 2000 of them located at its headquarters in Montreal. Its employees represent "more than 50 nationalities and speak 25 different languages," which could present challenges in developing a spirit of teamwork.

Teamwork, however, is what Cirque du Soleil does best. According to Lyn Heward, the company's director of creation, "no matter what your product is . . . your results lie in having a passionate strong team of people. People are the driving force. I think because the Cirque's product is the sum total of people, it's a little more evident." Heward notes the importance of building trust so that everyone can work together interdependently. Guy Laliberté, the founder and majority owner of Cirque, emphasizes that the whole is much bigger than the sum of the parts, as each individual employee is "but a quarter note in a grand symphony."

Cirque assesses 60 to 70 new candidates a year, trying to find individuals who will add to the many talented employees on board. Candidates are evaluated on a number of dimensions, but team skills are important. Specifically, recruiters evaluate whether individuals can effectively work in teams to solve problems and whether they generously share ideas with others.

For teams to excel, a number of conditions need to be met. Effective teams need wise leadership, a variety of resources, and a way to solve problems. Team members need to be dedicated, and they need to build trust. In this chapter, we examine when it's best to have a team, how to create effective teams, and how to deal with diversity on teams.

Teams vs. Groups: What's the Difference?

1 What are teams and groups?

There is some debate whether groups and teams are really separate concepts or whether the two terms can be used interchangeably. We think that there is a subtle difference between the terms. A **group** is two or more people with a common relationship. Thus a group could be co-workers, or people meeting for lunch or standing at the bus stop. Unlike teams, groups do not necessarily engage in collective work that requires interdependent effort.

A **team** is "a small number of people with complementary skills who are committed to a common purpose, performance goals, and approach for which they hold themselves mutually accountable."[2] Groups become teams when they meet the following conditions:[3]

- Team members share *leadership*.

- Both individuals and the team as a whole share *accountability* for the work of the team.

- The team develops its own *purpose* or *mission*.

- The team works on *problem-solving* continuously, rather than just at scheduled meeting times.

- The team's measure of *effectiveness* is the team's outcomes and goals, not individual outcomes and goals.

Thus, while not all groups are teams, all teams can be considered groups. Much of what we discuss in this chapter applies equally well to both. We will offer some suggestions on creating effective teams later in the chapter.

Why Have Teams Become So Popular?

How do we explain the current popularity of teams? As organizations have restructured themselves to compete more effectively and efficiently, they have turned to teams as a better way to use employee talents. Management has found that teams are more flexible and responsive to changing events than are traditional departments or other forms of permanent groupings. Teams have the capability to quickly assemble, deploy, refocus, and disband. Teams also can be more motivational. Recall from the job characteristics model in Chapter 14 that having greater task identity is one way of increasing motivation. Teams allow for greater task identity, with team members working on tasks together.

Research suggests that teams typically outperform individuals when the tasks being done require multiple skills, judgment, and experience.[4] However, teams are not necessarily appropriate in every situation. Are teams truly effective? What conditions affect their potential? How do members work together? These are some of the questions we will answer in this chapter.

Types of Teams

Teams can be classified based on their objective. The four most common kinds of teams you are likely to find in an organization are

- Problem-solving (or process-improvement) teams

- Self-managed (or self-directed) teams

- Cross-functional (or project) teams

- Virtual teams

The types of relationships that members within each team have to one another are shown in Exhibit 18-1.

group Two or more people with a common relationship.

team A small number of people who work closely together toward a common objective and are accountable to one another.

EXHIBIT 18-1 Four Types of Teams

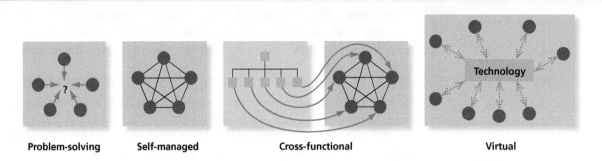

| Problem-solving | Self-managed | Cross-functional | Virtual |

Problem-Solving Teams

A **problem-solving (or process-improvement) team** is typically made up of 5 to 12 employees from the same department who meet for a few hours each week to discuss ways of improving quality, efficiency, and the work environment.[5] Such teams can also be planning teams, task forces, or committees that are organized to get tasks done. During meetings, members share ideas or offer suggestions on how to improve work processes and methods. Rarely, however, are these teams given the authority to unilaterally implement any of their suggested actions. Montreal-based Clairol Canada is an exception. When a Clairol employee identifies a problem, he or she has the authority to call together an ad hoc group to investigate, and then define and implement solutions. Clairol presents GOC (Group Operating Committee) Awards to teams for their efforts.

Self-Managed Teams

Problem-solving teams were on the right track, but they did not go far enough in involving employees in work-related decisions and processes. This led to experiments with truly autonomous teams that could not only solve problems but also implement solutions and assume responsibility for outcomes.

A **self-managed (or self-directed) team** is typically made up of 10 to 15 employees. The employees perform highly related or interdependent jobs and take on many

At the Louis Vuitton factory in Ducey, France, all employees work in problem-solving teams, with each team focusing on one product at a time. Team members are encouraged to suggest improvements in manufacturing work methods and processes as well as product quality. When a team was asked to make a test run on a prototype of a new handbag, team members discovered that decorative studs were causing the bag's zipper to bunch up. The team alerted managers, who had technicians move the studs away from the zipper, which solved the problem.

problem-solving (or process-improvement) team A group of 5 to 12 employees from the same department who meet for a few hours each week to discuss ways of improving quality, efficiency, and the work environment.

self-managed (or self-directed) team A group of 10 to 15 employees who take on many of the responsibilities of their former managers.

of the responsibilities of their former managers.[6] Typically, this includes planning and scheduling of work, assigning tasks to members, making operating decisions, taking action on problems, and working with suppliers and customers. Fully self-managed teams even select their own members and leader and have the members evaluate one another's performance. Supervisory positions can take on decreased importance and may even be eliminated.

Research on the effectiveness of self-managed work teams has not been uniformly positive.[7] When disputes arise, members stop cooperating and power struggles ensue, which leads to lower group performance.[8] Moreover, although individuals on these teams do tend to report higher levels of job satisfaction compared with other individuals, they also sometimes have higher absenteeism and turnover rates.

Cross-Functional Teams

As vice-president, operations and special projects for Mississauga, Ontario-based Walmart Canada, Don Swann used a **cross-functional (or project) team** to develop Walmart's Supercentre format for Canada. The team has representatives from all parts of retail business, "including store design, replenishment, systems, merchandising, marketing, operations, HR and finance." He created the cross-functional team because he knew that "we couldn't take a Supercentre from the U.S. and 'drop' it into the Canadian market. We needed to create a Supercentre that was uniquely Canadian."[9]

Cross-functional teams are made up of employees from about the same hierarchical level, but from different work areas, who come together to accomplish a task.[10] For instance, if a business school wanted to design a new integrated curriculum in business for undergraduates, it might bring together a group of faculty members, each of whom represents one discipline (for example, finance, accounting, marketing, and organizational behaviour) to work together to design the new program. Each individual would be expected to contribute knowledge of his or her field, and ways to package together the knowledge in a more integrated fashion.

Cross-functional teams are an effective means for allowing people from diverse areas within an organization (or even between organizations) to exchange information, develop new ideas, solve problems, and coordinate complex projects. Of course, cross-functional teams are not easy to manage.[11] Their early stages of development are often time-consuming as members learn to work with diversity and complexity. It takes time to build trust and teamwork, especially among people from different backgrounds, with different experiences and perspectives.

Skunkworks Skunkworks are cross-functional teams that develop spontaneously to create new products or work on complex problems. Such teams are typically found in the high-tech sector, and are generally sheltered from other organizational members. This gives the team the ability to work on new ideas in isolation, without being watched over by organization members, during creative stages. Skunkworks are thus able to ignore the structure and bureaucratic rules of the organization while they work.

The first skunkworks team appeared in the 1940s, at Lockheed Aerospace Corporation.[12] The team was to create a jet fighter as fast as possible, and avoid bureaucratic delays. In just 43 days, the team of 23 engineers and a group of support personnel put together the first American fighter to fly at more than 800 kilometres an hour.

Not all skunkworks projects are as successful. Many companies, including IBM and Xerox, have had mixed results in using them. Still, skunkworks do offer companies an alternative approach to teamwork when speed is an important factor.

Virtual Teams

Problem-solving, self-managed, and cross-functional teams do their work face to face. **Virtual teams** use computer technology to tie together physically dispersed members

cross-functional (or project) team A group of employees at about the same hierarchical level, but from different work areas, who come together to accomplish a task.

virtual team A team that uses computer technology to tie together physically dispersed members in order to achieve a common goal.

Queen's School of Business started an innovative executive MBA program in 2011 that relies on a virtual team of students. While there are three residential sessions during the program, most courses are taught in virtual boardroom sessions with students participating from home. "The program offers the same real-time connectivity and interactivity as our boardroom learning centres, but offers more accessibility to a top-ranked program to participants who wouldn't otherwise have the time or be able to physically be in a boardroom location on weekends," said Gloria Saccon, director of the executive MBA program.[13]

in order to achieve a common goal.[14] They allow people to collaborate online—using communication links such as wide-area networks, video conferencing, and email—whether they are only a room away or continents apart. Virtual teams are so pervasive, and technology has advanced so far, that it's probably a bit of a misnomer to call these teams "virtual." Nearly all teams today do at least some of their work remotely.

Despite their ubiquity, virtual teams face special challenges. They may suffer because there is less social rapport and less direct interaction among members. They are not able to duplicate the normal give-and-take of face-to-face discussion. Especially when members have not personally met, virtual teams tend to be more task oriented and exchange less social-emotional information than face-to-face teams. Not surprisingly, virtual team members report less satisfaction with the group interaction process than do face-to-face teams. An additional concern about virtual teams is whether members are able to build the same kind of trust that face-to-face teams build.

For virtual teams to be effective, management should ensure that (1) trust is established among team members (one inflammatory remark in a team member email can severely undermine team trust); (2) team progress is monitored closely (so the team does not lose sight of its goals and no team member "disappears"); and (3) the efforts and products of the virtual team are publicized throughout the organization (so the team does not become invisible).[15]

From Individual to Team Member

Ellie Syracopoulos is the manager of Cirque du Soleil's graphic communications team.[16] Her team works behind the scenes to create promotional materials that make Cirque du Soleil's "charm jump out from the page." To achieve the high-quality production she expects, Syracopoulos emphasizes a work environment that encourages creativity. She finds that "open communication, flexibility and gratitude" form the building blocks for that environment.

She insists that when her team is working, they must be focused on each other and the job at hand, and not be confronted with external distractions. Her basic instructions to her team are as follows:

- "Turn off email notifications
- Turn down your phone ringer

2 How does one become a team player?

- Do not bring your cell phone to a meeting
- Block off time each day to focus on hot projects, and stick to it!"

How can individual team members actually become a team?

For either a group or a team to function, individuals have to achieve some balance between their own needs and the needs of the group. When individuals come together to form groups and teams, they bring with them their personalities and all their previous experiences. They also bring their tendencies to act in different ways at different times, depending on the effects that different situations and different people have on them.

One way to think of these differences is in terms of possible pressures that individual group members put on one another through roles, norms, and status expectations. As we consider the process of how individuals learn to work in groups and teams, we will use the terms interchangeably. Many of the processes that each go through are the same, with the major difference being that teams within the workplace are often set up on a nonpermanent basis, in order to accomplish projects.

Roles

Shakespeare said, "All the world's a stage, and all the men and women merely players." Using the same metaphor, all group members are actors, each playing a **role**. By this term, we mean a set of expected behaviour patterns of a person in a given position in a social unit. The understanding of role behaviour would be dramatically simplified if each of us chose one role and "played it out" regularly and consistently. Unfortunately, we are required to play a number of diverse roles, both on and off our jobs.

As we will see, one of the tasks in understanding behaviour is grasping the role that a person is currently playing. For example, on the job a person might have the roles of electrical engineer, member of middle management, and primary company spokesperson in the community. Off the job, there are still more roles: spouse, parent, church member, food bank volunteer, and coach of the softball team. Many of these roles are compatible; some create conflicts. For instance, how does one's religious involvement influence managerial decisions regarding meeting with clients on the Sabbath? We address role conflict below.

Role Conflict

Most roles are governed by **role expectations**, that is, how others believe a person should act in a given situation. When an individual is confronted by conflicting role expectations, the result is role conflict. **Role conflict** exists when an individual finds that complying with one role requirement may make it more difficult to comply with another.[17] At the extreme, it can include situations in which two or more role expectations are mutually contradictory!

All of us have faced and will continue to face role conflicts. The critical issue, from our standpoint, is how conflicts imposed by different expectations within the organization affect behaviour. Certainly, they increase internal tension and frustration. There are a number of behavioural responses individuals may engage in. They may, for example, give a formalized bureaucratic response. The conflict is then resolved by relying on the rules, regulations, and procedures that govern organizational activities.

For example, an employee faced with the conflicting requirements imposed by the corporate controller's office and his own plant manager decides in favour of his immediate boss—the plant manager. Other behavioural responses may include withdrawal, stalling, negotiation, or redefining the facts or the situation to make them appear congruent.

Role Ambiguity

Role ambiguity exists when a person is unclear about the expectations of his or her role. In teams, role ambiguity can lead to confusion, stress, and even bad feelings. For

role A set of expected behaviours of a person in a given position in a social unit.

role expectations How others believe a person should act in a given situation.

role conflict A situation in which an individual finds that complying with one role requirement may make it more difficult to comply with another.

role ambiguity A person is unclear about his or her role.

instance, suppose two group members each think that the other one is responsible for preparing the first draft of a report. At the next group meeting, neither brings a draft report, and both are annoyed that the other person did not do the work.

Groups benefit when individuals know their roles. Roles within groups and teams should be balanced. Edgar Schein suggests that **role overload** occurs when what is expected of a person "far exceeds what he or she is able to do."[18] **Role underload** occurs when too little is expected of someone, and that person feels that he or she is not contributing to the group.

Norms

Have you ever noticed that golfers don't speak while their partners are putting on the green, or that employees don't criticize their bosses in public? Why? The answer is "norms!"

Norms are acceptable standards of behaviour within a group that are shared by the group's members. All groups have established norms that tell members what they ought and ought not to do under certain circumstances. When agreed to and accepted by the group, norms act as a means of influencing the behaviour of group members, with a minimum of external controls. Norms differ among groups, communities, and societies, but all of these entities have norms.[19]

Formalized norms are written up in organizational manuals that set out rules and procedures for employees to follow. But, by far, most norms in organizations are informal. You don't need someone to tell you that throwing paper airplanes or engaging in prolonged gossip sessions at the water cooler is an unacceptable behaviour when the "big boss from Toronto" is touring the office. Similarly, we all know that when we are in an employment interview discussing what we did not like about our previous job, there are certain things we should not talk about (such as difficulty in getting along with co-workers or our manager). There are other things it's appropriate to talk about (inadequate opportunities for advancement, or unimportant and meaningless work).

Norms can cover virtually any aspect of group behaviour.[20] Some of the most common norms have to do with issues such as

- *Performance.* How hard to work, the level of output, what kind of quality, levels of tardiness

- *Appearance.* Dress codes, when to look busy, when to "goof off," how to show loyalty

- *Social arrangement.* With whom to eat lunch, whether to form friendships on and off the job

- *Allocation of resources.* Pay, assignments, allocation of tools and equipment

The "How" and "Why" of Norms

How do norms develop? Why are they enforced? A review of the research allows us to answer these questions.[21]

Norms typically develop gradually as group members learn what behaviours are necessary for the team to function effectively. Of course, critical events in the group might short-circuit the process and quickly prompt new norms. Most norms develop in one or more of the following four ways:

- *Explicit statements made by a group member.* Often, instructions from the group's supervisor or a powerful member establish norms. The team leader might specifically say that no personal phone calls are allowed during working hours or that coffee breaks must be no longer than 10 minutes.

role overload Too much is expected of someone.

role underload Too little is expected of someone, and that person feels that he or she is not contributing to the group.

norms Acceptable standards of behaviour within a group that are shared by the group's members.

- *Critical events in the group's history.* These set important precedents. A bystander is injured while standing too close to a machine and, from that point on, members of the work group regularly monitor one another to ensure that no one other than the operator gets within two metres of any machine.

- *Primacy.* The first behavioural pattern that emerges in a group frequently sets team expectations. Groups of students who are friends often choose seats near one another on the first day of class and become upset if an outsider takes "their" seats in a later class.

- *Carry-over behaviours from past situations.* Group members bring expectations with them from other groups to which they have belonged. Thus, work groups typically prefer to add new members who are similar to current ones in background and experience. This is likely to increase the probability that the expectations they bring are consistent with those already held by the group.

Groups don't establish or enforce norms for every conceivable situation, however. The norms that the groups will enforce tend to be those that are important to them.[22] What makes a norm important?

- *It facilitates the group's survival.* Groups don't like to fail, so they seek to enforce any norm that increases their chances for success. This means that groups try to protect themselves from interference from other groups or individuals.

- *It increases the predictability of group members' behaviours.* Norms that increase predictability enable group members to anticipate one another's actions and to prepare appropriate responses.

- *It reduces embarrassing interpersonal problems for group members.* Norms are important if they ensure the satisfaction of their members and prevent as much interpersonal discomfort as possible.

- *It allows members to express the central values of the group and clarify what is distinctive about the group's identity.* Norms that encourage expression of the group's values and distinctive identity help solidify and maintain the group.

Conformity

As a group member, you desire acceptance by the group. Because of your desire for acceptance, you are susceptible to conforming to the group's norms. Considerable evidence shows that the group can place strong pressures on individual members to change their attitudes and behaviours to conform to the group's standard.[23]

The impact that group pressures for **conformity** can have on an individual member's judgment and attitudes was demonstrated in the now classic studies of noted social psychologist Solomon Asch.[24] Asch found that subjects gave answers that they knew were wrong, but that were consistent with the replies of other group members, about 35 percent of the time. The results suggest that group norms can pressure us toward conformity. We desire to be one of the group and avoid being visibly different.

Research by University of British Columbia professor Sandra Robinson and colleague Anne O'Leary-Kelly indicates that conformity may explain why some work groups are more prone to antisocial behaviour than others.[25] Individuals working with others who exhibited antisocial behaviour at work were more likely to engage in antisocial behaviour themselves. Of course, not all conformity leads to negative behaviour. Other research has indicated that work groups can have more positive influences, leading to more prosocial behaviour in the workplace.[26]

Overall, research continues to indicate that conformity to norms is a powerful force in groups and teams.

conformity Adjusting one's behaviour to align with the norms of the group.

Stages of Group and Team Development

> As Cirque du Soleil's creative team and cast prepared for the October 2011 opening of *Michael Jackson: The Immortal World Tour*, they faced a number of questions. Would the show capture the magic of Michael Jackson? What was the show's writer and director, Jamie King, going to be like? Who would fill some of the key roles in the show? What would it be like to produce a show unlike any other that Cirque had done in the past? Could the team all work well together? To build a successful team that produces a high-quality, creative performance, Cirque's cast members had to go through several stages. So what stages do teams go through as they develop?

③ Do teams go through stages while they work?

When people get together for the first time with the purpose of achieving some objective, they discover that acting as a team is not something simple, easy, or genetically programmed. Working in a group or team is often difficult, particularly in the initial stages, when people don't necessarily know one another. As time passes, groups and teams go through various stages of development, although the stages are not necessarily exactly the same for each group or team. In this section, we discuss two models of group development. The five-stage model describes the standardized sequence of stages groups pass through. The punctuated-equilibrium model describes the pattern of development specific to temporary groups with deadlines. These models can be applied equally to groups and teams.

The Five-Stage Model

From the mid-1960s, it was believed that groups passed through a standard sequence of five stages.[27] As shown in Exhibit 18-2, these five stages have been labelled *forming, storming, norming, performing,* and *adjourning.* Although we now know that not all groups pass through these stages in a linear fashion, the five-stage model of group development can still help in addressing any anxieties you might have about working in groups and teams. The model shows how individuals move from being independent to working interdependently with group members.

- *Stage I: Forming.* Think about the first time you met with a new team. Do you remember how some people seemed silent and others felt confused about the task you were to accomplish? Those feelings arise during the first stage of group development, known as **forming**. Forming is characterized by a great deal of uncertainty about the team's purpose, structure, and leadership. Members are "testing the waters" to determine what types of behaviour are acceptable. This stage is complete when members have begun to think of themselves as part of a team.

- *Stage II: Storming.* Do you remember how some people in your team just did not seem to get along, and sometimes power struggles even emerged? These reactions are typical of the **storming** stage, which is one of intragroup conflict. Members accept the existence of the team, but resist the constraints that the team imposes on individuality. Furthermore, there is conflict over who will control the team. When this stage is complete, a relatively clear hierarchy of leadership will emerge within the team.

    Some teams never really emerge from the storming stage, or they move back and forth through storming and the other stages. A team that remains forever planted in the storming stage may have less ability to complete the task because of all the interpersonal problems.

- *Stage III: Norming.* Many teams resolve the interpersonal conflict and reach the third stage, in which close relationships develop and the team demonstrates cohesiveness. There is now a strong sense of team identity and camaraderie. This **norming** stage is complete when the team structure solidifies, and the

forming The first stage in group development, characterized by much uncertainty.

storming The second stage in group development, characterized by intragroup conflict.

norming The third stage in group development, characterized by close relationships and cohesiveness.

EXHIBIT 18-2 Stages of Group Development and Accompanying Issues

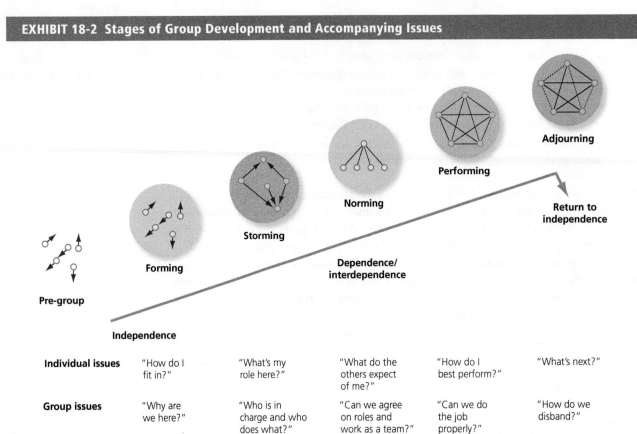

Individual issues	"How do I fit in?"	"What's my role here?"	"What do the others expect of me?"	"How do I best perform?"	"What's next?"
Group issues	"Why are we here?"	"Who is in charge and who does what?"	"Can we agree on roles and work as a team?"	"Can we do the job properly?"	"How do we disband?"

team has assimilated a common set of expectations of what defines correct member behaviour.

- *Stage IV: Performing.* Next, and you may have noticed this in some of your own team interactions, some teams just seem to come together well and start to do their work. This fourth stage, when significant task progress is being made, is called **performing**. The structure at this point is fully functional and accepted. Team energy has moved from getting to know and understand one another to performing the task at hand.

- *Stage V: Adjourning.* For permanent work groups and teams, performing is the last stage in their development. However, for temporary committees, teams, task forces, and similar groups that have a limited task to perform, there is an **adjourning** stage. In this stage, the group prepares for its disbandment. High task performance is no longer the group's top priority. Instead, attention is directed toward wrapping up activities. Group members' responses vary at this stage. Some members are upbeat, basking in the group's accomplishments. Others may be depressed over the loss of camaraderie and friendships gained during the work group's life.

 For some teams, the end of one project may mean the beginning of another. In this case, a team has to transform itself in order to get on with a new project that may need a different focus and different skills, and may need to take on new members. Thus the adjourning stage may lead to renewal of the team to get the next project started.

performing The fourth stage in group development, when the group is fully functional.

adjourning The final stage in group development for temporary groups, where attention is directed toward wrapping up activities rather than task performance.

Putting the Five-Stage Model into Perspective

Many interpreters of the five-stage model have assumed that a group becomes more effective as it progresses through the first four stages. This assumption may be generally true, but what makes a group effective is more complex than this model acknowledges.[28] Under some conditions, high levels of conflict are conducive to high group performance, as long as the conflict is directed toward the task and not toward group members. So we might expect to find situations where groups in Stage II outperform those in Stages III or IV. Similarly, groups do not always proceed clearly from one stage to the next. Sometimes, in fact, several stages go on simultaneously, as when groups are storming and performing at the same time. Teams even occasionally go backwards to previous stages. Therefore, you should not assume that all groups follow the five-stage process precisely, or that Stage IV is always the most preferable.

The five-stage model also ignores organizational context.[29] For instance, a study of a cockpit crew in an airliner found that, within 10 minutes, three strangers assigned to fly together for the first time had become a high-performing team. How could a team come together so quickly? The answer lies in the strong organizational context surrounding the tasks of the cockpit crew. This context provided the rules, task definitions, information, and resources needed for the team to perform. They did not need to develop plans, assign roles, determine and allocate resources, resolve conflicts, and set norms the way the five-stage model predicts.

The Punctuated-Equilibrium Model

Temporary groups with deadlines don't seem to follow the previous model. Studies indicate that temporary groups with deadlines have their own unique sequence of action (or inaction):[30]

- The first meeting sets the group's direction.

- The first phase of group activity is one of inertia.

- A transition takes place at the end of the first phase, which occurs exactly when the group has used up half its allotted time.

- The transition initiates major changes.

- A second phase of inertia follows the transition.

- The group's last meeting is characterized by markedly accelerated activity.

This pattern is called the punctuated-equilibrium model, developed by Professor Connie Gersick, a Visiting Scholar at the Yale University School of Management, and is shown in Exhibit 18-3.[31] It is important for you to understand these shifts in group behaviour, if for no other reason than when you are in a group that is not working well or one that has gotten off to a slow start, you can start to think of ways to help the group move to a more productive phase.

Ever wonder what causes flurries of activity in groups?

Phase 1

As both a team member and possibly a team leader, it's important that you recognize that the first meeting sets the team's direction. A framework of behavioural patterns and assumptions through which the team will approach its project emerges in this first meeting. These lasting patterns can appear as early as the first few seconds of the team's life.

Once set, the team's direction becomes "written in stone" and is unlikely to be re-examined throughout the first half of the team's life. This is a period of inertia—that is, the team tends to stand still or become locked into a fixed course of action. Even if it gains new insights that challenge initial patterns and assumptions, the team is incapable of acting on these new insights in Phase 1. You may recognize that in some teams, during the early period of trying to get things accomplished, no one really did his or her assigned tasks. You may also recognize this phase as one where everyone carries out the

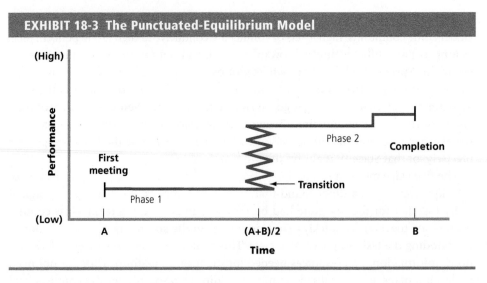

EXHIBIT 18-3 The Punctuated-Equilibrium Model

tasks, but not in a very coordinated fashion. Thus, the team is performing at a relatively low state. This does not necessarily mean that it is doing nothing at all, however.

Phase 2

At some point, the team moves out of the inertia stage and recognizes that work needs to get completed. One of the more interesting discoveries made in these studies was that each team experienced its transition at the same point in its calendar—precisely halfway between its first meeting and its official deadline.[32] The similarity occurred despite the fact that some teams spent as little as an hour on their project, while others spent six months. It was as if the teams universally experienced a midlife crisis at this point. The midpoint appears to work like an alarm clock, heightening members' awareness that their time is limited and that they need to "get moving." When you work on your next team project, you might want to examine when your team starts to "get moving."

This transition ends Phase 1 and is characterized by a concentrated burst of changes, dropping of old patterns, and adoption of new perspectives. The transition sets a revised direction for Phase 2, which is a new equilibrium or period of inertia. In this phase, the team executes plans created during the transition period. The team's last meeting is characterized by a final burst of activity to finish its work. There have been a number of studies that support the basic premise of punctuated equilibrium, though not all of them found that the transition in the team occurred exactly at the midpoint.[33]

Applying the Punctuated-Equilibrium Model

We can use this model to describe typical experiences of student teams created for doing group term projects. At the first meeting, a basic timetable is established. Members size up one another. They agree they have nine weeks to do their project. The instructor's requirements are discussed and debated. From that point, the group meets regularly to carry out its activities. About four or five weeks into the project, however, problems are confronted. Criticism begins to be taken seriously. Discussion becomes more open. The group reassesses where it has been and aggressively moves to make necessary changes. If the right changes are made, the next four or five weeks find the group developing a first-rate project. The group's last meeting, which will probably occur just before the project is due, lasts longer than the others. In it, all final issues are discussed and details resolved.

In summary, the punctuated-equilibrium model characterizes deadline-oriented teams as exhibiting long periods of inertia, interspersed with brief revolutionary changes triggered primarily by their members' awareness of time and deadlines. To use the terminology of the five-stage model, the team begins by combining the *forming* and *norming* stages, then goes through a period of *low performing*, followed by *storming*, then a period of *high performing*, and, finally, *adjourning*.

Several researchers have suggested that the five-stage and punctuated-equilibrium models are at odds with each other.[34] However, it makes more sense to view the models as complementary: The five-stage model considers the interpersonal process of the group, while the punctuated-equilibrium model considers the time challenges that the group faces.[35]

Creating Effective Teams

Cirque du Soleil has a multicultural workforce, with employees representing over 60 different cultures.[36] The company recognizes that it can use this diversity to its advantage by developing and sharing the cultural assets the employees bring to the workplace. Lyn Heward, the company's director of creation, notes that Cirque can draw on "Brazilian percussion and capoeira, Australian didgeridoo, Ukrainian and African dancing, Wushu, Peking Opera and Kung Fu" through the cultural backgrounds of its employees. Diversity can make it harder to be cohesive when teams first develop. Thus, Cirque holds training "boot camps," where new recruits are pushed to their limits. The goal, according to stage director Franco Dragone, is to "turn athletes into artists and form a cohesive team of brothers." What other factors might contribute to the effectiveness of the Cirque du Soleil performers?

4 How do we create effective teams?

When we consider team effectiveness, we refer to such objective measures as the team's productivity, managers' ratings of the team's performance, and aggregate measures of member satisfaction. Some of the considerations necessary to create effective teams are outlined next. However, we are also interested in team process. Exhibit 18-4 lists the characteristics of an effective team.

There is no shortage of efforts that try to identify the factors that lead to team effectiveness.[37] However, studies have taken what was once a "veritable laundry list of characteristics"[38] and organized them into a relatively focused model with four general categories summarized in Exhibit 18-5:[39]

- Resources and other contextual influences that make teams effective

- Team composition

- Work design

- Team process (those things that go on in the team that influence how effective the team is)

Keep in mind two caveats as you review the issues that lead to effective teams:

- First, teams differ in form and structure. Since the model we present attempts to generalize across all varieties of teams, you need to be careful not to rigidly apply the model's predictions to all teams.[40] The model should be used as a guide, not as an inflexible prescription.

- Second, the model assumes that it's already been determined that teamwork is preferable over individual work. Creating "effective" teams in situations where individuals can do the job better is equivalent to solving the wrong problem perfectly.

You might want to evaluate your own team experience against this checklist to give you some idea of how well your team is functioning, or to understand what might be causing problems for your team. Then consider the factors that lead to more effective teams below.

EXHIBIT 18-4 Characteristics of an Effective Team

1.	**Clear purpose**	The vision, mission, goal, or task of the team has been defined and is now accepted by everyone. There is an action plan.
2.	**Informality**	The climate tends to be informal, comfortable, and relaxed. There are no obvious tensions or signs of boredom.
3.	**Participation**	There is much discussion, and everyone is encouraged to participate.
4.	**Listening**	The members use effective listening techniques such as questioning, paraphrasing, and summarizing to get out ideas.
5.	**Civilized disagreement**	There is disagreement, but the team is comfortable with this and shows no signs of avoiding, smoothing over, or suppressing conflict.
6.	**Consensus decisions**	For important decisions, the goal is substantial but not necessarily unanimous agreement through open discussion of everyone's ideas, avoidance of formal voting, or easy compromises.
7.	**Open communication**	Team members feel free to express their feelings on the tasks as well as on the group's operation. There are few hidden agendas. Communication takes place outside of meetings.
8.	**Clear rules and work assignments**	There are clear expectations about the roles played by each team member. When action is taken, clear assignments are made, accepted, and carried out. Work is distributed among team members.
9.	**Shared leadership**	While the team has a formal leader, leadership functions shift from time to time depending on the circumstances, the needs of the group, and the skills of the members. The formal leader models the appropriate behaviour and helps establish positive norms.
10.	**External relations**	The team spends time developing key outside relationships, mobilizing resources, and building credibility with important players in other parts of the organization.
11.	**Style diversity**	The team has a broad spectrum of team-player types including members who emphasize attention to task, goal setting, focus on process, and questions about how the team is functioning.
12.	**Self-assessment**	Periodically, the team stops to examine how well it is functioning and what may be interfering with its effectiveness.

Source: G. M. Parker, *Team Players and Teamwork: The New Competitive Business Strategy* (San Francisco: Jossey-Bass, 1990), Table 2, p. 33. Copyright © 1990 by Jossey-Bass Inc., Publishers. Reprinted by permission of John Wiley & Sons, Inc.

Context

Teams can require a great deal of maintenance to function properly. They need management support, as well as an organizational structure that supports teamwork. The four contextual factors that appear to be most significantly related to team performance are the presence of adequate resources, effective leadership, a climate of trust, and a performance evaluation and reward system that reflects team contributions.

Adequate Resources

All work teams rely on resources outside the team to sustain them. A scarcity of resources directly reduces the ability of a team to perform its job effectively. As one set of researchers concluded, after looking at 13 factors potentially related to team performance, "perhaps one of the most important characteristics of an effective work group is the support the group receives from the organization."[41] This support includes technology, adequate staffing, administrative assistance, encouragement, and timely information.

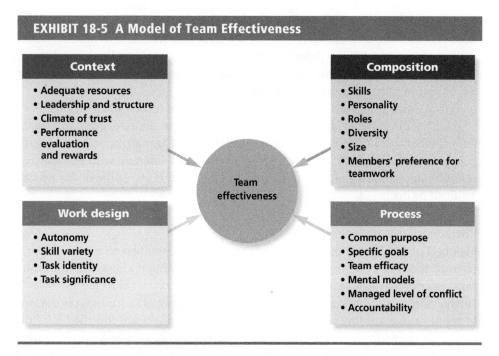

EXHIBIT 18-5 A Model of Team Effectiveness

Context
- Adequate resources
- Leadership and structure
- Climate of trust
- Performance evaluation and rewards

Composition
- Skills
- Personality
- Roles
- Diversity
- Size
- Members' preference for teamwork

Work design
- Autonomy
- Skill variety
- Task identity
- Task significance

Process
- Common purpose
- Specific goals
- Team efficacy
- Mental models
- Managed level of conflict
- Accountability

Team effectiveness

Teams must receive the necessary support from management and the larger organization if they are going to succeed in achieving their goals.

Leadership and Structure

Leadership plays a crucial role in the development and success of teams.

Professor Richard Hackman of Harvard University, who is the leading expert on teams, suggests that the role of team leader involves the following:[42]

- Creating a real team rather than a team in name only

- Setting a clear and meaningful direction for the team's work

- Making sure that the team structure will support working effectively

- Ensuring that the team operates within a supportive organizational context

- Providing expert coaching

There are some practical problems that must be resolved when a team first starts working together. Team members must agree on who is to do what, and ensure that all members contribute equally in sharing the workload. The team also needs to determine how schedules will be set, what skills need to be developed, how the team will resolve conflicts, and how the team will make and modify decisions. Agreeing on the specifics of work and how they fit together to integrate individual skills requires team leadership and structure. This leadership, incidentally, can be provided by management or by the team members themselves. Although you might think there is no role for leaders in self-managed teams, that could not be further from the truth. It is true that, in self-managed teams, team members absorb many of the duties typically assumed by managers. However, a manager's job becomes managing *outside* (rather than inside) the team.

Kerry Molinaro, President of Burlington, Ontario-based IKEA Canada, believes that teams are the best way to bring employees together. IKEA's leadership style is informal, and the company values people who are humble and trustworthy. These qualities also make them good team members.

Leadership is especially important in **multi-team systems**—where different teams need to coordinate their efforts to produce a desired outcome. In such systems, leaders need to empower teams by delegating responsibility to them, and they need to play the role of facilitator, making sure the teams are coordinating their efforts so that they work together rather than against one another.[43]

Recent research suggests that women may make better team leaders than men.

A leader, of course, is not always needed. For instance, the evidence indicates that self-managed teams often perform better than teams with formally appointed leaders.[44] Leaders can also obstruct high performance when they interfere with self-managed teams.[45] On self-managed teams, team members absorb many of the duties typically assumed by managers.

Climate of Trust

Members of effective teams trust one another. For team members to achieve a climate of trust, they must feel that the team is capable of getting the task done, and they must believe that "the team will not harm the individual or his or her interests."[46] Interpersonal trust among team members facilitates cooperation, reduces the need to monitor one another's behaviour, and bonds members around the belief that others on the team won't take advantage of them. Team members are more likely to take risks and expose vulnerabilities when they believe they can trust others on their team.

Team members must also trust their leaders.[47] Trust in leadership is important in that it allows the team to be willing to accept and commit to their leader's goals and decisions. Management at Mississauga, Ontario-based Flynn Canada invests in employees to help them become good team players. The company also helps employees build trust in one another so that they can learn to work effectively. Employees are encouraged to take pride in their work and successful outcomes. They are also encouraged to be open with one another. "Personally, what attracted me to Flynn is that it's got scale and horsepower but it has a heart and soul; it's not just another corporate entity. We are authentic in our interactions with each other. What you see is what you get," says Gerard Montocchio, vice-president of human resources."[48]

Performance Evaluation and Rewards

How do you get team members to be both individually and jointly accountable? The traditional individually oriented evaluation must be modified to reflect team performance.[49]

Individual performance evaluations, fixed hourly wages, individual incentives, and the like are not consistent with the development of high-performance teams. So in addition to evaluating and rewarding employees for their individual contributions, management should consider group-based appraisals, profit sharing, gainsharing, small-group incentives, and other system modifications that will reinforce team effort and commitment. Managers need to carefully consider the balance between paying on the basis of group performance[50] and the level of trust among team members. Recent research found that when team members did not trust their colleagues' ability, honesty, and dependability, they preferred individual-based rewards rather than team-based rewards. Even when trust improved over time from working together, there was still a preference for individual-based rewards, suggesting that "teams must have a very high level of trust for members to truly embrace group-based pay."[51]

One additional consideration when deciding whether and how to reward team members is the effect of pay dispersion on team performance. Research by Nancy Langton,

Should individuals be paid for their "teamwork" or their individual performance?

multi-team systems Systems in which different teams need to coordinate their efforts to produce a desired outcome.

your Vancouver-based author, shows that when there is a large discrepancy in wages among group members, collaboration is lowered.[52] A study of baseball player salaries also found that teams where players were paid more similarly often outperformed teams with highly paid "stars" and lowly paid "scrubs."[53]

Composition

This category includes variables that relate to how teams should be staffed. In this section, we will address the skills, personality, and roles of team members, the diversity and size of the team, and members' preference for teamwork.

Skills

To perform effectively, a team requires three different types of skills:

1. It needs people with *technical expertise*.

2. It needs people with the *problem-solving* and *decision-making skills* to be able to identify problems, generate alternatives, evaluate those alternatives, and make competent choices.

3. It needs people with good listening, feedback, conflict resolution, and other *interpersonal skills*.[54]

No team can achieve its performance potential without developing all three types of skills. The right mix is crucial. Too much of one at the expense of others will result in lower team performance. But teams don't need to have all the complementary skills in place at the beginning. It's not uncommon for one or more members to take responsibility to learn the skills in which the group is deficient, thereby allowing the team to reach its full potential. Exhibit 18-6 identifies some important teamwork skills that help teams function well.

Personality

Teams have different needs, and people should be selected for the team on the basis of their personalities and preferences, as well as the team's needs for diversity and specific roles. We demonstrated in Chapter 2 that personality has a significant influence on individual employee behaviour. This can also be extended to team behaviour.

> Why do some teams seem to get along better than others?

Many of the dimensions identified in the Big Five Personality Model have been shown to be relevant to team effectiveness. A recent review of the literature suggests that three of the Big Five traits are especially important for team performance.[55] Specifically, teams that rate higher on mean levels of conscientiousness and openness to experience tend to perform better. Moreover, a 2011 study found that the level of team member agreeableness also matters: Teams did worse when they had one or more highly disagreeable members.[56] Perhaps one bad apple *can* spoil the whole bunch!

Research has also provided us with a good idea about why these personality traits are important to teams. Conscientious people are valuable in teams because they are good at backing up other team members, and they are also good at sensing when that support is truly needed. Open team members communicate better with one another and throw out more ideas, which leads teams composed of open people to be more creative and innovative.[57]

Even if an organization does a really good job of selecting individuals for team roles, most likely they will find there are not enough, say, conscientious people to go around. Suppose an organization needs to create 20 teams of 4 people each and has

EXHIBIT 18-6 **Teamwork Skills**	
Orients team to problem-solving situation	Assists the team in arriving at a common understanding of the situation or problem. Determines the important elements of a problem situation. Seeks out relevant data related to the situation or problem.
Organizes and manages team performance	Helps team establish specific, challenging, and accepted team goals. Monitors, evaluates, and provides feedback on team performance. Identifies alternative strategies or reallocates resources to address feedback on team performance.
Promotes a positive team environment	Assists in creating and reinforcing norms of tolerance, respect, and excellence. Recognizes and praises other team members' efforts. Helps and supports other team members. Models desirable team member behaviour.
Facilitates and manages task conflict	Encourages desirable and discourages undesirable team conflict. Recognizes the type and source of conflict confronting the team and implements an appropriate resolution strategy. Employs "win-win" negotiation strategies to resolve team conflicts.
Appropriately promotes perspective	Defends stated preferences, argues for a particular point of view, and withstands pressure to change position for another that is not supported by logical or knowledge-based arguments. Changes or modifies position if a defensible argument is made by another team member. Projects courtesy and friendliness to others while arguing position.

Source: G. Chen, L. M. Donahue, and R. J. Klimoski, "Training Undergraduates to Work in Organizational Teams," *Academy of Management Learning & Education* 3, no. 1 (March 2004), p. 40. Copyright © Academy of Management, 2002.

40 highly conscientious people and 40 who score low on conscientiousness. Would the organization be better off (a) putting all the conscientious people together (forming 10 teams with the highly conscientious people and 10 teams of members low on conscientiousness) or (b) "seeding" each team with 2 people who scored high and 2 who scored low on conscientiousness?

Perhaps surprisingly, the evidence tends to suggest that option (a) is the best choice; performance across the teams will be higher if the organization forms 10 highly conscientious teams and 10 teams low in conscientiousness. "This may be because, in such teams, members who are highly conscientious not only must perform their own tasks but also must perform or re-do the tasks of low-conscientious members. It may also be because such diversity leads to feelings of contribution inequity."[58]

Roles

Teams have different needs, and members should be selected to ensure all the various roles are filled. A study of 778 major league baseball teams over a 21-year period highlights the importance of assigning roles appropriately.[59] As you might expect, teams with more experienced and skilled members performed better. However, the experience and skill of those in core roles who handle more of the workflow of the team, and who are central to all work processes (in this case, pitchers and catchers), were especially vital. In other words, put your most able, experienced, and conscientious workers in the most central roles in a team.

Within almost any group, two sets of role relationships need to be considered: task-oriented roles and maintenance roles. **Task-oriented roles** are performed by group members to ensure that the tasks of the group are accomplished. These roles include initiators, information seekers, information providers, elaborators, summarizers, and consensus makers. **Maintenance roles** are carried out to ensure that group members maintain good relations. These roles include harmonizers, compromisers, gatekeepers, and encouragers.

Effective teams maintain some balance between task orientation and maintenance of relations. Exhibit 18-7 identifies a number of task-oriented and maintenance behaviours

task-oriented roles Roles performed by group members to ensure that the tasks of the group are accomplished.

maintenance roles Roles performed by group members to maintain good relations within the group.

in the key roles that you might find in a team.

On many teams, there are individuals who will be flexible enough to play multiple roles and/or complete one another's tasks. This is an obvious plus to a team because it greatly improves its adaptability and makes it less reliant on any single member.[60] Selecting members who themselves value flexibility, and then cross-training them to be able to do one another's jobs, should lead to higher team performance over time.

Diversity

Group diversity refers to the presence of a heterogeneous mix of individuals within a group.[61] Individuals can be different not only in functional characteristics (jobs, positions, or work experiences) but also in demographic or cultural characteristics (age, race, sex, and citizenship). Many of us hold the optimistic view that diversity should be a good thing—diverse teams should benefit from differing perspectives and do better. Two meta-analytic reviews of the research literature show, however, that demographic diversity is essentially unrelated to team performance overall.[62] One qualifier is that gender and ethnic diversity have more negative effects in occupations dominated by white or male employees, but in more demographically balanced occupations, diversity is less of a problem. Diversity in function and expertise are positively related to group performance, but these effects are quite small and depend on the situation.

One of the pervasive challenges with teams is that while diversity may have real potential benefits, a team is deeply focused on commonly held information. But to realize their creative potential, diverse teams need to focus not on their similarities but on their differences. Some evidence suggests that when team members believe others have more expertise, they will work to support those members, leading to higher levels of effectiveness.[63] The key is for members of diverse teams to communicate what they uniquely know and also what they don't know. Proper leadership can also improve the performance of diverse teams. When leaders provide an inspirational common goal for members with varying types of education and knowledge, teams are very creative. When leaders don't provide such goals, diverse teams fail to take advantage of their unique skills and are actually *less* creative than teams with homogeneous skills.

Size

Generally speaking, the most effective teams have five to nine members. And experts suggest using the smallest number of people who can do the task. Unfortunately, there is a pervasive tendency for managers to err on the side of making teams too large. While a minimum of four or five may be necessary to develop diversity of views and skills, managers seem to seriously underestimate how coordination problems can dramatically increase as team members are added. When teams have excess members, cohesiveness and mutual accountability decline, social loafing increases, and more and more people do less talking compared with others. So in designing effective teams, managers should try to keep the number of members to less than 10. If a work unit is larger and you want a team effort, consider breaking the unit into subteams.[64] Uneven numbers in teams may help provide a mechanism to break ties and resolve conflicts, while an even number of team members may foster the need to create more consensus.

Size and Social Loafing

One of the most important findings related to the size of a team has been labelled **social loafing**. Social loafing is the tendency for individuals to expend less effort when working collectively than when working individually.[65] It directly challenges the logic that the productivity of the team as a whole should at least equal the sum of the productivity of each individual in that team. Research looking at

group diversity The presence of a heterogeneous mix of individuals within a group.

social loafing The tendency for individuals to expend less effort when working collectively than when working individually.

EXHIBIT 18-7 Roles Required for Effective Team Functioning			
	Function	**Description**	**Example**
Roles that build task accomplishment	*Initiating*	Stating the goal or problem, making proposals about how to work on it, setting time limits.	"Let's set up an agenda for discussing each of the problems we have to consider."
	Seeking information and opinions	Asking group members for specific factual information related to the task or problem, or for their opinions about it.	"What do you think would be the best approach to this, Jack?"
	Providing information and opinions	Sharing information or opinions related to the task or problems.	"I worked on a similar problem last year and found..."
	Clarifying	Helping one another understand ideas and suggestions that come up in the group.	"What you mean, Sue, is that we could . . . ?"
	Elaborating	Building on one another's ideas and suggestions.	"Building on Don's idea, I think we could . . ."
	Summarizing	Reviewing the points covered by the group and the different ideas stated so that decisions can be based on full information.	Appointing a recorder to take notes on a blackboard.
	Consensus taking	Providing periodic testing on whether the group is nearing a decision or needs to continue discussion.	"Is the group ready to decide about this?"
Roles that build and maintain a team	*Harmonizing*	Mediating conflict among other members, reconciling disagreements, relieving tensions.	"Don, I don't think you and Sue really see the question that differently."
	Compromising	Admitting error at times of group conflict.	"Well, I'd be willing to change if you provided some help on . . ."
	Gatekeeping	Making sure all members have a chance to express their ideas and feelings and preventing members from being interrupted.	"Sue, we haven't heard from you on this issue."
	Encouraging	Helping a group member make his or her point. Establishing a climate of acceptance in the group.	"I think what you started to say is important, Jack. Please continue."

teams working on a rope-pulling task showed, the larger the team, the less individual effort expended.[66] One person pulling on a rope alone exerted an average of 63 kilograms of force. In groups of three, per-person force dropped to 53 kilograms. And in groups of eight, it fell to only 31 kilograms per person. Other research supports these findings.[67] More may be better in the sense that the total productivity of a group of four is greater than that of one or two people, but the individual productivity of each group member declines.

What causes this social loafing effect? It may be due to a belief that others in the team are not carrying their fair share. If you view others as lazy or inept, you can

Employees in Taigu County, China, are collecting harvest grapes for the production of red wine. In collectivist societies such as China, employees perform better in a group than when working alone and they are less likely to engage in social loafing. Unlike individualistic cultures such as the United States, where people are dominated by self-interest, the Chinese are motivated by in-group goals.

re-establish equity by reducing your effort. Another explanation is the dispersion of responsibility. Because the results of the team cannot be attributed to any single person, the relationship between an individual's input and the team's output is clouded. In such situations, individuals may be tempted to become "free riders" and coast on the team's efforts. In other words, there will be a reduction in efficiency when individuals believe that their contribution cannot be measured. To reduce social loafing, teams should not be larger than necessary, and individuals should be held accountable for their actions.

> Why don't some team members pull their weight?

Members' Preference for Teamwork

Not every employee is a team player. Given the option, many employees will "select themselves out" of team participation. When people who would prefer to work alone are required to team up, there is a direct threat to the team's morale.[68] This suggests that, when selecting team members, individual preferences should be considered, as well as abilities, personalities, and skills. High-performing teams are likely to be composed of people who prefer working as part of a team.

Work Design

Effective teams need to work together and take collective responsibility to complete significant tasks. They must be more than a "team-in-name-only."[69] The work design category includes variables such as freedom and autonomy, the opportunity to utilize different skills and talents, the ability to complete a whole and identifiable task or product, and the participation in a task or project that has a substantial impact on others. The evidence indicates that these characteristics enhance member motivation

At the Olympic Village for the 2010 Winter Games in Vancouver, teams were housed in apartment buildings. In short order, teams put up their country's flags on balconies in a display of team spirit. The Australian team, however, also put up their boxing Kangaroo flag. The International Olympic Committee asked them to take it down because the flag is a commercial trademark, but the team refused, as they viewed it as their good luck charm. Many Canadians in Vancouver sided with the Australians, and the Australians' iconic flag did not come down.

and increase team effectiveness.[70] These work design characteristics motivate teams because they increase members' sense of responsibility and ownership over the work, and because they make the work more interesting to perform.[71] These recommendations are consistent with the job characteristics model we presented in Chapter 14.

Process

Process variables make up the final component of team effectiveness. The process category includes member commitment to a common purpose, establishment of specific goals, team efficacy, shared mental models, a managed level of conflict, and a system of accountability. These will be especially important in larger teams, and in teams that are highly interdependent.[72]

Why are processes important to team effectiveness? We learned from social loafing that 1 + 1 + 1 does not necessarily add up to 3. When each member's contribution is not clearly visible, individuals tend to decrease their effort. Social loafing, in other words, illustrates a process loss from using teams. But teams should create outputs greater than the sum of their inputs, as when a diverse group develops creative alternatives. Exhibit 18-8 illustrates how group processes can have an impact on a group's actual effectiveness.[73] Scientists often work in teams because they can draw on the diverse skills of various individuals to produce more meaningful research than could be generated by all the researchers working independently—that is, they produce positive synergy, and their process gains exceed their process losses.

Common Purpose

Effective teams begin by analyzing the team's mission, developing goals to achieve that mission, and creating strategies for achieving the goals. Teams that establish a clear sense of what needs to be done and how consistently perform better.[74] Members of successful teams put a tremendous amount of time and effort into discussing, shaping, and agreeing upon a purpose that belongs to them both collectively and individually. This common purpose, when accepted by the team, becomes the equivalent of what celestial navigation is to a ship captain—it provides direction and guidance under any and all conditions. Like a ship following the wrong course, teams that don't have good planning skills are doomed; perfectly executing the wrong plan is a lost cause.[75] Effective teams also show **reflexivity**, meaning that they reflect on and adjust their master plan when necessary. A team has to have a good plan, but it also has to be willing and able to adapt when conditions call for it.[76]

reflexivity A team characteristic of reflecting on and adjusting the master plan when necessary.

EXHIBIT 18-8 Effects of Group Processes

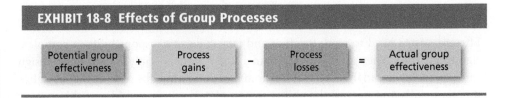

| Potential group effectiveness | + | Process gains | − | Process losses | = | Actual group effectiveness |

A study of 23 National Basketball Association teams found that "shared experience"—tenure on the team and time on court—tended to improve turnover and boost win-loss performance significantly. Why do you think teams that stay together longer tend to play better?

Specific Goals

Successful teams translate their common purpose into specific, measurable, and realistic performance goals. Just as we demonstrated in Chapter 13, how goals lead individuals to higher performance, goals also energize teams. These specific goals facilitate clear communication. They also help teams maintain their focus on achieving results.

Consistent with the research on individual goals, team goals should be challenging. Difficult goals have been found to raise team performance on those criteria for which they are set. So, for instance, goals for quantity tend to raise quantity, goals for speed tend to raise speed, goals for accuracy tend to raise accuracy, and so on.[77]

Team Efficacy

Effective teams have confidence in themselves. They believe they can succeed. We call this team *efficacy*.[78] Teams that have been successful raise their beliefs about future success, which, in turn, motivates them to work harder.

One of the factors that helps teams build their efficacy is **cohesiveness**—the degree to which members are attracted to one another and are motivated to stay on the team.[79] Though teams differ in their cohesiveness, it is important because it has been found to be related to the team's productivity.[80]

Studies consistently show that the relationship of cohesiveness and productivity depends on the performance-related norms established by the group.[81] If performance-related norms are high (for example, high output, quality work, cooperation with individuals outside the group), a cohesive group will be more productive than a less cohesive group. If cohesiveness is high and performance norms are low, productivity will be low. If cohesiveness is low and performance norms are high, productivity increases—but less than in the high cohesiveness–high norms situation. Where cohesiveness and performance-related norms are both low, productivity will tend to fall into the low-to-moderate range. These conclusions are summarized in Exhibit 18-9.

cohesiveness The degree to which team members are attracted to one another and are motivated to stay on the team.

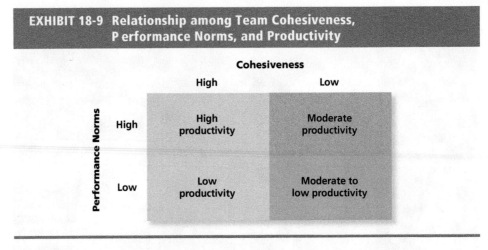

EXHIBIT 18-9 **Relationship among Team Cohesiveness, Performance Norms, and Productivity**

Most studies of cohesiveness focus on socio-emotional cohesiveness, the "sense of togetherness that develops when individuals derive emotional satisfaction from group participation."[82] There is also instrumental cohesiveness: the "sense of togetherness that develops when group members are mutually dependent on one another because they believe they could not achieve the group's goal by acting separately." Teams need to achieve a balance of these two types of cohesiveness to function well.

What, if anything, can management do to increase team efficacy? Two possible options are helping the team to achieve small successes and skill training. Small successes build team confidence. As a team develops an increasingly stronger performance record, it also increases the collective belief that future efforts will lead to success. In addition, managers should consider providing training to improve members' technical and interpersonal skills. The greater the abilities of team members, the greater the likelihood that the team will develop confidence and the capability to deliver on that confidence.

Mental Models

Effective teams have accurate and common **mental models**—knowledge and beliefs (a "psychological map") about how the work gets done. If team members have the wrong mental models, which is particularly likely to happen with teams under acute stress, their performance suffers.[83] For example, in the Iraq war, many military leaders said they underestimated the power of the insurgency and the infighting among Iraqi religious sects. The similarity of team members' mental models matters, too. If team members have different ideas about how to do things, the teams will fight over how to do things rather than focus on what needs to be done.[84]

Managed Level of Conflict

Conflict on a team is not necessarily bad. Though relationship conflicts—those based on interpersonal incompatibilities, tension, and animosity toward others—are almost always dysfunctional, teams that are completely void of conflict are likely to be less effective, with the members becoming withdrawn and only superficially harmonious.[85] On teams performing nonroutine activities, disagreements among members about task content (called *task conflicts*) stimulate discussion, promote critical assessment of problems and options, and can lead to better team decisions. The way conflicts are resolved can also make the difference between effective and ineffective teams. Effective teams resolved conflicts by explicitly discussing the issues, whereas ineffective teams had conflicts focused more on personalities and the way things were said.[86]

Kathleen Eisenhardt of the Stanford Graduate School of Business and her colleagues studied top management teams in technology-based companies to understand how they manage conflict.[87] Their research identified six tactics that helped teams successfully

mental models Team members' knowledge and beliefs about how the work gets done by the team.

manage the interpersonal conflict that can accompany group interactions. By handling the interpersonal conflict well, these groups were able to achieve their goals without letting conflict get in the way.

Groups need mechanisms by which they can manage the conflict, however.[88] From the research reported above, we could conclude that sharing information and goals, and striving to be open and get along, are helpful strategies for negotiating our way through the maze of conflict. A sense of humour, and a willingness to understand the points of others without insisting that everyone agree on all points, are also important. Group members should try to focus on the issues, rather than on personalities, and strive to achieve fairness and equity in the group process.

Accountability

Successful teams make members individually and jointly accountable for the team's purpose, goals, and approach.[89] They clearly define what they are individually responsible for and what they are jointly responsible for. This reduces the ability for individuals to engage in social loafing.

Beware! Teams Aren't Always the Answer

Despite considerable success in the use of teams, they are not necessarily appropriate in all situations, as Exhibit 18-10 suggests. Teamwork takes more time and often more resources than individual work. Teams have increased communication demands, conflicts to be managed, and meetings to be run. So the benefits of using teams have to exceed the costs, and that is not always the case.[90] A study done by Statistics Canada found that the introduction of teamwork lowered turnover in the service industries, for both high- and low-skilled employees. However, manufacturing companies experienced higher turnover if they introduced teamwork and formal teamwork training, compared with not doing so (15.8 percent vs. 10.7 percent).[91]

5 Are teams always the answer?

How do you know if the work of your group would be better done in teams? It's been suggested that three tests be applied to see if a team fits the situation:[92]

- *Can the work be done better by more than one person?* Simple tasks that don't require diverse input are probably better left to individuals.

- *Does the work create a common purpose or set of goals for the people in the group that is more than the sum of individual goals?* For instance, the service departments of many new-car dealers have introduced teams that link customer service personnel, mechanics, parts specialists, and sales representatives. Such teams can better manage collective responsibility for ensuring that customers' needs are properly met.

- *Are the members of the group interdependent?* Teams make sense where there is interdependence between tasks—where the success of the whole depends on the success of each one, and the success of each one depends on the success of the others. Soccer, for instance, is an obvious *team* sport because of the interdependence of the players. Swim teams, by contrast, except for relays, rely heavily on

EXHIBIT 18-10

Source: Dilbert, reprinted by permission of Universal Uclick.

LESSONS LEARNED

- A good team will achieve balance between individual needs and team needs.
- To create effective teams, members should be rewarded for engaging in team behaviour rather than individual behaviour.
- Teams should not be created for tasks that could be better done by individuals.

individual performance to win a meet. They are groups of individuals performing individually, whose total performance is merely the aggregate summation of their individual performances.

GLOBAL IMPLICATIONS

Research on global considerations in the use of teams is just beginning, but four areas are particularly worth mentioning: the extent of teamwork, self-managed teams, team cultural diversity, and group cohesiveness.

Extent of Teamwork

One study comparing US workers to Canadian and Asian workers revealed that 51 percent of workers in Asian-Pacific countries and 48 percent of Canadian employees report high levels of teamwork. But only 32 percent of US employees say their organization has a high level of teamwork.[93] Thus, Canadians engage in a great deal more teamwork than do Americans.

Self-Managed Teams

Evidence suggests self-managed teams have not fared well in Mexico, largely due to that culture's low tolerance of ambiguity and uncertainty and employees' strong respect for hierarchical authority.[94] Thus, in countries relatively high in power distance—where roles of leaders and followers are clearly delineated—a team may need to be structured so leadership roles are spelled out and power relationships identified.

Team Cultural Diversity and Team Performance

How do teams composed of members from different countries perform? The evidence indicates that the cultural diversity of team members interferes with team processes, at least in the short term.[95] However, cultural diversity does seem to be an asset for tasks that call for a variety of viewpoints. But culturally heterogeneous team members have more difficulty learning to work with one another and solving problems. The good news is while newly formed culturally diverse teams underperform newly formed culturally homogeneous teams, the differences disappear after about three months.[96] Fortunately, some team performance–enhancing strategies seem to work well in many cultures. One study found that teams in the European Union made up of members from collectivistic and individualistic countries benefited equally from group goals.[97]

Group Cohesiveness

Researchers studied teams from an international bank with branches in the United States (an individualistic culture) and in Hong Kong (a collectivistic culture) to determine the factors that affected group cohesiveness.[98] Teams were entirely composed of individuals from the branch country. The results showed that, regardless of what culture the teams were from, giving teams difficult tasks and more freedom to accomplish those tasks created a more tight-knit group. Consequently, team performance was enhanced.

However, the teams differed in the extent to which increases in task complexity and autonomy resulted in greater group cohesiveness. Teams in individualistic cultures responded more strongly than did teams in collectivistic cultures, became more united and committed, and, as a result, received higher performance ratings from their supervisors than did teams from collectivistic cultures.

These findings suggest that individuals from collectivistic cultures already have a strong predisposition to work together as a group, so there is less need for increased cohesiveness. However, managers in individualistic cultures may need to work harder to increase team cohesiveness. One way to do this is to give teams more challenging assignments and provide them with more independence.

Communication

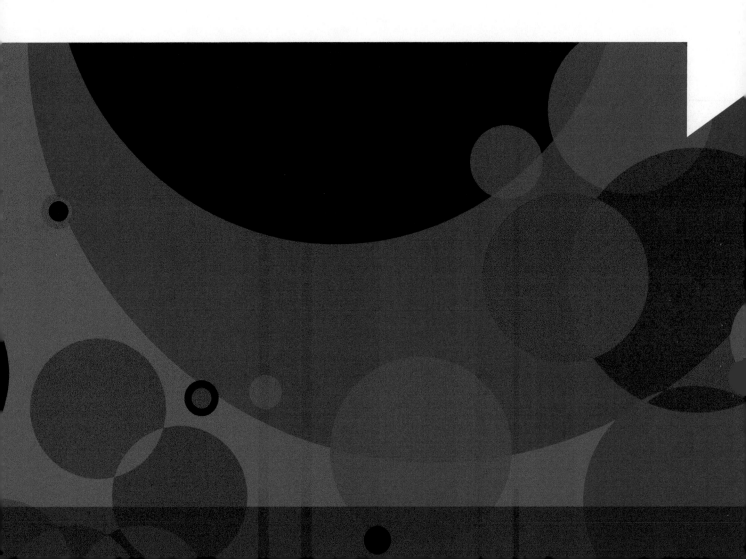

Ted Reeve Arena, one of 48 community arenas owned by the city of Toronto, is run by a volunteer board that decides how to allocate ice time to hockey leagues in the community.[1] Players and coaches from the Toronto Leaside Girls Hockey Association (TLGHA) felt they received limited access to the arena, especially compared with some other leagues. This was costing the Association an average of $200 000 in fees to rent ice time elsewhere. In the fall of 2009, TLGHA decided to fight back and launched an extensive communication campaign to let the community know about its concerns. The main goal was to force the city of Toronto to enforce its ice allocation policy at all publicly owned arenas.

In developing its communication campaign, the TLGHA carefully considered its target audience: the city's then mayor David Miller; members of Toronto city council; the TLGHA players and their families and fans; and the news media. The intent was to communicate effectively with these different groups to gain their support.

In this chapter, we explore the foundations of communication. By learning how to communicate effectively with others, we can improve our relationships with those around us, and work more effectively on teams.

The Communication Process

1 How does communication work?

Individuals spend nearly 70 percent of their waking hours communicating—writing, reading, speaking, listening—which means that they have many opportunities in which to engage in poor communication. Communication is an important consideration for organizations and individuals alike. Communication is a foundation for many things that happen among groups and within the workplace—from motivating, to providing information, to controlling behaviour, to expressing emotion. Good communication skills are very important to your career success. A recent study of recruiters found that they rated communication skills as *the* most important characteristic of an ideal job candidate.[2]

No group can exist without **communication**, which is the *transfer* and *understanding* of a message between two or more people. Communication can be thought of as a process, or flow, as shown in Exhibit 19-1. The *sender* initiates a message by encoding a thought. The *message* is the actual physical product of the sender's *encoding*. When we speak, the speech is the message. When we write, the writing is the message. When we gesture, the movements of our arms and the expressions on our faces are the message. The *channel* is the medium through which the message travels. The sender selects it, determining whether to use a formal or informal channel. **Formal channels** are established by the organization and transmit messages related to the professional activities of members. They traditionally follow the authority chain within the organization. Other forms of messages, such as personal or social, follow **informal channels**, which are spontaneous and emerge as a response to individual choices.[3] The *receiver* is the person(s) to whom the message is directed, who must first translate the symbols into understandable form. This step is the *decoding* of the message. *Noise* represents communication barriers that distort the clarity of the message, such as perceptual problems, information overload, semantic difficulties, or cultural differences. The final link in the communication process is a feedback loop. *Feedback* is the check on how successful we have been in transferring our messages as originally intended. It determines whether understanding has been achieved.

The model indicates that communication is both an interactive and iterative process. The sender has to keep in mind the receiver (or audience), and in finalizing the communication may decide to revisit decisions about the message, the encoding, and/or the feedback.

Choosing a Channel

Why do people choose one **channel** of communication over another; for instance, a phone call instead of a face-to-face talk? One answer might be anxiety! An estimated 5 to 20 percent of the population[4] suffers from debilitating **communication apprehension**, or anxiety, which is undue tension and anxiety about oral communication, written communication, or both. We all know people who dread speaking in front of a group, but some people may find it extremely difficult to talk with others face to face

communication The transfer and understanding of a message between two or more people.

formal channels Communication channels established by an organization to transmit messages related to the professional activities of members.

informal channels Communication channels that are created spontaneously and that emerge as responses to individual choices.

channel The medium through which a message travels.

communication apprehension Undue tension and anxiety about oral communication, written communication, or both.

EXHIBIT 19-1 The Communication Process Model

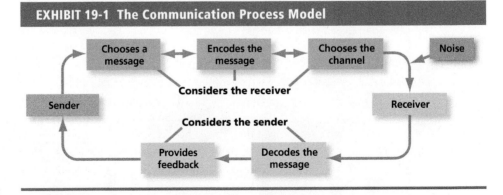

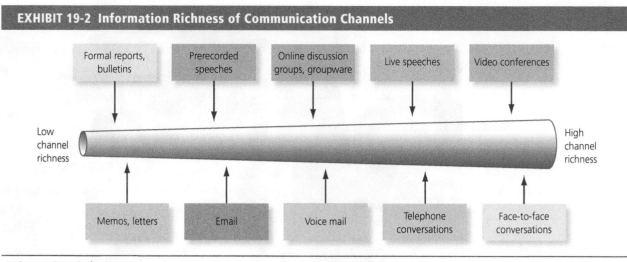

EXHIBIT 19-2 Information Richness of Communication Channels

Formal reports, bulletins
Prerecorded speeches
Online discussion groups, groupware
Live speeches
Video conferences

Low channel richness

High channel richness

Memos, letters
Email
Voice mail
Telephone conversations
Face-to-face conversations

Source: From Daft. *Organizational Behavior*, 1E. © 2001 South-Western, a part of Cengage Learning, Inc. Reproduced by permission. www.cengage.com/permissions.

or become extremely anxious when they have to use the telephone. As a result, they may rely on memos, letters, or email to convey messages when a phone call would not only be faster but also more appropriate.

But what about the 80 to 95 percent of the population who don't suffer from this problem? Is there any general insight we might be able to provide regarding choice of communication channel? The answer is a qualified "yes." A model of media richness has been developed to explain channel selection among managers.[5]

Research has found that channels differ in their capacity to convey information. Some are rich in that they have the ability to (1) handle multiple cues simultaneously, (2) facilitate rapid feedback, and (3) be very personal. Others are lean in that they score low on these three factors. As Exhibit 19-2 illustrates, face-to-face conversation scores highest in terms of **channel richness** because it provides for the maximum amount of information to be transmitted during a communication episode. That is, it offers multiple information cues (words, postures, facial expressions, gestures, intonations), immediate feedback (both verbal and nonverbal), and the personal touch of "being there." Mississauga, Ontario-based Phonak Canada, a manufacturer of advanced hearing systems, holds monthly town-hall meetings for all staff. The firm shares information, introduces new employees, and recognizes notable achievements. It provides an opportunity to make sure that everyone in the company is on the same page.[6]

Impersonal written media such as formal reports and bulletins rate lowest in richness. Two students were suspended from class for choosing YouTube, a very rich channel, to distribute their message. Their actions also raised concerns about privacy in the classroom.

The choice of one channel over another depends on whether the message is routine or nonroutine. Routine messages tend to be straightforward and have a minimum of ambiguity. Nonroutine messages are likely to be complicated and have the potential for misunderstanding. Individuals can communicate routine messages efficiently through channels that are lower in richness. However, they communicate nonroutine messages more effectively by selecting rich channels. Evidence indicates that high-performing managers tend to be more media sensitive than low-performing managers.[7] That is, they are better able to match appropriate media richness with the ambiguity involved in the communication. Rob Sobey, president of the Dartmouth, Nova Scotia-based Lawtons Drugs chain, knows that memos do not help in a crisis when staff morale needs boosting. "A memo never motivates. A memo can thank and compliment, but you need the town hall meeting [in a true crisis]. You have to put yourself out there in the flesh."[8]

channel richness The amount of information that can be transmitted during a communication episode.

According to Rob Sobey, president of Lawtons Drugs, a memo never motivates. It can thank and compliment, but in a true crisis, you need to hold a town hall meeting to communicate seminal information. Use of a rich communication channel to communicate a nonroutine message is more likely to be successful.

One study found that managers preferred delivering bad news (layoffs, promotion denials, and negative feedback) via email, and that the messages were delivered more accurately this way. However, sending negative information through email is generally not recommended. One of the co-authors of the study noted that "offering negative comments face-to-face is often taken as a sign that the news is important and the deliverer cares about the recipient."[9] It appears that a CEO's use of a channel relatively low in richness (email) to convey a nonroutine and complex message did a lot of harm to his company.

The media richness model is consistent with organizational trends and practices of the past decade. It is not just coincidence that more and more senior managers use meetings to facilitate communication and regularly leave the isolated sanctuary of their executive offices to manage by walking around. These executives are relying on richer channels of communication to transmit the more ambiguous messages they need to convey. The past decade has been characterized by organizations closing facilities, imposing large layoffs, restructuring, merging, consolidating, and introducing new products and services at an accelerated pace—all nonroutine messages high in ambiguity and requiring the use of channels that can convey a large amount of information. It is not surprising, therefore, to see the most effective managers expanding their use of rich channels.

Barriers to Effective Communication

 What are the barriers to communication?

When the Toronto Leaside Girls Hockey Association (TLGHA) decided to launch its campaign to get more ice time, it faced significant challenges.[10] There were sexist attitudes toward girls' and women's hockey to overcome. As Ward 30 councillor Paula Fletcher noted, the anti-female attitudes were "left over from the past" and "need[ed] to change. It's just shocking that in this day and age, girls' hockey is being treated so poorly."

Because of such difficulties, the communication team for TLGHA had to consider the best way to deliver the message of change. Approaching the volunteer-run boards of the arenas did appear to be a good strategy, as the problem was a city-wide issue. Therefore, the association threatened to launch a human-rights complaint against the city in a letter sent to the mayor. Are there other things the communication team might have considered to make sure everyone was ready to listen to their concerns?

A number of factors have been identified as barriers to communication. This section presents the most prominent ones.

Filtering

Filtering occurs when a sender manipulates information so that the receiver will view it more favourably. For example, when a manager tells a senior executive what the manager feels the executive wants to hear, the manager is filtering information. The more vertical levels in the organization's hierarchy, the more opportunities there are for filtering. But some filtering will occur wherever there are status differences. Factors such as fear of conveying bad news and the desire to please the boss often lead employees to tell their superiors what they think they want to hear, thus distorting upward communications.

Selective Perception

Receivers in the communication process selectively see and hear based on their needs, motivations, experience, background, and other personal characteristics. Receivers also project their interests and expectations into communications as they decode them. For example, the employment interviewer who believes that young people are more interested in spending time on leisure and social activities than working extra hours to further their careers is likely to be influenced by that stereotype when interviewing young job applicants. As we discussed in Chapter 2, we don't see reality; rather, we interpret what we see and call it "reality." One 2011 study found that people perceived that they communicated better with people with whom they were close (friends and partners) than with strangers. However, in ambiguous conversations, it turned out that their ability to communicate with close friends was no better than their ability to communicate with strangers.[11]

Defensiveness

When people feel that they are being threatened, they tend to react in ways that reduce their ability to achieve mutual understanding. That is, they become defensive—engaging in behaviours such as verbally attacking others, making sarcastic remarks, being overly judgmental, and questioning others' motives. So when individuals interpret another's message as threatening, they often respond in ways that hinder effective communication.

Emotions

You may interpret the same message differently when you are angry or distraught than when you are happy. Extreme emotions such as jubilation or depression are most likely to hinder effective communication. In such instances, we are most prone to disregard our rational and objective thinking processes and substitute emotional judgments.

Information Overload

Individuals have a finite capacity for processing data. When the information we have to work with exceeds our ability to process it, the result is **information overload**. With emails, phone calls, faxes, meetings, and the need to keep current in one's field, more and more employees are saying that they are suffering from too much information. The information can be distracting as well. A recent study of employees who have tracking software on their computers found that they clicked on their email program more than 50 times in the course of a day, and used instant messaging 77 times. The study also found that, on average, employees visited 40 websites during the workday.[12]

What happens when individuals have more information than they can sort out and use? They tend to select out, ignore, pass over, or forget information. Or they may put off further processing until the overload situation is over. Regardless, the result is lost information and less effective communication.

filtering A sender's manipulation of information so that it will be seen more favourably by the receiver.

information overload The state of having more information than one can process.

Language

Even when we are communicating in the same language, words mean different things to different people. Age and context are two of the biggest factors that influence such differences.

When Michael Schiller, a business consultant, was talking with his 15-year-old daughter about where she was going with her friends, he told her, "You need to recognize your ARAs and measure against them." Schiller said that in response, his daughter "looked at him like he was from outer space." (For the record, *ARA* stands for accountability, responsibility, and authority.) Those new to corporate lingo may find acronyms such as *ARA*, words such as *skeds* (schedules), and phrases such as *bake your noodle* (provide a service) bewildering, in the same way parents may be mystified by teen slang.[13]

In short, our use of language is far from uniform. If we knew how each of us modified the language, we could minimize communication difficulties, but we usually don't know. Senders tend to assume that the words and terms they use mean the same to the receiver as to them.

Silence

It's easy to ignore silence or lack of communication, precisely because it is defined by the absence of information. However, research suggests silence and withholding communication are both common and problematic.[14] One survey found over 85 percent of managers reported remaining silent about at least one issue of significant concern.[15] Employee silence means managers lack information about ongoing operational problems. Moreover, silence regarding discrimination, harassment, corruption, and misconduct means top management cannot take action to eliminate this behaviour. Finally, employees who are silent about important issues may also experience psychological stress.

A study looking at the human factors that caused airline accidents found that pilots who had "take charge" attitudes with their crews were more likely to make wrong decisions than pilots who were more inclusive and consulted with their crews before deciding what to do.[16] It was the communication style of the pilot that affected the crew's behaviour. Crew members were not willing to intervene, even when they had

Call-centre operators at Convergys Corp. in New Delhi, India, speak English in serving their customers from North America and the United Kingdom. But even though the operators and customers speak a common language, communication barriers exist because of differences in the countries' cultures and language accents. To overcome these barriers, the operators receive training in North American and British pop culture so they can make small talk and are taught to speak with Western accents so they can be more easily understood by the calling clients.

necessary information, when they regularly worked under "decisive" pilots. That kind of silence can be fatal. In his book *Outliers*, Malcolm Gladwell noted, "The kinds of errors that cause plane crashes are invariably errors of teamwork and communication. One pilot knows something important and somehow doesn't tell the other pilot."

Silence is less likely where minority opinions are treated with respect, work group identification is high, and high procedural justice prevails.[17] Practically, this means managers must make sure they behave in a supportive manner when employees voice divergent opinions or express concerns, and they must take these concerns under advisement. One act of ignoring or belittling an employee for expressing concerns may well lead the employee to withhold important information in the future.

Professors Craig Pinder of the Peter B. Gustavson School of Business at the University of Victoria and Karen Harlos of the Desautels Faculty of Management at McGill University have noted that silence generally has often been thought to represent *inaction* or *nonbehaviour*, much as we saw with the airline pilots. But silence is not necessarily inaction, nor a failure to communicate. Silence can, in fact, be a powerful form of communication.[18] It can mean someone is thinking or contemplating a response to a question. It can mean a person is anxious and fearful of speaking. It can signal agreement, dissent, frustration, or anger.

Failing to pay close attention to the silent portion of a conversation can result in missing a vital part of the message. Astute communicators watch for gaps, pauses, and hesitations. They hear and interpret silence. They treat pauses, for instance, as analogous to a flashing yellow light at an intersection—they pay attention to what comes next. Is the person thinking, deciding how to frame an answer? Is the person suffering from communication apprehension? Sometimes the real message in a communication is buried in the silence.

Nonverbal Communication

Every time we deliver a verbal message, we also impart a nonverbal message.[19] Sometimes the nonverbal component may stand alone. Anyone who has ever paid a visit to a singles bar or a nightclub is aware that communication need not be verbal to convey a message. A glance, a stare, a smile, a frown, a provocative body movement—they all convey meaning. This example illustrates that no discussion of communication would be complete without a discussion of **nonverbal communication**. This type of communication includes body movements, facial expressions, and the physical distance between the sender and receiver.

Does body language really make a difference?

It has been argued that every body movement has a meaning and that no movement is accidental.[20] Through body language, we can say such things as, "Help me, I'm confused," or "Leave me alone, I'm really angry." Rarely do we send our messages consciously. We act out our state of being with nonverbal body language, even if we are not aware of doing so. We lift one eyebrow for disbelief. We rub our noses for puzzlement. We clasp our arms to isolate ourselves or to protect ourselves. We shrug our shoulders for indifference, wink one eye for intimacy, tap our fingers for impatience, slap our forehead for forgetfulness.[21]

The two most important messages that body language conveys are (1) the extent to which an individual likes another and is interested in his or her views and (2) the relative perceived status between a sender and receiver.[22] For instance, we are more likely to position ourselves closer to people we like and to touch them more often. Similarly, if you feel that you are of higher status than another, you are more likely to display body movements—such as crossed legs or a slouched seated position—that reflect a casual and relaxed manner.[23]

nonverbal communication Messages conveyed through body movements, facial expressions, and the physical distance between the sender and receiver.

While we may disagree with the specific meaning of certain movements (and different cultures may interpret specific body movements differently), body language adds to and often complicates verbal communication. For instance, if you read the transcript of a meeting, you do not grasp the impact of what was said in the same way you would if you had been there or had seen the meeting on video. Why? There is no record of nonverbal communication. The *intonations*, or emphasis, given to words or phrases is missing.

The *facial expression* of a person also conveys meaning. A snarling face says something different from a smile. Facial expressions, along with intonations, can show arrogance, aggressiveness, fear, shyness, and other characteristics that would never be communicated if you read a transcript of the meeting.

The way individuals space themselves in terms of *physical distance*, commonly called **proxemics**, also has meaning. What is considered proper spacing is largely dependent on cultural norms. For instance, studies have shown that those from "contact" cultures (for example, Arabs, Latin Americans, southern Europeans) are more comfortable with body closeness and touch than those from "noncontact" cultures (for example, Asians, North Americans, northern Europeans).[24] These differences can lead to confusion. If someone stands closer to you than expected according to your cultural norms, you may interpret the action as an expression of aggressiveness or sexual interest. However, if the person stands farther away than you expect, you might think he or she is displeased with you or uninterested. Someone whose cultural norms differ from yours might be very surprised by your interpretation.

It's important for the receiver to be alert to these nonverbal aspects of communication. You should look for nonverbal cues, as well as listen to the literal meaning of a sender's words. In particular, you should be aware of contradictions between the messages. The manager may say that she is free to talk to you about that raise you have been seeking, but you may see nonverbal signals (such as looking at her watch) that suggest this is not the time to discuss the subject. It's not uncommon for people to express one emotion verbally and another nonverbally. These contradictions often suggest that actions speak louder (and more accurately) than words.

We should also monitor body language with some care. For instance, while it is often thought that people who cross their arms in front of their chest are showing resistance to a message, individuals might also do this if they are feeling cold, regardless of their reaction to a message.

Stress

One of the most difficult times to communicate properly is when one is under stress. One consultant has identified several tips for communicating under stress. These tips are also appropriate for encouraging less stressful communication.[25]

- *Speak clearly.* Be direct about what you want to say, and avoid hiding behind words. For instance, as difficult as it might be to say, "You did not receive the position," the listener is better able to process the information when it is spoken that directly.

How can you communicate better when you are stressed out?

- *Be aware of the nonverbal part of communicating.* Tone, facial expression, and body language send signals that may or may not be consistent with your message. In a stressful situation, it is best to speak in a neutral manner.

- *Think carefully about how you state things.* In many situations, it is better to be restrained so that you do not offend your listener. For instance, when you threaten someone if they do not do exactly what you want ("I insist on speaking

proxemics The study of physical space in interpersonal relationships.

to your manager this minute"), you simply escalate the situation. It is better to state what you want calmly, so that you can be heard accurately.

Organizational Communication

How an organization communicates with its constituents plays an important role in whether the constituents actually hear the message.[26] Writing a letter to the mayor threatening a human rights complaint was certainly provocative. But this was not the only communication the Toronto Leaside Girls Hockey Association (TLGHA) launched. The association set other communication targets: reach 10 million people through the media (including a feature in the *Toronto Star*), get 900 Facebook fans, and get 2000 signatures on a petition.

The tactics the association used included the association president sending emails to parents to explain the plan of action; developing a Facebook fan page ("Fairness for Girls' Hockey in Toronto"); and conducting interviews on radio and television, and with the major local newspapers. TLGHA also created an online petition, which was ranked among "the top five most popular petitions on ipetitions.com." The association updated its Facebook page daily and included a "petition quote of the day."

What was the result of all of this attention to communication? When Toronto city council finally debated the issue, it was long and rancorous. The seven-hour debate took place over four days. Then-mayor David Miller sided with TLGHA, saying that the girls did not get enough ice time. The volunteer boards of the eight arenas were "ordered to allocate their ice equitably." So what can organizations do to make communication more effective?

3 How does communication flow in organizations?

In this section, we explore ways that communication occurs in organizations, including the direction of communication, formal small-group networks, the grapevine, and electronic communications.

Direction of Communication

Communication can flow downward, upward, and/or laterally in organizations.[27] We will explore each of these directional flows and their implications.

Downward

Communication that flows from one level of a group or organization to a lower level is downward communication. When we think of managers communicating with employees, the downward pattern is the one we usually have in mind. Group leaders and managers use this approach to assign goals, provide job instructions, inform employees of policies and procedures, identify problems that need attention, and offer feedback about performance.

When engaging in downward communication, managers must explain the reasons *why* a decision was made. One study found that employees were twice as likely to be committed to changes when the reasons behind them were fully explained. Although this may seem like common sense, many managers feel they are too busy to explain things, or that explanations will "open up a big can of worms." Evidence clearly indicates, though, that explanations increase employee commitment and support of decisions.[28] Toronto-based RL Solutions, a health care software developer, shares all of its performance and financial information with employees, so that everyone feels that they are in the loop.[29]

Upward

Upward communication flows to a higher level in the group or organization. It's used to provide feedback to higher-ups, inform them of progress toward goals, and relay current problems. Upward communication keeps managers aware of how employees feel about their jobs, co-workers, and the organization in general. Managers also rely on upward communication for ideas on how things can be improved. Port Coquitlam, BC-based

Benefits by Design, a benefits administration agency, encourages an open-door policy so that staff members can take their concerns to their managers as soon as possible.[30]

Given that job responsibilities of most managers and supervisors have expanded, upward communication is increasingly difficult because managers are overwhelmed and easily distracted. As well, sometimes managers subtly (or not so subtly) discourage employees from speaking up.[31] To engage in effective upward communication, try to reduce distractions (meet in a conference room if you can, rather than your boss's office or cubicle), communicate in headlines, not paragraphs (your job is to get your boss's attention, not to engage in a meandering discussion), support your headlines with actionable items (what you believe should happen), and prepare an agenda to make sure you use your boss's attention well.[32]

In general, few Canadian firms rely on upward communication. In their study of 375 Canadian organizations, David Saunders, dean of Queen's School of Business, and Joanne Leck, associate dean (research) at the University of Ottawa School of Management, found that unionized organizations were more likely to use upward communication.[33] The form of upward communication most used was grievance procedures.

Lateral

When communication occurs among members of the same work group, among members of work groups at the same level, among managers at the same level, or among any horizontally equivalent employees, we describe it as lateral (or horizontal) communication.

Horizontal communication is often necessary to save time and to ease coordination. In some cases, lateral relationships are formally sanctioned. Often, they are informally created to short-circuit the vertical hierarchy and speed up action. So lateral communication can, from management's perspective, be good or bad. Because strict adherence to the formal vertical structure for all communications can slow the efficient and accurate transfer of information, lateral communication can be beneficial. In such cases, it occurs with the knowledge and support of managers. But it can create dysfunctional conflicts when the formal vertical channels are breached, when members go above or around their managers to get things done, or when employers find out that actions have been taken or decisions made without their knowledge.

Small-Group Networks

Communication networks define the channels by which information flows. These channels are one of two varieties—either formal or informal. **Formal networks** are typically vertical, follow the authority chain, and are limited to task-related communications. Exhibit 19-3 illustrates three common formal small-group networks: *chain*, *wheel*, and *all-channel*. The chain network rigidly follows the formal chain of command. The wheel network relies on the leader to act as the central conduit for all the group's communication. The all-channel network permits all group members to communicate actively with one another. As Exhibit 19-3 illustrates, the effectiveness of each network depends on the dependent variable you are concerned about. For instance, the structure of the wheel network facilitates the emergence of a leader, the all-channel network is best if high member satisfaction is most important, and the chain network is best if accuracy is most important. Thus, we conclude that no single network is appropriate for all occasions.

The Grapevine

The most common **informal network** in the organization is the **grapevine**. Research has found that 75 percent of employees hear about matters first through rumours on the grapevine.[34] A recent study shows that grapevine or word-of-mouth information

communication networks Channels by which information flows.

formal networks Task-related communications that follow the authority chain.

informal networks Communications that flow along social and relational lines.

grapevine The organization's most common informal network.

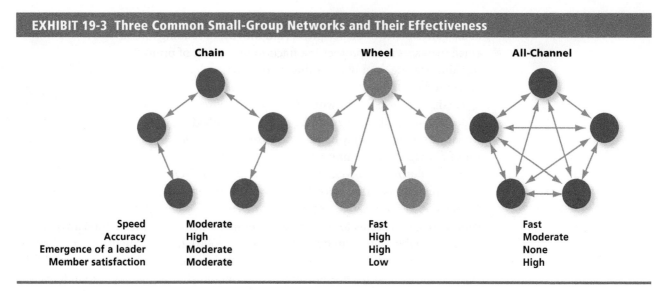

EXHIBIT 19-3 Three Common Small-Group Networks and Their Effectiveness

	Chain	Wheel	All-Channel
Speed	Moderate	Fast	Fast
Accuracy	High	High	Moderate
Emergence of a leader	Moderate	High	None
Member satisfaction	Moderate	Low	High

from peers about a company has important effects on whether job applicants join an organization.[35] Thus it is an important source of information for many employees.

The grapevine has three main characteristics.[36] First, it is not controlled by management. Second, most employees perceive it as more believable and reliable than formal communiqués issued by top management. Finally, it is largely used to serve the interests of the people within it.

Is the information that flows along the grapevine accurate? The evidence indicates that about 75 percent of what is carried is accurate.[37] But what conditions foster an active grapevine? What gets the rumour mill rolling?

It is frequently assumed that rumours start because they make titillating gossip. Research indicates that rumours emerge as a response to situations that are important to us, where there is ambiguity, and under conditions that arouse anxiety.[38] The secrecy and competition that typically prevail in large organizations around such issues as the appointment of new senior managers, the relocation of offices, and the realignment of work assignments create conditions that encourage and sustain rumours on the grapevine. A rumour will persist either until the wants and expectations creating the uncertainty underlying the rumour are fulfilled or until the anxiety is reduced.

What can we conclude from this discussion? Certainly the grapevine is an important part of any group's or organization's communication network and well worth understanding.[39] It gives managers a feel for the morale of their organization, identifies issues employees consider important, and helps tap into employee anxieties. The grapevine also serves employees' needs: Small talk creates a sense of closeness and friendship among those who share information, although research suggests it often does so at the expense of those in the "out" group.[40] Managers can reduce the negative consequences of rumours by explaining decisions and openly discussing worst-case possibilities.[41]

Electronic Communications

An indispensable—and in about 71 percent of cases, the primary—medium of communication in today's organizations is electronic. Electronic communications—which include email, instant messaging, text messaging, social networking sites, and blogs—make it possible for you to work, even if you are away from your workstation.

Email

Email's growth has been spectacular, and its use is now so pervasive that it's hard to imagine life without it. As a communication tool, email has a long list of benefits. Email messages can be quickly written, edited, and stored. They can be distributed to one person or thousands with a click of a mouse. They can be read, in their entirety, at the convenience of the recipient. And the cost of sending formal email messages to employees is a fraction of the cost of printing, duplicating, and distributing a comparable letter or brochure.[42]

Email, of course, is not without drawbacks. Email has added considerably to the number of hours worked per week, according to a study by Christina Cavanagh, professor of management communications at the Richard Ivey School of Business, University of Western Ontario.[43] One researcher suggests that knowledge workers devote about 28 percent of their day to email.[44] While the increase in the volume of email seems to have slowed, up just 9 percent between 2006 and 2007 (compared with 26 percent between 2005 and 2006), the volume of junk mail shows no let-up.[45] Canadians divert 42 percent of their email directly to "junk mail" folders, according to an Ipsos Reid study. Over one-third of the survey respondents said they had trouble handling all of their email, and only 43 percent thought that email increased efficiency at work.

> Ever notice that communicating via email can lead to misunderstandings?

The following are some of the most significant limitations of email and what organizations should do to reduce or eliminate these problems:

- *Misinterpreting the message.* It's true that we often misinterpret verbal messages, but the potential for misinterpretation with email is even greater. One research team found that we can accurately decode an email's intent and tone only 50 percent of the time, yet most of us vastly overestimate our ability to send and interpret clear messages. If you are sending an important message, make sure you reread it for clarity. Moreover, if you are upset about the presumed tone of someone else's message, keep in mind that you may be misinterpreting it.[46]

- *Communicating negative messages.* When companies have negative information to communicate, managers need to think carefully. Email may not be the best way to communicate the message. When RadioShack decided to lay off

Toronto-based Upverter was started by three friends (left to right) Zak Homuth, Stephen Hamer, and Michael Woodworth (shown here at the Maker Faire, an event that showcases grassroots innovation). The three, all trained as electrical engineers, wanted to create a network for online collaboration for hardware designers. They launched a "crowd-sourced library of parts and design tools," and the company took off quickly after they demonstrated the service at DemoFall 2011 in Santa Clara, California.

400 employees, it was widely criticized for doing it via email. Employees need to be careful communicating negative messages via email, too. Justen Deal, 22, wrote an email critical of some strategic decisions made by his employer, pharmaceutical giant Kaiser Permanente. In the email, he criticized the "misleadership" of Kaiser CEO George Halvorson and questioned the financing of several information technology projects. Within hours, Deal's computer was seized; he was later fired.[47]

- *Time-consuming nature of email.* An estimated 6 trillion emails are sent every year, of which approximately 60 percent, or 36 trillion, are nonspam messages,[48] and someone has to answer all those nonspam messages! A survey of Canadian managers revealed 58 percent spent 2 to 4 hours per day reading and responding to emails. The average worker checks his or her email 50 times a day. Some people, such as venture capitalist and Dallas Mavericks owner Mark Cuban, receive more than 1000 messages a day (Cuban says 10 percent are of the "I want" variety). Although you probably don't receive *that* many, most of us have trouble keeping up with all email, especially as we advance in our career. Experts suggest the following strategies:

  - *Do not check email in the morning.* Take care of important tasks before getting ensnared in emails. Otherwise, you may never get to those tasks.

  - *Check email in batches.* Don't check email continually throughout the day. Some experts suggest twice a day. "You wouldn't want to do a new load of laundry every time you have a dirty pair of socks," says one expert.

  - *Unsubscribe.* Stop newsletters and other subscriptions you don't really need.

  - *Stop sending email.* The best way to receive lots of email is to send lots of email, so send less. Shorter emails garner shorter responses. "A well-written message can and should be as concise as possible," says one expert.

  - *Declare email bankruptcy.* Some people, like recording artist Moby and venture capitalist Fred Wilson, become so overwhelmed by email they declare "email bankruptcy." They wipe out their entire inbox and start over.

    Although some of these steps may not work for you, keep in mind that email can be less productive than it seems: We often seem busy but get less accomplished through email than we might think.[49]

- *Email emotions.* We tend to think of email as a sort of sterile, faceless form of communication. Some researchers say the lack of visual and vocal cues means emotionally positive messages, such as those including praise, will be seen as more emotionally neutral than the sender intended.[50] But, as you no doubt know, emails are often highly emotional. One CEO said, "I've seen people not talk to each other, turf wars break out and people quit their jobs as a result of emails." Email tends to make senders feel free to write things they would never be comfortable saying in person. Facial expressions tend to temper our emotional expressions, but in email, there is no other face to look at, and so many of us fire away. An increasingly common way of communicating emotions in email is with emoticons (see Exhibit 19-4). For example, Yahoo!'s email software allows users to pick from 75 graphical emoticons. Although emoticons used to be considered for personal use only, adults are increasingly using them in business emails. Still, some see them as too informal for business use.

    If you find yourself angry or upset as you write an email, save it as a draft, and look at it again once you are on a more even keel. When others send flaming messages, remain calm and try not to respond in kind. And, as hard

EXHIBIT 19-4 Showing Emotions in Email

Email need not be emotion-free. Over the years, email users have developed a way of displaying text, as well as a set of symbols (emoticons) for expressing emotions. For instance, the use of all caps (as in THIS PROJECT NEEDS YOUR IMMEDIATE ATTENTION!) is the email equivalent of shouting. The following highlights some emoticons:

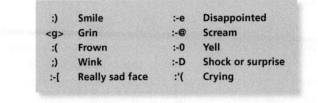

:)	Smile	:-e	Disappointed
<g>	Grin	:-@	Scream
:(	Frown	:-0	Yell
;)	Wink	:-D	Shock or surprise
:-[	Really sad face	:'(	Crying

as it might sometimes be, try to see the flaming message from the other party's point of view. That in itself may calm your nerves.[51]

- *Privacy concerns.* There are two privacy issues with email. First, you need to be aware that your emails may be, and often are, monitored. Also, you cannot always trust that the recipient of your email will keep it confidential. For these reasons, you should not write anything you would not want made public. Second, you need to exercise caution in forwarding email from your company's email account to a personal, or "public" (for example, Gmail, Yahoo!, MSN), email account. These accounts often are not as secure as corporate accounts, so when you forward a company email to them, you may be violating your organization's policy or unintentionally disclosing confidential data. Many employers hire vendors to sift through emails, using software to catch not only the obvious keywords ("insider trading") but also the vague ("that thing we talked about") or guilt ridden ("regret"). One survey found that nearly 40 percent of companies have employees whose only job is to read other employees' email. You are being watched—so be careful what you email![52]

Ann Cavoukian, Information and Privacy Commissioner of Ontario, notes that "employees deserve to be treated like adults and companies should limit surveillance to rare instances, such as when there is suspicion of criminal activity or harassment."[53] She suggests that employers use respect and courtesy when dealing with employees' email, and she likens email to office phone calls, which generally are not monitored by the employer. It is clearly important, in any event, that employees be aware of their company's policy on email.

Instant Messaging and Text Messaging

Instant messaging (IM) and text messaging (TM), which have been popular among teens for more than a decade, are now rapidly moving into business.[54]

The growth of IM and TM has been spectacular. In 2002, Canadians sent 174 million text messages, while the estimate for 2011 is 72.6 billion, a staggering increase.[55] More people use IM than email as their primary communication tool at work.[56]

IM and TM represent fast and inexpensive means for managers to stay in touch with employees and for employees to stay in touch with one another. In an increasing number of cases, this is not just a luxury, it is a business imperative.

Despite the advantages of IM and TM, email is still probably a better device for conveying long messages that need to be saved. IM is preferable for one- or two-line messages that would just clutter up an email inbox. On the downside, some IM/TM users find the technology intrusive and distracting. Its continual presence can make it hard for employees to concentrate and stay focused. For example, a survey of managers revealed that in 86 percent of meetings, at least some participants checked TM, and another survey revealed 20 percent of managers report having been reprimanded for using wireless devices during meetings.[57] Finally, because instant messages can be intercepted easily, many organizations are concerned about the security of IM/TM.[58]

One other point: It's important to not let the informality of text messaging ("omg! r u serious? brb") spill over into business emails. Many prefer to keep business communication relatively formal. A survey of employers revealed that 58 percent rate grammar, spelling, and punctuation as "very important" in email messages.[59] By making sure your professional communications are, well, professional, you will show yourself to be mature and serious. Avoid jargon and slang, use formal titles, use formal email addresses for yourself (lose that partygirl@yahoo.com address), and take care to make your message concise and well written. That does not mean, of course, that you have to give up TM or IM; you just need to maintain the boundaries between how you communicate with your friends and how you communicate professionally.

Social Networking

Nowhere has communication been more transformed than in social networking. You are doubtless familiar with and perhaps a user of social networking platforms such as Facebook. LinkedIn, XING, and ZoomInfo are all professional websites that allow users to set up lists of contacts and do everything from casually "pinging" them with updates to hosting chat rooms for all or some of the users' contacts. Some companies, such as IBM, have their own social networks. IBM is selling its BluePages tool to companies and individual users. Microsoft is doing the same thing with its SharePoint tool.

To get the most out of social networks and avoid irritating your contacts, use them for high-value items only—not as an everyday or even every-week tool. Remember that a prospective employer might check your Facebook entry. Some entrepreneurs have developed software that mines such websites for companies (or individuals) that want to check up on a job applicant (or potential date). So keep in mind that what you post may be read by people other than your intended contacts.[60] Employees have been disciplined for Facebook postings.

Blogs

Peter Aceto, CEO of Toronto-based ING Direct Canada, is a big fan of the **blog (web log)**, a website about a single person or company that is usually updated daily. He encourages his employees to have blogs and has one himself (http://blog.ingdirect.ca/author/paceto/). Aceto allows readers to post comments and rate his blog entries.

Obviously, Aceto is not the only fan of blogs. Experts estimate that more than 112 million blogs and more than 350 million blog entries are now read daily. While most blogs are written by individuals, many organizations and organizational leaders have blogs that speak for the organization.

As a variant of blogs (which are generally either personal or company-owned), Twitter is a service that allows users to post "micro-blog" entries about any topic, including work. Many organizational leaders send Twitter messages ("tweets"), but they can come from any employee about any work topic, leaving organizations with less control over the communication of important or sensitive information. While many CEOs worry about the use of Twitter, Peter Aceto posts to Twitter at least five times a day. One of his tweets in November 2010 informed his 3785 Twitter followers that his daughter had just scored her first goal. Aceto uses social media because "I felt my personal involvement in being transparent would be important for our brand."[61] A 2010 study found that only 8 percent of CEOs at the world's largest companies have Twitter accounts, while 64 percent have no social media presence at all.[62]

blog (web log) A website where entries are written, and generally displayed in reverse chronological order, about news, events, and personal diary entries.

Managing Information

④ How is information managed?

We all have more information at our disposal than ever. It brings us many benefits, but also three important challenges: information overload, being always on call, and information security. We consider each in turn.

Dealing with Information Overload

Do you find yourself bombarded with information—from email, blogs, Internet surfing, IMs, cellphones, and television? You are not alone. Basex, a company that looks at worker efficiency, found the largest part of an average employee's day—43 percent—is spent on matters that are neither important nor urgent, such as responding to non-crucial emails and surfing the web. (In fairness to email, Basex also found 25 percent of an employee's time was spent composing and responding to important email.[63])

Semiconductor manufacturer Intel designed an 8-month experiment to see how limiting information overload might aid productivity. One group of employees was told to limit both digital and in-person contact for 4 hours on Tuesdays, while another group followed its usual routine. The first group was more productive, and 75 percent of its members suggested the program be expanded.[64] "It's huge. We were expecting less," remarked Nathan Zeldes, an Intel engineer who led the experiments. "When people are uninterrupted they can sit back and design chips and really think."[65]

Some of the biggest technology companies, including Microsoft, Intel, Google, and IBM, are banding together to study the issue more systematically. As one of the team members, IBM's John Tang, noted, "There's a competitive advantage to figuring out how to address this problem."[66]

We have already reviewed some ways of reducing the time sunk into emails. More generally, as the Intel study shows, it may make sense to connect to technology less frequently, to, in the words of one article, "avoid letting the drumbeat of digital missives constantly shake up and reorder to-do lists." Lynaia Lutes, an account supervisor for a small Texas company, was able to think much more strategically by taking a break from digital information each day. In the past, she said, "I basically completed an assignment" but didn't approach it strategically. By creating such breaks for yourself, you may be better able to prioritize and think about the big picture and, thereby, be more effective.[67]

Being Always on Call

As information technology and immediate communication have become a more prevalent component of modern organizational life, more employees find they are never able to get offline. The addictive potential of constant communication is so great that some harried managers jokingly refer to their BlackBerrys as "Crackberries."[68] Some business travellers were disappointed when airlines began offering wireless Internet connections in flight because they could no longer use their time in flight as a rare opportunity to relax without a constant barrage of organizational communications. The negative impacts of these communication devices can spill over into employees' personal lives as well. Both employees and their spouses relate the use of electronic communication technologies outside of work to higher levels of work-life conflict.[69] Employees must balance the need for constant communication with their own personal need for breaks from work, or they risk burnout from being on call 24 hours a day.

Information Security

Security is a huge concern for nearly all organizations with private or proprietary information about clients, customers, and employees. A Merrill Lynch survey of 50 executives found 52 percent rated leaks of company information as their number one information security concern, topping viruses and hackers. In response, most companies actively monitor employee Internet use and email records, and some even use video surveillance and record phone conversations. Necessary though they may be, such practices may seem invasive to employees. An organization can buttress employee concerns by involving them in the creation of information-security policies and giving them some control over how their personal information is used.[70]

GLOBAL IMPLICATIONS

Effective communication is difficult under the best of conditions. Cross-cultural factors clearly create the potential for increased communication problems.

Cultural Barriers to Communication

Researchers have identified four specific problems related to language difficulties in cross-cultural communication.[71] First, there are *barriers caused by semantics*. As we have noted previously, words mean different things to different people. This is particularly true for people from different national cultures. Some words, for instance, don't translate between cultures. Understanding the word *sisu* will help you communicate with people from Finland, but this word does not have an exact translation in English. It means something akin to "guts" or "dogged persistence." Similarly, the new capitalists in Russia may have difficulty communicating with their English-speaking counterparts because English terms such as *efficiency*, *free market*, and *regulation* cannot be directly translated into Russian.

Second, there are *barriers caused by word connotations*. Words imply different things in different languages. The Japanese word *hai* translates as "yes," but its connotation may be "yes, I'm listening," rather than "yes, I agree." Western executives may be hampered in their negotiations if they don't understand this connotation.

Third are *barriers caused by tone differences*. In some cultures, language is formal; in others, it's informal. In some cultures, the tone changes depending on the context: People speak differently at home, in social situations, and at work. Using a personal, informal style in a situation where a more formal style is expected can be embarrassing and offensive.

Fourth are *differences in tolerance for conflict and methods for resolving conflicts*. Individuals from individualist cultures tend to be more comfortable with direct conflicts and will make the source of their disagreements overt. Collectivists are more likely to acknowledge conflict only implicitly and avoid emotionally charged disputes. They may attribute conflicts to the situation more than to the individuals and therefore may not require explicit apologies to repair relationships, whereas individualists prefer explicit statements accepting responsibility for conflicts and public apologies to restore relationships.

Cultural Context

Cultures tend to differ in the degree to which context influences the meaning individuals take from communication.[72] In **high-context cultures** like China, Vietnam, and Saudi Arabia, people rely heavily on nonverbal and subtle situational cues when communicating with others. What is not said may be more significant than what is said. A person's official status, place in society, and reputation carry considerable weight in communications. In contrast, people from Europe and North America reflect their **low-context cultures**. They rely essentially on words to convey meaning. Body language or formal titles are secondary to spoken and written words (see Exhibit 19-5).

high-context cultures Cultures that rely heavily on nonverbal and subtle situational cues in communication.

low-context cultures Cultures that rely heavily on words to convey meaning in communication.

What do these contextual differences mean in terms of communication? Actually, quite a lot! Communication in high-context cultures implies considerably more trust by both parties.

What may appear, to an outsider, as a casual and insignificant conversation is important because it reflects the desire to build a relationship and create trust. Oral agreements imply strong commitments in high-context cultures. Also, who you are—your age, seniority, rank in the organization—are highly valued and heavily influence your credibility. But in low-context cultures, enforceable contracts will tend to be in writing, precisely worded, and highly legalistic. Similarly, low-context cultures value directness. Managers are expected to be explicit and precise in conveying intended meaning. It's quite different in high-context cultures, where managers tend to "make suggestions" rather than give orders.

A Cultural Guide

When communicating with people from a different culture, what can you do to reduce misperceptions, misinterpretations, and misevaluations? Following these four rules can be helpful:[73]

> How can you improve cross-cultural communication?

- *Assume differences until similarity is proven.* Most of us assume that others are more similar to us than they actually are. But people from different countries often are very different from us. So you are far less likely to make an error if you assume that others are different from you, rather than assuming similarity until difference is proven.

- *Emphasize description rather than interpretation or evaluation.* Interpreting or evaluating what someone has said or done, in contrast with describing, is based more on the observer's culture and background than on the observed situation. As a result, delay judgment until you have had sufficient time to

Globalization has changed the way Toyota Motor Corporation provides employees with the information they need for decision making. In the past, Toyota transferred employee knowledge on the job from generation to generation through "tacit understanding," a common communication method used in the conformist and subdued Japanese culture. Today, however, as a global organization, Toyota transfers knowledge of its production methods to overseas employees by bringing them to its training centre in Japan, shown here, to teach them production methods by using how-to manuals, practice drills, and lectures.

EXHIBIT 19-5 High- vs. Low-Context Cultures

High
context

→ Chinese
Korean
Japanese
Vietnamese
Arab
Greek
Spanish
Italian
English
North American
Scandinavian

Low
context

↓ Swiss
German

observe and interpret the situation from the differing perspectives of all the cultures involved.

- *Practise empathy.* Before sending a message, put yourself in the recipient's shoes. What are his or her values, experiences, and frames of reference? What do you know about his or her education, upbringing, and background that can give you added insight? Try to see the other person as he or she really is.

- *Treat your interpretations as a working hypothesis.* Once you have developed an explanation for a new situation, or think you empathize with someone from a foreign culture, treat your interpretation as a hypothesis that needs further testing rather than as a certainty. Carefully assess the feedback provided by recipients to see if it confirms your hypothesis. For important decisions or communiqués, you can also check with other foreign and home-country colleagues to ensure that your interpretations are on target.

LESSONS LEARNED

- Just because something is said, it does not mean that it was heard.
- Communication is rarely "objective." Both the sender's and receiver's reality affects the framing and understanding of the message.
- Information overload is a serious problem for most individuals.

Ottawa-based Donna Cona made history when it designed and installed the computer network for the government of Nunavut. Two-thirds of the firm's software engineers are Aboriginal. Peter Baril, Nunavut's director of information technology operations, notes: "Donna Cona's quiet and knowledgeable approach was perhaps the most important skill brought to our project. No other style could have worked in this predominantly Aboriginal environment."

20

Leadership

Leadership in a team setting is something that Lieutenant Colonel Maryse Carmichael knows a lot about.[1] Since May 2010 she has been the Commanding Officer (CO) of the 431 Air Demonstration Squadron, better known as Canada's Snowbirds. Carmichael is responsible for 14 pilots and 71 ground employees, and she knows the importance of maintaining strong relationships with her staff. In fact, it was the military's desire to promote strong relationships that led to the creation of her position.

Previously, the squadron's CO had always been a Major and a flying member of the demonstration team. With so many staff on the ground, however, it became hard to manage personnel effectively while on the road. The Canadian Forces created a new CO role at the Lieutenant Colonel level, responsible for administration and command of the fleet, maintenance, and personnel. Carmichael's two decades of experience with the Canadian Air Force in a number of flying and non-flying roles made her a natural choice for the newly defined position. She entered the job having established the trust and respect of both pilots and ground personnel, since she had proven herself in both areas.

Carmichael believes that working with the Snowbirds provides an opportunity for leadership at two levels. "For me it is about looking at the overall operations of the entire squadron and the future of the squadron." But it is also about a broader kind of leadership. "We demonstrate to the Canadian public the skills, professionalism, and teamwork of the Canadian Forces." For Carmichael, it is not enough to inspire her own team; she seeks to inspire an entire nation.

In this chapter, we review leadership studies to determine what makes an effective leader. We consider factors that affect one's ability to lead and examine inspirational leadership and self-management. Finally, we discuss contemporary issues in leadership.

Are Managers and Leaders the Same?

1 What is the difference between a manager and a leader?

Leadership and *management* are two terms that are often confused. What is the difference between them?

John Kotter of the Harvard Business School argues that "managers promote stability while leaders press for change and only organizations that embrace both sides of the contradiction can survive in turbulent times."[2]

McGill University professor Rabindra Kanungo notes there is a growing consensus emerging "among management scholars that the concept of 'leadership' must be distinguished from the concept of 'supervision/management.'"[3] Exhibit 20-1 illustrates Kanungo's distinctions between leadership and management. Leaders establish direction by developing a vision of the future; then they align people by communicating this vision and inspiring them to overcome hurdles. In other words, leaders need to develop followers. Managers implement the vision and strategy provided by leaders, coordinate and staff the organization, and handle day-to-day problems. Organizations need strong leadership *and* strong management for optimal effectiveness.

In our discussion of leadership, we will focus on two major tasks of those who lead in organizations: managing those around them to get the day-to-day tasks done, and inspiring others to do the extraordinary. It will become clear that successful leaders rely on a variety of interpersonal skills in order to encourage others to perform at their best. It will also become clear that, no matter the place in the hierarchy, from CEO to team leader, a variety of individuals can be called on to perform leadership roles.

Leadership as Supervision

2 Are there specific traits, behaviours, and situations that affect how one leads?

Lt.-Col. Maryse Carmichael served as a Snowbird pilot from early 2000 until late 2001, at which point she received a promotion to an Executive Officer role, followed by relocation to the air force base at Bagotville, Quebec.[4] She says that returning to the Snowbirds as Commanding Officer has given her a new perspective on leadership: "This time around it is really about the entire squadron, about leading the men and women of 431 Squadron to accomplish our mission every day. So it has a broader focus this time."

EXHIBIT 20-1 Distinguishing Leadership from Management	
Management	**Leadership**
1. Engages in day-to-day caretaker activities: Maintains and allocates resources	Formulates long-term objectives for reforming the system: Plans strategy and tactics
2. Exhibits supervisory behaviour: Acts to make others maintain standard job behaviour	Exhibits leading behaviour: Acts to bring about change in others congruent with long-term objectives
3. Administers subsystems within organizations	Innovates for the entire organization
4. Asks how and when to engage in standard practice	Asks what and why to change standard practice
5. Acts within established culture of the organization	Creates vision and meaning for the organization
6. Uses transactional influence: Induces compliance in manifest behaviour using rewards, sanctions, and formal authority	Uses transformational influence: Induces change in values, attitudes, and behaviour using personal examples and expertise
7. Relies on control strategies to get things done by subordinates	Uses empowering strategies to make followers internalize values
8. Status quo supporter and stabilizer	Status quo challenger and change creator

Source: Copyright 1998, Canadian Psychological Association. Permission granted for use of material.

Her focus on the big picture makes sense in more ways than one. Military jobs are unique in that roles and responsibilities are highly formalized and defined in great detail, and the level of compliance with policies and procedures is extremely high. Penalties for non-compliance are also highly formalized and follow standardized procedures. This helps senior officers maintain a strong focus on strategic decision making rather than on acting as supervisors, since lower level employees have full information and very little ambiguity about managing their day-to-day tasks. So, what makes an effective leader?

In this section, we discuss theories of leadership that were developed before 1980. These early theories focused on the supervisory nature of leadership—that is, how individuals managed the day-to-day functioning of employees. The theories took different approaches in understanding how best to lead in a supervisory capacity. The three general types of theories that emerged were (1) trait theories, which propose leaders have a particular set of traits that makes them different from nonleaders; (2) behavioural theories, which propose that particular behaviours make for better leaders; and (3) contingency theories, which propose the situation has an effect on leaders. When you think about these theories, remember that although they have been considered "theories of leadership," they rely on an older understanding of what "leadership" means, and they don't convey Kanungo's distinction between leadership and supervision.

Trait Theories: Are Leaders Different from Others?

Have you ever wondered whether there is some fundamental personality difference that makes some people "born leaders"? **Trait theories of leadership** focus on personal qualities and characteristics. We recognize leaders like South Africa's Nelson Mandela, Virgin Group CEO Richard Branson, and Apple co-founder Steve Jobs as *charismatic*, *enthusiastic*, and *courageous*. Trait theory emerged in the hope that if it were possible to identify the traits of leaders, it would be easier to select people to fill leadership roles. Being able to select good leaders is important because not all people know how to be good leaders.

Research efforts at isolating leadership traits resulted in a number of dead ends. For instance, a review in the late 1960s of 20 studies identified nearly 80 leadership traits, but only 5 of these traits were common to 4 or more of the investigations.[5] By the 1990s, after numerous studies and analyses, about the best thing that could be said was that most "leaders are not like other people," but the particular traits that were isolated varied a great deal from review to review.[6] It was a pretty confusing state of affairs.

A breakthrough, of sorts, came when researchers began organizing traits around the Big Five Personality Model (see Chapter 2).[7] Most of the dozens of traits in various leadership reviews fit under one of the Big Five (ambition and energy are part of extraversion, for instance), giving strong support to traits as predictors of leadership.

A comprehensive review of the leadership literature, when organized around the Big Five, found extraversion to be the most important trait of effective leaders[8] but more strongly related to leader emergence than to leader effectiveness. Sociable and dominant people are more likely to assert themselves in group situations, but leaders need to make sure they are not too assertive—one study found that leaders who scored very high on assertiveness were less effective than those who were moderately high.[9]

Unlike agreeableness and emotional stability, conscientiousness and openness to experience also showed strong and consistent relationships to leadership, though not quite as strong as extraversion. Overall, the trait approach does have something to offer. Leaders who like being around people and are able to assert themselves (extraverted), are disciplined and keep commitments they make (conscientious), and are creative and flexible (open) do have an advantage when it comes to leadership, suggesting that good leaders do have key traits in common.

One reason is that conscientiousness and extraversion are positively related to leaders' self-efficacy, which explained most of the variance in subordinates' ratings of

trait theories of leadership
Theories that consider personal qualities and characteristics that differentiate leaders from nonleaders.

leader performance.[10] People are more likely to follow someone who is confident that she is going in the right direction.

Another trait that may indicate effective leadership is emotional intelligence (EI), discussed in Chapter 2. Advocates of EI argue that without it, a person can have outstanding training, a highly analytical mind, a compelling vision, and an endless supply of terrific ideas but still not make a great leader. This may be especially true as individuals move up in an organization.[11] Why is EI so critical to effective leadership? A core component of EI is empathy. Empathetic leaders can sense others' needs, listen to what followers say (and don't say), and read the reactions of others. As one leader noted, "The caring part of empathy, especially for the people with whom you work, is what inspires people to stay with a leader when the going gets rough. The mere fact that someone cares is more often than not rewarded with loyalty."[12]

The link between EI and leadership effectiveness is still much less investigated than other traits. One reviewer noted, "Speculating about the practical utility of the EI construct might be premature. Despite such warnings, EI is being viewed as a panacea for many organizational malaises with recent suggestions that EI is essential for leadership effectiveness."[13] But until more rigorous evidence accumulates, we cannot be confident about the connection.

Based on the latest findings, we offer two conclusions. First, traits can predict leadership. Twenty years ago, the evidence suggested otherwise. But this was probably because of the lack of a valid framework for classifying and organizing traits. The Big Five seem to have rectified that. Second, traits do a better job at predicting the emergence of leaders and the appearance of leadership than in actually distinguishing between *effective* and *ineffective* leaders.[14] The fact that an individual exhibits the traits and others consider that person to be a leader does not necessarily mean that the leader is successful at getting his or her group to achieve its goals.

Behavioural Theories: Do Leaders Behave in Particular Ways?

The failures of early trait studies led researchers in the late 1940s through the 1960s to go in a different direction. They wondered whether there was something unique in the way that effective leaders behave. Trait research provides a basis for *selecting* the right people for leadership. In contrast, behavioural theories implied we could *train* people to be leaders. Many argued that **behavioural theories of leadership** had advantages over trait theories.

The Ohio State Studies

The most comprehensive and replicated behavioural theories resulted from the Ohio State Studies in the late 1940s,[15] which sought to identify independent dimensions of leader behaviour. Beginning with more than a thousand dimensions, the studies narrowed the list to two that substantially accounted for most of the leadership behaviour described by employees. Researchers called these *initiating structure* and *consideration*. **Initiating structure** is the extent to which a leader is likely to define and structure his or her role and those of employees in order to attain goals; it includes behaviour that attempts to organize work, work relationships, and goals. A leader high in initiating structure is someone who "assigns group members to particular tasks," "expects workers to maintain definite standards of performance," and "emphasizes the meeting of deadlines."

Consideration is the extent to which a leader's job relationships are characterized by mutual trust, respect for employees' ideas, and regard for their feelings. A leader high in consideration helps employees with personal problems, is friendly and approachable, treats all employees as equals, and expresses appreciation and support. In a recent

behavioural theories of leadership Theories that propose that specific behaviours differentiate leaders from nonleaders.

initiating structure The extent to which a leader is likely to define and structure his or her role and the roles of employees in order to attain goals.

consideration The extent to which a leader is likely to have job relationships characterized by mutual trust, respect for employees' ideas, and regard for their feelings.

survey, when asked to indicate the factors that most motivated them at work, 66 percent of employees mentioned appreciation.[16]

The Michigan Studies

Leadership studies at the University of Michigan's Survey Research Center had similar objectives: to locate behavioural characteristics of leaders that appeared related to performance effectiveness.[17] The Michigan group also came up with two behavioural dimensions: the **employee-oriented leaders** emphasized interpersonal relations by taking a personal interest in the needs of employees and accepting individual differences among them; the **production-oriented leaders** emphasized the technical or task aspects of the job—focusing on accomplishing the group's task. These dimensions are closely related to the Ohio State dimensions. Employee-oriented leadership is similar to consideration, and production-oriented leadership is similar to initiating structure. In fact, most leadership researchers use the terms synonymously.[18]

At one time, the results of testing behavioural theories were thought to be disappointing. One 1992 review concluded, "Overall, the research based on a two-factor conceptualization of leadership behavior has added little to our knowledge about effective leadership."[19] However, a more recent review of 160 studies found the followers of leaders high in consideration were more satisfied with their jobs, were more motivated, and had more respect for their leader. Initiating structure was more strongly related to higher levels of group and organization productivity and more positive performance evaluations.

employee-oriented leader A leader who emphasizes interpersonal relations.

production-oriented leader A leader who emphasizes the technical or task aspects of the job.

RESEARCH FINDINGS:
Behavioural Theories of Leadership

While the results of the behavioural studies have been somewhat mixed,[20] a careful evaluation of the situations that leaders face provides some insights into when leaders should be production-oriented and when they should be people-oriented:[21]

- When subordinates experience a lot of pressure because of deadlines or unclear tasks, leaders who are people-oriented will increase employee satisfaction and performance.

- When the task is interesting or satisfying, there is less need for leaders to be people-oriented.

- When it's clear how to perform the task and what the goals are, leaders who are people-oriented will increase employee satisfaction, while those who are task-oriented will increase dissatisfaction.

- When people don't know what to do, or individuals don't have the knowledge or skills to do the job, it's more important for leaders to be production-oriented than people-oriented.

The followers of leaders who are high in people orientation are more satisfied with their jobs, more motivated, and also have more respect for their leaders. Leaders who are high in task orientation show higher levels of group and organizational productivity and receive more positive performance evaluations.

Sally Jewell, CEO of Recreational Equipment (REI), is an employee-oriented leader. During her tenure as CEO, Jewell has turned a struggling company into one with record sales. But she credits REI's success to the work of employees, stating that she does not believe in "hero CEOs." Jewell respects each employee's contribution to the company and includes in her leadership people who are very different from herself. Described as a leader high in consideration, she listens to employees' ideas and empowers them in performing their jobs.

Contingency Theories: Does the Situation Matter?

Some leaders may have the right traits or display the right behaviours and still fail.[22] Moreover, many leaders who leave while their organizations are still successful—such as GE's Jack Welch or Procter & Gamble's A. G. Lafley—have their legacies clouded by events after their departure. As important as traits and behaviours are in identifying effective or ineffective leaders, they do not guarantee success. The context matters, too.

The relationship between leadership style and effectiveness suggests that there is no one right style, but that style *depends* upon the situation the leader faces. There has been no shortage of studies attempting to isolate critical situational factors that affect leadership effectiveness. The volume of studies is illustrated by the number of moderating variables that researchers have identified in their discussions of **situational, or contingency, theories**. These variables include the degree of structure in the task being performed, the quality of leader-member relations; the leader's position power; the clarity of the employee's role; group norms; information availability; employee acceptance of the leader's decisions; and employee maturity.[23]

> Have you ever wondered if there was one *right* way to lead?

We consider four situational theories below: the Fiedler contingency model, Hersey and Blanchard's Situational Leadership®, path-goal theory, and substitutes for leadership.

Fiedler Contingency Model

The first comprehensive contingency model for leadership was developed by Fred Fiedler.[24] The **Fiedler contingency model** proposes that effective group performance depends on the proper match between the leader's style and the degree to which the situation gives the leader control.

Fiedler created the *least preferred co-worker (LPC)* questionnaire to determine whether individuals were primarily interested in good personal relations with co-workers, and thus *relationship-oriented*, or primarily interested in productivity, and thus *task-oriented*. Fiedler assumed that an individual's leadership style is fixed. Therefore, if a situation requires a task-oriented leader and the person in that leadership position is relationship-oriented, either the situation has to be modified or the leader must be removed and replaced for optimum effectiveness to be achieved.

After assessing an individual's basic leadership style through an LPC questionnaire, the next step is to match the leader with the situation. Fiedler identified three contingency dimensions that determine the situation a leader faces. That situation will then affect the leader's effectiveness:

- *Leader-member relations.* The degree of confidence, trust, and respect members have for their leader.

- *Task structure.* The degree to which job assignments are procedurized (that is, structured or unstructured).

- *Position power.* The degree of influence a leader has over power-based activities such as hiring, firing, discipline, promotions, and salary increases.

The next step is to evaluate the situation in terms of these three variables. Fiedler stated that the better the leader-member relations, the more highly structured the job, and the stronger the position power, the more control the leader has. A very favourable situation (in which the leader has a great deal of control) might include a payroll manager who is well respected and whose employees have confidence in her (good leader-member relations); activities to be done—such as wage computation, cheque writing, and report filing—that are specific and clear (high task structure); and provision of considerable freedom to reward and punish employees (strong position power). An

situational, or contingency, theories Theories that propose leadership effectiveness is dependent on the situation.

Fiedler contingency model A leadership theory that proposes that effective group performance depends on the proper match between the leader's style and the degree to which the situation gives the leader control.

unfavourable situation might be that of the disliked chairperson of a volunteer United Way fundraising team. In this job, the leader has very little control.

Fiedler suggested that task-oriented leaders perform best in situations of high and low control, while relationship-oriented leaders perform best in moderate control situations.[25] In a high control situation, a leader can "get away" with task orientation, because the relationships are good, and followers are easily influenced.[26] In a low control situation (which is characterized by poor relations, ill-defined task, and low influence), task orientation may be the only thing that makes it possible to get something done. In a moderate control situation, being relationship-oriented may smooth the way to getting things done.

How would you apply Fiedler's findings? You would match leaders with the type of situation—in terms of leader-member relations, task structure, and position power—for which they were best suited. Because Fiedler views an individual's leadership style as fixed, there are only two ways to improve leader effectiveness.

First, you can change the leader to fit the situation—as a baseball manager puts a right- or left-handed pitcher into the game depending on the hitter. If a group situation rates highly unfavourable but is currently led by a relationship-oriented manager, the group's performance could be improved under a manager who is task-oriented. The second alternative is to change the situation to fit the leader, by restructuring tasks or increasing or decreasing the leader's power to control factors such as salary increases, promotions, and disciplinary actions.

Fiedler's theory has been found to be more difficult to apply in the workplace than some of the other contingency theories we review.[27]

Hersey and Blanchard's Situational Leadership®

Paul Hersey and Ken Blanchard's **Situational Leadership® (SL)**, which focuses on followers, has been incorporated into the leadership system of more than 700 of the *Fortune* 1000 companies, and more than a million managers a year from a wide variety of organizations are being taught its basic elements.[28]

SL says successful leadership is achieved by selecting the right leadership style contingent on the followers' *readiness*, or the extent to which they are willing and able to accomplish a specific task. A leader should choose one of four behaviours, depending on follower readiness. This idea is illustrated in Exhibit 20-2.

If followers are *unable* and *unwilling* to do a task, the leader needs to give clear and specific directions; if they are *unable* and *willing*, the leader needs to display high task orientation to compensate for followers' lack of ability and high relationship orientation to get them to "buy into" the leader's desires. If followers are *able* and *unwilling*, the leader needs to use a supportive and participative style; if they are both *able* and *willing*, the leader does not need to do much.

SL has intuitive appeal. It acknowledges the importance of followers and builds on the logic that leaders can compensate for their limited ability and motivation. Yet research efforts to test and support the theory have generally been disappointing.[29] Why? Possible explanations include internal ambiguities and inconsistencies in the model itself as well as problems with research methodology in tests. So despite its intuitive appeal and wide popularity, any endorsement must be cautious for now.

Path-Goal Theory

Developed by University of Toronto professor Martin Evans in the late 1960s and subsequently expanded upon by Robert House (formerly at the University of Toronto, but now at the Wharton School of Business at the University of Pennsylvania), **path-goal theory** extracts elements from the Ohio State leadership research on initiating structure and consideration and the expectancy theory of motivation.[30] It says that it's the leader's job to provide followers with the information, support, or other resources necessary to achieve their goals. (The term *path-goal* implies effective leaders clarify followers' paths to their work goals and make the journey easier by reducing roadblocks.)

Situational Leadership® (SL) A leadership theory that focuses on the readiness of followers.

path-goal theory A leadership theory that says it is the leader's job to assist followers in attaining their goals and to provide the necessary direction and/or support to ensure that their goals are compatible with the overall objectives of the group or organization.

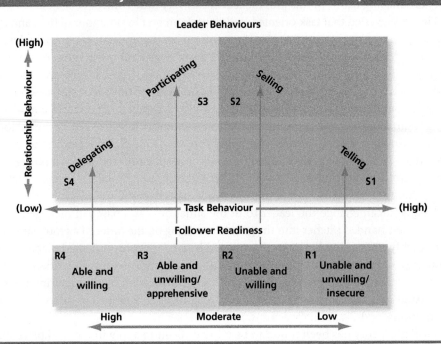

EXHIBIT 20-2 Hersey and Blanchard's Situational Leadership®

According to this theory, leaders should follow three guidelines to be effective:[31]

- *Determine the outcomes subordinates want.* These might include good pay, job security, interesting work, and autonomy to do one's job.

- *Reward individuals with their desired outcomes* when they perform well.

- *Let individuals know what they need to do to receive rewards* (that is, the path to the goal), remove any barriers that would prevent high performance, and express confidence that individuals have the ability to perform well.

Path-goal theory identifies four leadership behaviours that might be used in different situations to motivate individuals:

- The *directive leader* lets followers know what is expected of them, schedules work to be done, and gives specific guidance as to how to accomplish tasks. This closely parallels the Ohio State dimension of initiating structure. This behaviour is best used when individuals have difficulty doing tasks or the tasks are ambiguous. It would not be very helpful when used with individuals who are already highly motivated, have the skills and abilities to do the task, and understand the requirements of the task.

- The *supportive leader* is friendly and shows concern for the needs of followers. This is essentially synonymous with the Ohio State dimension of consideration. This behaviour is often recommended when individuals are under stress, or otherwise show that they need to be supported.

- The *participative leader* consults with followers and uses their suggestions before making a decision. This behaviour is most appropriate when individuals need to buy in to decisions.

- The *achievement-oriented leader* sets challenging goals and expects followers to perform at their highest level. This behaviour works well with individuals who like challenges and are highly motivated. It would be less effective with less capable individuals, or those who are highly stressed from overwork.

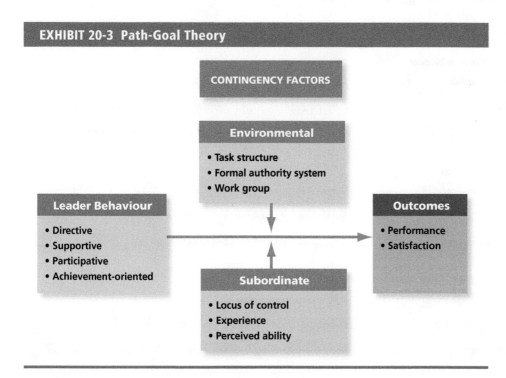

EXHIBIT 20-3 Path-Goal Theory

CONTINGENCY FACTORS

Environmental
- Task structure
- Formal authority system
- Work group

Leader Behaviour
- Directive
- Supportive
- Participative
- Achievement-oriented

Subordinate
- Locus of control
- Experience
- Perceived ability

Outcomes
- Performance
- Satisfaction

As Exhibit 20-3 illustrates, path-goal theory proposes two types of contingency variables that affect the leadership behaviour-outcome relationship: environmental variables that are outside the control of the employee and variables that are part of the personal characteristics of the employee. The theory proposes that employee performance and satisfaction are likely to be positively influenced when the leader compensates for what is lacking in either the employee or the work setting. However, the leader who spends time explaining tasks when those tasks are already clear or when the employee has the ability and experience to handle them without interference is likely to be ineffective because the employee will see such directive behaviour as redundant or even insulting.

RESEARCH FINDINGS: Path-Goal Theory

Testing path-goal theory has not been easy. A review of the evidence suggests mixed support, which indicates "that either effective leadership does not rest in the removal of roadblocks and pitfalls to employee path instrumentalities as path-goal theories propose or that the nature of these hindrances is not in accord with the proposition of the theories."[32] Another review found the lack of support to be "shocking and disappointing."[33] Others argue that adequate tests of the theory have yet to be conducted.[34] Thus, the jury is out. Because path-goal theory is so complex to test, that may remain the case for some time.

One of the dangers of any theory of situational leadership is the assumption that the behaviour of the leader should adjust to meet followers' needs. It may be that leaders act on employees' perceived needs rather than their real needs. Recall from Chapter 2 that "perceptions are reality." A 2010 study found that "if managers view followers positively—that they are good citizens, industrious, enthusiastic—they will treat their employees positively. If they think of their employees negatively—that they are conforming, insubordinate and incompetent—they will treat them that way."[35] By extension, managers may not adopt the appropriate situational leadership behaviour if they have incorrect perceptions of their employees.

EXHIBIT 20-4 Substitutes and Neutralizers for Leadership

Characteristics of Individual	Effect on Leadership
Experience/training	Substitutes for task-oriented leadership
Professionalism	Substitutes for relationship-oriented and task-oriented leadership
Indifference to rewards	Neutralizes relationship-oriented and task-oriented leadership

Characteristics of Job	
Highly structured task	Substitutes for task-oriented leadership
Provides its own feedback	Substitutes for task-oriented leadership
Intrinsically satisfying	Substitutes for relationship-oriented leadership

Characteristics of Organization	
Explicit formalized goals	Substitutes for task-oriented leadership
Rigid rules and procedures	Substitutes for task-oriented leadership
Cohesive work groups	Substitutes for relationship-oriented and task-oriented leadership

Source: Based on S. Kerr and J. M. Jermier, "Substitutes for Leadership: Their Meaning and Measurement," *Organizational Behavior and Human Performance*, December 1978, p. 378.

Substitutes for Leadership

The previous three theories argue that leaders are needed, but that leaders should consider the situation in determining which style of leadership to adopt. However, numerous studies collectively demonstrate that, in many situations, leaders' actions are irrelevant. Experience and training are among the *substitutes* that can replace the need for a leader's support or ability to create structure. Organizational characteristics such as explicit formalized goals, rigid rules and procedures, and cohesive work groups can also replace formal leadership, while indifference to organizational rewards can neutralize its effects. *Neutralizers* make it impossible for leader behaviour to make any difference to follower outcomes. These are shown in Exhibit 20-4.[36]

This observation should not be surprising. After all, we have introduced a number of variables—such as attitudes, personality, ability, and group norms—that affect employee performance and satisfaction. It's simplistic to think employees are guided to goal accomplishments solely by the actions of their leader. Leadership is simply another independent variable in our overall OB model.

There are many possible substitutes for and neutralizers of many different types of leader behaviours across many different situations. Moreover, sometimes the difference between substitutes and neutralizers is fuzzy. If I am working on a task that is intrinsically enjoyable, theory predicts that leadership will be less important because the task itself provides enough motivation. But does that mean intrinsically enjoyable tasks neutralize leadership effects, or substitute for them, or both? Another problem is that while substitutes for leadership (such as employee characteristics, the nature of the task, and so forth) matter to performance, that does not necessarily mean that leadership does not matter to performance.[37]

Inspirational Leadership

How does a leader lead with vision?

Lt.-Col. Maryse Carmichael's leadership role extends out into the community, where the Snowbirds are a source of inspiration and wonder (not to mention an important tool used for recruitment purposes).[38] "If I can influence not only young girls but boys to follow their passion then that's great," Carmichael says. That is why she ensures that new candidates for pilot jobs are not screened solely on the basis on flying ability. "Teamwork is so important," she adds, noting that to a large degree teamwork is what defines the Snowbirds. But the desire and ability to engage with communities and do public relations work is critical too. After all, for many Canadians, the Snowbirds are the face of the military. "People often hear about Canadian Forces in Afghanistan but you rarely get to meet them. We get to meet Canadians on a daily basis." She vividly remembers her own first experience seeing the Snowbirds at a show in Beauport, Quebec, when she was five years old. "It's sometimes hard to quantify what we do," she says. "How can you explain that we motivate young people to dream?" What does it take to be an inspiring leader?

The leadership theories we have discussed above ignore the importance of the leader as a communicator who inspires others to act beyond their immediate self-interests. In this section, we present two contemporary leadership theories with a common theme. They view leaders as individuals who inspire followers through their words, ideas, and behaviours. These theories are charismatic leadership and transformational leadership.

Charismatic Leadership

The following individuals are frequently cited as being charismatic leaders: Frank Stronach of Aurora, Ontario-based Magna International; Mogens Smed, CEO of Calgary-based DIRTT (Doing It Right This Time); Pierre Trudeau, the late prime minister; René Lévesque, the late Quebec premier; Lucien Bouchard, former Bloc Québécois leader; Michaëlle Jean, former Governor General; and Craig Kielburger, who founded Kids Can Free the Children as a teenager. So what do they have in common?

What Is Charismatic Leadership?

Max Weber, a sociologist, defined *charisma* (from the Greek for "gift") more than a century ago as "a certain quality of an individual personality, by virtue of which he or she is set apart from ordinary people and treated as endowed with supernatural, superhuman, or at least specifically exceptional powers or qualities. These are not accessible to the ordinary person and are regarded as of divine origin or as exemplary, and on the basis of them the individual concerned is treated as a leader."[39] Weber argued that charismatic leadership was one of several ideal types of authority.

The first researcher to consider charismatic leadership in terms of OB was Robert House. According to House's **charismatic leadership theory**, followers make attributions of heroic or extraordinary leadership abilities when they observe certain behaviours.[40] A number of studies have attempted to identify the characteristics of the charismatic leader and have documented four—they have a vision, they are willing to take personal risks to achieve that vision, they are sensitive to followers' needs, and they exhibit behaviours that are out of the ordinary (see Exhibit 20-5).[41]

How Charismatic Leaders Influence Followers

How do charismatic leaders actually influence followers? The evidence suggests a four-step process.[42] It begins by the leader articulating an appealing **vision**, a long-term strategy for how to attain a goal by linking the present with a better future for the organization. Desirable visions fit the times and circumstances and reflect the uniqueness of the organization. Steve Jobs championed the iPod, noting, "It's as Apple as anything Apple has ever done." People in the organization must also believe the vision is challenging yet attainable. The creation of the iPod achieved Apple's goal of offering groundbreaking and easy-to-use technology.

Second, a vision is incomplete without an accompanying **vision statement**, a formal articulation of an organization's vision or mission. Charismatic leaders may use vision statements to imprint on followers an overarching goal and purpose. They then com-

charismatic leadership theory A leadership theory that states that followers make attributions of heroic or extraordinary leadership abilities when they observe certain behaviours.

vision A long-term strategy for attaining a goal or goals.

vision statement A formal articulation of an organization's vision or mission.

> ### EXHIBIT 20-5 Key Characteristics of Charismatic Leaders
>
> 1. *Vision and articulation.* Has a vision—expressed as an idealized goal—that proposes a future better than the status quo; and is able to clarify the importance of the vision in terms that are understandable to others.
>
> 2. *Personal risk.* Willing to take on high personal risk, incur high costs, and engage in self-sacrifice to achieve the vision.
>
> 3. *Sensitivity to followers' needs.* Perceptive of others' abilities and responsive to their needs and feelings.
>
> 4. *Unconventional behaviour.* Engages in behaviours that are perceived as novel and counter to norms.
>
> *Source:* Based on J. A. Conger and R. N. Kanungo, *Charismatic Leadership in Organizations* (Thousand Oaks, CA: Sage, 1998), p. 94.

municate high performance expectations and express confidence that followers can attain them. This enhances follower self-esteem and self-confidence.

Next, through words and actions, the leader conveys a new set of values and sets an example for followers to imitate. One study of Israeli bank employees showed, for example, that charismatic leaders were more effective because their employees personally identified with them.[43] Charismatic leaders also set a tone of cooperation and mutual support. A study of 115 government employees found they had a stronger sense of personal belonging at work when they had charismatic leaders, increasing their willingness to engage in helping and compliance-oriented behaviour.[44]

Finally, the charismatic leader engages in emotion-inducing and often unconventional behaviour to demonstrate courage and convictions about the vision. Followers "catch" the emotions their leader is conveying.[45]

What are examples of visions? The late Steve Jobs' vision of elegance in design influenced how all of Apple's products were built. Facebook founder and CEO Mark Zuckerberg's vision for his company is to have it be a one-stop place for everyone's communication needs, including text messaging.

RESEARCH FINDINGS: Charismatic Leadership

Research shows impressive correlations between charismatic leadership and high performance and satisfaction among followers.[46] People working for charismatic leaders are motivated to exert extra work effort and, because they like and respect their leader, express greater satisfaction. It also appears that organizations with charismatic CEOs are more profitable. And charismatic professors enjoy higher course evaluations.[47]

However, charisma may not always be generalizable; its effectiveness may depend on the situation. Charisma appears to be most successful when the follower's task has an ideological component or when the environment involves a high degree of stress and uncertainty.[48] Even in laboratory studies, when people are psychologically aroused, they are more likely to respond to charismatic leaders.[49] This may explain why charismatic leaders tend to surface in politics, religion, wartime, or a business firm that is in its infancy or facing a life-threatening crisis.

People are especially receptive to charismatic leadership when they sense a crisis, when they are under stress, or when they fear for their lives. More generally, some people's personalities are especially susceptible to charismatic leadership.[50] Consider self-esteem. If a person lacks self-esteem and questions his or her self-worth, that person

The creative vision of Steve Jobs, Apple's charismatic co-founder, was to make state-of-the-art technology that is easy for people to use. As Apple CEO, Jobs inspired, motivated, and led employees to develop products such as Macintosh computers, iPod music players, iPads, and iPhones. "The iPhone is like having your life in your pocket," said Jobs. In October 2011, Jobs passed away, and Apple employees and others paid tribute to him as the ultimate consumer-electronics visionary.

is more likely to absorb a leader's direction rather than establish his or her own way of leading or thinking.

A 2010 study found that it is possible for a person to learn how to communicate charismatically, which would then lead that person to be perceived more as a leader. People who are perceived to be charismatic show empathy, enthusiasm, and self-confidence; have good speaking and listening skills; and make eye contact.[51]

The Dark Side of Charismatic Leadership

When organizations are in need of great change, charismatic leaders are often able to inspire their followers to meet the challenges of change. Be aware that a charismatic leader may become a liability to an organization once the crisis is over and the need for dramatic change subsides.[52] Why? Because then the charismatic leader's overwhelming self-confidence can be a liability. He or she is unable to listen to others, becomes uncomfortable when challenged by aggressive employees, and begins to hold an unjustifiable belief in his or her "rightness" on issues. Some would argue that Stephane Dion's behaviour after the Liberal party lost 19 seats in the 2008 federal election, first refusing to step down, and then trying to form a coalition government shortly thereafter, would fit this description.

Many have argued that the financial scandals and large losses experienced by investors in North America, including the ponzi scheme created by Bernie Madoff and the near bankruptcy of the Caisse de dépôt et placement du Québec because of the "audacious investment strategies" of Henri-Paul Rousseau, point to some of the dangers of charismatic leadership.[53]

Charismatic leadership, by its very nature, silences criticism. Thus, employees follow the lead of their visionary CEOs unquestioningly. Professor David Leighton, of the Richard Ivey School of Business at the University of Western Ontario, notes that even boards of directors and auditors are reluctant to challenge these CEOs. He finds that Canada's "more balanced culture" is less likely to turn CEOs into heroes.[54]

A study of 29 companies that went from good to great (their cumulative stock returns were all at least three times better than the general stock market over 15 years) found that a key difference in successful charismatic leaders may be the *absence* of being ego-driven.[55] Although the leaders of these firms were fiercely ambitious and driven, their ambition was directed toward their company rather than themselves. They took responsibility for mistakes and poor results but gave credit for successes to other people. These individuals are called **level 5 leaders** because they have four basic leadership qualities—individual capability, team skills, managerial competence, and the ability to stimulate others to high performance—plus a fifth quality: a paradoxical blend of personal humility and professional will. Level 5 leaders channel their ego needs away from themselves and into the goal of building a great company while getting little notoriety in the business press.

Transformational Leadership

A stream of research has focused on differentiating transformational from transactional leaders.[56] The Ohio and Michigan State studies, the Fiedler contingency model, and path-goal theory describe **transactional leaders**—those who guide their followers toward established goals by clarifying role and task requirements. **Transformational leaders** inspire followers to transcend their self-interests for the good of the organization, and can have an extraordinary effect on their followers.[57] Andrea Jung at Avon, Richard Branson of the Virgin Group, and Jim McNerney of Boeing are all examples of transformational leaders. They pay attention to the concerns and developmental needs of individual followers; they change followers' awareness of issues by helping them to look at old problems in new ways; and they excite and inspire followers to put out extra effort to achieve group goals. Exhibit 20-6 briefly identifies and defines the characteristics that differentiate these two types of leaders.

Transactional and transformational leadership are not opposing approaches to getting things done.[58] They complement each other, though they are not equally important. Transformational leadership *builds on* transactional leadership and produces levels of follower effort and performance that go beyond what transactional leadership alone can do. But the reverse is not true. So if you are a good transactional leader but do not have transformational qualities, you will likely only be a mediocre leader. The best leaders are transactional *and* transformational.

Full Range of Leadership Model

Exhibit 20-7 shows the full range of leadership model. Laissez-faire is the most passive and therefore the least effective of the leader behaviours.[59] Management by exception—active or passive—is slightly better than laissez-faire, but it's still considered ineffective. Management by exception leaders tend to be available only when there is a problem, which is often too late. Contingent reward leadership can be an effective style of leadership, but will not get employees to go above and beyond the call of duty.

Only with the four remaining leadership styles—all aspects of transformational leadership—are leaders able to motivate followers to perform above expectations and transcend their own self-interest for the sake of the organization. Individualized consideration, intellectual stimulation, inspirational motivation, and idealized influence all result in extra effort from employees, higher productivity, higher morale and satisfaction, higher organizational effectiveness, lower turnover, lower absenteeism, and greater organizational adaptability. Based on this model, leaders are generally most effective when they regularly use each of the four transformational behaviours.

How Transformational Leadership Works

Transformational leaders are more effective because they themselves are more creative and also because they encourage those who follow them to be creative, too.[60] In companies with transformational leaders, there is greater decentralization of responsibility, managers have more propensity to take risks, and compensation plans are geared toward long-term results, all of which facilitate corporate entrepreneurship.[61]

level 5 leaders Leaders who are fiercely ambitious and driven, but their ambition is directed toward their company rather than themselves.

transactional leaders Leaders who guide or motivate their followers in the direction of established goals by clarifying role and task requirements.

transformational leaders Leaders who inspire followers to transcend their own self-interests and who are capable of having a profound and extraordinary effect on followers.

EXHIBIT 20-6 Characteristics of Transactional and Transformational Leaders

Transactional Leader

Contingent reward: Contracts exchange of rewards for effort, promises rewards for good performance, recognizes accomplishments.

Management by exception (active): Watches and searches for deviations from rules and standards, takes corrective action.

Management by exception (passive): Intervenes only if standards are not met.

Laissez-faire: Abdicates responsibilities, avoids making decisions.

Transformational Leader

Idealized influence: Provides vision and sense of mission, instills pride, gains respect and trust.

Inspirational motivation: Communicates high expectations, uses symbols to focus efforts, expresses important purposes in simple ways.

Intellectual stimulation: Promotes intelligence, rationality, and careful problem solving.

Individualized consideration: Gives personal attention, treats each employee individually, coaches, advises.

Source: Reprinted from B. M. Bass, "From Transactional to Transformational Leadership: Learning to Share the Vision," *Organizational Dynamics,* Winter 1990, p. 22, with permission from Elsevier.

Companies with transformational leaders also show greater agreement among top managers about the organization's goals, which yields superior organizational performance.[62] Similar results, showing that transformational leaders improve performance by building consensus among group members, have been demonstrated in the Israeli military.[63] Transformational leaders are able to increase follower self-efficacy, giving the group a "can do" spirit.[64] Followers of transformational leaders are more likely to pursue ambitious goals, be familiar with and agree on the strategic goals of the organization, and believe that the goals they are pursuing are personally important.[65]

EXHIBIT 20-7 Full Range of Leadership Model

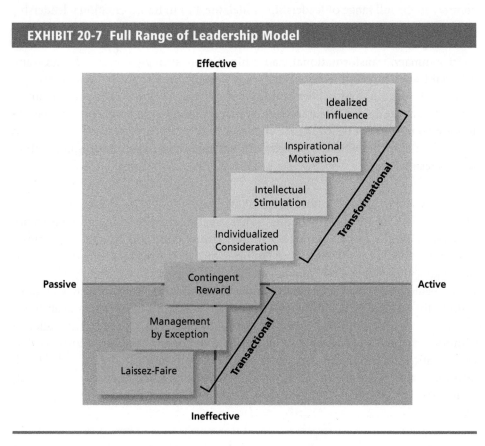

Research has shown that vision explains part of the effect of transformational leadership. One study found that vision was even more important than a charismatic (effusive, dynamic, lively) communication style in explaining the success of entrepreneurial firms.[66] Finally, transformational leadership also engenders commitment on the part of followers and instills in them a greater sense of trust in the leader.[67]

RESEARCH FINDINGS: Transformational Leadership

Transformational leadership has been impressively supported at various job levels and in disparate occupations (school principals, marine commanders, ministers, presidents of MBA associations, military cadets, union shop stewards, schoolteachers, sales reps). One recent study of R & D firms found that teams whose project leaders scored high on transformational leadership produced better-quality products as judged one year later and were more profitable five years later.[68] A review of 87 studies testing transformational leadership found that it was related to the motivation and satisfaction of followers and to the higher performance and perceived effectiveness of leaders.[69]

Transformational leadership is not equally effective in all situations, however. It has a greater impact on the bottom line in smaller, privately held firms than in more complicated organizations.[70] The personal nature of transformational leadership may be most effective when leaders can directly interact with the workforce and make decisions than when they report to an external board of directors or deal with a complex bureaucratic structure. Another study showed transformational leaders were more effective in improving group potency in teams higher in power distance and collectivism.[71] Where group members are highly individualistic and don't readily cede decision-making authority, transformational leadership might not have much impact.

Transformational leadership theory is not perfect. There are concerns about whether contingent reward leadership is strictly a characteristic of transactional leaders only. And contrary to the full range of leadership model, the 4 *I*'s in transformational leadership are not always superior in effectiveness to transactional leadership (contingent reward leadership sometimes works as well as transformational leadership).

In summary, transformational leadership is more strongly correlated than transactional leadership with lower turnover rates, higher productivity, lower employee stress and burnout, and higher employee satisfaction.[72] Like charisma, it can be learned. One study of Canadian bank managers found that branches managed by those who underwent transformational leadership training performed significantly better than branches whose managers did not receive training. Other studies show similar results.[73]

Transformational Leadership vs. Charismatic Leadership

There is some debate about whether transformational leadership and charismatic leadership are the same. Researcher Robert House considers them synonymous, calling the differences "modest" and "minor." McGill University professor Rabindra Kanungo agrees.[74] However, one researcher who disagrees says, "The purely charismatic [leader] may want followers to adopt the charismatic's world view and go no further; the transformational leader will attempt to instill in followers the ability to question not only established views but eventually those established by the leader."[75] Although many researchers believe that transformational leadership is broader than charismatic leadership, a leader who scores high on transformational leadership is also likely to score high on charisma. Therefore, in practice, they may be roughly equivalent.

Contemporary Leadership Roles

The military may be a surprising place to find self-directed leadership, given the rigid formality of the hierarchy and role definitions.[76] However, senior leaders still find ways to create opportunities to take initiative. For example, retired Snowbird Dan Dempsey notes that historic Snowbird team pictures were scattered about the base but not organized or protected in a systematic way. With the support of base command, Dempsey started a museum in the squadron, eventually collecting enough material to fill a book. "I was able to find, through a vast myriad of collections, a whole bunch of old-timers and pioneers who started the air-show industry in Canada and adapt their personal accounts." By enabling this self-directed project, the Snowbird team ended up with both a museum and a book that continue to help them address public relations and community engagement goals. What can formal leaders do to help foster self-directed leadership among employees?

4 Are there leadership roles for nonmanagers?

Transformational leadership theory focuses on heroic leaders, leaders at the top echelons of the organization, and also on individuals rather than teams. However, the notion of "leader at the top" does not adequately reflect what is happening in some workplaces today, where there is less hierarchy and more connections, both inside and outside of the organization. There is a need for more "distributed leadership." In this form, leadership is "distributed across many players, both within and across organizations, up and down the hierarchy, wherever information, expertise, vision, and new ways of working together reside."[77]

Can anyone be a leader?

The following sections aim to explain how leadership can be spread throughout the organization through mentoring, self-leadership, team leadership, online leadership, and leading without authority. Even if you are not a manager or someone thinking about leadership in a corporate situation, this discussion offers important insights into how you can take on a leadership role in an organization.

mentor A senior employee who sponsors and supports a less-experienced employee.

Mentoring

Many leaders take responsibility for developing future leaders through mentoring relationships. A **mentor** is a senior employee who sponsors and supports a less-experienced employee (a protégé). The mentoring role includes coaching, counselling, and sponsorship to help protégés develop skills, to provide support and help bolster protégés' self-confidence, and to lobby so that protégés get good assignments, promotions, and salary increases.[78] Successful mentors are good teachers. They present ideas clearly, listen well, and empathize with protégés' problems.

Traditional informal mentoring relationships develop when leaders identify a less experienced, lower-level employee who appears to have potential for future development.[79] The protégé will often be tested with a particularly challenging assignment. If he or she performs acceptably, the mentor will develop the relationship, informally showing the protégé how the organization *really* works outside its formal structures and procedures. Protégés can also learn how the mentor

N. R. Narayana Murthy is one of the founders of Infosys in Bangalore, India. He has served the firm as chairman and chief mentor of the board, where he has shared his experiences, knowledge, and lessons learned while building Infosys for over three decades into a company with 142 000 employees globally and annual sales of over $6 billion. In August 2011, Mr. Murthy retired from Infosys and is currently Chairman Emeritus of the company. He is shown here with Infosys employees at the company's Bangalore campus, which is also its corporate headquarters.

has navigated early career issues or led effectively and how to work through problems with minimal stress.

Why would a leader want to be a mentor?[80] Many feel they have something to share with the younger generation and want to provide a legacy. Mentoring provides unfiltered access to the attitudes of lower-ranking employees, and protégés can be an excellent source of early warning signals that identify potential organizational problems.

Are all employees in an organization equally likely to participate in a mentoring relationship? Unfortunately, no.[81] The evidence indicates that minorities and women are less likely to be chosen as protégés than are white males. Mentors tend to select protégés who are similar to themselves on criteria such as background, education, gender, race, ethnicity, and religion. "People naturally move to mentor and can more easily communicate with those with whom they most closely identify."[82] Senior male managers may also select male protégés to minimize problems such as sexual attraction or gossip.

Many organizations have created formal programs to ensure mentoring relationships are equally available to minorities and women.[83] Although begun with the best intentions, these formal relationships are not as effective as informal ones.[84]

Poor planning and design may often be the reason. Mentor commitment is critical to a program's effectiveness; mentors must see the relationship as beneficial to themselves and the protégé. The protégé, too, must feel he or she has input into the relationship; someone who feels it's foisted on him or her will just go through the motions.[85] Formal mentoring programs are also most likely to succeed if they appropriately match the work style, needs, and skills of protégé and mentor.[86]

You might assume that mentoring is valuable for career success, but the research suggests the gains are primarily psychological. Benefits to objective outcomes like compensation and job performance are very small. One study concluded, "Though mentoring may not be properly labeled an utterly useless concept to careers, neither can it be argued to be as important as the main effects of other influences on career success such as ability and personality."[87] It may *feel* nice to have a mentor, but it does not appear that having a mentor, or even having a good mentor who provides both support and advice, is critical to one's career. Mentors may be effective not because of the functions they provide but because of the resources they can obtain: A mentor connected to a powerful network can build relationships that will help the protégé advance. Most evidence suggests that network ties, whether built through a mentor or not, are a significant predictor of career success.[88] If a mentor is not well connected or not a very strong performer, the best mentoring advice in the world will not be very beneficial.

Self-Leadership (or Self-Management)

A growing trend in organizations is the focus on self-leadership, or self-management, where individuals and teams set goals, plan and implement tasks, evaluate performance, solve their own problems, and motivate themselves.[89] (Recall our discussion of self-managed teams in Chapter 18.)

How do you manage yourself?

Reduced levels of supervision, offices in the home, teamwork, and growth in service and professional employment have increased the demand for self-leadership. Self-management can also be a substitute or neutralizer for leadership from others.

Despite the lack of studies of self-management techniques in organizational settings, self-management strategies have been shown to be successful in nonorganizational settings.[90] Those who practise self-management look for opportunities to be more effective in the workplace and improve their career success and provide their own sense of reward and feedback after carrying out their accomplishments. Moreover, self-reinforced behaviour is often maintained at a higher rate than behaviour that is externally regulated.[91]

How do leaders create self-leaders? The following approaches have been suggested:[92]

- *Model self-leadership.* Practise self-observation, setting challenging personal goals, self-direction, and self-reinforcement. Then display these behaviours, and encourage others to rehearse and then produce them.

- *Encourage employees to create self-set goals.* Support employees in developing quantitative, specific goals; having such goals is the most important part of self-leadership.

- *Encourage the use of self-rewards to strengthen and increase desirable behaviours.* By contrast, limit self-punishment only to occasions when the employee has been dishonest or destructive.

- *Create positive thought patterns.* Encourage employees to use mental imagery and self-talk to further stimulate self-motivation.

- *Create a climate of self-leadership.* Redesign the work to increase the natural rewards of a job and focus on these naturally rewarding features of work to increase motivation.

- *Encourage self-criticism.* Encourage individuals to be critical of their own performance.

The underlying assumptions behind self-leadership are that people are responsible, capable, and able to exercise initiative without the external constraints of bosses, rules, or regulations. Given the proper support, individuals can monitor and control their own behaviour.

Team Leadership

Leadership is increasingly taking place within a team context. As teams grow in popularity, the role of the leader in guiding team members takes on heightened importance.[93] Also, because of its more collaborative nature, the role of team leader is different from the traditional leadership role performed by first-line supervisors.

Many leaders are not equipped to handle the change to team leader. As one prominent consultant noted, "Even the most capable managers have trouble making the transition because all the command-and-control type things they were encouraged to do before are no longer appropriate. There's no reason to have any skill or sense of this."[94] This same consultant estimated that "probably 15 percent of managers are natural team leaders; another 15 percent could never lead a team because it runs counter to their personality. [They're unable to sublimate their dominating style for the good of the team.] Then there's that huge group in the middle: team leadership doesn't come naturally to them, but they can learn it."[95]

Effective team leaders need to build commitment and confidence, remove obstacles, create opportunities, and be part of the team.[96] They have to learn skills such as the patience to share information, the willingness to trust others, the ability to give up authority, and an understanding of when to intervene. New team leaders may try to retain too much control at a time when team members need more autonomy, or they may abandon their teams at times when the teams need support and help.[97]

Roles of Team Leaders

A study of 20 organizations that reorganized themselves around teams found certain common responsibilities that all leaders had to assume. These included coaching, facilitating, training, communicating, handling disciplinary problems, and reviewing team/individual performance.[98] Many of these responsibilities apply to managers in general. A more meaningful way to describe the team leader's job is to focus on two priorities: managing the team's external boundary and facilitating the team process.[99] We have divided these priorities into four specific roles that team leaders play:

- *Liaisons with external constituencies.* Outsiders include upper management, other internal teams, customers, and suppliers. The leader represents the team to other constituencies, secures needed resources, clarifies others' expectations of the team, gathers information from the outside, and shares this information with team members.

- *Troubleshooters.* When the team has problems and asks for assistance, team leaders sit in on meetings and try to help resolve the problems. This rarely relates to technical or operational issues because the team members typically know more about the tasks being done than does the team leader. The leader contributes by asking penetrating questions, by helping the team discuss problems, and by getting needed resources from external constituencies. For instance, when a team in an aerospace firm found itself short-handed, its team leader took responsibility for getting more staff. He presented the team's case to upper management and got the approval through the company's human resource department.

- *Conflict managers.* When disagreements surface, team leaders help process the conflict. What is the source of the conflict? Who is involved? What are the issues? What resolution options are available? What are the advantages and disadvantages of each? By getting team members to address questions such as these, the leader minimizes the disruptive aspects of intrateam conflicts.

- *Coaches.* They clarify expectations and roles, teach, offer support, cheerlead, and do whatever else is necessary to help team members improve their work performance.

Exhibit 20-8 offers a lighthearted look at what it means to be a team leader.

Online Leadership

How do you lead people who are physically separated from you and with whom you communicate electronically? This question has received minimal attention from organizational behaviour researchers.[100] But today's managers and their employees are increasingly being linked by networks rather than geographical proximity. Obvious examples include managers who regularly use email to communicate with their staff,

EXHIBIT 20-8

Source: Dilbert, reprinted by permission of Universal Uclick.

managers who oversee virtual projects or teams, and managers whose teleworking employees are linked to the office by an Internet connection.

Electronic communication is a powerful channel that can build and enhance leadership effectiveness. But when misused, it can undermine much of what a leader has achieved through verbal communication. In face-to-face communications, harsh *words* can be softened by nonverbal action. A smile and comforting gestures, for instance, can lessen the blow behind strong words like *disappointed, unsatisfactory, inadequate,* or *below expectations.* That nonverbal component does not exist with online interactions. The *structure* of words in electronic communication has the power to motivate or demotivate the receiver. We propose that online leaders have to think carefully about what actions they want their digital messages to initiate.

Jane Howell at the Richard Ivey School of Business, University of Western Ontario, and one of her students, Kate Hall-Merenda, considered the issues of leading from a distance.[101] They note that physical distance can create many potential problems, with team members feeling isolated, forgotten, and perhaps not cared about. It may result in lowered productivity. Their study of 109 business leaders and 371 followers in a large financial institution found that physical distance makes it more difficult to develop high-quality relationships.

Howell and Hall-Merenda suggest that some of the same characteristics of transformational leaders are appropriate for long-distance managing. In particular, they emphasize the need to articulate a compelling vision and to communicate that vision in an inspiring way. Encouraging employees to think about ways to strive toward that vision is another important task of the leader.

Online leaders confront unique challenges, the greatest of which appears to be developing and maintaining trust. **Identification-based trust**, based on a mutual understanding of each other's intentions and appreciation of the other person's wants and desires, is particularly difficult to achieve without face-to-face interaction.[102] Online negotiations can also be hindered because parties express lower levels of trust.[103] It's not clear whether it's even possible for employees to identify with or trust leaders with whom they only communicate electronically.[104]

This discussion leads us to the tentative conclusion that, for an increasing number of managers, good leadership skills may include the abilities to communicate support, trust, and inspiration through keyboarded words and accurately read emotions in others' messages. In electronic communication, writing skills are likely to become an extension of interpersonal skills.

Leading without Authority

Can you lead, even if you don't have the authority (or a formal appointment)? For instance, what if you wanted to convince the dean to introduce more relevant business courses, or you wanted to convince the president of the company where you work to use more environmentally friendly strategies in dealing with waste? How do you effectively lead in a student group, when everyone is a peer?

Leadership at the grassroots level does happen. Rosabeth Moss Kanter, in her book *The Change Masters*,[105] discusses examples of employees who saw something that needed changing and took on the responsibility to do so. Employees were more likely to do this when organizations permitted initiative at all levels of the organization, rather than making it a tool of senior executives only.

Leading without authority means exhibiting leadership behaviour even though you do not have a formal position or title. Neither Martin Luther King Jr. nor Nelson Mandela operated from a position of authority, yet each was able to inspire many to follow him in the quest for social justice. The workplace can be an opportunity for leading without authority as well. As Ronald Heifetz of Harvard's Kennedy School of Government notes, "Leadership means taking responsibility for hard problems beyond anyone's expectations."[106] It also means not waiting for the coach's call.[107]

identification-based trust Trust based on a mutual understanding of each other's intentions and appreciation of each other's wants and desires.

What are the benefits of leading without authority? Heifetz has identified three:[108]

- *Latitude for creative deviance.* It's easier to raise harder questions and look for less traditional solutions when a person is not locked into the trappings that go with authority.

- *Issue focus.* Individuals can focus on a single issue, rather than be concerned with the myriad issues that those in authority face.

- *Front-line information.* An individual is closer to the detailed experiences of some of the stakeholders and thus, more information is available.

Not all organizations support this type of leadership, and some have been known to actively suppress it. Still, you may want to reflect on the possibility of engaging in leadership behaviour because you see a need, rather than because you are required to act.

Contemporary Issues in Leadership

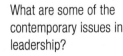

5 What are some of the contemporary issues in leadership?

When Lt.-Col. Maryse Carmichael watched her first air show at age five, she was inspired to fly planes herself one day.[109] At the time, however, becoming a Snowbird pilot seemed like an impossible dream. Females in the Canadian military were barred from pilot training until the mid-1980s. It is therefore not surprising that she is the first female Commanding Officer in the group's 41 year history.

Despite being the first female CO of her squadron, Carmichael downplays gender, finding team familiarity and fit to be more important to her acceptance as a leader. "At my level perhaps it is a new thing to have a woman as a CO," she says, "but for me it's been my entire career working with these people. I don't see anything different." She also takes equal joy in the thought of inspiring young boys and girls and is quick to point out that she is not the first female flight squadron leader in the military, only the most visible. In fact Carmichael sees the Snowbirds' show as an equalizing force in communities. "That is the beauty . . . if you are looking up at the display you wouldn't know if it is a man or a woman flying. All that matters is that you can do the job." Does gender impact leadership style?

What is authentic leadership? Is there a moral dimension to leadership? Do men and women rely on different leadership styles, and if so, is one style inherently superior to the other? In this section, we briefly address these contemporary issues in leadership.

Authentic Leadership

Douglas R. Conant is not your typical CEO. His style is decidedly understated. When asked to reflect on the strong performance of Campbell Soup, he says, "We're hitting our stride a little bit more [than our peers]." He regularly admits mistakes and often says, "I can do better." Conant appears to be a good example of authentic leadership.[110]

Authentic leaders know who they are, know what they believe in and value, and act on those values and beliefs openly and candidly. Their followers consider them to be ethical people. The primary quality produced by authentic leadership is trust. Authentic leaders share information, encourage open communication, and stick to their ideals. The result: People come to have faith in them.

Because the concept is so recent, there has been little research on authentic leadership.[111] However, it's a promising way to think about ethics and trust in leadership because it focuses on the moral aspects of being a leader. Transformational or charismatic leaders can have a vision and communicate it persuasively, but sometimes the vision is wrong (as in the case of Hitler), or the leader is more concerned with his own needs or pleasures, as in the case of business leaders Dennis Kozlowski (ex-CEO of Tyco International) and Jeffrey Skilling (ex-CEO of Enron).[112]

authentic leaders Leaders who know who they are, know what they believe in and value, and act on these values and beliefs openly and candidly. Their followers could consider them to be ethical people.

Moral Leadership

Only recently have ethicists and leadership researchers begun to consider the ethical implications in leadership.[113] Why now? One reason may be the growing interest in ethics throughout the field of management. Another reason may be that ethical lapses by business leaders are never absent from the headlines. Another may be the discovery that many past leaders—such as Martin Luther King Jr. and John F. Kennedy—suffered ethical shortcomings. Some companies, like Boeing, are tying executive compensation to ethics to reinforce the idea that, in CEO Jim McNerney's words, "there's no compromise between doing things the right way and performance."[114]

Ethics and leadership intersect in a number of ways. Transformational leaders have been described as fostering moral virtue when they try to change the attitudes and behaviours of followers.[115] Charisma, too, has an ethical component. Unethical leaders use their charisma to enhance power over followers, directed toward self-serving ends. Ethical leaders use it in a socially constructive way to serve others.[116] Leaders who treat their followers with fairness, especially by providing honest, frequent, and accurate information, are seen as more effective.[117] Because top executives set the moral tone for an organization, they need to set high ethical standards, demonstrate those standards through their own behaviour, and encourage and reward integrity in others while avoiding abuses of power such as giving themselves large raises and bonuses while seeking to cut costs by laying off long-time employees.

Leadership is not value-free. In assessing its effectiveness we need to address the *means* that a leader uses in trying to achieve goals, as well as the content of those goals. Scholars have tried to integrate ethical and charismatic leadership by advancing the idea of **socialized charismatic leadership**—leadership that conveys other-centred (not self-centred) values by leaders who model ethical conduct.[118] Socialized charismatic leaders are able to bring employee values in line with their own values through their words and actions.[119]

One researcher suggests that there are four cornerstones to a "moral foundation of leadership":[120]

Bill Young created Toronto-based Social Capital Partners to help businesses hire the hard to employ: youths, single mothers, Aboriginal people, new immigrants, and those with disabilities or substance abuse. His goal is to help people who are struggling get back into the economic mainstream.

- *Truth telling.* Leaders who tell the truth as they see it allow for a mutual, fair exchange to occur.

- *Promise keeping.* Leaders need to be careful of the commitments they make, and then careful of keeping those commitments.

- *Fairness.* Leaders who are equitable ensure that followers get their fair share for their contributions to the organization.

- *Respect for the individual.* Leaders who tell the truth, keep promises, and are fair show respect for followers. Respect means treating people with dignity.

Moral leadership comes from within the individual, and in general means treating people well, and with respect. This chapter's raises some provocative issues about whether we should consider just the ends toward which a leader strives, or the means as well.

Gender and Leadership

How Many Women Make It to the Top?

The following statistics give the picture for women in Canada in 2010. Women made up 50.4 percent of the Canadian population.[121] More women (71 percent) than men (65 percent) aged 25 to 44 years had completed a post-secondary education.[122] Women

socialized charismatic leadership A leadership concept that states that leaders convey values that are other-centred vs. self-centred and who role model ethical conduct.

George Cooke, CEO of Toronto-based Dominion of Canada General Insurance, believes in promoting women to senior positions. He is noteworthy for this: Dominion is well above the national average in the percentage of women who have made it to the executive ranks of Canada's top companies: 54 percent of senior management (VP and up) are female and 78 percent of officers are female.

made up 47.3 percent of the labour force in Canada, but they held only 36.8 percent of managerial roles and 31.9 percent of senior management roles. Women held 14 percent of the board seats and 17.7 percent of the highest corporate titles—CEO, chief financial officer, or chief operating officer—of the *Financial Post* 500.[123]

Despite women's low representation in large companies, they are highly involved in smaller companies. Industry Canada reports that in 2007, 46 percent of all small- to medium-sized enterprises had at least one female owner.[124] Moreover, women start almost half of all small businesses in Canada today and, among young people, women start almost 80 percent of small businesses.[125]

Similarities and Differences in Women's and Men's Leadership Styles

Do men and women lead differently? An extensive review of the literature suggests two conclusions.[126] First, most recent evidence suggests that there is a great deal of overlap between males and females in their leadership styles. Second, what differences there are seem to be that women fall back on a more democratic leadership style, while men feel more comfortable with a directive style.

Do men and women lead differently?

A recent review of 45 organizations found female leaders were more transformational than males. The authors concluded, "These data attest to the ability of women to perform very well in leadership roles in contemporary organizations."[127] However, women who demonstrate stereotypical male behaviours (self-confidence, assertiveness, and dominance) can face "backlash" at work for not fitting the female stereotype for behaviour. A 2011 study found that "women who displayed male characteristics and self-monitored their behavior were more likely to be promoted than those who did not self-monitor."[128] One of the authors of the study explained: "Working women face a real dilemma: if they are seen to behave in a stereotypically male way, they may damage their chances of promotion, even though these traits are synonymous with successful managers. These findings suggest if these women learn how to self-monitor their behavior, they have a better chance of promotion."[129]

Despite the previous conclusion, studies indicate some differences in the inherent leadership styles of women and men. A Conference Board of Canada study found that "women are particularly strong in managing interpersonal relationships and their approach is more consensual."[130] Other studies have shown that women tend to adopt a style of shared leadership. They encourage participation, share power and information, and attempt to enhance followers' self-worth. They prefer to lead through inclusion and rely on their charisma, expertise, contacts, and interpersonal skills to influence others. Men, on the other hand, are more likely to use a directive command-and-control style. They rely on the formal authority of their position for their influence base.

Although it's interesting to see how men's and women's leadership styles differ, a more important question is whether they differ in effectiveness. Although some researchers have shown that men and women tend to be equally effective as leaders,[131] an increasing number of studies have shown that women executives, when rated by their peers, employees, and bosses, score higher than their male counterparts on a wide variety of measures, including getting extra effort from subordinates and overall effectiveness in leading. Subordinates also report more satisfaction with the leadership given by women.[132]

We know that there is no one best style for all situations. Instead, which leadership style is effective will depend on the situation. So even if men and women differ in their leadership styles, we should not assume that one is always preferable to the other. In today's organizations, flexibility, teamwork, trust, and information sharing are replacing rigid structures, competitive individualism, control, and secrecy. The best leaders listen, motivate, and provide support to their people.

GLOBAL IMPLICATIONS

Most of the research discussed in this chapter was conducted in English-speaking countries. We know very little about how culture might influence the validity of the theories, particularly in Eastern cultures. However, a recent analysis of the Global Leadership and Organizational Behavior Effectiveness (GLOBE) research program (see Chapter 3 for more details) has produced some useful preliminary insights about how to manage in Brazil, France, Egypt, and China.[133] Let's consider each.

- *Brazil* Based on the values of Brazilian employees, a manager leading a team in Brazil would need to be team oriented, participative, and humane. Leaders high on consideration who emphasize participative decision making and have high LPC scores would be best suited to managing employees in this culture. As one Brazilian manager said in the study, "We do not prefer leaders who take self-governing decisions and act alone without engaging the group. That's part of who we are."

- *France* French employees have a more bureaucratic view of leaders and are less likely to expect them to be humane and considerate than Canadian and American employees. A leader high on initiating structure (relatively task oriented) will do best and can make decisions in a relatively autocratic manner. A manager who scores high on consideration (people oriented) may find that style backfiring in France.

- *Egypt* Employees in Egypt are more likely to value team-oriented and participative leadership than Canadian and American employees. However, Egypt is also a relatively high-power-distance culture, meaning status differences between leaders and followers are expected. To be participative yet demonstrate one's status, the leader should ask employees for their opinions, try to minimize conflicts, and not be afraid to take charge and make the final decision (after consulting team members).

- *China* According to the GLOBE study, Chinese culture emphasizes being polite, considerate, and unselfish, but it also has a high performance orientation. These two factors suggest consideration and initiating structure may both be important. Although Chinese culture is relatively participative compared with the cultures of Canada and the United States, there are also status differences between leaders and employees. These findings suggest that a moderately participative style may work best with Chinese employees.

While the idea of charismatic leadership was developed based on North American observations, professors Dale Carl of the Faculty of Management at Ryerson University and Mansour Javidan at the University of Calgary found that transformational leadership is expressed relatively similarly in a variety of countries, including Canada, Hungary, India, Turkey, Austria, Singapore, Sweden, and Venezuela. The transformational leadership traits that appear to be universal are vision, foresight, providing encouragement, trustworthiness, dynamism, positiveness, and proactiveness. The two concluded that "effective business leaders in any country are expected by their subordinates to provide a powerful and proactive vision to guide the company into the future, strong motivational skills to stimulate all employees to fulfill the vision, and excellent planning skills to assist in implementing the vision."[134]

A vision is important in any culture, then, but how it is formed and communicated may still need to vary by culture. A GE executive who used his US leadership style in Japan recalls, "Nothing happened. I quickly realized that I had to adapt my approach, to act more as a consultant to my colleagues and to adopt a team-based motivational decision-making process rather than the more vocal style which tends to be common in the West. In Japan the silence of a leader means far more than a thousand words uttered by somebody else."[135]

LESSONS LEARNED

- Leaders provide vision and strategy; managers implement that vision and strategy.
- Leaders need to have a vision, they need to communicate that vision, and they must have followers.
- Leaders need to adjust their behaviours, depending on the situation and the needs of employees.

21 Human Resources Planning

SECTION EIGHT

HR PLANNING

AND

EMPLOYEE RELATIONS

The Strategic Importance of Human Resources Planning

Human resources planning (HRP) is the process of forecasting future human resources requirements to ensure that the organization will have the required number of employees with the necessary skills to meet its strategic objectives. HRP is a proactive process, which both anticipates and influences an organization's future by systematically forecasting the supply of and demand for employees under changing conditions and by developing plans and activities to satisfy these needs. Effective HRP helps an organization achieve its strategic goals and objectives, achieve economies in hiring new workers, make major labour market demands more successfully, anticipate and avoid shortages and surpluses of human resources, as well as control or reduce labour costs.

HRP has recently become a key strategic priority not just for HR departments but for strategic business planners as well. The existing labour shortage in Canada is forecast to increase to 1 million workers over the next 15 years.[1] Currently, Canada is in the beginning stages of a major labour shortage. As the baby boom generation begins to retire, there are not enough candidates to fill vacant positions.[2] On average, two out of every three job openings over the next decade will be focused on replacing retiring workers. In addition, fertility rates in Canada continue to decline, resulting in fewer possible workers for the future labour force. Combined, these conditions create a situation of fierce labour competition, further increasing the importance of effective HRP.

> **human resources planning (HRP)**
> The process of forecasting future human resources requirements to ensure that the organization will have the required number of employees with the necessary skills to meet its strategic objectives.

EXHIBIT 21-1 Occupations Currently Showing or Expected to Show Labour Shortages

Occupation	Normalized future labour market situation (NFLMS)	The increase in the number of school leavers and immigrants needed to restore balance between expected supply and demand (annually)
Contractors & Supervisors, Trades & Related	4.2	509%
Contractors / Operators / Supervisors: Agriculture	4.1	305%
Facility Operation & Maintenance Managers	3.9	335%
Health / Education / Social & Community Services Managers	5.0	156%
Legislators & Senior Management	5.5	250%
Managers in Communication (Except Broadcasting)	3.6	217%
Managers in Construction & Transportation	4.5	521%
Managers in Protective Service	5.2	226%
Managers in Public Administration	6.6	355%
Optometrists / Chiropractors / Other Health Professions	3.5	124%
Supervisors, Railway & Motor Transportation	5.5	1090%
Supervisors, Assembly & Fabrication	4.3	294%
Supervisors, Mining / Oil / Gas	3.2	338%
Supervisors, Processing Occupations	4.8	403%
Train Crew Operating Occupations	4.0	1062%

Source: Looking-Ahead: A 10-Year Outlook for the Canadian Labour Market (2006–2015), http://www.hrsdc.gc.ca/eng/publications_resources/research/categories/labour_market_e/sp_615_10_06/la06-shortages-29jan07.pdf, Human Resources and Social Development in Canada, 2007. Reproduced with the permission of the Minister of Public Works and Government Services Canada, 2012.

Exhibit 21-1 highlights occupations that are currently facing a labour shortage or ones that are expected to face a labour shortage by 2015. HRP will be absolutely essential for successful strategy implementation.[3]

As illustrated in Exhibit 21-2, key steps in the HRP process include analyzing forecasted labour supply, forecasting labour demands, and then planning and implementing HR programs to balance supply and demand.

Lack of or inadequate human resources planning within an organization can result in significant costs when unstaffed positions create costly inefficiencies and when severance pay is required for large numbers of employees being laid off. It can also create situations in which one department is laying off employees while another is hiring individuals with similar skills, which can reduce morale or productivity and can often result in turnover. The greater concern is that ineffective HRP can lead to an organization's inability to accomplish short-term operational plans or long-range strategic plans.

The Relationship between HRP and Strategic Planning

An HR plan (HRP) does not occur independently of the other departments within an organization (such as finance, marketing, research and development). The HRP must align with the overall goals of the organization as well as both the long-term and short-term strategic plans set by the organization. Fundamental to the business planning process is the impact and alignment of HRP. An organization's strategic decision to expand, redirect, diverge, divest, partner, or merge will have an associated effect on the HR expectations and plans of the organization.

Failure to integrate HRP and strategic planning can have very serious consequences. For example, in Ontario, a fifth year of high school called the Ontario Academic Credit (OAC) year (often referred to as Grade 13) was abolished in 2003 as an effort to cut provincial government costs. As a result, there was a double cohort of students (from both Grade 12 and Grade 13) graduating and wanting to attend postsecondary institutions. Most universities and colleges adopted a strategic decision to significantly increase

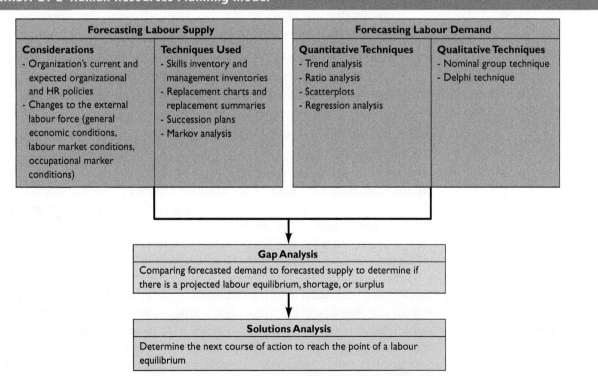

EXHIBIT 21-2 Human Resources Planning Model

Forecasting Labour Supply		Forecasting Labour Demand	
Considerations	**Techniques Used**	**Quantitative Techniques**	**Qualitative Techniques**
- Organization's current and expected organizational and HR policies - Changes to the external labour force (general economic conditions, labour market conditions, occupational marker conditions)	- Skills inventory and management inventories - Replacement charts and replacement summaries - Succession plans - Markov analysis	- Trend analysis - Ratio analysis - Scatterplots - Regression analysis	- Nominal group technique - Delphi technique

Gap Analysis

Comparing forecasted demand to forecasted supply to determine if there is a projected labour equilibrium, shortage, or surplus

Solutions Analysis

Determine the next course of action to reach the point of a labour equilibrium

admissions in 2003 to accommodate for the double cohort. Postsecondary institutions that aligned their HRP with the strategy of increased admissions benefited from an associated increase in labour. Organizations that did not link their strategic decision with HRP struggled with supporting the increased number of students inside the classroom (professors and teaching assistants) and outside of the classroom (libraries, career and learning centres, cafeterias, and so on). Thus, alignment of HR planning to strategic decisions is essential to an organization's success.

The Importance of Environmental Scanning

Environmental scanning is a critical component of HRP and strategic planning processes; the most successful organizations are prepared for changes before they occur. **Environment scanning** involves assessing factors that affect the external labour market as well as an organization's ability to find and secure talent from outside of the organization. The external environmental factors most frequently monitored include

- economic conditions (local, regional, national, international); for example, if the unemployment rate in a region is low, an organization would have to be more aggressive in recruiting talent, as selection may be more scarce

- market and competitive trends; for example, compensation policies that lag behind competitors' policies may result in higher turnover or more difficulties in attracting talent

- new or revised laws and the decisions of courts and quasi-judicial bodies; for example, a raise in the minimum wage rate can inflate the cost of labour in an organization, therefore creating budgetary pressure to reduce labour expenses

- social concerns such as healthcare, childcare, and educational priorities; for example, a trend toward securing higher education can reduce the size of the available external workforce in the short run, but in the longer run can result in retaining applicants with more specialized training

- technological changes affecting processes, products, and people; for example, a new technology developed at a local university can be implemented in the organization and significantly reduce labour demands through automation of a previously labour-intensive process

- demographic trends of an internal and external labour force; for example, if an organization is situated in a community largely inhabited by senior citizens, it may face difficulties securing a diverse or full-time workforce from the local area

Steps in Human Resources Planning

HRP is critical to an organization's success as it aligns forecasted labour supply (provided by the human resources department) with the predicted labour demands of the organization (such as the number of employees needed and the skill sets required). An element of HR planning that is often taken for granted is the availability and accuracy of information regarding the current HR situation. Understanding the internal labour force in the present is the basis for a number of demand and supply estimates. Therefore, before embarking on an HR planning exercise, current HR levels must be assessed.

There are numerous sources of information for identifying existing talent and human resources in an organization. An organization chart can provide HR planners and managers with an understanding of the organizational structure, business units, and possible career paths. This macro-level information can be linked to more micro-level information, such as how many employees the company currently has at each level, what existing skill sets the employees have, as well as the demographic information and job-related information about the existing employee base.

environment scanning An assessment of external factors influencing the organizations ability to find and secure talent from the external labour market including economic, competitive, legislative, social, technological and demographic trends.

An organization must forecast future HR demand (the number of employees and the skill sets needed in the future) and forecast future HR supply (internal availability of workers). These two forecasts can occur simultaneously or one after the other depending on the resources available (time, money, people, and so on). Only after demand and supply is forecast can an organization identify potential labour imbalance issues, which leads to the development and implementation of plans to balance HR.

Forecasting the Availability of Candidates (Supply)

Short-term and long-range HR demand forecasts only provide half of the staffing equation by answering the question, "How many employees will we need?" The next major concern is how projected openings will be filled. There are two sources of supply:

1. *Internal*—present employees who can be trained, transferred, or promoted to meet anticipated needs

2. *External*—people in the labour market not currently working for the organization, including those who are employed elsewhere and those who are unemployed who can be expected to join the organization to meet anticipated needs

While internal forecasting identifies which members of the internal workforce will remain within the organization and where, an awareness of the external labour force can aid organizations in identifying challenges that may occur with expected recruitment of candidates into the internal labour force, such as the number of graduates in a specific program that acts as a significant source of talent, the literacy levels of the local or target population, as well as general economic trends. These external factors can impact how much compensation an organization must provide to secure top talent. As well, in times of low unemployment the internal workforce may be more inclined to seek employment elsewhere, if there is a general labour shortage for employees with their specific skill set. Therefore, trends in the external labour force have a direct impact on projections of the internal labour force.

Forecasting the Supply of Internal Candidates

Before estimating how many external candidates will need to be recruited and hired, management must determine how many candidates for projected openings will likely come from within the firm. This is the purpose of forecasting the supply of internal candidates.

Skills Inventories and Management Inventories

Skills inventories contain comprehensive information about the capabilities of current employees. Data gathered for each employee include name, age, date of employment, current position, present duties and responsibilities, educational background, previous work history, skills, abilities, and interests. Information about current performance and readiness for promotion is generally included as well. Data pertaining to managerial staff are compiled in **management inventories**. Records summarizing the background, qualifications, interests, and skills of management employees, as well as information about managerial responsibilities and management training, are used to identify internal candidates eligible for promotion or transfer opportunities.

To be useful, skills and management inventories must be updated regularly. Failure to do so can lead to present employees being overlooked for job openings. Updating every two years is generally adequate if employees are encouraged to report significant qualifications changes (such as new skills learned or courses completed) to the HR department as they occur.

skills inventories Manual or computerized records summarizing employees' education, experience, interests, skills, and so on, which are used to identify internal candidates eligible for transfer or promotion.

management inventories Records summarizing the qualifications, interests, and skills of management employees, along with the number and types of employees supervised, duties of such employees, total budget managed, previous managerial duties and responsibilities, and managerial training received.

Replacement Charts and Replacement Summaries

Replacement charts are typically used to keep track of potential internal candidates for the firm's most critical positions. It assumes that the organization chart will remain static for a long period of time and usually identifies three potential candidates for a top-level position, should it become vacant. As can be seen in Exhibit 21-3, such charts typically indicate the age of potential internal candidates (which cannot be used as a criterion in making selection or promotion decisions but is necessary to project retirement dates), the current performance level of the employee, and his or her promotion potential. The latter is based on the employee's future career aspirations and a supervisory assessment of readiness for promotion.

To provide a more objective estimate of future potential this information may be supplemented by results of psychological tests, interviews with HR specialists, and other selection techniques.

Although replacement charts provide an excellent quick reference tool, they contain very little information. For that reason, many firms prefer to use **replacement summaries**. Such summaries list likely replacements for each position and their relative strengths and weaknesses, as well as information about current position, performance, promotability, age, and experience. These additional data can be extremely helpful to decision makers, although caution must be taken to ensure that no discrimination occurs on the basis of age, sex, and so on.

Cenera
www.cenera.ca

replacement charts Visual representations of who will replace whom in the event of a job opening. Likely internal candidates are listed, along with their age, present performance rating, and promotability status.

replacement summaries Lists of likely replacements for each position and their relative strengths and weaknesses, as well as information about current position, performance, promotability, age, and experience.

EXHIBIT 21-3 Management Replacement Chart

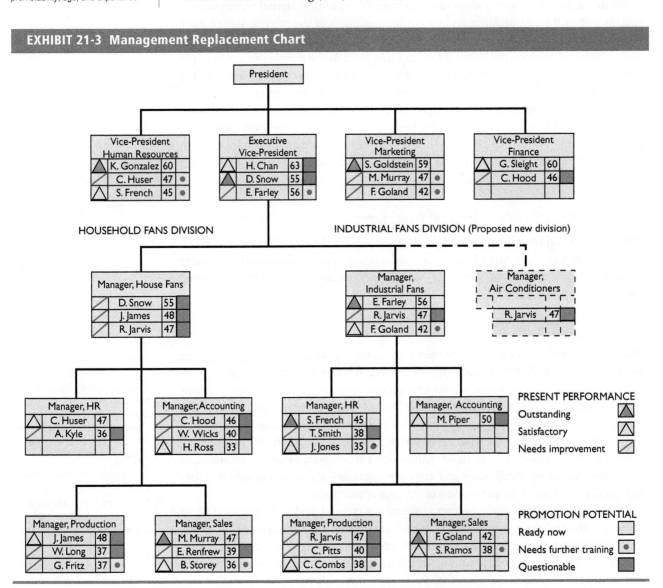

Succession Plans

Forecasting the availability of inside candidates is particularly important in succession planning. In a nutshell, **succession planning** refers to the plans a company makes to fill its most important executive positions. It extends beyond the replacement chart by focusing on developing people rather than simply identifying potential replacements. As a result, there is a stronger focus on skills development for a specific list of potential successors within an organization.

In the days when companies were hierarchical and employees tended to remain with a firm for years, executive succession was often straightforward: Staff climbed the ladder one rung at a time, and it wasn't unusual for someone to start on the shop floor and end up in the president's office. Although that kind of ascent is still possible, employee turnover and flatter structures mean that the lines of succession are no longer as direct. For example, potential successors for top positions might be routed through the top jobs at several key divisions, as well as overseas, and sent through a university graduate-level, advanced management program.

Succession planning is extremely important today, affecting both large and small organizations. The Entrepreneurs and HR box highlights some of the challenges that entrepreneurial organizations often face with succession planning. Because succession planning requires balancing the organization's top management needs with the potential career aspirations of available candidates, succession should include these activities:

- analysis of the demand for managers and professionals in the company

- audit of existing executives and projection of likely future supply

- planning of individual career paths based on objective estimates of future needs, performance appraisal data, and assessments of potential

- career counselling and performance-related training and development to prepare individuals for future roles

- accelerated promotions, with development targeted at future business needs

- planned strategic recruitment aimed at obtaining people with the potential to meet future needs as well as filling current openings[4]

It should be noted that replacement charts, replacement summaries, and succession plans are considered highly confidential in most organizations.

An Ethical | Dilemma

You were recently asked to identify one employee you manage as a top performer to align with a new company program offering top performers intensive management skills training. The employee you identified for this role is unaware of the program. This morning, she confided in you that she just applied for graduate school and will find out if she has been accepted five months from now, with the intent to start the program one month after that. Would you change the identification of who was the top performer in your team based on this information? Why or why not?

Tips | FOR THE FRONT LINE

Markov Analysis

Estimating internal supply involves much more than simply calculating the number of employees. Some firms use the **Markov analysis** technique to track the pattern of employee movements through various jobs and develop a transitional probability matrix for forecasting internal supply by specific categories, such as position and gender. As illustrated in Exhibit 21-4, such an analysis shows the actual number (and percentage) of employees who remain in each job from one year to the next, as well as the proportions promoted, demoted, transferred, and leaving the organization. These proportions (probabilities) are used to forecast human resources supply.

In the example provided, there were 35 employees in the foreperson occupation in 2013. Out of these, 82 percent (28 employees) are expected to remain in that position next year (based on past levels of activity). The organization can anticipate that 8 percent of the foreperson population (which would be 3 out of the 35 employees in 2013) would be promotable to the role of plant manager. In addition, the past trends

succession planning The process of ensuring a suitable supply of successors for current and future senior or key jobs so that the careers of individuals can be effectively planned and managed.

Markov analysis A method of forecasting internal labour supply that involves tracking the pattern of employee movements through various jobs and developing a transitional probability matrix.

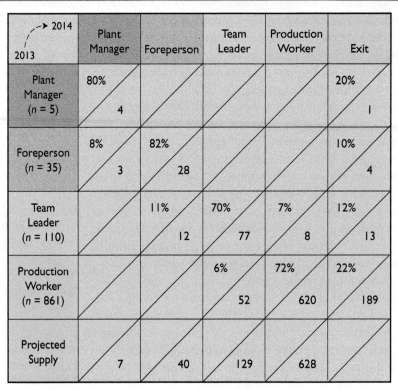

EXHIBIT 21-4 Hypothetical Markov Analysis for a Manufacturing Operation

2013 → 2014	Plant Manager	Foreperson	Team Leader	Production Worker	Exit
Plant Manager (n = 5)	80% / 4				20% / 1
Foreperson (n = 35)	8% / 3	82% / 28			10% / 4
Team Leader (n = 110)		11% / 12	70% / 77	7% / 8	12% / 13
Production Worker (n = 861)			6% / 52	72% / 620	22% / 189
Projected Supply	7	40	129	628	

Percentages represent transitions (previous year's actuals).
Actual numbers of employees are shown as whole numbers in each block
(projections for 2014 based on current staffing).

show that 10 percent of employees at this level are lost to turnover (representing four employees who are expected to leave the organization before the start of next year). In addition, out of the 110 team leaders (the level below), 11 percent (12 employees) would be eligible for promotion to a foreperson position. Therefore, next year's projected supply of forepersons would be the 28 from this year who are projected to stay in that role plus the 12 team leaders who are projected to be eligible for promotion over the year, for a total supply of 40 forepersons.

In addition to such quantitative data, the skills and capabilities of current employees must be assessed and skills inventories prepared. From this information, replacement charts or summaries and succession plans can be developed.

Forecasting the Supply of External Candidates

Some jobs cannot be filled with internal candidates because no current employees are qualified (such as entry-level jobs) or they are jobs that experience significant growth. In these situations, the firm looks for external candidates. Employer growth is primarily responsible for the number of entry-level openings. A key factor in determining the number of positions that must be filled externally is the effectiveness of the organization's training, development, and career-planning initiatives. If employees are not encouraged to expand their capabilities, they may not be ready to fill vacancies as they arise, and external sources must be tapped.

To project the supply of outside candidates, employers assess general economic conditions, labour market conditions, and occupational market conditions.

General Economic Conditions

General economic conditions refer to the impact of natural fluctuations in economic activity, which impacts all businesses. These include factors such as interest rates, wage rates, rate of inflation, and unemployment rates. In general terms, the lower the rate of unemployment, the smaller the labour supply and the more difficult it will be to recruit employees. It is important to note that unemployment rates vary by occupation and geographic location and can result in an organization's inability to fill certain positions.

Labour Market Conditions

Labour market conditions refer to the demographics of those in the population, such as education levels, age, gender, marital status, and so on. Demographic conditions remain stable and can be forecast with a relatively high degree of accuracy. Fortunately, a wealth of national labour market information is available from Statistics Canada and other government or private sources. Regional chambers of commerce and provincial/ local development and planning agencies can be excellent sources of local labour market information.

Statistics Canada
www.statcan.gc.ca

A crucial reality is that a large portion of the population is expected to retire over the next decade, significantly decreasing the size of the labour force. Graduating students (from any level of education) who are just joining the workforce are projected to account for 550 000 new entrants to the labour market a year.[5] In contrast, new immigrants are expected to account for 131 500 new entrants to the labour market a year.

Occupational Market Conditions

In addition to looking at the overall labour market, organizations also generally want to forecast the availability of potential candidates in specific occupations (engineers, drill press operators, accountants, and so on) for which they will be recruiting. Alberta has recently faced a severe labour shortage of workers in the oil and gas sector.[6] Furthermore, the mining industry, the construction industry, the electricity industry, the manufacturing industry, as well as the non-profit sector are also experiencing significant labour shortages.[7] A shortage of information technology workers is projected to cost the Canadian economy $10 billion per year until it is resolved.[8] Shortages of civil service workers, accountants, lawyers, engineers, meteorologists, funeral directors (to bury the baby boomers), and hospitality industry workers are also expected.[9]

In recent years, the information, communication, and technology sectors (ICT) have suffered from a significant skills shortage, where the demand for ICT workers exceeds the supply. This shortage is expected to continue until 2016.

Forecasting Future Human Resources Needs (Demand)

A key component of HRP is forecasting the number and type of people needed to meet organizational objectives. Managers should consider several factors when forecasting such requirements. From a practical point of view, the demand for the organization's product or service is paramount. Thus, in a manufacturing firm, sales are projected first. Then the volume of production required to meet these sales requirements is determined. Finally, the staff needed to maintain this volume of output is estimated. In addition to this "basic requirement" for staff, several other factors should be considered, including

1. *Projected turnover* as a result of resignations or terminations

2. *Quality and nature of employees* in relation to what management sees as the changing needs of the organization

3. *Decisions to upgrade* the quality of products or services *or enter into new markets*, which might change the required employee skill mix

4. *Planned technological and administrative changes aimed at increasing productivity and reducing employee head count,* such as the installation of new equipment or introduction of a financial incentive plan

5. The *financial resources* available to each department; for example, a budget increase may enable managers to pay higher wages or hire more people; conversely, a budget crunch might result in wage freezes or layoffs

In large organizations, needs forecasting is primarily quantitative in nature and is the responsibility of highly trained specialists. *Quantitative techniques* for determining human resources requirements include trend analysis, ratio analysis, scatter plot analysis, and regression analysis. These are often viewed as numerically or mathematically grounded, and therefore more objective in nature. *Qualitative approaches* to forecasting range from sophisticated analytical models to informal expert opinions about future needs, often involving subjective interpretations or estimates, such as the nominal group technique or the Delphi technique.

Quantitative Approaches

Trend Analysis

Trend analysis involves studying the firm's employment levels over the last three to five years to predict future needs. The purpose is to identify employment trends that might continue into the future, assuming that the past is a strong predictor of the future. Trend analysis is valuable as an initial estimate only, since employment levels rarely depend solely on the passage of time. Other factors (like changes in sales volume and productivity) will also affect future staffing needs.

Ratio Analysis

Ratio analysis involves making forecasts based on the ratio between some causal factor (such as sales volume) and the number of employees required (for example, the number of salespeople). Ratio analysis can also be used to help forecast other employee requirements. Like trend analysis, ratio analysis assumes that productivity remains about the same. For example, suppose a salesperson traditionally generates $500 000 in sales and that plans call for increasing the firm's sales by $3 million next year. Then, if the sales revenue–salespeople ratio remains the same, six new salespeople would be required (each of whom produces an extra $500 000 in sales).

The Scatter Plot

Scatter plots can be used to determine whether two factors—a measure of business activity and staffing levels—are related. If they are, then when the measure of business activity is forecast, HR requirements can also be estimated.

An example to illustrate follows. Legislative changes to the healthcare system require that two 500-bed Canadian hospitals be amalgamated. Both previously had responsibility for acute, chronic, and long-term care. The government's plan is for Hospital A to specialize in acute care while Hospital B assumes responsibility for chronic and long-term care. In general, providing acute care requires staffing with registered nurses (RNs), while chronic and long-term care facilities can be staffed primarily with registered practical nurses (RPNs).

By the end of the calendar year, 200 beds at Hospital A must be converted from chronic and long-term care beds to facilities for acute patients. At the same time, Hospital A's 200 chronic and long-term patients must be transferred to Hospital B. In a joint meeting, the directors of nursing and HR decide that a good starting point in the planning process would be to calculate the relationship between hospital size (in terms of number of acute beds) and the number of RNs required. After placing telephone calls to their counterparts at eight hospitals in larger centres across the country, they obtain the following information:

trend analysis The study of a firm's past employment levels over a period of years to predict future needs.

ratio analysis A forecasting technique for determining future staff needs by using ratios between some causal factor (such as sales volume) and the number of employees needed.

scatter plot A graphical method used to help identify the relationship between two variables.

Size of Hospital (Number of Acute Beds)	Number of Registered Nurses
200	240
300	260
400	470
500	500
600	620
700	660
800	820
900	860

To determine how many RNs would be needed, they use the data obtained to draw the scatter plot shown in EXHIBIT 21-5, in which hospital size is shown on the horizontal axis and number of RNs is shown on the vertical axis. If the two factors are related, then the points will tend to fall along a straight line, as they do in this case. Carefully drawing a line that minimizes the distances between the line and each of the plotted points (the line of best fit) permits an estimate of the number of nurses required for hospitals of various sizes. Thus, since Hospital A will now have 500 acute-care beds, the estimated number of RNs needed is 500.

Regression Analysis

Regression analysis is a more sophisticated statistical technique to determine the line of best fit, often involving multiple variables (rather than just two, as per the example above). As a statistical tool used to investigate the effect of one variable on another, the investigator is able to determine the magnitude and direction of the relationship between variables to develop future predictions. In the context of HRP, it involves the use of a mathematical formula to project future demands based on an established relationship between an organization's employment level (dependent variable) and some measurable factors of output (independent variables), such as revenue, sales, or production level.

EXHIBIT 21-5 Determining the Relationship between Hospital Size and Number of Registered Nurses

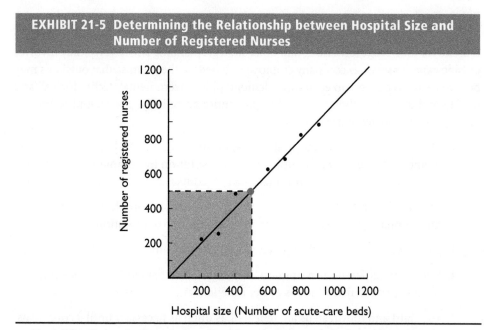

Note: After fitting the line, the number of employees needed, given the projected volume, can be extrapolated (projected).

regression analysis A statistical technique involving the use of a mathematical formula to project future demands based on an established relationship between an organization's employment level (dependent variable) and some measurable factor of output (independent variable).

Qualitative Approaches

In contrast to quantitative approaches, which use statistical formulas, qualitative techniques rely solely on expert judgments. Two approaches used to forecast human resources demand (or supply) are the nominal group and Delphi techniques. Although managerial judgment is central to qualitative forecasting, it also plays a key role when quantitative techniques are used. It's rare that any historical trend, ratio, or relationship will continue unchanged into the future. Judgment is therefore needed to modify the forecast based on anticipated changes.

Nominal Group Technique

The **nominal group technique** involves a group of experts (such as first-line supervisors and managers) meeting face to face. Although one of its uses is human resources demand forecasting, this technique is used to deal with issues and problems ranging from identifying training needs to determining safety program incentives. The steps involved are as follows:[10]

1. Each member of the group independently writes down his or her ideas on the problem or issue (in this case, estimates of demand).

2. Going around the table, each member then presents one idea. This process continues until all ideas have been presented and recorded, typically on a flip-chart or chalkboard. No discussion is permitted during this step.

3. Clarification is then sought, as necessary, followed by group discussion and evaluation.

4. Finally, each member is asked to rank the ideas. This is done independently and in silence.

The advantages of this technique include involvement of key decision makers, a future focus, and the fact that the group discussion involved in the third step can facilitate the exchange of ideas and greater acceptance of results. Drawbacks include subjectivity and the potential for group pressure to lead to a less accurate assessment than could be obtained through other means.

Delphi Technique

Although short-term forecasting is generally handled by managers, the **Delphi technique** is useful for long-range forecasting and other strategic planning issues. It typically involves outside experts as well as company employees, based on the premise that outsiders may be able to assess changes in economic, demographic, governmental, technological, and social conditions, and their potential impact more objectively. The Delphi technique involves the following steps:[11]

1. The problem is identified (in this case, estimates of demand) and each group member is requested to submit a potential solution by completing a carefully designed questionnaire. Direct face-to-face contact is not permitted.

2. After each member independently and anonymously completes the initial questionnaire, the results are compiled at a centralized location.

3. Each group member is then given a copy of the results.

4. If there are differences in opinion, each individual uses the feedback from other experts to fine-tune his or her independent assessment.

5. The third and fourth steps are repeated as often as necessary until a consensus is reached.

nominal group technique A decision-making technique that involves a group of experts meeting face to face. Steps include independent idea generation, clarification and open discussion, and private assessment.

Delphi technique A judgmental forecasting method used to arrive at a group decision, typically involving outside experts as well as organizational employees. Ideas are exchanged without face-to-face interaction and feedback is provided and used to fine-tune independent judgments until a consensus is reached.

EXHIBIT 21-6 A Sample Staffing Table

Job Title (As on Job Description)	Department	Anticipated Openings												
		Total	Jan.	Feb.	Mar.	Apr.	May	June	July	Aug.	Sept.	Oct.	Nov.	Dec.
General Manager	Administration	1					1							
Director of Finance	Administration	1												1
Human Resources Officer	Administration	2	1					1						
Collection Clerk	Administration	1		1										
Groundskeeper	Maintenance	4						1	1					2
Service and Maintenance Technician	Maintenance	5	1			2					2			
Water Utility Engineer	Operations	3									2			1
Apprentice Lineperson	Operations	10	6						4					
Water Meter Technician	Operations	1												1
Engineering Technician	Operations	3			2							1		
Field Technician	Operations	8						8						
Senior Programmer/ Analyst	Systems	2					1			1				
Programmer/Operator	Systems	4		2						1			1	
Systems Operator	Systems	5						2					3	
Customer Service Representative	Sales	8	4					3				1		

Springbrook Utilities Commission Staffing Table
Date compiled:_____

As with the nominal group technique, the advantages of the Delphi technique include involvement of key decision makers and a future focus; in addition, though, it permits the group to critically evaluate a wider range of views. Drawbacks include the fact that judgments may not efficiently use objective data, the time and costs involved, and the potential difficulty in integrating diverse opinions.

Gap Analysis: Summarizing Human Resources Requirements

The end result of the forecasting process is an estimate of short-term and long-range HR requirements. Long-range plans are general statements of potential staffing needs and may not include specific numbers.

Short-term plans—although still approximations—are more specific and are often depicted in a **staffing table**. As illustrated in Exhibit 21-6, a staffing table is a pictorial representation of all jobs within the organization, along with the number of current incumbents and future employment requirements (monthly or yearly) for each.

Planning and Implementing HR Programs to Balance Supply and Demand

Once the supply and demand of human resources have been estimated, program planning and implementation begin. To successfully fill positions internally, organizations must manage performance and careers. Performance is managed through effectively designing jobs and quality-of-working-life initiatives; establishing performance standards and goals; coaching, measuring, and evaluating; and implementing a suitable reward structure (compensation and benefits).

staffing table A pictorial representation of all jobs within the organization, along with the number of current incumbents and future employment requirements (monthly or yearly) for each.

EXHIBIT 21-7 Balancing Supply and Demand Considerations

Conditions	Possible Solutions
Labour Equilibrium (when labour demand equals labour supply)	• Vacancies are filled internally through training, transfers, or promotions or externally through hiring
Labour Surplus (when labour demand is less than labour supply)	• Hiring freeze: reassign current workers to job openings • Attrition: standard employee resignation, retirement, or death • Early retirement buyout programs: entice those close to retirement to retire early with a buyout program, access to full or reduced pension, and/or continuation of benefits • Job sharing, work sharing, or reduced workweek programs: reducing work from the standard full-time workload to a less than full-time work • Layoff: temporary or permanent withdrawal of employment due to business or economic reasons • Termination: permanent separation from the organization because of job performance reasons • Leave of absence: voluntary, temporary withdrawal of employment with guaranteed job upon return
Labour Shortage (when labour demand is greater than labour supply)	• Scheduling overtime hours • Hiring temporary workers • Subcontracting work • External recruitment • Internal promotions or transfers

To manage careers effectively, policies and systems must be established for recruitment, selection and placement (including transfer, promotion, retirement, and termination), and training and development. Policies and systems are also required for job analysis, individual employee assessment, replacement and succession planning, and career tracking, as well as career planning and development.

Specific strategies must be formulated to balance supply and demand considerations. As illustrated in Exhibit 21-7, there are three possible scenarios:

1. projected labour demand matches projected labour supply (equilibrium)

2. projected labour supply exceeds projected demand (surplus)

3. projected labour demand exceeds projected supply (shortage)

Labour Equilibrium

Although it is extremely rare to have a labour equilibrium, when the expected supply matches the actual demand organizations do not need to change their course of action. Existing plans to replace outgoing employees should be maintained by promoting or transferring internal members of the organization as well as recruiting external labourers.

Labour Surplus

A labour surplus exists when the internal supply of employees exceeds the organization's demand. Most employers respond initially by instituting a **hiring freeze**, which means that openings are filled by reassigning current employees and no outsiders are hired. The surplus is slowly reduced through **attrition**, which is the normal separation of employees because of resignation, retirement, or death. When employees leave, the

hiring freeze A common initial response to an employee surplus; openings are filled by reassigning current employees and no outsiders are hired.

attrition The normal separation of employees from an organization because of resignation, retirement, or death.

ensuing vacancies are not filled and the staffing level decreases gradually without any involuntary terminations. In addition to the time it takes, a major drawback of this approach is that the firm has no control over who stays and who leaves.

Some organizations attempt to accelerate attrition by offering incentives to employees to leave, such as **early retirement buyout programs**. Staffing levels are reduced and internal job openings created by offering attractive buyout packages or the opportunity to retire on full pension with an attractive benefits package at a relatively early age (often 50 or 55). To be successful, buyouts must be handled carefully. Selection criteria should be established to ensure that key people who cannot be easily replaced do not leave the firm. A drawback of buyouts and early retirement packages is that they often require a great deal of money upfront. Care must also be taken to ensure that early retirement is voluntary, since forced early retirement is a contravention of human rights legislation.

Another strategy used to deal with an employee surplus involves reducing the total number of hours worked. **Job sharing** involves dividing the duties of a single position between two or more employees. Reducing full-time positions to *part-time work* is sometimes more effective, especially if there are peak demand periods. Creating a job-share position or offering part-time employment can be win–win strategies, since layoffs can be avoided. Although the employees involved work fewer hours and thus have less pay, they are still employed, and they may enjoy having more free time at their disposal; the organization benefits by retaining good employees.

Twenty-five years ago, the federal government introduced a **work-sharing** scheme, a layoff-avoidance strategy that involves employees working three or four days a week and receiving employment insurance (EI) benefits on their non-workday(s). The program was temporarily extended to provide 52 weeks of benefits from February 1, 2009, to April 3, 2010, during the recent economic slowdown.[12] Similar to work sharing, but without a formal arrangement with the government regarding EI benefits, is a **reduced workweek**. Employees simply work fewer hours and receive less pay. The organization retains a skilled workforce, lessens the financial and emotional impact of a full layoff, and reduces production costs. One potential drawback is that it is sometimes difficult to predict in advance, with any degree of accuracy, how many hours of work should be scheduled each week.

Another strategy used to manage employee surplus is a **layoff**; the temporary withdrawal of employment to workers for economic or business reasons. Layoffs may be short in duration (for example, when a plant closes for brief periods in order to adjust inventory levels or to retool for a new product line), but can last months or even years at a time if the organization is negatively affected by a major change in the business cycle. However, layoffs are often permanent in nature. Layoffs are not easy for managers, who have to reduce the number of employees to the required level, or for workers, but are usually necessary to ultimately reduce the impact of the organization's economic downturn. Layoffs and terminations are discussed in depth in Chapter 23.

Termination is a broad term that encompasses permanent separation of the worker from the organization. Termination is often triggered by a management decision to sever the employment relationship due to reasons that are related to job performance. Purging poorly performing employees is often an ongoing activity in any organization, regardless of any projected labour surpluses; however, the rate of termination may increase if there is a projected surplus of labour.

The option of a voluntary **leave of absence** can also be used if the labour surplus is temporary in nature. A leave of absence allows those who may be interested in time off for personal, educational, or other reasons to have a set period of time away from their position, with a guarantee that their job will be available upon their return. A leave of absence can be paid or unpaid, but often seniority and benefits remain intact. Terms of the leave and expected return must be clearly outlined, including potential conflicts of interest and mutual expectations from each party.

Hints | TO ENSURE LEGAL COMPLIANCE

Tips | FOR THE FRONT LINE

early retirement buyout programs Strategies used to accelerate attrition that involve offering attractive buyout packages or the opportunity to retire on full pension with an attractive benefits package.

job sharing A strategy that involves dividing the duties of a single position between two or more employees.

work sharing Employees work three or four days a week and receive EI benefits on their non-workday(s).

reduced workweek Employees work fewer hours and receive less pay.

layoff The temporary or permanent withdrawal of employment to workers for economic or business reasons.

termination Permanent separation from the organization for any reason

leave of absence Allows those who may be interested in taking time away from work for a variety of reasons (e.g. personal, educational, etc.) to have a set period of time aware from their position without pay, but with a guarantee that their job will be available upon their return.

Research | INSIGHT

Easing the Pain of Labour Surplus Management

Although restructuring initiatives, ranging from layoffs to mergers and acquisitions, were prevalent in the last two decades, organizations that engaged in layoffs were not consistently achieving the desired goals or financial benefits of their decisions. In a study of 6418 workforce reductions in Fortune 500 firms over 18 years, researchers found no consistent evidence that downsizing led to improved financial performance.[13]

A primary reason for this is the high cost associated with **survivor syndrome**, a range of emotions that can include feelings of betrayal or violation, guilt, or detachment. The remaining employees, anxious about the next round of terminations, often suffer stress symptoms, including depression, increased errors, and reduced performance.

To ease the financial burden of layoffs, some organizations offer **supplemental unemployment benefits (SUBs)**, which are a top-up of EI benefits to bring income levels of temporarily laid-off workers closer to their regular, on-the-job pay. SUB programs are generally negotiated through collective bargaining between the employee and employer. Benefits are payable until the pool of funds set aside has been exhausted.

An Ethical | Dilemma

How much time, effort, and money should firms devote to helping "surviving" employees deal with downsizing? With mergers and acquisitions?

A **severance package** is typically provided when employees are being terminated through no fault of their own in order to avoid wrongful dismissal lawsuits. Severance pay is legally required in certain situations, such as mass layoffs.

In addition to pay, severance packages often include the continuation of benefits for a specified period. In determining the appropriate package, employers should take salary, years of service, the employee's age, and his or her likelihood of obtaining another job into consideration.[14] Executives may be protected by a *golden parachute clause* in their contract of employment, which is a guarantee by the employer to pay specified compensation and benefits in the case of termination because of downsizing or restructuring. To soften the blow of termination, *outplacement assistance*, generally offered by an outside agency, can assist affected employees in finding employment elsewhere. The issues and processes related to managing a labour surplus legally and fairly are provided in significant detail in Chapter 23 (managing employee terminations).

Hints | TO ENSURE LEGAL COMPLIANCE

survivor syndrome A range of negative emotions experienced by employees remaining after a major restructuring initiative, which can include feelings of betrayal or violation, guilt, or detachment, and can result in stress symptoms, including depression, increased errors, and reduced performance.

supplemental unemployment benefits (SUBs) A top-up of EI benefits to bring income levels closer to what an employee would receive if on the job.

severance package A lump-sum payment, continuation of benefits for a specified period of time, and other benefits that are provided to employees who are being terminated.

transfer Movement of an employee from one job to another that is relatively equal in pay, responsibility, or organizational level.

promotion Movement of an employee from one job to another that is higher in pay, responsibility, or organizational level, usually based on merit, seniority, or a combination of both.

Labour Shortage

A labour shortage exists when the internal supply of human resources cannot meet the organization's needs. Scheduling overtime hours is often the initial response. Employers may also subcontract work on a temporary or permanent basis. Another short-term solution is to hire temporary employees.

As vacancies are created within the firm, opportunities are generally provided for employee transfers and promotions, which necessitate performance management, training (and retraining), and career development. Of course, internal movement does not eliminate a shortage, which means that recruitment will be required. It is hoped, though, that resultant vacancies will be for entry-level jobs, which can be filled more easily externally.

Internal Solutions to a Labour Shortage

A **transfer** involves a lateral movement from one job to another that is relatively equal in pay, responsibility, or organizational level. Transfers can lead to more effective use of human resources, broaden an employee's skills and perspectives, and help make him or her a better candidate for future promotions. Transfers also offer additional technical and interpersonal challenges and increased variety of work, which may enhance job satisfaction and motivation.

A **promotion** involves the movement of an employee from one job to another that is higher in pay, responsibility, or organizational level. Such a move may be based on merit, seniority, or a combination of both. Merit-based promotions are awarded in recognition of a person's outstanding performance in his or her present job or as an assessment of his or her future potential.

A focus on employee retention initiatives can also mitigate potential labour shortages. The HRP process often highlights challenges the organization is having with turnover or retention at specific levels. This may warrant further investigation into why employees are leaving and which types of employees are leaving. Rather than a broad focus on retention, organizations can benefit from focusing on retaining key employees or employees with strong job performance. A discussion of career planning to assist with internal solutions regarding a labour shortage are provided in Chapters 11 and 12 (career development and performance management).

External Solutions to a Labour Shortage

External solutions to managing a labour shortage involve recruiting the right quality and quantity of talent needed in an organization to meet the long-term goals and strategy of the company. Chapter 8 extensively discusses the recruitment process, methods of recruitment, and strategies of determining recruitment targets. Options for recruitment and selection related to managing a labour shortage are provided in Chapters 8 and 9 (recruitment and selection).

22

Occupational Health and Safety

Strategic Importance of Occupational Health and Safety

Health and safety initiatives are part of a strategic approach to human resources management. Service provided to clients and customers is a function of how employees are treated, and employee health, safety, and wellness management are important determinants of employee perceptions regarding fair treatment by the organization. Further, investment in disability management and proactive wellness programs create measurable bottom-line returns.[1]

Another reason that safety and accident prevention concerns managers is that the work-related accident figures are staggering. **Lost-time injury rate** measures any occupational injury or illness resulting in an employee being unable to fulfill the work full work assignments, not including any fatalities. According to the Association of Workers' Compensation Boards of Canada, in 2007 there were 1 055 deaths and 317 524 injuries resulting from accidents at work. Thus, on average, more than three Canadian workers died each working day.[2] These figures do not include minor injuries that do not involve time lost from work beyond the day of the accident. Moreover, these figures do not tell the full story. They do not reflect the human suffering incurred by injured or ill workers and their families. On April 28 each year, a day of mourning is observed for Canadian workers killed or injured on the job.

Workplace health concerns are also widespread. Surveys have shown that 61 percent of Canadians believe that workplace accidents are inevitable.[3] According to the Canadian Centre for Justice Statistics, 17 percent of all self-reported incidents of violent victimization, including sexual assault, robbery, and physical assault, occur at the respondents' place of work, representing over 356 000 violent workplace incidents in Canada in one year alone.[4] This statistic is particularly disturbing because workplace accidents are largely preventable.

Ceremonies are held across Canada every April 28 to mark the National Day of Mourning for workers killed or injured on the job. In Moncton, New Brunswick, Pauline Farrell lays roses in memory of her late husband, Bill Kelly, who was killed more than 30 years ago.

Basic Facts About Occupational Health and Safety Legislation

All provinces, territories, and the federal jurisdiction have **occupational health and safety legislation** based on the principle of joint responsibility. There is an implicit and explicit expectation that both workers and employers must maintain a hazard-free work environment and enhance the health and safety of workers.[5]

Lost-time injury rate Measures any occupational injury or illness resulting in an employee being unable to fulfill the work full work assignments, not including any fatalities.

occupational health and safety legislation Laws intended to protect the health and safety of workers by minimizing work-related accidents and illnesses.

Purpose

These laws fall into three categories: general health and safety rules, rules for specific industries (for example, mining), and rules related to specific hazards (for example, asbestos). In some jurisdictions, these are combined into one overall law with regulations for specific industries and hazards, while in others they remain separate. The regulations are very complex and cover almost every conceivable hazard in great detail, as shown in Exhibit 22-1. Provisions of occupational health and safety legislation differ significantly across Canada but most have certain basic features in common.

EXHIBIT 22-1 Ontario Occupational Health and Safety Act—Construction Regulations

O.REG.213/91

68. A sign used to direct traffic,

(a) shall be diamond shaped, 450 millimetres wide and 450 millimetres long, with the diamond mounted at one corner on a pole 1.2 metres long; (b) shall be made of material that has at least the rigidity of six millimetres thick plywood; (c) shall be reflective fluorescent and coloured, (i) red-orange on one side with the corner areas coloured black, so that the red-orange area forms a regular eight-sided figure, with the word "STOP" written in legible white letters 150 millimetres high in a central position on the sign, and (ii) chartreuse on one side, with the word "SLOW" written in legible black letters 150 millimetres high in a central position on the sign; and (d) shall be maintained in a clean condition.

Source: Ontario Health and Safety Act © Queen's Printer for Ontario, 2011.

Responsibilities and Rights of Employers and Employees

In all jurisdictions, employers are responsible for taking every reasonable precaution to ensure the health and safety of their workers. This is called the "due diligence" requirement. Specific duties of the employer include filing government accident reports, maintaining records, ensuring that safety rules are enforced, and posting safety notices and legislative information.[6] A recent Ontario court decision suggests that employers must enforce safe work procedures through a progressive discipline process to establish a defence of due diligence when workers do not follow safety rules and are injured on the job.[7]

Employees are responsible for taking reasonable care to protect their own health and safety and, in most cases, that of their co-workers. Specific requirements include wearing protective clothing and equipment and reporting any contravention of the law or regulations. Employees have three basic rights under the joint responsibility model: (1) the right to know about workplace safety hazards, (2) the right to participate in the occupational health and safety process, and (3) the right to refuse unsafe work if they have "reasonable cause" to believe that the work is dangerous. "Reasonable cause" usually means that a complaint about a workplace hazard has not been satisfactorily resolved, or a safety problem places employees in immediate danger. If performance of a task would adversely affect health and safety, a worker cannot be disciplined for refusing to do the job.

Joint Health and Safety Committees

The function of joint health and safety committees is to provide a non-adversarial atmosphere where management and labour can work together to ensure a safe and healthy workplace. Most jurisdictions require a joint health and safety committee to be established in each workplace with a minimum number of workers (usually 10 or 20). In the other jurisdictions, the government has the power to require a committee to be formed. Committees are usually required to consist of between 2 and 12 members, at least half of whom must represent workers. In small workplaces, one health and safety representative may be required.

The committee is generally responsible for making regular inspections of the workplace to identify potential health and safety hazards, evaluate the hazards, and implement solutions. Hazard control can be achieved by addressing safety issues before an accident or injury happens, identifying ways in which a hazardous situation can be prevented from harming workers, and establishing procedures to ensure that a potential hazard will not recur. Health and safety committees are also responsible for investigating employee complaints, accident investigation, development and promotion of measures to protect health and safety, and dissemination of information about health and safety laws and regulations. In Ontario, at least one management and one labour representative must be certified in occupational health and safety through a provincial training program. Committees are often more effective if the company's health and safety manager acts as an independent expert rather than as a management representative.[8]

The Supervisor's Role in Safety

Most jurisdictions impose a personal duty on supervisors to ensure that workers comply with occupational health and safety regulations. They place a specific obligation on supervisors to advise and instruct workers about safety, to ensure that all reasonable precautions have been taken to provide for the safety of all employees, and to minimize risk of injuries or illness.

Safety-minded managers must aim to instill in their workers the desire to work safely. Minimizing hazards (by ensuring that spills are wiped up, machine guards are adequate, and so forth) is important, but no matter how safe the workplace is, there will be accidents unless workers want to and do act safely. Of course, supervisors try to watch each employee closely, but most managers know that this will not work. In the final analysis, the best (and perhaps only) alternative is to get workers to want to work safely. Then, when needed, safety rules should be enforced.[9]

Enforcement of Occupational Health and Safety Laws

In all Canadian jurisdictions, occupational health and safety law provides for government inspectors to periodically carry out safety inspections of workplaces. Health and safety inspectors have wide powers to conduct inspections in any workplace at any time without a warrant or prior notification and may engage in any examination and inquiry that they believe necessary to ascertain whether the workplace is in compliance with the law. Safety inspectors may order a variety of actions on the part of employers and employees, including orders to stop work or stop using tools, install first aid equipment, and stop emission of contaminants. Governments have been criticized for weak enforcement of health and safety laws, and several provinces have recently strengthened their inspection services.[10]

Penalties consist of fines and/or jail terms. Governments across Canada are increasingly turning to prosecutions as a means of enforcing health and safety standards. In 2008, Alberta imposed a record $5 million in penalties against companies for health and safety violations.[11] Other provinces are increasing the number of charges laid against both individual managers and organizations.[12]

Canadian corporate executives and directors may be held directly responsible for workplace injuries, and in some cases corporate officers have been convicted and received prison sentences for health and safety violations.[13] The Criminal Code includes a criminal offence (known as Bill C-45 amendments, and commonly referred to as "corporate killing") that imposes criminal liability on "all persons" who direct the work of other employees and fail to ensure an appropriate level of safety in the workplace. Criminal Code convictions can be penalized by incarceration up to life in prison, and financial fines can be imposed on guilty parties.

The first company to be charged with and plead guilty to criminal negligence causing death of a worker was Transpavé, a concrete block manufacturer in Quebec. The incident involved a young employee who was crushed by heavy machinery when he tried to remove debris jamming a stacking machine. The machine did have a safety guard device, but the device had been disabled almost two years prior to the accident. In addition, the court found that the company had inadequate programs to ensure safe operations of the machine, and there was a lack of training regarding safety and hazards in the workplace. As a result, the company was found to be negligent in its responsibility of safety in the workplace and the company was fined $110 000.[14]

Control of Toxic Substances

Most occupational health and safety laws require basic precautions with respect to toxic substances, including chemicals, biohazards (such as HIV/AIDS and SARS), and physical agents (such as radiation, heat, and noise). An accurate inventory of these substances must be maintained, maximum exposure limits for airborne concentrations of these agents adhered to, the substances tested, and their use carefully controlled.

The **Workplace Hazardous Materials Information System (WHMIS)** is a Canada-wide, legally mandated system designed to protect workers by providing crucial information about hazardous materials or substances in the workplace. WHMIS was the outcome of a cooperative effort among the federal, provincial, and territorial governments together with industry and organized labour. The WHMIS legislation has three components:[15]

1. Labelling of hazardous material containers to alert workers that there is a potentially hazardous product inside (see Exhibit 22-2 for examples of hazard symbols).

2. Material safety data sheets (MSDS) to outline a product's potentially hazardous ingredients and the procedures for safe handling of the product (see Exhibit 22-3 for a sample MSDS).

3. Employee training to ensure that employees can identify WHMIS hazard symbols, read WHMIS supplier and workplace labels, and read and apply the information on an MSDS.

WHMIS Training
www.whmis.net

Occupational Health and Safety and Other Legislation

Health and safety, human rights, labour relations, and employment standards laws are in force in every jurisdiction in Canada in an interlaced web of legislation. For example, Bill 168 came into effect in June 2010 as an amendment to the Ontario Occupational Health and Safety Act. The amendment has specific legislation requiring the employer to develop violence and harassment policies/programs, report and investigate violence and harassment situations, develop violence-related emergency response procedures, and deal with complaints, incidents, and threats of violence through a formalized process. Such changes to legislation may be specific or vague, local or national, and short or long term, but the role of HR in addressing and responding to changing occupational health and safety legislation will remain critical.

In addition, situations arise in which it is difficult to know which law is applicable, or which one takes precedence over another. For example, are the human rights of one employee to wear a ceremonial knife related to his or her religion more important than the safety of other employees? How much discipline is acceptable to labour arbitrators for health and safety violations? Should fights in the workplace be considered a safety hazard? Is sexual harassment a safety hazard? And how long does an employer have to tolerate poor performance from an alcoholic employee whose attempts at treatment fail? In Saskatchewan, human rights and occupational health and safety legislation overlap because sexual harassment is considered to be a workplace hazard.[16]

At DuPont, safety is the company's highest value, and its accident rate worldwide has been much lower than that of the chemical industry as a whole. As the DuPont safety philosophy states, "Safety management is an integral part of our business and is built

Workplace Hazardous Materials Information System (WHMIS) A Canada-wide, legally mandated system designed to protect workers by providing information about hazardous materials in the workplace.

EXHIBIT 22-2 WHMIS Symbols

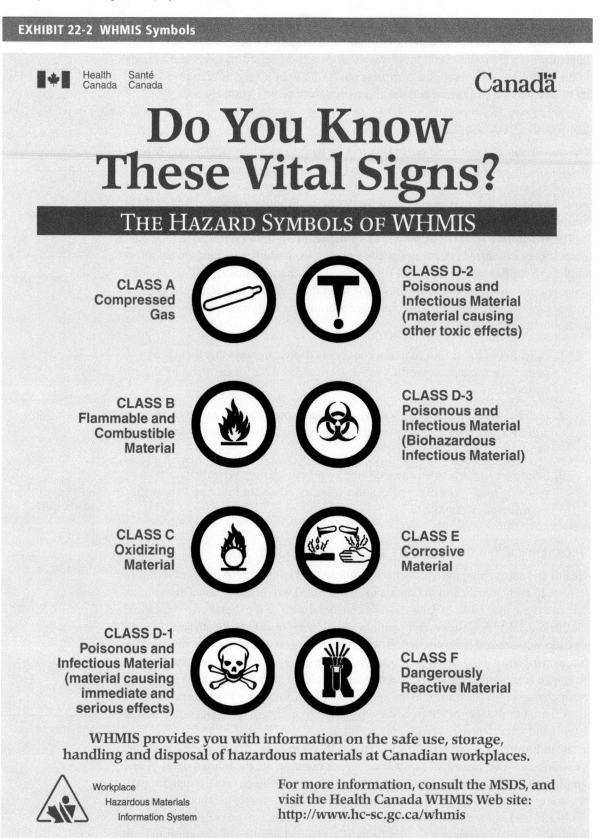

Source: The Hazard Symbols of WHMIS, http://www.hc-sc.gc.ca/ewh-semt/alt_formats/hecs-sesc/pdf/occup-travail/whmis-simdut/ poster_symbols-eng.pdf, Health Canada 2011 ©. Adapted and reproduced with the permission of the Minister of Public Works and Government Services Canada, 2012.

EXHIBIT 22-3 **Material Safety Data Sheet (MSDS)**

NORTH ATLANTIC REFINING LTD.
MATERIAL SAFETY DATA SHEET

PREPARED: July 26, 2008

SECTION 1. PRODUCT INFORMATION

Product Identifier: **Propane**

Application and Use: Multiple use fuel gas.

Product Description: A colourless gas composed primarily of C3 hydrocarbons and handled as a liquid under pressure.

REGULATORY CLASSIFICATION
W.H.M.I.S.
CLASS A: COMPRESSED GAS
CLASS B1: FLAMMABLE GAS

MANUFACTURER/SUPPLIER:

NORTH ATLANTIC REFINING LTD.	CONTACT BETWEEN
COME BY CHANCE, NFLD. A0B 1N0	07:30–1600 HRS N.S.T.
TEL: (709) 463-8811 (24 hrs.)	Plant Industrial Hygienist
FAX: (709) 463-8076	
AFTER HOURS:	Plant Security

USE IN CASE OF A DANGEROUS GOODS EMERGENCY:
CANUTEC: (613) 996 6666

SECTION 2. REGULATED COMPONENT

THE FOLLOWING ARE DEFINED IN ACCORDANCE WITH SUBPARAGRAPH 13 (a)(I) TO (iv) OR PARAGRAPH 14(a) OF THE HAZARDOUS PRODUCTS ACT:

Name	%	CAS #
CONTROLLED INGREDIENTS		
PROPANE	90 to 95 v/v	74-98-6
ETHANE	0 to 5 v/v	74-84-0
PROPYLENE	0 to 5 v/v	115-07-1
BUTANE	1 to 2.5 v/v	106-97-8

Manufacturer recommended TWA: 1000 ppm

SECTION 3. HAZARDS IDENTIFICATION

Potential Acute Health Effects:
Inhalation: Low toxicity. This gas may displace oxygen and cause suffocation (asphyxiant)
Eye Contact: Exposure to rapidly expanding gases may cause frostbite and permanent eye injury.
Skin Contact: Exposure to rapidly expanding gases may cause frostbite.
Ingestion: Not considered a hazard.

Potential Chronic Health Effects:
None established

SECTION 4. TYPICAL PHYSICAL AND CHEMICAL PROPERTIES

Physical state:	Gas
Odour and appearance:	Colourless gas; may be odorized
Odour threshold:	Not available
Density:	0.51 g/cc @ 15 °C
Vapour pressure:	92000 kPa @ 16 °C
Vapour density:	1.52 (Air = 1)
Evaporation rate:	>1
Boiling point:	−42 °C

Freezing/melting point:	Not available
pH:	Not applicable
Coefficient of water/oil distribution:	Not available
Solubility in water:	0 %

SECTION 5. FIRST AID MEASURES

EYE CONTACT:
In case of cold burns or frostbite of the eye, get prompt medical attention.

SKIN CONTACT:
In case of cold burns or frostbite to the skin, get prompt seek medical attention.

INGESTION:
First aid is not applicable.

INHALATION:
In emergence situations, use proper respiratory protection to remove the victim from the hazard. Allow the victim to rest in a well-ventilated area. If victim is not breathing, perform mouth-to-mouth resuscitation. Seek immediate medical attention.

SECTION 6. FIRE AND EXPLOSION DATA

Fire Fighting Instructions: Flammable gas, insoluble in water. Use water spray to cool fire-exposed surfaces and to protect personnel. Shut off fuel to fire if it is possible to do so without hazard. If a leak or spill has not ignited, use water spray to disperse the vapours. Remotely disconnect or shut off the power sources. Either, allow the fire to burn out under controlled conditions or extinguish with foam, dry chemicals or other approved extinguishing medium. Try to cover spilled liquid with foam. Respiratory, eye and body protection is required for fire fighting personnel. Response to small fire with extinguishers will usually be done upwind and only if considered safe. Personal protective equipment is usually not required when using portable extinguishers. Response to larger (catastrophic) fires should only be attempted by trained fire fighters.

Flammability:	Extremely flammable
Auto-Ignition Temperature:	432 °C
Flammable Limits:	Approx. 2.4 LEL, 9.5 UEL
Products of Combustion:	CO_X, and Smoke
Conditions of Flammability:	Heat and ignition source, flame or electric spark.
Explosion Hazards:	Not believed to be sensitive to mechanical agitation. May accumulate static charge.
Auto-refrigerant:	Rapidly expanding gases may cause ice to form. Drains and valves may become inoperable due to ice formation.

SECTION 7. ACCIDENTAL RELEASE MEASURES

Small Spill: Eliminate sources of ignition. Keep people away. Prevent additional discharge. Warn downwind occupant of hazard.

continued

EXHIBIT 22-3 (Continued)

Large Spill: Eliminate sources of ignition. Keep people away. Prevent additional discharge. Warn downwind occupant of hazard. Seek advice from the appropriate authorities.

SECTION 8. REACTIVITY DATA

Stability:	Product is stable.
Conditions for instability:	Not available.
Conditions to avoid:	Avoid excessive heat, sources of ignition product extremely flammable
Incompatibility:	Highly reactive with oxidising agents such as peroxides, perchlorates.
Decomposition products:	CO_X, and Smoke.

SECTION 9. PREVENTATIVE MEASURES

Personal Protective Equipment: A full-face shield is recommended to protect eyes and face. Chemically resistant gloves (with a thermal liner) and impervious clothing should be worn at all times while handling the product. When eye or skin contact may occur during short and/or periodic events, long sleeves, chemical-resistant gloves (thermal liner) and a face shield are required. A full-face respirator may be necessary to prevent overexposure by inhalation.

Engineering Controls: Highly recommended for all indoor situations to control fugitive emissions. Electrical and mechanical equipment should be explosion proof Concentrations should be maintained below the lower explosion limit at all times or below the recommended threshold limit value if unprotected personnel are involved. For personnel entry into a confined space (i.e. bulk storage tanks), a proper confined space entry must be followed, including ventilation and testing of tank atmosphere. Make up air should always be supplied to balance air exhausted.

Land Spill: Allow gases to dissipate. Eliminate any sources of ignition. Keep the public away. Prevent additional discharge of material if possible to do so without hazard. Consult an expert on disposal of recovered material. Ensure disposal is performed in compliance with government regulations. Notify the appropriate authorities. For spills over 70L in Canada contact the Canadian Coast Guard, 1-800-563-2444. Take additional action to prevent and remedy the adverse effects of the spill.

Water Spill: Allow gases to dissipate. Eliminate all sources of ignition. Prevent additional discharge of material. Consult an expert on disposal of recovered material. Ensure disposal is performed in compliance with government regulations. Notify the appropriate authorities. For all spills in Canada contact the Canadian Coast Guard, 1-800-563-2444. Take additional action to prevent and remedy the adverse effects of the spill.

Storage and handling: Combustible, store in a cool, dry, well ventilated area away from heat sources.

Keep containers closed. Handle and open propane containers with care.

The information contained herein is based on the data available to us and is believed to be correct. However, North Atlantic Refining Limited makes no warranty, expressed or implied regarding the accuracy of these data or results to be obtained from the use thereof. North Atlantic Refining Limited assumes no responsibility for injury from the use of the product described herein.

Prepared by:
Paul Sullivan
North Atlantic Refining Limited
P.O. Box 40
Come By Chance, Newfoundland, Canada
A0B 1N0
Phone: 709-463-8811 ext 306
FAX: 709-463-3489

on the belief that all injuries and occupational illnesses are preventable; that we are all responsible for our safety and also that of our fellow employees; and that managers are responsible for the safety of those in their organizations."[17]

Without full commitment at all levels of management, any attempts to reduce unsafe acts by workers will meet with little success. The first-line supervisor is a critical link in the chain of management. If the supervisor does not take safety seriously, it is likely that those under him or her will not either.

What Causes Accidents?

Workplace accidents have three basic causes: (1) chance occurrences, (2) unsafe conditions, and (3) unsafe acts on the part of employees.

Chance Occurrences

Chance occurrences (such as walking past a plate-glass window just as someone hits a ball through it) contribute to accidents but are more or less beyond management's control. We will therefore focus on *unsafe conditions* and *unsafe acts*.

Unsafe Conditions

Unsafe conditions are one main cause of accidents. They include such factors as improperly guarded equipment; defective equipment; hazardous procedures in, on, or around machines or equipment; unsafe storage (congestion, overloading); improper illumination (glare, insufficient light); and improper ventilation (insufficient air change, impure air source).[18] In addition, a number of factors have been found to increase the risk of violence in the workplace. These are highlighted in Exhibit 22-4.

Canada Safety Council
www.canadasafetycouncil.org

The basic remedy here is to eliminate or minimize the unsafe conditions. Government standards address the mechanical and physical conditions that cause accidents. Furthermore, a checklist of unsafe conditions can be used to conduct a job hazard analysis. Common indicators of job hazards include increased numbers of accidents, employee complaints, poor product quality, employee modifications to workstations, and higher levels of absenteeism and turnover.[19]

In addition to unsafe conditions, three other work-related factors contribute to accidents: the *job itself,* the *work schedule,* and the *psychological climate* of the workplace. Certain jobs are inherently more dangerous than others. According to one study, for example, the job of crane operator results in about three times more accident-related hospital visits than does the job of supervisor. Similarly, the work of some departments is inherently safer than that of others. An accounting department usually has fewer accidents than a shipping department.

Tips | **FOR THE FRONT LINE**

Work schedules and fatigue also affect accident rates. Accident rates usually do not increase too noticeably during the first five or six hours of the workday. Beyond that, however, the accident rate increases quickly as the number of hours worked increases. This is due partly to fatigue. It has also been found that accidents occur more often during night shifts.

Finally, many experts believe that the psychological climate of the workplace affects the accident rate. For example, accidents occur more frequently in plants with a high seasonal layoff rate and those where there is hostility among employees, many garnished wages, and blighted living conditions. Temporary stress factors, such as high workplace temperature, poor illumination, and a congested workplace, are also related to accident rates. It appears that workers who work under stress or who consider their jobs to be threatened or insecure have more accidents than those who do not work under these conditions.[20]

EXHIBIT 22-4 Who Is at Risk From Workplace Violence?

Violence can happen in any workplace. However, people whose jobs involve any of the following factors are at increased risk of workplace violence:

- Contact with the public
- Exchange of money
- Delivery of passengers, goods, or services
- Having a mobile workplace (such as a vehicle)
- Working with unstable or volatile people
- Working alone or in small numbers
- Working late at night or during early morning hours
- Guarding valuable property or possessions
- Working in community-based settings (e.g., home care)

Source: Workplace Safety and Insurance Board Ontario, "Who Is at Risk from Workplace Violence?" www.wsib.on.ca/en/community/WSIB/230/ArticleDetail/24338?vgnextoid=bb194c23529d7210VgnV CM100000449c710aRCRD (accessed July 10, 2012).

Unsafe Acts

Most safety experts and managers know that it is impossible to eliminate accidents just by improving unsafe conditions. People cause accidents, and no one has found a sure-fire way to eliminate *unsafe acts* by employees, such as

- throwing materials

- operating or working at unsafe speeds (either too fast or too slow)

- making safety devices inoperative by removing, adjusting, or disconnecting them

- using unsafe equipment or using equipment unsafely

- using unsafe procedures in loading, placing, mixing, and combining

- taking unsafe positions under suspended loads

- lifting improperly

- distracting, teasing, abusing, startling, quarrelling, and instigating horseplay

Such unsafe acts as these can undermine even the best attempts to minimize unsafe conditions, and the progressive discipline system should be used in such situations.

Personal Characteristics

A model summarizing how personal characteristics are linked to accidents is presented in Exhibit 22-5. Personal characteristics (personality, motivation, and so on) can serve as the basis for certain undesirable attitudes and behaviour tendencies, such as the tendency to take risks. These behaviour tendencies can, in turn, result in unsafe acts, such as inattention and failure to follow procedures. It follows that such unsafe acts increase the probability of someone having an accident.[21]

Research | **INSIGHT**

Years of research have failed to unearth any set of traits that accident repeaters seem to have in common. Instead, the consensus is that the person who is accident prone on one job may not be that way on a different job—that accident proneness is *situational*. For example, *personality traits* (such as emotional stability) may distinguish accident-prone workers on jobs involving risk; and *lack of motor skills* may distinguish accident-prone workers on jobs involving coordination. In fact, many human traits have been found to be related to accident repetition in specific situations, as the following discussion illustrates.[22]

Vision

Vision is related to accident frequency for many jobs. For example, passenger car drivers, intercity bus drivers, and machine operators who have high visual skills have fewer injuries than those who do not.[23]

Literacy

The risk of accidents is higher for employees who cannot read and understand machinery operating instructions, safety precautions, equipment and repair manuals, first aid instructions, or organizational policies on workplace health and safety. Low literacy skills potentially put workers and their co-workers in harm's way and increase the likelihood of work stoppages due to accidents or errors.[24] This situation is complicated by the fact that most workers with low literacy skills believe that their skills are good or excellent.[25]

A report by the Conference Board of Canada concluded that employers can reduce accidents by improving employees' literacy skills. They found an inverse relationship between industries requiring a high level of health and safety and investment in literacy skills.[26] This finding, together with the reality that people with lower levels of literacy

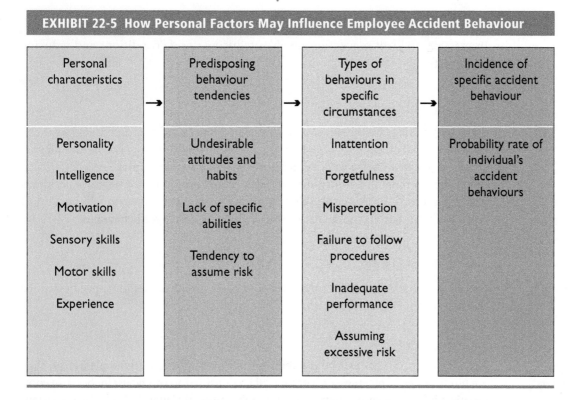

EXHIBIT 22-5 How Personal Factors May Influence Employee Accident Behaviour

Personal characteristics		Predisposing behaviour tendencies		Types of behaviours in specific circumstances		Incidence of specific accident behaviour
Personality	→	Undesirable attitudes and habits	→	Inattention	→	Probability rate of individual's accident behaviours
Intelligence				Forgetfulness		
Motivation		Lack of specific abilities		Misperception		
Sensory skills				Failure to follow procedures		
Motor skills		Tendency to assume risk		Inadequate performance		
Experience				Assuming excessive risk		

often end up in more dangerous occupations like trucking, manufacturing, or construction, where literacy requirements are low compared to more intellectual jobs, clearly indicates the need for action to heighten literacy skills of workers.

Age

Accidents are generally most frequent among people between the ages of 17 and 28, declining thereafter to reach a low in the late 50s and 60s. Although different patterns might be found with different jobs, this age factor repeats year after year. Across Canada, young workers between the ages of 15 and 24 (often students in low-paying summer jobs) are over five times more likely to be injured during their first four weeks on the job than others, which raises questions about the supervision and training of young workers.[27] Suggestions regarding training of young workers are provided in the Workforce Diversity box.

Canadian LifeQuilt
www.youngworkerquilt.ca

Perceptual versus Motor Skills

If a worker's perceptual skill is greater than or equal to his or her motor skill, the employee is more likely to be a safe worker than another worker whose perceptual skill is lower than his or her motor skill.[28] In other words, a worker who reacts more quickly than he or she can perceive is more likely to have accidents.

In summary, these findings provide a partial list of the human traits that have been found to be related to higher accident rates, and they suggest that, for specific jobs, it seems to be possible to identify accident-prone individuals and to screen them out. Overall, it seems that accidents can have multiple causes. With that in mind, accident prevention will be discussed.

Jessica DiSabatino, with a picture of her 18-year-old brother David Ellis who was killed on his second day on the job in 1999, wants employers to take young worker safety seriously.

How to Prevent Accidents

In practice, accident prevention involves reducing unsafe conditions and reducing unsafe acts.

Reducing Unsafe Conditions

Reducing unsafe conditions is an employer's first line of defence. Safety engineers can design jobs to remove or reduce physical hazards. In addition, supervisors and managers play a role in reducing unsafe conditions by ensuring that employees wear personal protective equipment, an often difficult chore. However, only 4 percent of accidents stem from unsafe working conditions, and therefore more attention will be paid to accident prevention methods that focus on changing employee behaviours.

Reducing Unsafe Acts

Reducing unsafe acts is the second basic approach, and there are four specific actions that can help to reduce unsafe acts.

Selection Testing

Employee Reliability Inventory
www.eri.com

Certain selection tests can help screen out accident-prone individuals before they are hired. For example, measures of muscular coordination can be useful because coordination is a predictor of safety for certain jobs. Tests of visual skills can be important because good vision plays a part in preventing accidents in many occupations, including operating machines and driving. A test called the Employee Reliability Inventory (ERI), which measures reliability dimensions such as emotional maturity, conscientiousness, safe job performance, and courteous job performance, can also be helpful in selecting employees who are less likely to have accidents.

Research | **INSIGHT**

A Canadian study conducted in a major industrial plant compared injury costs for a group of employees that were subjected to post-offer screening to assess their physical capability to perform job duties, and another group that did not receive post-offer screening. Injury costs over five years for the screened group were $6 500 and for the non-screened group were $2 073 000—a highly significant difference.[29]

Hints | **TO ENSURE LEGAL COMPLIANCE**

Many employers would like to inquire about applicants' workers' compensation history before hiring, in part to avoid habitual workers' compensation claimants and accident-prone individuals. However, inquiring about an applicant's workers' compensation injuries and claims can lead to allegations of discrimination based on disability. Similarly, applicants cannot be asked whether they have a disability, nor can they be asked to take tests that tend to screen out those with disabilities.

Employers can ask each applicant whether he or she has the ability to perform the essential duties of the job and ask, "Do you know of any reason why you would not be able to perform the various functions of the job in question?" Candidates can also be asked to demonstrate job-related skills, provided that every applicant is required to do so. Any selection test that duplicates the physical requirements of the job at realistic levels and the type of work expected does not violate human rights law, as long as it is developed and imposed honestly and in good faith to test whether or not the applicant can meet production requirements.[30]

Top-Management Commitment

Studies consistently find that successful health and safety programs require a strong management commitment. An example of the importance of top-management commitment is provided in the Strategic HR box. This commitment manifests itself in senior managers being personally involved in safety activities on a routine basis, giving safety matters high priority in company meetings and production scheduling, giving the company safety officer high rank and status, and including safety training in new workers' training. For example, linking managers' bonuses to safety improvements can reinforce a firm's commitment to safety and encourage managers to emphasize safety. HR managers have an important role to play in communicating the importance of health and safety to senior management by demonstrating how it affects the bottom line.

Training and Education

Safety training is another technique for reducing accidents. The Canadian Centre for Occupational Health and Safety and several safety associations, such as the Industrial Accident Prevention Association (IAPA), are available to partner in training efforts. The Canadian Federation of Independent Business offers online training leading to a Small Business Health and Safety (SBHS) certificate.

All employees should be required to participate in occupational health and safety training programs, and opportunities for employee input into the content and design of such programs is advisable. The training should include a practical evaluation process to ensure that workers are applying the acquired knowledge and following recommended safety procedures. Such training is especially appropriate for new employees.

Industrial Accident Prevention Association
www.iapa.ca

Safety posters can also help reduce unsafe acts. However, posters are no substitute for a comprehensive safety program; instead, they should be combined with other techniques, like screening and training, to reduce unsafe conditions and acts. Posters with pictures may be particularly valuable for immigrant workers if their first language is not the language of the workplace.

An Ethical | Dilemma

Is it ethical to provide safety training in English to immigrant workers who speak little English in order to reduce costs?

Positive Reinforcement

Safety programs based on positive reinforcement can improve safety behaviour at work. Employees often receive little or no positive reinforcement for performing safely. One approach is to establish and communicate a reasonable goal (in terms of observed incidents performed safely) so that workers know what is expected of them in terms of good performance. Employees are encouraged to increase their performance to the new safety goal for their own protection and to decrease costs for the company. Various observers (such as safety coordinators and senior managers) walk through the plant regularly, collecting safety data. The results are then posted on a graph charting the percentage of incidents performed safely by the group as a whole, thus providing workers with feedback on their safety performance. Workers can compare their current safety performance with their assigned goal. In addition, supervisors should praise workers when they perform selected activities safely.[31]

For example, UPS Canada honours drivers who have achieved 25 years or more of safe driving with a special badge to add to their uniform. The drivers are part of UPS's prestigious Circle of Honour, the company's highest level of driving recognition.[32]

Controlling Workers' Compensation Costs

Workers' compensation costs are often the most expensive benefit provided by an employer. For example, the average workplace injury in Ontario costs more than $59 000 in workers' compensation benefits. Indirect costs are estimated to be about four times the direct costs.[33] Each firm's workers' compensation premiums are proportional to its workers' compensation experience rate. Thus, the more claims a firm has, the more the firm will pay in premiums. A new online tool is available for small businesses in Ontario to calculate the true costs of a workplace injury.

Association of Workers' Compensation Boards of Canada
www.awcbc.org

Canadian Injured Workers Alliance
www.ciwa.ca

Before the Accident

The appropriate time to begin "controlling" workers' compensation claims is before the accident happens, not after. This involves taking all the steps previously summarized. For example, firms should remove unsafe conditions, screen out employees who might be accident-prone for the job in question (without violating human rights legislation), and establish a safety policy and loss control goals.

After the Accident—Facilitating the Employee's Return to Work

Employers should provide first aid, make sure that the worker gets quick medical attention, make it clear that they are interested in the injured worker and his or her fears and questions, document the accident, file any required accident reports, and encourage a speedy return to work. Perhaps the most important and effective thing an employer can do to reduce costs is to develop an aggressive return-to-work program.

The National Institute of Disability Management and Research (NIDMAR) in Victoria, British Columbia, recommends following the three Cs: (1) *commitment* to keeping in touch with the worker and ensuring his or her return to work; (2) *collaboration* among the parties involved, including medical, family, and workers' compensation; and (3) *creativity* in focusing on how to use the worker's remaining abilities on the job.[34]

Specific actions to encourage early return to work can be internal or external to the organization. Internally, an employer can set up rehabilitation committees to identify modified work, including relevant stakeholders, such as the employee and his or her colleagues, HR professionals, union representatives, and managers.

Functional abilities evaluations (FAEs) are an important step in facilitating the return to work. The FAE is conducted by a healthcare professional with an aim to

- improve the chances that the injured worker will be safe on the job

- help the worker's performance by identifying problem areas of work that can be addressed by physical therapy or accommodated through job modification

- determine the level of disability so that the worker can either go back to his or her original job or be accommodated[35]

Externally, the employer can work with the employee's family to ensure that they are supportive, mobilize the resources of the EAP to help the employee, ensure that physical and occupational therapists are available, and make the family physician aware of workplace accommodation possibilities.

Occupational Health and Safety Challenges in Canada

A number of health-related issues and challenges can undermine employee performance at work. These include alcoholism and substance abuse, stress and burnout, repetitive strain injuries, workplace toxins, workplace smoking, influenza pandemics, and workplace violence.

Substance Abuse

The effects of substance abuse on the employee and his or her work are severe. Both the quality and quantity of work decline sharply, and safety may be compromised. When dealing with alcohol and substance abuse on the job, employers must balance conflicting legal obligations. On the one hand, under human rights laws, alcoholism and drug addiction are considered to be disabilities. On the other hand, under occupational health and safety legislation, employers are responsible for maintaining due diligence. As a result, employers worry that when they accommodate an employee with an addiction, they may not be ensuring a safe work environment for other employees.[36]

Further, drug and alcohol testing in Canada is only legal in situations where three conditions determined by the Supreme Court are met:

1. The test is rationally connected to the performance of the job.

2. The test is adopted in an honest and good-faith belief that it is necessary for the fulfillment of a legitimate work-related purpose.

3. The test is reasonably necessary to the accomplishment of the work-related purpose.[37]

Random drug tests do not measure actual impairment and are therefore unjustifiable. Arbitrary alcohol testing of one or more employees but not others is not usually justifiable, but for employees in safety-sensitive positions, such as airline pilots, it may be justifiable. "For cause" and "post-incident" testing for either alcohol or drugs may be acceptable in specific circumstances. Positive test results should generally result in accommodation of the employee. Immediate dismissal is not generally justifiable.[38]

Recognizing the substance abuser on the job can pose a problem. The early symptoms can be similar to those of other problems and thus hard to classify. Problems range from tardiness to prolonged, unpredictable absences in later stages of addiction. Supervisors should be the company's first line of defence in combating substance abuse in the workplace, but they should not try to be company detectives or medical diagnosticians. Guidelines for supervisors should include the following:[39]

- If an employee appears to be under the influence of drugs or alcohol, ask how the employee feels and look for signs of impairment, such as slurred speech. An employee judged to be unfit for duty may be sent home but not fired on the spot.

- Make a written record of observed behaviour and follow up each incident. In addition to issuing a written reprimand, managers should inform workers of the number of warnings that the company will tolerate before requiring termination. Regardless of any suspicion of substance abuse, concerns should be focused on work performance, expected changes, and available options for help.

- Troubled employees should be referred to the company's employee assistance program.

Bellwood Health Services Inc.
www.bellwood.ca

Shepell.fgi
www.shepellfgi.com

The four traditional techniques for dealing with substance abuse are discipline, discharge, in-house counselling, and referral to an outside agency. Discharge is used to deal with alcoholism and drug problems only after repeated attempts at rehabilitation have failed. In-house counselling can be offered by the employer's medical staff or the employee assistance plan. External agencies such as Alcoholics Anonymous can also be used.

In Grande Prairie, Alberta, a clinic was established by the Alberta Alcohol and Drug Abuse Commission as a result of requests from the business community for a treatment centre that could deal with workplace-specific issues. It offers quick enrollment in its 30-day alcohol treatment program or the 50-day cocaine treatment program for $175 per day, plus months of follow-up, helping 180 clients a year return to work as soon as possible.[40]

Job-Related Stress

Workplace stress is a pervasive problem that is getting worse. Job stress has serious consequences for both the employee and the organization. The human consequences of job stress include anxiety, depression, anger, and various physical consequences, such as cardiovascular disease, headaches, and accidents. In Canada, the total cost of mental health problems approximates 17 percent of payroll, and the overall economic impact of work-related mental health problems is estimated to be $51 billion annually.[41] Stress also has serious consequences for the organization, including reductions in productivity and increased absenteeism and turnover.[42] Lost productivity at work due to health-related issues can cost the average Canadian organization up to $10 million each year.[43] Mental health issues are the leading cause of both short- and long-term disability claims.[44] Many organizations make physical safety a priority, but too often work environments that clearly have the potential for serious consequences from stress are simply tolerated.[45] Perhaps this reflects the fact that two-thirds of companies underestimate the prevalence of mental illness in the workplace, and only 13 percent of senior executives have a strong awareness of the impact of mental health on their workplaces.[46] As reflected in Exhibit 22-6, there are common indicators that a colleague is reaching their stress threshold.

Organizations begin to suffer when too many employees feel that the relentless pace of work life is neither sustainable nor healthy. Why is this happening? Employees are being asked to do more with less, creating work overload, increased time pressures, and tighter deadlines (almost one-third of Canadian workers consider themselves workaholics).[47] More people are working in "precarious" employment, such as temporary or part-time work with no benefits.[48] The sheer volume of email imposes terrific amounts of pressure and distraction on employees, taking a toll on their emotional equilibrium. Psychopathic bosses with no consciences, called "snakes in suits," can wreak havoc with other employees. The result is a corporate climate characterized by fatigue, depression, and anxiety.[49]

Job stress has two main sources: environmental factors and personal factors. First, a variety of external, *environmental factors* can lead to job stress. Two factors are particularly stress-inducing. The first is a high-demand job, such as one with constant deadlines coupled with low employee control. The second is high levels of mental and physical effort combined with low rewards in terms of compensation or acknowledgement.[50] Healthcare workers, whose jobs typically include these factors, are more stressed than any other group.[51] However, no two people react to the same job in an identical way, since *personal factors* also influence stress. For example, Type A personalities—people who are workaholics and who feel driven to always be on time and meet deadlines—normally place themselves under greater stress than do others. Similarly, one's patience, tolerance for ambiguity, self-esteem, health and exercise, and work and sleep patterns can also affect how one reacts to stress. Add to job stress the stress caused by non-job-related issues like divorce, postpartum depression, seasonal affective disorder, and work–family conflict, and many workers are problems waiting to happen.

EXHIBIT 22-6 Warning Signs: How Can You Tell if an Employee Is Reaching Their Stress Threshold?

How can you tell if a colleague has reached the breaking point? Experts note some possible indicators:

- Skipping group lunches: a signal someone feels demoralized and not part of their work community
- Coming to work late: one of the first hints that stress is eating away at motivation
- Calling in sick frequently: if people feel they aren't getting a break at work, they may start taking them on their own
- Withdrawing: when someone uncharacteristically retreats from water cooler talk and office banter, it may indicate an unhealthy distancing from colleagues
- Obsessing: if colleagues focus on seemingly insignificant matters or isolated incidents, it may mean they are angry or can no longer cope with the big picture

Source: Mitchell Messer, director of the Anger Institute in Chicago; R. Brayton Bowen, president of The Howland Group, a management-consulting firm. Printed in "Stressed Out: Can Workplace Stress Get Worse?" *Wall Street Journal* (January 16, 2001), p. 1.

Yet stress is not necessarily dysfunctional. Too little stress creates boredom and apathy. Performance is optimal at a level of stress that energizes but does not wear someone out.[52] Others find that stress may result in a search that leads to a better job or to a career that makes more sense given the person's aptitudes. A modest level of stress may even lead to more creativity if a competitive situation results in new ideas being generated.

Reducing Job Stress

There are things that a person can do to alleviate stress, ranging from commonsense remedies, such as getting more sleep, eating better, and taking vacation time, to more exotic remedies, such as biofeedback and meditation. Finding a more suitable job, getting counselling through an EAP or elsewhere, and planning and organizing each day's activities are other sensible responses.[53]

The organization and its HR specialists and supervisors can also play a role in identifying and reducing job stress. Offering an EAP is a major step toward alleviating the pressure on managers to try to help employees cope with stress. About 40 percent of EAP usage is related to stress at work. For the supervisor, important activities include monitoring each employee's performance to identify symptoms of stress and then informing the person of the organizational remedies that may be available, such as EAPs, job transfers, or other counselling. Also important are fair treatment and permitting the employee to have more control over his or her job.[54]

An Ethical | Dilemma

Is it ethical for an organization to ignore the issue of job stress entirely?

The importance of control over a job was illustrated by the results of a study in which the psychological strain caused by job stress was reduced by the amount of control that employees had over their job. The less stressful jobs did have high demands in terms of quantitative workload, the amount of attention that the employees had to pay to their work, and work pressure; however, they also ranked high in task clarity, job control, supervisory support, and employee skill utilization. The researchers conclude that "to achieve a balanced system, that is, to reduce psychological strain, [job] demands and [ambiguity regarding the future of the job] need to be lowered, while skill utilization, task clarity, job control, and supervisor support need to be increased."[55]

HR executives need to become advocates for employee mental health within the senior management team. Today's highly valued employees who are driving corporate productivity, innovation, and performance tend to be young knowledge workers, precisely the type of worker most prone to depression and stress.[56]

Burnout

Many people fall victim to **burnout**—the total depletion of physical and mental resources—because of excessive striving to reach an unrealistic work-related goal. Burnout begins with cynical and pessimistic thoughts and leads to apathy, exhaustion, withdrawal into isolation, and eventually depression.[57] Burnout is often the result of too much job stress, especially when that stress is combined with a preoccupation with attaining unattainable work-related goals. Burnout victims often do not lead well-balanced lives; virtually all of their energies are focused on achieving their work-related goals to the exclusion of other activities, leading to physical and sometimes mental collapse. This need not be limited to upwardly mobile executives; for instance, social workers caught up in their clients' problems are often burnout victims.

What can a candidate for burnout do? Here are some suggestions:

- *Break patterns.* First, survey how you spend your time. Are you doing a variety of things, or the same thing over and over? The more well-rounded your life is, the better protected you are against burnout. If you have stopped trying new activities, start them again—for instance, travel or new hobbies.

burnout The total depletion of physical and mental resources caused by excessive striving to reach an unrealistic work-related goal.

- *Get away from it all periodically.* Schedule occasional periods of introspection during which you can get away from your usual routine, perhaps alone, to seek a perspective on where you are and where you are going.

- *Reassess goals in terms of their intrinsic worth.* Are the goals that you have set for yourself attainable? Are they really worth the sacrifices that you will have to make?

- *Think about work.* Could you do as good a job without being so intense or while also pursuing outside interests?

- *Reduce stress.* Organize your time more effectively, build a better relationship with your boss, negotiate realistic deadlines, find time during the day for detachment and relaxation, reduce unnecessary noise around your office, and limit interruptions.

Workers' Compensation and Stress-Related Disability Claims

All Canadian jurisdictions provide benefits for post-traumatic stress caused by a specific and sudden workplace incident. However, when it comes to chronic stress, there is very limited or no coverage, depending on the jurisdiction.[58] The rationale is that stress has multiple causes, including family situations and personal disposition. Research, however, that a significant portion of chronic stress is often work related. In particular, high-demand/low-control jobs (such as an administrative assistant with several demanding bosses) are known to be "psychotoxic." Consequently, employees who are denied workers' compensation benefits for chronic stress that they believe to be work related are suing their employers. The courts are recognizing these claims and holding employers responsible for actions of supervisors who create "poisoned work environments" through harassment and psychological abuse. Courts are finding that a fundamental implied term of any employment relationship is that the employer will treat the employee fairly and with respect and dignity and that the due diligence requirement includes protection of employees from psychological damage as well as physical harm.[59]

Repetitive Strain Injuries

RSI Clinic
www.treatpain.ca/RSI_CLINIC.html

Human Systems Inc.
www.humansys.com

Human Factors and Ergonomics Society
wwww.hfes.org

Repetitive strain injuries (RSIs) are rapidly becoming the most prevalent work-related injury because of the increasing number of "knowledge" workers who use computers. RSI is an umbrella term for a number of "overuse" injuries affecting muscles, tendons, and nerves of the neck, back, chest, shoulders, arms, and hands. Typically arising as aches and pains, these injuries can progress to become crippling disorders that prevent sufferers from working and from leading normal lives. Warning signs of RSI include tightness or stiffness in the hands, elbow, wrists, shoulders, and neck; numbness and tingling in the fingertips; hands falling asleep; and frequent dropping of tools.[60]

A variety of workplace factors can play a role in the development of RSIs, including repetition, work pace, awkward or fixed positions, forceful movements, vibration, cold temperatures, and insufficient recovery time. RSIs are costly for employers in terms of compensation claims, overtime, equipment modification, retraining, and lost productivity. As with any other workplace safety issue, employers are required under occupational health and safety law to put controls in place to prevent RSIs. British Columbia has the most rigorous requirements regarding protection of workers against RSIs, and unions are calling for other provinces to follow suit. Employers must advise and train workers about the risk of RSIs from workplace activity, identify and assess job-related RSI risk factors, encourage workers to report RSI symptoms early, and use ergonomic interventions.[61]

repetitive strain injuries (RSIs)
Activity-related soft-tissue injuries of the neck, shoulders, arms, wrists, hands, back, and legs.

Ergonomics

Poorly designed workstations, bad posture, and long periods of time working on computers are common conditions leading to RSIs, and these are easily preventable. **Ergonomics** is the art of fitting the workstation and work tools to the individual, which is necessary because there is no such thing as an average body. Exhibit 22-7 illustrates ergonomic factors at a computer workstation. The most important preventive measure is to have employees take short breaks every half-hour or hour to do simple stretches at their workstations.[62]

Ergonomically designed workstations have been found to increase productivity and efficiency, as well as reduce injuries. The Institute for Work and Health studied 200 tax collectors who were in sedentary, computer-intensive jobs. Workers who were given a highly adjustable chair combined with a 90-minute ergonomics training session reported less musculoskeletal pain over their workday, compared with workers who received just the training or nothing at all. Productivity increased nearly 18 percent because of the reduction in pain and more effective use of workspaces.[63]

Ergonomics will become more and more important as the workforce ages, and the physical demands of work will need to be adapted to accommodate some of the many physical changes typically associated with aging, including changes in muscular strength, hand function, cardiovascular capacity, vision, and hearing.

Video Display Terminals

The physical demands of new technologies have brought a new set of RSIs. The fact that many workers today must spend hours each day working with video display terminals (VDTs) is creating new health problems at work. Short-term eye problems, like burning, itching, and tearing, as well as eyestrain and eye soreness are common complaints among video display operators. Backaches and neck aches are also widespread among display users. These often occur because employees try to compensate for display problems like glare and immovable keyboards by manoeuvring into awkward body positions.

Researchers also found that employees who used VDTs and had heavy workloads were prone to psychological distress, such as anxiety, irritability, and fatigue. There is also a tendency for computer users to suffer from RSIs, such as *carpal tunnel syndrome* (a tingling or numbness in the fingers caused by the narrowing of a tunnel of bones and ligaments in the wrist) caused by repetitive use of the hands and arms at uncomfortable angles.[64]

General recommendations regarding the use of VDTs include giving employees rest breaks every hour, designing maximum flexibility into the workstation so that it can be adapted to the individual operator, reducing glare with devices, such as shades over windows and terminal screens, and giving VDT workers a complete pre-placement vision exam to ensure that vision is properly corrected to reduce visual strain.[65]

Tips | FOR THE FRONT LINE

Workplace Toxins

The leading cause of work-related deaths around the world is cancer. Hundreds of Canadian workers die from occupational cancer each year.[66] There is an erroneous perception that cancer-causing agents in the workplace are disappearing. Employers often face significant costs to eliminate carcinogens in the workplace, and unions are often so preoccupied with wage and benefit increases that they don't bring the issue to the bargaining table (although the Canadian Labour Congress has launched an initiative to reduce work-related cancers by releasing an information kit for workers on cancer-causing materials on the job).[67] In addition to known carcinogens, such as asbestos and benzene, new chemicals and substances are constantly being introduced into the workplace without adequate testing.[68] Workers' compensation laws in several provinces have been amended to provide benefits to firefighters who develop specific job-related cancers.[69]

ergonomics An interdisciplinary approach that seeks to integrate and accommodate the physical needs of workers into the design of jobs. It aims to adapt the entire job system—the work, environment, machines, equipment, and processes—to match human characteristics.

EXHIBIT 22-7 Computer Ergonomics

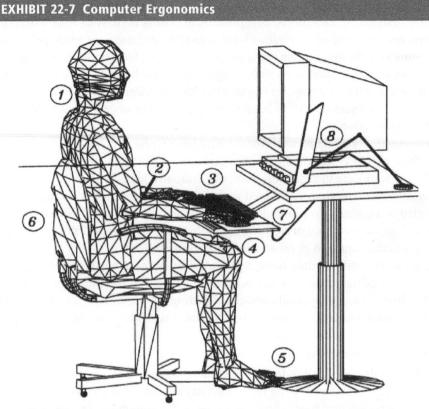

Note: This diagram is just an example. Workstation set ups will vary according to the particular desk style, monitor, tray mount, or other accessories used.

1) The monitor should be set at a height so that your neck will be straight.
2) Your elbow joints should be at about 90 degrees, with the arms hanging naturally at the sides.
3) Keep your hands in line with the forearms, so the wrists are straight, not bending up, down, or to either side.
4) Thighs should be roughly parallel to the floor, with your feet flat on the floor or footrest.
5) If necessary, use a footrest to support your feet.
6) Your chair should be fully adjustable (i.e., for seat height, backrest height and seat pan tilt, and, preferably, armrests). It should have a well-formed lumbar (lower back) support to help maintain the lumbar curve.
7) There should be enough space to use the mouse. Use a wrist rest or armrest so that your wrist is straight and your arm muscles are not overworked.
8) Use an adjustable document holder to hold source documents at the same height, angle, and distance as the monitor.

Source: Computer Ergonomics: Workstation Layout and Lighting (Toronto, ON: Ontario Ministry of Labour Health and Safety Guidelines, 2004). © Queen's Printer for Ontario, 2004. Reproduced with permission.

Workplace Smoking

Smoking is a serious problem for employees and employers. Employers face higher costs for healthcare and disability insurance, as smoking is associated with numerous health problems. Employees who smoke have reduced productivity and a significantly greater risk of occupational accidents than do non-smokers. Employees who smoke also expose non-smoking co-workers to toxic second-hand smoke.

Smokers who are also exposed to other carcinogens in the workplace, such as asbestos, have dramatically higher rates of lung cancer. The effects of on-the-job exposure to radon on lung cancer rates were found to last up to 14 years, and the cancer rates were greatly increased for smokers.[70]

Most Canadian jurisdictions have banned smoking in workplaces. Health Canada is urging employers to implement smoking cessation programs for employees to achieve better health for employees, better business results, legislative compliance, increased employee satisfaction (especially for the 80 percent of Canadians who do not smoke), and avoidance of litigation.[71]

Viral Pandemic

Recent major outbreaks of viral diseases like influenza have alarmed people around the world and reminded everyone that a major viral pandemic is inevitable at some time in the future. A 2006 study by the Conference Board of Canada found that although almost 80 percent of executives are concerned about the impact of a pandemic on their organization, only 4 percent of their organizations had developed a pandemic preparedness plan.[72]

HR will be a key player in responding to a pandemic as most employers are planning to continue their business operations using the existing workforce—in other words, with substantially fewer employees. Immediate decisions will be required regarding telecommuting and working at remote worksites, compensation for absent employees, and maintenance of occupational health for employees who are working on company premises.[73] Even in the plans that do exist, there is little detail on the status of quarantined employees, compensating employees who cover for absent co-workers, responding to employee refusals to work in an unsafe environment, and business shutdown if health and safety officers declare the entire workplace to be unsafe.[74]

A pandemic preparedness plan should address prevention, containment, response to employee work refusals, creation of a pandemic preparation and response team, viability of continuing company operations, security of company premises, sickness/disability coverage, leaves to care for sick family members or children at home if schools are closed, and visitors to company premises.[75] Communication will be a critical component of pandemic management (likely using email, intranet, and hotlines), particularly if travel bans are imposed.[76] Unionized organizations will also need to consult their collective agreements and may wish to consult with the union when making pandemic preparedness plans.[77]

The Canadian Pandemic Influenza Plan
www.phac-aspc.gc.ca/cpip-pclcpi

Recently amended Ontario legislation provides that if an emergency is declared by the government, then 10 unpaid days of leave will be available to employees who need to care for sick family members, in addition to the already existing 10 unpaid days available in these circumstances.[78]

Although the risk of a pandemic occurring in any one year may be small, the potential consequences are so serious that business leaders are well advised to prepare their organizations.[79]

Violence at Work

Workplace violence is defined by the International Labour Organization (ILO) as incidents in which an employee is abused, threatened, or assaulted in circumstances relating to work, and it includes harassment, bullying, intimidation, physical threats, assaults, and robberies. Most workplace violence arises from members of the public—customers or strangers—rather than co-workers. Canada is the fourth-worst country in the world for workplace violence (the United States is seventh) according to ILO data.[80]

Health Minister Leona Aglukkaq speaking at a news conference in Ottawa about the swine flu outbreak. Employers that lack pandemic plans should start putting them together now, according to experts.

The first-ever Statistics Canada report on criminal victimization in the workplace, released in 2007, indicated that one in every five violent incidents in Canada (such as physical and sexual assault, or armed robbery) occurred in the workplace. Physical assault was the most common violent incident, representing 71 percent of all incidents of workplace violence.[81] Violence against employees at work is particularly prevalent for women in healthcare professions. More than one-third of nurses are physically assaulted and almost half suffer emotional abuse.[82] Reports of abuse of nurses by clinical area of practice are shown in Exhibit 22-8.

Workplace Violence and the Law

Most Canadian jurisdictions now have workplace violence legislation in place covering physical violence, and some include psychological/emotional violence as well. Human rights laws across the country prohibit various forms of harassment and bullying. Employers may be found vicariously liable for the violent acts of their employees on the basis that the employer negligently hired or negligently retained someone whom they should reasonably have known could cause the violent act; employers may also be found liable when they are aware of violent incidents and fail to respond.[83]

Prevention and Control of Workplace Violence

There are several concrete steps that employers can take to reduce the incidence of workplace violence. These include identifying jobs with high risk of violence, instituting a workplace violence policy, creating a healthy work environment, heightening security measures, training for violence reduction, and improving employee screening.

Identify Jobs with High Risk of Violence Kevin Kelloway, a researcher at Saint Mary's University in Halifax, has identified three job characteristics that are reliable predictors of workplace violence. First, the instigator of the violence specifically enters the work environment with the intent to engage in criminal behaviour (theft, for instance) and generally has no other legitimate reason to be in the workplace; most at risk are jobs like taxi drivers or gas station attendants. Second, the instigator is the recipient of a service or object offered at the targeted workplace (for example, a nurse or social worker). Third, the risk of violence from a potential or former employee is increased (for example, a disgruntled employee). Identifying and redressing these hazards and risk factors, such as installing safety shields for taxi drivers and bus drivers, can help to reduce victimization.[84]

Canadian Initiative on Workplace Violence
www.workplaceviolence.ca

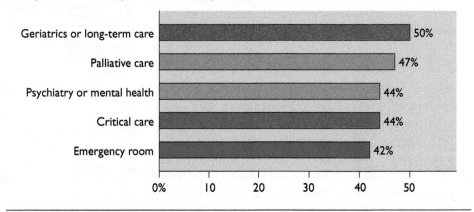

EXHIBIT 22-8 Reports of Abuse by Clinical Area of Practice

Reports of abuse by clinical area of practice

Clinical area	Percent
Geriatrics or long-term care	50%
Palliative care	47%
Psychiatry or mental health	44%
Critical care	44%
Emergency room	42%

Source: Statistics Canada, Factors Related to On-the-Job Abuse of Nurses by Patients, *Health Reports*, 20, no. 2 (2009), pp. 7–19.

Institute a Workplace Violence Policy Firms should develop, support, and communicate a workplace violence policy that clearly communicates management's commitment to preventing violent incidents. The policy should state that no degree or type of violence is acceptable in the workplace; provide definitions of prohibited conduct; specify consequences of violating the policy; encourage reporting of violent incidents; include prohibitions and sanctions for retaliation or reprisal; and specify that all physical assaults will be reported to police.[85]

Create a Healthy Work Environment According to Julian Barling, a researcher at Queen's University, a healthy work environment with professional supervision is the best way to reduce violence on the part of employees. Leaders, managers, and supervisors should express real concern for employees and treat people fairly, as acts of revenge typically occur in response to perceived injustice.[86]

Heighten Security Measures Security precautions to reduce the risk of workplace violence include improving external lighting, using drop safes to minimize cash on hand and posting signs noting that only a limited amount of cash is on hand, installing silent alarms and surveillance cameras, increasing the number of staff members on duty, and closing establishments during high-risk hours late at night and early in the morning. In workplaces serving members of the public, some important precautions for employee safety include providing staff training in conflict resolution and defusing anger; having security staff to refuse admittance to anyone who appears intoxicated, visibly angry, or threatening; and instituting a recognizable "help" signal to alert other staff members that assistance is required.[87]

Provide Workplace Violence Training Workplace violence training explains what workplace violence is, identifies its causes and signs, and offers tips on how to prevent it and what to do when it occurs. Supervisors can also be trained to identify the typical perpetrator—male, aged 25 to 40, bad at handling stress, a constant complainer, has a tendency to make verbal threats and physical or verbal outbursts, harbours grudges, and brandishes weapons to gain attention.[88]

Improve Employee Screening Screening out potentially violent applicants means instituting a sound pre-employment investigation of all information provided. Sample interview questions to ask might include "What frustrates you?" and "Who was your worst supervisor and why?"[89] As sensible as it is to try to screen out potentially violent employees, doing so incurs the risk of liability and lawsuits. Human rights legislation limits the use of criminal records in hiring decisions.

Employee Wellness Programs

There are three elements in a healthy workplace: the physical environment, the social environment, and health practices. **Employee wellness programs** take a proactive approach to all these areas of employee well-being (as opposed to EAPs, which provide reactive management of employee health problems). Wellness should be viewed as a management strategy to achieve measurable outcomes related to productivity, cost reduction, recruitment/retention, and profit, as shown in Exhibit 22-9. TELUS has a 50-year-old wellness program in which managers are held accountable—if absenteeism increases in their department, their bonus decreases![90] The company believes that a focus on wellness and enhancing corporate competitiveness are one and the same. Its long-term experience has netted a savings of three dollars for every dollar spent on wellness.

Experience has shown that wellness programs are very effective; there is overwhelming evidence that money invested in a wellness program is returned many times over.[91] For example, Seven Oaks General Hospital in Winnipeg, which has a 10-year-old Wellness Institute, reports a turnover rate of 4.5 percent, well under half of the industry average in Winnipeg of 11.9 percent.[92] A study of heart health wellness initiatives

Strength Tek
www.strengthtek.com

Healthy Workplace Month
www.healthyworkplacemonth.ca

employee wellness program A program that takes a proactive approach to employee health and well-being.

PRODUCTIVITY
- Reduced absenteeism
- Reduced distractions
- Improved performance
- Improved skills

COST REDUCTION
- Reduced workplace accidents and injuries
- Reduced compensation claims
- Reduced benefits costs

RECRUITMENT AND RETENTION
- Improved retention rates
- Improved employee engagement

PROFIT
- Reduced turnover costs
- Improved customer service and retention
- Improved recruitment competitiveness

Source: Daniel Munro, *Healthy People, Healthy Performances, Healthy Profits: The Case for Business Action on the Socio-Economic Determinants of Health* (Ottawa, ON: Conference Board of Canada, 2008). Reprinted by permission of The Conference Board of Canada, Ottawa.

reported a return on investment of 415 percent.[93] NCR Canada saved $600 000 in direct and indirect costs during the first year of its wellness program; absenteeism was cut by more than half after 12 months and was still one-third lower after 36 months.[94]

One expert predicts that, over the next 25 years, prevention and wellness will be the next great leap forward in healthcare, as employees become more broadly recognized as the most important assets of organizations. A focus on wellness will also be driven by the shrinking workforce, an increase in postponed retirement, increased awareness of mental health, and medical and technological advances.[95]

Wellness initiatives often include stress management, nutrition and weight management, smoking cessation programs, tai chi, heart health (such as screening cholesterol and blood pressure levels), physical fitness programs, and workstation wellness through ergonomics. Even simple things like providing safe bicycle lockup and change rooms or making fresh fruit and water available can make a difference.[96] Wellness and prevention efforts need to be understood and undertaken as a process—a long-term commitment to a holistic focus on the total person.

23 Managing Employee Separations

Foundations of Employee Engagement,
Communication, and Turnover Management

The Importance of Managing Employee Separations

Issues of recruitment and selection focus on growing the human resource talent within an organization. The role of HRM is often overlooked in managing employee engagement and communication during a time of employee separations. Who leaves, how they are treated during the exit, what the cause or nature of the exit is, and how remaining employees perceive this all impacts the long-term sustainability of the organization.

This chapter first reviews employee separations by categorizing the possible causes and consequences of employee separations. Methods of reducing turnover and the negative implications of turnover on remaining employees (including legal compliance, two-way communication, and fair treatment programs) will be explored later in the chapter.

Managing Turnover

Employee exits can become a huge challenge for organizations. The time, money, and resources invested in recruiting, training, and maintaining employees is lost when employees exit a firm. Additionally, employee exits disrupt the organization's ability to produce and maintain the right quantity and quality of talent and derail the organization's focus on larger strategic issues. For example, the retail sector often has high turnover levels, with very few long-tenured employees. Similarly, in the hospitality industry, one in every five employees leaves the company in any given year.[1]

An organization's labour force is in constant fluctuation as employees continuously enter and exit the workforce. **Turnover** refers to the termination of an individual's employment with an organization. Turnover can be either permanent or temporary and can be a result of action taken by either the employee or employer. There are many possible reasons for an employee to separate from a firm. An online study of over 1 000 Canadians asked people why they left their last employer. Results are highlighted in Exhibit 23-1 on the next page. The most common reason given by those interviewed was downsizing or restructuring activity, followed by a desire to find new challenges, then ineffective leadership.

Overall, the reasons for turnover can be classified into two subgroups: voluntary and involuntary. **Voluntary turnover** is employee initiated, usually in the form of quits or retirement. The decision to discontinue employment with the firm is made by the employee, without management enticement. **Involuntary turnover** is employer initiated and is usually in the form of dismissals or layoffs. Regardless, the employee has little or no personal say in this turnover decision. Employee exits from a firm are usually a mix of voluntary and involuntary turnover.

A study of over 34 000 workers in the Canadian labour force examined voluntary and involuntary turnover from 2000–2004. As an employee gains tenure in a company, his or her likelihood of quitting or being dismissed or laid off is significantly reduced. Additionally, individuals who hold occupations in management and administration-related positions are less likely to be laid off than individuals in other occupations. However, on average, the personality characteristics of employees who get laid off in relation to those who quit are opposite. For example, higher education reduces the likelihood that an employee will be laid off, but increases the probability that they will quit. Employees in the goods industry are more likely to experience a layoff, whereas employees in the service industry are more likely to voluntarily leave their job via quitting.[2]

The Cost of Turnover

In Canada, from 1978–1995, the temporary employment separation rate per year ranged from 18.9 to 23.8 percent, while the layoff rate ranged from 12.6 to 16.4 percent per year. Combined, these statistics suggest that temporary and permanent rates of employee separation have affected 30 to 40 percent of employees annually. Turnover

Research INSIGHT

turnover The termination of an individual's employment with an organization.

voluntary turnover Employee-initiated termination of employment, such as quits, retirement, or resignation.

involuntary turnover Employer-initiated termination of employment, such as dismissal or layoff.

EXHIBIT 23-1 Reasons for Turnover

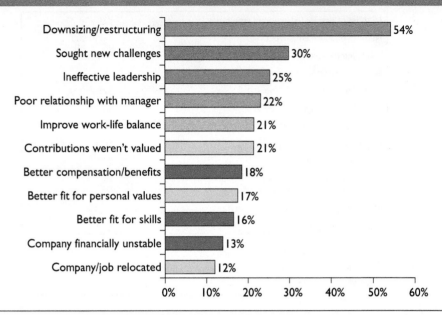

Reason	%
Downsizing/restructuring	54%
Sought new challenges	30%
Ineffective leadership	25%
Poor relationship with manager	22%
Improve work-life balance	21%
Contributions weren't valued	21%
Better compensation/benefits	18%
Better fit for personal values	17%
Better fit for skills	16%
Company financially unstable	13%
Company/job relocated	12%

Source: News 4, "Reasons for Turnover," *Canadian HR Reporter,* June 16, 2008. Reprinted by permission of Canadian HR Reporter. © Copyright Thomson Reuters Canada Ltd., (2012) Toronto, Ontario, 1-800-387-5164. Web: www.hrreporter.com.

rates vary by industry (for example, the construction industry and consumer services industries typically have the highest turnover levels in Canada, while public services has the lowest turnover levels), by the size of the company (smaller organizations typically have higher turnover rates), and by age (older workers are less likely to experience turnover than younger workers).[3]

It is not surprising that over 50 percent of Canadian organizations admit that they experience difficulties recruiting and retaining talent.[4] Some companies are in a constant search for talent, like supermarkets, where the industry-wide turnover rate for courtesy clerks or cashiers is 300 percent.[5] Translated, that means that, on average, each cashier will work for four months at a time before the position will be vacated. The challenge is that the cost of turnover ranges from 150 percent of salary to 250 percent of salary.[6] Ultimately, the combination of having a company incur the cost of turnover as well as the cost of day-to-day operations can be economically damaging. As highlighted in Exhibit 23-2, the estimated direct cost of turnover per year can reach $1.4 billion, and the impact on customer loyalty can be two to three times the direct cost of loyalty. Reducing turnover even 10 percent could potentially result in direct savings of roughly $140 million per year.

Direct costs associated with turnover are often easier to estimate given that they are more visible (for example, cost of advertising and interviewing, cost of moving expenses offered to the new candidate), while indirect costs associated with turnover are often overlooked, but are still considerable (for example, lost productivity during the employment gap, training curve productivity losses). There are four main components associated with the cost of the turnover:

- Separation costs—the cost of exit interviews, administrative functions associated with the turnover, and separation or severance pay

- Vacancy costs—the net savings or cost incurred of increased overtime, the use of temporary workers, and the loss of sales associated with the vacancy

- Replacement costs—the cost of recruiting and hiring a replacement to fill the vacant position (including the cost of interviews, testing, administrative expenses, travel/moving expenses, and so on)

Tips FOR THE FRONT LINE

EXHIBIT 23-2 The Estimated Direct Cost of Turnover

Number of terminated/resigned employees	725 000
Number of active employees	1 300 000
Employee turnover	55.7%
But for every ONE employee who leaves:	
Cost of recruiting/advertising	$25
Cost of interviewing	$60
Cost of orientation	$60
Cost of training	$600
Administrative cost	$20
Hourly wage of a new employee (not including payroll costs, benefits, etc.)	$6
Total direct cost for ONE new employee	$1950
Total direct cost of all employee turnover	$1.4 billion

Source: A. Heller, "The People Factor: Supermarkets Investment in "Return On People" Provides Results in a Changing Labor Environment" *Supermarket News*, 52, no. 18 (May 3, 2004), p. 32.

- Training costs—formal and informal training (including the performance differential between employees exiting the organization and their replacements)[7]

Voluntary Turnover

Voluntary turnover includes quitting, resignations, and retirements, presenting a specific and immediate challenge to organizational success. In voluntary turnover, the employee initiates the termination of employment. Often, departing employees migrate to competing firms and create situations where their knowledge, skills, and abilities developed within the firm can be used to disadvantage the firm. As a result, voluntary turnover presents unanticipated challenges of replacing and retraining employees.

Research | INSIGHT

A review of turnover research identifies predictors of voluntary turnover. Individual-level variables found to have a statistically significant relationship with voluntary job loss are (1) low organizational commitment, (2) low role clarity, (3) low tenure, (4) high role conflict, and (5) low overall job satisfaction. Additionally, age and marital status were negatively correlated with voluntary turnover, while education was positively correlated with voluntary turnover.[8]

The biggest challenge of voluntary turnover is the lack of managerial control. Voluntary turnover can be functional (where bad performers leave and good performers stay), which can help reduce suboptimal organizational performance, or dysfunctional (where good performers leave and bad performers stay), which can be detrimental to a firm's success.[9]

Two researchers, Abbasi and Hollman, argue that eroding employee loyalty has the potential to radically affect a firm's ability to prosper in today's competitive economy, leaving even the most ambitious firms struggling to keep the most productive and talented employees. They highlight five reasons for employee turnover within an organization:[10]

(1) suboptimal hiring practices

(2) difficult managerial style

(3) lack of recognition

(4) lack of competitive compensation systems

(5) toxic workplace environments

In addition to the reasons outlined above, voluntary turnover also includes unexplained reasons, known as the "hobo phenomena."[11]

While an employer cannot always predict the reasoning behind voluntary turnover, it is important to try to understand which types of employees are likely to leave and why. This helps manage and prevent dysfunctional or excessive turnover. This information can be collected in exit interviews, staff surveys, and annual HR reviews.[12] Collecting this type of information can lead to trends that companies can use to screen certain types of individuals in the selection process. Additionally, these trends may lead organizations to develop methods of reducing turnover amongst current employees. In doing so, organizations obtain the information required to reduce turnover, retain effective employees, and decrease direct costs associated with turnover.

Tips | FOR THE FRONT LINE

Quits

Quitting is legally recognized as a voluntary resignation in which the employee terminates the employment relationship, often in the form of a resignation letter. In Canada, employment-related legislation clearly identifies employer responsibilities at the time of involuntary turnover (such as minimum notice periods and severance pay), but there exist no equivalent employer-oriented protections in the case of employee-initiated turnover.

Employees often elect to leave a company based on work-related factors (for example, the employee dislikes the boss, too much pressure or stress), or non-work-related factors (return to school, moving).[13] Either way, employee quits are most often caused by low job satisfaction.[14]

Competitive factors often play a significant role in a person's desire to resign from a company, including opportunities for employment in other organizations. Consequently, perceived job alternatives and high labour demands influence an employee's perception of ease of employment in other organizations, and are often carefully considered by the employee prior to resignation. Globalization, technological advancements, and market pressures have created an increasingly turbulent economy, and over the last few decades large-scale labour mobility has become the norm. The result has been a decline in employee job tenure and job stability.

To adapt to a constantly changing environment, individual employees are more willing to look for horizontal and vertical career advancement opportunities outside of the organization. The notion of "cradle-to-grave" jobs that permeated the employment relationship prior to the 1980s no longer exists. A leading researcher best captures this change: "If the traditional, lifetime employment relationship was like a marriage, then the new employment relationship is like a lifetime of divorces and remarriages."[15]

Retirement

The origins of mandatory retirement in Canada are largely routed in the industrial revolution of the late 1800s and early 1900s. At a time when the skilled workforce was being replaced by an unskilled, assembly and task-oriented workforce, employers were forcing employees to take retirement at age 65 so they could replace older and often more expensive workers with younger and less costly labour. Governments responded by introducing a series of acts aimed at providing financial support for people reaching "retirement age" to prevent poverty amongst the oldest generation. In the early 1900s, average male life expectancy was 47 years and female life expectancy was 50 years.[16] As a result, mandatory retirement at the age of 65 was not a reality for a significant portion of the workforce. Medical discoveries, eradication of infectious diseases, and implementation of public health measures (like water chlorination) have resulted in a significant increase in average lifespan on an international scale. According to Statistics Canada, average life expectancy for men in 2011 was 78.3 years, while average life expectancy for women was 83 years.

quitting Voluntary, employee-initiated resignation.

However, a combination of legal advancements on anti-discriminatory employment policies (such as age-based discrimination), labour scarcity, and peoples' desires to choose their own lifestyle, circumstances, and priorities has resulted in the abolishment of mandatory retirement in Canada.

The result has been a shift from categorizing retirement as voluntary turnover rather than as a form of involuntary turnover. The average age of retirement for public sector employees is 60 years of age and 62 for private sector employees. However, there is a large range of possible retirement ages, with some 40 year olds eligible to retire from their organization while some 87 year olds continue to be employed.[17]

retirees on call A program where retirees can continue to work on a part-time or as needed basis post-retirement.

phased retirement potential retirees gradually reduce the number of hours worked per week over time.

pre-retirement counselling Counselling provided to employees some months (or even years) before retirement, which covers such matters as benefits advice, second careers, and so on.

One of the challenges associated with the retirement of employees, from an organizational standpoint, is the difficulty in predicting when employees will retire. Developing succession or replacement plans around potential retires and finding ways to their transfer tacit and social knowledge becomes paramount to how an organization deals with retirement. Some companies are managing the labour shortage created by retiring employees by offering "**retirees on call**" programs, where retirees can come back on a part-time or as-needed basis, or by offering "**phased retirement**," where employees gradually reduce the number of hours that they work.[18]

Court decisions have confirmed that employers do have some legal responsibility to help employees prepare for retirement.[19] Most employers provide some type of formal **pre-retirement counselling** aimed at easing the passage of their employees into retirement.[20] Retirement education and planning firms provide services to assist upcoming retirees with such issues as lifestyle goals (including part-time or volunteer work, or moving to another country), financial planning, relationship issues, and health issues. Both individual and group transition counselling are offered in seminars and workshops featuring workbooks, questionnaires, discussions, group exercises, and software products.[21]

The Retirement Education Centre
www.iretire.org

The Financial Education Institute of Canada
www.financialknowledgeinc.com

T.E. Financial Consultants
www.tefinancial.com

Involuntary Turnover

There are many reasons why an organization might engage in involuntary turnover. Job performance may be below acceptable standards and the organization decides to dismiss an employee. Economic or financial pressures may result in a decision to downsize through mass layoffs. The organization may be engaging in a new strategic direction and has choosen to close down or outsource one or more business units. In any of these cases, the decision to terminate employment is made by the organization and its agents, not by the individual employee. Employee dismissal and downsizing are two of the most common situations in which employees perceive that they are treated unfairly. This reaction is not surprising given the negative ramifications to the employee in each case (job loss). Thus, it is important for all managers and HR professionals to be aware of how to conduct involuntary turnover fairly and legally.

An employee contemplating different retirement options

Specifically, employer-initiated termination should be fair and occur after all reasonable steps to rehabilitate or salvage the employment relationship through employee discipline have failed. The legal system in Canada has repeatedly articulated the rights of employees to fair treatment, not only during the term of employment but also during the discipline and dismissal process. A fair and just disciplinary process is based on three foundations: rules and regulations, progressive discipline, and an appeals process.

Hints | **TO ENSURE LEGAL COMPLIANCE**

Rules and Regulations

A set of clear expectations informs employees ahead of time as to what is and is not considered acceptable behaviour in the workplace. Employees must be informed, preferably in writing, of what behaviours or actions are not permitted. This is usually done during the employee's orientation (and included in the employee orientation handbook), or when rules or regulations in the workplace change. Examples of such rules include:

- Poor work performance is not acceptable. Each employee is expected to perform his or her work properly and efficiently, and to meet established standards of quality.

- Liquor and drug use is not permitted on work premises. The use of either during working hours or working under the influence of drugs or alcohol is strictly prohibited.

- Safety rules must be followed at all times.

Progressive Discipline

A system of progressive penalties is the second foundation of effective discipline. Penalties may range from verbal warnings, to written warnings, to suspension (paid or unpaid) from the job, and finally to dismissal. The severity of the penalty is usually a function of the type of offence and the number of times the offence has occurred. For example, most companies issue warnings for the first instance of unexcused lateness. However, for chronic lateness, dismissal is the more usual disciplinary action.

Finally, there should be an appeals process as part of the disciplinary process; this helps to ensure procedural fairness.

Dismissal for Just Cause

Dismissal is the most drastic disciplinary step that can be taken toward an employee and one that must be handled with deliberate care. While dismissals damage the goodwill of a company as well as sever the employment relationship, there are undoubtedly times when dismissal is required, and in these instances it should be carried out forthrightly.[22] In cases where an employee was **dismissed for just cause**, it is considered an employer-initiated termination based on an employee's poor behaviours, therefore no severance, reasonable notice periods, or additional payments beyond what the employee has already earned are owed (for example, earned vacation time that is unused must be paid out). In cases of dismissal for just cause, the onus of proof lies on management to prove that performance in the past was below acceptable levels and that the organization provided feedback and allowed for opportunities to correct behaviours that led to poor performance (as discussed in detail in Chapter 12). In Canada, research finds that the group of employees who lose their jobs due to dismissal are no different in terms of age, gender, education, occupation, and industry than those who remain employed (no turnover).[23]

There is no clear definition of what behaviour constitutes "just cause" for dismissal.[24] Any allegation of just cause must be considered using a contextual approach, looking at not only the alleged behaviour, but the entirety of the employment relationship.[25] If an employer is considering making an allegation of just cause, it is crucial to investigate fully and fairly before any decision is made. The fundamental question is whether or not the employee has irreparably harmed the relationship to the point that it would be unreasonable to expect the employer to continue the employment relationship.[26]

Just cause can often be demonstrated in cases of disobedience, incompetence, dishonesty, insubordination, fighting, and persistent absence or lateness.[27] However, just cause cannot be assessed in isolation and may vary depending on the possible consequences of the misconduct, the status of the employee, and the circumstances of the case. The burden of proof rests with the employer in cases of dismissal or layoff. In Canada, courts often do not accept the assertion of just cause by the employer, and unions almost never do—one union alleged that a death threat made by an employee to his supervisor was "mild insubordination."[28]

Tips FOR THE FRONT LINE

An Ethical | Dilemma

Is it ethical to apply disciplinary action in cases of ongoing absenteeism and tardiness because of family responsibilities? What other approach could be used?

Research INSIGHT

dismissal Involuntary termination of an employee's employment.

dismissal for just cause An employer-initiated termination based on an employee's poor behaviours; in these situations, no severance, reasonable notice periods, or additional payments beyond what the employee has already earned are owed.

Employee misconduct (including theft, expense account fraud, abuse of sick leave, and so on) is a fundamental violation of the employment relationship and can constitute just cause.[29] Unfortunately, the prevalence of theft behaviour is alarming. For example, an Ernst & Young study estimated that 47 percent of retail "inventory shrinkage" is attributable to employees, and the Retail Council of Canada estimates that employee theft costs Canadian businesses about $1 billion per year.[30] Air Canada estimates that it loses up to 9 percent of its cabin stock each year to employee theft, or about $9 per day per employee.[31]

Insubordination is a form of misconduct that often provides grounds for just cause dismissal, although it may be relatively difficult to describe and to prove. To that end, it is important to communicate to employees that some acts are considered insubordinate whenever and wherever they occur. These generally include the following:[32]

1. Direct disregard of the boss' authority; refusal to obey the boss' reasonable instructions—particularly in front of others.

2. Deliberate defiance of clearly stated company policies, rules, regulations, and procedures.

3. Public criticism of the boss; contradicting or arguing with him or her.

4. Contemptuous display of disrespect—making insolent comments and portraying these feelings in terms of the employee's attitude on the job.

5. Disregard for the chain of command, shown by going around the immediate supervisor or manager with a complaint, suggestion, or political manoeuvre.

6. Participation in (or leadership of) an effort to undermine and remove the boss from power.

A recent example of dismissal for just cause based on insubordination involved a Calgary stockbroker who was fired after he brought a prostitute to his office after hours and left her there alone following a dispute about payment. The woman was left alone in the reception area where she could have accessed confidential client and company data after he left. She showed up at the office the next day demanding payment, which resulted in the dismissal of the stockbroker. The court said the stockbroker's conduct exhibited contempt for his employer, his co-workers, and their reputation in the business community.[33]

Exhibit 23-3 provides guidelines on insubordination used by the Saskatchewan government to assist managers and supervisors in dealing with insubordination.

Layoff

As organizations adapt to ever-changing demands, markets, technologies, and competitors, layoffs have become an accepted and familiar organizational activity. "Downsizing" refers to an intentional decision made by executives within the organization that involves a reduction of the workforce to improve efficiency or effectiveness of the organization by affecting the work process.[34] A **layoff**, in which workers are sent home for a period of time (often undefined), is a situation in which three conditions are present: (1) There is no work available for the employees, (2) management expects the no-work situation to be temporary and probably short term, and (3) management intends to recall the employees when work is again available.[35] Alternative names for layoffs include downsizing, rightsizing, reduction in workforce, and mass terminations, to list just a few. Layoffs that involve unionized employees are almost always based on seniority or conditions outlined in the collective bargaining agreement. However, layoffs that occur in non-unionized environments or affect non-unionized employees occur regularly and are not significantly standardized or influenced by third-party limitations.

insubordination Wilful disregard or disobedience of the boss' authority or legitimate orders; criticizing the boss in public.

layoff The temporary withdrawal of employment to workers for economic or business reasons.

Many employers today recognize the enormous investments that organizations have in recruiting, screening, and training their employees. As a result, they are more hesitant to lay off employees at the first signs of business decline. Instead, they are using new approaches to either limit the effects of a layoff or eliminate the layoffs entirely.

There are several alternatives to layoffs. One such alternative is a voluntary reduction in pay, where all employees agree to reductions in their pay to keep everyone working. Other employers arrange to have all or most of their employees accumulate their vacation time and to concentrate their vacations during slow periods. Other employees agree to take voluntary time off, which again has the effect of reducing the employer's payroll and avoiding the need for a layoff. Another way to avoid layoffs is the use of contingent employees hired with the understanding that their work is temporary and they may be laid off at any time.[36] Finally, the work-sharing program, available through Service Canada, allows employers to reduce the workweek by one to three days, and employees can claim employment insurance for the time not worked.

EXHIBIT 23-3 Saskatchewan Public Service Commission Corrective Discipline Guidelines for Insubordination

Saskatchewan Public Service Commission	**Human Resource Manual** www.gov.sk.ca/psc/hrmanual
	Section: PS 803-Guidelines
Corrective Discipline Guidelines Part E: Insubordination	Date issued: 1982 11 17 Revision date: 1990 09 30

The following sets out guidelines to assist managers and supervisors in dealing with the discipline situation.

1. **Insubordination - A Special Case**

   Insubordination is defined as the refusal of an employee to carry out the order of a supervisor. Employees are required, under the Public Service Employment Regulations Section 15.1, to carry out such orders. Employees may disagree with such orders. However, the proper employee response is to obey the order and seek redress via grievance action. The rule of "obey now - grieve later" is well founded in arbitration decisions.

   Note however, that the "obey now - grieve later" rule does not apply to all orders given by supervisors. Some exceptions are as follows:

   - where the order given is not related to work, e.g., deliver my personal mail as opposed to deliver departmental mail, etc. An employee may be directed and is required to perform work duties not found in his job description. However, the employee may later grieve the assignment of these duties.

   - where the employee has reasonable grounds for believing that obeying the order given would endanger health and/or safety.

   - where the order given is illegal.

   - where the order is given by someone without authority. Note however that all orders need not be given by one's immediate supervisor. Where the employee knows that the order is being given by his supervisor's superior, such orders must be followed.

   - where the order interferes with personal appearance or privacy, e.g., a search of one's personal effects where there is suspected theft, that one shave a beard, cut ones hair, wear certain clothes, etc. Note however that appearance or clothing rules may apply where they are a direct job requirement, e.g., uniforms for regulatory staff, cleanliness when preparing food, etc. The refusal of an employee to submit himself to a search of personal effects when management has reasonable grounds for such a request should be recorded. Inform the employee discipline action may be taken; consult with your personnel advisor on how to proceed.

   - where the employee has a reasonable personal excuse, e.g., the employee was provoked into refusing the order, where the employee has a legitimate and reasonable personal excuse and gives it at the time of refusal - personal illness, death in the family, etc. Note however that mere personal inconvenience is not acceptable, e.g., I'm on my break, it's my bowling night, etc.

continued

EXHIBIT 23-3 (Continued)

**Saskatchewan
Public Service
Commission**

Human Resource Manual
www.gov.sk.ca/psc/hrmanual

Section: PS 803-Guidelines

2. Insubordination - How to Handle

Among disciplinary offenses, insubordination is common. To have an employee refuse an order can be unsettling for a supervisor. As a result, the following approach is suggested:

- give the order in the normal manner, e.g., would you be kind enough to help out. The employee refuses.

- determine the employee's reason for refusal.

- determine if the employee's refusal is valid.

- if not, inform the employee you will give a formal order and failure to comply could result in disciplinary action.

- if feasible, inform the employee you will give him three (3) to five (5) minutes to consider his response to the order you will give.

- on return or when you give the order, it is desirable to be accompanied by another supervisory representative or employee if possible. This person will act as a witness.

- clearly repeat the order, e.g., as your supervisor I am ordering you to help out; failure could result in disciplinary action.

- if the employee continues to refuse, inform him that the matter will be investigated further and disciplinary action could result.

- record all of the above in writing immediately after the event; note complete details, i.e., the exact order you gave, the exact words of refusal, the time of the order, etc. Have your witness add his comments.

- initiate the employer's policy of Corrective Discipline.

Source: Human Resources Manual, Saskatchewan Public Service Commission, www.psc.gov.sk.ca/ Default.aspx?DN=6acee10d-6c70-4392-a536-9aac55f273e5 (accessed July 17, 2009).

Fairness In Employee Separations

Research INSIGHT

A study of 996 recently fired or laid off workers found that wrongful dismissal claims were strongly correlated with the way workers felt they had been treated at the time of termination. They also found a "vendetta effect," where the instances of wrongful dismissal claims became stronger as negative treatment became more extreme, as shown in Exhibit 23-4. The researchers concluded that many wrongful dismissal lawsuits could be avoided if effective human resource practices, specifically treating employees fairly, were employed. Providing clear, honest explanations of termination decisions, and handling the termination in a way that treats people with dignity and respect can be especially favourable to the company's reputation, as well as reduce the employee's negative feelings toward themselves and the company.[37]

Over 30 years of organizational research clearly indicates that employees are sensitive to the treatment they receive, and that they have strong perceptions regarding the fairness of their experiences at work.[38] In respect to employee relations, experts generally define organizational justice in terms of three components: distributive justice, procedural justice, and interactional justice. **Distributive justice** refers to the fairness and justice of the outcome of a decision (Would a comparable employee have the same outcome related to the employee separation?). **Procedural justice** refers to the fairness of the process (Is the process my company uses to make decisions about terminations or employee separations fair?). **Interactional justice** refers to the manner in which managers conduct their interpersonal dealings with employees and, in particular, the degree to which they treat employees with dignity and respect as opposed to abuse or disrespect (Does my supervisor treat me with respect when assessing factors related to the separation?).

distributive justice Fairness of a decision outcome.

procedural justice Fairness of the process used to make a decision.

interactional justice Fairness in interpersonal interactions by treating others with dignity and respect.

EXHIBIT 23.4 Fair Treatment and Wrongful Dismissal Claims: The Vendetta Effect

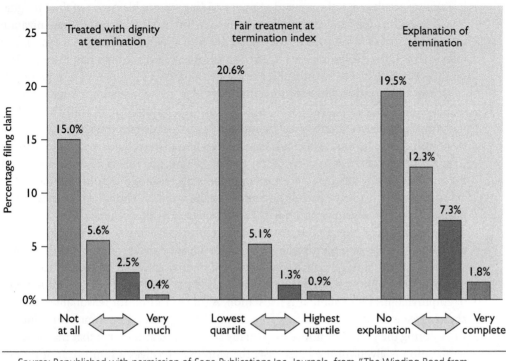

Source: Republished with permission of Sage Publications Inc. Journals, from "The Winding Road from Employee to Complainant: Situational and Psychological Determinants of Wrongful-Termination Claims," by E.A. Lind, J. Greenberg, K.S. Scott, and T.D. Welchans. *Administrative Science Quarterly*, (September 2000) p. 557–590; permission conveyed through Copyright Clearance Center, Inc.

While a focus on fairness perceptions of employees who exit an organization through employee separations is important from a legal and ethical perspective, perceptions of whether exiting employees were treated fairly and justly also affect employees who remain with the organization. For example, fair treatment of employees whose jobs are lost in layoffs is important for maintaining employee engagement on the part of the "survivors" who continue to come to work in these difficult circumstances. Communicating the news of impending layoffs is a difficult task, but ensuring interactional justice when doing so is critical to maintaining engagement on the part of the employees who will continue working for the organization.

Effectively managing employee separations in Canada includes a focus on both exiting employees (including legal compliance with reasonable notice periods) and remaining employees (employee engagement), as well as effective communication to all employees.

Providing Reasonable Notice

In Canada, the employer–employee relationship is governed by an employment contract—a formal agreement (in writing or based on mutual understanding) made between the two parties. If the contract is for a specific length of time, the contract ends at the expiration date and the employee cannot be prematurely dismissed without just cause.

More commonly, employees are hired under an implied contract where the understanding is that employment is for an indefinite period of time and may be terminated by either party only when reasonable notice is given.[39] Employers cannot hire and fire employees at will, as is the case in the United States. Canadian employers can only terminate an employee's employment without reasonable notice when just cause exists. If there is no employment contract and just cause is not present, then a termination without reasonable notice is considered unfair and is known as **wrongful dismissal**. Although it is rare for employees to be accused of not providing reasonable notice of their resignation, if they don't they may be forced to pay out a reimbursement fee to the organization in compensation for the profits lost during the employee's absence. As an example, a manager in British Columbia was ordered to compensate his former employer for lost profits when he left without providing any notice and went to work for a competitor.[40]

Group termination laws require employers who are terminating a large group of employees to give employees more notice than that required on termination of an individual employee. The laws are intended to assist employees in situations of plant closings and large downsizings. Most jurisdictions in Canada require employers who are terminating a group of employees (some specify 10 or more, others 25 or more) within a short time to give advance notice to employees and sometimes to their union. The amount of notice varies by jurisdiction and with the number of employees being terminated, but it generally ranges from 6 to 18 weeks. The laws do not prevent the employer from closing down, nor do they require saving jobs; they simply give employees time to seek other work or retraining by giving them advance notice of their termination.

Often, the amount of notice considered reasonable when an employer decides to terminate the employment relationship is beyond the minimum notice requirements of employment/labour standards legislation. A rule of thumb for reasonable notice is about three to four weeks per year of service. The employee sometimes continues to work during the period of notice but usually ceases work at the time that the notice of termination is given. In the latter case, the employee receives a lump-sum of money equal to his or her pay for the period of notice. Payments are often conditional on the employee signing a general release of all legal claims against the employer.

The employee can accept the notice given (and sign any required release form) or can sue for wrongful dismissal if the notice is considered unacceptable. The court will review the circumstances of the dismissal and make a final decision on the amount of notice to be provided. The courts generally award a period of notice based on their assessment of how long it will take the employee to find alternative employment, taking into account the employee's age, salary, length of service, the level of the job, and other factors. Rarely have notice periods exceeded 24 months.[41]

Another important factor in determining notice periods is whether the dismissed employee was induced or lured away from stable employment elsewhere and then terminated because of a business downturn. For example, a senior marketing manager who had worked for Bell Canada for 20 years was urged by two former co-workers to join them at Alcatel. She joined Alcatel with a 50 percent salary increase to offset her pension loss at Bell. She was terminated after 21 months, sued for wrongful dismissal, and was awarded nine months' notice due to the inducement.[42]

Bad-Faith Damages

In 1997, "bad-faith conduct" on the part of the employer in dismissing an employee was added as another factor considered by the courts in determining the period of reasonable notice.[43] At a minimum, employers are required to be candid, reasonable, honest, and forthright with their employees in the course of dismissal and should refrain from engaging in conduct that is unfair or in bad faith, such as being untruthful, misleading, or unduly insensitive. The resulting additional periods of notice are unpredictable, often around three to four months, but sometimes considerably higher.[44] A significant change to the assessment of bad-faith damages was established by a 2008 decision by the Supreme Court of Canada, which ruled that bad-faith damages apply to only the most extreme conduct and that damages should not be provided by extending the notice period but by compensation for actual damages suffered by the employee.[45] Nevertheless, it is still clear that employers must treat employees with dignity and respect at all times, especially at the time of dismissal.[46]

wrongful dismissal An employee dismissal that does not comply with the law or does not comply with a written or implied contractual arrangement.

group termination laws Laws that require an employer to notify employees in the event that they decide to terminate a group of employees.

Punitive Damages

In extreme cases, employers may also be ordered to pay punitive damages for harsh and vindictive treatment of an employee, or damages for aggravated or mental distress if the employee suffered undue distress from not being given adequate notice of termination.[47] In 2005, the largest punitive damage award in Canadian history was handed down when Honda Canada was ordered to pay $500 000 to a terminated employee for its mistreatment of the employee, who was disabled due to chronic fatigue syndrome.[48] The amount was later reduced to $100 000 by an appeal court and eliminated entirely by the Supreme Court of Canada, who ruled in 2008 that punitive damages should only apply in exceptional cases with wrongful acts by the employer that are truly malicious and outrageous.[49]

Constructive Dismissal

Constructive dismissal is considered to occur when the employer makes unilateral changes in the employment contract that are recognized as unacceptable according to the employee, even though the employee has not been formally terminated.[50] The most common changes in employment status that are considered to constitute constructive dismissal are demotion, reduction in pay and benefits, forced resignation, forced early retirement, forced transfer, and changes in job duties and responsibilities. An employee who believes that he or she has been constructively dismissed can sue the employer for wrongful dismissal. If the judge agrees that constructive dismissal occurred, then a period of notice to be provided to the employee can be determined.

For example, a long-term employee of Ontario Power Generation was affected by a shift in the company's focus that largely eliminated his responsibilities for business development. He was told that he would be "underutilized for the foreseeable future" and that if he didn't like the changes, he could resign or retire. He resigned shortly thereafter and sued for constructive dismissal. The court found that the essential terms of his employment had been substantially changed. The court also discovered that the company had no plan to provide him with work and that he had been constructively dismissed. He was awarded 24 months' pay.[51]

The definition of constructive dismissal was expanded in a recent case where an employee was given two years' notice of a change to his written employment agreement that would reduce the amount in the termination pay clause. The employee disagreed with the change and was told two years later that he had to accept the new terms or "we do not have a job for you." The employee left the company and successfully sued for constructive dismissal.[52]

Avoiding Wrongful Dismissal Suits

Dismissals for cause may result in the employee filing a wrongful dismissal lawsuit. A wrongful dismissal accusation is one in which the terminated employee contends that the employer terminated the employment relationship in violation of relevant law (based on age, gender, or other protected grounds), the contract of employment (implied or explicit), or the employer's own dismissal procedures. More recent accusations have stemmed from how the dismissal was carried out (perceptions of fairness) or employee perception that the reason for the termination did not qualify as "just cause."

There are several steps that can be taken to avoid wrongful dismissal suits:[53]

Hints TO ENSURE LEGAL COMPLIANCE

1. Use employment contracts with a termination clause and with wording clearly permitting the company to dismiss without cause during the probationary period.

2. Document all disciplinary action.

3. Do not allege just cause for dismissal unless it can be proven.

constructive dismissal When the employer makes unilateral changes in the employment contract that are unacceptable to the employee, even though the employee has not been formally terminated.

4. Time the termination so that it does not conflict with special occasions, such as birthdays or holidays.

5. Use termination letters in all cases, clearly stating the settlement offer.

6. Schedule the termination interview in a private location at a time of day that will allow the employee to clear out belongings with a minimal amount of contact with other employees.

7. Include two members of management in the termination meeting.

If a wrongful dismissal suit is made against the company, the firm should:[54]

- Review the claim carefully before retaining an employment lawyer, and investigate for other improper conduct; ask for a legal opinion on the merits of the case; work with the lawyer and provide all relevant facts and documentation; and discuss any possible letter of reference with the lawyer.

- Never allege cause if none exists, and avoid defamatory statements.

- Consider mediation as an option, or offer to settle to save time and money.

Tips | **FOR THE FRONT LINE**

Outplacement Counselling

Outplacement counselling provides career counselling and job search skills training for terminated employees. The counselling itself is done either by the employer's in-house specialist or by outside consultants. Outplacement counselling is considered part of the terminated employee's severance package.[55]

Outplacement counselling is usually conducted by outplacement firms, such as Drake Beam Morin and Right Management. Middle- and upper-level managers who are dismissed will typically have office space and secretarial services that they can use at local offices of such firms, in addition to the counselling services.

The Termination Interview

Dismissing an employee is one of the most difficult tasks that a manager will face at work.[56] The dismissed employee, even if warned many times in the past, will often still react with total disbelief or even violence. Guidelines for the **termination interview** itself follow.

1. *Plan the interview.* Carefully schedule the meeting on a day early in the week, and try to avoid Fridays, pre-holidays, and vacation times. Have the employee agreement, human resources file, and release announcement (internal and external) prepared in advance. Be available at a time after the interview in case questions or problems arise, and have phone numbers ready for medical or security emergencies.

2. *Get to the point.* As soon as the employee arrives, give the person a moment to get comfortable and then inform him or her of the decision.

3. *Describe the situation briefly.* In three or four sentences, explain why the person is being let go. For instance, "Production in your area is down 4 percent, and we are continuing to have quality problems. We have talked about these problems several times in the past three months, and the solutions are not being followed through. We have to make a change."[57] Remember to describe the situation rather than attacking the employee personally.

4. Listen. It is important to continue the interview until the person appears to be talking freely and seems reasonably calm about the reasons for his or her termination and the severance package that he or she is to receive. Behavioural

outplacement counselling A systematic process by which a terminated person is trained and counselled in the techniques of self-appraisal and securing a new position.

termination interview The interview in which an employee is informed of the fact that he or she has been dismissed.

indications can be used to help gauge the person's reaction and to decide how best to proceed. Five major reactions often occur:

- First, some employees will be *hostile and angry*, expressing hurt and disappointment. In such cases, remain objective while providing information on any outplacement or career counselling to be provided, being careful to avoid being defensive or confronting the person's anger.

- Second, some employees may react in a *defensive, bargaining* manner, based on their feelings of fear and disbelief. In this case, it is important to acknowledge that this is a difficult time for the employee and then provide information regarding outplacement counselling without getting involved in any bargaining discussions.

Termination interviews are among the most difficult tasks that managers face, but there are guidelines for making them less painful for both parties.

- Third, the employee may proceed in a *formal, controlled* manner, indicative of a suppressed, vengeful reaction and the potential for legal action. In this case, allow the employee to ask any questions pertaining to his or her case (avoiding side issues) in a formal tone while leading into information about the outplacement counselling to be provided.

- Fourth, some employees will maintain a *stoic* façade, masking their shock, disbelief, and numbness. In this case, communicate to the employee that his or her shock is recognized and that the details can be handled later if the employee prefers. Answer any questions arising at that point and provide information on outplacement counselling.

- A fifth reaction is an *emotional* one involving tears and sadness, indicating grief and worry on the part of the employee. Allow the person to cry and provide tissues. When the person regains his or her composure, explain the outplacement counselling process.

5. *Review all elements of the severance package.* Describe severance payments, benefits, and the way in which references will be handled. However, under no conditions should any promises or benefits beyond those already in the severance package be implied. The termination should be complete when the person leaves.

6. *Identify the next step.* The terminated employee may be disoriented, so explain where he or she should go on leaving the interview. Remind the person whom to contact at the company regarding questions about the severance package or references.

An Ethical | Dilemma

Is it ethical to "buy out" an undesirable employee with severance pay and a good letter of reference in order to avoid prolonged wrongful dismissal litigation, even if you know the letter is misleading to potential future employers?

Effective Employee Communication

Employee Engagement

Employee engagement is a positive, fulfilling, work-related state of mind characterized by vigour, dedication, and absorption.[58] It is a heightened emotional and intellectual connection that an employee has for his or her job, organization, manager, or co-workers, that in turn influences the employee to apply additional discretionary effort.[59] Engaged employees feel a vested interest in the company's success and are both willing and motivated to perform to levels that exceed the stated job requirements (see Exhibit 23-5).[60]

employee engagement The emotional and intellectual involvement of employees in their work, such as intensity, focus, and involvement in his or her job and organization.

EXHIBIT 23.5 Top Drivers of Attraction, Retention, and Engagement in Canada

	TOP FIVE DRIVERS	
Top Attraction Drivers	**Top Retention Drivers**	**Top Engagement Drivers**
Competitive base pay	Have excellent career advancement opportunities	Senior management sincerely interested in employee well-being
Vacation/paid time off	Satisfaction with the organization's people decisions	Organization's reputation for social responsibility
Competitive health care benefits	Ability to balance my work/personal life	Input into decision making in my department
Challenging work	Fairly compensated compared to others doing similar work in my organization	Improved my skills and capabilities over the last year
Career advancement opportunities	Understand potential career track within organization	Understand potential career track within organization

Source: *Closing the Engagement Gap: A Road Map for Driving Superior Business Performance.* Towers Perrin Workforce Study 2007–2008, p. 21. Copyright 2009 Towers Perrin. Used with permission.

A closer look at the drivers of employee engagement reveals the importance of fair treatment. Senior management that are concerned about the well-being of their employees, tell the truth, and communicate difficult messages well are treating employees with dignity and respect, which is the cornerstones of interactional justice. Opportunities for growth and development, including increased autonomy and participation in day-to-day decision making, are manifestations of procedural justice. Organizations that strive for excellence and maintain high levels of distributive fairness ensure that their employees' career objectives are clear and their performances are compensated.

One of the most important drivers of employee engagement is effective communication, because an engaged employee is an informed employee who feels valued and critical to their organization's success.[61] It is important for managers to deliver information (facts) about individual performance and organizational success to their employees in combination with effective communication and feedback to maximize employee engagement. It is also important to maximize face-to-face opportunities when delivering information from members of the senior management team.[62]

To increase employee engagement, many firms give employees extensive data on the performance of and prospects for their operations.[63] It must be remembered that employee communication requires careful consideration, as Chrysler found out in early 2009 when it sent a letter to unionized employees outlining the serious challenges the company was facing and the need to reduce labour costs. Within hours, workers in Windsor, Ontario, spilled out of the plant to burn the letter in protest. The union called the letter a "clear attempt to sidestep and undermine" them.[64]

Suggestion Programs

Employees can often offer well-informed, thoughtful, and creative suggestions regarding issues ranging from malfunctioning vending machines to unlit parking lots to a manager spending too much of the department's money on travel. Dofasco Inc.'s suggestion program has been a success story for decades. Employees can receive cash awards of up to $50 000, depending on the savings realized by implementing the suggestion. Suggestion programs like these have several benefits. They let management continually monitor employees' feelings and concerns while making it clear that employees have several channels through which to communicate concerns and get responses. The net effect is less likelihood that minor employee issues will manifest themselves into organizational concerns.

Employee Opinion Surveys

Many firms also administer periodic anonymous **employee opinion surveys**. For maximum benefit, surveys should be conducted regularly and the results must be provided to participants.[65] An employee satisfaction survey, called the Employee Feedback System (EFS), has been developed by the National Quality Institute and the Workplace Health Research Unit at Brock University.[66] The EFS examines 16 areas ranging from job satisfaction and co-worker cohesion to quality focus and employee commitment.

Recently, employees began to use blogs to express opinions about their employers, and employer concerns arose about damage to their reputation and possible disclosure of confidential company information. Some corporations, such as IBM, Cisco, and Sun Microsystems, have chosen to trust their employees and have suggested guidelines and specific tactics so that employees can blog without causing themselves or their employers any grief.[67] However, there are also cases where employees have been terminated for posting negative opinions about their employer, and arbitration boards have upheld the terminations, finding that postings about managers, co-workers, and the work environment are sufficient grounds for discharge.[68] A blogging policy is recommended by legal experts and should include directions to refrain from disclosing any confidential company information or embarrassing or demeaning information about the company and its employees.[69]

Employee Feedback System
**www.thcu.ca/workplace/sat/pubs/
sat_0065_v102.pdf**

Communication from Management

To increase employee engagement, many firms give employees extensive data on the performance of and prospects for their operations. Traditionally, newsletters and verbal presentations were the most effective methods used to disseminate information from the company to employees. More recently, organizations have used videos, email, and intranets.[70] Blogs can also be used by senior managers to connect with employees. When Jim Estill sold his company and became CEO of the larger combined operation, he found employees of the acquiring company "treated me like I was some sort of Martian." He started a blog (80 percent company-related content and 20 percent personal) and soon overcame the problem—staff even sent him pictures from their kids' birthday parties! In addition, staff sent the blog to vendors and customers, which elevated him in their eyes as well.[71] One Canadian company used improved management communication to drive huge increases in employee engagement as well as a turnaround in financial results.

employee opinion surveys
Communication devices that use questionnaires to ask for employees' opinions about the company, management, and work life.

24 Labour Relations

Introduction to Labour Relations

A **labour union** (or **union**) is an officially recognized body representing a group of employees who have joined together to present a collective voice in dealing with management. The purposes of unionization are to influence HR policies and practices that affect bargaining unit members, such as pay and benefits; to achieve greater control over the jobs being performed, greater job security, and improved working conditions; and to increase job satisfaction and meet employees' affiliation needs. The term **labour–management relations** refers to the ongoing interactions between labour unions and management in organizations.

The presence of a labour union alters the relationship between employees and the firm and has implications for planning and implementing a business strategy. Managerial discretion and flexibility in dealing with employees and in implementing and administering HR policies and procedures are reduced. For example, union seniority provisions in the **collective bargaining agreement (union contract)**, negotiated through **collective bargaining**, govern the selection of employees for transfers, promotions, and training programs and specify the order in which employees can be laid off and recalled. Many other terms and conditions of employment for **bargaining unit** members are determined and standardized through collective bargaining, rather than being left to management's discretion.

An organization's *labour relations (LR) strategy*, one component of its HR strategy, is its overall plan for dealing with unions, which sets the tone for its union–management relationship. The decision to accept or avoid unions is the basis of an organization's LR strategy.[1]

Managers in firms choosing a *union acceptance strategy* view the union as the legitimate representative of the firm's employees. Such a relationship can lead to innovative initiatives and win–win outcomes. Managers select a *union avoidance strategy* when they believe that it is preferable to operate in a non-unionized environment. Walmart is well known for its preference to remain non-union (and has even closed stores that have attempted to unionize).[2] To avoid unions, companies can either adopt a *union substitution approach*, in which they become so responsive to employee needs that there is no incentive for them to unionize (as is the case at Dofasco), or adopt a *union suppression approach* when there is a desire to avoid a union at all costs (Walmart challenged the constitutionality of Saskatchewan's labour laws all the way to the Supreme Court of Canada, but lost).[3]

Canada's Labour Laws

Canadian labour laws have two general purposes:

1. To provide a common set of rules for fair negotiations

2. To protect the public interest by preventing the impact of labour disputes from inconveniencing the public.

As with other employment-related legislation, there are 13 provincial/territorial jurisdictions, as well as federal labour relations legislation for employees subject to federal jurisdiction. There are a number of common characteristics in the LR legislation across Canada, which can be summarized as follows:

- Procedures for the certification of a union

- The requirement that a collective agreement be in force for a minimum of one year

- Procedures that must be followed by one or both parties before a strike or lockout is legal

- The prohibition of strikes or lockouts during the life of a collective agreement

---

Canadian Labour and Business Centre
www.clbc.ca

Ontario Ministry of Labour
www.labour.gov.on.ca

Canadian LabourWatch Association
www.labourwatch.com

labour union (union) An officially recognized association of employees practising a similar trade or employed in the same company or industry who have joined together to present a united front and collective voice in dealing with management.

labour–management relations The ongoing interactions between labour unions and management in organizations.

collective bargaining agreement (union contract) A formal agreement between an employer and the union representing a group of employees regarding terms and conditions of employment.

collective bargaining Negotiations between a union and an employer to arrive at a mutually acceptable collective agreement.

bargaining units The group of employees in a firm, a plant, or an industry that has been recognized by an employer or certified by a labour relations board (LRB) as appropriate for collective bargaining purposes.

- The requirement that disputes over matters arising from interpretation of the collective agreement be settled by final and binding arbitration

- Prohibition of certain specified "unfair practices" on the part of labour and management

- Establishment of a labour relations board or the equivalent; labour relations boards are tripartite—made up of representatives of union and management, as well as a neutral chair or a vice-chair, typically a government representative.

Chrysler workers at the company's assembly plant in Windsor, Ontario, burn letters they received from management. The letters outlined a number of concessions the company is requesting of employees.

Labour relations legislation attempts to balance employees' rights to engage in union activities with employers' rights to manage. For example, managers are prohibited from interfering with and discriminating against employees who are exercising their rights under the LR legislation. One restriction on unions is that they are prohibited from calling or authorizing an unlawful strike.

The Labour Movement in Canada Today

The primary goal of labour unions active in Canada today is to obtain economic benefits and improved treatment for their members. It may involve lobbying for legislative changes pertaining to these issues. This union philosophy, with its emphasis on economic and welfare goals, has become known as **business unionism**. Unions strive to ensure *job security* for their members and to attain *improved economic conditions* and *better working conditions* for their members. Most unions today also become involved in broader political and social issues affecting their members. Activities aimed at influencing government economic and social policies are known as **social (reform) unionism**. For example, unions have recognized the special circumstances of Aboriginal workers.

Construction Labour Relations
www.clra.org

International Labour News
www.labourstart.org

Types of Unions

The labour unions in Canada can be classified according to the following characteristics:

1. *Type of worker eligible for membership.* All the early trade unions in Canada were **craft unions**—associations of persons performing a certain type of skill or trade (for example, carpenters or bricklayers). Examples in today's workforce include the British Columbia Teachers' Federation and the Ontario Nurses' Association. An **industrial union** is a labour organization comprising all the workers eligible for union membership in a particular company or industry, irrespective of the type of work performed.

2. *Geographical scope.* Labour unions with head offices in other countries (most often theUnited States) that charter branches in both Canada and one or more countriesare known as *international unions.* Labour unions that charter branches in Canada only and have their head office in this country are known as *national unions.* A small number of employees belong to labour unions that are purely *local* in geographical scope.

3. *Labour congress affiliation.* A third way of distinguishing among labour unions is according to affiliation with one or another central labour organization. These central organizations include the following:

   - *Canadian Labour Congress (CLC).* The CLC is the major central labour organization in Canada and has over 3 million affiliated union members. Most international and national unions belong to the CLC, as well as all directly

business unionism The activities of labour unions focusing on economic and welfare issues, including pay and benefits, job security, and working conditions.

social (reform) unionism Activities of unions directed at furthering the interests of their members by influencing the social and economic policies of governments at all levels, such as speaking out on proposed legislative reforms.

craft union Traditionally, a labour organization representing workers practising the same craft or trade, such as carpentry or plumbing.

industrial union A labour organization representing all workers eligible for union membership in a particular company or industry, including skilled trades people.

chartered local unions, local/district labour councils, and provincial/territorial federations of labour.

- *Confédération des syndicats nationaux (CSN)*—in English, Confederation of National Trade Unions (CNTU). This organization is the Quebec counterpart of the CLC and has more than 300 000 members.

- *American Federation of Labor and Congress of Industrial Organizations (AFL–CIO).* The American counterpart of the CLC is the AFL–CIO. The two organizations operate independently, but since most international unions in the CLC are also members of the AFL–CIO, a certain degree of common interest exists.

American Federation of Labor and Congress of Industrial Organizations (AFL–CIO)
www.aflcio.org

The basic unit of the labour union movement in Canada is the **local**, formed in a particular location. For HR managers and front-line supervisors, the union locals are generally the most important part of the union structure. Key players within the local are the elected officials known as **union stewards**, who are responsible for representing the interests and protecting the rights of bargaining unit employees in their department or area.

Membership Trends

As of 2010, 31.5 percent of Canadian employees were unionized. The membership in unions as a percentage of the labour force has been steadily decreasing, as shown in Exhibit **24-1**. Various factors are responsible for membership decline, including a dramatic increase in service sector and white-collar jobs, combined with a decrease in employment opportunities in industries that have traditionally been highly unionized, such as manufacturing. More effective HR practices in non-unionized firms are another contributing factor.[4]

Traditionally, unions have targeted full-time, manufacturing workers (which used to be almost exclusively older males) for membership. Canadian unions are unique in that they have managed to refocus their target on membership to better align with workforce realities. As a result, the rate of decline in union membership is not nearly as significant in Canada as it is elsewhere (for example, the United States). This can be attributed to three significant issues: global competition, demographics, and unionization of white-collar workers in Canada.

Global Competition

Globalization is transforming the dynamics of labour relations in Canada such that employers are being forced to become more militant, and unions are struggling to maintain their influence at the bargaining table.[5] Some unions face the difficult choice of negotiating concessions or watching jobs go to lower-cost countries.

Demographics

The focus of union collective bargaining efforts must align with the workplace demographics. The aging of the workforce and pending labour shortage affects unions as well as HR managers.[6] It has been suggested that unions and management may need to work together to attract and retain workers. Retention concerns may make employers more willing to offer job security in exchange for promises of productivity and flexibility from unions. Pensions and benefits for older workers and retirees has also become more of a union priority.

Unionization of White-Collar Employees

Difficulties in attempting to resolve grievances and lack of job security have led to increased interest in unionization among white-collar workers. Service sector workers, such as those in retail stores, fast-food chains, and government agencies, as well as managers and professionals (including university/college faculty), have been targeted for organizing campaigns. Since these jobs tend to have more women and young people

local A group of unionized employees in a particular location.

union steward A union member elected by workers in a particular department or area of a firm to act as their union representative.

EXHIBIT 24-1 Unionization Rate in Canada, 1997–2010 (Percentage of Employed Workers)

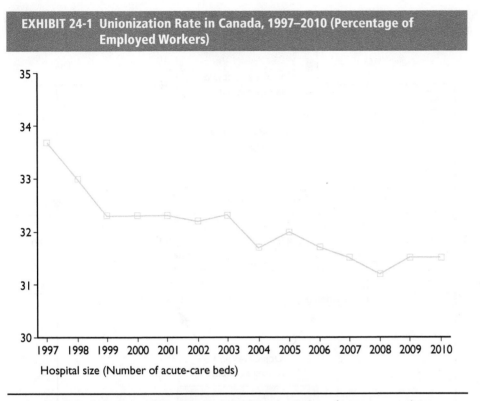

Hospital size (Number of acute-care beds)

Note: HRSDC calculations based on Statistics Canada, "Labour force survey estimates (LFS), employees by union coverage, North American Industry Classification System (NAICS), sex and age group, annual" (CANSIM Table 282-0078). Ottawa, ON: Statistics Canada, 2011.

Source: Work-Unionization Rates, http://www4.hrsdc.gc.ca/.3ndic.1t.4r@-eng.jsp?iid=17, Human Resources and Skills Development Canada, 2012. Reproduced with the permission of the Minister of Public Works and Government Services Canada, 2012.

than manufacturing jobs, unions are now focusing more on work–family issues as well as the health and safety risks associated with white-collar jobs, such as the potential for repetitive strain injuries from working at video display terminals (computers or laptops).[7]

The Labour Relations Process

As illustrated in Exhibit 24-2, the labour relations process consists of five steps:

1. Employees decide to seek collective representation.

2. The union organizing campaign begins.

3. The union receives official recognition.

4. Union and management negotiate a collective agreement.

5. Day-to-day contract administration begins.

Each of these five steps will now be reviewed in detail.

Step 1: Desire for Collective Representation

Based on a review of 36 research studies internationally, three classifications were developed to explain why individuals join unions:[8]

- *Dissonance-based reasons.* When expectations of work (work should be enjoyable and rewarding, for example) and the experience of work (the work environment is unpleasant and pay is low) are in conflict, the desire to join

EXHIBIT 24-2 An Overview of the Labour Relations Process

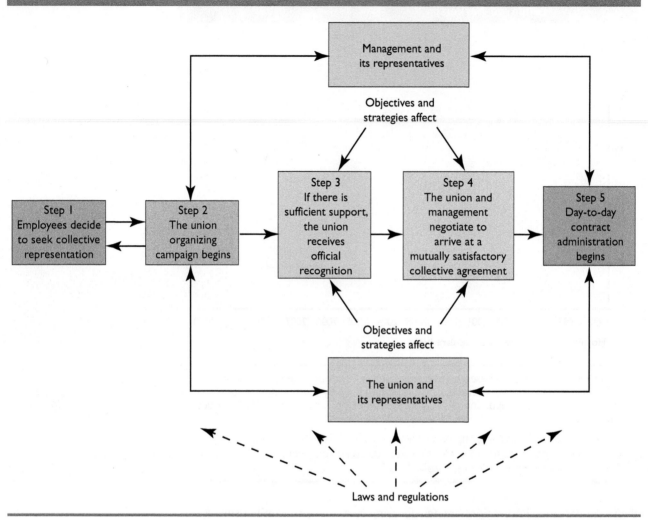

a union is triggered. However if dissonance is the reason why employees want to unionize, then they will only do so if they think the union will be effective in remedying the associated discontent or frustration with the work expectations versus experiences dissonance.

- *Utility-based reasons.* An individual's decision to join a union can also be attributed to a rational calculation of the costs and benefits of unionization, where individuals compare the costs and benefits of remaining non-unionized versus becoming unionized. The selection of which decision to make is largely based on the calculation of the cost/benefit analysis.[9]

- *Political/ideological reasons.* An individual's political or ideological beliefs may influence their understanding of and desire for collective versus individual negotiation of employment terms.[10]

Numerous studies suggest that age, gender, education levels, and other demographic factors are highly correlated with the desire to join a union. However, there is little consistency with the findings of the studies, with the exception of two groups: People over the age of 60 and black workers are consistently likely to have a desire to join a union.[11] It has been theorized that this is largely due to perceptions of employment related discrimination. It has also been suggested that each workplace is unique, so the demographic characteristics of one workforce may impact the desire to join a union in a way that isn't highly generalizable or applicable to a larger population.

Given the fact that, in 2007, the average wage rate for unionized employees was significantly higher than non-unionized employees (average hourly rate full time: unionized = $24.15, non-unionized = $20.55: average hourly rate part time: unionized = $19.99, non-unionized = $12.56) and average hours worked per week was significantly higher for unionized employees in Canada (unionized = 19.3 hours, non-unionized = 16.9), these expectations seem quite justifiable. Being a union member also has an impact on female workers' ability to achieve pay equity. On average, full-time female unionized workers earned 94 percent of the hourly wages of their male counterparts, and part-time female unionized workers earned 14 percent more than their male counterparts.[12]

However, research studies have made it clear that dissatisfaction alone will not lead to unionization. More important seems to be the employees' belief that it is only through unity that they can protect themselves from the arbitrary whims of management. In other words, it is only when workers are dissatisfied and believe that they are without the ability to change the factors causing dissatisfaction, except through collective action, that they become interested in unionizing.[13]

Step 2: Union Organizing Campaign

Once interest in joining a union has been aroused, the union organizing process begins. There are five steps typically involved in this process:

Promoting the benefits of unionization.

1. *Employee/union contact.* A formal organizing campaign may be initiated by a union organizer or by employees acting on their own behalf. Most organizing campaigns are begun by employees who get in touch with an existing union.[14] However, large unions have a number of *union organizers* on staff who are responsible for identifying organizing opportunities and launching organizing campaigns. During these initial discussions, employees investigate the advantages of union representation, and the union officials start to gather information about the employees' sources of dissatisfaction.

2. *Initial organizational meeting.* The union organizer then schedules an initial meeting with the individuals who first expressed an interest in unionization and co-workers who subsequently express their support. The aim is to identify employees who would be willing to help the organizer direct the campaign.

3. *Formation of an in-house organizing committee.* This committee comprises a group of employees who are dedicated to the goal of unionization and who are willing to assist the union organizer.

4. *The organizing campaign.* Members of the in-house committee then contact employees, present the case for unionization, and encourage as many employees as possible to sign an **authorization card**, indicating their willingness to be represented by the union in collective bargaining with the employer.

5. *The outcome.* There are a number of possible outcomes to a unionization campaign, including rejection by the majority of eligible employees. For a union to become the bargaining unit for a group of employees, it must be certified by a labour relations board (LRB) or receive official recognition from the employer.

Signs of Organizing Activity

Managers who suspect that a unionization attempt may be underway should watch for a number of the following signs:[15]

- Disappearance of employee lists or directories

- More inquiries than usual about benefits, wages, promotions, and other HR policies and procedures

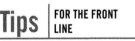

authorization card A card signed by an employee that indicates his or her willingness to have the union act as his or her representative for purposes of collective bargaining.

- Questions about their opinions of unions

- An increase in the number or nature of employee complaints or grievances

- A change in the number, composition, and size of informal groups at lunch and coffee breaks

- The sudden popularity of certain employees (especially if they are the informal leaders)

- The sudden cessation of employee conversation when a member of management approaches, or an obvious change in employees' behaviour toward members of management, expressed either formally or informally

- The appearance of strangers in the parking lot

- The distribution of cards, flyers, or pro-union buttons

Employer Response to an Organizing Campaign

Labour Relations (Ontario)
www.labour.gov.on.ca/english/lr

If the employer prefers that the group seeking unionization retain its non-union status, a careful campaign is usually mounted to counteract the union drive. Normally, HR department staff members head up the campaign, although they may be assisted by a consultant or labour lawyer. Absolutely critical to the success of a company's counter-campaign is supervisory training. Supervisors need to be informed about what they can and cannot do or say during the organizing campaign to ensure that they avoid actions that might directly or inadvertently provide fuel for the union's campaign and refrain from violating LR legislation.

An Ethical | Dilemma

Knowing that head office plans to close your facility if a unionization bid is successful, how should you, as a manager, respond to inquiries from employees about the impact of a union?

As much information about the union as possible should be obtained pertaining to dues, strike record, salaries of officers, and any other relevant facts that might cause employees to question the benefits of unionization. Communication strategies can be planned, with the aim of reminding employees about the company's good points, pointing out disadvantages of unionization, and refuting any misleading union claims. The employer's case for remaining non-union should be presented in a factual, honest, and straightforward manner.

Under the law, employers are granted the right to do the following:

Hints | TO ENSURE LEGAL COMPLIANCE

- Express their views and opinions regarding unions

- State their position regarding the desirability of remaining non-union

- Prohibit distribution of union literature on company property on company time

- Increase wages, make promotions, and take other HR actions, as long as they would do so *in the normal course of business*. In most jurisdictions, however, once an application for certification is received by the LRB, wages, benefits, and working conditions are frozen until the application is dealt with.

- Assemble employees during working hours to state the company's position, as long as employees are advised of the purpose of the meeting in advance, attendance is optional, and threats and promises are avoided (employers have no obligation to give the union the same opportunity).

Step 3: Union Recognition

A union can obtain recognition as a bargaining unit for a group of workers in three basic ways: (1) voluntary recognition, (2) the regular certification process, and (3) a pre-hearing vote. Bargaining rights can also be terminated in various ways.

Voluntary Recognition

An employer in every Canadian jurisdiction, except Quebec, can voluntarily recognize a union as the bargaining agent for a group of its employees. Although fairly rare, this may occur if an employer has adopted a union acceptance strategy and believes that employees want to be represented by that union.

Regular Certification

The normal union certification procedure is for the union to present evidence of at least a minimum level of membership support for a bargaining unit that they have defined, in the form of signed authorization cards, to the appropriate LRB, along with an application for **certification**. The minimum level of support required to apply for certification varies by jurisdiction, from 25 percent of the bargaining unit in Saskatchewan to 65 percent in Manitoba.[16] The LRB then determines whether the bargaining unit defined by the union is appropriate for collective bargaining purposes.

In most jurisdictions LRBs can grant *automatic certification* without a vote if the applicant union can demonstrate a high enough level of support for the proposed bargaining unit (generally 50 or 55 percent). Automatic certification may also be granted in some jurisdictions if the employer has engaged in unfair practices. If the level of support is not sufficient for automatic certification, but is above a specified minimum level (between 25 and 45 percent, depending on jurisdiction), the LRB will order and supervise a **representation vote**.[17] Eligible employees have the opportunity to cast a secret ballot, indicating whether or not they want the union to be certified. In some jurisdictions, to gain certification the voting results must indicate that *more than 50 percent of the potential bargaining unit members* are in support of the union. In other jurisdictions, the standard is the support of *more than 50 percent of those voting*.[18] If the union loses, another election cannot be held among the same employees for at least one year. Only about 20 percent of certifications are the result of a vote—roughly four out of five certifications are the result of authorization cards alone.[19]

Pre-Hearing Votes

In most jurisdictions, a **pre-hearing vote** may be conducted where there is evidence of violations of fair labour practices early in an organizing campaign. In such a case, the LRB may order a vote before holding a hearing to determine the composition of the bargaining unit. The intent is to determine the level of support for the union as quickly as possible, before the effect of any irregularities can taint the outcome. The ballot box is then sealed until the LRB determines whether the bargaining unit is appropriate and, if so, which employees are eligible for membership. If the bargaining unit is deemed appropriate by the LRB, only the votes of potential bargaining unit members are counted, and if the majority of the ballots cast support the union, it is certified.

Termination of Bargaining Rights

All labour relations acts provide procedures for workers to apply for the **decertification** of their unions. Generally, members may apply for decertification if the union has failed to negotiate a collective agreement within one year of certification, or if they are dissatisfied with the performance of the union. The LRB holds a secret-ballot vote, and if more than 50 percent of the ballots cast (or bargaining unit members, depending on jurisdiction) are in opposition to the union, the union will be decertified. A labour union also has the right to notify the LRB that it no longer wants to continue to represent the employees in a particular bargaining unit. This is known as "termination on abandonment." Once the LRB has declared that the union no longer represents the bargaining unit employees, any collective agreement negotiated between the parties is void.

certification The procedure whereby a labour union obtains a certificate from the relevant LRB declaring that the union is the exclusive bargaining agent for a defined group of employees in a bargaining unit that the LRB considers appropriate for collective bargaining purposes.

representation vote A vote conducted by the LRB in which employees in the bargaining unit indicate, by secret ballot, whether or not they want to be represented, or continue to be represented, by a labour union.

pre-hearing vote An alternative mechanism for certification, used in situations in which there is evidence of violations of fair labour practices early in the organizing campaign.

decertification The process whereby a union is legally deprived of its official recognition as the exclusive bargaining agent for a group of employees.

Step 4: Collective Bargaining

Collective bargaining is the process by which a formal collective agreement is established between labour and management. The collective agreement is the cornerstone of the Canadian LR system. Both union and management representatives are required to bargain in good faith. This means that they must communicate and negotiate, that proposals must be matched with counterproposals, and that both parties must make every reasonable effort to arrive at an agreement.

Steps typically involved in the collective bargaining process include (1) preparation for bargaining, (2) face-to-face negotiations, and (3) obtaining approval for the proposed contract. There are two possible additional steps. First, when talks break down, third-party assistance is required by law in every jurisdiction except Saskatchewan.[20] The second additional step is a strike/lockout or interest arbitration if the parties arrive at a bargaining impasse. Each of these steps will be described next.

Preparation for Negotiations

Good preparation leads to a greater likelihood that desired goals will be achieved. Preparation for negotiations involves planning the bargaining strategy and process and assembling data to support bargaining proposals. Both union and management will gather data on general economic trends, analyze other collective agreements and trends in collective bargaining, conduct an analysis of grievances, review the existing contract or the union's organizing campaign promises, conduct wage and salary surveys at competitor organizations, prepare cost estimates of monetary proposals, and make plans for a possible strike or lockout. In addition, management negotiators will obtain input from supervisors. Union negotiators will obtain input from union stewards, obtain the company's financial information (if it is a public company), gather demographic information on their membership, and obtain input from members.

International Labour Organization
www.ilo.org

Once these steps are completed, each side forms a negotiating team and an initial bargaining plan/strategy is prepared. Initial proposals are then finalized and presented for approval by either senior management or the union membership.

Face-to-Face Negotiations

Under LR legislation, representatives of either union or management can give written notice to the other party of their desire to negotiate a first collective agreement or renew an existing one. Early in the negotiating process, demands are exchanged—often before the first bargaining session. Then both negotiating teams can make a private assessment of the other team's demands. Usually, each team finds some items with which they can agree quite readily and others on which compromise seems likely. Tentative conclusions are also made regarding which items, if any, are potential strike or lockout issues.

caucus session A session in which only the members of one's own bargaining team are present.

Location, Frequency, and Duration of Meetings Negotiations are generally held at a neutral, offsite location, such as a hotel meeting room, so that there is no psychological advantage for either team and so that interruptions and work distractions can be kept to a minimum. Each side generally has another room in which intra-team meetings, known as **caucus sessions**, are held.

Generally, meetings are held as often as either or both parties consider desirable, and they last as long as progress is being made. Marathon bargaining sessions, such as those lasting all night, are not typical until conciliation has been exhausted and the clock is ticking rapidly toward the strike/lockout deadline.

Initial Bargaining Session The initial meeting of the bargaining teams is extremely important in establishing the climate that will prevail during the negotiating sessions that follow. A cordial attitude can help to relax tension and ensure that negotiations proceed smoothly. Generally,

Negotiating a collective agreement.

the first meeting is devoted to an exchange of demands (if this has not taken place previously) and the establishment of rules and procedures that will be used during negotiations.

Subsequent Bargaining Sessions In traditional approaches to bargaining, each party argues for its demands and resists those of the other at each negotiating session. At the same time, both are looking for compromise alternatives that will enable an agreement to be reached. Every proposal submitted must be either withdrawn temporarily or permanently, accepted by the other side in its entirety, or accepted in a modified form. Ideally, both sides should come away from negotiations feeling that they have attained many of their basic bargaining goals and confident that the tentative agreement reached will be acceptable to senior management and the members of the bargaining unit.

For each issue on the table to be resolved satisfactorily, the point at which agreement is reached must be within limits that the union and employer are willing to accept, often referred to as the **bargaining zone**. As illustrated in Exhibit 24-3, if the solution desired by one party exceeds the limits of the other party, then it is outside of the bargaining zone. Unless that party modifies its demands sufficiently to bring them within the bargaining zone, or the other party extends its limits to accommodate such demands, a bargaining deadlock is the inevitable result.

Distributive bargaining is an approach often typified as "win–lose" bargaining because the gains of one party are normally achieved at the expense of the other.[21] It is appropriately involved when the issues being discussed pertain to the distribution of things that are available in fixed amounts, such as wage increases and benefits improvements. However, it may also be used when there is a history of distrust and adversarial relations, even when dealing with issues on which a more constructive approach is possible.

As indicated in Exhibit 24-3, distributive bargaining is characterized by three distinct components: the initial point, the target point, and the resistance point. The initial point for the union is usually higher than what the union expects to receive from management. The union target point is next, and represents the negotiating team's assessment of what is realistically achievable from management. The union's bargaining zone limit is its resistance point, which represents its minimally acceptable level.

These points are essentially reversed for management. The management team's initial point is its lowest level, which is used at the beginning of negotiations. Next is its target point, the desired agreement level. Management's resistance point forms the other boundary of the bargaining zone.

EXHIBIT 24-3 The Bargaining Zone and Characteristics of Distributive Bargaining

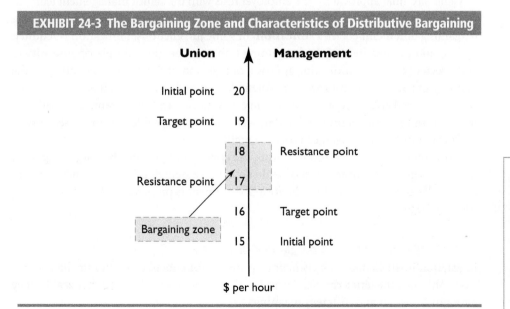

bargaining zone The area defined by the bargaining limits (resistance points) of each side, in which compromise is possible, as is the attainment of a settlement satisfactory to both parties.

distributive bargaining A win–lose negotiating strategy where one party gains at the expense of the other.

Integrative bargaining is an approach that assumes that a win–win solution can be found but also acknowledges that one or both sides can be losers if the bargaining is not handled effectively.[22] Integrative bargaining strategies require that both management and union negotiators adopt a genuine interest in the joint exploration of creative solutions to common problems.

Issues pertaining to work rules, job descriptions, and contract language can often be handled effectively by using an integrative approach; these are situations in which management negotiators are not intent on retaining management rights and both sides are committed to seeking a win–win solution. Wage rates and vacation entitlements are more likely to be fixed-sum issues that are handled by a distributive approach.

The objective of integrative bargaining is to establish a creative negotiating relationship that benefits labour and management. Becoming increasingly popular these days is a relatively new integrative approach known as **mutual gains (interest-based) bargaining**, which is another win–win approach to LR issues. All key union and management negotiators are trained in the fundamentals of effective problem solving and conflict resolution. Such training is often extended to other employees to ensure that the principles of mutual gains (interest-based) bargaining are incorporated into the organization's value system and that cooperation becomes a year-round corporate objective.[23]

Solutions must take the interests of each party into account. A joint sense of accountability is fostered and ongoing joint union–management initiatives can result from the negotiating process. In addition, the tools that are used at the bargaining table can be applied to the resolution of all workplace issues. Although mutual gains (interest-based) bargaining has been put into practice in about 40 percent of Canadian negotiations, experts warn that implementation is difficult, as it requires a grassroots culture change.[24]

Thus, the negotiating process is far more complex than it may appear to a casual observer. There are different types of bargaining strategies involved, and each side arrives at the bargaining table with political and organizational interests at stake.

The Contract Approval Process

As mentioned previously, collective agreements must be written documents. However, the parties do not normally execute a formal written document until after the bargaining process has been completed. Instead, the terms and conditions agreed to by the parties are usually reduced to a **memorandum of settlement** and submitted to the constituent groups for final approval.

Generally, final approval for the employer rests with the senior management team. In most cases, the union bargaining team submits the memorandum of settlement to the bargaining unit members for **ratification**. In some jurisdictions, ratification is required by law, and all members of the bargaining unit must be given ample opportunity to cast a secret-ballot vote indicating approval or rejection of the proposed contract. If the majority of bargaining unit members vote in favour of the proposal, it goes into effect. If the proposed collective agreement is rejected, union and management negotiators must return to the bargaining table and seek a more acceptable compromise. In such instances, third-party assistance is often sought.

Once approval has been received from the constituent groups, the bargaining team members sign the memorandum of settlement. Once signed, this memorandum serves as the collective agreement until the formal document is prepared and contract administration begins.

Third-Party Assistance and Bargaining Impasses

Legislation in all Canadian jurisdictions provides for conciliation and mediation services. Although the terms *conciliation* and *mediation* are often used interchangeably, they have quite distinct and different meanings.

integrative bargaining A negotiating strategy in which the possibility of win–win, lose–win, win–lose, and lose–lose outcomes is recognized, and there is acknowledgement that achieving a win–win outcome will depend on mutual trust and problem solving.

mutual gains (interest-based) bargaining A win–win negotiating approach based on training in the fundamentals of effective problem solving and conflict resolution, in which the interests of all stakeholders are taken into account.

memorandum of settlement A summary of the terms and conditions agreed to by the parties that is submitted to the constituent groups for final approval.

ratification Formal approval by secret-ballot vote of the bargaining unit members of the agreement negotiated between union and management.

Conciliation is the intervention of a neutral third party whose primary purpose is to bring the parties together and keep them talking so they can reach a mutually satisfactory collective agreement. The only means available to a conciliator to bring the parties to agreement is persuasion—he or she is not permitted to have any direct input into the negotiation process or to impose a settlement. Conciliation is typically requested after the parties have been negotiating for some time and are starting to reach a deadlock, or after talks have broken down. The aim of conciliation is to try to help the parties avoid the hardship of a strike or lockout.

In all jurisdictions except Saskatchewan, strikes and lockouts are prohibited until third-party assistance has been undertaken (Conciliation is required in all but two jurisdictions.) In most jurisdictions in which third-party assistance is mandatory, strikes/lockouts are prohibited until conciliation efforts have failed and a specified time period has elapsed.[25]

Mediation is the intervention of a neutral third party whose primary purpose is to help the parties fashion a mutually satisfactory agreement. Mediation is usually a voluntary process, typically occurring during the countdown period prior to a strike or lockout or during the strike or lockout itself. The mediator's role is an active one. It often involves meeting with each side separately and then bringing them together in an attempt to assist them in bridging the existing gaps. He or she is allowed to have direct input into the negotiation process but cannot impose a settlement.

When the union and management negotiating teams are unable to reach an agreement, and once the conciliation process has been undertaken (where required), the union may exercise its right to strike or request interest arbitration, and the employer may exercise its right to lock out the bargaining unit members. Alternatively, bargaining unit members may continue to work without a collective agreement once the old one has expired until talks resume and an agreement is reached.

Strikes A **strike** can be defined as a temporary refusal by bargaining unit members to continue working for the employer. When talks are reaching an impasse, unions will often hold a **strike vote**. Legally required in some jurisdictions, such a vote seeks authorization from bargaining unit members to strike if necessary. A favourable vote does not mean that a strike is inevitable. In fact, a highly favourable strike vote is often used as a bargaining ploy to gain concessions that will make a strike unnecessary. The results of a strike vote also help the union negotiating team members determine their relative bargaining strength. Unless strike action is supported by a substantial majority of bargaining unit members, union leaders are rarely prepared to risk a strike and must therefore be more willing to compromise, if necessary, to avoid a work stoppage.

Since a strike can have serious economic consequences for bargaining unit members, the union negotiating team must carefully analyze the prospects for its success. Striking union members receive no wages and often have no benefits coverage until they return to work, although they may draw some money from the union's strike fund. Work stoppages are also costly for employers, customers, and suppliers.

When a union goes on strike, bargaining unit members often **picket** the employer. To ensure as many picketers as possible, the union may make strike pay contingent on picket duty. Picketers stand at business entrances, carrying signs advertising the issues in dispute, and attempt to discourage people from entering or leaving the premises.

Another economic weapon available to unions is a **boycott**, which is a refusal to patronize the employer. A boycott occurs when a union asks its members, other union members, the employer's customers/clients, and supporters in the general public not to patronize the business involved in the labour dispute. Such action can harm the employer if the union is successful in gaining a large number of supporters. As with a strike, a boycott can have long-term consequences if former customers/clients develop a bias against the employer's products or services or make a change in buying habits or service provider that is not easily reversed.

Ontario Ministry of labour—Conciliation
www.labour.gov.on.ca/english/lr/faqs/lr_faq2.php

conciliation The often mandatory use of a neutral third party who has no direct input on the negotiation process to help an organization and the union representing a group of its employees communicate more effectively with the aim of coming to a mutually satisfactory collective agreement.

mediation The often voluntary use of a neutral third party who has direct input on the negotiation process to help an organization and the union representing its employees to reach a mutually satisfactory collective agreement.

strike The temporary refusal by bargaining unit members to continue working for the employer.

strike vote Legally required in some jurisdictions, it is a vote seeking authorization from bargaining unit members to strike if necessary. A favourable vote does not mean that a strike is inevitable.

picket Stationing groups of striking employees, usually carrying signs, at the entrances and exits of the struck operation to publicize the issues in dispute and discourage people from entering or leaving the premises.

boycott An organized refusal of bargaining unit members and supporters to buy the products or use the services of the organization whose employees are on strike in an effort to exert economic pressure on the employer.

Striking members of the Canadian Union of Public Employees, local 3903, picket at York University in Toronto.

An Ethical | Dilemma

Is it ethical for a firm to close the establishment during a labour dispute if that results in non-striking employees being laid off?

Public Service Grievance Board—
Arbitration
**www.psab.gov.on.ca/english/psgb/
Arbitration.htm**

lockout The temporary refusal of a company to continue providing work for bargaining unit employees involved in a labour dispute, which may result in closure of the establishment for a time.

wildcat strike A spontaneous walkout, not officially sanctioned by the union leadership, which may be legal or illegal, depending on its timing.

arbitration The use of an outside third party to investigate a dispute between an employer and union and impose a settlement.

interest arbitration The imposition of the final terms of a collective agreement.

interest dispute A dispute between an organization and the union representing its employees over the terms of a collective agreement.

The duration and ultimate success of a strike depends on the relative strength of the parties. Once a strike is settled, striking workers return to their jobs. During a labour dispute many people are put under remarkable pressure, and relationships essential to effective post-settlement work dynamics can be tarnished—especially in firms that rely heavily on teamwork. Post-settlement work environments are often riddled with tension, derogatory remarks, and hostility.

Lockout Although not a widely used strategy in Canada, a lockout is legally permissible. This involves the employer prohibiting the bargaining unit employees from entering the company premises as a means of putting pressure on the union to agree to the terms and conditions being offered by management. Sometimes the employer chooses to close operations entirely, which means that non-striking employees are also affected. Most employers try to avoid this option, since doing so means that the well-being of innocent parties is threatened, and a lockout may damage the firm's public image. Employees at forest products company Stora Enso in Port Hawkesbury, Nova Scotia, were locked out in 2006 after 20 months of bargaining when the union refused to accept a wage rollback of 10 percent, contracting out, and loss of seniority rights. An agreement was ratified five months later, just before the mill closure deadline set by the company.[26]

Unlawful Strikes and Lockouts An unlawful strike is one that contravenes the relevant LR legislation and lays the union and its members open to charges and possible fines or periods of imprisonment if found guilty. For example, it is illegal for a union to call a strike involving employees who do not have the right to strike because of the essential nature of their services, such as nurses or police officers. In all jurisdictions, it is illegal to call a strike during the term of an existing collective agreement.

A **wildcat strike** is a spontaneous walkout, not officially sanctioned by the union leaders, that is illegal if it occurs during the term of a collective agreement. For example, hotel workers at a Holiday Inn in Toronto, many of them new Canadians in low-end jobs, staged a wildcat walkout for about 45 minutes in November 2007 to protest lagging contract talks.[27]

Interest Arbitration Arbitration involves the use of an outside third party to investigate a dispute between an employer and union and impose a settlement. A sole arbitrator or three-person arbitration board may be involved. Arbitrators listen to evidence, weigh it impartially and objectively, and make a decision based on the law or the contract language. An arbitrator is not a judge, however. First, arbitration hearings tend to be much more informal than courtroom proceedings. Second, the arbitrator is not bound by precedents to the extent that a judge is usually held.[28] Third, both the law and court decisions have given the arbitration function considerable power and freedom. Arbitration decisions are final and binding and cannot be changed or revised.

Interest arbitration may be used to settle an **interest dispute** regarding the terms of a collective agreement by imposing the terms of the collective agreement. The right to interest arbitration is legally mandated for workers who are not permitted to strike, such as hospital and nursing home employees, police officers and firefighters in most jurisdictions, and some public servants.[29] Interest arbitration is also involved when special legislation is passed ordering striking or locked-out parties back to work because of public hardship.

The Collective Agreement: Typical Provisions

The eventual outcome of collective bargaining, whether negotiated by the parties or imposed by an arbitrator, is a formal, written collective agreement.

Union Recognition Clause A *union recognition clause* clarifies the scope of the bargaining unit by specifying the employee classifications included therein or listing those excluded.

Union Security/Checkoff Clause All Canadian jurisdictions permit the inclusion of a **union security clause** in the collective agreement to protect the interests of the labour union. This clause deals with the issue of membership requirements and, often, the payment of union dues. There are various forms of union security clauses:[30]

- A *closed shop* is the most restrictive form of union security. Only union members in good standing may be hired by the employer to perform bargaining unit work. This type of security clause is common in the construction industry.

- In a *union shop*, membership and dues payment are mandatory conditions of employment. Although individuals do not have to be union members at the time that they are hired, they are required to join the union on the day on which they commence work or on completion of probation.

- In a *modified union shop*, the individuals who were bargaining unit members at the time of certification or when the collective agreement was signed are not obliged to join the union, although they must pay dues, but all subsequently hired employees must do both.

- Under a *maintenance-of-membership arrangement*, individuals voluntarily joining the union must remain members during the term of the contract. Membership withdrawal is typically permitted during a designated period around the time of contract expiration. Dues payment is generally mandatory for all bargaining unit members.

An Ethical | Dilemma

Given the fact that some workers have religious or other objections to unions, is the Rand formula ethical?

- The *Rand formula* is the most popular union security arrangement. It does not require union membership, but it does require that all members of the bargaining unit pay union dues. It is a compromise arrangement that recognizes the fact that the union must represent all employees in the bargaining unit and should therefore be entitled to their financial support, but also provides the choice to join or not join the union.

- An *open shop* is a type of security arrangement whereby union membership is voluntary and non-members are not required to pay dues.

No-Strike-or-Lockout Provision There must be a clause in every contract in Canada forbidding strikes or lockouts while the collective agreement is in effect. The intent is to guarantee some degree of stability in the employment relationship during the life of the collective agreement, which must be at least one year. Saskatchewan and Quebec are the only jurisdictions that impose a maximum duration of three years.[31] In general, the duration of collective agreements in Canada is increasing.[32] Halifax police accepted a 12-year agreement in 2003.[33]

Management Rights Clause The management rights clause clarifies the areas in which management may exercise its exclusive rights without agreement from the union, and the issues that are not subject to collective bargaining. It typically refers to the rights of management to operate the organization, subject to the terms of the collective agreement. Any rights not limited by the clause are reserved to management.

Arbitration Clause All Canadian jurisdictions require that collective agreements contain a clause providing for the final and binding settlement, by arbitration, of all disputes

union security clause The contract provisions protecting the interests of the labour union, dealing with the issue of membership requirements and, often, the payment of union dues.

arising during the term of a collective agreement. Such disputes may relate to the application, interpretation, or administration of the agreement, as well as alleged contraventions by either party.

Step 5: Contract Administration

After a collective agreement has been negotiated and signed, the contract administration process begins. Both union and management are required to abide by the contract provisions. It is also in day-to-day contract administration that the bulk of labour–management relations occurs. Regardless of the amount of time and effort put into the wording of the contract, it is almost inevitable that differences of opinion will arise regarding the application and interpretation of the agreement. Seniority and discipline issues tend to be the major sources of disagreement between union and management.

Seniority

Unions typically prefer to have employee-related decisions determined by **seniority**, which refers to length of service in the bargaining unit. In many collective agreements, seniority is the governing factor in layoffs and recalls (the most senior employees are the last to be laid off and the first to be recalled) and a determining factor in transfers and promotions. In some collective agreements, seniority is also the determining factor in decisions pertaining to work assignments, shift preferences, allocation of days off, and vacation time.

Unions prefer the principle of seniority as an equitable and objective decision-making criterion, ensuring that there is no favouritism. Managers often prefer to place greater weight on ability or merit.

Discipline

Almost all collective agreements give the employer the right to make reasonable rules and regulations governing employees' behaviour and to take disciplinary action if the rules are broken. In every collective agreement, bargaining unit members are given the right to file a grievance if they feel that any disciplinary action taken was too harsh or without just cause.

Most collective agreements restrict an employer's right to discipline employees by requiring proof of just cause for the disciplinary action imposed. Since just cause is open to different interpretations, disciplinary action is a major source of grievances. Thus, disciplinary issues must be handled in accordance with the terms of the collective agreement and backed by carefully documented evidence. Even when disciplinary action is handled carefully, the union may argue that there were extenuating circumstances that should be taken into consideration. Supervisors have to strike a delicate balance between fairness and consistency.

When discipline cases end up at arbitration, two independent decisions are made. The first is whether the employee actually engaged in some form of misconduct. Then, if that question is answered in the affirmative, an assessment must be made of whether such misconduct warrants the particular discipline imposed, as well as whether such disciplinary action violated the collective agreement.

Grievance Resolution and Rights Arbitration

A **grievance** is a written allegation of a contract violation relating to a disagreement about its application or interpretation. When such alleged violations or disagreements arise, they are settled through the grievance procedure. A multistep grievance procedure, the last step of which is final and binding arbitration, is found in virtually all collective agreements. Such procedures have been very effective in resolving day-to-day problems arising during the life of the collective agreement.

seniority Length of service in the bargaining unit.

grievance A written allegation of a contract violation, filed by an individual bargaining unit member, the union, or management.

The primary purpose of the grievance procedure is to ensure the application of the contract with a degree of justice for both parties. Secondary purposes include providing the opportunity for the interpretation of contract language, such as the meaning of "sufficient ability"; serving as a communications device through which managers can become aware of employee concerns and areas of dissatisfaction; and bringing to the attention of both union and management those areas of the contract requiring clarification or modification in subsequent negotiations.

Steps in the Grievance Procedure The grievance procedure involves systematic deliberation of a complaint at progressively higher levels of authority in the company and union, and most provide for arbitration as a final step. Grievances are usually filed by individual bargaining unit members. If the issue in contention is one that may affect a number of union members, either at that time or in the future, the union may file a *policy grievance.* Management also has the right to use the grievance procedure to process a complaint about the union, although such use is rare. Although the number of steps and people involved at each grievance procedure vary, **Exhibit 24-4** illustrates a typical sequence.

As illustrated in Exhibit 24-4, the typical first step of the grievance procedure is the filing of a written complaint with the employee's immediate supervisor. If the problem is not resolved to the satisfaction of the employee at the first step, he or she may then take the problem to the next higher managerial level designated in the contract, and so on through all the steps available. Time limits are typically provided for resolution at each step. Failure to respond within the specified time limit may result in the grievance being automatically processed at the next step or being deemed to have been withdrawn or resolved. Ninety percent or more of all grievances are settled, abandoned, or withdrawn before arbitration.

Rights Arbitration Grievances relating to the interpretation or administration of the collective agreement are known as **rights disputes**. If these cannot be resolved internally, they must be referred to arbitration for a final and binding decision. The process involved in resolving such issues is known as **rights arbitration**.

A written arbitration award is issued at the conclusion of most rights arbitration cases, indicating that the grievance has been upheld or overturned. In disciplinary cases, it is also possible for an arbitration award to substitute a penalty that is more or less severe than the one proposed by union or management.

The Impact of Unionization on Hrm

Unionization results in a number of changes relating to HRM, all relating back to the requirements of the collective agreement. A union does have an impact on the way in which managers perform their HR responsibilities; when union leaders are treated as partners, they can provide a great deal of assistance with HR functions.

Once an organization is unionized, the HR department is typically expanded by the addition of an LR specialist or section. In a large firm with a number of bargaining units, human resources and labour relations may form two divisions within a broader department, often called industrial relations or labour relations.

In a unionized setting, management has less freedom to make unilateral decisions. This change may lead managers and supervisors to feel that they have lost some of their authority, which can cause resentment, especially since they inevitably find that unionization results in an increase in their responsibilities. Supervisors are often required to produce more written records than ever before, since documentation is critical at grievance and arbitration hearings.

All HR policies must be consistent with the terms of the collective agreement. Union representatives are often involved in the formulation of any policies that affect bargain-

rights dispute A disagreement between an organization and the union representing its employees regarding the interpretation or application of one or more clauses in the current collective agreement.

rights arbitration The process involved in the settlement of a rights dispute.

EXHIBIT 24-4 A Typical Grievance Procedure

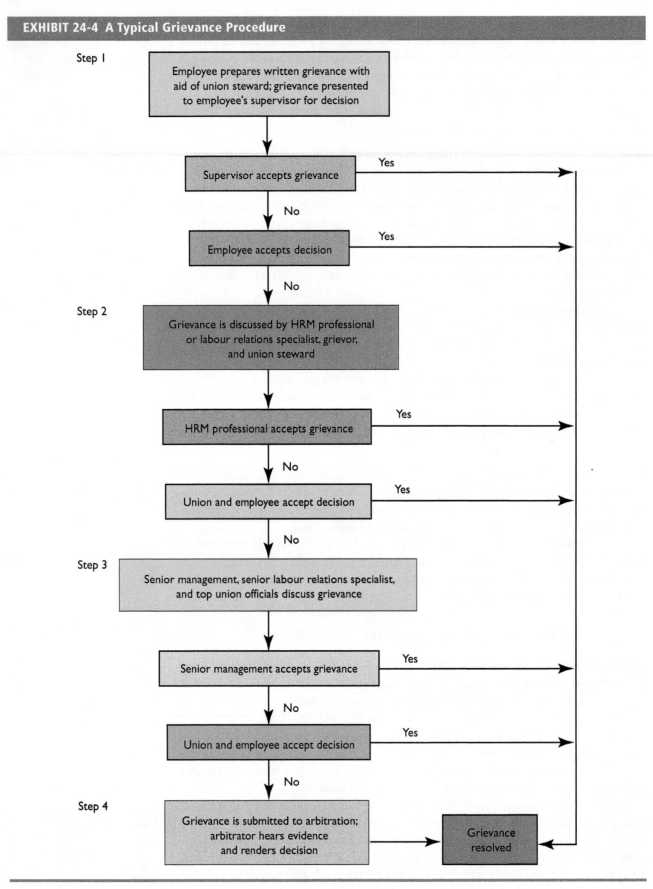

ing unit members—such as those pertaining to disciplinary rules and regulations—or are at least consulted as such policies are being drafted. Unionization also generally results in greater centralization of employee record keeping, which helps to ensure consistency and uniformity.

Building Effective Labour–Management Relations

One of the biggest challenges to HRM in unionized organizations is to build a cooperative and harmonious working relationship between management and union leaders. The result can be a win–win situation. There are a number of ways to promote cooperation between management and labour.

Instituting an Open-Door Policy

When the key managers involved in labour–management relations welcome employees into their offices to discuss any problems or concerns, and when employees feel comfortable in doing so, many issues can be resolved informally. For example, if the president of the local knows that he or she can approach the LR manager "off the record" and that anything discussed in such sessions will be kept strictly confidential, fewer grievances and more trusting and harmonious relationships often result.

Extending the Courtesy of Prior Consultation

Although not every management decision requires union approval, if any actions that might affect union members are discussed with the union executive first, the likelihood of grievances is greatly reduced.

Demonstrating Genuine Concern for Employee Well-Being

When managers are genuinely concerned about employee well-being and demonstrate that concern, mutual trust and respect are often established. This involves fair treatment and communication going well above and beyond the requirements of the collective agreement.

Forming Joint Committees and Holding Joint Training Programs

Forming labour–management committees to investigate and resolve complex issues can lead to innovative and creative solutions, as well as to a better relationship. When a contract is first signed, it can be beneficial to hold a joint training program to ensure that supervisors and union stewards are familiar with the terms and conditions specified therein and that they understand the intent of the negotiating teams. Such training can reduce misunderstandings and the likelihood of disagreement regarding interpretation of contract language.

Meeting Regularly

Whether required by the collective agreement or voluntarily instituted, regularly scheduled union–management meetings can result in more effective communication and the resolution of problems/concerns before they become formal grievance issues.

Using Third-Party Assistance

To build a better relationship, it is often beneficial to bring in a consultant or a government agency representative to help identify common goals and objectives and ways in which trust and communication can be strengthened.

25

Power and Politics

Arch and Anne Jollymore are not happy with Tim Hortons' senior management.[1] The couple, who own several Tim Hortons franchises, brought a class action lawsuit against the company that was heard in August 2011. They argued that the company's management forced changes in the production of donuts and other baked goods that enriched management and shareholders at the expense of the franchise owners.

One of the key complaints is the move to using "flash frozen" baked goods in the coffee shops in 2002. Before then, each Tim Hortons store had its own baker, who made all the baked goods from scratch, and baked them on the premises. The move has made donut production more expensive.

The franchise owners who signed on to the lawsuit complain bitterly about what they see as the company's abuse of power. An email sent to Roland Walton, head of Tim Hortons' Canadian operations, shortly after the lawsuit was launched, explained the power differential between management and franchisees: "[T]he feeling is that [the company's] attitude is 'We're still the best game in town, if you don't like it or aren't happy, there is a waiting list to get stores.'"

A major theme throughout this chapter is that power and politics are a natural process in any group or organization. Although you might have heard the saying "Power corrupts, and absolute power corrupts absolutely," power is not always bad.

Understanding how to use power and politics effectively makes organizational life more manageable, because it can help you gain the support you need to do your job effectively.

A Definition of Power

  What is power?

Power refers to a capacity that A has to influence the behaviour of B, so that B acts in accordance with A's wishes.[2] This definition implies that there is a *potential* for power if someone is dependent on another. But one can have power and not impose it.

Probably the most important aspect of power is that it is a function of **dependency**. The more that B depends on A, the more power A has in the relationship. Dependence, in turn, is based on the alternatives that B perceives and the importance that B places on the alternative(s) that A controls. A person can have power over you only if he or she controls something you desire. If you are attending college or university on funds totally provided by your parents, you probably recognize the power that your parents hold over you. You are dependent on them for financial support. But once you are out of school, have a job, and are making a good income, your parents' power is reduced significantly. Who among us, though, has not known or heard of the rich relative who is able to control a large number of family members merely through the implicit or explicit threat of "writing them out of the will"?

Within larger organizations, the information technology (IT) group often has considerable power, because everyone, right up to the CEO, is dependent on this group to keep computers and networks running. Since few people have the technical expertise to do so, IT personnel end up being viewed as irreplaceable. This gives them a lot of power within the organization.

Power makes people uncomfortable.[3] People who have power deny it, people who want it try not to look like they are seeking it, and those who are good at getting it are secretive about how they do so.[4] Commenting on a recent study, one researcher noted, "A person's sense of power is an extremely pervasive feeling in everyday life."[5]

Part of the discomfort about power may have to do with how people perceive those in power. A 2011 study found that people who behave rudely—putting their feet up on a chair, ordering a meal brusquely—were believed by those watching this behaviour to be more likely to "get to make decisions" and able to "get people to listen to what [they] say" than people who behave politely. The researchers concluded that "norm violators are perceived as having the capacity to act as they please."[6] As a result, they seem more powerful. A 2010 study found that people who have power judged others much more negatively for speeding, dodging taxes, and keeping a stolen bike than if they engaged in this behaviour themselves. The researchers found that those who had legitimate power were even more likely to indulge in moral hypocrisy than those who did not feel personally entitled to their power.[7]

Power should not be considered a bad thing, however. "Power, if used appropriately, should actually be a positive influence in your organization," says Professor Patricia Bradshaw of the Schulich School of Business at York University. "Having more power doesn't necessarily turn you into a Machiavellian monster. It can help your team and your organization achieve its goals and increase its potential."[8]

A major theme of this chapter is that power and political behaviour are natural processes in any group or organization. By learning how power works in organizations, you will be better able to use your knowledge to become a more effective manager.

power A capacity that A has to influence the behaviour of B, so that B acts in accordance with A's wishes.

dependency B's relationship to A when A possesses something that B requires.

Bases of Power

  How does one get power?

Where does power come from? What is it that gives an individual or a group influence over others? The answer to these questions was developed by social scientists John French and Bertrand Raven, who first presented a five-category classification scheme of sources or bases of power: coercive, reward, legitimate, expert, and referent.[9] They subsequently added one new dimension, information power, to that schema (see Exhibit 25-1).[10]

EXHIBIT 25-1 Measuring Bases of Power	

Does a person have one or more of the six bases of power? These descriptions help identify the person's power base.

Power Base	Statement
Coercive	The person can make things difficult for people, and you want to avoid getting him or her angry.
Reward	The person is able to give special benefits or rewards to people, and you find it advantageous to trade favours with him or her.
Legitimate	The person has the right, considering his or her position and your job responsibilities, to expect you to comply with legitimate requests.
Expert	The person has the experience and knowledge to earn your respect, and you defer to his or her judgment in some matters.
Referent	You like the person and enjoy doing things for him or her.
Information	The person has data or knowledge that you need.

Source: Adapted from G. Yukl and C. M. Falbe, "Importance of Different Power Sources in Downward and Lateral Relations," *Journal of Applied Psychology*, June 1991, p. 417.

Coercive Power

Coercive power is defined by French and Raven as dependent on fear of the negative results that might occur if one fails to comply. It rests on the application, or the threat of the application, of physical sanctions such as the infliction of pain, the generation of frustration through restriction of movement, or the controlling by force of basic physiological or safety needs.

At the organizational level, A has coercive power over B if A can dismiss, suspend, or demote B, assuming that B values his or her job. Similarly, if A can assign B work activities that B finds unpleasant or treat B in a manner that B finds embarrassing, A possesses coercive power over B.

Reward Power

The opposite of coercive power is **reward power**. People will go along with the wishes or directives of another if doing so produces positive benefits; therefore, someone who can distribute rewards that others view as valuable will have power over those others. These rewards can be either financial—such as controlling pay rates, raises, and bonuses—or nonfinancial, including offering recognition, promotions, interesting work assignments, friendly colleagues, and preferred work shifts or sales territories.[11]

Legitimate Power

In formal groups and organizations, probably the most frequent access to one or more of the bases of power is through a person's structural position. This is called **legitimate power**. It represents the power a person receives as a result of his or her position in the formal hierarchy of an organization.

Legitimate power is broader than the power to coerce and reward. Specifically, it includes acceptance by members of an

coercive power Power that is based on fear.

reward power Power that achieves compliance based on the ability to distribute rewards that others view as valuable.

legitimate power Power that a person receives as a result of his or her position in the formal hierarchy of an organization.

In India, Naina Lal Kidwai is a powerful woman in the banking industry. She derives her power as managing director and vice chairman of HSBC Securities and Capital Markets, a group within the Hongkong and Shanghai Banking Corporation. Kidwai's formal power is based on her position at the bank.

"I was just going to say 'Well, I don't make the rules.' But, of course, I do make the rules."

Source: © Leo Cullum/ The New Yorker Collection/ www.cartoonbank.com

organization of the authority of a position. We associate power so closely with the concept of hierarchy that just drawing longer lines in an organization chart leads people to infer that the leaders are especially powerful, and when a powerful executive is described, people tend to put the person at a higher position when drawing an organization chart.[12] When school principals, bank presidents, or generals speak (assuming that their directives are viewed to be within the authority of their positions), teachers, tellers, and privates listen and usually comply. You will note in Exhibit 25-2 that one of the men in the meeting identifies himself as the rule maker, which means that he has legitimate power.

Expert Power

Expert power is influence based on expertise, special skills, or knowledge. Expertise has become one of the most powerful sources of influence as the world has become more technologically oriented. While it is generally acknowledged that physicians have expertise and hence expert power—most of us follow the advice that our doctor gives us—you should also recognize that computer specialists, tax accountants, economists, and other specialists can have power as a result of their expertise. Young people may find they have increased power in the workplace these days because of their technical knowledge and expertise that Baby Boomer managers may not have.

Referent Power

Referent power develops out of admiration of another and a desire to be like that person. Sometimes teachers and coaches have referent power because of our admiration of them. Referent power explains why celebrities are paid millions of dollars to endorse products in commercials. Mississauga, Ontario-based Alexis Life Sciences uses endorsements from Don Cherry of *Hockey Night in Canada* and popular athletes such

expert power Influence based on special skills or knowledge.

referent power Influence based on possession by an individual of desirable resources or personal traits.

as Alexandre Bilodeau, Clara Hughes, and Joannie Rochette to convince people to buy COLD-FX, its cold and flu product. Similarly, Nike Canada uses sports celebrities, such as Montreal Canadiens defenceman P. K. Subban, to promote its products.

Information Power

Information power comes from access to and control over information. People in an organization who have data or knowledge that others need can make those others dependent on them. Managers, for instance, because of their access to privileged sales, cost, salary, profit, and similar data, can use this information to control and shape subordinates' behaviour. Similarly, departments that possess information that is critical to a company's performance in times of high uncertainty—for example, the legal department when a firm faces a major lawsuit or the human resource department during critical labour negotiations—will gain increased power in their organization until those uncertainties are resolved. Withholding information can result in poor-quality performance by those who need the information.[13]

Evaluating the Bases of Power

Generally, people will respond in one of three ways when faced with those who use the bases of power described above:

- *Commitment.* The person is enthusiastic about the request, and shows initiative and persistence in carrying it out.

- *Compliance.* The person goes along with the request grudgingly, puts in minimal effort, and takes little initiative in carrying out the request.

- *Resistance.* The person is opposed to the request and tries to avoid it with such tactics as refusing, stalling, or arguing about it.[14]

A review of the research on the effectiveness of these forms of power finds that they differ in their impact on a person's performance.[15] Exhibit 25-3 summarizes some of this research. Coercive power leads to resistance from individuals, decreased satisfaction, and increased mistrust. Reward power results in compliance if the rewards are consistent with what individuals want as rewards. Legitimate power also results in compliance, but it does not generally result in increased commitment. In other words,

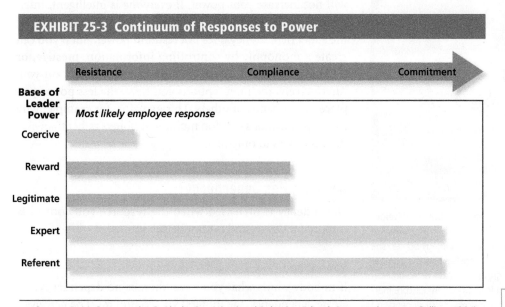

EXHIBIT 25-3 Continuum of Responses to Power

Resistance   Compliance   Commitment

Bases of Leader Power

Most likely employee response

Coercive

Reward

Legitimate

Expert

Referent

Source: R. M. Steers and J. S. Black, *Organizational Behavior*, 5th ed. (New York: HarperCollins, 1994), p. 487. Reprinted by permission of Pearson Education Inc., Upper Saddle River, New Jersey.

information power Power that comes from access to and control over information.

legitimate power does not inspire individuals to act beyond the basic level. Expert and referent powers are the most likely to lead to commitment from individuals. Ironically, the least effective bases of power for improving commitment—coercive, reward, and legitimate—are the ones most often used by managers, perhaps because they are the easiest to introduce.[16] Research shows that deadline pressure increases group members' reliance on individuals with expert and information power.[17]

Dependency: The Key to Power

3 How does dependency affect power?

Franchisees are at the heart of Tim Hortons' business model.[18] To acquire a store, an owner pays a start-up fee of nearly a half-million dollars. Owners buy all of their supplies from the company (which ensures that products taste the same throughout the country). They also pay a percentage of yearly sales to cover "rent, royalties and advertising." Franchisees have very limited autonomy in running their franchise. For example, when the company introduced its "Always Fresh" baking system, franchisees had no choice but to buy the pre-baked products sold by Maidstone Bakeries in Brantford, Ontario. The purchased donuts cost more than the donuts baked in-store. There was no other supplier, and thus no real way to force the company to lower its charges for supplies. What factors might lead one entity (a person or an organization) to have greater power over another?

In this section, we show how an understanding of dependency is central to furthering your understanding of power itself.

The General Dependency Postulate

Let's begin with a general postulate: *The greater B's dependency on A, the greater the power A has over B*. When you possess anything that others require but that you alone control, you make them dependent upon you and, therefore, you gain power over them.[19] Another way to frame dependency is to think about a relationship in terms of "who needs whom?" The person who has most need is the one most dependent on the relationship.[20]

Dependency is inversely proportional to the alternative sources of supply. If something is plentiful, possession of it will not increase your power. If everyone is intelligent, intelligence gives no special advantage. Similarly, in the circles of the super rich, money does not result in power. But if you can create a monopoly by controlling information, prestige, or anything that others crave, they become dependent on you. Alternatively, the more options you have, the less power you place in the hands of others. This explains, for example, why most organizations develop multiple suppliers rather than give their business to only one.

What Creates Dependency?

Dependency is increased when the resource you control is important, scarce, and cannot be substituted.[21]

Importance

If nobody wants what you have, there is no dependency. To create dependency, the thing(s) you control must be perceived as important. In some organizations, people who control the

Because Xerox Corporation has staked its future on development and innovation, Sophie Vanderbroek is in a position of power at Xerox. As the company's chief technology officer, she manages Xerox's 4000 scientists and engineers at the company's global research centres. The group's mission is "to pioneer high-impact technologies that enable us to lead in our core markets and to create future markets for Xerox." Xerox depends on Vanderbroek to make that mission a reality.

budget have a great deal of importance. In other organizations, those who possess the knowledge to keep technology working smoothly are viewed as important. What is important is situational. It varies among organizations and undoubtedly also varies over time within any given organization.

Have you ever wondered how you might increase your power?

Scarcity

As noted previously, if something is plentiful, possession of it will not increase your power. A resource must be perceived as scarce to create dependency.

Scarcity can help explain how low-ranking employees gain power if they have important knowledge not available to high-ranking employees. Possession of a scarce resource—in this case, important knowledge—makes those who don't have it dependent on those who do. Thus, an individual might refuse to show others how to do a job or might refuse to share information, thereby increasing his or her importance.

The scarcity-dependency relationship can further be seen in the power of occupational categories. For example, college and university administrators have no problem finding English instructors to staff classes. There are more individuals who have degrees enabling them to work as English instructors than there are positions available in Canada. The market for corporate finance professors, by contrast, is extremely tight, with the demand high and the supply limited. The result is that the bargaining power of finance faculty allows them to negotiate higher salaries, lighter teaching loads, and other benefits.

Nonsubstitutability

The fewer substitutes there are for a resource, the more power comes from control over that resource. During his tenure as CEO, the common belief at Apple Computer, for example, was that Steve Jobs was not replaceable. His passing in October 2011 means that Apple now has to contend with replacing the company's charismatic figurehead. The unanswered question at the time of his death was whether Apple could continue to be innovative and edgy without Jobs at the helm. In another example, when a union goes on strike and management is not permitted to replace the striking employees, the union has considerable control over the organization's ability to carry out its tasks.

People are often able to ask for special rewards (higher pay or better assignments) because they have skills that others do not.

Influence Tactics

Tim Hortons' management used a number of influence tactics to persuade its franchisees to adopt the "Always Fresh" baking system in their stores.[22] Management started with a taste test at the 2000 annual convention, an inspirational appeal that convinced some of the franchisees that the taste was much better. Management then used rational persuasion to convince owners that the increased cost was worth the gain in convenience. Under the in-house baking system, franchise owners were paying about 5 to 9 cents to make one donut. According to some franchisees, they were told that the new process would result in donuts that cost about 11.5 cents to produce. "We all knew that that was more than we were paying to bake in-house, but we all felt the same," Ottawa franchisee Greg Gilson said. "The convenience of it would be worth the offset of the three to four cents." Thus, management further influenced the decisions of the franchisees by emphasizing convenience. However, when the final cost turned out to be about 18 cents per donut, head office used its legitimate power to require the owners to buy the "flash frozen" donuts from Maidstone Bakeries. So how and why do influence tactics work?

4 What tactics can be used to increase power?

How do individuals translate their bases of power into specific, desired actions? Research indicates that people use common tactics to influence outcomes.[23] One study identified the nine influence tactics managers and employees use to increase their power:[24]

1. *Rational persuasion.* Using facts and data to make a logical or rational presentation of ideas.

2. *Inspirational appeals.* Appealing to values, ideals, and goals when making a request.

3. *Consultation.* Getting others involved to support one's objectives.

4. *Ingratiation.* Using flattery, creating goodwill, and being friendly prior to making a request.

5. *Personal appeals.* Appealing to loyalty and friendship when asking for something.

6. *Exchange.* Offering favours or benefits in exchange for support.

7. *Coalitions.* Getting the support of other people to provide backing when making a request.

8. *Pressure.* Using demands, threats, and reminders to get someone to do something.

9. *Legitimacy.* Claiming the authority or right to make a request, or showing that it supports organizational goals or policies.

Some tactics are more effective than others. Rational persuasion, inspirational appeals, and consultation tend to be the most effective, especially when the audience is highly interested in the outcomes of a decision process. Pressure tends to frequently backfire and is typically the least effective of the nine tactics.[25] You can also increase your chance of success by using more than one type of tactic at the same time or sequentially, as long as your choices are compatible.[26] For instance, using both ingratiation and legitimacy can lessen the negative reactions that might come from appearing to "dictate" outcomes, but only when the audience does not really care about the outcomes of a decision process or the policy is routine.[27]

The effectiveness of some influence tactics depends on the direction of influence.[28] Studies have found that rational persuasion is the only tactic that is effective across organizational levels. Inspirational appeals work best as a downward-influencing tactic with subordinates. When pressure works, it's generally only to achieve downward influence. The use of personal appeals and coalitions is most effective with lateral influence attempts. In addition to the direction of influence, a number of other factors have been found to affect which tactics work best. These include the sequencing of tactics, a person's skill in using the tactic, and the culture of the organization.

You are more likely to be effective if you begin with "softer" tactics that rely on personal power such as personal and inspirational appeals, rational persuasion, and consultation. If these fail, you can move to "harder" tactics (which emphasize formal power and involve greater costs and risks), such as exchange, coalitions, and pressure.[29] Interestingly, it has been found that using a single soft tactic is more effective than using a single hard tactic, and that combining two soft tactics or a soft tactic and rational persuasion is more effective than any single tactic or a combination of hard tactics.[30] The effectiveness of tactics depends on the audience.[31] People especially likely to comply with soft power tactics tend to be more reflective, are intrinsically motivated, have high self-esteem, and have greater desire for control. People especially likely to comply with hard power tactics are more action oriented and extrinsically motivated and are more focused on getting along with others than with getting their own way.

People differ in their **political skill**, or the ability to influence others in such a way as to enhance their own objectives. Those who are politically skilled are more effective in their use of influence tactics, regardless of the tactics they are using. Political skill also appears to be more effective when the stakes are high—such as when the individual is accountable for important organizational outcomes. Finally, the politically skilled are able to exert their influence without others detecting it, which is a key element in being effective (it's damaging to be labelled political).[32]

Finally, we know that cultures within organizations differ markedly—for example, some are warm, relaxed, and supportive; others are formal and conservative. The organizational culture in which a person works, therefore, will have a bearing on defining which tactics are considered appropriate. Some cultures encourage the use of participation and consultation, some encourage reason, and still others rely on pressure. People who fit the culture of the organization tend to obtain more influence.[33] Specifically, extraverts tend to be more influential in team-oriented organizations, and highly conscientious people are more influential in organizations that value working alone on technical tasks. Part of the reason people who fit the culture are influential is that they are able to perform especially well in the domains deemed most important for success. In other words, they are influential because they are competent. So the organization itself will influence which subset of influence tactics is viewed as acceptable for use. The kinds of tactics used have also changed over time.

Empowerment: Giving Power to Employees

Thus far, our discussion has implied—to some extent, at least—that power is something that is more likely to reside in the hands of managers, to be used as part of their interaction with employees. However, in today's workplace, there is a movement toward sharing more power with employees by putting them in teams and also by making them

5 What does it mean to be empowered?

WestJet has an empowerment culture. As Sean Durfy, WestJet's former president and CEO, notes: "If you empower people to do the right things, then they will. If you align the interests of the people with the interests of the company, it's very powerful. That's what we do." WestJet's empowerment culture is admired by others as well. In 2011, the company was named one of "Canada's Most Admired Corporate Cultures for Western Canada" by Waterstone Human Capital. Two years earlier, WestJet was named to Waterstone Human Capital's Inaugural Hall of Fame after having placed on its "Canada's 10 Most Admired Corporate Cultures" list four times in a row, including three times in a row at number one.

political skill The ability to influence others in such a way as to enhance one's objectives.

responsible for some of the decisions regarding their jobs. For instance, at Vancouver-based iQmetrix Software Development, employees are part of a results-only workplace, where they are encouraged to make their own decisions.[34] Organizational specialists refer to this increasing responsibility as *empowerment*.

Definition of Empowerment

The definition of *empowerment* that we use here refers to the freedom and the ability of employees to make decisions and commitments.[35] Unfortunately, neither managers nor researchers agree on the definition of empowerment. One study found that executives were split about 50-50 in their definition.[36] One group of executives "believed that empowerment was about delegating decision making within a set of clear boundaries." Empowerment would start at the top, specific goals and tasks would be assigned, responsibility would be delegated, and people would be held accountable for their results. The other group believed that empowerment was "a process of risk-taking and personal growth." This type of empowerment starts at the bottom, with considering the employees' needs, showing them what empowered behaviour looks like, building teams, encouraging risk-taking, and demonstrating trust in employees' ability to perform.

One difficulty with empowerment is that managers often give lip service to the idea,[37] with organizations telling employees that they have decision-making responsibility, but not giving them the authority to carry out their decisions. This leads to a great deal of cynicism in many workplaces, particularly when "empowered" employees are micromanaged. For an employee to be fully empowered, he or she needs access to the information required to make decisions; rewards for acting in appropriate, responsible ways; and the authority to make the necessary decisions. Empowerment means that employees understand how their job fits into the organization and are able to make decisions regarding job action guided by the organization's purpose and mission.

Not every employee appreciates being empowered, however. One study found that sometimes empowerment can make employees ill if they are put in charge at work but lack the confidence to handle their responsibilities.[38]

At Vancouver-based Great Little Box Company (GLBC), which designs and manufactures corrugated containers, employees are given the freedom to do whatever they feel is necessary and appropriate to make customers happy. If a customer is dissatisfied with the product, the employee can say, "OK, I'll bring this product back and return it for you," without having to get prior authorization.

EXHIBIT 25-4 Characteristics of Empowered People

Robert E. Quinn and Gretchen M. Spreitzer, in their research on the characteristics of empowered people (through both in-depth interviews and survey analysis), found four characteristics that most empowered people have in common:

- Empowered people have a sense of *self-determination* (this means that they are free to choose how to do their work; they are not micromanaged).
- Empowered people have a sense of *meaning* (they feel that their work is important to them; they care about what they are doing).
- Empowered people have a sense of *competence* (this means that they are confident about their ability to do their work well; they know they can perform).
- Empowered people have a sense of *impact* (this means that people believe they can have influence on their work unit; others listen to their ideas).

Source: Reprinted from R. E. Quinn and G. M. Spreitzer, "The Road to Empowerment: Seven Questions Every Leader Should Consider," *Organizational Dynamics*, Autumn 1997, p. 41, with permission from Elsevier.

When employees are empowered, it means that they are expected to act, at least in a small way, as owners of the company, rather than just employees. Ownership is not necessary in the financial sense, but in terms of identifying with the goals and mission of the organization. For employees to be empowered, however, and have an ownership mentality, four conditions need to be met, according to Professor Dan Ondrack at the Rotman School of Management at the University of Toronto:[39]

What do you need to be truly empowered?

- There must be a clear definition of the values and mission of the company.
- The company must help employees acquire the relevant skills.
- Employees need to be supported in their decision making, and not criticized when they try to do something extraordinary.
- Employees need to be recognized for their efforts.

Exhibit 25-4 outlines what two researchers discovered in studying the characteristics of empowered people.

The Abuse of Power

Studies indicate that when someone is in a position of power, he or she may be more willing to exert that power.[40]

6 How are power and harassment related?

Below we examine ways in which power can be unacceptably exhibited at work.

Harassment in the Workplace

People who engage in harassment in the workplace are typically abusing their power position. The manager-employee relationship best characterizes an unequal power relationship, where position power gives the manager the capacity to reward and coerce. Managers give employees their assignments, evaluate their performance, make recommendations for salary adjustments and promotions, and even decide whether employees retain their job. These decisions give a manager power. Since employees want favourable performance reviews, salary increases, and the like, it's clear that managers control the resources that most employees consider important and scarce.

Although co-workers do not have position power, they can have influence and use it to harass peers. In fact, although co-workers appear to engage in somewhat less severe forms of harassment than do managers, co-workers are the most frequent perpetrators of harassment, particularly sexual harassment, in organizations. How do co-workers exercise power? Most often they provide or withhold information, cooperation, and support.

Some categories of harassment have long been illegal in Canada, including those based on race, religion, and national origin, as well as sexual harassment. Unfortunately, some types of harassment that occur in the workplace are not deemed illegal, even if they create problems for employees and managers. We focus here on two types of harassment that have received considerable attention in the press: workplace bullying and sexual harassment.

Workplace Bullying

Many of us are aware, anecdotally if not personally, of managers who harass employees, demanding overtime without pay or excessive work performance. Further, some of the recent stories of workplace violence have reportedly been the result of an employee feeling intimidated at work. In research conducted in the private and public sector in southern Saskatchewan, Céleste Brotheridge, a professor at the Université du Québec à Montréal, found that bullying was rather prevalent in the workplace. Forty percent of the respondents noted that they had experienced one or more forms of bullying weekly in the past six months. Ten percent experienced bullying at a much greater level: five or more incidents a week. Brotheridge notes that bullying has a negative effect on the workplace: "Given bullying's deleterious effects on employee health, it is reason for concern."[41]

There is no clear definition of workplace bullying, and Marilyn Noble, a Fredericton-based adult educator, remarks that in some instances there can be a fine line between managing and bullying. However, recent research suggests that bosses who feel inadequate or overwhelmed are more likely to bully.[42] As one of the study's co-authors explained: "The combination of having a high-power role and fearing that one is not up to the task . . . causes power holders to lash out."[43]

The effects of bullying can be devastating. Professors Sandy Hershcovis of the University of Manitoba and Julian Barling of Queen's University found that the consequences of bullying were more harmful to its victims than those who suffered sexual harassment. Bullied employees more often quit their jobs, were less satisfied with their jobs, and had more difficult relationships with their supervisors.[44]

Quebec introduced the first anti-bullying labour legislation in North America on June 1, 2004. The legislation defines psychological harassment as "any vexatious behaviour in the form of repeated and hostile or unwanted conduct, verbal comments, actions or gestures that affect an employee's dignity or psychological or physical integrity and that results in a harmful work environment for the employee."[45] Under the Quebec law, bullying allegations will be sent to mediation, where the accuser and the accused will work with an independent third party to try to resolve the problem. If mediation fails, employers who have allowed psychological harassment can be fined up to $10 000 and ordered to pay financial damages to the victim.

Sexual Harassment

Sexual harassment is wrong. It can also be costly to employers. Just ask executives at Walmart, the World Bank, and the United Nations.[46] The Supreme Court of Canada defines **sexual harassment** as unwelcome behaviour of a sexual nature in the workplace that negatively affects the work environment or leads to adverse job-related consequences for the employee.[47] Despite the legal framework for defining sexual harassment, there continues to be disagreement as to what *specifically* constitutes sexual

sexual harassment Unwelcome behaviour of a sexual nature in the workplace that negatively affects the work environment or leads to adverse job-related consequences for the employee.

harassment. Sexual harassment includes unwanted physical touching, recurring requests for dates when it is made clear the person is not interested, and coercive threats that a person will lose her or his job if she or he refuses a sexual proposition. The problems of interpreting sexual harassment often surface around some of its more subtle forms— unwanted looks or comments, off-colour jokes, sexual artifacts such as nude calendars in the workplace, sexual innuendo, or misinterpretations of where the line between "being friendly" ends and "harassment" begins. Most studies confirm that the concept of power is central to understanding sexual harassment.[48] It's about an individual controlling or threatening another individual. This seems to be true whether the harassment comes from a manager, a co-worker, or an employee.

Because of power inequities, sexual harassment by a manager typically creates great difficulty for an employee being harassed. If there are no witnesses, it's the manager's word against the employee's word. Are there others whom this manager has harassed, and if so, will they come forward? Because of the manager's control over resources, many of those who are harassed are afraid of speaking out for fear of retaliation by the manager.

Workplaces are not the only place where sexual harassment occurs. While nonconsensual sex between professors and students is rape and subject to criminal charges, it's harder to evaluate apparently consensual relationships that occur outside the classroom. There is some argument over whether truly consensual sex is ever possible between students and professors. In an effort to underscore the power discrepancy and potential for abuse of it by professors, in 2009 Yale University implemented a policy forbidding romantic relationships between professors and undergraduate students.[49] Deputy Provost Charles Long explained the university's decision: "I think we have a responsibility to protect students from behavior that is damaging to them and to the objectives for their being here." Most universities have been unwilling to adopt such an extreme stance, and it's not clear that in Canada such a policy would stand up in the courts. Carleton University does not prohibit relationships between individuals in authority and those who are not, but does include the following statement in its sexual harassment policy: "No individual in a position of authority is permitted to grade or supervise the performance of any student, or evaluate an employee or a colleague, with whom they are sexually involved or have been within the past five years."[50]

One recent study found that nearly two-thirds of university students experience some type of sexual harassment, but most of these incidents go unreported.[51] However, much of this harassment comes from student-on-student incidents. Matt Abbott, a student at the University of New Brunswick, says that "certain aspects of sexual violence are almost normal within the dating culture in campus communities." A University of British Columbia student, Anoushka Ratnarajah, notes that "'the line' with respect to sexual harassment and the issue of consent are still fuzzy for many students."[52]

A recent review of the literature shows the damage caused by sexual harassment. As you would expect, individuals who are sexually harassed report more negative job attitudes (such as lower job satisfaction, diminished organizational commitment) as a result. This review also revealed that sexual harassment undermines the victims' mental and physical health. However, sexual harassment also negatively affects the group in which the victim works, lowering its level of productivity. The authors of this study conclude that sexual harassment "is significantly and substantively associated with a host of harms."[53]

We have seen how sexual harassment can wreak havoc on an organization, not to mention on the victims themselves. But it can be avoided. A manager's role in preventing sexual harassment is critical. Some ways managers can protect themselves and their employees from sexual harassment are as follows:

- Make sure an active policy defines what constitutes sexual harassment, informs employees that they can be fired for sexually harassing another employee, and establishes procedures for how complaints can be made.

- Assure employees that they will not encounter retaliation if they issue a complaint.

- Investigate every complaint and include the legal and human resource departments.

- Make sure that offenders are disciplined or terminated.

- Set up in-house seminars to raise employee awareness about the issues surrounding sexual harassment.

Politics: Power in Action

7 Why do people engage in politics?

Archibald Jollymore was a senior executive at Tim Hortons before he retired and became the owner of a franchise in Burlington, Ontario.[54] His cousin is Ron Joyce, co-founder of Tim Hortons. Joyce sold the company to Wendy's in 1995 and regrets doing so. There is speculation that Joyce is the financial backer behind the lawsuit, although neither Joyce nor Jollymore confirms this. Joyce does not like the direction the company has taken under his successor, Paul D. House, and is vocal in his complaints about the executive team. With respect to the "Always Fresh" donuts, Joyce said publicly, "This is not a philosophy that I would have embraced if I still owned the company." Thus, politics, rather than money, may be part of the reason behind the lawsuit.

The lawsuit has also pitted franchise operators against one another. Some claim that they lost money with the "Always Fresh" baking system, while others suggest that it was "a welcome transition." Some franchisees even launched a website to encourage others to stand up against the lawsuit. "How comfortable are you sharing your profitability with the media?" the website asks. "Do we want the press reporting about the Tim Hortons' brand in a negative way?" In other words, the franchise owners are forming coalitions to either foster or hinder the lawsuit, depending on their perspective on the matter. Why is politics so prevalent in organizations? Is it merely a fact of life?

When people get together in groups, power will be exerted. People want to carve out a niche from which to exert influence, to earn awards, and to advance their careers.[55] When employees in organizations convert their power into action, we describe them as being engaged in politics. Those with good political skills have the ability to use their bases of power effectively.[56] In this section, we look at political behaviour, the types of political activity people use to try to influence others, and impression management. Political skills are not confined to adults, of course. Even young children are quite adept at waging careful, deliberate campaigns to wear their parents down, so that they can get things that they want.

Definition of Political Behaviour

There has been no shortage of definitions for organizational politics. One clever definition of politics comes from Tom Jakobek, Toronto's former budget chief, who said, "In politics, you may have to go from A to C to D to E to F to G and then to B."[57]

For our purposes, we will define **political behaviour** in organizations as those activities that are outside one's formal role, and that influence, or attempt to influence, the distribution of advantages and disadvantages within the organization.[58]

This definition encompasses key elements from what most people mean when they talk about organizational politics. Political behaviour is outside one's specified job requirements. The behaviour requires some attempt to use one's bases of power. Our definition also encompasses efforts to influence the goals, criteria, or processes used for decision making when we state that politics is concerned with "the distribution of advantages and disadvantages within the organization." Our definition is broad

political behaviour Those activities that influence, or attempt to influence, the distribution of advantages and disadvantages within the organization.

enough to include such varied political behaviours as withholding key information from decision makers, joining a coalition, whistle-blowing, spreading rumours, leaking confidential information about organizational activities to the media, exchanging favours with others in the organization for mutual benefit, and lobbying on behalf of or against a particular individual or decision alternative. Exhibit 25-5 provides a quick measure to help you assess how political your workplace is.

Political behaviour is not confined to just individual hopes and goals. Politics might also be used to achieve organizational goals. For instance, if a CEO wants to change the way employees are paid, say from salaries to commissions, this change might not be a popular choice for employees. While it might make good organizational sense to make this change (perhaps the CEO believes doing so will increase productivity), simply imposing the change through the use of power ("go along with this or you are

---

EXHIBIT 25-5 A Quick Measure of How Political Your Workplace Is

How political is your workplace? Answer the 12 questions using the following scale:

SD = Strongly disagree

D = Disagree

U = Uncertain

A = Agree

SA = Strongly agree

1. Managers often use the selection system to hire only people who can help them in their future. _____

2. The rules and policies concerning promotion and pay are fair; it's how managers carry out the policies that is unfair and self-serving. _____

3. The performance ratings people receive from their managers reflect more of the managers' "own agenda" than the actual performance of the employee. _____

4. Although a lot of what my manager does around here appears to be directed at helping employees, it's actually intended to protect my manager. _____

5. There are cliques or "in-groups" that hinder effectiveness around here. _____

6. My co-workers help themselves, not others. _____

7. I have seen people deliberately distort information requested by others for purposes of personal gain, either by withholding it or by selectively reporting it. _____

8. If co-workers offer to lend some assistance, it is because they expect to get something out of it. _____

9. Favouritism rather than merit determines who gets ahead around here. _____

10. You can usually get what you want around here if you know the right person to ask. _____

11. Overall, the rules and policies concerning promotion and pay are specific and well-defined. _____

12. Pay and promotion policies are generally clearly communicated in this organization. _____

This questionnaire taps the three salient dimensions that have been found to be related to perceptions of politics: manager behaviour; co-worker behaviour; and organizational policies and practices. To calculate your score for items 1–10, give yourself 1 point for Strongly disagree; 2 points for Disagree; and so forth (through 5 points for Strongly agree). For items 11 and 12, reverse the score (that is, 1 point for Strongly agree, etc.). Sum up the total: The higher the total score, the greater the degree of perceived organizational politics.

Source: G. R. Ferris, D. D. Frink, D. P. S. Bhawuk, J. Zhou, and D. C. Gilmore, "Reactions of Diverse Groups to Politics in the Workplace," *Journal of Management* 22, no. 1 (1996), pp. 32–33. Reprinted by permission of SAGE Publications.

fired") might not be very popular. Instead, the CEO may try to pitch the reasons for the change to sympathetic managers and employees, trying to get them to understand the necessity for the change. Burnaby, BC-based TELUS used a direct approach with its employees after four-and-a-half years of unsuccessful bargaining with union leaders. Management became frustrated with the impasse and explained their wage and benefit offer directly to employees in the hopes of getting the employees to side with management rather than their union leaders. The union was outraged by this behaviour, and it took several more months for union members and management to finally complete a new collective agreement in fall 2005.

The Reality of Politics

Why, you may wonder, must politics exist? Isn't it possible for an organization to be politics-free? It's *possible*, but most unlikely. Organizations are made up of individuals and groups with different values, goals, and interests.[59] This sets up the potential for conflict over resources. Organizational members sometimes disagree about the allocation of resources such as departmental budgets, space allocations, project responsibilities, and salary adjustments.

Resources in organizations are also limited, which often turns potential conflict into real conflict. If resources were abundant, all the constituencies within the organization could satisfy their goals. Because they are limited, not everyone's interests can be provided for. Furthermore, whether true or not, gains by one individual or group are often *perceived* as being at the expense of others within the organization. These forces create a competition among members for the organization's limited resources.

Maybe the most important factor behind politics within organizations is the realization that most of the "facts" that are used to allocate the limited resources are open to interpretation. What, for instance, is *good* performance? What is an *adequate* improvement? What constitutes an *unsatisfactory* job? It's in this large and ambiguous middle ground of organizational life—where the facts *don't* speak for themselves—that politics flourish.

When American figure skater Johnny Weir's low scores were announced at the men's 2010 Olympic Figure Skating finals, almost the entire crowd booed the judges in the Vancouver stadium. Some thought that the judges were engaging in politics to send a message to him that his style of artistic skating was not "masculine" enough for the sport.

Finally, because most decisions must be made in a climate of ambiguity—where facts are rarely fully objective, and thus are open to interpretation—people within organizations will use whatever influence they can to spin the facts to support their goals and interests. That, of course, creates the activities we call *politicking*. For more about how one engages in politicking.

Therefore, to answer the earlier question about whether it is possible for an organization to be politics-free, we can say "yes"—but only if all the members of that organization hold the same goals and interests, organizational resources are not scarce, and performance outcomes are completely clear and objective. However, that does not describe the organizational world that most of us live in.

RESEARCH FINDINGS: Politicking

Our earlier discussion focused on the favourable outcomes for individuals who successfully engage in politicking. But for most people—who have modest political skills or are unwilling to play the politics game—outcomes tend to be predominantly negative.[60] There is, for instance, very strong evidence indicating that perceptions of organizational politics are negatively related to job satisfaction.[61] The perception of politics also tends to increase job anxiety and stress. This seems to be because of the perception that, by not engaging in politics, a person may be losing ground to others who are active politickers, or, conversely, because of the additional pressures individuals feel because of having entered into and competing in the political arena.[62] Not surprisingly, when politicking becomes too much to handle, it can lead employees to quit.[63] Finally, there is preliminary evidence suggesting that politics leads to self-reported declines in employee performance.[64] Perceived organizational politics appears to have a demotivating effect on individuals, and thus leads to decreased performance levels.

Types of Political Activity

Within organizations, we can find a variety of political activities in which people engage. These include the following:[65]

- *Attacking or blaming others.* Used when trying to avoid responsibility for failure.

- *Using information.* Withholding or distorting information, particularly to hide negative information.

- *Managing impressions.* Bringing positive attention to oneself or taking credit for positive accomplishments of others.

- *Building support for ideas.* Making sure that others will support one's ideas before they are presented.

- *Praising others.* Making important people feel good.

- *Building coalitions.* Joining with other people to create a powerful group.

- *Associating with influential people.* Building support networks.

- *Creating obligations.* Doing favours for others so they will owe you favours later.

Individuals will use these political activities for different purposes. Some of these activities (such as attacking or blaming others) are more likely to be used to defend one's position, while other activities (such as building support for ideas and managing impressions) are meant to enhance one's image.

Impression Management

The process by which individuals attempt to control the impression others form of them is called **impression management**.[66] Being perceived positively by others should have benefits for people in organizations. It might, for instance, help them initially to get the jobs they want in an organization and, once hired, to get favourable evaluations, superior salary increases, and more rapid promotions. In a political context, it might help bring more advantages their way.

Why do some people seem to engage in politics more than others?

Impression management does not imply that the impressions people convey are necessarily false (although, of course, they sometimes are).[67] Some activities may be done with great sincerity. For instance, you may *actually* believe that ads contribute little to sales in your region or that you are the key to the tripling of your division's sales. However, if the image claimed is false, you may be discredited.[68] The impression manager must be cautious not to be perceived as insincere or manipulative.[69]

RESEARCH FINDINGS

RESEARCH FINDINGS:
Impression Management Techniques

Most of the studies undertaken to test the effectiveness of impression management techniques have related it to two criteria: interview success and performance evaluations. Let's consider each of these.

The evidence indicates that most job applicants use impression management techniques in interviews[70] and that, when impression management behaviour is used, it works.[71] In one study, for instance, interviewers felt that applicants for a position as a customer-service representative who used impression management techniques performed better in the interview, and they seemed somewhat more inclined to hire these people.[72] Moreover, when the researchers considered applicants' credentials, they concluded that it was the impression management techniques alone that influenced the interviewers. That is, it did not seem to matter if applicants were well or poorly qualified. If they used impression management techniques, they did better in the interview.

In what situations does impression management work best?

Research indicates that some impression management techniques work better than others in an interview. Researchers have compared applicants who used techniques that focused on promoting one's accomplishments (called *self-promotion*) to applicants who used techniques that focused on complimenting the interviewer and finding areas of agreement (referred to as *ingratiation*). In general, applicants appear to use self-promotion more than ingratiation.[73] What is more, self-promotion tactics may be more important to interviewing success. Applicants who work to create an appearance of competence by enhancing their accomplishments, taking credit for successes, and explaining away failures do better in interviews. These effects reach beyond the interview: Applicants who use more self-promotion tactics also seem to get more follow-up job-site visits, even after adjusting for grade-point average, gender, and job type. Ingratiation also works well in interviews, meaning that applicants who compliment the interviewer, agree with his or her opinions, and emphasize areas of fit do better than those who don't.[74]

In terms of performance ratings, the picture is quite different. Ingratiation is positively related to performance ratings, meaning that those who ingratiate with their supervisors get higher performance evaluations. However, self-promotion appears to backfire: Those

impression management The process by which individuals attempt to control the impression others form of them.

who self-promote actually seem to receive *lower* performance evaluations.[75] There is an important qualifier to this general result. It appears that individuals high in political skill are able to translate impression management into higher performance appraisals, whereas those lower in political skill are more likely to be hurt by their attempts at impression management.[76]

What explains these results? If you think about them, they make sense. Ingratiating always works because everyone—both interviewers and supervisors—likes to be treated nicely. However, self-promotion may work only in interviews and backfire on the job because, whereas the interviewer has little idea whether you are blowing smoke about your accomplishments, the supervisor knows because it's his or her job to observe you. Thus, if you are going to self-promote, remember that what works in an interview will not always work once you are on the job.

Making Office Politics Work

One thing to be aware of is that extreme office politics can have a negative effect on employees. Researchers have found that organizational politics is associated with less organizational commitment,[77] lower job satisfaction,[78] and decreased job performance.[79] Individuals who experience greater organizational politics are more likely to report higher levels of job anxiety,[80] and they are more likely to consider leaving the organization.[81]

Is there an effective way to engage in office politics that is less likely to be disruptive or negative? We discuss different negotiation strategies in Chapter 9, including a *win-lose* strategy, which means if I win, you lose, and a *win-win* strategy, which means creating situations where both of us can win. *Fast Company*, a business magazine, identifies several rules that may help improve the climate of the organization while negotiating through the office politics maze:[82]

- *Nobody wins unless everybody wins.* The most successful proposals look for ways to acknowledge, if not include, the interests of others. This requires building support for your ideas across the organization. "Real political skill isn't about campaign tactics," says Lou Di Natale, a veteran political consultant at the University of Massachusetts. "It's about pulling people toward your ideas and then pushing those ideas through to other people." When ideas are packaged

General Electric wants its managers to share their power with employees. GE is breaking down autocratic barriers between labour and management that "cramp people, inhibit creativity, waste time, restrict visions, smother dreams, and above all, slow things down." GE expects managers to behave more democratically by fostering teamwork and rewarding employees who suggest ideas for improvement. This photo illustrates GE's move toward democracy, as a manager and an employee at the company's plant in Louisville, Kentucky, work together to improve the plant's profitability.

to look like they are best for the organization as a whole and will help others, it is harder for others to counteract your proposal.

- *Don't just ask for opinions—change them.* It's helpful to find out what people think and then, if necessary, set out to change their opinions so that they can see what you want to do. It's also important to seek out the opinions of those you don't know well, or who are less likely to agree with you. Gathering together people who always support you is often not enough to build an effective coalition.

- *Everyone expects to be paid back.* In organizations, as in life, we develop personal relationships with those around us. It's those personal relationships that affect much of the behaviour in organizations. By building good relationships with colleagues, supporting them in their endeavours, and showing appreciation for what they accomplish, you are building a foundation of support for your own ideas.

- *Success can create opposition.* As part of the office politics, success can be viewed as a *win-lose* strategy, which we identified above. Some people may feel that your success comes at their expense. So, for instance, your higher profile may mean that a project of theirs will be received less favourably. You have to be prepared to deal with this opposition.

GLOBAL IMPLICATIONS

Although culture might enter any of the topics we have covered to this point, three questions are particularly important: (1) Does culture influence views on empowerment? (2) Does culture influence perceptions of politics? And (3) Does culture affect the influence tactics people prefer to use?

Views on Empowerment

Four US researchers investigated the effects of empowerment on employees of a multinational firm by looking at four of the company's comparable plants: one in the Midwestern United States, one in central Mexico, one in west-central India, and one in the south of Poland.[83] These four locations were chosen because they differed on power distance and individualism (concepts we discussed in Chapter 3). India and Mexico are considered high in power distance, and the United States is considered the lowest in power distance. Mexico and India are high in collectivity, the United States is highly individualistic, and Poland is moderately individualistic.

The findings showed that Indian employees gave their supervisors low ratings when empowerment was high, while employees in the other three countries rated their supervisors favourably when empowerment was high. In both the United States and Mexico, empowerment had no effect on satisfaction with co-workers. However, satisfaction with co-workers was higher when employees were empowered in Poland. In India, empowerment led to lower satisfaction with co-workers.

Similar findings in a study comparing empowerment in the United States, Brazil, and Argentina suggest that in hierarchical societies, empowerment may need to be introduced with care.[84] Employees in those countries may be more used to working in teams, but they also expect their manager to be the person with all the answers. Professor Marylène Gagné of Concordia's John Molson School of Business, who has studied empowerment cross-culturally,[85] notes that "in some cultures, bosses can't ask the opinion of subordinates, because it makes them appear weak. So managers in these environments have to find other ways to make people feel autonomous. There is no simple recipe."[86]

Perceptions of Politics

We have already noted that (based on research conducted mostly in the United States) when people see their work environment as political, the effect on their overall work attitudes and behaviours is usually negative. When employees of two agencies in a recent study in Nigeria viewed their work environments as political, they reported higher levels of job distress and were less likely to help their co-workers. Thus, although developing countries such as Nigeria are perhaps more ambiguous and more political environments in which to work, the negative consequences appear to be the same as in the United States.[87]

Preference for Influence Tactics

Evidence indicates that people in different countries tend to prefer different influence tactics.[88] A study comparing managers in the United States and China found that US managers prefer rational appeal, whereas Chinese managers prefer coalition tactics.[89] These differences tend to be consistent with the values in these two countries. Reason is consistent with the US preference for direct confrontation and the use of rational persuasion to influence others and resolve differences. Similarly, coalition tactics are consistent with the Chinese preference for using indirect approaches for difficult or controversial requests. Research also has shown that individuals in Western, individualistic cultures tend to engage in more self-enhancement (such as self-promotion) behaviours than individuals in Eastern, more collectivistic cultures.[90]

A study of Swedish, German, Czech, Polish, and Finnish managers found that Swedish managers saw mere differences in opinion as conflicts, so they adopted a conflict-avoidant strategy that emphasized more passive forms of persuasion.[91] German managers, on the other hand, saw disagreement as a useful opportunity to gain new knowledge and fostered some rational discussion as an influence technique. Finnish managers preferred discussion-oriented influence tactics as well. Czech and Polish managers believed managers were under pressure to halt conflicts quickly when they arose, since conflict resolution is time consuming. Therefore, the Czech and Polish managers switched to more autocratic, power-oriented influence styles.

Are the same influence tactics equally effective across a country? Though researchers usually compare two very different cultures, it is also important to examine differences within a given culture, because those differences can sometimes be greater than differences between cultures. China is a big country with different cultures and traditions. A recent study of mainland Chinese, Taiwanese, and Hong Kong managers explored how the three cultural subgroups differ according to the influence tactics they prefer to use.[92] Though managers from all three places believe that rational persuasion and exchange are the most effective influence tactics, managers in Taiwan tend to use inspirational appeals and ingratiation more than managers from either mainland China or Hong Kong. The study also found that managers from Hong Kong rate pressure as more effective in influencing others than do managers in Taiwan or mainland China. Such differences have implications for business relationships. For example, Taiwanese or mainland Chinese managers may be taken aback by the use of pressure tactics by a Hong Kong manager. Likewise, managers from Hong Kong may not be persuaded by managers from Taiwan, who tend to use ingratiating tactics. Such differences in influence tactics may make business dealings difficult. Companies should address these issues, perhaps making their managers aware of the differences within cultures.

LESSONS LEARNED

- Effective leaders use expert and/or referent power.
- To maximize your power, increase others' dependence on you.
- Politics is inevitable; managing politics well is a skill.

26 Conflict and Negotiation

O n August 20, 2011, one day before the opening of the Vancouver-based Pacific National Exhibition's (PNE's) annual fair, talks between management and the union representing PNE's 4000 employees broke down.[1] PNE employees, including ride operators, maintenance personnel, administrators, games operators, ushers, and parking lot attendants, had been without a contract since the start of the year. It was the first time in 25 years that a contract agreement had not been reached prior to the opening of the fair.

The local chapter of CUPE (1004) was seeking more job security, cost of living wage increases totalling 7.5 percent over three years, and improved equity for their lowest paid employees, many of whom earned less than $10 per hour. Unionized employees rejected PNE's offer of a 3.75 percent raise over three years. They confirmed their position in a strike vote that took place in mid-September, in which 92 percent of employees supported a strike.

Despite the fact that the fair was over when the vote took place, a number of important upcoming events were scheduled at the PNE, including professional hockey and soccer games and a Pearl Jam concert. With staff on strike, those events were at risk of being cancelled. "If the new [contract agreement] talks broke down on Monday or Tuesday and everyone was annoyed . . . we could serve strike notice in time for the Giant's game on Friday" observed CUPE business agent Steve Varty after the mid-September vote.

In this chapter, we look at sources of conflict and strategies for resolving conflict, including negotiation.

Conflict Defined

1 What is conflict?

Several common themes underlie most definitions of conflict.[2] Conflict must be perceived by the parties to it; if no one is aware of a conflict, then it is generally agreed that no conflict exists. Conflict also involves opposition or incompatibility, and some form of interaction between the parties.[3] These factors set the conditions that determine the beginning point of the conflict process. We can define **conflict**, then, as a process that begins when one party perceives that another party has negatively affected, or is about to negatively affect, something that the first party cares about.[4]

This definition is deliberately broad. It describes that point in any ongoing activity when an interaction "crosses over" to become an interparty conflict. It encompasses the wide range of conflicts that people experience in groups and organizations—incompatibility of goals, differences over interpretations of facts, disagreements based on behavioural expectations, and the like. Finally, our definition is flexible enough to cover the full range of conflict levels—from subtle forms of disagreement to overt and violent acts.

Conflict has positive sides and negative sides, which we will discuss further when we cover functional and dysfunctional conflict.

Functional vs. Dysfunctional Conflict

The general view on conflict is that not all conflict is bad.[5] Some conflicts support the goals of the group and improve its performance; these are **functional**, or constructive, forms of conflict. But there are conflicts that hinder group performance; these are **dysfunctional**, or destructive, forms of conflict. The criterion that differentiates functional from dysfunctional conflict is group performance. If a group is unable to achieve its goals because of conflict, then the conflict is dysfunctional.

Is conflict always bad?

Exhibit 26-1 provides a way of visualizing conflict behaviour. All conflicts exist somewhere along this continuum. At the lower part of the continuum, we have conflicts characterized by subtle, indirect, and highly controlled forms of tension. An illustration might be a student politely objecting to a point the instructor has just made in class. Conflict intensities escalate as they move upward along the continuum,

conflict A process that begins when one party perceives that another party has negatively affected, or is about to negatively affect, something that the first party cares about.

functional conflict Conflict that supports the goals of the group and improves its performance.

dysfunctional conflict Conflict that hinders group performance.

EXHIBIT 26-1 Conflict Intensity Continuum

Annihilatory conflict — Overt efforts to destroy the other party

Aggressive physical attacks

Threats and ultimatums

Assertive verbal attacks

Overt questioning or challenging of others

No conflict — Minor disagreements or misunderstandings

Sources: Based on S. P. Robbins, *Managing Organizational Conflict: A Nontraditional Approach* (Upper Saddle River, NJ: Prentice Hall, 1974), pp. 93–97; and F. Glasl, "The Process of Conflict Escalation and the Roles of Third Parties," in *Conflict Management and Industrial Relations*, ed. G. B. J. Bomers and R. Peterson (Boston: Kluwer-Nijhoff, 1982), pp. 119–140.

until they become highly destructive. Strikes and lockouts, riots, and wars clearly fall in this upper range. For the most part, you should assume that conflicts that reach the upper ranges of the continuum are almost always dysfunctional. Functional conflicts are typically confined to the lower range of the continuum.

RESEARCH FINDINGS: Cognitive and Affective Conflict

Research on conflict has yet to clearly identify those situations where conflict is more likely to be constructive than destructive. However, there is growing evidence that the source of the conflict is a significant factor determining functionality.[6] **Cognitive conflict**, which is task-oriented and occurs because of differences in perspectives and judgments, can often result in identifying potential solutions to problems. Thus it would be regarded as functional conflict. **Affective conflict**, which is emotional and aimed at a person rather than an issue, tends to be dysfunctional conflict.

One study of 53 teams found that cognitive conflict, because it generates more alternatives, led to better decisions, more acceptance of the decisions, and ownership of the decisions. Teams experiencing affective conflict, where members had personality incompatibilities and disputes, had poorer decisions and lower levels of acceptance of the decisions.[7] It also appears that the friction and interpersonal hostilities inherent in affective conflicts increase personality clashes and decrease mutual understanding, which hinders the completion of organizational tasks. Unfortunately, managers spend a lot of effort resolving personality conflicts among staff members; one survey indicated this task consumes 18 percent of their time.[8]

Because conflict can involve our emotions in a variety of ways, it can also lead to stress. You may want to refer to *OB on the Edge—Stress at Work* on pages 154–161 to get some ideas on how to manage the stress that might arise from conflicts you experience.

Resolution-Focused View of Conflict

Researchers have begun to recognize some problems with encouraging conflict.[9] As we will see, there are some very specific cases in which conflict can be beneficial. However, workplace conflicts are not productive, they take time away from job tasks or interacting with customers, and hurt feelings and anger often linger after conflicts appear to be over. People seldom can wall off their feelings into neat categories of "task" or "relationship" disagreements, so task conflicts sometimes escalate into relationship conflicts.[10] Conflicts produce stress, which may lead people to become more close minded and adversarial.[11] Studies of conflict in laboratories also fail to take account of the reductions in trust and cooperation that occur even with relationship conflicts. Longer-term studies show that all conflicts reduce trust, respect, and cohesion in groups, which reduces their long-term viability.[12]

In light of these findings, researchers have started to focus more on managing the whole context in which conflicts occur, both before and after the behavioural stage of conflict occurs. A growing body of research suggests we can minimize the negative effects of conflict by focusing on preparing people for conflicts, developing resolution strategies, and facilitating open discussion.

Sources of Conflict

There are a number of conditions that can give rise to conflict. They *need not* lead directly to conflict, but at least one of these conditions is necessary if conflict is to surface. For simplicity's sake, these conditions (which we can also look at as causes or sources of conflict) have been condensed into three general categories: communication, structure, and personal variables.[13]

cognitive conflict Conflict that is task-oriented and related to differences in perspectives and judgments.

affective conflict Conflict that is emotional and aimed at a person rather than an issue.

A lack of functional conflict among General Motors management in the past decades resulted in concessions to union demands for general health benefits and pensions. Burdened by health costs that GM provided to more than 1 million employees, retirees, and dependants, the automaker was forced into bankruptcy and more mass layoffs even after it closed factories as part of its cost-cutting strategy. The Chevy Blazer SUV shown here was one of the last GM vehicles to roll off the assembly line at a plant in Linden, New Jersey. GM closed the plant after 68 years of operation, which marked the end of automobile manufacturing in a state where the industry once employed thousands of workers and helped fuel the state's economic engine.

Communication

As we saw in Chapter 19, communication can be a source of conflict through semantic difficulties, misunderstandings, and "noise" in the communication channels.[14]

A review of the research suggests that differing word connotations, jargon, insufficient exchange of information, and noise in the communication channel are all barriers to communication and potential antecedent conditions to conflict. Research has further demonstrated a surprising finding: The potential for conflict increases when either too little or too much communication takes place. Apparently, an increase in communication is functional up to a point, whereupon it is possible to overcommunicate, with a resultant increase in the potential for conflict.

Structure

Conflicts between two people can be structural in nature; that is, they can be the consequence of the requirements of the job or the workplace more than personality. For instance, it is not uncommon for the sales department to be in conflict with the production department, if sales perceives that products will be delivered late to customers. The term *structure* in this context includes variables such as size of the group, degree of specialization in the tasks assigned to group members, composition of the group, jurisdictional clarity, reward systems, leadership style, goal compatibility, and the degree of dependence between groups.

A review of structural variables that can lead to conflict in the workplace suggests the following:[15]

- *Size, specialization, and composition* of the group act as forces to stimulate conflict. The larger the group and the more specialized its activities, the greater the likelihood of conflict. The potential for conflict tends to be greatest where group members are younger and where turnover is high.

- *The greater the ambiguity* in precisely defining where responsibility for actions lies, the greater the potential for conflict to emerge. Such jurisdictional ambiguities increase intergroup fighting for control of resources and territory.

- *Reward systems* create conflict when one member's gain is at another's expense. Similarly, the performance evaluation process can create conflict when individuals feel that they are unfairly evaluated, or when managers and employees have differing ideas about the employees' job responsibilities.

- *Leadership style* can create conflict if managers tightly control and oversee the work of employees, allowing employees little discretion in how they carry out tasks.

- *The diversity of goals* among groups is a major source of conflict. When groups within an organization seek diverse ends, some of which are inherently at odds—such as when the sales team promises products that the development team has not yet finalized—opportunities for conflict increase.

- *If one group is dependent on another* (in contrast to the two being mutually independent), or if interdependence allows one group to gain at another's expense, opposing forces are stimulated.

Personal Variables

Have you ever met people to whom you take an immediate dislike? You disagree with most of their opinions. The sound of their voice, their smirk when they smile, and their personality annoy you. We have all met people like that. When you have to work with such individuals, there is often the potential for conflict.

Our last category of potential sources of conflict is personal variables, which include personality, emotions, and values. Personality does appear to play a role in the conflict process: Some people just tend to get in conflicts a lot. In particular, people high in the personality traits of disagreeableness, neuroticism, or self-monitoring are prone to tangle with other people more often, and to react poorly when conflicts occur.[16] Emotions can also cause conflict. An employee who shows up to work irate from her hectic morning commute may carry that anger with her to her 9:00 a.m. meeting. The problem? Her anger can annoy her colleagues, which can result in a tension-filled meeting.[17]

Conflict Resolution

Each side in the PNE dispute used the media to influence public opinion, and there were mutual accusations of bad faith bargaining, so some hard feelings were inevitable.[18] CUPE 1004 and the PNE recognized they could not solve the impasse alone. When talks resumed after the strike vote in September 2011, a mediator was called in to assist the process. What other approaches might the parties use to try to resolve a conflict?

2 How can conflict be resolved?

Conflict in the workplace can affect the effectiveness of individuals, teams, and the entire organization.[19] One study found that 20 percent of managers' time is spent managing conflict.[20]

Once conflict arises, what can be done to resolve it? The way a conflict is defined goes a long way toward establishing the sort of outcomes that might settle it. For instance, if I define our salary disagreement as a zero-sum or *win-lose situation*—that is, if you get the increase in pay you want, there will be just that amount less for me—I am going to be far less willing to look for mutual solutions than if I frame the conflict as a potential *win-win situation*. So individual attitudes toward a conflict are important, because attitudes typically define the set of possible settlements.

Conflict Management Strategies

Conflict researchers often use *dual concern theory* to describe people's conflict management strategies.[21] Dual concern theory considers how one's degree of *cooperativeness* (the degree to which one tries to satisfy the other person's concerns) and *assertiveness* (the degree to which one tries to satisfy one's own concerns) determine how a conflict is handled.[22] The five conflict-handling strategies identified by the theory are as follows:

- *Forcing.* Imposing one's will on the other party.

- *Problem solving.* Trying to reach an agreement that satisfies both one's own and the other party's aspirations as much as possible.

- *Avoiding.* Ignoring or minimizing the importance of the issues creating the conflict.

- *Yielding.* Accepting and incorporating the will of the other party.

- *Compromising.* Balancing concern for oneself with concern for the other party in order to reach a solution.

Forcing is a win-lose solution, as is yielding, while problem solving seeks a win-win solution. Avoiding conflict and pretending it does not exist, and compromising, so that neither person gets what they want, can yield lose-lose solutions. Exhibit 26-2 illustrates these five strategies, along with specific actions that one might take when using them.

Choosing a particular strategy for resolving conflict depends on a variety of factors. Research shows that while people may choose among the strategies, they have an underlying disposition to handle conflicts in certain ways.[24] In addition, some situations call for particular strategies. For instance, when a small child insists on trying to run into the street, a parent may need a forcing strategy to restrain the child. Co-workers who are having a conflict over setting deadlines to complete a project on time may decide that problem solving is the best strategy to use.

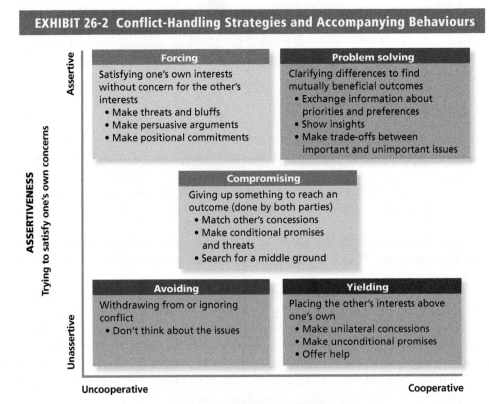

EXHIBIT 26-2 Conflict-Handling Strategies and Accompanying Behaviours

Forcing
Satisfying one's own interests without concern for the other's interests
- Make threats and bluffs
- Make persuasive arguments
- Make positional commitments

Problem solving
Clarifying differences to find mutually beneficial outcomes
- Exchange information about priorities and preferences
- Show insights
- Make trade-offs between important and unimportant issues

Compromising
Giving up something to reach an outcome (done by both parties)
- Match other's concessions
- Make conditional promises and threats
- Search for a middle ground

Avoiding
Withdrawing from or ignoring conflict
- Don't think about the issues

Yielding
Placing the other's interests above one's own
- Make unilateral concessions
- Make unconditional promises
- Offer help

ASSERTIVENESS — Trying to satisfy one's own concerns (Assertive / Unassertive)

COOPERATIVENESS — Trying to satisfy the other person's concerns (Uncooperative / Cooperative)

Sources: Based on K. W. Thomas, "Conflict and Negotiation Processes in Organizations," in *Handbook of Industrial and Organizational Psychology*, vol. 3, 2nd ed., ed. M. D. Dunnette and L. M. Hough (Palo Alto, CA: Consulting Psychologists Press, 1992), p. 668; C. K. W. De Dreu, A. Evers, B. Beersma, E. S. Kluwer, and A. Nauta, "A Theory-Based Measure of Conflict Management Strategies in the Workplace," *Journal of Organizational Behavior* 22, no. 6 (September 2001), pp. 645–668; and D. G. Pruitt and J. Rubin, *Social Conflict: Escalation, Stalemate and Settlement* (New York: Random House, 1986).

What Can Individuals Do to Manage Conflict?

There are a number of conflict resolution techniques that individuals can use to try to defuse conflict inside and outside of the workplace. These include the following:[25]

- *Problem solving.* Requesting a face-to-face meeting to identify the problem and resolve it through open discussion.

- *Developing overarching goals.* Creating a shared goal that requires both parties to work together, and motivates them to do so.

- *Smoothing.* Playing down differences while emphasizing common interests with the other party.

- *Compromising.* Agreeing with the other party that each will give up something of value to reach an accord.

- *Avoidance.* Withdrawing from or suppressing the conflict.

The choice of technique may depend on how serious the issue is to you, whether you take a win-win or a win-lose approach, and your preferred conflict management style.

When the conflict is specifically work-related, there are additional techniques that might be used:

- *Expansion of resources.* The scarcity of a resource—say, money, promotion opportunities, office space—can create conflict. Expansion of the resource can create a win-win solution.

- *Authoritative command.* Management can use its formal authority to resolve the conflict and then communicate its desires to the parties involved.

- *Altering the human variable.* Behavioural change techniques such as human relations training can alter attitudes and behaviours that cause conflict.

- *Altering the structural variables.* The formal organization structure and the inter-action patterns of conflicting parties can be changed through job redesign, transfers, creation of coordinating positions, and the like.

Resolving Personality Conflicts

Personality conflicts are an everyday occurrence in the workplace. A 2011 study found that Canadian supervisors spend about 16 percent of their time handling disputes among employees.[26] A variety of factors lead to personality conflicts at work, including the following:[27]

- Misunderstandings based on age, race, or cultural differences

- Intolerance, prejudice, discrimination, or bigotry

- Perceived inequities

- Misunderstandings, rumours, or falsehoods about an individual or group

- Blaming for mistakes or mishaps (finger-pointing)

Personality conflicts can result in lowered productivity when people find it difficult to work together. The individuals experiencing the conflict may seek sympathy from other members of the work group, causing co-workers to take sides. The ideal solution would be for the two people having a conflict to work it out between themselves, without involving others, but this does not always happen.

EXHIBIT 26-3 Strategies for Dealing with Intercultural Conflict

Behaviour	Rank
Listening rather than talking	1
Being sensitive to others' needs	2 (tie)
Being cooperative rather than competitive	2 (tie)
Being an inclusive leader	4
Compromising rather than domineering	5
Trying to engage in rapport	6
Being compassionate and understanding	7
Emphasizing harmony by avoiding conflict	8
Nurturing people	9

Source: Adapted from R. L. Tung, "American Expatriates Abroad: From Neophytes to Cosmopolitans," *Journal of World Business* 33, no. 2 (Summer 1998), p. 136, Table 6. With permission from Elsevier.

Resolving Intercultural Conflicts

While some personality conflicts may be stimulated by cultural differences, it's important to consider intercultural conflicts as a separate form of conflict. Canada is a multicultural society, and its organizations increasingly interact in a global environment, setting up alliances and joint ventures with partners from other parts of the world. Greater contact with people from other cultures can lead to greater understanding, but it can also lead to misunderstanding when individuals ignore the different perspectives that might result from cultural differences.

In Chapter 19, we discussed the idea that people from high- and low-context cultures have different expectations about how to interact with one another. In high-context cultures, communication is based on nonverbal and subtle situational cues. Status and one's place in society are also very important. Low-context cultures, such as those in North America, rely more on words and less on subtle situational cues. In low-context cultures, there is also less formality when communicating with people of different status. As a result of these differences, people from one cultural context may misinterpret the actions of those from another, which could produce conflict.

Professor Rosalie Tung of the Business School at Simon Fraser University studied 409 Canadian and American expatriates who were living in 51 different countries worldwide to determine the factors that made it easier (or harder) to adjust to living in a foreign culture.[29] As part of that study, she asked expatriates to identify the characteristics that they thought best facilitated interaction with the host country's nationals. The list, presented in Exhibit 26-3, provides some guidance for what behaviours individuals might try when dealing with conflict with someone from another culture. The list is ordered from the attribute ranked most important to least important.

RESEARCH FINDINGS: Cultural Views on Conflict

Across cultures, people have different ideas about the appropriateness and effects of conflict. For instance, Mexicans expect conflict to be kept private, while Americans expect conflict to be dealt with directly and openly.[30] We suggest in Exhibit 26-4 that there is an optimal level of conflict in the workplace to maximize productivity, but this is decidedly a North American viewpoint. Many Asian cultures believe that conflict almost always has a negative effect on the work unit.[31]

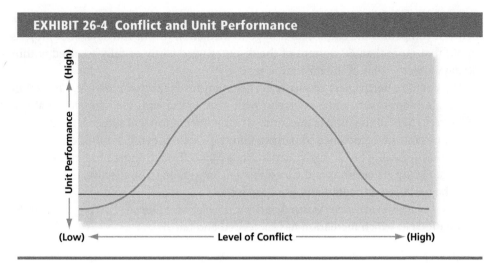

| EXHIBIT 26-4 Conflict and Unit Performance |

Collectivistic cultures value harmony among members more than individualistic cultures do. Consistent with this idea, research shows that those from Asian cultures show a preference for conflict avoidance, compared with Americans and Britons.[32] Research also shows that Chinese and East Asian managers prefer compromising as a strategy,[33] even though from a North American perspective, this might be viewed as suboptimal. Compromise may be viewed as a way of saving face, so that each party gets to preserve pride and dignity.[34]

Studies show that North Americans prefer a problem-solving approach to conflicts, because this presents both parties with a win-win solution.[35] Win-win solutions are less likely to be achieved in Asian cultures, however. East Asian managers tend to ignore conflict rather than make it public,[36] and more often than not, Japanese managers tend to choose nonconfrontational styles.[37] Chinese managers prefer compromising and avoiding to manage conflict.[38] These preferences make it difficult to negotiate a win-win solution. In general, Westerners are more comfortable with competition, which may explain why research finds that Westerners are more likely to choose forcing as a strategy than are Asians.[39]

Taken together, these research findings suggest the importance of being aware of cultural differences with respect to conflict. Using one's own culture's conflict resolution strategies may result in even greater conflict.[40] Some individuals and some cultures prefer harmonious relations over asserting themselves, and may not react well to the confrontational dynamics more common among North Americans. Similarly, North Americans expect that negotiations may lead to a legal contract, whereas Asian cultures rely less on legal contracts and more on relational contracts.

Third-Party Conflict Resolution

Occasionally, individuals or group representatives reach a stalemate and are unable to resolve their differences. In such cases, they may turn to alternative dispute resolution (ADR), where a third party helps both sides find a solution outside a courtroom. There are four basic third-party roles: mediator, arbitrator, conciliator, and consultant.[41]

Can someone else be asked to help resolve a conflict?

Mediator

A **mediator** is a neutral third party who facilitates a negotiated solution by using reasoning and persuasion, suggesting alternatives, and the like. Mediators can be much more aggressive in proposing solutions than conciliators. Mediators are widely used in labour-management negotiations and in civil court disputes. British Columbia's Motor

mediator A neutral third party who facilitates a negotiated solution by using reasoning, persuasion, and suggestions for alternatives.

Vehicle Branch uses mediation to help settle accident claims. In Ontario, all disputes between companies and employees now go to mediation within 100 days. Pilot projects found that more than 60 percent of the disputes were partly or fully resolved within 60 days after the start of the mediation session.[42]

The overall effectiveness of mediated negotiations is fairly impressive. The settlement rate is approximately 60 percent, with satisfaction with the mediator at about 75 percent. But the situation is the key to whether mediation will succeed; the conflicting parties must be motivated to bargain and resolve their conflict. Additionally, conflict intensity cannot be too high; mediation is most effective under moderate levels of conflict. Finally, perceptions of the mediator are important; to be effective, the mediator must be perceived as neutral and noncoercive.

Case Incident—Mediation: Master Solution to Employment Disputes? on page 352 looks at situations in which mediation has succeeded and failed.

Arbitrator

An **arbitrator** is a third party with the authority to dictate an agreement. Arbitration can be voluntary (requested by the parties) or compulsory (forced on the parties by law or contract).

The big advantage of arbitration over mediation is that it always results in a settlement. Whether or not there is a negative side depends on how "heavy-handed" the arbitrator appears. If one party is left feeling overwhelmingly defeated, that party is certain to be dissatisfied and unlikely to accept the arbitrator's decision graciously. Therefore, the conflict may resurface at a later time.

Conciliator

A **conciliator** is a trusted third party who provides an informal communication link between the negotiator and the opponent. Conciliation is used extensively in international, labour, family, and community disputes. In practice, conciliators typically act as more than mere communication conduits. They also engage in fact-finding, interpreting messages, and persuading disputants to develop agreements.

In Canada, the first step in trying to resolve a labour relations dispute can be to bring in a conciliation officer when agreement cannot be reached. This may be a good faith effort to resolve the dispute. Sometimes, however, it is used so that the union can reach a legal strike position or management can engage in a lockout. Provinces vary somewhat in how they set out the ability to engage in a strike after going through a conciliation process. For instance, in Nova Scotia, once the conciliation officer files a report that the dispute cannot be resolved through conciliation, there is a 14-day waiting period before either party can give 48 hours' notice of either a strike or a lockout.[43]

arbitrator A third party to a negotiation who has the authority to dictate an agreement.

conciliator A trusted third party who provides an informal communication link between the negotiator and the opponent.

consultant An impartial third party, skilled in conflict management, who attempts to facilitate creative problem solving through communication and analysis.

Consultant

A **consultant** is a skilled and impartial third party who attempts to facilitate problem solving through communication and analysis, aided by a knowledge of conflict management. Unlike other third parties, the consultant does not try to settle the issues but rather works to improve relationships between the conflicting parties so they can reach a settlement themselves. Instead of putting forward specific solutions, the consultant tries to help the parties learn to understand and work with each other. This approach has a longer-term focus: to build new and positive perceptions and attitudes between the conflicting parties.

Conflict Outcomes

 3 What are the effects of conflict?

One of the unfortunate side effects of the dispute between PNE and CUPE 1004 was a loss of mutual trust, especially since it was the first time an agreement was not reached prior to the start of the fair. This conflict deepened the existing divide between unionized employees and management, with strong potential for negative impact on employees' work values. Is there a way to minimize these negative outcomes when conflict becomes inevitable? How could the situation have been handled differently to reduce the impact on employee attitudes once the issue is resolved?

As Exhibit 26-4 on page 332 demonstrates, conflict can be functional and improve group performance, or it can be dysfunctional and hinder group performance. As well, we see there is an optimal level of conflict that results in the highest level of unit performance.

Conflict is constructive when it improves the quality of decisions, stimulates creativity and innovation, encourages interest and curiosity among group members, provides the medium through which problems can be aired and tensions released, and fosters an environment of self-evaluation and change. The evidence suggests that conflict can improve the quality of decision making by allowing all points to be weighed in important decisions, particularly the ones that are unusual or held by a minority.[44] Conflict can prevent groupthink (discussed in Chapter 5). It does not allow the group passively to "rubber-stamp" decisions that may be based on weak assumptions, inadequate consideration of relevant alternatives, or other problems. Conflict challenges the status quo and therefore supports the creation of new ideas, promotes reassessment of group goals and activities, and increases the probability that the group will respond to change. An open discussion focused on higher-order goals can make these functional outcomes more likely. Groups that are extremely polarized do not manage their underlying disagreements effectively and tend to accept suboptimal solutions, or they tend to avoid making decisions altogether rather than working out the conflict.[45]

Dean Tjosvold of Lingnan University in Hong Kong suggests three desired outcomes for conflict:[46]

- *Agreement.* Equitable and fair agreements are the best outcome. If agreement means that one party feels exploited or defeated, this will likely lead to further conflict later.

- *Stronger relationships.* When conflict is resolved positively, this can lead to better relationships and greater trust. If the parties trust each other, they are more likely to keep the agreements they make.

- *Learning.* Handling conflict successfully teaches one how to do it better next time. It gives an opportunity to practise the skills one has learned about handling conflict.

Below we examine what research tells us about the constructive effects of conflict.

RESEARCH **FINDINGS:**
The Constructive Effects of Conflict

Research studies in diverse settings confirm that conflict can be functional and improve productivity. For instance, studies demonstrate that groups composed of members with different interests tend to produce higher-quality solutions to a variety of problems than do homogeneous groups.[47] Team members with greater differences in work styles and experience also tend to share more information with one another.[48] One study found that high-conflict groups improved their decision-making ability 73 percent more than groups characterized by low-conflict conditions.[49] An investigation of 22 teams of systems analysts found that the more incompatible team members were, the more likely they were to be more productive.[50] Research and development scientists have been found to be most productive when a certain amount of intellectual conflict exists.[51]

The above research findings suggest that conflict within a group can lead to strength rather than weakness. However, factors such as personality, social support, and communication moderate how well groups can deal with internal conflict. At an individual level, both a person's personality (agreeableness) and his or her level of social support influence that person's response to conflict. Agreeable employees and those with lower levels of social support respond to conflict more negatively.[52]

Open communication is important to resolving conflict. Group members who discuss differences of opinion openly and are prepared to manage conflict when it arises resolve conflicts successfully.[53] Group members with cooperative conflict styles and a strong underlying identification to the overall group goals are more effective than those with a more competitive style.[54] Managers need to emphasize shared interests in resolving conflicts, so group members who disagree with one another don't become too entrenched in their points of view and start to take the conflicts personally.

Unfortunately, not all conflict results in positive outcomes. A substantial body of literature documents how dysfunctional conflict can reduce group effectiveness.[55] Among the more undesirable outcomes are stopping communication, reducing group cohesiveness, and subordinating group goals due to infighting among members. At the extreme, conflict can bring group functioning to a halt and potentially threaten the group's survival.

④ How does one negotiate effectively?

Negotiation

The dispute between PNE and CUPE 1004 was resolved on September 23, 2011, when over 80 percent of unionized employees accepted a negotiated deal that included raises of 1.5 percent a year over three years and improved contracting and scheduling regulations.[56] It was a very different story four years earlier when CUPE 1004 used a mediator to assist with strike negotiations with the City of Vancouver. The city's outdoor employees had been on strike for 82 days when they voted on whether to accept a mediator's recommendations to resolve the dispute. Two-thirds of the membership needed to accept the deal for it to go through. The outdoor employees rejected the mediator's recommendations, largely due to perceived unfairness. "There's just no way that our members can accept returning to work with less than what other civic workers have negotiated in this round of bargaining," said Mike Jackson, CUPE 1004 president. "After almost three months on strike, it is an insult to be offered less than other civic workers in the region. . . . We're also baffled at why CUPE 15 got the same Olympic agreement that we had tabled to the mediator and we got an inferior agreement," stated Jackson. Why did these two negotiations end so differently? How do perceptions of fairness influence the negotiation process?

Earlier in the chapter, we reviewed a number of conflict resolution strategies. One well-developed strategy is to negotiate a resolution. Negotiation permeates the interactions of almost everyone in groups and organizations: Labour bargains with management; managers negotiate with employees, peers, and senior management; salespeople negotiate with customers; purchasing agents negotiate with suppliers; employees agree to cover for one another for a few minutes in exchange for some past or future benefit. In today's loosely structured organizations, in which members work with colleagues over whom they have no direct authority and with whom they may not even share a common boss, negotiation skills become critical for teams to work together effectively.

We define **negotiation** as a process in which two or more parties try to agree on the exchange rate for goods or services they are trading.[57] Note that we use the terms *negotiation* and *bargaining* interchangeably.

Within a negotiation, be aware that individuals have issues, positions, and interests. *Issues* are items that are specifically placed on the bargaining table for discussion.

negotiation A process in which two or more parties exchange goods or services and try to agree on the exchange rate for them.

Negotiation skills are critical in the buyer-seller relationship. At this open-air cheese market in Alkmaar, Netherlands, two purchasing agents for food buyers taste a sample of Edam cheese before they negotiate prices with the seller of the cheese.

Positions are the individual's stand on the issues. For instance, salary may be an issue for discussion. The salary you hope to receive is your position. Finally, *interests* are the underlying concerns that are affected by the negotiation resolution. For instance, the reason that you might want a six-figure salary is that you are trying to buy a house in Vancouver, and that is your only hope of being able to make mortgage payments.

Negotiators who recognize the underlying interests of themselves and the other party may have more flexibility in achieving a resolution. For instance, in the example just given, an employer who offers you a mortgage at a lower rate than the bank does, or who provides you with an interest-free loan that can be used against the mortgage, may be able to address your underlying interests without actually meeting your salary position. You may be satisfied with this alternative, if you understand what your interest is.

Interest-based bargaining enabled the Information Services Corporation (ISC) to sign a mutually beneficial three-year contract with the Saskatchewan Government and General Employees' Union (SGEU) Local 2214 in May 2010, after nine days of bargaining. The agreement provided for wage and pension increases plus greater dental plan benefits for employees and efficiencies in recruitment and leave for the government.[58] ISC union chairperson Barb Wright called the result "a true testament to the interest-based bargaining process."[59]

Below we discuss bargaining strategies and how to negotiate.

Bargaining Strategies

There are two general approaches to negotiation—*distributive bargaining* and *integrative bargaining*.[60] These are compared in Exhibit 26-5.

Distributive Bargaining

Distributive bargaining is a negotiating strategy that operates under zero-sum (win-lose) conditions. That is, any gain I make is at your expense, and vice versa. You see a used car advertised for sale online. It appears to be just what you have been looking to buy. You go out to see the car. It's great, and you want it. The owner tells you the asking price. You don't want to pay that much. The two of you then

Should you try to win at any cost when you bargain?

distributive bargaining Negotiation that seeks to divide up a fixed amount of resources; a win-lose solution.

EXHIBIT 26-5 Distributive vs. Integrative Bargaining		
Bargaining Characteristic	**Distributive Bargaining**	**Integrative Bargaining**
Available resources	Fixed amount of resources to be divided	Variable amount of resources to be divided
Primary motivations	I win, you lose	I win, you win
Primary interests	Opposed to each other	Convergent or congruent with each other
Focus of relationships	Short-term	Long-term

Source: Based on R. J. Lewicki and J. A. Litterer, *Negotiation* (Homewood, IL: Irwin, 1985), p. 280.

negotiate over the price. Every dollar you can get the seller to cut from the car's price is a dollar you save, and every dollar more the seller can get from you comes at your expense. So the essence of distributive bargaining is negotiating over who gets what share of a fixed pie. By **fixed pie**, we mean a set amount of goods or services to be divided up. When the pie is fixed, or parties believe it is, they tend to bargain distributively.

A party engaged in distributive bargaining focuses on trying to get the opponent to agree to a specific target point, or to get as close to it as possible. Examples of this tactic are persuading your opponent of the impossibility of reaching his or her target point and the advisability of accepting a settlement near yours; arguing that your target is fair, while your opponent's is not; and attempting to get your opponent to feel emotionally generous toward you and thus accept an outcome close to your target point.

When engaged in distributive bargaining, one of the best things you can do is to make the first offer, and to make it an aggressive one. Research consistently shows that the best negotiators are those who make the first offer, and whose initial offer has very favourable terms. Why is this so? One reason is that making the first offer shows power; research shows that individuals in power are much more likely to make initial offers, speak first at meetings, and thereby gain the advantage. Another reason is the anchoring bias (the tendency for people to fixate on initial information). Once that anchoring point is set, people fail to adequately adjust it based on subsequent information. A savvy negotiator sets an anchor with the initial offer, and scores of negotiation studies show that such anchors greatly favour the person who sets it.[61]

For example, say you have a job offer, and your prospective employer asks you what sort of starting salary you would be looking for. You have just been given a great gift—you have a chance to set the anchor, meaning that you should ask for the highest salary that you think the employer could reasonably offer. For most of us, asking for a million dollars is only going to make us look ridiculous, which is why we suggest being on the high end of what you think is *reasonable*. Too often, we err on the side of caution, being afraid of scaring off the employer, and thus settle for too little. It *is* possible to scare off an employer, and it's true that employers do not like candidates to be overly aggressive in salary negotiations, but liking is not the same as respect or doing what it takes to hire or retain someone.[62] What happens much more often is that we ask for less than what we could have gotten.

Another distributive bargaining tactic is revealing a deadline. Negotiators who reveal deadlines speed concessions from their negotiating counterparts, making them reconsider their position. And even though negotiators don't *think* this tactic works, in reality, negotiators who reveal deadlines do better.[63]

Integrative Bargaining

In contrast to distributive bargaining, **integrative bargaining** operates under the assumption that there exists one or more settlements that can create a win-win solution. In terms of intraorganizational behaviour, all things being equal, integrative bargaining is preferable to distributive bargaining. Why? Because the former builds long-term

fixed pie The belief that there is only a set amount of goods or services to be divvied up between the parties.

integrative bargaining Negotiation that seeks one or more settlements that can create a win-win solution.

relationships and makes working together in the future easier. It bonds negotiators and allows both sides to leave the bargaining table feeling that they have achieved a victory. For instance, in union-management negotiations, both sides might sit down to figure out other ways to reduce costs within an organization, so that it is possible to have greater wage increases. Distributive bargaining, on the other hand, leaves one party a loser. It tends to build animosities and deepen divisions when people must work together on an ongoing basis.

Research shows that over repeated bargaining episodes, when the "losing" party feels positive about the negotiation outcome, the party is much more likely to bargain cooperatively in subsequent negotiations. This points to the important advantage of integrative negotiations: Even when you "win," you want your opponent to feel positively about the negotiation.[64]

Why, then, don't we see more integrative bargaining in organizations? The answer lies in the conditions necessary for this type of negotiation to succeed. These include parties who are open with information and candid about their concerns, sensitivity by both parties to the other's needs, the ability to trust one another, and a willingness by both parties to maintain flexibility.[65] Because these conditions often don't exist in organizations, it isn't surprising that negotiations often take on a win-at-any-cost dynamic.

There are ways to achieve more integrative outcomes. Individuals who bargain in teams reach more integrative agreements than those who bargain individually. This happens because more ideas are generated when more people are at the bargaining table. So try bargaining in teams.[66] Another way to achieve higher joint-gain settlements is to put more issues on the table. The more negotiable issues that are introduced into a negotiation, the more opportunity there is for "logrolling," where issues are traded because of differences in preferences. This approach creates better outcomes for each side than if each issue were negotiated individually.[67]

Finally, you should realize that compromise may be your worst enemy in negotiating a win-win agreement. This is because compromising reduces the pressure to bargain integratively. After all, if you or your opponent caves in easily, it does not require anyone to be creative to reach a settlement. Thus, people end up settling for less than they could have obtained if they had been forced to consider the other party's interests, trade off issues, and be creative.[68] Think of the classic example where two sisters are arguing over who gets an orange. Unknown to them, one sister wants the orange to drink the juice, whereas the other sister wants the orange peel to bake a cake. If one sister simply gives in and gives the other sister the orange, then they will not be forced to explore their reasons for wanting the orange, and thus they will never find the win-win solution: They could each have the orange because they want different parts of it! A poor compromise may sometimes be the result of negotiation anxiety. A 2011 study found that negotiators who feel anxious "expect lower outcomes, make lower first offers, respond more quickly to offers, exit bargaining situations earlier, and ultimately obtain worse outcomes." If self-efficacy is high, this will moderate some of the harmful effects of anxiety.[69] So it is important to feel prepared, and do what you can to reduce anxiety before negotiating a deal.

How does anxiety affect negotiating outcomes?

How to Negotiate

Exhibit 26-6 provides a simplified model of the negotiation process. It views negotiation as made up of five steps: (1) developing a strategy; (2) defining ground rules; (3) clarification and justification; (4) bargaining and problem solving; and (5) closure and implementation.

EXHIBIT 26-6 The Negotiation

- Developing a strategy
- Defining ground rules
- Clarification and justification
- Bargaining and problem solving
- Closure and implementation

Source: This model is based on R. J. Lewicki, "Bargaining and Negotiation," *Exchange: The Organizational Behavior Teaching Journal* 6, no. 2 (1981), pp. 39–40.

BATNA The *best alternative to a negotiated agreement;* the outcome an individual faces if negotiations fail.

bargaining zone The zone between each party's resistance point, assuming that there is overlap in this range.

Developing a Strategy

Before you start negotiating, you need to do your homework. What is the nature of the conflict? What is the history leading up to this negotiation? Who is involved, and what are their perceptions of the conflict? What do you want from the negotiation? What are *your* goals? It often helps to put your goals in writing and develop a range of outcomes—from "most hopeful" to "minimally acceptable"—to keep your attention focused.

You also want to prepare an assessment of what you think are the other party's goals.[70] What are they likely to ask for? How entrenched are they likely to be in their position? What intangible or hidden interests may be important to them? On what terms might they be willing to settle? When you can anticipate your opponent's position, you are better equipped to counter arguments with the facts and figures that support your position. You might also be able to anticipate better negotiating options for yourself, as *Case Incident—David Out-Negotiating Goliath: Apotex and Bristol-Myers Squibb* on page 351 shows. You want to be sure, however, that the information that you consider regarding your opponent is relevant to the negotiation. A 2011 study found that too much of the wrong kind of information can make for worse bargaining outcomes. In some cases, the person with extraneous information stopped looking for mutually beneficial outcomes earlier than those who did not have this information.[71]

In determining goals, parties are well advised to consider their "target and resistance" points, as well as their *best alternative to a negotiated agreement* (**BATNA**).[72] The buyer and the seller are examples of two negotiators. Each has a *target point* that defines what he or she would like to achieve. Each also has a *resistance point*, which marks the lowest outcome that is acceptable—the point below which each would break off negotiations rather than accept a less favourable settlement. The area between these two points makes up each negotiator's aspiration range. As long as there is some overlap between the buyer's and seller's aspiration ranges, there exists a **bargaining zone** where each side's aspirations can be met. Referring to Exhibit 26-7, if the buyer's resistance point is $450, and the seller's resistance point is $500, then the two may not be able to reach agreement because there is no overlap in their aspiration ranges.

One's BATNA represents the alternative that an individual will face if negotiations fail. For instance, during the PNE and CUPE 1004 negotiations, for both the unionized employees and PNE management, the BATNA was the loss of revenue from sport and entertainment events and the fair of the following year. In the end, both sides must have concluded that it was preferable to get the conflict resolved.

As part of your strategy, you should determine not only your BATNA but also some estimate of the other side's as well.[73] If you go into your negotiation having a good idea of what the other party's BATNA is, even if you are not able to meet theirs, you might

EXHIBIT 26-7 Staking Out the Bargaining Zone

$400	$475	$525	$600
Buyer's target point	Seller's resistance point	Buyer's resistance point	Seller's target point

be able to get them to change it. Think carefully about what the other side is willing to give up. People who underestimate their opponent's willingness to give on key issues before the negotiation even starts end up with lower outcomes from a negotiation.[74]

Defining Ground Rules

Once you have done your planning and developed a strategy, you are ready to begin defining the ground rules and procedures with the other party over the negotiation itself. Who will do the negotiating? Where will it take place? What time constraints, if any, will apply? To what issues will negotiation be limited? Will there be a specific procedure to follow if an impasse is reached? During this phase, the parties will also exchange their initial proposals or demands. *From Concepts to Skills* on pages 353–354 directly addresses some of the actions you should take to improve the likelihood that you can achieve a good agreement.

Clarification and Justification

When initial positions have been exchanged, both you and the other party will explain, amplify, clarify, bolster, and justify your original demands. This part of the process need not be confrontational. Rather, it's an opportunity for educating and informing each other on the issues, why they are important, and how each arrived at their initial demands. This is the point at which you might want to provide the other party with any documentation that helps support your position. The *Ethical Dilemma Exercise* on page 350 considers whether it is ever appropriate to lie during negotiations.

Bargaining and Problem Solving

The essence of the negotiation process is the actual give and take in trying to hash out an agreement. A 2011 study found that those who used competing and collaborating (essentially a combination of the forcing and problem solving conflict resolution styles discussed earlier in the chapter) as part of their strategy to gain a higher starting salary were more successful (and received higher increases) than those who used compromising and accommodating strategies.[75] The study looked at the influence of individual differences and negotiation strategies on starting salary outcomes based on a sample of 149 newly hired employees in various industry settings. Results indicated that those who chose to negotiate increased their starting salaries by an average of $5000. Individuals who negotiated by using competing and collaborating strategies, characterized by an open discussion of one's positions, issues, and perspectives, further increased their salaries as compared with those who used compromising and accommodating strategies. Individual differences, including risk aversion and integrative attitudes, played a significant role in predicting whether individuals negotiated, and if so, what strategies they used.

Closure and Implementation

The final step in the negotiation process is formalizing the agreement that has been worked out and developing procedures that are necessary for implementation and monitoring. For major negotiations—which would include everything from labour-management negotiations, to bargaining over lease terms, to buying real estate, to negotiating a job offer for a senior management position—this will require hammering out the specifics in a formal contract. For most cases, however, closure of the negotiation process is nothing more formal than a handshake.

Individual Differences in Negotiation Effectiveness

Are some people better negotiators than others? The answer is more complex than you might think. Three factors influence how effectively individuals negotiate: personality, mood/emotions, and gender.

 How do individual differences influence negotiations?

Personality Traits in Negotiation

Can you predict an opponent's negotiating tactics if you know something about his or her personality? Because personality and negotiation outcomes are related but only weakly, the answer is, at best, "sort of." Negotiators who are agreeable or extraverted are not very successful in distributive bargaining. Why? Because extraverts are outgoing and friendly, they tend to share more information than they should. And agreeable people are more interested in finding ways to cooperate rather than to butt heads. These traits, while slightly helpful in integrative negotiations, are liabilities when interests are opposed. So the best distributive bargainer appears to be a disagreeable introvert—someone more interested in his or her own outcomes than in pleasing the other party and having a pleasant social exchange. People who are highly interested in having positive relationships with other people, and who are not very concerned about their own outcomes, are especially poor negotiators. These people tend to be very anxious about disagreements and plan to give in quickly to avoid unpleasant conflicts even before negotiations start.[76]

Research also suggests intelligence predicts negotiation effectiveness, but, as with personality, the effects are not especially strong.[77] In a sense, these weak links are good news because they mean you are not severely disadvantaged, even if you are an agreeable extravert, when it comes time to negotiate. We all can learn to be better negotiators. In fact, people who think so are more likely to do well in negotiations because they persist in their efforts even in the face of temporary setbacks.[78]

Moods/Emotions in Negotiation

Do moods and emotions influence negotiation? They do, but the way they do appears to depend on the type of negotiation.[79] In distributive negotiations, it appears that negotiators in a position of power or equal status who show anger negotiate better outcomes because their anger induces concessions from their opponents. This appears to hold true even when the negotiators are instructed to show anger despite not being truly angry. On the other hand, for those in a less powerful position, displaying anger leads to worse outcomes. So if you are a boss negotiating with a peer or a subordinate, displaying anger may help you, but if you are an employee negotiating with a boss, it might hurt you.

In integrative negotiations, in contrast, positive moods and emotions appear to lead to more integrative agreements (higher levels of joint gain).

Gender Differences in Negotiation

Do men and women negotiate differently? And does gender affect negotiation outcomes? The answer to the first question appears to be no.[80] The answer to the second is a qualified yes.[81]

Ever wonder if men and women negotiate differently?

A popular stereotype is that women are more cooperative and pleasant in negotiations than are men. The evidence doesn't support this belief. However, men have been found to negotiate better outcomes than women, although the difference is relatively small. It's been postulated that men and women place divergent values on outcomes. "It is possible that a few hundred dollars more in salary or the corner office is less important to women than forming and maintaining an interpersonal relationship."[82]

The belief that women are "nicer" than men in negotiations is probably due to a confusion between gender and the lower degree of power women typically hold in most large organizations. Because women are expected to be "nice" and men "tough," research shows women are penalized when they initiate negotiations.[83] Moreover, when women and men actually do conform to these stereotypes—women act "nice" and men "tough"—it becomes a self-fulfilling prophecy, reinforcing the stereotypical gender differences between male and female negotiators.[84] Thus, one of the reasons negotiations favour men is that women are "damned if they do, damned if they don't." Negotiate tough, and they are penalized for violating a gender stereotype. Negotiate nice, and it only reinforces and lets others take advantage of the stereotype.

Evidence also suggests women's own attitudes and behaviours hurt them in negotiations. Managerial women demonstrate less confidence in anticipation of negotiating and are less satisfied with their performance afterward, even when their performance and the outcomes they achieve are similar to those for men.[85] Women are also less likely than men to see an ambiguous situation as an opportunity for negotiation. It appears that women may unduly penalize themselves by failing to engage in negotiations when such action would be in their best interests.

The outcomes of negotiations for women and men also seem to differ. One researcher found that when women negotiated to buy a car, the opening offer by the salesperson was higher than it was for men.[86] In a study of salary offers, researchers found that men were offered higher starting salaries in a negotiating process than were women.[87] While in each of these instances the opening offers were just that, offers to be negotiated, women also fared less well than men at the end of the negotiating process, even when they used the same negotiating tactics as men. A 2011 study found that during negotiations, particularly for salary, women may desire social approval, and thus bargain less assertively. The same women were much more assertive when bargaining on behalf of someone else.[88] A 2011 study by professor Linda Schweitzer of the Sprott School of Business, Carleton University, and three colleagues found that women tended to have lower expectations about salaries and promotions as they enter the workforce.[89]

The results of these studies may shed some light on the pay and promotion discrepancies between men and women, which we discuss in Chapter 20. If women expect and then negotiate even slightly lower starting salaries, then over time, with raises based on percentages of salaries, the gap between men's and women's salaries can grow quite substantially.

Respected for her intelligence, confident negotiating skills, and successful outcomes, Christine Lagarde is the managing director of the International Monetary Fund (IMF). Prior to that she was the minister for the economy, finance, and employment in France, where she used her negotiating skills to boost French exports by 10 percent. She is also known for her much earlier work as a labour and antitrust lawyer for the global law firm Baker & McKenzie, during which she negotiated with France's trade unions to change the country's labour laws, including ending the 35-hour limit on the workweek, to help boost the nation's sluggish economy.

GLOBAL IMPLICATIONS

Below we look at (1) how conflict is handled in different cultures, (2) whether there are differences in negotiating styles across cultures, and (3) how the display of emotions affects negotiations in different cultures.

Conflict Resolution and Culture

Research suggests that differences across countries in conflict resolution strategies may be based on collectivistic tendencies and motives.[90] Collectivistic cultures see people as deeply embedded in social situations, whereas individualistic cultures see people as autonomous. As a result, collectivists are more likely to seek to preserve relationships and promote the good of the group as a whole than individualists. To preserve peaceful relationships, collectivists will avoid direct expression of conflicts, preferring to use more indirect methods for resolving differences of opinion. Collectivists may also be more interested in demonstrations of concern and working through third parties to resolve disputes, whereas individualists will be more likely to confront differences of opinion directly and openly.

Some research supports this theory. Compared with collectivistic Japanese negotiators, individualistic US negotiators are more likely to see offers from their counterparts as unfair and reject them. Another study revealed that while US managers are more likely to use competing tactics when faced with a conflict, Chinese managers are more likely to use compromising and avoiding.[91] Interview data, however, suggest top management teams in Chinese high-technology firms prefer integration even more than compromising and avoiding.[92]

Cultural Differences in Negotiating Style

Negotiating styles vary across national cultures, as the following examples suggest:[93]

- *France.* The French like conflict. They frequently gain recognition and develop their reputations by thinking and acting against others. As a result, the French tend to take a long time in negotiating agreements, and they are not overly concerned about whether their opponents like or dislike them.[94]

- *China.* The Chinese draw out negotiations because they believe negotiations never end. Just when you think you have pinned down every detail and reached a final solution with a Chinese executive, that executive might smile and start the process all over again. The Chinese negotiate to develop a relationship and a commitment to work together rather than to tie up every loose end.[95]

- *Japan.* The Japanese also negotiate to develop relationships and a commitment to work together. One study compared US and Japanese negotiators and found that the Japanese negotiators tend to communicate indirectly and adapt their behaviours to the situation. A follow-up study showed that early offers by US negotiators led to the anchoring effect (see the "Distributive Negotiation" section), whereas early offers by Japanese negotiators led to more information sharing and better integrative outcomes.[96]

- *United States.* Americans are known around the world for their impatience and their desire to be liked. Astute negotiators from other countries often turn these characteristics to their advantage by dragging out negotiations and making friendship conditional on the final settlement.

The cultural context of a negotiation significantly influences the amount and type of preparation for bargaining, the relative emphasis on task vs. interpersonal relationships, the tactics used, and even the place where the negotiation should be conducted. Exhibit 26-8 identifies whether countries focus more on win-win or win-lose solutions. These findings are based on research on 300 negotiators in 12 countries. As you will note, 100 percent of Japanese negotiators said they focus on finding a win-win solution. By contrast, only 37 percent of Spanish negotiators said the same.[97]

Culture, Negotiations, and Emotions

As a rule, no one likes to face an angry counterpart in negotiations. However, East Asian negotiators may respond less favourably than people from other cultures.[98]

Two separate studies found that East Asian negotiators were less likely to accept offers from negotiators who displayed anger during negotiations. Another study explicitly compared how US and Chinese negotiators react to an angry counterpart. When confronted with an angry negotiator, Chinese negotiators increased their use of distributive negotiating tactics, whereas US negotiators decreased their use of these tactics.

LESSONS LEARNED

- A medium level of conflict often results in higher productivity than an absence of conflict.
- Negotiators should identify their BATNA (best alternative to negotiated agreement).
- In relationships with long-term consequences, it is best to use a win-win strategy in bargaining.

EXHIBIT 26-8 Negotiating Attitude: Win-Win or Win-Lose?											
Country	Japan	China	Argentina	France	India	US	UK	Mexico	Germany	Nigeria	Brazil	Spain
Negotiator focuses on win-win solution (%)	100	82	81	80	78	71	59	50	55	47	44	37

Source: Based on J. W. Salacuse, "Ten Ways That Culture Affects Negotiating Style: Some Survey Results," *Negotiation Journal,* July 1998, pp. 221–240.

Why might East Asian and Chinese negotiators respond more negatively to angry negotiators? The authors of the research speculated that because their cultures emphasize respect and deference, they may be particularly likely to perceive angry behaviour as disrespectful, and thus deserving of uncooperative tactics in response.

ORAL PRESENTATION SKILLS[1]

Most adults fear speaking in public. Nevertheless, a study conducted by AT&T and Stanford University revealed that it is the top predictor of success and upward mobility in organizations.[2] Unfortunately, this skill is often lacking in new managers and college graduates.[3] This appendix will provide ideas on three skills necessary for making effective oral presentations: managing anxiety, planning and preparing, and delivery of the presentation.

Managing Anxiety

Stage fright is a normal reaction. Almost every speaker, actor, musician, or performer experiences some degree of stage fright. Although anxiety never goes away entirely, you

EXHIBIT A-1   Tips for Overcoming Stage Fright

- *Know your material well.*   Being the expert gives you confidence because you know more than the audience does.

- *Practice.*   Practice your presentation and, if possible, videotape yourself so that you know how you look to others.

- *Get audience participation.*   It shifts attention from you to the audience and generates more of an easy-going conversational atmosphere.

- *Use names and eye contact.*   These establish rapport. It is easier to talk to friends than strangers.

- *Check the facilities and audiovisual equipment in advance.*   Beforehand checking eliminates worry about whether the equipment works, and you avoid having to figure things out in front of the audience if it does not work.

- *Research your audience.*   Being familiar with your audience gives you confidence because you know their needs. You might even discover that you have friends in the audience who will support you.

- *Relax.*   Take time out right before your presentation to relax. Different things will relax different people. Some concentrate on breathing deeply. Others visualize themselves successfully presenting. Some do progressive muscle relaxation (i.e., focus on relaxing specific muscle groups one at a time: neck, shoulders, arms, legs).

- *Dress comfortably and appropriately.*   The way you dress can help you avoid anxiety about your image.

- *Use your own style.*   You do not need the stress of trying to imitate someone else.

- *Use audiovisual aids.*   They can reduce anxiety by providing prompts and taking the visual impact off you personally for a while.

Source: D. A. Level and W. P. Galle, Jr., *Managerial Communications* (San Diego, CA: Business Publications, Inc., 1988) 44.

can learn to manage your fear so that it can actually help you perform better.[4] Exhibit A-1 provides 10 tips for overcoming stage fright.

Planning and Preparing

Once you have your stage fright under control, the success of your public speaking is determined primarily by the time you spend preparing before you step in front of your audience. You want to avoid speeches that are too long, too detailed, confusing, vague, boring, or off-track. The following steps will help you prepare an effective presentation.

Identify the Purpose

The first and most critical step in preparation is understanding the "what" and the "why" of your presentation. Your *purpose* is the broad general outcome you want the presentation to achieve. Ask yourself three questions to clarify the objective of your presentation:

- *Why* am I giving this presentation: to persuade, to explain, to instruct, to report on something?

- *What* do I want the audience to know or do at the end of the presentation?

- *How* do I want the audience to feel?

Analyze Your Audience

After you are clear on what you want to accomplish, mold your presentation to fit the specific characteristics of the audience. You can acquire information about your audience by

- *Asking the presentation host* about the audience.

- *Talking to people who will be in the audience.*

- *Talking to other speakers* who have spoken to the same group.

Organize the Presentation

Once you know your audience and are clear about your purpose and objectives, you are ready to start organizing your presentation. The first step is to find your focus or the "big idea" of your material. The second is to develop an outline so that you can visualize the flow of your presentation.

The Big Idea

What is the power punch of your presentation—the one thing you want your audience to walk away with? Say, for example, that you are going to explain a new marketing plan to your company's board of directors. It probably has several sections that are supported by reams of documented research and facts, but you only have 20 to 30 minutes to summarize the plan in a way that will gain the board's approval. What is it about the plan that will capture their imagination? A new theme? A new program? A high payoff possibility?

How well you translate your message into benefits for the audience determines its effectiveness. You need to structure your presentation so that it supports your one big idea. Of course, your message will contain more than one idea but they should all reinforce the primary focus.

Develop an Outline

One way to make sure you are clear on your focus is to develop a basic outline for your presentation. Begin by listing no more than five independent ideas that the audience must understand for the objectives to be accomplished. Then outline your plan for presenting the detail and persuasive material needed to allow your audience to understand those points. For the most effective delivery, break your presentation down into its three main parts: the introduction, body, and conclusion.

The Introduction   It is important to write out your introduction completely, word-for-word. This part of your presentation is too important to leave to chance, hoping you have the right words when you get there. It also acts as a security blanket. If you can get through those first few minutes, the butterflies will settle down and the rest of the presentation will flow more easily. The introduction should take 5 to 15 percent of the allowed speaking time, and it should prepare the audience for the main points of the presentation.[5]

- ***Start the introduction with a bang.***   At this point you need to get the audience's attention and convince them to listen to you. Grab the audience with something vitally interesting to them. Give them an interesting story or example that ties into your focus. Or you might use a strong, meaningful quotation, a startling statistic, or appropriate humor that makes a relevant point.

- ***Increase your credibility.***   Relate something about your background and experience that makes you an expert on the topic you are speaking about. This point, of course, is one of the purposes of having someone share your credentials when they introduce you before the talk. But, referring to a time when you successfully applied your expertise provides a relevant example and further amplifies your credibility.

- ***Present your agenda.***   Keep in mind the familiar slogan "Tell them what you are going to tell them, tell them, and then tell them what you just told them."

- ***Share what you expect of the audience.***   At the beginning of your presentation, tell listeners about the question-and-answer session at the end, or the ensuing reception, or the cards you want them to fill out before they leave.

- ***Use icebreakers if appropriate.***   In some presentations it is helpful to do an opening icebreaker to set an emotional climate for the presentation. The most common icebreaker is having people introduce themselves and explain their reason for attending the presentation. Make sure your icebreakers are short, appropriate, and participative.[6] They should last no longer than 5 to 10 minutes, have something to do with the topic, and be something that each person can, and wants to, get involved with.

The Main Message   Once you have gotten the audience's attention, you need to deliver what you promised in the shortest, most interesting way possible. Keep two things in mind as you structure your message: the attention cycle of your audience and pace of your speech.[7]

Material at the beginning and end of a presentation will be remembered more than the material in the middle.[8] Our attention span lasts only for a short time and then it tapers off. When we sense the end of a message, we pull our attention back in time to catch the last material. Fluctuation of the attention cycle is one of the main reasons we put such emphasis on the introduction and conclusion.

You can also change the pace every 10 to 15 minutes to break up your talk and keep attention riveted. You can create this change by including appropriate humor, stories, exercises requiring people to move their bodies (even if it is just raising their hands), or calls for a verbal response.

Other things you do can help retention. First, use repetition. Your main ideas need to be communicated several times to make sure they get through accurately and are remembered. Second, use stories and analogies to associate and connect your ideas to something the listeners already understand. Third, change the intensity in the pitch, tone, and loudness of your voice to focus audience attention. Fourth, use audience involvement. Use visual aids, questions, hand gestures, and sound effects, anything that gets the audience involved with the message.

The Conclusion   Your conclusion should repeat your main ideas to reinforce your objectives and expectations for the audience. It should be strong, succinct, and persuasive. Many speakers consider this section almost as important as the introduction and they write it out word-for-word.

Practice and Visualize Success[9]

You know your audience. You know your material. You have written a dynamite speech. The last step is to practice delivering it. The following guidelines may assist you in the process.

Rehearse

Rehearse aloud at least four or five times in order to check your timing (you read out loud slower than you read in your mind), and to make sure your presentation flows and sounds the way you want it to. You should feel comfortable explaining all of your ideas. Do not try to memorize your speech. You may end up sounding stale, as if you are reciting or reading.

Rehearse in the actual location of the presentation, if possible. It is better to work out the technicalities of visual aids, sound equipment, outlets, and positioning during a rehearsal, rather than be surprised on the day of your presentation.

You can get used to public speaking through rehearsing with family or friends. Ask them to explain what they heard. This feedback will give you a chance to make sure your message is clear. Ask them whether your visual aids are effective and whether they make your message more understandable. Ask them what you can do better.

Visualize

Once you have rehearsed your presentation and feel comfortable with the material, visualize yourself presenting it successfully. Olympic athletes use visualization to reach their peak performance. Studies have shown that visualized practice has a similar effect to actual practice. Visualizing a successful conclusion to any activity gives you a chance to experience success and become more confident in your delivery.

Delivery of the Presentation

Planning and rehearsing are necessary, but not sufficient to ensure a successful presentation. No matter how well organized, logical, and supported with visual aids, if a presentation is poorly delivered it is doomed to failure. Following are some guidelines for using delivery to enhance your presentation.[10]

Be Enthusiastic

Students usually forgive a teacher's lack of platform skills if he or she appears devoted to the subject and is trying to share that appreciation with them. Similarly, an audience can become oblivious to similar speaker deficiencies if his or her gestures, vocal intonations, and attitude convey enthusiasm for the message. Your interest in your topic tends to be contagious. An enthusiastic introduction will perk audience interest to learn why you are so enthusiastic. Speak as if you are in a lively conversation with friends, but avoid shouting or preaching.

Maintain Eye Contact

Eye contact enhances audience involvement. It makes the audience feel that they are being spoken to personally and that you are sincere. It is most effective to rotate looking at audience members one at a time on a random basis.

Use Proxemics

The arrangement and use of physical space can enhance or detract from your presentation. It is better not to hide behind a podium. Eliminate distracting items from the area such as unnecessary equipment, furniture, papers, writings on the board, and irrelevant signs. You want to keep the audience's attention on you.

Body movement keeps the audience's attention. It can emphasize key points, build rapport, and signal transitions. Variety is the key, so keep alternating standing, moving, sitting, speaking, listening, and gesturing. Move closer to the audience to build rapport with particular members and make points. Back off when you are awaiting responses or addressing the entire group.

Use Appropriate Gestures

You should obviously avoid alienating or distracting gestures such as jingling keys, twisting hair, or adjusting notes. Appropriate gestures appear to be spontaneous and accentuate your verbal message. Small audiences can pick up minor variances in facial expression and hand movements, but with large audiences, your gestures need to be more accentuated and dramatic.

Never Apologize

Do not apologize for the way you look or sound, do not apologize for not being the best speaker in the world, do not apologize because your slides are upside down . . . do not apologize for anything! The minute you apologize, your ability to influence your audience is decreased. Start your speech with power. Make your audience think they are going to be informed, entertained, or enlightened. . . . Do not let them think they are getting anything except your best.

Concept Quiz

Complete the following true-false quiz by circling the correct answer. Answers are at the end of the quiz. After marking your answers, remember to go back and check your understanding of any answers you missed.

True or False	1. The three main sections of an oral presentation are the big idea, the introduction, and the conclusion.
True or False	2. Because you are the expert, it is not a good idea to involve the audience in your presentation.
True or False	3. You should never apologize during oral presentations.
True or False	4. You can minimize anxiety by dressing comfortably and appropriately.
True or False	5. An army colonel should avoid using technical military jargon when addressing the general public.
True or False	6. You should never use gestures because they are confusing.
True or False	7. Being enthusiastic about your topic can discredit your presentation.
True or False	8. Proxemics is the use of body language to convey messages.
True or False	9. You should not check on the technological capabilities of the place where you are speaking because they are your host's responsibility.
True or False	10. Preparing by practicing out loud can be detrimental and throw you off during the actual presentation.

Answers.   (1) False; (2) False; (3) True; (4) True; (5) True; (6) False; (7) False; (8) True; (9) False; (10) False

Behavioral Checklist

The following skills are important to effective formal oral and written communication. Use them when evaluating your communication skills and those of others.

The Effective Oral Presenter

- Includes content appropriate for the audience.
- Determines the presentation's purpose and behavioral objectives.
- Productively manages anxiety.
- Includes an introduction, body, and conclusion.
- Speaks clearly and enthusiastically.
- Effectively uses visual aids.
- Utilizes space for maximum impact.
- Maintains eye contact and uses appropriate gestures.

ENDNOTES

Chapter 1

1 S. Dobson, "Business Acumen Critical for HR: Survey," *Canadian HR Reporter* (May 9, 2011).

2 P. Verge and G. Vallee, "Un droit du travail? Essai sur la spicifite du droit du travail," Editions Yvon Blais, Cowansville, (1997).

3 J. Sack, "U.S. and Canadian Labour Law: Significant Distinctions", *ABA Journal of Labor & Employment Law*, 25, no. 2 (2010), pp. 241–259.

4 Canadian Charter of Rights and Freedoms, as part of the Constitution Act of 1982.

5 Canadian Charter of Rights and Freedoms, Section 15(1).

6 *Annual Report of the Canadian Human Rights Commission* (Ottawa, ON: Government of Canada, 1991), p. 65.

7 A.P. Aggarwal, *Sex Discrimination: Employment Law and Practices* (Toronto, ON: Butterworths Canada, 1994).

8 H.J. Jain, "Human Rights: Issues in Employment," *Human Resources Management in Canada* (Toronto, ON: Prentice-Hall Canada, 1995), p. 50.

9 Ontario Human Rights Commission, *Human Rights at Work* (Toronto, ON: Government of Ontario, 1999), pp. 63–64.

10 S. Rudner, "Just Cause—Back from the Dead?" *Canadian HR Reporter* (September 22, 2008); M. Bélanger and R. Ravary, "Supreme Court of Canada Sets Limits on Employer's Duty to Accommodate," *McCarthy Tétrault e-Alert* (July 24, 2008); D. Elenbaas, "Undue Hardship: Supreme Court of Canada Clarifies the Standard—or Does it?" *Ultimate HR Manual*, 39 (August 2008), pp. 1–3.

11 According to Raj Anand, partner with WeirFoulds LLP and former chief commissioner of the Ontario Human Rights Commission. Presentation on "Equity, Diversity and Accommodation" at Osgoode Hall Law School, April 7, 2011.

12 "Policy and Guidelines on Disability and the Duty to Accommodate," Ontario Human Rights Commission (December, 2009), www.ohrc.on.ca/en/resources/Policies/PolicyDisAccom2/pdf (accessed September 26, 2011).

13 British Columbia (Public Service Employee Relations Commission) v. BCGSEU, [1999] 3 S.C.R. 3 at para. 68.

14 According to the US National Library of Medicine, www.ncbi.nlm.nih.gov/pubmedhealth/PMH0001295.

15 "Disability and the Duty to Accommodate: Your Rights and Responsibilities," Ontario Human Rights Commission, www.ohrc.on.ca/en/issues/disability (accessed November 23, 2011).

16 J.R. Smith, "Bipolar Employee Awarded $80,000" *Canadian HR Reporter* (April 7, 2008); C. Hall, "Just Because You Can't See Them Doesn't Mean They're Not There: 'Invisible Disabilities,'" *Ultimate HR Manual*, 34 (March 2008), pp. 1–3; "Duty to Accommodate Mental Health Disability Upheld in Landmark Ontario Human Rights Decision," *Ultimate HR Manual*, 33 (February 2008), p. 6.

17 According to the Supreme Court Ruling by Brian Dickson Chief Justice of Canadia, Janzen v. Platy Enterprises Ltd., 1989.

18 S. Klie, "Harassment Twice as Bad for Minority Women," *Canadian HR Reporter* (April 10, 2006).

19 S. Dobson, "Tackling the Bullies," *Canadian HR Reporter* (March 9, 2009).

20 B. Kuretzky, "When Push Comes to Shove," *Workplace News* (November/December 2005), p. 22; U. Vu, "Employers Waiting for Courts to Define Bullying," *Canadian HR Reporter* (September 12, 2005), pp. 1, 13.

21 "Saskatchewan's Anti-Bullying Law Now in Effect," *Canadian HR Reporter* (October 4, 2007); S. Rudner, "Psychological Harassment Hurts Employees, Productivity," *Canadian HR Reporter* (October 21, 2007).

22 J.R. Smith, "Employers: Don't Let Workplace Harassment Catch You Off Guard," *Canadian HR Reporter* (October 22, 2007); *Anti-Harassment Policies for the Workplace: An Employer's Guide* (Canadian Human Rights Commission, March 2006), p. 3.

23 J.R. Smith, "Employer's Damage Control Leads to Big-Time Damages," *Canadian HR Reporter* (June 1, 2009); "Employer Vicariously Liable for Supervisor's Abusive Conduct," *Ultimate HR Manual*, 49 (June 2009), p. 7.

24 A.P. Aggarwal, *Sexual Harassment in the Workplace*, 2nd ed. (Toronto, ON: Butterworths Canada, 1992), pp. 10–11.

25 N.C. MacDonald, "Keeping the Bedroom out of the Boardroom," *Canadian HR Reporter* (October 22, 2007).

26 *Anti-Harassment Policies for the Workplace: An Employer's Guide* (Canadian Human Rights Commission, March 2006), pp. 16–25.

27 "Construction Firms Fight B.C. Human Rights Ruling," *HR Professional* (April/May 2009), p. 13.

28 S. Klie, "Muslims Face Discrimination in Workplace," *Canadian HR Reporter* (February 27, 2006).

29 "Key Provisions of Ottawa's Same-Sex Legislation," *Canadian HR Reporter* (March 27, 2000), p. 11.

30 Canadian Human Rights Commission, www.chrc-ccdp.ca/adr/settlements/archives2/page5-en.asp (accessed August 13, 2006).

31 Canadian Human Rights Commission, www.chrc-ccdp.ca/discrimination/age-en.asp (accessed August 13, 2006).

32 Ontario Human Rights Commission, www.ohrc.on.ca/english/publicatoins/age-policy_5.shtml (accessed June 2, 2006).

33 H. Levitt and L-K Hum, "Accommodating Family Status," *Canadian HR Reporter* (January 12, 2009).

34 L. Corrente, "Accommodating Family Status," Torkin Maines Presentation (June 8, 2005).

35 R.S. Abella, *Equality in Employment: A Royal Commission Report* (Ottawa, ON: Supply and Services Canada, 1984).

36 A.B. Bakan and A. Kobyashi, *Employment Equity Policy in Canada: An Interprovincial Comparison* (Ottawa, ON: Status of Women Canada, March 2000), pp. 9–10.

37 *Women in Canada: Work Chapter Updates*, Statistics Canada, Catalogue No. 89F0133XIE, 2006.

38 S. Klie, "Feds Discriminated Against Nurses," *Canadian HR Reporter* (February 25, 2008).

39 K.A. Zavitz, "Intolerance Costly Problem for Employers," *Canadian HR Reporter* (December 15, 2008).

40 C. Williams, "Disability in the Workplace," *Perspectives on Labour and Income* 7, no. 2 (February 2006), pp. 16–23.

41 "2006 Census: Ethnic Origin, Visible Minorities, Place of Work and Mode of Transportation," Statistics Canada (April 2, 2008), www.statcan.gc.ca/daily-quotidien/080402/dq080402a-eng.htm (accessed September 26, 2011).

42 W. Cukier and M. Yap, *DiverseCity Counts: A Snapshot of Diversity in the Greater Toronto Area.* (Toronto, ON: The Diversity Institute, Ryerson University, May 2009).

43 P. Israel, "Employee Misconduct . . . Employer Responsibility?" *Canadian HR Reporter* (May 20, 2002), p. 5.

44 P. Israel, "Spying on Employees . . . and It's Perfectly Legal," *Canadian HR Reporter* (April 21, 2003), p. 5.

45 M. Draaisma, "Computer Use Policy in Workplace Is a Must, Says Toronto Lawyer," *Ultimate HR Manual* (May 2009), pp. 1–4.

46 A.P. Cleek, "Six Steps to an Effective Workplace Blogging Policy," *Ultimate HR Manual* (August 2007), pp. 6–7.

47 E. Kuzz, "More Rules for Employee Information Protection," *Canadian HR Reporter* (September 9, 2002), p. 16; D. Brown, "10 Months to Get Ready," *Canadian HR Reporter* (February 24, 2003), pp. 1, 11.

48 D. Fallows, "Technology Paves the Way for Big Brother," *Canadian HR Reporter* (April 9, 2007).

49 M. Draaisma, "Computer Use Policy in Workplace Is a Must, Says Toronto Lawyer," *Ultimate HR Manual* (May 2009), pp. 1–4; S. Rudner, "The High Cost of Internet, E-mail Abuse," *Canadian HR Reporter* (January 31, 2005), pp. R5–R6; N. MacDonald, "You've Got E-mail Problems," *Canadian HR Reporter* (March 10, 2003), pp. G5, G10.

50 K. Williams, "Privacy in a Climate of Electronic Surveillance," *Workplace News* (April 2005), p. 10; S. Hood, "What's Private, What's Not?" *HR Professional* (February/March 2006), pp. 20–28; P. Strazynski, "Falsely Accused Employee Gets $2.1 Million," *Canadian HR Reporter* (July 14, 2008).

Chapter 2

1 Vignette based on http://www.retailcouncil.org/news/media/press/2007/pr20070516.asp; "Wal-Mart Canada Named One of Canada's Best Employers," http://www.newswire.ca/en/releases/archive/January2007/02/c2780.html; "Walmart Canada to Open First Supercentre in Manitoba," *Canada NewsWire*, May 12, 2011; and C. Persaud, "Walmart Canada to Face Steep Competition Once Target Arrives," *MarketNews*, July 8, 2011, http://www.marketnews.ca/LatestNewsHeadlines/WalmartCanadatoFaceSteepCompetitionOnceTargetArrives.html; and http://www.workplaceinstitute.org/press-releases/2011-best-employers-awards-winners/

2 B. Nyhan and J. Reifler, "When Corrections Fail: The Persistence of Political Misperceptions" *Political Behavior* 32, no. 2 (2010), pp. 303–330.

3 D. Wood, P. Harms, and S. Vazire, "Perceiver Effects as Projective Tests: What Your Perceptions of Others Say About You," *Journal of Personality and Social Psychology* 99, no. 1 (2010), pp. 174–190.

4 H. H. Kelley, "Attribution in Social Interaction," in *Attribution: Perceiving the Causes of Behavior*, ed. E. Jones, D. Kanouse, H. Kelley, N. Nisbett, S. Valins, and B. Weiner (Morristown, NJ: General Learning Press, 1972).

5 See L. Ross, "The Intuitive Psychologist and His Shortcomings," in *Advances in Experimental Social Psychology*, vol. 10, ed. L. Berkowitz (Orlando, FL: Academic Press, 1977), pp. 174–220; and A. G. Miller and T. Lawson, "The Effect of an Informational Option on the Fundamental Attribution Error," *Personality and Social Psychology Bulletin*, June 1989, pp. 194–204.

6 M. J. Young, M. W. Morris, and V. M. Scherwin, "Managerial Mystique: Magical Thinking in Judgments of Managers' Vision, Charisma, and Magnetism," *Journal of Management*, May 2011, published online before print, http://jom.sagepub.com/content/early/2011/04/29/0149206311406284

7 Columbia Business School, "Dynamics behind Magical Thinking and Charismatic Leadership Revealed," *ScienceDaily*, July 15, 2011.

8 N. Epley and D. Dunning, "Feeling 'Holier Than Thou': Are Self-Serving Assessments Produced by Errors in Self- or Social Predictions?" *Journal of Personality and Social Psychology* 79, no. 6 (2000), pp. 861–875.

9 M. C. Frame, K. J. Roberto, A. E. Schwab, and C. T. Harris, "What Is Important on the Job? Differences across Gender, Perspective, and Job Level," *Journal of Applied Social Psychology* 40, no. 1 (January 2010), pp. 36–56.

10 See K. R. Murphy, R. A. Jako, and R. L. Anhalt, "Nature and Consequences of Halo Error: A Critical Analysis," *Journal of Applied Psychology*, April 1993, pp. 218–225; P. Rosenzweig, *The Halo Effect* (New York: Free Press, 2007); I. Dennis, "Halo Effects in Grading Student Projects," *Journal of Applied Psychology* 92, no. 4 (2007), pp. 1169–1176; and C. E. Naquin and R. O. Tynan, "The Team Halo Effect: Why Teams Are Not Blamed for Their Failures," *Journal of Applied Psychology*, April 2003, pp. 332–340.

11 S. E. Asch, "Forming Impressions of Personality," *Journal of Abnormal and Social Psychology*, July 1946, pp. 258–290.

12 http://www.timescolonist.com/entertainment/UVic+grad+student+launches+First+Nations+music+website/5594608/story.html#ixzz1bugKFx8q

13 See, for example, G. N. Powell, "The Good Manager: Business Students' Stereotypes of Japanese Managers versus Stereotypes of American Managers," *Group & Organization Management*, March 1992, pp. 44–56; C. Ostroff and L. E. Atwater, "Does Whom You Work with Matter? Effects of Referent Group Gender and Age Composition on Managers' Compensation," *Journal of Applied Psychology*, August 2003, pp. 725–740; M. E. Heilman, A. S. Wallen, D. Fuchs, and M. M. Tamkins, "Penalties for Success: Reactions to Women Who Succeed at Male Gender-Typed Tasks," *Journal of Applied Psychology*, June 2004, pp. 416–427; and R. A. Posthuma and M. A. Campion, "Age Stereotypes in the Workplace: Common Stereotypes, Moderators, and Future Research Directions," *Journal of Management* 35, no. 1 (2009), pp. 158–188.

14 J. L. Eberhardt, P. G. Davies, V. J. Purdie-Vaughns, and S. L. Johnson, "Looking Deathworthy: Perceived Stereotypicality of Black Defendants Predicts Capital-Sentencing Outcomes," *Psychological Science* 17, no. 5 (2006), pp. 383–386.

15 J. D. Remedios, A. L. Chasteen, and J. D. Paek, "Not All Prejudices Are Experienced Equally: Comparing Experiences of Racism and Sexism in Female Minorities," *Group Processes & Intergroup Relations*, June 11, 2011, published online before print, http://gpi.sagepub.com/content/early/2011/06/17/1368430211411594

16 K. A. Martin, A. R. Sinden, and J. C. Fleming, "Inactivity May Be Hazardous to Your Image: The Effects of Exercise Participation on Impression Formation," *Journal of Sport & Exercise Psychology* 22, no. 4 (December 2000), pp. 283–291.

17 F. Yuan and R. W. Woodman, "Innovative Behavior in the Workplace: The Role of Performance and Image Outcome Expectations," *Academy of Management Journal* 53, no. 2 (2010), pp. 323–342.

18 J. K. Harter, F. L. Schmidt, J. W. Asplund, E. A. Killham, and S. Agrawal, "Causal Impact of Employee Work Perceptions on the Bottom Line of Organizations," *Perspectives on Psychological Science* 5, no. 4 (2010), p. 378–389.

19 Y. H. Kim, C. Y. Chiu, and Z. Zou, "Know Thyself: Misperceptions of Actual Performance Undermine Achievement Motivation, Future Performance, and Subjective Well-Being," *Journal of Personality and Social Psychology* 99, no. 3 (2010), pp. 395–409.

20 H. G. Heneman III and T. A. Judge, *Staffing Organizations* (Middleton, WI: Mendota House, 2006).

21 J. Willis and A. Todorov, "First Impressions: Making Up Your Mind after a 100ms Exposure to a Face," *Psychological Science*, July 2006, pp. 592–598.

22 See, for example, E. C. Webster, *Decision Making in the Employment Interview* (Montreal: McGill University, Industrial Relations Center, 1964).

23 See, for example, K. F. E. Wong and J. Y. Y. Kwong, "Effects of Rater Goals on Rating Patterns: Evidence from an Experimental Field Study," *Journal of Applied Psychology* 92, no. 2 (2007), pp. 577–585; and S. E. DeVoe and S. S. Iyengar, "Managers' Theories of Subordinates: A Cross-Cultural Examination of Manager Perceptions of Motivation and Appraisal of Performance," *Organizational Behavior and Human Decision Processes*, January 2004, pp. 47–61.

24 D. B. McNatt and T. A. Judge, "Boundary Conditions of the Galatea Effect: A Field Experiment and Constructive Replication," *Academy of Management Journal*, August 2004, pp. 550–565; O. B. Davidson and D. Eden, "Remedial Self-Fulfilling Prophecy: Two Field Experiments to Prevent Golem Effects among Disadvantaged Women," *Journal of Applied Psychology*, June 2000, pp. 386–398; D. Eden, "Self-Fulfilling Prophecies in Organizations," in *Organizational Behavior: The State of the Science*, 2nd ed., ed. J. Greenberg (Mahwah, NJ: Lawrence Erlbaum, 2003), pp. 91–122; and G. Natanovich and D. Eden, "Pygmalion Effects among Outreach Supervisors and Tutors: Extending Sex Generalizability," *Journal of Applied Psychology* 93, no. 6 (2008), pp. 1382–1389.

25 See, for example, K. F. E. Wong and J. Y. Y. Kwong, "Effects of Rater Goals on Rating Patterns: Evidence from an Experimental Field Study," *Journal of Applied Psychology* 92, no. 2 (2007), pp. 577–585; and S. E. DeVoe and S. S. Iyengar, "Managers' Theories of Subordinates: A Cross-Cultural Examination of Manager Perceptions of Motivation and Appraisal of Performance," *Organizational Behavior and Human Decision Processes*, January 2004, pp. 47–61.

26 Vignette based on "Personality Counts: Walmart's Frugal, but Target Charms," *CNNMoney*, August 19, 2011, http://management.fortune.cnn.com/2011/08/19/personality-counts-walmart-is-frugal-but-target-charms/; and "Target Plans up to 135 Canadian Stores by 2013," *Toronto Star*, September 23, 2011, http://www.thestar.com/business/article/1058457—target-finalizes-its-canadian-stores-inks-deal-with-sobeys

27 G. W. Allport, *Personality: A Psychological Interpretation* (New York: Holt, Rinehart and Winston, 1937), p. 48.

28 K. I. van der Zee, J. N. Zaal, and J. Piekstra, "Validation of the Multicultural Personality Questionnaire in the Context of Personnel Selection," *European Journal of Personality* 17 (2003), pp. S77–S100.

29 S. A. Birkeland, T. M. Manson, J. L. Kisamore, M. T. Brannick, and M. A. Smith, "A Meta-analytic Investigation of Job Applicant Faking on Personality Measures," *International Journal of Selection and Assessment* 14, no. 14 (2006), pp. 317–335.

30 T. A. Judge, C. A. Higgins, C. J. Thoresen, and M. R. Barrick, "The Big Five Personality Traits, General Mental Ability, and Career Success across the Life Span," *Personnel Psychology* 52, no. 3 (1999), pp. 621–652.

31 See D. T. Lykken, T. J. Bouchard Jr., M. McGue, and A. Tellegen, "Heritability of Interests: A Twin Study," *Journal of Applied Psychology*, August 1993, pp. 649–661; R. D. Arvey and T. J. Bouchard Jr., "Genetics, Twins, and Organizational Behavior," in *Research in Organizational Behavior*, vol. 16, ed. B. M. Staw and L. L. Cummings (Greenwich, CT: JAI Press, 1994), pp. 65–66; D. Lykken and A. Tellegen, "Happiness Is a Stochastic Phenomenon," *Psychological Science*, May 1996, pp. 186–189; and W. Wright, *Born That Way: Genes, Behavior, Personality* (New York: Knopf, 1998).

32 S. Srivastava, O. P. John, and S. D. Gosling, "Development of Personality in Early and Middle Adulthood: Set Like Plaster or Persistent Change?" *Journal of Personality and Social Psychology*, May 2003, pp. 1041–1053; and B. W. Roberts, K. E. Walton, and W. Viechtbauer, "Patterns of Mean-Level Change in Personality Traits across the Life Course: A Meta-analysis of Longitudinal Studies," *Psychological Bulletin* 132, no. 1 (2006), pp. 1–25.

33 S. E. Hampson and L. R. Goldberg, "A First Large Cohort Study of Personality Trait Stability over the 40 Years between Elementary School and Midlife," *Journal of Personality and Social Psychology* 91, no. 4 (2006), pp. 763–779.

34 See A. H. Buss, "Personality as Traits," *American Psychologist*, November 1989, pp. 1378–1388; and D. G. Winter, O. P. John, A. J. Stewart, E. C. Klohnen, and L. E. Duncan, "Traits and Motives: Toward an Integration of Two Traditions in Personality Research," *Psychological Review*, April 1998, pp. 230–250.

35 See, for instance, G. W. Allport and H. S. Odbert, "Trait Names, A Psycholexical Study," *Psychological Monographs* 47, no. 211 (1936); and R. B. Cattell, "Personality Pinned Down," *Psychology Today*, July 1973, pp. 40–46.

36 R. B. Kennedy and D. A. Kennedy, "Using the Myers-Briggs Type Indicator in Career Counseling," *Journal of Employment Counseling*, March 2004, pp. 38–44.

37 G. N. Landrum, *Profiles of Genius* (New York: Prometheus, 1993).

38 See, for instance, D. J. Pittenger, "Cautionary Comments Regarding the Myers-Briggs Type Indicator," *Consulting Psychology Journal: Practice and Research*, Summer 2005, pp. 210–221; L. Bess and R. J. Harvey, "Bimodal Score Distributions and the Myers-Briggs Type Indicator: Fact or Artifact?" *Journal of Personality Assessment*, February 2002, pp. 176–186; R. M. Capraro and M. M. Capraro, "Myers-Briggs Type Indicator Score Reliability across Studies: A Meta-analytic Reliability Generalization Study," *Educational and Psychological Measurement*, August 2002, pp. 590–602; and R. C. Arnau, B. A. Green, D. H. Rosen, D. H. Gleaves, and J. G. Melancon, "Are Jungian Preferences Really Categorical? An Empirical Investigation Using Taxometric Analysis," *Personality and Individual Differences*, January 2003, pp. 233–251.

39 See, for example, J. M. Digman, "Personality Structure: Emergence of the Five-Factor Model," in *Annual Review of Psychology*, vol. 41, ed. M. R. Rosenzweig and L. W. Porter (Palo Alto, CA: Annual Reviews, 1990), pp. 417–440; D. B. Smith, P. J. Hanges, and M. W. Dickson, "Personnel Selection and the Five-Factor Model: Reexamining the Effects of Applicant's Frame of Reference," *Journal of Applied Psychology*, April 2001, pp. 304–315; and M. R. Barrick and M. K. Mount, "Yes, Personality Matters: Moving On to More Important Matters," *Human Performance* 18, no. 4 (2005), pp. 359–372.

40 J. B. Hirsh and J. B. Peterson, "Predicting Creativity and Academic Success with a 'Fake-Proof' Measure of the Big Five," *Journal of Research in Personality* 42 (2008), pp. 1323–1333.

41 "New Fake-Proof Personality Test Created," *ScienceDaily*, October 8, 2008, http://www.sciencedaily.com/releases/2008/10/081007102849.htm

42 See, for instance, M. R. Barrick and M. K. Mount, "The Big Five Personality Dimensions and Job Performance: A Meta-analysis," *Personnel Psychology*, Spring 1991, pp. 1–26; G. M. Hurtz and J. J. Donovan, "Personality and Job Performance: The Big Five Revisited," *Journal of Applied Psychology*, December

2000, pp. 869–879; J. Hogan and B. Holland, "Using Theory to Evaluate Personality and Job-Performance Relations: A Socioanalytic Perspective," *Journal of Applied Psychology*, February 2003, pp. 100–112; and M. R. Barrick and M. K. Mount, "Select on Conscientiousness and Emotional Stability," in *Handbook of Principles of Organizational Behavior*, ed. E. A. Locke (Malden, MA: Blackwell, 2004), pp. 15–28.

43 M. K. Mount, M. R. Barrick, and J. P. Strauss, "Validity of Observer Ratings of the Big Five Personality Factors," *Journal of Applied Psychology*, April 1994, p. 272. Additionally confirmed by G. M. Hurtz and J. J. Donovan, "Personality and Job Performance: The Big Five Revisited," *Journal of Applied Psychology* 85 (2000), pp. 869–879; and M. R. Barrick, M. K. Mount, and T. A. Judge, "The FFM Personality Dimensions and Job Performance: Meta-analysis of Meta-analyses," *International Journal of Selection and Assessment* 9 (2001), pp. 9–30.

44 A. E. Poropat, "A Meta-analysis of the Five-Factor Model of Personality and Academic Performance," *Psychological Bulletin* 135, no. 2 (2009), pp. 322–338.

45 F. L. Schmidt and J. E. Hunter, "The Validity and Utility of Selection Methods in *Personnel Psychology*: Practical and Theoretical Implications of 85 Years of Research Findings," *Psychological Bulletin*, September 1998, p. 272.

46 R. J. Foti and M. A. Hauenstein, "Pattern and Variable Approaches in Leadership Emergence and Effectiveness," *Journal of Applied Psychology*, March 2007, pp. 347–355.

47 L. I. Spirling and R. Persaud, "Extraversion as a Risk Factor," *Journal of the American Academy of Child and Adolescent Psychiatry* 42, no. 2 (2003), p. 130.

48 B. Weiss and R. S. Feldman, "Looking Good and Lying to Do It: Deception as an Impression Management Strategy in Job Interviews," *Journal of Applied Social Psychology* 36, no. 4 (2006), pp. 1070–1086.

49 J. A. LePine, J. A. Colquitt, and A. Erez, "Adaptability to Changing Task Contexts: Effects of General Cognitive Ability, Conscientiousness, and Openness to Experience," *Personnel Psychology* 53 (2000), pp. 563–595.

50 S. Clarke and I. Robertson, "An Examination of the Role of Personality in Accidents Using Meta-analysis," *Applied Psychology: An International Review* 57, no. 1 (2008), pp. 94–108.

51 B. Laursen, L. Pulkkinen, and R. Adams, "The Antecedents and Correlates of Agreeableness in Adulthood," *Developmental Psychology* 38, no. 4 (2002), pp. 591–603.

52 B. Barry and R. A. Friedman, "Bargainer Characteristics in Distributive and Integrative Negotiation," *Journal of Personality and Social Psychology*, February 1998, pp. 345–359.

53 T. Bogg and B. W. Roberts, "Conscientiousness and Health-Related Behaviors: A Meta-analysis of the Leading Behavioral Contributors to Mortality," *Psychological Bulletin* 130, no. 6 (2004), pp. 887–919.

54 S. Lee and H. J. Klein, "Relationships between Conscientiousness, Self-Efficacy, Self-Deception, and Learning over Time," *Journal of Applied Psychology* 87, no. 6 (2002), pp. 1175–1182; and G. J. Feist, "A Meta-analysis of Personality in Scientific and Artistic Creativity," *Personality and Social Psychology Review* 2, no. 4 (1998), pp. 290–309.

55 T. A. Judge and J. E. Bono, "A Rose by Any Other Name . . . Are Self-Esteem, Generalized Self-Efficacy, Neuroticism, and Locus of Control Indicators of a Common Construct?" in *Personality Psychology in the Workplace*, ed. B. W. Roberts and R. Hogan, pp. 93–118 (Washington, DC: American Psychological Association); and A. M. Grant and A. Wrzesniewski "I Won't Let You Down . . . or Will I? Core Self-Evaluations, Other-Orientation, Anticipated Guilt and Gratitude, and Job

Performance," *Journal of Applied Psychology* 95, no. 1 (2010), pp. 108–121.

56 A. Erez and T. A. Judge, "Relationship of Core Self-Evaluations to Goal Setting, Motivation, and Performance," *Journal of Applied Psychology* 86, no. 6 (2001), pp. 1270–1279.

57 A. N. Salvaggio, B. Schneider, L. H. Nishi, D. M. Mayer, A. Ramesh, and J. S. Lyon, "Manager Personality, Manager Service Quality Orientation, and Service Climate: Test of a Model," *Journal of Applied Psychology* 92, no. 6 (2007), pp. 1741–1750; B. A. Scott and T. A. Judge, "The Popularity Contest at Work: Who Wins, Why, and What Do They Receive?" *Journal of Applied Psychology* 94, no. 1 (2009), pp. 20–33; and T. A. Judge and C. Hurst, "How the Rich (and Happy) Get Richer (and Happier): Relationship of Core Self-Evaluations to Trajectories in Attaining Work Success," *Journal of Applied Psychology* 93, no. 4 (2008), pp. 849–863.

58 U. Malmendier and G. Tate, "CEO Overconfidence and Corporate Investment," *Journal of Finance* 60, no. 6 (December 2005), pp. 2661–2700.

59 J. J. Dahling, B. G. Whitaker, and P. E. Levy, "The Development and Validation of a New Machiavellianism Scale," *Journal of Management* 35, no. 2 (2009), pp. 219–257.

60 R. Christie and F. L. Geis, *Studies in Machiavellianism* (New York: Academic Press, 1970), p. 312; and N. V. Ramanaiah, A. Byravan, and F. R. J. Detwiler, "Revised Neo Personality Inventory Profiles of Machiavellian and Non-Machiavellian People," *Psychological Reports*, October 1994, pp. 937–938.

61 J. J. Dahling, B. G. Whitaker, and P. E. Levy, "The Development and Validation of a New Machiavellianism Scale," *Journal of Management* 35, no. 2 (2009), pp. 219–257.

62 R. Christie and F. L. Geis, *Studies in Machiavellianism* (New York: Academic Press, 1970).

63 C. Sedikides, E. A. Rudich, A. P. Gregg, M. Kumashiro, and C. Rusbult, "Are Normal Narcissists Psychologically Healthy?: Self-Esteem Matters," *Journal of Personality and Social Psychology* 87, no. 3 (2004), pp. 400–416, reviews some of the literature on narcissism.

64 M. Elias, "Study: Today's Youth Think Quite Highly of Themselves," *USA Today*, November 19, 2008, p. 7D; and K. H. Trzesniewski, M. B. Donnellan, and R. W. Robins, "Do Today's Young People Really Think They Are So Extraordinary?" *Psychological Science* 19, no. 2 (2008), pp. 181–188.

65 A. B. Brunell, S. Staats, J. Barden, and J. M. Hupp, "Narcissism and Academic Dishonesty: The Exhibitionism Dimension and the Lack of Guilt," *Personality and Individual Differences* 50, no. 3 (2011), pp. 323–328.

66 M. Maccoby, "Narcissistic Leaders: The Incredible Pros, the Inevitable Cons," *Harvard Business Review*, January–February 2000, pp. 69–77, http://www.maccoby.com/Articles/NarLeaders. shtml

67 W. K. Campbell and C. A. Foster, "Narcissism and Commitment in Romantic Relationships: An Investment Model Analysis," *Personality and Social Psychology Bulletin* 28, no. 4 (2002), pp. 484–495.

68 T. A. Judge, J. A. LePine, and B. L. Rich, "The Narcissistic Personality: Relationship with Inflated Self-Ratings of Leadership and with Task and Contextual Performance," *Journal of Applied Psychology* 91, no. 4 (2006), pp. 762–776.

69 J. Goncalo, F. J. Flynn, and S. H. Kim, "Are Two Narcissists Better Than One? The Link between Narcissism, Perceived Creativity, and Creative Performance," *Personality and Social Psychology Bulletin* 36, no. 11 (2010), pp. 1484–1495.

70 See M. Snyder, *Public Appearances/Private Realities: The Psychology of Self-Monitoring* (New York: W. H. Freeman, 1987); and

S. W. Gangestad and M. Snyder, "Self-Monitoring: Appraisal and Reappraisal," *Psychological Bulletin*, July 2000, pp. 530–555.

71 F. J. Flynn and D. R. Ames, "What's Good for the Goose May Not Be as Good for the Gander: The Benefits of Self-Monitoring for Men and Women in Task Groups and Dyadic Conflicts," *Journal of Applied Psychology* 91, no. 2 (2006), pp. 272–281; and M. Snyder, *Public Appearances/Private Realities: The Psychology of Self-Monitoring* (New York: W. H. Freeman, 1987).

72 H. Oh and M. Kilduff, "The Ripple Effect of Personality on Social Structure: Self-monitoring Origins of Network Brokerage," *Journal of Applied Psychology* 93, no. 5 (2008), pp. 1155–1164; and A. Mehra, M. Kilduff, and D. J. Brass, "The Social Networks of High and Low Self-Monitors: Implications for Workplace Performance," *Administrative Science Quarterly*, March 2001, pp. 121–146.

73 D. V. Day, D. J. Schleicher, A. L. Unckless, and N. J. Hiller, "Self-Monitoring Personality at Work: A Meta-analytic Investigation of Construct Validity," *Journal of Applied Psychology*, April 2002, pp. 390–401.

74 R. N. Taylor and M. D. Dunnette, "Influence of Dogmatism, Risk-Taking Propensity, and Intelligence on Decision-Making Strategies for a Sample of Industrial Managers," *Journal of Applied Psychology*, August 1974, pp. 420–423.

75 I. L. Janis and L. Mann, *Decision Making: A Psychological Analysis of Conflict, Choice, and Commitment* (New York: Free Press, 1977); W. H. Stewart Jr. and L. Roth, "Risk Propensity Differences between Entrepreneurs and Managers: A Meta-analytic Review," *Journal of Applied Psychology*, February 2001, pp. 145–153; J. B. Miner and N. S. Raju, "Risk Propensity Differences between Managers and Entrepreneurs and between Low- and High-Growth Entrepreneurs: A Reply in a More Conservative Vein," *Journal of Applied Psychology* 89, no. 1 (2004), pp. 3–13; and W. H. Stewart Jr. and P. L. Roth, "Data Quality Affects Meta-analytic Conclusions: A Response to Miner and Raju (2004) Concerning Entrepreneurial Risk Propensity," *Journal of Applied Psychology* 89, no. 1 (2004), pp. 14–21.

76 J. K. Maner, J. A. Richey, K. Cromer, M. Mallott, C. W. Lejuez, T. E. Joiner, and N. B. Schmidt, "Dispositional Anxiety and Risk-Avoidant Decision Making," *Personality and Individual Differences* 42, no. 4 (2007), pp. 665–675.

77 M. Friedman and R. H. Rosenman, *Type A Behavior and Your Heart* (New York: Knopf, 1974), p. 84.

78 M. Friedman and R. H. Rosenman, *Type A Behavior and Your Heart* (New York: Alfred A. Knopf, 1974), pp. 84–85.

79 K. W. Cook, C. A. Vance, and E. Spector, "The Relation of Candidate Personality with Selection-Interview Outcomes," *Journal of Applied Social Psychology* 30 (2000), pp. 867–885.

80 M. Friedman and R. H. Rosenman, *Type A Behavior and Your Heart* (New York: Knopf, 1974), p. 86.

81 J. M. Crant, "Proactive Behavior in Organizations," *Journal of Management* 26, no. 3 (2000), p. 436.

82 S. E. Seibert, M. L. Kraimer, and J. M. Crant, "What Do Proactive People Do? A Longitudinal Model Linking Proactive Personality and Career Success," *Personnel Psychology*, Winter 2001, p. 850.

83 T. S. Bateman and J. M. Crant, "The Proactive Component of Organizational Behavior: A Measure and Correlates," *Journal of Organizational Behavior*, March 1993, pp. 103–118; A. L. Frohman, "Igniting Organizational Change from Below: The Power of Personal Initiative," *Organizational Dynamics*, Winter 1997, pp. 39–53; and J. M. Crant and T. S. Bateman, "Charismatic Leadership Viewed from Above: The Impact of Proactive Personality," *Journal of Organizational Behavior*, February 2000, pp. 63–75.

84 J. M. Crant, "Proactive Behavior in Organizations," *Journal of Management* 26, no. 3 (2000), p. 436.

85 See, for instance, R. C. Becherer and J. G. Maurer, "The Proactive Personality Disposition and Entrepreneurial Behavior among Small Company Presidents," *Journal of Small Business Management*, January 1999, pp. 28–36.

86 S. E. Seibert, J. M. Crant, and M. L. Kraimer, "Proactive Personality and Career Success," *Journal of Applied Psychology*, June 1999, pp. 416–427; S. E. Seibert, M. L. Kraimer, and J. M. Crant, "What Do Proactive People Do? A Longitudinal Model Linking Proactive Personality and Career Success," *Personnel Psychology*, Winter 2001, p. 850; F. J. Flynn and D. R. Ames, "What's Good for the Goose May Not Be as Good for the Gander: The Benefits of Self-Monitoring for Men and Women in Task Groups and Dyadic Conflicts," *Journal of Applied Psychology* 91, no. 2 (2006), pp. 272–281; and J. D. Kammeyer-Mueller and C. R. Wanberg, "Unwrapping the Organizational Entry Process: Disentangling Multiple Antecedents and Their Pathways to Adjustment," *Journal of Applied Psychology* 88, no. 5 (2003), pp. 779–794.

87 Vignette based on "Trail Workers Test Walmart's Resistance to Unions," August 15, 2010, *Nelson Life*, http://nelsonlife.com/550/trail-workers-test-walmarts-resistance-to-unions/; and http://www.ratemyemployer.ca/employer/employer.aspx?empID=7575&l=en

88 See, for instance, C. D. Fisher and N. M. Ashkanasy, "The Emerging Role of Emotions in Work Life: An Introduction," *Journal of Organizational Behavior*, Special Issue (2000), pp. 123–129; N. M. Ashkanasy, C. E. J. Hartel, and W. J. Zerbe, eds., *Emotions in the Workplace: Research, Theory, and Practice* (Westport, CT: Quorum Books, 2000); N. M. Ashkanasy and C. S. Daus, "Emotion in the Workplace: The New Challenge for Managers," *Academy of Management Executive*, February 2002, pp. 76–86; and N. M. Ashkanasy, C. E. J. Hartel, and C. S. Daus, "Diversity and Emotion: The New Frontiers in Organizational Behavior Research," *Journal of Management* 28, no. 3 (2002), pp. 307–338.

89 See, for example, L. L. Putnam and D. K. Mumby, "Organizations, Emotion and the Myth of Rationality," in *Emotion in Organizations*, ed. S. Fineman (Thousand Oaks, CA: Sage, 1993), pp. 36–57; and J. Martin, K. Knopoff, and C. Beckman, "An Alternative to Bureaucratic Impersonality and Emotional Labor: Bounded Emotionality at the Body Shop," *Administrative Science Quarterly*, June 1998, pp. 429–469.

90 B. E. Ashforth and R. H. Humphrey, "Emotion in the Workplace: A Reappraisal," *Human Relations*, February 1995, pp. 97–125.

91 S. G. Barsade and D. E. Gibson, "Why Does Affect Matter in Organizations?" *Academy of Management Perspectives*, February 2007, pp. 36–59.

92 See N. H. Frijda, "Moods, Emotion Episodes and Emotions," in *Handbook of Emotions*, ed. M. Lewis and J. M. Haviland (New York: Guilford Press, 1993), pp. 381–403.

93 H. M. Weiss and R. Cropanzano, "Affective Events Theory," in *Research in Organizational Behavior*, vol. 18, ed. B. M. Staw and L. L. Cummings (Greenwich, CT: JAI Press, 1996), pp. 17–19.

94 See P. Ekman and R. J. Davidson, eds., *The Nature of Emotions: Fundamental Questions* (Oxford, UK: Oxford University Press, 1994).

95 N. H. Frijda, "Moods, Emotion Episodes and Emotions," in *Handbook of Emotions*, ed. M. Lewis and J. M. Haviland (New York: Guilford Press, 1993), pp. 381–403.

96 See P. Ekman and R. J. Davidson, eds., *The Nature of Emotions: Fundamental Questions* (Oxford, UK: Oxford University Press, 1994).

97 See J. A. Morris and D. C. Feldman, "Managing Emotions in the Workplace," *Journal of Managerial Issues* 9, no. 3 (1997), pp. 257–274; S. Mann, *Hiding What We Feel, Faking What We Don't: Understanding the Role of Your Emotions at Work* (New York: HarperCollins, 1999); and S. M. Kruml and D. Geddes,

"Catching Fire without Burning Out: Is There an Ideal Way to Perform Emotion Labor?" in *Emotions in the Workplace*, ed. N. M. Ashkansay, C. E. J. Hartel, and W. J. Zerbe (New York: Quorum Books, 2000), pp. 177–188.

98 P. Ekman, W. V. Friesen, and M. O'Sullivan, "Smiles When Lying," in *What the Face Reveals: Basic and Applied Studies of Spontaneous Expression Using the Facial Action Coding System (FACS)*, ed. P. Ekman and E. L. Rosenberg (London: Oxford University Press, 1997), pp. 201–216.

99 A. Grandey, "Emotion Regulation in the Workplace: A New Way to Conceptualize Emotional Labor," *Journal of Occupational Health Psychology* 5, no. 1 (2000), pp. 95–110; and R. Cropanzano, D. E. Rupp, and Z. S. Byrne, "The Relationship of Emotional Exhaustion to Work Attitudes, Job Performance, and Organizational Citizenship Behavior," *Journal of Applied Psychology*, February 2003, pp. 160–169.

100 A. R. Hochschild, "Emotion Work, Feeling Rules, and Social Structure," *American Journal of Sociology*, November 1979, pp. 551–575; W.-C. Tsai, "Determinants and Consequences of Employee Displayed Positive Emotions," *Journal of Management* 27, no. 4 (2001), pp. 497–512; M. W. Kramer and J. A. Hess, "Communication Rules for the Display of Emotions in Organizational Settings," *Management Communication Quarterly*, August 2002, pp. 66–80; and J. M. Diefendorff and E. M. Richard, "Antecedents and Consequences of Emotional Display Rule Perceptions," *Journal of Applied Psychology*, April 2003, pp. 284–294.

101 B. M. DePaulo, "Nonverbal Behavior and Self-Presentation," *Psychological Bulletin*, March 1992, pp. 203–243.

102 C. S. Hunt, "Although I Might Be Laughing Loud and Hearty, Deep Inside I'm Blue: Individual Perceptions Regarding Feeling and Displaying Emotions at Work" (paper presented at the Academy of Management Conference, Cincinnati, OH, August 1996), p. 3.

103 R. C. Solomon, "Back to Basics: On the Very Idea of 'Basic Emotions,'" *Journal for the Theory of Social Behaviour* 32, no. 2 (2002), pp. 115–144.

104 C. M. Brotheridge and R. T. Lee, "Development and Validation of the Emotional Labour Scale," *Journal of Occupational and Organizational Psychology* 76, no. 3 (September 2003), pp. 365–379.

105 A. A. Grandey, "When 'the Show Must Go On': Surface Acting and Deep Acting as Determinants of Emotional Exhaustion and Peer-Rated Service Delivery," *Academy of Management Journal*, February 2003, pp. 86–96; and A. A. Grandey, D. N. Dickter, and H. Sin, "The Customer Is Not Always Right: Customer Aggression and Emotion Regulation of Service Employees," *Journal of Organizational Behavior* 25, no. 3 (May 2004), pp. 397–418.

106 J. P. Trougakos, D. J. Beal, S. G. Green, and H. M. Weiss, "Making the Break Count: An Episodic Examination of Recovery Activities, Emotional Experiences, and Positive Affective Displays," *Academy of Management Journal* 51, no. 1 (2008), pp. 131–146.

107 S. Brassen, M. Gamer, and C. Büchel, "Anterior Cingulate Activation Is Related to a Positivity Bias and Emotional Stability in Successful Aging," *Biological Psychiatry* 70, no. 2 (2011), pp. 131–137.

108 A. R. Damasio, *Descartes' Error: Emotion, Reason, and the Human Brain* (New York: Quill, 1994).

109 N. M. Ashkanasy and C. S. Daus, "Emotion in the Workplace: The New Challenge for Managers," *Academy of Management Executive*, February 2002, pp. 76–86.

110 Based on D. R. Caruso, J. D. Mayer, and P. Salovey, "Emotional Intelligence and Emotional Leadership," in *Multiple Intelligences and Leadership*, ed. R. E. Riggio, S. E. Murphy, and F. J. Pirozzolo (Mahwah, NJ: Lawrence Erlbaum, 2002), p. 70.

111 This section is based on Daniel Goleman, *Emotional Intelligence* (New York: Bantam, 1995); P. Salovey and D. Grewal, "The Science of Emotional Intelligence," *Current Directions in Psychological Science* 14, no. 6 (2005), pp. 281–285; M. Davies, L. Stankov, and R. D. Roberts, "Emotional Intelligence: In Search of an Elusive Construct," *Journal of Personality and Social Psychology*, October 1998, pp. 989–1015; D. Geddes and R. R. Callister, "Crossing the Line(s): A Dual Threshold Model of Anger in Organizations," *Academy of Management Review* 32, no. 3 (2007), pp. 721–746; and J. Ciarrochi, J. P. Forgas, and J. D. Mayer, eds., *Emotional Intelligence in Everyday Life* (Philadelphia: Psychology Press, 2001).

112 M. Seo and L. F. Barrett, "Being Emotional During Decision Making—Good or Bad? An Empirical Investigation," *Academy of Management Journal* 50, no. 4 (2007), pp. 923–940.

113 E. H. O'Boyle, R. H. Humphrey, J. M. Pollack, T. H. Hawver, and P. A. Story, "The Relation between Emotional Intelligence and Job Performance: A Meta-analysis," *Journal of Organizational Behavior* 32, no. 5 (2011), pp. 788–818.

114 F. I. Greenstein, *The Presidential Difference: Leadership Style from FDR to Clinton* (Princeton, NJ: Princeton University Press, 2001).

115 M. Maccoby, "To Win the Respect of Followers, Leaders Need Personality Intelligence," *Ivey Business Journal* 72, no. 3 (2008); J. Reid, "The Resilient Leader: Why EQ Matters," *Business Journal* 72, no. 3 (2008); and P. Wieand, J. Birchfield, and M. C. Johnson III, "The New Leadership Challenge: Removing the Emotional Barriers to Sustainable Performance in a Flat World," *Ivey Business Journal* 72, no. 4 (2008).

116 P. Wieand, J. Birchfield, and M. C. Johnson III, "The New Leadership Challenge: Removing the Emotional Barriers to Sustainable Performance in a Flat World," *Ivey Business Journal* 72, no. 4 (2008).

117 C. Cherniss, "The Business Case for Emotional Intelligence," *Consortium for Research on Emotional Intelligence in Organizations*, 1999, http://www.eiconsortium.org/research/business_case_for_ei.pdf

118 K. S. Law, C. Wong, and L. J. Song, "The Construct and Criterion Validity of Emotional Intelligence and Its Potential Utility for Management Studies," *Journal of Applied Psychology* 89, no. 3 (2004), pp. 483–496.

119 H. A. Elfenbein and N. Ambady, "Predicting Workplace Outcomes from the Ability to Eavesdrop on Feelings," *Journal of Applied Psychology* 87, no. 5 (October 2002), pp. 963–971.

120 D. L. Van Rooy and C. Viswesvaran, "Emotional Intelligence: A Meta-analytic Investigation of Predictive Validity and Nomological Net," *Journal of Vocational Behavior* 65, no. 1 (August 2004), pp. 71–95.

121 R. Bar-On, D. Tranel, N. L. Denburg, and A. Bechara, "Exploring the Neurological Substrate of Emotional and Social Intelligence," *Brain* 126, no. 8 (August 2003), pp. 1790–1800.

122 P. A. Vernon, K. V. Petrides, D. Bratko, and J. A. Schermer, "A Behavioral Genetic Study of Trait Emotional Intelligence," *Emotion* 8, no. 5 (2008), pp. 635–642.

123 E. A. Locke, "Why Emotional Intelligence Is an Invalid Concept," *Journal of Organizational Behavior* 26, no. 4 (2005), pp. 425–431.

124 J. M. Conte, "A Review and Critique of Emotional Intelligence Measures," *Journal of Organizational Behavior* 26, no. 4 (2005), pp. 433–440; and M. Davies, L. Stankov, and R. D. Roberts, "Emotional Intelligence: In Search of an Elusive Construct," *Journal of Personality and Social Psychology* 75, no. 4 (1998), pp. 989–1015.

125 T. Decker, "Is Emotional Intelligence a Viable Concept?" *Academy of Management Review* 28, no. 2 (2003), pp. 433–440;

and M. Davies, L. Stankov, and R. D. Roberts, "Emotional Intelligence: In Search of an Elusive Construct," *Journal of Personality and Social Psychology* 75, no. 4 (1998), pp. 989–1015.

126 F. J. Landy, "Some Historical and Scientific Issues Related to Research on Emotional Intelligence," *Journal of Organizational Behavior* 26, no. 4 (June 2005), pp. 411–424.

127 S. L. Robinson and R. J. Bennett, "A Typology of Deviant Workplace Behaviors: A Multidimensional Scaling Study," *Academy of Management Journal*, April 1995, p. 556.

128 S. L. Robinson and R. J. Bennett, "A Typology of Deviant Workplace Behaviors: A Multidimensional Scaling Study," *Academy of Management Journal*, April 1995, pp. 555–572.

129 Based on A. G. Bedeian, "Workplace Envy," *Organizational Dynamics*, Spring 1995, p. 50.

130 A. G. Bedeian, "Workplace Envy," *Organizational Dynamics*, Spring 1995, p. 54.

131 S. C. Douglas, C. Kiewitz, M. Martinko, P. Harvey, Y. Kim, and J. U. Chun, "Cognitions, Emotions, and Evaluations: An Elaboration Likelihood Model for Workplace Aggression," *Academy of Management Review* 33, no. 2 (2008), pp. 425–451.

132 K. Lee and N. J. Allen, "Organizational Citizenship Behavior and Workplace Deviance: The Role of Affect and Cognition," *Journal of Applied Psychology* 87, no. 1 (2002), pp. 131–142; and T. A. Judge, B. A. Scott, and R. Ilies, "Hostility, Job Attitudes, and Workplace Deviance: Test of a Multilevel Model," *Journal of Applied Psychology* 91, no. 1 (2006), pp. 126–138.

133 H. M. Weiss and R. Cropanzano, "Affective Events Theory: A Theoretical Discussion of the Structure, Causes and Consequences of Affective Experiences at Work," in *Research in Organizational Behavior*, vol. 18, ed. B. M. Staw and L. L. Cummings (Greenwich, CT: JAI Press, 1996), pp. 17–19.

134 J. Basch and C. D. Fisher, "Affective Events-Emotions Matrix: A Classification of Work Events and Associated Emotions," in *Emotions in the Workplace*, ed. N. M. Ashkanasy, C. E. J. Hartel, and W. J. Zerbe (Westport, CN: Quorum Books, 2000), pp. 36–48.

135 See, for example, H. M. Weiss and R. Cropanzano, "Affective Events Theory: A Theoretical Discussion of the Structure, Causes and Consequences of Affective Experiences at Work," in *Research in Organizational Behavior*, vol. 18, ed. B. M. Staw and L. L. Cummings (Greenwich, CT: JAI Press, 1996), pp. 17–19; and C. D. Fisher, "Antecedents and Consequences of Real-Time Affective Reactions at Work," *Motivation and Emotion*, March 2002, pp. 3–30.

136 Based on H. M. Weiss and R. Cropanzano, "Affective Events Theory: A Theoretical Discussion of the Structure, Causes and Consequences of Affective Experiences at Work," in *Research in Organizational Behavior*, vol. 18, ed. B. M. Staw and L. L. Cummings (Greenwich, CT: JAI Press, 1996), p. 42.

137 N. M. Ashkanasy, C. E. J. Hartel, and C. S. Daus, "Diversity and Emotion: The New Frontiers in Organizational Behavior Research," *Journal of Management* 28, no. 3 (2002), p. 324.

138 C. West, "How Culture Affects the Way We Think," *APS Observer* 20, no. 7 (2007), pp. 25–26.

139 T. Masuda, R. Gonzalez, L. Kwan, and R. E. Nisbett, "Culture and Aesthetic Preference: Comparing the Attention to Context of East Asians and Americans," *Personality and Social Psychology Bulletin* 34, no. 9 (2008), pp. 1260–1275.

140 D. C. Park, "Developing a Cultural Cognitive Neuroscience of Aging," in *Handbook of Cognitive Aging*, ed. S. M. Hofer and D. F. Alwin (Thousand Oaks, CA: Sage Publications, 2008), pp. 352–367.

141 Q. Wang, "On the Cultural Constitution of Collective Memory," *Memory* 16, no. 3 (2008), pp. 305–317.

142 See, for instance, D. S. Krull, M. H.-M. Loy, J. Lin, C.-F. Wang, S. Chen, and X. Zhao, "The Fundamental Attribution Error: Correspondence Bias in Individualistic and Collectivist Cultures," *Personality and Social Psychology Bulletin*, October 1999, pp. 1208–1219; and F. F. T. Chiang and T. A. Birtch, "Examining the Perceived Causes of Successful Employee Performance: An East-West Comparison," *International Journal of Human Resource Management* 18, no. 2 (2007), pp. 232–248.

143 S. Nam, "Cultural and Managerial Attributions for Group Performance," unpublished doctoral dissertation, University of Oregon. Cited in R. M. Steers, S. J. Bischoff, and L. H. Higgins, "Cross-Cultural Management Research," *Journal of Management Inquiry*, December 1992, pp. 325–326.

144 T. Menon, M. W. Morris, C. Y. Chiu, and Y. Y. Hong, "Culture and the Construal of Agency: Attribution to Individual versus Group Dispositions," *Journal of Personality and Social Psychology* 76 (1999), pp. 701–717; and R. Friedman, W. Liu, C. C. Chen, and S. S. Chi, "Causal Attribution for Interfirm Contract Violation: A Comparative Study of Chinese and American Commercial Arbitrators," *Journal of Applied Psychology* 92, no. 3 (2007), pp. 856–864.

145 J. Spencer-Rodgers, M. J. Williams, D. L. Hamilton, K. Peng, and L. Wang, "Culture and Group Perception: Dispositional and Stereotypic Inferences About Novel and National Groups," *Journal of Personality and Social Psychology* 93, no. 4 (2007), pp. 525–543.

146 A. Zhang, C. Reyna, Z. Qian, and G. Yu, "Interpersonal Attributions of Responsibility in the Chinese Workplace: A Test of Western Models in a Collectivistic Context," *Journal of Applied Social Psychology* 38, no. 9 (2008), pp. 2361–2377; and A. Zhang, F. Xia, and C. Li, "The Antecedents of Help Giving in Chinese Culture: Attribution, Judgment of Responsibility, Expectation Change and the Reaction of Affect," *Social Behavior and Personality* 35, no. 1 (2007), pp. 135–142.

147 See, for instance, R. R. McCrae and P. T. Costa Jr., "Personality Trait Structure as a Human Universal," *American Psychologist*, May 1997, pp. 509–516; S. Yamagata, A. Suzuki, J. Ando, Y. Ono, K. Yutaka, N. Kijima, K. Yoshimura, F. Ostendorf, A. Angleitner, R. Riemann, F. M. Spinath, W. J. Livesley, and K. L. Jang, "Is the Genetic Structure of Human Personality Universal? A Cross-Cultural Twin Study from North America, Europe, and Asia," *Journal of Personality and Social Psychology* 90, no. 6 (2006), pp. 987–998; H. C. Triandis and E. M. Suh, "Cultural Influences on Personality," in *Annual Review of Psychology*, vol. 53, ed. S. T. Fiske, D. L. Schacter, and C. Zahn-Waxler (Palo Alto, CA: Annual Reviews, 2002), pp. 133–160; R. R. McCrae and J. Allik, *The Five-Factor Model of Personality across Cultures* (New York: Kluwer Academic/Plenum, 2002); and R. R. McCrae, P. T. Costa Jr., T. A. Martin, V. E. Oryol, A. A. Rukavishnikov, I. G. Senin, M. Hřebíčková, and T. Urbánek, "Consensual Validation of Personality Traits across Cultures," *Journal of Research in Personality* 38, no. 2 (2004), pp. 179–201.

148 A. T. Church and M. S. Katigbak, "Trait Psychology in the Philippines," *American Behavioral Scientist*, September 2000, pp. 73–94.

149 J. F. Salgado, "The Five Factor Model of Personality and Job Performance in the European Community," *Journal of Applied Psychology*, February 1997, pp. 30–43.

150 M. Eid and E. Diener, "Norms for Experiencing Emotions in Different Cultures: Inter- and International Differences," *Journal of Personality and Social Psychology* 81, no. 5 (2001), pp. 869–885.

151 S. Oishi, E. Diener, and C. Napa Scollon, "Cross-Situational Consistency of Affective Experiences across Cultures," *Journal of Personality and Social Psychology* 86, no. 3 (2004), pp. 460–472; and J. Leu, J. Wang, and K. Koo, "Are Positive Emotions Just as 'Positive' across Cultures?" *Emotion*, March 28, 2011, Epub ahead of print, http://www.ncbi.nlm.nih.gov/pubmed/21443338

152 M. Eid and E. Diener, "Norms for Experiencing Emotions in Different Cultures: Inter- and International Differences," *Journal of Personality and Social Psychology* 81, no. 5 (2001), pp. 869–885.

153 M. Eid and E. Diener, "Norms for Experiencing Emotions in Different Cultures: Inter- and International Differences," *Journal of Personality and Social Psychology* 81, no. 5 (2001), pp. 869–885.

154 B. E. Ashforth and R. H. Humphrey, "Emotion in the Workplace: A Reappraisal," *Human Relations*, February 1995, p. 104; B. Plasait, "Accueil des Touristes Dans les Grands Centres de Transit Paris," *Rapport du Bernard Plasait*, October 4, 2004, http://www.tourisme.gouv.fr/fr/navd/presse/dossiers/att00005767/dp_plasait.pdf; B. Mesquita, "Emotions in Collectivist and Individualist Contexts," *Journal of Personality and Social Psychology* 80, no. 1 (2001), pp. 68–74; and D. Rubin, "Grumpy German Shoppers Distrust the Wal-Mart Style," *Seattle Times*, December 30, 2001, p. A15.

Chapter 3

1 Vignette based on http://www.casinoregina.com/corporate/aboutus

2 M. Rokeach, *The Nature of Human Values* (New York: Free Press, 1973), p. 5.

3 See, for instance, B. Meglino and E. Ravlin, "Individual Values in Organizations," *Journal of Management* 24, no. 3 (1998), pp. 351–389.

4 M. Rokeach and S. J. Ball-Rokeach, "Stability and Change in American Value Priorities, 1968–1981," *American Psychologist*, May 1989, pp. 775–784.

5 M. Rokeach, *The Nature of Human Values* (New York: Free Press, 1973), p. 6.

6 M. Rokeach, *The Nature of Human Values* (New York: Free Press, 1973), p. 56.

7 M. Rokeach, *The Nature of Human Values* (New York: Free Press, 1973), p. 56.

8 J. M. Munson and B. Z. Posner, "The Factorial Validity of a Modified Rokeach Value Survey for Four Diverse Samples," *Educational and Psychological Measurement*, Winter 1980, pp. 1073–1079; and W. C. Frederick and J. Weber, "The Values of Corporate Managers and Their Critics: An Empirical Description and Normative Implications," in *Business Ethics: Research Issues and Empirical Studies*, ed. W. C. Frederick and L. E. Preston (Greenwich, CT: JAI Press, 1990), pp. 123–144.

9 W. C. Frederick and J. Weber, "The Values of Corporate Managers and Their Critics: An Empirical Description and Normative Implications," in *Business Ethics: Research Issues and Empirical Studies*, ed. W. C. Frederick and L. E. Preston (Greenwich, CT: JAI Press, 1990), pp. 123–144.

10 W. C. Frederick and J. Weber, "The Values of Corporate Managers and Their Critics: An Empirical Description and Normative Implications," in *Business Ethics: Research Issues and Empirical Studies*, ed. W. C. Frederick and L. E. Preston (Greenwich, CT: JAI Press, 1990), p. 132.

11 K. Hodgson, *A Rock and a Hard Place: How to Make Ethical Business Decisions When the Choices Are Tough* (New York: AMACOM, 1992), pp. 66–67.

12 Vignette based on http://www.casinoregina.com/corporate/aboutus

13 G. Hofstede, *Culture's Consequences: International Differences in Work-Related Values* (Beverly Hills, CA: Sage, 1980); G. Hofstede, *Cultures and Organizations: Software of the Mind* (London: McGraw-Hill, 1991); G. Hofstede, "Cultural Constraints in Management Theories," *Academy of Management Executive* 7,

no. 1 (1993), pp. 81–94; G. Hofstede and M. F. Peterson, "National Values and Organizational Practices," in *Handbook of Organizational Culture and Climate*, ed. N. M. Ashkanasy, C. M. Wilderom, and M. F. Peterson (Thousand Oaks, CA: Sage, 2000), pp. 401–416; and G. Hofstede, *Culture's Consequences: Comparing Values, Behaviors, Institutions, and Organizations Across Nations*, 2nd ed. (Thousand Oaks, CA: Sage, 2001). For criticism of this research, see B. McSweeney, "Hofstede's Model of National Cultural Differences and Their Consequences: A Triumph of Faith—A Failure of Analysis," *Human Relations* 55, no. 1 (2002), pp. 89–118.

14 G. Hofstede and M. H. Bond, "The Confucius Connection: From Cultural Roots to Economic Growth," *Organizational Dynamics*, Spring 1988, pp. 12–13.

15 M. H. Bond, "Reclaiming the Individual from Hofstede's Ecological Analysis—A 20-Year Odyssey: Comment on Oyserman et al. (2002)," *Psychological Bulletin* 128, no. 1 (2002), pp. 73–77; G. Hofstede, "The Pitfalls of Cross-National Survey Research: A Reply to the Article by Spector et al. on the Psychometric Properties of the Hofstede Values Survey Module 1994," *Applied Psychology: An International Review* 51, no. 1 (2002), pp. 170–178; and T. Fang, "A Critique of Hofstede's Fifth National Culture Dimension," *International Journal of Cross-Cultural Management* 3, no. 3 (2003), pp. 347–368.

16 See A. Harzing and G. Hofstede, "Planned Change in Organizations: The Influence of National Culture," in *Research in the Sociology of Organizations, Cross Cultural Analysis of Organizations*, vol. 14, ed. P. A. Bamberger, M. Erez, and S. B. Bacharach (Greenwich, CT: JAI Press, 1996), pp. 297–340. The five usual criticisms and Hofstede's responses (in parentheses) are (1) Surveys are not a suitable way to measure cultural differences (answer: they should not be the only way); (2) Nations are not the proper units for studying cultures (answer: they are usually the only kind of units available for comparison); (3) A study of the subsidiaries of one company cannot provide information about entire national cultures (answer: what was measured were differences among national cultures, and any set of functionally equivalent samples can supply information about such differences); (4) The IBM data are old and therefore obsolete (answer: the dimensions found are assumed to have century-old roots; they have been validated against all kinds of external measurements; and recent replications show no loss of validity); and (5) Four or five dimensions are not enough (answer: additional dimensions should be statistically independent of the dimensions defined earlier; they should be valid on the basis of correlations with external measures; and candidates are welcome to apply).

17 M. Javidan and R. J. House, "Cultural Acumen for the Global Manager: Lessons from Project GLOBE," *Organizational Dynamics* 29, no. 4 (2001), pp. 289–305; and R. J. House, P. J. Hanges, M. Javidan, and P. W. Dorfman, eds., *Leadership, Culture, and Organizations: The GLOBE Study of 62 Societies* (Thousand Oaks, CA: Sage, 2004).

18 P. C. Early, "Leading Cultural Research in the Future: A Matter of Paradigms and Taste," *Journal of International Business Studies*, September 2006, pp. 922–931; G. Hofstede, "What Did GLOBE Really Measure? Researchers' Minds versus Respondents' Minds," *Journal of International Business Studies*, September 2006, pp. 882–896; and M. Javidan, R. J. House, P. W. Dorfman, P. J. Hanges, and M. S. de Luque, "Conceptualizing and Measuring Cultures and Their Consequences: A Comparative Review of GLOBE's and Hofstede's Approaches," *Journal of International Business Studies*, September 2006, pp. 897–914.

19 B. Meglino, E. C. Ravlin, and C. L. Adkins, "A Work Values Approach to Corporate Culture: A Field Test of the Value Congruence Process and Its Relationship to Individual Outcomes," *Journal of Applied Psychology* 74 (1989), pp. 424–432.

20 B. Z. Posner, J. M. Kouzes, and W. H. Schmidt, "Shared Values Make a Difference: An Empirical Test of Corporate Culture," *Human Resource Management* 24 (1985), pp. 293–310; and A. L. Balazas, "Value Congruency: The Case of the 'Socially Responsible' Firm," *Journal of Business Research* 20 (1990), pp. 171–181.

21 C. A. O'Reilly, J. Chatman, and D. Caldwell, "People and Organizational Culture: A Q-Sort Approach to Assessing Person-Organizational Fit," *Academy of Management Journal* 34 (1991), pp. 487–516.

22 C. Enz and C. K. Schwenk, "Performance and Sharing of Organizational Values" (paper presented at the annual meeting of the Academy of Management, Washington, DC, 1989).

23 See, for example, *The Multigenerational Workforce* (Alexandria, VA: Society for Human Resource Management, 2009); and M. Adams, *Sex in the Snow* (Toronto: Penguin, 1997).

24 J. Timm, "Leadership Q&A: Robert Dutton," *Canadian Business*, June 22, 2011, http://www.canadianbusiness.com/article/30752—leadership-q-a-robert-dutton

25 K. W. Smola and C. D. Sutton, "Generational Differences: Revisiting Generational Work Values for the New Millennium," *Journal of Organizational Behavior* 23 (2002), pp. 363–382; and K. Mellahi and C. Guermat, "Does Age Matter? An Empirical Examination of the Effect of Age on Managerial Values and Practices in India," *Journal of World Business* 39, no. 2 (2004), pp. 199–215.

26 N. A. Hira, "You Raised Them, Now Manage Them," *Fortune*, May 28, 2007, pp. 38–46; R. R. Hastings, "Surveys Shed Light on Generation Y Career Goals," *SHRM Online*, March 2007, http://www.shrm.org; and S. Jayson, "The 'Millennials' Come of Age," *USA Today*, June 29, 2006, pp. 1D, 2D.

27 B. Tulgan, *Not Everyone Gets a Trophy: How to Manage Generation Y* (San Francisco, CA: Jossey-Bass, 2009).

28 Statistics Canada, "Census of Population," *The Daily*, February 11, 2003.

29 S. A. Hewlett, L. Sherbin, and K. Sumberg "How Gen Y & Boomers Will Reshape Your Agenda," *Harvard Business Review*, July/August 2009, pp. 71–76.

30 Statistics Canada, "2006 Census: Immigration, Citizenship, Language, Mobility and Migration," *The Daily*, December 4, 2007.

31 Statistics Canada, "Immigration in Canada: A Portrait of the Foreign-born Population, 2006 Census: Immigrants in Metropolitan Areas," http://www12.statcan.ca/english/census06/analysis/immcit/city_life.cfm

32 K. Young, "Language: Allophones on the Rise," *National Post*, December 4, 2007.

33 K. Young, "Language: Allophones on the Rise," *National Post*, December 4, 2007.

34 Statistics Canada, "Ethnic Diversity Survey, 2002," *The Daily*, September 29, 2003.

35 http://www.marketingcharts.com/television/american-vs-canadian-youth-lifestyles-values-differ-10588/

36 M. Adams, *Fire and Ice: The United States, Canada and the Myth of Converging Values* (Toronto: Penguin, 2003).

37 M. Adams, *Fire and Ice: The United States, Canada and the Myth of Converging Values* (Toronto: Penguin, 2003).

38 "The choice in Cuebec," *Maclean's*, October 30, 1995, pp. 18–33.

39 R. N. Kanungo and J. K. Bhatnagar, "Achievement Orientation and Occupational Values: A Comparative Study of Young French and English Canadians," *Canadian Journal of Behavioural Science* 12 (1978), pp. 384–392; M. W. McCarrey, S. Edwards, and R. Jones, "Personal Values of Canadian Anglophone and Francophone Employees and Ethnolinguistic Group

Membership, Sex and Position Level," *Journal of Psychology* 104 (1978), pp. 175–184; M. W. McCarrey, S. Edwards, and R. Jones, "The Influence of Ethnolinguistic Group Membership, Sex, and Position Level on Motivational Orientation of Canadian Anglophone and Francophone Employees," *Canadian Journal of Behavioural Science* 9 (1977), pp. 274–282; M. W. McCarrey, Y. Gasse, and L. F. Moore, "Work Value Goals and Instrumentalities: A Comparison of Canadian West-Coast Anglophone and Quebec City Francophone Managers," *International Review of Applied Psychology* 33 (1984), pp. 291–303; and S. C. Jain and D. A. Ralston, "The North American Free Trade Agreement: An Overview," in *NAFTA: A Three-Way Partnership for Free Trade and Growth*, ed. S. C. Jain and D. A. Ralston (Storrs, CT: University of Connecticut, 1996), pp. 3–7.

40 M. Major, M. McCarrey, P. Mercier, and Y. Gasse, "Meanings of Work and Personal Values of Canadian Anglophone and Francophone Middle Managers," *Canadian Journal of Administrative Sciences*, September 1994, pp. 251–263.

41 R. N. Kanungo and J. K. Bhatnagar, "Achievement Orientation and Occupational Values: A Comparative Study of Young French and English Canadians," *Canadian Journal of Behavioural Science* 12 (1978), pp. 384–392.

42 V. Mann-Feder and V. Savicki, "Burnout in Anglophone and Francophone Child and Youth Workers in Canada: A Cross-Cultural Comparison," *Child & Youth Care Forum* 32, no. 6 (2003), p. 345.

43 R. N. Kanungo and J. K. Bhatnagar, "Achievement Orientation and Occupational Values: A Comparative Study of Young French and English Canadians," *Canadian Journal of Behavioural Science* 12 (1978), pp. 384–392.

44 V. Mann-Feder and V. Savicki, "Burnout in Anglophone and Francophone Child and Youth Workers in Canada: A Cross-Cultural Comparison," *Child & Youth Care Forum* 32, no. 6 (2003), pp. 337–354.

45 N. J. Adler and J. L. Graham, "Cross-Cultural Interaction: The International Comparison Fallacy?" *Journal of International Business Studies* 20 (1989), pp. 515–537.

46 N. J. Adler, J. L. Graham, and T. S. Gehrke, "Business Negotiations in Canada, Mexico, and the United States," *Journal of Business Research* 15 (1987), pp. 411–429.

47 H. C. Jain, J. Normand, and R. N. Kanungo, "Job Motivation of Canadian Anglophone and Francophone Hospital Employees," *Canadian Journal of Behavioural Science*, April 1979, pp. 160–163; and R. N. Kanungo, G. J. Gorn, and H. J. Dauderis, "Motivational Orientation of Canadian Anglophone and Francophone Managers," *Canadian Journal of Behavioural Science*, April 1976, pp. 107–121.

48 M. Major, M. McCarrey, P. Mercier, and Y. Gasse, "Meanings of Work and Personal Values of Canadian Anglophone and Francophone Middle Managers," *Canadian Journal of Administrative Sciences*, September 1994, pp. 251–263.

49 K. L. Gibson, S. J. Mckelvie, and A. F. De Man, "Personality and Culture: A Comparison of Francophones and Anglophones in Québec," *Journal of Social Psychology* 148, no. 2 (2008), pp. 133–165.

50 G. Bouchard, F. Rocher, and G. Rocher, *Les Francophones Québécois* (Montreal: Bowne de Montréal, 1991).

51 K. L. Gibson, S. J. Mckelvie, and A. F. De Man, "Personality and Culture: A Comparison of Francophones and Anglophones in Québec," *Journal of Social Psychology* 148, no. 2 (2008), pp. 133–165.

52 C. P. Egri, D. A. Ralston, C. S. Murray, and J. D. Nicholson, "Managers in the NAFTA Countries: A Cross-Cultural Comparison of Attitudes toward Upward Influence Strategies," *Journal of International Management* 6, no. 2 (2000), pp. 149–171.

53 C. P. Egri, D. A. Ralston, C. S. Murray, and J. D. Nicholson, "Managers in the NAFTA Countries: A Cross-Cultural Comparison of Attitudes toward Upward Influence Strategies," *Journal of International Management* 6, no. 2 (2000), p. 164.

54 G. Hamilton, "B.C. First Nation Logging Firm Wins National Award," *Vancouver Sun*, July 14, 2011, p. C2.

55 G. Hamilton, "B.C. First Nation Logging Firm Wins National Award," *Vancouver Sun*, July 14, 2011, p. C2.

56 L. Redpath and M. O. Nielsen, "A Comparison of Native Culture, Non-Native Culture and New Management Ideology," *Canadian Journal of Administrative Sciences* 14, no. 3 (1997), p. 327.

57 G. C. Anders and K. K. Anders, "Incompatible Goals in Unconventional Organizations: The Politics of Alaska Native Corporations," *Organization Studies* 7 (1986), pp. 213–233; G. Dacks, "Worker-Controlled Native Enterprises: A Vehicle for Community Development in Northern Canada?" *Canadian Journal of Native Studies* 3 (1983), pp. 289–310; and L. P. Dana, "Self-Employment in the Canadian Sub-Arctic: An Exploratory Study," *Canadian Journal of Administrative Sciences* 13 (1996), pp. 65–77.

58 L. Redpath and M. O. Nielsen, "A Comparison of Native Culture, Non-Native Culture and New Management Ideology," *Canadian Journal of Administrative Sciences* 14, no. 3 (1997), p. 327.

59 R. B. Anderson, "The Business Economy of the First Nations in Saskatchewan: A Contingency Perspective," *Canadian Journal of Native Studies* 2 (1995), pp. 309–345.

60 E. Struzik, "'Win-Win Scenario' Possible for Resource Industry, Aboriginals," *Edmonton Journal*, April 6, 2003, p. A12.

61 http://www.highlevelwoodlands.com

62 http://www.cuslm.ca/foresterie/sfmn/nouvelles/LUM-Webb.pdf

63 Discussion based on L. Redpath and M. O. Nielsen, "A Comparison of Native Culture, Non-Native Culture and New Management Ideology," *Canadian Journal of Administrative Sciences* 14, no. 3 (1997), pp. 327–339.

64 Discussion based on L. Redpath and M. O. Nielsen, "A Comparison of Native Culture, Non-Native Culture and New Management Ideology," *Canadian Journal of Administrative Sciences* 14, no. 3 (1997), pp. 327–339.

65 D. Grigg and J. Newman, "Five Ways to Foster Bonds, Win Trust in Business," *Ottawa Citizen*, April 23, 2003, p. F12.

66 T. Chui, K. Tran, and J. Flanders, "Chinese Canadians: Enriching the Cultural Mosaic," *Canadian Social Trends*, no. 76, Spring 2005, pp. 26–34.

67 Statistics Canada, "Canada's Visible Minority Population in 2017," *The Daily*, March 22, 2005.

68 I. Y. M. Yeung and R. L. Tung, "Achieving Business Success in Confucian Societies: The Importance of Guanxi (Connections)," *Organizational Dynamics*, Special Report, 1998, pp. 72–83.

69 I. Y. M. Yeung and R. L. Tung, "Achieving Business Success in Confucian Societies: The Importance of Guanxi (Connections)," *Organizational Dynamics*, Special Report, 1998, p. 73.

70 Vignette based on K. Blevins, "Casino Workers in Regina Going Back to Work on Tuesday," *Leader-Post*, July 25, 2010, http://communities.canada.com/reginaleaderpost/print.aspx?postid=337941

71 D. A. Harrison, D. A. Newman, and P. L. Roth, "How Important Are Job Attitudes? Meta-analytic Comparisons of Integrative Behavioral Outcomes and Time Sequences," *Academy of Management Journal* 49, no. 2 (2006), pp. 305–325.

72 M. Riketta, "The Causal Relation between Job Attitudes and Performance: A Meta-analysis of Panel Studies," *Journal of Applied Psychology* 93, no. 2 (2008), pp. 472–481.

73 D. P. Moynihan and S. K. Pandey, "Finding Workable Levers over Work Motivation: Comparing Job Satisfaction, Job Involvement, and Organizational Commitment," *Administration & Society* 39, no. 7 (2007), pp. 803–832.

74 For problems with the concept of job satisfaction, see R. Hodson, "Workplace Behaviors," *Work and Occupations*, August 1991, pp. 271–290; and H. M. Weiss and R. Cropanzano, "Affective Events Theory: A Theoretical Discussion of the Structure, Causes and Consequences of Affective Experiences at Work," in *Research in Organizational Behavior*, vol. 18, ed. B. M. Staw and L. L. Cummings (Greenwich, CT: JAI Press, 1996), pp. 1–3.

75 J. Morrissy, "Canadian Workers among Most Dissatisfied in World," *Vancouver Sun*, June 25, 2011.

76 J. Barling, E. K. Kelloway, and R. D. Iverson, "High-Quality Work, Job Satisfaction, and Occupational Injuries," *Journal of Applied Psychology* 88, no. 2 (2003), pp. 276–283; and F. W. Bond and D. Bunce, "The Role of Acceptance and Job Control in Mental Health, Job Satisfaction, and Work Performance," *Journal of Applied Psychology* 88, no. 6 (2003), pp. 1057–1067.

77 S. E. Humphrey, J. D. Nahrgang, and F. P. Morgeson, "Integrating Motivational, Social, and Contextual Work Design Features: A Meta-analytic Summary and Theoretical Extension of the Work Design Literature," *Journal of Applied Psychology* 92, no. 5 (2007), pp. 1332–1356; and D. S. Chiaburu and D. A. Harrison, "Do Peers Make the Place? Conceptual Synthesis and Meta-analysis of Coworker Effect on Perceptions, Attitudes, OCBs, and Performance," *Journal of Applied Psychology* 93, no. 5 (2008), pp. 1082–1103.

78 E. Diener, E. Sandvik, L. Seidlitz, and M. Diener, "The Relationship between Income and Subjective Well-Being: Relative or Absolute?" *Social Indicators Research* 28 (1993), pp. 195–223.

79 E. Diener, E. Sandvik, L. Seidlitz, and M. Diener, "The Relationship Between Income and Subjective Well-Being: Relative or Absolute?" *Social Indicators Research* 28 (1993), pp. 195–223.

80 E. Diener, E. Sandvik, L. Seidlitz, and M. Diener, "The Relationship between Income and Subjective Well-Being: Relative or Absolute?" *Social Indicators Research* 28 (1993), pp. 195–223.

81 E. Diener and M. E. P. Seligman, "Beyond Money: Toward an Economy of Well-Being," *Psychological Science in the Public Interest* 5, no. 1 (2004), pp. 1–31; and A. Grant, "Money = Happiness? That's Rich: Here's the Science behind the Axiom," *The (South Mississippi) Sun Herald*, January 8, 2005.

82 T. A. Judge and C. Hurst, "The Benefits and Possible Costs of Positive Core Self-Evaluations: A Review and Agenda for Future Research," in *Positive Organizational Behavior*, ed. D. Nelson and C. L. Cooper (London, UK: Sage Publications, 2007), pp. 159–174.

83 M. T. Iaffaldano and M. Muchinsky, "Job Satisfaction and Job Performance: A Meta-analysis," *Psychological Bulletin*, March 1985, pp. 251–273.

84 T. A. Judge, C. J. Thoresen, J. E. Bono, and G. K. Patton, "The Job Satisfaction–Job Performance Relationship: A Qualitative and Quantitative Review," *Psychological Bulletin*, May 2001, pp. 376–407; and T. Judge, S. Parker, A. E. Colbert, D. Heller, and R. Ilies, "Job Satisfaction: A Cross-Cultural Review," in *Handbook of Industrial, Work, & Organizational Psychology*, vol. 2, ed. N. Anderson, D. S. Ones, H. K. Sinangil, and C. Viswesvaran (Thousand Oaks, CA: Sage, 2001), p. 41.

85 M. Riketta, "The Causal Relation between Job Attitudes and Performance: A Meta-analysis of Panel Studies," *Journal of Applied Psychology* 93, no. 2 (2008), pp. 472–481.

86 C. N. Greene, "The Satisfaction–Performance Controversy," *Business Horizons*, February 1972, pp. 31–41; E. E. Lawler III, *Motivation in Organizations* (Monterey, CA: Brooks/Cole, 1973); and M. M. Petty, G. W. McGee, and J. W. Cavender, "A Meta-analysis of the Relationship between Individual Job Satisfaction and Individual Performance," *Academy of Management Review*, October 1984, pp. 712–721.

87 C. Ostroff, "The Relationship between Satisfaction, Attitudes, and Performance: An Organizational Level Analysis," *Journal of Applied Psychology*, December 1992, pp. 963–974; A. M. Ryan, M. J. Schmit, and R. Johnson, "Attitudes and Effectiveness: Examining Relations at an Organizational Level," *Personnel Psychology*, Winter 1996, pp. 853–882; and J. K. Harter, F. L. Schmidt, and T. L. Hayes, "Business-Unit Level Relationship between Employee Satisfaction, Employee Engagement, and Business Outcomes: A Meta-analysis," *Journal of Applied Psychology*, April 2002, pp. 268–279.

88 D. W. Organ, *Organizational Citizenship Behavior: The Good Soldier Syndrome* (Lexington, MA: Lexington Books, 1988), p. 4.

89 D. W. Organ, *Organizational Citizenship Behavior: The Good Soldier Syndrome* (Lexington, MA: Lexington Books, 1988); C. A. Smith, D. W. Organ, and J. P. Near, "Organizational Citizenship Behavior: Its Nature and Antecedents," *Journal of Applied Psychology*, 1983, pp. 653–663.

90 J. Farh, C. Zhong, and D. W. Organ, "Organizational Citizenship Behavior in the People's Republic of China," *Academy of Management Proceedings*, 2000, pp. OB: D1–D6.

91 J. M. George and A. P. Brief, "Feeling Good-Doing Good: A Conceptual Analysis of the Mood at Work–Organizational Spontaneity Relationship," *Psychological Bulletin* 112 (2002), pp. 310–329; S. Wagner and M. Rush, "Altruistic Organizational Citizenship Behavior: Context, Disposition and Age," *Journal of Social Psychology* 140 (2002), pp. 379–391; and J. R. Spence, D. L. Ferris, D. J. Brown, and D. Heller, "Understanding Daily Citizenship Behaviors: A Social Comparison Perspective," *Journal of Organizational Behavior* 32, no. 4 (2011), pp. 547–571.

92 P. E. Spector, *Job Satisfaction: Application, Assessment, Causes, and Consequences* (Thousand Oaks, CA: Sage, 1997), pp. 57–58.

93 P. M. Podsakoff, S. B. MacKenzie, J. B. Paine, and D. G. Bachrach, "Organizational Citizenship Behaviors: A Critical Review of the Theoretical and Empirical Literature and Suggestions for Future Research," *Journal of Management* 26, no. 3 (2000), pp. 513–563.

94 B. J. Hoffman, C. A. Blair, J. P. Maeriac, and D. J. Woehr, "Expanding the Criterion Domain? A Quantitative Review of the OCB Literature," *Journal of Applied Psychology* 92, no. 2 (2007), pp. 555–566; and J. A. LePine, A. Erez, and D. E. Johnson, "The Nature and Dimensionality of Organizational Citizenship Behavior: A Critical Review and Meta-analysis," *Journal of Applied Psychology*, February 2002, pp. 52–65.

95 S. L. Blader and T. R. Tyler, "Testing and Extending the Group Engagement Model: Linkages between Social Identity, Procedural Justice, Economic Outcomes, and Extrarole Behavior," *Journal of Applied Psychology* 94, no. 2 (2009), pp. 445–464; J. Fahr, P. M. Podsakoff, and D. W. Organ, "Accounting for Organizational Citizenship Behavior: Leader Fairness and Task Scope Versus Satisfaction," *Journal of Management*, December 1990, pp. 705–722; and M. A. Konovsky and D. W. Organ, "Dispositional and Contextual Determinants of Organizational Citizenship Behavior," *Journal of Organizational Behavior*, May 1996, pp. 253–266.

96 D. S. Chiaburu and D. A. Harrison, "Do Peers Make the Place? Conceptual Synthesis and Meta-analysis of Coworker Effect on Perceptions, Attitudes, OCBs, and Performance," *Journal of Applied Psychology* 93, no. 5 (2008), pp. 1082–1103; and J. R. Spence, D. L. Ferris, D. J. Brown, and D. Heller, "Understanding Daily Citizenship Behaviors: A Social Comparison Perspective," *Journal of Organizational Behavior* 32, no. 4 (2011), pp. 547–571.

97 See, for instance, E. Naumann and D. W. Jackson Jr., "One More Time: How Do You Satisfy Customers?" *Business Horizons*, May–June 1999, pp. 71–76; D. J. Koys, "The Effects of Employee Satisfaction, Organizational Citizenship Behavior, and Turnover on Organizational Effectiveness: A Unit-Level, Longitudinal Study," *Personnel Psychology*, Spring 2001, pp. 101–114; J. Griffith, "Do Satisfied Employees Satisfy Customers? Support-Services Staff Morale and Satisfaction among Public School Administrators, Students, and Parents," *Journal of Applied Social Psychology*, August 2001, pp. 1627–1658; and C. Vandenberghe, K. Bentein, R. Michon, J. Chebat, M. Tremblay, and J. Fils, "An Examination of the Role of Perceived Support and Employee Commitment in Employee-Customer Encounters," *Journal of Applied Psychology* 92, no. 4 (2007), pp. 1177–1187.

98 M. J. Bitner, B. H. Booms, and L. A. Mohr, "Critical Service Encounters: The Employee's Viewpoint," *Journal of Marketing*, October 1994, pp. 95–106.

99 E. A. Locke, "The Nature and Causes of Job Satisfaction," in *Handbook of Industrial and Organizational Psychology*, ed. M. D. Dunnette (Chicago: Rand McNally, 1976), p. 1331; K. D. Scott and G. S. Taylor, "An Examination of Conflicting Findings on the Relationship between Job Satisfaction and Absenteeism: A Meta-analysis," *Academy of Management Journal*, September 1985, pp. 599–612; and R. Steel and J. R. Rentsch, "Influence of Cumulation Strategies on the Long-Range Prediction of Absenteeism," *Academy of Management Journal*, December 1995, pp. 1616–1634.

100 J. P. Hausknecht, N. J. Hiller, and R. J. Vance, "Work-Unit Absenteeism: Effects of Satisfaction, Commitment, Labor Market Conditions, and Time," *Academy of Management Journal* 51, no. 6 (2008), pp. 1123–1245.

101 W. Hom and R. W. Griffeth, *Employee Turnover* (Cincinnati, OH: South-Western Publishing, 1995); R. W. Griffeth, P. W. Hom, and S. Gaertner, "A Meta-analysis of Antecedents and Correlates of Employee Turnover: Update, Moderator Tests, and Research Implications for the Next Millennium," *Journal of Management* 26, no. 3 (2000), p. 479.

102 T. H. Lee, B. Gerhart, I. Weller, and C. O. Trevor, "Understanding Voluntary Turnover: Path-Specific Job Satisfaction Effects and the Importance of Unsolicited Job Offers," *Academy of Management Journal* 51, no. 4 (2008), pp. 651–671.

103 P. E. Spector, S. Fox, L. M. Penney, K. Bruursema, A. Goh, and S. Kessler, "The Dimensionality of Counterproductivity: Are All Counterproductive Behaviors Created Equal?" *Journal of Vocational Behavior* 68, no. 3 (2006), pp. 446–460; and D. S. Chiaburu and D. A. Harrison, "Do Peers Make the Place? Conceptual Synthesis and Meta-analysis of Coworker Effect on Perceptions, Attitudes, OCBs, and Performance," *Journal of Applied Psychology* 93, no. 5 (2008), pp. 1082–1103.

104 See D. Farrell, "Exit, Voice, Loyalty, and Neglect as Responses to Job Dissatisfaction: A Multidimensional Scaling Study," *Academy of Management Journal*, December 1983, pp. 596–606; C. E. Rusbult, D. Farrell, G. Rogers, and A. G. Mainous III, "Impact of Exchange Variables on Exit, Voice, Loyalty, and Neglect: An Integrative Model of Responses to Declining Job Satisfaction," *Academy of Management Journal*, September 1988, pp. 599–627; M. J. Withey and W. H. Cooper, "Predicting Exit, Voice, Loyalty, and Neglect," *Administrative Science Quarterly*, December 1989, pp. 521–539; J. Zhou and J. M. George, "When Job Dissatisfaction Leads to Creativity: Encouraging the Expression of Voice," *Academy of Management Journal*, August 2001, pp. 682–696; J. B. Olson-Buchanan and W. R. Boswell, "The Role of Employee Loyalty and Formality in Voicing Discontent," *Journal of Applied Psychology*, December 2002, pp. 1167–1174; and A. Davis-Blake, J. P. Broschak, and E. George, "Happy

Together? How Using Nonstandard Workers Affects Exit, Voice, and Loyalty among Standard Employees," *Academy of Management Journal* 46, no. 4 (2003), pp. 475–485.

105 R. B. Freeman, "Job Satisfaction as an Economic Variable," *American Economic Review*, January 1978, pp. 135–141.

106 K. Holland, "Inside the Minds of Your Employees," *New York Times*, January 28, 2007, p. B1; "Study Sees Link between Morale and Stock Price," *Workforce Management*, February 27, 2006, p. 15; and "The Workplace as a Solar System," *New York Times*, October 28, 2006, p. B5.

107 G. J. Blau and K. R. Boal, "Conceptualizing How Job Involvement and Organizational Commitment Affect Turnover and Absenteeism," *Academy of Management Review*, April 1987, p. 290.

108 N. J. Allen and J. P Meyer, "The Measurement and Antecedents of Affective, Continuance, and Normative Commitment to the Organization," *Journal of Occupational Psychology* 63 (1990), pp. 1–18; and J. P Meyer, N. J. Allen, and C. A. Smith, "Commitment to Organizations and Occupations: Extension and Test of a Three-Component Conceptualization," *Journal of Applied Psychology* 78 (1993), pp. 538–551.

109 M. Riketta, "Attitudinal Organizational Commitment and Job Performance: A Meta-analysis," *Journal of Organizational Behavior*, March 2002, pp. 257–266.

110 T. A. Wright and D. G. Bonett, "The Moderating Effects of Employee Tenure on the Relation between Organizational Commitment and Job Performance: A Meta-analysis," *Journal of Applied Psychology*, December 2002, pp. 1183–1190.

111 See, for instance, W. Hom, R. Katerberg, and C. L. Hulin, "Comparative Examination of Three Approaches to the Prediction of Turnover," *Journal of Applied Psychology*, June 1979, pp. 280–290; H. Angle and J. Perry, "Organizational Commitment: Individual and Organizational Influence," *Work and Occupations*, May 1983, pp. 123–146; J. L. Pierce and R. B. Dunham, "Organizational Commitment: Pre-Employment Propensity and Initial Work Experiences," *Journal of Management*, Spring 1987, pp. 163–178; and T. Simons and Q. Roberson, "Why Managers Should Care About Fairness: The Effects of Aggregate Justice Perceptions on Organizational Outcomes," *Journal of Applied Psychology* 88, no. 3 (2003), pp. 432–443.

112 Y. Gong, K. S. Law, S. Chang, and K. R. Xin, "Human Resources Management and Firm Performance: The Differential Role of Managerial Affective and Continuance Commitment," *Journal of Applied Psychology* 94, no. 1 (2009), pp. 263–275.

113 A. A. Luchak and I. R. Gellatly, "A Comparison of Linear and Nonlinear Relations between Organizational Commitment and Work Outcomes," *Journal of Applied Psychology* 92, no. 3 (2007), pp. 786–793.

114 J. R. Katzenback and J. A. Santamaria, "Firing up the Front Line," *Harvard Business Review*, May–June 1999, p. 109.

115 See, for example, J. M. Diefendorff, D. J. Brown, and A. M. Kamin, "Examining the Roles of Job Involvement and Work Centrality in Predicting Organizational Citizenship Behaviors and Job Performance," *Journal of Organizational Behavior*, February 2002, pp. 93–108.

116 Based on G. J. Blau and K. R. Boal, "Conceptualizing How Job Involvement and Organizational Commitment Affect Turnover and Absenteeism," *Academy of Management Review*, April 1987, p. 290.

117 G. Chen and R. J. Klimoski, "The Impact of Expectations on Newcomer Performance in Teams as Mediated by Work Characteristics, Social Exchanges, and Empowerment," *Academy of Management Journal* 46, no. 5 (2003), pp. 591–607; A. Ergeneli, G. Saglam, and S. Metin, "Psychological Empowerment and Its Relationship to Trust in Immediate Managers," *Journal of Business*

Research, January 2007, pp. 41–49; and S. E. Seibert, S. R. Silver, and W. A. Randolph, "Taking Empowerment to the Next Level: A Multiple-Level Model of Empowerment, Performance, and Satisfaction," *Academy of Management Journal* 47, no. 3 (2004), pp. 332–349.

118 J. M. Diefendorff, D. J. Brown, A. M. Kamin, and R. G. Lord, "Examining the Roles of Job Involvement and Work Centrality in Predicting Organizational Citizenship Behaviors and Job Performance," *Journal of Organizational Behavior*, February 2002, pp. 93–108.

119 M. R. Barrick, M. K. Mount, and J. P. Strauss, "Antecedents of Involuntary Turnover Due to a Reduction in Force," *Personnel Psychology* 47, no. 3 (1994), pp. 515–535.

120 D. R. May, R. L. Gilson, and L. M. Harter, "The Psychological Conditions of Meaningfulness, Safety and Availability and the Engagement of the Human Spirit at Work," *Journal of Occupational and Organizational Psychology* 77, no. 1 (2004), pp. 11–37.

121 B. L. Rich, J. A. Lepine, and E. R. Crawford, "Job Engagement: Antecedents and Effects on Job Performance," *Academy of Management Journal* 53, no. 3 (2010), pp. 617–635; and J. B. James, S. McKechnie, and J. Swanberg, "Predicting Employee Engagement in an Age-Diverse Retail Workforce," *Journal of Organizational Behavior* 32, no. 2 (2011), pp. 173–196.

122 "Building a Better Workforce," *PROFIT*, February 16, 2011, http://www.profitguide.com/article/10084—building-a-better-workforce—page0

123 J. K. Harter, F. L. Schmidt, and T. L. Hayes, "Business-Unit-Level Relationship between Employee Satisfaction, Employee Engagement, and Business Outcomes: A Meta-analysis," *Journal of Applied Psychology* 87, no. 2 (2002), pp. 268–279.

124 W. H. Macey and B. Schneider, "The Meaning of Employee Engagement," *Industrial and Organizational Psychology* 1 (2008), pp. 3–30.

125 A. Saks, "The Meaning and Bleeding of Employee Engagement: How Muddy Is the Water?" *Industrial and Organizational Psychology* 1 (2008), pp. 40–43.

126 A. B. Bakker, "An Evidence-Based Model of Work Engagement," *Current Directions in Psychological Science*, August 2011 (in press at time of writing).

127 Vignette based on "SaskGaming Is Proud to Support the Future of Saskatchewan," *Leader Post*, April 5, 2011, p. C8; and http://www.casinoregina.com/corporate/aboutus

128 See http://content.dell.com/ca/en/corp/d/corp-comm/cr-equal-employment-opportunity.aspx

129 N. Girouard, D. Stack, and M. O'Neill-Gilbert, "Ethnic Differences during Social Interactions of Preschoolers in Same-Ethnic and Cross-Ethnic Dyads," *European Journal of Developmental Psychology* 8, no. 2 (2011), pp. 185–202.

130 R. A. Roe and P. Ester, "Values and Work: Empirical Findings and Theoretical Perspective," *Applied Psychology: An International Review* 48 (1999), pp. 1–21.

131 A. Chapin, "Special Report: Diversity Knocks," *Canadian Business*, October 7, 2010.

132 D. A. Thomas and R. J. Ely, "Making Differences Matter: A New Paradigm for Managing Diversity," *Harvard Business Review* 74, no. 5 (1996), pp. 79–90; C. L. Holladay and M. A. Quiñones, "The Influence of Training Focus and Trainer Characteristics on Diversity Training Effectiveness," *Academy of Management Learning and Education* 7, no. 3 (2008), pp. 343–354; and R. Anand and M. Winters, "A Retrospective View of Corporate Diversity Training from 1964 to the Present," *Academy of Management Learning and Education* 7, no. 3 (2008), pp. 356–372.

133 L. Legault, J. Gutsell, and M. Inzlicht, "Ironic Effects of Anti-Prejudice Messages," *Psychological Science*, July 6, 2011, http://www.psychologicalscience.org/index.php/news/releases/ironic-effects-of-anti-prejudice-messages.html

134 Q. M. Roberson and C. K. Stevens, "Making Sense of Diversity in the Workplace: Organizational Justice and Language Abstraction in Employees' Accounts of Diversity-Related Incidents," *Journal of Applied Psychology* 91 (2006), pp. 379–391; and D. A. Harrison, D. A. Kravitz, D. M. Mayer, L. M. Leslie, and D. Lev-Arey, "Understanding Attitudes toward Affirmative Action Programs in Employment: Summary and Meta-analysis of 35 Years of Research," *Journal of Applied Psychology* 91 (2006), pp. 1013–1036.

135 A. Kalev, F. Dobbin, and E. Kelly, "Best Practices or Best Guesses? Assessing the Efficacy of Corporate Affirmative Action and Diversity Policies," *American Sociological Review* 71, no. 4 (2006), pp. 589–617.

136 For more examples, see D. Jermyn, "45 of Canada's Most Welcoming Places to Work," *Globe and Mail*, February 21, 2011, p. B14.

137 A. Pomeroy, "Cultivating Female Leaders," *HR Magazine*, February 2007, pp. 44–50.

138 L. Nguyen, "Banana Peel Thrown at Flyers' Wayne Simmonds Called a Wake-Up Call to NHL for More Ethnic Diversity," *Vancouver Sun*, September 23, 2011.

139 P. C. Earley and E. Mosakowski, "Cultural Intelligence," *Harvard Business Review* 82, no. 10 (October 2004), pp. 139–146.

140 S. S. Ramalu, R. C. Rose, N. Kumar, and J. Uli, "Doing Business in Global Arena: An Examination of the Relationship between Cultural Intelligence and Cross-Cultural Adjustment," *Asian Academy of Management Journal* 15, no. 1 (2010), pp. 79–97.

141 J. Sanchez-Burks, F. Lee, R. Nisbett, I. Choi, S. Zhao, and J. Koo, "Conversing across Cultures: East-West Communication Styles in Work and Nonwork Contexts," *Journal of Personality and Social Psychology* 85, no. 2 (2003), pp. 363–372.

142 M. J. Gelfand, M. Erez, and Z. Aycan, "Cross-Cultural Organizational Behavior," *Annual Review of Psychology* 58 (2007), pp. 479–514; and A. S. Tsui, S. S. Nifadkar, and A. Y. Ou, "Cross-National, Cross-Cultural Organizational Behavior Research: Advances, Gaps, and Recommendations," *Journal of Management*, June 2007, pp. 426–478.

143 M. Benz and B. S. Frey, "The Value of Autonomy: Evidence from the Self-Employed in 23 Countries," working paper 173, Institute for Empirical Research in Economics, University of Zurich, November 2003; and P. Warr, *Work, Happiness, and Unhappiness* (Mahwah, NJ: Laurence Erlbaum, 2007).

144 Based on E. Snape, C. Lo, and T. Redman, "The Three-Component Model of Occupational Commitment: A Comparative Study of Chinese and British Accountants," *Journal of Cross-Cultural Psychology*, November 2008, pp. 765–781; and Y. Cheng and M. S. Stockdale, "The Validity of the Three-Component Model of Organizational Commitment in a Chinese Context," *Journal of Vocational Behavior*, June 2003, pp. 465–489.

145 E. Bellman, "Reversal of Fortune Isolates India's Brahmins," *Wall Street Journal*, December 29, 2007, p. A4.

146 A. Sippola and A. Smale, "The Global Integration of Diversity Management: A Longitudinal Case Study," *International Journal of Human Resource Management* 18, no. 11 (2007), pp. 1895–1916.

Chapter 4

1 Opening vignette based on M. Parker, "Identifying Enablers and Blockers of Cultural Transformation," *Canadian Business*, May 17, 2007; E. Lazarus, "Building the Perfect Franchise," *PROFIT*, February 2006, p. 48ff; M. Parker, "Why Can't Employers See the Paradox?" *Financial Post*, March 19, 2008, p. WK7; Boston Pizza Press Kit, http://www.bostonpizza.com; and "Boston Pizza Reports Higher Second-Quarter Net Income, Same Store Sales," *Canadian Press*, August 10, 2011.

2 "Organization Man: Henry Mintzberg Has Some Common Sense Observations About the Ways We Run Companies," *Financial Post*, November 22/24, 1997, pp. 14–16.

3 K. McArthur, "Air Canada Tells Employees to Crack a Smile More Often," *Globe and Mail*, March 14, 2002, pp. B1, B2.

4 K. McArthur, "Air Canada Tells Employees to Crack a Smile More Often," *Globe and Mail*, March 14, 2002, pp. B1, B2.

5 See, for example, H. S. Becker, "Culture: A Sociological View," *Yale Review*, Summer 1982, pp. 513–527; and E. H. Schein, *Organizational Culture and Leadership* (San Francisco: Jossey-Bass, 1985), p. 168.

6 This seven-item description is based on C. A. O'Reilly III, J. Chatman, and D. F. Caldwell, "People and Organizational Culture: A Profile Comparison Approach to Assessing Person-Organization Fit," *Academy of Management Journal*, September 1991, pp. 487–516; and J. A. Chatman and K. A. Jehn, "Assessing the Relationship between Industry Characteristics and Organizational Culture: How Different Can You Be?" *Academy of Management Journal*, June 1994, pp. 522–553. For a description of other popular measures, see A. Xenikou and A. Furnham, "A Correlational and Factor Analytic Study of Four Questionnaire Measures of Organizational Culture," *Human Relations*, March 1996, pp. 349–371. For a review of cultural dimensions, see N. M. Ashkanasy, C. P. M. Wilderom, and M. F. Peterson, eds., *Handbook of Organizational Culture and Climate* (Thousand Oaks, CA: Sage, 2000), pp. 131–145.

7 E. Schein, "Coming to a New Awareness of Organizational Culture," *Sloan Management Review*, Winter 1984, pp. 3–16; E. Schein, *Organizational Culture and Leadership*, 2nd ed. (San Francisco, CA: Jossey-Bass, 1992); and E. Schein, "What Is Culture?" in *Reframing Organizational Culture*, ed. P. J. Frost, L. F. Moore, M. R. Louis, C. C. Lundberg, and J. Martin (Newbury Park, CA: Sage, 1991), pp. 243–253.

8 T. G. Stroup Jr., "Leadership and Organizational Culture: Actions Speak Louder Than Words," *Military Review* 76, no. 1 (January-February 1996), pp. 44–49; B. Moingeon and B. Ramanantsoa "Understanding Corporate Identity: The French School of Thought," *European Journal of Marketing* 31, no. 5/6 (1997), pp. 383–395; A. P. D. Van Luxemburg, J. M. Ulijn, and N. Amare, "The Contribution of Electronic Communication Media to the Design Process: Communicative and Cultural Implications," *IEEE Transactions on Professional Communication* 45, no. 4 (December 2002), pp. 250–264; L. D. McLean, "Organizational Culture's Influence on Creativity and Innovation: A Review of the Literature and Implications for Human Resource Development," *Advances in Developing Human Resources* 7, no. 2 (May 2005), pp. 226–246; and V. J. Friedman and A. B. Antal, "Negotiating Reality: A Theory of Action Approach to Intercultural Competence," *Management Learning* 36, no. 1 (2005), pp. 69–86.

9 See http://www.palliser.com/furniture/AboutUs/

10 See C. A. O'Reilly and J. A. Chatman, "Culture as Social Control: Corporations, Cultures, and Commitment," in *Research in Organizational Behavior*, vol. 18, ed. B. M. Staw and L. L. Cummings (Greenwich, CT: JAI Press, 1996), pp. 157–200.

11 T. E. Deal and A. A. Kennedy, "Culture: A New Look through Old Lenses," *Journal of Applied Behavioral Science*, November 1983, p. 501.

12 Y. Ling, Z. Simsek, M. H. Lubatkin, and J. F. Veiga, "Transformational Leadership's Role in Promoting Corporate Entrepreneurship: Examining the CEO-TMT Interface," *Academy of Management Journal* 51, no. 3 (2008), pp. 557–576; and

A. Malhotra, A. Majchrzak, and B. Rosen, "Leading Virtual Teams," *Academy of Management Perspectives* 21, no. 1 (2007), pp. 60–70.

13 D. Denison, "What Is the Difference between Organizational Culture and Organizational Climate? A Native's Point of View on a Decade of Paradigm Wars," *Academy of Management Review* 21 (1996) pp. 519–654; and L. R. James, C. C. Choi, C. E. Ko, P. K. McNeil, M. K. Minton, M. A. Wright, and K. Kim, "Organizational and Psychological Climate: A Review of Theory and Research," *European Journal of Work and Organizational Psychology* 17, no. 1 (2008), pp. 5–32.

14 J. Z. Carr, A. M. Schmidt, J. K. Ford, and R. P. DeShon, "Climate Perceptions Matter: A Meta-analytic Path Analysis Relating Molar Climate, Cognitive and Affective States, and Individual Level Work Outcomes," *Journal of Applied Psychology* 88, no. 4 (2003), pp. 605–619.

15 M. Schulte, C. Ostroff, S. Shmulyian, and A. Kinicki, "Organizational Climate Configurations: Relationships to Collective Attitudes, Customer Satisfaction, and Financial Performance," *Journal of Applied Psychology* 94, no. 3 (2009), pp. 618–634.

16 See, for example, Z. S. Byrne, J. Stoner, K. R. Thompson, and W. Hochwarter, "The Interactive Effects of Conscientiousness, Work Effort, and Psychological Climate on Job Performance," *Journal of Vocational Behavior* 66, no. 2 (2005), pp. 326–338; D. S. Pugh, J. Dietz, A. P. Brief, and J. W. Wiley, "Looking Inside and Out: The Impact of Employee and Community Demographic Composition on Organizational Diversity Climate," *Journal of Applied Psychology* 93, no. 6 (2008), pp. 1422–1428; and J. C. Wallace, E. Popp, and S. Mondore, "Safety Climate as a Mediator between Foundation Climates and Occupational Accidents: A Group-Level Investigation," *Journal of Applied Psychology* 91, no. 3 (2006), pp. 681–688.

17 The view that there will be consistency among perceptions of organizational culture has been called the "integration" perspective. For a review of this perspective and conflicting approaches, see D. Meyerson and J. Martin, "Cultural Change: An Integration of Three Different Views," *Journal of Management Studies*, November 1987, pp. 623–647; and P. J. Frost, L. F. Moore, M. R. Louis, C. C. Lundberg, and J. Martin, eds., *Reframing Organizational Culture* (Newbury Park, CA: Sage, 1991).

18 See J. M. Jermier, J. W. Slocum Jr., L. W. Fry, and J. Gaines, "Organizational Subcultures in a Soft Bureaucracy: Resistance Behind the Myth and Facade of an Official Culture," *Organization Science*, May 1991, pp. 170–194; S. A. Sackmann, "Culture and Subcultures: An Analysis of Organizational Knowledge," *Administrative Science Quarterly*, March 1992, pp. 140–161; R. F. Zammuto, "Mapping Organizational Cultures and Subcultures: Looking Inside and across Hospitals" (paper presented at the 1995 National Academy of Management Conference, Vancouver, BC, August 1995); and G. Hofstede, "Identifying Organizational Subcultures: An Empirical Approach," *Journal of Management Studies*, January 1998, pp. 1–12.

19 D. A. Hoffman and L. M. Jones, "Leadership, Collective Personality, and Performance," *Journal of Applied Psychology* 90, no. 3 (2005), pp. 509–522.

20 S. Hamm, "No Letup—and No Apologies," *BusinessWeek*, October 26, 1998, pp. 58–64.

21 See, for example, G. G. Gordon and N. DiTomaso, "Predicting Corporate Performance from Organizational Culture," *Journal of Management Studies*, November 1992, pp. 793–798; and J. B. Sorensen, "The Strength of Corporate Culture and the Reliability of Firm Performance," *Administrative Science Quarterly*, March 2002, pp. 70–91.

22 Y. Wiener, "Forms of Value Systems: A Focus on Organizational Effectiveness and Cultural Change and Maintenance," *Academy of Management Review*, October 1988, p. 536; and B. Schneider, A. N. Salvaggio, and M. Subirats, "Climate Strength: A New Direction for Climate Research," *Journal of Applied Psychology* 87 (2002), pp. 220–229.

23 R. T. Mowday, L. W. Porter, and R. M. Steers, *Employee-Organization Linkages: The Psychology of Commitment, Absenteeism, and Turnover* (New York: Academic Press, 1982); C. Vandenberghe, "Organizational Culture, Person-Culture Fit, and Turnover: A Replication in the Health Care Industry," *Journal of Organizational Behavior*, March 1999, pp. 175–184; and M. Schulte, C. Ostroff, S. Shmulyian, and A. Kinicki, "Organizational Climate Configurations: Relationships to Collective Attitudes, Customer Satisfaction, and Financial Performance," *Journal of Applied Psychology* 94, no. 3 (2009), pp. 618–634.

24 Vignette based on "Rising on Three Pillars Strategy; 10 Most Admired Corporate Cultures," *Financial Post*, November 26, 2008, p. WK4; M. Parker, "Why Can't Employers See The Paradox?" *Financial Post*, March 19, 2008, p. WK7; and M. Parker, "Identifying Enablers and Blockers of Cultural Transformation," *Canadian Business*, May 17, 2007.

25 R. Spence, "Telling Stories Makes for Happy Endings," *National Post (Financial Post)*, April 20, 2009, pp. FP4.

26 D. M. Boje, "The Storytelling Organization: A Study of Story Performance in an Office-Supply Firm," *Administrative Science Quarterly*, March 1991, pp. 106–126; and C. H. Deutsch, "The Parables of Corporate Culture," *New York Times*, October 13, 1991, p. F25.

27 A. M. Pettigrew, "On Studying Organizational Cultures," *Administrative Science Quarterly*, December 1979, p. 576.

28 A. M. Pettigrew, "On Studying Organizational Cultures," *Administrative Science Quarterly*, December 1979, p. 576. See also K. Kamoche, "Rhetoric, Ritualism, and Totemism in Human Resource Management," *Human Relations*, April 1995, pp. 367–385.

29 V. Matthews, "Starting Every Day with a Shout and a Song," *Financial Times*, May 2, 2001, p. 11; and M. Gimein, "Sam Walton Made Us a Promise," *Fortune*, March 18, 2002, pp. 121–130.

30 A. Rafaeli and M. G. Pratt, "Tailored Meanings: On the Meaning and Impact of Organizational Dress," *Academy of Management Review*, January 1993, pp. 32–55.

31 Thanks to an anonymous reviewer for adding these.

32 M. Pendergast, *Uncommon Grounds: The History of Coffee and How It Transformed Our World* (New York: Basic Books, 1999), p. 369.

33 Thanks to a reviewer for this story.

34 Vignette based on "Rising on Three Pillars Strategy; 10 Most Admired Corporate Cultures," *Financial Post*, November 26, 2008, p. WK4; and http://www.bostonpizza.com/en/about/PressKit.aspx

35 E. H. Schein, "The Role of the Founder in Creating Organizational Culture," *Organizational Dynamics*, Summer 1983, pp. 13–28.

36 http://bostonpizza.com/assets/mediacentre/documents/pdf/BP_ProfilePDF_WTreliving_FINAL.pdf

37 E. H. Schein, "Leadership and Organizational Culture," in *The Leader of the Future*, ed. F. Hesselbein, M. Goldsmith, and R. Beckhard (San Francisco: Jossey-Bass, 1996), pp. 61–62.

38 "PCL's Biggest Investment: Its People," *National Post*, September 2, 2008, p. FP10.

39 See, for example, J. R. Harrison and G. R. Carroll, "Keeping the Faith: A Model of Cultural Transmission in Formal Organizations," *Administrative Science Quarterly*, December 1991, pp. 552–582.

40 B. Schneider, H. W. Goldstein, and D. B. Smith, "The ASA Framework: An Update," *Personnel Psychology*, Winter 1995, pp. 747–773; D. M. Cable and T. A. Judge, "Interviewers' Perceptions of Person-Organization Fit and Organizational

Selection Decisions," *Journal of Applied Psychology*, August 1997, pp. 546–561; M. L. Verquer, T. A. Beehr, and S. H. Wagner, "A Meta-analysis of Relations between Person-Organization Fit and Work Attitudes," *Journal of Vocational Behavior*, December 2003, pp. 473–489; and W. Li, Y. Wang, P. Taylor, K. Shi, and D. He, "The Influence of Organizational Culture on Work-Related Personality Requirement Ratings: A Multilevel Analysis," *International Journal of Selection and Assessment* 16, no. 4 (2008), pp. 366–384.

41 "Building a Better Workforce," *PROFIT*, February 16, 2011, http://www.profitguide.com/article/10084--building-a-better-workforce--page0

42 "Building a Better Workforce," *PROFIT*, February 16, 2011, http://www.profitguide.com/article/10084--building-a-better-workforce--page0

43 D. C. Hambrick and P. A. Mason, "Upper Echelons: The Organization as a Reflection of Its Top Managers," *Academy of Management Review*, April 1984, pp. 193–206; B. P. Niehoff, C. A. Enz, and R. A. Grover, "The Impact of Top-Management Actions on Employee Attitudes and Perceptions," *Group & Organization Studies*, September 1990, pp. 337–352; and H. M. Trice and J. M. Beyer, "Cultural Leadership in Organizations," *Organization Science*, May 1991, pp. 149–169.

44 See, for instance, J. P. Wanous, *Organizational Entry*, 2nd ed. (New York: Addison Wesley, 1992); G. T. Chao, A. M. O'Leary-Kelly, S. Wolf, H. J. Klein, and P. D. Gardner, "Organizational Socialization: Its Content and Consequences," *Journal of Applied Psychology*, October 1994, pp. 730–743; B. E. Ashforth, A. M. Saks, and R. T. Lee, "Socialization and Newcomer Adjustment: The Role of Organizational Context," *Human Relations*, July 1998, pp. 897–926; D. A. Major, "Effective Newcomer Socialization into High-Performance Organizational Cultures," in *Handbook of Organizational Culture & Climate*, ed. N. M. Ashkanasy, C. P. M. Wilderom, and M. F. Peterson (Thousand Oaks, CA: Sage, 2000), pp. 355–368; and D. M. Cable and C. K. Parsons, "Socialization Tactics and Person-Organization Fit," *Personnel Psychology*, Spring 2001, pp. 1–23.

45 A. M. Saks and J. A. Gruman, "Organizational Socialization and Positive Organizational Behaviour: Implications for Theory, Research, and Practice," *Canadian Journal of Administrative Sciences* 28, no. 1 (2011), pp. 4–16.

46 J. Impoco, "Basic Training, Sanyo Style," *U.S. News & World Report*, July 13, 1992, pp. 46–48.

47 B. Filipczak, "Trained by Starbucks," *Training*, June 1995, pp. 73–79; and S. Gruner, "Lasting Impressions," *Inc.*, July 1998, p. 126.

48 "Building a Better Workforce," *PROFIT*, February 16, 2011, http://www.profitguide.com/article/10084--building-a-better-workforce---page0

49 J. Van Maanen and E. H. Schein, "Career Development," in *Improving Life at Work*, ed. J. R. Hackman and J. L. Suttle (Santa Monica, CA: Goodyear, 1977), pp. 58–62.

50 C. J. Collins, "The Interactive Effects of Recruitment Practices and Product Awareness on Job Seekers' Employer Knowledge and Application Behaviors," *Journal of Applied Psychology* 92, no. 1 (2007), pp. 180–190.

51 G. Chen and R. J. Klimoski, "The Impact of Expectations on Newcomer Performance in Teams as Mediated by Work Characteristics, Social Exchanges, and Empowerment," *Academy of Management Journal* 46 (2003), pp. 591–607; C. R. Wanberg and J. D. Kammeyer-Mueller, "Predictors and Outcomes of Proactivity in the Socialization Process," *Journal of Applied Psychology* 85 (2000), pp. 373–385; J. D. Kammeyer-Mueller and C. R. Wanberg, "Unwrapping the Organizational Entry Process: Disentangling Multiple Antecedents and Their Pathways to Adjustment," *Journal of Applied Psychology* 88 (2003),

pp. 779–794; and E. W. Morrison, "Longitudinal Study of the Effects of Information Seeking on Newcomer Socialization," *Journal of Applied Psychology* 78 (2003), pp. 173–183.

52 J. Van Maanen and E. H. Schein, "Career Development," in *Improving Life at Work*, ed. J. R. Hackman and J. L. Suttle (Santa Monica, CA: Goodyear, 1977), p. 59.

53 http://www.canadianbusiness.com/article/11442—the-brands-we-trust; and http://www.timhortons.com/us/en/about/3315.html

54 E. W. Morrison, "Newcomers' Relationships: The Role of Social Network Ties During Socialization," *Academy of Management Journal* 45 (2002), pp. 1149–1160.

55 A. M. Saks and J. A. Gruman, "Getting Newcomers Engaged: The Role of Socialization Tactics," *Journal of Managerial Psychology* 26 (2011), pp. 383–402.

56 T. N. Bauer, T. Bodner, B. Erdogan, D. M. Truxillo, and J. S. Tucker, "Newcomer Adjustment during Organizational Socialization: A Meta-analytic Review of Antecedents, Outcomes, and Methods," *Journal of Applied Psychology* 92, no. 3 (2007), pp. 707–721.

57 J. E. Sheridan, "Organizational Culture and Employee Retention," *Academy of Management Journal*, December 1992, pp. 1036–1056.

58 J. B. Sorensen, "The Strength of Corporate Culture and the Reliability of Firm Performance," *Administrative Science Quarterly*, March 2002, pp. 70–91.

59 See, for instance, D. Miller, "What Happens after Success: The Perils of Excellence," *Journal of Management Studies*, May 1994, pp. 11–38.

60 See T. Cox Jr., *Cultural Diversity in Organizations: Theory, Research & Practice* (San Francisco: Berrett-Koehler, 1993), pp. 162–170; L. Grensing-Pophal, "Hiring to Fit Your Corporate Culture," *HR Magazine*, August 1999, pp. 50–54; and D. L. Stone, E. F. Stone-Romero, and K. M. Lukaszewski, "The Impact of Cultural Values on the Acceptance and Effectiveness of Human Resource Management Policies and Practices," *Human Resource Management Review* 17, no. 2 (2007), pp. 152–165.

61 S. Cartwright and C. L. Cooper, "The Role of Culture Compatibility in Successful Organizational Marriages," *Academy of Management Executive*, May 1993, pp. 57–70; R. A. Weber and C. F. Camerer, "Cultural Conflict and Merger Failure: An Experimental Approach," *Management Science*, April 2003, pp. 400–412; and I. H. Gleibs, A. Mummendey, and P. Noack, "Predictors of Change in Postmerger Identification During a Merger Process: A Longitudinal Study," *Journal of Personality and Social Psychology* 95, no. 5 (2008), pp. 1095–1112.

62 K. W. Smith, "A Brand-New Culture for the Merged Firm," *Mergers and Acquisitions* 35, no. 6 (June 2000), pp. 45–50.

63 M. Raynaud and M. Teasdale, "Confusions & Acquisitions: Post-Merger Culture Shock and Some Remedies," *Communication World* 9, no. 6 (May–June 1992), pp. 44–45.

64 M. Raynaud and M. Teasdale, "Confusions & Acquisitions: Post-Merger Culture Shock and Some Remedies," *Communication World* 9, no. 6 (May–June 1992), pp. 44–45.

65 Vignette based on "Corporate Culture," *Canadian HR Reporter* 17, no. 21 (December 6, 2004), pp. 7–11; P. Kuitenbrouwer, "Making Money, and Enjoying It: Dingwall at the Mint," *Financial Post* (*National Post*), December 29, 2004, p. FP1; and C. Clark, "Dingwall Severance in the Works," *Globe and Mail*, September 30, 2005, p. A5.

66 J. P. Kotter, "Leading Changes: Why Transformation Efforts Fail," *Harvard Business Review*, March–April 1995, pp. 59–67; and J. P. Kotter, *Leading Change* (Boston: Harvard Business School Press, 1996).

67 See B. Victor and J. B. Cullen, "The Organizational Bases of Ethical Work Climates," *Administrative Science Quarterly*, March 1988, pp. 101–125; R. L. Dufresne, "An Action Learning Perspective on Effective Implementation of Academic Honor Codes," *Group & Organization Management*, April 2004, pp. 201–218; and A. Ardichvilli, J. A. Mitchell, and D. Jondle, "Characteristics of Ethical Business Cultures," *Journal of Business Ethics* 85, no. 4 (2009), pp. 445–451.

68 J. P. Mulki, J. F. Jaramillo, and W. B. Locander, "Critical Role of Leadership on Ethical Climate and Salesperson Behaviors," *Journal of Business Ethics* 86, no. 2 (2009), pp. 125–141; M. Schminke, M. L. Ambrose, and D. O. Neubaum, "The Effect of Leader Moral Development on Ethical Climate and Employee Attitudes," *Organizational Behavior and Human Decision Processes* 97, no. 2 (2005), pp. 135–151; and M. E. Brown, L. K. Treviño, and D. A. Harrison, "Ethical Leadership: A Social Learning Perspective for Construct Development and Testing," *Organizational Behavior and Human Decision Processes* 97, no. 2 (2005), pp. 117–134.

69 D. M. Mayer, M. Kuenzi, R. Greenbaum, M. Bardes, and S. Salvador, "How Low Does Ethical Leadership Flow? Test of a Trickle-Down Model," *Organizational Behavior and Human Decision Processes* 108, no. 1 (2009), pp. 1–13.

70 M. L. Gruys, S. M. Stewart, J. Goodstein, M. N. Bing, and A. C. Wicks, "Values Enactment in Organizations: A Multi-Level Examination," *Journal of Management* 34, no. 4 (2008), pp. 806–843.

71 D. L. Nelson and C. L. Cooper, eds., *Positive Organizational Behavior* (London: Sage, 2007); K. S. Cameron, J. E. Dutton, and R. E. Quinn, eds., *Positive Organizational Scholarship: Foundations of a New Discipline* (San Francisco: Berrett-Koehler, 2003); and F. Luthans and C. M. Youssef, "Emerging Positive Organizational Behavior," *Journal of Management*, June 2007, pp. 321–349.

72 J. Robison, "Great Leadership Under Fire," *Gallup Leadership Journal*, March 8, 2007, pp. 1–3.

73 R. Wagner and J. K. Harter, *12: The Elements of Great Managing* (New York: Gallup Press, 2006).

74 S. Fineman, "On Being Positive: Concerns and Counterpoints," *Academy of Management Review* 31, no. 2 (2006), pp. 270–291.

75 P. Dvorak, "A Firm's Culture Can Get Lost in Translation," *Wall Street Journal*, April 3, 2006, pp. B1, B3; K. Kranhold, "The Immelt Era, Five Years Old, Transforms GE," *Wall Street Journal*, September 11, 2006, pp. B1, B3; and S. McCartney, "Teaching Americans How to Behave Abroad," *Wall Street Journal*, April 11, 2006, pp. D1, D4.

76 D. J. McCarthy and S. M. Puffer, "Interpreting the Ethicality of Corporate Governance Decision in Russia: Utilizing Integrative Social Contracts Theory to Evaluate the Relevance of Agency Theory Norms," *Academy of Management Review* 33, no. 1 (2008), pp. 11–31.

Chapter 5

1 Vignette based on J. Warrillow, "Reframe a Supply Problem to Build Anticipation," *Globe and Mail*, October 5, 2011, http://www.theglobeandmail.com/report-on-business/small-business/sb-growth/day-today/reframe-a-supply-problem-to-build-antic-ipation/article2190385/; and J. Warrillow, *Built to Sell: Creating a Business That Can Thrive without You* (New York: Portfolio, 2011).

2 See H. A. Simon, "Rationality in Psychology and Economics," *Journal of Business*, October 1986, pp. 209–224; and A. Langley, "In Search of Rationality: The Purposes Behind the Use of Formal Analysis in Organizations," *Administrative Science Quarterly*, December 1989, pp. 598–631.

3 For a review of the rational decision-making model, see E. F. Harrison, *The Managerial Decision Making Process*, 5th ed. (Boston: Houghton Mifflin, 1999), pp. 75–102.

4 https://www.cibc.com/ca/inside-cibc/community-matters/funding-guidelines.html

5 J. G. March, *A Primer on Decision Making* (New York: Free Press, 1994), pp. 2–7.

6 Vignette based on J. Warrillow, "Reframe a Supply Problem to Build Anticipation," *Globe and Mail*, October 5, 2011, http://www.theglobeandmail.com/report-on-business/small-business/sb-growth/day-today/reframe-a-supply-problem-to-build-anticipation/article2190385/

7 D. L. Rados, "Selection and Evaluation of Alternatives in Repetitive Decision Making," *Administrative Science Quarterly*, June 1972, pp. 196–206.

8 M. Bazerman, *Judgment in Managerial Decision Making*, 3rd ed. (New York: Wiley, 1994), p. 5.

9 J. E. Russo, K. A. Carlson, and M. G. Meloy, "Choosing an Inferior Alternative," *Psychological Science* 17, no. 10 (2006), pp. 899–904.

10 See, for instance, L. R. Beach, *The Psychology of Decision Making* (Thousand Oaks, CA: Sage, 1997).

11 See H. A. Simon, *Administrative Behavior*, 4th ed. (New York: Free Press, 1997); and M. Augier, "Simon Says: Bounded Rationality Matters," *Journal of Management Inquiry*, September 2001, pp. 268–275.

12 G. Gigerenzer, "Why Heuristics Work," *Perspectives on Psychological Science* 3, no. 1 (2008), pp. 20–29; and A. K. Shah and D. M. Oppenheimer, "Heuristics Made Easy: An Effort-Reduction Framework," *Psychological Bulletin* 134, no. 2 (2008), pp. 207–222.

13 See T. Gilovich, D. Griffin, and D. Kahneman, *Heuristics and Biases: The Psychology of Intuitive Judgment* (New York: Cambridge University Press, 2002).

14 E. Dane and M. G. Pratt, "Exploring Intuition and Its Role in Managerial Decision Making," *Academy of Management Review* 32, no. 1 (2007), pp. 33–54.

15 P. D. Brown, "Some Hunches About Intuition," *New York Times* (November 17, 2007), p. B5.

16 See, for instance, L. A. Burke and M. K. Miller, "Taking the Mystery Out of Intuitive Decision Making," *Academy of Management Executive*, November 1999, pp. 91–99; N. Khatri and H. A. Ng, "The Role of Intuition in Strategic Decision Making," *Human Relations*, January 2000, pp. 57–86; J. A. Andersen, "Intuition in Managers: Are Intuitive Managers More Effective?" *Journal of Managerial Psychology* 15, no. 1–2 (2000), pp. 46–63; D. Myers, *Intuition: Its Powers and Perils* (New Haven, CT: Yale University Press, 2002); and L. Simpson, "Basic Instincts," *Training*, January 2003, pp. 56–59.

17 See, for instance, L. A. Burke and M. K. Miller, "Taking the Mystery Out of Intuitive Decision Making," *Academy of Management Executive*, November 1999, pp. 91–99.

18 B. D. Dunn and H. C. Galton, "Listening to Your Heart: How Interoception Shapes Emotion Experience and Intuitive Decision Making," *Psychological Science* 21 no. 12 (December 2010), pp. 1835–1844.

19 S. P. Robbins, *Decide & Conquer: Making Winning Decisions and Taking Control of Your Life* (Upper Saddle River, NJ: Financial Times/Prentice Hall, 2004), p. 13.

20 S. Plous, *The Psychology of Judgment and Decision Making* (New York: McGraw-Hill, 1993), p. 217.

21 S. Lichtenstein and B. Fischhoff, "Do Those Who Know More Also Know More About How Much They Know?" *Organizational Behavior and Human Performance*, December 1977, pp. 159–183.

22 B. Fischhoff, P. Slovic, and S. Lichtenstein, "Knowing with Certainty: The Appropriateness of Extreme Confidence," *Journal of Experimental Psychology: Human Perception and Performance,* November 1977, pp. 552–564.

23 J. Kruger and D. Dunning, "Unskilled and Unaware of It: How Difficulties in Recognizing One's Own Incompetence Lead to Inflated Self-Assessments," *Journal of Personality and Social Psychology,* November 1999, pp. 1121–1134.

24 B. Fischhoff, P. Slovic, and S. Lichtenstein, "Knowing with Certainty: The Appropriateness of Extreme Confidence," *Journal of Experimental Psychology* 3 (1977), pp. 552–564.

25 J. Kruger and D. Dunning, "Unskilled and Unaware of It: How Difficulties in Recognizing One's Own Incompetence Lead to Inflated Self-Assessments," *Journal of Personality and Social Psychology,* November 1999, pp. 1121–1134.

26 See, for instance, A. Tversky and D. Kahneman, "Judgment under Uncertainty: Heuristics and Biases," *Science,* September 1974, pp. 1124–1131.

27 J. S. Hammond, R. L. Keeney, and H. Raiffa, *Smart Choices* (Boston: HBS Press, 1999), p. 191.

28 R. Hastie, D. A. Schkade, and J. W. Payne, "Juror Judgments in Civil Cases: Effects of Plaintiff's Requests and Plaintiff's Identity on Punitive Damage Awards," *Law and Human Behavior,* August 1999, pp. 445–470.

29 C. Janiszewski and D. Uy, "Precision of the Anchor Influences the Amount of Adjustment," *Psychological Science* 19, no. 2 (2008), pp. 121–127.

30 See R. S. Nickerson, "Confirmation Bias: A Ubiquitous Phenomenon in Many Guises," *Review of General Psychology,* June 1998, pp. 175–220; and E. Jonas, S. Schultz-Hardt, D. Frey, and N. Thelen, "Confirmation Bias in Sequential Information Search after Preliminary Decisions," *Journal of Personality and Social Psychology,* April 2001, pp. 557–571.

31 B. Nyhan and J. Reifler, "When Corrections Fail: The Persistence of Political Misperceptions," *Political Behavior* 32, no. 2 (2010), pp. 303–330.

32 See A. Tversky and D. Kahneman, "Availability: A Heuristic for Judging Frequency and Probability," in *Judgment under Uncertainty: Heuristics and Biases,* ed. D. Kahneman, P. Slovic, and A. Tversky (Cambridge, UK: Cambridge University Press, 1982), pp. 163–178; and B. J. Bushman and G. L. Wells, "Narrative Impressions of Literature: The Availability Bias and the Corrective Properties of Meta-analytic Approaches," *Personality and Social Psychology Bulletin,* September 2001, pp. 1123–1130.

33 See B. M. Staw, "The Escalation of Commitment to a Course of Action," *Academy of Management Review,* October 1981, pp. 577–587; and H. Moon, "Looking Forward and Looking Back: Integrating Completion and Sunk-Cost Effects within an Escalation-of-Commitment Progress Decision," *Journal of Applied Psychology,* February 2001, pp. 104–113.

34 B. M. Staw, "Knee-Deep in the Big Muddy: A Study of Escalating Commitment to a Chosen Course of Action," *Organizational Behavior and Human Performance* 16 (1976), pp. 27–44; and B. M. Staw, "The Escalation of Commitment: An Update and Appraisal," in *Organizational Decision Making,* ed. Z. Shapira (New York; Cambridge University Press, 1997), pp. 121–215.

35 K. F. E. Wong and J. Y. Y. Kwong, "The Role of Anticipated Regret in Escalation of Commitment," *Journal of Applied Psychology* 92, no. 2 (2007), pp. 545–554.

36 K. F. E. Wong, J. Y. Y. Kwong, and C. K. Ng, "When Thinking Rationally Increases Biases: The Role of Rational Thinking Style in Escalation of Commitment," *Applied Psychology: An International Review* 57, no. 2 (2008), pp. 246–271.

37 See, for instance, A. James and A. Wells, "Death Beliefs, Superstitious Beliefs and Health Anxiety," *British Journal of Clinical Psychology,* March 2002, pp. 43–53.

38 http://lilomag.com/2011/06/04/10-most-superstitious-famous-athletes/

39 See, for example, D. J. Keys and B. Schwartz, "Leaky Rationality: How Research on Behavioral Decision Making Challenges Normative Standards of Rationality," *Psychological Science* 2, no. 2 (2007), pp. 162–180; and U. Simonsohn, "Direct Risk Aversion: Evidence from Risky Prospects Valued Below Their Worst Outcome," *Psychological Science* 20, no. 6 (2009), pp. 686–692.

40 J. K. Maner, M. T. Gailliot, D. A. Butz, and B. M. Peruche, "Power, Risk, and the Status Quo: Does Power Promote Riskier or More Conservative Decision Making," *Personality and Social Psychology Bulletin* 33, no. 4 (2007), pp. 451–462.

41 A. Chakraborty, S. Sheikh, and N. Subramanian, "Termination Risk and Managerial Risk Taking," *Journal of Corporate Finance* 13, (2007), pp. 170–188.

42 X. He and V. Mittal, "The Effect of Decision Risk and Project Stage on Escalation of Commitment," *Organizational Behavior and Human Decision Processes* 103, no. 2 (2007), pp. 225–237.

43 D. Kahneman and A. Tversky, "Prospect Theory: An Analysis of Decisions under Risk," *Econometrica* 47, no. 2 (1979), pp. 263–291; and P. Bryant and R. Dunford, "The Influence of Regulatory Focus on Risky Decision-Making," *Applied Psychology: An International Review* 57, no. 2 (2008), pp. 335–359.

44 A. J. Porcelli and M. R. Delgado, "Acute Stress Modulates Risk Taking in Financial Decision Making," *Psychological Science* 20, no. 3 (2009), pp. 278–283.

45 R. L. Guilbault, F. B. Bryant, J. H. Brockway, and E. J. Posavac, "A Meta-analysis of Research on Hindsight Bias," *Basic and Applied Social Psychology,* September 2004, pp. 103–117; and L. Werth, F. Strack, and J. Foerster, "Certainty and Uncertainty: The Two Faces of the Hindsight Bias," *Organizational Behavior and Human Decision Processes,* March 2002, pp. 323–341.

46 M. Gladwell, "Connecting the Dots," *New Yorker,* March 10, 2003.

47 See S. A. Mohrman, D. Finegold, and J. A. Klein, "Designing the Knowledge Enterprise: Beyond Programs and Tools," *Organizational Dynamics* 31, no. 2 (2002), pp. 134–150; and H. Dolezalek, "Collaborating in Cyberspace," *Training,* April 2003, pp. 32–37.

48 Cited in A. Cabrera and E. F. Cabrera, "Knowledge-Sharing Dilemmas," *Organization Studies* 5, 2002, p. 687.

49 B. Roberts, "Pick Employees' Brains," *HR Magazine,* February 2000, pp. 115–116; B. Fryer, "Get Smart," *Inc.,* September 1999, p. 65; and D. Zielinski, "Have You Shared a Bright Idea Today?" *Training,* July 2000, p. 65.

50 B. Fryer, "Get Smart," *Inc.,* September 1999, p. 63.

51 C. E. Connelly, D. Zweig, J. Webster, and J. P. Trougakos, "Knowledge Hiding in Organizations," *Journal of Organizational Behavior,* January 4, 2011, published online before print, http://onlinelibrary.wiley.com/doi/10.1002/job.737/abstract

52 J. Gordon, "Intellectual Capital and You," *Training,* September 1999, p. 33.

53 D. Zielinski, "Have You Shared a Bright Idea Today?" *Training,* July 2000, pp. 65–67.

54 See N. R. F. Maier, "Assets and Liabilities in Group Problem Solving: The Need for an Integrative Function," *Psychological Review,* April 1967, pp. 239–249; G. W. Hill, "Group versus Individual Performance: Are N+1 Heads Better Than One?" *Psychological Bulletin,* May 1982, pp. 517–539; M. D. Johnson and J. R. Hollenbeck, "Collective Wisdom as an Oxymoron:

Team-Based Structures as Impediments to Learning," in *Research Companion to the Dysfunctional Workplace: Management, Challenges and Symptoms*, ed. J. Langan-Fox, C. L. Cooper, and R. J. Klimoski (Northampton, MA: Edward Elgar Publishing, 2007), pp. 319–331; and R. F. Martell and M. R. Borg, "A Comparison of the Behavioral Rating Accuracy of Groups and Individuals," *Journal of Applied Psychology*, February 1993, pp. 43–50.

55 See, for example, W. C. Swap and Associates, *Group Decision Making* (Newbury Park, CA: Sage, 1984).

56 "Group Judgments," *Psychological Bulletin*, January 1997, pp. 149–167; and B. L. Bonner, S. D. Sillito, and M. R. Baumann, "Collective Estimation: Accuracy, Expertise, and Extroversion as Sources of Intra-Group Influence," *Organizational Behavior and Human Decision Processes* 103 (2007), pp. 121–133.

57 See, for example, W. C. Swap and Associates, *Group Decision Making* (Newbury Park, CA: Sage, 1984).

58 I. L. Janis, *Groupthink: Psychological Studies of Policy Decisions and Fiascoes*, 2nd ed. (Boston: Houghton Mifflin, 1982); W. Park, "A Review of Research on Groupthink," *Journal of Behavioral Decision Making*, July 1990, pp. 229–245; C. P. Neck and G. Moorhead, "Groupthink Remodeled: The Importance of Leadership, Time Pressure, and Methodical Decision Making Procedures," *Human Relations*, May 1995, pp. 537–558; and J. N. Choi and M. U. Kim, "The Organizational Application of Groupthink and Its Limits in Organizations," *Journal of Applied Psychology*, April 1999, pp. 297–306.

59 I. L. Janis, *Groupthink: Psychological Studies of Policy Decisions and Fiascoes*, 2nd ed. (Boston: Houghton Mifflin, 1982).

60 M. E. Turner and A. R. Pratkanis, "Mitigating Groupthink by Stimulating Constructive Conflict," in *Using Conflict in Organizations*, ed. C. De Dreu and E. Van de Vliert (London: Sage, 1997), pp. 53–71.

61 See N. R. F. Maier, *Principles of Human Relations* (New York: Wiley, 1952); N. Richardson Ahlfinger and J. K. Esser, "Testing the Groupthink Model: Effects of Promotional Leadership and Conformity Predisposition," *Social Behavior & Personality* 29, no. 1 (2001), pp. 31–41; and S. Schultz-Hardt, F. C. Brodbeck, A. Mojzisch, R. Kerschreiter, and D. Frey, "Group Decision Making in Hidden Profile Situations: Dissent as a Facilitator for Decision Quality," *Journal of Personality and Social Psychology* 91, no. 6 (2006), pp. 1080–1093.

62 J. N. Choi and M. U. Kim, "The Organizational Application of Groupthink and Its Limitations in Organizations," *Journal of Applied Psychology* 84 (1999), pp. 297–306.

63 J. Longley and D. G. Pruitt, "Groupthink: A Critique of Janis' Theory," in *Review of Personality and Social Psychology*, ed. L. Wheeler (Newbury Park, CA: Sage, 1980), pp. 507–513; and J. A. Sniezek, "Groups under Uncertainty: An Examination of Confidence in Group Decision Making," *Organizational Behavior & Human Decision Processes* 52, 1992, pp. 124–155.

64 C. McCauley, "The Nature of Social Influence in Groupthink: Compliance and Internalization," *Journal of Personality and Social Psychology* 57 (1989), pp. 250–260; P. E. Tetlock, R. S. Peterson, C. McGuire, S. Chang, and P. Feld, "Assessing Political Group Dynamics: A Test of the Groupthink Model," *Journal of Personality and Social Psychology* 63 (1992), pp. 781–796; S. Graham, "A Review of Attribution Theory in Achievement Contexts," *Educational Psychology Review* 3 (1991), pp. 5–39; and G. Moorhead and J. R. Montanari, "An Empirical Investigation of the Groupthink Phenomenon," *Human Relations* 39 (1986), pp. 399–410.

65 J. N. Choi and M. U. Kim, "The Organizational Application of Groupthink and Its Limitations in Organizations," *Journal of Applied Psychology* 84 (1999), pp. 297–306.

66 See D. J. Isenberg, "Group Polarization: A Critical Review and Meta-analysis," *Journal of Personality and Social Psychology*, December 1986, pp. 1141–1151; J. L. Hale and F. J. Boster,

"Comparing Effect Coded Models of Choice Shifts," *Communication Research Reports*, April 1988, pp. 180–186; and P. W. Paese, M. Bieser, and M. E. Tubbs, "Framing Effects and Choice Shifts in Group Decision Making," *Organizational Behavior & Human Decision Processes*, October 1993, pp. 149–165.

67 See, for example, N. Kogan and M. A. Wallach, "Risk Taking as a Function of the Situation, the Person, and the Group," in *New Directions in Psychology*, vol. 3 (New York: Holt, Rinehart and Winston, 1967); and M. A. Wallach, N. Kogan, and D. J. Bem, "Group Influence on Individual Risk Taking," *Journal of Abnormal and Social Psychology* 65 (1962), pp. 75–86.

68 R. D. Clark III, "Group-Induced Shift toward Risk: A Critical Appraisal," *Psychological Bulletin*, October 1971, pp. 251–270.

69 Z. Krizan and R. S. Baron, "Group Polarization and Choice-Dilemmas: How Important Is Self-Categorization?" *European Journal of Social Psychology* 37, no. 1 (2007), pp. 191–201.

70 N. W. Kohn and S. M. Smith, "Collaborative Fixation: Effects of Others' Ideas on Brainstorming," *Applied Cognitive Psychology* 25, no. 3 (May/June 2011), pp. 359–371.

71 N. L. Kerr and R. S. Tindale, "Group Performance and Decision-Making," *Annual Review of Psychology* 55 (2004), pp. 623–655.

72 N. W. Kohn and S. M. Smith, "Collaborative Fixation: Effects of Others' Ideas on Brainstorming," *Applied Cognitive Psychology* 25, no. 3 (May/June 2011), pp. 359–371; and S. M. Smith, "The Constraining Effects of Initial Ideas," in *Group Creativity*, ed. P. B. Paulus and B. A. Nijstad (New York: Oxford University Press, 2003), pp. 15–31.

73 R. C. Litchfield, "Brainstorming Reconsidered: A Goal-Based View," *Academy of Management Review* 33, no. 3 (2008), pp. 649–668.

74 See A. L. Delbecq, A. H. Van deVen, and D. H. Gustafson, *Group Techniques for Program Planning: A Guide to Nominal and Delphi Processes* (Glenview, IL: Scott, Foresman, 1975); and P. B. Paulus and H.-C. Yang, "Idea Generation in Groups: A Basis for Creativity in Organizations," *Organizational Behavior and Human Decision Processing*, May 2000, pp. 76–87.

75 C. Faure, "Beyond Brainstorming: Effects of Different Group Procedures on Selection of Ideas and Satisfaction with the Process," *Journal of Creative Behavior* 38 (2004), pp. 13–34.

76 See, for instance, A. R. Dennis and J. S. Valacich, "Computer Brainstorms: More Heads Are Better Than One," *Journal of Applied Psychology*, August 1993, pp. 531–537; R. B. Gallupe and W. H. Cooper, "Brainstorming Electronically," *Sloan Management Review*, Fall 1993, pp. 27–36; and A. B. Hollingshead and J. E. McGrath, "Computer-Assisted Groups: A Critical Review of the Empirical Research," in *Team Effectiveness and Decision Making in Organizations*, ed. R. A. Guzzo and E. Salas (San Francisco: Jossey-Bass, 1995), pp. 46–78.

77 B. B. Baltes, M. W. Dickson, M. P. Sherman, C. C. Bauer, and J. LaGanke, "Computer-Mediated Communication and Group Decision Making: A Meta-analysis," *Organizational Behavior and Human Decision Processes*, January 2002, pp. 156–179.

78 T. M. Amabile, "A Model of Creativity and Innovation in Organizations," in *Research in Organizational Behavior*, vol. 10, ed. B. M. Staw and L. L. Cummings (Greenwich, CT: JAI Press, 1988), p. 126; and J. E. Perry-Smith and C. E. Shalley, "The Social Side of Creativity: A Static and Dynamic Social Network Perspective," *Academy of Management Review*, January 2003, pp. 89–106.

79 G. J. Feist and F. X. Barron, "Predicting Creativity from Early to Late Adulthood: Intellect, Potential, and Personality," *Journal of Research in Personality*, April 2003, pp. 62–88.

80 R. W. Woodman, J. E. Sawyer, and R. W. Griffin, "Toward a Theory of Organizational Creativity," *Academy of Management Review*, April 1993, p. 298; J. M. George and J. Zhou, "When Openness to Experience and Conscientiousness Are Related to Creative Behavior: An Interactional Approach," *Journal of*

Applied Psychology, June 2001, pp. 513–524; and E. F. Rietzschel, C. K. W. de Dreu, and B. A. Nijstad, "Personal Need for Structure and Creative Performance: The Moderating Influence of Fear of Invalidity," *Personality and Social Psychology Bulletin*, June 2007, pp. 855–866.

81 Cited in C. G. Morris, *Psychology: An Introduction*, 9th ed. (Upper Saddle River, NJ: Prentice Hall, 1996), p. 344.

82 This section is based on T. M. Amabile, "Motivating Creativity in Organizations: On Doing What You Love and Loving What You Do," *California Management Review* 40, no. 1 (Fall 1997), pp. 39–58.

83 G. Keenan, "GM Shows a Nimble Touch in Oshawa," *Globe and Mail*, March 27, 2010. Caption from GM: "Auto workers at the General Motors Canada assembly line in Oshawa, Ont."

84 M. Baas, C. K. W. De Dreu, and B. A. Nijstad, "A Meta-analysis of 25 Years of Mood-Creativity Research: Hedonic Tone, Activation, or Regulatory Focus?" *Psychological Bulletin* 134, no. 6 (2008), pp. 779–806.

85 J. Zhou, "When the Presence of Creative Coworkers Is Related to Creativity: Role of Supervisor Close Monitoring, Developmental Feedback, and Creative Personality," *Journal of Applied Psychology* 88, no. 3 (June 2003), pp. 413–422.

86 J. E. Perry-Smith, "Social Yet Creative: The Role of Social Relationships in Facilitating Individual Creativity," *Academy of Management Journal* 49, no. 1 (2006), pp. 85–101.

87 G. Park, D. Lubinski, and C. P. Benbow, "Contrasting Intellectual Patterns Predict Creativity in the Arts and Sciences," *Psychological Science* 18, no. 11 (2007), pp. 948–952.

88 W. J. J. Gordon, *Synectics* (New York: Harper & Row, 1961).

89 See C. E. Shalley, J. Zhou, and G. R. Oldham, "The Effects of Personal and Contextual Characteristics on Creativity: Where Should We Go from Here?" *Journal of Management*, November 2004, pp. 933–958; G. Hirst, D. Van Knippenberg, and J. Zhou, "A Cross-Level Perspective on Employee Creativity: Goal Orientation, Team Learning Behavior, and Individual Creativity," *Academy of Management Journal* 52, no. 2 (2009), pp. 280–293; and C. E. Shalley, L. L. Gilson, and T. C. Blum, "Interactive Effects of Growth Need Strength, Work Context, and Job Complexity on Self-Reported Creative Performance," *Academy of Management Journal* 52, no. 3 (2009), pp. 489–505.

90 Cited in T. Stevens, "Creativity Killers," *IndustryWeek*, January 23, 1995, p. 63.

91 Vignette based on A. Trang, "'Kick Ass' Coffee," *Advantage*, November–December 2011, pp. 75–76; and http://www.kickinghorsecoffee.com/en/story

92 P. L. Schumann, "A Moral Principles Framework for Human Resource Management Ethics," *Human Resource Management Review* 11 (Spring–Summer 2001), pp. 93–111; M. G. Velasquez, *Business Ethics*, 4th ed. (Upper Saddle River, NJ: Prentice Hall, 1998), Chapter 2; and G. F. Cavanagh, D. J. Moberg, and M. Valasquez, "The Ethics of Organizational Politics," *Academy of Management Journal*, June 1981, pp. 363–374.

93 P. L. Schumann, "A Moral Principles Framework for Human Resource Management Ethics," *Human Resource Management Review* 11 (Spring–Summer 2001), pp. 93–111.

94 See, for example, T. Machan, ed., *Commerce and Morality* (Totowa, NJ: Rowman and Littlefield, 1988).

95 L. K. Trevino, "Ethical Decision Making in Organizations: A Person-Situation Interactionist Model," *Academy of Management Review*, July 1986, pp. 601–617; and L. K. Trevino and S. A. Youngblood, "Bad Apples in Bad Barrels: A Causal Analysis of Ethical Decision Making Behavior," *Journal of Applied Psychology*, August 1990, pp. 378–385.

96 See L. Kohlberg, *Essays in Moral Development: The Philosophy of Moral Development*, vol. 1 (New York: Harper and Row, 1981); L. Kohlberg, *Essays in Moral Development: The Psychology of Moral Development*, vol. 2 (New York: Harper and Row, 1984); and R. S. Snell, "Complementing Kohlberg: Mapping the Ethical Reasoning Used by Managers for Their Own Dilemma Cases," *Human Relations*, January 1996, pp. 23–49.

97 L. Kohlberg, *Essays in Moral Development: The Philosophy of Moral Development*, vol. 1 (New York: Harper and Row, 1981); L. Kohlberg, *Essays in Moral Development: The Psychology of Moral Development*, vol. 2 (New York: Harper and Row, 1984); and R. S. Snell, "Complementing Kohlberg: Mapping the Ethical Reasoning Used by Managers for Their Own Dilemma Cases," *Human Relations*, January 1996, pp. 23–49.

98 J. Weber, "Managers' Moral Reasoning: Assessing Their Responses to Three Moral Dilemmas," *Human Relations*, July 1990, pp. 687–702; and S. B. Knouse and R. A. Giacalone, "Ethical Decision-Making in Business: Behavioral Issues and Concerns," *Journal of Business Ethics*, May 1992, pp. 369–377.

99 R. Teper, M. Inzlicht, and E. Page-Gould, "Are We More Moral Than We Think? Exploring the Role of Affect in Moral Behavior and Moral Forecasting," *Psychological Science*, April 2011.

100 This discussion is based on G. F. Cavanagh, D. J. Moberg, and M. Valasquez, "The Ethics of Organizational Politics," *Academy of Management Journal*, June 1981, pp. 363–374.

101 Vignette based on J. Warrillow, "Reframe a Supply Problem to Build Anticipation," *Globe and Mail*, October 5, 2011, http://www.theglobeandmail.com/report-on-business/small-business/sb-growth/day-today/reframe-a-supply-problem-to-build-anticipation/article2190385/

102 J. Castaldo, "Those Emotional Canadians!" *Canadian Business*, May 10, 2010, pp. 32–33.

103 M. McClearn, "Brands We Trust: On a First-Name Basis," *Canadian Business*, April 7, 2011.

104 M. Friedman, *Capitalism and Freedom* (Chicago: University of Chicago Press, 1962).

105 J. Bakan, *The Corporation* (Toronto: Big Picture Media Corporation, 2003).

106 J. Nelson, "The CEO Poll: Should Companies Give to Charity?" *Canadian Business*, April 7, 2011.

107 J. Castaldo, "The CEO Poll: The Trouble with Outsourcing," *Canadian Business*, April 7, 2011.

108 http://www.greenbiz.com/news/2006/10/26/survey-shows-mba-students-believe-business-should-be-agent-social-change

109 M. J. Gelfand, M. Erez, and Z. Aycan, "Cross-Cultural Organizational Behavior," *Annual Review of Psychology*, January 2007, pp. 479–514; and A. S. Tsui, S. S. Nifadkar, and A. Y. Ou, "Cross-National, Cross-Cultural Organizational Behavior Research: Advances, Gaps, and Recommendations," *Journal of Management*, June 2007, pp. 426–478.

110 N. J. Adler, *International Dimensions of Organizational Behavior*, 4th ed. (Cincinnati, OH: South-Western Publishing, 2002), pp. 182–189.

111 T. Jackson, "Cultural Values and Management Ethics: A 10-Nation Study," *Human Relations*, October 2001, pp. 1267–1302; see also J. B. Cullen, K. P. Parboteeah, and M. Hoegl, "Cross-National Differences in Managers' Willingness to Justify Ethically Suspect Behaviors: A Test of Institutional Anomie Theory," *Academy of Management Journal*, June 2004, pp. 411–421.

112 W. Chow Hou, "To Bribe or Not to Bribe?" *Asia, Inc.*, October 1996, p. 104.

113 P. Digh, "Shades of Gray in the Global Marketplace," *HR Magazine*, April 1997, p. 91.

114 T. Donaldson, "Values in Tension: Ethics Away from Home," *Harvard Business Review*, September–October 1996, pp. 48–62.

115 http://www.transparency.org/content/download/61106/978536

Chapter 6

1 Vignette based on D. Veale, "The Only True Test Is Success in the Marketplace," *Telegraph Journal*, November 10, 2011, http://telegraphjournal.canadaeast.com/rss/article/1454583

2 See, for instance, R. L. Daft, *Organization Theory and Design*, 6th ed. (Cincinnati, OH: South Western College, 1998).

3 C. Hymowitz, "Managers Suddenly Have to Answer to a Crowd of Bosses," *Wall Street Journal*, August 12, 2003, p. B1.

4 See, for instance, L. Urwick, *The Elements of Administration* (New York: Harper and Row, 1944), pp. 52–53.

5 J. Child and R. G. McGrath, "Organizations Unfettered: Organizational Form in an Information-Intensive Economy," *Academy of Management Journal*, December 2001, pp. 1135–1148.

6 G. Morgan, *Images of Organization* (Newbury Park, CA: Sage, 1986), p. 21.

7 H. Mintzberg, *Structure in Fives: Designing Effective Organizations* (Englewood Cliffs, NJ: Prentice Hall, 1983), p. 157.

8 J. Davis, "Governing the Family-Run Business," *Harvard Business School Working Knowledge*, September 4, 2001.

9 D. Miller, L. Steier, and I. Le Breton-Miller, "Lost in Time: Intergenerational Succession, Change, and Failure in Family Business," *Journal of Business Venturing*, July 2003, pp. 513–531.

10 J. J. Chrisman, J. H. Chua, and L. P. Steier, "An Introduction to Theories of Family Business," *Journal of Business Venturing*, July 2003, pp. 441–448.

11 K. Knight, "Matrix Organization: A Review," *Journal of Management Studies*, May 1976, pp. 111–130; and L. R. Burns and D. R. Wholey, "Adoption and Abandonment of Matrix Management Programs: Effects of Organizational Characteristics and Interorganizational Networks," *Academy of Management Journal*, February 1993, pp. 106–138.

12 See, for instance, S. M. Davis and P. R. Lawrence, "Problems of Matrix Organization," *Harvard Business Review*, May–June 1978, pp. 131–142.

13 Vignette based on D. Veale, "The Only True Test Is Success in the Marketplace," *Telegraph Journal*, November 10, 2011, http://telegraphjournal.canadaeast.com/rss/article/1454583; http://www.t4g.com/Newsroom/News-Article/April-2011/T4G-in-Top-10-of-Canada-s-Best-Workplaces.aspx; and http://leadingthinkers.t4g.com/about.html

14 J. R. Galbraith and E. E. Lawler III, "Effective Organizations: Using the New Logic of Organizing," in *Organizing for the Future: The New Logic for Managing Complex Organizations*, ed. J. R. Galbraith, E. E. Lawler III, and Associates (San Francisco: Jossey-Bass, 1993).

15 G. G. Dess, A. M. A. Rasheed, K. J. McLaughlin, and R. Priem, "The New Corporate Architecture," *Academy of Management Executive*, August 1995, pp. 7–18; and C. Y. Baldwin and K. B. Clark, "Managing in an Age of Modularity," *Harvard Business Review*, September–October 1997, pp. 84–93.

16 M. Kaeter, "The Age of the Specialized Generalist," *Training*, December 1993, pp. 48–53.

17 See, for instance, R. E. Miles and C. C. Snow, "The New Network Firm: A Spherical Structure Built on Human Investment Philosophy," *Organizational Dynamics*, Spring 1995, pp. 5–18; D. Pescovitz, "The Company Where Everybody's a Temp," *New York Times Magazine*, June 11, 2000, pp. 94–96; B. Hedberg, G. Dahlgren, J. Hansson, and N. Olve, *Virtual Organizations and Beyond* (New York: Wiley, 2001); N. S. Contractor, S. Wasserman, and K. Faust, "Testing Multitheoretical, Multilevel Hypotheses About Organizational Networks: An Analytic Framework and Empirical Example," *Academy of Management Review* 31, no. 3 (2006), pp. 681–703; and Y. Shin, "A Person-Environment Fit Model for Virtual Organizations," *Journal of Management*, October 2004, pp. 725–743.

18 G. G. Dess, A. M. A. Rasheed, K. J. McLaughlin, and R. Priem, "The New Corporate Architecture," *Academy of Management Executive*, August 1995, pp. 7–18.

19 J. Bates, "Making Movies and Moving On," *Los Angeles Times*, January 19, 1998, p. A1.

20 "Why Do Canadian Companies Opt for Cooperative Ventures?" *Micro: The Micro-Economic Research Bulletin* 4, no. 2 (1997), pp. 3–5.

21 C. B. Gibson and J. L. Gibbs, "Unpacking the Concept of Virtuality: The Effects of Geographic Dispersion, Electronic Dependence, Dynamic Structure, and National Diversity on Team Innovation," *Administrative Science Quarterly* 51, no. 3 (2006), pp. 451–495; and H. M. Latapie and V. N. Tran, "Subculture Formation, Evolution, and Conflict Between Regional Teams in Virtual Organizations," *Business Review*, Summer 2007, pp. 189–193.

22 "GE: Just Your Average Everyday $60 Billion Family Grocery Store," *IndustryWeek*, May 2, 1994, pp. 13–18.

23 The following is based on D. D. Davis, "Form, Function and Strategy in Boundaryless Organizations," in *The Changing Nature of Work*, ed. A. Howard (San Francisco: Jossey-Bass, 1995), pp. 112–138; P. Roberts, "We Are One Company, No Matter Where We Are. Time and Space Are Irrelevant," *Fast Company*, April–May 1998, pp. 122–128; R. L. Cross, A. Yan, and M. R. Louis, "Boundary Activities in 'Boundaryless' Organizations: A Case Study of a Transformation to a Team-Based Structure," *Human Relations*, June 2000, pp. 841–868; and R. Ashkenas, D. Ulrich, T. Jick, and S. Kerr, *The Boundaryless Organization: Breaking the Chains of Organizational Structure*, revised and updated (San Francisco: Jossey-Bass, 2002).

24 R. Blackwell, "For Cisco, a Canadian's Global Aspirations," *Globe and Mail*, June 26, 2011, http://www.theglobeandmail.com/report-on-business/careers/careers-leadership/at-the-top/article2076260.ece; "Cisco to Kill Flip Cam," *Globe and Mail*, April 12, 2011, http://www.theglobeandmail.com/news/technology/tech-news/cisco-to-kill-flip-cam/article1981650/

25 "At Starbucks, Baristas Told No More Than Two Drinks," *Wall Street Journal*, October 13, 2010, http://online.wsj.com/article/SB10001424052748704164004575548403514060736.html?mod=e2tw; and J. Jargon, "Latest Starbucks Buzzword: 'Lean' Japanese Techniques," *Wall Street Journal*, August 4, 2009.

26 See J. P. Guthrie and D. K. Datta, "Dumb and Dumber: The Impact of Downsizing on Firm Performance as Moderated by Industry Conditions," *Organization Science* 19, no. 1 (2008), pp. 108–123; W. F. Cascio, C. E. Young, and J. R. Morris, "Financial Consequences of Employment-Change Decisions in Major U.S. Corporations," *Academy of Management Journal* 40 (1997), pp. 1175–1189; and K. P. De Meuse, T. J. Bergmann, P. A. Vanderheiden, and C. E. Roraff, "New Evidence Regarding Organizational Downsizing and a Firm's Financial Performance: A Long-Term Analysis," *Journal of Managerial Issues* 16, no. 2 (2004), pp. 155–177.

27 See, for example, C. O. Trevor and A. J. Nyberg, "Keeping Your Headcount When All About You Are Losing Theirs: Downsizing, Voluntary Turnover Rates, and the Moderating Role of HR Practices," *Academy of Management Journal* 51, no. 2 (2008), pp. 259–276; S. Moore, L. Grunberg, and E. Greenberg, "Surviving Repeated Waves of Organizational Downsizing: The Recency, Duration, and Order Effects Associated with

Different Forms of Layoff Contact," *Anxiety, Stress & Coping: An International Journal* 19, no. 3 (2006), pp. 309–329; T. M. Probst, S. M. Stewart, M. L. Gruys, and B. W. Tierney, "Productivity, Counterproductivity and Creativity: The Ups and Downs of Job Insecurity," *Journal of Occupational and Organizational Psychology* 80, no. 3 (2007), pp. 479–497; and J. E. Ferrie, M. J. Shipley, M. G. Marmot, P. Martikainen, S. Stansfeld, and G. D. Smith, "Job Insecurity in White-Collar Workers: Toward an Explanation of Associations with Health," *Journal of Occupational Health Psychology* 6, no. 1 (2001), pp. 26–42.

28 C. D. Zatzick and R. D. Iverson, "High-Involvement Management and Workforce Reduction: Competitive Advantage or Disadvantage?" *Academy of Management Journal* 49, no. 5 (2006), pp. 999–1015; A. Travaglione and B. Cross, "Diminishing the Social Network in Organizations: Does There Need to Be Such a Phenomenon as 'Survivor Syndrome' After Downsizing?" *Strategic Change* 15, no. 1 (2006), pp. 1–13; and J. D. Kammeyer-Mueller, H. Liao, and R. D. Arvey, "Downsizing and Organizational Performance: A Review of the Literature from a Stakeholder Perspective," *Research in Personnel and Human Resources Management* 20 (2001), pp. 269–329.

29 T. Burns and G. M. Stalker, *The Management of Innovation* (London: Tavistock, 1961); and J. A. Courtright, G. T. Fairhurst, and L. E. Rogers, "Interaction Patterns in Organic and Mechanistic Systems," *Academy of Management Journal*, December 1989, pp. 773–802.

30 This analysis is referred to as a contingency approach to organization design. See, for instance, J. M. Pennings, "Structural Contingency Theory: A Reappraisal," in *Research in Organizational Behavior*, vol. 14, ed. B. M. Staw and L. L. Cummings (Greenwich, CT: JAI Press, 1992), pp. 267–309; J. R. Hollenbeck, H. Moon, A. P. J. Ellis, B. J. West, D. R. Ilgen, L. Sheppard, C. O. L. H. Porter, and J. A. Wagner III, "Structural Contingency Theory and Individual Differences: Examination of External and Internal Person-Team Fit," *Journal of Applied Psychology*, June 2002, pp. 599–606; and A. Drach-Zahavy and A. Freund, "Team Effectiveness under Stress: A Structural Contingency Approach," *Journal of Organizational Behavior* 28, no. 4 (2007), pp. 423–450.

31 The strategy-structure thesis was originally proposed in A. D. Chandler Jr., *Strategy and Structure: Chapters in the History of the Industrial Enterprise* (Cambridge, MA: MIT Press, 1962). For an updated analysis, see T. L. Amburgey and T. Dacin, "As the Left Foot Follows the Right? The Dynamics of Strategic and Structural Change," *Academy of Management Journal*, December 1994, pp. 1427–1452.

32 See R. E. Miles and C. C. Snow, *Organizational Strategy, Structure, and Process* (New York: McGraw-Hill, 1978); D. C. Galunic and K. M. Eisenhardt, "Renewing the Strategy-Structure-Performance Paradigm," in *Research in Organizational Behavior*, vol. 16, ed. B. M. Staw and L. L. Cummings (Greenwich, CT: JAI Press, 1994), pp. 215–255; I. C. Harris and T. W. Ruefli, "The Strategy/Structure Debate: An Examination of the Performance Implications," *Journal of Management Studies*, June 2000, pp. 587–603; and S. M. Toh, F. P. Morgeson, and M. A. Campion, "Human Resource Configurations: Investigating Fit with the Organizational Context," *Journal of Applied Psychology* 93, no. 4 (2008), pp. 864–882.

33 See, for instance, P. M. Blau and R. A. Schoenherr, *The Structure of Organizations* (New York: Basic Books, 1971); D. S. Pugh, "The Aston Program of Research: Retrospect and Prospect," in *Perspectives on Organization Design and Behavior*, ed. A. H. Van de Ven and W. F. Joyce (New York: Wiley, 1981), pp. 135–166; R. Z. Gooding and J. A. Wagner III, "A Meta-analytic Review of the Relationship between Size and Performance: The Productivity and Efficiency of Organizations and Their Subunits," *Administrative Science Quarterly*, December 1985, pp. 462–481; and A. C. Bluedorn, "Pilgrim's Progress: Trends and Convergence in Research on Organizational Size and Environments," *Journal of Management*, Summer 1993, pp. 163–192.

34 See C. Perrow, "A Framework for the Comparative Analysis of Organizations," *American Sociological Review*, April 1967, pp. 194–208; J. Hage and M. Aiken, "Routine Technology, Social Structure, and Organizational Goals," *Administrative Science Quarterly*, September 1969, pp. 366–377; C. C. Miller, W. H. Glick, Y. Wang, and G. P. Huber, "Understanding Technology-Structure Relationships: Theory Development and Meta-analytic Theory Testing," *Academy of Management Journal*, June 1991, pp. 370–399; and W. D. Sine, H. Mitsuhashi, and D. A. Kirsch, "Revisiting Burns and Stalker: Formal Structure and New Venture Performance in Emerging Economic Sectors," *Academy of Management Journal* 49, no. 1 (2006), pp. 121–132.

35 See F. E. Emery and E. Trist, "The Causal Texture of Organizational Environments," *Human Relations*, February 1965, pp. 21–32; P. Lawrence and J. W. Lorsch, *Organization and Environment: Managing Differentiation and Integration* (Boston: Harvard Business School, Division of Research, 1967); M. Yasai-Ardekani, "Structural Adaptations to Environments," *Academy of Management Review*, January 1986, pp. 9–21; A. C. Bluedorn, "Pilgrim's Progress: Trends and Convergence in Research on Organizational Size and Environments," *Journal of Management*, Summer 1993, pp. 163–192; and M. Arndt and B. Bigelow, "Presenting Structural Innovation in an Institutional Environment: Hospitals' Use of Impression Management," *Administrative Science Quarterly*, September 2000, pp. 494–522.

36 See F. E. Emery and E. Trist, "The Causal Texture of Organizational Environments," *Human Relations*, February 1965, pp. 21–32; P. Lawrence and J. W. Lorsch, *Organization and Environment: Managing Differentiation and Integration* (Boston: Harvard Business School, Division of Research, 1967); M. Yasai-Ardekani, "Structural Adaptations to Environments," *Academy of Management Review*, January 1986, pp. 9–21; and A. C. Bluedorn, "Pilgrim's Progress: Trends and Convergence in Research on Organizational Size and Environments," *Journal of Management*, Summer 1993, pp. 163–192.

37 G. G. Dess and D. W. Beard, "Dimensions of Organizational Task Environments," *Administrative Science Quarterly*, March 1984, pp. 52–73; E. A. Gerloff, N. K. Muir, and W. D. Bodensteiner, "Three Components of Perceived Environmental Uncertainty: An Exploratory Analysis of the Effects of Aggregation," *Journal of Management*, December 1991, pp. 749–768; and O. Shenkar, N. Aranya, and T. Almor, "Construct Dimensions in the Contingency Model: An Analysis Comparing Metric and Non-Metric Multivariate Instruments," *Human Relations*, May 1995, pp. 559–580.

38 C. S. Spell and T. J. Arnold, "A Multi-Level Analysis of Organizational Justice and Climate, Structure, and Employee Mental Health," *Journal of Management* 33, no. 5 (2007), pp. 724–751; and M. L. Ambrose and M. Schminke, "Organization Structure as a Moderator of the Relationship Between Procedural Justice, Interactional Justice, Perceived Organizational Support, and Supervisory Trust," *Journal of Applied Psychology* 88, no. 2 (2003), pp. 295–305.

39 See, for instance, L. W. Porter and E. E. Lawler III, "Properties of Organization Structure in Relation to Job Attitudes and Job Behavior," *Psychological Bulletin*, July 1965, pp. 23–51; L. R. James and A. P. Jones, "Organization Structure: A Review of Structural Dimensions and Their Conceptual Relationships with Individual Attitudes and Behavior," *Organizational Behavior and Human Performance*, June 1976, pp. 74–113; C. S. Spell and T. J. Arnold, "A Multi-Level Analysis of Organizational Justice Climate, Structure, and Employee Mental Health," *Journal of Management* 33, no. 5 (2007), pp. 724–751; and J. D. Shaw and N. Gupta, "Job Complexity, Performance, and Well-Being: When

Does Supplies-Values Fit Matter?" *Personnel Psychology* 57, no. 4 (2004), pp. 847–879.

40 See, for instance, B. Schneider, H. W. Goldstein, and D. B. Smith, "The ASA Framework: An Update," *Personnel Psychology* 48, no. 4 (1995), pp. 747–773; and R. E. Ployhart, J. A. Weekley, and K. Baughman, "The Structure and Function of Human Capital Emergence: A Multilevel Examination of the Attraction-Selection-Attrition Model," *Academy of Management Journal* 49, no. 4 (2006), pp. 661–677.

41 P. Dvorak, "Making U.S. Management Ideas Work Elsewhere," *Wall Street Journal*, May 22, 2006, p. B3.

42 See, for example, P. R. Harris and R. T. Moran, *Managing Cultural Differences*, 5th ed. (Houston, TX: Gulf Publishing, 1999).

OB on the Edge: Stress at Work

1 Based on J. Newman and D. Grigg, "Road to Health Pays Off for B.C. Trucking Firm," *Edmondon Journal*, July 2, 2011, p. C5.

2 Paragraph based on D. Hansen, "Worker Who Felt 'Thrown Away' Wins," *Vancouver Sun*, August 16, 2006.

3 Statistics Canada, "Perceived Life Stress, Quite a Lot, by Sex, by Province and Territory, 2010," http://www40.statcan.ca/l01/cst01/health107b-eng.htm

4 K. MacQueen, "Workplace Stress Costs Us Dearly, and Yet Nobody Knows What It Is or How to Deal with It," *Maclean's*, October 15, 2007.

5 K. MacQueen, "Workplace Stress Costs Us Dearly, and Yet Nobody Knows What It Is or How to Deal with It," *Maclean's*, October 15, 2007.

6 L. Duxbury and C. Higgins, "2001 National Work-Life Conflict Study," as reported in J. Campbell, "'Organizational Anorexia' Puts Stress on Employees," *Ottawa Citizen*, July 4, 2002.

7 K. Harding, "Balance Tops List of Job Desires," *Globe and Mail*, May 7, 2003, pp. C1, C6.

8 V. Galt, "Productivity Buckling under the Strain of Stress, CEOs Say," *Globe and Mail*, June 9, 2005, p. B1.

9 "Canadian Workers among Most Stressed," *Worklife Report* 14, no. 2 (2002), pp. 8–9.

10 N. Ayed, "Absenteeism Up Since 1993," *Canadian Press Newswire*, March 25, 1998.

11 N. Ayed, "Absenteeism Up Since 1993," *Canadian Press Newswire*, March 25, 1998.

12 Adapted from R. S. Schuler, "Definition and Conceptualization of Stress in Organizations," *Organizational Behavior and Human Performance*, April 1980, p. 189. For an updated review of definitions, see C. L. Cooper, P. J. Dewe, and M. P. O'Driscoll, *Organizational Stress: A Review and Critique of Theory, Research, and Applications* (Thousand Oaks, CA: Sage, 2002).

13 See, for instance, M. A. Cavanaugh, W. R. Boswell, M. V. Roehling, and J. W. Boudreau, "An Empirical Examination of Self-Reported Work Stress among U.S. Managers," *Journal of Applied Psychology*, February 2000, pp. 65–74.

14 N. P. Podsakoff, J. A. LePine, and M. A. LePine, "Differential Challenge-Hindrance Stressor Relationships with Job Attitudes, Turnover Intentions, Turnover, and Withdrawal Behavior: A Meta-analysis," *Journal of Applied Psychology* 92, no. 2 (2007), pp. 438–454; and J. A. LePine, M. A. LePine, and C. L. Jackson, "Challenge and Hindrance Stress: Relationships with Exhaustion, Motivation to Learn, and Learning Performance," *Journal of Applied Psychology*, October 2004, pp. 883–891.

15 Based on *Health* magazine as it appeared in Centers for Disease Control and Prevention, US Department of Health and Human Services, "*Helicobacter pylori* and Peptic Ulcer Disease—Myths," http://www.cdc.gov/ulcer/myth.htm

16 S. Gilboa, A. Shirom, Y. Fried, and C. Cooper, "A Meta-analysis of Work Demand Stressors and Job Performance: Examining Main and Moderating Effects," *Personnel Psychology* 61, no. 2 (2008), pp. 227–271.

17 J. C. Wallace, B. D. Edwards, T. Arnold, M. L. Frazier, and D. M. Finch, "Work Stressors, Role-Based Performance, and the Moderating Influence of Organizational Support," *Journal of Applied Psychology* 94, no. 1 (2009), pp. 254–262.

18 L. W. Hunter and S. M. B. Thatcher, "Feeling the Heat: Effects of Stress, Commitment, and Job Experience on Job Performance," *Academy of Management Journal* 50, no. 4 (2007), pp. 953–968.

19 J. de Jonge and C. Dormann, "Stressors, Resources, and Strain at Work: A Longitudinal Test of the Triple-Match Principle," *Journal of Applied Psychology* 91, no. 5 (2006), pp. 1359–1374; K. Daniels, N. Beesley, A. Cheyne, and V. Wimalasiri, "Coping Processes Linking the Demands-Control-Support Model, Affect and Risky Decisions at Work," *Human Relations* 61, no. 6 (2008), pp. 845–874; and M. van den Tooren and J. de Jonge, "Managing Job Stress in Nursing: What Kind of Resources Do We Need?" *Journal of Advanced Nursing* 63, no. 1 (2008), pp. 75–84.

20 This section is adapted from C. L. Cooper and R. Payne, *Stress at Work* (London: Wiley, 1978); S. Parasuraman and J. A. Alutto, "Sources and Outcomes of Stress in Organizational Settings: Toward the Development of a Structural Model," *Academy of Management Journal* 27, no. 2 (June 1984), pp. 330–350; and P. M. Hart and C. L. Cooper, "Occupational Stress: Toward a More Integrated Framework," in *Handbook of Industrial, Work and Organizational Psychology*, vol. 2, ed. N. Anderson, D. S. Ones, H. K. Sinangil, and C. Viswesvaran (London: Sage, 2001), pp. 93–114.

21 E. A. Rafferty and M. A. Griffin, "Perceptions of Organizational Change: A Stress and Coping Perspective," *Journal of Applied Psychology* 71, no. 5 (2007), pp. 1154–1162.

22 See, for example, M. L. Fox, D. J. Dwyer, and D. C. Ganster, "Effects of Stressful Job Demands and Control of Physiological and Attitudinal Outcomes in a Hospital Setting," *Academy of Management Journal*, April 1993, pp. 289–318.

23 G. W. Evans and D. Johnson, "Stress and Open-Office Noise," *Journal of Applied Psychology*, October 2000, pp. 779–783.

24 T. M. Glomb, J. D. Kammeyer-Mueller, and M. Rotundo, "Emotional Labor Demands and Compensating Wage Differentials," *Journal of Applied Psychology*, August 2004, pp. 700–714; and A. A. Grandey, "When 'The Show Must Go On': Surface Acting and Deep Acting as Determinants of Emotional Exhaustion and Peer-Rated Service Delivery," *Academy of Management Journal*, February 2003, pp. 86–96.

25 S. Lim, L. M. Cortina, and V. J. Magley, "Personal and Workgroup Incivility: Impact on Work and Health Outcomes," *Journal of Applied Psychology* 93, no. 1 (2008), pp. 95–107; N. T. Buchanan and L. F. Fitzgerald, "Effects of Racial and Sexual Harassment on Work and the Psychological Well-Being of African American Women," *Journal of Occupational Health Psychology* 13, no. 2 (2008), pp. 137–151; C. R. Willness, P. Steel, and K. Lee, "A Meta-analysis of the Antecedents and Consequences of Workplace Sexual Harassment," *Personnel Psychology* 60, no. 1 (2007), pp. 127–162; and B. Moreno-Jiménez, A. Rodríguez-Muñoz, J. C. Pastor, A. I. Sanz-Vergel, and E. Garrosa, "The Moderating Effects of Psychological Detachment and Thoughts of Revenge in Workplace Bullying," *Personality and Individual Differences* 46, no. 3 (2009), pp. 359–364.

26 V. S. Major, K. J. Klein, and M. G. Ehrhart, "Work Time, Work Interference with Family, and Psychological Distress," *Journal of Applied Psychology*, June 2002, pp. 427–436; see also P. E. Spector, C. L. Cooper, S. Poelmans, T. D. Allen, M. O'Driscoll,

J. I. Sanchez, O. L. Siu, P. Dewe, P. Hart, L. Lu, L. F. R. De Moraes, G. M. Ostrognay, K. Sparks, P. Wong, and S. Yu, "A Cross-National Comparative Study of Work-Family Stressors, Working Hours, and Well-Being: China and Latin America versus the Anglo World," *Personnel Psychology*, Spring 2004, pp. 119–142.

27 D. L. Nelson and C. Sutton, "Chronic Work Stress and Coping: A Longitudinal Study and Suggested New Directions," *Academy of Management Journal*, December 1990, pp. 859–869.

28 H. Selye, *The Stress of Life* (New York: McGraw-Hill, 1976).

29 FactBox based on A. Picard, "The Working Wounded," *Globe and Mail*, June 22, 2008; and Statistics Canada, "Study: Work Absences in 2010," *The Daily*, May 25, 2011, http://www.statcan.gc.ca/daily-quotidien/110525/dq110525e-eng.htm; Statistics Canada, "Perceived Life Stress, 2009," http://www.statcan. gc.ca/pub/82-229-x/2009001/status/pls-eng.htm; Canadian Newswire, "Vacation Deprivation Continues but Canadians Still Value Vacations in Today's Economy, Expedia.ca Survey Finds," May 13, 2009, http://www.newswire.ca/en/releases/archive/May2009/13/c2818.html

30 R. S. Schuler, "Definition and Conceptualization of Stress in Organizations," *Organizational Behavior and Human Performance*, April 1980, p. 191; and R. L. Kahn and P. Byosiere, "Stress in Organizations," *Organizational Behavior and Human Performance*, April 1980, pp. 604–610.

31 See T. A. Beehr and J. E. Newman, "Job Stress, Employee Health, and Organizational Effectiveness: A Facet Analysis, Model, and Literature Review," *Personnel Psychology*, Winter 1978, pp. 665–699; and B. D. Steffy and J. W. Jones, "Workplace Stress and Indicators of Coronary-Disease Risk," *Academy of Management Journal*, September 1988, pp. 686–698.

32 J. Schaubroeck, J. R. Jones, and J. L. Xie, "Individual Differences in Utilizing Control to Cope with Job Demands: Effects on Susceptibility to Infectious Disease," *Journal of Applied Psychology*, April 2001, pp. 265–278.

33 KPMG Canada, compensation letter, July 1998.

34 B. D. Steffy and J. W. Jones, "Workplace Stress and Indicators of Coronary-Disease Risk," *Academy of Management Journal* 31 (1988), p. 687.

35 C. L. Cooper and J. Marshall, "Occupational Sources of Stress: A Review of the Literature Relating to Coronary Heart Disease and Mental Ill Health," *Journal of Occupational Psychology* 49, no. 1 (1976), pp. 11–28.

36 J. R. Hackman and G. R. Oldham, "Development of the Job Diagnostic Survey," *Journal of Applied Psychology*, April 1975, pp. 159–170.

37 J. L. Xie and G. Johns, "Job Scope and Stress: Can Job Scope Be Too High?" *Academy of Management Journal*, October 1995, pp. 1288–1309.

38 S. J. Motowidlo, J. S. Packard, and M. R. Manning, "Occupational Stress: Its Causes and Consequences for Job Performance," *Journal of Applied Psychology*, November 1987, pp. 619–620.

39 See, for instance, R. C. Cummings, "Job Stress and the Buffering Effect of Supervisory Support," *Group & Organization Studies*, March 1990, pp. 92–104; M. R. Manning, C. N. Jackson, and M. R. Fusilier, "Occupational Stress, Social Support, and the Cost of Health Care," *Academy of Management Journal*, June 1996, pp. 738–750; and P. D. Bliese and T. W. Britt, "Social Support, Group Consensus and Stressor-Strain Relationships: Social Context Matters," *Journal of Organizational Behavior*, June 2001, pp. 425–436.

40 R. Williams, *The Trusting Heart: Great News About Type A Behavior* (New York: Times Books, 1989).

41 D. C. Ganster, W. E. Sime, and B. T. Mayes, "Type A Behavior in the Work Setting: A Review and Some New Data," in *In Search of Coronary-Prone Behavior: Beyond Type A*, ed. A. W. Siegman and T. M. Dembroski (Hillsdale, NJ: Erlbaum, 1989), pp. 117–118; and B. K. Houston, "Cardiovascular and Neuroendocrine Reactivity, Global Type A, and Components of Type A," in *Type A Behavior Pattern: Research, Theory, and Intervention*, ed. B. K. Houston and C. R. Snyder (New York: Wiley, 1988), pp. 212–253.

42 T. H. Macan, "Time Management: Test of a Process Model," *Journal of Applied Psychology*, June 1994, pp. 381–391.

43 See, for example, G. Lawrence-Ell, *The Invisible Clock: A Practical Revolution in Finding Time for Everyone and Everything* (Seaside Park, NJ: Kingsland Hall, 2002).

44 S. A. Devi, "Aging Brain: Prevention of Oxidative Stress by Vitamin E and Exercise," *ScientificWorldJournal* 9 (2009), pp. 366–372. See also J. Kiely and G. Hodgson, "Stress in the Prison Service: The Benefits of Exercise Programs," *Human Relations*, June 1990, pp. 551–572.

45 E. J. Forbes and R. J. Pekala, "Psychophysiological Effects of Several Stress Management Techniques," *Psychological Reports*, February 1993, pp. 19–27; and G. Smith, "Meditation, the New Balm for Corporate Stress," *BusinessWeek*, May 10, 1993, pp. 86–87.

46 J. Lee, "How to Fight That Debilitating Stress in Your Workplace," *Vancouver Sun*, April 5, 1999, p. C3. Reprinted with permission.

47 H. Staseson, "Can Perk Help Massage Bottom Line? On-Site Therapeutic Sessions Are Used by an Increasingly Diverse Group of Employers Hoping to Improve Staff Performance," *Globe and Mail*, July 3, 2002, p. C1.

48 Health Canada, "Wellness Programs Offer Healthy Return, Study Finds," *Report Bulletin*, #224, October 2001, p. 1.

49 H. Staseson, "Can Perk Help Massage Bottom Line? On-Site Therapeutic Sessions Are Used by an Increasingly Diverse Group of Employers Hoping to Improve Staff Performance," *Globe and Mail*, July 3, 2002, p. C1.

50 "Cdn Employers Not Measuring Wellness Outcomes: Survey," *Benefits Canada*, May 4, 2011, http://www.benefitscanada.com/news/cnd-employers-not-measuring-wellness-outcomes-survey-16510

51 P. M. Wright, "Operationalization of Goal Difficulty as a Moderator of the Goal Difficulty-Performance Relationship," *Journal of Applied Psychology*, June 1990, pp. 227–234; E. A. Locke and G. P. Latham, "Building a Practically Useful Theory of Goal Setting and Task Motivation: A 35-Year Odyssey," *American Psychologist* 57, no. 9 (2002), pp. 705–717; K. L. Langeland, C. M. Johnson, and T. C. Mawhinney, "Improving Staff Performance in a Community Mental Health Setting: Job Analysis, Training, Goal Setting, Feedback, and Years of Data," *Journal of Organizational Behavior Management*, 1998, pp. 21–43.

52 E. R. Greenglass and L. Fiksenbaum, "Proactive Coping, Positive Affect, and Well-Being: Testing for Mediation Using Path Analysis," *European Psychologist* 14, no. 1 (2009), pp. 29–39; and P. Miquelon and R. J. Vallerand, "Goal Motives, Well-Being, and Physical Health: Happiness and Self-Realization as Psychological Resources under Challenge," *Motivation and Emotion* 30, no. 4 (2006), pp. 259–272.

53 Based on S. Martin, "Money Is the Stressor for Americans," *Monitor on Psychology*, December 2008, pp. 28–29; *Helicobacter pylori and Peptic Ulcer Disease*, Centers for Disease Control and Prevention, U.S. Department of Health and Human Services, http://www.cdc.gov/ulcer; and M. Maynard, "Maybe the Toughest Job Aloft," *New York Times*, August 15, 2006, pp. C1, C6.

54 S. E. Jackson, "Participation in Decision Making as a Strategy for Reducing Job-Related Strain," *Journal of Applied Psychology*, February 1983, pp. 3–19.

55 S. Greengard, "It's About Time," *IndustryWeek*, February 7, 2000, pp. 47–50; and S. Nayyar, "Gimme a Break," *American Demographics*, June 2002, p. 6.

56 See, for instance, B. Leonard, "Health Care Costs Increase Interest in Wellness Programs," *HR Magazine*, September 2001, pp. 35–36; and "Healthy, Happy and Productive," *Training*, February 2003, p. 16.

57 K. M. Richardson and H. R. Rothstein, "Effects of Occupational Stress Management Intervention Programs: A Meta-analysis," *Journal of Occupational Health Psychology* 13, no. 1 (2008), pp. 69–93.

Chapter 7

1 R. I. Henderson (ed.), *Compensation Management in a Knowledge-Based World* (Upper Saddle River, NJ: Prentice-Hall, 2003), pp. 135–138.; See also P.W. Wright and K. Wesley, "How to Choose the Kind of Job Analysis You Really Need," *Personnel*, 62 (May 1985), pp. 51–55; C.J. Cranny and M.E. Doherty, "Importance Ratings in Job Analysis: Note on the Misinterpretation of Factor Analyses," *Journal of Applied Psychology* (May 1988), pp. 320–322.

2 J. Heerwagen, K. Kelly, and K. Kampschroer, "The Changing Nature of Organizations, Work, and Workplace," *Whole Building Design Group (WBDG), National Institute of Building Sciences* (February 2006).

3 C. Babbage, *On the Economy of Machinery and Manufacturers* (London: Charles Knight, 1832), pp. 169–176; reprinted in Joseph Litterer, *Organizations* (New York: John Wiley and Sons, 1969), pp. 73–75.

4 F. Herzberg, "One More Time, How Do You Motivate Employees?" *Harvard Business Review*, 46 (January–February 1968), pp. 53–62.

5 Next two sections based on Jeffrey Shippmann et al., "The Practice of Competency Modeling," *Personnel Psychology*, 53, no. 3 (2000), p. 703; P. Singh, "Job Analysis for a Changing Workplace," *Human Resource Management Review*, 18 (2008), pp. 87–99.

6 Adapted from Richard Mirabile, "Everything You Wanted to Know About Competency Modeling," *Training and Development*, 51, no. 8 (August 1997), pp. 73–78.

7 Dennis Kravetz, "Building a Job Competency Database: What the Leaders Do," Kravetz Associates (Bartlett, Illinois, 1997).

8 G.M. Parker, *Cross-Functional Teams: Working with Allies, Enemies and Other Strangers* (San Francisco: Jossey-Bass, 2003), p. 68.

9 "Collaboration for Virtual Teams," *HR Professional* (December 2002/January 2003), p. 44.

10 Note that the PAQ (and other quantitative techniques) can also be used for job evaluation.

11 E. Cornelius III, F. Schmidt, and T. Carron, "Job Classification Approaches and the Implementation of Validity Generalization Results," *Personnel Psychology*, 37 (Summer 1984), pp. 247–260; E. Cornelius III, A. DeNisi, and A. Blencoe, "Expert and Naïve Raters Using the PAQ: Does It Matter?" *Personnel Psychology*, 37 (Autumn 1984), pp. 453–464; L. Friedman and R. Harvey, "Can Raters with Reduced Job Description Information Provide Accurate Position Analysis Questionnaire (PAQ) Ratings?" *Personnel Psychology*, 34 (Winter 1986), pp. 779–789; R. J. Harvey et al., "Dimensionality of the Job Element Inventory: A Simplified Worker-Oriented Job Analysis Questionnaire," *Journal of Applied Psychology* (November 1988), pp. 639–646; S. Butler and R. Harvey, "A Comparison of Holistic versus Decomposed Rating of Position Analysis Questionnaire Work Dimensions," *Personnel Psychology* (Winter 1988), pp. 761–772.

12 This discussion is based on H. Olson et al., "The Use of Functional Job Analysis in Establishing Performance Standards for Heavy Equipment Operators," *Personnel Psychology*, 34 (Summer 1981), pp. 351–364.

13 Human Resources Development Canada, *National Occupation Classification Career Handbook*, (2006).

14 R. J. Plachy, "Writing Job Descriptions That Get Results," *Personnel* (October 1987), pp. 56–58. See also M. Mariani, "Replace with a Database," *Occupational Outlook Quarterly*, 43 (Spring 1999), pp. 2–9.

15 J. Evered, "How to Write a Good Job Description," *Supervisory Management* (April 1981), p. 16.

16 Ibid, p. 18.

17 P.H. Raymark, M.J. Schmidt, and R.M. Guion, "Identifying Potentially Useful Personality Constructs for Employee Selection," *Personnel Psychology* 50 (1997), pp. 723–726.

Chapter 8

1 G. Bouchard, "Strong Employer Brand Can Tap Scarce Resource: Talent," *Canadian HR Reporter* (November 19, 2007), p. 10.

2 "Effective Recruiting Tied to Stronger Financial Performance," *WorldatWork Canadian News* (Fourth Quarter, 2005), pp. 18–19.

3 K. Peters, "Public Image Ltd," *HR Professional* (December 2007/January 2008), pp. 24–30; S. Klie, "Getting Employees to Come to You," *Canadian HR Reporter* (November 19, 2007), pp. 9–10; S. Klie, "Tuning into TV's Recruitment Reach," *Canadian HR Reporter* (September 25, 2006).

4 G. Bouchard, "Strong Employer Brand Can Tap Scarce Resource: Talent," *Canadian HR Reporter* (November 19, 2007), p. 10.

5 K. Peters, "Public Image Ltd," *HR Professional* (December 2007/January 2008), pp. 24–30; G. Bouchard, "Strong Employer Brand Can Tap Scarce Resource: Talent," *Canadian HR Reporter* (November 19, 2007), p. 10; M. Morra, "Best in Show," *Workplace News* (September/October 2006), pp. 17–21; M. Shuster, "Employment Branding: The Law of Attraction!" *Workplace* (January/February 2008), pp. 14–15.

6 M. Morra, "Best in Show," *Workplace News* (September/October 2006), pp. 17–21.

7 G. Bouchard, "Strong Employer Brand Can Tap Scarce Resource: Talent," *Canadian HR Reporter* (November 19, 2007), p. 10.

8 S. Klie, "Getting Employees to Come to You," *Canadian HR Reporter* (November 19, 2007), pp. 9–10; M. Shuster, "Employment Branding: The Law of Attraction!" *Workplace* (January/February 2008), pp. 14–15.

9 K. Peters, "Public Image Ltd," *HR Professional* (December 2007/January 2008), pp. 24–30; S. Dobson, "The Little School Bus Company That Could," *Canadian HR Reporter* (April 23, 2007).

10 M. Shuster, "Employment Branding: The Law of Attraction!" *Workplace* (January/February 2008), pp. 14–15.

11 A. Watanabe, "From Brown to Green, What Colour Is Your Employment Brand?" *HR Professional* (February/March 2008), pp. 47–49.

12 M. Morra, "Best in Show," *Workplace News* (September/October 2006), pp. 17–21.

13 R. Milgram, "Getting the Most Out of Online Job Ads," *Canadian HR Reporter* (January 28, 2008).

14 K. Peters, "Public Image Ltd," *HR Professional* (December 2007/January 2008), pp. 24–30; S. Klie, "Getting Employees to Come to You," *Canadian HR Reporter* (November 19, 2007), pp. 9–10.

15 S. Klie, "Getting Employees to Come to You," *Canadian HR Reporter* (November 19, 2007), pp. 9–10; M. Shuster, "Employment Branding: The Law of Attraction!" *Workplace* (January/February 2008), pp. 14–15.

16 "Recruitment Tops HR Areas Expecting 'Enormous Change,'" *Canadian HR Reporter* (December 6, 2004), p. G3; *Hewitt Associates Timely Topic Survey* (February 2004).

17 H.N. Chait, S.M. Carraher, and M.R. Buckley, "Measuring Service Orientation with Biodata," *Journal of Management Issues* (Spring 2000), pp. 109–120; V.M. Catano, S.F. Cronshaw, R.D. Hackett, L.L. Methot, and W.H. Weisner, *Recruitment and Selection in Canada*, 2nd ed. (Scarborough, ON: Nelson Thomson Learning, 2001), p. 307; J.E. Harvey-Cook and R.J. Taffler, "Biodata in Professional Entry-Level Selection: Statistical Scoring of Common-Format Applications," *Journal of Occupational and Organizational Psychology* (March 1, 2000), pp. 103–118; Y.Y. Chung, "The Validity of Biographical Inventories for the Selection of Salespeople," *International Journal of Management* (September 2001).

18 L. Petrecca, "With 3000 Job Applications a Day, Google Can Be Picky," *USA Today* (May 18, 2010), (accessed September 9, 2012). http://www.usatoday.com/money/workplace/2010-05-19-jobs19_VA_N.htm

19 D. Dahl and P. Pinto, "Job Posting, an Industry Survey," *Personnel Journal* (January 1977), pp. 40–41.

20 J. Daum, "Internal Promotion—Psychological Asset or Debit? A Study of the Effects of Leader Origin," *Organizational Behavior and Human Performance*, 13 (1975), pp. 404–413.

21 See, for example, A. Harris, "Hiring Middle Management: External Recruitment or Internal Promotion?" *Canadian HR Reporter* (April 10, 2000), pp. 8–10.

22 M. Sharma, "Welcome Back!" *HR Professional* (February/March 2006), pp. 38–40; E. Simon, "You're Leaving the Company? Well, Don't Be a Stranger," *Globe and Mail* (December 22, 2006), p. B16.

23 U. Vu, "Encana Builds Talent Pipeline into High School Classrooms," *Canadian HR Reporter* (April 11, 2005), p. 3.

24 Halifax Career Fair, www.halifaxcareerfairs.com (accessed May 31, 2009).

25 Career Edge, www.careeredge.ca (accessed May 31, 2009).

26 N. Laurie and M. Laurie, "No Holds Barred in Fight for Students to Fill Internship Programs," *Canadian HR Reporter* (January 17, 2000), pp. 15–16.

27 Human Resources Professionals Association of Ontario, www.hrpao.org (accessed June 25, 2003).

28 D. Hurl, "Letting the Armed Forces Train Your Managers," *Canadian HR Reporter* (December 3, 2001), pp. 8–9.

29 L. MacGillivray, "Cashing in on the Canadian Forces," *Workplace Today* (October 2001), pp. 40–41.

30 L. Blake, "Ready-Trained, Untapped Source of Skilled Talent—Courtesy Canadian Forces," *Workplace*, www.workplace-mag.com (accessed December 2, 2008).

31 U. Vu, "Security Failures Expose Résumés," *Canadian HR Reporter* (May 24, 2003); P. Lima, "Talent Shortage? That Was Yesterday. Online Recruiters Can Deliver More Candidates for Your Job Openings and Help You Find Keepers," *Profit: The Magazine for Canadian Entrepreneurs* (February/March 2002), pp. 65–66; "Online Job Boards," *Canadian HR Reporter* (February 11, 2002), pp. G11–G15.

32 U. Vu, "Security Failures Expose Résumés," *Canadian HR Reporter* (May 24, 2003).

33 S. Bury, "Face-Based Recruiting," *Workplace* (September/October 2008), pp. 19–21.

34 G. Stanton, "Recruiting Portals Take Centre Stage in Play for Talent," *Canadian HR Reporter* (September 25, 2000), pp. G1–G2.

35 A. da Luz, "Video Enhances Online Job Ads," *Canadian HR Reporter* (February 11, 2008).

36 D. Brown, "Canadian Government Job Boards Lag on Best Practices," *Canadian HR Reporter* (January 13, 2003), p. 2.

37 T. Martell, "Résumé Volumes Push Firms to Web," *ComputerWorld Canada* (April 7, 2000), p. 45.

38 A. Altass, "E-Cruiting: A Gen X Trend or Wave of the Future?" *HR Professional* (June–July 2000), p. 33.

39 "Corporate Spending Millions on Ineffective Web Recruiting Strategies," *Canadian HR Reporter* (September 25, 2000), p. G5.

40 A. Snell, "Best Practices for Web Site Recruiting," *Canadian HR Reporter* (February 26, 2001), pp. G7, G10.

41 D. Brown, "Who's Looking Online? Most Firms Don't Know," *Canadian HR Reporter* (August 13, 2001), pp. 2, 12; "Corporate Spending Millions on Ineffective Web Recruiting Strategies," *Canadian HR Reporter* (September 25, 2000), p. G5; A. Snell, "Best Practices for Web Site Recruiting," *Canadian HR Reporter* (February 26, 2001), pp. G7, G10.

42 Service Canada, Job Bank, http://jb-ge.hrdc-drhc.gc.ca (accessed May 31, 2009).

43 J.A. Parr, "7 Reasons Why Executive Searches Fail," *Canadian HR Reporter* (March 12, 2001), pp. 20, 23.

44 Association of Canadian Search, Employment and Staffing Services (ACSESS), www.acsess.org (accessed August 8, 2006).

45 Statistics Canada, *The Daily* (April 8, 2005); Association of Canadian Search, Employment and Staffing Services (ACSESS), "Media Kit: Media Fact Sheet," www.acsess.org/NEWS/factsheet.asp (accessed May 31, 2009).

46 A. Doran, "Technology Brings HR to Those Who Need It," *Canadian HR Reporter* (October 6, 1997), p. 8.

47 S. Bury, "Face-Based Recruiting," *Workplace* (September/October 2008), pp. 19–21.

48 D. Harder, "Recruiting in Age of Social Networking," *Canadian HR Reporter* (April 21, 2008).

49 L. Barrington and J. Shelp, "Looking for Employees in All the Right Places," *The Conference Board Executive Action Series* (December 2005).

50 A. Pell, *Recruiting and Selecting Personnel* (New York, NY: Regents, 1969), pp. 16–34.

51 T. Lende, "Workplaces Looking to Hire Part-Timers," *Canadian HR Reporter* (April 22, 2002), pp. 9, 11.

52 K. LeMessurier, "Temp Staffing Leaves a Permanent Mark," *Canadian HR Reporter* (February 10, 2003), pp. 3, 8.

53 A. Ryckman, "The 5 Keys to Getting Top Value from Contractors," *Canadian HR Reporter* (December 2, 2002), p. 25; S. Purba, "Contracting Works for Job Hunters," *Globe and Mail* (April 24, 2002).

54 "Flexible Staffing in the Aerospace Industry," *Airfinance Journal I Aircraft Economic Yearbook* (2001), pp. 14–17.

55 M. Potter, "A Golden Opportunity for Older Workers to Energize Firms," *Canadian HR Reporter* (April 25, 2005), p. 13.

56 L. Cassiani, "Looming Retirement Surge Takes on New Urgency," *Canadian HR Reporter* (May 21, 2001), pp. 1, 10.

57 O. Parker, *Too Few People, Too Little Time: The Employer Challenge of an Aging Workforce* (Ottawa, ON: The Conference Board of Canada Executive *Action*, July 2006).

58 K. Thorpe, *Harnessing the Power: Recruiting, Engaging, and Retaining Mature Workers*. (Ottawa, ON: Conference Board of Canada, 2008).

59 S.B. Hood, "Generational Diversity in the Workplace," *HR Professional* (June/July 2000), p. 20.

60 G. Kovary and A. Buahene, "Recruiting the Four Generations," *Canadian HR Reporter* (May 23, 2005), p. R6.

61 S. Klie, "Firm Asks Students: What Do You Want?" *Canadian HR Reporter* (May 5, 2008).

62 Inclusion Network, www.inclusionnetwork.ca (accessed May 31, 2009); Aboriginal Human Resource Council, http://aboriginalhr.ca (accessed May 31, 2009).

63 Society for Canadian Women in Science and Technology, www.harbour.sfu.ca/scwist/index_files/Page1897.htm (accessed May 31, 2009); C. Emerson, H. Matsui, and L. Michael, "Progress Slow for Women in Trades, Tech, Science," *Canadian HR Reporter* (February 14, 2005), p. 11.

64 WORKInk, www.workink.com (accessed May 31, 2009).

Chapter 9

1 D. Brown, "Waterloo Forced to Fire Top Bureaucrat Weeks After Hiring," *Canadian HR Reporter* (October 11, 2004), p. 3.

2 British Columbia Criminal Records Review Act, www.pssg.gov.bc.ca/criminal-records-review/index.htm (accessed May 31, 2009).

3 C. Kapel, "Giant Steps," *Human Resources Professional* (April 1993), pp. 13–16.

4 P. Lowry, "The Structured Interview: An Alternative to the Assessment Center?" *Public Personnel Management*, 23, no. 2 (Summer 1994), pp. 201–215.

5 Steps two and three are based on the Kepner-Tregoe Decision-Making Model.

6 S.A. Way and J.W. Thacker, "Selection Practices: Where Are Canadian Organizations?" *HR Professional* (October/November 1999), p. 34.

7 L.J. Katunich, "How to Avoid the Pitfalls of Psych Tests," *Workplace News Online* (July 2005), p. 5; *Testing and Assessment—FAQ/Finding Information About Psychological Tests*, APA Online, www.apa.org/science/faq-findtests.html (accessed August 1, 2006).

8 M. McDaniel et al., "The Validity of Employment Interviews: A Comprehensive Review and Meta-analysis," *Journal of Applied Psychology*, 79, no. 4 (1994).

9 "Hiring: Psychology and Employee Potential," *HR Professional* (August/September 2008), p. 16.

10 Ibid.

11 S. Bakker, "Psychometric Selection Assessments," *HR Professional* (April/May 2009), p. 21.

12 Canadian Psychological Association, *Guidelines for Educational and Psychological Testing*, www.cpa.ca/documents/PsyTest.html (accessed May 31, 2009).

13 R.M. Yerkes, "Psychological Examining in the U.S. Army: Memoirs of the National Academy of Sciences," Washington DC: U.S. Government Printing Office, Vol. 15 (1921).

14 F.L. Schmidt and J. Hunter, "General Mental Ability in the World of Work: Occupational Attainment and Job Performance," *Journal of Personality and Social Psychology*, 86, no. 1 (2004), 162–173.

15 M. Zeidner, I. G. Matthews, and R.D. Roberts, "Emotional Intelligence in the Workplace: A Critical Review" *Applied Psychology: An International Review*, 53, no.3 (2004), pp. 371–399

16 "Emotional Intelligence Testing," *HR Focus* (October 2001), pp. 8–9.

17 Results of meta-analyses in one recent study indicated that isometric strength tests were valid predictors of both supervisory ratings of physical performance and performance on work simulations. See B.R. Blakley, M. Quinones, M.S. Crawford, and I.A. Jago, "The Validity of Isometric Strength Tests," *Personnel Psychology*, 47 (1994), pp. 247–274.

18 C. Colacci, "Testing Helps You Decrease Disability Costs," *Canadian HR Reporter* (June 14, 1999), p. G4.

19 K. Gillin, "Reduce Employee Exposure to Injury with Pre-Employment Screening Tests," *Canadian HR Reporter* (February 28, 2000), p. 10.

20 This approach calls for construct validation, which, as was pointed out, is extremely difficult to demonstrate.

21 Myers-Briggs Type Indicator (MBTI) Assessment, www.cpp.com/products/mbti/index.asp (accessed May 31, 2009).

22 See, for example, D. Cellar et al., "Comparison of Factor Structures and Criterion Related Validity Coefficients for Two Measures of Personality Based on the Five-Factor Model," *Journal of Applied Psychology*, 81, no. 6 (1996), pp. 694–704; J. Salgado, "The Five Factor Model of Personality and Job Performance in the European Community," *Journal of Applied Psychology*, 82, no. 1 (1997), pp. 30–43.

23 M.R. Barrick and M.K. Mount, "The Big Five Personality Dimensions and Job Performance: A Meta-Analysis," *Personnel Psychology*, 44 (Spring 1991), pp. 1–26.

24 C. Robie, K. Tuzinski, and P. Bly, "A Survey of Assessor Beliefs and Practices Related to Faking," *Journal of Managerial Psychology* (October 2006), pp. 669–681.

25 C. Robie, "Effects of Perceived Selection Ratio on Personality Test Faking," *Social Behavior and Personality*, 34, no. 10 (2006), 1233–1244.

26 E. Silver and C. Bennett, "Modification of the Minnesota Clerical Test to Predict Performance on Video Display Terminals," *Journal of Applied Psychology*, 72, no. 1 (February 1987), pp. 153–155.

27 L. Siegel and I. Lane, *Personnel and Organizational Psychology* (Homewood, IL: Irwin, 1982), pp. 182–183.

28 J. Weekley and C. Jones, "Video-Based Situational Testing," *Personnel Psychology*, 50 (1997), p. 25.

29 Ibid, pp. 26–30.

30 D. Chan and N. Schmitt, "Situational Judgment and Job Performance," *Human Performance*, 15, no. 3 (2002), pp. 233–254.

31 S. Klie, "Screening Gets More Secure," *Canadian HR Reporter* (June 19, 2006).

32 Canadian Human Rights Commission, *Canadian Human Rights Commission Policy on Alcohol and Drug Testing* (June 2002).

33 M. McDaniel et al., "The Validity of Employment Interviews: A Comprehensive Review and Meta-Analysis," *Journal of Applied Psychology*, 79, no. 4 (1994), p. 599.

34 J.G. Goodale, *The Fine Art of Interviewing* (Englewood Cliffs, NJ: Prentice Hall Inc., 1982), p. 22; see also R.L. Decker, "The Employment Interview," *Personnel Administrator*, 26 (November 1981), pp. 71–73.

35 M. Campion, E. Pursell, and B. Brown, "Structured Interviewing: Raising the Psychometric Properties of the Employment Interview," *Personnel Psychology*, 41 (1988), pp. 25–42.

36 M. McDaniel et al., "The Validity of Employment Interviews: A Comprehensive Review and Meta-Analysis," *Journal of Applied Psychology*, 79, no. 4 (1994).

37 D.S. Chapman and P.M. Rowe, "The Impact of Video Conferencing Technology, Interview Structure, and Interviewer Gender on Interviewer Evaluations in the Employment Interview: A Field Experiment," *Journal of Occupational and Organizational Psychology*, 74 (September 2001), pp. 279–298.

38 M. McDaniel et al., "The Validity of Employment Interviews: A Comprehensive Review and Meta-Analysis," *Journal of Applied Psychology*, 79, no. 4 (1994), p. 601.

39 Ibid.

40 "Lights, Camera...Can I Have a Job?" *Globe and Mail* (March 2, 2007), p. C1; A. Pell, *Recruiting and Selecting Personnel* (New York, NY: Regents, 1969), p. 119.

41 J.G. Goodale, *The Fine Art of Interviewing* (Englewood Cliffs, NJ: Prentice Hall Inc., 1982), p. 26.

42 See R.D. Arvey and J.E. Campion, "The Employment Interview: A Summary and Review of Recent Research," *Personnel Psychology*, 35 (1982), pp. 281–322; M. Heilmann and L. Saruwatari, "When Beauty Is Beastly: The Effects of Appearance and Sex on Evaluation of Job Applicants for Managerial and Nonmanagerial Jobs," *Organizational Behavior and Human Performance*, 23 (June 1979), pp. 360–722; C. Marlowe, S. Schneider, and C. Nelson, "Gender and Attractiveness Biases in Hiring Decisions: Are More Experienced Managers Less Biased?" *Journal of Applied Psychology*, 81, no. 1 (1996), pp. 11–21; V. Galt, "Beauty Found Not Beastly in the Job Interview," *Globe and Mail* (April 15, 2002).

43 A. Pell, "Nine Interviewing Pitfalls," *Managers* (January 1994), p. 29; T. Dougherty, D. Turban, and J. Callender, "Confirming First Impressions in the Employment Interview: A Field Study of Interviewer Behavior," *Journal of Applied Psychology*, 79, no. 5 (1994), p. 663.

44 See A. Pell, "Nine Interviewing Pitfalls," *Managers* (January 1994), p. 29; P. Sarathi, "Making Selection Interviews Effective," *Management and Labor Studies*, 18, no. 1 (1993), pp. 5–7; J. Shetcliffe, "Who, and How, to Employ," *Insurance Brokers' Monthly* (December 2002), pp. 14–16.

45 G.J. Sears and P.M. Rowe, "A Personality-Based Similar-to-Me Effect in the Employment Interview: Conscientious, Affect-versus-Competence Mediated Interpretations, and the Role of Job Relevance," *Canadian Journal of Behavioural Sciences*, 35 (January 2003), p. 13.

46 This section is based on E.D. Pursell, M.A. Campion, and S.R. Gaylord, "Structured Interviewing: Avoiding Selection Problems," *Personnel Journal*, 59 (1980), pp. 907–912; G.P. Latham, L.M. Saari, E.D. Pursell, and M.A. Campion, "The Situational Interview," *Journal of Applied Psychology*, 65 (1980), pp. 422–427; see also M. Campion, E. Pursell, and B. Brown, "Structured Interviewing: Raising the Psychometric Properties of the Employment Interview," *Personnel Psychology*, 41 (1988), pp. 25–42; J.A. Weekley and J.A. Gier, "Reliability and Validity of the Situational Interview for a Sales Position," *Journal of Applied Psychology*, 72 (1987), pp. 484–487.

47 A. Pell, *Recruiting and Selecting Personnel* (New York, NY: Regents, 1969), pp. 103–115.

48 W.H. Wiesner and R.J. Oppenheimer, "Note-Taking in the Selection Interview: Its Effect upon Predictive Validity and Information Recall," *Proceedings of the Annual Conference Meeting. Administrative Sciences Association of Canada* (Personnel and Human Resources Division, 1991), pp. 97–106.

49 V. Tsang, "No More Excuses," *Canadian HR Reporter* (May 23, 2005); L.T. Cullen, "Getting Wise to Lies," *TIME* (May 1, 2006), p. 27.

50 Ibid.

51 L. Fischer, "Gatekeeper," *Workplace News* (August 2005), pp. 10–11.

52 "Background Checks," *HR Professional* (June/July 2008), p. 16.

53 T. Humber, "Recruitment Isn't Getting Any Easier," *Canadian HR Reporter* (May 23, 2005).

54 C. Hall and A. Miedema, "But I Thought You Checked?" *Canadian HR Reporter* (May 21, 2007).

55 R. Zupek, "Is Your Future Boss Researching You Online?" CareerBuilder.ca, www.careerbuilder.ca/blog/2008/10/09/cb-is-your-future-boss-researching-you-online (accessed May 24, 2009).

56 J.R. Smith, "Damaging Reference Survives Alberta Privacy Challenge," *Canadian HR Reporter* (January 28, 2008).

57 A.C. Elmslie, "Writing a Reference Letter—Right or Wrong?" *Ultimate HR Manual*, 44 (January 2009), pp. 1–3.

58 A. Moffat, "The Danger of Digging too Deep," *Canadian HR Reporter* (August 11, 2008); see also P. Israel, "Providing References to Employees: Should You or Shouldn't You?" *Canadian HR Reporter* (March 24, 2003), pp. 5–6; T. Humber, "Name, Rank and Serial Number," *Canadian HR Reporter* (May 19, 2003), pp. G1, G7.

59 J.A. Breaugh, "Realistic Job Previews: A Critical Appraisal and Future Research Directions," *Academy of Management Review*, 8, no. 4 (1983), pp. 612–619.

60 P. Buhler, "Managing in the '90s: Hiring the Right Person for the Job," *Supervision* (July 1992), pp. 21–23; S. Jackson, "Realistic Job Previews Help Screen Applicants and Reduce Turnover," *Canadian HR Reporter* (August 9, 1999), p. 10.

61 S. Jackson, "Realistic Job Previews Help Screen Applicants and Reduce Turnover," *Canadian HR Reporter* (August 9, 1999), p. 10.

62 B. Kleinmutz, "Why We Still Use Our Heads Instead of Formulas: Toward an Integrative Approach," *Psychological Bulletin*, 107 (1990), pp. 296–310.

Chapter 10

1 M. Akdere and S. Schmidt, "Measuring the Effects of Employee Orientation Training on Employee Perception," *The Business Review* (Summer 2007), pp. 322–327.

2 B.W. Pascal, "The Orientation Wars," *Workplace Today* (October 2001), p. 4.

3 B. Pomfret, "Sound Employee Orientation Program Boosts Productivity and Safety," *Canadian HR Reporter* (January 25, 1999), pp. 17–19.

4 L. Shelat, "First Impressions Matter—A Lot," *Canadian HR Reporter* (May 3, 2004), pp. 11, 13.

5 For a recent discussion of socialization, see, for example, G. Chao et al., "Organizational Socialization: Its Content and Consequences," *Journal of Applied Psychology*, 79, no. 5 (1994), pp. 730–743.

6 S. Jackson, "After All That Work in Hiring, Don't Let New Employees Dangle," *Canadian HR Reporter* (May 19, 1997), p. 13.

7 A. Macaulay, "The Long and Winding Road," *Canadian HR Reporter* (November 16, 1998), pp. G1–G10.

8 R. Biswas, "Employee Orientation: Your Best Weapon in the Fight for Skilled Talent," *Human Resources Professional* (August/September 1998), pp. 41–42.

9 "Employee Onboarding Guides New Hires," *Workspan* (January 2009), p. 119.

10 D. Chhabra, "What Web-Based Onboarding Can Do for Your Company," *Workspan* (May 2008), pp. 111–114.

11 R. Harrison, "Onboarding: The First Step in Motivation and Retention," *Workspan* (September 2007), pp. 43–45.

12 D. Barnes, "Learning Is Key to Post-Merger Success," *Canadian HR Reporter* (July 12, 1999), pp. 16–17.

13 C. Gibson, "Online Orientation: Extending a Welcoming Hand to New Employees," *Canadian HR Reporter* (November 30, 1998), pp. 22–23.

14 "Onboarding: Virtual Orientation at IBM," *HR Professional* (August/September 2008), p. 12.

15 D. Brown, "Execs Need Help Learning the Ropes Too," *Canadian HR Reporter* (April 22, 2002), p. 2.

16 Ibid.

17 "The Critical Importance of Executive Integration," *Drake Business Review* (December 2002), pp. 6–8.

18 S. Mingail, "Employers Need a Lesson in Training," *Canadian HR Reporter* (February 11, 2002), pp. 22–23.

19 U. Vu, "Trainers Mature into Business Partners," *Canadian HR Reporter* (July 12, 2004), pp. 1–2.

20 S. Klie, "Training Isn't Always the Answer," *Canadian HR Reporter* (December 5, 2005), pp. 13–14.

21 V. Galt, "Training Falls Short: Study," *Globe and Mail* (July 9, 2001), p. M1.

22 D. Harder, "Sierra Systems Earns Top Marks for Training," *Canadian HR Reporter* (February 2, 2009).

23 *Knowledge Matters: Skills and Learning for Canadians* (Government of Canada, 2002), p. 3, www11.sdc.gc.ca/sl-ca/doc/summary. shtml (accessed June 7, 2006).

24 A. Tomlinson, "More Training Critical in Manufacturing," *Canadian HR Reporter* (November 4, 2002), p. 2.

25 D. Brown, "PM Calls for Business to Spend More on Training," *Canadian HR Reporter* (December 16, 2002), pp. 1, 11; D. Brown, "Budget Should Include More for Training: Critics," *Canadian HR Reporter* (March 10, 2003), pp. 1–2; D. Brown, "Legislated Training, Questionable Results," *Canadian HR Reporter* (May 6, 2002), pp. 1, 12.

26 N.L. Trainor, "Employee Development the Key to Talent Attraction and Retention," *Canadian HR Reporter* (November 1, 1999), p. 8.

27 Bank of Montreal, www.bmo.com (accessed May 31, 2009).

28 L. Johnston, "Employees Put High Price on Learning, Development," *Canadian HR Reporter* (November 3, 2008); S. Klie, "Higher Education Leads to Higher Productivity," *Canadian HR Reporter* (December 3, 2007).

29 D. LaMarche-Bisson, "There's More than One Way to Learn," *Canadian HR Reporter* (November 18, 2003), p. 7.

30 M. Belcourt, P.C. Wright, and A.M. Saks, *Managing Performance through Training and Development*, 2nd ed. (Toronto, ON: Nelson Thomson Learning, 2000); see also A.M. Saks and R.R. Haccoun, "Easing the Transfer of Training," *Human Resources Professional* (July–August 1996), pp. 8–11.

31 J.A. Colquitt, J.A. LePine, and R.A. Noe, "Toward an Integrative Theory of Training Motivation: A Meta-Analytic Path Analysis of 20 Years of Research," *Journal of Applied Psychology*, 85 (2000), pp. 678–707.

32 M. Georghiou, "Games, Simulations Open World of Learning," *Canadian HR Reporter* (May 5, 2008).

33 K.A. Smith-Jentsch et al., "Can Pre-Training Experiences Explain Individual Differences in Learning?" *Journal of Applied Psychology*, 81, no. 1 (1986), pp. 100–116.

34 J.A. Cannon-Bowers et al., "A Framework for Understanding Pre-Practice Conditions and Their Impact on Learning," *Personnel Psychology*, 51 (1988), pp. 291–320.

35 Based on K. Wexley and G. Latham, *Developing and Training Human Resources in Organizations* (Glenview, IL: Scott, Foresman, 1981), pp. 22–27.

36 G. Na, "An Employer's Right to Train," *Canadian HR Reporter* (October 6, 2008).

37 B.M. Bass and J.A. Vaughan, "Assessing Training Needs," in C. Schneier and R. Beatty, *Personnel Administration Today* (Reading, MA: Addison-Wesley, 1978), p. 311; see also R. Ash and E. Leving, "Job Applicant Training and Work Experience Evaluation: An Empirical Comparison of Four Methods," *Journal of Applied Psychology*, 70, no. 3 (1985), pp. 572–576; J. Lawrie, "Break the Training Ritual," *Personnel Journal*, 67, no. 4

(April 1988), pp. 95–77; T. Lewis and D. Bjorkquist, "Needs Assessment—A Critical Reappraisal," *Performance Improvement Quarterly*, 5, no. 4 (1992), pp. 33–54.

38 See, for example, G. Freeman, "Human Resources Planning—Training Needs Analysis," *Human Resources Planning*, 39, no. 3 (Fall 1993), pp. 32–34.

39 J.C. Georges, "The Hard Realities of Soft Skills Training," *Personnel Journal*, 68, no. 4 (April 1989), pp. 40–45; R.H. Buckham, "Applying Role Analysis in the Workplace," *Personnel*, 64, no. 2 (February 1987), pp. 63–65; J.K. Ford and R. Noe, "Self-Assessed Training Needs: The Effects of Attitudes towards Training, Management Level, and Function," *Personnel Psychology*, 40, no. 1 (Spring 1987), pp. 39–54.

40 K. Wexley and G. Latham, *Developing and Training Human Resources in Organizations* (Glenview, IL: Scott, Foresman, 1981), p. 107.

41 "German Training Model Imported," *BNA Bulletin to Management* (December 19, 1996), p. 408; L. Burton, "Apprenticeship: The Learn While You Earn Option," *Human Resources Professional* (February/March 1998), p. 25; H. Frazis, D.E. Herz, and M.W. Harrigan, "Employer-Provided Training: Results from a New Survey," *Monthly Labor Review*, 118 (1995), pp. 3–17.

42 "Apprenticeship Grant Gets Going," *Canadian HR Reporter* (January 25, 2007); "New Funding for Apprenticeships," *Canadian HR Reporter* (May 3, 2004), p. 2; "Ontario Boosts Apprenticeship Program with $37 Million Investment," *Canadian HR Reporter* (April 7, 2000); ThinkTrades (Alberta Aboriginal Apprenticeship Project), www.thinktrades.com/candidates.htm (accessed June 13, 2006).

43 N. Day, "Informal Learning Gets Results," *Workforce* (June 1998), p. 31.

44 S. Williams, "'Classroom' Training Alive and Changing," *Canadian HR Reporter* (October 6, 2008).

45 M. Emery and M. Schubert, "A Trainer's Guide to Video-conferencing," *Training* (June 1993), p. 60.

46 G.N. Nash, J.P. Muczyk, and F.L. Vettori, "The Role and Practical Effectiveness of Programmed Instruction," *Personnel Psychology*, 24 (1971), pp. 397–418.

47 K. Wexley and G. Latham, *Developing and Training Human Resources in Organizations* (Glenview, IL: Scott, Foresman, 1981), p. 141; see also R. Wlozkowski, "Simulation," *Training and Development Journal*, 39, no. 6 (June 1985), pp. 38–43.

48 "Pros and Cons of E-learning," *Canadian HR Reporter* (July 16, 2001), pp. 11, 15; D. Murray, *E-learning for the Workplace* (Ottawa, ON: Conference Board of Canada, 2001); see also M. Rueda, "How to Make E-Learning Work for Your Company," *Workspan* (December 2002), pp. 50–53; U. Vu, "Technology-Based Learning Comes of Age," *Canadian HR Reporter* (April 21, 2003), pp. 3, 17.

49 S. Mingail, "Good E-Learning Built on Good Instructional Design," *Canadian HR Reporter* (March 22, 2004), p. 12.

50 S. Carliner, M. Ally, N. Zhao, L. Bairstow, S. Khoury, and L. Johnston, *A Review of the State of the Field of Workplace Learning: What We Need to Know About Competencies, Diversity, E-Learning, and Human Performance Impact* (Canadian Society for Training and Development, 2006).

51 G. Siemens, "5 Things to Watch in E-learning," *Canadian HR Reporter* (October 6, 2008).

52 See, for example, T. Falconer, "No More Pencils, No More Books!" *Canadian Banker* (March/April 1994), pp. 21–25.

53 M. Georghiou, "Games, Simulations Open World of Learning," *Canadian HR Reporter* (May 5, 2008).

54 W. Powell, "Like Life?" *Training & Development* (February 2002), pp. 32–38; see also A. Macaulay, "Reality-Based Computer

Simulations Allow Staff to Grow through Failure," *Canadian HR Reporter* (October 23, 2000), pp. 11–12.

55 S. Klie, "L'Oreal Plays Games with Training," *Canadian HR Reporter* (October 6, 2008).

56 A. Czarnecki, "Interactive Learning Makes Big Dent in Time, Money Requirements for T&D," *Canadian HR Reporter* (November 18, 1996), pp. L30–L31.

57 L. Young, "Self-Directed Computer-Based Training That Works," *Canadian HR Reporter* (April 24, 2000), pp. 7–8.

58 F. Manning, "The Misuse of Technology in Workplace Learning," *Canadian HR Reporter* (April 24, 2000), pp. 7, 10; T. Purcell, "Training Anytime, Anywhere," *Canadian HR Reporter* (July 16, 2001), pp. 11, 15; L. Cassini, "Student Participation Thrives in Online Learning Environments," *Canadian HR Reporter* (May 2, 2001), p. 2.

59 O. Diss, "Deploying a New E-Learning Program?" *HR Professional* (October–November 2005), p. 16.

60 P. Weaver, "Preventing E-Learning Failure," *Training & Development* (August 2002), pp. 45–50; K. Oakes, "E-Learning," *Training & Development* (March 2002), pp. 73–75; see also P. Harris, "E-Learning: A Consolidation Update," *Training & Development* (April 2002), pp. 27–33; C.R. Taylor, "The Second Wave," *Training & Development* (October 2002), pp. 24–31; E. Wareham, "The Educated Buyer," *Computing Canada* (February 18, 2000), p. 33; A. Tomlinson, "E-Learning Won't Solve All Problems," *Canadian HR Reporter* (April 8, 2002), pp. 1, 6.

61 P. Weaver, "Preventing E-Learning Failure," *Training & Development* (August 2002), pp. 45–50.

62 M. Belcourt, P.C. Wright, and A.M. Saks, *Managing Performance through Training and Development*, 2nd ed. (Toronto, ON: Nelson Thomson Learning, 2002), pp. 188–202.

63 Ibid, p. 9.

64 D. Kirkpatrick, "Effective Supervisory Training and Development," Part 3, "Outside Programs," *Personnel*, 62, no. 2 (February 1985), pp. 39–42. Among the reasons training might not pay off on the job are a mismatching of courses and trainees' needs, supervisory slip-ups (with supervisors signing up trainees and then forgetting to have them attend the sessions when the training session is actually given), and lack of help in applying skills on the job.

65 N.L. Trainor, "Evaluating Training's Four Levels," *Canadian HR Reporter* (January 13, 1997), p. 10.

66 C. Knight, "Awards for Literacy Announced," *Canadian HR Reporter* (December 29, 1997), p. 10.

67 *Reading the Future: Planning to Meet Canada's Future Literacy Needs* (Ottawa, ON: Canadian Council on Learning, 2008).

68 "New Report Reveals the Future of Literacy in Canada's Largest Cities," Canadian Council on Learning, www.ccl-cca.ca/CCL/Newsroom/Releases/20100908literacy2031.html (accessed July 7, 2011).

69 S. Coulombe, J-F. Tremblay, and S. Marchand, *International Adult Literacy Study: Literacy Scores, Human Capital and Growth Across 14 OECD Countries*, Statistics Canada, Catalogue No. 89-552-MIE, 2004; S. Mingal, "Tackling Workplace Literacy a No-Brainer," *Canadian HR Reporter* (November 22, 2004), pp. G3, G10; D. Brown, "Poor Reading, Math Skills a Drag on Productivity, Performance," *Canadian HR Reporter* (February 28, 2005), pp. 1, 10.

70 U. Vu, "Workplace Language Training Gets Cash Boost," *Canadian HR Reporter* (May 19, 2008); K. Wolfe, "Language Training for the Workplace," *Canadian HR Reporter* (June 6, 2005), pp. 1, 13.

71 R. Rosen and P. Digh, "Developing Globally Literate Leaders," *Training & Development* (May 2001), pp. 70–81.

72 B. Siu, "Cross-Cultural Training and Customer Relations: What Every Manager Should Know," *Canadian HR Reporter* (November 15, 1999), pp. G3, G15.

73 D. Roberts and B. Tsang, "Diversity Management Training Helps Firms Hone Competitive Edge," *Canadian HR Reporter* (June 19, 1995), pp. 17–18.

74 L. Young, "Retail Sector Seeks to Upgrade Education, Training to Solve Human Resource Woes," *Canadian HR Reporter* (February 8, 1999), p. 11; see also B. Nagle, "Superior Retail Training Blends Customer Service, Product Knowledge," *Canadian HR Reporter* (July 15, 2002), pp. 7–8; D. Brown, "Is Retail Ready to Buy Training?" *Canadian HR Reporter* (July 15, 2002), pp. 7–8.

75 Canadian Retail Institute, www.retaileducation.ca/cms/sitem.cfm/certification_&_training (accessed May 31, 2009).

76 Based on J. Laabs, "Team Training Goes Outdoors," *Personnel Journal* (June 1991), pp. 56–63; see also S. Caudron, "Teamwork Takes Work," *Personnel Journal*, 73, no. 2 (February 1994), pp. 41–49.

77 B. Donais, "Training Managers in Handling Conflict," *Canadian HR Reporter* (March 12, 2007); A. Tomlinson, "A Dose of Training for Ailing First-Time Managers," *Canadian HR Reporter* (December 3, 2001), pp. 7, 10.

78 L.C. McDermott, "Developing the New Young Managers," *Training & Development* (October 2001), pp. 42–48; A. Tomlinson, "A Dose of Training for Ailing First-Time Managers," *Canadian HR Reporter* (December 3, 2001), pp. 7, 10.

Chapter 11

1 Towers Perrin, *Talent Management: The State of the Art* (Toronto, ON: Towers Perrin, 2005); E. Chadnick, "Is HR Prepared to Keep the Keepers?" *Canadian HR Reporter* (January 29, 2007).

2 S. O'Neal and J. Gebauer, "Talent Management in the 21st Century: Attracting, Retaining and Engaging Employees of Choice," *WorldatWork Journal* (First Quarter, 2006), pp. 6–17.

3 Quoted from F. Otte and P. Hutcheson, *Helping Employees Manage Careers* (Englewood Cliffs, NJ: Prentice Hall, 1992), pp. 5–6.

4 M. Duarte, "O indivíduo e a organização: Perspectivas de desenvolvimento" (The Individual and the Organization: Perspectives of Development)," *Psychologica (Extra-Série)* (2004), pp. 549–557.

5 M. Savickas, L. Nota, J. Rossier, J. Dauwalder, M. Duarte, J. Guichard, S. Soresi, R. Van Esbroeck, and A. Van Vianen, "Life Designing: A Paradigm for Career Construction in the 21st Century," *Journal of Vocational Behavior* (May 2009), pp. 239–250.

6 M. Duarte, "O indivíduo e a organização: Perspectivas de desenvolvimento" (The Individual and the Organization: Perspectives of Development)," *Psychologica (Extra-Série)* (2004), pp. 549–557.

7 W. Enelow, *100 Ways to Recession-Proof Your Career* (Toronto, ON: McGraw-Hill, 2002), p. 1.

8 P. Linkow, "Winning the Competition for Talent: The Role of the New Career Paradigm in Total Rewards," *Workspan* (October 2006), pp. 28–32.

9 M. Watters and L. O'Connor, *It's Your Move: A Personal and Practical Guide to Career Transition and Job Search for Canadian Managers, Professionals and Executives* (Toronto, ON: HarperCollins, 2001).

10 For example, one survey of Baby Boomers concluded that "allowed to excel" was the most frequently mentioned factor in overall job satisfaction in an extensive attitude survey of Canadian supervisors and middle managers between

30 and 45 years of age; J. Rogers, "Baby Boomers and Their Career Expectations," *Canadian Business Review* (Spring 1993), pp. 13–18.

11 See, for example, R. Chanick, "Career Growth for Baby Boomers," *Personnel Journal*, 71, no. 1 (January 1992), pp. 40–46.

12 R. Sheppard, "Spousal Programs and Communication Curb Relocation Rejections," *Canadian HR Reporter* (November 1, 1999), p. 17.

13 D. Quinn Mills, *Labor–Management Relations* (New York, NY: McGraw-Hill, 1986), pp. 387–396.

14 G. Dessler, *Winning Commitment* (New York, NY: McGraw-Hill, 1993), pp. 144–149.

15 See J. Famularo, *Handbook of Modern Personnel Administration* (New York, NY: McGraw-Hill, 1972), p. 17.

16 J. Swain, "Dispelling Myths about Leadership Development," *Canadian HR Reporter* (June 3, 2002), p. 27.

17 J. Cooper, "Succession Planning: It's Not Just for Executives Anymore," *Workspan* (February 2006), pp. 44–47.

18 Ibid.

19 P. Cantor, "Succession Planning: Often Requested, Rarely Delivered," *Ivey Business Journal* (January/February 2005), pp.1–11.

20 R. Cheloha and J. Swain, "Talent Management System Key to Effective Succession Planning," *Canadian HR Reporter* (October 10, 2005), pp. 5, 8.

21 U. Vu, "Beware the Plan That's Led Too Much by HR," *Canadian HR Reporter* (October 10, 2005), pp. 6–7.

22 For discussions of the steps in succession planning, see, for example, K. Nowack, "The Secrets of Succession," *Training and Development* (November 1994), pp. 49–55; D. Brookes, "In Management Succession, Who Moves Up?" *Human Resources* (January/February 1995), pp. 11–13.

23 "Half of Companies Fail to Update Succession Plans," *Workplace e-Newsletter*, www.workplace-mag.com/Half-of-companies-fail-to-update-succession-plans.html (accessed May 31, 2009).

24 K. Spence, "The Employee's Role in Succession Planning," *Canadian HR Reporter* (February 14, 2000), p. 13.

25 J. Orr, "Job Rotations Give Future Leaders the Depth They Need," *Canadian HR Reporter* (January 30, 2006), pp. 17, 20.

26 D. Yoder, H.G. Heneman, J. Turnbull, and C.H. Stone, *Handbook of Personnel Management and Labor Relations* (New York, NY: McGraw Hill, 1958); see also J. Phillips, "Training Supervisors Outside the Classroom," *Training and Development Journal*, 40, no. 2 (February 1986), pp. 46–49.

27 K. Wexley and G. Latham, *Developing and Training Human Resources in Organizations* (Glenview, IL: Scott, Foresman, 1981), p. 207.

28 D. Brown, "Action Learning Popular in Europe, Not Yet Caught on in Canada," *Canadian HR Reporter* (April 25, 2005), pp. 1–17.

29 IPM Management Training and Development, "Workplace.ca," www.workplace.ca (accessed March 31, 2003).

30 L. Cassiani, "Taking Team Building to New Heights," *Canadian HR Reporter* (February 26, 2001), pp. 8, 17.

31 J. Famularo, *Handbook of Modern Personnel Administration* (New York, NY: McGraw-Hill, 1972), pp. 21.7–21.8.

32 L. Morin and S. Renaud, "Corporate University Basics," *Workplace Gazette*, 7, no. 4, pp. 61–71.

33 E. Lazarus, "Corporate University," *HR Professional* (June/July 2006), pp. 28–29; "City of Richmond Wins International Award," www.richmond.ca/__shared/printpages/page4754.htm (accessed May 8, 2009).

34 Based on A. Kraut, "Developing Managerial Skill via Modeling Techniques: Some Positive Research Findings—A Symposium," *Personnel Psychology*, 29, no. 3 (Autumn 1976), pp. 325–361.

35 K. Wexley and G. Latham, *Developing and Training Human Resources in Organizations* (Glenview, IL: Scott, Foresman, 1981), p. 193.

36 J. Hinrichs, "Personnel Testing," in M. Dunnette (ed.), *Handbook of Industrial and Organizational Psychology* (Chicago, IL: Rand McNally, 1976), p. 855.

37 J. Kay, "At Harvard on the Case," *National Post Business* (March 2003), pp. 68–78.

38 A.M. Young and P.L. Perrewé, "What Did You Expect? An Examination of Career-Related Support and Social Support Among Mentors and Protégés," *Journal of Management*, 20 (2000), pp. 611–632; "Mentoring Makes Better Employees," *Workplace Today* (June 2001), p. 12; S. Butyn, "Mentoring Your Way to Improved Retention," *Canadian HR Reporter* (January 27, 2003), pp. 13, 15.

39 S. Klie, "Mentoring Accelerates Leadership Development," *Canadian HR Reporter* (March 23, 2009).

40 A.K. Buahene and G. Kovary, "Reversing the Roles: Why Gen Ys Can Make Great Mentors," *Canadian HR Reporter* (May 4, 2009).

41 D. Crisp, "Leadership Values Evolving," *Canadian HR Reporter* (September 8, 2008); S. Klie, "Holistic Approach to Developing Leaders Best," *Canadian HR Reporter* (October 27, 2008).

42 D. Brown, "Banking on Leadership Development," *Canadian HR Reporter* (January 17, 2005), pp. 7, 9.

43 Maple Leaf Foods, "Developing Leaders," www.mapleleaf.com/Working/YourDevelopment.aspx (accessed June 13, 2006).

44 R.J. Kramer, "Growing the New Business Leader," *The Conference Board Executive Action Series*, no. 208 (September 2006).

45 E. Chadnick, "Is HR Prepared to Keep the Keepers?" *Canadian HR Reporter* (January 29, 2007).

46 L. Finkelstein, "Coaching SaskEnergy to Higher Performance," *Canadian HR Reporter* (December 1, 2008).

47 Banff Centre, www.banffcentre.ca/departments/leadership/programs/framework.asp#model (accessed May 31, 2009).

Chapter 12

1 J.T. Rich, "The Solutions for Employee Performance Management," *Workspan* (February 2002), pp. 32–37.

2 J.A. Rubino, "Aligning Performance Management and Compensation Rewards Successfully," *WorldatWork Canadian News* (Fourth Quarter, 2004), pp. 12–16.

3 P. Nel, O. Van Dyk, G. Haasbroek, H. Schultz, T. Sono, and A. Werner, *Human Resource Management*, (Cape Town, South Africa: Oxford University Press, 2004).

4 D. Brown, "HR Improving at Performance Management," *Canadian HR Reporter* (December 2, 2002), pp. 1, 14.

5 "The Performance-Management Process," *Workspan* (October 2006), p. 96.

6 R. Thorndike, "Concepts of Culture-Fairness," *Journal of Educational Measurement* (Summer, 1971), pp. 63–70.

7 S. Motowidlo and J. Van Scotter, "Evidence That Task Performance Should Be Distinguished from Contextual Performance," *Journal of Applied Psychology* (November 1993), pp. 475–480.

8 R. Tett, K. Fox, and P. Palmer, "Task and Contextual Performance as Formal and Expected Work Behaviors," Paper presented at the 18th annual Society of Industrial Organizational Psychologists conference (Orlando, FL, April, 2002).

9 A. Sung and E. Todd, "Line of Sight: Moving Beyond the Catchphrase," *Workspan* (October 2004), pp. 65–69.

10 For further discussion, see G. English, "Tuning Up for Performance Management," *Training and Development Journal* (April 1991), pp. 56–60.

11 C.L. Hughes, "The Bell-Shaped Curve That Inspires Guerrilla Warfare," *Personnel Administrator* (May 1987), pp. 40–41.

12 R. Girard, "Are Performance Appraisals Passé?" *Personnel Journal*, 67, no. 8 (August 1988), pp. 89–90.

13 D. Bernardin and P. Smith, "A Clarification of Some Issues Regarding the Development and Use of Behaviorally Anchored Ratings Scales (BARS)," *Journal of Applied Psychology* (August 1981), pp. 458–463.

14 D. Bownas and H. Bernardin, "Critical Incident Technique," in S. Gael (Ed.), *The Job Analysis Handbook for Business, Industry, and Government* (New York, NY: Wiley, 1988), pp. 1120–1137.

15 N. Hauenstein, R. Brown, and A. Sinclair, "BARS and Those Mysterious, Missing Middle Anchors," *Journal of Business and Psychology* (May 2010), pp. 663–672.

16 J. Goodale and R. Burke, "Behaviorally Based Rating Scales Need Not Be Job Specific," *Journal of Applied Psychology*, 60 (June 1975).

17 K.R. Murphy and J. Constans, "Behavioral Anchors as a Source of Bias in Rating," *Journal of Applied Psychology*, 72, no. 4 (November 1987), pp. 573–577.

18 E. Mone and M. London, *Employee Engagement through Effective Performance Management: A Manager's Guide* (New York, NY: Routledge, 2009).

19 S. Kerr and S. Landouer, "Using Stretch Goals to Promote Organizational Effectiveness and Personal Growth: General Electric and Goldman Sachs," *Academy of Management Executive* (November 2004), pp. 134–138.

20 C. Maslach and M. Leiter, "Early Predictors of Job Burnout and Engagement," *Journal of Applied Psychology* (May 2008), pp. 498–512.

21 M. Levy, "Almost-Perfect Performance Appraisals," *Personnel Journal*, 68, no. 4 (April 1989), pp. 76–83.

22 P. Loucks, "Plugging into Performance Management," *Canadian HR Reporter* (February 26, 2007).

23 C. Howard, "Appraise This!" *Canadian Business* (May 23, 1998), p. 96.

24 E. Farndale, V. Hope-Hailey, and C. Kelliher, "High Commitment Performance Management: The Roles of Justice and Trust," *Personnel Review* (2011), pp. 5–23.

25 E. Mone, C. Eisinger, K. Guggenheim, B. Price, and C. Stine, "Performance Management at the Wheel: Driving Employee Engagement in Organizations," *Journal of Business and Psychology* (May 2011), pp. 205–212.

26 K.S. Teel, "Performance Appraisal: Current Trends, Persistent Progress," *Personnel Journal*, 59, no. 4 (April 1980), pp. 296–316.

27 D. Brown, "Performance Management Systems Need Fixing: Survey," *Canadian HR Reporter* (April 11, 2005), pp. 1, 10; M. Waung and S. Highhouse, "Fear of Conflict and Empathic Buffering: Two Explanations for the Inflation of Performance Feedback," *Organizational Behavior and Human Decision Processes*, 71 (1997), pp. 37–54.

28 Y. Ganzach, "Negativity (and Positivity) in Performance Evaluation: Three Field Studies," *Journal of Applied Psychology*, 80 (1995), pp. 491–499.

29 T.J. Maurer and M.A. Taylor, "Is Sex by Itself Enough? An Exploration of Gender Bias Issues in Performance Appraisal," *Organizational Behavior and Human Decision Processes*, 60 (1994), pp. 231–251; see also C.E. Lance, "Test for Latent Structure of

Performance Ratings Derived from Wherry's (1952) *Theory of Ratings*," *Journal of Management*, 20 (1994), pp. 757–771.

30 S.E. Scullen, M.K. Mount, and M. Goff, "Understanding the Latent Structure of Job Performance Ratings," *Journal of Applied Psychology*, 85 (2001), pp. 956–970.

31 A.M. Saks and D.A. Waldman, "The Relationship between Age and Job Performance Evaluations for Entry-Level Professionals," *Journal of Organizational Behavior*, 19 (1998), pp. 409–419.

32 W.C. Borman, L.A. White, and D.W. Dorsey, "Effects of Ratee Task Performance and Interpersonal Factors in Supervisor and Peer Performance Ratings," *Journal of Applied Psychology*, 80 (1995), pp. 168–177.

33 K. Murphy, W. Balzer, M. Lockhart, and E. Eisenman, "Effects of Previous Performance on Evaluations of Present Performance," *Journal of Applied Psychology*, 70, no. 1 (1985), pp. 72–84; see also K. Williams, A. DeNisi, B. Meglino, and T. Cafferty, "Initial Decisions and Subsequent Performance Ratings," *Journal of Applied Psychology*, 71, no. 2 (May 1986), pp. 189–195.

34 S. Appelbaum, M. Roy, and T. Gillilan, "Globalization of Performance Appraisals: Theory and Applications," *Management Decision* (2011), pp. 570–585.

35 J. Hedge and M. Cavanagh, "Improving the Accuracy of Performance Evaluations: Comparison of Three Methods of Performance Appraiser Training," *Journal of Applied Psychology*, 73, no. 1 (February 1988), pp. 68–73.

36 B. Davis and M. Mount, "Effectiveness of Performance Appraisal Training Using Computer Assistance Instruction and Behavior Modeling," *Personnel Psychology*, 37 (Fall 1984), pp. 439–452.

37 T. Athey and R. McIntyre, "Effect of Rater Training on Rater Accuracy: Levels of Processing Theory and Social Facilitation Theory Perspectives," *Journal of Applied Psychology*, 72, no. 4 (November 1987), pp. 567–572.

38 M.M. Greller, "Participation in the Performance Appraisal Review: Inflexible Manager Behavior and Variable Worker Needs," *Human Relations*, 51 (1998), pp. 1061–1083.

39 R. Arvey, and J. Campion, (1982). "The Employment Interview: A Summary and Review of Recent Research," *Personnel Psychology* (June 1982), pp. 281–322; W. Wiesner and S. Cronshaw, "A Meta-Analytic Investigation of the Impact of Interview Format and Degree of Structure on the Validity of the Employment Interview," *Journal of Occupational Psychology* (1988), pp. 275–290; K. Murphy, and J. Cleveland, *Understanding Performance Appraisal: Social, Organizational, and Goal-Based Perspectives* (Thousand Oaks, CA: Sage, 1995).

40 B.D. Cawley, L.M. Keeping, and P.E Levy, "Participation in the Performance Appraisal Process and Employee Reactions: A Meta-Analytic Review of Field Investigations," *Journal of Applied Psychology*, 83 (1998), pp. 615–633.

41 J.W. Lawrie, "Your Performance: Appraise It Yourself!" *Personnel*, 66, no. 1 (January 1989), pp. 21–33; includes a good explanation of how self-appraisals can be used at work; see also A. Furnham and P. Stringfield, "Congruence in Job-Performance Ratings: A Study of 360° Feedback Examining Self, Manager, Peers, and Consultant Ratings," *Human Relations*, 51 (1998), pp. 517–530.

42 P.A. Mabe III and S.G. West, "Validity of Self-Evaluation of Ability: A Review and Meta-Analysis," *Journal of Applied Psychology*, 67, no. 3 (1982), pp. 280–296.

43 J. Russell and D. Goode, "An Analysis of Managers' Reactions to Their Own Performance Appraisal Feedback," *Journal of Applied Psychology*, 73, no. 1 (February 1988), pp. 63–67; M.M. Harris and J. Schaubroeck, "A Meta-Analysis of Self–Supervisor, Self–Peer, and Peer–Supervisor Ratings," *Personnel Psychology*, 41 (1988), pp. 43–62.

44 V.V. Druskat and S.B. Wolff, "Effects and Timing of Developmental Peer Appraisals in Self-Managing Work Groups," *Journal of Applied Psychology*, 84 (1999), pp. 58–74.

45 M.M. Harris and J. Schaubroeck, "A Meta-Analysis of Self–Supervisor, Self–Peer, and Peer–Supervisor Ratings," *Personnel Psychology*, 41 (1988), pp. 43–62.

46 W.C. Borman, "The Rating of Individuals in Organizations: An Alternate Approach," *Organizational Behavior and Human Performance*, 12 (1974), pp. 105–124.

47 H.J. Bernardin and R.W. Beatty, "Can Subordinate Appraisals Enhance Managerial Productivity?" *Sloan Management Review* (Summer 1987), pp. 63–73.

48 M. London and A. Wohlers, "Agreement between Subordinate and Self-Ratings in Upward Feedback," *Personnel Psychology*, 44 (1991), pp. 375–390.

49 Ibid, p. 376.

50 D. Antonioni, "The Effects of Feedback Accountability on Upward Appraisal Ratings," *Personnel Psychology*, 47 (1994), pp. 349–355.

51 T.J. Maurer, N.S. Raju, and W.C. Collins, "Peer and Subordinate Performance Appraisal Measurement Equivalence," *Journal of Applied Psychology*, 83 (1998), pp. 693–702.

52 R. Reilly, J. Smither, and N. Vasilopoulos, "A Longitudinal Study of Upward Feedback," *Personnel Psychology*, 49 (1996), pp. 599–612.

53 K. Nowack, "360-Degree Feedback: The Whole Story," *Training and Development* (January 1993), p. 69; for a description of some of the problems involved in implementing 360-degree feedback, see M. Budman, "The Rating Game," *Across the Board*, 31, no. 2 (February 1994), pp. 35–38.

54 C. Romano, "Fear of Feedback," *Management Review* (December 1993), p. 39; see also M.R. Edwards and A.J. Ewen, "How to Manage Performance and Pay with 360-Degree Feedback," *Compensation and Benefits Review*, 28, no. 3 (May/June 1996), pp. 41–46.

55 G.P. Latham, J. Almost, S. Mann, and C. Moore, "New Developments in Performance Management," *Organizational Dynamics*, 34, no. 1 (2005), pp. 77–87; R. Brillinger, "The Many Faces of 360-Degree Feedback," *Canadian HR Reporter* (December 16, 1996), p. 21.

56 J.F. Milliman, R.A. Zawacki, C. Norman, L. Powell, and J. Kirksey, "Companies Evaluate Employees from All Perspectives," *Personnel Journal*, 73, no. 11 (November 1994), pp. 99–103.

57 R. Brillinger, "The Many Faces of 360-Degree Feedback," *Canadian HR Reporter* (December 16, 1996), p. 20.

58 Ibid.

59 D.A. Waldman, L.A. Atwater, and D. Antonioni, "Has 360-Degree Feedback Gone Amok?" *Academy of Management Executive*, 12 (1998), pp. 86–94.

60 P.E. Levy, B.D. Cawley, and R.J. Foti, "Reactions to Appraisal Discrepancies: Performance Ratings and Attributions," *Journal of Business and Psychology*, 12 (1998), pp. 437–455.

61 M. Derayeh and S. Brutus, "Learning from Others' 360-Degree Experiences," *Canadian HR Reporter* (February 10, 2003), pp. 18, 23.

62 A.S. DeNisi and A.N. Kluger, "Feedback Effectiveness: Can 360-Degree Appraisal Be Improved?" *Academy of Management Executive*, 14 (2000), pp. 129–139.

63 T. Bentley, "Internet Addresses 360-Degree Feedback Concerns," *Canadian HR Reporter* (May 8, 2000), pp. G3, G15.

64 D. Brown, "Performance Management Systems Need Fixing: Survey," *Canadian HR Reporter* (April 1, 2005), pp. 1, 10.

65 See also J. Greenberg, "Using Explanations to Manage Impressions of Performance Appraisal Fairness," *Employee Responsibilities and Rights Journal*, 4, no. 1 (March 1991), pp. 51–60.

66 R.G. Johnson, *The Appraisal Interview Guide*, Chapter 9 (New York, NY: AMACOM, 1979).

67 J. Block, *Performance Appraisal on the Job: Making It Work* (New York, NY: Executive Enterprises Publications, 1981), pp. 58–62; see also T. Lowe, "Eight Ways to Ruin a Performance Review," *Personnel Journal*, 65, no. 1 (January 1986).

68 J.W. Smither and M. London, "Best Practices in Performance Management," in J.W. Smither & M. London (Eds.), *Performance Management: Putting Research into Action* (San Francisco, CA: Jossey-Bass, 2009).

69 J. Block, *Performance Appraisal on the Job: Making It Work* (New York, NY: Executive Enterprises Publications, 1981), pp. 58–62.

70 M. Feinberg, *Effective Psychology for Managers* (New York, NY: Simon & Schuster, 1976).

71 J. Pearce and L. Porter, "Employee Response to Formal Performance Appraisal Feedback," *Journal of Applied Psychology*, 71, no. 2 (May 1986), pp. 211–218.

72 D.B. Jarvis and R.E. McGilvery, "Poor Performers," *HR Professional* (June/July 2005), p. 32.

73 L. Axline, "Ethical Considerations of Performance Appraisals," *Management Review* (March 1994), p. 62.

74 M. McDougall and L. Cassiani, "HR Cited in Unfair Performance Review," *Canadian HR Reporter* (September 10, 2001), pp. 1, 6.

75 "Health Worker's Performance Review Unfair," *Workplace Today* (June 2001), p. 23.

76 G. Barrett and M. Kernan, "Performance Appraisal and Terminations: A Review of Court Decisions Since Brito v. Zia with Implications for Personnel Practices," *Personnel Psychology*, 40, no. 3 (Autumn 1987), pp. 489–504.

77 J. Kochnarski and A. Sorenson, "Managing Performance Management," *Workspan* (September 2005), pp. 20–37.

78 E.E. Lawler and M. McDermott, "Current Performance Management Practices," *WorldatWork Journal*, 12, no. 2, pp. 49–60.

79 D. Bell, J. Blanchet, and N. Gore, "Performance Management: Making It Work Is Worth the Effort," *WorldatWork Canadian News*, 12, no. 11 (Fourth Quarter, 2004), pp. 1, 27–28.

Chapter 13

1 Vignette based on N. Watts, "Chan Finishes Off Podium in Fifth, Lysacek Takes Gold," *Toronto Observer*, February 19, 2010, http://www.torontoobserver.ca/2010/02/19/chan-finishes-off-podium-in-fifth-lysacek-takes-gold/; and L. Ewing, "Figure Skating's Code of Points Practically Takes a Statistician to Decipher," *Canadian Press*, February 8, 2010.

2 See, for instance, T. R. Mitchell, "Matching Motivational Strategies with Organizational Contexts," in *Research in Organizational Behavior*, vol. 19, ed. L. L. Cummings and B. M. Staw (Greenwich, CT: JAI Press, 1997), pp. 60–62.

3 D. Gregor, *The Human Side of Enterprise* (New York: McGraw-Hill, 1960). For an updated analysis of Theory X and Theory Y constructs, see R. J. Summers and S. F. Cronshaw, "A Study of McGregor's Theory X, Theory Y and the Influence of Theory X, Theory Y Assumptions on Causal Attributions for Instances of Worker Poor Performance," in *Organizational Behavior*, ed. S. L. McShane, ASAC Conference Proceedings, vol. 9, part 5, Halifax, 1988, pp. 115–123.

4 K. W. Thomas, *Intrinsic Motivation at Work* (San Francisco: Berrett-Koehler, 2000); and K. W. Thomas, "Intrinsic Motivation and How It Works," *Training*, October 2000, pp. 130–135.

5 A. Kohn, *Punished by Rewards* (Boston: Houghton Mifflin, 1993).

6 A. H. Maslow, *Motivation and Personality* (New York: Harper and Row, 1954).

7 C. Conley, *Peak: How Great Companies Get Their Mojo from Maslow* (San Francisco: Jossey-Bass, 2007).

8 K. Korman, J. H. Greenhaus, and I. J. Badin, "Personnel Attitudes and Motivation," in *Annual Review of Psychology*, ed. M. R. Rosenzweig and L. W. Porter (Palo Alto, CA: Annual Reviews, 1977), p. 178; and M. A. Wahba and L. G. Bridwell, "Maslow Reconsidered: A Review of Research on the Need Hierarchy Theory," *Organizational Behavior and Human Performance*, April 1976, pp. 212–240.

9 L. Tay and E. Diener, "Needs and Subjective Well-Being around the World," *Journal of Personality and Social Psychology*, June 20, 2011, published online before print, http://psycnet.apa.org/?fa=main.doiLanding&doi=10.1037/a0023779

10 C. P. Alderfer, "An Empirical Test of a New Theory of Human Needs," *Organizational Behavior and Human Performance*, May 1969, pp. 142–175.

11 C. P. Schneider and C. P. Alderfer, "Three Studies of Measures of Need Satisfaction in Organizations," *Administrative Science Quarterly*, December 1973, pp. 489–505; and I. Borg and M. Braun, "Work Values in East and West Germany: Different Weights, but Identical Structures," *Journal of Organizational Behavior* 17, Special Issue (1996), pp. 541–555.

12 F. Herzberg, B. Mausner, and B. Snyderman, The Motivation to Work (New York: Wiley, 1959).

13 R. J. House and L. A. Wigdor, "Herzberg's Dual-Factor Theory of Job Satisfaction and Motivations: A Review of the Evidence and Criticism," *Personnel Psychology*, Winter 1967, pp. 369–389; D. P. Schwab and L. L. Cummings, "Theories of Performance and Satisfaction: A Review," *Industrial Relations*, October 1970, pp. 403–430; R. J. Caston and R. Braito, "A Specification Issue in Job Satisfaction Research," *Sociological Perspectives*, April 1985, pp. 175–197; and J. Phillipchuk and J. Whittaker, "An Inquiry into the Continuing Relevance of Herzberg's Motivation Theory," *Engineering Management Journal* 8, no. 1 (1996), pp. 15–20.

14 R. J. House and L. A. Wigdor, "Herzberg's Dual-Factor Theory of Job Satisfaction and Motivations: A Review of the Evidence and Criticism," *Personnel Psychology*, Winter 1967, pp. 369–389; D. P. Schwab and L. L. Cummings, "Theories of Performance and Satisfaction: A Review," *Industrial Relations*, October 1970, pp. 403–430; and R. J. Caston and R. Braito, "A Specification Issue in Job Satisfaction Research," *Sociological Perspectives*, April 1985, pp. 175–197.

15 D. C. McClelland, *The Achieving Society* (New York: Van Nostrand Reinhold, 1961); J. W. Atkinson and J. O. Raynor, *Motivation and Achievement* (Washington, DC: Winston, 1974); D. C. McClelland, *Power: The Inner Experience* (New York: Irvington, 1975); and M. J. Stahl, *Managerial and Technical Motivation: Assessing Needs for Achievement, Power, and Affiliation* (New York: Praeger, 1986).

16 D. C. McClelland, *The Achieving Society* (New York: Van Nostrand Reinhold, 1961).

17 D. C. McClelland and D. G. Winter, *Motivating Economic Achievement* (New York: The Free Press, 1969); and J. B. Miner, N. R. Smith, and J. S. Bracker, "Role of Entrepreneurial Task Motivation in the Growth of Technologically Innovative Firms: Interpretations from Follow-up Data," *Journal of Applied Psychology*, October 1994, pp. 627–630.

18 D. C. McClelland, *Power: The Inner Experience* (New York: Irvington, 1975); D. C. McClelland and D. H. Burnham, "Power Is the Great Motivator," *Harvard Business Review*, March–April 1976, pp. 100–110; and R. E. Boyatzis, "The Need for Close Relationships and the Manager's Job," in *Organizational Psychology: Readings on Human Behavior in Organizations*, 4th ed.,

ed. D. A. Kolb, I. M. Rubin, and J. M. McIntyre (Upper Saddle River, NJ: Prentice Hall, 1984), pp. 81–86.

19 D. G. Winter, "The Motivational Dimensions of Leadership: Power, Achievement, and Affiliation," in *Multiple Intelligences and Leadership*, ed. R. E. Riggio, S. E. Murphy, and F. J. Pirozzolo (Mahwah, NJ: Lawrence Erlbaum, 2002), pp. 119–138.

20 J. B. Miner, *Studies in Management Education* (New York: Springer, 1965).

21 Vignette based on P. J. Kwong, "With Lessons Learned, Chan Ready to Defend His Title," *cbcsports.ca*, July 11, 2011, http://www.cbc.ca/sports/blogs/pjkwong/2011/07/with-lessons-learned-chan-ready-to-defend-his-title.html; and "Chan Wins World Figure Skating Title," *Toronto Sun*, http://www.torontosun.com/2011/04/28/chan-wins-world-figure-skating-title

22 V. H. Vroom, *Work and Motivation* (New York: Wiley, 1964).

23 R. Sinclair, "A&A: LPGA Golfer Alena Sharp," *CBC.ca*, February 18, 2011, http://www.cbc.ca/sports/moresports/ story/2011/02/13/sp-lpga-sharp.html

24 See http://www.radical.ca

25 See, for example, H. G. Heneman III and D. P. Schwab, "Evaluation of Research on Expectancy Theory Prediction of Employee Performance," *Psychological Bulletin*, July 1972, pp. 1–9; T. R. Mitchell, "Expectancy Models of Job Satisfaction, Occupational Preference and Effort: A Theoretical, Methodological and Empirical Appraisal," *Psychological Bulletin*, November 1974, pp. 1053–1077; and L. Reinharth and M. A. Wahba, "Expectancy Theory as a Predictor of Work Motivation, Effort Expenditure, and Job Performance," *Academy of Management Journal*, September 1975, pp. 502–537.

26 See, for example, L. W. Porter and E. E. Lawler III, *Managerial Attitudes and Performance* (Homewood, IL: Richard D. Irwin, 1968); D. F. Parker and L. Dyer, "Expectancy Theory as a Within-Person Behavioral Choice Model: An Empirical Test of Some Conceptual and Methodological Refinements," *Organizational Behavior and Human Performance*, October 1976, pp. 97–117; H. J. Arnold, "A Test of the Multiplicative Hypothesis of Expectancy-Valence Theories of Work Motivation," *Academy of Management Journal*, April 1981, pp. 128–141; and W. Van Eerde and H. Thierry, "Vroom's Expectancy Models and Work-Related Criteria: A Meta-analysis," *Journal of Applied Psychology*, October 1996, pp. 575–586.

27 P. C. Earley, *Face, Harmony, and Social Structure: An Analysis of Organizational Behavior across Cultures* (New York: Oxford University Press, 1997); R. M. Steers and C. Sanchez-Runde, "Culture, Motivation, and Work Behavior," in *Handbook of Cross-Cultural Management*, ed. M. Gannon and K. Newman (London: Blackwell, 2001), pp. 190–215; and H. C. Triandis, "Motivation and Achievement in Collectivist and Individualistic Cultures," in *Advances in Motivation and Achievement*, vol. 9, ed. M. Maehr and P. Pintrich (Greenwich, CT: JAI Press, 1995), pp. 1–30.

28 J. S. Lublin, "It's Shape-up Time for Performance Reviews," *Wall Street Journal*, October 3, 1994, p. B1.

29 Much of this section is based on H. H. Meyer, "A Solution to the Performance Appraisal Feedback Enigma," *Academy of Management Executive*, February 1991, pp. 68–76.

30 T. D. Schelhardt, "It's Time to Evaluate Your Work, and All Involved Are Groaning," *Wall Street Journal*, November 19, 1996, p. A1.

31 R. J. Burke, "Why Performance Appraisal Systems Fail," *Personnel Administration*, June 1972, pp. 32–40.

32 B. D. Cawley, L. M. Keeping, and P. E. Levy, "Participation in the Performance Appraisal Process and Employee Reactions: A Meta-analytic Review of Field Investigations," *Journal of Applied Psychology*, August 1998, pp. 615–633; and P. E. Levy and J. R. Williams, "The Social Context of Performance Appraisal: A Review

and Framework for the Future," *Journal of Management* 30, no. 6 (2004), pp. 881–905.

33 List directly quoted from R. Kreitner and A. Kinicki, *Organizational Behavior*, 6th ed. (New York: McGraw-Hill/Irwin, 2004), p. 335 (emphasis added).

34 P. C. Earley, P. Wojnaroski, and W. Prest, "Task Planning and Energy Expended: Exploration of How Goals Influence Performance," *Journal of Applied Psychology*, February 1987, pp. 107–114.

35 See, for instance, D. Morisano, J. B. Hirsh, J. B. Peterson, R. O. Pihl, and B. M. Shore, "Setting, Elaborating, and Reflecting on Personal Goals Improves Academic Performance," *Journal of Applied Psychology* 95, no. 2 (2010), pp. 255–264.

36 "KEY Group Survey Finds Nearly Half of All Employees Have No Set Performance Goals," *IPMA-HR Bulletin*, March 10, 2006, p. 1; S. Hamm, "SAP Dangles a Big, Fat Carrot," *BusinessWeek*, May 22, 2006, pp. 67–68; and "P&G CEO Wields High Expectations but No Whip," *USA Today*, February 19, 2007, p. 3B.

37 Based on L. Bourgon, "The End of Clock-Punching?" *Canadian Business*, September 27, 2010; "Building a Better Workforce," *PROFIT*, February 16, 2011, http://www.profitguide.com/article/10084—building-a-better-workforce—page0; and C. Ressler and J. Thompson, *Why Work Sucks and How to Fix It* (New York: Penguin, 2008).

38 M. Craemer, "Motivating Employees in the 21st Century," *Seattle Post Intelligence*, April 5, 2010, http://blog.seattlepi.com/workplacewrangler/2010/04/05/motivating-employees-in-the-21st-century/

39 E. A. Locke and G. P. Latham, *A Theory of Goal Setting and Task Performance* (Englewood Cliffs, NJ: Prentice Hall, 1980).

40 E. A. Locke, K. N. Shaw, L. M. Saari, and G. P. Latham, "Goal Setting and Task Performance," *Psychological Bulletin*, January 1981, pp. 125–152; and A. J. Mento, R. P. Steel, and R. J. Karren, "A Meta-Analytic Study of the Effects of Goal Setting on Task Performance: 1966–1984," *Organizational Behavior and Human Decision Processes*, February 1987, pp. 52–83.

41 R. E. Wood, A. J. Mento, and E. A. Locke, "Task Complexity as a Moderator of Goal Effects: A Meta-analysis," *Journal of Applied Psychology*, August 1987, pp. 416–425.

42 P. M. Wright, "Operationalization of Goal Difficulty as a Moderator of the Goal Difficulty-Performance Relationship," *Journal of Applied Psychology*, June 1990, pp. 227–234; E. A. Locke and G. P. Latham, "Building a Practically Useful Theory of Goal Setting and Task Motivation: A 35-Year Odyssey," *American Psychologist* 57, no. 9 (2002): pp. 705–717.

43 P. M. Wright, J. R. Hollenbeck, S. Wolf, and G. C. McMahan, "The Effects of Varying Goal Difficulty Operationalizations on Goal Setting Outcomes and Processes," *Organizational Behavior and Human Decision Processes*, January 1995, pp. 28–43.

44 K. L. Langeland, C. M. Johnson, and T. C. Mawhinney, "Improving Staff Performance in a Community Mental Health Setting: Job Analysis, Training, Goal Setting, Feedback, and Years of Data," *Journal of Organizational Behavior Management*, 1998, pp. 21–43.

45 J. M. Ivancevich and J. T. McMahon, "The Effects of Goal Setting, External Feedback, and Self-Generated Feedback on Outcome Variables: A Field Experiment," *Academy of Management Journal*, June 1982, pp. 359–372; and E. A. Locke, "Motivation Through Conscious Goal Setting," *Applied and Preventive Psychology* 5 (1996), pp. 117–124.

46 E. A. Locke and G. P. Latham, *A Theory of Goal Setting and Task Performance* (Englewood Cliffs, NJ: Prentice Hall, 1990).

47 M. Erez, P. C. Earley, and C. L. Hulin, "The Impact of Participation on Goal Acceptance and Performance: A Two-Step Model," *Academy of Management Journal*, March 1985, pp. 50–66.

48 E. A. Locke, "The Motivation to Work: What We Know," *Advances in Motivation and Achievement* 10 (1997), pp. 375–412; and G. P. Latham, M. Erez, and E. A. Locke, "Resolving Scientific Disputes by the Joint Design of Crucial Experiments by the Antagonists: Application to the Erez-Latham Dispute Regarding Participation in Goal Setting," *Journal of Applied Psychology*, November 1988, pp. 753–772.

49 H. J. Klein, M. J. Wesson, J. R. Hollenbeck, P. M. Wright, and R. D. DeShon, "The Assessment of Goal Commitment: A Measurement Model Meta-analysis," *Organizational Behavior and Human Decision Processes* 85, no. 1 (2001), pp. 32–55.

50 J. R. Hollenbeck, C. R. Williams, and H. J. Klein, "An Empirical Examination of the Antecedents of Commitment to Difficult Goals," *Journal of Applied Psychology*, February 1989, pp. 18–23. See also J. C. Wofford, V. L. Goodwin, and S. Premack, "Meta-analysis of the Antecedents of Personal Goal Level and of the Antecedents and Consequences of Goal Commitment," *Journal of Management*, September 1992, pp. 595–615; M. E. Tubbs, "Commitment as a Moderator of the Goal-Performance Relation: A Case for Clearer Construct Definition," *Journal of Applied Psychology*, February 1993, pp. 86–97; and J. E. Bono and A. E. Colbert, "Understanding Responses to Multi-Source Feedback: The Role of Core Self-evaluations," *Personnel Psychology*, Spring 2005, pp. 171–203.

51 See R. E. Wood, A. J. Mento, and E. A. Locke, "Task Complexity as a Moderator of Goal Effects: A Meta-analysis," *Journal of Applied Psychology*, August 1987, pp. 416–425; R. Kanfer and P. L. Ackerman, "Motivation and Cognitive Abilities: An Integrative/Aptitude-Treatment Interaction Approach to Skill Acquisition," *Journal of Applied Psychology* (monograph) 74 (1989), pp. 657–690; T. R. Mitchell and W. S. Silver, "Individual and Group Goals When Workers Are Interdependent: Effects on Task Strategies and Performance," *Journal of Applied Psychology*, April 1990, pp. 185–193; and A. M. O'Leary-Kelly, J. J. Martocchio, and D. D. Frink, "A Review of the Influence of Group Goals on Group Performance," *Academy of Management Journal*, October 1994, pp. 1285–1301.

52 G. P. Latham and E. A. Locke, "Enhancing the Benefits and Overcoming the Pitfalls of Goal Setting," *Organizational Dynamics* 35, no. 6 (2006), pp. 332–340; L. D. Ordóñez, M. E. Schweitzer, A. D. Galinsky, and M. Bazerman, "Goals Gone Wild: The Systematic Side Effects of Overprescribing Goal Setting," *Academy of Management Perspectives* 23, no.1 (2009), pp. 6–16; and E. A. Locke and G. P. Latham, "Has Goal Setting Gone Wild, or Have Its Attackers Abandoned Good Scholarship?" *Academy of Management Perspectives* 23, no. 1 (2009), pp. 17–23.

53 A. Bandura, *Self-Efficacy: The Exercise of Control* (New York: Freeman, 1997). See also M. Salanova, S. Llorens, and W. Schaufeli, "'Yes, I Can, I Feel Good, and I Just Do It!' On Gain Cycles and Spirals of Efficacy Beliefs, Affect, and Engagement," *Applied Psychology: An International Review* 60, no. 2 (2011), pp. 255–285.

54 A. D. Stajkovic and F. Luthans, "Self-Efficacy and Work-Related Performance: A Meta-analysis," *Psychological Bulletin*, September 1998, pp. 240–261; and A. Bandura, "Cultivate Self-Efficacy for Personal and Organizational Effectiveness," in *Handbook of Principles of Organizational Behavior*, ed. E. Locke (Malden, MA: Blackwell, 2004), pp. 120–136.

55 A. Bandura and D. Cervone, "Differential Engagement in Self-Reactive Influences in Cognitively-Based Motivation," *Organizational Behavior and Human Decision Processes*, August 1986, pp. 92–113.

56 A. Bandura, *Self-Efficacy: The Exercise of Control* (New York: Freeman, 1997).

57 C. L. Holladay and M. A. Quiñones, "Practice Variability and Transfer of Training: The Role of Self-Efficacy Generality," *Journal of Applied Psychology* 88, no. 6 (2003), pp. 1094–1103.

58 R. C. Rist, "Student Social Class and Teacher Expectations: The Self-Fulfilling Prophecy in Ghetto Education," *Harvard Educational Review* 70, no. 3 (2000), pp. 266–301.

59 D. Eden, "Self-Fulfilling Prophecies in Organizations," in *Organizational Behavior: The State of the Science*, 2nd ed., ed. J. Greenberg (Mahwah, NJ: Erlbaum, 2003), pp. 91–122.

60 E. Eden, "Self-Fulfilling Prophecies in Organizations," in *Organizational Behavior: The State of the Science*, 2nd ed., ed. J. Greenberg (Mahwah, NJ: Erlbaum, 2003), pp. 91–122.

61 T. A. Judge, C. L. Jackson, J. C. Shaw, B. Scott, and B. L. Rich, "Self-Efficacy and Work-Related Performance: The Integral Role of Individual Differences," *Journal of Applied Psychology* 92, no. 1 (2007), pp. 107–127.

62 T. A. Judge, C. L. Jackson, J. C. Shaw, B. Scott, and B. L. Rich, "Self-Efficacy and Work-Related Performance: The Integral Role of Individual Differences," *Journal of Applied Psychology* 92, no. 1 (2007), pp. 107–127.

63 Vignette based on C. Cole, "Figure Skating's Code of Points System Has Opened Up the Podium," *Vancouver Sun*, February 6, 2010, http://www.vancouversun.com/news/regional/Figure+skating+Code+Points+system+opened+podium/2532110/story.html

64 J. S. Adams, "Inequity in Social Exchanges," in *Advances in Experimental Social Psychology*, ed. L. Berkowitz (New York: Academic Press, 1965), pp. 267–300.

65 P. S. Goodman, "An Examination of Referents Used in the Evaluation of Pay," *Organizational Behavior and Human Performance*, October 1974, pp. 170–195; S. Ronen, "Equity Perception in Multiple Comparisons: A Field Study," *Human Relations*, April 1986, pp. 333–346; R. W. Scholl, E. A. Cooper, and J. F. McKenna, "Referent Selection in Determining Equity Perception: Differential Effects on Behavioral and Attitudinal Outcomes," *Personnel Psychology*, Spring 1987, pp. 113–127; T. P. Summers and A. S. DeNisi, "In Search of Adams' Other: Reexamination of Referents Used in the Evaluation of Pay," *Human Relations*, June 1990, pp. 497–511; S. Werner and N. P. Mero, "Fair or Foul? The Effects of External, Internal, and Employee Equity on Changes in Performance of Major League Baseball Players," *Human Relations*, October 1999, pp. 1291–1312; and R. W. Griffeth and S. Gaertner, "A Role for Equity Theory in the Turnover Process: An Empirical Test," *Journal of Applied Social Psychology*, May 2001, pp. 1017–1037.

66 C. T. Kulik and M. L. Ambrose, "Personal and Situational Determinants of Referent Choice," *Academy of Management Review*, April 1992, pp. 212–237.

67 C. Ostroff and L. E. Atwater, "Does Whom You Work with Matter? Effects of Referent Group Gender and Age Composition on Managers' Compensation," *Journal of Applied Psychology* 88, no. 4 (2003), pp. 725–740.

68 "Women in the Workforce: Still a Long Way from Equality," *Canadian Labour Congress*, May 5, 2008, http://canadianlabour.ca/en/women-workforce-still-a-long-way-equality

69 See, for example, E. Walster, G. W. Walster, and W. G. Scott, *Equity: Theory and Research* (Boston: Allyn and Bacon, 1978); and J. Greenberg, "Cognitive Reevaluation of Outcomes in Response to Underpayment Inequity," *Academy of Management Journal*, March 1989, pp. 174–184.

70 P. S. Goodman and A. Friedman, "An Examination of Adams' Theory of Inequity," *Administrative Science Quarterly*, September 1971, pp. 271–288; R. P. Vecchio, "An Individual-Differences Interpretation of the Conflicting Predictions Generated by Equity Theory and Expectancy Theory," *Journal of Applied Psychology*, August 1981, pp. 470–481; R. T. Mowday, "Equity Theory Predic-tions of Behavior in Organizations," in *Motivation and Work Behavior*, 6th ed., ed. R. Steers, L. W. Porter, and G. Bigley (New York: McGraw-Hill, 1996), pp. 111–131; R. W. Griffeth and S. Gaertner, "A Role for Equity Theory in the Turnover Process: An Empirical Test," *Journal of Applied Social Psychology*, May 2001, pp. 1017–1037; and L. K. Scheer, N. Kumar, and J.-B. E. M. Steenkamp, "Reactions to Perceived Inequity in U.S. and Dutch Interorganizational Relationships," *Academy of Management* 46, no. 3 (2003), pp. 303–316.

71 See, for example, R. C. Huseman, J. D. Hatfield, and E. W. Miles, "A New Perspective on Equity Theory: The Equity Sensitivity Construct," *Academy of Management Journal*, April 1987, pp. 222–234; K. S. Sauley and A. G. Bedeian, "Equity Sensitivity: Construction of a Measure and Examination of Its Psychometric Properties," *Journal of Management* 26, no. 5 (2000), pp. 885–910; and J. A. Colquitt, "Does the Justice of One Interact with the Justice of Many? Reactions to Procedural Justice in Teams," *Journal of Applied Psychology* 89, no. 4 (2004), pp. 633–646.

72 J. Greenberg and S. Ornstein, "High Status Job Title as Compensation for Underpayment: A Test of Equity Theory," *Journal of Applied Psychology*, May 1983, pp. 285–297; and J. Greenberg, "Equity and Workplace Status: A Field Experiment," *Journal of Applied Psychology*, November 1988, pp. 606–613.

73 See, for instance, J. Greenberg, *The Quest for Justice on the Job* (Thousand Oaks, CA: Sage, 1996); R. Cropanzano and J. Greenberg, "Progress in Organizational Justice: Tunneling through the Maze," in *International Review of Industrial and Organizational Psychology*, vol. 12, ed. C. L. Cooper and I. T. Robertson (New York: Wiley, 1997); J. A. Colquitt, D. E. Conlon, M. J. Wesson, C. O. L. H. Porter, and K. Y. Ng, "Justice at the Millennium: A Meta-analytic Review of the 25 Years of Organizational Justice Research," *Journal of Applied Psychology*, June 2001, pp. 425–445; T. Simons and Q. Roberson, "Why Managers Should Care About Fairness: The Effects of Aggregate Justice Perceptions on Organizational Outcomes," *Journal of Applied Psychology*, June 2003, pp. 432–443; and G. P. Latham and C. C. Pinder, "Work Motivation Theory and Research at the Dawn of the Twenty-First Century," *Annual Review of Psychology* 56, 2005, pp. 485–516.

74 O. Janssen, C. K. Lam, and X. Huang, "Emotional Exhaustion and Job Performance: The Moderating Roles of Distributive Justice and Positive Affect," *Journal of Organizational Behavior* 31, no. 6 (2010), pp. 787–809.

75 K. Leung, K. Tong, and S. S. Ho, "Effects of Interactional Justice on Egocentric Bias in Resource Allocation Decisions," *Journal of Applied Psychology* 89, no. 3 (2004), pp. 405–415.

76 "Americans Feel They Pay Fair Share of Taxes, Says Poll," *NaturalNews.com*, May 2, 2005, http://www.naturalnews.com/007297.html

77 R. E. Johnson, C.-H. Chang, and C. Rosen, "'Who I Am Depends on How Fairly I'm Treated': Effects of Justice on Self-Identity and Regulatory Focus," *Journal of Applied Social Psychology* 40, no. 12 (2010), pp. 3020–3058.

78 G. S. Leventhal, "What Should Be Done with Equity Theory? New Approaches to the Study of Fairness in Social Relationships," in *Social Exchange: Advances in Theory and Research*, ed. K. Gergen, M. Greenberg, and R. Willis (New York: Plenum, 1980), pp. 27–55.

79 D. P. Skarlicki and R. Folger, "Retaliation in the Workplace: The Roles of Distributive, Procedural, and Interactional Justice," *Journal of Applied Psychology* 82, no. 3 (1997), pp. 434–443.

80 R. Cropanzano, C. A. Prehar, and P. Y. Chen, "Using Social Exchange Theory to Distinguish Procedural from Interactional Justice," *Group & Organization Management* 27, no. 3 (2002), pp. 324–351; and S. G. Roch and L. R. Shanock, "Organizational Justice in an Exchange Framework: Clarifying Organizational Justice Dimensions," *Journal of Management*, April 2006, pp. 299–322.

81 J. A. Colquitt, D. E. Conlon, M. J. Wesson, C. O. L. H. Porter, and K. Y. Ng, "Justice at the Millennium: A Meta-Analytic Review of the 25 Years of Organizational Justice Research," *Journal of Applied Psychology*, June 2001, pp. 425–445.

82 D. P. Skarlicki and R. Folger, "Retaliation in the Workplace: The Roles of Distributive, Procedural and Interactional Justice," *Journal of Applied Psychology* 82, no. 3 (1997), pp. 434–443.

83 E. Deci and R. Ryan, eds., *Handbook of Self-Determination Research* (Rochester, NY: University of Rochester Press, 2002); R. Ryan and E. Deci, "Self-Determination Theory and the Facilitation of Intrinsic Motivation, Social Development, and Well-Being," *American Psychologist* 55, no. 1 (2000), pp. 68–78; and M. Gagné and E. L. Deci, "Self-Determination Theory and Work Motivation," *Journal of Organizational Behavior* 26, no. 4 (2005), pp. 331–362.

84 E. L. Deci, R. Koestner, and R. M. Ryan, "A Meta-analytic Review of Experiments Examining the Effects of Extrinsic Rewards on Intrinsic Motivation," *Psychological Bulletin* 125, no. 6 (1999), pp. 627–668; N. Houlfort, R. Koestner, M. Joussemet, A. Nantel-Vivier, and N. Lekes, "The Impact of Performance-Contingent Rewards on Perceived Autonomy and Competence," *Motivation & Emotion* 26, no. 4 (2002), pp. 279–295; G. J. Greguras and J. M. Diefendorff, "Different Fits Satisfy Different Needs: Linking Person-Environment Fit to Employee Commitment and Performance Using Self-Determination Theory," *Journal of Applied Psychology* 94, no. 2 (2009), pp. 465–477; and M. P. Moreno-Jiménez and M. C. H. Villodres, "Prediction of Burnout in Volunteers," *Journal of Applied Social Psychology* 40, no. 7 (2010), pp. 1798–1818. This work studies the personal experience of volunteering and several antecedent and consequent variables. We studied the effect of the amount of time dedicated to the organization, motivation, social support, integration in the organization, self-efficacy, and characteristics of the work on a consequent variable of the volunteering experience; that is, burnout, with its 3 components of efficacy, cynicism, and exhaustion. The statistical analysis shows that the time dedicated to volunteering and the extrinsic motivations (i.e., social and career) predicts higher levels of burnout, whereas intrinsic motivations (i.e., values and understanding), life satisfaction, and integration in the organization are negatively related to burnout.

85 R. Eisenberger and L. Rhoades, "Incremental Effects of Reward on Creativity," *Journal of Personality and Social Psychology* 81, no. 4 (2001), pp. 728–741; and R. Eisenberger, W. D. Pierce, and J. Cameron, "Effects of Reward on Intrinsic Motivation—Negative, Neutral, and Positive: Comment on Deci, Koestner, and Ryan (1999)," *Psychological Bulletin* 125, no. 6 (1999), pp. 677–691.

86 M. Burgess, M. E. Enzle, and R. Schmaltz, "Defeating the Potentially Deleterious Effects of Externally Imposed Deadlines: Practitioners' Rules-of-Thumb," *Personality and Social Psychology Bulletin* 30, no. 7 (2004), pp. 868–877.

87 K. M. Sheldon, A. J. Elliot, and R. M. Ryan, "Self-Concordance and Subjective Well-Being in Four Cultures," *Journal of Cross-Cultural Psychology* 35, no. 2 (2004), pp. 209–223.

88 K. M. Sheldon, A. J. Elliot, and R. M. Ryan, "Self-Concordance and Subjective Well-Being in Four Cultures," *Journal of Cross-Cultural Psychology* 35, no. 2 (2004), pp. 209–223.

89 J. E. Bono and T. A. Judge, "Self-Concordance at Work: Toward Understanding the Motivational Effects of Transformational Leaders," *Academy of Management Journal* 46, no. 5 (2003), pp. 554–571.

90 B. J. Calder and B. M. Staw, "Self-Perception of Intrinsic and Extrinsic Motivation," *Journal of Personality and Social Psychology*, April 1975, pp. 599–605; and J. Pfeffer, *The Human Equation: Building Profits by Putting People First* (Boston: Harvard Business School Press, 1998), p. 217.

91 B. M. Staw, "Motivation in Organizations: Toward Synthesis and Redirection," in *New Directions in Organizational Behavior*, ed. B. M. Staw and G. R. Salancik (Chicago: St. Clair, 1977), p. 76.

92 K. W. Thomas, E. Jansen, and W. G. Tymon Jr., "Navigating in the Realm of Theory: An Empowering View of Construct Development," in *Research in Organizational Change and Development*, vol. 10, ed. W. A. Pasmore and R. W. Woodman (Greenwich, CT: JAI Press, 1997), pp. 1–30.

93 Vignette based on "I Need to Do Double Quad, Says Plushenko," *Reuters*, February 20, 2010, http://www.reuters.com/article/2010/02/20/olympics-figureskating-plushenko-idUSLDE61J0FH20100220; and P. J. Kwong, "With Lessons Learned, Chan Ready to Defend His Title," *cbcsports.ca*, July 11, 2011, http://www.cbc.ca/sports/blogs/pjkwong/2011/07/with-lessons-learned-chan-ready-to-defend-his-title.html

94 R. Kreitner and A. Kinicki, *Organizational Behavior*, 6th ed. (New York: McGraw-Hill, 2004), p. 345. See also J. W. Donahoe, "The Unconventional Wisdom of B. F. Skinner: The Analysis-Interpretation Distinction," *Journal of the Experimental Analysis of Behavior*, September 1993, pp. 453–456.

95 B. F. Skinner, *Contingencies of Reinforcement* (East Norwalk, CT: Appleton-Century-Crofts, 1971).

96 F. Luthans and R. Kreitner, *Organizational Behavior Modification and Beyond*, 2nd ed. (Glenview, IL: Scott, Foresman, 1985); and A. D. Stajkovic and F. Luthans, "A Meta-analysis of the Effects of Organizational Behavior Modification on Task Performance, 1975–95," *Academy of Management Journal*, October 1997, pp. 1122–1149.

97 This section based on C. Michaelson, "Meaningful Motivation for Work Motivation Theory," *Academy of Management Review* 30, no. 2 (2005), pp. 235–238; and R. M. Steers, R. T. Mowday, and D. L. Shapiro, "Response to Meaningful Motivation for Work Motivation Theory," *Academy of Management Review* 30, no. 2 (2005), p. 238.

98 C. Michaelson, "Meaningful Motivation for Work Motivation Theory," *Academy of Management Review* 30, no. 2 (2005), p. 237.

99 N. J. Adler, *International Dimensions of Organizational Behavior*, 4th ed. (Cincinnati, OH: South-Western Publishing, 2002), p. 174.

100 G. Hofstede, "Motivation, Leadership, and Organization: Do American Theories Apply Abroad?" *Organizational Dynamics*, Summer 1980, p. 55.

101 G. Hofstede, "Motivation, Leadership, and Organization: Do American Theories Apply Abroad?" *Organizational Dynamics*, Summer 1980, p. 55.

102 D. F. Crown, "The Use of Group and Groupcentric Individual Goals for Culturally Heterogeneous and Homogeneous Task Groups: An Assessment of European Work Teams," *Small Group Research* 38, no. 4 (2007), pp. 489–508; J. Kurman, "Self-Regulation Strategies in Achievement Settings: Culture and Gender Differences," *Journal of Cross-Cultural Psychology* 32, no. 4 (2001), pp. 491–503; and M. Erez and P. C. Earley, "Comparative Analysis of Goal-Setting Strategies across Cultures," *Journal of Applied Psychology* 72, no. 4 (1987), pp. 658–665.

103 C. Sue-Chan and M. Ong, "Goal Assignment and Performance: Assessing the Mediating Roles of Goal Commitment and Self-Efficacy and the Moderating Role of Power Distance," *Organizational Behavior and Human Decision Processes* 89, no. 2 (2002), pp. 1140–1161.

104 J. K. Giacobbe-Miller, D. J. Miller, and V. I. Victorov, "A Comparison of Russian and U.S. Pay Allocation Decisions, Distributive Justice Judgments, and Productivity Under Different Payment Conditions," *Personnel Psychology*, Spring 1998, pp. 137–163.

105 S. L. Mueller and L. D. Clarke, "Political-Economic Context and Sensitivity to Equity: Differences between the United States and the Transition Economies of Central and Eastern Europe," *Academy of Management Journal*, June 1998, pp. 319–329.

106 Based on S. E. DeVoe and S. S. Iyengar, "Managers' Theories of Subordinates: A Cross-Cultural Examination of Manager Perceptions of Motivation and Appraisal of Performance," *Organizational Behavior and Human Decision Processes*, January 2004, pp. 47–61.

107 I. Harpaz, "The Importance of Work Goals: An International Perspective," *Journal of International Business Studies*, First Quarter 1990, pp. 75–93.

108 G. E. Popp, H. J. Davis, and T. T. Herbert, "An International Study of Intrinsic Motivation Composition," *Management International Review*, January 1986, pp. 28–35.

109 R. Fischer and P. B. Smith, "Reward Allocation and Culture: A Meta-analysis," *Journal of Cross-Cultural Psychology* 34, no. 3 (2003), pp. 251–268.

110 F. T. Chiang and T. Birtch, "The Transferability of Management Practices: Examining Cross-National Differences in Reward Preferences," *Human Relations* 60, no. 9 (2007), pp. 1293–1330; A. E. Lind, T. R. Tyler, and Y. J. Huo, "Procedural Context and Culture: Variation in the Antecedents of Procedural Justice Judgments," *Journal of Personality and Social Psychology* 73, no. 4 (1997), pp. 767–780; and M. J. Gelfand, M. Erez, and Z. Aycan, "Cross-Cultural Organizational Behavior," *Annual Review of Psychology* 58 (2007), pp. 479–514.

Chapter 14

1 Vignette based on T. W. Martin, "Whole Foods to Sell 31 Stores in FTC Deal," *Wall Street Journal*, March 7, 2009, p. B5; and C. Tobias, "Whole Foods Controversy," *Canadian Business*, May 2, 2011, http://www.canadianbusiness.com/article/11666—whole-foods-controversy

2 D. W. Krueger, "Money, Success, and Success Phobia," in *The Last Taboo: Money as a Symbol and Reality in Psychotherapy and Psychoanalysis*, ed. D. W. Krueger (New York: Brunner/Mazel, 1986), pp. 3–16.

3 J. Nelson, "Payday Woes," *Canadian Business*, April 8, 2011.

4 T. R. Mitchell and A. E. Mickel, "The Meaning of Money: An Individual-Difference Perspective," *Academy of Management*, July 1999, pp. 568–578.

5 T. A. Judge, R. F. Piccolo, J. C. Podsakoff, and B. L. Rich, "The Relationship between Pay Satisfaction and Job Satisfaction," *Journal of Vocational Behavior* 77 (2010), 157–167.

6 R. Fischer and D. Boer, "What Is More Important for National Well-Being: Money or Autonomy? A Meta-analysis of Well-Being, Burnout, and Anxiety across 63 Societies," *Journal of Personality and Social Psychology*, July 2011, pp. 164–184.

7 S. A. Hewlett, L. Sherbin, and K. Sumberg "How Gen Y & Boomers Will Reshape Your Agenda," *Harvard Business Review*, July/August 2009, pp. 71–76.

8 This paragraph is based on T. R. Mitchell and A. E. Mickel, "The Meaning of Money: An Individual-Difference Perspective," *Academy of Management*, July 1999, pp. 568–578. The reader may want to refer to the myriad of references cited in the article.

9 S. A. Hewlett, L. Sherbin, and K. Sumberg "How Gen Y & Boomers Will Reshape Your Agenda," *Harvard Business Review*, July/August 2009, pp. 71–76.

10 Vignette based on M. Kliger and S. Tweraser, "Motivating Front Line Staff for Bottom Line Results," *McKinsey.com*, http:// www.mckinsey.com/practices/retail/knowledge/articles/Motivatingfrontlinestaff.pdf

11 http://www.wholefoodsmarket.com/company/declaration.php

12 http://www.wholefoodsmarket.com/company/declaration.php

13 E. White, "Opportunity Knocks, and It Pays a Lot Better," *Wall Street Journal*, November 13, 2006, p. B3.

14 M. Sabramony, N. Krause, J. Norton, and G. N. Burns, "The Relationship between Human Resource Investments and Organizational Performance: A Firm-Level Examination of Equilibrium Theory," *Journal of Applied Psychology* 93, no. 4 (2008), pp. 778–788.

15 Based on J. R. Schuster and P. K. Zingheim, "The New Variable Pay: Key Design Issues," *Compensation & Benefits Review*, March–April 1993, p. 28; K. S. Abosch, "Variable Pay: Do We Have the Basics in Place?" *Compensation & Benefits Review*, July–August 1998, pp. 12–22; and K. M. Kuhn and M. D. Yockey, "Variable Pay as a Risky Choice: Determinants of the Relative Attractiveness of Incentive Plans," *Organizational Behavior and Human Decision Processes*, March 2003, pp. 323–341.

16 "Canada's General Motors Workers to Get Up to 16 Per Cent of Salary in Bonuses," *Canadian Press*, February 14, 2011.

17 J. Ratner, "Dofasco Boss Took Home Biggest Pay," *National Post*, February 1, 2006, p. WK3.

18 "Canada's General Motors Workers to Get Up to 16 Per Cent of Salary in Bonuses," *Canadian Press*, February 14, 2011.

19 "2010 Global Salary Increase & Variable Pay Budget Trends," http://compforce.typepad.com/compensation_force/2010/02/2010-global-salary-increase-variable-pay-budget-trends.html

20 B. Wysocki, Jr., "Chilling Reality Awaits Even the Employed," *Wall Street Journal*, November 5, 2001, p. A1.

21 O. Bertin, "Is There Any Merit in Giving Merit Pay?" *Globe and Mail*, January 31, 2003, pp. C1, C7.

22 E. Willes "Give Buono Credit for Lions Revival," *Gazette* (Montreal), September 25, 2011.

23 E. Arita, "Teething Troubles Aside, Merit-Based Pay Catching On," *Japan Times*, April 23, 2004, http://search.japantimes.co.jp/cgi-bin/nb20040423a3.html

24 G. D. Jenkins Jr., N. Gupta, A. Mitra, and J. D. Shaw, "Are Financial Incentives Related to Performance? A Meta-analytic Review of Empirical Research," *Journal of Applied Psychology*, October 1998, pp. 777–787; and S. L. Rynes, B. Gerhart, and L. Parks, "Personnel Psychology: Performance Evaluation and Pay for Performance," *Annual Review of Psychology* 56, no. 1 (2005), pp. 571–600.

25 "Many Companies Fail to Achieve Success with Pay-for-Performance Programs," *Hewitt & Associates News and Information*, June 9, 2004; and J. Pfeffer, *What Were They Thinking? Unconventional Wisdom About Management* (Boston: Harvard Business School Press, 2007).

26 E. J. Castilla and S. Benard, "The Paradox of Meritocracy in Organizations," *Administrative Science Quarterly* 55, no. 4 (2010), pp. 543–576.

27 "Bonus Pay in Canada," *Manpower Argus*, September 1996, p. 5; E. White, "Employers Increasingly Favor Bonuses to Raises," *Wall Street Journal*, August 28, 2006, p. B3; and J. S. Lublin, "Boards Tie CEO Pay More Tightly to Performance," *Wall Street Journal*, February 21, 2006, pp. A1, A14.

28 N. Byrnes, "Pain, But No Layoffs at Nucor," *BusinessWeek*, March 26, 2009, http://www.businessweek.com

29 G. E. Ledford Jr., "Paying for the Skills, Knowledge, and Competencies of Knowledge Workers," *Compensation & Benefits Review*, July–August 1995, pp. 55–62; B. Murray and B. Gerhart, "An Empirical Analysis of a Skill-Based Pay Program and Plant

Performance Outcomes," *Academy of Management Journal*, February 1998, pp. 68–78; J. R. Thompson and C. W. LeHew, "Skill-Based Pay as an Organizational Innovation," *Review of Public Personnel Administration*, Winter 2000, pp. 20–40; and J. D. Shaw, N. Gupta, A. Mitra, and G. E. Ledford Jr., "Success and Survival of Skill-Based Pay Plans," *Journal of Management*, February 2005, pp. 28–49.

30 See, for instance, S. C. Hanlon, D. G. Meyer, and R. R. Taylor, "Consequences of Gainsharing," *Group & Organization Management*, March 1994, pp. 87–111; J. G. Belcher Jr., "Gainsharing and Variable Pay: The State of the Art," *Compensation & Benefits Review*, May–June 1994, pp. 50–60; and T. M. Welbourne and L. R. Gomez Mejia, "Gainsharing: A Critical Review and a Future Research Agenda," *Journal of Management* 21, no. 3 (1995), pp. 559–609.

31 Employment Policy Foundation, *U.S. Wage and Productivity Growth Attainable through Gainsharing*, May 10, 2000.

32 T. M. Welbourne and C. J. Ferrante, "To Monitor or Not to Monitor: A Study of Individual Outcomes from Monitoring One's Peers under Gainsharing and Merit Pay," *Group & Organization Management* 33, no. 2 (2008), pp. 139–162.

33 T. M. Welbourne and L. R. Gomez-Mejia, "Gainsharing: A Critical Review and a Future Research Agenda," *Journal of Management* 21, no. 3 (1995), pp. 559–609.

34 B. Jang, "WestJet Charts Bold New Path," *Globe and Mail*, March 27, 2010.

35 M. Gooderham, "A Piece of the Pie as Motivational Tool," *Globe and Mail*, November 20, 2007, p. B8.

36 R. J. Long, "Patterns of Workplace Innovations in Canada," *Relations Industrielles* 44, no. 4 (1989), pp. 805–826; R. J. Long, "Motives for Profit Sharing: A Study of Canadian Chief Executive Officers," *Relations Industrielles* 52, no. 4 (1997), pp. 712–723; and T. H. Wagar and R. J. Long, "Profit Sharing in Canada: Incidences and Predictors," *Proceedings of the Administrative Sciences Association of Canada* (Human Resources Division), 1995, pp. 97–105.

37 N. Chi and T. Han, "Exploring the Linkages between Formal Ownership and Psychological Ownership for the Organization: The Mediating Role of Organizational Justice," *Journal of Occupational and Organizational Psychology* 81, no. 4 (2008), pp. 691–711.

38 See K. M. Young, ed., *The Expanding Role of ESOPs in Public Companies* (New York: Quorum, 1990); J. L. Pierce and C. A. Furo, "Employee Ownership: Implications for Management," *Organizational Dynamics*, Winter 1990, pp. 32–43; J. Blasi and D. L. Druse, *The New Owners: The Mass Emergence of Employee Ownership in Public Companies and What It Means to American Business* (Champaign, IL: Harper Business, 1991); F. T. Adams and G. B. Hansen, *Putting Democracy to Work: A Practical Guide for Starting and Managing Worker-Owned Businesses* (San Francisco: Berrett-Koehler, 1993); and A. A. Buchko, "The Effects of Employee Ownership on Employee Attitudes: An Integrated Causal Model and Path Analysis," *Journal of Management Studies*, July 1993, pp. 633–656.

39 K. Vermond, "Worker as Shareholder: Is It Worth It?" *Globe and Mail*, March 29, 2008, p. B21.

40 A. A. Buchko, "The Effects of Employee Ownership on Employee Attitudes: An Integrated Causal Model and Path Analysis," *Journal of Management Studies*, July 1993, pp. 633–656.

41 K. Vermond, "Worker as Shareholder: Is It Worth It?" *Globe and Mail*, March 29, 2008, p. B21.

42 J. L. Pierce and C. A. Furo, "Employee Ownership: Implications for Management," *Organizational Dynamics*, Winter 1990, pp. 32–43; and S. Kaufman, "ESOPs' Appeal on the Increase," *Nation's Business*, June 1997, p. 43.

43 See data in D. Stamps, "A Piece of the Action," *Training*, March 1996, p. 66.

44 X. Zhang, K. M. Bartol, K. G. Smith, M. D. Pfarrer, and D. M. Khanin, "CEOs on the Edge: Earnings Manipulation and Stock-Based Incentive Misalignment," *Academy of Management Journal* 51, no. 2 (2008), pp. 241–258.

45 C. G. Hanson and W. D. Bell, *Profit Sharing and Profitability: How Profit Sharing Promotes Business Success* (London: Kogan Page, 1987); M. Magnan and S. St-Onge, "Profit Sharing and Firm Performance: A Comparative and Longitudinal Analysis" (paper presented at the 58th annual meeting of the Academy of Management, San Diego, CA, August 1998); and D. D'Art and T. Turner, "Profit Sharing, Firm Performance, and Union Influence in Selected European Countries," *Personnel Review* 33, no. 3 (2004), pp. 335–350.

46 T. M. Welbourne and L. R. Gomez-Mejia, "Gainsharing: A Critical Review and a Future Research Agenda," *Journal of Management* 21, no. 3 (1995), pp. 559–609.

47 E. P. Lazear, "Performance Pay and Productivity," *American Economic Review* 90, no. 5 (December 2000), pp. 1346–1361. See also S. Oah, and J.-H. Lee. "Effects of Hourly, Low-Incentive, and High-Incentive Pay on Simulated Work Productivity: Initial Findings with a New Laboratory Method," *Journal of Organizational Behavior Management* 31, no. 1 (2011), pp. 21–42.

48 C. B. Cadsby, F. Song, and F. Tapon, "Sorting and Incentive Effects of Pay for Performance: An Experimental Investigation," *Academy of Management Journal* 50, no. 2 (2007), pp. 387–405.

49 J. Pfeffer and N. Langton, "The Effects of Wage Dispersion on Satisfaction, Productivity, and Working Collaboratively: Evidence from College and University Faculty," *Administrative Science Quarterly* 38, no. 3 (1983), pp. 382–407.

50 "Risk and Reward: More Canadian Companies Are Experimenting with Variable Pay," *Maclean's*, January 8, 1996, pp. 26–27.

51 "Hope for Higher Pay: The Squeeze on Incomes Is Gradually Easing Up," *Maclean's*, November 25, 1996, pp. 100–101.

52 "Risk and Reward: More Canadian Companies Are Experimenting with Variable Pay," *Maclean's*, January 8, 1996, pp. 26–27.

53 B. E. Wright, "Work Motivation in the Public Sector," *Academy of Management Proceedings*, 2001, pp. PNP: D1–5.

54 B. E. Wright, "Work Motivation in the Public Sector," *Academy of Management Proceedings*, 2001, pp. PNP: D1–5.

55 S. Greenhouse, "Suits Say Wal-Mart Forces Workers to Toil Off the Clock," *New York Times*, June 25, 2002, http://www.nytimes.com/2002/06/25/national/25WALM.html?pagewanted=1

56 See, for instance, M. W. Barringer and G. T. Milkovich, "A Theoretical Exploration of the Adoption and Design of Flexible Benefit Plans: A Case of Human Resource Innovation," *Academy of Management Review*, April 1998, pp. 305–324; D. Brown, "Everybody Loves Flex," *Canadian HR Reporter*, November 18, 2002, p. 1; J. Taggart, "Putting Flex Benefits through Their Paces," *Canadian HR Reporter*, December 2, 2002, p. G3; and N. D. Cole and D. H. Flint, "Perceptions of Distributive and Procedural Justice in Employee Benefits: Flexible versus Traditional Benefit Plans," *Journal of Managerial Psychology* 19, no. 1 (2004), pp. 19–40.

57 D. A. DeCenzo and S. P. Robbins, *Human Resource Management*, 7th ed. (New York: Wiley, 2002), pp. 346–348.

58 Cited in S. Caudron, "The Top 20 Ways to Motivate Employees," *IndustryWeek*, April 3, 1995, pp. 15–16. See also B. Nelson, "Try Praise," *Inc.*, September 1996, p. 115.

59 Our definition of a formal recognition system is based on S. E. Markham, K. D. Scott, and G. H. McKee, "Recognizing Good Attendance: A Longitudinal, Quasi-Experimental Field Study," *Personnel Psychology*, Autumn 2002, p. 641.

60 S. J. Peterson and F. Luthans, "The Impact of Financial and Nonfinancial Incentives on Business Unit Outcomes over Time," *Journal of Applied Psychology* 91, no. 1 (2006), pp. 156–165.

61 "Building a Better Workforce," *PROFIT*, February 16, 2011, http://www.profitguide.com/article/10084--building-a-better-workforce--page0; and http://www.rlsolutions.com/Careers/Benefits.aspx

62 B. Scudamore, "Pump up Employee Passion," *PROFIT*, October 13, 2010, http://www.profitguide.com/article/6574--pump-up-employee-passion

63 Hewitt Associates, "Employers Willing to Pay for High Performance," news release, September 8, 2004, http://was4.hewitt.com/hewitt/resource/newsroom/pressrel/2004/09-08-04eng.htm

64 S. Kerr, "On the Folly of Rewarding A, While Hoping for B," *Academy of Management Executive* 9, no. 1 (1995), pp. 7–14.

65 "More on the Folly," *Academy of Management Executive* 9, no. 1 (1995), pp. 15–16.

66 M. Parker, "Strategies for Creating a Culture of Innovation," *Canadian Business Online*, August 29, 2007.

67 A. Kohn, *Punished by Rewards* (Boston: Houghton Mifflin, 1999), p. 181.

68 A. Kohn, *Punished by Rewards* (Boston: Houghton Mifflin, 1993), p. 186. See also Peter R. Scholtes, "An Elaboration of Deming's Teachings on Performance Appraisal," in *Performance Appraisal: Perspectives on a Quality Management Approach*, ed. Gary N. McLean, Susan R. Damme, and Richard A. Swanson (Alexandria, VA: American Society for Training and Development, 1990); H. H. Meyer, E. Kay, and J. R. P. French Jr., "Split Roles in Performance Appraisal," *Harvard Business Review*, 1965, excerpts reprinted in "HBR Retrospect," *Harvard Business Review*, January–February 1989, p. 26; W.-U. Meyer, M. Bachmann, U. Biermann, M. Hempelmann, F.-O. Ploeger, and H. Spiller, "The Informational Value of Evaluative Behavior: Influences of Praise and Blame on Perceptions of Ability," *Journal of Educational Psychology* 71, 1979, pp. 259–268; and A. Halachmi and M. Holzer, "Merit Pay, Performance Targetting, and Productivity," *Review of Public Personnel Administration* 7 (1987), pp. 80–91.

69 A. S. Blinder, "Introduction," in *Paying for Productivity: A Look at the Evidence*, ed. A. S. Blinder (Washington, DC: Brookings Institution, 1990).

70 A. Kohn, *Punished by Rewards* (Boston: Houghton Mifflin, 1999), p. 187.

71 D. Tjosvold, *Working Together to Get Things Done: Managing for Organizational Productivity* (Lexington, MA: Lexington Books, 1986); P. R. Scholtes, *The Team Handbook: How to Use Teams to Improve Quality* (Madison, WI: Joiner Associates, 1988); and A. Kohn, *No Contest: The Case Against Competition*, rev. ed. (Boston: Houghton Mifflin, 1992).

72 E. L. Deci, "Applications of Research on the Effects of Rewards," in *The Hidden Costs of Rewards: New Perspectives on the Psychology of Human Motivation*, ed. M. R. Lepper and D. Green (Hillsdale, NJ: Erlbaum, 1978).

73 S. E. Perry, *San Francisco Scavengers: Dirty Work and the Pride of Ownership* (Berkeley: University of California Press, 1978).

74 A. Kohn, *Punished by Rewards* (Boston: Houghton Mifflin, 1999), p. 192.

75 T. H. Naylor, "Redefining Corporate Motivation, Swedish Style," *Christian Century*, May 30–June 6, 1990, pp. 566–570; R. A. Karasek, T. Thorell, J. E. Schwartz, P. L. Schnall, C. F. Pieper, and J. L. Michela, "Job Characteristics in Relation to the Prevalence of Myocardial Infarction in the US Health Examination Survey (HES) and the Health and Nutrition Examination Survey (HANES)," *American Journal of Public Health* 78 (1988), pp. 910–916; and D. P. Levin, "Toyota Plant in Kentucky Is Font of Ideas for the U.S.," *New York Times*, May 5, 1992, pp. A1, D8.

76 M. Bosquet, "The Prison Factory," reprinted from *Le Nouvel Observateur* in *Working Papers for a New Society*, Spring 1973, pp. 20–27; J. Holusha, "Grace Pastiak's 'Web of Inclusion,'" *New York Times*, May 5, 1991, pp. F1, F6; J. Simmons and W. Mares, *Working Together: Employee Participation in Action* (New York: New York University Press, 1985); D. I. Levine and L. D'Andrea Tyson, "Participation, Productivity, and the Firm's Environment," in *Paying for Productivity: A Look at the Evidence*, ed. A. S. Blinder (Washington, DC: Brookings Institution, 1990); and W. F. Whyte, "Worker Participation: International and Historical Perspectives," *Journal of Applied Behavioral Science* 19, 1983, pp. 395–407.

77 J. R. Hackman and G. R. Oldham, "Motivation through the Design of Work: Test of a Theory," *Organizational Behavior and Human Performance*, August 1976, pp. 250–279.

78 J. R. Hackman, "Work Design," in *Improving Life at Work*, ed. J. R. Hackman and J. L. Suttle (Santa Monica, CA: Goodyear, 1977), p. 129.

79 D. A. Light, "Human Resources: Recruiting Generation 2001," *Harvard Business Review*, July–August 1998, pp. 13–16.

80 See "Job Characteristics Theory of Work Redesign," in *Theories of Organizational Behavior*, ed. J. B. Miner (Hinsdale, IL: Dryden Press, 1980), pp. 231–266; B. T. Loher, R. A. Noe, N. L. Moeller, and M. P. Fitzgerald, "A Meta-analysis of the Relation of Job Characteristics to Job Satisfaction," *Journal of Applied Psychology*, May 1985, pp. 280–289; S. J. Behson, E. R. Eddy, and S. J. Lorenzet, "The Importance of the Critical Psychological States in the Job Characteristics Model: A Meta-analytic and Structural Equations Modeling Examination," *Current Research in Social Psychology*, May 2000, pp. 170–189; T. A. Judge, "Promote Job Satisfaction through Mental Challenge," in *Handbook of Principles of Organizational Behavior*, ed. E. A. Locke, pp. 75–89 (Hoboken, NJ: Wiley-Blackwell, 2003); S. E. Humphrey, J. D. Nahrgang, and F. P. Morgeson, "Integrating Motivational, Social, and Contextual Work Design Features: A Meta-analytic Summary and Theoretical Extension of the Work Design Literature," *Journal of Applied Psychology* 92, no. 5 (2007), pp. 1332–1356; R. F. Piccolo, R. Greenbaum, D. N. D. Hartog, and R. Folger, "The Relationship between Ethical Leadership and Core Job Characteristics," *Journal of Organizational Behavior* 31, no. 2/3 (2010), pp. 259–278; D. J. Holman, C. M. Axtell, C. A. Sprigg, P. Totterdell, and T. D. Wall, "The Mediating Role of Job Characteristics in Job Redesign Interventions: A Serendipitous Quasi-Experiment," *Journal of Organizational Behavior* 31, no. 1 (2010), pp. 84–105; and M. Gagné and D. Bhave, "Autonomy in the Workplace: An Essential Ingredient to Employee Engagement and Well-Being in Every Culture?" in *Human Autonomy in Cross-Cultural Context: Perspectives on the Psychology of Agency, Freedom, and Well-Being*, ed. V. I. Chirkov, R. M. Ryan, and K. M. Sheldon (Berlin, Germany: Springer, 2011).

81 T. A. Judge, S. K. Parker, A. E. Colbert, D. Heller, and R. Ilies, "Job Satisfaction: A Cross-Cultural Review," in *Handbook of Industrial, Work and Organizational Psychology*, vol. 2, ed. N. Anderson and D. S. Ones (Thousand Oaks, CA: Sage Publications, 2002), pp. 25–52.

82 See, for example, J. R. Hackman and G. R. Oldham, *Work Redesign* (Reading, MA: Addison Wesley, 1980); J. B. Miner, *Theories of Organizational Behavior* (Hinsdale, IL: Dryden Press, 1980), pp. 231–266; R. W. Griffin, "Effects of Work Redesign on Employee Perceptions, Attitudes, and Behaviors: A Long-Term Investigation," *Academy of Management Journal*, June 1991, pp. 425–435; and G. Johns, "Some Unintended Consequences of Job Design," *Journal of Organizational Behavior* 31, no. 2/3 (2010), pp. 361–369.

83 J. R. Hackman, "Work Design," in *Improving Life at Work*, ed. J. R. Hackman and J. L. Suttle (Santa Monica, CA: Goodyear, 1977), p. 129.

84 J. P. Wanous, "Individual Differences and Reactions to Job Characteristics," *Journal of Applied Psychology*, October 1974, pp. 616–622; and H. P. Sims and A. D. Szilagyi, "Job Characteristic Relationships: Individual and Structural Moderators," *Organizational Behavior and Human Performance*, June 1976, pp. 211–230.

85 F. Pomeroy, "Workplace Change: A Union Perspective," *Canadian Business Review* 22, no. 2 (1995), pp. 17–19.

86 J. E. Rigdon, "Using Lateral Moves to Spur Employees," *Wall Street Journal*, May 26, 1992, p. B1.

87 N. Leckie, A. Léonard, J. Turcotte, and D. Wallace, *Employer and Employee Perspectives on Human Resource Practices*, Report 71-584-MIE no. 1 (Ottawa: Ministry of Industry, 2001).

88 J. Ortega, "Job Rotation as a Learning Mechanism," *Management Science*, October 2001, pp. 1361–1370.

89 J. R. Hackman and G. R. Oldham, *Work Redesign* (Reading, MA: Addison-Wesley, 1980).

90 A. M. Grant, E. M. Campbell, G. Chen, K. Cottone, D. Lapedis, and K. Lee, "Impact and the Art of Motivation Maintenance: The Effects of Contact with Beneficiaries on Persistence Behavior," *Organizational Behavior and Human Decision Processes* 103 (2007), pp. 53–67.

91 A. M. Grant, J. E. Dutton, and B. D. Rosso, "Giving Commitment: Employee Support Programs and the Prosocial Sensemaking Process," *Academy of Management Journal* 51, no. 5 (2008), pp. 898–918.

92 See, for example, J. R. Hackman and G. R. Oldham, *Work Redesign* (Reading, MA: Addison-Wesley, 1980); J. B. Miner, *Theories of Organizational Behavior* (Hinsdale, IL: Dryden Press, 1980), pp. 231–266; R. W. Griffin, "Effects of Work Redesign on Employee Perceptions, Attitudes, and Behaviors: A Long-Term Investigation," *Academy of Management Journal* 34, no. 2 (1991), pp. 425–435; and J. L. Cotton, *Employee Involvement* (Newbury Park, CA: Sage, 1993), pp. 141–172.

93 R. D. Pritchard, M. M. Harrell, D. DiazGrandos, and M. J. Guzman, "The Productivity Measurement and Enhancement System: A Meta-analysis," *Journal of Applied Psychology* 93, no. 3 (2008), pp. 540–567.

94 F. P. Morgeson, M. D. Johnson, M. A. Campion, G. J. Medsker, and T. V. Mumford, "Understanding Reactions to Job Redesign: A Quasi-Experimental Investigation of the Moderating Effects of Organizational Contact on Perceptions of Performance Behavior," *Personnel Psychology* 39 (2006), pp. 333–363.

95 F. W. Bond, P. E. Flaxman, and D. Bunce, "The Influence of Psychological Flexibility on Work Redesign: Mediated Moderation of a Work Reorganization Intervention," *Journal of Applied Psychology* 93, no. 3 (2008), pp. 645–654.

96 Statistics Canada, "Part-Time Work and Family-Friendly Practices," *The Daily*, June 26, 2003.

97 L. Rubis, "Fourth of Full-Timers Enjoy Flexible Hours," *HR Magazine*, June 1998, pp. 26–28.

98 See, for example, D. A. Ralston and M. F. Flanagan, "The Effect of Flextime on Absenteeism and Turnover for Male and Female Employees," *Journal of Vocational Behavior*, April 1985, pp. 206–217; D. A. Ralston, W. P. Anthony, and D. J. Gustafson, "Employees May Love Flextime, but What Does It Do to the Organization's Productivity?" *Journal of Applied Psychology*, May 1985, pp. 272–279; D. R. Dalton and D. J. Mesch, "The Impact of Flexible Scheduling on Employee Attendance and Turnover," *Administrative Science Quarterly*, June 1990, pp. 370–387; B. B. Baltes, T. E. Briggs, J. W. Huff, J. A. Wright, and G. A. Neuman, "Flexible and Compressed Workweek Schedules: A Meta-analysis of Their Effects on Work-Related Criteria," *Journal of Applied Psychology* 84, no. 4 (1999), pp. 496–513; K. M. Shockley and T. D. Allen, "When Flexibility Helps: Another Look at the Availability of Flexible Work Arrangements and Work-Family Conflict," *Journal of Vocational Behavior* 71, no. 3 (2007), pp. 479–493; and J. G. Grzywacz, D. S. Carlson, and S. Shulkin, "Schedule Flexibility and Stress: Linking Formal Flexible Arrangements and Perceived Flexibility to Employee Health," *Community, Work, and Family* 11, no. 2 (2008), pp. 199–214.

99 D. Keevil, *The Flexible Workplace Study: Asking the Experts About Flexible Policies and Workplace Performance* (Halifax: Halifax YWCA in cooperation with Status of Women Canada, 1996).

100 L. Duxbury and G. Haines, "Predicting Alternative Work Arrangements from Salient Attitudes: A Study of Decision Makers in the Public Sector," *Journal of Business Research*, August 1991, pp. 83–97.

101 J. E. Fast and J. A. Frederick, "Working Arrangements and Time Stress," *Canadian Social Trends*, Winter 1996, pp. 14–19.

102 A. Sisco and R. Nelson, *From Vision to Venture: An Account of Five Successful Aboriginal Businesses* (Ottawa: The Conference Board of Canada, 2008).

103 S. Schieman and M. Young, "Is There a Downside to Schedule Control for the Work-Family Interface?" *Journal of Family Issues* 31, no. 10 (2010), pp. 1391–1414.

104 T. Grant, "Job Sharing," *Globe and Mail*, May 16, 2009, p. B14.

105 Society for Human Resource Management, *2008 Employee Benefits* (Alexandria, VA: Author, 2008).

106 S. Shellenbarger, "Two People, One Job: It Can Really Work," *Wall Street Journal*, December 7, 1994, p. B1.

107 T. Grant, "Job Sharing," *Globe and Mail*, May 16, 2009, p. B1.

108 C. Dawson, "Japan: Work-Sharing Will Prolong the Pain," *BusinessWeek*, December 24, 2001, p. 46.

109 Government of Canada, *The Next Phase of Canada's Economic Action Plan: A Low-Tax Plan for Jobs and Growth, Chapter 3: Canada's Economic Action Plan*. Tabled in the House of Commons by the Honourable James M. Flaherty, PC, MP, Minister of Finance, June 6, 2011, http://www.budget.gc.ca/2011/plan/chap3-eng.html; and S. Chase and O. Moore, "Canadian Workers Cozy Up to Job-Sharing," September 29, 2009, http://www.theglobeandmail.com/news/politics/canadian-workers-cozy-up-to-job-sharing/article1304955/

110 T. Grant, "Job Sharing," *Globe and Mail*, May 16, 2009, p. B1.

111 D. Hodges, "New Nunavut: Canada's Newest Territory Faces the Daunting Task of Creating a New Health Bureaucracy While Dealing with Traditional Recruitment Problems in the Arctic," *Medical Post*, November 13, 2001, p. 31.

112 See, for example, K. E. Pearlson and C. S. Saunders, "There's No Place Like Home: Managing Telecommuting Paradoxes," *Academy of Management Executive*, May 2001, pp. 117–128; S. J. Wells, "Making Telecommuting Work," *HR Magazine*, October 2001, pp. 34–45; E. J. Hill, M. Ferris, and V. Martinson, "Does It Matter Where You Work? A Comparison of How Three Work Venues (Traditional Office, Virtual Office, and Home Office) Influence Aspects of Work and Personal/Family Life," *Journal of Vocational Behavior* 63, no. 2 (2003), pp. 220–241; Anonymous, "Labour Movement," *The Economist*, April 12, 2008, p. 5; and J. Berkow, "Telework: The New Labour Force Norm," *Postmedia News*, July 7, 2011.

113 D. Bradbury, "Nothing to Fear from Teleworking," *Financial Post*, March 16, 2010, http://www.financialpost.com/story.html?id=2689687; V. Galt, "Telecommute—and Save the Environment," *Globe and Mail*, April 27, 2007, http://www.ivc.ca/media/articles/savetheenvironment.html

114 J. Berkow, "Telework: The New Labour Force Norm," *Postmedia News*, July 7, 2011.

115 "Canadian Studies on Telework," *InnoVisions Canada*, http://www.ivc.ca/studies/canada/

116 J. Berkow, "Telework: The New Labour Force Norm," *Postmedia News*, July 7, 2011.

117 J. Budak, "Work-Life: Better Working through Living," *Canadian Business*, April 5, 2011.

118 Cited in R. W. Judy and C. D'Amico, *Workforce 2020* (Indianapolis, IL: Hudson Institute, 1997), p. 58.

119 P. Lima, "The Next Best Thing to Being There," *Globe and Mail*, April 26, 2006, p. 31.

120 L. Arnold, "Geographical, Organisational and Social Implications of Teleworking—Emphasis on the Social Perspectives" (paper presented at the 29th Annual Meeting of the Canadian Sociological and Anthropological Association, Calgary, June 1994); K. S. Devine, L. Taylor, and K. Haryett, "The Impact of Teleworking on Canadian Employment," in *Good Jobs, Bad Jobs, No Jobs: The Uncertain Future of Employment* in Canada, ed. A. Duffy, D. Glenday, and N. Pupo (Toronto: Harcourt Brace, 1997); C. A. Hamilton, "Telecommuting," *Personnel Journal*, April 1987, pp. 91–101; and I. U. Zeytinoglu, "Employment Conditions in Telework: An Experiment in Ontario," *Proceedings of the 30th Conference of the Canadian Industrial Relations Association*, 1992, pp. 281–293.

121 L. Arnold, "Geographical, Organisational and Social Implications of Teleworking—Emphasis on the Social Perspectives" (paper presented at the 29th Annual Meeting of the Canadian Sociological and Anthropological Association, Calgary, June 1994).

122 I. U. Zeytinoglu, "Employment Conditions in Telework: An Experiment in Ontario," *Proceedings of the 30th Conference of the Canadian Industrial Relations Association*, 1992, pp. 281–293; and K. S. Devine, L. Taylor, and K. Haryett, "The Impact of Teleworking on Canadian Employment," in *Good Jobs, Bad Jobs, No Jobs: The Uncertain Future of Employment in Canada*, ed. A. Duffy, D. Glenday, and N. Pupo (Toronto: Harcourt Brace, 1997).

123 I. U. Zeytinoglu, "Employment Conditions in Telework: An Experiment in Ontario," *Proceedings of the 30th Conference of the Canadian Industrial Relations Association*, 1992, pp. 281–293.

124 K. S. Devine, L. Taylor, and K. Haryett, "The Impact of Teleworking on Canadian Employment," in *Good Jobs, Bad Jobs, No Jobs: The Uncertain Future of Employment in Canada*, ed. A. Duffy, D. Glenday, and N. Pupo (Toronto: Harcourt Brace, 1997); and C. A. Hamilton, "Telecommuting," *Personnel Journal*, April 1987, pp. 91–101.

125 E. E. Kossek, B. A. Lautsch, and S. C. Eaton, "Telecommuting, Control, and Boundary Management: Correlates of Policy Use and Practice, Job Control, and Work-Family Effectiveness," *Journal of Vocational Behavior* 68, no. 2 (2006), pp. 347–367; and K. L. Fonner and M. E. Roloff, "Why Teleworkers Are More Satisfied with Their Jobs than Are Office-Based Workers: When Less Contact Is Beneficial," *Journal of Applied Communication Research* 38, no. 4 (2010), pp. 336–361.

126 J. M. Stanton and J. L. Barnes-Farrell, "Effects of Electronic Performance Monitoring on Personal Control, Task Satisfaction, and Task Performance," *Journal of Applied Psychology*, December 1996, pp. 738–745; B. Pappas, "They Spy," *Forbes*, February 8, 1999, p. 47; S. Armour, "More Bosses Keep Tabs on Telecommuters," *USA Today*, July 24, 2001, p. 1B; and D. Buss, "Spies Like Us," *Training*, December 2001, pp. 44–48.

127 J. Welch and S. Welch, "The Importance of Being There," *BusinessWeek*, April 16, 2007, p. 92; Z. I. Barsness, K. A. Diekmann, and M. L. Seidel, "Motivation and Opportunity: The Role of Remote Work, Demographic Dissimilarity, and Social Network Centrality in Impression Management," *Academy of Management Journal* 48, no. 3 (2005), pp. 401–419.

128 P. Glavin, S. Schieman, and S. Reid, "Boundary-Spanning Work Demands and Their Consequences for Guilt and Psychological Distress," *Journal of Health and Social Behavior* 52, no. 1 (2011), pp. 43–57.

129 F. P. Morgeson and S. E. Humphrey, "The Work Design Questionnaire (WDQ): Developing and Validating a Comprehensive Measure for Assessing Job Design and the Nature of Work," *Journal of Applied Psychology* 91, no. 6 (2006), pp. 1321–1339; S. E. Humphrey, J. D. Nahrgang, and F. P. Morgeson, "Integrating Motivational, Social, and Contextual Work Design Features: A Meta-analytic Summary and Theoretical Extension of the Work Design Literature," *Journal of Applied Psychology* 92, no. 5 (2007), pp. 1332–1356; and R. Takeuchi, D. P. Lepak, H. Wang, and K. Takeuchi, "An Empirical Examination of the Mechanisms Mediating Between High-Performance Work Systems and the Performance of Japanese Organizations," *Journal of Applied Psychology* 92, no. 4 (2007), pp. 1069–1083.

130 Vignette based on M. Kliger and S. Tweraser, "Motivating Front Line Staff for Bottom Line Results," *McKinsey.com*, http://www.mckinsey.com/practices/retail/knowledge/articles/Motivatingfrontlinestaff.pdf

131 See, for example, the increasing body of literature on empowerment, such as W. A. Randolph, "Re-Thinking Empowerment: Why Is It So Hard to Achieve?" *Organizational Dynamics* 29, no. 2 (2000), pp. 94–107; K. Blanchard, J. P. Carlos, and W. A. Randolph, *Empowerment Takes More Than a Minute*, 2nd ed. (San Francisco: Berrett-Koehler, 2001); D. P. Ashmos, D. Duchon, R. R. McDaniel Jr., and J. W. Huonker, "What a Mess! Participation as a Simple Managerial Rule to 'Complexify' Organizations," *Journal of Management Studies*, March 2002, pp. 189–206; and S. E. Seibert, S. R. Silver, and W. A. Randolph, "Taking Empowerment to the Next Level: A Multiple-Level Model of Empowerment, Performance, and Satisfaction," *Academy of Management Journal* 47, no. 3 (2004), pp. 332–349.

132 F. Heller, E. Pusic, G. Strauss, and B. Wilpert, *Organizational Participation: Myth and Reality* (Oxford, UK: Oxford University Press, 1998).

133 See, for instance, K. L. Miller and P. R. Monge, "Participation, Satisfaction, and Productivity: A Meta-analytic Review," *Academy of Management Journal*, December 1986, pp. 727–753; J. A. Wagner III, "Participation's Effects on Performance and Satisfaction: A Reconsideration of Research Evidence," *Academy of Management Review*, April 1994, pp. 312–330; C. Doucouliagos, "Worker Participation and Productivity in Labor-Managed and Participatory Capitalist Firms: A Meta-analysis," *Industrial and Labor Relations Review*, October 1995, pp. 58–77; J. A. Wagner III, C. R. Leana, E. A. Locke, and D. M. Schweiger, "Cognitive and Motivational Frameworks in U.S. Research on Participation: A Meta-analysis of Primary Effects," *Journal of Organizational Behavior* 18 (1997), pp. 49–65; E. A. Locke, M. Alavi, and J. A. Wagner III, "Participation in Decision Making: An Information Exchange Perspective," in *Research in Personnel and Human Resource Management*, vol. 15, ed. G. R. Ferris (Greenwich, CT: JAI Press, 1997), pp. 293–331; and J. A. Wagner III and J. A. LePine, "Effects of Participation on Performance and Satisfaction: Additional Meta-analytic Evidence," *Psychological Reports*, June 1999, pp. 719–725.

134 D. K. Datta, J. P. Guthrie, and P. M. Wright, "Human Resource Management and Labor Productivity: Does Industry Matter?" *Academy of Management Journal* 48, no. 1 (2005), pp. 135–145; C. M. Riordan, R. J. Vandenberg, and H. A. Richardson, "Employee Involvement Climate and Organizational

Effectiveness" *Human Resource Management* 44, no. 4 (2005), pp. 471–488.

135 J. L. Cotton, *Employee Involvement* (Newbury Park, CA: Sage, 1993), pp. 141–172.

136 See, for example, M. Gilman and P. Marginson, "Negotiating European Works Council: Contours of Constrained Choice," *Industrial Relations Journal*, March 2002, pp. 36–51; J. T. Addison and C. R. Belfield, "What Do We Know About the New European Works Council? Some Preliminary Evidence from Britain," *Scottish Journal of Political Economy*, September 2002, pp. 418–444; and B. Keller, "The European Company Statute: Employee Involvement—and Beyond," *Industrial Relations Journal*, December 2002, pp. 424–445.

137 J. L. Cotton, *Employee Involvement* (Newbury Park, CA: Sage, 1993), pp. 141–172.

138 J. L. Cotton, *Employee Involvement* (Newbury Park, CA: Sage, 1993), pp. 141–172.

139 N. Nohria, B. Groysberg, and L.-E. Lee, "Employee Motivation: A Powerful New Model," *Harvard Business Review* 86, no. 7–8 (July–August 2008), pp. 78–84.

140 P. R. Lawrence and N. Nohria, *Driven: How Human Nature Shapes Our Choices* (San Francisco: Jossey-Bass, 2002).

141 S. C. L. Fong and M. A. Shaffer, "The Dimensionality and Determinants of Pay Satisfaction: A Cross-Cultural Investigation of a Group Incentive Plan," *International Journal of Human Resource Management*, June 2003, pp. 559–580.

142 D. Brown, "Everybody Loves Flex," *Canadian HRReporter*, November 18, 2002, p. 1.

143 E. Unsworth, "U.K. Employers Find Flex Benefits Helpful: Survey," *Business Insurance*, May 21, 2001, pp. 19–20.

144 R. S. Schuler and N. Rogovsky, "Understanding Compensation Practice Variations across Firms: The Impact of National Culture," *Journal of International Business Studies* 29, no. 1 (First Quarter 1998), pp. 159–177.

145 M. Erez, "Culture and Job Design," *Journal of Organizational Behavior* 31, no. 2/3 (2010), pp. 389–400.

146 B. M. Meglino and A. M. Korsgaard, "The Role of Other Orientation in Reactions to Job Characteristics," *Journal of Management*, February 2007, pp. 57–83.

147 M. F. Peterson and S. A. Ruiz-Quintanilla, "Cultural Socialization as a Source of Intrinsic Work Motivation," *Group & Organization Management*, June 2003, pp. 188–216.

148 P. Peters and L. den Dulk, "Cross Cultural Differences in Managers' Support for Home-Based Telework: A Theoretical Elaboration," *International Journal of Cross Cultural Management*, December 2003, pp. 329–346.

149 See, for instance, A. Sagie and Z. Aycan, "A Cross-Cultural Analysis of Participative Decision-Making in Organizations," *Human Relations*, April 2003, pp. 453–473; and J. Brockner, "Unpacking Country Effects: On the Need to Operationalize the Psychological Determinants of Cross-National Differences," in *Research in Organizational Behavior*, vol. 25, ed. R. M. Kramer and B. M. Staw (Oxford, UK: Elsevier, 2003), pp. 336–340.

150 C. Robert, T. M. Probst, J. J. Martocchio, R. Drasgow, and J. J. Lawler, "Empowerment and Continuous Improvement in the United States, Mexico, Poland, and India: Predicting Fit on the Basis of the Dimensions of Power Distance and Individualism," *Journal of Applied Psychology*, October 2000, pp. 643–658.

151 Z. X. Chen and S. Aryee, "Delegation and Employee Work Outcomes: An Examination of the Cultural Context of Mediating Processes in China," *Academy of Management Journal* 50, no. 1 (2007), pp. 226–238.

Chapter 15

1 S. O'Neal, "Total Rewards and the Future of Work," *Workspan* (January 2005), pp. 18–26; S. Watson, "Total Rewards: Building a Better Employment Deal," *Workspan* (December 2003), pp. 48–51.

2 S. O'Neal, "Total Rewards and the Future of Work," *Workspan* (January 2005), pp. 18–26; L. Wright, "Total Rewards Can Mean More HR Work than You Think," *Canadian HR Reporter* (October 6, 2003), pp. 9, 12; K.D. Scott, D. Morajda, and J.W. Bishop, "Increase Company Competitiveness: 'Tune Up' Your Pay System," *WorldatWork Journal* (First Quarter, 2002), pp. 35–42.

3 *Towers Perrin 2007–2008 Global Workforce Study* (Stamford CT: Towers Perrin, 2008), www.towersperrin.com/tp/getwebcachedoc?webc=HRS/USA/2008/200802/GWS_handout_web.pdf (accessed September 26, 2011).

4 "Employee Attraction and Retention," Western Compensation and Benefits Consultants, www.wcbc.ca/news/attractionretention (accessed September 26, 2011).

5 J. Dawe, "Compassionate Care Benefit: A New Alternative for Family Caregivers," *Workplace Gazette* (Summer 2004); S. Klie, "Feds Expand Eligibility for Compassionate Care," *Canadian HR Reporter* (July 17, 2006).

6 "GM, Daimler-Chrysler Workers Ratify Agreements," *Workplace Today* (December 1999), p. 11.

7 Harold Jones, "Union Views on Job Evaluations: 1971 vs. 1978," *Personnel Journal*, 58 (February 1979), pp. 80–85.

8 R. Sahl, "Job Content Salary Surveys: Survey Design and Selection Features," *Compensation and Benefits Review* (May–June 1991), pp. 14–21.

9 M.A. Thompson, "Rewards, Performance Two Biggest Words in HR Future," *WorldatWork Canadian News*, 10 (2002), pp. 1, 2, 11.

10 E. Sibray and J.B. Cavallaro, "Case Study: Market Data and Job Evaluation Equals the Best of Both Worlds," *Workspan*, (July 2007), pp. 27–30.

11 Job analysis can be a useful source of information on compensable factors, as well as on job descriptions and job specifications. For example, a quantitative job analysis technique like the position analysis questionnaire generates quantitative information on the degree to which the following five basic factors are present in each job: having decision making/communication/social responsibilities, performing skilled activities, being physically active, operating vehicles or equipment, and processing information. As a result, a job analysis technique like the PAQ is actually also appropriate as a job evaluation technique (or, some say, more appropriate), in that jobs can be quantitatively compared with one another on those five dimensions, and their relative worth thus ascertained.

12 H. Risher, "Job Evaluation: Validity and Reliability," *Compensation and Benefits Review*, 21 (January–February 1989), pp. 22–36.

13 S. Werner, R. Konopaske, and C. Touhey, "Ten Questions to Ask Yourself about Compensation Surveys," *Compensation and Benefits Review*, 31 (May/June 1999), pp. 54–59.

14 P. Cappelli, *The New Deal at Work: Managing the Market-Driven Workforce* (Boston, MA: Harvard Business School Press, 1999).

15 S. Werner, R. Konopaske, and C. Touhey, "Ten Questions to Ask Yourself about Compensation Surveys," *Compensation and Benefits Review*, 31 (May/June 1999), pp. 54–59.

16 "Compensation Surveys on the Internet," *Canadian HR Reporter* (February 10, 1997), p. 6.

17 F.W. Cook, "Compensation Surveys Are Biased," *Compensation and Benefits Review* (September–October 1994), pp. 19–22.

18 K.R. Cardinal, "The Art and Science of the Match, or Why Job Matching Keeps Me Up at Night," *Workspan* (February 2004),

pp. 53–56; S. Werner, R. Konopaske, and C. Touhey, "Ten Questions to Ask Yourself about Compensation Surveys," *Compensation and Benefits Review*, 31 (May/June 1999), pp. 1–6; see also U. Vu, "Know-How Pays in Comp Surveys," *Canadian HR Reporter* (April 7, 2003), p. 13.

19 D. Hofrichter, "Broadbanding: A 'Second Generation' Approach," *Compensation and Benefits Review* (September–October 1993), pp. 53–58; see also G. Bergel, "Choosing the Right Pay Delivery System to Fit Banding," *Compensation and Benefits Review*, 26 (July–August 1994), pp. 34–38.

20 C. Bacca and G. Starzmann, "Clarifying Competencies: Powerful Tools for Driving Business Success," *Workspan* (March 2006), pp. 44–46.

21 Ibid.

22 P.K. Zingheim and J.R. Schuster, "Reassessing the Value of Skill-Based Pay," *WorldatWork Journal* (Third Quarter, 2002).

23 R. Long, "Paying for Knowledge: Does It Pay?" *Canadian HR Reporter* (March 28, 2005), pp. 12–13.

24 S. St.-Onge, "Competency-Based Pay Plans Revisited," *Human Resources Professional* (August/September 1998), pp. 29–34; J. Kochanski and P. Leblanc, "Should Firms Pay for Competencies: Competencies Have to Help the Bottom Line," *Canadian HR Reporter* (February 22, 1999), p. 10.

25 F. Giancola, "Skill-Based Pay—Issues for Consideration," *Benefits & Compensation Digest*, 44, no. 5 (May 2007), pp. 10–15.

26 D. Tyson, *Canadian Compensation Handbook* (Toronto, ON: Aurora Professional Press, 2002).

27 P.K. Zingheim, J.R. Schuster, and M.G. Dertien, "Measuring the Value of Work: The 'People-Based' Pay Solution," *WorldatWork Journal* (Third Quarter, 2005), pp. 42–49.

28 D. Yoder, *Personnel Management and Industrial Relations* (Englewood Cliffs, NJ: Prentice Hall, 1970), pp. 643–645.

29 B.R. Ellig, "Executive Pay: A Primer," *Compensation & Benefits Review* (January–February 2003), pp. 44–50.

30 "The Top 1000: Top 50 Highest Paid Executives, 2007," www.reportonbusiness.com/v5/content/tp1000-2007/index.php?view-top_50_execs (accessed November 26, 2008).

31 H.L. Tosi, S. Werner, J.P. Katz, and L.R. Gomez-Mejia, "How Much Does Performance Matter? A Meta-Analysis of CEO Pay Studies," *Journal of Management*, 26 (2000), pp. 301–339.

32 M.A. Thompson, "Investors Call for Better Disclosure of Executive Compensation in Canada," *Workspan Focus Canada* (2006), pp. 5–6.

33 P. Moran, "Equitable Salary Administration in High-Tech Companies," *Compensation and Benefits Review*, 18 (September–October 1986), pp. 31–40.

34 R. Sibson, *Compensation* (New York, NY: AMACOM, 1981), p. 194.

35 B. Bridges, "The Role of Rewards in Motivating Scientific and Technical Personnel: Experience at Elgin AFB," *National Productivity Review* (Summer 1993), pp. 337–348.

36 M. Drolet, "The Male–Female Wage Gap," *Perspectives*, Statistics Canada (Spring 2002), pp. 29–37; E. Carey, "Gender Gap in Earnings Staying Stubbornly High," *Toronto Star* (March 12, 2003), p. A9.

37 "Female Grads Make Less than Males," *Canadian HR Reporter* (April 19, 2004), p. 2.

38 D. Brown, "StatsCan Unable to Explain Gender Wage Gap," *Canadian HR Reporter* (January 31, 2000), p. 3.

39 "PSAC Prepares for Federal Court of Appeal Hearing on Pay Equity Complaint at Canada Post," (July 10, 2008), www.psac.com/news/2008/what/2080710-e.shtml (accessed March 23, 2009).

40 "Air Canada Loses Pay Equity Decision, For Now," *Canadian HR Reporter* (February 13, 2006), p. 2.

41 D. Brown, "StatsCan Unable to Explain Gender Wage Gap," *Canadian HR Reporter* (January 31, 2000), p. 3.

Chapter 16

1 A. Cowan, *Compensation Planning Outlook 2011* (Ottawa, ON: Conference Board of Canada, 2011).

2 P.K. Zingheim and J.R. Schuster, *Pay People Right! Breakthrough Reward Strategies to Create Great Companies* (San Francisco, CA: Jossey-Bass, 2000); D. Brown, "Top Performers Must Get Top Pay," *Canadian HR Reporter* (May 8, 2000), pp. 7, 10; V. Dell'Agnese, "Performance-Based Rewards, Line-of-Sight Foster Ownership Behaviour in Staff," *Canadian HR Reporter* (October 8, 2001), p. 10.

3 S. Klie, "'Employees First' at CPX," *Canadian HR Reporter* (September 26, 2005), pp. 1, 3.

4 R. Henderson, *Compensation Management* (Reston, VA: Reston, 1979), p. 363. For a discussion of the increasing use of incentives for blue-collar employees, see, for example, R. Henderson, "Contract Concessions: Is the Past Prologue?" *Compensation and Benefits Review*, 18, no. 5 (September–October 1986), pp. 17–30; see also A.J. Vogl, "Carrots, Sticks and Self-Deception," *Across-the-Board*, 3, no. 1 (January 1994), pp. 39–44.

5 D. Belcher, *Compensation Administration* (Englewood Cliffs, NJ: Prentice Hall, 1973), p. 314.

6 For a discussion of these, see T. Wilson, "Is It Time to Eliminate the Piece Rate Incentive System?" *Compensation and Benefits Review* (March–April 1992), pp. 43–49.

7 Measured day work is a third type of individual incentive plan for production workers. See, for example, M. Fein, "Let's Return to MDW for Incentives," *Industrial Engineering* (January 1979), pp. 34–37.

8 A. Saunier and E. Hawk, "Realizing the Potential of Teams through Team-Based Rewards," *Compensation and Benefits Review* (July–August 1994), pp. 24–33; S. Caudron, "Tie Individual Pay to Team Success," *Personnel Journal*, 73, no. 10 (October 1994), pp. 40–46.

9 Some other suggestions are equal payments to all members on the team; differential payments to team members based on their contributions to the team's performance; differential payments determined by a ratio of each group member's base pay to the total base pay of the group. See K. Bartol and L. Hagmann, "Team-Based Pay Plans: A Key to Effective Teamwork," *Compensation and Benefits Review* (November–December 1992), pp. 24–29.

10 J. Nickel and S. O'Neal, "Small Group Incentives: Gainsharing in the Microcosm," *Compensation and Benefits Review* (March–April 1990), p. 24; see also J. Pickard, "How Incentives Can Drive Teamworking," *Personnel Management* (September 1993), pp. 26–32; S. Caudron, "Tie Individual Pay to Team Success," *Personnel Journal* (October 1994), pp. 40–46; For an explanation of how to develop a successful group incentive program, see K.D. Scott and T. Cotter, "The Team That Works Together Earns Together," *Personnel Journal*, 63 (March 1984), pp. 59–67.

11 L.N. McClurg, "Team Rewards: How Far Have We Come?" *Human Resource Management*, 40 (Spring 2001), pp. 73–86; see also A. Gostick, "Team Recognition," *Canadian HR Reporter* (May 21, 2001), p. 15.

12 W.E. Reum and S. Reum, "Employee Stock Ownership Plans: Pluses and Minuses," *Harvard Business Review*, 55 (July–August 1976), pp. 133–143; R. Bavier, "Managerial Bonuses," *Industrial Management* (March–April 1978), pp. 1–5; see also J. Thompson,

L. Murphy Smith, and A. Murray, "Management Performance Incentives: Three Critical Issues," *Compensation and Benefits Review*, 18, no. 5 (September–October 1986), pp. 41–47.

13 A. Cowan, *Compensation Planning Outlook 2009* (Ottawa, ON: Conference Board of Canada, 2009).

14 B.R. Ellig, "Incentive Plans: Short-Term Design Issues," *Compensation Review*, 16, no. 3 (Third Quarter, 1984), pp. 26–36; B. Ellig, *Executive Compensation—A Total Pay Perspective* (New York, NY: McGraw-Hill, 1982), p. 187.

15 F.D. Hildebrand Jr., "Individual Performance Incentives," *Compensation Review*, 10 (Third Quarter, 1978), p. 32.

16 Ibid., pp. 28–33.

17 P. Brieger, "Shareholders Target CEO Compensation," *Financial Post* (April 7, 2003), p. FP5; see also S.M. Van Putten and E.D. Graskamp, "End of an Era? The Future of Stock Options," *Compensation and Benefits Review* (September–October 2002), pp. 29–35; N. Winter, "The Current Crisis in Executive Compensation," *WorldatWork Canadian News* (Fourth Quarter, 2002), pp. 1–3; R.M. Kanungo and M. Mendonca, *Compensation: Effective Reward Management* (1997), p. 237.

18 A. Cowan, *Compensation Planning Outlook 2011* (Ottawa, ON: Conference Board of Canada, 2011).

19 R. Levasseur and D. D'Alessandro, "Preparing for Changes in Executive Compensation," *Workspan Canada: Workspan Focus* (January 2009), pp. 101–104.

20 A. Cowan, *Compensation Planning Outlook 2011* (Ottawa, ON: Conference Board of Canada, 2011).

21 R. Murrill, "Executive Share Ownership," *Watson Wyatt Memorandum*, 11, no. 1 (March 1997), p. 11.

22 R.J. Long, "Ensuring Your Executive Compensation Plan Is an Asset Rather Than a Liability," *Canadian HR Reporter* (October 19, 1998), pp. 15–16; see also D. Brown, "Bringing Stock Options Back to the Surface," *Canadian HR Reporter* (May 7, 2001), p. 2.

23 I. Huss and M. Maclure, "Broad-Based Stock Option Plans Take Hold," *Canadian HR Reporter* (July 17, 2000), p. 18; J. Staiman and C. Thompson, "Designing and Implementing a Broad-Based Stock Option Plan," *Compensation and Benefits Review* (July–August 1998), p. 23.

24 *CPP Investment Board Proxy Voting Principles and Guidelines* (February 7, 2006).

25 R. Levasseur and D. D'Alessandro, "Preparing for Changes in Executive Compensation," *Workspan Canada: Workspan Focus* (January 2009), pp. 101–104.

26 P. Singh and N.C. Agarwal, "Executive Compensation: Examining an Old Issue from New Perspectives," *Compensation and Benefits Review* (March/April 2003), pp. 48–54.

27 R. Levasseur and D. D'Alessandro, "Preparing for Changes in Executive Compensation," *Workspan Canada: Workspan Focus* (January 2009), pp. 101–104.

28 J. Tallitsch and J. Moynahan, "Fine-Tuning Sales Compensation Programs," *Compensation and Benefits Review*, 26, no. 2 (March–April 1994), pp. 34–37.

29 Straight salary by itself is not, of course, an incentive compensation plan as we use the term in this chapter; J. Steinbrink, "How to Pay Your Sales Force," *Harvard Business Review*, 57 (July–August 1978), pp. 111–122.

30 T.H. Patten, "Trends in Pay Practices for Salesmen," *Personnel*, 43 (January–February 1968), pp. 54–63; see also C. Romano, "Death of a Salesman," *Management Review*, 83, no. 9 (September 1994), pp. 10–16.

31 D. Harrison, M. Virick, and S. William, "Working Without a Net: Time, Performance, and Turnover Under Maximally Contingent Rewards," *Journal of Applied Psychology*, 81 (1996), pp. 331–345.

32 G. Stewart, "Reward Structure as Moderator of the Relationship between Extroversion and Sales Performance," *Journal of Applied Psychology*, 81 (1996), pp. 619–627.

33 In the salary plus bonus plan, salespeople are paid a basic salary and are then paid a bonus for carrying out specified activities. For a discussion of how to develop a customer-focused sales compensation plan, see, for example, M. Blessington, "Designing a Sales Strategy with the Customer in Mind," *Compensation and Benefits Review* (March–April 1992), pp. 30–41; S.S. Sands, "Ineffective Quotas: The Hidden Threat to Sales Compensation Plans," *Compensation and Benefits Review* (March/April 2000), pp. 35–42.

34 E. Maggio, "Compensation Strategies Pulling You in Different Directions?" *Canadian HR Reporter* (October 4, 1999), pp. 11, 19; see also B. Serino, "Non-Cash Awards Boost Sales Compensation Plans," *Workspan* (August 2002), pp. 24–27.

35 B. Weeks, "Setting Sales Force Compensation in the Internet Age," *Compensation and Benefits Review* (March/April 2000), pp. 25–34.

36 See, for example, W. Kearney, "Pay for Performance? Not Always," *MSU Business Topics* (Spring 1979), pp. 5–16; see also H. Doyel and J. Johnson, "Pay Increase Guidelines with Merit," *Personnel Journal*, 64 (June 1985), pp. 46–50.

37 J. Pfeffer and R.I. Sutton, *Hard Facts, Dangerous Half-Truths, and Total Nonsense* (Boston MA: Harvard Business School Press, 2006).

38 W. Seithel and J. Emans, "Calculating Merit Increases: A Structured Approach," *Personnel*, 60, no. 5 (June 1985), pp. 56–68; D. Gilbert and G. Bassett, "Merit Pay Increases Are a Mistake," *Compensation and Benefits Review*, 26, no. 2 (March–April 1994), pp. 20–25.

39 S. Minken, "Does Lump Sum Pay Merit Attention?" *Personnel Journal* (June 1988), pp. 77–83; J. Newman and D. Fisher, "Strategic Impact Merit Pay," *Compensation and Benefits Review* (July–August 1992), pp. 38–45.

40 Based primarily on R. Sibson, *Compensation* (New York, NY: AMACOM, 1981), pp. 189–207; C. Shelton and L. Shelton, "What HR Can Do about the 'Opt-Out' Revolution (Guest Commentary)," *Canadian HR Reporter* (May 8, 2006).

41 A. Cowan, *Compensation Planning Outlook 2009* (Ottawa, ON: Conference Board of Canada, 2009).

42 B. Duke, "Are Profit-Sharing Plans Making the Grade?" *Canadian HR Reporter* (January 11, 1999), pp. 8–9.

43 D.E. Tyson, *Profit-Sharing in Canada: The Complete Guide to Designing and Implementing Plans That Really Work* (Toronto, ON: Wiley, 1996), pp. 200–207.

44 C. Baarda, *Compensation Planning Outlook 2006* (Ottawa, ON: Conference Board of Canada, 2006).

45 R. Murrill, "Executive Share Ownership," *Watson Wyatt Memorandum*, 11, no. 1 (March 1997), p. 11.

46 P. Robertson, "Increasing Productivity through an Employee Share Purchase Plan," *Canadian HR Reporter* (September 20, 1999), pp. 7, 9.

47 C. Beatty, "Our Company: Employee Ownership May Sound Drastic, but It Can Work," *HR Professional* (June/July 2004), p. 20.

48 B.W. Thomas and M.H. Olson, "Gainsharing: The Design Guarantees Success," *Personnel Journal* (May 1988), pp. 73–79; see also "Aligning Compensation with Quality," *Bulletin to Management, BNA Policy and Practice Series* (April 1, 1993), p. 97.

49 See T.A. Welbourne and L. Gomez Mejia, "Gainsharing Revisited," *Compensation and Benefits Review* (July–August 1988), pp. 19–28.

50 Paraphrased from W. Imberman, "Boosting Plant Performance with Gainsharing," *Business Horizons* (November–December 1992), p. 77; for other examples, see T. Ross and L. Hatcher, "Gainsharing Drives Quality Improvement," *Personnel Journal* (November 1992), pp. 81–89; see also J. McAdams, "Employee Involvement and Performance Reward Plans: Design, Implementation, and Results," *Compensation and Benefits Review*, 27, no. 2 (March 1995), pp. 45–55.

51 P.K. Zingheim and J.R. Schuster, "Value Is the Goal," *Workforce* (February 2000), pp. 56–61.

52 "US Airways Employees to Get Profit Sharing Checks," *Entertainment Close-Up* (March 19, 2011).

53 R.J. Long, "Ensuring Your Executive Compensation Plan Is an Asset Rather Than a Liability," *Canadian HR Reporter* (October 19, 1998), pp. 15–16; see also D. Brown, "Bringing Stock Options Back to the Surface," *Canadian HR Reporter* (May 7, 2001), p. 2.

54 J. Cameron and W.D. Pierce, *Rewards and Intrinsic Motivation: Resolving the Controversy* (Westport, CT: Bergin & Garvey, 2002); see also G. Bouchard, "When Rewards Don't Work," *Globe and Mail* (September 25, 2002), p. C3.

55 P.K. Zingheim and J.R. Schuster, *Pay People Right! Breakthrough Reward Strategies to Create Great Companies* (San Francisco, CA: Jossey-Bass, 2000).

56 S. Gross and J. Bacher, "The New Variable Pay Programs: How Some Succeed, Why Some Don't," *Compensation and Benefits Review* (January–February 1993), pp. 55–56; see also G. Milkovich and C. Milkovich, "Strengthening the Pay-Performance Relationship: The Research," *Compensation and Benefits Review* (November–December 1992), pp. 53–62; J. Schuster and P. Zingheim, "The New Variable Pay: Key Design Issues," *Compensation and Benefits Review* (March–April 1993), pp. 27–34.

57 D. Belcher, *Compensation Administration* (Englewood Cliffs, NJ: Prentice Hall, 1973), pp. 309–310.

58 A. Avalos, "Recognition: A Critical Component of the Total Rewards Mix," *Workspan* (July 2007), pp. 32–35.

59 K. Izuma, D.N. Saito, and N. Sadato, "Processing of Social and Monetary Rewards in the Human Striatum," *Neuron*, 58, no. 2 (April 24, 2008), pp. 284–294.

60 J. Mills, "Gratitude à la carte," *Workplace News* (January 2005), p. 12; L. McKibbon-Brown, "Beyond the Gold Watch: Employee Recognition Today," *Workspan* (April 2003), pp. 44–46.

61 A. Welsh, "The Give and Take of Recognition Programs," *Canadian HR Reporter* (September 22, 1997), pp. 16–17, 22; J.M. Kouzas and B.Z. Posner, *Encouraging the Heart: A Leader's Guide to Rewarding and Recognizing Others* (San Francisco, CA: Wiley, 2003); D. Brown, "Canada Wants Nurses Again, but Will Anyone Answer the Call?" *Canadian HR Reporter* (January 15, 2001), pp. 1, 14, 15.

62 J.M. Kouzas and B.Z. Posner, *Encouraging the Heart: A Leader's Guide to Rewarding and Recognizing Others* (San Francisco, CA: Wiley, 2003); see also B. Nelson, "Why Managers Don't Recognize Employees," *Canadian HR Reporter* (March 11, 2002), p. 9; L. Cassiani, "Lasting Impressions through Recognition," *Canadian HR Reporter* (March 12, 2001), p. 7; J. Mills, "A Matter of Pride: Rewarding Team Success," *Canadian HR Reporter* (March 8, 1999), p. 16; L. Young, "How Can I Ever Thank You?" *Canadian HR Reporter* (January 31, 2000), pp. 7, 9.

63 E. Wright and K. Ryan, "Thanks a Million (More or Less)," *Canadian HR Reporter* (March 9, 1998), pp. 19, 21, 23; see also "How to Sell Recognition to Top Management," *Canadian HR Reporter* (June 1, 1998), p. 21; B. Nelson, "Cheap and Meaningful Better than Expensive and Forgettable," *Canadian HR Reporter* (August 13, 2001), p. 22.

64 L. Davidson, "The Power of Personal Recognition," *Workforce* (July 1999), pp. 44–49; see also A. Gostick and C. Elton, "Show Me the Rewards," *Canadian HR Reporter* (March 12, 2001), pp. 7, 10; V. Scott and B. Phillips, "Recognition Program Links Achievement to Corporate Goals," *Canadian HR Reporter* (December 14, 1998), pp. 22–23; R. Clarke, "Building a Recognition Program: Alternatives and Considerations," *Canadian HR Reporter* (November 2, 1998), pp. 17, 19; E. Wright and K. Ryan, "Thanks a Million (More or Less)," *Canadian HR Reporter* (March 9, 1998), pp. 19, 21, 23; L. Davidson, "The Power of Personal Recognition," *Workforce* (July 1999), pp. 44–49; D. Brown, "Recognition an Integral Part of Total Rewards," *Canadian HR Reporter* (August 12, 2002), pp. 25, 27.

65 U. Vu, "Green Recognition a Mere Whisper," *Canadian HR Reporter* (August 11, 2008); U. Vu, "What Green Recognition Looks Like," *Canadian HR Reporter* (August 11, 2008).

66 J. Jackson, "The Art of Recognition," *Canadian HR Reporter* (January 15, 2001), p. 22; see also B.P. Keegan, "Incentive Programs Boost Employee Morale," *Workspan* (March 2002), pp. 30–33; S. Nador, "Beyond Trinkets and Trash," *Canadian HR Reporter* (May 20, 2002), pp. 15, 19.

67 H. Hilliard, "How to Reward Top Performers When Money Is No Object," *Canadian HR Reporter* (August 13, 2001), pp. 21, 23.

68 A. Welsh, "The Give and Take of Recognition Programs," *Canadian HR Reporter* (September 22, 1997), pp. 16–17, 22; E. Wright and K. Ryan, "Thanks a Million (More or Less)," *Canadian HR Reporter* (March 9, 1998).

69 L.J. Blake, "Montana's Cookhouse Serves Up Recognition," *Workplace* (September–October 2008), pp. 14–16; D. Irvine, "Bring Back that Lovin' Feeling," *Canadian HR Reporter* (November 3, 2008); T. Humber, "Beyond the Gold Watch," *Canadian HR Reporter* (January 30, 2006), pp. 23, 29; S. Singh, "'Tis the Season for Recognition," *Canadian HR Reporter* (December 5, 2005), pp. 19–20.

Chapter 17

1 Based on F. Hills, T. Bergmann, and V. Scarpello, *Compensation Decision Making* (Fort Worth, TX: The Dryden Press, 1994), p. 424; see also L.K. Beatty, "Pay and Benefits Break Away from Tradition," *HR Magazine*, 39 (November 1994), pp. 63–68.

2 R.K. Platt, "A Strategic Approach to Benefits," *Workspan* (July 2002), pp. 23–24.

3 S. Beech and J. Tompkins, "Do Benefits Plans Attract and Retain Talent?" *Benefits Canada* (October 2002), pp. 49–53.

4 F. Holmes, "Talking about an Evolution," *Benefits Canada* (September 2001), pp. 30–32; J. Thomas and M. Chilco, "Coming of Age," *Benefits Canada* (March 2001), pp. 36–38.

5 "EI Top-Ups Common—Survey," *Canadian HR Reporter* (February 23, 1998), p. 15.

6 S. Klie, "Feds Expand Eligibility for Compassionate Care," *Canadian HR Reporter* (July 17, 2006).

7 "Tragedy Leaves of Absence," *HR Professional* (October/November 2008), p. 16.

8 D. Gunch, "The Family Leave Act: A Financial Burden?" *Personnel Journal* (September 1993), p. 49.

9 H. Amolins, "Workers Must Cooperate in Return to Work," *Canadian HR Reporter* (November 3, 1997), p. 8; C. Knight, "Ontario Businesses Ready for New WCB," *Canadian HR Reporter* (November 17, 1997), p. 9.

10 U. Vu, "How Purolator Dealt with Skyrocketing Costs," *Canadian HR Reporter* (March 13, 2006).

11 S. Pellegrini, "Considering Critical," *Benefits Canada* (April 2002), pp. 71–73.

12 "Employee Benefits in Small Firms," *BNA Bulletin to Management* (June 27, 1991), pp. 196–197.

13 "Employee Benefits," *Commerce Clearing House Ideas and Trends in Personnel* (January 23, 1991), pp. 9–11.

14 S. Dobson, "Health-Care Costs Maintain Dramatic Rise," *Canadian HR Reporter* (July 13, 2009).

15 *Canadian Health Care Trend Survey Results 2009* (Toronto, ON: Buck Consultants).

16 C. Kapel, "Unitel Asks Employees to Share Costs," *Canadian HR Reporter* (June 17, 1996), p. 17; see also J. Sloane and J. Taggart, "Runaway Drug Costs," *Canadian HR Reporter* (September 10, 2001), pp. 17–18; "Deductibles Could Be Making a Comeback," *Canadian HR Reporter* (February 26, 2001), pp. 2, 16.

17 J. Norton, "The New Drug Invasion," *Benefits Canada* (June 1999), pp. 29–32.

18 S. Felix, "Healthy Alternative," *Benefits Canada* (February 1997), p. 47; A. Dimon, "Money Well Spent," *Benefits Canada* (April 1997), p. 15.

19 A. Dimon, "Money Well Spent," *Benefits Canada* (April 1997), p. 15.

20 D. Jones, "Accounting for Health: The Present and Future of HCSAs and Other Consumer-Driven Health Care Products in Canada," *Benefits Canada* (January 2009), pp. 21–23.

21 J. Taggart, "Health Spending Accounts: A Prescription for Cost Control," *Canadian HR Reporter* (October 22, 2001), pp. 16, 18; see also "How Spending Accounts Work," *Canadian HR Reporter* (February 24, 2003), p. 16.

22 K. Gay, "Post-Retirement Benefits Costing Firms a Fortune," *Financial Post* (June 2, 1995), p. 18; S. Lebrun, "Turning a Blind Eye to Benefits," *Canadian HR Reporter* (February 24, 1997), p. 2; S. Pellegrini, "Keep Benefits Costs Low by Assessing Retiree Health," *Canadian HR Reporter* (June 14, 1999), pp. 9–10; M. Warren, "Uncovering the Costs," *Benefits Canada* (November 1996), p. 41; G. Dufresne, "Financing Benefits for Tomorrow's Retirees," *Canadian HR Reporter* (April 6, 1998), p. 11.

23 A. Khemani, "Post-Retirement Benefits Liability Grows," *Canadian HR Reporter* (November 4, 1996), p. 17; see also M. Warren, "Retiree Benefits Come of Age," *Benefits Canada* (May 2000), pp. 73–77.

24 *2008 Post-Retirement Trends* (Toronto, ON: Mercer Human Resources Consulting).

25 W. Pyper, "Aging, Health and Work," *Perspectives on Labour and Income* (Spring 2006), p. 48; S. Klie, "Private Health Coverage Enters Benefits Realm," *Canadian HR Reporter* (September 12, 2005), pp. 1, 22.

26 "Managing Episodic Disabilities Course," *HR Professional* (February–March 2009), p. 18.

27 A. Blake, "A New Approach to Disability Management," *Benefits Canada* (March 2000), pp. 58–64; P. Kulig, "Returning the Whole Employee to Work," *Canadian HR Reporter* (March 9, 1998), p. 20; see also A. Gibbs, "Gearing Disability Management to the Realities of Working Life," *Canadian HR Reporter* (December 2, 2002), p. G7.

28 J. Curtis and L. Scott, "Making the Connection," *Benefits Canada* (April 2003), pp. 75–79.

29 N. Rankin, "A Guide to Disability Management," *Canadian HR Reporter* (March 22, 1999), pp. 14–15.

30 *Staying@Work: Effective Presence at Work*, 2007 Survey Report-Canada (Toronto, ON: Watson Wyatt); "Mental Health Claims on the Rise in Canada," *WorldatWork Canadian News* (Third Quarter, 2005), pp. 15–16; D. Brown, "Mental Illness a Top Concern but Only Gets Band-Aid Treatment," *Canadian HR Reporter* (May 9, 2005), pp. 1, 3; "Mental Health Biggest Workplace Barrier, Women Say," *Canadian HR Reporter* (January 17, 2005), p. 2.

31 P. Weiner, "A Mental Health Priority for Canada's Employers," *Workspan* (January 2009), pp. 91–95.

32 J. Melnitzer, "Down and Out," *Workplace News* (September/October 2005), pp. 20–23; M. Burych, "Baby Blues," *Benefits Canada* (October 2000), pp 33–35.

33 B. Hayhoe, "The Case for Employee Retirement Planning," *Canadian HR Reporter* (May 20, 2002), p. 18.

34 J. Nunes, "Defined Benefit or Defined Contribution, It's Always Costly," *Canadian HR Reporter* (November 5, 2001), pp. 7, 9.

35 Ibid.

36 S. Klie, "Little guarantee for Ontario pensions," *Canadian HR Reporter* (May 4, 2009); S. Dobson, "Costs top list of concerns for DB plan sponsors: Survey," *Canadian HR Reporter* (March 24, 2008).

37 A. Scappatura, "DB Plans Endangered," *Canadian HR Reporter* (June 15, 2009); T. Humber, "The Death of the DB Pension," *Canadian HR Reporter* (March 23, 2009); S. Dobson, "Ottawa Provides Pension Relief," *Canadian HR Reporter* (December 15, 2008); D. Birschel, "Alberta and British Columbia Provide Pension Solvency Relief," *Benefits Quarterly*, 25, no. 2 (2009), p. 66.

38 S. Dobson, "Workers Postpone Retirement to Save Money," *Canadian HR Reporter* (May 18, 2009); "Canadians Delaying Retirement Due to Economic Slowdown," *Workspan* (January 2009), pp. 106–107; S. Klie, "Workers Delay Retirement as Economy Tanks," *Canadian HR Reporter* (January 26, 2009).

39 T. Piskorski, "Minimizing Employee Benefits Litigation through Effective Claims Administration Procedures," *Employee Relations Law Journal*, 20, no. 3 (Winter 1994–95), pp. 421–431.

40 A. Rappaport, "Phased Retirement: An Important Part of the Evolving Retirement Scene," *Benefits Quarterly*, 25, no. 2 (2009), pp. 38–50; R. Castelli, "Phased Retirement Plans, *HR Professional* (December 2008/January 2009), p. 23.

41 D. Brown, "New Brunswick Nurses Find Phased Retirement Solution," *Canadian HR Reporter* (September 22, 2003), pp. 1, 12; Y. Saint-Cyr, "Phased Retirement Agreements," *Canadian Payroll and Employment Law News*, www.hrpao.org/HRPAO/HRResourceCentre/LegalCentre/ (accessed July 11, 2005).

42 *Towers Perrin 2004 SERP Report: Supplementary Pensions Under Pressure* (Toronto, ON: Towers Perrin).

43 L. Burger, "Group Legal Service Plans: A Benefit Whose Time Has Come," *Compensation and Benefits Review*, 18 (July–August 1986), pp. 28–34.

44 "Financial Distress Impacts Health and Productivity: Employees Turning to EAP for Help," Shepell-fgi Research Group, 2009 Series, 5, no. 1; A. Scappatura, "EAP Use Soars as Economy Tanks: Study," *Canadian HR Reporter* (March 23, 2009); "Requests for Help through EAP Up Significantly," *Workspan* (February 2009), p. 13.

45 J. Hobel, "EAPs Flounder without Manager Support," *Canadian HR Reporter* (June 2, 2003), p. 7; P. Davies, "Problem Gamblers in the Workplace," *Canadian HR Reporter* (November 4, 2002), p. 17; A. Sharratt, "When a Tragedy Strikes," *Benefits Canada* (November 2002), pp. 101–105.

46 R. Csiernik, "The Great EAP Question: Internal or External?" *Canadian HR Reporter* (August 20, 2007).

47 R. Csiernik, "What to Look for in an External EAP Service," *Canadian HR Reporter* (May 31, 2004), p. 7; D. Sharar, "With HR Chasing Lowest Price, EAPs Can't Improve Quality," *Canadian HR Reporter* (May 31, 2004), pp. 6, 8; A. Davis, "Helping Hands," *Benefits Canada* (November 2000), pp. 117–121.

48 "100 Best Companies to Work For," *Fortune* (January 2000), http://money.cnn.com/magazines/fortune/fortune_archive/2000/01/10/271718/index.htm (accessed September 4, 2012).

49 C. Foster, "Workers Don't Leave Problems at Home," *Canadian HR Reporter* (May 7, 2007).

50 S. Dobson, "Is Backup Care Worth the Investment?" *Canadian HR Reporter* (November 3, 2008); D. Brown, "Bringing the Family to Work," *Canadian HR Reporter* (November 6, 2000), pp. 19–20.

51 "Employer-Sponsored Child Care Can Be Instrumental in Attraction and Retention," *Workspan* (January 2009), p. 10.

52 D. McCloskey, "Caregiving and Canadian Families," *Transition Magazine* (Summer 2005), p. 1; B. Parus, "Who's Watching Grandma? Addressing the Eldercare Dilemma," *Workspan* (January 2004), pp. 40–43.

53 "Elder Care to Eclipse Child Care, Report Says," *Canadian HR Reporter* (August 14, 1995), p. 11; A. Vincola, "Eldercare—What Firms Can Do to Help," *Canadian HR Reporter* (June 5, 2000), p. G3.

54 S. Klie, "Employers Can Help with 'Long Goodbye'," *Canadian HR Reporter* (August 13, 2007).

55 D. Dyck, "Make Your Workplace Family-Friendly," *Canadian HR Reporter* (December 13, 1999), pp. G5, G10.

56 E.E. Kossek and C. Ozeki, "Work-Family Conflict, Policies, and the Job-Life Satisfaction Relationship: A Review and Direction for Organizational Behavior–Human Resources Research," *Journal of Applied Psychology*, 83, (1998), pp. 139–149.

57 B. Ellig, *Executive Compensation—A Total Pay Perspective* (New York, NY: McGraw-Hill, 1982), p. 141.

58 B. Jaworski, "'I'll Have My People Call Your People '" *Canadian HR Reporter* (March 27, 2006).

59 W. White and J. Becker, "Increasing the Motivational Impact of Employee Benefits," *Personnel* (January–February 1980), pp. 32–37; B. Olmsted and S. Smith, "Flex for Success!" *Personnel*, 66, no. 6 (June 1989), pp. 50–55.

60 B. McKay, "The Flexible Evolution," *Workplace News* (January/February 2006), pp. 14–15.

61 Ibid.

62 D. Brown, "Everybody Loves Flex," *Canadian HR Reporter* (November 18, 2002), pp. 1, 11; R. Dawson and B. McKay, "The Flexibility of Flex," *WorldatWork Canadian News* (Fourth Quarter, 2005), pp. 1, 6–13

63 J. Tompkins, "Moving Out: A Look at Comprehensive Benefits Outsourcing," *Canadian HR Reporter* (May 5, 1997), p. 9.

64 N. Chaplick, "Enter at Your Own Risk," *Benefits Canada* (May 2000), pp. 37–39; see also M. Reid, "Legal Aid," *Benefits Canada* (June 2000), pp. 46–48; S. Deller, "Five Hot Survival Tips for Communicating Benefits," *Canadian HR Reporter* (July 13, 1998), pp. 9, 19.

65 C. Davenport, "Employers Twig to Value of Ongoing Pension Communication," *Canadian HR Reporter* (December 16, 1996), p. 33.

Chapter 18

1 Opening vignette is based on http://www.cirquedusoleil.com; "Cirque du Soleil on Teamwork and Creativity," *Business Banter*, June 28, 2011, http://businessbanter.wordpress.com/2011/06/28/cirque-du-soleil-on-teamwork-and-creativity/; G. Collins, "Run Away to the Circus? No Need. It's Staying Here," *New York Times*, April 29, 2009, p. C1; and A. Tesolin, "Igniting the Creative Spark at Cirque du Soleil—Arupa Tesolin Interviews Lyn Heward Creative Leader at Cirque," *SelfGrowth.com*, http://www.selfgrowth.com/articles/Igniting_the_Creative_Spark_at_Cirque_du_Soleil.html

2 J. R. Katzenback and D. K. Smith, *The Wisdom of Teams: Creating the High-Performance Organization* (New York: Harper Business, 1999), p. 45.

3 J. R. Katzenback and D. K. Smith, *The Wisdom of Teams: Creating the High-Performance Organization* (New York: Harper Business, 1999), p. 214.

4 See, for example, D. Tjosvold, *Team Organization: An Enduring Competitive Advantage* (Chichester, UK: Wiley, 1991); S. A. Mohrman, S. G. Cohen, and A. M. Mohrman Jr., *Designing Team-Based Organizations* (San Francisco: Jossey-Bass, 1995); P. MacMillan, *The Performance Factor: Unlocking the Secrets of Teamwork* (Nashville, TN: Broadman and Holman, 2001); and E. Salas, C. A. Bowers, and E. Edens, eds., *Improving Teamwork in Organizations: Applications of Resource Management Training* (Mahwah, NJ: Erlbaum, 2002).

5 J. H. Shonk, *Team-Based Organizations* (Homewood, IL: Business One Irwin, 1992); and M. A. Verespej, "When Workers Get New Roles," *IndustryWeek*, February 3, 1992, p. 11.

6 See, for example, C. C. Manz and H. P. Sims Jr., *Business without Bosses: How Self-Managing Teams Are Building High Performance Companies* (New York: Wiley, 1993); J. R. Barker, "Tightening the Iron Cage: Concertive Control in Self-Managing Teams," *Administrative Science Quarterly*, September 1993, pp. 408–437; and S. G. Cohen, G. E. Ledford Jr., and G. M. Spreitzer, "A Predictive Model of Self-Managing Work Team Effectiveness," *Human Relations*, May 1996, pp. 643–676.

7 See, for instance, J. L. Cordery, W. S. Mueller, and L. M. Smith, "Attitudinal and Behavioral Effects of Autonomous Group Working: A Longitudinal Field Study," *Academy of Management Journal*, June 1991, pp. 464–476; R. A. Cook and J. L. Goff, "Coming of Age with Self-Managed Teams: Dealing with a Problem Employee," *Journal of Business and Psychology*, Spring 2002, pp. 485–496; and C. W. Langfred, "Too Much of a Good Thing? Negative Effects of High Trust and Individual Autonomy in Self-Managing Teams," *Academy of Management Journal*, June 2004, pp. 385–399.

8 A. Mehra, M. Kilduff, and D. J. Brass, "At the Margins: A Distinctiveness Approach to the Social Identity and Social Networks of Underrepresented Groups," *Academy of Management Journal* 41, no. 4 (1998), pp. 441–452.

9 J. Tutunjian, "Interview with Don Swann," *Canadian Grocer* 121, no. 10 (December 2007–January 2008), pp. 18–19.

10 G. Taninecz, "Team Players," *IndustryWeek*, July 15, 1996, pp. 28–32; D. R. Denison, S. L. Hart, and J. A. Kahn, "From Chimneys to Cross-Functional Teams: Developing and Validating a Diagnostic Model," *Academy of Management Journal*, August 1996, pp. 1005–1023; and A. R. Jassawalla, "Building Collaborative Cross-Functional New Product Teams," *Academy of Management Executive*, August 1999, pp. 50–63.

11 "Cross-Functional Obstacles," *Training*, May 1994, pp. 125–126.

12 P. Gwynne, "Skunk Works, 1990s-Style," *Research Technology Management*, July–August 1997, pp. 18–23.

13 "Virtual Teams a First in Canada," January 19, 2011, http://business.financialpost.com/2011/01/19/mba-virtual-teams-a-first-in-canada/

14 See, for example, M. E. Warkentin, L. Sayeed, and R. Hightower, "Virtual Teams versus Face-to-Face Teams: An Exploratory Study of a Web-Based Conference System," *Decision Sciences*, Fall 1997, pp. 975–993; A. M. Townsend, S. M. DeMarie, and A. R. Hendrickson, "Virtual Teams: Technology and the Workplace of the Future," *Academy of Management Executive*, August 1998, pp. 17–29; D. Duarte and N. T. Snyder, *Mastering*

Virtual Teams: Strategies, Tools, and Techniques (San Francisco: Jossey-Bass, 1999); M. L. Maznevski and K. M. Chudoba, "Bridging Space over Time: Global Virtual Team Dynamics and Effectiveness," *Organization Science*, September–October 2000, pp. 473–492; and J. Katzenbach and D. Smith, "Virtual Teaming," *Forbes*, May 21, 2001, pp. 48–51.

15 A. Malhotra, A. Majchrzak, and B. Rosen, "Leading Virtual Teams," *Academy of Management Perspectives*, February 2007, pp. 60–70; and J. M. Wilson, S. S. Straus, and B. McEvily, "All in Due Time: The Development of Trust in Computer Mediated and Face-to-Face Teams," *Organizational Behavior and Human Decision Processes* 19 (2006), pp. 16–33.

16 Vignette based on E. Syracopoulos, "#FocusFriday: How Cirque du Soleil's Graphics Team Stays Focused Off Stage," *Xerox Blogs*, July 29, 2011, http://realbusinessatxerox.blogs.xerox.com/2011/07/29/focusfriday-how-cirque-du-soleil%E2%80%99s-graphics-team-stays-focused-off-stage/; http://www.cirquedusoleil.com

17 See M. F. Peterson, P. B, Smith, A. Akande, S. Ayestaran, S. Bochner, V. Callan, N. Guk Cho, J. C. Jesuino, M. D'Amorim, P.-H. Francois, K. Hofmann, P. L. Koopman, K. Leung, T. K. Lim, and S. Mortaz, "Role Conflict, Ambiguity, and Overload: A 21-Nation Study," *Academy of Management Journal*, April 1995, pp. 429–452.

18 E. H. Schein, *Organizational Psychology*, 3rd ed. (Englewood Cliffs, NJ: Prentice Hall, 1980), p. 145.

19 For a recent review of the research on group norms, see J. R. Hackman, "Group Influences on Individuals in Organizations," in *Handbook of Industrial & Organizational Psychology*, vol. 3, 2nd ed., ed. M. D. Dunnette and L. M. Hough (Palo Alto, CA: Consulting Psychologists Press, 1992), pp. 235–250.

20 Adapted from P. S. Goodman, E. Ravlin, and M. Schminke, "Understanding Groups in Organizations," in *Research in Organizational Behavior*, vol. 9, ed. L. L. Cummings and B. M. Staw (Greenwich, CT: JAI Press, 1987), p. 159.

21 D. C. Feldman, "The Development and Enforcement of Group Norms," *Academy of Management Journal*, January 1984, pp. 47–53; and K. L. Bettenhausen and J. K. Murnighan, "The Development of an Intragroup Norm and the Effects of Interpersonal and Structural Challenges," *Administrative Science Quarterly*, March 1991, pp. 20–35.

22 D. C. Feldman, "The Development and Enforcement of Group Norms," *Academy of Management Journal*, January 1984, pp. 47–53; and K. L. Bettenhausen and J. K. Murnighan, "The Development of an Intragroup Norm and the Effects of Interpersonal and Structural Challenges," *Administrative Science Quarterly*, March 1991, pp. 20–35.

23 C. A. Kiesler and S. B. Kiesler, *Conformity* (Reading, MA: Addison Wesley, 1969).

24 S. E. Asch, "Effects of Group Pressure upon the Modification and Distortion of Judgments," in *Groups, Leadership and Men*, ed. H. Guetzkow (Pittsburgh, PA: Carnegie Press, 1951), pp. 177–190; and S. E. Asch, "Studies of Independence and Conformity: A Minority of One Against a Unanimous Majority," *Psychological Monographs: General and Applied* 70, no. 9 (1956), pp. 1–70.

25 S. L. Robinson and A. M. O'Leary-Kelly, "Monkey See, Monkey Do: The Influence of Work Groups on the Antisocial Behavior of Employees," *Academy of Management Journal* 41 (1998), pp. 658–672.

26 J. M. George, "Personality, Affect and Behavior in Groups," *Journal of Applied Psychology* 78 (1993), pp. 798–804; and J. M. George and L. R. James, "Personality, Affect, and Behavior in Groups Revisited: Comment on Aggregation, Levels of Analysis, and a Recent Application of Within and Between Analysis," *Journal of Applied Psychology* 78 (1993), pp. 798–804.

27 B. W. Tuckman, "Developmental Sequences in Small Groups," *Psychological Bulletin*, June 1965, pp. 384–399; B. W. Tuckman

and M. C. Jensen, "Stages of Small-Group Development Revisited," *Group and Organizational Studies*, December 1977, pp. 419–427; and M. F. Maples, "Group Development: Extending Tuckman's Theory," *Journal for Specialists in Group Work*, Fall 1988, pp. 17–23.

28 J. F. George and L. M. Jessup, "Groups over Time: What Are We Really Studying?" *International Journal of Human-Computer Studies* 47, no. 3 (1997), pp. 497–511.

29 R. C. Ginnett, "The Airline Cockpit Crew," in *Groups That Work (and Those That Don't)*, ed. J. R. Hackman (San Francisco: Jossey-Bass, 1990).

30 C. J. G. Gersick, "Time and Transition in Work Teams: Toward a New Model of Group Development," *Academy of Management Journal*, March 1988, pp. 9–41; C. J. G. Gersick, "Marking Time: Predictable Transitions in Task Groups," *Academy of Management Journal*, June 1989, pp. 274–309; E. Romanelli and M. L. Tushman, "Organizational Transformation as Punctuated Equilibrium: An Empirical Test," *Academy of Management Journal*, October 1994, pp. 1141–1166; B. M. Lichtenstein, "Evolution or Transformation: A Critique and Alternative to Punctuated Equilibrium," in *Academy of Management Best Paper Proceedings*, ed. D. P. Moore (National Academy of Management Conference, Vancouver, 1995), pp. 291–295; and A. Seers and S. Woodruff, "Temporal Pacing in Task Forces: Group Development or Deadline Pressure?" *Journal of Management* 23, no. 2 (1997), pp. 169–187.

31 C. J. G. Gersick, "Time and Transition in Work Teams: Toward a New Model of Group Development," *Academy of Management Journal*, March 1988, pp. 9–41; and M. J. Waller, J. M. Conte, C. B. Gibson, and M. A. Carpenter, "The Effect of Individual Perceptions of Deadlines on Team Performance," *Academy of Management Review*, October 2001, pp. 586–600.

32 C. J. G. Gersick, "Time and Transition in Work Teams: Toward a New Model of Group Development," *Academy of Management Journal*, March 1988, pp. 9–41; and C. J. G. Gersick, "Marking Time: Predictable Transitions in Task Groups," *Academy of Management Journal*, June 1989, pp. 274–309.

33 A. Chang, P. Bordia, and J. Duck, "Punctuated Equilibrium and Linear Progression: Toward a New Understanding of Group Development," *Academy of Management Journal* 46, no. 1 (2003), pp. 106–117.

34 K. L. Bettenhausen, "Five Years of Groups Research: What We Have Learned and What Needs to be Addressed," *Journal of Management* 17, 1991, pp. 345–381; and R. A. Guzzo and G. P. Shea, "Group Performance and Intergroup Relations in Organizations," in *Handbook of Industrial and Organizational Psychology*, vol. 3, 2nd ed., ed. M. D. Dunnette and L. M. Hough (Palo Alto, CA: Consulting Psychologists Press, 1992), pp. 269–313.

35 A. Chang, P. Bordia, and J. Duck, "Punctuated Equilibrium and Linear Progression: Toward a New Understanding of Group Development," *Academy of Management Journal* 46, no. 1 (2003), pp. 106–117; and S. G. S. Lim and J. K. Murnighan, "Phases, Deadlines, and the Bargaining Process," *Organizational Behavior and Human Decision Processes* 58 (1994), pp. 153–171.

36 Vignette based on A. Tesolin, "Igniting the Creative Spark at Cirque du Soleil—Arupa Tesolin Interviews Lyn Heward Creative Leader at Cirque," *SelfGrowth.com*, http://www.selfgrowth.com/articles/Igniting_the_Creative_Spark_at_Cirque_du_Soleil.html; and M. Baghai and J. Quigley, "Cirque du Soleil: A Very Different Vision of Teamwork," *Fast Company*, February 4, 2011.

37 See, for instance, D. L. Gladstein, "Groups in Context: A Model of Task Group Effectiveness," *Administrative Science Quarterly*, December 1984, pp. 499–517; J. R. Hackman, "The Design of Work Teams," in *Handbook of Organizational Behavior*, ed. J. W. Lorsch (Englewood Cliffs, NJ: Prentice Hall, 1987), pp. 315–342; M. A. Campion, G. J. Medsker, and

C. A. Higgs, "Relations between Work Group Characteristics and Effectiveness: Implications for Designing Effective Work Groups," *Personnel Psychology*, 1993; and R. A. Guzzo and M. W. Dickson, "Teams in Organizations: Recent Research on Performance and Effectiveness," in *Annual Review of Psychology*, vol. 47, ed. J. T. Spence, J. M. Darley, and D. J. Foss, 1996, pp. 307–338.

38 D. E. Hyatt and T. M. Ruddy, "An Examination of the Relationship between Work Group Characteristics and Performance: Once More into the Breech," *Personnel Psychology*, Autumn 1997, p. 555.

39 This model is based on M. A. Campion, E. M. Papper, and G. J. Medsker, "Relations between Work Team Characteristics and Effectiveness: A Replication and Extension," *Personnel Psychology*, Summer 1996, pp. 429–452; D. E. Hyatt and T. M. Ruddy, "An Examination of the Relationship between Work Group Characteristics and Performance: Once More into the Breech," *Personnel Psychology*, Autumn 1997, pp. 553–585; S. G. Cohen and D. E. Bailey, "What Makes Teams Work: Group Effectiveness Research from the Shop Floor to the Executive Suite," *Journal of Management* 23, no. 3 (1997), pp. 239–290; G. A. Neuman and J. Wright, "Team Effectiveness: Beyond Skills and Cognitive Ability," *Journal of Applied Psychology*, June 1999, pp. 376–389; and L. Thompson, *Making the Team* (Upper Saddle River, NJ: Prentice Hall, 2000), pp. 18–33.

40 See M. Mattson, T. V. Mumford, and G. S. Sintay, "Taking Teams to Task: A Normative Model for Designing or Recalibrating Work Teams" (paper presented at the National Academy of Management Conference, Chicago, August 1999); and G. L. Stewart and M. R. Barrick, "Team Structure and Performance: Assessing the Mediating Role of Intrateam Process and the Moderating Role of Task Type," *Academy of Management Journal*, April 2000, pp. 135–148.

41 Based on W. G. Dyer, R. H. Daines, and W. C. Giauque, *The Challenge of Management* (New York: Harcourt Brace Jovanovich, 1990), p. 343.

42 J. R. Hackman, *Leading Teams* (Boston: Harvard Business School Press, 2002).

43 P. Balkundi and D. A. Harrison, "Ties, Leaders, and Time in Teams: Strong Inference About Network Structure's Effects on Team Viability and Performance," *Academy of Management Journal* 49, no. 1 (2006), pp. 49–68; G. Chen, B. L. Kirkman, R. Kanfer, D. Allen, and B. Rosen, "A Multilevel Study of Leadership, Empowerment, and Performance in Teams," *Journal of Applied Psychology* 92, no. 2 (2007), pp. 331–346; L. A. DeChurch and M. A. Marks, "Leadership in Multiteam Systems," *Journal of Applied Psychology* 91, no. 2 (2006), pp. 311–329; A. Srivastava, K. M. Bartol, and E. A. Locke, "Empowering Leadership in Management Teams: Effects on Knowledge Sharing, Efficacy, and Performance," *Academy of Management Journal* 49, no. 6 (2006), pp. 1239–1251; J. E. Mathieu, K. K. Gilson, and T. M. Ruddy, "Empowerment and Team Effectiveness: An Empirical Test of an Integrated Model," *Journal of Applied Psychology* 91, no. 1 (2006), pp. 97–108; and K. J. Klein, A. P. Knight, J. C. Ziegert, B. C. Lim, and J. L. Saltz, "When Team Members' Values Differ: The Moderating Role of Team Leadership," *Organizational Behavior & Human Decision Processes* 114, no. 1 (2011), pp. 25–36.

44 R. I. Beekun, "Assessing the Effectiveness of Sociotechnical Interventions: Antidote or Fad?" *Human Relations*, October 1989, pp. 877–897.

45 S. G. Cohen, G. E. Ledford, and G. M. Spreitzer, "A Predictive Model of Self-Managing Work Team Effectiveness," *Human Relations*, May 1996, pp. 643–676.

46 D. R. Ilgen, J. R. Hollenbeck, M. Johnson, and D. Jundt, "Teams in Organizations: From Input-Process-Output Models to IMOI Models," *Annual Review of Psychology* 56, no. 1 (2005), pp. 517–543.

47 K. T. Dirks, "Trust in Leadership and Team Performance: Evidence from NCAA Basketball," *Journal of Applied Psychology*, December 2000, pp. 1004–1012; and M. Williams, "In Whom We Trust: Group Membership as an Affective Context for Trust Development," *Academy of Management Review*, July 2001, pp. 377–396.

48 "Relationship Building Breeds Success," *National Post*, August 11, 2008, p. FP7.

49 See S. T. Johnson, "Work Teams: What's Ahead in Work Design and Rewards Management," *Compensation & Benefits Review*, March–April 1993, pp. 35–41; and A. M. Saunier and E. J. Hawk, "Realizing the Potential of Teams through Team-Based Rewards," *Compensation & Benefits Review*, July–August 1994, pp. 24–33.

50 M. J. Pearsall, M. S. Christian, A. P. J. Ellis, "Motivating Interdependent Teams: Individual Rewards, Shared Rewards, or Something in Between?" *Journal of Applied Psychology* 95, no. 1 (2010), pp. 183–191.

51 K. Merriman, "Low-Trust Teams Prefer Individualized Pay," *Harvard Business Review* 86, no. 11 (November 2008), p. 32.

52 J. Pfeffer and N. Langton, "The Effect of Wage Dispersion on Satisfaction, Productivity, and Working Collaboratively: Evidence from College and University Faculty," *Administrative Science Quarterly* 38, 1993, pp. 382–407.

53 M. Bloom, "The Performance Effects of Pay Dispersion on Individuals and Organizations," *Academy of Management Journal* 42, 1999, pp. 25–40.

54 For a more detailed breakdown on team skills, see M. J. Stevens and M. A. Campion, "The Knowledge, Skill, and Ability Requirements for Teamwork: Implications for Human Resource Management," *Journal of Management*, Summer 1994, pp. 503–530.

55 S. T. Bell, "Deep-Level Composition Variables as Predictors of Team Performance: A Meta-analysis," *Journal of Applied Psychology* 92, no. 3 (2007), pp. 595–615; and M. R. Barrick, G. L. Stewart, M. J. Neubert, and M. K. Mount, "Relating Member Ability and Personality to Work-Team Processes and Team Effectiveness," *Journal of Applied Psychology*, June 1998, pp. 377–391.

56 K. Tasa, G. J. Sears, and A. C. H. Schat, "Personality and Teamwork Behavior in Context: The Cross-Level Moderating Role of Collective Efficacy," *Journal of Organizational Behavior* 32, no. 1 (2011), pp. 65–85.

57 A. Ellis, J. R. Hollenbeck, D. R. Ilgen, C. O. Porter, B. West, and H. Moon, "Team Learning: Collectively Connecting the Dots," *Journal of Applied Psychology* 88 (2003), pp. 821–835; C. O. L. H. Porter, J. R. Hollenbeck, and D. R. Ilgen, "Backing up Behaviors in Teams: The Role of Personality and Legitimacy of Need," *Journal of Applied Psychology* 88, no. 3 (June 2003), pp. 391–403; A. Colquitt, J. R. Hollenbeck, and D. R. Ilgen, "Computer-Assisted Communication and Team Decision-Making Performance: The Moderating Effect of Openness to Experience," *Journal of Applied Psychology* 87, no. 2 (April 2002), pp. 402–410; J. A. LePine, J. R. Hollenbeck, D. R. Ilgen, and J. Hedlund, "The Effects of Individual Differences on the Performance of Hierarchical Decision Making Teams: Much More Than G," *Journal of Applied Psychology* 82 (1997), pp. 803–811; C. L. Jackson and J. A. LePine, "Peer Responses to a Team's Weakest Link," *Journal of Applied Psychology* 88, no. 3 (2003), pp. 459–475; and M. R. Barrick, G. L. Stewart, J. M. Neubert, and M. K. Mount, "Relating Member Ability and Personality to Work-Team Processes and Team Effectiveness," *Journal of Applied Psychology* 83, no. 3 (1998), pp. 377–391.

58 M. A. Neale, G. B. Northcraft, and K. A. Jehn, "Exploring Pandora's Box: The Impact of Diversity and Conflict on Work Group Performance," *Performance Improvement Quarterly* 12, no. 1 (1999), pp. 113–126.

59 S. E. Humphrey, F. P. Morgeson, and M. J. Mannor, "Developing a Theory of the Strategic Core of Teams: A Role Composition

Model of Team Performance," *Journal of Applied Psychology* 94, no. 1 (2009), pp. 48–61.

60 E. Sundstrom, K. P. Meuse, and D. Futrell, "Work Teams: Applications and Effectiveness," *American Psychologist*, February 1990, pp. 120–133.

61 See, for instance, M. Sashkin and K. J. Kiser, *Putting Total Quality Management to Work* (San Francisco: Berrett-Koehler, 1993); and J. R. Hackman and R. Wageman, "Total Quality Management: Empirical, Conceptual and Practical Issues," *Administrative Science Quarterly*, June 1995, pp. 309–342.

62 A. Joshi and H. Roh, "The Role of Context in Work Team Diversity Research: A Meta-analytic Review," *Academy of Management Journal* 52, no. 3 (2009), pp. 599–627; and S. K. Horwitz and I. B. Horwitz, "The Effects of Team Diversity on Team Outcomes: A Meta-analytic Review of Team Demography," *Journal of Management* 33, no. 6 (2007), pp. 987–1015.

63 G. S. Van Der Vegt, J. S. Bunderson, and A. Oosterhof, "Expertness Diversity and Interpersonal Helping in Teams: Why Those Who Need the Most Help End Up Getting the Least," *Academy of Management Journal* 49, no. 5 (2006), pp. 877–893.

64 "Is Your Team Too Big? Too Small? What's the Right Number?" *Knowledge@Wharton*, June 14, 2006, pp. 1–5.

65 See D. R. Comer, "A Model of Social Loafing in Real Work Groups," *Human Relations*, June 1995, pp. 647–667.

66 W. Moede, "Die Richtlinien der Leistungs-Psychologie," *Industrielle Psychotechnik* 4 (1927), pp. 193–207. See also D. A. Kravitz and B. Martin, "Ringelmann Rediscovered: The Original Article," *Journal of Personality and Social Psychology*, May 1986, pp. 936–941.

67 See, for example, J. A. Shepperd, "Productivity Loss in Performance Groups: A Motivation Analysis," *Psychological Bulletin*, January 1993, pp. 67–81; and S. J. Karau and K. D. Williams, "Social Loafing: A Meta-analytic Review and Theoretical Integration," *Journal of Personality and Social Psychology*, October 1993, pp. 681–706.

68 D. E. Hyatt and T. M. Ruddy, "An Examination of the Relationship between Work Group Characteristics and Performance: Once More into the Breech," *Personnel Psychology*, Autumn 1997, p. 555; and J. D. Shaw, M. K. Duffy, and E. M. Stark, "Interdependence and Preference for Group Work: Main and Congruence Effects on the Satisfaction and Performance of Group Members," *Journal of Management* 26, no. 2 (2000), pp. 259–279.

69 R. Wageman, "Critical Success Factors for Creating Superb Self-Managing Teams," *Organizational Dynamics*, Summer 1997, p. 55.

70 M. A. Campion, E. M. Papper, and G. J. Medsker, "Relations between Work Team Characteristics and Effectiveness: A Replication and Extension," *Personnel Psychology*, Summer 1996, p. 430.

71 M. A. Campion, E. M. Papper, and G. J. Medsker, "Relations between Work Team Characteristics and Effectiveness: A Replication and Extension," *Personnel Psychology*, Summer 1996, p. 430.

72 J. A. LePine, R. F. Piccolo, C. L. Jackson, J. E. Mathieu, and J. R. Saul, "A Meta-analysis of Teamwork Processes: Tests of a Multidimensional Model and Relationships with Team Effectiveness Criteria," *Personnel Psychology* 61 (2008), pp. 273–307.

73 I. D. Steiner, *Group Processes and Productivity* (New York: Academic Press, 1972).

74 J. A. LePine, R. F. Piccolo, C. L. Jackson, J. E. Mathieu, and J. R. Saul, "A Meta-analysis of Teamwork Processes: Tests of a Multidimensional Model and Relationships with Team Effectiveness Criteria," *Personnel Psychology* 61 (2008), pp. 273–307; and J. E. Mathieu and T. L. Rapp, "Laying the Foundation for Successful Team Performance Trajectories: The Roles of Team Charters and Performance Strategies," *Journal of Applied Psychology* 94, no. 1 (2009), pp. 90–103.

75 J. E. Mathieu and W. Schulze, "The Influence of Team Knowledge and Formal Plans on Episodic Team Process—Performance Relationships," *Academy of Management Journal* 49, no. 3 (2006), pp. 605–619.

76 A. Gurtner, F. Tschan, N. K. Semmer, and C. Nagele, "Getting Groups to Develop Good Strategies: Effects of Reflexivity Interventions on Team Process, Team Performance, and Shared Mental Models," *Organizational Behavior and Human Decision Processes* 102 (2007), pp. 127–142; M. C. Schippers, D. N. Den Hartog, and P. L. Koopman, "Reflexivity in Teams: A Measure and Correlates," *Applied Psychology: An International Review* 56, no. 2 (2007), pp. 189–211; and C. S. Burke, K. C. Stagl, E. Salas, L. Pierce, and D. Kendall, "Understanding Team Adaptation: A Conceptual Analysis and Model," *Journal of Applied Psychology* 91, no. 6 (2006), pp. 1189–1207.

77 E. Weldon and L. R. Weingart, "Group Goals and Group Performance," *British Journal of Social Psychology*, Spring 1993, pp. 307–334.

78 K. Tasa, S. Taggar, and G. H. Seijts, "The Development of Collective Efficacy in Teams: A Multilevel and Longitudinal Perspective," *Journal of Applied Psychology* 92, no. 1 (2007), pp. 17–27; C. B. Gibson, "The Efficacy Advantage: Factors Related to the Formation of Group Efficacy," *Journal of Applied Social Psychology*, October 2003, pp. 2153–2086; and D. I. Jung and J. J. Sosik, "Group Potency and Collective Efficacy: Examining Their Predictive Validity, Level of Analysis, and Effects of Performance Feedback on Future Group Performance," *Group & Organization Management*, September 2003, pp. 366–391.

79 For some of the controversy surrounding the definition of cohesion, see J. Keyton and J. Springston, "Redefining Cohesiveness in Groups," *Small Group Research*, May 1990, pp. 234–254.

80 C. R. Evans and K. L. Dion, "Group Cohesion and Performance: A Meta-analysis," *Small Group Research*, May 1991, pp. 175–186; B. Mullen and C. Cooper, "The Relation between Group Cohesiveness and Performance: An Integration," *Psychological Bulletin*, March 1994, pp. 210–227; S. M. Gully, D. J. Devine, and D. J. Whitney, "A Meta-analysis of Cohesion and Performance: Effects of Level of Analysis and Task Interdependence," *Small Group Research*, 1995, pp. 497–520; and P. M. Podsakoff, S. B. MacKenzie, and M. Ahearne, "Moderating Effects of Goal Acceptance on the Relationship between Group Cohesiveness and Productivity," *Journal of Applied Psychology*, December 1997, pp. 974–983.

81 A. Chang and P. Bordia, "A Multidimensional Approach to the Group Cohesion-Group Performance Relationship," *Small Group Research*, August 2001, pp. 379–405.

82 Paragraph based on R. Kreitner and A. Kinicki, *Organizational Behavior*, 6th ed. (New York: Irwin, 2004), pp. 459–461.

83 A. P. J. Ellis, "System Breakdown: The Role of Mental Models and Transactive Memory on the Relationships between Acute Stress and Team Performance," *Academy of Management Journal* 49, no. 3 (2006), pp. 576–589.

84 S. W. J. Kozlowski and D. R. Ilgen, "Enhancing the Effectiveness of Work Groups and Teams," *Psychological Science in the Public Interest*, December 2006, pp. 77–124; and B. D. Edwards, E. A. Day, W. Arthur Jr., and S. T. Bell, "Relationships among Team Ability Composition, Team Mental Models, and Team Performance," *Journal of Applied Psychology* 91, no. 3 (2006), pp. 727–736.

85 K. M. Eisenhardt, J. L. Kahwajy, and L. J. Bourgeois III, "How Management Teams Can Have a Good Fight," *Harvard Business Review*, July–August 1997, p. 78.

86 K. J. Behfar, R. S. Peterson, E. A. Mannix, and W. M. K. Trochim, "The Critical Role of Conflict Resolution in Teams: A Close

Look at the Links between Conflict Type, Conflict Management Strategies, and Team Outcomes," *Journal of Applied Psychology* 93, no. 1 (2008), pp. 170–188.

87 K. M. Eisenhardt, J. L. Kahwajy, and L. J. Bourgeois III, "How Management Teams Can Have a Good Fight," *Harvard Business Review*, July–August 1997, p. 78.

88 K. A. Jehn, S. Rispens, and S M. B. Thatcher, "The Effects of Conflict Asymmetry on Work Group and Individual Outcomes," *Academy of Management Journal* 53, no. 3 (2010), pp. 596–616.

89 K. Hess, *Creating the High-Performance Team* (New York: Wiley, 1987).

90 C. E. Naquin and R. O. Tynan, "The Team Halo Effect: Why Teams Are Not Blamed for Their Failures," *Journal of Applied Psychology*, April 2003, pp. 332–340.

91 D. Brown, "Innovative HR Ineffective in Manufacturing Firms," *Canadian HR Reporter*, April 7, 2003, pp. 1–2.

92 A. B. Drexler and R. Forrester, "Teamwork—Not Necessarily the Answer," *HR Magazine*, January 1998, pp. 55–58.

93 "Watson Wyatt's Global Work Studies," http://www.watsonwyatt.com/research/featured/workstudy.asp

94 C. E. Nicholls, H. W. Lane, and M. Brehm Brechu, "Taking Self-Managed Teams to Mexico," *Academy of Management Executive* 13, no. 3 (1999), pp. 15–27.

95 W. E. Watson, K. Kumar, and L. K. Michaelsen, "Cultural Diversity's Impact on Interaction Process and Performance: Comparing Homogeneous and Diverse Task Groups," *Academy of Management Journal*, June 1993, pp. 590–602; P. C. Earley and E. Mosakowski, "Creating Hybrid Team Cultures: An Empirical Test of Transnational Team Functioning," *Academy of Management Journal*, February 2000, pp. 26–49; and S. Mohammed and L. C. Angell, "Surface- and Deep-Level Diversity in Workgroups: Examining the Moderating Effects of Team Orientation and Team Process on Relationship Conflict," *Journal of Organizational Behavior*, December 2004, pp. 1015–1039.

96 W. E. Watson, K. Kumar, and L. K. Michaelsen, "Cultural Diversity's Impact on Interaction Process and Performance: Comparing Homogeneous and Diverse Task Groups," *Academy of Management Journal*, June 1993, pp. 590–602.

97 D. F. Crown, "The Use of Group and Groupcentric Individual Goals for Culturally Heterogeneous and Homogeneous Task Groups: An Assessment of European Work Teams," *Small Group Research* 38, no. 4 (2007), pp. 489–508.

98 Based on D. Man and S. S. K. Lam, "The Effects of Job Complexity and Autonomy on Cohesiveness in Collectivist and Individualistic Work Groups: A Cross-Cultural Analysis," *Journal of Organizational Behavior*, December 2003, pp. 979–1001.

Chapter 19

1 Vignette based on http://www.iabc.com/awards/gq/judging/WPMgt.htm

2 "Employers Cite Communication Skills, Honesty/Integrity as Key for Job Candidates," *IPMA-HR Bulletin*, March 23, 2007, p. 1.

3 J. Langan-Fox, "Communication in Organizations: Speed, Diversity, Networks, and Influence on Organizational Effectiveness, Human Health, and Relationships," in *Handbook of Industrial, Work and Organizational Psychology*, vol. 2, ed. N. Anderson, D. S. Ones, H. K. Sinangil, and C. Viswesvaran (Thousand Oaks, CA: Sage, 2001), p. 190.

4 J. C. McCroskey, J. A. Daly, and G. Sorenson, "Personality Correlates of Communication Apprehension," *Human Communication Research*, Spring 1976, pp. 376–380.

5 See R. L. Daft and R. H. Lengel, "Information Richness: A New Approach to Managerial Behavior and Organization Design," in *Research in Organizational Behavior*, vol. 6, ed. B. M. Staw and L. L. Cummings (Greenwich, CT: JAI Press, 1984), pp. 191–233; R. E. Rice and D. E. Shook, "Relationships of Job Categories and Organizational Levels to Use of Communication Channels, Including Electronic Mail: A Meta-analysis and Extension," *Journal of Management Studies*, March 1990, pp. 195–229; R. E. Rice, "Task Analyzability, Use of New Media, and Effectiveness," *Organization Science*, November 1992, pp. 475–500; S. G. Straus and J. E. McGrath, "Does the Medium Matter? The Interaction of Task Type and Technology on Group Performance and Member Reaction," *Journal of Applied Psychology*, February 1994, pp. 87–97; and J. Webster and L. K. Trevino, "Rational and Social Theories as Complementary Explanations of Communication Media Choices: Two Policy-Capturing Studies," *Academy of Management Journal*, December 1995, pp. 1544–1572.

6 "Building a Better Workforce," *PROFIT*, February 16, 2011, http://www.profitguide.com/article/10084--building-a-better-workforce--page0

7 R. L. Daft, R. H. Lengel, and L. K. Trevino, "Message Equivocality, Media Selection, and Manager Performance: Implications for Information Systems," *MIS Quarterly*, September 1987, pp. 355–368.

8 P. Brent, "How to Arm, Not Alarm, Your Staff in Crisis," *Canadian Business*, March 14, 2011, p. 68.

9 "Virtual Pink Slips Start Coming Online," *Vancouver Sun*, July 3, 1999, p. D15.

10 Vignette based on M. Ormsby, "Brawl Brewing In Girls' Hockey," *Toronto Star*, November 11, 2009.

11 K. Savitsky, B. Keysar, N. Epley, T. Carter, and A. Swanson, "The Closeness-Communication Bias: Increased Egocentrism among Friends versus Strangers," *Journal of Experimental Social Psychology* 47, no. 1 (2011), pp. 269–273.

12 M. Richtel, "Lost in E-mail, Tech Firms Face Self-Made Beast," *New York Times*, June 14, 2008.

13 J. Sandberg, "The Jargon Jumble," *Wall Street Journal*, October 24, 2006, p. B1.

14 E. W. Morrison and F. J. Milliken, "Organizational Silence: A Barrier to Change and Development in a Pluralistic World," *Academy of Management Review* 25, no. 4 (2000), pp. 706–725; and B. E. Ashforth and V. Anand, "The Normalization of Corruption in Organizations," *Research in Organizational Behavior* 25 (2003), pp. 1–52.

15 F. J. Milliken, E. W. Morrison, and P. F. Hewlin, "An Exploratory Study of Employee Silence: Issues That Employees Don't Communicate Upward and Why," *Journal of Management Studies* 40, no. 6 (2003), pp. 1453–1476.

16 This paragraph is based on J. O'Toole and W. Bennis, "What's Needed Next: A Culture of Candor," *Harvard Business Review*, June 2009, pp. 54–61.

17 S. Tangirala and R. Ramunujam, "Employee Silence on Critical Work Issues: The Cross-Level Effects of Procedural Justice Climate," *Personnel Psychology* 61, no. 1 (2008), pp. 37–68; and F. Bowen and K. Blackmon, "Spirals of Silence: The Dynamic Effects of Diversity on Organizational Voice," *Journal of Management Studies* 40, no. 6 (2003), pp. 1393–1417.

18 C. G. Pinder and K. P. Harlos, "Silent Organizational Behavior" (paper presented at the Western Academy of Management Conference, March 2000).

19 L. S. Rashotte, "What Does That Smile Mean? The Meaning of Nonverbal Behaviors in Social Interaction," *Social Psychology Quarterly*, March 2002, pp. 92–102.

20 R. L. Birdwhistell, *Introduction to Kinesics* (Louisville, KY: University of Louisville Press, 1952).

21 J. Fast, *Body Language* (Philadelphia, PA: M. Evan, 1970), p. 7.

22 A. Mehrabian, *Nonverbal Communication* (Chicago: Aldine-Atherton, 1972).

23 N. M. Henley, "Body Politics Revisited: What Do We Know Today?" in *Gender, Power, and Communication in Human Relationships*, ed. P. J. Kalbfleisch and M. J. Cody (Hillsdale, NJ: Erlbaum, 1995), pp. 27–61.

24 E. T. Hall, *The Hidden Dimension*, 2nd ed. (Garden City, NY: Anchor Books/Doubleday, 1966).

25 H. Weeks, "Taking the Stress Out of Stressful Conversations," *Harvard Business Review*, July–August 2001, pp. 112–119.

26 Vignette based on S.-A. Levy, "City Offside in Shuffling Ice Time," *Toronto Sun*, May 6, 2010; and http://www.iabc.com/awards/gq/judging/WPMgt.htm

27 R. L. Simpson, "Vertical and Horizontal Communication in Formal Organizations," *Administrative Science Quarterly*, September 1959, pp. 188–196; and B. Harriman, "Up and Down the Communications Ladder," *Harvard Business Review*, September–October 1974, pp. 143–151.

28 P. Dvorak, "How Understanding the 'Why' of Decisions Matters," *Wall Street Journal*, March 19, 2007, p. B3.

29 "Building a Better Workforce," *PROFIT*, February 16, 2011, http://www.profitguide.com/article/10084--building-a-better-workforce--page0

30 "Building a Better Workforce," *PROFIT*, February 16, 2011, http://www.profitguide.com/article/10084--building-a-better-workforce--page0

31 J. R. Detert and L. K. Treviño, "Speaking Up to Higher-Ups: How Supervisors and Skip-Level Leaders Influence Employee Voice," *Organization Science* 21, no. 1 (2010), pp. 249–270.

32 E. Nichols, "Hyper-Speed Managers," *HR Magazine*, April 2007, pp. 107–110.

33 D. M. Saunders and J. D. Leck, "Formal Upward Communication Procedures: Organizational and Employee Perspectives," *Revue Canadienne des Sciences de l'Administration*, September 1993, pp. 255–268.

34 "Heard It through the Grapevine," *Forbes*, February 10, 1997, p. 22.

35 G. Van Hoye and F. Lievens, "Tapping the Grapevine: A Closer Look at Word-of-Mouth as a Recruitment Source," *Journal of Applied Psychology* 94, no. 2 (2009), pp. 341–352.

36 See, for instance, J. W. Newstrom, R. E. Monczka, and W. E. Reif, "Perceptions of the Grapevine: Its Value and Influence," *Journal of Business Communication*, Spring 1974, pp. 12–20; and S. J. Modic, "Grapevine Rated Most Believable," *IndustryWeek*, May 15, 1989, p. 14.

37 K. Davis cited in R. Rowan, "Where Did That Rumor Come From?" *Fortune*, August 13, 1979, p. 134.

38 Based on L. Hirschhorn, "Managing Rumors," in *Cutting Back*, ed. L. Hirschhorn (San Francisco: Jossey-Bass, 1983), pp. 54–56.

39 R. L. Rosnow and G. A. Fine, *Rumor and Gossip: The Social Psychology of Hearsay* (New York: Elsevier, 1976).

40 See, for instance, J. G. March and G. Sevon, "Gossip, Information and Decision Making," in *Decisions and Organizations*, ed. J. G. March (Oxford: Blackwell, 1988), pp. 429–442; M. Noon and R. Delbridge, "News from Behind My Hand: Gossip in Organizations," *Organization Studies* 14, no. 1 (1993), pp. 23–36; and N. DiFonzo, P. Bordia, and R. L. Rosnow, "Reining in Rumors," *Organizational Dynamics*, Summer 1994, pp. 47–62.

41 J. K. Bosson, A. B. Johnson, K. Niederhoffer, and W. B. Swann Jr., "Interpersonal Chemistry through Negativity: Bonding by Sharing Negative Attitudes About Others," *Personal Relationships* 13 (2006), pp. 135–150.

42 B. Gates, "How I Work," *Fortune*, April 17, 2006, http://money.cnn.com

43 "Email Brings Costs and Fatigue," *Western News (UWO)*, July 9, 2004, http://communications.uwo.ca/com/western_news/stories/email_brings_costs_and_fatigue_20040709432320/

44 K. Macklem, "You've Got Too Much Mail," *Maclean's*, January 30, 2006, pp. 20–21.

45 "Overloaded Canadians Trash 42% of All E-Mails: Study," *Ottawa Citizen*, June 26, 2008, p. D5.

46 D. Brady, "*!#?@ the E-mail. Can We Talk?" *BusinessWeek*, December 4, 2006, p. 109.

47 E. Binney, "Is E-mail the New Pink Slip?" *HR Magazine*, November 2006, pp. 32–33; and R. L. Rundle, "Critical Case: How an Email Rant Jolted a Big HMO," *Wall Street Journal*, April 24, 2007, pp. A1, A16.

48 S. Hourigan, "62 Trillion Spam Emails Cause Huge Carbon Footprint," *Courier Mail*, April 17, 2009, http://www.news.com.au/couriermail

49 R. Stross, "The Daily Struggle to Avoid Burial by E-Mail," *New York Times*, April 21, 2008, p. BU5; and H. Rhodes, "You've Got Mail . . . Again," *Gainesville Sun*, September 29, 2008, pp. 1D, 6D.

50 C. Byron, "Carrying Too Heavy a Load? The Communication and Miscommunication of Emotion by Email," *Academy of Management Review* 33, no. 2 (2008), pp. 309–327.

51 D. Goleman, "Flame First, Think Later: New Clues to E-mail Misbehavior," *New York Times*, February 20, 2007, p. D5; and E. Krell, "The Unintended Word," *HR Magazine*, August 2006, pp. 50–54.

52 R. Zeidner, "Keeping E-mail in Check," *HR Magazine*, June 2007, pp. 70–74; "E-mail May Be Hazardous to Your Career," *Fortune*, May 14, 2007, p. 24; and J. D. Glater, "Open Secrets," *New York Times*, June 27, 2008, pp. B1, B5.

53 E. Church, "Employers Read E-mail as Fair Game," *Globe and Mail*, April 14, 1998, p. B16.

54 A. Harmon, "Appeal of Instant Messaging Extends into the Workplace," *New York Times*, March 11, 2003, p. A1.

55 http://www.cwta.ca/CWTASite/english/industryfacts.html

56 J. Bow, "Business Jumps on Text-Messaging Wave," *Business Edge*, April 5, 2007, p. 12.

57 A. Williams, "Mind Your BlackBerry or Mind Your Manners," *New York Times*, June 21, 2009, http://www.nytimes.com

58 "Survey Finds Mixed Reviews on Checking E-mail During Meetings," *IPMA-HR Bulletin*, April 27, 2007, p. 1.

59 K. Gurchiek, "Shoddy Writing Can Trip Up Employees, Organizations," *SHRM Online*, April 27, 2006, pp. 1–2.

60 D. Lidsky, "It's Not Just Who You Know," *Fast Company*, May 2007, p. 56.

61 J. Castaldo, "Are You Sure You Really Want To Tweet That, Boss?" *Canadian Business*, November 22, 2010.

62 J. Castaldo, "Are You Sure You Really Want To Tweet That, Boss?" *Canadian Business*, November 22, 2010.

63 M. Richtel, "Lost in E-mail, Tech Firms Face Self-Made Beast," *New York Times*, June 14, 2008, pp. A1, A14.

64 J. B. Spira and C. Burke, "Intel's War on Information Overload: A Case Study," copyright © 2009 Basex, Inc.

65 M. Richtel, "Lost in E-mail, Tech Firms Face Self-Made Beast," *New York Times*, June 14, 2008, pp. A1, A14.

66 M. Richtel, "Lost in E-mail, Tech Firms Face Self-Made Beast," *New York Times*, June 14, 2008, pp. A1, A14.

67 Based on M. Conlin and M. MacMillan, "Managing the Tweets," *BusinessWeek*, June 1, 2009, pp. 20–21; H. Green and R. D. Hof, "Six Million Users: Nothing to Twitter At," *BusinessWeek*,

March 16, 2009, pp. 51–52; and A. Hawkins, "Shut Up, Already," *Forbes*, April 7, 2008, p. 44.

68 D. Harris, "Crackberry Addiction: Gadget Users Compared to Drug Users for Excessive Behavior," *ABCNews Online*, August 23, 2006, http://abcnews.go.com/WNT/Technology/story?id=2348779

69 W. R. Boswell and J. B. Olson-Buchanan, "The Use of Communication Technologies After Hours: The Role of Work-Attitudes and Work-Life Conflict," *Journal of Management* 33, no. 4 (2007), pp. 592–610.

70 "At Many Companies, Hunt for Leakers Expands Arsenal of Monitoring Tactics," *Wall Street Journal*, September 11, 2006, pp. B1, B3; and B. J. Alge, G. A. Ballinger, S. Tangirala, and J. L. Oakley, "Information Privacy in Organizations: Empowering Creative and Extrarole Performance," *Journal of Applied Psychology* 91, no. 1 (2006), pp. 221–232.

71 See M. Munter, "Cross-Cultural Communication for Managers," *Business Horizons*, May–June 1993, pp. 75–76; and H. Ren and B. Gray, "Repairing Relationship Conflict: How Violation Types and Culture Influence the Effectiveness of Restoration Rituals," *Academy of Management Review* 34, no. 1 (2009), pp. 105–126.

72 See E. T. Hall, *Beyond Culture* (Garden City, NY: Anchor Press/Doubleday, 1976); E. T. Hall and M. R. Hall, *Understanding Cultural Differences* (Yarmouth, ME: Intercultural Press, 1990); W. L. Adair, "Integrative Sequences and Negotiation Outcome in Same- and Mixed-Culture Negotiations," *International Journal of Conflict Management* 14, no. 3–4 (2003), pp. 1359–1392; W. L. Adair and J. M. Brett, "The Negotiation Dance: Time, Culture, and Behavioral Sequences in Negotiation," *Organization Science* 16, no. 1 (2005), pp. 33–51; E. Giebels and P. J. Taylor, "Interaction Patterns in Crisis Negotiations: Persuasive Arguments and Cultural Differences," *Journal of Applied Psychology* 94, no. 1 (2009), pp. 5–19; and Y. Fujimoto, N. Bahfen, J. Fermelise, and C. E. J. Härtel, "The Global Village: Online Cross-Cultural Communication and HRM," *Cross Cultural Management* 14, no. 1 (2007), pp. 7–22.

73 N. Adler, *International Dimensions of Organizational Behavior*, 3rd ed. (Cincinnati, OH: South Western College, 1997), pp. 87–88.

Chapter 20

1 Vignette based on National Defence, "Canadian Forces Snowbirds to Gain Leadership Depth," (news release), January 9, 2010, http://www.snowbirds.dnd.ca/v2/nr-sp/nr-sp-eng.asp?cat=2&id=321; J. Graham, "She's the Boss: Snowbirds First Female Pilot to Lead Aerobatic Squad," *Canadian Press*, May 2, 2010, http://www.cbc.ca/canada/saskatchewan/story/2010/05/02/sask-snowbirds.html#ixzz0mv2nPxRr; and C. Coward, "Five Questions with a Snowbird," *Hamilton Spectator*, November 5, 2011, http://www.thespec.com/localprofile/article/620542--five-questions-with-a-snowbird

2 J. P. Kotter, "What Leaders Really Do," *Harvard Business Review*, May–June 1990, pp. 103–111.

3 R. N. Kanungo, "Leadership in Organizations: Looking Ahead to the 21st Century," *Canadian Psychology* 39, no. 1–2 (1998), p. 77. For more evidence of this consensus, see N. Adler, *International Dimensions of Organizational Behavior*, 3rd ed. (Cincinnati, OH: South Western, 1997); R. J. House, "Leadership in the Twenty-First Century," in *The Changing Nature of Work*, ed. A. Howard (San Francisco: Jossey-Bass, 1995), pp. 411–450; R. N. Kanungo and M. Mendonca, *Ethical Dimensions of Leadership* (Thousand Oaks, CA: Sage, 1996); and A. Zaleznik, "The Leadership Gap," *Academy of Management Executive* 4, no. 1 (1990), pp. 7–22.

4 Vignette based on J. Graham, "She's the Boss: Snowbirds First Female Pilot to Lead Aerobatic Squad," *Canadian Press*, May 2, 2010, http://www.cbc.ca/canada/saskatchewan/story/2010/05/02/sask-snowbirds.html#ixzz0mv2nPxRr

5 J. G. Geier, "A Trait Approach to the Study of Leadership in Small Groups," *Journal of Communication*, December 1967, pp. 316–323.

6 S. A. Kirkpatrick and E. A. Locke, "Leadership: Do Traits Matter?" *Academy of Management Executive*, May 1991, pp. 48–60; and S. J. Zaccaro, R. J. Foti, and D. A. Kenny, "Self-Monitoring and Trait-Based Variance in Leadership: An Investigation of Leader Flexibility across Multiple Group Situations," *Journal of Applied Psychology*, April 1991, pp. 308–315.

7 See T. A. Judge, J. E. Bono, R. Ilies, and M. Werner, "Personality and Leadership: A Review" (paper presented at the 15th Annual Conference of the Society for Industrial and Organizational Psychology, New Orleans, 2000); and T. A. Judge, J. E. Bono, R. Ilies, and M. W. Gerhardt, "Personality and Leadership: A Qualitative and Quantitative Review," *Journal of Applied Psychology*, August 2002, pp. 765–780.

8 T. A. Judge, J. E. Bono, R. Ilies, and M. Werner, "Personality and Leadership: A Review" (paper presented at the 15th Annual Conference of the Society for Industrial and Organizational Psychology, New Orleans, 2000).

9 D. R. Ames and F. J. Flynn, "What Breaks a Leader: The Curvilinear Relation between Assertiveness and Leadership," *Journal of Personality and Social Psychology* 92, no. 2 (2007), pp. 307–324.

10 K. Ng, S. Ang, and K. Chan, "Personality and Leader Effectiveness: A Moderated Mediation Model of Leadership Self-Efficacy, Job Demands, and Job Autonomy," *Journal of Applied Psychology* 93, no. 4 (2008), pp. 733–743.

11 This section is based on D. Goleman, "What Makes a Leader?" *Harvard Business Review*, November–December 1998, pp. 93–102; J. M. George, "Emotions and Leadership: The Role of Emotional Intelligence," *Human Relations*, August 2000, pp. 1027–1055; C.-S. Wong and K. S. Law, "The Effects of Leader and Follower Emotional Intelligence on Performance and Attitude: An Exploratory Study," *Leadership Quarterly*, June 2002, pp. 243–274; and D. R. Caruso and C. J. Wolfe, "Emotional Intelligence and Leadership Development," in *Leader Development for Transforming Organizations: Growing Leaders for Tomorrow*, ed. D. David and S. J. Zaccaro (Mahwah, NJ: Lawrence Erlbaum, 2004), pp. 237–263.

12 J. Champy, "The Hidden Qualities of Great Leaders," *Fast Company*, November 2003, p. 135.

13 J. Antonakis, "Why 'Emotional Intelligence' Does Not Predict Leadership Effectiveness: A Comment on Prati, Douglas, Ferris, Ammeter, and Buckley (2003)," *International Journal of Organizational Analysis* 11 (2003), pp. 355–361. See also M. Zeidner, G. Matthews, and R. D. Roberts, "Emotional Intelligence in the Workplace: A Critical Review," *Applied Psychology: An International Review* 53 (2004), pp. 371–399; and F. Walter, M. S. Cole, and R. H. Humphrey, "Emotional Intelligence: Sine Qua Non of Leadership or Folderol?" *Academy of Management Perspectives* 25, no. 1 (2011), pp. 45–59.

14 T. A. Judge, J. E. Bono, R. Ilies, and M. Werner, "Personality and Leadership: A Review" (paper presented at the 15th Annual Conference of the Society for Industrial and Organizational Psychology, New Orleans, 2000); R. G. Lord, C. L. DeVader, and G. M. Alliger, "A Meta-analysis of the Relation between Personality Traits and Leadership Perceptions: An Application of Validity Generalization Procedures," *Journal of Applied Psychology*, August 1986, pp. 402–410; and J. A. Smith and R. J. Foti, "A Pattern Approach to the Study of Leader Emergence," *Leadership Quarterly*, Summer 1998, pp. 147–160.

15 R. M. Stogdill and A. E. Coons, eds., *Leader Behavior: Its Description and Measurement*, Research Monograph no. 88 (Columbus: Ohio State University, Bureau of Business Research, 1951).

This research is updated in C. A. Schriesheim, C. C. Cogliser, and L. L. Neider, "Is It 'Trustworthy'? A Multiple-Levels-of-Analysis Reexamination of an Ohio State Leadership Study, with Implications for Future Research," *Leadership Quarterly*, Summer 1995, pp. 111–145; and T. A. Judge, R. F. Piccolo, and R. Ilies, "The Forgotten Ones? The Validity of Consideration and Initiating Structure in Leadership Research," *Journal of Applied Psychology*, February 2004, pp. 36–51.

16 D. Akst, "The Rewards of Recognizing a Job Well Done," *Wall Street Journal*, January 31, 2007, p. D9.

17 R. Kahn and D. Katz, "Leadership Practices in Relation to Productivity and Morale," in *Group Dynamics: Research and Theory*, 2nd ed., ed. D. Cartwright and A. Zander (Elmsford, NY: Row, Paterson, 1960).

18 T. A. Judge, R. F. Piccolo, and R. Ilies, "The Forgotten Ones? The Validity of Consideration and Initiating Structure in Leadership Research," *Journal of Applied Psychology*, February 2004, pp. 36–51.

19 G. Yukl and D. D. Van Fleet, "Theory and Research on Leadership in Organizations," in *Handbook of Industrial and Organizational Psychology*, vol. 2, ed. M. D. Dunnette and L. M. Hough (Palo Alto, CA: Consulting Psychologists Press, 1992), pp. 147–197.

20 For a critical review, see A. K. Korman, "'Consideration,' 'Initiating Structure' and Organizational Criteria—A Review," *Personnel Psychology* 19 (1966), pp. 349–361. For a more supportive review, see S. Kerr and C. Schriesheim, "Consideration, Initiating Structure, and Organizational Criteria—An Update of Korman's 1966 Review," *Personnel Psychology* 27 (1974), pp. 555–568.

21 Based on G. Johns and A. M. Saks, *Organizational Behaviour*, 5th ed. (Toronto: Pearson Education Canada, 2001), p. 276.

22 A. J. Mayo and N. Nohria, "Zeitgeist Leadership," *Harvard Business Review* 83, no. 10 (2005), pp. 45–60.

23 See, for instance, P. M. Podsakoff, S. B. MacKenzie, M. Ahearne, and W. H. Bommer, "Searching for a Needle in a Haystack: Trying to Identify the Illusive Moderators of Leadership Behavior," *Journal of Management* 1, no. 3 (1995), pp. 422–470.

24 F. E. Fiedler, *A Theory of Leadership Effectiveness* (New York: McGraw-Hill, 1967).

25 Cited in R. J. House and R. N. Aditya, "The Social Scientific Study of Leadership: Quo Vadis?" *Journal of Management* 23, no. 3 (1997), p. 422.

26 G. Johns and A. M. Saks, *Organizational Behaviour*, 5th ed. (Toronto: Pearson Education Canada, 2001), pp. 278–279.

27 For controversy surrounding the Fiedler LPC scale, see A. Bryman, "Leadership in Organizations," in *Handbook of Organization Studies*, ed. S. R. Clegg, C. Hardy, and W. R. Nord (London: Sage, 1996), pp. 279–280; A. Bryman, *Leadership and Organizations* (London: Routledge and Kegan Paul, 1986); and T. Peters and N. Austin, *A Passion for Excellence* (New York: Random House, 1985). For supportive evidence on the Fiedler model, see L. H. Peters, D. D. Hartke, and J. T. Pohlmann, "Fiedler's Contingency Theory of Leadership: An Application of the Meta-analysis Procedures of Schmidt and Hunter," *Psychological Bulletin*, March 1985, pp. 274–285; C. A. Schriesheim, B. J. Tepper, and L. A. Tetrault, "Least Preferred Co-Worker Score, Situational Control, and Leadership Effectiveness: A Meta-analysis of Contingency Model Performance Predictions," *Journal of Applied Psychology*, August 1994, pp. 561–573; and R. Ayman, M. M. Chemers, and F. Fiedler, "The Contingency Model of Leadership Effectiveness: Its Levels of Analysis," *Leadership Quarterly*, Summer 1995, pp. 147–167. For evidence that LPC scores are not stable, see, for instance, R. W. Rice, "Psychometric Properties of the Esteem for the Least Preferred Coworker (LPC) Scale," *Academy of Management Review*, January 1978, pp. 106–118; C. A. Schriesheim, B. D. Bannister, and

W. H. Money, "Psychometric Properties of the LPC Scale: An Extension of Rice's Review," *Academy of Management Review*, April 1979, pp. 287–290; and J. K. Kennedy, J. M. Houston, M. A. Korgaard, and D. D. Gallo, "Construct Space of the Least Preferred Co-worker (LPC) Scale," *Educational & Psychological Measurement*, Fall 1987, pp. 807–814. For difficulty in applying Fiedler's model, see E. H. Schein, *Organizational Psychology*, 3rd ed. (Englewood Cliffs, NJ: Prentice Hall, 1980), pp. 116–117; and B. Kabanoff, "A Critique of Leader Match and Its Implications for Leadership Research," *Personnel Psychology*, Winter 1981, pp. 749–764. For evidence that Hersey and Blanchard's model has received little attention from researchers, see R. K. Hambleton and R. Gumpert, "The Validity of Hersey and Blanchard's Theory of Leader Effectiveness," *Group & Organization Studies*, June 1982, pp. 225–242; C. L. Graeff, "The Situational Leadership Theory: A Critical View," *Academy of Management Review*, April 1983, pp. 285–291; R. P. Vecchio, "Situational Leadership Theory: An Examination of a Prescriptive Theory," *Journal of Applied Psychology*, August 1987, pp. 444–451; J. R. Goodson, G. W. McGee, and J. F. Cashman, "Situational Leadership Theory: A Test of Leadership Prescriptions," *Group & Organization Studies*, December 1989, pp. 446–461; W. Blank, J. R. Weitzel, and S. G. Green, "A Test of the Situational Leadership Theory," *Personnel Psychology*, Autumn 1990, pp. 579–597; and W. R. Norris and R. P. Vecchio, "Situational Leadership Theory: A Replication," *Group & Organization Management*, September 1992, pp. 331–342. For evidence of partial support for the theory, see R. P. Vecchio, "Situational Leadership Theory: An Examination of a Prescriptive Theory," *Journal of Applied Psychology*, August 1987, pp. 444–451; and W. R. Norris and R. P. Vecchio, "Situational Leadership Theory: A Replication," *Group & Organization Management*, September 1992, pp. 331–342; and for evidence of no support for Hersey and Blanchard, see W. Blank, J. R. Weitzel, and S. G. Green, "A Test of the Situational Leadership Theory," *Personnel Psychology*, Autumn 1990, pp. 579–597.

28 P. Hersey and K. H. Blanchard, "So You Want to Know Your Leadership Style?" *Training and Development Journal*, February 1974, pp. 1–15; and P. Hersey, K. H. Blanchard, and D. E. Johnson, *Management of Organizational Behavior: Leading Human Resources*, 8th ed. (Upper Saddle River, NJ: Prentice Hall, 2001), cited in C. F. Fernandez and R. P. Vecchio, "Situational Leadership Theory Revisited: A Test of an ACROSS-Jobs Perspective," *Leadership Quarterly* 8, no. 1 (1997), p. 67. See also http://www.situational.com/leadership.htm

29 See, for instance, C. F. Fernandez and R. P. Vecchio, "Situational Leadership Theory Revisited: A Test of an ACROSS-Jobs Perspective," *Leadership Quarterly* 8, no. 1 (1997), pp. 67–84; C. L. Graeff, "Evolution of Situational Leadership Theory: A Critical Review," *Leadership Quarterly* 8, no. 2 (1997), pp. 153–170; and R. P. Vecchio and K. J. Boatwright, "Preferences for Idealized Styles of Supervision," *Leadership Quarterly*, August 2002, pp. 327–342.

30 M. G. Evans, "The Effects of Supervisory Behavior on the Path-Goal Relationship," *Organizational Behavior and Human Performance* 5 (1970), pp. 277–298; M. G. Evans, "Leadership and Motivation: A Core Concept," *Academy of Management Journal* 13 (1970), pp. 91–102; R. J. House, "A Path-Goal Theory of Leader Effectiveness," *Administrative Science Quarterly*, September 1971, pp. 321–338; R. J. House and T. R. Mitchell, "Path-Goal Theory of Leadership," *Journal of Contemporary Business*, Autumn 1974, p. 86; M. G. Evans, "Leadership," in *Organizational Behavior*, ed. S. Kerr (Columbus, OH: Grid Publishing, 1979); R. J. House, "Retrospective Comment," in *The Great Writings in Management and Organizational Behavior*, 2nd ed., ed. L. E. Boone and D. D. Bowen (New York: Random House, 1987), pp. 354–364; and M. G. Evans, *"Fuhrungstheorien, Weg-ziel-theorie,"* in *Handworterbuch Der Fuhrung*, 2nd ed., ed. A. Kieser, G. Reber,

and R. Wunderer, trans. G. Reber (Stuttgart, Germany: Schaffer Poeschal Verlag, 1995), pp. 1075–1091.

31 G. R. Jones, J. M. George, C. W. L. Hill, and N. Langton, *Contemporary Management* (Toronto: McGraw-Hill Ryerson, 2002), p. 392.

32 J. C. Wofford and L. Z. Liska, "Path-Goal Theories of Leadership: A Meta-analysis," *Journal of Management* 19, no. 4 (1993), pp. 857–876.

33 P. M. Podsakoff, S. B. MacKenzie, and M. Ahearne, "Searching for a Needle in a Haystack: Trying to Identify the Illusive Moderators of Leadership Behaviors," *Journal of Management* 21 (1995), pp. 423–470.

34 J. R. Villa, J. P. Howell, and P. W. Dorfman, "Problems with Detecting Moderators in Leadership Research Using Moderated Multiple Regression," *Leadership Quarterly* 14 (2003), pp. 3–23; C. A. Schriesheim and L. Neider, "Path-Goal Leadership Theory: The Long and Winding Road," *Leadership Quarterly* 7 (1996), pp. 317–321; and M. G. Evans, "R. J. House's 'A Path-Goal Theory of Leader Effectiveness,'" *Leadership Quarterly* 7 (1996), pp. 305–309.

35 T. Sy, "What Do You Think of Followers? Examining the Content, Structure, and Consequences of Implicit Followership Theories," *Organizational Behavior and Human Decision Processes* 113, no. 2 (2010), pp. 73–84.

36 S. Kerr and J. M. Jermier, "Substitutes for Leadership: Their Meaning and Measurement," *Organizational Behavior and Human Performance*, December 1978, pp. 375–403; J. P. Howell and P. W. Dorfman, "Substitutes for Leadership: Test of a Construct," *Academy of Management Journal*, December 1981, pp. 714–728; J. P. Howell, P. W. Dorfman, and S. Kerr, "Leadership and Substitutes for Leadership," *Journal of Applied Behavioral Science* 22, no. 1 (1986), pp. 29–46; J. P. Howell, D. E. Bowen, P. W. Dorfman, S. Kerr, and P. M. Podsakoff, "Substitutes for Leadership: Effective Alternatives to Ineffective Leadership," *Organizational Dynamics*, Summer 1990, pp. 21–38; P. M. Podsakoff, B. P. Niehoff, S. B. MacKenzie, and M. L. Williams, "Do Substitutes for Leadership Really Substitute for Leadership? An Empirical Examination of Kerr and Jermier's Situational Leadership Model," *Organizational Behavior and Human Decision Processes*, February 1993, pp. 1–44; P. M. Podsakoff and S. B. MacKenzie, "An Examination of Substitutes for Leadership within a Levels-of-Analysis Framework," *Leadership Quarterly*, Fall 1995, pp. 289–328; P. M. Podsakoff, S. B. MacKenzie, and W. H. Bommer, "Transformational Leader Behaviors and Substitutes for Leadership as Determinants of Employee Satisfaction, Commitment, Trust, and Organizational Citizenship Behaviors," *Journal of Management* 22, no. 2 (1996), pp. 259–298; P. M. Podsakoff, S. B. MacKenzie, and W. H. Bommer, "Meta-analysis of the Relationships between Kerr and Jermier's Substitutes for Leadership and Employee Attitudes, Role Perceptions, and Performance," *Journal of Applied Psychology*, August 1996, pp. 380–399; and J. M. Jermier and S. Kerr, "'Substitutes for Leadership: Their Meaning and Measurement'— Contextual Recollections and Current Observations," *Leadership Quarterly* 8, no. 2 (1997), pp. 95–101.

37 S. D. Dionne, F. J. Yammarino, L. E. Atwater, and L. R. James, "Neutralizing Substitutes for Leadership Theory: Leadership Effects and Common-Source Bias," *Journal of Applied Psychology* 87 (2002), pp. 454–464; and J. R. Villa, J. P. Howell, P. W. Dorfman, and D. L. Daniel, "Problems with Detecting Moderators in Leadership Research Using Moderated Multiple Regression," *Leadership Quarterly* 14 (2002), pp. 3–23.

38 Vignette based on J. Graham, "She's the Boss: Snowbirds First Female Pilot to Lead Aerobatic Squad," *Canadian Press*, May 2, 2010, http://www.cbc.ca/canada/saskatchewan/story/2010/05/02/sask-snowbirds.html#ixzz0mv2nPxRr; and C. Coward, "Five Questions with a Snowbird," *Hamilton Spectator*, November 5, 2011, http://www.thespec.com/localprofile/article/620542--five-questions-with-a-snowbird

39 M. Weber, *The Theory of Social and Economic Organization*, trans. A. M. Henderson and T. Parsons (New York: The Free Press, 1947).

40 J. A. Conger and R. N. Kanungo, "Behavioral Dimensions of Charismatic Leadership," in *Charismatic Leadership*, ed. J. A. Conger and R. N. Kanungo (San Francisco: Jossey-Bass, 1988), p. 79.

41 J. A. Conger and R. N. Kanungo, *Charismatic Leadership in Organizations* (Thousand Oaks, CA: Sage, 1998); and R. Awamleh and W. L. Gardner, "Perceptions of Leader Charisma and Effectiveness: The Effects of Vision Content, Delivery, and Organizational Performance," *Leadership Quarterly*, Fall 1999, pp. 345–373.

42 B. Shamir, R. J. House, and M. B. Arthur, "The Motivational Effects of Charismatic Leadership: A Self-Concept Theory," *Organization Science*, November 1993, pp. 577–594.

43 R. Kark, B. Shamir, and G. Chen, "The Two Faces of Transformational Leadership: Empowerment and Dependency," *Journal of Applied Psychology* 88, no. 2 (2003), pp. 246–255.

44 D. N. Den Hartog, A. H. B. De Hoogh, and A. E. Keegan, "The Interactive Effects of Belongingness and Charisma on Helping and Compliance," *Journal of Applied Psychology* 92, no. 4 (2007), pp. 1131–1139.

45 A. Erez, V. F. Misangyi, D. E. Johnson, M. A. LePine, and K. C. Halverson, "Stirring the Hearts of Followers: Charismatic Leadership as the Transferal of Affect," *Journal of Applied Psychology* 93, no. 3 (2008), pp. 602–615. For reviews on the role of vision in leadership, see S. J. Zaccaro, "Visionary and Inspirational Models of Executive Leadership: Empirical Review and Evaluation," in *The Nature of Executive Leadership: A Conceptual and Empirical Analysis of Success*, ed. S. J. Zaccaro (Washington, DC: American Psychological Association, 2001), pp. 259–278; and M. Hauser and R. J. House, "Lead through Vision and Values," in *Handbook of Principles of Organizational Behavior*, ed. E. A. Locke (Malden, MA: Blackwell, 2004), pp. 257–273.

46 D. A. Waldman, B. M. Bass, and F. J. Yammarino, "Adding to Contingent-Reward Behavior: The Augmenting Effect of Charismatic Leadership," *Group & Organization Studies*, December 1990, pp. 381–394; and S. A. Kirkpatrick and E. A. Locke, "Direct and Indirect Effects of Three Core Charismatic Leadership Components on Performance and Attitudes," *Journal of Applied Psychology*, February 1996, pp. 36–51.

47 A. H. B. de Hoogh, D. N. den Hartog, P. L. Koopman, H. Thierry, P. T. van den Berg, and J. G. van der Weide, "Charismatic Leadership, Environmental Dynamism, and Performance," *European Journal of Work & Organizational Psychology*, December 2004, pp. 447–471; S. Harvey, M. Martin, and D. Stout, "Instructor's Transformational Leadership: University Student Attitudes and Ratings," *Psychological Reports*, April 2003, pp. 395–402; and D. A. Waldman, M. Javidan, and P. Varella, "Charismatic Leadership at the Strategic Level: A New Application of Upper Echelons Theory," *Leadership Quarterly*, June 2004, pp. 355–380.

48 R. J. House, "A 1976 Theory of Charismatic Leadership," in *Leadership: The Cutting Edge*, ed. J. G. Hunt and L. L. Larson (Carbondale, IL: Southern Illinois University Press, 1977), pp. 189–207; and Robert J. House and Ram N. Aditya, "The Social Scientific Study of Leadership," *Journal of Management* 23, no. 3 (1997), p. 441.

49 J. C. Pastor, M. Mayo, and B. Shamir, "Adding Fuel to Fire: The Impact of Followers' Arousal on Ratings of Charisma," *Journal of Applied Psychology* 92, no. 6 (2007), pp. 1584–1596.

50 F. Cohen, S. Solomon, M. Maxfield, T. Pyszczynski, and J. Greenberg, "Fatal Attraction: The Effects of Mortality Salience on Evaluations of Charismatic, Task-Oriented, and Relationship-Oriented Leaders," *Psychological Science*, December 2004, pp. 846–851; and M. G. Ehrhart and K. J. Klein, "Predicting Followers' Preferences for Charismatic Leadership: The Influence of Follower Values and Personality," *Leadership Quarterly*, Summer 2001, pp. 153–179.

51 K. Levine, R. Muenchen, and A. Brooks, "Measuring Transformational and Charismatic Leadership: Why Isn't Charisma Measured?" *Communication Monographs* 77, no. 4 (2010), pp. 576–591.

52 J. A. Conger, *The Charismatic Leader: Behind the Mystique of Exceptional Leadership* (San Francisco: Jossey-Bass, 1989); R. Hogan, R. Raskin, and D. Fazzini, "The Dark Side of Charisma," in *Measures of Leadership*, ed. K. E. Clark and M. B. Clark (West Orange, NJ: Leadership Library of America, 1990); D. Sankowsky, "The Charismatic Leader as Narcissist: Understanding the Abuse of Power," *Organizational Dynamics*, Spring 1995, pp. 57–71; and J. O'Connor, M. D. Mumford, T. C. Clifton, T. L. Gessner, and M. S. Connelly, "Charismatic Leaders and Destructiveness: An Historiometric Study," *Leadership Quarterly*, Winter 1995, pp. 529–555.

53 K. Yakabuski, "Henri-Paul Rousseau Was the King of Quebec's Pension Fund and His Returns the Envy of Many," *Globe and Mail*, January 31, 2009, p. B1.

54 G. Pitts, "Scandals Part of Natural Cycles of Excess," *Globe and Mail*, June 28, 2002, pp. B1, B5.

55 J. Collins, "Level 5 Leadership: The Triumph of Humility and Fierce Resolve," *Harvard Business Review*, January 2001, pp. 67–76; J. Collins, "Good to Great," *Fast Company*, October 2001, pp. 90–104; J. Collins, "The Misguided Mix-up," *Executive Excellence*, December 2002, pp. 3–4; and H. L. Tosi, V. F. Misangyi, A. Fanelli, D. A. Waldman, and F. J. Yammarino, "CEO Charisma, Compensation, and Firm Performance," *The Leadership Quarterly* 15 (2004), pp. 405–420.

56 See, for instance, B. M. Bass, B. J. Avolio, D. I. Jung, and Y. Berson, "Predicting Unit Performance by Assessing Transformational and Transactional Leadership," *Journal of Applied Psychology*, April 2003, pp. 207–218; and T. A. Judge and R. F. Piccolo, "Transformational and Transactional Leadership: A Meta-analytic Test of Their Relative Validity," *Journal of Applied Psychology*, October 2004, pp. 755–768.

57 N.-W. Chi, Y.-Y. Chung, and W.-C. Tsai, "How Do Happy Leaders Enhance Team Success? The Mediating Roles of Transformational Leadership, Group Affective Tone, and Team Processes," *Journal of Applied Social Psychology* 41, no. 6 (2011), pp. 1421–1454.

58 B. M. Bass, "Leadership: Good, Better, Best," *Organizational Dynamics*, Winter 1985, pp. 26–40; and J. Seltzer and B. M. Bass, "Transformational Leadership: Beyond Initiation and Consideration," *Journal of Management*, December 1990, pp. 693–703.

59 T. R. Hinkin and C. A. Schriesheim, "An Examination of 'Nonleadership': From Laissez-Faire Leadership to Leader Reward Omission and Punishment Omission," *Journal of Applied Psychology* 93, no. 6 (2008), pp. 1234–1248.

60 S. J. Shin and J. Zhou, "Transformational Leadership, Conservation, and Creativity: Evidence from Korea," *Academy of Management Journal*, December 2003, pp. 703–714; V. J. García-Morales, F. J. Lloréns-Montes, and A. J. Verdú-Jover, "The Effects of Transformational Leadership on Organizational Performance Through Knowledge and Innovation," *British Journal of Management* 19, no. 4 (2008), pp. 299–313; and S. A. Eisenbeiss, D. van Knippenberg, and S. Boerner, "Transformational Leadership and Team Innovation: Integrating Team Climate Principles," *Journal of Applied Psychology* 93, no. 6 (2008), pp. 1438–1446.

61 Y. Ling, Z. Simsek, M. H. Lubatkin, and J. F. Veiga, "Transformational Leadership's Role in Promoting Corporate Entrepreneurship: Examining the CEO-TMT Interface," *Academy of Management Journal* 51, no. 3 (2008), pp. 557–576.

62 A. E. Colbert, A. E. Kristof-Brown, B. H. Bradley, and M. R. Barrick, "CEO Transformational Leadership: The Role of Goal Importance Congruence in Top Management Teams," *Academy of Management Journal* 51, no. 1 (2008), pp. 81–96.

63 D. Zohar and O. Tenne-Gazit, "Transformational Leadership and Group Interaction as Climate Antecedents: A Social Network Analysis," *Journal of Applied Psychology* 93, no. 4 (2008), pp. 744–757.

64 F. O. Walumbwa, B. J. Avolio, and W. Zhu, "How Transformational Leadership Weaves Its Influence on Individual Job Performance: The Role of Identification and Efficacy Beliefs," *Personnel Psychology* 61, no. 4 (2008), pp. 793–825.

65 J. E. Bono and T. A. Judge, "Self-Concordance at Work: Toward Understanding the Motivational Effects of Transformational Leaders," *Academy of Management Journal*, October 2003, pp. 554–571; Y. Berson and B. J. Avolio, "Transformational Leadership and the Dissemination of Organizational Goals: A Case Study of a Telecommunication Firm," *Leadership Quarterly*, October 2004, pp. 625–646; and J. Schaubroeck, S. S. K. Lam, and S. E. Cha, "Embracing Transformational Leadership: Team Values and the Impact of Leader Behavior on Team Performance," *Journal of Applied Psychology* 92, no. 4 (2007), pp. 1020–1030.

66 J. R. Baum, E. A. Locke, and S. A. Kirkpatrick, "A Longitudinal Study of the Relation of Vision and Vision Communication to Venture Growth in Entrepreneurial Firms," *Journal of Applied Psychology*, February 2000, pp. 43–54.

67 B. J. Avolio, W. Zhu, W. Koh, and P. Bhatia, "Transformational Leadership and Organizational Commitment: Mediating Role of Psychological Empowerment and Moderating Role of Structural Distance," *Journal of Organizational Behavior*, December 2004, pp. 951–968; and T. Dvir, N. Kass, and B. Shamir, "The Emotional Bond: Vision and Organizational Commitment Among High-Tech Employees," *Journal of Organizational Change Management* 17, no. 2 (2004), pp. 126–143.

68 R. T. Keller, "Transformational Leadership, Initiating Structure, and Substitutes for Leadership: A Longitudinal Study of Research and Development Project Team Performance," *Journal of Applied Psychology* 91, no. 1 (2006), pp. 202–210.

69 T. A. Judge and R. F. Piccolo, "Transformational and Transactional Leadership: A Meta-analytic Test of Their Relative Validity," *Journal of Applied Psychology*, October 2004, pp. 755–768.

70 Y. Ling, Z. Simsek, M. H. Lubatkin, and J. F. Veiga, "The Impact of Transformational CEOs on the Performance of Small- to Medium-Sized Firms: Does Organizational Context Matter?" *Journal of Applied Psychology* 93, no. 4 (2008), pp. 923–934.

71 J. Schaubroeck, S. S. K. Lam, and S. E. Cha, "Embracing Transformational Leadership: Team Values and the Impact of Leader Behavior on Team Performance," *Journal of Applied Psychology* 92, no. 4 (2007), pp. 1020–1030.

72 H. Hetland, G. M. Sandal, and T. B. Johnsen, "Burnout in the Information Technology Sector: Does Leadership Matter?" *European Journal of Work and Organizational Psychology* 16, no. 1 (2007), pp. 58–75; and K. B. Lowe, K. G. Kroeck, and N. Sivasubramaniam, "Effectiveness Correlates of Transformational and Transactional Leadership: A Meta-analytic Review of the MLQ Literature," *Leadership Quarterly*, Fall 1996, pp. 385–425.

73 See, for instance, J. Barling, T. Weber, and E. K. Kelloway, "Effects of Transformational Leadership Training on Attitudinal and Financial Outcomes: A Field Experiment," *Journal of Applied Psychology*, December 1996, pp. 827–832; T. Dvir, D. Eden, and B. J. Avolio, "Impact of Transformational Leadership on

Follower Development and Performance: A Field Experiment," *Academy of Management Journal*, August 2002, pp. 735–744; and R. A. Hassan, B. A. Fuwad, and A. I. Rauf, "Pre-Training Motivation and the Effectiveness of Transformational Leadership Training: An Experiment," *Academy of Strategic Management Journal* 9, no. 2 (2010), pp. 1–8.

74 R. N. Kanungo, "Leadership in Organizations: Looking Ahead to the 21st Century," *Canadian Psychology* 39, no. 1–2 (1998), p. 78.

75 B. J. Avolio and B. M. Bass, "Transformational Leadership, Charisma and Beyond," working paper, School of Management, State University of New York, Binghamton, 1985, p. 14.

76 Vignette based on A. McCuaig, "Pilot Flies into Literary World," *Medicine Hat News*, http://www.medicinehatnews.com/local-entertainment/pilot-flies-into-literary-world-11252011.html

77 D. Ancona, E. Backman, and H. Bresman, "X-Teams: New Ways of Leading in a New World," *Ivey Business Journal* 72, no. 3 (May–June 2008), http://www.iveybusinessjournal.com/article.asp?intArticle_ID=755

78 See, for example, L. J. Zachary, *The Mentor's Guide: Facilitating Effective Learning Relationships* (San Francisco: Jossey-Bass, 2000); M. Murray, *Beyond the Myths and Magic of Mentoring: How to Facilitate an Effective Mentoring Process*, rev. ed. (New York: Wiley, 2001); and F. Warner, "Inside Intel's Mentoring Movement," *Fast Company*, April 2002, pp. 116–120.

79 B. R. Ragins and J. L. Cotton, "Easier Said Than Done: Gender Differences in Perceived Barriers to Gaining a Mentor," *Academy of Management Journal* 34, no. 4 (1993), pp. 939–951; C. R. Wanberg, E. T. Welsh, and S. A. Hezlett, "Mentoring Research: A Review and Dynamic Process Model," in *Research in Personnel and Human Resources Management*, vol. 22, ed. G. R. Ferris and J. J. Martocchio (Greenwich, CT: Elsevier Science, 2003), pp. 39–124; and T. D. Allen, "Protégé Selection by Mentors: Contributing Individual and Organizational Factors," *Journal of Vocational Behavior* 65, no. 3 (2004), pp. 469–483.

80 T. D. Allen, M. L. Poteet, J. E. A. Russell, and G. H. Dobbins, "A Field Study of Factors Related to Supervisors' Willingness to Mentor Others," *Journal of Vocational Behavior* 50, no. 1 (1997), pp. 1–22; S. Aryee, Y. W. Chay, and J. Chew, "The Motivation to Mentor among Managerial Employees in the Maintenance Career Stage: An Interactionist Perspective," *Group and Organization Management* 21, no. 3 (1996), pp. 261–277; L. T. Eby, A. L. Lockwood, and M. Butts, "Perceived Support for Mentoring: A Multiple Perspectives Approach," *Journal of Vocational Behavior* 68, no. 2 (2006), pp. 267–291; and T. D. Allen, E. Lentz, and R. Day, "Career Success Outcomes Associated with Mentoring Others: A Comparison of Mentors and Nonmentors," *Journal of Career Development* 32, no. 3 (2006), pp. 272–285.

81 See, for example, D. A. Thomas, "The Impact of Race on Managers' Experiences of Developmental Relationships: An Intra-Organizational Study," *Journal of Organizational Behavior*, November 1990, pp. 479–492; K. E. Kram and D. T. Hall, "Mentoring in a Context of Diversity and Turbulence," in *Managing Diversity*, ed. E. E. Kossek and S. A. Lobel (Cambridge, MA: Blackwell, 1996), pp. 108–36; M. N. Ruderman and M. W. Hughes-James, "Leadership Development across Race and Gender," in *The Center for Creative Leadership Handbook of Leadership Development*, ed. C. D. McCauley, R. S. Moxley, and E. Van Velsor (San Francisco: Jossey-Bass, 1998), pp. 291–335; and B. R. Ragins and J. L. Cotton, "Mentor Functions and Outcomes: A Comparison of Men and Women in Formal and Informal Mentoring Relationships," *Journal of Applied Psychology*, August 1999, pp. 529–550.

82 J. A. Wilson and N. S. Elman, "Organizational Benefits of Mentoring," *Academy of Management Executive*, November 1990, p. 90.

83 See, for instance, K. Houston-Philpot, "Leadership Development Partnerships at Dow Corning Corporation," *Journal of Organizational Excellence*, Winter 2002, pp. 13–27.

84 B. R. Ragins and J. L. Cotton, "Mentor Functions and Outcomes: A Comparison of Men and Women in Formal and Informal Mentoring Relationships," *Journal of Applied Psychology*, August 1999, pp. 529–550; and C. M. Underhill, "The Effectiveness of Mentoring Programs in Corporate Settings: A Meta-analytical Review of the Literature," *Journal of Vocational Behavior* 68, no. 2 (2006), pp. 292–307.

85 T. D. Allen, E. T. Eby, and E. Lentz, "The Relationship between Formal Mentoring Program Characteristics and Perceived Program Effectiveness," *Personnel Psychology* 59 (2006), pp. 125–153; T. D. Allen, L. T. Eby, and E. Lentz, "Mentorship Behaviors and Mentorship Quality Associated with Formal Mentoring Programs: Closing the Gap between Research and Practice," *Journal of Applied Psychology* 91, no. 3 (2006), pp. 567–578; and M. R. Parise and M. L. Forret, "Formal Mentoring Programs: The Relationship of Program Design and Support to Mentors' Perceptions of Benefits and Costs," *Journal of Vocational Behavior* 72, no. 2 (2008), pp. 225–240.

86 L. T. Eby and A. Lockwood, "Protégés' and Mentors' Reactions to Participating in Formal Mentoring Programs: A Qualitative Investigation," *Journal of Vocational Behavior* 67, no. 3 (2005), pp. 441–458; G. T. Chao, "Formal Mentoring: Lessons Learned from Past Practice," *Professional Psychology: Research and Practice* 40, no. 3 (2009), pp. 314–320; C. R. Wanberg, J. D. Kammeyer-Mueller, and M. Marchese, "Mentor and Protégé Predictors and Outcomes of Mentoring in a Formal Mentoring Program," *Journal of Vocational Behavior* 69 (2006), pp. 410–423.

87 T. D. Allen, L. T. Eby, M. L. Poteet, L. Mark, E. Lentz, and L. Lizzette, "Career Benefits Associated with Mentoring for Protégés: A Meta-analysis," *Journal of Applied Psychology*, February 2004, pp. 127–136; and J. D. Kammeyer-Mueller and T. A. Judge, "A Quantitative Review of the Mentoring Literature: Test of a Model," *Journal of Vocational Behavior* 72 (2008), pp. 269–283.

88 M. K. Feeney and B. Bozeman, "Mentoring and Network Ties," *Human Relations* 61, no. 12 (2008), pp. 1651–1676; N. Bozionelos, "Intra-Organizational Network Resources: How They Relate to Career Success and Organizational Commitment," *Personnel Review* 37, no. 3 (2008), pp. 249–263; and S. A. Hezlett and S. K. Gibson, "Linking Mentoring and Social Capital: Implications for Career and Organization Development," *Advances in Developing Human Resources* 9, no. 3 (2007), pp. 384–412.

89 C. C. Manz and H. P. Sims Jr., *The New SuperLeadership: Leading Others to Lead Themselves* (San Francisco: Berrett-Koehler Publishers, 2001).

90 A. Bandura, "Self-Reinforcement: Theoretical and Methodological Considerations," *Behaviorism* 4 (1976), pp. 135–155; P. W. Corrigan, C. J. Wallace, and M. L. Schade, "Learning Medication Self-Management Skills in Schizophrenia; Relationships with Cognitive Deficits and Psychiatric Symptom," *Behavior Therapy*, Winter 1994, pp. 5–15; A. S. Bellack, "A Comparison of Self-Reinforcement and Self-Monitoring in a Weight Reduction Program," *Behavior Therapy* 7 (1976), pp. 68–75; T. A. Eckman, W. C. Wirshing, and S. R. Marder, "Technique for Training Schizophrenic Patients in Illness Self-Management: A Controlled Trial," *American Journal of Psychiatry* 149 (1992), pp. 1549–1555; J. J. Felixbrod and K. D. O'Leary, "Effect of Reinforcement on Children's Academic Behavior as a Function of Self-Determined and Externally Imposed Contingencies," *Journal of Applied Behavior Analysis* 6 (1973), pp. 141–150; A. J. Litrownik, L. R. Franzini, and D. Skenderian, "The Effects of Locus of Reinforcement Control on a Concept Identification Task," *Psychological Reports* 39 (1976), pp. 159–165; P. D. McGorry, "Psychoeducation in First-Episode Psychosis: A Therapeutic Process," *Psychiatry*, November 1995, pp. 313–328; G. S. Parcel,

P. R. Swank, and M. J. Mariotto, "Self-Management of Cystic Fibrosis: A Structural Model for Educational and Behavioral Variables," *Social Science and Medicine* 38 (1994), pp. 1307–1315; and G. E. Speidel, "Motivating Effect of Contingent Self-Reward," *Journal of Experimental Psychology* 102 (1974), pp. 528–530.

91 D. B. Jeffrey, "A Comparison of the Effects of External Control and Self-Control on the Modification and Maintenance of Weight," *Journal of Abnormal Psychology* 83 (1974), pp. 404–410.

92 C. C. Manz and H. P. Sims Jr., *The New SuperLeadership: Leading Others to Lead Themselves* (San Francisco: Berrett-Koehler, 2001).

93 See, for instance, J. H. Zenger, E. Musselwhite, K. Hurson, and C. Perrin, *Leading Teams: Mastering the New Role* (Homewood, IL: Business One Irwin, 1994); and M. Frohman, "Nothing Kills Teams Like Ill-Prepared Leaders," *IndustryWeek*, October 2, 1995, pp. 72–76.

94 See, for instance, M. Frohman, "Nothing Kills Teams Like Ill-Prepared Leaders," *IndustryWeek*, October 2, 1995, p. 93.

95 See, for instance, M. Frohman, "Nothing Kills Teams Like Ill-Prepared Leaders," *IndustryWeek*, October 2, 1995, p. 100.

96 J. R. Katzenbach and D. K. Smith, *The Wisdom of Teams: Creating the High-Performance Organization* (Boston: Harvard Business School Press, 1993).

97 N. Steckler and N. Fondas, "Building Team Leader Effectiveness: A Diagnostic Tool," *Organizational Dynamics*, Winter 1995, p. 20.

98 R. S. Wellins, W. C. Byham, and G. R. Dixon, *Inside Teams* (San Francisco: Jossey-Bass, 1994), p. 318.

99 N. Steckler and N. Fondas, "Building Team Leader Effectiveness: A Diagnostic Tool," *Organizational Dynamics*, Winter 1995, p. 21.

100 L. A. Hambley, T. A. O'Neill, and T. J. B. Kline, "Virtual Team Leadership: The Effects of Leadership Style and Communication Medium on Team Interaction Styles and Outcomes," *Organizational Behavior and Human Decision Processes* 103 (2007), pp. 1–20; and B. J. Avolio and S. S. Kahai, "Adding the 'E' to E-Leadership: How It May Impact Your Leadership," *Organizational Dynamics* 31, no. 4 (2003), pp. 325–338.

101 J. Howell and K. Hall-Merenda, "Leading from a Distance," in *Leadership: Achieving Exceptional Performance*, A Special Supplement Prepared by the Richard Ivey School of Business, *Globe and Mail*, May 15, 1998, pp. C1, C2.

102 S. J. Zaccaro and P. Bader, "E-Leadership and the Challenges of Leading E-Teams: Minimizing the Bad and Maximizing the Good," *Organizational Dynamics* 31, no. 4 (2003), pp. 381–385.

103 C. E. Naquin and G. D. Paulson, "Online Bargaining and Interpersonal Trust," *Journal of Applied Psychology*, February 2003, pp. 113–120.

104 B. Shamir, "Leadership in Boundaryless Organizations: Disposable or Indispensable?" *European Journal of Work and Organizational Psychology* 8, no. 1 (1999), pp. 49–71.

105 R. M. Kanter, *The Change Masters, Innovation and Entrepreneurship in the American Corporation* (New York: Simon and Schuster, 1983).

106 R. A. Heifetz, *Leadership without Easy Answers* (Cambridge, MA: Harvard University Press, 1996), p. 205.

107 R. A. Heifetz, *Leadership without Easy Answers* (Cambridge, MA: Harvard University Press, 1996), p. 205.

108 R. A. Heifetz, *Leadership without Easy Answers* (Cambridge, MA: Harvard University Press, 1996), p. 188.

109 Vignette based on C. Coward, "Five Questions with a Snowbird," *Hamilton Spectator*, November 5, 2011, http://www.thespec.com/localprofile/article/620542--five-questions-with-a-snowbird; and J. Graham, "She's the Boss: Snowbirds First Female Pilot to Lead Aerobatic Squad," *Canadian Press*, May 2, 2010, http://www.cbc.ca/canada/saskatchewan/story/2010/05/02/sask-snowbirds.html#ixzz0mv2nPxRr

110 C. Tan, "CEO Pinching Penney in a Slowing Economy," *Wall Street Journal*, January 31, 2008, pp. 1–2; and A. Carter, "Lighting a Fire under Campbell," *BusinessWeek*, December 4, 2006, pp. 96–101.

111 F. O. Walumbwa, F. Luthans, J. B. Avey, and A. Oke, "Authentically Leading Groups: The Mediating Role of Collective Psychological Capital And Trust," *Journal of Organizational Behavior* 32, no. 1 (2011), pp. 4–24.

112 R. Ilies, F. P. Morgeson, and J. D. Nahrgang, "Authentic Leadership and Eudaemonic Wellbeing: Understanding Leader-Follower Outcomes," *Leadership Quarterly* 16 (2005), pp. 373–394.

113 This section is based on E. P. Hollander, "Ethical Challenges in the Leader–Follower Relationship," *Business Ethics Quarterly*, January 1995, pp. 55–65; J. C. Rost, "Leadership: A Discussion About Ethics," *Business Ethics Quarterly*, January 1995, pp. 129–142; L. K. Treviño, M. Brown, and L. P. Hartman, "A Qualitative Investigation of Perceived Executive Ethical Leadership: Perceptions from Inside and Outside the Executive Suite," *Human Relations*, January 2003, pp. 5–37; and R. M. Fulmer, "The Challenge of Ethical Leadership," *Organizational Dynamics* 33, no. 3 (2004), pp. 307–317.

114 J. L. Lunsford, "Piloting Boeing's New Course," *Wall Street Journal*, June 13, 2006, pp. B1, B3.

115 J. M. Burns, *Leadership* (New York: Harper and Row, 1978).

116 J. M. Howell and B. J. Avolio, "The Ethics of Charismatic Leadership: Submission or Liberation?" *Academy of Management Executive*, May 1992, pp. 43–55.

117 D. van Knippenberg, D. De Cremer, and B. van Knippenberg, "Leadership and Fairness: The State of the Art," *European Journal of Work and Organizational Psychology* 16, no. 2 (2007), pp. 113–140.

118 M. E. Brown and L. K. Treviño, "Socialized Charismatic Leadership, Values Congruence, and Deviance in Work Groups," *Journal of Applied Psychology* 91, no. 4 (2006), pp. 954–962.

119 M. E. Brown and L. K. Treviño, "Leader-Follower Values Congruence: Are Socialized Charismatic Leaders Better Able to Achieve It?" *Journal of Applied Psychology* 94, no. 2 (2009), pp. 478–490.

120 J. G. Clawson, *Level Three Leadership* (Upper Saddle River, NJ: Prentice Hall, 1999), pp. 46–49.

121 http://www.statcan.gc.ca/daily-quotidien/110726/dq110726a-eng.htm

122 HRSDC calculations based on Statistics Canada, *Labour Force Survey Estimates (LFS), by Educational Attainment, Sex and Age Group, Annual*, CANSIM Table 282-0004 (Ottawa: Statistics Canada, 2011).

123 All labour force data based on "Women in Management in Canada (2010)," *Catalyst*, http://www.catalyst.org/publication/247/women-in-management-in-canada

124 Industry Canada, "Key Small Business Statistics—July 2010," http://www.ic.gc.ca/eic/site/sbrp-rppe.nsf/eng/rd02504.html

125 L. Ramsay, "A League of Their Own," *Globe and Mail*, November 23, 2002, p. B11.

126 The material in this section is based on J. Cliff, N. Langton, and H. Aldrich, "Walking the Talk? Gendered Rhetoric vs. Action in Small Firms," *Organizational Studies* 26, no. 1 (2005), pp. 63–91; J. Grant, "Women as Managers: What They Can Offer to Organizations," *Organizational Dynamics*, Winter 1988, pp. 56–63; S. Helgesen, *The Female Advantage: Women's Ways of Leadership* (New York: Doubleday, 1990); A. H. Eagly and B. T. Johnson, "Gender and Leadership Style: A Meta-analysis," *Psychological Bulletin*, September 1990, pp. 233–256; A. H. Eagly and S. J. Karau, "Gender and the Emergence of Leaders: A Meta-analysis," *Journal of Personality and Social Psychology*, May 1991, pp. 685–710; J. B. Rosener, "Ways

Women Lead," *Harvard Business Review*, November–December 1990, pp. 119–125; "Debate: Ways Men and Women Lead," *Harvard Business Review*, January–February 1991, pp. 150–160; A. H. Eagly, M. G. Makhijani, and B. G. Klonsky, "Gender and the Evaluation of Leaders: A Meta-analysis," *Psychological Bulletin*, January 1992, pp. 3–22; A. H. Eagly, S. J. Karau, and B. T. Johnson, "Gender and Leadership Style among School Principals: A Meta-analysis," *Educational Administration Quarterly*, February 1992, pp. 76–102; L. R. Offermann and C. Beil, "Achievement Styles of Women Leaders and Their Peers," *Psychology of Women Quarterly*, March 1992, pp. 37–56; T. Melamed and N. Bozionelos, "Gender Differences in the Personality Features of British Managers," *Psychological Reports*, December 1992, pp. 979–986; G. N. Powell, *Women & Men in Management*, 2nd ed. (Thousand Oaks, CA: Sage, 1993); R. L. Kent and S. E. Moss, "Effects of Size and Gender Role on Leader Emergence," *Academy of Management Journal*, October 1994, pp. 1335–1346; C. Lee, "The Feminization of Management," *Training*, November 1994, pp. 25–31; H. Collingwood, "Women as Managers: Not Just Different, Better," *Working Woman*, November 1995, p. 14; and J. B. Rosener, *America's Competitive Secret: Women Managers* (New York: Oxford University Press, 1995).

127 A. H. Eagly, "Female Leadership Advantage and Disadvantage: Resolving the Contradictions," *Psychology of Women Quarterly*, March 2007, pp. 1–12; and A. H. Eagly, M. C. Johannesen-Schmidt, and M. L. van Engen, "Transformational, Transactional, and Laissez-Faire Leadership Styles: A Meta-analysis Comparing Women and Men," *Psychological Bulletin*, July 2003, pp. 569–591.

128 O. A. O'Neill and C. A. O'Reilly III, "Reducing the Backlash Effect: Self-Monitoring and Women's Promotions," *Journal of Occupational and Organizational Psychology*, January 11, 2011, published online before print.

129 "'Macho' Women Face Backlash at Work, Researchers Find," *ScienceDaily*, http://www.sciencedaily.com/releases/2011/01/110119114954.htm

130 B. Orser, *Creating High Performance Organizations: Leveraging Women's Leadership* (Ottawa: The Conference Board of Canada, 2000).

131 J. M. Norvilitis and H. M. Reid, "Evidence for an Association between Gender-Role Identity and a Measure of Executive Function," *Psychological Reports*, February 2002, pp. 35–45; W. H. Decker and D. M. Rotondo, "Relationships among Gender, Type of Humor, and Perceived Leader Effectiveness," *Journal of Managerial Issues*, Winter 2001, pp. 450–465; H. Aguinis and S. K. R. Adams, "Social-Role versus Structural Models of Gender and Influence Use in Organizations: A Strong Inference Approach," *Group & Organization Management*, December 1998, pp. 414–446; and A. H. Eagly, S. J. Karau, and M. G. Makhijani, "Gender and the Effectiveness of Leaders: A Meta-analysis," *Psychological Bulletin* 117 (1995), pp. 125–145.

132 A. H. Eagly, M. C. Johannesen-Schmidt, and M. L. van Engen, "Transformational, Transactional, and Laissez-Faire Leadership Styles: A Meta-analysis Comparing Women and Men," *Psychological Bulletin* 129, no. 4 (July 2003), pp. 569–591; K. M. Bartol, D. C. Martin, and J. A. Kromkowski, "Leadership and the Glass Ceiling: Gender and Ethnic Influences on Leader Behaviors at Middle and Executive Managerial Levels," *Journal of Leadership & Organizational Studies*, Winter 2003, pp. 8–19; and R. Sharpe, "As Leaders, Women Rule," *BusinessWeek*, November 20, 2000, pp. 74–84.

133 M. Javidan, P. W. Dorfman, M. S. de Luque, and R. J. House, "In the Eye of the Beholder: Cross Cultural Lessons in Leadership from Project GLOBE," *Academy of Management Perspectives*, February 2006, pp. 67–90.

134 D. E. Carl and M. Javidan, "Universality of Charismatic Leadership: A Multi-Nation Study" (paper presented at the National Academy of Management Conference, Washington, DC,

August 2001), p. 29; and R. J. House, M. Javidan, P. Hanges, and P. Dorfman, "Understanding Cultures and Implicit Leadership Theories across the Globe: An Introduction to Project GLOBE," *Journal of World Business*, Spring 2002, pp. 3–10.

135 N. Beccalli, "European Business Forum Asks: Do Companies Get the Leaders They Deserve?" *European Business Forum*, 2003, www.pwcglobal.com/extweb/pwcpublications.nsf/DocID/D1EC3380F589844585256D7300346A1B

Chapter 21

1 *Performance and Potential 2000–2001: Seeking Made in Canada Solutions* (Ottawa, ON: Conference Board of Canada, 2000), p. 51.

2 HRSDC, Looking Ahead: A 10-Year Outlook for the Canadian Labour Market (2006–2015), Statistics Canada, January 29, 2007), www.hrsdc.gc.ca/eng/publications_resources/research/categories/labour_market_e/sp_615_10_06/supply.shtml (accessed September 26, 2011).

3 S. Klie, "Guesses Just Don't Cut It Anymore," *Canadian HR Reporter* (March 24, 2008).

4 This is a modification of a definition found in P. Wallum, "A Broader View of Succession Planning," *Personnel Management* (September 1993), pp. 43–44.

5 HRSDC, Looking Ahead: A 10-Year Outlook for the Canadian Labour Market (2006–2015), Statistics Canada, (January 29, 2007), www.hrsdc.gc.ca/eng/publications_resources/research/categories/labour_market_e/sp_615_10_06/supply.shtml (accessed September 26, 2011).

6 A. Coughlin, *Alberta's Labour Shortage Just the Tip of the Iceberg* (Conference Board of Canada Executive Action, 2006); G. Hodgson and G. McGowan, "Taking Sides: Is Alberta's Labour Shortage a Doomsday Scenario?" *Canadian HR Reporter* (July 17, 2006); P. Brethour, "Oil Patch Labour Crisis Seen Spreading to Rest of Country; "Husky Head Raises Alarm Over Rising Costs, Saying Projects at Risk," *Globe and Mail* (April 20, 2006), http://www.theglobeandmail.com/report-on-business/oil-patch-labour-crisis-seen-spreading-to-rest-of-country/article707140/ (accessed September 9, 2012).

7 "Mining Industry Needs 80,000 Workers," *Canadian HR Reporter* (March 26, 2007), p. 2; S. Klie, "Construction Demand Outpaces Labour Growth," *Canadian HR Reporter* (September 10, 2007); "Non-profits Facing Labour Shortage," *Canadian HR Reporter* (July 9, 2007); U. Vu, "Mounties Prepare For Recruiting Spree," *Canadian HR Reporter* (October 23, 2006); "Manufacturing Sector Labours to Address Human Resources Issues," Conference Board of Canada, *InsideEdge* (Spring 2008), p. 18; S. Klie, "Short Circuiting Labour Supply," *Canadian HR Reporter* (December 15, 2008).

8 *Canadian Perspectives on ICT Outsourcing and Offshoring* (Toronto ON: IDC, 2007); S. Klie, "IT Offshoring Growing," *Canadian HR Reporter* (October 22, 2007); L. Young, "IT University Enrolment Plunges," *Canadian HR Reporter* (December 3, 2007); S; Klie, "Price Tag of IT Shortage: $10 Billion Per Year," *Canadian HR Reporter* (February 11, 2008); S. Klie, "Women Could Solve IT Worker Shortage," *Canadian HR Reporter* (October 20, 2008).

9 H. Sokoloff, "Legal Exodus," *National Post* (March 17, 2005), p. FP3; "Baby Boomers an HR Problem for Funeral Services," *Canadian HR Reporter* (January 16, 2006), p. 2; "Today's Forecast: Meteorologist Shortage," *Canadian HR Reporter* (December 5, 2005), p. 2; "Engineers in Short Supply," *Canadian HR Reporter* (November 21, 2005), p. 2; S. Klie, "Fewer Accountants Is a Bad Thing—Really," *Canadian HR Reporter* (February 13, 2006), p. 3; "Alberta Labour Shortage Draining Civil Service," *Canadian HR Reporter* (January 30, 2006), p. 2.

10 A.L. Delbecq, A.H. Van DelVen, and D.H. Gustafson, *Group Techniques for Program Planning: A Guide to Nominal and Delphi Processes* (Glenview, IL: Scott Foresman, 1975).

11 G. Milkovich, A.J. Annoni, and T.A. Mahoney, "The Use of Delphi Procedures in Manpower Forecasting," *Management Science* (1972), pp. 381–388.

12 "Feds Help Employers Avoid Layoffs," *HR Professional* (June/July 2009), p. 12.

13 W.F. Cascio and C.E. Young, "Financial Consequences of Employment Change Decisions in Major U.S. Corporations: 1982–2000," in K.P. DeMeuse and M.L. Marks (eds.), *Resizing the Organization*, pp. 131–156 (San Francisco, CA: Jossey-Bass, 2003).

Chapter 22

1 D. Brown, "Wellness Programs Bring Healthy Bottom Line," *Canadian HR Reporter* (December 17, 2001), pp. 1, 14.

2 Association of Workers' Compensation Boards of Canada, www.awcbc.ca (accessed July 15, 2009); "Working to Death—Millions Die Each Year Due to Work-Related Accidents and Diseases," *IAPA Press Release* (April 19, 2006), www.iapa.ca/about_iapa/2006_apr19_press.asp (accessed June 20, 2006).

3 H. Bryan, "Attitude Is Everything," *WorkSafe Magazine* (October 2005), p. 18.

4 S. De Léséleuc, "Criminal Victimization in the Workplace," Canadian Centre for Justice Statistics Profile Series (2004), http://downloads.workplaceviolencenews.com/criminal_victimization_in_the_workplace.pdf (accessed September 26, 2011).

5 Based on T.A. Opie and L. Bates, *1997 Canadian Master Labour Guide* (CCH Canada Inc.), pp. 1015–1034.

6 C.A. Edwards and C.E. Humphrey, *Due Diligence Under the Occupational Health and Safety Act: A Practical Guide* (Toronto, ON: Carswell/Thomson Canada, 2000).

7 N. Keith, "The Omniscient Employer: The Need to See the Unforeseeable," *Workplace* (March/April 2008), pp. 16–19.

8 M. Pilger, "Conducting a Hygiene Assessment," *Canadian HR Reporter* (April 10, 2000), pp. G3, G4; J. Montgomery, *Occupational Health and Safety* (Toronto, ON: Nelson Canada, 1996), p. 97; D. Brown, "Joint H&S Committees: An Opportunity, Not a Nuisance," *Canadian HR Reporter* (October 20, 2002), pp. 7, 10.

9 P. Strahlendorf, "What Supervisors Need to Know," *OH&S Canada* (January/February 1996), pp. 38–40; N. Tompkins, "Getting the Best Help from Your Safety Committee," *HR Magazine*, 40, no. 4 (April 1995), p. 76.

10 J. Grant and D. Brown, "The Inspector Cometh," *Canadian HR Reporter* (January 31, 2005), pp. 13, 17; "It's Time to Wake Up to Health and Safety: Ministry of Labour Increases Number of Inspectors," *Safety Mosaic*, 8 (Spring 2005), pp. 5–6.

11 "Alberta Imposes Record Penalties for OH&S Violations," *Workplace*, www.workplace-mag.com/Alberta-imposes-record-penalties-for-ohs-violations.html (accessed July 16, 2009).

12 S. Klie, "Individuals Targeted under OHS," *Canadian HR Reporter* (March 12, 2007); R. Stewart, "Legal Duties of the Front Line," *Canadian HR Reporter* (March 12, 2007).

13 "Employer Jailed for H&S Violation," *Canadian HR Reporter* (April 8, 2002), p. 2; see also T. Humber, "Putting the Boss Behind Bars?" *Canadian HR Reporter* (April 7, 2003).

14 "Quebec Employer First to Be Criminally Convicted in Death of Worker," *Canadian HR Reporter* (February 7, 2008); "C-45 Conviction Nets $110K Fine," *Canadian HR Reporter* (April 7, 2008).

15 J. Montgomery, *Occupational Health and Safety* (Toronto, ON: Nelson Canada, 1996), p. 34.

16 K. Prisciak, "Health, Safety & Harassment?" *OH&S Canada* (April/May 1997), pp. 20–21.

17 Dupont Canada, www2.dupont.com/DuPont_Home/en_CA/index.html (accessed June 20, 2006).

18 *A Safety Committee Man's Guide*, Aetna Life and Casualty Insurance Company, Catalog 872684.

19 J. Roughton, "Job Hazard Analysis," *OH&S Canada* (January/February 1996), pp. 41–44.

20 A. Fowler, "How to Make the Workplace Safer," *People Management*, 1, no. 2 (January, 1995), pp. 38–39.

21 List of unsafe acts from *A Safety Committee Man's Guide*, Aetna Life and Casualty Insurance Company; E. McCormick and J. Tiffin, *Industrial Psychology* (Englewood Cliffs, NJ: Prentice Hall, 1974).

22 E. McCormick and J. Tiffin, *Industrial Psychology* (Englewood Cliffs, NJ: Prentice Hall, 1974), pp. 522–523; David DeJoy, "Attributional Processes and Hazard Control Management in Industry," *Journal of Safety Research*, 16 (Summer 1985), pp. 61–71.

23 E. McCormick and J. Tiffin, *Industrial Psychology* (Englewood Cliffs, NJ: Prentice Hall, 1974), p. 523.

24 A. Campbell, *All Signs Point to Yes: Literacy's Impact on Workplace Health and Safety* (Ottawa, ON: The Conference Board of Canada, 2008).

25 S. Dobson, "Evidence of Link between Literacy, Safety," *Canadian HR Reporter* (December 1, 2008).

26 A. Campbell, *All Signs Point to Yes: Literacy's Impact on Workplace Health and Safety* (Ottawa, ON: The Conference Board of Canada, 2008).

27 "IAPA Wins First Place at International Film and Multimedia Festival," *Workplace* e-newsletter (July 18, 2008).

28 M. Blum and J. Nayler, *Industrial Psychology* (New York, NY: Harper & Row, 1968), p. 522.

29 L. Scott, "Measuring Employee Abilities," *Benefits Canada* (September 2002), pp. 41–49.

30 K. Gillin, "Reduce Employee Exposure to Injury with Pre-Employment Screening Tests," *Canadian HR Reporter* (February 28, 2000), p. 10.

31 M. Shaw, "Rewarding Health and Safety," *Canadian HR Reporter* (December 2, 2002), pp. 19–20.

32 "Rewarding Safety: 70 Million Kilometres and Counting," *Workplace* (November/December 2008).

33 M. Morra, "Fun, with Caution," *Workplace* (March/April 2008), pp. 1; L. Scott, "Measuring Employee Abilities," *Benefits Canada* (September 2002), pp. 41–49.

34 A. Dunn, "Back in Business," *Workplace News* (April 2005), pp. 16–17.

35 Ergomed Solutions, http://ergomedsolutions.com/functionalabilitiesevaluationsp17.php (accessed July 15, 2009); C. Colacci, "Meet Your Return to Work Obligations with a Functional Abilities Evaluation," *Canadian HR Reporter* (April 10, 2000), p. G5.

36 C. Hall, "Sobering Advice," *Workplace News*, 11, no. 10 (November/December 2005), pp. 11–12.

37 *British Columbia (Public Service Employee Relations Commission) v. B.C.G.S.E.U.*, (1999) 176 D.L.R. (4th) 1 (S.C.C.) [*Meiorin*].

38 Policy on Drug and Alcohol Testing, Ontario Human Rights Commission, www.ohrc.on.ca/en/resources/Policies/PolicyDrugAlch (accessed July 16, 2009).

39 D. McCutcheon, "Confronting Addiction," *HR Professional* (June/July 2009), p. 39.

40 D. O'Meara, "Sober Second Chance," *Alberta Venture*, 9, no. 2 (March 2005), http://albertaventure.com/2005/03/sober-second-chance/?year=2005 (accessed September 4, 2012).

41 A. Nicoll, *Time for Action: Managing Mental Health in the Workplace* (Toronto, ON: Mercer Human Resources Consulting), (2008); L. Duxbury and C. Higgins, *Exploring the Link between Work–Life Conflict and Demands on Canada's* Health *Care System: Report Three* (Public Health Agency of Canada: March 2004).

42 *Mental Health at Work: Booklet 1*. IRSST (Laval University, 2005).

43 *Staying@Work: Effective Presence at Work: 2007 Survey Report:Canada* (Toronto, ON: Watson Wyatt).

44 Ibid.

45 D. Crisp, "Leaders Make the Difference," in A. Shaw, "Toxic Workplaces as Bad as Unsafe Ones," *Canadian HR Reporter* (April 21, 2008).

46 A. Nicoll, *Time for Action: Managing Mental Health in the Workplace* (Toronto, ON: Mercer Human Resources Consulting), (2008).

47 Statistics Canada, "Study: Workaholics and Time Perception," *The Daily* (May 15, 2007).

48 "Is Your Job Making You Sick?" *Canadian HR Reporter* (September 17, 2008).

49 J.W. Simpson, "Psychopaths Wear Suits, Too," *National Post* (May 10, 2006), p. WK6; A. Gill, "The Psychopath in the Corner Office," *Globe and Mail* (May 27, 2006), p. F1; "Push for Productivity Taking its Toll," *Canadian HR Reporter* (November 6, 2001), p. 15; D. Brown, "Doing More with Less Hurts Employees and Productivity," *Canadian HR Reporter* (October 7, 2002), pp. 3, 13; A. Sharratt, "Silver Linings," *Benefits Canada* (March 2003), pp. 51–53.

50 J. Santa-Barbara, "Preventing the Stress Epidemic," *Canadian HR Reporter* (March 8, 1999), p. 19; see also A. Chiu, "Beyond Physical Wellness: Mental Health Issues in the Workplace," *Canadian HR Reporter* (February 26, 2001), p. 4; L. Hyatt, "Job Stress: Have We Reached the Breaking Point?" *Workplace Today* (January 2002), pp. 14, 15, 37.

51 "Health Care Workers Most Stressed," *Canadian HR Reporter* (November 15, 2007)

52 P. Crawford-Smith, "Stressed Out," *Benefits Canada* (November 1999), pp. 115–117.

53 *Stress at Work: Taking Control* (Industrial Accident Prevention Association, 2002); J. Newman and T. Beehr, "Personal and Organizational Strategies for Handling Job Stress: A Review of Research and Opinion," *Personnel Psychology* (Spring 1979), pp. 1–43; see also Bureau of National Affairs, "Work Place Stress: How to Curb Claims," *Bulletin to Management* (April 14, 1988), p. 120.

54 T. Humber, "Stress Attack," *Canadian HR Reporter* (February 10, 2002), pp. G1, G10; M. Shain, "Stress and Satisfaction," *OH&S Canada* (April/May 1999), pp. 38–47.

55 P. Carayon, "Stressful Jobs and Non-Stressful Jobs: A Cluster Analysis of Office Jobs," *Ergonomics*, 37, no. 2 (1994), pp. 311–323.

56 *Workplace Mental Health Indicators: An EAP's Perspective*, Shepell-fgi Research Group, 2005, Series 1, Vol. 1, Issue 1.

57 A. Pihulyk, "When the Job Overwhelms," *Canadian HR Reporter* (January 14, 2002), p. 11.

58 P. Kishchuk, *Yukon Workers' Compensation Act Subsection 105.1 Research Series: Expansion of the Meaning of Disability* (March 2003).

59 M. Gibb-Clark, "The Case for Compensating Stress Claims," *Globe and Mail* (June 14, 1999), p. M1; L. Young, "Stressed Workers Are Suing Employers," *Canadian HR Reporter* (May 3, 1999), pp. 1, 6; D. Brown, "Liability Could Extend to Mental Damage," *Canadian HR Reporter* (October 9, 2000), pp. 1, 8.

60 OPSEU Online, "International RSI Awareness Day—February 28, 2006," www.opseu.org/hands/rsi2006.htm (accessed May 18, 2006); J. Hampton, "RSIs: The Biggest Strain Is on the Bottom Line," *Canadian HR Reporter* (February 10, 1997), pp. 15, 19; see also G. Harrington, "Pushing Ergonomics into Place," *Canadian HR Reporter* (April 24, 1995), pp. 11–12.

61 "Prevent Workplace Pains and Strains! It's Time to Take Action!" Ontario Ministry of Labour, www.labour.gov.on.ca/english/hs/ergonomics/is_ergonomics.html (accessed May 25, 2006).

62 S.B. Hood, "Repetitive Strain Injury," *Human Resources Professional* (June/July 1997), pp. 29–34.

63 "Ergonomic Intervention Improves Worker Health and Productivity," *Institute for Work and Health* (December 15, 2003), www.iwh.on.ca/media/ergonomic.php (accessed July 8, 2006); "Ergonomic Intervention Improves Worker Health and Productivity," *Workplace News* (February 2004), p. 16.

64 J.A. Savage, "Are Computer Terminals Zapping Workers' Health?" *Business and Society Review* (1994).

65 "Office Ergonomics and Repetitive Strain Injuries: What You Need to Know," Ottawa Valley Physiotherapy, www.ovphysio.com (accessed May 25, 2006); Occupational Health and Safety Agency for Healthcare in British Columbia, www.ohsah.bc.ca/templates/index.php?section_copy_id=5396 (accessed May 25, 2006); S. Tenby, "Introduction to Ergonomics: How to Avoid RSI—Repetitive Strain Injury," Disabled Women's Network Ontario, http://dawn.thot.net/cd/20.html (accessed May 25, 2006).

66 U. Vu, "Steel Union Gathers Workplace Cancer Data," *Canadian HR Reporter* (June 2, 2008).

67 "Unions Stress Cancer Prevention," *Canadian HR Reporter* (February 28, 2005), p. 2.

68 D. Brown, "Killer Toxins in the Workplace," *Canadian HR Reporter* (April 23, 2001), pp. 1, 12.

69 A. Scappatura, "Enhanced Coverage for Firefighters," *Canadian HR Reporter* (May 18, 2009).

70 "EI Granted in Second-Hand Smoke Case," *Canadian HR Reporter* (May 19, 2003), p. 3; see also M.M. Finklestein, "Risky Business," *OH&S Canada* (September/October 1996), pp. 32–34.

71 T. Humber, "Snuffing Out Smoking," *Canadian HR Reporter* (April 11, 2005), p. 19, 23; *Towards Healthier Workplaces and Public Places* (Health Canada, 2004).

72 C. Hallamore, *A State of Unpreparedness: Canadian Organizations' Readiness for a Pandemic* (Ottawa, ON: The Conference Board of Canada, June 2006).

73 C.C. Cavicchio, "Action Plan for Dealing with a Global Pandemic," *The Conference Board Executive Action Series* (May 2009).

74 C. Hallamore, *A State of Unpreparedness: Canadian Organizations' Readiness for a Pandemic* (Ottawa, ON: The Conference Board of Canada, June 2006).

75 R.A. Macpherson, E. Ringsels, and H. Singh, "Swine Influenza: Advice for Employers Preparing for a Pandemic," *McCarthy Tetrault e-Alert* (April 29, 2009), http://news.mccarthy.ca/en/news_template_full.asp?pub_code=4502&news_code=1066 (accessed April 29, 2009).

76 C.C. Cavicchio, "Action Plan for Dealing with a Global Pandemic," *The Conference Board Executive Action Series* (May 2009).

77 D.J. McKeown and K. Ford, "The Importance of People-Focused Pandemic Planning," *Workplace News* (September/October 2006).

78 Ibid.

79 C. Harden, "Preparing for a Pandemic: The Total Rewards Angle," *Workspan* (July 2006).

80 *Violence in the Workplace*, Canadian Association of University Teachers (October 4, 2004); W.H. Glenn, "Workplace Violence: An Employees' Survival Guide," *OH&S Canada* (April/May 2002), pp. 26–31.

81 S. De Leseleuc, *Criminal Victimization in the Workplace* (Canadian Centre for Justice Statistics, Catalogue No. 85F0033MIE – No. 013, 2004).

82 "Male Nurses More Likely to Be Assaulted by Patients: StatsCan," *Canadian HR Reporter* (April 16, 2009).

83 S. Dobson, "Sexual Assault Prompts OHS Charge," *Canadian HR Reporter* (December 15, 2008); L. De Piante, "Watch Out for Dangerous Employees," *Canadian HR Reporter* (October 22, 2007); A. Feliu, "Workplace Violence and the Duty of Care: The Scope of an Employer's Obligation to Protect against the Violent Employee," *Employee Relations Law Journal*, 20, no. 3 (Winter 1994/95), pp. 381–406; G. French and P. Morgan, "The Risks of Workplace Violence," *Canadian HR Reporter* (December 18, 2000), pp. 27–28.

84 M.M. LeBlanc and E.K. Kelloway, "Predictors and Outcomes of Workplace Violence and Aggression, *Journal of Applied Psychology*, 87, no. 3 (June 2002), 444–453.

85 L. De Piante, "Watch Out for Dangerous Employees," *Canadian HR Reporter* (October 22, 2007).

86 S. Klie, "Screening New Hires Won't End Workplace Violence, Study Says," *Canadian HR Reporter* (November 21, 2005), pp. 1, 3; K. Acquino et al., "How Employees Respond to Personal Offense: The Effect of the Blame Attribution, Victim Status, and Offender Status on Revenge and Reconciliation in the Workplace," *Journal of Applied Psychology*, 86, no. 1 (2001), pp. 52–59.

87 A. Tomlinson, "Re-evaluating Your Workplace: Is It Safe and Secure?" *Canadian HR Reporter* (February 25, 2002), pp. 3, 12; L. Martin and D. Tona, "Before It's Too Late," *OH&S Canada* (April/May 2000), pp. 52–53.

88 P. Viollis and C. Mathers, "Companies Need to Re-engineer Their Cultural Thinking About Workplace Violence," *Canadian HR Reporter* (March 14, 2005), p. 19; D. Anfuso, "Workplace Violence," *Personnel Journal* (October 1994), p. 71; see also L. Martin and D. Tona, "Before It's Too Late," *OH&S Canada* (April/May 2000), pp. 52–53; H. Bloom, "Workplace Violence: The Myth That We're Helpless," *Workplace Today* (January 2002), pp. 36–37; W.H. Glenn, "Workplace Violence: An Employees' Survival Guide," *OH&S Canada* (April/May 2002), pp. 26–31.

89 D. Anfuso, "Workplace Violence," *Personnel Journal* (October 1994), pp. 66–77.

90 L. Young, "Managers at B.C. Telus Held Accountable for Wellness," *Canadian HR Reporter* (February 28, 2000), p. 9.

91 J. Taggart and J. Farrell, "Where Wellness Shows Up on the Bottom Line," *Canadian HR Reporter* (October 20, 2003), pp. 12, 15.

92 S. Klie, "Seven Oaks Hospital Relies on Healthy Staff," *Canadian HR Reporter* (October 23, 2006).

93 E. Buffett, "Healthy Employees Translate into Profits," *Canadian HR Reporter* (April 9, 2007).

94 A. Tomlinson, "Healthy Living a Remedy for Burgeoning Employee Absentee Rates," *Canadian HR Reporter* (March 25, 2002), pp. 3, 12.

95 S. Pellegrini, "The Next 25 Years: Wellness," *Benefits Canada* (June 2002), pp. 83–85.

96 C. Warren, "Healthy Competition Boosts Workplace Wellness," *Workplace News* (November/December 2007).

Chapter 23

1 Compdata Surveys, www.compdatasurveys.com/Products/Compensation.

2 N. Chhinzer and K. Ababneh, "Characteristics of the Unemployed in Canada: Leavers, Losers, and Layoffs," *International Business & Economics Research Journal*, 9, no. 12 (2010), pp. 1–15.

3 Statistics Canada, "Permanent Layoffs, Quits and Hirings in the Canadian Economy 1978 to 1995," Business and Labour Market Analysis Division, www.statcan.gc.ca/pub/71-539-x/71-539-x1995001-eng.pdf (accessed September 26, 2011).

4 A. Cowan and N. Stewart, "Compensation Planning Outlook 2011: Playing It Safe in the Face of an Unsteady Economic Recovery," The Conference Board of Canada (October 2010).

5 A. Heller, "The People Factor: Supermarkets' Investment in Return on People Provides Results in a Changing Labour Environment," *Supermarket News* (May 2004), http://subscribers.supermarketnews.com/mag/people_factor, (accessed September 26, 2011).

6 W.F. Cascio, *Responsible Restructuring: Creative and Profitable Alternatives to Layoffs* (San Fransico, CA: Barrett-Koehler, 2002).

7 W.F. Cascio, *Costing human resources: The financial impact of behavior in Organizations* (Boston, MA: PWS-Kent, 1991).

8 R.W. Griffeth, P.W. Hom, and S. Gaertner, "A Meta-Analysis of Antecedents and Correlates of Employee Turnover: Update, Moderator Tests, and Research Implications for the Next Millennium," *Journal of Management*, 26, no. 3 (June 2006), pp. 463–488.

9 J. Johnson, R.W. Griffeth, and M. Griffin, "Factors Discrimination Functional and Dysfunctional Sales Force Turnover," *Journal of Business & Industrial Marketing*, 15, no. 6 (January 2000), pp. 399–415.

10 S. Abbasi and K. Hollman, "Turnover: The Real Bottom-Line," *Public Personnel Management*, 29, no. 3 (2000), pp. 333–342.

11 S. Hartman and A. Yrle, "Can the Hobo Phenomenon Help Explain Voluntary Turnover?" *International Journal of Contemporary Hospitality Management*, 8, no. 4 (August 1996), pp. 11–16.

12 M. Stovel and N. Bontis, "Voluntary Turnover: Knowledge Management Friend or Foe?" *Journal of Intellectual Capital*, 3, no. 3 (2002), pp. 303–322.

13 W.H. Mobley, R.W. Griffeth, H.H. Hand, and B.M. Meglino, "Review and Conceptual Analysis of the Employee Turnover Process," *Psychological Bulletin*, 86, no. 3 (May 1979), pp. 493–522.

14 P.W. Hom and A.J. Kinicki, "Toward a Greater Understanding of How Dissatisfaction Drives Employee Turnover," *Academy of Management Journal*, 44, no. 5 (October, 2001), pp. 975–987.

15 P. Cappelli, *The New Deal at Work: Managing the Market-Driven Workforce* (Boston, MA: Harvard Business School Press, 1999).

16 S. Norris, and T. Williams, "Healthy Aging: Adding Years to Life and Life to Years," Government of Canada (October 27, 2000), http://dsp-psd.pwgsc.gc.ca/Collection-R/LoPBdP/BP/prb0023-e.htm (accessed September 26, 2011).

17 "Mandatory Retirement Fades in Canada," CBC News (October 18, 2010), www.cbc.ca/news/canada/story/2009/08/20/mandatory-retirement-explainer523.html (accessed September 26, 2011).

18 Ibid.

19 G. Golightly, "Preparing Employees for Retirement Transitions," *HR Professional* (December 1999/January 2000), pp. 27–33.

20 *1995 Canadian Dismissal Practices Survey* (Toronto, ON: Murray Axmith & Associates).

21 G. Golightly, "Preparing Employees for Retirement Transitions," *HR Professional* (December 1999/January 2000), pp. 27–33.

22 J. Famularo, *Handbook of Modern Personnel Administration* (New York, NY: McGraw-Hill, 1972), pp. 65.3–65.5.

23 N. Chhinzer and K. Ababneh, "Characteristics of the Unemployed in Canada: Leavers, Losers, and Layoffs," *International Business & Economics Research Journal*, 9, no. 12 (December 2010), pp. 1–15

24 N.C. MacDonald, "Progressing towards Just Cause," *Canadian HR Reporter* (September 22, 2008).

25 S. Rudner, "Just Cause Termination Still Not Clearcut," *Canadian HR Reporter* (March 23, 2009).

26 D. Bambrough and M. Certosimo, "Worker Fraud Usually Justifies Dismissal," *Canadian HR Reporter* (October 23, 2006).

27 L. Cassiani, "Dishonesty Not Always Enough to Terminate," *Canadian HR Reporter* (August 13, 2001), pp. 3, 6; P. Israel, "Firing an Employee for Dishonesty? Put Things in Context First," *Canadian HR Reporter* (August 12, 2002), p. 5.

28 "Proving Cause for Termination Getting Harder," *Workplace Today* (January 2001), p. 17; L. Harris, "High Standards Allow Employer to Fire Threatening Employee," *Canadian HR Reporter* (October 22, 2001), pp. 8, 10.

29 D. Bambrough and M. Certosimo, "Worker Fraud Usually Justifies Dismissal," *Canadian HR Reporter* (October 23, 2006).

30 A. Britnell, "Stop Employee Theft," *Canadian Business Online* (July 16, 2003), www.canadianbusiness.com (accessed May 29, 2006); J. Towler, "Dealing with Employees Who Steal," *Canadian HR Reporter* (September 23, 2002), p. 4.

31 "Air Canada Searches Employee Rooms," *Canadian HR Reporter* (February 10, 2003), p. 2.

32 J. Famularo, *Handbook of Modern Personnel Administration* (New York, NY: McGraw-Hill, 1972), pp. 65.4–65.5.

33 "Good Broker, Bad Decision," *Canadian HR Reporter* (July 17, 2006).

34 K.S. Cameron. "Investigating Organizational Downsizing: Fundamental Issues," *Human Resource Management*, 33 (1994), pp. 183–188.

35 Ibid.

36 Commerce Clearing House, *Personnel Practices/Communications* (Chicago, IL: CCH, 1992), p. 1410.

37 E.A. Lind, J. Greenberg, K.S. Scott, and T.D. Welchans, "The Winding Road from Employee to Complainant: Situational and Psychological Determinants of Wrongful Dismissal Claims," *Administrative Science Quarterly*, 45 (2000), pp. 557–590.

38 Y. Cohen-Charash and P. E. Spector, "The Role of Justice in Organizations: A Meta-Analysis," *Organizational Behavior and Human Decision Processes*, 86 (November 2001), pp. 278–321.

39 E.E. Mole, *Wrongful Dismissal Practice Manual*, Chapter 7 (Toronto, ON: Butterworths Canada, 1993).

40 J.R. Smith, "Worker Ordered to Pay $41.5 Million," *Canadian HR Reporter* (December 1, 2008).

41 K. Blair, "Sports Editor Scores 28-Month Severance," *Canadian HR Reporter* (April 7, 1997), p. 5.

42 M. Fitzgibbon, "Desperate for Workers? Watch Your Step," *Canadian HR Reporter* (January 28, 2008).

43 J. McAlpine, "Don't Add Bad Faith to Wrongful Dismissal," *Canadian HR Reporter* (May 6, 2002), p. 7; P. Israel, "Cut Down on Lawsuits Just by Being Nice," *Canadian HR Reporter* (November 18, 2002), p. 5.

44 N.C. MacDonald, "Record-Setting Wallace Award Overturned," *Canadian HR Reporter* (September 11, 2006).

45 J.R. Smith, "Top Court Strips Out Damages in *Keays*," *Canadian HR Reporter* (July 14, 2008); T. Giesbrecht, K. McDermott, and K. McNeill, "*Keays v. Honda Canada Inc.*" www.mccarthy.ca/article_detail.aspx?id=4053 (accessed June 27, 2008).

46 M.J. MacKillop, "The Perils of Dismissal: The Impact of the Wallace Decision on Reasonable Notice." Paper presented at the Human Resources Professionals Association of Ontario Employment Law Conference (Toronto, ON, October 1999), p. 18.

47 K. Blair, "Pay in Lieu Just the Beginning," *Canadian HR Reporter* (July 14, 1997), p. 5; see also K. Blair, "Dismissal Damages, Thy Name Is Mitigation," *Canadian HR Reporter* (February 9, 1998), p. 5.

48 M. MacKillop and L. Jessome, "Manage Disability Claims with Care," *HR Professional* (August/September 2005), p. 30; J.M. Carvalho, "$500,000 Punitive Damages Award Shocks Honda," *McCarthy Tetrault Report on Canadian Labour and Employment Law* (September 2005).

49 N.C. MacDonald, "The *Keays* to Punitive Damages," *Canadian HR Reporter* (November 20, 2006); T. Giesbrecht, K. McDermott, and K. McNeill, "*Keays v. Honda Canada Inc.*" www.mccarthy.ca/article_detail.aspx?id=4053 (accessed June 27, 2008).

50 E.E. Mole, *Wrongful Dismissal Practice Manual*, Chapter 3 (Toronto, ON: Butterworths Canada, 1993).

51 H.A.Levitt and V. Michaelidis, "Ex-Employee Granted $800,000 in Constructive Dismissal Case," *Workplace* (March/April 2008), p. 11.

52 H. Nieuwland, "Changing Employment Contracts," *HR Professional* (October/November 2008), p. 21.

53 J. McApline, "10 Steps for Reducing Exposure to Wrongful Dismissal," *Canadian HR Reporter* (May 6, 2002), p. 8.

54 E. Caruk, "What to Do If a Wrongful Dismissal Action Hits," *Canadian HR Reporter* (May 6, 2002), p. 10.

55 Sonny Weide, "When You Terminate an Employee," *Employment Relations Today* (August 1994), pp. 287–293.

56 D. Bell, "No Easy Way to Say 'You're Fired'," *Canadian HR Reporter* (June 15, 2009); J. Coil, III and C. Rice, "Three Steps to Creating Effective Employee Releases," *Employment Relations Today* (Spring 1994), p. 92.

57 S. Milne, "The Termination Interview," *Canadian Manager* (Spring 1994), pp. 15–16.

58 A. Saks, "Engagement: The Academic Perspective," *Canadian HR Reporter* (January 26, 2009).

59 J. Gibbons, *Employee Engagement: A Review of Current Research and Its Implications* (New York, NY: The Conference Board, 2006).

60 *Engaging Employees to Drive Global Business Success: Insights from Mercer's What's Working*™ *Research* (New York, NY: Mercer, 2007).

61 S. O'Neal and J. Gebauer, "Talent Management in the 21st Century: Attracting, Retaining and Engaging Employees of Choice," *WorldatWork Journal*, 15, no. 1 (2006), pp. 6–17.

62 J. Shaffer, "Measurable Payoff: How Employee Engagement Can Boost Performance and Profits," *Communication World* (July–August 2004).

63 Based on D. McElroy, "High Tech with High Touch: A New Communication Contract," *Canadian HR Reporter* (April 7, 1997), p. G6.

64 "Chrysler Workers Furious over CEO's Letter," *Canadian HR Reporter* (May 4, 2009).

65 D. Jones, "What If You Held a Survey and No-One Came?" *Canadian HR Reporter* (July 16, 2001), pp. 19, 22.

66 D. Brown, "Getting the Hard Facts in Employee Attitude and Satisfaction," *Canadian HR Reporter* (November 1, 1999), p. 2.

67 A. Massey, "Blogging Phobia Hits Employers," *Canadian HR Reporter* (September 26, 2005), pp. 15, 17.

68 L. Harris, "Staffer Fired after Bad-Mouthing Colleagues, Management in Blog," *Canadian HR Reporter* (September 8, 2008); S.E. Sorenson, "Employee Blogging," *HR Professional* (April/May 2008), p. 16.

69 L. De Piante, "Blogging Guidelines for Employees: A Necessity in the Workplace," *Canadian HR Reporter* (April 23, 2007); S. Crossley and M. Torrance, "Indiscriminate Blogging and the Workplace," *Workplace News* (November/December 2007), pp. 12–13.

70 Based on D. McElroy, "High Tech with High Touch: A New Communication Contract," *Canadian HR Reporter* (April 7, 1997), p. G6.

71 S. Klie, "Blogs Connect CEOs with Employees, Clients," *Canadian HR Reporter* (November 17, 2008).

Chapter 24

1 T.T. Delaney, "Unions and Human Resource Policies," in K. Rowland and G. Ferris (eds.), *Research in Personnel and Human Resources Management* (Greenwich, CT: JAI Press, 1991).

2 S. Klie, "Wal-Mart Closes Union Shop in Quebec," *Canadian HR Reporter* (November 3, 2008).

3 L. Harris, "Union-Proof: How Some Employers Avoid Organized Labour," *Canadian HR Reporter* (October 22, 2007).

4 R. Morissette, G. Shellenberg, and A. Johnson, "Diverging Trends in Unionization," *Perspectives on Labour and Income*, 17, no. 2, Statistics Canada (Summer 2005); U. Vu, "Low Membership Keeps Unions on the Defensive," *Canadian HR Reporter* (February 13, 2006), pp. 4, 9.

5 C. Hallamore, "Globalization Shifts the Ground in Labour Relations," *Inside Edge* (Spring 2006), p. 14; see also C. Hallamore, *Industrial Relations Outlook 2006: Shifting Ground, Shifting Attitudes* (Ottawa, ON: Conference Board of Canada, 2006).

6 C. Hallamore, *Industrial Relations Outlook 2007: Finding Common Ground through the War for Workers* (Ottawa, ON: The Conference Board of Canada, 2007); S. Klie, "Labour Market Should Unite Business, Unions," *Canadian HR Reporter* (February 27, 2007).

7 L. Harris, "Unions Taking Up the Mantle of Women's Issues," *Canadian HR Reporter* (August 11, 2008); L. Harris, "Youthful Proposition from Unions," *Canadian HR Reporter* (October 20, 2008).

8 H.N. Wheeler and J.A. McClendon, "The Individual Decision to Unionise," in G. Strauss et. al., (eds.), *The State of the Unions* (Madison, WI: Industrial Relations Research Association, 1991).

9 H.S. Farber and D.H. Saks, "Why Workers Want Unions: The Role of Relative Wages and Job Characteristics," *Journal of Political Economy*, 88, no. 21 (April, 1980), pp. 349–369.

10 J. Kelly, *Rethinking Industrial Relations: Mobilization, Collectivism, and Long Waves* (London, UK: Routledge, 1998).

11 H.N. Wheeler and J.A. McClendon, "The Individual Decision to Unionise," in G. Strauss et. al., (eds.), *The State of the Unions* (Madison, WI: Industrial Relations Research Association, 1991).

12 Statistics Canada, "Unionization Rates in First Half of 2007 and 2008," (March, 3, 2010), www.statcan.gc.ca/pub/75-001-x/topics-sujets/unionization-syndicalisation/unionization-syndicalisation-2008-eng.htm (accessed September 26, 2011).

13 C. Fullager and J. Barling, "A Longitudinal Test of a Model of the Antecedents and Consequences of Union Loyalty," *Journal of Applied Psychology*, 74, no. 2 (April 1989), pp. 213–227; A. Eaton, M. Gordon, and J. Keefe, "The Impact of Quality of Work-Life Programs and Grievance Systems Effectiveness on Union Commitment," *Industrial and Labor Relations Review*, 45, no. 3 (April 1992), pp. 592–604.

14 L. Young, "Union Drives: Initiated Within, Prevented Within," *Canadian HR Reporter* (November 29, 1999), pp. 2, 14.

15 Based in part on L. Field, "Early Signs," *Canadian HR Reporter* (November 29, 1999), p. 14.

16 *Canadian Master Labour Guide*, 16th ed. (Toronto, ON: CCH Canadian, 2002).

17 A.W.J. Craig and N.A. Solomon, *The System of Industrial Relations in Canada*, 5th ed. (Toronto, ON: Prentice Hall Canada, 1996), p. 217.

18 Ibid., p. 218.

19 Ibid., p. 216.

20 J. Peirce, *Canadian Industrial Relations* (Toronto, ON: Prentice Hall Canada, 2000), p. 431.

21 The section on distributive bargaining is based on R.E. Walton and R.B. McKersie, *A Behavioral Theory of Labor Negotiations* (New York, NY: McGraw-Hill, 1965), pp. 4–6.

22 The section on integrative bargaining is based on R.E. Walton and R.B. McKersie, *A Behavioral Theory of Labor Negotiations* (New York, NY: McGraw-Hill, 1965), pp. 4–6.

23 Based on C. Kapel, "The Feeling's Mutual," *Human Resources Professional* (April 1995), pp. 9–13; see also S.D. Smith, "Taking the Confrontation out of Collective Bargaining," *Canadian HR Reporter* (September 10, 2001), pp. 11, 13.

24 U. Vu, "Interest Wanes on Interest-Based?" *Canadian HR Reporter* (February 28, 2006), pp. 6, 9.

25 J. Peirce, *Canadian Industrial Relations* (Toronto, ON: Prentice Hall Canada, 2000), p. 431.

26 C. Spurr, "A 'Perfect Storm': Stora Enso Lockout in Nova Scotia," *Shunpiking Online*, 3, no. 4 (May 3, 2006), www.shunpiking.com/o10304/0304-AC-CS-perfectstrom.htm (accessed June 1, 2006); "Keep Stora off Campaign Agenda: Mayor," *CBC News* (May 26, 2006), www.cbc.ca/ns/story/nsv-stora20060526.html (accessed June 1, 2006).

27 L. Diebel, "45-Minute Job Action Staged for International Hotel Workers' Day," *Toronto Star* (November 11, 2007), www.thestar.com/printArticle/275447 (accessed July 21, 2009).

28 See J.E. Grenig, "Stare Decisis, Re Judicata and Collecteral Estoppel and Labour Arbitration," *Labour Law Journal*, 38 (April 1987), pp. 195–205.

29 Based on M. Gunderson and D.G. Taras, *Union–Management Relations in Canada* (Toronto, ON: Pearson Education Canada, 2001), p. 429; J. Peirce, *Canadian Industrial Relations* (Toronto, ON: Prentice Hall Canada, 2000), p. 431.

30 M. Hebert, "Length of Collective Agreements," *Workplace Gazette*, 7, no. 4 (Winter 2004), p. 27.

31 *Canadian Master Labour Guide*, 16th ed. (Toronto, ON: CCH Canadian Ltd., 2002).

32 M. Hebert, "Length of Collective Agreements," *Workplace Gazette*, 7, no. 4 (Winter 2004), p. 27.

33 G. Sova, "How Long a Contract Should You Sign?" *Canadian HR Reporter* (February 28, 2005), p. 9.

Chapter 25

1 Vignette based on "Tim Hortons' Extra-Large Trouble Trouble," *Macleans.ca*, September 7, 2010, http://www2.macleans.ca/2010/09/07/extra-large-trouble-trouble; and M. Friscolanti, "Tim Hortons: Rolling in Dough," *Macleans.ca*, September 6, 2011, http://www2.macleans.ca/2011/09/06/rolling-in-dough

2 Based on B. M. Bass, *Bass & Stogdill's Handbook of Leadership*, 3rd ed. (New York: Free Press, 1990).

3 D. H. Gruenfeld, M. E. Inesi, J. C. Magee, and A. D. Galinsky, "Power and the Objectification of Social Targets," *Journal of Personality and Social Psychology* 95, no. 1 (2008), pp. 111–127; A. D. Galinsky, J. C. Magee, D. H. Gruenfeld, J. A. Whitson, and K. A. Liljenquist, "Power Reduces the Press of the Situation: Implications for Creativity, Conformity, and Dissonance," *Journal of Personality and Social Psychology* 95, no. 6 (2008), pp. 1450–1466; and J. C. Magee and C. A. Langner, "How Personalized and Socialized Power Motivation Facilitate Antisocial and Prosocial Decision-Making," *Journal of Research in Personality* 42, no. 6 (2008), pp. 1547–1559.

4 R. M. Kanter, "Power Failure in Management Circuits," *Harvard Business Review*, July–August 1979, p. 65.

5 "Power Outage: A Loss of Social Power Distorts How Money Is Represented," *ScienceDaily*, July 26, 2010, http://www.sciencedaily.com/releases/2010/06/100607151320.htm; and D. Dubois, D. D. Rucker, and A. D. Galinsky, "The Accentuation Bias: Money Literally Looms Larger (and Sometimes Smaller) to the Powerless," *Social Psychological and Personality Science* 1, no. 3 (2010), pp. 199–205.

6 G. A. Van Kleef, A. C. Homan, C. Finkenauer, S. Gundemir, and E. Stamkou, "Breaking the Rules to Rise to Power: How Norm Violators Gain Power in the Eyes of Others," *Social Psychological and Personality Science*, January 26, 2011, published online before print, http://spp.sagepub.com/content/early/2011/01/20/1948550611398416

7 J. Lammers, D. A. Stapel, and A. Galinsky, "Power Increases Hypocrisy: Moralizing in Reasoning, Immunity and Behavior," *Psychological Science* 21, no. 5 (2010), pp. 737–744.

8 S. Prashad, "Fill Your Power Gap," *Globe and Mail*, July 23, 2003, p. C3.

9 J. R. P. French Jr. and B. Raven, "The Bases of Social Power," in *Studies in Social Power*, ed. D. Cartwright (Ann Arbor, MI: University of Michigan, Institute for Social Research, 1959), pp. 150–167. For an update on French and Raven's work, see D. E. Frost and A. J. Stahelski, "The Systematic Measurement of French and Raven's Bases of Social Power in Workgroups," *Journal of Applied Social Psychology*, April 1988, pp. 375–389; T. R. Hinkin and C. A. Schriesheim, "Development and Application of New Scales to Measure the French and Raven (1959) Bases of Social Power," *Journal of Applied Psychology*, August 1989, pp. 561–567; and G. E. Littlepage, J. L. Van Hein, K. M. Cohen, and L. L. Janiec, "Evaluation and Comparison of Three Instruments Designed to Measure Organizational Power and Influence Tactics," *Journal of Applied Social Psychology*, January 16–31, 1993, pp. 107–125.

10 B. H. Raven, "Social Influence and Power," in *Current Studies in Social Psychology*, ed. I. D. Steiner and M. Fishbein (New York: Holt, Rinehart, Winston, 1965), pp. 371–382.

11 E. A. Ward, "Social Power Bases of Managers: Emergence of a New Factor," *Journal of Social Psychology*, February 2001, pp. 144–147.

12 S. R. Giessner and T. W. Schubert, "High in the Hierarchy: How Vertical Location and Judgments of Leaders' Power Are Interrelated," *Organizational Behavior and Human Decision Processes* 104, no. 1 (2007), pp. 30–44.

13 D. Hickson, C. Hinings, C. Lee, R. Schneck, and J. Pennings, "A Strategic Contingencies Theory of Intra-Organizational Power," *Administrative Science Quarterly* 16, 1971, pp. 216–229; and J. W. Dean Jr. and J. R. Evans, *Total Quality: Management, Organization, and Strategy* (Minneapolis-St. Paul, MN: West, 1994).

14 G. Yukl, H. Kim, and C. M. Falbe, "Antecedents of Influence Outcomes," *Journal of Applied Psychology* 81, no. 3 (1996), pp. 309–317.

15 P. P. Carson, K. D. Carson, and C. W. Roe, "Social Power Bases: A Meta-analytic Examination of Interrelationships and Outcomes," *Journal of Applied Social Psychology* 23, no. 14 (1993), pp. 1150–1169.

16 C. M. Falbe and G. Yukl, "Consequences for Managers of Using Single Tactics and Combinations of Tactics," *Academy of Management Journal* 35, 1992, pp. 638–652.

17 Cited in J. R. Carlson, D. S. Carlson, and L. L. Wadsworth, "The Relationship between Individual Power Moves and Group Agreement Type: An Examination and Model," *SAM Advanced Management Journal* 65, no. 4 (2000), pp. 44–51.

18 Vignette based on "Tim Hortons' Extra-Large Trouble Trouble," *Macleans.ca*, September 7, 2010, http://www2.macleans.ca/2010/09/07/extra-large-trouble-trouble

19 R. E. Emerson, "Power-Dependence Relations," *American Sociological Review* 27 (1962), pp. 31–41.

20 Thanks are due to an anonymous reviewer for supplying this insight.

21 H. Mintzberg, *Power in and Around Organizations* (Englewood Cliffs, NJ: Prentice Hall, 1983), p. 24.

22 Vignette based on M. Friscolanti, "Tim Hortons: Rolling in Dough," *Macleans.ca*, September 6, 2011, http://www2.macleans.ca/2011/09/06/rolling-in-dough

23 See, for example, D. Kipnis, S. M. Schmidt, C. Swaffin-Smith, and I. Wilkinson, "Patterns of Managerial Influence: Shotgun Managers, Tacticians, and Bystanders," *Organizational Dynamics*, Winter 1984, pp. 58–67; T. Case, L. Dosier, G. Murkison, and B. Keys, "How Managers Influence Superiors: A Study of Upward Influence Tactics," *Leadership and Organization Development Journal* 9, no. 4 (1988), pp. 25–31; D. Kipnis and S. M. Schmidt, "Upward-Influence Styles: Relationship with Performance Evaluations, Salary, and Stress," *Administrative Science Quarterly*, December 1988, pp. 528–542; G. Yukl and C. M. Falbe, "Influence Tactics and Objectives in Upward, Downward, and Lateral Influence Attempts," *Journal of Applied Psychology*, April 1990, pp. 132–140; B. Keys and T. Case, "How to Become an Influential Manager," *Academy of Management Executive*, November 1990, pp. 38–51; D. A. Ralston, D. J. Gustafson, L. Mainiero, and D. Umstot, "Strategies of Upward Influence: A Cross-National Comparison of Hong Kong and American Managers," *Asia Pacific Journal of Management*, October 1993, pp. 157–175; G. Yukl, H. Kim, and C. M. Falbe, "Antecedents of Influence Outcomes," *Journal of Applied Psychology*, June 1996, pp. 309–317; K. E. Lauterbach and B. J. Weiner, "Dynamics of Upward Influence: How Male and Female Managers Get Their Way," *Leadership Quarterly*, Spring 1996, pp. 87–107; K. R. Xin and A. S. Tsui, "Different Strokes for Different Folks? Influence Tactics by Asian-American and Caucasian-American Managers," *Leadership Quarterly*, Spring 1996, pp. 109–132; and S. J. Wayne, R. C. Liden, I. K. Graf, and G. R. Ferris, "The Role of Upward Influence Tactics in Human Resource Decisions," *Personnel Psychology*, Winter 1997, pp. 979–1006.

24 This section adapted from G. Yukl, C. M. Falbe, and J. Y. Youn, "Patterns of Influence Behavior for Managers," *Group & Organization Studies* 18, no. 1 (March 1993), p. 7.

25 G. Yukl, *Leadership in Organizations*, 5th ed. (Upper Saddle River, NJ: Prentice Hall, 2002), pp. 141–174; G. R. Ferris, W. A. Hochwarter, C. Douglas, F. R. Blass, R. W. Kolodinksy, and D. C. Treadway, "Social Influence Processes in Organizations and Human Resource Systems," in *Research in Personnel and Human Resources Management*, vol. 21, ed. G. R. Ferris and J. J. Martocchio (Oxford, UK: JAI Press/Elsevier, 2003), pp. 65–127; and C. A. Higgins, T. A. Judge, and G. R. Ferris, "Influence Tactics and Work Outcomes: A Meta-analysis," *Journal of Organizational Behavior*, March 2003, pp. 89–106.

26 C. M. Falbe and G. Yukl, "Consequences for Managers of Using Single Influence Tactics and Combinations of Tactics," *Academy of Management Journal*, July 1992, pp. 638–653.

27 R. E. Petty and P. Briñol, "Persuasion: From Single to Multiple to MetaCognitive Processes," *Perspectives on Psychological Science* 3, no. 2 (2008), pp. 137–147.

28 I. Stern and J. D. Westphal, "Stealthy Footsteps to the Boardroom: Executives' Backgrounds, Sophisticated Interpersonal Influence Behavior, and Board Appointments," *Administrative Science Quarterly* 55, no. 2 (2010), pp. 278–319; and G. Yukl, *Leadership in Organizations*, 5th ed. (Upper Saddle River, NJ: Prentice Hall, 2002), pp. 141–174.

29 N. K. Grant, L. R. Fabrigar, and Heidi Lim, "Exploring the Efficacy of Compliments as a Tactic for Securing Compliance," *Basic & Applied Social Psychology* 32, no. 3 (2010), pp. 226–233.

30 C. M. Falbe and G. Yukl, "Consequences for Managers of Using Single Influence Tactics and Combinations of Tactics," *Academy of Management Journal*, July 1992, pp. 638–653.

31 A. W. Kruglanski, A. Pierro, and E. T. Higgins, "Regulatory Mode and Preferred Leadership Styles: How Fit Increases Job Satisfaction," *Basic and Applied Social Psychology* 29, no. 2 (2007), pp. 137–149; and A. Pierro, L. Cicero, and B. H. Raven, "Motivated Compliance with Bases of Social Power," *Journal of Applied Social Psychology* 38, no. 7 (2008), pp. 1921–1944.

32 G. R. Ferris, D. C. Treadway, P. L. Perrewé, R. L. Brouer, C. Douglas, and S. Lux, "Political Skill in Organizations," *Journal of Management*, June 2007, pp. 290–320; K. J. Harris, K. M. Kacmar, S. Zivnuska, and J. D. Shaw, "The Impact of Political Skill on Impression Management Effectiveness," *Journal of Applied Psychology* 92, no. 1 (2007), pp. 278–285; W. A. Hochwarter, G. R. Ferris, M. B. Gavin, P. L. Perrewé, A. T. Hall, and D. D. Frink, "Political Skill as Neutralizer of Felt Accountability–Job Tension Effects on Job Performance Ratings: A Longitudinal Investigation," *Organizational Behavior and Human Decision Processes* 102 (2007), pp. 226–239; D. C. Treadway, G. R. Ferris, A. B. Duke, G. L. Adams, and J. B. Tatcher, "The Moderating Role of Subordinate Political Skill on Supervisors' Impressions of Subordinate Ingratiation and Ratings of Subordinate Interpersonal Facilitation," *Journal of Applied Psychology* 92, no. 3 (2007), pp. 848–855.

33 C. Anderson, S. E. Spataro, and F. J. Flynn, "Personality and Organizational Culture as Determinants of Influence," *Journal of Applied Psychology* 93, no. 3 (2008), pp. 702–710.

34 "Building a Better Workforce," *PROFIT*, February 16, 2011, http://www.profitguide.com/article/10084—building-a-better-workforce—page0

35 This is the definition given by R. Forrester, "Empowerment: Rejuvenating a Potent Idea," *Academy of Management Executive*, August 2000, pp. 67–80.

36 R. E. Quinn and G. M. Spreitzer, "The Road to Empowerment: Seven Questions Every Leader Should Consider," *Organizational Dynamics*, Autumn 1997, p. 38.

37 C. Argyris, "Empowerment: The Emperor's New Clothes," *Harvard Business Review*, May–June 1998.

38 J. Schaubroeck, J. R. Jones, and J. L. Xie, "Individual Differences in Utilizing Control to Cope with Job Demands: Effects on Susceptibility to Infectious Disease," *Journal of Applied Psychology* 86, no. 2 (2001), pp. 265–278.

39 "Delta Promotes Empowerment," *Globe and Mail*, May 31, 1999, Advertising Supplement, p. C5.

40 R. Sutton, "How to Be a Good Boss in a Bad Economy," *Harvard Business Review* 87, no. 6 (2009), pp. 42–50.

41 T. Lee and C. M. Brotheridge, "When the Prey Becomes the Predator: Bullying as Predictor of Reciprocal Bullying, Coping, and Well-Being" (working paper, University of Regina, Regina, 2005).

42 N. J. Fast and S. Chen, "When the Boss Feels Inadequate: Power, Incompetence, and Aggression," *Psychological Science* 20, no. 11 (2009), pp. 1406–1413.

43 University of California-Berkeley, "Bosses Who Feel Inadequate Are More Likely to Bully," *ScienceDaily*, October 15, 2009, http://www.sciencedaily.com /releases/2009/10/091014102209.htm

44 M. S. Hershcovis and J. Barling, "Comparing the Outcomes of Sexual Harassment and Workplace Aggression: A Meta-analysis" (paper presented at the Seventh International Conference on Work, Stress and Health, Washington, DC, March 8, 2008).

45 Quebec Labour Standards, s. 81.18, *Psychological Harassment at Work.*

46 S. Stecklow, "Sexual-Harassment Cases Plague U.N.," *Wall Street Journal*, May 21, 2009, p. A1.

47 *Janzen v. Platy Enterprises Ltd.* [1989] 10 C.H.R.R. D/6205 SCC.

48 The following section is based on J. N. Cleveland and M. E. Kerst, "Sexual Harassment and Perceptions of Power: An Under-Articulated Relationship," *Journal of Vocational Behavior*, February 1993, pp. 49–67.

49 C. Bass, "University Bans Faculty-Student Sex," *Yale Alumni Magazine*, March/April 2010, http://yalealumnimagazine.com/issues/2010_03/lv_sex015.html

50 http://www2.carleton.ca/equity/human-rights/policy/1307-2/#SEXUAL%20HARASSMENT

51 C. Hill and E. Silva, *Drawing the Line: Sexual Harassment on Campus* (Washington, DC: American Association of University Women, 2005).

52 H. Burnett-Nichols, "Don't Touch, Do Tell," *University Affairs*, March 8, 2010, http://www.universityaffairs.ca/dont-touch-do-tell.aspx

53 C. R. Willness, P. Steel, and K. Lee, "A Meta-analysis of the Antecedents and Consequences of Workplace Sexual Harassment," *Personnel Psychology* 60 (2007), pp. 127–162.

54 Vignette based on "Tim Hortons' Extra-Large Trouble Trouble," *Macleans.ca*, September 7, 2010, http://www2.macleans.ca/2010/09/07/extra-large-trouble-trouble

55 S. A. Culbert and J. J. McDonough, *The Invisible War: Pursuing Self-Interest at Work* (New York: Wiley, 1980), p. 6.

56 H. Mintzberg, *Power in and Around Organizations* (Englewood Cliffs, NJ: Prentice Hall, 1983), p. 26.

57 T. Cole, "Who Loves Ya?" *Report on Business Magazine*, April 1999, p. 54.

58 D. Farrell and J. C. Petersen, "Patterns of Political Behavior in Organizations," *Academy of Management Review*, July 1982, p. 405. For a thoughtful analysis of the academic controversies underlying any definition of organizational politics, see A. Drory and T. Romm, "The Definition of Organizational Politics: A Review," *Human Relations*, November 1990, pp. 1133–1154; and R. S. Cropanzano, K. M. Kacmar, and D. P. Bozeman, "Organizational Politics, Justice, and Support: Their Differences and Similarities," in *Organizational Politics, Justice and Support: Managing Social Climate at Work*, ed. R. S. Cropanzano and K. M. Kacmar (Westport, CT: Quorum Books, 1995), pp. 1–18.

59 J. Pfeffer, *Power in Organizations* (Marshfield, MA: Pittman, 1981).

60 G. R. Ferris, G. S. Russ, and P. M. Fandt, "Politics in Organizations," in *Impression Management in Organizations*, ed. R. A. Giacalone and P. Rosenfeld (Newbury Park, CA: Sage, 1989), pp. 143–170; and K. M. Kacmar, D. P. Bozeman, D. S. Carlson, and W. P. Anthony, "An Examination of the Perceptions of Organizational Politics Model: Replication and Extension," *Human Relations*, March 1999, pp. 383–416.

61 K. M. Kacmar and R. A. Baron, "Organizational Politics: The State of the Field, Links to Related Processes, and an Agenda for Future Research," in *Research in Personnel and Human Resources*

Management, vol. 17, ed. G. R. Ferris (Greenwich, CT: JAI Press, 1999); and M. Valle and L. A. Witt, "The Moderating Effect of Teamwork Perceptions on the Organizational Politics-Job Satisfaction Relationship," *Journal of Social Psychology*, June 2001, pp. 379–388.

62 G. R. Ferris, D. D. Frink, M. C. Galang, J. Zhou, K. M. Kacmar, and J. L. Howard, "Perceptions of Organizational Politics: Prediction, Stress-Related Implications, and Outcomes," *Human Relations*, February 1996, pp. 233–266; K. M. Kacmar, D. P. Bozeman, D. S. Carlson, and W. P. Anthony, "An Examination of the Perceptions of Organizational Politics Model; Replication and Extension," *Human Relations*, March 1999, p. 388; and J. M. L. Poon, "Situational Antecedents and Outcomes of Organizational Politics Perceptions," *Journal of Managerial Psychology* 18, no. 2 (2003), pp. 138–155.

63 C. Kiewitz, W. A. Hochwarter, G. R. Ferris, and S. L. Castro, "The Role of Psychological Climate in Neutralizing the Effects of Organizational Politics on Work Outcomes," *Journal of Applied Social Psychology*, June 2002, pp. 1189–1207; and J. M. L. Poon, "Situational Antecedents and Outcomes of Organizational Politics Perceptions," *Journal of Managerial Psychology* 18, no. 2 (2003), pp. 138–155.

64 K. M. Kacmar and R. A. Baron, "Organizational Politics: The State of the Field, Links to Related Processes, and an Agenda for Future Research," in *Research in Personnel and Human Resources Management*, vol. 17, ed. G. R. Ferris (Greenwich, CT: JAI Press, 1999); and M. Valle and L. A. Witt, "The Moderating Effect of Teamwork Perceptions on the Organizational Politics-Job Satisfaction Relationship," *Journal of Social Psychology*, June 2001, pp. 379–388.

65 R. W. Allen, D. L. Madison, L. W. Porter, P. A. Renwick, and B. T. Mayes, "Organizational Politics: Tactics and Characteristics of Its Actors," *California Management Review*, Fall 1979, pp. 77–83.

66 See, for instance, W. L. Gardner and M. J. Martinko, "Impression Management in Organizations," *Journal of Management*, June 1988, pp. 321–338; M. C. Bolino and W. H. Turnley, "More Than One Way to Make an Impression: Exploring Profiles of Impression Management," *Journal of Management* 29, no. 2 (2003), pp. 141–160; S. Zivnuska, K. M. Kacmar, L. A. Witt, D. S. Carlson, and V. K. Bratton, "Interactive Effects of Impression Management and Organizational Politics on Job Performance," *Journal of Organizational Behavior*, August 2004, pp. 627–640; and M. C. Bolino, K. M. Kacmar, W. H. Turnley, and J. B. Gilstrap, "A Multi-Level Review of Impression Management Motives and Behaviors," *Journal of Management* 34, no. 6 (2008), pp. 1080–1109.

67 M. R. Leary and R. M. Kowalski, "Impression Management: A Literature Review and Two-Component Model," *Psychological Bulletin*, January 1990, p. 40.

68 W. L. Gardner and M. J. Martinko, "Impression Management in Organizations," *Journal of Management*, June 1988, p. 333.

69 R. A. Baron, "Impression Management by Applicants during Employment Interviews: The 'Too Much of a Good Thing' Effect," in *The Employment Interview: Theory, Research, and Practice*, ed. R. W. Eder and G. R. Ferris (Newbury Park, CA: Sage, 1989), pp. 204–215.

70 A. P. J. Ellis, B. J. West, A. M. Ryan, and R. P. DeShon, "The Use of Impression Management Tactics in Structural Interviews: A Function of Question Type?" *Journal of Applied Psychology*, December 2002, pp. 1200–1208.

71 C. K. Stevens and A. L. Kristof, "Making the Right Impression: A Field Study of Applicant Impression Management during Job Interviews," *Journal of Applied Psychology* 80 (1995), pp. 587–606; L. A. McFarland, A. M. Ryan, and S. D. Kriska, "Impression Management Use and Effectiveness across Assessment Methods," *Journal of Management* 29, no. 5 (2003), pp. 641–661; C. A. Higgins and T. A. Judge, "The Effect of Applicant

Influence Tactics on Recruiter Perceptions of Fit and Hiring Recommendations: A Field Study," *Journal of Applied Psychology* 89, no. 4 (2004), pp. 622–632; and W. C. Tsai, C. C. Chen, and S. F. Chiu, "Exploring Boundaries of the Effects of Applicant Impression Management Tactics in Job Interviews," *Journal of Management*, February 2005, pp. 108–125.

72 D. C. Gilmore and G. R. Ferris, "The Effects of Applicant Impression Management Tactics on Interviewer Judgments," *Journal of Management*, December 1989, pp. 557–564.

73 C. K. Stevens and A. L. Kristof, "Making the Right Impression: A Field Study of Applicant Impression Management during Job Interviews," *Journal of Applied Psychology* 80 (1995), pp. 587–606.

74 C. A. Higgins, T. A. Judge, and G. R. Ferris, "Influence Tactics and Work Outcomes: A Meta-analysis," *Journal of Organizational Behavior*, March 2003, pp. 89–106.

75 C. A. Higgins, T. A. Judge, and G. R. Ferris, "Influence Tactics and Work Outcomes: A Meta-analysis," *Journal of Organizational Behavior*, March 2003, pp. 89–106.

76 K. J. Harris, K. M. Kacmar, S. Zivnuska, and J. D. Shaw, "The Impact of Political Skill on Impression Management Effectiveness," *Journal of Applied Psychology* 92, no. 1 (2007), pp. 278–285; and D. C. Treadway, G. R. Ferris, A. B. Duke, G. L. Adams, and J. B. Thatcher, "The Moderating Role of Subordinate Political Skill on Supervisors' Impressions of Subordinate Ingratiation and Ratings of Subordinate Interpersonal Facilitation," *Journal of Applied Psychology* 92, no. 3 (2007), pp. 848–855.

77 J. M. Maslyn and D. B. Fedor, "Perceptions of Politics: Does Measuring Different Foci Matter?" *Journal of Applied Psychology* 84 (1998), pp. 645–653; and L. G. Nye and L. A. Witt, "Dimensionality and Construct Validity of the Perceptions of Organizational Politics Scale," *Educational and Psychological Measurement* 53 (1993), pp. 821–829.

78 G. R. Ferris, D. D. Frink, D. Bhawuk, J. Zhou, and D. C. Gilmore, "Reactions of Diverse Groups to Politics in the Workplace," *Journal of Management* 22 (1996), pp. 23–44; K. M. Kacmar, D. P. Bozeman, D. S. Carlson, and W. P. Anthony, "An Examination of the Perceptions of Organizational Politics Model: Replication and Extension," *Human Relations* 52 (1999), pp. 383–416.

79 T. P. Anderson, "Creating Measures of Dysfunctional Office and Organizational Politics: The DOOP and Short-Form DOOP Scales," *Psychology: A Journal of Human Behavior* 31 (1994), pp. 24–34.

80 G. R. Ferris, D. D. Frink, D. Bhawuk, J. Zhou, and D. C. Gilmore, "Reactions of Diverse Groups to Politics in the Workplace," *Journal of Management* 22 (1996), pp. 23–44; K. M. Kacmar, D. P. Bozeman, D. S. Carlson, and W. P. Anthony, "An Examination of the Perceptions of Organizational Politics Model: Replication and Extension," *Human Relations* 52 (1999), pp. 383–416.

81 K. M. Kacmar, D. P. Bozeman, D. S. Carlson, and W. P. Anthony, "An Examination of the Perceptions of Organizational Politics Model: Replication and Extension," *Human Relations* 52 (1999), pp. 383–416; J. M. Maslyn and D. B. Fedor, "Perceptions of Politics: Does Measuring Different Foci Matter?" *Journal of Applied Psychology* 84 (1998), pp. 645–653.

82 M. Warshaw, "The Good Guy's (and Gal's) Guide to Office Politics," *Fast Company*, April 1998, p. 156.

83 C. Robert, T. M. Probst, J. J. Martocchio, F. Drasgow, and J. J. Lawler, "Empowerment and Continuous Improvement in the United States, Mexico, Poland, and India: Predicting Fit on the Basis of the Dimensions of Power Distance and Individualism," *Journal of Applied Psychology* 85 (2000), pp. 643–658.

84 W. A. Randolph and M. Sashkin, "Can Organizational Empowerment Work in Multinational Settings?" *Academy of Management Executive*, February 2002, pp. 102–115.

85 M. Gagné and D. Bhave, "Autonomy in the Workplace: An Essential Ingredient to Employee Engagement and Well-Being in Every Culture?" in *Human Autonomy in Cross-Cultural Context: Perspectives on the Psychology of Agency, Freedom, and Well-Being*, ed. V. I. Chirkov, R. M. Ryan, and K. M. Sheldon (Berlin, Germany: Springer, 2011).

86 Concordia University, "Freedom's Just Another Word for Employee Satisfaction," *ScienceDaily*, January 24, 2011, http://www.sciencedaily.com/releases/2011/01/110124102944.htm

87 O. J. Labedo, "Perceptions of Organisational Politics: Examination of the Situational Antecedent and Consequences among Nigeria's Extension Personnel," *Applied Psychology: An International Review* 55, no. 2 (2006), pp. 255–281.

88 P. P. Fu and G. Yukl, "Perceived Effectiveness of Influence Tactics in the United States and China," *Leadership Quarterly*, Summer 2000, pp. 251–266; O. Branzei, "Cultural Explanations of Individual Preferences for Influence Tactics in Cross-Cultural Encounters," *International Journal of Cross Cultural Management*, August 2002, pp. 203–218; G. Yukl, P. P. Fu, and R. McDonald, "Cross-Cultural Differences in Perceived Effectiveness of Influence Tactics for Initiating or Resisting Change," *Applied Psychology: An International Review*, January 2003, pp. 66–82; and P. P. Fu, T. K. Peng, J. C. Kennedy, and G. Yukl, "Examining the Preferences of Influence Tactics in Chinese Societies: A Comparison of Chinese Managers in Hong Kong, Taiwan, and Mainland China," *Organizational Dynamics* 33, no. 1 (2004), pp. 32–46.

89 P. P. Fu and G. Yukl, "Perceived Effectiveness of Influence Tactics in the United States and China," *Leadership Quarterly*, Summer 2000, pp. 251–266.

90 S. J. Heine, "Making Sense of East Asian Self-Enhancement," *Journal of Cross-Cultural Psychology*, September 2003, pp. 596–602.

91 E. Szabo, "Meaning and Context of Participation in Five European Countries," *Management Decision* 44, no. 2 (2006), pp. 276–289.

92 P. P. Fu, T. K. Peng, J. C. Kennedy, and G. Yukl, "A Comparison of Chinese Managers in Hong Kong, Taiwan, and Mainland China," *Organizational Dynamics*, February 2004, pp. 32–46.

Chapter 26

1 Vignette based on B. Mackin, "PNE Workers Vote to Strike," *Vancouver Courier*, September 16, 2011, http://www.vancourier.com/news/workers+vote+strike/5408991/story.html

2 See, for instance, C. F. Fink, "Some Conceptual Difficulties in the Theory of Social Conflict," *Journal of Conflict Resolution*, December 1968, pp. 412–460. For an updated review of the conflict literature, see J. A. Wall Jr. and R. R. Callister, "Conflict and Its Management," *Journal of Management* 21, no. 3 (1995), pp. 515–558.

3 L. L. Putnam and M. S. Poole, "Conflict and Negotiation," in *Handbook of Organizational Communication: An Interdisciplinary Perspective*, ed. F. M. Jablin, L. L. Putnam, K. H. Roberts, and L. W. Porter (Newbury Park, CA: Sage, 1987), pp. 549–599.

4 K. W. Thomas, "Conflict and Negotiation Processes in Organizations," in *Handbook of Industrial and Organizational Psychology*, 2nd ed., vol. 3, ed. M. D. Dunnette and L. M. Hough (Palo Alto, CA: Consulting Psychologists Press, 1992), pp. 651–717.

5 For a comprehensive review of this approach, also called the interactionist approach, see C. De Dreu and E. Van de Vliert, eds., *Using Conflict in Organizations* (London: Sage, 1997).

6 K. Jehn, "A Multimethod Examination of the Benefits and Detriments of Intragroup Conflict," *Administrative Science Quarterly*, June 1995, pp. 256–282; K. A. Jehn, "A Qualitative

Analysis of Conflict Types and Dimensions in Organizational Groups," *Administrative Science Quarterly*, September 1997, pp. 530–557; K. A. Jehn and E. A. Mannix, "The Dynamic Nature of Conflict: A Longitudinal Study of Intragroup Conflict and Group Performance," *Academy of Management Journal*, April 2001, pp. 238–251; C. K. W. De Dreu and A. E. M. Van Vianen, "Managing Relationship Conflict and the Effectiveness of Organizational Teams," *Journal of Organizational Behavior*, May 2001, pp. 309–328; and K. A. Jehn and C. Bendersky, "Intragroup Conflict in Organizations: A Contingency Perspective on the Conflict-Outcome Relationship," in *Research in Organizational Behavior*, vol. 25, ed. R. M. Kramer and B. M. Staw (Oxford, UK: Elsevier, 2003), pp. 199–210.

7 A. C. Amason, "Distinguishing the Effects of Functional and Dysfunctional Conflict on Strategic Decision Making: Resolving a Paradox for Top Management Teams," *Academy of Management Journal* 39, no. 1 (1996), pp. 123–148.

8 "Survey Shows Managers Have Their Hands Full Resolving Staff Personality Conflicts," *IPMA-HR Bulletin*, November 3, 2006.

9 C. K. W. De Dreu, "The Virtue and Vice of Workplace Conflict: Food for (Pessimistic) Thought," *Journal of Organizational Behavior* 29, no. 1 (2008), pp. 5–18.

10 R. S. Peterson and K. J. Behfar, "The Dynamic Relationship between Performance Feedback, Trust, and Conflict in Groups: A Longitudinal Study," *Organizational Behavior and Human Decision Process* 92, no. 1–2 (2003), pp. 102–112.

11 L. M. Penny and P. E. Spector, "Job Stress, Incivility, and Counterproductive Work Behavior: The Moderating Role of Negative Affectivity," *Journal of Organizational Behavior* 26, no. 7 (2005), pp. 777–796.

12 K. A. Jehn, L. Greer, S. Levine, and G. Szulanski, "The Effects of Conflict Types, Dimensions, and Emergent States on Group Outcomes," *Group Decision and Negotiation* 17, no. 6 (2008), pp. 465–495.

13 This section is based on S. P. Robbins, *Managing Organizational Conflict: A Nontraditional Approach* (Englewood Cliffs, NJ: Prentice Hall, 1974), pp. 31–55; and J. A. Wall Jr. and R. R. Callister, "Conflict and Its Management," *Journal of Management* 21, no. 3 (1995), pp. 517–523.

14 R. S. Peterson and K. J. Behfar, "The Dynamic Relationship between Performance Feedback, Trust, and Conflict in Groups: A Longitudinal Study," *Organizational Behavior and Human Decision Processes*, September–November 2003, pp. 102–112.

15 See K. A. Jehn, "A Multimethod Examination of the Benefits and Detriments of Intragroup Conflict," *Administrative Science Quarterly*, June 1995, pp. 256–282.

16 T. M. Glomb and H. Liao, "Interpersonal Aggression in Work Groups: Social Influence, Reciprocal, and Individual Effects," *Academy of Management Journal* 46, no. 4 (2003), pp. 486–496; and V. Venkataramani and R. S. Dalal, "Who Helps and Who Harms? Relational Aspects of Interpersonal Helping and Harming in Organizations," *Journal of Applied Psychology* 92, no. 4 (2007), pp. 952–966.

17 R. Friedman, C. Anderson, J. Brett, M. Olekalns, N. Goates, and C. C. Lisco, "The Positive and Negative Effects of Anger on Dispute Resolution: Evidence from Electronically Mediated Disputes," *Journal of Applied Psychology*, April 2004, pp. 369–376.

18 Vignette based on B. Mackin, "PNE Workers Vote to Strike," *Vancouver Courier*, September 16, 2011, http://www.vancourier.com/news/workers+vote+strike/5408991/story.html

19 D. Tjosvold, "Cooperative and Competitive Goal Approach to Conflict: Accomplishments and Challenges," *Applied Psychology: An International Review* 47, no. 3 (1998), pp. 285–342.

20 K. W. Thomas, "Conflict and Negotiation Processes in Organizations," in *Handbook of Industrial and Organizational Psychology*,

2nd ed., vol. 3, ed. M. D. Dunnette and L. M. Hough (Palo Alto, CA: Consulting Psychologists Press, 1992), pp. 651–717.

21 C. K. W. De Dreu, A. Evers, B. Beersma, E. S. Kluwer, and A. Nauta, "A Theory-Based Measure of Conflict Management Strategies in the Workplace," *Journal of Organizational Behavior* 22, no. 6 (September 2001), pp. 645–668. See also D. G. Pruitt and J. Rubin, *Social Conflict: Escalation, Stalemate and Settlement* (New York: Random House, 1986).

22 C. K. W. De Dreu, A. Evers, B. Beersma, E. S. Kluwer, and A. Nauta, "A Theory-Based Measure of Conflict Management Strategies in the Workplace," *Journal of Organizational Behavior* 22, no. 6 (September 2001), pp. 645–668.

23 Based on K. W. Thomas, "Toward Multidimensional Values in Teaching: The Example of Conflict Behaviors," *Academy of Management Review*, July 1977, p. 487; and C. K. W. De Dreu, A. Evers, B. Beersma, E. S. Kluwer, and A. Nauta, "A Theory-Based Measure of Conflict Management Strategies in the Workplace," *Journal of Organizational Behavior* 22, no. 6 (September 2001), pp. 645–668.

24 R. A. Baron, "Personality and Organizational Conflict: Effects of the Type A Behavior Pattern and Self-Monitoring," *Organizational Behavior and Human Decision Processes*, October 1989, pp. 281–296; A. Drory and I. Ritov, "Effects of Work Experience and Opponent's Power on Conflict Management Styles," *International Journal of Conflict Management* 8 (1997), pp. 148–161; R. J. Sternberg and L. J. Soriano, "Styles of Conflict Resolution," *Journal of Personality and Social Psychology*, July 1984, pp. 115–126; and R. J. Volkema and T. J. Bergmann, "Conflict Styles as Indicators of Behavioral Patterns in Interpersonal Conflicts," *Journal of Social Psychology*, February 1995, pp. 5–15.

25 These ideas are based on S. P. Robbins, *Managing Organizational Conflict: A Nontraditional Approach* (Upper Saddle River, NJ: Prentice Hall, 1974), pp. 59–89.

26 "Managers Spend More Than 6 Hours Per Week Handling Staff Conflicts: Survey," hrreporter.com, March 23, 2011.

27 R. D. Ramsey, "Interpersonal Conflicts," *SuperVision* 66, no. 4 (April 2005), pp. 14–17.

28 R. L. Tung, "American Expatriates Abroad: From Neophytes to Cosmopolitans," *Journal of World Business* 33, no. 2 (Summer 1998), pp. 125–144.

29 "Negotiating South of the Border," *Harvard Management Communication Letter* 2, no. 8 (August 1999), p. 12.

30 F. W. Swierczek, "Culture and Conflict in Joint Ventures in Asia," *International Journal of Project Management* 12, no. 1 (1994), pp. 39–47.

31 P. S. Kirkbride, S. Tang, and R. I. Westwood, "Chinese Conflict Preferences and Negotiation Behavior: Cultural and Psychological Influences," *Organization Studies* 12, no. 3 (1991), pp. 365–386; S. Tang, and P. Kirkbride, "Development of Conflict Management Skills in Hong Kong: An Analysis of Some Cross-Cultural Implications," *Management Education and Development* 17, no. 3 (1986), pp. 287–301; P. Trubisky, S. Ting-Toomey, and S. L. Lin, "The Influence of Individualism-Collectivism and Self-monitoring on Conflict Styles," *International Journal of Intercultural Relations* 15 (1991), pp. 65–84; and K. I. Ohbuchi and Y. Takahashi, "Cultural Styles of Conflict Management in Japanese and Americans: Passivity, Covertness, and Effectiveness of Strategies," *Journal of Applied Social Psychology* 24 (1994), pp. 1345–1366.

32 P. S. Kirkbride, S. Tang, and R. I. Westwood, "Chinese Conflict Preferences and Negotiation Behavior: Cultural and Psychological Influences," *Organization Studies* 12 (1991), pp. 365–386; and F. W. Swierczek, "Culture and Conflict in Joint Ventures in Asia," *International Journal of Project Management* 12 (1994), pp. 39–47.

33 C. L. Wang, X. Lin, A. K. K. Chan, and Y. Shi, "Conflict Handling Styles in International Joint Ventures: A Cross-Cultural and Cross-National Comparison," *Management International Review* 45, no. 1 (2005), pp. 3–21.

34 M. A. Rahim, "A Measure of Styles of Handling Interpersonal Conflict," *Academy of Management Journal* 26 (1983), pp. 368–376; and C. H. Tinsley, "Model of Conflict Resolution in Japanese, German, and American Cultures," *Journal of Applied Psychology* 83 (1998), pp. 316–323.

35 R. T. Moran, J. Allen, R. Wichman, T. Ando, and M. Sasano, "Japan," in *Global Perspectives on Organizational Conflict*, ed. M. A. Rahim and A. A. Blum (Westport, CT: Praeger 1994), pp. 33–52.

36 D. C. Barnlund, *Communicative Styles of Japanese and Americans: Images and Realities* (Belmont, CA: Wadsworth 1989); and K. I. Ohbuchi and Y. Takahashi, "Cultural Styles of Conflict Management in Japanese and Americans: Passivity, Covertness, and Effectiveness of Strategies," *Journal of Applied Social Psychology* 24 (1994), pp. 1345–1366.

37 Z. Ma, "Chinese Conflict Management Styles and Negotiation Behaviours: An Empirical Test," *International Journal of Cross Cultural Management*, April 2007, pp. 101–119.

38 K. Leung, "Some Determinants of Reactions to Procedural Models for Conflict Resolution: A Cross-National Study," *Journal of Personality and Social Psychology* 53 (1987), pp. 898–908; K. Leung and E. A. Lind, "Procedure and Culture: Effects of Culture, Gender, and Investigator Status on Procedural Preferences," *Journal of Personality and Social Psychology* 50 (1986), pp. 1134–1140; M. W. Morris, K. Y. Williams, K. Leung, R. Larrick, M. T. Mendoza, D. Bhatnagar, J. Li, M. Kondo, J. Luo, and J. Hu, "Conflict Management Style: Accounting for Cross-National Differences," *Journal of International Business Studies* 29 (1998), pp. 729–747; and F. W. Swierczek, "Culture and Conflict in Joint Ventures in Asia," *International Journal of Project Management* 12 (1994), pp. 39–47.

39 J. S. Black and M. Mendenhall, "Resolving Conflicts with the Japanese: Mission Impossible?" *Sloan Management Review* 34 (1993), pp. 49–59.

40 J. A. Wall Jr. and M. W. Blum, "Negotiations," *Journal of Management*, June 1991, pp. 283–287; and R. Kreitner and A. Kinicki, *Organizational Behavior*, 6th ed. (New York: McGraw-Hill, 2004), p. 502.

41 C. Olsheski, "Resolving Disputes Has Just Become More Efficient," *Financial Post (National Post)*, August 16, 1999, p. D9.

42 http://www.caut.ca/aufa/newsletter/0504/prescomm.htm

43 See, for instance, R. A. Cosier and C. R. Schwenk, "Agreement and Thinking Alike: Ingredients for Poor Decisions," *Academy of Management Executive*, February 1990, pp. 69–74; K. A. Jehn, "Enhancing Effectiveness: An Investigation of Advantages and Disadvantages of Value-Based Intragroup Conflict," *International Journal of Conflict Management*, July 1994, pp. 223–238; R. L. Priem, D. A. Harrison, and N. K. Muir, "Structured Conflict and Consensus Outcomes in Group Decision Making," *Journal of Management* 21, no. 4 (1995), pp. 691–710; and K. A. Jehn and E. A. Mannix, "The Dynamic Nature of Conflict: A Longitudinal Study of Intragroup Conflict and Group Performance," *Academy of Management Journal*, April 2001, pp. 238–251.

44 B. A. Nijstad and S. C. Kaps, "Taking the Easy Way Out: Preference Diversity, Decision Strategies, and Decision Refusal in Groups," *Journal of Personality and Social Psychology* 94, no. 5 (2008), pp. 860–870.

45 Based on D. Tjosvold, *Learning to Manage Conflict: Getting People to Work Together Productively* (New York: Lexington Books, 1993), pp. 12–13.

46 R. L. Hoffman, "Homogeneity of Member Personality and Its Effect on Group Problem-Solving," *Journal of Abnormal and Social*

Psychology, January 1959, pp. 27–32; and R. L. Hoffman and N. R. F. Maier, "Quality and Acceptance of Problem Solutions by Members of Homogeneous and Heterogeneous Groups," *Journal of Abnormal and Social Psychology*, March 1961, pp. 401–407.

47 M. E. Zellmer-Bruhn, M. M. Maloney, A. D. Bhappu, and R. Salvador, "When and How Do Differences Matter? An Exploration of Perceived Similarity in Teams," *Organizational Behavior and Human Decision Processes* 107, no. 1 (2008), pp. 41–59.

48 J. Hall and M. S. Williams, "A Comparison of Decision-Making Performances in Established and Ad-Hoc Groups," *Journal of Personality and Social Psychology*, February 1966, p. 217.

49 R. E. Hill, "Interpersonal Compatibility and Work Group Performance among Systems Analysts: An Empirical Study," *Proceedings of the Seventeenth Annual Midwest Academy of Management Conference*, Kent, OH, April 1974, pp. 97–110.

50 D. C. Pelz and F. Andrews, *Scientists in Organizations* (New York: Wiley, 1966).

51 R. Ilies, M. D. Johnson, T. A. Judge, and J. Keeney, "A Within-Individual Study of Interpersonal Conflict as a Work Stressor: Dispositional and Situational Moderators," *Journal of Organizational Behavior* 32, no. 1 (2011), pp. 44–64.

52 K. J. Behfar, R. S. Peterson, E. A. Mannix, and W. M. K. Trochim, "The Critical Role of Conflict Resolution in Teams: A Close Look at the Links between Conflict Type, Conflict Management Strategies, and Team Outcomes," *Journal of Applied Psychology* 93, no. 1 (2008), pp. 170–188; A. G. Tekleab, N. R. Quigley, and P. E. Tesluk, "A Longitudinal Study of Team Conflict, Conflict Management, Cohesion, and Team Effectiveness," *Group and Organization Management* 34, no. 2 (2009), pp. 170–205; and E. Van de Vliert, M. C. Euwema, and S. E. Huismans, "Managing Conflict with a Subordinate or a Superior: Effectiveness of Conglomerated Behavior," *Journal of Applied Psychology* 80 (1995), pp. 271–281.

53 A. Somech, H. S. Desivilya, and H. Lidogoster, "Team Conflict Management and Team Effectiveness: The Effects of Task Interdependence and Team Identification," *Journal of Organizational Behavior* 30, no. 3 (2009), pp. 359–378.

54 See J. A. Wall Jr. and R. R. Callister, "Conflict and Its Management," *Journal of Management* 21, no. 3 (1995), pp. 523–526 for evidence supporting the argument that conflict is almost uniformly dysfunctional.

55 Vignette based on CUPE, "Foley Recommends Don't Pass CUPE 1004 Vote," *CUPE LOCAL 1004*, October 9, 2007, http://cupe.ca/communications/Foleys_recommendatio

56 J. A. Wall Jr., *Negotiation: Theory and Practice* (Glenview, IL: Scott, Foresman, 1985).

57 http://www.gov.sk.ca/news?newsId=db80bb4e-28ae-49d0-819f-bb9e328081bd

58 http://www.gov.sk.ca/news?newsId=9c8ad8fa-d115-479a-8937-2ecfeaad195e

59 This model is based on R. J. Lewicki, "Bargaining and Negotiation," *Exchange: The Organizational Behavior Teaching Journal* 6, no. 2 (1981), pp. 39–40; and B. S. Moskal, "The Art of the Deal," *IndustryWeek*, January 18, 1993, p. 23.

60 J. C. Magee, A. D. Galinsky, and D. H. Gruenfeld, "Power, Propensity to Negotiate, and Moving First in Competitive Interactions," *Personality and Social Psychology Bulletin*, February 2007, pp. 200–212.

61 H. R. Bowles, L. Babcock, and L. Lei, "Social Incentives for Gender Differences in the Propensity to Initiative Negotiations: Sometimes It Does Hurt to Ask," *Organizational Behavior and Human Decision Processes* 103 (2007), pp. 84–103.

62 Based on G. Ku, A. D. Galinsky, and J. K. Murnighan, "Starting Low but Ending High: A Reversal of the Anchoring Effect in

Auctions," *Journal of Personality and Social Psychology* 90, June 2006, pp. 975–986; K. Sherstyuk, "A Comparison of First Price Multi-Object Auctions," *Experimental Economics* 12, no. 1 (2009), pp. 42–64; and R. M. Isaac, T. C. Salmon, and A. Zillante, "A Theory of Jump Bidding in Ascending Auctions," *Journal of Economic Behavior & Organization* 62, no. 1 (2007), pp. 144–164.

63 D. A. Moore, "Myopic Prediction, Self-Destructive Secrecy, and the Unexpected Benefits of Revealing Final Deadlines in Negotiation," *Organizational Behavior and Human Decision Processes*, July 2004, pp. 125–139.

64 J. R. Curhan, H. A. Elfenbein, and H. Xu, "What Do People Value When They Negotiate? Mapping the Domain of Subjective Value in Negotiation," *Journal of Personality and Social Psychology* 91, no. 3 (2007), pp. 493–512.

65 K. W. Thomas, "Conflict and Negotiation Processes in Organizations," in *Handbook of Industrial and Organizational Psychology*, 2nd ed., vol. 3, ed. M. D. Dunnette and L. M. Hough (Palo Alto, CA: Consulting Psychologists Press, 1992), pp. 651–717.

66 P. M. Morgan and R. S. Tindale, "Group vs. Individual Performance in Mixed-Motive Situations: Exploring an Inconsistency," *Organizational Behavior and Human Decision Processes*, January 2002, pp. 44–65.

67 C. E. Naquin, "The Agony of Opportunity in Negotiation: Number of Negotiable Issues, Counterfactual Thinking, and Feelings of Satisfaction," *Organizational Behavior and Human Decision Processes*, May 2003, pp. 97–107.

68 C. K. W. De Dreu, L. R. Weingart, and S. Kwon, "Influence of Social Motives on Integrative Negotiation: A Meta-analytic Review and Test of Two Theories," *Journal of Personality and Social Psychology*, May 2000, pp. 889–905.

69 A. W. Brooks and M. E. Schweitzer, "Can Nervous Nelly Negotiate? How Anxiety Causes Negotiators to Make Low First Offers, Exit Early, and Earn Less Profit," *Organizational Behavior and Human Decision Processes* 115, no. 1 (2011), pp. 43–54.

70 D, Malhotra and M. Bazerman, "Investigative Negotiation," *Harvard Business Review*, September 2007, pp. 72–78.

71 S. S. Wiltermuth and M. A. Neale, "Too Much Information: The Perils of Nondiagnostic Information in Negotiations," *Journal of Applied Psychology* 96, no. 1 (2011), pp. 192–201.

72 R. Fisher and W. Ury, *Getting to Yes: Negotiating Agreement without Giving In*, 2nd ed. (New York: Penguin, 1991).

73 M. H. Bazerman and M. A. Neale, *Negotiating Rationally* (New York: Free Press, 1992), pp. 67–68.

74 R. P. Larrick and G. Wu, "Claiming a Large Slice of a Small Pie: Asymmetric Disconfirmation in Negotiation," *Journal of Personality and Social Psychology* 93, no. 2 (2007), pp. 212–233.

75 M. Marks and C. Harold, "Who Asks and Who Receives in Salary Negotiation," *Journal of Organizational Behavior* 32, no. 3 (2011), pp. 371–394.

76 E. T. Amanatullah, M. W. Morris, and J. R. Curhan, "Negotiators Who Give Too Much: Unmitigated Communion, Relational Anxieties, and Economic Costs in Distributive and Integrative Bargaining," *Journal of Personality and Social Psychology* 95, no. 3 (2008), pp. 723–738.

77 B. Barry and R. A. Friedman, "Bargainer Characteristics in Distributive and Integrative Negotiation," *Journal of Personality and Social Psychology*, February 1998, pp. 345–359.

78 L. J. Kray and M. P. Haselhuhn, "Implicit Negotiations Beliefs and Performance: Experimental and Longitudinal Evidence," *Journal of Personality and Social Psychology* 93, no. 1 (2007), pp. 49–64.

79 S. Kopelman, A. S. Rosette, and L. Thompson, "The Three Faces of Eve: Strategic Displays of Positive, Negative, and Neutral Emotions in Negotiations," *Organizational Behavior and Human*

Decision Processes 99 (2006), pp. 81–101; G. A. Gan Kleef and S. Côté, "Expressing Anger in Conflict: When It Helps and When It Hurts," *Journal of Applied Psychology* 92, no. 6 (2007), pp. 1157–1569; and J. M. Brett, M. Olekalns, R. Friedman, N. Goates, C. Anderson, and C. C. Lisco, "Sticks and Stones: Language, Face, and Online Dispute Resolution," *Academy of Management Journal* 50, no. 1 (2007), pp. 85–99.

80 C. Watson and L. R. Hoffman, "Managers as Negotiators: A Test of Power Versus Gender as Predictors of Feelings, Behavior, and Outcomes," *Leadership Quarterly*, Spring 1996, pp. 63–85.

81 A. E. Walters, A. F. Stuhlmacher, and L. L. Meyer, "Gender and Negotiator Competitiveness: A Meta-analysis," *Organizational Behavior and Human Decision Processes*, October 1998, pp. 1–29; and A. F. Stuhlmacher and A. E. Walters, "Gender Differences in Negotiation Outcome: A Meta-analysis," *Personnel Psychology*, Autumn 1999, pp. 653–677.

82 A. F. Stuhlmacher and A. E. Walters, "Gender Differences in Negotiation Outcome: A Meta-analysis," *Personnel Psychology*, Autumn 1999, pp. 655.

83 H. R. Bowles, L. Babcock, and L. Lei, "Social Incentives for Gender Differences in the Propensity to Initiative Negotiations: Sometimes It Does Hurt to Ask," *Organizational Behavior and Human Decision Processes* 103 (2007), pp. 84–103.

84 L. J. Kray, A. D. Galinsky, and L. Thompson, "Reversing the Gender Gap in Negotiations: An Exploration of Stereotype Regeneration," *Organizational Behavior and Human Decision Processes*, March 2002, pp. 386–409.

85 D. A. Small, M. Gelfand, L. Babcock, and H. Gettman, "Who Goes to the Bargaining Table? The Influence of Gender and Framing on the Initiation of Negotiation," *Journal of Personality and Social Psychology* 93, no. 4 (2007), pp. 600–613; and C. K. Stevens, A. G. Bavetta, and M. E. Gist, "Gender Differences in the Acquisition of Salary Negotiation Skills: The Role of Goals, Self-Efficacy, and Perceived Control," *Journal of Applied Psychology* 78, no. 5 (October 1993), pp. 723–735.

86 I. Ayres, "Further Evidence of Discrimination in New Car Negotiations and Estimates of Its Cause," *Michigan Law Review* 94, no. 1 (October 1995), pp. 109–147.

87 B. Gerhart and S. Rynes, "Determinants and Consequences of Salary Negotiations by Male and Female MBA Graduates," *Journal of Applied Psychology* 76, no. 2 (April 1991), pp. 256–262.

88 E. T. Amanatullah and M. W. Morris, "Negotiating Gender Roles: Gender Differences in Assertive Negotiating Are Mediated By Women's Fear of Backlash and Attenuated When Negotiating on Behalf of Others," *Journal of Personality and Social Psychology* 98, no. 2 (2010), pp. 256–267.

89 L. Schweitzer, E. Ng, S. Lyons, and L. Kuron, "Exploring the Career Pipeline: Gender Differences in Pre-Career Expectations," *Relations Industrielles/Industrial Relations* 66, no. 3 (2011), pp. 422–444.

90 H. R. Markus and S. Kitayama, "Culture and the Self: Implications for Cognition, Emotion, and Motivation," *Psychological Review* 98, no. 2 (1991), pp. 224–253; and H. Ren and B. Gray, "Repairing Relationship Conflict: How Violation Types and Culture Influence the Effectiveness of Restoration Rituals," *Academy of Management Review* 34, no. 1 (2009), pp. 105–126.

91 M. J. Gelfand, M. Higgins, L. H. Nishii, J. L. Raver, A. Dominguez, F. Murakami, S. Yamaguchi, and M. Toyama, "Culture and Egocentric Perceptions of Fairness in Conflict and Negotiation," *Journal of Applied Psychology*, October 2002, pp. 833–845; and Z. Ma, "Chinese Conflict Management Styles and Negotiation Behaviours: An Empirical Test," *International Journal of Cross Cultural Management*, April 2007, pp. 101–119.

92 P. P. Fu, X. H. Yan, Y. Li, E. Wang, and S. Peng, "Examining Conflict-Handling Approaches by Chinese Top Management Teams in IT Firms," *International Journal of Conflict Management* 19, no. 3 (2008), pp. 188–209.

93 See N. J. Adler, *International Dimensions of Organizational Behavior*, 4th ed. (Cincinnati, OH: South Western, 2002), pp. 208–256; W. L. Adair, T. Okurmura, and J. M. Brett, "Negotiation Behavior When Cultures Collide: The United States and Japan," *Journal of Applied Psychology*, June 2001, pp. 371–385; and L. A. Liu, C. H. Chua, and G. K. Stahl, "Quality of Communication Experience: Definition, Measurement, and Implications for Intercultural Negotiations," *Journal of Applied Psychology* 95, no. 3 (2010), pp. 469-487.

94 K. D. Schmidt, *Doing Business in France* (Menlo Park, CA: SRI International, 1987).

95 Y. Chen, E. A. Mannix, and T. Okumura, "The Importance of Who You Meet: Effects of Self—versus Other—Concerns among Negotiators in the United States, the People's Republic of China, and Japan," *Journal of Experimental Social Psychology*, January 2003, pp. 1–15; Z. Ma, "Chinese Conflict Management Styles and Negotiation Behaviours: An Empirical Test," *International Journal of Cross Cultural Management*, April 2007, pp. 101–119; and S. Lubman, "Round and Round," *Wall Street Journal*, December 10, 1993, p. R3.

96 W. L. Adair, T. Okumura, and J. M. Brett, "Negotiation Behavior When Cultures Collide: The United States and Japan," *Journal of Applied Psychology*, June 2001, pp. 371–385; and W. L. Adair, L. Weingart, and J. Brett, "The Timing and Function of Offers in U.S. and Japanese Negotiations," *Journal of Applied Psychology* 92, no. 4 (2007), pp. 1056–1068.

97 Y. Chen, E. A. Mannix, and T. Okumura, "The Importance of Who You Meet: Effects of Self—versus Other—Concerns among Negotiators in the United States, the People's Republic of China, and Japan," *Journal of Experimental Social Psychology*, January 2003, pp. 1–15; and J. W. Salacuse, "Ten Ways That Culture Affects Negotiating Style: Some Survey Results," *Negotiation Journal*, July 1998, pp. 221–240.

98 Based on S. Kopelman and A. S. Rosette, "Cultural Variation in Response to Strategic Emotions in Negotiations," *Group Decision and Negotiation* 17, no. 1 (2008), pp. 65–77; and M. Liu, "The Intrapersonal and Interpersonal Effects of Anger on Negotiation Strategies: A Cross-Cultural Investigation," *Human Communication Research* 35, no. 1 (2009), pp. 148–169.

PHOTO CREDITS

Chapter 1

Page 3 Orange Line Media/Shutterstock Page 14 © Nataq/Dreamstime.com Page 20 © Lisa F. Young/ iStockphoto.com

Chapter 2

Page 27, CP Images/Mario Beauregard; Page 32, Wavebreakmediamicro / Dreamstime.com /Get-Stock.com; Page 33, Courtesy of Winnipeg's Most; Page 34, Nathan Denette/National Post; Page 38, Peanuts, reprinted by permission of Universal Uclick; Page 41, CP Images/AP Photo/Manish Swarup; Page 42, CP Images/Frank Gunn

Chapter 3

Page 57, Courtesy of SaskGaming; Page 63, Courtesy of RONA INC.; Page 64, CP PHOTO/Larry MacDougal; Page 71, © Britta Kasholm-Tengve/ iStock; Page 73 CP Images/Photo by Rex Features; Page 76, CP Images/AP Photo/Katsumi Kasahara; Page 79, Courtesy of Toon Boom;

Chapter 4

Page 85, Courtesy of Boston Pizza International; Page 87, Steve Bosch/Vancouver Sun; Page 90, CP Images/AP Photo/Elaine Thompson; Page 91, Southwest Airlines; Page 92, CP Images/AP Photo/ Nam Y. Huh; Page 95, CP Images/Mario Beauregard; Page 96, © Mick Stevens/ The New Yorker Collection/ www.cartoonbank.com; Page 97, Jin Lee/Bloomberg via Getty Images; Page 98, © Michael Christopher Brown/Corbis

Chapter 5

Page 107, Kicking Horse Coffee; Page 109, CP PHOTO/Adrian Wyld; Page 117, THE CANADIAN PRESS/Ryan Remiorz; Page 121, The Canadian Press Images/Maclean's Magazine/Andrew Tolson; Page 123, Stuart Davis/PNG; Page 124, Courtesy of Steward Leibl; Page 127, Courtesy of DumpRunner Waste Systems. Photo by Paul Nielsen

Chapter 6

Page 131, Courtesy of Geoff Flood, T4G; Page 133, © Shen Bohan/Xinhua Press/Corbis; Page 134, THE CANADIAN PRESS IMAGES/Graham Hughes; Page 137, Dilbert, reprinted by permission of Universal Uclick; Page 136, Courtesy of RCMP, Surrey, BC; Page 138, © Vittoriano Rastelli/CORBIS; Page 139, Courtesy of Furlani's; Page 145, CP Images/AP Photo/Eckehard Schulz

Chapter 7

Page 163 Alexander Raths/Shutterstock Page 172 Andy Levin/Photo Researchers, Inc.

Chapter 8

Page 189 Gemenacom/Shutterstock Page 201 © Spencer Grant/PhotoEdit Page 207 © Willie B. Thomas/iStockphoto Page 208 Toronto Star/Get-Stock.com

Chapter 9

Page 211 © Yuri Arcurs/Fotolia Page 221 Lewis J Merrim/Photo Researchers/Getty Images Page 222 © Chris Howes/Wild Places Photography/Alamy Page 223 © Gina Sanders/Fotolia Page 226 © Michael Newman/PhotoEdit Page 228 Yuri Arcurs/ Shutterstock

Chapter 10

Page 235 Goodluz/Shutterstock Page 237 © goodluz/Fotolia Page 246 © Steven Rubin/The Image Works Page 249 NASA

Chapter 11

Page 257 Sergej Khakimullin/Shutterstock Page 266 © ESLINE/Fotolia Page 268 Nyul/Dreamstime. com/GetStock Page 269 © Jami Garrison/iStockphoto.com

Chapter 12

Page 273 Dmitriy Shironosov/Shutterstock Page 284 Monty Rakusen/Cultura/Getty Images Page 288 auremar/Shutterstock

Chapter 13

Page 299, CP Images/AP Photo/Mark Baker; Page 305, CP Images/AP Photo/Nick Ut; Page 308, CP Images/AP Photo/Kevork Djansezian; Page 309, THE CANADIAN PRESS/Tom Hanson; Page 310, © Reuters/CORBIS

Chapter 14

Page 329, CP Images/AP Photo/Richard Drew; Page 343, Barrett & MacKay/All Canada Photos; Page 347, CP PHOTO/Larry MacDougal; Page 348, CP PHOTO/Jonathan Hayward

Chapter 15

Page 355 Solidsdman/Dreamstime.com/GetStock Page 359 The Canadian Press(Frank Gunn) Page 361 Yuri Arcurs/Shutterstock Page 370 Jupiter/Comstock Page 373 Regina Leader-Post/Patrick Pettit

Chapter 16

Page 375 Mangostock/Dreamstime.com/GetStock. com Page 380 The Canadian Press(Dave Chidley)

Chapter 17

Page 395 Dmitry Kalinovsky/Shutterstock Page 403 Paha_l/Dreamstime.com/GetStock Page 408 Dan Janisse/The Windsor Star Page 411 © Ariel Skelley/ Terra/Corbis Page 412 © Ed Kashi/Corbis News Premium/Corbis

Chapter 18

Page 417, CP Images/yy/ChinaFotoPress; Page 419, © Alexandra Boulat/VII/Corbis; Page 421, Courtesy of Queen's School of Business, Queen's University; Page 431, Courtesy of Ikea; Page 437, Gamma-Rapho via Getty Images; Page 438, CP Images/AP Photo/Jae C. Hong; Page 439, THE CANADIAN PRESS/Darren Calabrese; Page 441, Dlibert, reprinted by permission of Universal Uclick

Chapter 19

Page 257, Steve Russell / GetStock.com; Page 448, Courtesy of Lawtons Drugs; Page 450, CP Images/ AP Photo/Gurinder Osan; Page 456, Courtesy of Upverter; Page 462, Courtesy of Toyota Motor Corporation; Page 463, Courtesy of Donna Cona Inc.

Chapter 20

Page 465, THE CANADIAN PRESS/Troy Fleece, Page 469, CP Images/AP Photo/Scott Cohen; Page 477, CP Images/AP Photo/Paul Sakuma; Page 481, Courtesy of Infosys Limited; Page 484, Dilbert, reprinted by permission of Universal Uclick; Page 487, Courtesy of Bill Young, founder of Social Capital Partners; Page 488, Fred Lum/The Globe and Mail

Chapter 21

Page 493 Losevsky Photo and Video/Shutterstock Page 501 Stewart Cohen/Photolibrary/Getty Images

Chapter 22

Page 511 zulufoto/Shutterstock Page 512 Greg Agnew/Moncton Times and Transcript Page 521 Todd Humber/Canadian HR Reporter Page 531 Blair Gable/Reuters/Landov

Chapter 23

Page 537 Goldenkb/Dreamstime.com/GetStock Page 542 © Helder Almeida/Fotolia Page 551 iStockphoto/Thinkstock

Chapter 24

Page 555 The Canadian Press(Sean Kilpatrick) Page 557 Dan Janisse/The Windsor Star Page 561 Dick Hemingway Page 564 © Francisco Cruz/SuperStock Page 568 The Canadian Press(Frank Gunn)

Chapter 25

Page 575, The Canadian Press Images/Bayne Stanley; Page 577, Adeel Halim/Bloomberg via Getty Images; Page 578, © Leo Cullum/ The New Yorker Collection/ www.cartoonbank.com; Page 580, Courtesy of Xerox Corporation; Page 583, CP Photo; Page 584, Courtesy Great Little Box Company; Page 590, CP Images/AP Photo/Mark Baker; Page 593, Tobey Sanford/Courtesy of General Electric Company

Chapter 26

Page 597, John Lehmann/Globe and Mail/CP Images; Page 600, CP Images/AP Photo/Mike Derer; Page 609, David Robertson / Alamy; Page 615, YURI GRIPAS/Reuters /Landov; Page 356, John Kenney, The (Montreal) Gazette © 2010